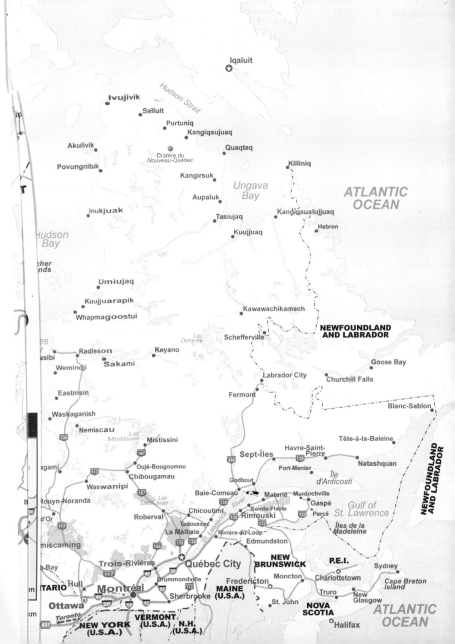

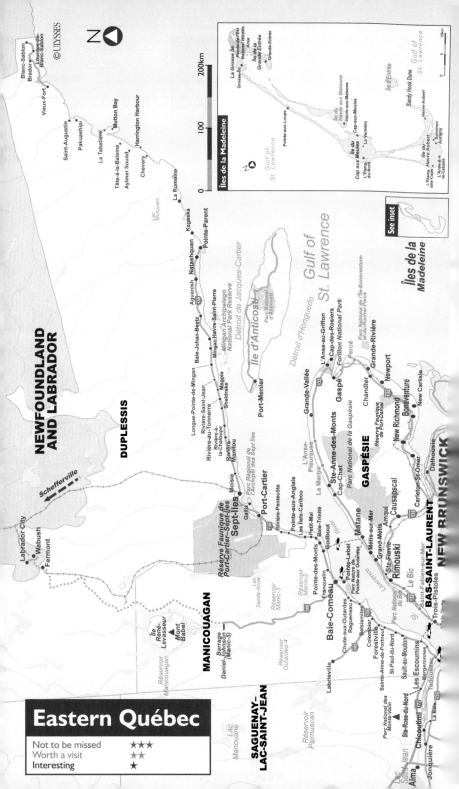

Québec

Eighth Edition

Eastward, the view down the St. Lawrence towards the Gulf is the finest of all, scarcely surpassed by anything in the world. Your eye follows the range of lofty mountains until their blue summits are blended and lost in the blue of the sky.

Susanna Moodie, *Roughing it in the Bush* (1852)

Travel better, enjoy more

ULYSSES

Travel Guides

Guide Update
Pierre Ledoux

Research and Writing
François Rémillard (Exploring)
Benoit Prieur (Portrait)

Additional research and writing:
Gabriel Audet, Caroline Béliveau, Julie
Brodeur, Alexandre Chouinard, Daniel
Desjardins, Alexandra Gilbert, Olivier
Gougeon, Élodie Luquet, Stéphane G.
Marceau, Jacqueline Grekin, François Hénault,
Judith Lefebvre, Alain Legault, Claude
Morneau, Yves Ouellet, Joël Pomerleau,
Sylvie Rivard, Yves Séguin, Marcel Verreault.

Previous Contributors
Virginie Bonneau, Nathalie Boucher, Catherine
Desforges, Simon Dubé, Claude Feuiltault,
Annie Frenette, Séverine Giroux, Isabel
Gosselin, Alain Legault, Jennifer McMorran,
Francis Plourde, Marc Rigole, Steve Rioux,
Christian Roy, Maxime Soucy, Christopher
Woodward.

Publisher
Olivier Gougeon

Production Director
André Duchesne

Copy Editing
Cindy Garayt

Computer Graphics
Marie-France Denis
Isabelle Lalonde

Cartographers
Pascal Biet
Bradley Fenton

Photography
Cover page
François Rivard / ATR Charlevoix
Inside pages
Patrick Escudero
Philippe Renault

Acknowledgements

We acknowledge the financial support of the Government of Canada through the Book
Publishing Industry Development Program (BPIDP) for our publishing activities. We would also
like to thank the Government of Québec for its tax credit for book publishing administered by
SODEC.

Library and Archives Canada Cataloguing in Publication

Main entry under title :

　　　　Québec

　　　　(Ulysses travel guide)
　　　　Translation of: Le Québec.
　　　　Includes index.

　　　　ISSN 1486-3502
　　　　ISBN 2-89464-711-5

　　　　1. Québec (Province) - Guidebooks. I. Series.

FC2907.Q4913　　917.1404'5　　C99-301663-4

Table of Contents

Table of Contents

List of Maps

List of Maps

Map Symbols

★	Attractions	⊘	Beach	①	Metro station
▲	Accommodations	🚲	Bike path	▲	Mountain
●	Restaurants	⊠	Border crossing	🏛	Museum
	Sea, lake, river	▪	Building		Optional tour
	Forest or park	🚌	Bus station	P	Parking
	Place	🚗	Car ferry		Passenger ferry
✪	National capital	✝	Church	🎿	Ski resort
✪	Provincial or state capital	H	Hospital	≡	Stairs
▬ ▬ ▬	International border	✚	First aid		Suggested tour
	Provincial or regional border	⸰	Golf course	❶	Tourist information
	Train track	✈	International airport		Train station
	Tunnel	☀	Lookout		ULYSSES bookstore
		⚓	Marina		

Symbols Used In This Guide

≡	Air conditioning
bkfst incl.	Breakfast included
♠	Casino
⌁	Fan
🗏	Fax number
⌂	Fireplace
🛏	Fitness centre
fb	Full board (lodging + 3 meals)
½b	Half board (lodging + 2 meals)
●	Kitchenette
@	Internet access in the room
#	Mosquito net
P	Parking
🐾	Pets allowed
≋	Pool
❄	Refrigerator
⚊	Restaurant
)))	Sauna
sb	Shared bathroom
⅄	Spa
☎	Telephone number
🚲	Travel by bike
🚌	Travel by bus
🚗	Travel by car
人	Travel by foot
Ⓜ	Travel by metro
	Ulysses favourite
♿	Wheelchair access
@	Whirlpool

Attraction Classification

★ ★ ★	Not to be missed
★ ★	Worth a visit
★	Interesting

Accommodation Classification

Unless otherwise noted, all prices indicated in this guide apply to a standard room for two people in peak season.

$	less than $60
$$	from $60 to $100
$$$	from $101 to $150
$$$$	from $151 to $225
$$$$$	more than $225

Restaurant Classification

Prices in this guide are for a meal for one person, excluding taxes and tip.

$	less than $15
$$	$15 to $25
$$$	$26 to $50
$$$$	more than $50

All prices in this guide are in Canadian dollars.

This guide's practical section features a grey border and lists this destination's useful addresses. You can refer to the following pictograms to find the information you need:

▲	Accommodations
⚊	Restaurants
♪	Entertainment
🛍	Shopping

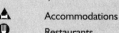

QUÉBEC'S TOURIST REGIONS

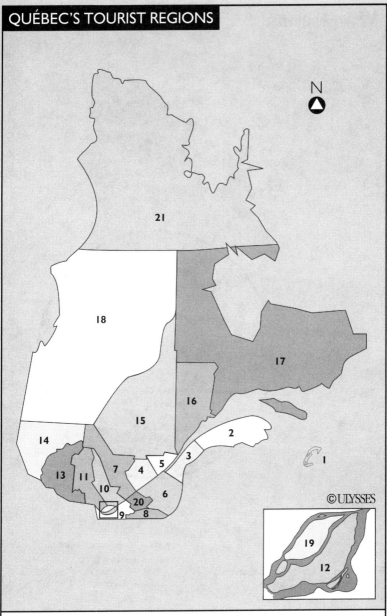

© ULYSSES

1.	Îles de la Madeleine	**9.**	Montérégie
2.	Gaspésie	**10.**	Lanaudière
3.	Bas-Saint-Laurent	**11.**	Laurentides (Laurentians)
4.	Québec City Region	**12.**	Montréal
5.	Charlevoix	**13.**	Outaouais
6.	Chaudière-Appalaches	**14.**	Abitibi-Témiscamingue
7.	Mauricie	**15.**	Saguenay–Lac-Saint-Jean
8.	Cantons-de-l'Est (Eastern Townships)	**16.**	Côte-Nord: Manicouagan

17.	Côte-Nord: Duplessis
18.	Baie-James (James Bay)
19.	Laval
20.	Centre-du-Québec
21.	Nunavik

Where is Québec?

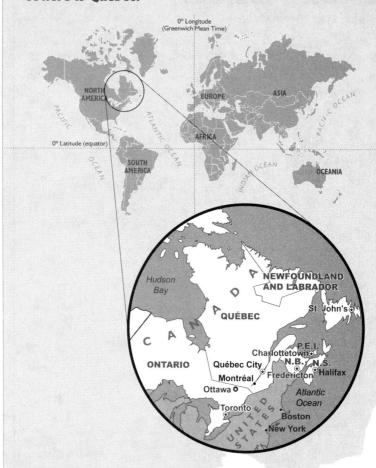

Québec

Area
1,668,000km²

Population
over 7,5 million inhabitants

Population Density
4,9 inhab./km²

Capital
Québec City

Time Zone
GMT –5

Currency
Canadian Dollar

Language
Official Language: French

French speakers: 81.2%
English speakers: 8.0%
Others: 10%

Climate
(Average temperatures)
Montréal:
Winter: -11°C to -3°C
Summer: 16°C to 26°C
Québec City
Winter: -13°C to -5°C
Summer: 14°C to 25°C

Highest Point
Mont d'Iberville (1,652m) in
the Nunavik region

Portrait

S ituated in the extreme northeast of North America, Québec is Canada's largest province. It covers a surface area of 1,668,000km², roughly equivalent to the size of France, Germany and the Iberian peninsula put together.

With the exception of certain southern regions, Québec is sparsely populated and is characterized by an expansive wilderness of lakes, rivers and forests. The province forms a huge northern peninsula, with James Bay and Hudson Bay to the west, Hudson Strait and Ungava Bay to the north, and the Gulf of St. Lawrence to the east. Québec also has very long land borders that it shares with Ontario to the west, New Brunswick and the U.S. state of Maine to the southeast, the states of New York, Vermont and New Hampshire to the south and the province of Newfoundland and Labrador to the northeast.

Québec's borders changed several times prior to 1927, when the province was defined as we know it today. With Canadian Confederation in 1867, Québec occupied the territory previously known as Lower Canada, which corresponds to what is now southern Québec. Soon, Québec expanded northward. By 1898, it included the region between Abitibi and the Rivière Eastmain, and in 1912, the province grew once again, when Nouveau Québec was added in the north. In 1927, London's Privy Council decided in favour of Newfoundland in its dispute with Québec over the immense territory of Labrador, in the northeast.

Geography

Québec's geography is dominated by the St. Lawrence River, the Appalachian Mountain range and the Canadian Shield, three of the most distinct geographical formations in North America. More than 1,000km long, the St. Lawrence is the largest river leading to the Atlantic Ocean on the continent. The river has its source at the Great Lakes and is also fed by a number of major waterways, such as the Ottawa, the Richelieu, the Saguenay and the Manicouagan. Traditionally the primary route into the continent, the St. Lawrence played a central part in Québec's development. Even today, the majority of the province's population lives along the river, particularly in the Montréal region, where nearly half of Québec's population resides. To the south, near the U.S. border, the Appalachian Mountains cross the St. Lawrence lowlands from southeastern Québec to the Gaspé peninsula. The hilly scenery of these regions is very similar to that of New England, although the mountains rarely exceed 1,000m in height. The remaining 80% of Québec's land mass is part of the Canadian Shield, a very old, heavily eroded mountain range extending over all of northern Québec. This region of the province has a tiny population and abundant natural resources, including vast forests and mighty rivers, some of which are used in the production of hydroelectric power.

■ Settling the Land

Traces of the seigneurial system used by the first colonists to settle the land can still be seen today in the St. Lawrence lowlands. Land was divided into long tracts running inland from the water in order to give the maximum number of colonists access to the river, which was the only thoroughfare navigable by canoe in the summer and by sled in the winter. When all the land near the river had been settled, another set of tracts was cleared along a road, called a *rang* (row), at the far end of the previously established tracts. Today, much of the land remains divided like this, and farmers still live as they would have all those years ago, working long, narrow fields. In certain other regions close to the U.S. border, the first European settlers were British and they cleared the land according to a system of townships, which involved dividing the territory into squares. This system survives in some parts of the Cantons de l'Est (which literally translates to Eastern Townships).

Flora

As a result of climatic differences, the vegetation in northern Québec is sparse, while in the south it is quite lush (at least in the summer). Québec's flora can be divided into four zones from north to south: the tundra, the taiga, the boreal forest and the deciduous forest.

The tundra occupies the northernmost reaches of Québec, principally along Hudson Bay and Ungava Bay. With a short month-long growing season and severe winters, when the ground is frozen several metres deep, vegetation in the tundra is limited to mosses, lichens and very small trees.

The taiga, an area of transition between the tundra and the boreal forest, covers more than a third of Québec and is characterized by sparse, slow-growing trees such as spruce and larch.

The boreal forest covers a huge section of the province, from the edge of the taiga to the banks of the St. Lawrence in some regions. This is a very homogeneous zone made up of coniferous trees, primarily white pine, black pine, grey pine, balsam fir and larch. This forest is an important source of lumber and wood pulp.

The deciduous forest is actually made up of coniferous and deciduous trees and covers the regions south of the St. Lawrence River, all the way to the U.S. border. Along with a variety of coniferous trees, this zone is rich in maple, birch, spruce and aspen.

Fauna

Québec's vast and varied wilderness boasts a richly diverse fauna. A multitude of animal species populates its immense forests, plains and arctic regions, while its seas, lakes and rivers are teeming with fish and aquatic animals. Please refer to the colour section on Québec's wildlife for more information.

History

By the time European settlers arrived in the New World, a mosaic of indigenous peoples had already been living on the continent for thousands of years. The ancestors of these people were nomads who began to cross the Bering Strait from northern Asia toward the end of the ice age, more than 12,000 years ago, and slowly populated the continent. Over the following millennia, as the glaciers receded, some of these groups began to settle in the northernmost parts of the continent, including the peninsula now known as Québec. A variety of native peoples belonging to three language groups (Algonquian, Iroquoian and Inuit) were thus sharing the territory when the Europeans first began to explore North America. Established societies with very diverse ways of life occupied this vast region. For example, native peoples occupying the valley of the St. Lawrence River lived primarily on fish, game and food they grew themselves, while communities farther north depended mostly on meat gathered during hunting expeditions. All, however, made ample use of the canoe as a means of travelling along the "paths that walk," and maintained very close trade relations with the neighbouring nations. These societies, which were well adapted to the rigours and distinctive features of the territory, were quickly marginalized with the onset of European colonization at the beginning of the 16th century.

Portrait - History

■ New France

During his first exploration of the mouth of the St. Lawrence and the shores of what is now Newfoundland, French explorer Jacques Cartier came into contact with fishermen from various parts of Europe. In fact, these waters were first explored by the Vikings sometime around the year 900, and were being visited regularly by European cod fishermen and whalers. However, Jacques Cartier's three voyages, which began in 1534, did represent an important step forward, as they established the first official contact between France and the peoples and territory of this part of North America. On these expeditions, the Breton navigator sailed far up the St. Lawrence to the villages of Stadacona (now Québec City) and Hochelaga (on the island of Montréal). However, since Cartier's mandate from the king of France had been to find gold or a passage to Asia, his discoveries were considered unimportant. For several decades after this "failure," the French crown forgot about this distant, inhospitable place.

French interest in North America was rekindled when fur coats and hats became increasingly fashionable and therefore profitable in Europe. The fur trade requiring a direct and constant link with local suppliers, a permanent presence in the New World was indispensable. Until the end of the 16th century, various unsuccessful attempts at setting up trading posts on the Atlantic coast and in the interior of the continent were made. Finally, in 1608, under the leadership of Samuel de Champlain, the first permanent outpost was set up. Champlain and his men chose a location at the foot of a large cliff overlooking a considerable narrowing of the St. Lawrence. The collection of fortified buildings they constructed was named the Abitation de Québec (*kebec* is an Algonquian word meaning "where the river narrows"). During that first harsh winter in Québec, 20 of the 28 men posted there died of scurvy or malnutrition before ships carrying fresh supplies arrived in the spring of 1609. When Samuel de Champlain died on Christmas Day, 1635, there were about 300 pioneers living in New France.

Between 1627 and 1663, the Compagnie des Cent Associés held a monopoly on the fur trade and ensured the slow growth of the colony. Meanwhile, French religious orders became more and more interested in New France. The Récollets arrived first, in 1615, and were then replaced by the Jesuits, who began arriving in 1632. Determined to convert the natives, the Jesuits settled deep in the interior of the continent, near the shores of Georgian Bay, where they founded the Sainte-Marie-des-Hurons mission. The Huron people, it can be assumed, put up with the presence of the Jesuits to maintain the trading arrangements they had established with the French. The mission was nevertheless abandoned after five Jesuits were killed during the Huron-Iroquois war of 1648-1649. This war was part of an extensive offensive campaign launched by the powerful Iroquois Five Nations between 1645 and 1655 that intended on wiping out all rival nations. The Huron, Pétun, Neutrals and Erie nations, each at least 10,000 strong, were almost completely annihilated within 10 years. The offensive also threatened the existence of the French colony. In 1660 and 1661, Iroquois warriors mounted strikes all over New France, destroying crops and bringing about a decline in the fur trade. Louis XIV, the king of France, decided to take the situation in hand. In 1663, he dissolved the Compagnie des Cent Associés and took on the responsibility of administering the colony himself, officially declaring New France, with its 3,000 settlers (or *habitants*), a French province.

Emigration to New France continued under the royal regime. Most people sent over were agricultural workers, though some also belonged to the military. In 1665, for example, the Carignan-Salières regiment was dispatched to the New World to fight the Iroquois. The Crown also took steps to encourage the natural growth of the population, which had theretofore been hindered by the lack of unmarried female immigrants. Between 1663 and 1673, 800 young women, known as the *filles du roi* ("king's daughters"), and each provided with a dowry, were sent to find husbands in the New World. This period of the history of New France was also the glorious era of the *coureurs des bois*, or "travellers of the woods". Abandoning their land for the fur trade, these intrepid young men travelled into the heart of the continent to deal directly with native trappers. The primary occupation of most colonists, however, remained farming.

The *Coureur des Bois*

The *coureur des bois* is a legendary figure in Québec culture. When the colony was first established, Champlain left a young man named Étienne Brûlé in this region. Brûlé learned the language of the Algonquins and travelled inland. In those days, men like him—who in some way illustrated the impact that the French had on the natives, be it positive or negative—were known as *truchements*.

Upon his return, Champlain found Brûlé dressed like the Aboriginals and completely adapted to their way of life. The *truchements* originally adopted the native lifestyle for economic reasons, as they did not want to offend their hosts and thus imperil the fur trade. However, as months went by, they came to appreciate the Aboriginals' daily routines, which were in direct response to the environment. They thus learned to eat corn, wear snowshoes and use bark canoes. They also started using toboggans to carry their cargo.

Removed from church and state as they were, however, these *truchements* did have a tendency to let themselves go altogether, and their unfettered freedom led to some rather dubious practices. This side of their life is clearly exemplified by Étienne Brûlé's death; he was killed and eaten by the Hurons, with whom he had lived over a long period.

Over time, the *truchements*' reputation improved, thanks in large part to the wisdom of a number of men who played a crucial role in the development of the new colony. The *truchements* came to be known as *coureurs des bois*. The two most illustrious figures of this new generation were Médard Chouart Des Groseillers and Pierre-Esprit Radisson. Thanks to their bravery and ingenuity, these men established ties with the Aboriginals. Radisson learned the ropes by being captured, tortured and then finally adopted by the Iroquois. He even joined them on an expedition, wielding a tomahawk and returning with scalps and prisoners in the purest Iroquois tradition.

Des Groseilliers and Radisson extended the fur-trading routes as far as lakes Michigan and Superior, where they set up trading posts. In 1654, however, the governor established a permit system for the fur trade, putting an end to their plans to push on past the Great Lakes, where the Aboriginals hunted. In 1661, Des Groseilliers and Radisson, unable to reach an agreement with the governor, ran off without an official permit. They returned two years later with a sizeable load of furs, having learned of a land route to Hudson Bay. They expected to be welcomed as pioneers, but instead found themselves faced with a fine. Refusing to hang their heads, the two proud men switched over to the English camp and helped found the Hudson's Bay Company, a move that revived the negative image of the *coureurs des bois*.

Be that as it may, the *truchements*-turned-*coureurs-des-bois* were still the first Europeans to adopt and begin to understand the traditional native way of life. They chose this lifestyle because it corresponded to the geographic, climatic, economic and social conditions of the New World. Their behaviour may not have always been exemplary but they nevertheless played a crucial role in Canada's development by serving as a link between the European and Aboriginal cultures.

Portrait - History

Society revolved around the seigneurial system. Land in New France was divided into seigneuries, which in turn were divided into *roture*s. The long narrow lots running perpendicular to the rivers (most notably the St. Lawrence) gave everyone access to the water. Serfs were expected to pay an annual sum to their seigneur and accomplish certain obligations for them. Since the territory was so vast and sparsely populated, however, colonists in New France enjoyed much higher profits once their debts were paid than their counterparts in France.

The territorial claims made by the French in North America increased rapidly during this era as a result of expeditions made by religious orders, *coureurs des bois* and explorers, to whom we owe the discovery of most of the North American continent. New France reached its peak at the beginning of the 18th century. At this time, it had a monopoly on the North American fur trade, control of the St. Lawrence and was beginning to develop Louisiana. New France was thus able to contain the expansion of the more populous British colonies located between the Atlantic and the Appalachians. But this changed following military defeat in Europe and the Treaty of Utrecht (1713), when France relinquished control of Hudson Bay, Newfoundland and Acadia to the British. France thereby lost a large stake in the fur trade, as well as certain strategic military locations, all of which severely weakened its position in North America and marked the beginning of the end of New France.

Over the following years, the stakes continued to mount. In 1755, British colonel Charles Lawrence took what he viewed as preventive measures and ordered the deportation of the Acadians, French-speaking settlers living in what is now Nova Scotia. At least 7,000 Acadians, who had been considered British citizens since 1713, were displaced as a result of this directive. In 1758, some 3,500 Acadians were also deported from Île Saint-Jean (present-day Prince Edward Island).

The fight for control of the colony came to an end several years later. Though Montréal was the last to fall in 1760, it was the infamous battle of the Plains of Abraham a year before, where Montcalm's and Wolfe's troops met, that sealed the fate of New France with the loss of Québec City. At the time of the British conquest, the population of the colony had risen to 60,000. Of this number, 8,967 lived in Québec City and 5,733 lived in Montréal.

■ British Rule

A result of the Treaty of Paris in 1763, French Canada, holdings east of the Mississippi and what remained of Acadia were officially ceded to England. For former subjects of the French crown, the first years under British rule were difficult ones. Territorial divisions dictated by the Royal Proclamation of 1763 denied the colony control of the fur trade, the most dynamic sector of its economy. In addition, the introduction of British civil law and the refusal to recognize the authority of the Pope put an end to both the seigneurial system and the Catholic hierarchy, the pillars on which French colonial society had been based. Finally, the Test Oath, required of anyone in a high-ranking administrative position, discriminated against French Canadians since it denied the transubstantiation of the Eucharist and the authority of the Pope. A large segment of the French elite returned to France, while English merchants gradually took control of most businesses.

England, however, soon agreed to do away with the Royal Proclamation. To better resist the push towards independence of its 13 colonies to the south, it sought to secure its place in Canada by gaining the favour of the population. In 1774, the Québec Act replaced the Royal Proclamation, introducing policies that were much more appropriate to a French Catholic colony. Important powers were given to the Catholic church, which they managed to hold onto until 1963.

The Canadian population remained mostly of French origin until the end of the American Revolution, when Canada experienced the arrival of a first big wave of Anglo-Saxon colonists. The new arrivals were Loyalists, Americans wishing to remain faithful to the British crown. Most moved to the Maritimes (formerly Acadia) and around Lake Ontario, but some also settled in regions strictly inhabited by Francophones. With the arrival of these new colonists, British authorities passed the Constitution Act of 1791, dividing Canada into two provinces. Upper Canada, situated west of the Ottawa River and mainly populated by Anglophones, would be governed by British civil law. Lower Canada, which was mostly francophone, would be governed according to the French tradition of common law. In addition, the Act planted the seeds of a parliamentary system in Canada by creating a Legislative Assembly in each province.

Meanwhile, Napoleon's Continental System forced Britain to get its lumber from Canada. From an economic standpoint, this was good for the colony. The development of a new industry was especially timely, as the fur trade, the original reason for the colony's existence, was in steady decline. In 1821, the takeover of the Montréal-based Northwest Company by the Hudson's Bay Company marked the end of Montréal as the centre of the North American fur trade. Meanwhile, rural Québec suffered an agricultural crisis caused by the exhaustion of farmlands and a rapid population growth resulting from high birth rates among French-Canadian families, whose diet during the crisis consisted almost entirely of pea soup and buckwheat pancakes.

These economic difficulties and the struggle for power between Francophones and Anglophones in Lower Canada combined to spark the *Patriotes* rebellion of 1837 and 1838. The period of political conflict that fuelled the rebellion was initiated by the 1834 publication of the *Quatre-Vingt-Douze Résolutions* (92 Resolutions), a scathing indictment of British colonial policy. Its authors, a group of parliamentarians led by Louis-Joseph Papineau, decided to hold back from voting on the budget until Britain addressed their demands. Britain's response came in 1837 in the form of the *10 Resolutions*, written by Lord Russell, which categorically refused any compromise with their opponents in Lower Canada. In the fall of 1837, Montréal was the scene of violent clashes between the *Fils de la Liberté* (Sons of Liberty), made up of young French Canadians, and the Doric Club, comprised of Loyalists. Further confrontations occurred in the Richelieu valley region and in the county of Deux-Montagnes, where small insurgent groups stood up to the British army before being crushed.

The following year, in an attempt to rekindle the rebellion, a group of *Patriotes* met with the same fate in Napierville, where they confronted 7,000 British troops. This time, however, colonial authorities sent a strong message to prospective rebels. In 1839, they hanged 12 *Patriotes* and deported many others.

When hostilities first broke out, London sent an emissary, Lord Durham, to study the problems in the colonies. Expecting to find a population rebelling against colonial authority, Durham found instead two peoples, one French and one British, in battle. The solution he later proposed in his report, known as the Durham Report, was radical. He suggested to authorities in Britain that gradual efforts be made to assimilate French Canadians.

The Union Act, laid down by the British government in 1840, was largely based on the conclusions of the Durham Report. A new parliamentary system was introduced, giving the two former colonies the same number of delegates, despite the fact that Lower Canada had a much larger population than Upper Canada. Financial responsibilities were also divided equally between the provinces, and English was made the sole official language. Since armed insurrection had proven futile in the past, French Canada's political class sought to align itself with progressive Anglophones in an attempt to resist these changes. Later, the struggle for responsible government became the central goal of this coalition.

Furthermore, the agricultural crisis remained as severe as ever in Lower Canada. Intensified by the constant arrival of immigrants and by the high birth rate, the situation resulted in a massive emigration of French Canadians to the United States. Between 1840 and 1850, 40,000 French Canadians left the country to seek employment in the factories of New England. To counteract this exodus, the Catholic Church and the government launched an extensive campaign to colonize outlying regions, such as Lac Saint-Jean. The harsh life in these newly settled regions, where colonists worked as farmers in the summer and lumberjacks in the winter, is poignantly depicted in Louis Hémon's novel *Maria Chapdelaine*. Nevertheless, the mass exodus from Québec did not stop until the beginning of the next century. It is estimated that about 750,000 French Canadians left the province between 1840 and 1930. From this point of view, the colonization campaign, which doubled the amount of farmland in Lower Canada, was a failure. The swelling population of rural

Québec was not effectively absorbed until several decades later, with the start of industrialization.

The Canadian economy received a serious blow during this era when Britain abandoned its policy of mercantilism and preferential tariffs for its colonies. To cushion the effects of this change in British policy, United Canada signed a treaty in 1854, making it possible for certain goods to enter the United States without import duties. Canada's economy began to recover slightly but the treaty was revoked in 1866, under pressure from U.S. industrialists. Resolving these economic difficulties was the impetus behind Canadian Confederation in 1867.

■ Confederation

Under Canadian Confederation, Lower Canada became the Province of Québec. Three other provinces, Nova Scotia, New Brunswick and Ontario (formerly Upper Canada) joined the Confederation, which would eventually unite a vast territory stretching from the Atlantic to the Pacific oceans. For French Canadians, this new political system reinforced their minority status, which began with the Union Act of 1840. The creation of two levels of government did, however, grant Québec jurisdiction over education, culture and civil law.

Confederation was slow to bring about positive economic change. The economy fluctuated for three decades before experiencing a real boom. The first years after Confederation did, however, see the development of local industry (thanks to the implementation of protective tariffs), the creation of a large, unified market and the development of the railway system across the territory. The industrial revolution that had begun in the mid-19th century picked up again in the 1880s. While Montréal remained the undisputed centre of this movement, it was felt in many smaller towns.

The lumber industry, which had been one of the mainsprings of the economy during the 19th century, began exporting more cut wood than raw lumber, giving rise to a processing industry. Montréal was also the hub of the expanding railroad, leading the city to specialize in the production of rolling stock. The leather goods, clothing and food industries also enjoyed significant growth in Québec. In addition, this period of growth was marked by the emergence of the brand-new textile industry, which would remain Québec's flagship industry for many years. Benefitting from a huge pool of unskilled labour, the textile industry initially employed mostly women and children.

This wave of industrialization accelerated the pace of urbanization and created a large, poor working class clustered near the factories. Montréal's working-class neighbourhoods were terribly unhealthy; infant mortality in these areas was twice that of wealthy neighbourhoods.

As Québec's cities were going through tremendous changes, the situation in rural areas finally began to improve. Dairy production gradually replaced subsistence farming, contributing to an improved standard of living among farmers.

In 1885, the tragic hanging of Louis Riel once again highlighted the opposition between Canada's two language groups. Having led Métis and aboriginal rebels in the western part of the country, Riel, a French-speaking, Catholic Métis (a semi-nomadic group descended from French traders and Aboriginals) was found guilty of high treason and sentenced to death. French-Canadian public opinion was strongly in favour of a commuted sentence, while Anglophones took the opposite view. The federal government, under John A. Macdonald, ultimately went ahead with the execution, and the reaction was quick and angry among the people of Québec.

Important Dates in Québec's History

Over 12,000 years ago: Nomads from Northern Asia begin to cross the Bering Strait and gradually populate the Americas. With the melting of the glaciers, some of them settle on the peninsula now known as Québec; these are the ancestors of the Aboriginal people.

1534: Jacques Cartier, a navigator from Saint-Malo in Brittany, France, makes the first of three explorations of the Gulf and St. Lawrence River. These were the first official French expeditions to this territory.

1608: Samuel de Champlain and his men found Québec City, marking the beginning of a permanent French presence in North America.

1663: New France officially becomes a French province. Colonization continues.

1759: Québec City falls to British forces. Four years later, the King of France officially relinquishes all of New France, which now has a population of about 60,000 colonists of French origin.

1837-1838: The British army suppresses the Patriotes rebellion.

1840: Following the Durham Report, the Union Act seeks to create an English majority and eventually assimilate French Canadians.

1867: The Canadian Confederation is born. Four provinces, including Québec, sign the agreement. Six others eventually follow suit.

■ The Golden Age of Economic Liberalism

In the early 20th century, a period of prodigious economic growth in Québec started and lasted until the Great Depression of the 1930s. Sharing the optimism and euphoria of Canadians, Prime Minister Wilfrid Laurier predicted that the 20th century would be Canada's century.

Québec manufacturers profited during this period of growth. Thanks to new technologies and markets, the province's abundance of natural resources became the principal catalyst of this second wave of industrialization. Central to the new era was the production of electric power. With its numerous powerful rivers, Québec became a major producer of hydroelectric power in a matter of years. The resulting availability of affordable energy attracted industries with large electricity needs. Aluminum smelters and chemical plants were constructed in the vicinity of hydroelectric power stations, and the mining industry also began to enjoy modest growth during this period with the development of asbestos mines in the Eastern Townships and copper, gold, zinc and silver mines in Abitibi. Above all, Québec's pulp and paper industry found huge markets in the United States due to the depletion of U.S. forests and the rise of the popular press. To promote the development of processing industries in Québec, the exportation of logs was forbidden by the provincial government in 1910.

This new period of industrialization differed from the first one in several ways. Taking place largely outside the major cities, it led to an increase in urban growth in outlying regions. In some cases, cities sprang up within few years. Unlike the manufacturing industries, the exploitation of natural resources required more qualified workers and a level of financing far beyond local means. Britain's stake in the economy, which until now had been the largest, gave way to the triumphant rise of U.S. capitalism.

Despite rapid changes in Québec society (by 1921, half the population was living in urban centres), the church was still highly influential. With 85% of the overall population, including virtually all French Canadians, as members, the Catholic Church was a major political force in the province. Because of the control it wielded over education, health care and social services, its authority was inescapable. The Catholic Church, moreover, did not hesitate to intervene in the political arena, often confronting politicians it considered too liberal.

When World War I began, the Canadian government gave its full support to Britain without hesitation. A significant number of French Canadians voluntarily enrolled in the army, although the percentage of volunteers per capita was far lower than in other provinces. This lack of enthusiasm could undoubtedly be attrib-

1914-1918: Canada participates in World War I. Anglophones and Francophones disagree about conscription. Canada comes out of the conflict very divided.

1929-1939: The stock market crash and Great Depression hit Québec hard. In 1933, unemployment reaches 27%.

1939-1945: Canada participates in World War II. Once again, Anglophones and Francophones are divided on the issue of conscription.

1944-1959: Premier Maurice Duplessis leads Québec with a strong hand. This period is known as the "*grande noirceur*," or "great darkness."

1960: The Liberal Party is elected, marking the beginning of the *Révolution tranquille*, or Quiet Revolution.

October 1970: A small terrorist group, the Front de Libération du Québec (FLQ), kidnaps a British diplomat and a Québec cabinet minister, igniting a serious political crisis.

November 1976: The Parti Québécois, a party favouring independence for Québec, wins the provincial election.

May 1980: A majority of Québec's population votes against holding negotiations aimed at Québec independence.

1982: The Canadian Constitution is repatriated without Québec's consent.

June 1990: The failure of the Meech Lake Accord on the Canadian Constitution is poorly accepted in Québec. Following this, opinion polls show that a majority of Quebecers are in favour of Québec sovereignty.

October 22, 1992: The federal government and the provin-

uted both to Québec's long-severed ties with France and, more importantly, to Francophones' somewhat ambivalent feelings toward Britain. Canada soon set a goal of inducting 500,000 men. Since there were not enough volunteers, the government voted, in 1917, to introduce conscription. Reaction to this in Québec was violent and marked by fights, bombings and riots. In the end, conscription failed to appreciably increase the number of French-Canadian recruits. Instead, it simply underlined once again the ongoing friction between English and French Canada.

■ The Great Depression

Between 1929 and 1945, two international-scale events, the Depression and World War II, greatly disrupted the country's political, economic and social progress. The Great Depression of the 1930s, originally viewed as a cyclical, temporary crisis, lengthened into a decade-long nightmare and put an end to Québec's rapid economic expansion. With Canada strongly dependent on foreign markets, the country as a whole was hit hard by the international stock market crash.

Québec was unevenly affected. With its economy based to a large extent on exports, Montréal, along with towns dependent on the development of natural resources, suffered the hardest blow. The textile and food industries, which sold to the Canadian market, held up better during the first years of the Depression, before foundering as well. The trend towards urbanization slowed as people began to view the countryside as a refuge where they could grow their own food. Poverty became more and more widespread, and unemployment levels reached 27% in 1933.

Governments were at a loss in the face of this crisis, which they had expected to be short-lived. The Québec government started introducing massive public works projects to provide jobs for the unemployed. As this proved insufficient, more direct help was gradually given. Very timidly put forward at first, since unemployment had always been considered a personal problem, these measures later helped many Quebecers. The federal government was also compelled to question the merits of economic liberalism and to redefine the role of the state. Part of this trend included establishing the Bank of Canada in 1935, which permitted greater control over the monetary and financial system. However, it was not until the ensuing war years that a full-scale welfare state was created. In the meantime, the crisis led to the proliferation of political ideologies in Québec. The most popular of these, traditional nationalism, put great emphasis on values such as rural life, family, religion and language.

ces organize a referendum on new constitutional offers. Considered unacceptable, these are rejected by a majority of Quebecers and Canadians.

October 30, 1995: The Parti Québécois government holds a referendum on Québec sovereignty: 49.4% of Quebecers vote "yes" to sovereignty and 50.6% vote "no."

■ World War II

World War II began in 1939, and Canada became officially involved on September 10th of that year. The Canadian economy received a much-needed boost as industry set out to modernize the country's military equipment and to meet the requirements of the Allies. Canada's close ties to Great Britain and the United States gave it an important diplomatic role, as indicated by the conferences held in Québec in 1943 and 1944.

Early in the war, however, the problem of conscription surfaced again. While the federal government wanted to avoid the issue, mounting pressure from the country's Anglophones forced a plebiscite on the question. The results once again showed the division between Francophones and Anglophones: 80% of English Canadians voted in favour of conscription, while the same percentage of French Canadians were opposed to the idea. Mixed feelings toward Britain and France left French Canadians very reluctant to become involved in the fighting. However, they were forced to follow the will of the majority, and in the end, 600,000 Canadians were recruited, 42,000 of whom died in action.

Québec was profoundly changed by the war. Its economy became much stronger and more diversified than before. As far as relations between Ottawa and Québec City were concerned, the federal government's massive intervention during the war marked the beginning of its increased role in the economy and of the relative marginalization of provincial governments. In addition, the contact thousands of Quebecers had with European life and the jobs women held in the factories modified people's expectations. The winds of change were blowing, but they were to face a serious obstacle: Premier Maurice Duplessis and his political allies.

■ 1945-1960: The Duplessis Era

The end of World War II signalled a period of considerable economic growth during which consumer demands, repressed by the economic crisis and wartime rationing, could finally be satisfied. Despite a few fluctuations, the economy performed spectacularly until 1957. However, this prosperity affected Québec's various social and ethnic groups unequally. Many workers, particularly non-unionized ones, continued to receive relatively low wages. Furthermore, the anglophone minority in Québec still enjoyed a far superior standard of living than the francophone majority. Indeed, a francophone employee with the same skills and experience as an anglophone employee was usually paid less. With an economy largely controlled by English Canadians and Americans, French Canadians were held back. To some degree, Francophones lived as second-class citizens in their own province.

Be that as it may, the economic growth encouraged a stable political environment, such that the leader of the Union Nationale Party, Maurice Duplessis, remained in power as Premier of Québec from 1944 until he died in 1959. Duplessis's influence characterized this era, often referred to as *la grande noirceur*, or the great darkness. The Duplessis ideology was based on a sometimes paradoxical amalgam of traditional nationalism, conservatism and unbridled capitalism. He professed a respect for rural life, religion and authority, while at the same time provided major foreign business interests with highly favourable opportunities to exploit Québec's natural resources. In his mind, a cheap work force was one of those resources and it had to be preserved. To this end, he fought fiercely against unionization, not hesitating to use intimidation tactics when he felt it necessary. Those years were marked by many strikes but it was the asbestos strike of 1949 that most influenced the collective conscience.

Portrait - History

While Maurice Duplessis was the dominant personality of this period, his rule could only have been sustained by the tacit collaboration of much of the traditional and business elite, both francophone and anglophone. The church, seemingly at the height of its glory during these years, felt its authority weakening, prompting it to support the Duplessis government in full measure.

Despite Duplessis's iron hand, opposing voices nonetheless emerged. The Liberal Party of Québec had difficulty getting organized, so opposition came mainly from outside the parliamentary structure. Artists and writers made their anger known by publishing the *Refus Global*, a bitter attack on the repressive atmosphere in Québec. The most organized opposition came from union leaders, journalists and the intellectual community. All of these groups wanted modernization for Québec and endorsed the same neo-liberalist economic credo favouring a strong welfare system. However, from quite early on, two different camps developed among these reformists. Certain individuals, such as Gérard Pelletier and Pierre Trudeau, believed modernization would come from a strong federal government, while neo-nationalists like André Laurendeau wanted change through a more powerful provincial government. The two groups, which quickly overshadowed traditionalism during the Quiet Revolution, would remain at odds with each other throughout modern Québec history.

■ The Quiet Revolution

In 1960, the Liberal Party under Jean Lesage was elected on a platform of change and stayed in power until 1966. This period, referred to as the Révolution tranquille, or Quiet Revolution, was indeed marked by a veritable race for modernism.

Over the course of just a few years, Québec caught up to the modern world. Control of education, health care and social services meant the provincial government played a bigger role in society. The church, stripped of its main spheres of influence, lost its authority and eventually its following, as dissatisfied Québec Catholics strayed from the church.

State control of the production of hydroelectricity increased the provincial government's interests in the economy. Powerful economic resources finally allowed the government to establish itself, and French Canadians in general, in the business world. The great vitality brought to Québec society during the Quiet Revolution was symbolized by two events of international scope that took place in Montréal: Expo '67 and the 1976 Olympics.

The lively nature of Québec society in the 1960s engendered a number of new ideological movements, particularly on the left. The extreme was the Front de Libération du Québec (FLQ), a small group of radicals who wanted to "decolonize" Québec and who launched a series of terrorist strikes in Montréal. In October 1970, the FLQ abducted James Cross, a British diplomat, and Pierre Laporte, a Québec cabinet minister. The Canadian Prime Minister at the time, Pierre Elliot Trudeau, fearing a political uprising, called for the War Measures Act to be enforced. The Canadian army took to the streets of Montréal, thousands of searches were carried out and hundreds of innocent people were temporarily imprisoned. Shortly afterward, Pierre Laporte was found dead. The crisis finally ended when James Cross's kidnappers agreed to let him go in exchange for their safe conduct to Cuba. During this entire crisis, and long afterwards, Trudeau was severely criticized for invoking the War Measures Act. Some accused him of having done so mainly to quash the growing Québec independence movement.

The most significant political phenomenon in Québec between 1960 and 1980 was the rapid rise of moderate nationalism. Breaking with the traditionalism of the past, this new vision of nationalism championed a strong, open and modern Québec with increased powers for the provincial government, and, ultimately, political independence for the province.

Portrait - History

The nationalist forces rallied around René Lévesque, founder of the Mouvement Souveraineté-Association and then, in 1968, the Parti Québécois. After two elections, which saw only a handful of its representatives elected to Parliament, a stunning 1976 victory brought the Parti Québécois to power. Right away, in 1977, the new government voted in Bill 101, which made French the sole official language in Québec. In response, many Anglophones left the province, mainly for Ontario.

With a mandate to negotiate sovereignty for Québec, the party called a referendum in 1980. From the beginning, the referendum campaign revived the division between Québec sovereigntists and federalists. The struggle was intense and mobilized the entire population right up until the vote. Finally, after a campaign based on promises of a new style of federalism, the "No" (No to Sovereignty Association) side won with 60% of the vote. Despite this loss, sovereigntists were consoled by how far their cause had come in only a few years. From a marginal trend in the 1960s, nationalism quickly proved itself to be a major political movement. The night of the defeat, Parti Québécois leader René Lévesque, charisma intact, vowed to his supporters that victory would be their's "next time."

■ Since 1980: Breaks and Continuity

The independence movement and desire for self-determination amongst Quebecers, brought about by the Quiet Revolution, suffered a great setback with the loss of the referendum on sovereignty. For many, the 1980s began with a post-referendum depression, accentuated by a period of economic crisis in Canada that had been unseen since the 1930s. As the economy improved slightly over time, the unemployment rate remained very high and government spending resulted in a massive deficit. Like many other Western governments, Québec had to reassess the policies of the past, though some feared that the new chosen direction would sacrifice the achievements of the Quiet Revolution.

The 1980s and early 1990s were a time of streamlining and saw the creation of global markets and the consolidation of large economic blocks. Canada and the United States signed the Free-Trade Agreement in 1989. The 1994 North American Free Trade Agreement (NAFTA) brought Mexico into this market, creating the largest tariff-free market in the world.

From a political standpoint, the question of Québec's political status surfaced again. In the early 1990s, the sovereigntist movement regained surprising momentum, spurred along by Quebecers' resentment at the failure in June 1990 of the Meech Lake Accord, an agreement aimed at reintegrating Québec into the "constitutional family" by giving it special status. The governing bodies involved, in an attempt to resolve this impasse, called for a Canada-wide referendum on a new constitutional offer, held on October 26, 1992. The offer was flatly rejected everywhere in Canada, but for differing reasons. The federal election of October 25, 1993, saw the sovereigntist Bloc Québécois win two thirds of the ridings in Québec and form the official opposition in the Canadian Parliament. The next year, the Parti Québecois was elected in Québec; high on its agenda was the holding of a referendum on the sovereignty of Québec.

Less than one year after its election, the Parti Québecois launched a referendum campaign, as promised, for the sovereignty of Québec. As with the first referendum held 15 years earlier, the Québec population was very divided on the issue. This time, however, the results were unbelievably close. The suspense lasted right until the last ballot was counted on referendum night, October 30, 1995. The results told of a population divided: 49.4% of Quebecers voted "yes" to Québec sovereignty and 50.6% voted "no." The profound question of Québec's political status thus remained unresolved following this referendum, which in effect only served to underline the division within the population. In recent years, opinion polls have indicated that Quebecers are more interested in discussing other matters of public policy, such as the economy and the environment, yet the "national question" will likely remain an issue in Québec politics for quite a while.

Portrait · History

Municipal Mergers

In 2001, the Québec government passed a law requiring many of Québec's municipalities to merge with their neighbours in order to create larger regional entities. On January 1, 2002, several towns and villages lost their official name and became part of a bigger city. However, on June 20, 2004, Québec's then-new Liberal government allowed for a referendum to be held in those cities that wished to reverse the mergers. The "new" city of Montréal, for example, which included all of the communities on the island, was re-divided. Of the 27 boroughs that made up the city at the time of the referendums, only a dozen or so chose to remain part of Montréal; most of the boroughs that chose to regain their independence were located in the rich, English-speaking West Island area. In Québec City, most of the cities that were part of the Communauté urbaine de Québec opted against the "de-merger" and remain part of the city. The mergers involved plenty of hiccups, and the process is far from being complete. This is why we have decided, for the time being, not to modify most town names in this guide. In most towns that must be renamed, the choice of a new name is much cause for debate, and we believe that it is still too soon to use place names that will actually take years to be adopted. Nevertheless, you will have no trouble finding your way around the province of Québec.

Politics

The British North America Act is the constitutional document on which Canadian Confederation is based. It creates a division of powers between the levels of government. In addition to a central government based in Ottawa, each of the 10 Canadian provinces has a government with the power to legislate in certain domains. The constitutional conflict between Québec and the Canadian government is largely a product of disagreements over precisely how these powers should be divided.

Based on the British model, Canada's and Québec's political systems give legislative power to a parliament elected by universal suffrage. In Québec, the Parliament is called the Assemblée nationale. It has 125 seats, each representing a riding in the province. In Ottawa, power belongs to the House of Commons, with members from regions across the country. The federal government also has an Upper Chamber, the Senate. This institution has gradually had all its real power reduced and its future is now unclear.

In an election, the party with the most elected representatives forms the government. These elections are held about every four years and function according to the single-ballot majority system. This kind of system generally leaves room for only two major political parties. It also, however, has the advantage of ensuring great stability between each election, while making it possible to identify each member of Parliament with a particular riding.

■ Federal Politics

At the federal level, two parties, the Liberal Party and the Conservative Party, have each governed the country at various times since Confederation in 1867. Quebecers and French-speaking Canadians in general have, until recently, strongly supported the Liberal Party. The first three French-speaking Prime Ministers of Canada, for example, represented this party.

The Conservative Party, long associated with British imperialism and the implementation of conscription in 1917, has traditionally made little room for Francophones. Recently, however, the Conservative Party has shown signs of greater openness. In 1984, the party was voted into power in a federal election and retained that power in the next election in 1988, with tremendous support from Québec. It was, however, defeated by the Liberal Party in the election of October 25, 1993, which placed Jean Chrétien at the head of the Canadian government.

This election led to a spectacular rearrangement of Canada's political map and signalled the rise of two new federal political parties: the Reform Party and the Bloc Québécois. The Reform Party, a populist right-wing party, elected 52 Members of Parliament, almost exclusively from Western Canada. The Bloc Québécois won 54 seats, or more than two thirds of the seats in Québec. Born out of the Meech Lake fiasco, the Bloc Québécois's goal is to promote Québec sovereignty at the federal level.

The results of the 1993 federal election were confirmed during the spring of 1997 election. The Liberal Party was re-elected, though with a smaller majority despite massive support from Ontario, the most populous Canadian province. The Reform Party was once again the big winner in the West, claiming even more seats than in the previous election and ousting the Bloc Québécois from official opposition status.

During the November 2000 elections, the Reform Party was replaced by the Canadian Alliance, which became the Liberal government's official opposition. The Liberal Party once again claimed a landslide victory over the other parties, with the Bloc Québécois losing several seats in Parliament. Jean Chrétien was thus elected Prime Minister of Canada for a third consecutive term.

In 2003, the Canadian Alliance united with the Conservative Party of Canada (CPC). This new federal party chose the keep the name of the CPC, much to the displeasure of several Alliance and Conservative strong liners. Stephen Harper is at the head of this new party. Also in 2003, Jean Chrétien resigned from his post as Prime Minister, clearing the way for Paul Martin as chief of the Liberal Party of Canada.

The Liberal Party's mandate was renewed during the June 2004 elections, but this time as a minority government, with the CPC finishing second and the Bloc Québécois taking back some of the headway it had gained in 1993. The Liberal Party was now standing on shaky ground, especially following a widely publicized scandal that revolved around federal sponsorship funds being diverted back into the Liberal Party's coffers during the 1995 referendum on Québec sovereignty, and the subsequent Gomery Commission inquiry into the affair. The scandal led to the opposing parties tabling a non-confidence motion in the House of Commons on November 28, 2005. The minority parliament was thus dissolved the next day and federal elections were set for January 23, 2006. The head of Canada's current minority Conservative government is Prime Minister Stephen Harper.

■ Provincial Politics

In 2001, Bernard Landry, the head of the Parti Québécois (PQ), replaced Lucien Bouchard as Prime Minister of Québec. Bouchard had held the post from 1996 to 2001, succeeding Jacques Parizeau who had been elected in 1994.

The April 2003 provincial elections brought the Québec Liberal Party to power, making Jean Charest the new Prime Minister. Parti Québécois head Bernard Landry became the official leader of the opposition, but he resigned from his post in 2005 and was replaced by André Boisclair, following a tight leadership race within the party.

The PQ, a relatively young party, previously led the provincial government from 1976 to 1985, with the charismatic René Lévesque as its leader. The Liberal victory promises to change the playing field when it comes to the major source of disagreement between the two parties: the political status of Québec. Since it was founded, the PQ has pursued the objective of gaining political sovereignty for Québec. The Liberal Party, on the other hand, has sought more power for the provincial government, though it remains loyal to the Canadian federalist system.

A third party, the Action démocratique du Québec (ADQ), led by Mario Dumont, is now on the scene. Despite some major victories in a 2002 bi-election, its performance in the 2003 election was less impressive.

■ Federal-Provincial Relations

Over the course of the last 40 years, federal-provincial relations and the conflicts between federalists and Québec sovereigntists have dominated politics in Canada. This ongoing dispute continues to fuel public debate. Since the Quiet Revolution, successive Québec governments have all considered themselves representatives of a distinct society, demanding special status for Québec and greater independence from the federal government. Faced with the prospect of Québec autonomy, the federal government has resisted vigorously, arguing that there is only one Canada and that Québec is a province like the others. During this same 30-year period, the federal government was attempting to repatriate the Canadian constitution in London, a task that required the support of the provinces. While Québec did not oppose the repatriation of the constitution, it decided that such a development could be an opportunity to bring about a major revision of its place in the country and an increase of its powers. However, the province's demands were never met by the federal government, and Québec, long supported by other provinces, responded by blocking the repatriation of the Constitution at the federal-provincial conferences of 1964 and 1971.

■ The 1980 Referendum

The stakes became much higher when the Parti Québécois took power in 1976. This party, whose reason for being was the creation of a sovereign Québec, worried the federal government and Québec's federalist forces. In 1980, the PQ decided to hold a referendum on sovereignty, asking Quebecers to give the party a mandate to negotiate a sovereignty-association with the rest of the country. The referendum campaign that followed was a showdown between federalist forces, represented by the Liberal Party of Québec and the Canadian government, and sovereigntist forces, represented by the Parti Québécois.

This clash of the two main views that had defined the contemporary political scene in Québec also took on the appearance of a fight to the finish between two men: Pierre Elliot Trudeau and René Lévesque. After a long battle, marked by a good deal of demagoguery, the campaign concluded on May 20, 1980, with 60% of Quebecers voting against the negotiation of sovereignty-association. Taking into account the anglophone vote, the results showed that the francophone population was about evenly split on the issue. The vote came as a serious jolt to those who had dreamed of an independent state with a francophone majority in North America. On referendum day 1980, a majority of Quebecers decided to give federalism another chance and placed their future in Pierre Elliot Trudeau's hands. Trudeau, without being very specific about what he meant, promised that voting No in the referendum meant voting Yes to a new Canada.

Quebecers were quick to discover, however, that Trudeau's new federalism did not address their province's traditional demands. In November 1981, Trudeau called a federal-provincial conference with the goal of repatriating the Constitution. Québec, with the support of certain other provinces, intended to block the federal project, but a spectacular turnaround occurred in a late-night meeting to which Québec was not invited. Following this event, which became known as the "night of the long knives," the federal government imposed a new constitutional pact on Québec in 1982, knowing full well that the Québec

National Assembly was fiercely opposed to signing it. Not only were Québec's language laws placed in jeopardy and provincial powers not increased, but the new constitutional pact also removed the Québec government's veto right on all constitutional amendments. Having won the referendum victory, the federalists thus attempted to silence Québec's separatist impulses once and for all.

■ From Meech Lake to Charlottetown

After a break of several years, the constitutional saga entered a new and tumultuous era with the elections of Brian Mulroney in Ottawa (1984) and the Liberal Party led by Robert Bourassa in Québec (1985). Bringing Québec back into the constitutional fold with "honour and enthusiasm" became a priority for the new Canadian Prime Minister. In 1987, the federal government and the 10 provinces drew up an agreement, known as the Meech Lake Accord, which called for constitutional changes in response to a minimum of Québec's traditional demands. To become official, the Accord had to be ratified by the Legislative Assemblies of the 10 provinces before June 24, 1990. This seemed simple enough. However, the situation turned into a monumental fiasco when certain provincial premiers were elected out of office and replaced by opponents of the deal, when the Premier of Newfoundland changed his mind on the matter, and when public opinion in English Canada turned against the agreement, considered too advantageous to Québec. After a number of hopeless attempts to save it, what was to have been a "great national reconciliation" ended in resounding failure. In an attempt to avert a major swing towards sovereignty, Premier Bourassa resolved to present the federal government with an ultimatum. He announced that a referendum would be held before October 26, 1992, either on an acceptable federalist offer or on the proposition of sovereignty for Québec. Until the last moment, Robert Bourassa truly believed the other provinces and the federal government would produce, for the first time in the recent history of the country, an agreement responding to the demands of a majority of Quebecers. However, as the referendum date came near and it became clear that this was not going to happen, he put aside his threats and once again entered into negotiations with the other provinces and the federal government.

A general agreement, the Charlottetown Accord, was thrown together in a few days. This was presented not only as a response to Québec's aspirations, but also to those of the other Canadian provinces and Canada's aboriginal peoples. To be ratified, however, this agreement had to be accepted by a majority of the population of each province. October 26, 1992, the date originally set for a provincial referendum on Québec's future, was kept as the date for this Canada-wide referendum.

Bourassa promised to succeed in "selling" the package to the people of Québec. However, from the beginning, a majority of Quebecers were fiercely opposed to the deal and Bourassa even lost the support of certain militants within his own party. The rejection of the agreement by Quebecers was therefore no surprise. It was rejected by a number of other provinces as well, though for completely opposite reasons. The matter of Québec's political status thus remained unresolved.

■ The 1995 Referendum

Tired of the endless discussions throughout Canada on the Québec issue, Quebecers were anxious for the situation to be resolved. The opportunity presented itself in the shape of the 1993 federal election. With the election of the Bloc Québécois as official opposition in the Canadian Parliament, sovereignist Quebecers could now show their support for Québec sovereignty at the federal level. In the beginning, the Bloc only expected a small showing, enough to make the sovereigntist case in Ottawa, the federal capital, but what occurred was a veritable landslide in Québec. The party won two thirds of the province's ridings and became the official opposition in Ottawa.

The following year, the Québec population was called upon to elect a new provincial government, and it chose the Parti Québecois, the principal proponent of Québec sovereignty for the last quarter of the 20th century. And so, with a strong sovereignist force in the Canadian Parliament and the Parti Québecois at the head of the Québec government, Quebecers would once again be given a choice between sovereignty and Canadian federalism.

After a few months a referendum was set for October 30, 1995. Fifteen years after the 1980 referendum, federalists and sovereigntists once again found themselves engaged in the campaign of their lives, one whose outcome would determine the nature of Québec's political status. From the start of the campaign, both sides realized that the population was divided. No one could have predicted such a close race, however. The night of the referendum, every single ballot had to be counted before the results became known: 50.6% of Quebecers voted "no" to sovereignty while 49.4% voted "yes." A mere 28,000 votes separated the two options; Québec was literally split right down the middle. Although the leaders of the sovereignty movement announced on the night of the vote that another referendum would be called very soon, the movement seems to have lost its momentum and the recent victory of the Liberals, for whom sovereignty is not a goal, precludes the possibility of another referendum in the immediate future.

The Economy

Long avoided by a majority of Francophones, the world of business now occupies a particularly important place within Québec society. Since the 1960s, it has become a vehicle through which Francophones have sought to take control of their own destiny, something that represents a significant social change.

Until the Quiet Revolution, French-speaking students usually studied law or medicine, or joined the clergy. The business world, seen as shallow and controlled by Anglophones, seemed largely inaccessible. But Francophones' attitudes have changed drastically in the last 40 years: indifference has given way to a clear desire for direct involvement in Québec's economy.

Today, a large proportion of students in the province study business administration. In fact, Québec is now turning out more graduates in this field than any other province. Media attention on the success of Québec entrepreneurs has helped to fuel this trend. Increased business activity among Francophones has overshadowed Anglo-Canadian and U.S. interests in the province, and over the last few years, there has been a reduction in the foreign presence, particularly from the United States, in Québec's economy. This is explained by many factors, including a climate of political uncertainty, the energy of local entrepreneurs, federal laws controlling investments by outsiders and the decline in certain sectors controlled by U.S. investors.

■ The Government's Role

As in many Western countries, government influence over business has been reduced over the past few decades. Despite this trend, the government remains in many ways an important player in the development of the economy. In fact, it is now the largest employer in Québec, boasting many highly qualified management-level employees, as well as being active in stimulating the economy.

The expansion of Hydro-Québec is a good example of the Québec government's successful intervention in business. From the time of Premier Jean Lesage, Hydro-Québec has had an almost exclusive monopoly on the production and distribution of hydroelectricity in Québec. This vital public enterprise, through the great sweep of its activities, has propelled the success of many private businesses in Québec. Certain engineering firms also owe their growth, in Québec and beyond, to experience gained through participation in the construction of Hydro-Québec's immense hydroelectric projects.

Over the last few decades, the Québec government has also had at its disposal a number of powerful investment tools for economic development, the most famous being the Caisse de Dépôt et de Placement. This institution, which manages capital from the retirement funds of a huge number of Québec workers, has become a financial giant. While making only modest investments in its first few years, the Caisse de Dépôt et de Placement began to provide massive support for Québec businesses after the Parti Québécois came to power in 1976.

Today, the CDPQ has one of the biggest stock portfolios in Canada. Presently, there is a concern that too much public intervention can be bad for an economy, but in a small economy like Québec's, the need for strong state involvement is generally agreed on.

■ Québec's Economic Future

Québec's economy is going through a period of great change, largely resulting from a move away from industrialization, as is seen in many Western countries. The effects have been a diversification of the economy, a reduction in mining and the decline of certain traditional industries. At the same time, there has been growth in several new and promising sectors. Because of its abundance of affordable electric power, Québec has become the world's third-largest producer of molten aluminium and is an important centre for the processing of other metals. Also, industries creating finished products in the fields of transportation, machinery and electrical appliances are important to Québec's economy. The Bombardier company, for example, which began as a family snowmobile business, has expanded to become a major producer of rail–and air–transport products.

Despite recent trends, natural resources remain a key asset for Québec. By harnessing certain powerful rivers in northern Québec, Hydro-Québec produces a colossal amount of electrical power: 37,500MW. Forest industries continue to have a significant place in Québec's economy, providing 160,000 jobs and representing 4% of the province's GDP. Lastly, the decline in the metal market around the world has resulted in a decrease in the once profitable mining of iron, asbestos, copper and zinc.

Population

As is the case in the rest of America, the people of Québec have a diverse ancestry. The aboriginal peoples were joined by French colonists in the 16th century, the descendants of whom represent a majority of the current population. Over the last two centuries, Québec has experienced waves of immigration from all over the world, particularly from Britain and the United States. The latest census figures show a provincial population of over 7,5 million inhabitants.

■ Aboriginal Peoples

The original inhabitants of Québec, the Inuit and 10 other First Nations, now represent a small fraction of Québec's total population. The ancestors of these peoples began to cross the Bering Strait from Northern Asia more than 12,000 years ago and moved into the region that would come to be known as Québec in successive waves several thousand years later.

When Jacques Cartier "discovered" the region around the Gulf of St. Lawrence in the name of François I, the King of France, the area had already been home to a number of civilizations for thousands of years. During that period, the territory was populated by a complex mosaic of indigenous cultures, each with its own language, way of life and religious practices. With lifestyles adapted to the climate and the particularities of the landscape, northern populations survived by hunting and fishing, while the peoples of the St. Lawrence valley grew much of their food. The Aboriginal population of Québec did not have a written language. Its history comes to us through oral tradition, from explorers' journals and anthropological research.

With the arrival of the first European colonists in the 16th century, these ancient civilizations went into decline. Unlike the European conquest of certain other regions in the Americas, clashes between colonists and Aboriginals are not common to Québec history. The low population density of the vast territory allowed the first settlers to establish their small colonies without directly challenging the indigenous population, which for a long time was numerous.

However, the First Nations of Québec did suffer enormously during the first years of European colonization as a result of the introduction of certain illnesses, such as influenza, measles and tuberculosis. In some areas, nearly half the Aboriginal population was wiped out because of these diseases.

Further devastation resulted as Aboriginal peoples engaged in bloody warfare against each other (using firearms provided by colonists) for control of the fur trade, a business introduced by the Europeans. Between 1645 and 1665, the Iroquois Confederacy nearly wiped out all other Aboriginal peoples. The destruction of Aboriginal civilizations continued with territorial losses to the unrelenting spread of colonization. While the Aboriginals of Québec were rarely the target of European military aggression, they were nevertheless soon overpowered by the colonists.

Today, three quarters of Québec's Aboriginal population lives in small communities scattered across the province. Though some of these groups live in areas where they can hunt and fish, in most cases traditional lifestyles have not survived. With the loss of their culture and the resulting sense of alienation, Aboriginals endure major social problems.

In recent years, however, Aboriginals living in Québec have managed to attract increased attention from the media, leading to a sensitization on the part of the government and the rest of the population to their issues. Aboriginal land claims and issues of self-government have attracted significant attention, particularly during the summer of 1990, when, for two months, armed Mohawks barricaded one of the main bridges connecting Montréal to the south shore of the St. Lawrence. The incident forced native concerns to the forefront, though the resulting political crisis may have represented a short-term setback for their cause.

Today, native causes generally enjoy the support of most Canadians, and various agreements granting Aboriginals more autonomy have been signed in recent years.

Québec's 11 First Nations are part of three distinct cultural families. The Abenaki, Algonquin, Attikamek, Cree, Malecite, Micmac, Montagnais and Naskapi are all part of the Algonquian culture, while the Wendat-Huron and the Mohawk are Iroquoian. The Inuit, for their part, form an entirely distinct culture. The following is a brief description of each of Québec's 11 First Nations.

Originally occupying the region that is now New England, where many still live, the **Waban Aki (Abenaki)** settled first in Sillery (near Québec City) around 1675, then in 1684 next to falls of the Rivière Chaudière. The Abenaki had close ties with the French colonists and shared many of their ancestral skills with them, including, it seems, the art of making maple syrup. During the colonial wars, the Waban Aki sided with the French and also participated in the defence of the colony against British invaders, who were established to the south. In 1700, a group of them settled permanently in Odanak, a village that was later sacked during the British conquest in 1759. Today, there are two Waban Aki villages

Aboriginal Art

Aboriginal works of art were once considered anthropological specimens and collected almost exclusively by ethnological museums. It was only in the latter 20th century that they gradually obtained the status of "art." Since First Nations did not traditionally disassociate art from everyday objects, their work did not measure up to the canons of conventional European art. It was only after many struggles, some of which have yet to be won, that Aboriginal works were introduced in art museums. Canadians have showed an increased interest in Aboriginal art since the 1960s and 1970s, with over 100 Canadian museums today displaying various collections. While artistic practices vary greatly from region to region, the differences between First Nations and Inuit art are the most marked.

Inuit art is very popular in Canada; it is regularly exhibited in museums and appreciated by numerous collectors. Cooperatives were formed in the 1950s to promote and disseminate the arts of the Far North, a major turning point in the history of Inuit art. Before this time, the objects created were small: toys, tools and sacred amulets. Near the end of the 1940s, however, sculptures began to appear as they do today, sometimes reaching one metre in height and assuming a variety of shapes and colours. These sculptures were made of bone, ivory (its use is forbidden today), and, occasionally, antler or wood. The most popular material, however, remains stone, which has been sculpted by the Inuit for millennia. Also known as "soapstone," this rock comes from the steatite family and its colour varies from grey, green and black; the darker the stone, the higher its density. Stonecut printing is a recent practice that has become popular due to the simplicity of the lines and the quality of the product. Some Inuit art forms are practiced exclusively by women, such as basketry, doll-making, sewing, embroidery and beadwork, as well as hide and leather work.

The Inuit call their art *sananquaq*, which means "small portrayal of reality." For the artists, who are often hunters and fishers, the best works are those that faithfully capture human or animal movement. Sculptures, like carvings, tell stories that are part of a heritage passed down through the oral tradition: myths and legends, dreams, the forces of nature, relationships between people and animals and the work of daily life. Themes and styles vary from one region to another.

First Nations peoples produce fewer sculptures than their northern neighbours, except for those on the West Coast, a region renowned for its totemic art. While those in eastern and northern Canada preferred creating small items, perhaps because most First Nations peoples were nomadic, it was quite the opposite for those on the Pacific coast. Their totems, which represented the lineage of different tribes, could reach heights of 20 to 25m. The motifs were inspired by the spirit world, the animal world, as well as mythology. Totemic culture has existed for thousands of years, but the only totems we now see are those preserved in museums or in parks. The oldest of them is about 300 years old. Generally speaking, the works of First Nations artists were made with materials such as wood, leather or cloth. They also created many three-dimensional works (masks, dream catchers, decorated objects), silk-screen prints and works on paper.

Portrait - Population

in Québec–Odanak and Wôlinak–located on the south shore of the St. Lawrence between the cities of Sorel and Bécancour. Of the 2,000 Waban Aki living in Québec, about 350 live in one of the two villages. The baskets woven of hay and ash, for which the Waban Aki are famous, are still made in these villages; however, most Waban Aki work in the neighbouring cities or elsewhere in Québec. The Waban Aki language has practically disappeared.

Having lived in more or less remote areas away from the city centres, the **Anishnabe (Algonquin)** were able to preserve their nomadic way of life, living off the land, hunting, fishing and gathering. The traditional activities of the Algonquin were upset by the arrival of lumberjacks and prospectors to the Abitibi region in the middle of the 19th century. Their way of life thus became less nomadic. In Québec, there are approximately 9,900 Anishnabe, 5,000 of which live in the communities of Kitcisakik (Grand-Lac-Victoria), Kitiganik (Lac-Rapide) and Kitigan Zibi (Maniwaki), in the Outaouais region, and Hunter's Point, Kebaowek, Simo Sagigan (Lac-Simon), Abitibiwinni (Pikogon), Timiskaming (Notre-Dame-du-Nord) and Winneway, in Abitibi-Témiscamingue. The Anishnabe language is still used in most of these communities.

Almost completely decimated during the 17th century as a result of epidemics and Iroquois wars, the **Attikamekw** took refuge with the Cree or Montagnais peoples before integrating a group from Lake Superior known as the O'pimittish Ininivac, who later settled in Haute-Mauricie. The 5,000 Attikamekw in Québec still live in this region, mainly in the villages of Manawan, Wemotaci and Obedjiwan. The Attikamekw have remained close to nature–working in forestry and advocating the development of resources while preserving the balance of nature. The Attikamekw language, which is similar to Montagnais, is still spoken by the populations of all three communities.

Remarkably well adapted to the land and the rigours of the climate, the **Cree** have lived in Northern Québec for about 5,000 years. Despite their remote isolation, the Cree came into regular contact with Europeans very early. From the 17th century on, fur trading with non-native merchants constituted one of the principal economic activities of the Cree nation. The decline in the fur trade and the Canadian and Québec governments' increased interest in the development of Québec's far north, starting in the 1950s, have had a profound effect on the interaction between the Cree and their environment. However, it was the signing in 1975 of the James Bay and Northern Québec Agreement by the governments of Québec and Canada that really changed the Cree way of life. This signing allowed Hydro-Québec to construct hydroelectric dams on some of the most powerful rivers of the region; in exchange, the Cree were given $225 million, ownership of 13,696km^2 and exclusive hunting and fishing rights in a territory covering 151,580km^2. The Agreement provided the Cree with the resources to take an active part in the economic development of their region, as shown by the number of dynamic enterprises undertaken by this nation in the last 10 years or so. The 13,000 Cree of Québec today live in nine villages: Waskaganish, Eastmain, Wemindji and Chisasibi, on the shores of James Bay; Whapmagoostui, near Hudson Bay; Nemiscau, Waswanipi and Mistissini, in the interior; and Oujé-Bougoumou, near the city of Chibougamau. The Cree language is still used by most of the population.

The **Inuit** have lived for about 4,500 years in the extreme north of Québec, in a region known in Inuktitut as Nunavik, which means "land to live off." Right up to the beginning of the 20th century, the Inuit still lived as their ancestors had, hunting with traditional weapons and living in igloos. The adaptation to a more modern lifestyle only occurred in the last few decades, and is still very new.

Like the Cree, the Inuit also signed the James Bay and Northern Québec Agreement. Among other things, this convention granted the Inuit a greater degree of independence and self-government. They administer most of the services in Nunavik and will eventually receive a regional government. The monetary compensation received by the Inuit is managed by the Société Makivik, and provides the Inuit with the tools necessary to play a larger role in the economic development of their region. In fact, thanks to Société Makivik, the Inuit of Québec are the owners of the Air Inuit and First Air airline companies, which play a dominant role in air transport in Northern Canada. The 9,000 Inuit in Québec live in 14 villages located on the shores of Hudson Bay (Kuujjuarapik, Umiujaq, Inukjuak, Payungnituk, Akulivik), Hudson Strait (Ivujivik, Salluit, Kangiqsujjuag, Quaqtag) and Ungava Bay (Kangirsuk, Aupaluk, Tasiujaq, Kuujjuaq and Kangiqsualujjuaq). A few dozen Inuit live in Chisasibi. The language of the Inuit, Inuktitut, is still used in these communities. In Inuit schools it is the only language of instruction from kindergarten to third grade. Even though the Inuit have adopted a more modern lifestyle, their ancestral culture and values remain significant.

Scattered across the territory, the **Welustuk (Malecite)**, who were for a long time known as Etchemins, number only about 750 in Québec. They are also the only Aboriginal nation that does not have its own village. However, in 1827, the government created the first native reserve for them, on the shores of the Rivière Verte, in the Bas-St-Laurent region. The reserve was eventually bought back by the government because the Welustuk hardly ever used it and preferred to remain nomadic. In the end, the Welustuk never settled down in one community, and were eventually integrated into neighbouring non-native communities. Even though the language is no longer spoken and no village exists, the Welustuk have had a chief and band-council since 1987.

The **Mi'gmaq (Micmac)**, who number just over 4,800 in Québec, settled in the Gaspésie region and formed the villages of Restigouche and Gesgapegiag, or lived with non-natives in Gaspé and the surroundings. One of the first Aboriginal nations, if not the first, to come into contact with Europeans, the Mi'gmaq were living on the shores of the St. Lawrence and the coast of the Atlantic Ocean when the colonists arrived. Known as accomplished seamen, the Mi'gmaq also established temporary and permanent camps on various islands in the Gulf of St. Lawrence. With the economic development of the region, many Mi'gmaq became lumberjacks and labourers. A considerable number of Mi'gmaq still speak the language, which is now taught in the two communities' schools.

When the Europeans arrived, the **Kanien'Kahaka (Mohawks)** formed one of the five Iroquois nations of the powerful Five-Nation Confederation, which was at the heart of the fur-trade war in the 17th century. Despite their association with this sophisticated political system, the Kanien'Kahaka were still very independent and ambitious. Later, after they had become more sedentary, many became very skilled craftsmen, particularly as specialized steel workers. The Kanien'Kahaka have an international reputation, even today, as expert steel craftsmen for skyscrapers and bridges. Numbering around 16,000, the Kanien'Kahaka are the largest group of Aboriginals in Québec. They live mainly in three villages: Kahnawake, located close to Montréal, on the south shore of the St. Lawrence; Akwesasne, in the southwest corner of the province, overlapping the borders of Québec, Ontario and the state of New York; and Kanesatake, about 50km west of Montréal, on the shores of Lac des Deux Montagnes. Land claims by the Kanesatake Kanien'Kahaka were at the centre of a crisis during the summer of 1990. Though many Kanien'Kahaka have adapted to modern North American culture, others still live according to their ancestral teachings, based on the Great Law of Peace. Kanien'Kahaka society is traditionally matriarchal, and as such the clan mothers choose the chief. The Kanien'Kahaka (Mohawk) language is still spoken by several members of the communities.

Isolated across the vast regions of the Côte-Nord and the Basse-Côte-Nord, the **Innus (Montagnais)** lived essentially by hunting, fishing, gathering and by the fur trade up until the beginning of the 20th century. The arrival of the mining and forestry industries, as well as the construction of hydroelectric dams, completely disrupted their way of life. Their culture remains nevertheless very vibrant, and the Innuat language is still spoken in most communities, especially the more isolated ones. The success in Europe and America of musical group Kashtin, from Uashat-Maliotenam, is proof positive of the vital culture of this nation, as was the recent publication of the first Montagnais-French dictionary. Numbering 15,000, the Innus form the second-largest Aboriginal nation in Québec. They live in nine communities: Les Escoumins, Betsiamites and Uashat-Maliotenam in the Côte-Nord; Mingan, Natashquan, La Romaine and Pakuashipi in the Basse-Côte-Nord; Mashteuiatsh in Lac-Saint-Jean, and Matimekosh near Schefferville.

The **Naskapi** nation has only one village in Canada—Kawawachikamach—founded in 1984 and located in northern Québec, a few kilometres from Schefferville. In accordance with the Northeastern Québec Agreement, the 775 Naskapis of Kawawachikamach own 285km^2 of territory and have exclusive hunting, fishing and trapping rights on a 4,144km^2 territory. The Naskapis, who have only recently embraced modern culture, still hunt cari-

Portrait - Population

bou, whose flesh and fur allow them to survive the harsh conditions of the arctic tundra. The Naskapi language is still spoken by the entire population.

When the first French colonists arrived, the **Wendat-Huron** inhabited about 20 large villages in central Ontario on the shores of Georgian Bay. Besides being excellent farmers, they controlled an extensive commercial empire, which stretched from the Great Lakes to the Rivière Saguenay and Hudson Bay, and quite naturally became the main trading partners of the French merchants in the early years of colonization. However, this economically profitable relationship did not last, for within a few years the Wendat-Huron population was decimated, first by epidemics in 1634 and 1639, then by repeated Iroquois attacks starting in 1640. In 1649 the remaining 300 Wendat-Hurons took refuge on the outskirts of Québec City, then settled on Île d'Orléans in 1657, and finally near the Rivière Saint-Charles in 1697, where the village of Wendake still sits. Located near Loretteville, this economically flourishing community is the only Wendat-Huron village in Québec. Of the approximate 3,000 Wendat-Hurons who live in Québec, about 1,300 live in Wendake. Some of the goods produced in Wendake, such as moccasins, canoes and snowshoes, are known worldwide. The Huron language is no longer used in Québec.

■ Francophones

A large percentage of Québec's Francophones are descendants of the original French colonists who gradually arrived in the country between 1608 and 1759. By 1663, there were only 3,000 settlers in New France. With an increased number of immigrants arriving and settlers starting families, the population of Québec stood at about 60,000 at the time of the British conquest in 1759. The settlers were mostly farmers from western France.

Today, after just over two centuries, the descendants of these 60,000 French-Canadians number in the millions, seven million of whom still live in Canada. Some interesting comparisons have been made between Québec's sharp rate of population growth and the growth rates seen elsewhere between 1760 and 1960. For example, while the population of the world during this same 200-year period grew three times, and the population of Europe grew five times, the population of francophone Canada grew 80 times. This statistic is particularly surprising given that immigration from France had dwindled to almost nothing and that there were very few marriages between British and French families (with the exception of a number of Irish-French unions). In addition, between 1840 and 1930, about 900,000 Quebecers, most of them francophone, left Canada for the United States.

This phenomenal growth of Canada's French population resulted largely from a remarkably high birth rate. Indeed, for a long time, French-Canadian women had an average of eight children, and families of 15 or 20 children were not unusual. This trend can be attributed to the influence of the Catholic Church, which sought to counterbalance the growth of the Protestant church in Canada. Interestingly, francophone Quebecers now have one of the lowest birth rates in the world, similar to Germany and other Western European countries.

The French majority in Québec has long been deprived of control over the economy of the province. In 1960, Francophones earned on average 66% of what Anglophones did. With the Quiet Revolution, Francophones began to take control of their economy. At the same time, they stopped thinking of themselves as French-Canadians and began to define themselves as *Québécois*. Québec's total population, 80% of which is francophone, is characterized by an increasing number of immigrants.

■ Anglophones

Anglophones were for a long time stereotyped as Protestant and rich. In reality, Anglo-Quebecers have always been a diversified group. While Anglophones may have been paid more on average, there have always been Anglophones in every socio-economic group.

Glossary of Unique Québecois Expressions

achaler: to bother someone

blonde: girlfriend

breuvage: in general, all non-alcoholic beverages

carosse: an airport or store cart

cenne: a penny

c'est pas pire: an expression warning of the banality of a situation or thing; also means: that's not too bad (according to the tone of voice)

char: automobile

chum: friend, buddy, boyfriend; ex: *mon chum* for a male friend and *ma chumme* for a female friend

dépanneur: a convenience store (*en panne* means out of order, not working)

dispendieux(euse): something that is expensive; ex: a car that is *dispendieuse*

donner un bec: to give a friendly kiss, the word *bec* means "mouth" or "beak" in a figurative sense; ex: *se sucrer le bec* means to eat sweets

être tanné: to have enough of a situation, to be at the end of one's rope

jaser: to chat

le fun: a good time, to be good or great or fun

liqueur: soft drink

niaiseux(euse): a stupid person or situation; ex: *une personne niaiseuse, une situation niaiseuse*

plate: used to describe an unpleasant situation; ex: missing the bus, *c'est plate!*

piastre: dollar (pronounced *"piasse"*)

se tasser: to make room for somebody, to move over

The integration of anglophone immigrants from many backgrounds into Québec society has created a particularly heterogeneous minority.

The first anglophone settlers arrived in Québec after the Conquest of 1759. Most were merchants and represented a small fraction of the total population. A second wave of English-speaking immigrants arrived from the United States between 1783 and the beginning of the 19th century. Of this group, many were British Loyalists, others were simply farmers looking for land. Throughout the 19th century, immigrants from the British Isles arrived in Québec in great numbers. These British, Scottish and Irish arrivals, who were often dispossessed in their own country or victims of famine, generally settled in the Eastern Townships, the Outaouais region and Montréal. The declining number of immigrants from Great Britain at the end of the 19th century has been made up for by the integration of newcomers from a variety of other places. Immigrants from countries other than France and Great Britain have generally preferred to adopt the English language, feeling that this is necessary for economic success.

For the same reason, a number of Francophones have become assimilated into Québec's anglophone culture. A breakdown of the anglophone population according to origin shows that 60% of the population have British origins, 15% have French origins, 8% have Jewish origins and 3% have Italian origins.

English-speaking Quebecers currently represent just over 10% of the total population of the province. Three quarters of this group live in Montréal, most in the west end of the city.

Portrait - Population

They have their own institutions (schools, universities, hospitals, media), which function just as francophone institutions do.

Anglophones represent a fairly large economic force, though unlike several decades ago, they no longer dominate Québec's economy. The rise of the independence movement, Québec Francophones increasing role in the economy and the creation of linguistic laws aimed at protecting the French language have shaken up the anglophone community. Though many have simply left the province, the majority has stayed and adapted. For example, 60% of Anglophones surveyed say that they can speak French. This demonstrates a marked increase. Francophones and Anglophones may differ on certain issues, but Anglophones generally feel a profound attachment to Québec and particularly to Montréal, a city they played a major role in building.

■ Quebecers of Other Ethnic Origins

Immigrants from places other than France, Great Britain and the United States really only started to arrive at the beginning of the 20th century. In the first part of the century, before the economic crisis of the 1930s and World War II put a stop to immigration to Québec, most new arrivals were of Jewish and Italian descent. During the era of post-war prosperity, immigrants began to come in even greater numbers than before. Most originated from Southern and Eastern Europe. Starting in the 1960s, Québec began to see the arrival of immigrants from every continent. The greatest number came from Indochina and Haiti. At present, Quebecers of Italian, Jewish, Greek, British and French origin represent the largest ethnic minorities.

Even though these new arrivals tended to preserve their own culture as much as possible, they eventually adopted either the English or the French language, and were then integrated into that particular community. This integration was until recently the source of significant social tensions. Not so long ago, immigrants for the most part were assimilated into the anglophone community, which threatened to completely reverse the linguistic balance, and therefore create a split within Québec's population between Francophones and the rest of the population, known as allophones. Promoted in 1977, Bill 101 was intended to remedy this situation by encouraging immigrants to integrate into the language of the majority by forcing new arrivals into French schools.

Architecture

■ The 17th and 18th Centuries

A Vast Territory to Defend and Develop

During the Age of Enlightenment, the immense French territory in America was quite impressive. In 1750, New France stretched from Acadia to the estuary of the Mississippi and from the foothills of the Appalachians to those of the Rockies. Explorers and soldiers who forged these unknown territories were usually content just to bury plaques of tin or terracotta in significant places (promontories, river mouths), claiming them for the King of France. Sometimes a small fort was erected to defend a critical pass. These buildings occasionally gave rise to villages, which years later grew into the large cities of the American Midwest, such as Detroit and Pittsburgh.

The hinterland remained for the most part untouched. This was native territory, visited sporadically by white fur trappers and Jesuit missionaries. The population of French origin, which reached about 60,000 in 1759, was concentrated in the valley of the St. Lawrence between Tadoussac and Montréal. Close to a quarter of this total lived in the three towns that lined the river (Québec City: pop. 8,400, Trois-Rivières: pop. 650 and Montréal:

pop. 5,200). This represented a higher proportion of urban population than in France at the same time (22% in Canada compared to only 17% in France).

The feeling of insecurity on the part of inhabitants, as well as the King's desire to protect his colony, led the citizens of the towns and villages of New France to surround their settlements with fortified enclosures made of stone or wood, designed according to the principles of Vauban, military engineer of Louis XIV. These strongholds, financially supported by the Crown, were completed by a network of forts intended to slow the advance of the enemy. Their walls had to be designed to withstand both surprise attacks by hostile native tribes and the British Army, who were arriving by sea in warships equipped with heavy artillery weapons. By the end of the French Regime, Montréal and Québec City were both typical French provincial towns, well protected within their walls. Inside, streets were lined with churches whose steeples reached above the walls, convents, colleges, hospitals and a few aristocratic and bourgeois homes surrounded by French gardens. Added to that was be a *place d'armes* (parade ground) and a market square.

For a long time, the rivers, in particular the St. Lawrence, were the roads of New France. These waterways became punctuated by portage routes, which often developed into tiny hamlets with little else besides an inn and a chapel. It was not until 1734 that a land route suitable for vehicles between Montréal and Québec City was opened. The Chemin du Roy (more or less present-day Route 138), as it was called, was only passable in summer; during the winter the frozen river once again became the main thoroughfare. In 1750, the trip from Québec City to Montréal along Chemin du Roy took five days.

The banks of the St. Lawrence River and Rivière Richelieu were slowly cleared and farmed. The King of France, who had chosen the seigneurial system to develop Canada, conceded long rectangles of land, perpendicular to the water, to individuals and religious communities, who in exchange kept hearth and home and recruited new colonists. These new colonists in turn promised to pay the *cens* (tax) and swear *foi et hommage* (faith and homage) to their seigneur.

Under the French Regime, few seigneurs actually fulfilled their obligations, finding their land too isolated and exposed to Iroquois and British attacks, while others used their land as hunting grounds or for speculation. It was not until the end of the 18th century that most of the seigneuries granted between 1626 and 1758 were actually cleared and planted.

The seigneuries were developed according to a strict model, which shaped the countryside of the valley of the St. Lawrence River and of the Richelieu. Close to the river that supplied the seigneury would sit the seigneur's *domaine*, which included the manor house and a wind or water mill intended to grind the grains harvested by the workers into flour. The *commune*, a common pasture land, was also located on the river bank. A small village would be located to the side, generally including a simple church and five or six stone or wooden houses. The rest of the seigneury consisted of long, narrow strips of land, laid out in successive rows, called *rangs*, and conceded to the colonists parcel by parcel as the number of families grew. Each strip was linked to the other by *côtes*, roads bordering the narrow edge of the land concessions, and by *montées*, which traversed the seigneury perpendicularly to the *rangs* and the *côtes*. The seigneurial system was abolished in 1854 but the division of land in *rangs* is still visible today.

French Architecture Adapted to the Québec Context

Of all enemies to battle, the cold was without a doubt the most dreaded. After rather difficult and often tragic beginnings, during which some colonists froze to death because their only shelter was a rickety wooden cabin with paper windows, French architecture slowly adapted to the long winters. It had to overcome the shortage of skilled workers, in particular stone-cutters, as well as the lack of necessary materials on the local market, like glass for the windows and slate for the roofs, which otherwise had to be shipped in

Portrait - Architecture

at great expense. As such, the architecture of the French Regime is an architecture of colonization, pure and economic, where each element has a specific function that is essential to the well-being of inhabitants.

The French Regime house consisted of a modest rubble-stone rectangle squared off by two chimneys and topped with a double-sloped roof covered with cedar shingles. Openings in the walls were few and far between and filled with small casement windows, since larger pieces of glass did not usually survive their ocean voyage. The door was made of moulded panels. The interior remained rustic since the priority was heating. The number of rooms was limited to the number of chimneys, as each room had to be heated. Starting in 1740, several buildings were equipped with cast-iron stoves, forged at the Saint-Maurice ironworks. Occasionally, stone sinks and built-in cupboards were found, and even more rarely, Louis XV-style panelling. Seigneurial manors were architecturally similar to the houses of prosperous farms. There were exceptions, particularly for busy seigneurs or religious communities where the manor also served as a convent. These manors took on the look and style of veritable castles.

The architecture of the towns varied little from that of the country. The first priority remained, of course, the eternal battle against the cold. Added to this, however, was the prevention of fire, which could easily result in tragedy in the absence of an effective fire-fighting system. Two edicts written by New France Intendants in 1721 and in 1727 pertained to construction inside the town walls. Wooden houses with mansard roofs and their dangerous wooden shingles were forbidden; all buildings had to be made of stone and equipped with fire-break walls; attic floors had to be covered with terracotta tiles. Those who could not afford to obey such strict standards built small communities outside the walls. Few examples remain of these wood houses, whose architecture was sober and functional.

Some buildings were more sophisticated. As expected in this colony settled by a devout society, the churches and chapels were the most elaborate. Some were even adorned with beautiful baroque facades of cut stone. Even more important, though, were the bright interiors, decorated with numerous Louis XIV- and Louis XV-style wood embellishments, painted white and gold leafed, which appeared in the first half of the 18th century. Most of the churches and chapels in the cities therefore were built with respect to classic French urban perspectives. Unfortunately, these perspectives were eliminated during the 19th century to ease traffic circulation. In the cities you might come upon *hôtels particuliers* with yards and gardens, but more prominent were three- and four-storey buildings, occupied by businesses and built close to the street. These occasionally included a workshop and stone-vaulted basements for storing merchandise. A few beautiful examples of these basements can be found surrounding the Place Royale in Québec City.

After the Conquest

New France was devastated by the Seven Years War, leaving many of its most beautiful buildings in ruins. And what the British conquest of 1759 did not succeed in destroying, the American invasion of 1775 and the War of 1812 did. Despite the political turmoil, however, the architectural vocabulary remained the same up until the end of the 18th century because the British population was too small to have an impact, and all the businessmen and labourers remained essentially French Canadian. The English Palladian style of architecture, influenced by the work of Andreo Palladio in Italy, was only visible after 1780, following the construction of a few homes for British dignitaries and high-ranking military officers posted in Québec City.

■ The 19th Century

The Evolution of a Tradition

The combination of the French Regime and Palladian architectural styles, as well as the Regency trend, formed the basis of traditional Québec architecture, which reached its peak in the 19th century. It differed from the style of the previous century mainly by a lengthening of the drip moulding, which extended out to cover the long balcony across the front of the house. The elaborate and gabled drip mouldings of Regency cottages, inspired by Oriental architecture, found a new function here. The balconies served as a halfway point between inside and outside, and as a place to relax in the summer. They also prevented snow from blocking windows and doors in the winter.

Other particularly useful innovations were the decreased slope of the roofs, which avoided the inevitable wall of snow that would come falling down each time an unlucky inhabitant stepped outside, the raising of the masonry brick foundation to separate the house from the ground, and the installation of chimneys against the walls instead of in the middle, thereby creating a better distribution of heat.

The windows remained French but became more numerous, and the number of panes decreased from 12 to 6; a storm window was added in the winter and a screen in the summer for the maximum comfort of those inside. Around 1820, the summer kitchen was introduced, a sort of lean-to positioned on the north side of the house, exposed to cool winds. This room was cooler in summer and closed in winter. It was used to store perishables, while at the same time protecting the main house from chilly winter winds. Eventually, the shingle roof was replaced by sheet metal, a material that is both resistant and inflammable and which was used also on steeples and churches.

Churches also benefitted from the contribution of Palladianism, thanks mostly to the Baillargé family from Québec City, who revolutionized the art of building churches in Québec. This dynasty of architects added Palladian windows and pediments to the facades. They also added Louis XVI elements to the liturgical furniture. At the other end of the scale, Louis-Amable Quévillon (1749-1823) assembled every sumptuous element of the French Regime to create his highly decorated diamond-and star-patterned ceilings.

The population in the villages of Québec was growing rapidly, leading to the enlargement or replacement of several churches of the French Regime. The Catholic nuns built convents and colleges for the education of boys and girls. In every region, a new class of professionals, including notaries, lawyers and doctors, was building large homes.

Traditional Québec villages established in this era differed from Ontarian and American villages; they consisted of country-style homes located very close together, so close they were almost duplexes; commercial buildings were rare, so boutiques and stores were located in buildings that resembled the residential dwellings. This style is explained by the townspeople's fear of fire (most of these village homes were made of wood), and by the Catholic Church's negative attitude towards the expansion of commerce.

American and British Immigration

Following the signing of the Treaty of Versailles in 1783, recognizing the independence of the United States, a number of Americans loyal to the crown of England took refuge in what remained of British North America, namely Canada. They brought with them a decidedly Georgian style of architecture from New England, characterized by the use of red brick and white wooden accents. These new arrivals settled in areas left vacant by the French Regime, which the British colonial government divided into townships in the first half of the 19th century. Most of these townships are located in the Eastern Townships and the Outaouais (Ottawa Valley) regions.

Portrait - Architecture

Québec City and Montréal also welcomed a large number of Scottish and Irish immigrants between 1800 and 1850. They brought with them a severe but elegant neoclassical style of architecture, such as is seen in Dublin and Glasgow. As a result, cut stone definitively replaced rubble stone around 1810. Sash windows and columned porticoes became more common in urban settings, as did all manner of Greek- and ancient Roman-inspired architectural styles (pediments, Tuscan pilasters and parapets with palmettes).

The first democratically elected municipal governments undertook the lighting and paving of the streets. This was also the era of large-scale engineering projects such as the dredging of the Canal de Lachine (1821-1825) and the appearance of shipyards larger than any ever seen before. This bustle of economic activity also attracted the rural French-Canadian population to the cities, such that the population of Montréal surpassed that of Québec City around 1830, and reached the 100,000 mark in 1860.

The Reign of Historicism

The building of the Protestant orphanage in Québec City in 1823, and in particular that of the Église Notre-Dame in Montréal between 1824 and 1829, both of which are Gothic Revival in style, announced the arrival of historicism in Québec architecture. Originally quite marginal, historicism would come to dominate the skyline of Québec's cities and towns in the second half of the 19th century. It is defined by the use of decorative elements taken from different architectural epochs in history, which were popularized thanks to archeological discoveries, the invention of photography, and the popularity of historical novels across the world.

An array of architectural styles influenced by ancient trends appeared almost simultaneously just before, and during, the reign of Queen Victoria (1837-1901), which explains why all these styles, so different from one another, are all united under the simplified architectural term "Victorian." America, being sufficiently removed from the Middle Ages and the Renaissance, was not affected by the pastiche elements that for so long influenced Europe. As such, North-American Victorian architecture was altogether new. It employed a backward-looking style that was meaningful only to North Americans.

The Gothic Revival style, with its pointed arches, pinnacles and battlements, was for a long time reserved for churches, since the Middle Ages, from which it originated, was a period of great religious fervour. Similarly, the Renaissance Revival style was favoured by the bourgeois class for the building of sumptuous residences, since the Italian Renaissance corresponded to the birth of a powerful middle class. The Second Empire style is associated with Napoleon III's refinement of Paris. The mansard roofs, covered in slate, were used repeatedly in Québec residential architecture and in a series of public buildings. Their popularity is a result of the French heritage of Québec society, but also the vogue of the style throughout North America between 1865 and 1900. Also not to be forgotten are the Romanesque Revival style characterized by compound arches and short, squat columns, the Queen Anne style, used in the suburbs of the new middle class, and in particular the Château style, a mixture of the architecture of Scottish manors and Loire châteaux, which became, over the years, a sort of Canadian "national style."

Victor Bourgeau (in the region of Montréal) and Joseph Ferdinand Peachy (in the region of Québec City) showed their talents well in the building of innumerable historicistic parochial churches of different styles, from economical to elaborate. Bourgeau originally worked with a neoclassical vocabulary, as much a product of Brit John Ostell as the church architecture of the French Regime, before gradually turning towards Gothic Revival, and then Romanesque Revival. Peachy left his mark through a series of Renaissance Revival and Second Empire works.

Industrialization and Comfort

The Victorian era might seem contradictory; while it looked backward in terms of its architectural style, it looked decidedly forward when it came to comfort. As such, the technological innovations that made life much more pleasant are often overlooked: running water, automatic hot water heaters, more washrooms, central heating, telephones and electricity. Among the permanent changes to the buildings that are of note were the popularity of bay windows, bow-windows and box-windows, as well as the use of flat roofs covered with tar and pebbles, which retained the snow until it melted, creating a natural insulator. Some of the more complex roofs belonging to religious and public buildings were covered with richly ornamented copper, which over the years acquired a rich green hue as a result of oxidation (verdigris).

In the second half of the 19th century, the railroad finally linked the major centres effectively. The railway also led to the development of land north of the St. Lawrence (Saguenay–Lac-Saint-Jean, Laurentians and Témiscamingue), thereby helping French-Canadian farmers extend the boundary of settled land in Québec.

The Industrial Revolution transformed the cities into manufacturing centres for primary goods. Workers' neighbourhoods sprouted like weeds around the factories, well serviced by a network of tramways, originally horse-drawn (1861), then electric (1892). The cities of Montréal and Québec City became bustling and business oriented. Large stores, theatres, bank and insurance-company headquarters opened their doors, attracting even more workers. Meanwhile, the rest of Québec, essentially agriculturally oriented, was still anchored in tradition, and would remain relatively isolated up until the middle of the 20th century.

■ The 20th Century

The Standard Urban Dwelling

The record birth rate in rural Québec around 1900, when families with 12 children were common, began to overburden the land. New regions such as Abitibi were opened up for settlement by the clergy, yet the attraction of the city proved insurmountable, despite meagre wages. These uprooted workers longed for aspects of their country homes in the city: galleries and balconies, numerous well-lit rooms, a lot of storage space, which might also serve as henhouse or stables if necessary. It all had to be inexpensive to heat and relatively easy to maintain. Thus, the Montréal-style dwelling was born.

Its outdoor staircases, which wound their way tightly to the second floor in the limited space between the sidewalk and balcony, avoided the need to heat an interior stairwell. The balconies were reminiscent of rural galleries, leading directly into the homes (one or two per floor), which each had their own exterior entrance. Between 1900 and 1930, thousands of these duplexes, triplexes, quadruplexes and quintuplexes were built along Montréal's straight streets. These two- and three-storey buildings, with wooden frames and built on top of each other, were covered either with local limestone or brick. Even though the dwelling was supposed to be economical, each one was adorned with a decorative cornice or parapet, balconies with Tuscan columns and beautiful *art nouveau*-inspired stained-glass windows.

During the same era, a whole series of single-industry towns (paper or mining) were born across Québec. These urban areas were created by the industries, and therefore laid out with a precise urban plan from the beginning. This included a well-designed public and residential architecture, renowned architectural works, modelled after English city-gardens.

Portrait - Architecture

Back to Basics

The École des Beaux-Arts de Paris, whose teachings engendered rigorous principles of architectural composition (symmetry, monumentalism), as well as a blend of French classicism, received a positive response among enlightened French-Canadians at the beginning of the 20th century. They sought to make a torch of the Beaux-Arts style, signalling the French presence in America. Twin columns, wrought-iron balconies supported by stone brackets and decorated railings were also found in the wealthy Anglo-Saxon neighbourhoods, for whom the Beaux-Arts style represented the tradition of Parisian refinement.

This timid back-to-basics movement on the part of French Canadians took on much larger proportions with the descendants of English and Scottish merchants, making pilgrimages back across the Atlantic to rediscover the ruins of such and such Welsh Manor, or such and such Scottish farm-house where Grandfather grew up. The British Arts and Crafts Movement found among these people enthusiasts of Herefordshire tiles, Elizabethan wainscotting and Tudor chimneys. These people, who were sensitized to Great Britain's rural architecture and planned to reproduce it in Québec, were ironically the first to attempt to save some of the rural architecture of the French Regime, which was in sad decline in 1920.

At the beginning of the 1930s, some new buildings inspired by New France styling were being constructed. The Quiet Revolution during the 1960s fortunately awakened a larger portion of the population to the importance of the traditions of their French heritage. It was the beginning of an era of painstaking restoration. However, while a part of the heritage was put on a pedestal, another part, that of the 19th century, was shoved off by the wrecking ball. The destruction went on until the 1980s. Efforts continue today to stave off the deterioration caused by the massive wave of demolition whose results have been compared to those of a military bombardment, and which left vacant lots scattered across cities.

North American Influence

The favourable contacts that Québec architects and artists maintained with their colleagues in Paris, Brussels and London did not deter them from opting out for America at the beginning of the 20th century. And so the first skyscrapers pierced the Montréal sky in 1928, following the definitive repeal of a ruling limiting the height of buildings to 10 storeys. Celebrated architects from the United States designed many of Montréal's towers, giving the downtown core its present, decidedly North-American skyline. The geometric and aerodynamic French Art-Deco style, of which there are several examples in all regions of Québec, was replaced by Modern American architecture following the Second World War. Expo '67 presented the perfect opportunity to provide Montréal and the whole province with bold, representative examples of international architecture.

The Quiet Revolution of the 1960s corresponded to a massive expansion of the suburbs and the construction of major public infrastructures. Since then, new highways have crisscrossed Québec; huge schools, hospitals, cultural centres and museums opened in towns where before there was only a church and a convent. Northern Québec received considerably more attention with the construction of major hydroelectric complexes. Cities underwent radical transformations in these respects: construction of the métro (subway system) in Montréal, vast modern government complexes in Québec City, etc.

At the beginning of the 1980s, the weariness resulting from the *ad nauseam* repetition of the same formulas put forward by the modernists provoked a return to the styles of the past by way of post-modernism, which freely combined reflective glass and polished granite in compositions that echo Art Deco and neoclassicism. The 1990s for their part presented two opposing ideas: the culmination of post-modernism, in the form of a Romantic architecture, and the search for a new ultra-modern style of architecture, making use of new materials, computers and electronics.

The Arts

The aspirations and the concerns of a society are reflected in the work of its artists. For a long time, artistic expression in Québec presented an image of a people constantly on the defensive, tormented by an unsatisfactory situation and filled with doubt over the future. However, after World War II, and particularly after the Quiet Revolution, Québec culture evolved and became more affirming. Open to outside influences, and often very innovative, Québec culture is now remarkably vital.

■ Québec Literature in French

Literary output in Québec began with the writings of early explorers, like Jacques Cartier, and members of religious communities. These manuscripts were usually intended to describe the New World to authorities back in France. The lifestyles of the Aboriginals, the geography of the region and the beginnings of colonization were the topics most often covered by authors of the period, such as Père Sagard (*Le Grand Voyage au Pays des Hurons*, 1632) and Baron de La Hontan (*Nouveaux Voyages en Amérique Septentrionale*, 1703).

The oral tradition dominated literature during the 18th century and the beginning of the 19th century. Later, the legends that had been passed down over generations, involving such things as ghosts, werewolves and pacts with the devil, were put down on paper. It was not until the end of the 19th century that Québec produced a more advanced literary movement. Most of the literary output of this period dealt with the theme of survival and reflected nationalist, religious and conservative values. The romanticizing of life in the country, far from the temptations of the city, was a common element. Glorifying the past, particularly the period of French rule, was another common theme in the literature of the time. With the exception of certain works, most of the novels from this period are only of socio-historic interest.

Traditionalism continued to profoundly influence literary creation until 1930, when certain new literary movements began to emerge. The École Littéraire de Montréal (Montréal Literary School), and particularly the works of the poet Émile Nelligan, who was inspired by Baudelaire, Rimbaud, Verlaine and Rodenbach, stood in contrast to the prevailing style of the time. Nelligan, who still remains a mythical figure, wrote poetry at a very young age before falling prey to mental illness. Rural life remained an important ingredient of Québec fiction during this period, though certain authors began to put country life in a different light. Louis Hémon, in *Maria Chapdelaine* (1916), presented rural life more realistically, while Albert Laberge (*La Scouine*, 1918) presented the mediocrity of a country existence.

During the Great Depression and World War II, Québec literature began to reflect modernism. Literature with a rural setting, which continued to dominate, gradually began to incorporate themes of alienation. Another major step was taken when cities, where most of Québec's population actually lived, began to be used as settings in francophone fiction, in books such as *Bonheur d'Occasion* (*The Tin Flute*, 1945), by Franco-Manitoban Gabrielle Roy.

Modernism became a particularly strong literary force with the end of the war, despite Maurice Duplessis's repressive administration. Two genres of fiction dominated during this period: the urban novel and the psychological novel. Québec poetry entered a golden era distinguished by the work of a multitude of writers such as Gaston Miron, Alain Grandbois, Anne Hébert, Rina Lasnier and Claude Gauvreau. This era essentially saw the birth of Québec theatre, as well. With regard to essay writing, the *Refus Global* (1948), signed by a group of painters, was the most incisive of many diatribes critical of the Duplessis administration.

Québec writers gained greater prominence with the political and social vitality brought about by the Quiet Revolution in the 1960s. A great number of political essays, such as *Nègres Blancs d'Amérique* (1968), by Pierre Vallières, reflected an era of reappraisal, conflict and cultural upheaval. Through the plays of Marcel Dubé and those of rising talents such as Michel Tremblay, Québec theatre truly came into its own during this period. The use by novelists, poets and dramatists of idiomatic French-Canadian speech, called *joual*, was an important literary breakthrough of the time.

Contemporary literature is rich and diversified. Writers such as Victor-Lévy Beaulieu, Jacques Godbout, Alice Parizeau, Roch Carrier, Jacques Poulin, Louis Caron, Yves Beauchemin, Suzanne Jacob and, more recently, Louis Hamelin, Robert Lalonde, Gaetan Soucy, Christian Mistral, Dany Laferrière, Ying Chen, Sergio Kokis, Arlette Cousture, Raymond Soucy, Marie Laberge, Gil Courtemanche and Yann Martel have joined the ranks of previously established authors.

■ Québec Literature in English

Québec's English-language literary soul is located in Montréal and its best-known author was Mordecai Richler (1931-2001), whose sharply comic prose, as salty as smoked meat on rye, depicts life in the cold-water flats and kosher delis of mid-town Montréal in the 1950s. Novels such as *The Apprenticeship of Duddy Kravitz* (1959), *The Street* (1969) and *St. Urbain's Horseman* (1971) portray a neighbourhood whose face is now changed but still recognizable on certain street corners, such as Clark and Fairmount. Richler was also a frequent contributor to the *New Yorker*, with his crusty and controversial accounts of Québec politics.

Other well-known literary voices of English Montréal include poet Irving Layton, gravel-throated crooner/poet Leonard Cohen, novelist and essayist Hugh MacLennan and poet and novelist Mavis Gallant. On the stage, playwright David Fennario's *Balconville* (1979), which examines the lives of middle-class Anglophones and Francophones in Montréal, is one of the city's best-known works in English.

Montreal's latest literary star is writer Yann Martel. Born in Spain in 1963 to diplomat parents, Martel won the prestigious Booker Prize in 2002 for his novel *Life of Pi*, a fish tale of a story about a teenaged Indian boy shipwrecked on a lifeboat with a Bengal tiger.

■ Theatre

Québec theatre made a name for itself in the 1980s, with the staging of numerous big productions, several of which incorporated different forms of artistic expression (dance, singing, video). As a result, many small theatres sprang up in Montréal. Among Québec's brightest stars in contemporary theatre are Troupe Carbone 14 and directors André Brassard, Robert Lepage, Lorraine Pintal, René-Richard Cyr, and authors René-Daniel Dubois, Michel-Marc Bouchard, Jean-Pierre Ronfard and Wajdi Mouhawad.

■ Music and Song

Music entered a modern era in Québec after World War II. In 1961, Québec hosted an international festival of *musique actuelle* (experimental music). Also in the 1960s, large orchestras, most notably the Orchestre Symphonique de Montréal (OSM), began to attract bigger crowds.

Several important music festivals are held throughout Québec, including the Festival international de musique actuelle in Victoriaville and the summer festival in the Lanaudière region.

Popular song, which has always been important to Québec folk culture, gained further popularity after World War I thanks to the rise of radio and the improved quality of music recordings. The greatest success was known by La Bolduc (Marie Travers), who sang popular songs in idiomatic French. In the 1950s, the prevailing popular music trend involved adapting American songs or reinterpreting songs from France. As a result, certain talented Québec songwriters working at the time, like Raymond Lévesque and Félix Leclerc, were virtually ignored until the 1960s.

With the Quiet Revolution, songwriting in Québec entered a new and vital era. Singers like Claude Léveillé, Jean-Pierre Ferland, Gilles Vigneault and Claude Gauthier won over crowds with nationalist and culturally significant lyrics. In 1968, Robert Charlebois made an important contribution to the Québec music scene by producing the first French-language rock album.

Currently, established performers like Plume Latraverse, Michel Rivard, Diane Dufresne, Pauline Julien, Ginette Reno, Jim Corcoran, Claude Dubois, Richard Séguin, Paul Piché and Marjo are joined by more recent artists as diverse as Jean Leloup, Richard Desjardins, Daniel Bélanger, Dan Bigras, Bruno Pelletier, Kevin Parent, Lynda Lemay, Luce Dufault, Daniel Boucher and Isabelle Boulay. The most well-known name on the international scene these days is Céline Dion, who sings in both French and English. Her amazing voice has made her *the* pop diva around the world. There is also the particular achievement of songwriter Luc Plamondon and his participation in the production of *Starmania* and *Notre-Dame de Paris*. In addition, certain non-francophone artists, like Leonard Cohen, Corey Hart, Bran Van 3000 and the Arcade Fire have enjoyed a strong international reputation.

■ Visual Arts

Visual art in Québec through most of the 19th century displayed a rather antiquated aesthetic. With the support of major art collectors in Montréal, Québec artists began to experiment somewhat towards the end of the 19th century and the beginning of the 20th century. Landscape artists, including Lucius R. O'Brien, achieved certain success during this period. The Barbizon school, characterized by representations of rural life, was also influential. Inspired by the La Haye school, painters like Edmund Morris began to introduce a suggestion of subjectivism into their work.

The works of Ozias Leduc, which were influenced by Symbolism, began to show a tendency towards the subjective interpretation of reality, as did the sculptures of Alfred Laliberté at the beginning of the 20th century. Some works completed around this time exhibit a certain receptiveness of European styles, among them the paintings of Suzor-Côté. It is, however, in the work of James Wilson Morrice, who was inspired by Matisse, that the influence of the European School is most explicitly detectable. Morrice, who died in 1924, is considered by most as the forerunner of modern art in Québec. It would, however, take several years, marked notably by the work of landscape and urban artist Marc-Aurèle Fortin, before the visual arts in Québec were in line with contemporary trends.

Québec modern art began to affirm itself during World War II thanks to the leaders of the movement, Alfred Pellan and Paul-Émile Borduas. In the 1950s, two major trends developed in Québec's art community. The most significant of these involved non-figurative works, of which there were two general categories: abstract expressionism, as seen in the works of Marcelle Ferron, Marcel Barbeau, Pierre Gauvreau and Jean-Paul Riopelle, and geometric abstraction, represented by artists such as Jean-Paul Jérôme, Fernand Toupin, Louis Belzile and Rodolphe de Repentigny. The other major trend in art was a new wave of figurative painting by artists like Jean Dallaire and Jean-Paul Lemieux.

Post-war trends continued into the 1960s. The emergence of new painters, such as Guido Molinari, Claude Tousignant and Yves Gaucher brought increased attention to the geometric abstraction style. Engraving and print-making became more common mediums of expression, art "happenings" were frequent and artists began to be asked to provide work for public places. Styles and influences diversified greatly in the early 1970s, resulting in the eclectic art scene found in Québec today.

Portrait - The Arts

■ Cinema

While some full-length films were made earlier, the birth of Québec cinema really did not occur until after World War II. Between 1947 and 1953, independent producers brought a number of literary adaptations to the screen, including *Un Homme et son Péché* (1948), *Séraphin* (1949), *La Petite Aurore l'Enfant Martyre* (1951) and *Tit-Coq* (1952). However, the arrival of television in the early 1950s resulted in a 10-year period of stagnation for the Québec film industry.

A cinematic renaissance during the 1960s occurred largely thanks to the support of the National Film Board (NFB). With documentaries and realistic films, directors focused primarily on a critique of Québec society. Later, the full-length feature film dominated with the success of certain directors like Claude Jutra (*Mon Oncle Antoine*, 1971), Jean-Claude Lord (*Les Colombes*, 1972), Gilles Carle (*La Vraie Nature de Bernadette*, 1972), Michel Brault (*Les Ordres*, 1974), Jean Beaudin (*J.A. Martin Photographe*, 1977) and Frank Mankiewicz (*Les Bons Débarras*, 1979). The NFB and other government agencies provided most of the funding for these largely uncommercial works.

Important feature films of recent years include those of Denys Arcand (*Le déclin de l'Empire américain*, 1986, *Jésus de Montréal*, 1989, and *Les Invasions Barbares*, 2003, which received an Oscar for best foreign film), Jean-Claude Lauzon (*Un zoo la nuit*, 1987, and *Léolo*, 1992), Léa Pool (*À corps perdu*, 1988), Jean Beaudin (*Being at Home With Claude*, 1992) and François Girard (*Le Violon Rouge*, 1998). Director Frédérick Back won an Academy Award in 1982 for *Crac!* and another one in 1988 for his superbly animated film *L'Homme qui plantait des Arbres*.

Daniel Langlois has also made significant contributions to Québec cinema. A key player in the film industry, he has been very involved in the development of film centres and festivals. He founded Softimage, which designs special-effects software that has been used in several well-known feature-length films in the past several years. He has also opened the Ex-Centris cinema complex in Montréal.

Practical Information

The information in this chapter will help you plan your trip to Québec. It contains important details on entrance formalities, getting there and getting around, as well as other useful information for visitors. We also explain how to use this guide. Happy travels in Québec!

Entrance Formalities

■ Customs

If you are bringing gifts into Canada, remember that certain restrictions apply:

Smokers (legal age is 18) can bring in a maximum of 200 cigarettes, 50 cigars, 200g of tobacco and 200 tobacco sticks.

For **wine** and **liquor**, the limit is 1.5 litres. The limit for beer is 24 355ml cans or 341ml bottles.

There are very strict rules regarding the importation of **plants**, **flowers**, **food** and other **vegetation**; it is therefore not advisable to bring any of these types of products into the country.

If you are travelling with **pets**, you will need a health certificate (available from your veterinarian), as well as a rabies vaccination certificate. Remember that the vaccination must be carried out **at least** 30 days **before** your departure and should not have been administered more than one year ago.

For more information on travelling with animals, plants or food, contact the **Canadian Food Inspection Agency** *(www.cfia-acia.agr. ca)* or the Canadian embassy or consulate nearest you before your departure for Canada.

Tax reimbursements for visitors: it is possible to get reimbursed for the tax paid on purchases made in Québec (see p 64).

■ Passports

A valid passport is usually sufficient for most visitors planning to stay less than three months in Canada. U.S. citizens do not need a passport, but it is, however, a good form of identification. U.S. citizens and citizens of Western Europe do not need a visa. For a complete list of countries whose citizens require a visa, see the **Canadian Citizenship and Immigration** Web site *(www.cic.gc.ca)* or contact the Canadian embassy or consulate nearest you.

■ Extended Visits

Visitors must submit a request to extend their visit **in writing three weeks before** the expiration of their visa (the date is usually written on your passport) to a Canadian Citizenship and Immigration office. To make a request, you must present a valid passport, a return ticket, proof of sufficient funds to cover the stay, as well as the $75 non-refundable filing fee. In some cases (work, study), however, the request must be made **before** arriving to Canada.

Getting There and Getting Around

■ By Plane

Flying is by far the most expensive mode of transportation; however, some airline companies, especially regional ones, regularly offer special rates. It is wise to shop around and compare prices.

Air travel within Québec is provided by **Air Canada Jazz** (☎*888-247-2262, www.flyjazz. ca)*, a subsidiary of Air Canada that serves many destinations, such as Saguenay, Québec City, Gaspé and Îles de la Madeleine.

Northern Québec

Air Creebec
☎ (819) 825-8355 or 800-567-6567
🖷 (819) 825-0885
www.aircreebec.ca
Air Creebec serves Chibougamau, Chisasibi, Roberval and Wemindji, among others. Flights depart from Val-d'Or or Montréal.

Flying out of Montréal, **First Air** (☎*800-267-1247, www.firstair.ca*) serves Kuujjuak.

Air Inuit (☎*800-361-2965, www.airinuit.com*) flies to La Grande and several Inuit villages from Montréal and Québec City.

Airports

There is one major international airport in the province of Québec, located in **Dorval**. A second airport, in **Québec City**, is much smaller and serves only a limited number of destinations, although it does welcome some international flights.

The Mont-Tremblant ski resort (see p 255) has an international airport that handles flights from New York and Toronto.

Montréal-Pierre Elliott Trudeau International Airport

The Montréal-Dorval International Airport was recently renamed "Montréal-Pierre Elliott Trudeau International Airport" in honour of the former Canadian Prime Minister. The airport, which is also simply referred to as "Montréal-Trudeau" is located approximately 20km from downtown Montréal, some 20min by car. To get downtown from here, take Autoroute 20 E. to the junction of Autoroute 720 (the Ville-Marie), then follow signs for "Centre-ville, Vieux-Montréal."

For information regarding airport services (arrivals, departures, other information), contact the **Aéroports de Montréal (ADM)** information centre (☎*514-394-7377 or 800-465-1213, www.admtl.com*).

Shuttle Service

A shuttle service between the Montréal bus depot, a few major hotels and Montréal-Trudeau airport is provided by the **La Québécoise** bus company's **Aérobus** (☎*514-842-2281, www.autobus.qc.ca*). Tickets can be purchased at the airport or at the **Station Centrale** bus depot (*505 Boulevard de Maisonneuve Est; Berri-UQAM métro*).

From Montréal-Trudeau airport to downtown Montréal: the shuttle leaves the airport every 20 minutes, from 7am to 2am.

From downtown Montréal to Montréal-Trudeau airport: the shuttle leaves the Station Centrale bus depot every 20 minutes from 4am to 11pm. There are stops at five major hotels (Marriott Château Champlain, Delta Centre-Ville, Fairmont Reine-Élizabeth, Sheraton and Delta Montréal) before arriving at the Station Centrale bus depot or at the airport. Cost: $13 one-way or $22.75 return trip.

A free shuttle service is also provided between the Station Centrale bus depot and several other major downtown Montréal hotels. Reservations: ☎(514) 843-4938.

Public Transport

You can also use the **Société de Transport de Montréal (STM)** (☎*514-288-6287, www.stm.info*) public transport system to travel from the airport to downtown Montréal. From the airport, take the 204 bus east to the Dorval bus terminal. From there, the eastbound 211 bus will take you to the Lionel-Groulx métro station. To get to the airport, follow the route in the opposite direction from the Lionel-Groulx métro station.

Car Rentals

Major car-rental companies have offices at the airport.

Taxis

Taxi service is offered from 6am until the last flight. The rate is $31 for trips between the airport and downtown Montréal. All taxis serving Montréal-Trudeau International Airport accept credit cards.

Limousines

Fixed rate (*$47.70*) to downtown. For information: ☎(514) 633-3019.

Lost and Found

☎(514) 636-0499

Jean-Lesage International Airport (Québec City)

Québec City's airport is located on the periphery of Sainte-Foy and L'Ancienne-Lorette. To get there from Vieux-Québec, take Boulevard Laurier heading west to Autoroute Henri-IV (Autoroute 40 N). From there, take Boulevard Hamel going west and follow it to Route de l'Aéroport.

500 Rue Principale, Sainte-Foy
☎ (418) 640-2700
www.aeroportdequebec.com

Taxis

A taxi from the airport to Vieux-Québec costs $27, $12 to Sainte-Foy. Some cars can carry as many as six passengers.

Car Rentals

Most major car-rental agencies can be found at the airport.

Lost and Found

☎ (418) 640-2760

■ By Car

Travelling by car is an excellent way to discover Québec. Excellent road and regional maps published in Québec can be found in bookstores and in tourist-information centres.

Things to Consider

Driver's License: As a general rule, foreign driver's licenses are valid for six months from the arrival date in Canada.

Winter Driving: Although roads are generally in good condition, the dangers brought on by drastic climatic conditions must be taken into consideration. Roads are often transformed into virtual skating rinks by black ice. Wind is also a factor, causing blowing snow and reducing visibility. All these factors, which Quebecers are used to, require prudent driving. If you plan on driving through remote areas, be sure to bring along a blanket and some supplies should your car break down.

Driving and the Highway Code: Turning right on a red light in Québec is permitted everywhere in the province (unless otherwise indicated) **except on the island of Montréal**. Signs marked *Arrêt* or "Stop" against a red background must always be respected. Come to a complete stop even if there is no apparent danger.

When a school bus (usually yellow) has stopped and has its signals flashing, you must come to a complete stop, no matter what direction you are travelling in. Failing to stop at the flashing signals is considered a serious offense and carries a heavy penalty. Wearing seatbelts in the front and back seats is compulsory at all times.

Pay attention to reserved bus lanes! They are marked by a large white diamond shape and signs clearly indicating the hours you cannot drive in these lanes, except when making a right turn.

There are no tolls on Québec highways (*autoroutes*), and the speed limit on them is 100km/h (up to 119km/h is usually tolerated). The speed limit on secondary highways is 90km/h, and 50km/h in urban areas.

Car Rentals

To rent a car in Québec, you must be at least 21 years of age and have had a driver's license for **at least** one year.

A credit card is extremely useful for the deposit to avoid tying up large sums of money, and in some cases (gold cards) can cover the insurance.

Most rental cars have an automatic transmission; however, you can request a car with a manual shift. Child safety seats cost extra.

Renting an RV (Motorhome, Camper-Trailer or Caravan)

Although this is a fairly expensive way to get around, RVs are an excellent way to discover the great outdoors. As with car rental, however, a package deal organized through a travel agency is the most economical means of renting this type of vehicle. Your travel agent can provide you with more information.

Because of high demand and the short camping season, it is necessary to reserve early to get a good choice of trailers. When planning a summer holiday, it is best to reserve by January or February at the latest.

Remember to examine the insurance coverage carefully, as these vehicles are very expensive. Make sure kitchen utensils and bedding are included in the rental price.

Cruise Canada (☎*450-628-7093)* is a good company if you decide to rent on the spot. There are many other companies listed in the Yellow Pages phone book under the heading *Véhicules récréatifs* (recreational vehicles).

Accidents and Emergencies

In case of serious accident, fire or other emergency, dial **911** or **0**.

If you run into trouble on the highway, pull onto the shoulder of the road and turn the hazard lights on. If it is a rental car, contact the rental company as soon as possible. Always file an accident report. If a disagreement arises over who was at fault in an accident, ask for police help.

■ By Bus

While a car may be the easiest way to get around, buses are relatively cheap and provide access to most of Québec. With the exception of city buses, which are government run, long-distance bus companies are privately run.

In general, children under five travel free of charge and people aged 60 and over get significant discounts. It is recommended that you arrive at the bus station at least 45min prior to the scheduled departure time.

Travel Times and Adult Fares
for a One-Way Trip from Montréal:

Québec City: *3hrs 15min; $45*
Rimouski: *7hrs; $71*
Sherbrooke: *2hrs 10min; $29.25*

Bus Stations

Montréal
Station Centrale, 505 Boulevard de Maisonneuve Est, corner Berri (Berri-UQAM métro)
☎ (514) 842-2281

Québec City
Gare du Palais, 320 Rue Abraham-Martin
☎ (418) 525-3000

Bus Tours

Some companies also offer package deals on excursions of a day or more, which (depending on the length of the excursion) include accommodation and guided tours. For further information on these tours, contact the Centre Infotouriste in Montréal or in Québec City.

■ By Train

Travelling by train can be very interesting, particularly when covering great distances, as they provide an excellent level of comfort. **Via Rail Canada** *(www.viarail.com)* is the main passenger railway company in Canada.

■ By Boat

There is an almost endless list of possible cruises and boating excursions available throughout Québec. Riverboat trips on what are known as *bateau-mouche* (sightseeing boats) are also available. In some cases, naturalists are on board to give interesting presentations on the ecosystem of the area, providing insights into the flora and fauna. Check the "Getting There and Getting Around" section of the region you want to visit.

Whale-watching excursions in zodiacs, guided cruises around Montréal and Québec City as well as dinner cruises are offered by **Croisières AML** (*124 Rue Saint-Pierre, Québec,* ☎*418-692-2634 or 800-563-4643,* 🖵 *418-692-0845, www.croisieresaml.com).*

N/M Nordik Express *(☎418-723-8787, www.desgagnes.com)* provides trips along the Côte-Nord from Sept-Îles to Blanc-Sablon, passing by Île d'Anticosti, as well as through several small towns accessible only by boat.

CTMA Vacancier
☎ (418) 986-3278 or 888-986-3278
www.ctma.ca
This weekly sightseeing cruise departs Montréal Fridays at noon and arrives in Cap-aux-Meules Sundays at noon, with whale-watching and other stops scheduled along the way. The return trip to Montréal ends on Tuesday evening.

The *M/S Jacques-Cartier* (☎*819-375-3000 or 800-567-3737*, 🖳*819-375-1975, www. croisieres.qc.ca)* is a cruise ship that can welcome up to 400 passengers. Excursions are offered on several navigable rivers in Québec: the Outaouais, the St. Lawrence, the Richelieu and the Saguenay. Although its port of registry is located in Trois-Rivières, the *M/S Jacques Cartier* offers cruises from various cities in the province.

■ By Ferry

Ferries cross the St. Lawrence River and other waterways at several points. For further information, check the "Getting There and Getting Around" section of the guide on the region you want to visit.

www.traversiers.gouv.qc.ca

■ By Bicycle

Cycling is very popular in Québec, especially in cities like Montréal. Bicycle paths have been set up so that cyclists can get around easily and safely, but caution is always recommended, even on these paths. Bicycle touring is possible throughout Québec.

■ Hitchhiking and Ride Sharing

There are two types: "free" hitchhiking, which is prohibited on highways, and "organized" hitchhiking with a group called **Allo-Stop** *(www.allostop.com)*. "Free" hitchhiking is more common, especially during the summer, and easier to do outside large city centres.

"Organized" hitchhiking, or ride sharing, with Allo-Stop works very well in all seasons. This reputed company pairs drivers who want to share their car for a small payment with passengers needing a ride. A membership card is required and costs $6

for a passenger and $7 for a driver per year. The driver receives part (approximately 60%) of the fees paid by the passengers. Destinations include virtually everywhere in the province of Québec.

Children under five cannot travel with Allo-Stop because of a regulation requiring the use of child safety seats.

For registration and information:

Allo-Stop Montréal
4317 Rue Saint-Denis
☎ (514) 985-3032

Allo-Stop Québec
665 Rue Saint-Jean
☎ (418) 522-0056
2360 Chemin Ste-Foy
☎ (418) 522-0056

Allo-Stop Saguenay
☎ (418) 695-2322

Allo-Stop Jonquière
2370 Rue St-Dominique
☎ (418) 695-2322

Allo-Stop Rimouski
106 Rue St-Germain
☎ (418) 723-5248

Allo-Stop Sherbrooke
1204 Rue King Ouest
☎ (819) 821-3637

Useful Information, from A to Z

■ Accommodations

A wide choice of accommodations to fit every budget is available in most regions of Québec. Most places are very comfortable and can offer a number of extra services. Prices vary according to the type of accommodation, but remember to add the 7% GST (federal Goods and Services Tax) and the 7.5% provincial sales tax (PST). These taxes may however be refundable to non-residents (see p 64). A specific tax on accommodation rates in Québec, called Taxe Spécifique sur l'Hébergement, was introduced to support the tourist infrastructures of several regions. Visitors will thus incur this $2/night tax, regardless of the total of their bill.

The various services offered by each establishment are indicated by a small symbol, which is explained in the legend on the last page of this guidebook. By no means is this an exhaustive list of what the establishment offers, but rather the services we consider to be the most important.

Please note that the presence of a symbol does not mean that all the rooms have this service; you sometimes have to pay extra to get, for example, a whirlpool tub. Please note that unless otherwise indicated, all lodgings in this guide offer private bathrooms.

All the prices mentioned in this guide apply to a **standard room for two people in peak season**. Prices are indicated with the following symbols:

$	less than $60
$$	$60 to $100
$$$	$101 to $150
$$$$	$151 to $225
$$$$$	more than $225

The actual cost to guests is often lower than the prices quoted here, particularly for travel during the off-peak season. Also, many hotels and inns offer considerable discounts to employees of corporations or members of automobile clubs (CAA, AAA). Be sure to ask about corporate and other discounts, as they are often very easy to obtain.

Tourisme Québec, in collaboration with the Corporation de l'Industrie touristique du Québec, has set up a system for classifying lodging in Québec. The classification, which ranges from one to five stars, complies with international standards and provides visitors with a point of reference from which to judge the quality of the establishment. This system assesses the amenities and services available in the establishment by means of an objective point scale–the more amenities and services available, the more points awarded. The listed accommodations bear a plaque with *Hébergement Québec* inscribed on it.

Under the "Accommodations" headings of this guide, the quality of the lodgings is not defined according to the standards of Tourism Québec, but rather to the authors' judgement, taking into account such factors as quality of service, decor, location and value.

The Ulysses Label

The Ulysses Label appears next to our favourite accommodations. While every establishment recommended in this guide was included because of its high quality and/or uniqueness, as well as its high value, every once in a while we come across an establishment that absolutely wows us. These, our favourite establishments, are awarded a Ulysses Label. You'll find such labels in all price categories. Regardless of the price, each of these establishments offers the most for your money. Look for them first!

Reservations

Hospitality Canada has an office in Montréal which offers free reservation services for tourism and accommodation packages throughout Québec and the rest of Canada.

Hospitality Canada
651 Rue Notre-Dame Ouest, Suite 260, Montréal
☎ (514) 287-9049 or 866-363-6674
🖷 (514) 287-1220
www.hospitality-canada.com

Hotels

There are countless hotels across Québec, and they range from modest to luxurious. Most hotel rooms feature a private bathroom.

Bed and Breakfasts

Bed and breakfasts are well distributed throughout most of Québec, and besides the obvious price advantage is their unique family atmosphere. They also provide the opportunity to appreciate regional architecture and cultural exchange, as many of the small houses are quite picturesque. Credit cards are not always accepted in bed and breakfasts. Prices for a room also include breakfast. Unlike hotels, rooms in private homes do not always have private bathrooms.

In Québec, some bed and breakfasts are known as *gîtes et auberges du passant*. The term refers to bed and breakfasts that are members of the Fédération des Agricotours du Québec and that conform to their regulations and standards.

Motels

There are many motels throughout the province, but they tend to be cheaper and lacking in atmosphere. They are, however, particularly useful when pressed for time.

Youth Hostels

Youth hostel addresses are listed in the "Accommodations" section for the cities in which they are located. For more information, contact:

Tourisme Jeunesse
☎ (514) 252-3117
www.tourismej.qc.ca

University Residences

Due to certain restrictions, this can be a complicated alternative. Residences are only available during the summer (mid-May to mid-August); reservations must be made several months in advance, usually by paying the first night with a credit card. This type of accommodation, however, is less costly than "traditional" alternatives, and making the effort to reserve early can be worthwhile. Travellers can expect to pay between $30 and $45, before taxes. Bedding is included in the price, and there is usually a cafeteria in the building (meals are not included in the price).

Spas

Spas, known as *relais santé*, are becoming increasingly popular. Professionals provide treatments such as hydrotherapy, massage therapy and beauty care in establishments that differ according to their various menus, activities and services. For more information, or to choose the spa that best suits your needs:

Relais Santé
☎ 800-788-7594
www.relais-sante.com

Staying in Aboriginal Communities

The opportunities for staying in First Nations communities are limited but are becoming more popular. As the reserves are managed by Aboriginal groups, in some cases it is necessary to obtain authorization from the band council to visit.

www.staq.net

Camping

Next to being put up by friends, camping is the most inexpensive form of accommodation. Unfortunately, unless you have winter-camping gear, camping is limited to a short period of the year, from June to August. Services provided by campgrounds can vary considerably. Campsites can be either private or publicly owned. The prices listed in this guide apply to campsites without hookups for campers, and vary depending on additional services. Take note that campgrounds are not subject to the accommodation tax.

Fédération Québécoise de Camping et Caravaning
4545 Avenue Pierre-De Coubertin
C.P. 1000, Succursale M, Montréal, Québec, H1V 3R2
☎ (514) 252-3003 or 866-237-3722
🖷 (514) 254-0694
www.campingquebec.com

■ Bars and Nightclubs

Most pub-style bars do not charge a cover (although in winter there is usually a mandatory coat-check). Expect to pay a few dollars to get into nightclubs and shows on weekends. Québec nightlife is particularly lively, and it doesn't hurt that the sale of alcohol continues until 3am. Some bars remain open past this hour but serve only soft drinks. Drinking establishments that only have a tavern or brasserie permit must close at midnight. In small towns, restaurants also frequently serve as bars. Those seeking entertainment come nightfall should therefore consult the "Restaurant" section in every chapter, as well as the "Entertainment" section.

■ Business Hours and Holidays

Business Hours

The law respecting business hours allows stores to be open the following hours:

- Monday to Wednesday from 8am to 9pm, though most stores open at 10am and close at 6pm.

- Thursday and Friday from 8am to 9pm, though most open at 10am.

- Saturday from 8am to 5pm, though most open at 10am.

- Sunday from 8am to 5pm, though most open at noon. Not all stores are open on Sundays.

Dépanneurs (convenience stores that sell food) are found throughout Québec and stay open later, sometimes 24hrs a day.

Holidays

The following is a list of public holidays in Québec. Most government offices and banks are closed on these days.

January 1st and 2nd
New Year and the day after

Easter Monday

Monday immediately preceding May 25
Jour des Patriotes or Victoria Day

June 24
Saint-Jean-Baptiste Day, Québec's national holiday

July 1st
Canada Day

First Monday in September
Labour Day

Second Monday in October
Thanksgiving

November 11
Remembrance Day; only banks and federal government services are closed

December 25 and 26
Christmas and Boxing Day

■ Children

Children in Québec are treated like royalty. Facilities are available almost everywhere you go, whether it be transportation or leisure activities. Generally, children under five travel for free, and those under 12 are eligible for fare reductions. The same rules apply for various leisure activities and shows. Find out before you purchase tickets. High chairs and children's menus are available in many restaurants, while a few of the larger stores provide a babysitting service while parents shop.

■ Climate

Québec's seasonal extremes set the province apart from much of the world. Temperatures can rise above 30°C in summer and drop to -25°C in winter. Visiting Québec during the two "main" seasons (summer and winter) is like visiting two totally different countries, with the seasons influencing not only the scenery, but the lifestyles and behaviour of the province's residents.

Winter

"Mon pays ce n'est pas un pays, c'est l'hiver..."
("My country is not a country, it's winter...")
– Gilles Vigneault

Mid-November to the end of March is the best time for skiing, snowmobiling, ice-skating, snowshoeing and other winter sports. In general, there are five or six big snowstorms per winter. Howling winds often make the temperatures bitterly cold, causing "drifting snow" (very fine snow that is blown by the wind). One bright spot is that though it may be freezing, Québec gets more hours of winter sunshine than Europe.

Spring

Spring is short, lasting roughly from the end of March to the end of May, and heralded by the arrival of "slush," a mixture of melted snow and mud. As the snow disappears, long-buried plants and grass, yellowed by frost and mud, come to life again. Nature's welcomed reawakening is spectacular.

Summer

Summer in Québec blossoms from the end of May to the end of August and may surprise some who think of Québec as a land of snow and igloos. The heat can be quite extreme and often seems much hotter because of the accompanying humidity. The vegetation becomes lush, and don't be surprised to see red and green peppers or tomatoes growing in window boxes—the temperature is almost high enough to fool you into thinking you are in Mexico! City streets are decorated with flowers, and restaurant terraces are always full. It is also the season when many different festivals are held all across Québec (see the "Festivals and Events" section, p 55).

Fall

Fall colours can last from September to November. Maple trees form one of the most beautiful living pictures on the North American continent. Leaves are transformed into a kaleidoscope of colours from bright green to scarlet red to golden yellow. Temperatures will stay warm for a while, but eventually the days and especially the nights will become quite cool.

Indian Summer

This relatively short period (only a few days) in late fall feels like summer's triumphant return. Referred to as Indian Summer, it is in fact the result of warm air currents from the Gulf of Mexico. This time of the year is called Indian Summer because it marked the last hunt before winter. Aboriginals took advantage of the warm weather to stock up on provisions before the cold weather arrived.

Weather

For road conditions:
☎ (514) 284-2363 or 877-393-2363

For weather forecasts:
☎ (514) 283-3010
www.meteomedia.com

■ Drugs

Recreational drugs are against the law and not tolerated (even "soft" drugs). Anyone caught with drugs in their possession risks severe consequences.

■ Electricity

Voltage is 110 volts throughout Canada, the same as in the United States. Electricity plugs have two parallel, flat pins. Adaptors are available here.

■ Embassies and Consulates

For a complete list of Canadian embassies and consulates abroad, consult the following Government of Canada Web site: www.dfait-maeci.gc.ca.

Abroad

Great Britain

Canada High Commission
Macdonald House
One Grosvenor Square, London, W1K 4AB
☎ (207) 258 6600
🗐 (207) 258 6333
www.dfait-maeci.gc.ca/canadaeuropa/united_kingdom

United States

Canadian Embassy
501 Pennsylvania Ave. NW, Washington, DC, 20001
☎ (202) 682-1740
🗐 (202) 682-7701
www.canadianembassy.org

In Montréal

Great Britain

1000 de la Gauchetière Ouest, Suite 4200
Montréal, QC, H3B 4W5
☎ (514) 866-5863
🗐 (514) 866-0202
www.britainincanada.org/Contact/montreal.htm

United States

Place Félix-Martin, 1155 Rue Saint-Alexandre
☎ (514) 398-9695
Mailing address:
C.P. 65, Station Desjardins, Montréal, QC, H5B 1G1
www.usembassycanada.gov

In Québec City

United States

Consulate General
2 Place Terrasse Dufferin, Québec, QC, G1R 4T9
☎ (418) 692-2095
www.usembassycanada.gov

■ Exploring

Every chapter in this guide leads you through one or more of Québec's tourist regions. The name of each attraction is followed by its address and phone number. The prices indicated are admission fees for one adult. It is best to inquire, because most attractions offer discounts for children, students, senior citizens and families. Some attractions are only open during the summer, but may welcome groups upon request in the off-season. A wheelchair icon indicates those attractions that are accessible to travellers with disabilities.

Attractions are classified according to a star-rating system, so you can spot the must-sees at a glance.

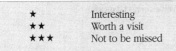

★	Interesting
★★	Worth a visit
★★★	Not to be missed

■ Festivals and Events

Québec's colourful history and distinct, culturally diverse population are well represented by a variety of cultural activities each year. Given the impressive number (over 170) of festivals, annual expositions, exhibitions, fairs, gatherings and other events, it is impossible to list them all. We have, however, selected a few of the highlights, which are described in the "Entertainment" section of each chapter, and in the section below.

Calendar of Events

February

Montréal
Fête des Neiges
www.fetedesneiges.com
(winter festival)

Gatineau – Ottawa (Outaouais)
Winterlude
www.canadascapital.gc.ca/winterlude

Québec City
Québec Winter Carnival
www.carnaval.qc.ca

Chicoutimi (Saguenay–Lac-Saint-Jean)
Carnaval-Souvenir de Chicoutimi

April

Plessisville (Centre-du-Québec)
Festival de l'érable de Plessisville
(maple festival)

May

Victoriaville (Centre-du-Québec)
Festival international de musique actuelle de Victoriaville
(International Festival of New Music)
www.fimav.qc.ca

June

Montréal
International Fireworks Competition
www.lemondialsaq.com
Canadian Grand Prix
www.grandprix.ca
Montreal International Jazz Festival
www.montrealjazzfest.com
(begins late June)

Saint-Jean-Port-Joli (Chaudière-Appalaches)
Internationale de la Sculpture
(International Sculpture Festival)

Matane (Gaspésie)
Festival de la Crevette
(shrimp festival)

Tadoussac (Manicouagan)
Festival de la Chanson de Tadoussac
(song festival)

Joliette (Lanaudière)
Festival de Lanaudière
www.lanaudiere.org

Saint-Irénée (Charlevoix)
Festival international du Domaine Forget
www.domaineforget.com

July

Montréal
International Fireworks Competition
www.lemondialsaq.com
Just for Laughs Comedy Festival
www.hahaha.com
Francofolies
www.francofolies.com
(French music festival)

Kahnawake (Montérégie)
Pow Wow

Saint-Hyacinthe (Montérégie)
Exposition agricole et alimentaire de Saint-Hyacinthe
(agricultural fair)

Sorel (Montérégie)
Festival de la Gibelotte de Sorel
(fish stew festival)

Salaberry-de-Valleyfield (Montérégie)
Valleyfield International Regatta
www.regates.ca

Orford (Eastern Townships)
Orford Festival
www.arts-orford.org

Drummondville (Centre-du-Québec)
Mondial des Cultures
www.mondialdescultures.com
(world folklore festival)

Québec City
Québec City Summer Festival
www.infofestival.com

Beauport (Québec City Region)
Grands feux Loto-Québec
www.lesgrandsfeux.com
(musical fireworks show)

Saint-Jean-Chrysostome (Chaudière-Appalaches)
Festivent
(wind festival)

Mont-Saint-Pierre (Gaspésie)
Fête du Vol Libre
(hang-gliding event)

Mont-Tremblant (Laurentians)
Festival de Blues de Mont-Tremblant
www.tremblant.com/bluesfestival
(blues festival)

Saint-Irénée (Charlevoix)
Festival international du Domaine Forget
www.domaineforget.com

Roberval (Saguenay–Lac-Saint-Jean)
Traversée internationale du lac Saint-Jean
www.traversee.qc.ca
(swimming marathon)

August

Montréal
World Film Festival (WFF)
www.ffm-montreal.org
Divers-cité
www.diverscite.org
(gay pride parade)

Chambly
Le Fort Chambly s'endimanche

Saint-Jean-sur-Richelieu (Montérégie)
International des montgolfières
www.montgolfieres.com
(hot-air balloon festival)

Orford (Eastern Townships)
Orford Festival
www.arts-orford.org

Trois-Rivières (Mauricie)
Grand Prix Automobile

Québec City
Expo-Québec
www.expocite.com

Rimouski (Bas-Saint-Laurent)
FestiJazz
www.festijazzrimouski.com

Beauport (Québec City Region)
Grands feux Loto-Québec
www.lesgrandsfeux.com
(musical fireworks show)

Île du Havre Aubert (Îles de la Madeleine)
Sand Castle Competition
www.artisansdusable.com

Saint-Irénée (Charlevoix)
Festival international du Domaine Forget
www.domaineforget.com

Baie-Saint-Paul (Charlevoix)
Symposium of Young Canadian Painters

September

Granby (Eastern Townships)
Festival de la chanson de Granby
(song festival)

Chambly (Montérégie)
Fête Bières et Saveurs

Saint-Donat (Lanaudière)
Autumn Colours Weekend

Laurentians
Festival des Couleurs
(autumn colours festival)

Mont-Tremblant (Laurentians)
Fête de la Musique

Montmagny (Chaudière-Appalaches)
Carrefour mondial de l'accordéon
http://accordeon.montmagny.com
(World Accordion Jamboree)

Val-Morin (Laurentians)
Les couleurs en vélo
(cycling event)

Gatineau (Outaouais)
Hot Air Balloon Festival
www.montgolfieresgatineau.com

Saint-Tite (Mauricie)
Western Festival
www.festivalwestern.com

Rimouski (Bas-Saint-Laurent)
Carrousel international du film de Rimouski
(film festival)

Baie-Saint-Paul (Charlevoix)
Rêves d'automne
(autumn dreams)

October

Montréal
Montreal International Festival of Cinema and New Media

Laurentians
Festival des couleurs
(autumn colours festival)

Rouyn-Noranda (Abitibi-Témiscamingue)
Festival du cinéma international
en Abitibi-Témiscamingue
(international film festival)

Trois-Rivières (Mauricie)
International Poetry Festival
www.fiptr.com

Montmagny (Chaudière-Appalaches)
Festival de l'Oie Blanche
(snow goose festival)

■ Folklore

Québec's rich folklore offers an interesting insight into the history and culture of the province. The organization below regroups various regional committees aimed at the preservation and development of folklore. Several activities are organized depending on the seasons and locations. For more information:

Association Québécoise des Loisirs Folkloriques
4545 Avenue Pierre-De Coubertin
C.P. 1000, Succursale M, Montréal, QC, H1V 3R2
☎ (514) 252-3022
www.quebecfolklore.qc.ca

■ Gay and Lesbian Life

In 1977, Québec became the second political entity in the world, after Holland, to include in its charter of rights the non-discrimination clause on the basis of sexual orientation. Quebecers' attitudes towards homosexuality are, in general, open and tolerant. Montréal and Québec City offer many services to the gay and lesbian community. In Montréal, most of these services are concentrated in the part of town known as **Le Village**, mainly located on Rue Sainte-Catherine, between Amherst and Papineau streets. The gay village in Québec City is found on Rue Saint-Jean-Baptiste, outside the walls of the old city.

The following telephone line provides details on activities in Montréal: **Gai Écoute** *(11am to 3am;* ☎*514-866-0103 or 888-505-1010).*

The **Centre Communautaire des Gais et Lesbiennes** *(2075 Rue Plessis,* ☎*514-528-8424, www.ccglm.org)* features a library specializing in gay and lesbian works.

The **Défilé de la Fierté Gaie et Lesbienne** (Pride Parade) takes place on the first Sunday of August on Boulevard René-Lévesque and ends with various performances *(Divers-Cité:* ☎*514-285-4011, www.diverscite.org).*

Several free monthly magazines containing information concerning the gay and lesbian communities are available in bars and other establishments serving them: *RG*, *Fugues* and *La Voix du Village*.

■ Guidebooks and Maps

There are various specialized guidebooks and maps that might prove very useful for visitors seeking more information on certain aspects of Québec.

Ulysses Travel Bookshop
4176 Rue Saint-Denis (métro Mont-Royal)
☎ (514) 843-9447
560 Avenue du Président-Kennedy (métro McGill)
☎ (514) 843-7222

■ Health

Vaccinations are not necessary for people coming from Europe, the United States or Australia. On the other hand, it is strongly suggested, particularly for medium or long-term stays, that visitors take out health and accident insurance. There are different types, so it is best to shop around. Bring along all medication, especially prescription drugs. Unless otherwise stated, the water is drinkable throughout Québec.

In the winter, moisturizing lotion and lip balm are useful for people with sensitive skin, since the air in many buildings is very dry.

During the summer, always protect yourself against sunburn. It is often hard to feel your skin getting burned by the sun on windy days, so do not forget to apply sun screen.

■ Insurance

Cancellation

Your travel agent will usually offer you cancellation insurance when you buy your airline ticket or vacation package. This insurance allows you to be reimbursed for the ticket or package deal if your trip must be cancelled due to serious illness or death. Travellers in good health usually do not need this type of insurance.

Theft

Most residential insurance policies protect some of your goods from theft, even if the theft occurs in a foreign country. To make a claim, you must fill out a police report. It may not be necessary to take out further insurance, depending on the amount covered by your current home policy. As policies vary considerably, you are advised to check with your insurance company. European visitors should take out baggage insurance.

Health

This is the most useful kind of insurance for travellers and should be purchased before your departure. Your insurance plan should be as complete as possible because health-care costs add up quickly. When buying insurance, make sure it covers all types of medical costs, such as hospitalization, nursing services and doctor's fees. Make sure your limit is high enough, as these expenses can be costly. A repatriation clause is also vital in case the required care is not available on site. Furthermore, since you may have to pay immediately, check your policy to see what provisions it includes for such situations. To avoid any problems during your vacation, always keep proof of your insurance policy on you.

■ Language

Language is a hot issue in Québec. Quebecers are very proud of their unique version of French and have struggled long and hard to preserve it while surrounded on all sides by English. The accent and vocabulary are different from European French, and can be surprising at first, but have a charm all their own.

French or English?

When writing a guide to a place where the use and preservation of language are part of daily life, certain decisions have to be made. We have tried to keep our combined use of English and French consistent throughout the guide. The official language in Québec is French, so when listing attractions and addresses, we have kept the titles in French, except with federal sites, which have official names in both languages, and with certain sites, in Montréal and the Eastern Townships, for example, which have two names as well. This will allow readers to make the connection between the guide and the signs they will be seeing. The terms used in these titles are in the glossary at the end of the guide, but we are confident that after a couple of days, you will not even need to check.

English style has been used in the text itself to preserve readability. In areas such as Montréal, Ottawa-Gatineau and the Eastern Townships, visitors will hear English almost as much as French. English-speaking visitors to these areas will often be able to take a break from practicing their French, if they want. Just remember, a valiant effort and a sincere smile go a long way! A complete list of all the local expressions would be too long to include in this guide. Travellers interested in knowing a bit more on the subject can refer to the *Canadian French for Better Travel* conversation guide, published by Ulysses Travel Guides.

Learning French

Travellers hoping to learn the language of Molière while in Québec can either absorb it as they go, or might prefer to take French lessons. In-depth courses are offered at Cégeps and universities, while private schools usually offer more courses of varying lengths and difficulties. Here are a few schools to check out:

Centre Linguista
☎ (514) 397-1736
www.centrelinguista.com

Language Studies Canada
☎ (514) 499-9911
www.lsc-canada.com

Berlitz Language Centre
☎ (514) 288-3111
www.berlitz.ca

Université Laval in Québec City and Université de Montréal in Montréal offer undergraduate French language courses for non-Francophones. The **Ecole des Langues Vivantes** (☎*418-656-2321, www.fl.ulaval.ca/elv*) also offers intensive summer courses.

■ Laundromats

Laundromats and dry cleaners are found almost everywhere in urban areas. In most cases, detergent is sold on site. Although change machines are sometimes provided, it is best to bring plenty of coins with you.

■ Money and Banking

Banks and Currency Exchange

Banks are open Monday to Friday, from 10am to 3pm. Many are also open Thursdays and Fridays until 6pm, and sometimes until 8pm.

Most bank services are available to tourists. Travellers who are planning extended stays should note however that non-residents cannot open a bank account. The best way to get money in this case is to carry traveller's cheques. Withdrawing money from your overseas account can be costly, as commission costs are high. However, some automatic teller machines accept foreign bank cards, allowing you to make withdrawals. The other choice is a postal money order, for which no commission is charged; however, they can be time-consuming to process. Those travellers who have gained resident status, permanent or not (such as immigrants or students), can open a bank account. To do so, be sure to bring your passport and proof of residence status with you to the bank.

Most banks readily exchange American and European currencies, but almost all will charge a **commission**. There are, however, exchange offices that do not charge commissions and keep longer hours. Just remember to **ask about fees** and **compare rates**.

Credit Cards

Most credit cards are accepted at stores, restaurants and hotels. While the main advantage of credit cards is that they allow visitors to avoid carrying large sums of money, using a credit card also makes leaving a deposit for car rental much easier and some cards, gold cards for example, automatically insure you when you rent a car. In addition, the exchange rate with a credit card is generally better. The most commonly accepted credit cards are Visa, MasterCard and American Express.

Exchange Rates*

$1 CAD	=	$0.87 USD
$1 CAD	=	£0.50
$1 CAD	=	0.72 euro
$1 USD	=	$1.14 CAD
£1	=	$2.00 CAD
1 euro	=	$1.39 CAD

*Samples only—rates fluctuate

Currency

The monetary unit is the dollar ($), which is divided into cents. One dollar = 100 cents (¢).

Bills come in 5, 10, 20, 50 and 100 dollar denominations, and coins come in 1, 5, 10 and 25 cent coins, as well as in 1 and 2 dollar coins.

Europeans may be surprised to hear of "pennies" ($0.01), "nickels" ($0.05), "dimes" ($0.10), "quarters" ($0.25), "loonies" ($1), and sometimes even "twoonies" ($2).

Traveller's Cheques

Traveller's cheques are accepted in most large stores and hotels; however, it is easier and to your advantage to change your cheques at an exchange office. For a better exchange rate, buy your traveller's cheques in Canadian dollars before leaving home.

■ Museums

Most museums charge admission; however, permanent exhibits at some museums are free on Wednesday evenings from 6pm to 9pm, while discounts are offered for temporary exhibits. Reduced prices are available for seniors, children and students. Call the museum for further details.

■ Newspapers

International newspapers can easily be found in the cities. Major Québec newspapers are: in French, *Le Devoir*, *La Presse* and *Le Journal de Montréal* in Montréal and *Le Soleil* in Québec City; and in English, *The Gazette* in Montréal. Four free weekly newspapers—*Voir* (in French—also Outaouais region and Québec City editions, *www.voir.ca*), *Ici* (French), the *Mirror* and *Hour*—are published in Montréal with information on restaurants, entertainment and other cultural activities.

■ Pets

Dogs on a leash are permitted in most public parks in cities. Québec's provincial parks, however, are definitely not pet-friendly (domestic animals are prohibited) and pets are not particularly welcome at federal parks in Québec either (although Forillon National Park is a pleasant surprise in this regard: dogs are permitted on beaches and hiking trails). Small pets are allowed on the public transportation systems in cities, as long as they are in a cage or small enough to remain in the arms of the owner. Pets are generally not allowed in stores or restaurants, although some establishments with terraces permit pets. Seeing Eye dogs are not subject to such restrictions.

■ Pharmacies

In addition to traditional pharmacies, there are several huge chain stores (medical- and beauty-product supermarkets) around so don't be surprised to find chocolates and detergent next to cough drops and headache medication.

■ Post Offices

Main post office branches are open from 9am to 5pm *(Canada Post: ☎800-267-1177)*. There are also several smaller postal outlets located in shopping malls, convenience stores and pharmacies throughout the province. These outlets often have extended opening hours.

■ Public Washrooms

Most shopping centres have public toilets, but if you cannot find one, you may be able to use the facilities in a bar or a restaurant.

■ Religion

Almost all religions are represented in the province. Unlike English Canada, the majority of the Québec population is Catholic, although most Quebecers are not practicing.

■ Restaurants

Though you may have learned differently in your French classes, Quebecers refer to breakfast as *déjeuner*, lunch as *dîner* and dinner as *souper*. Many restaurants offer a "daily special" (called *spécial du jour*), a complete meal for one price, which is usually less expensive than ordering individual items from the à-la-carte menu. Served only at lunch, the price usually includes a choice of appetizers and main dishes, plus coffee and sometimes dessert. In the evening, a table d'hôte (same formula but slightly more expensive) is also an attractive possibility.

Prices in this guide refer to the evening table d'hôte for one person, or an equivalent meal including appetizer, main course and dessert, before taxes and tip (See "Taxes and Tipping," p 64).

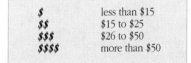

$	less than $15
$$	$15 to $25
$$$	$26 to $50
$$$$	more than $50

The Ulysses Label

The Ulysses Label appears next to our favourite restaurants. For more information, see p 51.

"Bring Your Own Wine" Restaurants

Québec features plenty of restaurants where you can bring your own wine. This is because in order to sell alcohol, a restaurant must have an alcohol permit, which is expensive. Restaurants who want to offer their clientele a less expensive menu opt for a special type of permit that allows their patrons to bring their own bottle of wine. In most cases, a sign in the restaurant window indicates whether alcohol can be purchased on the premises (*permis d'alcool*) or if you should bring your own (*apportez votre vin*). Besides the alcohol permit, there is also a bar permit. Restaurants with only the alcohol permit can sell alcohol, beer and wine, but only if they are accompanied by a meal. Restaurants with both permits can sell you just a drink, even if you do not order a meal.

Cafés

Many people in Québec are espresso connoisseurs. Numerous little restaurants with a relaxed, convivial atmosphere also serve as cafés. Every city has some, especially Montréal and Québec, and several are institutions in certain parts of the city. Coffee reigns supreme in these places, but good, small meals are also served, such as soup, salad and *croques-monsieur*, and, of course, croissants and desserts.

Québec Cuisine

Although many restaurant dishes are similar to those served in the rest of Canada or the United States, some of them are prepared in a typically Québécois way. These unique dishes should definitely be tasted:

La soupe aux pois
pea soup

La tourtière
meat pie

Le pâté chinois
(also known as shepherd's pie) layered pie consisting of ground beef, potatoes and corn

Les cretons
a type of pâté of ground pork cooked with onions in fat

Le jambon au sirop d'érable
ham with maple syrup

Maple Syrup

By the time the first colonists arrived in America, the territory's various indigenous cultures had already been enjoying maple syrup for a long time. In fact, it is impossible to determine exactly when the Aboriginals first discovered this sweet liquid. According to an Iroquois legend, it happened like this: Woksis, the Great Chief, headed out hunting one morning. The night had been cold, but the day promised to be warm. The day before, he had left his tomahawk stuck in a maple tree, and when he removed it, sap began to flow from the crack in the wood. The sap flowed into a bucket that happened to be sitting under the hole. Later, Woksis's wife needed water to prepare the evening meal. Upon seeing the bucket full of sap, she thought it would spare her a trip to the river. An intelligent and conscientious woman who hated waste, she tasted the water and found it a bit on the sweet side, but nevertheless good, and used it to make the meal. On his way home, Woksis smelled the sweet scent of maple from far away and knew something special was cooking. The sap had turned into syrup, making the meal positively succulent. And thus was born one of North America's sweetest traditions.

Natives did not have the necessary materials to heat a cauldron at very high temperatures, so they used heated rocks, which they dropped into the water to make it boil. Another method was to let the maple water freeze overnight, then remove the layer of ice the following morning, repeating this process until nothing remained but a thick syrup. Maple syrup played a prominent role in the Aboriginal diet, culture and religion. The syrup-making methods that are used today were handed down by Europeans, who taught them to the natives.

Technological advances have led to great changes in the way maple products are made. The sugar season is in the spring, when nighttime temperatures are still below zero and the days are warm, enabling the sap to flow more freely. Temperature thus plays a key role in the production of maple syrup. The first step is to carve a hole about 2.5cm deep in the maple tree, one metre above ground. A spout is then inserted in the hole and the sap flows either into a bucket or through a series of pipes leading to the sugar shack. For the former, the sap must be collected every morning. Of course, the latter system is more common, and only small outfits still use the traditional bucket method.

Once it reaches the sugar shack, the sap is boiled to reduce it to syrup. When the liquid reaches 7°C above boiling, it becomes maple syrup. If it is boiled longer, until it reaches 14.5°C above boiling, it becomes maple taffy (*tire*), a real treat when poured onto the snow. It is also possible to make other products, such as maple sugar, maple butter and maple candy, but these all require more careful preparation.

Come springtime, Quebecers head off to the woods to go sugaring-off and enjoy those mainstays of the sugar shack menu, *oreilles de Christ* (literally Christ's ears, but actually deep-fried lard), *œufs dans le sirop* (eggs in syrup) and *tire sur la neige* (maple taffy on snow).

Les fèves au lard
baked beans

Le ragoût de pattes de cochon
pigs' feet stew

Le cipaille
layered pie with different types of meat

La poutine
french fries served with gravy and cheese curds

La tarte aux pacanes
pecan pie

La tarte au sucre
sugar pie

La tarte aux bleuets
blueberry pie

Le sucre à la crème
rich maple-syrup fudge

In the countryside, you might also get the opportunity to enjoy some exceptional regional specialties like venison, hare, beaver, Atlantic salmon, Arctic char and Abitibi caviar.

Sugar Shack or Cabane à Sucre

Called "sugaring off" at the "sugar shack" in English, this is a true Québécois tradition. Sap begins to rise in maple trees at the beginning of the spring thaw, and taps are inserted in the trees in order to retrieve the sap. After a rather involved boiling process, the sap is transformed into a sugary syrup known as maple syrup. In the early spring, Quebecers from across the province venture off into the countryside, to the maple groves, to spend the day at the sugar shack, dining on such specialties as eggs with maple syrup and deep-fried lard (called *oreilles de crisse*). After the meal, it's time for *la tire*, hot maple syrup poured on snow, hardening into a delicious toffee that you roll onto a stick and enjoy!

■ Security

Violence is far less prevalent in Québec than in the United States. A genuine non-violence policy is advocated throughout the province. Visitors who take the same precautions they would at home have no need to be overly worried about personal security. In case of an emergency, call ☎*911*.

■ Senior Citizens

Seniors who would like to meet people their age can do so through the organization listed below. It provides information about activities and local clubs throughout Québec:

Fédération de l'Âge d'Or du Québec
4545 Avenue Pierre-De Coubertin
C.P. 1000, Succursale M, Montréal, QC, H1V 3R2
☎ (514) 252-3017 or 800-828-3344
▤ (514) 252-3154
www.fadoq.ca

Reduced transportation fares and entertainment tickets are often made available to seniors. Do not hesitate to ask.

■ Shopping

What to Buy?

Aboriginal Arts & Crafts

There are beautiful Aboriginal sculptures made from different types of stone that are generally quite expensive. Make sure the sculpture is authentic by asking for a certificate of authenticity issued by the Canadian government. Good quality imitations are widely available and are much less expensive.

Apple Cider

Apple Cider is made in the Montérégie region, along with many other apple-based products (vinegar, butter, alcohol, etc.).

Blueberry Wine

This wine is made from blueberries and is available in most stores of the Sociéte des Alcools du Québec (SAQ, liquor stores).

Books

Books by Québec francophone authors are ideal purchases for those interested in the francophone culture. English-language Quebecers and Canadian literature is easier to find here than elsewhere in the world. In addition, American books are sold in English bookstores throughout the province at better prices than in Europe. A wide selection of French-language books is also available.

Compact Discs

Compact discs are much less expensive than in Europe, however, they may be more expensive than in the United States.

Practical Information – Useful Information, from A to Z

Dandelion Wine

This dry white wine made from dandelion flowers is available in the Beauce region.

Electronics

Montréal is a major centre for telecommunications, therefore it might be a good idea to buy some gadgets such as answering machines, fax machines or cordless and cellular phones. However, be aware that these devices may require a special adaptor for use in your home country. Importing these items may also be illegal in certain European countries.

Furs and Leather

Clothes made from animal skins are of very good quality and their prices are relatively low. Approximately 80% of fur items sold in Canada are made in Montréal's "fur district."

Maple Syrup

There are many varieties of maple syrup. Some are thicker and more syrupy than others, some are dark and some are light in colour, and some have more sugar than others; in any case, it would be sinful to pass up a chance to try at least a few!

Mead

A honey wine, mead is produced in *hydromelleries* in certain parts of Québec, including Mirabel, just north of Montréal.

■ Smokers

Cigarette smoking is considered taboo and is prohibited in all public spaces since May 31, 2006 (including restaurants, bars and cafés). Cigarettes are sold in bars, grocery and convenience stores, and newspaper and magazine shops.

■ Taxes and Tipping

Taxes

The ticket price on items usually **does not include tax**. There are two taxes, the GST (federal Goods and Services Tax, TPS in French) of 7% and the PST (provincial sales tax, TVQ in French) at 7.5%, charged on all goods and services. They are cumulative and apply to most items and to restaurant and hotel prices. There is an additional tax on hotel rooms. See the "Accommodations" section on p 50 for more details.

There are some exceptions to this taxation system, such as books, which are only taxed 7%, and food (except for ready-made meals), which is not taxed at all.

Tax Refunds for Non-Residents

Non-residents can be refunded for the GST paid on purchases made while in Canada. To obtain a refund, it is important to keep your receipts. Note that to be eligible, your purchases must total at least $200. For further information on refunds of GST or PST, call ☎800-668-4748.

Tipping

In general, tipping applies to all table service in restaurants and to both table and bar service in bars and nightclubs (no tipping in fast-food restaurants). The tip is usually about 15% of the bill before taxes, but varies, of course, depending on the quality of service. Tipping is also standard in taxis and hair salons.

■ Telecommunications

Dialling the local area code is unnecessary if the call is within the same area code. However, within the greater Montréal area, the 10 digits must be dialled, including the area code (**514** or **438** for the island of Montréal and **450** for the surrounding suburbs). For long-distance calls, dial **1** for the United States and Canada, followed by the appropriate area code and the subscriber's number. The same goes for a fax. Phone numbers preceded by **800**, **877**, **866** or **888** are toll-free from Canada, and often from the U.S. as well. To contact an operator, dial **0**.

Considerably less expensive than in Europe, public phones are scattered throughout the city, easy to use and sometimes even accept credit cards. Local calls cost $0.25 for unlimited time. For long-distance calls, equip yourselves with quarters ($0.25 coins), or purchase a $10, $15 or $20 call card, on sale at newsstands, in convenience stores or at Bell Téléboutiques. Paying by credit card or with the prepaid "HELLO!" card is also possible, but be advised that they are considerably more expensive.

When calling abroad you can use a local operator and pay local phone rates. First dial *011*, then the international country code, then the phone number:

Australia	*61*
Belgium	*32*
Germany	*49*
Ireland	*353*
Italy	*39*
Netherlands	*31*
New Zealand	*64*
Spain	*34*
Switzerland	*41*
United Kingdom	*44*

For example, to call Great Britain, dial *011* + *44* + the area code (London *171* or *181*) + the number you are trying to reach.

■ Time Difference

Québec is six hours behind continental Europe and three hours ahead of the North American west coast. The entire province of Québec (save for the Îles de la Madeleine, which are an hour ahead) operates on Eastern Standard Time. Keep in mind that there are several time zones across Canada. Daylight Savings Time (+1hr) starts the first Sunday in April and ends the last Sunday in October (-1hr).

■ Tourist Information

Québec is divided into 21 tourist regions. Each region has its own regional tourist association, called the Associations Touristiques Régionales, or ATR, responsible for the distribution of information on the region. Basic information guides are published for each tourist region and are available free of charge from these associations and offices (addresses are provided in each region's chapter). In Montréal, Québec City and Laval, tourist information is available from municipal tourism offices.

In Canada and Abroad

Tourisme Québec
PO Box 979, Montréal, QC, H3C 2W3
☎ (514) 873-2015 or 877-266-5687
www.bonjourquebec.com

In Montréal

For detailed information, maps, flyers or accommodation information for Montréal and other tourist regions of Québec:

Centre Infotouriste
1255 Rue Peel
☎ (514) 873-2015

In Québec City

Centre Infotouriste
12 Rue Sainte-Anne
☎ 877-266-5687

Office du Tourisme et des Congrès de Québec
399 Rue Saint-Joseph Est, Québec, QC, G1K BE2
☎ (418) 641-6654
🖥 (418) 641-6578

In Toronto

Bureau du Québec
20 Queen St. W., Suite 1504, Toronto, ON, M5H 3S3
☎ (416) 977-6713
🖥 (416) 596-1407
www.saic.gouv.qc.ca/bureaux_du_quebec/bureau_quebec_toronto.htm

In Great Britain

Québec Government House
59 Pall Mall, London SW1Y 5JH
☎ (44) 207 766-5900
🖥 (44) 207 930-7938
www.mri.gouv.qc.ca/london/en/index.asp

In the United States

Québec Government House
One Rockefeller Plaza, 26th Floor
New York, NY 10020-2102
☎ (212) 397-0200 or 843-0950
🖥 (212) 757-4753 or 376-8984
www.mri.gouv.qc.ca/usa/en

■ Travellers with Disabilities

Kéroul, an association that specializes in tourism for people with disabilities, publishes a guide called *Accessible Québec*, which lists hotels, attractions and restaurants that are accessible to people with disabilities throughout the province. These places are listed by tourist region and the guide can be purchased at Ulysses' travel bookstore and in most other major bookstores.

Kéroul
4545 Avenue Pierre-De Coubertin
C.P. 1000, Succursale M, Montréal, QC, H1V 3R2
☎ (514) 252-3104
🖷 (514) 254-0766
www.keroul.qc.ca

Most of the regions also have associations that organize leisure and sports activities for people with disabilities. Contact the following organization for the addresses of these associations:

Association Québécoise de Loisir pour Personnes Handicapées
4545 Avenue Pierre-De Coubertin
C.P.1000, Succursale M, Montréal, QC, H1V 3R2
☎ (514) 252-3144
🖷 (514) 252-8360
www.aqlph.qc.ca

■ Wine, Beer and Alcohol

In Québec, the provincial government is responsible for regulating alcohol, sold in liquor stores known as Société des Alcools du Québec (SAQ). If you wish to purchase wine, imported beer or hard liquor, you must go to a branch of the SAQ. Some, known as "Sélection," offer a more varied and specialized selection of wines and spirits.

You must be at least 18 years old to purchase alcohol, the sale of which is not permitted after 11pm.

Beer

Two huge breweries share the largest part of the beer market in Québec: Labatt and Molson-O'Keefe. They each produce different types of beer, mostly lager, with varying levels of alcohol. In bars, restaurants, and nightclubs, draft beer is cheaper than bottled beer.

Besides these large breweries, some interesting independent micro-breweries have developed in the past few years. The variety and taste of these beers make them quite popular in Québec. However, because they are micro-brews, they are not available everywhere. Here are a few of Québec's micro-brewery beers: McAuslan (Griffon, St-Ambroise), Le Cheval Blanc (Coup de Grisou, Sainte-Paix), Les Brasseurs du Nord (Boréale) and GMT (Belle Gueule).

■ Work and Study

Studying in Québec

To study in Québec, individuals from outside Canada must first obtain a C.A.Q. (Certificat d'Acceptation du Québec), as well as a federal permit allowing an extended visit.

To obtain these documents, you must **first** be registered at a college or university for at least six months, with a minimum number of class hours per week. You must also provide proof of financial resources necessary to pay your living expenses and tuition. Moreover, you must have medical and hospitalization insurance, and a medical exam may be required.

Working in Québec

Student Employment

If you have obtained a residence permit to study in Québec, you have the right to work under certain conditions. Working on campus as a research assistant, or work providing experience in your field of study, are some of the possibilities offered to students.

Spouses of students admitted as visitors can also work for the duration of the student's stay. The laws, however, change regularly, so it is best to obtain information from the Délégation Générale du Québec or the Canadian consulate of your home country.

Temporary Work

All the necessary paperwork must be completed in your home country. Your Canadian employer must make a request at a Canada Employment Centre. If the job offer is deemed admissible, you will have to appear before a member of the Québec delegation who will evaluate your abilities and inform you as to the next steps to take.

Remember that if you have not received a working visa, it is against the law to work in the country. Also, the work permit is valid only for the job and the employer with which you applied, and were accepted, and only for the duration of this job.

Furthermore, authorization to work in Québec does **not** mean that you can stay on as an immigrant.

Au Pair Work

As with other temporary work, a request for a permit must be made by the employer, and is only valid for the specific job. The employee must reside with the employer.

Seasonal Work

This type of work is concentrated in the agricultural field and varies from apple-picking to agricultural training courses. Obtaining a work visa beforehand is required. Contact the Canadian embassy or consulate in your home country for additional information.

Internet Links

www.mcgill.ca/internationalstudents
www3.concordia.ca/info/students/prospective/international/
www.rhdcc.gc.ca
www.cic.gc.ca

Practical Information - Useful Information, from A to Z

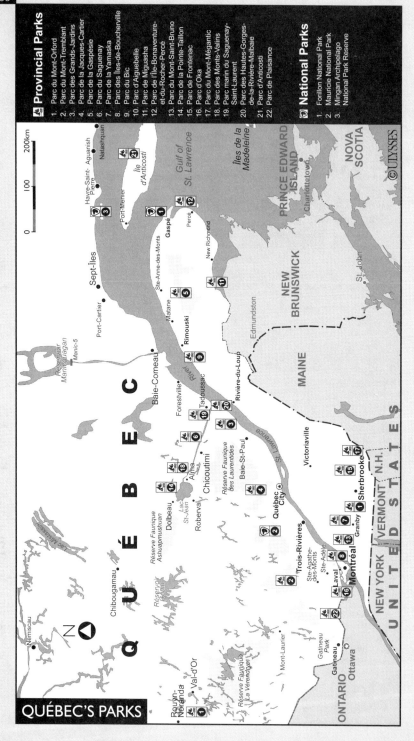

QUÉBEC'S PARKS

🏊 Provincial Parks

1. Parc du Mont-Orford
2. Parc du Mont-Tremblant
3. Parc des Grands-Jardins
4. Parc de la Jacques-Cartier
5. Parc de la Gaspésie
6. Parc du Saguenay
7. Parc de la Yamaska
8. Parc des Îles-de-Boucherville
9. Parc du Bic
10. Parc d'Aiguebelle
11. Parc de Miguasha
12. Parc de l'Île-Bonaventure-et-du-Rocher-Percé
13. Parc du Mont-Saint-Bruno
14. Parc de la Pointe-Taillon
15. Parc de Frontenac
16. Parc d'Oka
17. Parc du Mont-Mégantic
18. Parc des Monts-Valins
19. Parc marin du Saguenay-Saint-Laurent
20. Parc des Hautes-Gorges-de-la-Rivière-Malbaie
21. Parc d'Anticosti
22. Parc de Plaisance

🗺 National Parks

1. Forillon National Park
2. Mauricie National Park
3. Mingan Archipelago National Park Reserve

© ULYSSES

Outdoors

Q uébec's wide-open spaces and spectacular countryside make it ideal for all types of outdoor activities. This chapter outlines the various outdoor activities practiced in Québec.

What follows is in no way a complete list of the multitude of choices available to visitors in each region. For each activity or sport, the basic information needed to organize an outing is given, along with the address of the specific federation or organization in charge of the activity. Refer to the specific regional chapter to find out which activities can be enjoyed where. For clarity, we have categorized the activities as either winter or summer recreation.

Regroupement Loisir Québec

This private, non-profit organization groups together more than 100 provincial organizations (federations, movements, associations) responsible for the promotion of various sports and activities. Its goal is to provide these organizations with the financial and technical support they need. Most of the organization's offices are located at Montréal's Olympic Stadium.

Regroupement Loisir Québec
4545 Avenue Pierre-De Coubertin
C.P. 1000, Succursale M, Montréal, QC, H1V 3R2
☎ (514) 252-3126

Parks and Reserves

Throughout Québec are national parks administered by the federal government, and provincial parks administered by the Québec government. To make matters more confusing, since 2001, Québec's provincial parks are officially known as *parcs nationaux*, or national parks. For clarity, note that in this guidebook, the term "national park" refers to parks administered by the federal government. Most parks offer a variety of services and facilities: information centres, maps, nature-interpretation programs, guides and camping. Since these services often depend on the season and are not available in all parks, it is best to check with park offices ahead of time. It is possible to reserve campsites (except backwood sites), shelters and chalets (in provincial parks). Note that reservation policies for campsites in national parks vary from one to the other. Check with the park concerned or with Parks Canada (see below).

In most parks, networks of marked trails, many kilometres in length, traverse the area, permitting amateurs and experts alike to take advantage of the activities offered: hiking, canoeing, cross-country skiing and even snowmobiling. Backwood campsites and shelters are set up along the trails in some parks. Some of the backwood sites are quite basic, without even running water, so come well prepared. Some trails lead deep into forests far from civilization, so it is advisable to stick to the marked trails. Maps with the various trails, campsites and shelters are very helpful and available for most parks.

■ National Parks

There are four national parks in the province of Québec: Forillon National Park in the Gaspésie region, La Mauricie National Park in the Mauricie region, Mingan Archipelago National Park Reserve in the Duplessis region and the Saguenay–Saint-Laurent Marine Park. Beside these parks, the Canadian Parks Service also runs various National Historic Sites.

More information is available on these parks by contacting Parks Canada headquarters:

Parks Canada
25 Rue Eddy, Gatineau
☎ 888-733-8888
www.parkscanada.gc.ca

■ Provincial Parks

There are 23 provincial parks in Québec, including the Parc marin national du Saguenay–Saint-Laurent, which is under both federal and provincial jurisdictions.

Ministère des Ressources naturelles, de la Faune et des Parcs
☎800-561-1616
www.mrnfp.gouv.qc.ca

The Société des Établissements de Plein Air du Québec (Sépaq) manages around 50 outdoor establishments in Québec. The Sépaq's goal is to promote these sites while ensuring the conservation and preservation of their natural resources. For more information about the outdoor activities offered by Sépaq, as well as their sites, contact them at:

Sépaq
801 Chemin St-Louis, Bureau 180
Québec, QC, G1S 1C1
☎ (418) 686-4875
🖷 (418) 686-6160
www.sepaq.com

For reservations:

☎ (418) 890-6527 or 800-665-6527
www.sepaq.com

Sépaq Admission Fee

An admission fee is charged in all parks and wildlife reserves managed by the **Sépaq** (Société des Établissements de Plein Air du Québec), which includes most nature reserves in Québec. This fee is the same for all parks *($3.50 per adult)* and gives access to the park for the entire day. Annual passes are also available, either for the entire network of parks *($30)* or for one park that you may wish to visit at your leisure *($16.50)*.

■ Réserves Fauniques

Réserves Fauniques (provincial wildlife reserves) cover larger areas than the other parks. Organized fishing and hunting are permitted here. Québec has many provincial wildlife reserves, such as La Vérendrye, Saint-Maurice, Laurentides, Portneuf, Mastigouche, Rouge-Matawin, Papineau-Labelle and Chic-Chocs. They are also administered by the Sépaq (see above).

December 2005 saw the inauguration of the **Auberge de Montagne des Chic-Chocs** (see p 464) *(Réserve Faunique de Matane; transportation to the inn is provided from the Cap-Chat visitor centre; ☎800-665-3091)*. This inn will welcome the many visitors who come to the wildlife reserve to practice various outdoor activities: from wildlife observation to ski-mountaineering, snowshoeing, hiking, mountain biking and fishing.

■ Centres Touristiques

The **Société des Établissements de Plein Air du Québec** *(Sépaq; www.sepaq.com)* also manages eight tourist resorts *(centres touristiques)*. In addition to the many outdoor activities that can be enjoyed at these resorts, visitors can expect top-rate accommodations, quality restaurants and interesting historical attractions, all within a unique natural setting. Campers can also take advantage of the choice campgrounds that were set up at these resorts.

■ ZECs and Outfitters

The Zones d'Exploitation Contrôlée (ZEC), or controlled development zones, are also Québec government property. Unlike parks and wildlife reserves, they are not generally set up for visitors, but hunting and fishing are practiced here. Outfitters, called *pourvoiries* in Québec, are private establishments specially set up for hunting and fishing. Some offer only rustic huts while others feature luxurious inns with fancy restaurants.

■ Jardins du Québec

The province of Québec has wonderful gardens where it's a pleasure to discover landscapes of unparalleled beauty. Along with historic buildings, artwork and ances-

Outdoors – Parks and Reserves

tral traditions, gardens are considered an integral part of Québec's heritage.

In 1989, the Association des Jardins du Québec brought together the great gardens of Québec to promote ornamental horticulture and to let nature-lovers familiarize themselves with it. This association, in collaboration with Tourisme Québec, has also created a pamphlet describing the province's main gardens, as well as their location. So why not take a walk on these "garden paths"?

Summer Activities

As soon as the temperature inches above 0°C and the ice starts to melt, Quebecers and visitors alike start to look forward to days in the country. While your choice of clothing will vary with the season, don't forget that evenings and nights are often quite chilly (except in July and August). In certain regions of the province, regardless of the temperature, a long-sleeved shirt is indispensable unless you want to serve as dinner to the mosquitoes and black flies. If you plan on venturing into the woods in June, bring insect repellent and use it!

■ Beaches

The shores of Québec's rivers and countless lakes are lined with everything from fine white sand to pebbles to boulders. You should not have any trouble finding one that suits your sport or style of sunbathing. Unfortunately, swimming in the waters around the island of Montréal is no longer possible because of the pollution in the St. Lawrence and the Rivière des Prairies.

The city does, however, run a public beach on Île-Notre-Dame, where you can splash about in filtered river water. Beware though—this place is very popular and access is limited, so get there early.

■ Bird-Watching

In addition to national and provincial parks, there are many other interesting bird-watching spots throughout Québec. We recommend two interesting guides:

Les Meilleurs Sites d'Observation des Oiseaux du Québec, published by Éditions Québec-Science.

Peterson's Field Guide: All the Birds of Eastern and Central North America, published by Houghton Mifflin.

■ Canoeing

Québec's vast territory is dotted with a multitude of lakes and rivers, making it a canoe enthusiast's dream. Many of the parks and Réserves Fauniques are departure points for canoe trips of one or more days. For longer trips, backwoods campsites are available for canoeists. Maps of the canoe trips and trails, as well as canoe-rental services, are available at park information centres. River rafting is most popular in the springtime, when water levels are highest after the spring thaw.

An excellent map, *Les Parcours Canotables du Québec*, (Canoe Trips of Québec) is available in travel bookstores. A series of map-guides for rivers (up to 125 different maps) is available, as is a guide for beginners called *Guide Canot-Camping*, available only in French. For information, contact the Fédération Québécoise du Canot et du Kayak, which is part of Regroupement Loisir Québec (☎514-252-3001).

■ Canyoning

Canyoning is a hybrid sport that combines hiking, rappelling and swimming to travel along a waterway and the uneven relief that surrounds it. Canyoning can be practiced in canyons, gorges, waterfalls and narrows. A relatively recent sport in Québec, this activity is restricted to participants who are aged 10 and older, are in good physical condition, can swim and are comfortable with heights.

One of Québec's most popular canyoning spots for rappelling is at the foot of Mont Sainte-Anne, near Québec City: the Chute Jean-Larose and its three waterfalls plummet into crystal-clear waters and make for a perfect location to enjoy this sport. Other canyons are also located nearby: Canyon de la Vieille Rivière and Canyon des Éboulements. Contact the **Canyoning-Québec** association (*www.canyoning-quebec.com*), the

Respect the Forest!

As a hiker, it is important to realize your role in preserving and respecting the fragility of the ecosystem and to comprehend your impact on your surroundings. Here are a few guidelines:

First of all, stay on the trails even if they are covered in snow or mud in order to protect the ground vegetation and avoid widening the trail.

Unless you're heading off on a long trek, wear lightweight hiking boots, as they do less damage to vegetation. When in a group in alpine regions, spread out and walk on rocks as much as possible to avoid damaging vegetation.

It is just as important to protect waterways, bodies of water and the ground water when in mountainous regions. When digging back-country latrines, place them at least 30 metres from all water sources, and cover everything (paper included) with earth.

Never wash in lakes or streams.

At campsites dispose of waste water only in designated areas.

The water is not always potable and therefore should be boiled for at least 10 minutes before drinking.

Never leave any garbage behind.

Certain types of flowers are endangered, so do not pick any.

Leave everything as you find it so that those that follow can enjoy the beauty of nature as you did.

For safety reasons, always keep your dog on a leash, or leave it at home. Dogs that roam free have a tendency to wander off and chase wild animals. They have even been known to chase down bears and then take refuge with their masters. Warning: dogs are not allowed in the Parcs Québec network and must be kept on a leash in all federal parks.

only professional outfit of its kind in Québec, for more information.

■ Climbing

Climbing enthusiasts can practice their sport in summer and in winter, when there are ice walls for climbers of all levels. Adequate and reliable equipment (often rented on site) and a firm grasp of the basic techniques are crucial to this sport. Some climbing centres offer beginners' courses.

For information concerning ice-and rock-climbing activities, beginner courses and more advanced courses, contact the Fédération Québécoise de la Montagne, also part of Regroupement Loisir Québec (☎514-252-3004). A French-language magazine called *Le Mousqueton* (The Karabiner) is available free of charge from the Regroupement.

Outdoors - Summer Activities

■ Cycling

Exploring by bike is one of the most rewarding ways of discovering the diverse regions of Québec. There is quite a variety of publications to help organize your two-wheeled excursions. Ulysses Travel Guides publishes two French language guides: *Le Québec Cyclable* and *Cyclotourisme au Québec*, which list short and long bikepaths in Québec.

Mountain-bike trails have been cleared in most of the parks. Check with the information desk of the particular park.

Many bike shops have bicycles for rent. Check local tourist office to locate a place, or look in the *Yellow Pages* under "*Bicyclettes-Location*" or "Bicycle-Rental."

■ Golf

Groomed golf courses exist in all corners of Québec. A map called *Le Golf au Québec*, as well as the *Guide Maxi-Golf*, should provide all the teeing-off information necessary. Both are available in travel bookstores and at the Centre Infotouriste in Montréal and in Québec City.

■ Hang-Gliding and Paragliding

Hang-gliding has been practiced in Québec since the 1970s. The mountains and cliffs most conducive to this sport are located in the regions of Gaspésie, Charlevoix, the Appalachians and the Laurentians. Paragliding is a relatively new sport in Québec.

These sports are dangerous and can only be attempted after following a course given by an accredited instructor. For more information, contact the Association Québécoise de Vol Libre (The Québec Association of Hang-gliding and Paragliding) (☎*514-890-5276*).

■ Hiking

Hiking is accessible to all and is practiced all over Québec. Many parks have hiking trails of varying length and difficulty. A few have longer trails that head deep into the wilderness for 20 to 40km. Respect trail markings and always leave well prepared when you follow these trails. Maps that show the trails, campsites and shelters are available.

An excellent guide called *Hiking in Québec* (Ulysses Travel Guides) is available in bookstores and camping stores. A hiking guide with something for everyone, it suggests various trails and trips, and classifies them according to their length and level of difficulty. The Fédération Québécoise de la Marche *(Québec Hiking Federation;* ☎*514-252-3157)*, promotes hiking, snowshoeing and city walking, and can also provide information.

■ Horseback Riding

Many horse stables offer lessons or trail rides. Some even organize longer trips of more than one day. Both types of riding, English and Western, are available depending on the stable. Since the two styles are very different, check which one is offered when making reservations. Some provincial parks have horseback-riding trails.

Québec à Cheval (Québec on horseback) is an organization that promotes horseback riding. It distributes an annual French publication free of charge called *Découvrir le Québec à Cheval* (Discovering Québec on Horseback). Courses are also offered. For more information, check with Québec à Cheval, which is part of Regroupement Loisir Québec (☎*450-434-1433)*.

■ Hunting and Fishing

Hunting and fishing are both strictly regulated. Given the complexity of the regulations, it is a good idea to check with the **Société de la Faune et des Parcs** *(*☎*800-561-1616, www.fapaq.gouv.qc.ca)*. Free bilingual brochures containing the essentials about the hunting and fishing regulations and restrictions are available.

Residents and non-residents of Québec who wish to hunt or fish in the province must obtain a provincial hunting permit from an authorized dealer, such as: certain sporting goods stores, hardware stores, convenience stores and outfitters, as well as all ZECs and wildlife reserves operated by the Sépaq. To obtain a permit to hunt with a firearm, bow or crossbow, hunters must also obtain the proper permits pertaining to each piece of hunting equipment. Certain specific hunts, for example migratory bird hunting, may also require both a provincial and a federal hunting permit (provided by the Canadian Wildlife Service and sold in post offices).

The sport-fishing permit authorizes catches of most fish species in Québec, except for Atlantic salmon, which requires a special permit, also obtainable from the same authorized dealers. A single fishing permit authorizes several members of a same family to fish; if the holder of the permit does not accompany them, family members must be in possession of the permit and respect the quotas that are outlined on it. The same rules apply to salmon fishing, except only the children of a permit holder are authorized to use the same permit.

■ In-Line Skating

This relatively recent sport tides Quebecers over until they can lace up their ice skates again in winter. It takes a while to get comfortable on these skates, but once you're up and running (or rather, up and skating), you'll appreciate how quickly you can get around on them. In-line skating is mostly practiced on paved roads in urban areas. Several outfitters rent out all the necessary equipment. It is highly recommended that skaters wear knee and elbow pads, a protective helmet and gloves.

■ Kayaking

Kayaking isn't a new sport but its popularity has grown steadily in Québec. More and more people have discovered this wonderful way to travel on water in a safe and comfortable vessel at a pace that lets them appreciate the surrounding landscape. In fact, being in a kayak gives you the impression of sitting right on the water and being a part of nature: an experience that is both disorienting and fascinating! There are three types of kayaks with varying shapes: lake kayaks, river kayaks and sea kayaks. The latter can hold one or two people depending on the model, and is the most popular because it is the easiest to manoeuvre. Many companies offer kayak rentals and organize guided expeditions on Québec's waterways. For more infor-

mation, contact the **Fédération Québécoise du Canot et du Kayak** *(www.canot-kayak.qc.ca)*.

■ Nudism

Nudism is practiced in certain areas of Québec. The nudist federation, Fédération Québécoise de Naturisme, promotes these activities. Members of the International Federation of Nudists have certain privileges when they present their IFN card. For information, contact the federation itself or Regroupement Loisir Québec *(☎514-252-3014)*.

■ Pleasure Boating

La Fédération de Voile du Québec (Québec Sailing Federation) brings together clubs, schools and associations involved in sailing and pleasure boating. The federation offers courses and a database of important information. In addition to the *Annuaire de la Voile*, a French language listing of clubs and schools, they publish a seasonal bilingual periodical, *Le Bulletin Voile Québec*. For information, check with the federation itself, which is part of Regroupement Loisir Québec *(☎514-252-3097)*.

■ Rafting

Rafting, which involves tackling rapids in an inflatable dingy, is perfect for thrill-seekers. The rafts generally hold around 10 people and offer the strength and flexibility that are required to take on the rapids. The sport is particularly enjoyable in springtime, when river waters are high and the current is faster. A well-organized trip led by an experienced guide is the best way to enjoy this sport. Generally, companies that offer rafting excursions provide all the necessary equipment to ensure the comfort and safety of the participants.

■ Scuba Diving

Most of the regions of Québec feature dive sites, and there are at least 200 diving centres, schools or clubs in the province. For more complete information on diving in Québec, contact the Fédération Québécoise des Activités Subaquatiques (Québec Federation of Underwater Activities) *(☎514-252-3009)*.

Outdoors - Summer Activities

■ Tree-Top Adventure Courses

Tree-top forest adventure courses have gained much popularity in Québec in the last few years. Along the different courses, participants get to travel along various challenging suspended bridges, beams, nets, wood footbridges, Tyrolean traverses, zip lines and "Tarzan ropes." The courses take visitors to the top of the tree line, providing superb vantage points from which they get to admire Québec's rich forest environment.

■ Waterskiing

La Fédération Québécoise de Ski Nautique (Québec Federation of Waterskiing) provides information, guide-books and lessons. It also publishes a French-language newsletter called *Ski Nautique Québec*. For information, contact the federation through Regroupement Loisir Québec (☎514-252-3092).

■ Whale-Watching

The St. Lawrence is teeming with diverse marine life. A large part of it is made up of numerous marine mammals, including many species of whales (belugas, finback whales and blue whales). Whale-watching expeditions are popular in the tourist regions of Charlevoix, Saguenay–Lac-Saint-Jean, Bas-Saint-Laurent, Manicouagan, Duplessis and Gaspésie.

Winter Activities

A road map called *Sports d'Hiver Québec* (Québec Winter Sports) outlines the various winter sports practiced in Québec. It contains a list of facilities organized by location and sport, as well as directions on how to get there. This map is available in most travel bookstores and at the Centre Infotouriste in Montréal and in Québec City. The Ministry of Tourism also publishes a brochure describing various winter sports and activities.

■ Cross-Country Skiing

There are many parks and ski centres with well-kept cross-country trails in Québec. In most ski centres you can rent equipment by the day. Many places offer longer trails, with shelters alongside them offering accommodations for skiers. To ensure a spot in a shelter, reservations are required. Call ☎800-665-6527 or ☎(418) 890-6527, starting in mid-October. For skiers on longer trails, some ski centres offer a service that delivers food to the shelter by snowmobile.

■ Dogsledding

Used by the Inuit for transportation in the past, today dogsledding has become a respected sporting activity. Competitive events abound in northern countries all over the world. In recent years, tourist centres have started offering dogsledding trips lasting anywhere from a few hours to a few days. In the latter case, the tour organizer provides the necessary equipment and shelter. In general, you can expect to cover 30 to 60km per day, and since this sport is more demanding than it looks, good physical fitness is essential for long trips. Centres that offer dogsled trips are listed throughout the guide.

■ Downhill Skiing

There are many downhill-ski centres in Québec. Some of these have lighting systems and offer night skiing. Hotels located near the ski hills often offer package deals including accommodations, meals and lift tickets.

Lift tickets are very expensive; in an effort to accommodate all types of skiers, most centres offer half-day, whole-day and night passes. Some centres have even started offering skiing by the hour.

■ Ice Fishing

This sport has become more and more popular in recent years. The basic idea, as the name suggests, is to fish through the ice. A small wooden shack built on the ice keeps you warm during the long hours of waiting for the big one. The main regions for this sport are the Eastern Townships, Mauricie, Centre-du-Québec and Saguenay–Lac-Saint-Jean. This guide mentions various spots for ice fishing.

■ Skating

Most municipalities have public skating rinks set up in parks, on rivers or lakes. Some places have rental services and even a little hut where you and your skates can warm up.

■ Snowboarding

Contrary to popular belief, snowboarding is not only popular with youngsters and we often find more snowboarders than skiers on many slopes. It is recommended that beginners take a few lessons before taking their first run down the slopes. Most ski resorts offer lessons and rent out all the necessary equipment.

■ Snowmobiling

Now this is a popular Québec sport! It was, after all, a Quebecer named Joseph-Armand Bombardier who invented the snowmobile, giving life to one of the most important industries in Québec and now involved in the building of airplanes and railway materials.

A network of more than 26,000km of cleared snowmobile trails criss-crosses Québec. Trails cross diverse regions and lead adventurers into the heart of the wilderness. Along the trails are all the necessities for snowmobiling: repair services, heated sheds, fuel and food services. It is possible to rent a snowmobile and the ne-

cessary equipment in certain snowmobiling centres. The magazine *Motoneige Québec* is sold at newspaper stands. A map called *Sentiers de Motoneige à Travers le Québec* (Snowmobile Trails Across Quebec) is also available. It indicates the location of trails, service centres, and towns where equipment can be rented.

To use the trail, you must have the registration paper for your vehicle and a membership card. The membership card is available from the Fédération des Clubs de Motoneigistes. No-fault insurance is strongly recommended.

Certain safety rules apply. A helmet is mandatory and driving on public roads is forbidden unless the trail follows it. Headlights and brake lights must be lit at all times. The speed-limit is 60km/h. It is preferable to ride in groups. Lastly, always stick to cleared trails.

For information, contact the Fédération des Clubs de Motoneigistes du Québec, part of Regroupement Loisir Québec (☎*514-252-3076*).

■ Snowshoeing

Reinvented today as a leisure pastime, snowshoeing was first invented by Aboriginals as a means of transportation on deep snow. There is no association in Québec for enthusiasts of this sport, which is mainly practiced in cross-country-ski centres.

Outdoors - Winter Activities

THE ISLAND OF MONTRÉAL AND SURROUNDINGS

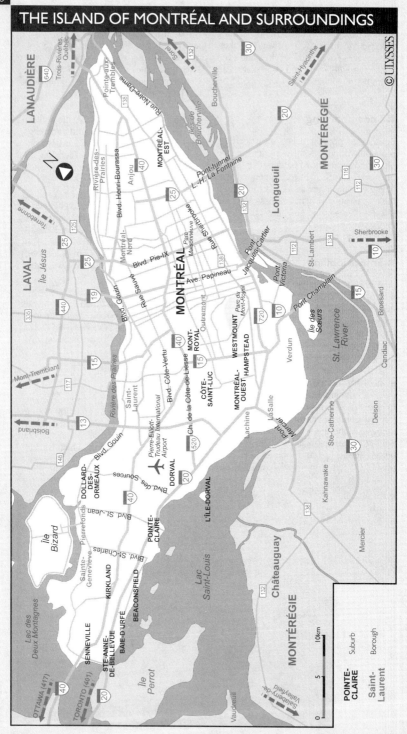

© ULYSSES

LANAUDIÈRE

Trois-Rivières, Québec

[640]

Pointe-aux-Trembles

[138] Rue Notre-Dame

Rivière-des-Prairies

MONTRÉAL-EST

Anjou

[40]

Blvd. Henri-Bourassa

[25]

Terrebonne

Pont-tunnel L.-H. La Fontaine

[125]

Montréal-Nord

LAVAL

Île Jésus

[25]

Blvd. Pie-IX

Parc Maisonneuve

Rue Sherbrooke

Blvd. Gouin

Rue Sauvé

[138]

[20]

[132]

[25]

MONTÉRÉGIE

Boucherville

Île de Boucherville

Saint-Hyacinthe

[30]

[132]

Sorel

[19]

[440]

[335]

Mont-Tremblant

[117]

[15]

Rivière des Prairies

MONTRÉAL

Ave. Papineau

OUTREMONT

Parc du Mont-Royal

Pont Jacques-Cartier

Pont Victoria

Longueuil

St-Lambert

[112]

Sherbrooke

[134]

[10]

Boisbriand

[13]

[148]

Saint-Laurent

Blvd. Gouin

Pierre-Elliott-Trudeau International Airport

Blvd. Côte-Vertu

[40]

MONT-ROYAL

[15]

CÔTE-SAINT-LUC

Ch. de la Côte-de-Liesse

[520]

WESTMOUNT

MONTRÉAL-OUEST HAMPSTEAD

[720]

[10]

Verdun

Île des Sœurs

Pont des Sœurs

Pont Champlain

St. Lawrence River

Brossard

[15]

Candiac

Delson

[30]

Île Bizard

Pierrefonds

DOLLARD-DES-ORMEAUX

Blvd. des Sources

Blvd. Gouin

[40]

DORVAL

[20]

L'ÎLE-DORVAL

LaSalle

Lachine

Pont Mercier

Ste-Catherine

Kahnawake

[138]

Mercier

Lac des Deux Montagnes

Sainte-Geneviève

Blvd. St-Jean

Blvd. St-Charles

KIRKLAND

BEACONSFIELD

POINTE-CLAIRE

Lac Saint-Louis

Châteauguay

[132]

MONTÉRÉGIE

SENNEVILLE

STE-ANNE-DE-BELLEVUE

BAIE-D'URFÉ

Île Perrot

Valleyfield

Valbert-de-Valleyfield

OTTAWA (417)

[40]

TORONTO (401)

[20]

Vaudreuil

Salaberry-de-Valleyfield

0   5   10 km

Montréal

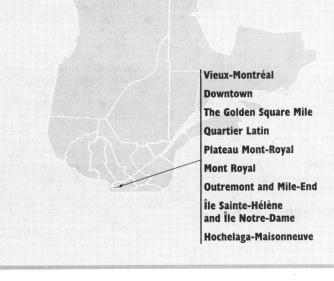

Vieux-Montréal

Downtown

The Golden Square Mile

Quartier Latin

Plateau Mont-Royal

Mont Royal

Outremont and Mile-End

**Île Sainte-Hélène
and Île Notre-Dame**

Hochelaga-Maisonneuve

Both Latin and Nordic, European and North American, cosmopolitan and metropolitan, the largest French-speaking city in the world after Paris and bilingual hub, **Montréal** ★ ★ ★ is definitely an exceptional city. Visitors to the city appreciate it for many different reasons; it succeeds in delighting American tourists with its European charm and also manages to surprise overseas travellers thanks its haphazard character and nonchalance. Above all, Montréal holds nothing back and visitors often find what they are looking for without having to search too far.

Montréal is a city that exists in a balance between several different worlds: firmly planted in America yet looking towards Europe, claimed by two lands, Québec and Canada, and always, it seems, in the midst of social, economic and demographic changes.

It is difficult to define this city, especially since no postcard or cliché truly succeeds in evoking an image of it that is realistic or honest. If Paris has its great boulevards and squares, New York its skyscrapers and celebrated Statue of Liberty, what best symbolizes Montréal? Perhaps its numerous and beautiful churches, its Olympic Stadium, or its opulent Victorian residences?

Despite Montréal's rich architectural heritage, it is above all its unique, engaging atmosphere that appeals to people. Montréal is an enchanting city to visit and an exhilarating place to discover; it is generous, friendly and not at all mundane.

And when the time comes to celebrate jazz, film, comedy, francophone singers or Saint-Jean-Baptiste Day, hundreds of thousands of people flood into the streets, turning events into warm public gatherings. There is no doubt that Montréal is a big city that has managed to keep its human touch. For while its towering glass-and-concrete silhouette gives it the appearance of a North-American metropolis, Montréal has trouble hiding the fact that it is primarily a city of small streets and unique neighbourhoods, each with its own church, businesses, restaurants, and bars—in short, its own personality, shaped over the years by the arrival of people from all corners of the globe.

Elusive and mysterious, Montréal is nevertheless genuine, and is as mystical for those who experience it on a daily basis as it is for visitors immersed in it for only a few days.

A Brief History of Montréal

During his second voyage to North America in 1535, Jacques Cartier sailed up the St. Lawrence River to Montréal, explored the shores of the island and climbed Mont Royal. While Cartier may not have been the first European to visit the island, which is located at the confluence of two rivers now known as the St. Lawrence and the Ottawa, he was nevertheless the first to report its existence. In those days, the Aboriginals referred to it as Hochelaga. At the time of Cartier's arrival, a large fortified town populated by about 1,000 Iroquois stretched across the slopes of Mont Royal. This town was evidently destroyed or abandoned a few years later, since when the great explorer Samuel de Champlain, founder of

Québec City, came here in 1611, he found no trace of it. He did note, however, that the island would make a very good spot for a trading post.

It was not the fur trade, however, that gave rise to the founding of Montréal. Originally named Ville-Marie, the city was established by a group of devout French citizens who came here in hopes of converting the Aboriginal people to Christianity. Under the direction of Paul de Chomedey, Sieur de Maisonneuve, 50 men and four women, including Jeanne Mance, founded Ville-Marie on May 18, 1642. Their plans soon came up against Iroquois opposition, however—so much so that until the signing of a peace treaty in 1701, the French and the Iroquois engaged in such constant conflict that the very existence of the settlement was threatened on a number of occasions.

Although Montréal was originally founded for the "glory of Christianity," merchants quickly replaced members of religious orders and other bearers of the "word." The numerous waterways leading deep into the hinterland provided easy access to rich hunting grounds. Montréal soon became an important business hub, and remained the main fur-trading centre in North America for nearly 150 years. The city also served as the starting point for the *coureurs des bois* (trappers) and explorers who set out to discover the vast territory stretching from Louisiana to Hudson Bay.

After the British army took Montréal in 1760, the Scots took over the fur trade from the French. The city became the country's metropolis during the 1820s, when its population surpassed that of Québec City. From that point on, Montréal underwent rapid changes; thousands of immigrants from the British Isles settled in the city, or simply passed through it on their way to other regions in North America. For a certain period of time, before the industrialization of the mid-19th century began attracting a continual influx of people from the Québec countryside, there was even a British majority here.

By the turn of the 20th century, Montréal had become a major industrial city, whose upper-class residents controlled 70% of the wealth in Canada. The industrial revolution had also generated a large working class, composed mainly of French Canadians and Irish, who lived in wretched conditions. Meanwhile, immigrants from outside Great Britain—particularly Jews from Eastern Europe, Germans and Italians—began to pour into the city, which was beginning to take on a cosmopolitan character.

During the 20th century, Montréal grew steadily, swallowing up neighbouring towns and villages due to the steady influx of both rural Quebecers and immigrants. Starting in the 1950s, the city even began spreading beyond the island itself, turning the adjacent countryside into a suburban zone. Its economic centre gradually shifted from Old Montréal to the area around Boulevard Dorchester (now Boulevard René-Lévesque), where glass and concrete skyscrapers have since sprung up.

In the 1960s and 1970s, Mayor Jean Drapeau, who has often been accused of megalomania, strengthened "his" city's international reputation by bringing about the construction of a subway (*métro*) system in 1966, and by organizing large-scale events. Montréal hosted the 1967 World Fair (Expo 67), the 1976 Summer Olympics and the 1980 Floralies Internationales.

Getting There and Getting Around

■ By Plane

Montréal-Pierre Elliott Trudeau International Airport

The Montréal-Dorval International Airport was recently renamed Montréal-Pierre Elliott Trudeau International Airport after the former Canadian Prime Minister. This airport, which is also simply refered to as "**Montréal-Trudeau**," is about a 20min drive from downtown Montréal. To reach the downtown area, take Highway 20 East to the junction with the Ville-Marie Highway (720) and follow directions to "Centre-ville, Vieux-Montréal."

For information regarding airport services (arrivals and departures), contact the **Aéroports de Montréal (ADM)** Information Centre (☎*514-394-7377 or 800-465-1213, www. admtl.com*).

Getting into the City

The **Aérobus**, affiliated to the **La Québécoise** bus company (☎*514-842-2281, www.autobus. qc.ca*), offers a shuttle service between the downtown area (Station Centrale), a few major hotels and the Montréal-Trudeau airport.

Car Rentals

Most major car-rental companies have offices at the Montréal-Trudeau airport.

Montréal - Getting There and Getting Around

■ By Car

Getting into the City

When coming from Québec City, there are two possible routes: take either Highway 20 West to the Champlain Bridge (*pont*), then Highway 10 (Autoroute Bonaventure), which leads directly downtown, or take Highway 40 West to Highway 15 South (Autoroute Décarie), and then follow the signs for downtown (*centre-ville*).

From Ottawa, take Highway 40 East to Highway 15 South (Autoroute Décarie), and then follow the signs for downtown (*centre-ville*).

Visitors arriving from Toronto will arrive via Highway 20 East. Continue along it and then take Autoroute 720 (the Ville-Marie) and follow the signs for downtown (*centre-ville*).

From the United States, via either Highway 10 or Highway 15, you will take the Champlain Bridge and Highway 10 (Autoroute Bonaventure).

Main Car Rental Companies

Avis	☎800-331-1212
	www.avis.com
Budget	☎800-268-8970
	www.budget.ca
Discount	☎888-310-2277
	www.discountcar.ca
Dollar	☎800-848-8268
	www.dollarcanada.ca
Enterprise	☎800-261-7331
	www.entreprise.com
Hertz	☎800-263-0678
	www.hertz.ca
National	☎800-227-7368
	www.nationalcar.ca
Thrifty	☎800-847-4389
	www.thryfty.com

■ By Bus

Station Centrale (*505 Boulevard de Maisonneuve Est, at the corner of Rue Berri,* ☎*514-842-2281; Berri-UQAM metro*) is Montréal's main bus station. It is served by such companies as **Greyhound** (☎*800-661-8747, www.greyhound. ca*) and **Orléans Express** (☎*888-999-3977, www.orleansexpress.com*), which link most major Canadian and American cities. The terminal is located in a building above the Berri-UQAM metro station and features a tourist-information desk and car-rental kiosks.

■ By Train

The Montréal train station, **Gare Centrale** (*895 rue De La Gauchetière O., metro Bonaventure,* ☎*514-989-2626 or 888-842-7245, www. viarail.ca*) is located right downtown.

■ Public Transportation

Bus and Metro

Visitors are strongly advised to take advantage of Montréal's public-transportation system, which consists of an extensive network of buses and subway trains (the metro) that serve the region well.

A pass entitling the holder to unlimited use of the public-transportation services of the **Société de Transport de Montréal (STM)** (*www.stm.info*) for one month costs $63 and $18.50 for one week. The monthly pass goes on sale a few days before the start of each month. Tourist cards, valid for one day (*$9*) or three consecutive days (*$17*) also entitle the holder to unlimited use of public-transportation services. For shorter stays or less moving about, visitors can purchase six tickets for $11.50, or single tickets at $2.50 each.

If a trip involves a transfer (from one bus to another, from the bus to the metro or vice versa), the passenger must ask the bus driver for a transfer ticket when getting on, or take one from a transfer machine in the metro station. Free subway maps are available inside all stations, as are timetables for the buses that stop at that station.

For more information on the public-transportation system and bus schedules, call

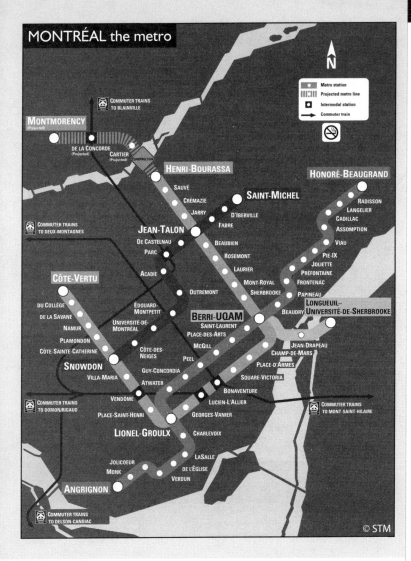

MONTRÉAL the metro

Legend:
- Metro station
- Projected metro line
- Intermodal station
- Commuter train

MONTMORENCY *(Projected)*

COMMUTER TRAINS TO BLAINVILLE

DE LA CONCORDE *(Projected)*

CARTIER *(Projected)*

CONSTRUCTION

HENRI-BOURASSA

SAUVÉ

CRÉMAZIE

JARRY

SAINT-MICHEL

D'IBERVILLE

FABRE

HONORÉ-BEAUGRAND

RADISSON
LANGELIER
CADILLAC
ASSOMPTION

COMMUTER TRAINS TO DEUX-MONTAGNES

JEAN-TALON

DE CASTELNAU

PARC

BEAUBIEN

ROSEMONT

VIAU

PIE-IX
JOLIETTE
PRÉFONTAINE
FRONTENAC

ACADIE

LAURIER

MONT-ROYAL

SHERBROOKE

PAPINEAU

CÔTE-VERTU

OUTREMONT

BEAUDRY

LONGUEUIL–
UNIVERSITÉ-DE-SHERBROOKE

DU COLLÈGE

DE LA SAVANE

ÉDOUARD-
MONTPETIT

BERRI-UQAM

SAINT-LAURENT
PLACE-DES-ARTS

NAMUR

UNIVERSITÉ-DE-
MONTRÉAL

McGILL

JEAN-DRAPEAU

PLAMONDON

CÔTE-SAINTE-CATHERINE

CÔTE-DES-
NEIGES

PEEL

CHAMP-DE-MARS

PLACE-D'ARMES

SNOWDON

VILLA-MARIA

GUY-CONCORDIA

ATWATER

SQUARE-VICTORIA

BONAVENTURE

COMMUTER TRAINS TO DORION/RIGAUD

VENDÔME

PLACE-SAINT-HENRI

LUCIEN-L'ALLIER

GEORGES-VANIER

COMMUTER TRAINS TO MONT-SAINT-HILAIRE

LIONEL-GROULX

CHARLEVOIX

JOLICOEUR

MONK

LaSALLE

DE L'ÉGLISE

VERDUN

ANGRIGNON

COMMUTER TRAINS TO DELSON-CANDIAC

© STM

☎(514) 786-4636 or 288-6287 (which corresponds to the word *AUTOBUS*, French for "bus," on a telephone dial pad) or visit the transit system's Web site: www.stm.info.

■ By Taxi

Taxi Co-op
☎(514) 725-9885
Taxi Diamond
☎(514) 273-6331
Taxi Royal
☎(514) 274-3333

■ By Bicycle

One of the most enjoyable ways to get around in the summer is by bicycle. Bike paths allow cyclists to explore various neighbourhoods in the city. To help you find your way around, a free map of paths is available at the tourist-information office. You can also purchase the booklet *Biking Montréal* (Ulysses Travel Guides).

The **Société de Transport de Montréal (STM)** *(☎514-786-4643, www.stm.info)* allows pas-

Montréal - Getting There and Getting Around

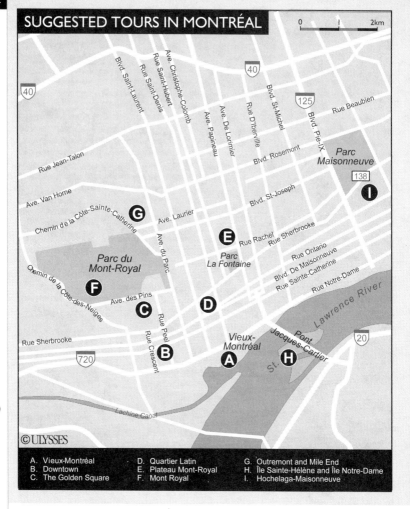

SUGGESTED TOURS IN MONTRÉAL

0 | 2km

©ULYSSES

A. Vieux-Montréal
B. Downtown
C. The Golden Square
D. Quartier Latin
E. Plateau Mont-Royal
F. Mont Royal
G. Outremont and Mile End
H. Île Sainte-Hélène and Île Notre-Dame
I. Hochelaga-Maisonneuve

sengers to board the metro with their bicycle. Certain restrictions apply.

Useful Information

■ Post Offices

The city's two largest post offices (see
below) are open Monday to Friday from
9am to 5:30pm *(Canada Post, ☎800-267-
1177, www.canadapost.ca)*. There are many
smaller post offices throughout Québec
located in shopping malls, *dépanneurs*
(convenience stores) and even drug stores;

these post offices are usually open much
later and sometimes even on Saturdays.

1250 Rue University
☎(514) 846-5401
1695 Rue Ste-Catherine Est
☎(514) 522-3220

■ Tourist Information

Centre Infotouriste de Montréal
*early Jun to early Sep 8:30am to 7:30pm, rest of
the year every day 9am to 6pm*
1255 Rue Peel, corner Rue Ste-Catherine
Peel metro
☎(514) 873-2015

The centre provides detailed information, maps, flyers and accommodation information for Montréal and all the tourist regions of Québec.

Bureau d'Accueil Touristique
du Vieux-Montréal (Old Montréal)
Jun to Sep every day 9am to 7pm, Sep to May
every day 9am to 1pm and 2pm to 5pm
174 Rue Notre-Dame Est
Champ-de-Mars metro
☎ (514) 874-1696

Exploring

Vieux-Montréal
★ ★ ★

 one day

During the 18th century, Montréal, like Québec City, was surrounded by stone fortifications. Between 1801 and 1817, these ramparts were demolished by local merchants who saw them as an obstacle to the city's development. The network of old streets, compressed after nearly a century of confinement, nevertheless remained in place. Today's Vieux-Montréal, or Old Montréal, thus corresponds quite closely to the area covered by the fortified city.

During the 19th century, this area became the hub of commercial and financial activity in Canada. Banks and insurance companies built sumptuous head offices here, leading to the demolition of almost all buildings erected under the French Regime.

The area was later abandoned for nearly 40 years in favour of today's modern downtown area. Finally, the long process of breathing new life into Old Montréal got underway during the preparations for Expo 67 and continues today with numerous conversion and restoration projects. This revitalization has even gotten a second wind since the late 1990s. In fact, several high-end hotels have been established in historic buildings, while many Montrealers have rejuvenated the neighbourhood by making it their home.

This tour starts at the western tip of Vieux-Montréal, on Rue Saint-Jacques (Square-Victoria metro). Square Victoria, located behind you, is described in the downtown Montréal tour.

Rue Saint-Jacques was the main artery of Canadian high finance for over a century. This role is reflected in its rich and varied architecture, which serves as a veritable encyclopedia of styles from 1830 to 1930. In those years, the banks, insurance companies and department stores, as well as the nation's railway and shipping companies, were largely controlled by Montrealers of Scottish extraction, who had come to the colonies to make their fortune.

Begun in 1928 according to plans by New York skyscraper specialists York and Sawyer, the former head office of the **Banque Royale / Royal Bank ★ ★** *(360 Rue St-Jacques; Square-Victoria metro)* was one of the last buildings erected during this era of prosperity. The 22-storey tower has a base inspired by Florentine palazzos, which corresponds to the scale of neighbouring buildings. Inside the tower, visitors can admire the high ceilings of this "temple of finance," built at a time when banks needed impressive buildings to win customers' confidence. The walls of the great hall are emblazoned with the heraldic insignia of eight of the 10 Canadian provinces, as well as those of Montréal (St. George's Cross) and Halifax (a yellow bird), where the bank was founded in 1861.

The **Banque Molson / Molson Bank ★** *(288 Rue Saint-Jacques; Square-Victoria metro)* was founded in 1854 by the Molson family, famous for the brewery established by their ancestor, John Molson (1763-1836), in 1786. The Molson Bank, like other banks at the time, even printed its own paper money—an indication of the power wielded by its owners, who contributed greatly to the city's development. The head office of the family business looks more like a patrician residence than an anonymous bank. Completed in 1866, it is one of the earliest examples of the Second Empire, or Napoleon III, style to have been erected in Canada. This French style, modelled on the Louvre and the Paris Opera, was extremely popular in North America between 1865 and 1890. Above the entrance, visitors will see the sandstone carvings of the heads of William Molson and two of his children.

Montréal - Exploring - Vieux-Montréal

The Molson Bank merged with the Bank of Montréal in 1925.

Walk along Rue Saint-Jacques; you'll soon reach Place d'Armes.

Under the French Regime, **Place d'Armes** ★★ *(Place-d'Armes metro)* was the heart of the city. Used for military manoeuvres and religious processions, the square was also the location of the Gadoys well, the city's main source of potable water. In 1847, the square was transformed into a lovely, fenced-in Victorian garden, which was destroyed at the beginning of the 20th century to make room for a tramway terminal. In the meantime, a **monument to Maisonneuve** ★★ was erected in 1895. Executed by sculptor Philippe Hébert, it shows the founder of Montréal, Paul de Chomedey, Sieur de Maisonneuve, surrounded by prominent figures from the city's early history, namely Jeanne Mance, founder of the Hôtel-Dieu hospital, Lambert Closse and his dog Pilote, and Charles LeMoyne, the head of a family of famous explorers. An Iroquois warrior completes the tableau.

The square, which is in fact shaped like a trapezoid, is surrounded by several noteworthy buildings. The **Banque de Montréal** ★★ *(119 Rue St-Jacques; Place-d'Armes metro)*, or Bank of Montreal, founded in 1817 by a group of merchants, is the country's oldest banking institution. Its present head office takes up an entire block on the north side of Place d'Armes. A magnificent building created by John Wells in 1847 and modelled after the Roman Pantheon, it occupies the place of honour in the centre of the block. Its Corinthian portico is a monument to the commercial power of the Scottish merchants who founded the institution. The columns' capitals, for their part,

were severely damaged by pollution and replaced in 1970 with aluminum replicas. The pediment includes a bas-relief depicting the bank's coat of arms carved out of Binney stone in Scotland by Her Majesty's sculptor, Sir John Steele.

The interior was almost entirely redone in 1904-05 by celebrated New York architects McKim, Mead and White (Boston Library, Columbia University in New York City). On this occasion, the bank was endowed with a splendid banking hall, designed in the style of a Roman basilica, with green syenite columns, gilded bronze ornamentation and beige marble counters. A small **Numismatic Museum** *(free admission; Mon-Fri 10am to 4pm)*, located in the lobby of the more recent building, displays bills from different eras, as well as an amusing collection of mechanical piggy banks. Across from the museum, visitors will find four bas-reliefs carved out of an artificial stone called *coade*, which once graced the facade of the bank's original head office. These were created in 1819, after drawings by English sculptor John Bacon.

The surprising red-sandstone tower at number 511 Place d'Armes was erected in 1888 for the New York Life insurance company by architects Babb, Cook and Willard. Although it only has eight floors, it is regarded as Montréal's first skyscraper. The stone used for the facing was imported from Scotland. At the time, this type of stone was transported in the holds of ships, where it served as ballast until it was sold to building contractors at the pier. The edifice next door *(507 Place-d'Armes)* is adorned with beautiful Art-Deco details. It was one of the first buildings over 10 stories to be erected in Montréal after a regula-

★ **ATTRACTIONS**

1.	BX	Banque Royale / Royal Bank
2.	BX	Banque Molson / Molson Bank
3.	CX	Place d'Armes / Monument to Maisonneuve
4.	CX	Banque de Montréal / Numismatic Museum
5.	CX	Basilique Notre-Dame
6.	CX	Vieux Séminaire Saint-Sulpice
7.	CY	Cours Le Royer
8.	CY	Place Royale
9.	CY	Pointe-à-Callière, Musée d'Archéologie et d'Histoire de Montréal / Maison de la Douane
10.	BY	Place D'Youville
11.	BY	Centre d'Histoire de Montréal
12.	BY	Hôpital Général des Sœurs Grises
13.	BZ	Musée Marc-Aurèle-Fortin
14.	DY	Vieux-Port de Montréal / Old Port
15.	CY	Centre des Sciences de Montréal
16.	DX	Palais de Justice
17.	DX	Édifice Ernest-Cormier
18.	DX	Palais de Justice (former)
19.	DX	Place Jacques-Cartier / Colonne Nelson
20.	DX	Hôtel de Ville
21.	DX	Place Vauquelin
22.	DX	Champ-de-Mars
23.	DX	Musée du Château Ramezay
24.	EX	Sir George-Étienne-Cartier National Historic Site
25.	EX	Cathédrale Schismatique Grecque Saint-Nicolas (former)
26.	EX	Gare Viger
27.	EX	Gare Dalhousie
28.	EX	Chapelle Notre-Dame-de-Bon-Secours / Musée Marguerite-Bourgeoys
29.	EX	Maison Papineau
30.	EY	Marché Bonsecours
31.	EY	Tour de l'Horloge

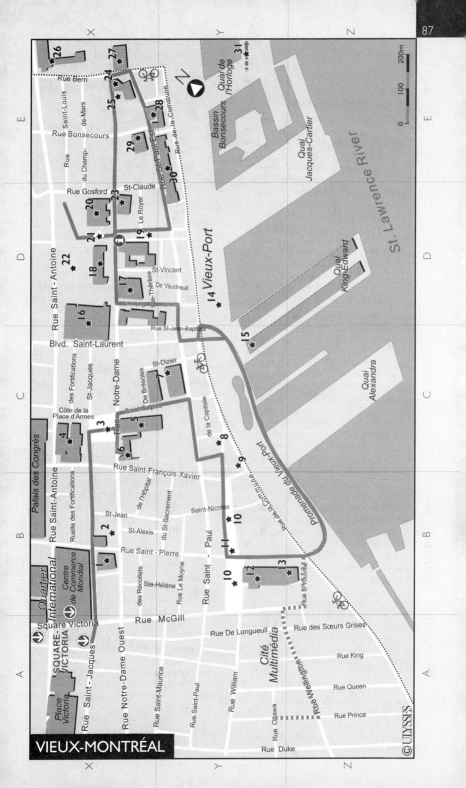

VIEUX-MONTRÉAL

© ULYSSES

tion restricting the height of structures was repealed in 1927.

On the south side of Place d'Armes, visitors will find the Basilique Notre-Dame and the Vieux Séminaire, which are described below.

In 1663, the seigneury of the island of Montréal was acquired by the Sulpicians from Paris, who remained its undisputed masters up until the British conquest of 1760. In addition to distributing land to colonists and laying out the city's first streets, the Sulpicians were responsible for the construction of a large number of buildings, including Montréal's first parish church (1673). Dedicated to *Notre Dame* (Our Lady), this church had a beautiful Baroque facade, which faced straight down the centre of the street of the same name, creating a pleasant perspective characteristic of classical French town-planning.

At the beginning of the 19th century, however, this rustic little church cut a sorry figure when compared to the Anglican cathedral on Rue Notre-Dame and the new Catholic cathedral on Rue Saint-Denis, neither of which still stands today. The Sulpicians therefore decided to make a move to surpass their rivals once and for all. In 1823, to the great displeasure of local architects, they commissioned New York architect James O'Donnell, who came from an Irish Protestant background, to design the largest and most original church north of Mexico.

Basilique Notre-Dame ★ ★ ★ *($4; Mon-Fri 8am to 4:30pm, Sat 8am to 4pm, Sun 12:30pm to 4pm; 110 Rue Notre-Dame Ouest,* ☎*514-842-2925 or 866-842-2925; Place-d'Armes metro)*, built between 1824 and 1829, is a true North-American masterpiece of Gothic Revival architecture. It should be seen not as a replica of a European cathedral, but rather as a fundamentally neoclassical structure characteristic of the Industrial Revolution, complemented by a medieval-style decor that foreshadowed the historicism of the Victorian era. These elements make the building simply remarkable.

O'Donnell was so pleased with his work that he converted to Catholicism before his death, so that he could be buried under the church. Between 1874 and 1880, the original interior, considered too austere, was replaced by the fabulous polychromatic

decorations found today. Executed by Victor Bourgeau, then the leading architect of religious buildings in the Montréal region, along with about 50 artists, it is made entirely of wood, painted and gilded with gold leaf.

Particularly noteworthy features include the baptistery, decorated with frescoes by Ozias Leduc, and the powerful electro-pneumatic Casavant organ with 7,000 pipes, often used during the numerous concerts given at the basilica. Lastly, there are the stained-glass windows by Francis Chigot, a master glass artist from France, which depict various episodes in the history of Montréal. They were installed in honour of the church's centennial.

To the right of the chancel, a passage leads to the Chapelle du Sacré-Cœur (Sacred Heart Chapel), added to the back of the church in 1888. Nicknamed *"Chapelle des Mariages"* (Wedding Chapel) because of the countless nuptials held there every year, it was seriously damaged by fire in 1978. The spiral staircases and the side galleries are all that remain of the exuberant, Spanish-style Gothic Revival decor of the original. Architects Jodoin, Lamarre and Pratte decided to tie in these vestiges with a modern design, completed in 1981, and included a lovely sectioned vault with skylights, a large bronze reredos by Charles Daudelin and a Guilbault-Thérien mechanical organ.

The **Vieux Séminaire Saint-Sulpice** ★ *(130 Rue Notre-Dame Ouest; Place-d'Armes metro)*, or old seminary, was built in 1683 in the style of a Parisian *hôtel particulier*, with a courtyard in front and a garden in back. It is the oldest building in the city. For more than three centuries, it has been occupied by Sulpician priests who, under the French Regime, used it as a manor from which they managed their vast seigneury. At the time of the building's construction, Montréal was home to barely 500 inhabitants and was constantly being terrorized by Iroquois attacks. Under those circumstances, the seminary, although modest in appearance, represented a precious haven of European civilization in the middle of the wilderness. The public clock at the top of the facade was installed in 1701, and may be the oldest one of its kind in the Americas.

Take Rue Saint-Sulpice, which runs alongside the basilica.

The immense warehouses of the **Cours Le Royer** ★ *(corner of Rue St-Sulpice and Rue St-Paul; Place-d'Armes metro)* belonged to the *religieuses hospitalières* (nursing sisters) of Saint-Joseph, who rented them out to importers. Designed between 1860 and 1871 by Michel Laurent and Victor Bourgeau, who seldom worked on commercial structures, they are located on the site of Montréal's first Hôtel-Dieu hospital, founded by Jeanne Mance in 1643. The warehouses, covering a total of 43,000m², were converted into apartments and offices between 1977 and 1986. The small Rue Le Royer was excavated to make room for an underground parking lot, now covered by a lovely pedestrian mall.

Turn right on Rue Saint-Paul, towards Place Royale, which lies on the left side of the street.

Rue Saint-Paul is Montréal's oldest street. It was drawn by land surveyor Bénigne de Basset in 1672 according to urban planner and historian Dollier de Casson's plans, and was Montréal's main commercial artery for a long time. It is probably Old Montréal's most emblematic street, lined with 19th-century stone buildings that are home to art galleries, arts-and-crafts shops and jazz clubs, making it a very pleasant place for a stroll.

Montréal's oldest public square, **Place Royale** *(Place-d'Armes metro)*, dates back to 1657. Originally a market square, it later became a pretty Victorian garden surrounded by a cast-iron fence. In 1991, it was raised in order to make room for an archaeological observation site. It now links the Musée d'Archéologie de Montréal to the **Maison de la Douane**, the former customs house, on the north side. The latter is a lovely example of British neoclassical architecture transplanted into a Canadian setting. The building's austere lines, accentuated by the facing of local grey stone, are offset by the appropriate proportions and simplified references to antiquity. The old customs house was built in 1836 by John Ostell, who had just arrived in Montréal. It is now an integral part of the Pointe-à-Callière museum.

Pointe-à-Callière, Musée d'Archéologie et d'Histoire de Montréal ★ ★ *($11; Sep to Jun Tue-Fri 10am to 5pm, Sat and Sun 11am to 5pm; Jul and Aug Mon-Fri 10am to 6pm, Sat and Sun 11am to 6pm; 350 Place Royale, Place-d'Armes metro, ☎514-872-9150, www.pacmusee.qc.ca)* is an archaeology and history museum that

lies on the exact site where Montréal was founded on May 18, 1642: **Pointe à Callière**.

The museum uses the most advanced techniques available to provide visitors with a survey of the city's history. Attractions include a multimedia presentation, a visit to the vestiges discovered on the site, excellent models illustrating the stages of Place Royale's development, holograms and thematic exhibitions. Designed by architect Dan Hanganu, the museum was established in 1992, the city's 350th anniversary.

Head towards Place d'Youville, west of the museum.

Stretching from Place Royale to Rue McGill, **Place d'Youville** owes its elongated shape to its location on top of the bed of the Rivière Saint-Pierre, which was canalized in 1832.

In the heart of Place d'Youville stands the former no. 3 fire station, one of Québec's rare examples of Flemish-inspired architecture. The station is now home to the **Centre d'Histoire de Montréal** ★ *($4.50; May to Aug Tue-Sun 10am to 5pm, Sep to Apr Wed-Sun 10am to 5pm; 335 Place d'Youville, ☎514-872-3207, www.ville.montreal.qc.ca/chm)*. A lovely exhibit showcasing various objects relating Montréal's history is presented on the first floor. Thanks to lively presentations, visitors can follow the city's evolution and learn about significant events, such as Expo 67, discover daily life in various eras, hear about major strikes in the city and see how several heritage buildings were demolished. Sound effects, among other things, play a particularly important role here, as you can hear taped testimonies of Montrealers of various origins talking about their city. On the top floors are temporary exhibits, as well as a glassed-in overpass from which you can admire Old Montréal.

Marché Sainte-Anne used to be located west of Rue Saint-Pierre and was the seat of the Province of Canada's Parliament from 1840 to 1849, when Orangemen burned the building down following the adoption of a compensatory law aimed at both English- and French-speaking victims of the 1837-1838 Rebellions. This marked the end of Montréal's political vocation: Canada's Parliament was subsequently moved to Toronto, then Québec City and, finally, Ottawa in 1847.

Montréal – Exploring – Vieux-Montréal

Turn left on Rue Saint-Pierre.

The Sœurs de la Charité (Sisters of Charity) are better known as the Sœurs Grises (Grey Nuns), a nickname given to these nuns who were falsely accused of selling alcohol to natives and getting them drunk (in French, *gris* means both grey and tipsy). In 1747, the founder of the community, Sainte Marguerite d'Youville, took charge of the former Hôpital des Frères Charon, established in 1693, and transformed it into the **Hôpital Général des Sœurs Grises** ★ *(138 Rue St-Pierre; Square-Victoria metro)*, a shelter for the city's homeless children. The west wing and the ruins of the chapel are all that remain of this complex, built during the 17th and 18th centuries in the shape of an *H*. The other part, which made up another of the old city's classical perspectives, was torn open when Rue Saint-Pierre was extended through the middle of the chapel. The right transept and part of the apse, visible on the right, have been reinforced in order to accommodate a work of art representing the text of the congregation's letters patent.

The small **Musée Marc-Aurèle-Fortin** *($5; Tue-Sun 11am to 5pm; 118 Rue St-Pierre, ☎514-845-6108, www.museemafortin.org; Square-Victoria metro)*, which has only a few rooms, is entirely dedicated to the work of Marc-Aurèle Fortin. Using his own unique style, Fortin painted picturesque Québec scenes. Paintings executed on a black background and majestic trees are just a few of his trademarks.

Cross Rue de la Commune to get to the Promenade du Vieux-Port, which runs alongside the St. Lawrence.

The port of Montréal is the largest inland port on the continent. It stretches 25km along the St. Lawrence River, from Cité du Havre to the refineries in the east end. The **Vieux-Port de Montréal / Old Port** ★ *(www.vieuxportdemontreal.com; Place-d'Armes or Champ-de-Mars metro)* corresponds to the historic portion of the port, located in front of the old city. Abandoned because of its obsolescence, it was revamped between 1983 and 1992, following the example of various other centrally located North-American ports. The old port encompasses a lovely park, laid out on the embankments and coupled with a promenade, which runs alongside the piers, or *quai*,

offering a "window" on the river and the few shipping activities that have fortunately been maintained. The layout emphasizes the view of the water, the downtown area and Rue de la Commune, whose wall of neoclassical grey-stone warehouses stands before the city, one of the only examples of so-called "waterfront planning" in North America.

From the port, visitors can set off on an excursion on the river and the Lachine Canal aboard the **Bateau-Mouche** *($20.65; mid-May to mid-Oct, departures every day at 10am, 11:30am, 1:30pm, 3pm and 4:30pm; quai Jacques-Cartier; ☎514-849-9952 or 800-361-9952, www.bateaumouche.ca)*, whose glass roof enables passengers to fully appreciate the beauty of the surroundings. These guided tours last 1.5hrs. At night, you can also enjoy dinner and dancing on the boat. The **navettes fluviales**, or river shuttles, *($5; ☎514-281-8000)* ferry passengers to Île Sainte-Hélène and Longueuil, offering a spectacular view of the old port and Old Montréal along the way.

On the right, directly in line with Rue Mc-Gill, visitors will find the mouth of the **Canal de Lachine / Lachine Canal** ★, inaugurated in 1825. This waterway made it possible to bypass the formidable rapids known as the Rapides de Lachine, upriver from Montréal, thus providing access to the Great Lakes and the American Midwest. The canal also became the cradle of the industrial revolution in Canada since spinning and flour mills were able to harness its power, as well as a direct means of taking in supplies and sending out shipments (from the boat to the factory and vice versa).

Closed in 1970, 11 years after the St. Lawrence seaway was opened in 1959, the canal was turned over to the Canadian Parks Service. A bicycle path now runs alongside it, continuing on to the Old Port. The locks, restored in 1991, lie adjacent to a park and a boldly designed lock-keeper's house. Behind the locks stands the last of the old port's towering **grain silos**. Erected in 1905, this reinforced concrete structure gained the admiration of Walter Gropius and Le Corbusier when they came here on a study trip. It is now illuminated as if it were a monument. In front, visitors will see the strange pile of cubes that form **Habitat 67** ★★ (see p 119) on the right, and the **Gare Maritime Iberville du Port de Montréal**

(☎514-286-7011), the harbour station for liners cruising the St. Lawrence, on the left.

The **Centre des Sciences de Montréal** *($10; May to Aug every day 10am to 6pm, Sep to Apr Mon-Fri 9am to 3:30pm, Sat-Sun 10am to 5pm; Quai King-Edward,* ☎*514-496-4724 or 877-496-4724, www.centredessciencesdemontreal.com; Place-d'Armes metro)* is an interactive science-and-entertainment complex set up in a modern building. The centre also features an IMAX theatre, the Immersion interactive cinema, restaurants and boutiques.

Walk along the promenade to **Boulevard Saint-Laurent** *(see p 100), where you will head north and and turn right on Rue Notre-Dame.*

Having passed through the financial and warehouse districts, visitors now enter an area dominated by civic and legal institutions; no fewer than three courthouses lie along Rue Notre-Dame. Inaugurated in 1971, the massive new **Palais de Justice** *(1 Rue Notre-Dame Est; Champ-de-Mars metro)*, or courthouse, dwarfs the surroundings. A sculpture by Charles Daudelin entitled *Allegropole* stands on its steps. A mechanism makes it possible to open and close this stylized "hand of justice."

From the time it was inaugurated in 1926 until it closed in 1970, the **Édifice Ernest-Cormier** ★★ *(100 Rue Notre-Dame Est; Champ-de-Mars metro)* was used for criminal proceedings. The former courthouse was converted into a conservatory and was named after its architect, the illustrious Ernest Cormier, who also designed the main pavilion of the Université de Montréal and the doors of the United Nations Headquarters in New York City. The Édifice Ernest-Cormier returned to its original use in 2004, as the Court of Appeal of Québec.

The former **Palais de Justice** ★ *(155 Rue Notre-Dame Est; Champ-de-Mars metro)*, the oldest courthouse in Montréal, was built between 1849 and 1856 by John Ostell and Henri-Maurice Perrault, on the site of the first courthouse, which was erected in 1800. It is another fine example of Canadian neoclassical architecture. After the courts were divided in 1926, the old Palais was used for civil cases, judged according to the Napoleonic Code. Since the opening of the new Palais to its left, the old Palais has been converted into an annex of city hall, located to the right.

Continue along Rue Notre-Dame. Place Jacques-Cartier will appear on your right.

Place Jacques-Cartier ★ *(Champ-de-Mars metro)* was laid out on the site once occupied by the Château de Vaudreuil, which burned down in 1803. The former Montréal residence of the governor of New France was without question the most elegant private home in the city. Designed by engineer Gaspard Chaussegros de Léry in 1723, it had a horseshoe-shaped staircase leading up to a handsome cut-stone portal, two projecting pavilions (one on each side of the main part of the building), and a formal garden that extended as far as Rue Notre-Dame. After the fire, the property was purchased by local merchants, who decided to give the government a small strip of land, on the condition that a public market be established there, thus increasing the value of the adjacent property that remained in private hands. This explains Place Jacques-Cartier's oblong shape.

Merchants of British descent sought various means of ensuring their visibility and publicly expressing their patriotism in Montréal. They quickly formed a much larger community in Montréal than in Québec City, where government and military headquarters were located. In 1809, they were the first in the world to erect a monument to Admiral Horatio Nelson, who defeated the combined French and Spanish fleets in the Battle of Trafalgar. Supposedly, they even got French-Canadian merchants drunk in order to extort a financial contribution from them for the project. The base of the **Colonne Nelson**, or Nelson Column, was designed and executed in London according to plans by architect Robert Mitchell. It is decorated with bas-relief depicting the exploits of the famous admiral at Abukir, Copenhagen, and of course Trafalgar. The statue of Nelson at the top was originally made of an artificial type of stone, but after being damaged time and time again by protestors, it was finally replaced by a fibre-glass replica in 1981. The column is the oldest extant monument in Montréal.

At the other end of Place Jacques-Cartier, visitors will see the **Quai Jacques-Cartier** and the river, while **Rue Saint-Amable** lies tucked away on the right, at the halfway mark.

Montréal - Exploring - Vieux-Montréal

During summer, artists and artisans gather on this little street, selling jewellery, drawings, etchings and caricatures.

Under the French Regime, Montréal, following the example of Québec City and Trois-Rivières, had its own governor, not to be confused with the governor of New France. The situation was the same under the English Regime. It wasn't until 1833 that the first elected mayor, Jacques Viger, took control of the city. This man, who was passionate about history, gave Montréal its motto (*Concordia Salus*) and coat of arms, composed of the four symbols of the "founding" peoples, namely the French *fleur de lys*, the Irish clover, the Scottish thistle and the English rose, all linked together by the Canadian beaver.

After occupying a number of inadequate buildings for decades (a notable example was the Hayes aqueduct, an edifice containing an immense reservoir of water, which one day cracked while a meeting was being held in the council chamber just below), the municipal administration finally moved into its present home in 1878. The **Hôtel de Ville** ★ *(275 Rue Notre-Dame Est; Champ-de-Mars metro)*, or city hall, a fine example of the Second Empire, or Napoleon III, style, is the work of Henri-Maurice Perrault, who also designed the neighbouring courthouse. In 1922, a fire destroyed the interior and roof of the building which was later restored in 1926 on the model of the city hall in Tours, France. Exhibitions are occasionally presented in the main hall, which is accessible via the main entrance. Visitors will also be interested to learn that it was from the balcony of this building that France's General de Gaulle cried out his famous "*Vive le Québec libre!*" ("Freedom for Québec!") in 1967, to the great delight of the crowd gathered in front of the building.

Head to the rear of the Hôtel de Ville by way of the lovely Place Vauquelin, the continuation of Place Jacques-Cartier.

The statue of Admiral Jean Vauquelin, defender of Louisbourg at the end of the French Regime, was probably put here to counterbalance the monument to Nelson, a symbol of British control over Canada. Go down the staircase leading to the **Champ-de-Mars**, modified in 1991 in order to reveal some vestiges of the fortifications that once surrounded Montréal. Gaspard Chaussegros de Léry designed Montréal's ramparts, erected between 1717 and 1745, as well as those of Québec City. The walls of Montréal, however, never lived through war, as the city's commercial calling and location ruled out such rash acts. The large, tree-lined lawns are reminders of the Champ-de-Mars' former vocation as a parade ground for military manoeuvres until 1924. A view of the downtown area's skyscrapers opens up through the clearing.

Head back to Rue Notre-Dame.

The **Musée du Château Ramezay** ★ ★ *($7.50; summer every day 10am to 6pm, rest of the year Tue-Sun 10am to 4:30pm; 280 Rue Notre-Dame Est, ☎514-861-3708, www.chateauramezay.qc. ca; Champ-de-Mars metro)* is located in the humblest of all the "châteaux" built in Montréal, and the only one still standing. The Château Ramezay was built in 1705 for the governor of Montréal, Claude de Ramezay, and his family. In 1745, it fell into the hands of the Compagnie des Indes Occidentales (The French West Indies Company), which made it its North-American headquarters. Precious Canadian furs were stored in its vaults awaiting shipment to France. After the conquest (1760), the British occupied the house, before being temporarily removed by American insurgents who wanted Québec to join the nascent United States. Benjamin Franklin even came to stay at the château for a few months in 1775, in an attempt to convince Montrealers to become American citizens.

In 1895, after serving as the first building of the Montréal branch of the Université Laval in Québec City, the château was converted into a museum, under the patronage of the Société d'Archéologie et de Numismatique de Montréal, founded by Jacques Viger. Visitors will still find a rich collection of furniture, clothing and everyday objects from the 18th and 19th centuries here, as well as many Aboriginal artifacts.

Walk along Rue Notre-Dame to Rue Berri.

At the corner of Rue Berri lies the **Sir George-Étienne-Cartier National Historic Site** ★ *($4; early Sep to late Dec and early Apr to late May Wed-Sun 10am to noon and 1pm to 5pm, late May to early Sep every day 10am to 6pm, closed Jan to Mar; 458 Rue Notre-Dame Est, ☎514-283-2282, www.pc.gc.ca/cartier; Champ-*

de-Mars métro), consisting of twin houses inhabited successively by George-Étienne Cartier, one of the Fathers of Canadian Confederation. Inside, visitors will find a reconstructed mid-19th-century French-Canadian bourgeois home.

The neighbouring building, at number 452, is the former **Cathédrale Schismatique Grecque Saint-Nicolas**, built around 1910 in the Romanesque-Byzantine Revival style.

Rue Berri marks the eastern border of Old Montréal, and thus the fortified city of the French Regime, beyond which extended the Faubourg Québec, excavated in the 19th century to make way for railroad lines. This explains the sharp difference in height between the hill known as Côteau Saint-Louis and the Viger and Dalhousie stations.

Gare Viger, visible on the left, was inaugurated by Canadian Pacific in 1897 in order to serve the eastern part of the country. Its resemblance to the Château Frontenac in Québec City is not a coincidence; both buildings were designed for the same railroad company and by the same architect, an American named Bruce Price. The Château-style station, closed in 1935, also included a prestigious hotel and large stained-glass train shed that has since been destroyed.

The smaller **Gare Dalhousie** *(514 Rue Notre-Dame Est; Champ-de-Mars métro)*, located near the Maison Cartier, was the first railway station built by Canadian Pacific, a company established for the purpose of building a Canadian transcontinental railroad. The station was the starting point of the first transcontinental train headed for Vancouver on June 28, 1886. Canadian Pacific seems to have had a weakness for foreign architects, since it was Thomas C. Sorby, Director of Public Works in England, who drew up the plans for this humble structure.

For a long time, Gare Dalhousie was home to the École Nationale de Cirque de Montréal, which recently moved to a building located in what is now known as TOHU, la Cité des Arts du Cirque, in the northern section of the island of Montréal. The Eloize circus company has since taken its place at Gare Dalhousie.

Turn right on Rue Berri, and right again on Rue Saint-Paul, which offers a lovely view of the Marché Bonsecours dome. Continue straight ahead to Chapelle Notre-Dame-de-Bonsecours.

This site was originally occupied by another chapel, built in 1658 upon the recommendation of Saint Marguerite Bourgeoys, founder of the congregation of Notre-Dame. The present **Chapelle Notre-Dame-de-Bonsecours** ★ *(400 Rue St-Paul Est; Champ-de-Mars métro)* dates back to 1771, when the Sulpicians wanted to establish a branch of the main parish in the eastern part of the fortified city. In 1890, the chapel was modified to suit contemporary tastes, and the present stone facade was added, along with the "aerial" chapel looking out on the port. Parishioners asked for God's blessing on ships and crews bound for Europe from this chapel. The interior, redone at the same time, contains a large number of votive offerings from sailors saved from shipwrecks. Some are in the form of model ships, hung from the ceiling of the nave.

Between 1996 and 1998, excavations below the chapel's nave uncovered several artifacts, including some dating from the colony's early days. Today, the **Musée Marguerite-Bourgeoys** ★ *($6; May to Oct every day 10am to 5:30pm, Nov to mid-Jan every day 11am to 3:30pm, Mar to late Apr every day 11am to 3:30pm, closed mid-Jan to early Mar; 400 Rue St-Paul Est, ☎514-282-8670, www.margueritebourgeoys.com)* displays these interesting archaeological finds. But there is even more to explore: adjoining the Notre-Dame-de-Bon-Secours chapel, it leads from the top of the tower, where the view is breathtaking, to the depths of the crypt, where the old stones tell their own story. Learn about the life of Marguerite Bourgeoys, a pioneer of education in Québec, admire her portrait and discover the mystery surrounding her. Guided tours of the archaeological site surrounding the foundations of the stone chapel, the oldest in Montréal, are offered.

Turn right on Rue Bonsecours.

Maison Papineau *(440 Rue Bonsecours; Champ-de-Mars métro)* was once inhabited by Louis-Joseph Papineau (1786-1871), a lawyer, politician and the head of the French-Canadian nationalist movement until the insurrection of 1837. Built in 1785 and covered with a wooden facing made to look like cut stone, it was one of the first buildings in Old Montréal to be restored (1962).

The **Marché Bonsecours** ★ ★ *(300 Rue St-Paul Est, www.marchebonsecours.qc.ca)* was erected between 1845 and 1850. The lovely greystone neoclassical edifice with sash windows is located between Rue Saint-Paul and Rue de la Commune. The building is adorned with a portico supported by cast-iron columns moulded in England, and topped by a silvery dome, which for many years served as the symbol of the city at the entrance to the port. The public market, closed in the early 1960s following the advent of the supermarket, was transformed into municipal offices, then an exhibition hall before finally partially reopening in 1996. The market now presents an exhibition and features arts-and-crafts shops. The building originally housed both the city hall and a concert hall upstairs. The market's old storehouses, recently renovated, can be seen on Rue Saint-Paul. From the large balcony on Rue de la Commune, you can see the partially reconstructed Bonsecours dock, where paddle-wheelers, full of farmers who came to the city to sell their produce, used to moor.

Walk to Place Jacques-Cartier and head down to the Old Port.

The **Tour de l'Horloge** ★ *(early May to late Sep; at the end of Quai de l'Horloge, ☎514-496-7678; Champ-de-Mars metro)* is visible to the east from the end of Quai Jacques-Cartier. Painted a pale yellow, the structure is actually a monument erected in 1922 in memory of merchant marine sailors who died during WWI. It was inaugurated by the Prince of Wales (who became Edward VIII) during one of his many visits to Montréal. An observatory at the top of the tower provides a clear view of Île Sainte-Hélène, the Jacques-Cartier bridge and the eastern part of Old Montréal. Standing on Place Belvédère at the base of the tower, one has the impression of standing on the deck of ship as it glides slowly down the St. Lawrence and out to the Atlantic Ocean.

To return to the metro, walk back up Place Jacques-Cartier, cross Rue Notre-Dame, Place Vauquelin and finally Champ-de-Mars, to the metro station of the same name.

Downtown
★ ★ ★

 one day

Downtown skyscrapers give Montréal a typically North-American look. Nevertheless, unlike most other cities on the continent, there is a certain Latin spirit here, which seeps in between the towering buildings, livening up this part of Montréal both day and night. Bars, cafés, department stores, shops and head offices, along with two universities and numerous colleges, all lie clustered within a limited area that neighbours Old Montréal.

At the beginning of the 20th century, Montréal's central business district gradually shifted from the old city to what was up until then a posh residential neighbourhood known as the **Golden Square Mile** (see p 102), inhabited by upper-class Canadians. Wide arterial streets such as Boulevard René-Lévesque (then known as Dorchester Street) were lined with palatial residences surrounded by shady gardens. The city centre underwent a radical transformation in a very short time (1960-1967), marked by the construction of Place Ville-Marie, the metro, the underground city, Place des Arts and various other infrastructures that still exert an influence on the area's development.

This tour kicks off underground at the Peel metro station. From here, head to Cours Mont-Royal and Rue Peel.

Montréal has the most extensive **underground city** in the world. Greatly appreciated in bad weather, it provides access to more than 2,000 shops and restaurants, as well as movie theatres, apartment and office buildings, hotels, parking lots, the train station, the bus station, Place des Arts and even the Université du Québec à Montréal (UQAM) via tunnels, atriums and indoor plazas.

The **Cours Mont-Royal** ★ ★ *(1455 Rue Peel; Peel metro)* are linked to this sprawling network, which centres around the various metro stations. A multi-purpose complex, Les Cours consists of four levels of stores, offices and apartments laid out inside the former Mount Royal Hotel. With its 1,100

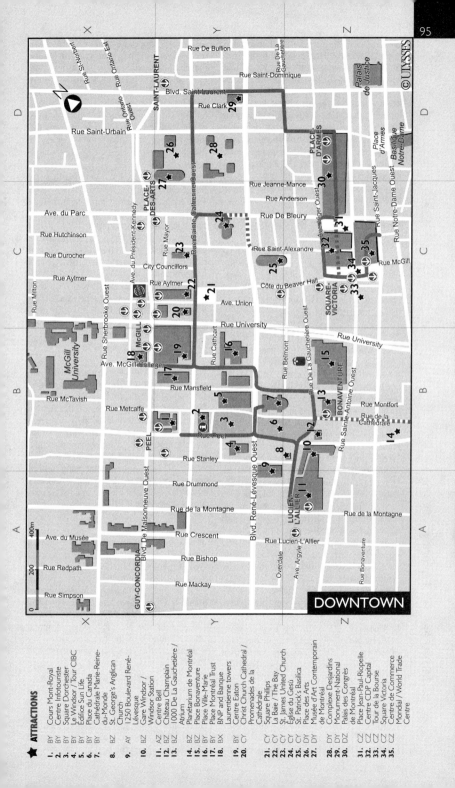

© ULYSSES

DOWNTOWN

Rue De Bullion
Rue De La Gauchetière
Palais de Justice
Rue Saint-Dominique
SAINT-LAURENT
Rue De Bullion
Rue Saint-Dominique
Blvd. Saint-Laurent
Rue Clark **29**
Place d'Armes
Rue St-Norbert
Rue Ontario Est
Rue Ontario Ouest
Rue Saint-Urbain **26**
28
PLACE D'ARMES **30**
Basilique Notre-Dame
Ave. du Parc
PLACE-DES-ARTS **27**
Rue Jeanne-Mance
Rue Anderson
Rue Hutchinson
Rue Durocher
Rue Mayor **23**
24
Rue Sainte-Catherine Ouest
Rue De Bleury
Ave. Ujer Ouest
Rue Saint-Jacques
Rue Notre-Dame Ouest
31
Rue Aylmer
City Councillors
Rue Saint-Alexandre
32
Ave. du Président-Kennedy
Rue Aylmer **22**
25
35
Rue Milton
21
34
Rue McGill
Ave. Union
Côte du Beaver Hall
33
Rue Sherbrooke Ouest
20
SQUARE VICTORIA
Rue University
McGill
Rue University
18
19
Rue Cathcart
16
Rue Belmont
15
Rue De La Gauchetière Ouest
McGill University
17
Rue Mansfield
Rue McTavish
5
BONAVENTURE
13
Rue Montfort
7
Rue Metcalfe
2
3
6
12
Rue Sainte-Antoine Ouest
Rue de la Cathédrale
PEEL
4
8
10
14
Rue Peel
9
Rue Stanley
11
Rue de la Montagne
Rue Drummond
LUCIEN-L'ALLIER
Rue de la Montagne
GUY-CONCORDIA
Rue de la Montagne
Blvd. René-Lévesque Ouest
Rue Crescent
Ave. du Musée
Rue Lucien-L'Allier
Rue Redpath
Overdale
Ave. Argyle
Rue Bonaventure
Rue Bishop
Rue Simpson
Rue Mackay
Blvd. De Maisonneuve Ouest

400m
200
0

rooms, this Jazz Age palace, inaugurated in 1922, was the largest hotel in the British Empire. Aside from the exterior, all that was preserved during the 1987 remodelling was a portion of the lobby's ceiling, from which the former chandelier of the Monte Carlo casino is suspended. The four 10-storey *cours* (inner courts) are definitely worth a visit, as is a stroll through what may be the best-designed shopping centre in the downtown area. The building that looks like a small Scottish manor across the street is the former head office of the Seagram distillery.

Head south on Rue Peel to Square Dorchester.

At Montreal's tourist office, the **Centre Info-touriste** *(1255 Rue Peel, corner Rue Ste-Catherine Ouest,* ☎877-266-5687, *www.tourisme-montreal.org; Peel metro)*, visitors will find representatives from a number of tourism-related enterprises.

From 1799 to 1854, **Square Dorchester** ★ *(Peel metro)* was occupied by Montréal's Catholic cemetery, which was later moved to Mount Royal, where it is still located. In 1872, the city turned the free space into two squares, one on either side of Dorchester Street (now Boulevard René-Lévesque). The northern portion is called Square Dorchester, while the southern part was renamed Place du Canada to commemorate the 100th anniversary of Confederation (1967). A number of monuments adorn Square Dorchester. In the centre is an equestrian statue dedicated to Canadian soldiers who died during the Boer War in South Africa, while around the perimeter stand a handsome statue of Scottish poet Robert Burns, styled after Bartholdi's Roaring Lion and donated by the Sun Life insurance company, and Émile Brunet's monument to Sir Wilfrid Laurier, Prime Minister of Canada from 1896 to 1911. The square also serves as the starting point for guided bus tours.

Le Windsor ★ *(1170 Rue Peel, www.lewindsor.com; Peel metro)*, the hotel where members of the royal family used to stay during their visits to Canada, no longer exists. The prestigious Second Empire–style edifice, built in 1878 by architect W. W. Boyington of Chicago, was ravaged by fire in 1957. All that remains is an annex erected in 1906, which was converted into an office building in 1986. The ballrooms and lovely Peacock Alley have, however, been pre-

served. An impressive atrium, visible from the upper floors, has been constructed for the building's tenants. The handsome **Tour CIBC**, designed by Peter Dickinson (1962), stands on the site of the old hotel. Its walls are faced with green slate, which blends harmoniously with the dominant colours of the buildings around the square, the greyish beige of stone and the green of oxidized copper.

The **Édifice Sun Life** ★★ *(1155 Rue Metcalfe; Peel metro)*, erected between 1913 and 1933 for the powerful Sun Life insurance company, was for many years the largest building in the British Empire. It was in this "fortress" of the Anglo-Saxon establishment, with its colonnades reminiscent of ancient mythology, that the British Crown Jewels were hidden during World War II. In 1977, the company's head office was moved to Toronto, in protest against provincial language laws excluding English. Fortunately, the chimes that ring at 5pm every day are still in place and remain an integral part of the neighbourhood's spirit.

Place du Canada ★ *(Bonaventure metro)*, the southern portion of Square Dorchester, is the setting for the annual Remembrance Day ceremony (November 11th), which honours Canadian soldiers killed in the two World Wars and the Korean War. Veterans reunite around the War Memorial, which occupies the place of honour in the centre of the square. A more imposing monument to Sir John A. Macdonald, Canada's first Prime Minister, elected in 1867, stands alongside Boulevard René-Lévesque.

A number of churches were clustered around Square Dorchester before it was even laid out in 1872. Unfortunately, only two of the eight churches built in the area between 1865 and 1875 have survived. One of these is **Cathédrale Marie-Reine-du-Monde** ★★ *(Boulevard René-Lévesque Ouest at the corner of Mansfield; Bonaventure metro)*, the seat of the archdiocese of Montréal and a reminder of the tremendous power wielded by the clergy up until the Quiet Revolution. It is exactly one third the size of St. Peter's in Rome.

In 1852, a terrible fire destroyed the Catholic cathedral on Rue Saint-Denis, so the ambitious Monseigneur Ignace Bourget (1799-1885), who was bishop of Montréal at the time, seized the opportunity to work out a grandiose scheme to outshine the Sulpicians' Basilique Notre-Dame and ensure the supremacy of the Catholic Church in Montréal. What could accomplish this better than a replica of Rome's St. Peter's, right in the middle of the Protestant neighbourhood? Despite reservations on the part of architect Victor Bourgeau, the plan was carried out. The bishop even sent Bourgeau to Rome to measure the venerable building. Construction began in 1870 and was finally completed in 1894. The copper statues of the 13 patron saints of Montréal's parishes were installed in 1900.

Modernized during the 1950s, the interior of the cathedral is no longer as harmonious as it once was. Nevertheless, there is a lovely replica of Bernini's baldaquin, executed by sculptor Victor Vincent. The bishops and archbishops of Montréal are interred in the mortuary chapel on the left, where the place of honour is occupied by the recumbent statue of Monseigneur Bourget. An outdoor monument reminds visitors of this individual, who did so much to strengthen the bonds between France and Canada.

Upon exiting the cathedral, turn left on Boulevard René-Lévesque and walk to Rue Peel and the splendid St. George's Anglican Church.

The beautiful Gothic Revival–style **St. George's Anglican Church**'s ★★ *(at the corner of Rue De La Gauchetière and Rue Peel; Bonaventure metro)* delicately sculpted sandstone exterior conceals an interior covered with lovely, dark woodwork. Particularly noteworthy are the remarkable ceiling, with its exposed framework, the woodwork in the chancel and the tapestry from Westminster Abbey, used during the coronation of Queen Elizabeth II.

The elegant 47-storey **1250 Boulevard René-Lévesque** ★ building *(1250 Boulevard René-Lévesque Ouest; Bonaventure metro)*, formerly the IBM-Marathon tower and forming part of the backdrop of St. George's, was completed in 1991 by famous New York architects Kohn, Pedersen and Fox. Its winter bamboo garden is open to the public.

In 1887, the head of Canadian Pacific, William Cornelius Van Horne, asked his New York friend Bruce Price (1845-1903) to draw up plans for **Gare Windsor / Windsor Station** ★★ *(at the corner of Rue De La Gauche-*

tière and Rue Peel; Bonaventure metro), a modern train station that would serve as the terminal for the transcontinental railroad, completed the previous year. At the time, Price was one of the most prominent architects in the eastern United States, where he worked on residential projects for high-society clients, as well as skyscrapers like the American Surety Building in Manhattan. Later, he was put in charge of building the Château Frontenac in Québec City, thus establishing the Château style in Canada.

The massive-looking Gare Windsor, with its corner buttresses, Roman arches outlined in stone and series of arcades, is Montréal's best example of the Romanesque Revival style as interpreted by American architect Henry Hobson Richardson. Its construction established the city as the country's railway centre and initiated the shift of commercial and financial activity from the old town to the Golden Square Mile. Abandoned in favour of the Gare Centrale after World War II, Windsor Station was used only for commuter trains up until 1993. Today, the Gare Windsor houses many stores and offices, and its waiting hall is used for various events.

Walk down Rue De La Gauchetière to get to the Centre Bell.

The **Centre Bell** *($8; 1hr 15min guided tours every day at 9:45am and 1:15pm; 1260 Rue De La Gauchetière Ouest, ☎514-932-2582; Bonaventure metro)*, built on the platforms of Windsor Station, now blocks all train access to the venerable old station. Opened in 1996 (when it was called the Molson Centre; Bell Canada purchased the rights in 2002), this immense, oddly shaped building succeeds the Forum on Sainte-Catherine as the home of the National Hockey League's Montréal Canadiens.

The amphitheatre can seat 21,247 people and boasts 138 glassed-in private boxes sold to Montréal companies for hefty sums. The National Hockey League's regular season runs from October to April, and playoffs can carry on into June. Two thousand tickets are sold at the Bell Centre on each game day, making it possible to get good last-minute seats. The Bell Centre also presents a wide array of concerts and family shows.

Retrace your steps to get to Château Champlain, which is located south of Place du Canada.

Built in 1966, the Marriott **Château Champlain** ★ *(1 Place du Canada; Bonaventure metro)*, nicknamed the "cheese grater" by Montrealers due to its many arched, convex openings, was designed by Québec architects Jean-Paul Pothier and Roger D'Astous. The latter is a disciple of American architect Frank Lloyd Wright, with whom he studied for several years. The hotel is not unlike some of the master's late works, characterized by rounded, fluid lines.

1000 De La Gauchetière *(1000 Rue De La Gauchetière; Bonaventure metro)*, a 51-storey skyscraper, was completed in 1992. It houses the terminus for buses linking Montréal to the South Shore, as well as the **Atrium**, an indoor skating rink open year-round *($5.50, skate rentals $5; schedule changes frequently; ☎514-395-0555, www.le1000.com)*. Its architects wanted to set the building apart from its neighbours by crowning it with a copper-covered point. Its total height is the maximum allowed by the city, namely the height of Mount Royal. The ultimate symbol of Montréal, the mountain may be not surpassed under any circumstances.

A short side trip from this tour leads to the Planétarium de Montréal. To get there, head south on Rue de la Cathédrale.

The **Planétarium de Montréal** ★ *($6.50; every day, presentations last 45min; schedule changes frequently; 1000 Rue Saint-Jacques Ouest, ☎514-872-4530; Bonaventure metro)* projects astronomy films onto a 20m hemispheric dome. The universe and its mysteries are explained in a way that makes this marvellous and often poorly understood world accessible to all.

Head onto Rue De La Gauchetière. Place Bonaventure will appear on your right.

An immense, grooved concrete block with no facade, **Place Bonaventure** ★ *(1 Place Bonaventure; Bonaventure metro)*, which was completed in 1966, is one of the most revolutionary works of modern architecture of its time. Designed by Montrealer Raymond Affleck, it is a multi-purpose complex built on top of the railway lines leading into the Gare Centrale. It contains a parking area, a bi-level shopping centre linked to the metro and the underground city, two large exhibition halls, wholesalers, offices and an intimate 400-room hotel laid out around a charming hanging garden, worth a short visit.

Head onto Rue Mansfield, which runs alongside Cathédrale Marie-Reine-du-Monde. The imposing Sun Life building can be seen in the background. Turn right on Boulevard René-Lévesque.

Place Ville-Marie ★ ★ ★ *(1 Place Ville-Marie; Bonaventure metro)* was erected above the northern part of the former open-air trench in 1959. Famous Chinese-American architect I.M. Pei (Louvre Pyramid, Paris; East Building of the National Gallery of Art, Washington, DC) designed the multipurpose complex built over the railway tracks and containing vast shopping arcades now linked to most of the surrounding edifices. It also encompasses a number of office buildings, including the famous cruciform aluminum tower, whose unusual shape enables natural light to penetrate all the way into the centre of the structure, while at the same time symbolizing Montréal, a Catholic city dedicated to the Virgin Mary.

In the middle of the public area, a granite compass card indicates true north, while **Avenue McGill College**, which leads straight toward the mountain, indicates "north" as it is perceived by Montrealers in their everyday life. This artery, lined with multicoloured skyscrapers, was still a narrow residential street in 1950. It now offers a wide view of Mount Royal, crowned by a **metal cross** (see p 114).

Cross Place Ville-Marie and take Avenue McGill College to Rue Sainte-Catherine Ouest.

Avenue McGill College was widened and entirely redesigned in the 1980s. Walking along it, visitors will see several examples of eclectic, polychromatic postmodern architecture composed largely of granite and reflective glass. **Place Montréal Trust** *(at the corner of Rue Sainte-Catherine; McGill metro)* is one of a number of Montréal shopping centres topped by an office building and linked to the underground city and the metro by corridors and private plazas.

The **twin BNP** and **Banque Laurentienne towers** ★ *(1981 Avenue McGill College; McGill metro)*, certainly the best designed buildings on Avenue McGill College, were built in 1981 by the architectural firm Webb, Zerafa, Menkès, Housden Partnership (Tour Elf-Aquitaine, Paris; Royal Bank, Toronto). Their bluish glass walls set off a sculpture entitled *La Foule Illuminée* (The Illuminated Crowd) by Franco-British artist Raymond Mason.

Return to Rue Sainte-Catherine.

Rue Sainte-Catherine is Montréal's main commercial artery. It stretches along 15km, changing in appearance several times along the way. Around 1870, it was still lined with row houses; by 1920, however, it had already become an integral part of life in Montréal. Since the 1960s, a number of shopping centres linking the street to the adjacent metro lines have sprouted up among the local businesses. The **Centre Eaton** *(705 Rue Ste-Catherine Ouest; McGill metro)* is the most recent of these. It is composed of a long, old-fashioned gallery lined with five levels of shops and restaurants, and is linked to Place Ville-Marie by a pedestrian tunnel.

The **Eaton** department store *(677 Rue Ste-Catherine Ouest; McGill metro)*, one of the largest department stores on Ste-Catherine and an institution across Canada, went bankrupt in 1999 and had to close its doors. The imposing nine-storey building now houses another department store, **Les Ailes de la Mode**. Its magnificent Art-Deco dining room on the ninth floor, designed by Jacques Carlu and completed in 1931, is a historic monument, but is not currently open to the public.

Montréal's first Anglican cathedral stood on Rue Notre-Dame, not far from Place d'Armes. After a fire in 1856, **Christ Church Cathedral** ★ ★ *(at the corner of Rue University; McGill metro)* was relocated to be closer to the community it served, in the heart of the nascent Golden Square Mile. Using the cathedral of his hometown, Salisbury, as his model, architect Frank Wills designed a flamboyant structure, with a single steeple rising above the transepts. The plain interior contrasts with the rich ornamentation of the Catholic churches included in this walking tour. A few beautiful stained-glass windows from the workshops of William Morris provide the only bit of colour. The steeple's stone spire was destroyed in 1927 and replaced by an aluminum replica; otherwise, it would have eventually caused the building to sink. The problem, linked

to the instability of the foundation, was not resolved, however, until a shopping centre, the **Promenades de la Cathédrale**, was constructed under the building in 1987. Christ Church Anglican Cathedral thus rests on the roof of the mall. At the same time, a postmodern glass skyscraper topped by a "crown of thorns" was erected behind the cathedral. At its base is a little garden that honours architect Raoul Wallenberg, a Swedish diplomat who saved several Hungarian Jews from Nazi deportation during the Second World War.

It was around **Square Phillips** ★ *(at the corner of Rue Union and Rue Ste-Catherine; McGill metro)* that the first stores appeared along Rue Sainte-Catherine, which was once strictly residential. Henry Morgan moved Morgan's Colonial House, now **La Baie / The Bay** *(McGill metro)*, here after the floods of 1886 in the old city. Henry Birks, descendant of a long line of English jewellers, arrived soon after, establishing his famous shop in a handsome beige sandstone building on the west side of the square. In 1914, a monument to King Edward VII, sculpted by Philippe Hébert, was erected in the centre of Square Phillips. Downtown shoppers and employees alike come here to relax.

A former Methodist church designed in the shape of an auditorium, **St. James United Church** ★ *(463 Rue Ste-Catherine Ouest; McGill metro)* originally had a complete facade looking out onto a garden. In 1926, in an effort to counter the decrease in its revenue, the community built a group of stores and offices along the front of the building on Rue Sainte-Catherine, leaving only a narrow passageway into the church. Visitors can still see the two Gothic Revival–style steeples set back from Rue Sainte-Catherine. St. James United Church recently underwent outdoor renovations to the tune of two million dollars. The removal of the shops and offices that hid its facade revealed an impressive structure. A large green space will be added in the coming years, greatly improving the quality of life of downtown residents.

Turn right on Rue De Bleury.

After a 40-year absence, the Jesuits returned to Montréal in 1842 at Monseigneur Ignace Bourget's invitation. Six years later, they founded Collège Sainte-Marie, where several generations of boys would receive an

Montréal - Exploring - Downtown

outstanding education. **Église du Gesù** ★★ *(1202 Rue De Bleury; Place-des-Arts metro)* was originally designed as the college chapel. The grandiose project begun in 1864 by architect Patrick C. Keely of Brooklyn, New York, was never completed, however, due to lack of funds. Consequently, the church's Renaissance Revival–style towers remain unfinished. The Jesuit college that was erected to the south of the church was demolished in 1975, but the church was fortunately saved and then restored in 1983.

Visitors can take a short side trip to St. Patrick's Basilica. To do so, head south on Rue de Bleury. Turn right on Boulevard René-Lévesque, then left on little Rue Saint-Alexandre. Enter the church through one of the side entrances.

Fleeing misery and potato blight, a large number of Irish immigrants came to Montréal between 1820 and 1860 and helped construct the Lachine Canal and the Victoria bridge. **St. Patrick's Basilica** ★★ *(460 Boulevard René-Lévesque Ouest; Place-des-Arts metro)*, was built to meet a pressing new demand for a church to serve the Irish-Catholic community. When it was inaugurated in 1847, St. Patrick's dominated the city below. Today, it is well hidden by the skyscrapers of the business centre.

Head back to Rue Sainte-Catherine.

During the rush of the Quiet Revolution, the government of Québec, inspired by cultural complexes like New York's Lincoln Center, built **Place des Arts** ★ *(175 Rue Sainte-Catherine Ouest, ☎514-842-2112, www. pda.qc.ca; Place-des-Arts metro)*, a collection of five halls for the performing arts. Salle Wilfrid Pelletier, in the centre, was inaugurated in 1963 (2,982 seats). It accommodates both the Montreal Symphony Orchestra and the Opéra de Montréal.

The cube-shaped Théâtre Maisonneuve, on the right, contains three theatres: Théâtre Maisonneuve (1,453 seats), Théâtre Jean-Duceppe (755 seats) and the intimate Studio-Théâtre (138 seats). The Cinquième Salle (350 seats) was built in 1992 during construction of the Musée d'Art Contemporain. Place des Arts is linked to the governmental section of the underground city, which stretches from the Palais des Congrès convention centre to Avenue du Président-Kennedy. Developed by the various levels of government, this portion of the underground network distinguishes itself from the private section, centered around Place Ville-Marie, farther west.

Place des Arts' esplanade also serves as a kind of cultural central square in the heart of the downtown sector. Many of Montréal's major cultural events are held here, and it's also where many of the Montréal International Jazz Festival's biggest outdoor shows are presented, attracting thousands of music fans.

The **Musée d'Art Contemporain de Montréal** ★★ *($8, free admission Wed 6pm to 9pm; Tue-Sun 11am to 6pm, Wed 11am to 9pm; 185 Rue Ste-Catherine Ouest, at the corner of Rue Jeanne-Mance, ☎514-847-6226, www.macm.org; Place-des-Arts metro)*, Montréal's museum of modern art, was moved to this site in 1992. Both its size and the sheer volume of its collection, which includes more than 7,000 works, make it the largest contemporary-art museum in Canada. The long, low building, erected on top of the Place des Arts parking lot, contains eight rooms where post-1940 works of art from both Québec and abroad are exhibited. The interior, which has a decidedly better design than the exterior, is laid out around a circular hall. The museum's permanent exhibit features the largest collection of works by Paul-Émile Borduas, while its temporary exhibits usually favour multimedia creations. Among the museum's other facilities are the Olivieri bookshop, which specializes in monographs on Canadian artists and essays on art, and the La Rotonde restaurant, located above the Place des Arts esplanade.

Since 1976, the head office of the Fédération des Caisses Populaires Desjardins, the credit union, has been located in the vast **Complexe Desjardins** ★ *(Rue Sainte-Catherine Ouest, www.complexedesjardins.com; Place-des-Arts metro)*, which also houses a large number of government offices. The building's large atrium surrounded by shops is very popular during the winter months. A variety of shows are presented in this space, which is surrounded by boutiques, a food court and the Hyatt Regency Montréal's adjacent tower.

Turn right on Boulevard Saint-Laurent.

Boulevard Saint-Laurent is commonly known to Montrealers as "The Main." At the end of the 18th century, the Faubourg Saint-Laurent sprung up along this street, which led inland from the river. In 1792, the city was officially divided into east and west sections, with this artery marking the boundary. Then, in the early 20th century, the addresses of east-west streets were re-assigned so that they all began at Boulevard Saint-Laurent.

Meanwhile, around 1880, French-Canadian high society came up with the idea of turning the boulevard into the "Champ-Élysées" of Montréal. The west side was destroyed in order to make the street wider and to reconstruct new buildings in Richardson's Romanesque Revival style, which was all the rage at the end of the 19th century. Populated by the successive waves of immigrants who arrived at the port, Boulevard Saint-Laurent never, however, attained the heights of glory anticipated by its developers. But the section between Boulevard René-Lévesque and Boulevard de Maisonneuve did become the hub of Montréal nightlife in the early 20th century. Indeed, the city's big theatres, like the Français, where Sarah Bernhardt performed, were located around here. During the Prohibition era (1919-1930), the area became run-down. Every week, thousands of Americans came here to frequent the cabarets and brothels, which abounded in this neighbourhood until the late 1950s.

Erected in 1893 for the Société Saint-Jean-Baptiste, which is devoted to protecting the rights of French-speakers, the **Monument-National** ★ *(1182 Boulevard St-Laurent; Saint-Laurent metro)* was intended to be a cultural centre dedicated to the French-Canadian cause. It offered business courses, became the favourite platform of political orators and presented shows of a religious nature. However, during the 1940s, it also hosted cabaret shows and plays, launching the career of many a Québec performer, including Olivier Guimond Sr. and Jr. The building was sold to the National Theatre School of Canada in 1971. As Canada's oldest theatre, it was artfully restored for its 100th anniversary.

Cross Boulevard René-Lévesque, then turn right on Rue De La Gauchetière.

Montréal's **Chinatown** ★ *(Rue De La Gauchetière; Place-d'Armes metro)* may be rather small, but it is nonetheless a lovely place to explore. A large number of the Chinese who came to Canada to help build the transcontinental railroad, completed in 1886, settled here at the end of the 19th century. Though they no longer live in the neighbourhood, they still come here on weekends to stroll about and stock up on traditional products. Rue De La Gauchetière has been converted into a pedestrian street lined with restaurants and framed by beautiful Chinese-style gates.

Turn left on Rue Saint-Urbain and enter the Palais des Congrès de Montréal, on the corner of Avenue Viger. This building is part of the new "Quartier International de Montréal" district.

The new **Quartier International de Montréal (QIM)** ★ ★ *(www.qimtl.qc.ca)* business sector is the result of a major overhaul of the area located between Saint-Urbain, Saint-Jacques, University and Viger streets. The QIM now serves as a window onto Montréal's international economic activities. The project entailed a profound urban restructuring effort that included the renovation of existing structures such as the Palais des Congrès, the addition of pedestrian walkways and green spaces and the construction of ultra-modern buildings to house new businesses and hotels, all with the mandate of attracting foreign investors and improving local residential spaces.

To the west of Rue Saint-Urbain lies Montréal's convention centre, the **Palais des Congrès de Montréal** ★ *(201 Avenue Viger Ouest, ☎514-871-3170, www.congresmtl.com; Place-d'Armes metro)*, a forbidding mass of concrete erected over the Ville-Marie highway, which contributes to the isolation of the old city from downtown. After an expansion in 2002, the Palais des Congrès doubled in size and now features two entrances.

The new section opens onto street level. Its huge coloured-glass facade, on Rue De Bleury, creates light effects both inside and outside the Palais des Congrès. It overlooks a new public square, **Place Jean-Paul-Riopelle** ★ ★, at the corner of Saint-Antoine and De Bleury streets, where you will find an immense bronze sculpture-fountain created by Riopelle himself and entitled *La Joute*, complete with water jets and flames. Facing it is a new building with a unique architectural style, the **Centre CDP Capital** ★, headquarters of the Caisse de Dépôt et Placement du Québec (CDP).

Turn left onto Avenue Viger and walk to Square Victoria. You can also reach the square by crossing the Centre CDP Capital building.

The **Tour de la Bourse** ★ *(Place Victoria, ☎514-871-2424)*, or the stock exchange tower, dominates the surroundings. It was erected in 1964 according to a design by famous Italian engineers Luigi Moretti and Pier Luigi Nervi, to whom we owe the Palazzo dello Sport (sports stadium) in Rome and the Exhibition Centre in Turin. The elegant 47-storey black tower that houses the stock exchange's offices and trading floor is one of several Montréal buildings that were designed by foreign architects. Initial plans had called for three identical towers, and its construction was meant to revitalize the city's financial district, which had been abandoned after economic activity was transferred to the area around Dorchester square after the 1929 crash.

In the 19th century, **Square Victoria** *(Square-Victoria metro)* was a Victorian garden surrounded by Second Empire and Renaissance Revival stores and office buildings. Only the narrow building at 751 Rue McGill remains from that era. Recently, Square Victoria was completely redesigned according to its original layout and has become one of the focal points in the Quartier International de Montréal. Square Victoria will eventually be given back its former shape and size, as well as its restored statue of Queen Victoria.

Recently, what is known as "Entourage Grimard" was officially reopened; named after architect Hector Grimard, who designed the gate to the Parisian "Metropolitain"— an Art-Nouveau piece that was created in the early 1900s—, it was loaned in 1966 by the Régie autonome des transports parisiens (RATP) to the Montréal metro so that it could be installed in one of its stations. During the inauguration of the "Entourage," which is set up at the outside entrance to the Square-Victoria metro, the RATP offered the gate as a gift to the Société de Transport de Montréal.

Enter the covered passageway of the Centre de Commerce Mondial.

World trade centres are exchange organizations intended to promote international trade. Montréal's **Centre de Commerce Mondial / World Trade Centre** ★ *(Rue McGill;*

Square-Victoria metro), completed in 1991, is a new structure hidden behind an entire block of old facades. An impressive glassed-in passageway stretches 180m through the centre of the building, along a portion of the Ruelle des Fortifications, a lane marking the former location of the northern wall of the fortified city. Alongside the passageway, visitors will find a portion of the Berlin Wall, a gift from the City of Berlin on the occasion of the 350th anniversary of Montréal's foundation.

*Exit via 363 Rue Saint-Jacques. This is where the **Vieux-Montréal** tour begins (see p 85). You can also get back on the metro at the Place-d'Armes station, which is connected to the World Trade Centre.*

The Golden Square Mile
★ ★

The Golden Square Mile was the residential neighbourhood of the Canadian upper class between 1850 and 1930. Since the early 20th century, the shady streets lined with sumptuous Victorian houses have gradually given way to the city's modern business centre. At its apogee, around 1900, the Golden Square Mile was bounded by Avenue Atwater to the west, Rue de Bleury to the east, Rue De La Gauchetière to the south and the mountain, Mount Royal, to the north. In those years, an estimated 70% of the country's wealth lay in the hands of local residents, the majority of whom were of Scottish descent. Only a few houses from this era remain, most of which are clustered north of Rue Sherbrooke, the Golden Square Mile's luxurious main street.

From the McGill metro station, head north on Avenue McGill College toward the campus of McGill University. The tour starts on Rue Sherbrooke.

The **Musée McCord d'Histoire Canadienne / McCord Museum of Canadian History** ★ ★ *($10, free admission first Sat of every month 10am to noon; Tue-Fri 10am to 6pm, Sat and Sun 10am to 5pm, Mon on holiday weekends and summer every day 10am to 5pm; 690 Rue Sherbrooke Ouest, ☎514-398-7100, www.musee-mccord. qc.ca; McGill metro and bus no 24)* occupies a building formerly used by the McGill University Students' Association. Designed by architect Percy Nobbs (1906), this hand-

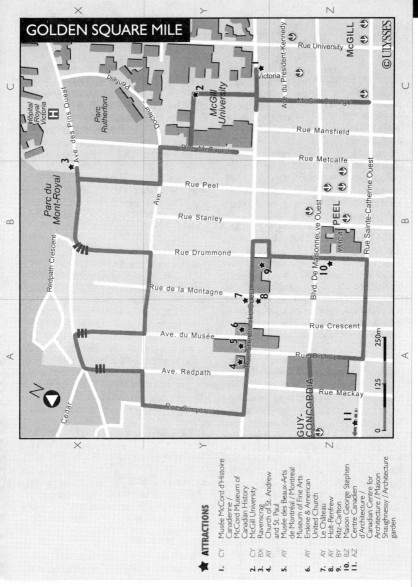

GOLDEN SQUARE MILE

★ ATTRACTIONS

1. CY   Musée McCord d'Histoire Canadienne / McCord Museum of Canadian History
2. CY   McGill University
3. BX   Ravenscrag
4. AY   Church of St. Andrew and St. Paul
5. AY   Musée des Beaux-Arts de Montréal / Montréal Museum of Fine Arts
6. AY   Erskine & American United Church
7. AY   Le Château
8. AY   Holt-Renfrew
9. BY   Ritz-Carlton
10. BZ Maison George Stephen
11. AZ Canadian Centre for Architecture / Centre Canadien d'Architecture / Maison Shaughnessy / Architecture garden

some building of English baroque inspiration was enlarged toward the back in 1991. Along Rue Victoria, visitors can see an interesting sculpture by Pierre Granche entitled *Totem Urbain/Histoire en Dentelle* ("Urban totem/History in lace"). For anyone interested in the First Nations and daily life in Canada in the 18th and 19th centuries, this is *the* museum to see in Montréal. It houses a large ethnographic collection, as well as collections of costumes, decora-

tive arts, paintings, prints and photographs, including the famous Notman photography collection, composed of 450,000 photos, including 200,000 glass negatives and constituting a veritable portrait of Canada at the end of the 19th century.

McGill University ★★ *(805 Rue Sherbrooke Ouest; McGill metro)* was founded in 1821, thanks to a donation by fur-trader James McGill. It is the oldest of Montréal's four universities. Throughout the 19th century, the institution was one of the finest jewels of the Golden Square Mile's Scottish bourgeoisie. The university's main campus lies nestled in greenery at the foot of Mount Royal. The entrance is located at the northernmost end of Avenue McGill College, at the Roddick Gates, which contain the university's clock and chimes. On the right are two Romanesque Revival buildings designed by Sir Andrew Taylor to house the physics (1893) and chemistry (1896) departments. The Faculty of Architecture now occupies the second building. A little farther along, visitors will see the Macdonald Engineering Building, a fine example of the English baroque-revival style, with a broken pediment adorning its rusticated portal (Percy Nobbs, 1908). At the end of the drive stands the oldest building on campus, the Arts Building (1839). For three decades, this austere neoclassical structure by architect John Ostell was McGill University's only building. It houses Moyse Hall, a lovely theatre dating back to 1926, with a design inspired by antiquity (Harold Lea Fetherstonaugh, architect).

Take the lane that leads to Rue McTavish. You'll notice the Ravenscrag building on the hillside.

During the 19th century, Montréal was not a political capital: it was above all a commercial city endowed with an important port. Its castle was not that of a king, but rather that of a financial and commercial magnate. **Ravenscrag ★★** *(1025 Avenue des Pins Ouest)* could indeed be labelled the castle of Montréal thanks to its prominent location overlooking the city, its exceptional size (originally over 60 rooms) and its history, which is rich in memorable receptions and prestigious hosts. This immense residence was built from 1861 to 1864 for the fabulously wealthy Sir Hugh Allan, who at the time had a near monopoly on sea transport between Europe and Canada. From the central tower of his house, this "monarch" could keep a close eye on the comings and goings of his ships at the port.

Head west on Avenue des Pins. Go down the stairway on your left to reach Avenue Redpath. Turn left onto Rue Sherbrooke.

The lovely presbyterian **Church of St. Andrew and St. Paul ★★** *(at the corner of Rue Redpath; Guy-Concordia metro)* was one of the most important institutions of the Scottish elite in Montréal. Built in 1932 by architect Harold Lea Fetherstonaugh as the community's third place of worship, it illustrates the endurance of the medieval style in religious architecture. The stone interior is graced with magnificent commemorative stained-glass windows. Those along the aisles came from the second church and are for the most part significant British pieces, such as the windows of Andrew Allan and his wife, produced by the workshop of William Morris after sketches by the famous English Pre-Raphaelite painter Edward Burne-Jones. The Scottish-Canadian Black Watch Regiment has been affiliated with the church ever since it was created in 1862.

The **Musée des Beaux-Arts de Montréal / Montreal Museum of Fine Arts ★★** *(free admission for the permanent collection; $12-$15 for temporary exhibitions, half-price Wed 5pm to 9pm; open Tue-Sun 11am to 5pm, Wed until 9pm; 1379-1380 Rue Sherbrooke Ouest, ☎514-285-2000, www.mbam.qc.ca; Guy-Concordia metro and bus no. 24),* located in the heart of the downtown area, is the oldest and largest museum in Québec. It houses a variety of collections that illustrate the evolution of the fine arts from antiquity to the present day. The museum occupies two separate buildings on either side of Rue Sherbrooke Ouest: the Michal and Renata Hornstein Pavilion and Liliane and David M. Stewart Pavilion at no. 1379 and the Jean-Noël Desmarais Pavilion at no. 1380.

Known until 1949 as the Art Association of Montreal, the museum was founded in 1860, when the city was at the height of its glory, by a group of affluent art-loving Montrealers of British origin.

The present Michal and Renata Hornstein Pavilion (formerly the Benaiah Gibb Pavilion), was inaugurated in 1912. Architects and brothers Edward and William Sutherland Maxwell graced it with an elegant, white Vermont-marble facade in the Classical Revival style, with lines reminiscent of ancient Rome. Expanded twice towards the back, in 1939 and in 1975, the building nonetheless ultimately proved to be too small.

Since demolishing the neighbouring buildings to the north and west was out of the question, the museum's directors turned their attention to the property across the street, proposing an original solution and offering quite a challenge to their architect, Moshe Safdie, already well known for designing Habitat 67 and the National Gallery in Ottawa. The new wing, named after Jean-Noël Desmarais, the father of arts patron Paul Desmarais, was inaugurated in 1991. On the left, it has a white marble facade that echoes the Maxwell brothers' museum, while incorporated into its right side is the red-brick facade of a former apartment building (1905). A series of underground passageways running beneath Rue Sherbrooke Ouest makes it possible to walk from the Jean-Noël Desmarais Pavilion to the Michal and Renata Hornstein Pavilion without ever stepping outside.

Among the museum's permanent collections, the most interesting are undoubtedly the **Old Masters collection** ★ ★ *(Jean-Noël Desmarais Pavilion, level 4)*, which includes paintings, furniture and sculptures from the Middle Ages, the Renaissance and the baroque and classical periods, offering a vast panorama of the history of European art from 1000 CE to the end of the 18th century; the **collection of Canadian Art** ★ ★ ★ *(Michal and Renata Hornstein Pavilion, level 2)*, the museum's true highlight; and the **Contemporary Decorative Arts collection** ★ ★ *(Liliane and David M. Stewart Pavilion, level 1)*, which features items by designers from around the world.

Built in 1892, the **Erskine & American United Church** ★ *(at the corner of Avenue du Musée)* is an excellent example of the Romanesque Revival style as interpreted by American architect Henry Hobson Richardson. The textured sandstone, large arches flanked by either squat or disproportionately elongated columns, and sequences of small, arched openings are typical of the style. The auditorium-shaped interior was remodelled in the style of the Chicago School in 1937. The lower chapel (along Avenue du Musée), contains lovely, brilliantly coloured Tiffany stained-glass windows.

A symbol of its era, **Le Château** ★ *(1321 Rue Sherbrooke Ouest; Guy-Concordia or Peel metro)*, a handsome Château-style building, was erected in 1925 for a French-Canadian businessman by the name of Pamphile du Tremblay, owner of the French-language newspaper *La Presse*. Architects Ross and Macdonald designed what was at the time the largest apartment building in Canada. The Royal Institute awarded these architects a prize for the design of the fashionable **Holt Renfrew** *(1300 Rue Sherbrooke Ouest)* store that stands across the street in 1937. With its rounded, horizontal lines, the store is a fine example of the streamlined Art Deco style.

The last of Montréal's old hotels, the **Ritz-Carlton** ★ *(1228 Rue Sherbrooke Ouest; Guy-Concordia or Peel metro)* was inaugurated in 1911 by César Ritz himself. For many years, it was the favourite gathering place of the Montréal bourgeoisie. Some people even stayed here year-round, living a life of luxury among the drawing rooms, garden and ballroom. The building was designed by Warren and Wetmore of New York City, the well-known architects of Grand Central Station on New York's Park Avenue. Many celebrities have stayed at this sophisticated luxury hotel over the years, including Richard Burton and Elizabeth Taylor, who were married here in 1964.

Turn right on Rue Drummond.

Lord Mount Stephen, born in Stephen Croft, Scotland, was a determined man. Co-founder and first president of Canadian Pacific, he built a transcontinental railroad stretching over 5,000km from New Brunswick to British Columbia. His house, **Maison George Stephen** ★ ★ *(1440 Rue Drummond; Peel metro)* is a veritable monument to Montréal's Scottish bourgeoisie. The house was built between 1880 and 1883 by William Tutin Thomas at a cost of $600,000, an astronomical sum at the time. Stephen called upon the best artisans in the world who covered the interior walls with marble, onyx and woodwork made of rare materials, such as English walnut, Cuban mahogany and Sri Lankan satinwood. The ceilings are so high that the house seems to have been built for giants. Since 1925, it has been owned by the Mount Stephen Club, a private club for business people.

At the end of Rue Drummond, you'll come upon **Rue Sainte-Catherine** (see p 99). Fifteen kilometres long, this is the city's main commercial thoroughfare.

Head west to get to Rue Crescent.

Montréal - Exploring - The Golden Square Mile

Rue Crescent ★ *(Guy-Concordia metro)* has a split personality. To the north of Boulevard de Maisonneuve, the street is lined with old row houses which now accommodate antique shops and luxury boutiques, while to the south, it is crowded with night clubs, restaurants and bars with sunny terraces lining the sidewalks. For many years, Rue Crescent was known as the English counterpart of Rue Saint-Denis. Though it is still a favourite among American visitors, its clientele is more diversified now.

Head west and turn onto Rue Saint-Marc, then Rue Baile to get to the Canadian Centre for Architecture.

Founded in 1979 by Phyllis Lambert, the **Centre Canadien d'Architecture / Canadian Centre for Architecture ★★★** *($10, free admission Thu 5:30pm to 9pm; Wed-Sun 10am to 5pm, Thu to 9pm; 1920 Rue Baile,* ☎*514-939-7026, www.cca.qc.ca; Guy-Concordia metro and bus no. 15 or 150)* is both a museum and a centre for the study of world architecture. Its collections of plans, drawings, models, books and photographs are the most important of their kind in the world.

The centre surrounds the **Maison Shaughnessy**, whose facade looks out onto Boulevard René-Lévesque Ouest. This house is in fact a pair of residences, built in 1874 by architect William Tutin Thomas. It is representative of the mansions that once lined Boulevard René-Lévesque (formerly Dorchester Street).

In 1974, it was at the centre of an effort to salvage the neighbourhood, which had been torn down in a number of places. The house, itself threatened by demolition, was purchased at the last moment by Phyllis Lambert; she set up the offices and reception rooms of the Canadian Centre for Architecture inside. The building was named after Sir Thomas Shaughnessy, a former president of the Canadian Pacific Railway Company, who lived in the house for several decades. Neighbourhood residents who formed an association subsequently chose to name the entire area after him.

The amusing **architecture garden ★** *(facing the Canadian Centre for Architecture, on the south side of Boulevard René-Lévesque)*, by artist Melvin Charney, lies across from Shaughnessy House between two highway on-

ramps. It illustrates the different stages of the neighbourhood's development using a portion of the Sulpicians' orchard on the left, stone lines to indicate borders of 19th-century properties and rose bushes reminiscent of the gardens of those houses. A promenade along the cliff that once separated the wealthy neighbourhood from the working-class sector below offers a view of the lower part of the city (Little Burgundy, Saint-Henri, Verdun) and the St. Lawrence River. Some of the highlights of this panorama are represented in a stylized manner, atop concrete posts.

To get back to the start of this tour, head east on either Boulevard De Maisonneuve or Rue Sainte-Catherine to the corner of Avenue McGill College, which is located near the McGill metro station.

Quartier Latin
★★

 three hours

People come to the Quartier Latin, a university neighbourhood centered around Rue Saint-Denis, for its theatres, cinemas and countless outdoor cafés, which offer a glimpse of its heterogeneous crowd of students and revellers. The area's origins date back to 1823, when Montréal's first Catholic cathedral, Église Saint-Jacques, was established on Rue Saint-Denis. This prestigious edifice quickly attracted the cream of French-Canadian society—mainly old noble families who had remained in Canada after the conquest—to the area. In 1852, a fire ravaged the neighbourhood, destroying the cathedral and Monseigneur Bourget's palace in the process. Painfully reconstructed in the second half of the 19th century, the area remained residential until the Université de Montréal was established here in 1893, marking the beginning of a period of cultural turmoil that would eventually lead to the Quiet Revolution of the 1960s. The Université du Québec à Montréal (UQAM), founded in 1969, has since taken over the Université de Montréal, which is now located on the north side of Mount Royal. The presence of the university has ensured the quarter's prosperity.

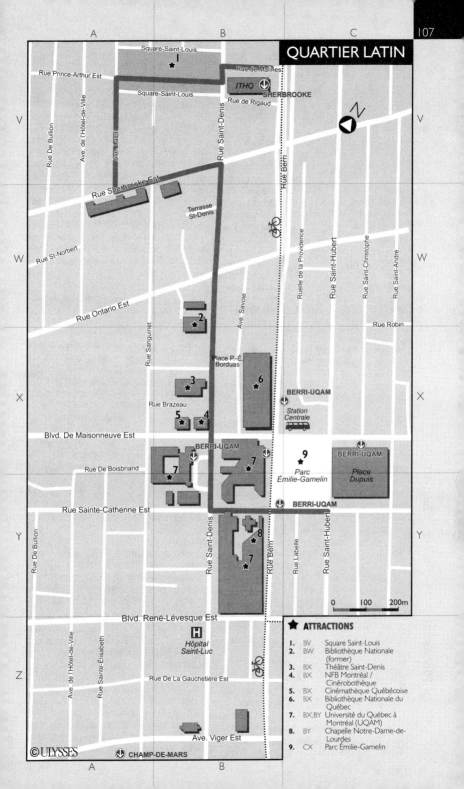

QUARTIER LATIN

Square-Saint-Louis

Rue Prince-Arthur Est

Square-Saint-Louis

Rue de Malines

ITHQ

SHERBROOKE

Rue de Rigaud

Rue Saint-Denis

Rue Berri

Rue De Bullion

Ave. de l'Hôtel-de-Ville

Ave. Laval

Rue Sherbrooke Est

Terrasse
St-Denis

Rue St-Norbert

Rue Ontario Est

Ruelle de la Providence

Rue Saint-Hubert

Rue Saint-Christophe

Rue Saint-André

Rue Robin

Rue Sanguinet

Ave. Savoie

Place P.-É.
Borduas

BERRI-UQAM

*Station
Centrale*

Rue Brazeau

Blvd. De Maisonneuve Est

BERRI-UQAM

Rue De Boisbriand

Rue Sainte-Catherine Est

*Parc
Émilie-Gamelin*

BERRI-UQAM

*Place
Dupuis*

BERRI-UQAM

Rue Saint-Denis

Rue Berri

Rue Labelle

Rue Saint-Hubert

Rue De Bullion

Blvd. René-Lévesque Est

Ave. de l'Hôtel-de-Ville

Rue Sainte-Élisabeth

H
*Hôpital
Saint-Luc*

Rue De La Gauchetière Est

Ave. Viger Est

CHAMP-DE-MARS

©ULYSSES

0   100   200m

★ ATTRACTIONS

1.	BV	Square Saint-Louis
2.	BW	Bibliothèque Nationale (former)
3.	BX	Théâtre Saint-Denis
4.	BX	NFB Montréal / Cinérobothèque
5.	BX	Cinémathèque Québécoise
6.	BX	Bibliothèque Nationale du Québec
7.	BX,BY	Université du Québec à Montréal (UQAM)
8.	BY	Chapelle Notre-Dame-de-Lourdes
9.	CX	Parc Émilie-Gamelin

This tour starts at the Sherbrooke metro station. Cross Rue-Saint Denis to get to Square Saint-Louis.

In 1848, the City of Montréal had a water reservoir built at the top of the hill known as Côte-à-Barron. In 1879, it was dismantled and the site was converted into a park by the name of **Square Saint-Louis ★★** *(Sherbrooke metro)*. Developers built beautiful Second Empire–style homes around the square, making it the nucleus of the French-Canadian bourgeois neighbourhood. These groups of houses give the area a certain harmonious quality that is rarely found in Montréal's urban landscape. **Rue Prince-Arthur** extends west from the square. This pedestrian street was Montréal's bastion of hippie culture during the 1960s. Here, visitors will find a cluster of family restaurants, with terraces stretching all the way to the middle of the street. On summer evenings, a dense crowd gathers between the buildings to applaud street performers.

Turn left onto **Avenue Laval**, one of the only streets in the city where the Belle Époque atmosphere is still very tangible. Abandoned by the French-Canadian bourgeoisie in 1920, the houses were converted into rooming houses before attracting the attention of local artists, who began restoring them one by one. Poet Émile Nelligan (1879-1941) lived at number 3688 with his family at the turn of the 20th century. A bronze bust by artist Roseline Granet in memory of the poet was recently inaugurated and stands at the corner of Avenue Laval and Square Saint-Louis.

The Union des Écrivains Québécois (Québec Writers' Association) house occupies number 3492, the former home of filmmaker Claude Jutra, who directed such films as *Mon Oncle Antoine*. A number of other artists, including singer Pauline Julien and her late husband, poet and politician Gérald Godin, writers Michel Tremblay and Yves Navarre, and pianist André Gagnon, live or have lived in the area around Square Saint-Louis and Avenue Laval.

Turn left on Rue Sherbrooke, then right on rue Saint-Denis and walk down the "Côte-à-Barron" toward the Université du Québec à Montréal.

The former **Bibliothèque Nationale ★** *(1704 Rue St-Denis; Berri-UQAM metro)*, or national library, was originally built for the Sulpi-

cians, who looked unfavourably upon the construction of a public library on Rue Sherbrooke. Even though many works were still on the *Index*, therefore forbidden reading for the clergy, the new library was seen as unfair competition. Known until 1967 as Bibliothèque Saint-Sulpice, this branch of the Bibliothèque Nationale du Québec was designed in the Beaux-Arts style by architect Eugène Payette in 1914. This style, a synthesis of classicism and French Renaissance architecture, was taught at the École des Beaux-Arts in Paris, hence its name in North America. The interior is graced with lovely stained-glass windows created by Henri Perdriau in 1915. The Bibliothèque Nationale's collections were transferred to its new location, at the corner of Rue Berri and Boulevard De Maisonneuve (see below).

The **Théâtre Saint-Denis** *(1594 Rue St-Denis, ☎514-790-1111; Berri-UQAM metro)* is made up of two theatres, which are among the most popular in the city. During summer, the Festival Juste pour Rire, also known as the Just for Laughs Festival, is presented here. The theatre opened in 1916, and has since welcomed big names in show business from the world over.

At the corner of Boulevard De Maisonneuve are the offices of **NFB Montréal** *(Tue-Sun noon to 9pm; 1564 Rue St-Denis, ☎514-496-6887, www.onf.ca)*, Montréal's distribution and consultation branch of the **National Film Board of Canada (NFB)**. NFB Montréal includes the **Cinérobothèque** *($5.50 for 2hrs, $3 for 1hr)*, which provides users with 21 viewing units (individual and double) so that they can view various films. In addition, the complex features two theatres that present documentaries and movies. You can also rent NFB archival films and get videocassettes and DVDs, as well as promotional products at the CinéBoutique.

A bit further west, the **Cinémathèque Québécoise ★** *(free admission to exhibits, $7 for screenings; closed Mon; 335 Boulevard De Maisonneuve Est, ☎514-842-9763, www.cinematheque.qc.ca)* is another great place for movie lovers. It features a collection of 25,000 Canadian, Québécois and foreign films, as well as several pieces of equipment that date back to the early days of cinema. The Cinémathèque contains, in addition, theatres, exhibit spaces, a "mediatheque" and a shop, as well as a café-bar.

Further east on Boulevard De Maisonneuve is the new **Bibliothèque Nationale du Québec** ★★ *(Tue-Fri 10am to 10pm, Sat-Sun 10am to 5pm; 475 Boulevard De Maisonneuve Est, ☎514-873-1100. www.bnquebec.ca)*, which opened on April 30, 2005 and is commonly known as "La Grande Bibliothèque." This major new addition to Montréal's cultural landscape cost nearly 100 million dollars and is housed in a bright and airy, luxurious six-storey building located on the site of the former Palais du Commerce. The edifice's design features contrasting wood and glass elements and the library contains over four million titles, making it the most important collection of books and multimedia documents in the province. Though some say the establishment's inauguration marks the death of neighbourhood libraries, others argue that it meets the modern needs of the major cultural metropolis that is Montréal, especially after UNESCO named it a "World Book Capital City" in 2005.

Unlike most North-American universities, whose buildings are contained within a specific campus, the campus of the **Université du Québec à Montréal (UQAM)** ★ *(Berri-UQAM metro)* is integrated into the city fabric like French and German universities built during the Renaissance. It is also linked to the underground city and the metro. The university is located on the site once occupied by the buildings of the Université de Montréal and the Église Saint-Jacques, which was reconstructed after the fire of 1852. Only the wall of the right transept and the Gothic Revival steeple were integrated into the Pavillon Judith-Jasmin (1979), and these elements have since become the symbol of the university. UQAM is part of the Université du Québec, founded in 1969 and established in cities across the province. Every year, over 40,000 students attend this flourishing institution of higher learning.

Artist Napoléon Bourassa lived in a large house on Saint-Denis Street (no. 1242): note the facade and its "tête à Papineau." **Chapelle Notre-Dame-de-Lourdes** ★ *(430 Rue Ste-Catherine Est; Berri-UQAM metro)*, erected in 1876, was his greatest achievement. It was commissioned by the Sulpicians, who wanted to secure their presence in this part of the city. Its Roman-Byzantine style is in some way a summary of its author's travels. The little chapel's recently restored interior,

adorned with Bourassa's vibrantly coloured frescoes, is a must-see.

Follow Rue Sainte-Catherine Est until you reach Rue Berri.

Parc Émilie-Gamelin ★ *(at the corner of Rue Berri and Rue Ste-Catherine; Berri-UQAM metro)*, laid out in 1992 for Montréal's 350th anniversary, is a large public space that honours the memory of the founder of the Soeurs de la Providence religious order, whose asylum occupied this site until 1960. At the north end, visitors will find a few unusual metal sculptures by Melvin Charney, who also designed the garden of the **Canadian Centre for Architecture** ★★★ (see p 106).

North of the park lies the bus terminal (Station Centrale), built on top of the Berri-UQAM metro station where three of the city's four metro lines converge. To the east, Place Dupuis, with stores, offices and a hotel, is located on the site of the former Dupuis Frères department store. A few businesses that are dear to Montrealers, such as the Archambault record shop, still grace Rue Sainte-Catherine Est. The part of this street between Rue Amherst and Avenue Papineau is known as Montréal's **Gay Village**.

The Berri-UQAM metro station is located right by Parc Émilie-Gamelin.

Plateau Mont-Royal
★★

 three hours

If there is one neighbourhood that best defines Montréal, it is definitely the Plateau Mont-Royal. Thrown into the spotlight by writer Michel Tremblay, one of its illustrious sons, the "Plateau" is a neighbourhood of penniless intellectuals, young professionals and old French-speaking working-class families. Its long streets are lined with duplexes and triplexes adorned with amusingly contorted exterior staircases leading up to the long, narrow apartments that are so typical of Montréal. Flower-decked balconies made of wood or wrought iron provide front-row seats from which to watch the activity on the street below.

The Plateau is traversed by a few major streets lined with cafés and theatres, such as Rue Saint-Denis and Avenue Papineau, but is a tranquil area on the whole. A stroll through this area is a must for visitors who want to grasp the spirit of Montréal.

This tour starts at the exit of the Mont-Royal metro station. Turn right on Avenue du Mont-Royal.

The **Sanctuaire du Saint-Sacrement** ★ *(500 Avenue du Mont-Royal Est; Mont-Royal metro)* and its church, Église Notre-Dame-du-Très-Saint-Sacrement, were built at the end of the 19th century for the community of priests of the same name. The somewhat austere facade of the church conceals an extremely colourful interior with an Italian-style decor designed by Jean-Baptiste Resther. This sanctuary, dedicated to the "Eternal Exhibition and Adoration of the Eucharist," is open for prayer and contemplation every day of the week. Baroque music concerts are also occasionally presented here.

Continue heading east on **Avenue du Mont-Royal**, blending in with the neighbourhood's widely varied inhabitants on their way in and out of an assortment of businesses, ranging from shops selling knick-knacks for a dollar to used records and books.

Turn right on Rue Fabre.

Rue Fabre features some good examples of Montréal-style housing. Built between 1900 and 1925, the houses contain between two and five apartments, all with private outdoor entrances. Decorative details vary from one building to the next. Visitors will see Art-Nouveau stained glass, parapets, cornices made of brick or sheet metal, balconies with Tuscan columns and ornamental ironwork shaped in ringlets and cables.

At the end of Rue Fabre, visitors will find **Parc La Fontaine** ★ *(Sherbrooke metro)*, the Plateau's main green space, laid out in 1908 on the site of an old military shooting range. Monuments to Sir Louis-Hippolyte

La Fontaine, Félix Leclerc and Dollard des Ormeaux have been erected here. The park covers an area of 36ha and is embellished with two artificial lakes and shaded paths for pedestrians and cyclists. There are tennis courts and bowling greens for summer-sports enthusiasts, and in the winter, the frozen lakes form a large rink that is illuminated at night. The Théâtre de Verdure outdoor theatre is also located here. Every weekend, the park is crowded with people from the neighbourhood who come here to make the most of beautiful sunny days.

The monument to Sir Louis-Hippolyte La Fontaine (1807-1864), after whom the park was named, is located in the southern part of the park. Regarded as the father of responsible government in Canada, La Fontaine was also one of the main defenders of the French language in the country's institutions. You'll pass **École Le Plateau** (1930) at 3700 Avenue Calixa-Lavallée. This Art-Deco building was designed by architects Perrault and Gadbois. An obelisk dedicated to Général de Gaulle, by French artist Olivier Debré, towers over the long **Place Charles-de-Gaulle** *(at the corner of Avenue Émile-Duployé; Sherbrooke metro)*, located alongside Rue Sherbrooke. The monument is made of blue granite and stands 17m high. It was given to the City of Montréal by the City of Paris in 1992, on the occasion of Montréal's 350th anniversary. **Hôpital Notre-Dame**, one of the city's major hospitals, stands across the street. From here, you'll also notice the stately building that housed the former **Bibliothèque Centrale de Montréal** ★ *(1210 Rue Sherbrooke Est)*. The library's collection has since been moved to the new **Bibliothèque Nationale du Québec** ★ ★ (see p 109), which opened in April of 2005 in the Quartier Latin neighbourhood.

Head onto Rue Cherrier, which branches off from Rue Sherbrooke across from the monument.

Rue Cherrier, along with Square Saint-Louis at its west end, once formed the nucleus of the French-Canadian bourgeois neighbourhood. At number 840, visitors will find the **Agora de la Danse**, where the studios of

★ **ATTRACTIONS**

1.	AW	Sanctuaire du Saint-Sacrement
2.	CY	Parc La Fontaine
3.	CY	École Le Plateau
4.	CZ	Place Charles-de-Gaulle
5.	CZ	Hôpital Notre-Dame

6.	BZ	Bibliothèque Centrale de Montréal (former)
7.	BZ	Agora de la Danse
8.	AZ	Église Saint-Louis-de-France
9.	AZ	Institut des Sourdes-Muettes (former)
10.	AX	Église Saint-Jean-Baptiste

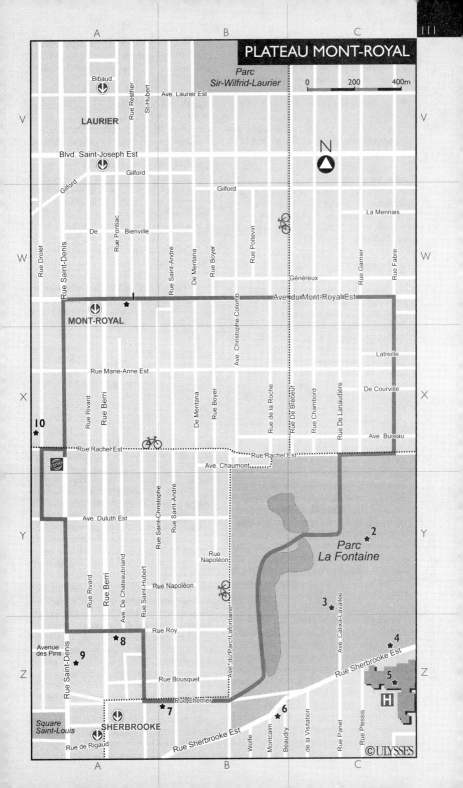

various dance companies are located. The red-brick building, completed in 1919, originally served as the Palestre Nationale, a sports centre for neighbourhood youth and the scene of many tumultuous public gatherings during the 1930s.

Turn right on Rue Saint-Hubert, lined with fine examples of vernacular architecture. Turn left on Rue Roy.

Église Saint-Louis-de-France was built in 1936 as a replacement for the original church, destroyed by fire in 1933. From here you'll notice the **Parc du Mont-Royal ★ ★ ★** (see p 114), which stands over the city, in the background.

At the corner of Rue Saint-Denis stands the former **Institut des Sourdes-Muettes** *(3725 Rue St-Denis, at the corner of Avenue des Pins; Sherbrooke metro)*, a large, grey-stone building made up of numerous wings and erected in stages between 1881 and 1900. Built in the Second Empire style, it covers an entire block and is typical of institutional architecture of that period in Québec. It once took in the region's deaf and mute girls and women. The strange chapel with cast-iron columns, as well as the sacristy, with its tall wardrobes and surprising spiral staircase, are now where special masses for deaf people are celebrated.

Head north on Rue Saint-Denis.

Between Boulevard De Maisonneuve, to the south, and Boulevard Saint-Joseph, to the north, **Rue Saint-Denis** is lined with numerous outdoor cafés and beautiful shops, established inside Second Empire–style residences built during the second half of the 19th century. Visitors will also find many bookstores, tea rooms and restaurants that have become veritable Montréal institutions over the years.

Turn left on Avenue Duluth and then right on Rue Drolet.

Rue Drolet offers a good example of the working-class dwellings that were built in the Plateau area during the 1870s and 1880s before the advent of the typical two- and three-storey houses with exterior staircases that we've already seen on Rue Fabre. The colourful houses may surprise you, with their light green, salmon pink, dark blue or violet ivy-covered brick exteriors. Continue north to the corner of Rachel and Drolet streets to get to Église Saint-Jean-Baptiste.

Église Saint-Jean-Baptiste ★ ★ *(309 Rue Rachel; Mont-Royal metro)*, dedicated to the patron saint of French Canadians, is a gigantic symbol of the solid faith of the Catholic working-class inhabitants of the Plateau Mont-Royal at the turn of the 20th century who, despite their poverty and large families, managed to amass considerable amounts of money for the construction of sumptuous churches. The exterior was built in 1874 by architect Émile Vanier. The interior was redone after a fire and is now a veritable Baroque Revival masterpiece designed by Casimir Saint-Jean that should not be missed.

Before heading north on Rue Saint-Denis to get to Avenue du Mont-Royal and the metro station, why not stop by **Ulysses' travel bookstore** *(4176 Rue St-Denis)?*

Mont Royal
★ ★

 one day

Montréal's central neighbourhoods were built around Mount Royal, an important landmark in the cityscape. Known simply as "the mountain" by Montrealers, this squat mass, measuring 233m at its highest point, is composed of intrusive rock. It is in fact one of the seven hills of the St. Lawrence plain in the Montérégie region. A "green lung" rising up at the far end of downtown streets, it exerts a positive influence on Montrealers who, as a result, never really lose touch with nature.

The mountain actually has three summits; the first is occupied by Parc du Mont-Royal, the second by the Université de Montréal, and the third by Westmount, a wealthy neighbourhood with lovely English-style homes which, up until recently, was an independent city. In addition to these areas, there are Catholic, Protestant and Jewish cemeteries, which, considered as a whole, form the largest necropolis in North America.

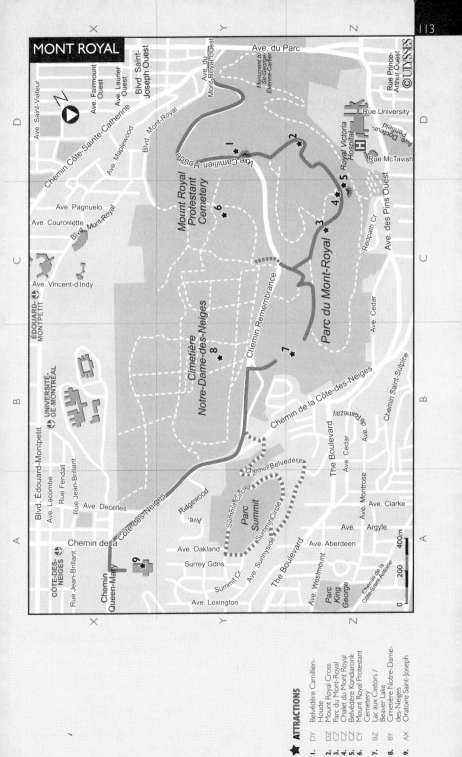

MONT ROYAL

© ULYSSES

Places labeled on map:

- Ave. Saint-Viateur
- Ave. Fairmount Ouest
- Ave. Laurier Ouest
- Blvd. Saint-Joseph Ouest
- Ave. du Parc
- Rue Prince-Arthur Ouest
- Chemin Côte-Sainte-Catherine
- Ave. Maplewood
- Blvd. Mont-Royal
- Ave. du Mont-Royal Ouest
- Monument to Sir-George-Étienne-Cartier
- Voie Camillien-Houde
- Rue University
- Royal Victoria Hospital
- Rue McTavish
- Ave. Docteur-Penfield
- Ave. Pagnuelo
- Ave. Courcelette
- Blvd. Mont-Royal
- Mount Royal Protestant Cemetery
- Ave. Vincent-d'Indy
- ÉDOUARD-MONTPETIT
- Chemin Remembrance
- Parc du Mont-Royal
- Redpath Cr.
- Ave. des Pins Ouest
- Ave. Cedar
- UNIVERSITÉ DE-MONTRÉAL
- Cimetière Notre-Dame-des-Neiges
- Chemin de la Côte-des-Neiges
- Chemin Saint-Sulpice
- Rue de Ramezay
- Blvd. Édouard-Montpetit
- Ave. Lacombe
- Rue Fendall
- Rue Jean-Brillant
- Ave. Decelles
- The Boulevard
- Ave. Cedar
- Ave. Montrose
- CÔTE-DES-NEIGES
- Ridgewood Ave.
- Chemin Belvédère
- Summit Circle
- Parc Summit
- Summit Circle
- Ave. Clarke
- Ave. Argyle
- Rue Jean-Brillant
- Chemin Queen-Mary
- Chemin de la Côte-des-Neiges
- Ave. Oakland
- Surrey Gdns.
- Ave. Sunnyside
- Ave. Aberdeen
- Ave. Westmount
- The Boulevard
- Chemin de la Côte-Saint-Antoine
- Ave. Lexington
- Summit Cr.
- Parc King George
- 400m / 200 / 0

ATTRACTIONS

1. DY Belvédère Camillien-Houde
2. DZ Mount Royal Cross
3. CZ Parc du Mont-Royal
4. CZ Chalet du Mont Royal
5. CZ Belvédère Kondiaronk
6. CY Mount Royal Protestant Cemetery
7. BZ Lac aux Castors / Beaver Lake
8. BY Cimetière Notre-Dame-des-Neiges
9. AX Oratoire Saint-Joseph

To reach the starting point of the tour, take bus no. 11 from the Mont-Royal metro station, located on the Plateau Mont-Royal, and get off at the Belvédère Camillien-Houde.

From the **Belvédère Camillien-Houde** ★ ★ *(Voie Camillien-Houde)*, a lovely scenic lookout, visitors can look out over the entire eastern portion of Montréal. The Plateau Mont-Royal lies in the foreground, a uniform mass of duplexes and triplexes, dominated in a few places by the oxidized copper bell towers of parish churches, while the Rosemont and Maisonneuve districts lie in the background as the Olympic Stadium towers over them.

Climb the staircase at the south end of the parking lot and follow Chemin Olmsted on the left, which leads to the chalet and main lookout. You will pass the mountain's cross on the way.

The **Mount Royal Cross** stands on the side of Chemin Oldsted and commemorates the moment when the city's founder, Paul Chomedey, Sieur de Maisonneuve, scaled the mountain in January of 1643 to place a wooden cross in thanks to the Virgin Mary for sparing the fort of Ville-Marie from a devastating flood.

Pressured by the residents of the Golden Square Mile, who saw their favourite playground being deforested by various firewood companies, the City of Montréal created **Parc du Mont-Royal** ★ ★ ★ *(www.lemontroyal.qc.ca)* in 1870. Frederick Law Olmsted (1822-1903), the celebrated designer of New York's Central Park, was commissioned to design the park. He decided to preserve the site's natural character, limiting himself to a few lookout points linked by winding paths. Inaugurated in 1876, the park, which covers 101ha on the southern part of the mountain, is cherished by Montrealers as a place to enjoy fresh air. Since 2003, Mount Royal and its three summits are protected by the Government of Québec as a historic and natural district.

The **Chalet du Mont Royal** ★ ★ ★ *(Mon-Sat 10:30am to 8pm; Parc du Mont-Royal, ☎514-872-3911)*, located in the centre of the park, was designed by Aristide Beaugrand-Champagne in 1932 as a replacement for the original structure, which was about to collapse. During the 1930s and 1940s, big bands gave moonlit concerts on the steps of the building. The interior is decorated with 17 remounted paintings depicting scenes from Canadian history. They were commissioned from some of Québec's great painters, such as Marc-Aurèle Fortin and Paul-Émile Borduas. The chalet underwent major renovations in 2003, and its paintings were restored.

Nevertheless, people go to the chalet mainly to stroll along the lookout and take in the exceptional view of downtown from the **Belvédère Kondiaronk** ★ ★ ★ (named after the Huron-Wendat chief who negotiated the Great Peace treaty in 1701). The view is at its best in the late afternoon and evening, when the skyscrapers light up the darkening sky.

Take the gravel road that leads to the parking lot of the chalet and Voie Camillien-Houde. One of the entrances to the Mount Royal Protestant Cemetery lies on the right.

The **Mount Royal Protestant Cemetery** ★ ★ *(Voie Camillien Houde)* ranks among the most beautiful spots in the city. Designed as an Eden for the living visiting the deceased, it is laid out like a landscape garden in an isolated valley, giving visitors the impression that they are a thousand miles from the city, though they are in fact right in the centre of it. The wide variety of hardwood and fruit trees attract species of birds found nowhere else in Québec. Founded by the Anglican, Presbyterian, Unitarian, Methodist and Baptist churches, the cemetery opened in 1852. Some of its monuments are true works of art, executed by celebrated artists. The families and eminent personalities buried here include the Molson brewers, who have the most impressive and imposing mausoleum, shipowner Sir Hugh Allan, and numerous other figures from the footnotes and headlines of history, such as Anna Leonowens, governess of the King of Siam in the 19th century and the inspiration for the play *The King and I*.

The small **Lac aux Castors / Beaver Lake** *(alongside Chemin Remembrance)* was created in 1958 in what used to be a swamp. In winter, it becomes a lovely skating rink. This part of the park also has grassy areas and a sculpture garden. It is laid out in a more conventional manner than the rest, violating Olmsted's purist directives.

The **Cimetière Notre-Dame-des-Neiges** ★ ★ *(Chemin Remembrance, www.cimetierenddn.*

Montréal – **Exploring** - Mont Royal

org; bus no. 11), Montréal's largest cemetery, is a veritable city of the dead, as more than 800,000 people have been buried here since it opened in 1855. It replaced the cemetery in Square Dominion (now Square Dorchester), which was deemed too small. Unlike the Protestant cemetery, it has a conspicuously religious character, clearly identifying it with the Catholic faith. Accordingly, two heavenly angels flanking a crucifix greet visitors at the main entrance on Chemin de la Côte-des-Neiges.

The "two solitudes" (Canadians of French Catholic and Anglo-Saxon Protestant extraction) thus remain separated even in death. The tombstones read like a who's who in the fields of business, arts, politics and science in Québec. An obelisk dedicated to the Patriotes of the rebellion of 1837-38 and numerous monuments executed by renowned sculptors lie scattered alongside the 55km of roads and paths that criss-cross the cemetery. Both the cemetery and the roads leading to it offer a number of views of the Oratoire Saint-Joseph.

Upon exiting the cemetery on Chemin Remembrance, take bus no. 11 to get to Oratoire Saint-Joseph.

Oratoire Saint-Joseph ★ ★ *(free admission; every day 7am to 8:30pm, Mass every day, Christmas manger from Nov to Mar; 3800 Chemin Queen Mary, ☎514-733-8211, www.saint-joseph.org; Côte-des-Neiges metro).* The enormous oratory, topped with a copper dome, is the second-largest dome in the world after that of St. Peter's in Rome and stands on a hillside, accentuating its mystical aura. From the gate at the entrance, there are over 300 steps to climb to reach the oratory. The oratory was built between 1924 and 1967, thanks to the efforts of the blessed Frère André, porter of Collège Notre-Dame (across the street), to whom many miracles are attributed. A veritable religious complex, the oratory is dedicated to both Saint Joseph and its humble creator. It includes the lower and upper basilicas, the crypt of Frère André and a museum. Visitors will also find the porter's first chapel, built in 1904, a cafeteria, a hostelry and a store selling devotional articles.

The oratory is one of the most important centres of worship and pilgrimage in North America. Each year, it attracts some 2,000,000 visitors. The building's neoclas-

sical exterior was designed by Dalbé Viau and Alphonse Venne, while the essentially modern interior is the work of Lucien Parent and French Benedictine monk Dom Paul Bellot, the author from Saint-Benoît-du-Lac in the Eastern Townships. It is well worth visiting the upper basilica to see the stained-glass windows by Marius Plamondon, the altar and crucifix by Henri Charlier, and the astonishing gilded chapel at the back. The oratory has an imposing Beckerath-style organ, which can be heard on Wednesday evenings in summer. Outside, visitors can also see the chimes, made by Paccard et Frères and originally intended for the Eiffel Tower, as well as the beautiful Chemin de Croix (Way of the Cross) by Louis Parent and Ercolo Barbieri, in the gardens on the side of the mountain. Measuring 263m, the oratory's observatory, which commands a sweeping view of the entire city, is the highest point on the island.

Outremont and Mile-End
★

 three to four hours

On the other side of Mount Royal is the borough of **Outremont**, which, like Westmount (its anglophone counterpart on the south side of the mountain), clings to the side of the mountain and has, over the course of its development, welcomed a fairly well-off population, including many influential Quebecers.

Outremont was once a municipality and has long been a sought-after residential area. In fact, recent research suggests that the mysterious Aboriginal village of Hochelaga, which disappeared between the voyages of Jacques Cartier and De Maisonneuve (16th and 17th centuries), was probably situated in this region. Furthermore, Chemin de la Côte-Sainte-Catherine, the main road around which Outremont developed, supposedly attests to Aboriginal activity in the area and follows a former communication route cleared by Aboriginals to enable them to skirt the mountain.

The Europeans first used the territory known today as Outremont for market gardening during the 17th and 18th centuries.

Montréal - **Exploring** - Outremont and Mile-End

It was later used for horticultural purposes and, being a rural area close to the city, as a vacation spot for middle-class Montrealers in the 19th century. Agricultural goods produced here at the time were popular and served at important tables throughout the American Northeast. Montréal's urban expansion brought an end to Outremont's agricultural vocation in the late 19th century and led to the development of the essentially residential municipality that is found here today.

Our suggested tour of Outremont runs along Chemin de la Côte-Sainte-Catherine, beginning at the corner of Avenue du Mont-Royal (Mont-Royal metro and bus no. 11).

A means of circling the mountain, **Chemin de la Côte-Sainte-Catherine** curves for a good part of its length, at an angle from the grid network of local streets. The *côte*, or slope, serves as the border between two types of terrain, while at the same time separating what has come to be known as "Outremont-en-haut" (Upper Outremont), perched atop the mountain, from the rest of the borough. Initially, many imposing residences were built along this large boulevard in order to take advantage of the sharp incline of the south side (the homes of the heirs of the famous cigar manufacturer Grothé are located at numbers 96 and 98).

For the past 30 years, however, the sporadic and controversial development of prestigious high-rises on the north side has somewhat altered the general appearance of the street, or at least the section between Boulevard Mont-Royal and Avenue Laurier.

Walk to the corner of Avenue Bloomfield and Avenue Laurier.

At the corner of Laurier and Bloomfield, visitors will find the **Église Saint-Viateur ★**, which dates back to the 1910s. Its remarkable interior, inspired by the Gothic Revival style, was decorated by artists renowned in the fields of painting (Guido Nincheri), glass-working (Henri Perdriau), cabinet-making (Philibert Lemay) and sculpting (Médard Bourgault and Olindo Gratton). The ceiling vaults, covered with paintings depicting the life of Saint Viateur, are quite exceptional.

Avenue Laurier ★ is one of three trendy shopping streets in the municipality that are popular among well-off Outremont and Montréal residents. The avenue has been given a facelift, contributing a certain stylishness to the local specialty shops.

Don't hesitate to venture east beyond Avenue du Parc to Boulevard Saint-Laurent, with Avenue Fairmount and Avenue Saint-Viateur to the north. You're now within the heart of the **Mile-End ★** district, a bustling bourgeois-bohemian neighbourhood that has welcomed several waves of immigration in the past. Mile-End is very representative of Montréal's cultural diversity, as much for its residents as for its many businesses, including cafés, restaurants and boutiques that are frequented by a multilingual, eclectic clientele. The neighbourhood has a distinctly working-class flavour, as many factories set up here during the 19th century, most notably quarries and tanneries.

The best way to get a feel for the area is probably to simply stroll down its main streets and savour its eclectic atmosphere. At the corner of Avenue Laurier and Boulevard Saint-Laurent you'll come upon a strange castle set up amidst residential buildings. It was built in 1905 and has served several different functions: it has been Saint-Louis-du-Mile-End's city hall, a bank, a post office, a prison and now a fire station. Across Boulevard Saint-Laurent, to the south, is Parc Lahaie, which borders a Baroque-style church: **Église Saint-Enfant-Jésus du Mile-End ★** *(5039 Rue St-Dominique)*. The church was designed by architect Victor Bourgeau during the 19th century and its dome contains artworks by Ozias Leduc. If there's one church you should visit in the Mile-End, however, it's the **Church of Saint Michael's and Saint Anthony's ★** *(5580 Rue St-Urbain)*. The church's construction was overseen by architect Aristide Beaugrand-Champagne, who, surprisingly enough, chose a Byzantine-inspired style for this Catholic church that contrasts sharply with the surrounding working-class residential area.

If you've been exploring the Mile-End district, head back to Avenue Laurier near Église Saint-Viateur and turn onto Avenue Bloomfield.

The overall layout of Avenue Bloomfield is very pleasant, with large trees, spacious

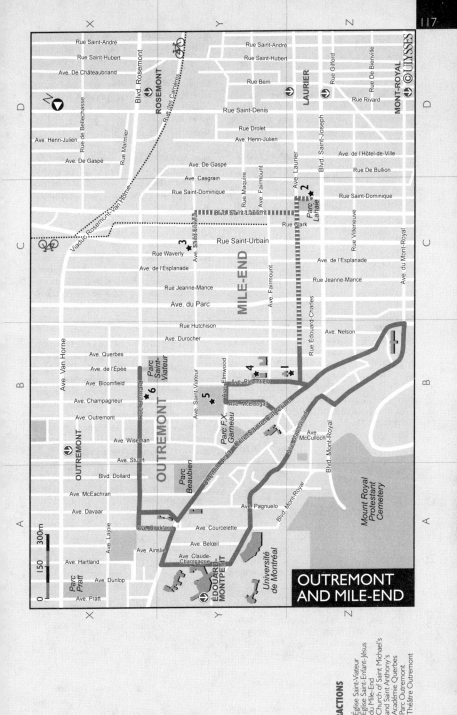

© ULYSSES

OUTREMONT AND MILE-END

ATTRACTIONS

1.	BZ	Église Saint-Viateur
2.	CZ	Église Saint-Enfant-Jésus du Mile-End
3.	CY	Church of Saint Michael's and Saint Anthony's
4.	BY	Académie Querbes
5.	BY	Parc Outremont
6.	BX	Théâtre Outremont

front yards and distinctive architecture. Several buildings are worth a look. The **Académie Querbes**, from numbers 215 to 235, was built in 1914. The architectural detail—monumental entrance and stone galleries reaching all the way to the third floor—is quite original for the period. Furthermore, the facilities were ahead of their time, including a swimming pool, bowling alley and gymnasium. The canopy-shaped balconies over the entrances of numbers 249 and 253 have been unusually styled as loggias. The building at number 261 was designed by the same architect as the latter two houses, and was once the home of Canon Lionel Groulx, a priest, writer, history professor and prominent Québec nationalist. The building now houses a foundation bearing his name. Number 262 stands out for its facade, made of alternating red brick and grey stone.

Turn left on Avenue Elmwood.

Parc Outremont is one of the municipality's many popular parks, used for both sports and leisure activities. Laid out a century ago on swamplands supplied with water by a stream flowing from the neighbouring hills, it gives the area a serene beauty. Occupying the place of honour in the middle of the Bassin McDougall is a fountain resembling the *Groupes d'Enfants* that adorns the grounds of the Château de Versailles in Paris. A monument to the citizens of Outremont who died during World War I faces the street.

Turn left on Avenue McDougall and then right on Chemin de la Côte-Sainte-Catherine.

This area of Chemin de la Côte-Sainte-Catherine once again becomes lined with homes, some of undeniable architectural interest. This is certainly the case for number 325, which has a very large balcony and numerous ornamental details, and number 356, home of architect Roger D'Astous, who added an aviary. D'Astous, a student of celebrated architect Frank Lloyd Wright, came up with the designs for Montréal's Olympic Village and Château Champlain.

Go down Avenue Davaar to Avenue Bernard.

Avenue Bernard ★ *(Outremont metro)* is lined with shops, offices, apartment buildings and houses. This wide avenue with large, grassy medians, curbside landscaping and stately buildings, appears quite imposing and reflects the will of an era to clearly affirm the growing municipality's prestige. The **Théâtre Outremont** *(1234-1248 Avenue Bernard, ☎514-495-9944, www.theatreoutremont.ca)*, once a very popular repertory theatre currently serving as a concert hall, is located on the street. Its interior was designed by Emmanuel Briffa.

Head back onto Chemin de la Côte-Sainte-Catherine and walk to Avenue Claude-Champagne. At the end of this avenue, turn left on Boulevard Mont-Royal and continue straight ahead at the traffic lights to Avenue Maplewood.

Also known as the "avenue of power," **Avenue Maplewood** ★ *(Édouard-Montpetit metro)* forms the central axis of the area referred to as "Outremont-en-haut," where various opulent-looking houses with distinctive architecture lie perched in a very hilly landscape, occupied in both the past and the present by influential Quebecers.

Beyond Avenue McCulloch (where the late former Prime Minister of Canada Pierre Elliott Trudeau lived for a time at number 84), Avenue Maplewood becomes even more picturesque. Its slight slope and gentle twists and turns, combined with the beauty of the residences and careful landscaping of the yards, are examples of how appealing "Outremont-en-haut" has always been for the Québec intelligentsia.

Take the footpath between numbers 54 and 52, which leads to Boulevard Mont-Royal via the lane of the same name.

Boulevard du Mont-Royal is the second major artery of "Outremont-en-haut." It was thus named because the first section of the road led to the Cimetière Protestant Mont-Royal.

From the end of the street (at the bend in the road) is a beautiful view of the eastern part of Montréal (Plateau Mont-Royal), which also reveals the radical difference between this part of Outremont and the city at its feet.

The **Mount Royal Protestant Cemetery** ★★ (see p 114) can be reached via Boulevard Mont-Royal and is described in the Mont Royal tour.

Return to Boulevard du Mont-Royal and head to the corner of Chemin de la Côte-Sainte-Catherine to get back on bus no. 11, which can either take you to the Mont-Royal metro station, in the Plateau Mont-Royal area, or to Parc du Mont-Royal, above the city.

Île Sainte-Hélène and Île Notre-Dame
★ ★

 one day

When Samuel de Champlain reached the island of Montréal in 1611, he found a small rocky archipelago located in front of it. He named the largest of these islands in the channel after his wife, Hélène Boulé. Île Sainte-Hélène later became part of the seigneury of Longueuil. Around 1720, the Baroness of Longueuil chose the island as the site for a country house surrounded by a garden. It is also worth noting that in 1760, the island was the last foothold of French troops in New France, commanded by Chevalier François de Lévis.

Recognizing Île Saint-Hélène's strategic importance, the British army built a fort on the eastern part of the island at the beginning of the 19th century. The threat of armed conflict with the United States having diminished, the Canadian government rented Île Sainte-Hélène to the City of Montréal in 1874, at which time the island was turned into a park and linked to Old Montréal by ferry and, in 1930, by the Jacques-Cartier bridge.

In the early 1960s, Montréal was chosen as the site of the 1967 World's Fair (Expo 67). The city wanted to set up the event on a large, attractive site near the downtown area; a site such as this, however, did not exist. So it became necessary to build one: using soil excavated during the construction of the metro tunnel, Île Notre-Dame was created, doubling the area of Île Sainte-Hélène. From April to November 1967, 45 million visitors passed through Cité-du-Havre, the gateway to the fairground, and criss-crossed both islands. Expo, as Montrealers still refer to it, was more than a jumble of assorted objects; it was Montréal's awakening, during which the city opened itself to the world, and visitors from all

over discovered a new art of living, including mini-skirts, colour television, hippies, flower power and protest rock.

It is not easy to reach Cité du Havre from downtown. The best way is to take Rue Mill, then Chemin des Moulins, which runs below Autoroute Bonaventure to Avenue Pierre-Dupuy. This last road leads to Pont de la Concorde and then over the St. Lawrence to the islands. It is also possible to take bus no. 168 from the McGill metro station.

Tropique Nord, **Habitat 67** and **Parc de la Cité-du-Havre ★ ★** were all built on a spit of land created to protect the port of Montréal from ice and currents. This site also offers lovely views of the city and the water. The administrative offices of the port are located at the entrance to the area, along with a group of buildings that once housed the Expo-Théâtre and Musée d'Art Contemporain. A little farther on, visitors will spot the large glass wall of Tropique Nord, a residential complex composed of apartments with a view of the outdoors on one side and an interior tropical garden on the other.

Next, visitors will see Habitat 67, an experimental housing development built for Expo 67 in order to illustrate construction techniques using prefabricated concrete slabs, and to herald a new art of living. Its architect, Moshe Safdie, was only 23 years old when he drew up the plans. Habitat 67 looks like a gigantic cluster of cubes, each containing one or two rooms. The apartments are as highly prized as ever and are inhabited by a number of notable Quebecers.

At Parc de la Cité du Havre, visitors will find 12 panels containing a brief description of the history of the St. Lawrence River. A section of the bicycle path leading to Île Notre-Dame and Île Sainte-Hélène passes through the park.

Cross Pont de la Concorde. From spring to autumn, Île Sainte-Hélène can also be reached by river shuttle from Montréal's Old Port ($5; ☎514-281-8000).

Parc Jean-Drapeau ★ ★ *(☎514-872-6120, www.parcjeandrapeau.com; Jean-Drapeau metro)* lies on Île Notre-Dame and Île Sainte-Hélène. The latter originally covered an area of 50ha but was enlarged to over 120ha for Expo 67. The original portion corresponds to the raised area studded with breccia boulders. Peculiar to this island, breccia is a very hard, ferrous stone that takes on an orange colour when exposed to air for a long time. In 1992, the western part was transformed into a vast open-air amphitheatre where large-scale shows are presented. In this lovely riverside park, visitors will find *L'Homme*, a large metal sculpture by Alexander Calder, created for Expo 67.

Follow the signs for the Fort de l'Île Sainte-Hélène.

After the War of 1812 between the United States and Great Britain, the **Fort de l'Île Sainte-Hélène** ★★ *(Jean-Drapeau metro)* was built so that Montréal could be properly defended if ever a new conflict were to erupt. Its construction, supervised by military engineer Elias Walker Durnford, was completed in 1825. Built of breccia stone, the fort is in the shape of a jagged *U*, surrounding a drill ground, used today by the Compagnie Franche de la Marine and the 78th Regiment of the Fraser Highlanders as a parade ground. These two costumed mock regiments delight visitors by reviving Canada's French and Scottish military traditions. The drill ground also offers a lovely view of both the port and Pont Jacques-Cartier, inaugurated in 1930 and straddling the island, separating the park from La Ronde.

The fort's arsenal is now occupied by the **Musée Stewart** ★★ *($10; mid-Oct to late May Wed-Mon 10am to 5pm, late May to mid-Oct every day 10am to 5pm; ☎514-861-6701, www.stewart-museum.org; Jean-Drapeau metro)*, which is dedicated to colonial history and the exploration of the New World. The museum exhibits objects from past centuries, including interesting collections of maps, firearms, and scientific and navigational instruments collected by Montréal industrialist David Stewart and his wife Liliane.

La Ronde ★ *($34; mid-May to late Oct, for schedules call ☎514-397-7777; ☎514-872-2000, www.laronde.com; Jean-Drapeau metro and bus no. 167)*, an amusement park set up for Expo 67 on the former Île Ronde, opens its doors to both the young and the not-so-young every summer. For Montrealers, an annual trip to La Ronde has almost become a pilgrimage. The **L'International des Feux Loto-Québec** (see p 141) international fireworks competition is held here during the months of June and July.

Head toward the Biosphere on the road that runs along the south shore of the island.

The **Biosphère** ★★ *($9.78; late Jun to mid-Sep every day 10am to 6pm; mid-Sep to late Jun Mon, Wed, Thu, Fri 12am to 5pm, Sat-Sun and holidays 10am to 5pm; ☎514-283-5000, www.biosphere.ec.gc.ca; Jean-Drapeau metro)*, built of tubular aluminum and measuring 80m in diameter, unfortunately lost its translucent acrylic skin in a fire back in 1976. An environmental interpretive centre on the St. Lawrence River, the Great Lakes and the different Canadian ecosystems is now located in the dome. The permanent exhibit aims to sensitize the public on issues of sustainable development and the conservation of water as a precious resource. There are several interactive galleries with giant screens and hands-on displays to explore and delight in.

Cross over to Île Notre-Dame on the Passerelle du Cosmos.

Île Notre-Dame emerged from the waters of the St. Lawrence in just 10 months, with the help of 15 million tons of rock and soil transported here from the metro construction site. Because it is an artificial island, its creators were able to give it a fanciful form by shaping both the soil and water. The island is traversed by charming **canals and gardens** ★★ *(Jean-Drapeau metro and bus no. 167)*, laid out for the 1980 Floralies Internationales, an international flower show. Boats can be rented here, enabling visitors to explore the canals.

The **Casino de Montréal** ★ *(see also p 142; free admission, parking and coat check; every day 24hrs; ☎514-392-2746 or 800-665-2274; Jean-Drapeau metro and bus no. 167)* occupies the former French and Québec pavilions of Expo 67. The main building corresponds to the old **French Pavilion** ★, an aluminum structure designed by architect Jean Faugeron. The upper galleries offer some lovely views of downtown Montréal and the St. Lawrence Seaway. Immediately to the west of the former French pavilion, the building shaped like a truncated pyramid is the former **Québec Pavilion** ★ *(every day 9am to 3am)*.

Nearby, visitors will find the entrance to the **Plage de l'Île Notre-Dame** *($7.50, $4.50 after 4pm; mid-Jun to mid-Aug every day 10am to 7pm; ☎514-872-6120; Jean-Drapeau metro and bus no. 167)*, a beach enabling Mont-

ÎLE SAINTE-HÉLÈNE AND ÎLE NOTRE-DAME

MONTRÉAL

Rue University

Rue Notre-Dame

Vieux-Montréal

Vieux-Port

Quai Jacques-Cartier

Quai King-Edward

Quai Alexandra

Canal de Lachine

Rue Mill

Rue de la commune

Ave Pierre-Dupuy

Chemin des Moulins

Autoroute Bonaventure

Pont Victoria

St. Lawrence River

Pont de la Concorde

Quai de l'Horloge

ÎLE SAINTE-HÉLÈNE

Parc Jean-Drapeau

Pont des Îles

JEAN-DRAPEAU

Passerelle du Cosmos

St. Lawrence Seaway

ÎLE NOTRE-DAME

Parc Jean-Drapeau

Lac des Régates

Olympic Basin

La Ronde Marina

Lac des Dauphins

Pont Jacques-Cartier

Longueuil (in season)

LONGUEUIL-UNIVERSITÉ-DE-SHERBROOKE

Longueuil

Saint-Lambert

© ULYSSES

1000m   500   0

ATTRACTIONS

1. AY Tropique Nord
2. BY Habitat 67
3. BY Parc de la Cité-du-Havre

île Sainte-Hélène

4. CY Parc Jean-Drapeau
5. DX Fort de l'île Sainte-Hélène / Musée Stewart / Le Festin du Gouverneur
6. DX La Ronde / L'International des Feux Loto-Québec
7. CY Biosphère

île Notre-Dame

8. CY Canals and gardens
9. CZ Casino de Montréal
10. BZ Plage de l'île Notre-Dame

realers to lounge on real sand right in the middle of the St. Lawrence. A natural filtering system keeps the water in the small lake clean, with no need for chemical additives. The number of swimmers allowed on the beach is strictly regulated, however, so as not to disrupt the balance of the system.

To return to downtown Montréal, take the metro from the Jean-Drapeau station.

Hochelaga-Maisonneuve
★ ★

 one day

In 1883, the city of Maisonneuve was founded in eastern Montréal by farmers and French-Canadian merchants; port facilities expanded into the area in 1889 and the city's development picked up. Then, in 1918, the formerly autonomous city was annexed to Montréal, becoming one of its major working-class neighbourhoods, with a 90% francophone population. In the course of its history, Maisonneuve has been profoundly influenced by men with grand ideas who wanted to make this part of the province a place where people could thrive together. Upon taking office at the Maisonneuve town hall in 1910, brothers Marius and Oscar Dufresne instituted a rather ambitious policy of building prestigious Beaux-Arts–style public buildings intended to make "their" city a model of development for French Québec. Then, in 1931, Brother Marie-Victorin founded Montréal's Jardin Botanique (botanical garden) in Maisonneuve; it is still one of the largest in the world today. The last major episode in the area's history took place in 1971, when Mayor Jean Drapeau initiated construction of the immense sports complex that was used for the 1976 Olympic Games.

From the Pie-IX metro station, climb the hill that leads to the corner of Rue Sherbrooke.

The **Jardin Botanique de Montréal** and **Insectarium de Montréal ★ ★ ★** *($11.75, $8.75 in low season, combined ticket for the Biôdome and the Tour de Montréal (Olympic Tower) $28.50, valid for 30 days; Nov to mid-May Tue-Sun 9am to 5pm, until 9pm early Sep to late Oct; mid-May to early Sep every day 9am to 6pm; 4101*

Rue Sherbrooke Est, ☎514-872-1400, www. ville.montreal.qc.ca; Pie-IX metro). The Jardin Botanique de Montréal, covering an area of 73ha, was first created during the economic crisis of the 1930s on the site of Mont-de-La-Salle, home base of the brothers of the Écoles Chrétiennes, by Brother Marie-Victorin, a well-known Québécois botanist. Behind the Art Deco building occupied by the Université de Montréal's institute of biology, visitors will find a stretch of 10 connected greenhouses open year-round, which shelter, most notably, a precious collection of orchids and the largest grouping of bonsais and *penjings* outside of Asia. The latter includes the famous Wu collection, given to the garden by master Wu Yee-Sun of Hong Kong in 1984. The cucurbitaceae family of vegetables takes the spotlight in the main greenhouse in October: over 600 pumpkins are dressed up to celebrate Halloween, much to the joy of the many young and not-so-young visitors who drop by for this event *(Le Grand Bal des Citrouilles / The Great Pumpkin Ball; Oct every day 9am to 9pm).*

Thirty outdoor gardens, open from spring to autumn and designed to educate and amaze visitors, stretch to the north and west of the greenhouses. Particularly noteworthy are a beautiful rosary, the Japanese garden and its *sukiya*-style tea pavilion, as well as the very beautiful Chinese Lac de Rêve, or Jardin de Chine, garden, whose pavilions were designed by artisans who came here from China specifically for the task. Since Montréal is the twin city of Shanghai, it was deemed appropriate that it should have the largest such garden outside of Asia. During late-summer nights, the Chinese Garden is decorated with hundreds of Chinese lanterns that create a wonderful fairytale-like setting of light and flowers *(La Magie des Lanternes; mid-Sep to late Oct every day 9am to 9pm).*

Another must-see is the First Nations Garden. Québec's 11 First Nations are represented in their natural habitat zones: deciduous forest, coniferous forest and the Arctic zone. An exhibition pavilion completes the tour.

The **Insectarium de Montréal** *(☎514-872-1400)* is located to the east of the greenhouses. This innovative, living museum invites visitors to discover the fascinating world of insects through short films, inter-

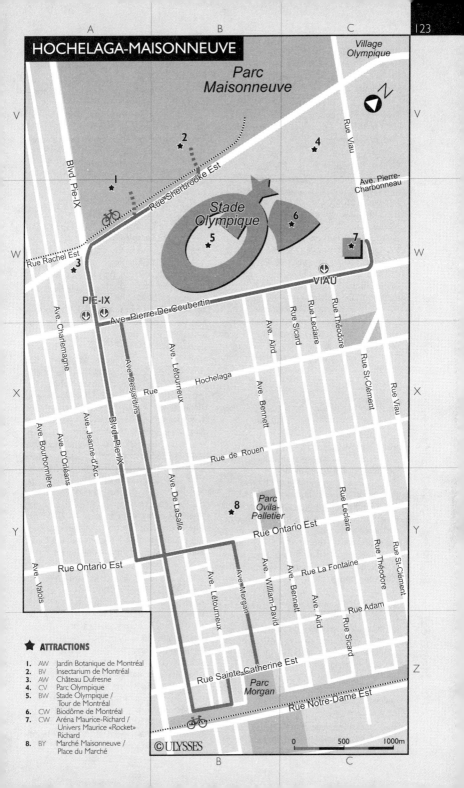

active games and an impressive collection of insects. Watch for the various activities organized throughout the year. You could, for instance, sample edible insects, if you're so inclined.

Return to Boulevard Pie-IX. On the western side of the boulevard, just south of Rue Sherbrooke, is Château Dufresne.

Château Dufresne ★★ *($6; Thu-Sun 10am to 5pm; 2929 Rue Jeanne-d'Arc, ☎514-259-9201, www.chateaudufresne.qc.ca; Pie-IX metro)* is in fact two 22-room private mansions behind the same facade, built in 1916 for brothers Marius and Oscar Dufresne, shoe manufacturers and authors of a grandiose plan to develop Maisonneuve. The plan was abandoned after the onset of World War I, causing the municipality to go bankrupt. Their home, designed by Marius Dufresne and Parisian architect Jules Renard, was supposed to be the nucleus of a residential upper-class neighbourhood, which never materialized. It is one of the best examples of Beaux-Arts architecture in Montréal. Château Dufresne now houses temporary exhibitions as well as a collection of furniture.

Head back downhill on Boulevard Pie-IX, then turn left on Avenue Pierre-De Coubertin.

Jean Drapeau was mayor of Montréal from 1954 to 1957, as well as from 1960 to 1986. He dreamed of great things for "his" city. Endowed with an exceptional power of persuasion and unfailing determination, he saw a number of important projects through to a successful conclusion, including the construction of Place des Arts, the metro, Expo 67 and, of course, the 1976 Summer Olympics.For this last international event, however, it was necessary to equip the city with the appropriate facilities.

In spite of the controversy it caused, the city hired Parisian visionary Roger Taillibert, who also designed the Parc des Princes stadium in Paris, to design something completely original. A billion dollars later, the **Parc Olympique** stunned everyone with its curving, organic concrete shapes, and remains one of this renowned architect's major works.

The **Stade Olympique** ★★★ *($7.50; guided tours, regular departures from 10am; 4141 Avenue Pierre-De Coubertin, ☎514-252-4737 or 877-997-0919, www.rio.gouv.qc.ca; Viau metro)* is also known as the Olympic Stadium, a 56,000-seat oval stadium that features a 175m leaning tower. In the distance, visitors will see the two pyramid-shaped towers of the Olympic Village, where athletes were housed in 1976. Each year, the stadium hosts different events. The Montréal Expos professional baseball team played its home games here from 1977 to 2004, when the team was transferred to Washington, DC.

The stadium's tower, which is the tallest leaning tower in the world, was renamed the **Tour de Montréal**. A funicular *($13; every day 9am to 5pm in high season, closed early Jan to mid-Feb)* climbs the structure to an interior observation deck that commands a view of the eastern part of Montreal. On the second floor of the observatory are various exhibits, and there is also a rest area known as Salon Montréal. The foot of the tower houses the swimming pools of the Olympic Complex and a cinema.

The former cycling track, known as the Vélodrome, located nearby, has been converted into an artificial habitat for plants and animals called the **Biodôme de Montréal** ★★★ *($10.50; late Jun to early Sep every day 9am to 6pm, early Sep to late Jun Tue-Sun 9am to 5pm; 4777 Avenue Pierre-De Coubertin, ☎514-868-3000, www.biodome.qc.ca; Viau metro)*. This new type of museum, associated with the Jardin Botanique, contains four very different ecosystems—the Tropical Rainforest, the Laurentian Forest, the St. Lawrence Marine Ecosystem and the Polar World—within a space of 10,000m². These are complete micro-climates, including plants, mammals and free-flying birds, and close to real climatic conditions.

As for the **Aréna Maurice-Richard** *(2800 Rue Viau, ☎514-872-6666; Viau metro)*, it preceded the Olympic Village, with which it is now affiliated, by 20 years. Its rink is the only one in Eastern Canada whose area respects international norms. Canada's Olympic speed-skating team practices here, as do several figure-skating champions. A statue of Maurice Richard has stood in front of the entrance to the arena since 1998. Measuring 2.5m in height and cast at the Inverness Atelier du Bronze, it is the work of sculptors Annick Bourgeau and Jules Lasalle. Ice hockey holds a special place in the hearts of Quebecers and many consider Maurice "The Rocket" Richard (1921-2000) the greatest hockey player of all time. **Univers Maurice "Rocket" Richard** *(free admission; Tue-Sun noon to 6pm; 2800 Rue Viau,* ☎*514-251-9930; Viau metro)* is a small museum in his honour. Located in the arena that bears his name, next to the Olympic facilities, the museum contains equipment, trophies and other significant memorabilia that once belonged to this hero of hockey who played for the Canadiens from 1942 to 1960. The museum also has a small boutique with hockey paraphernalia.

Return to Boulevard Pie-IX and head south to Rue Ontario, where you will turn left.

In 1912, the Dufresne administration kicked off its policy of grandeur by building the **Hôtel de Ville** ★ *(4120 Rue Ontario Est)*, a city hall designed by architect Cajetan Dufort. From 1925 to 1967, the building was occupied by the Institut du Radium, which specialized in cancer research. Since 1981, the edifice has served as the Bibliothèque Maisonneuve, which houses one of the City of Montréal's neighbourhood cultural centres. On the second floor, a 1915 bird's-eye-view drawing of Maisonneuve shows the prestigious buildings as they stood back then, as well as those that remained only on paper.

Built directly in line with Avenue Morgan in 1914, the **Marché Maisonneuve** ★ *(4445 Rue Ontario Est,* ☎*514-937-7754, www.marchespublics-mtl.com)* is one of Montréal's many lovely public markets. Since 1995, it has occupied a much newer building than the one next door, where it was once established. The Marché Maisonneuve is in keeping with a concept of urban design inherited from the teachings of the École des Beaux-Arts in Paris, known as the City Beautiful movement in North America. It is a mixture of parks, classical perspectives and civic and sanitary facilities. Designed by Cajetan Dufort, the market was Dufresne's most ambitious project. The centre of **Place du Marché** is adorned with an important work by sculptor Alfred Laliberté entitled *La Fermière* (The Woman Farmer).

Parks

There are parks all over the island of Montréal providing great opportunities to enjoy a thousand and one activities. In all seasons, Montrealers flock to these green spaces to get away from the urban hustle and bustle while staying close to their city. Nature parks, large and small urban parks, neighbourhood parks and recreational parks are open to all, in both summer and winter.

Parc La Fontaine ★ *(bordered by Avenue du Parc-La Fontaine, Rue Sherbrooke Est, Rue Rachel and Avenue Papineau; Plateau Mont-Royal; see p 110)* and **Parc René-Lévesque** ★★ *(at the western tip of the Lachine Canal)* are lovely spots for a bit of relaxation. In addition, both parks, as well as other parks in Montréal, are linked to the **Route Verte**, a 3,000km bike path that crosses the province of Québec.

Parc Jeanne-Mance *(bordered by Avenue de l'Esplanade, Place du Parc, Avenue du Mont-Royal Ouest and Avenue des Pins; Plateau Mont-Royal)* covers nearly 15ha and offers Montréal residents numerous equipments and facilities: playgrounds for children and toddlers, including a paddling pool, sports grounds for soccer and tennis, skating rinks and a snowshoeing area.

Parc Angrignon ★★ *(bordered by Boulevard La-Salle, Boulevard des Trinitaires and Boulevard La Vérendrye;* ☎*514-872-3066; Angrignon metro)*, covering 110ha, was originally created to feature a large zoo. Its network of pedestrian and cross-country ski trails stretches along some 10km, and a narrow, sinewy road also crosses the park. A trail that links the park to the Lachine Canal bike trail was added in June 2005.

Covering 268ha, **Parc Jean-Drapeau** *(*☎*514-872-6120; Jean-Drapeau metro; see p 119)* encompasses both **Île Sainte-Hélène** and **Île Notre-Dame**. In summer, Montrealers flock here on sunny days to enjoy the beach. Footpaths, in-line skating and bicycle trails criss-cross the park. **The Fête des Neiges** (see p 141) is held here in winter, and the park also welcomes the **Grand Prix of Canada** (see p 142) and the **L'International des Feux Loto-Québec** (see p 141) fireworks competition in summer.

Montrealers come to **Parc du Mont-Royal** ★★★ *(to get there, take Avenue du Parc and then Voie Camillien-Houde, or the no. 11 bus from the Mont-Royal metro station;* ☎*514-843-8240)*, a huge green expanse in the middle of the city, to enjoy a wide range of athletic activities all year-round. During summer, footpaths are open to hikers, and mountain biking is only permitted on Chemin Olmsted. In winter, the paths serve as cross-country ski trails, leading across the snowy slopes of the mountain, and Lac aux Castors becomes a big, beautiful skating rink. In summer, the park's eastern section, along Avenue du Parc near the Sir George Étienne Cartier monument, livens up on Sundays thanks to the sounds of percussionists. An eccentric crowd gathers here to have fun in a warm, friendly atmosphere.

Parc Maisonneuve ★ *(bordered by Boulevard Pie-IX, Rue Sherbrooke E., Boulevard Rosemont and Rue Viau; 4601 Rue Sherbrooke Est, ☎514-872-6555; Pie-IX or Viau metro)*, a large green space, is ideal for a stroll or a picnic in summer. In winter, a lovely skating rink and cross-country ski trails delight Montrealers.

Outdoor Activities

■ Cross-Country Skiing

There are nearly 6km of trails in the **Jardin Botanique de Montréal** (see p 122), offering skiers a chance to familiarize themselves with its many different kinds of trees.

Parc Maisonneuve (see above) has about 10km of trails, enabling skiers to go all the way around the park, while admiring the Olympic Stadium tower.

Skiers can also explore **Parc du Mont-Royal** (see p 114), the city's green lung or, perhaps more appropriately, "white lung" in winter, on over 25km of trails that provide exceptional views of the city.

Île Notre-Dame and **Île Sainte-Hélène** (see p 119) are accessible from Old Montréal. The path runs through an industrial area, then through the Cité du Havre before reaching the islands (cyclists can cross the river on the Pont de la Concorde). It is easy to ride from one island to the other. The islands are well maintained and are a great place to relax, stroll and admire Montréal's skyline.

Bicycle Rentals

Bicycletterie J.R.
151 Rue Rachel Est, Plateau Mont-Royal
☎ (514) 843-6989

Ça Roule Montréal
27 Rue de la Commune Est, Vieux-Montréal
☎ (514) 866-0633
www.caroulemontreal.com

■ Cycling

La Maison des Cyclistes *(1251 Rue Rachel Est, ☎514-521-8356)* provides various services. In addition to a café, it also features a specialized bike shop.

Vélo Montréal *(3880 Rue Rachel Est, ☎514-259-7272, www.velomontreal.com)* specializes in bicycle touring and organizes guided tours of the island.

A lovely bike path was laid out alongside the **Lachine Canal**. Very popular with Montrealers, especially on Sundays, the path leads from the Old Port to **Parc René-Lévesque** (see p 125), a narrow strip of land jutting out into Lac Saint-Louis that offers splendid views of the lake and its surroundings.

■ Ice Skating

A number of public skating rinks are set up in the city during the winter. Some of the best ones include **Lac aux Castors** *(Parc du Mont-Royal, see p 114)*, **Parc La Fontaine** (see p 110), **Bassin Bonsecours** *($4; rental; Vieux-Port, Champ-de-Mars metro, ☎514-496-7678, www.vieuxportdemontreal.com)* and **Parc Maisonneuve** (see above).

The **Atrium** *($5.50; $5 for rental; 1000 Rue De la Gauchetière Ouest, ☎514-395-0555)* is located at 1000 De la Gauchetière and houses a large year-round skating rink.

■ Swimming

On **Île Notre-Dame** (see p 119), the water at the **Parc Jean-Drapeau** ★★ (see p 119) beach is naturally filtered, allowing beachgoers to swim in clean, chemical-free water. If you're heading to the beach on a particularly sunny day, we recommend you arrive early, as the number of bathers admitted on site is limited.

Accommodations

The **Fédération des Agricotours** produces an annual guide entitled *Inns and Bed & Breakfasts Québec*, which lists the names and telephone numbers of the federation's member establishments that provide rooms for travellers. The rooms have been selected according to the federation's standards of quality and are also fairly economical. The book is available in bookstores throughout Canada, the United States and Great Britain.

Réseau de Gîtes Centre-ville de Montréal
$$ bkfst incl.
3458 Avenue Laval
☎ (514) 289-9749 or 800-267-5180
🖷 (514) 287-7386
www.bbmontreal.qc.ca

Since its first days of existence, almost 25 years ago, the Réseau de Gîtes Centreville de Montréal collaborates with bed and breakfasts in the downtown, Old Montréal, Quartier Latin and Plateau Mont-Royal districts. It brings together about 80 establishments, a large number of which are located in Victorian homes. In order to make sure that all rooms are comfortable and satisfactory, the organization takes the time to visit each B&B. Reservations are required.

Vieux-Montréal

L'Auberge Alternative
$ bkfst incl.
sb
358 Rue St-Pierre
☎ (514) 282-8069
www.auberge-alternative.qc.ca

Located in Old Montréal and opened in 1996, L'Auberge Alternative is run by a young couple and housed in a renovated building dating from 1875. The 34 beds in the rooms and dormitories are rudimentary but comfortable, and the bathrooms are very clean. A friendly atmosphere is provided by brightly coloured walls, lots of space and a large common room and kitchen with stone walls and old wooden floors. Guests have laundry machines at their disposal. Twenty-four-hour access.

Les Passants du Sans-Soucy
$$$-$$$$ bkfst incl.
≡ @ @
171 Rue St-Paul Ouest
☎ (514) 842-2634
🖷 (514) 842-2912
www.lesanssoucy.com

Les Passants du Sans-Soucy is a lovely inn set in the heart of the old city whose nine charming rooms are furnished with antiques. Built in 1723, the building was renovated about 15 years ago. Reservations required. No smoking in the establishment.

Hôtel Inter-Continental Montréal
$$$$-$$$$$
≋ ⚊ ♨ ⟩⟩⟩ ≡ ⚲ ⛟ @
360 Rue St-Antoine Ouest
☎ (514) 987-9900 or 800-361-3600
🖷 (514) 847-8730
www.montreal.intercontinental.com

This hotel, located on the edge of Old Montréal, is linked to the Centre de Commerce Mondial (World Trade Centre) and several shops. The Palais des Congrès (convention centre) is right nearby. The hotel

has an original look thanks to its turret with multiple windows, where the living rooms of the suites are located. The 357 rooms are tastefully decorated with simple furniture. Each one is equipped with a spacious bathroom, among other nice touches. Business people will enjoy all the necessary services, such as computer hook-ups, fax machines and photocopiers. Service is attentive and professional.

Auberge-Restaurant Pierre du Calvet
$$$$$ bkfst incl.
▲ ≡ ♨
405 Rue Bonsecours
☎ (514) 282-1725 or 866-544-1725
🖷 (514) 282-0456
www.pierreducalvet.ca

Located near the Champde-Mars metro station, this establishment is set in one of Montréal's oldest homes (1725), discretely tucked away at the intersection of Bonsecours and Saint-Paul streets. It has recently been entirely renovated, as have many other older houses in the neighbourhood. The nine rooms, all different and featuring a fireplace, exude a refined charm with lovely antique wood panelling accentuated by stained glass and beautiful antiques. Furnishings include canopy beds and mahogany armoires with gold leaf. Moreover, the bathrooms are tiled in Italian marble. A pretty indoor courtyard and day room allow guests to escape from the crowds. Breakfast is served in a lovely Victorian greenhouse, and service is attentive and meticulous. This inn, located in the heart of the city's historic district, is a real gem that

Montréal - Accommodations - Vieux-Montréal

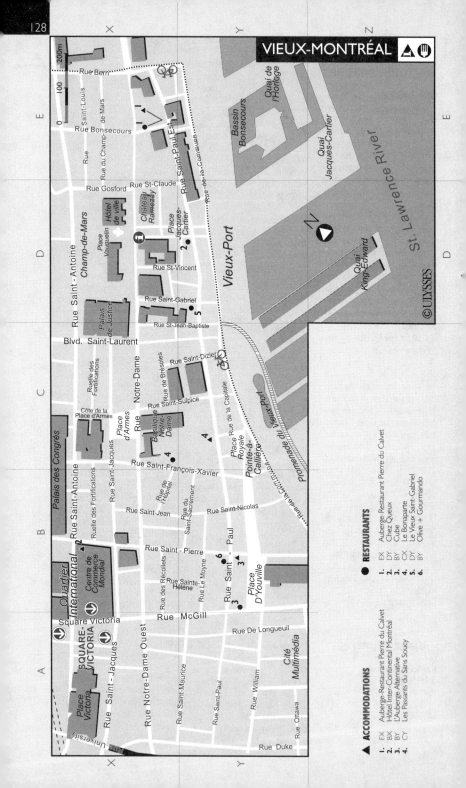

will make your stay absolutely unforgettable.

Downtown and Golden Square Mile

Auberge de Jeunesse
$-$$
☻ ≡

1030 Rue Mackay
☎ (514) 3843-3317
▤ (514) 934-3251
www.hostellingmontreal.com
This youth hostel, located a stone's throw from the downtown area, offers 250 beds in rooms for four to 10 people, as well as 15 private rooms equipped with bathrooms. This is one of the cheapest establishments in Montréal. Guests have the use of a washer and dryer, as well as a kitchen, a luggage check-room, a TV room and a pool table. This is a non-smoking hostel.

Le Manoir Ambrose
$$-$$$ bkfst incl.
pb/sb ≡ @
3422 Rue Stanley
☎ (514) 288-6922
▤ (514) 288-5757
www.manoirambrose.com
Le Manoir Ambrose is set in two Victorian houses, side by side on a peaceful street. It has 22 small rooms scattered all over the house, 20 of which feature private bathrooms. The outdated decor will amuse some guests, but the renovated rooms are well kept and the service is friendly. Laundry service for a fee. This is a non-smoking establishment.

Castel Durocher
$$$ bkfst incl. rooms
$$$$$ bkfst incl. apartments
pb/sb @ ≡ ☻
3488 Rue Durocher
☎ (514) 282-1697
▤ (514) 282-0025
www.casteldurocher.com
This elegant Queen Anne-style dwelling was built in 1898 and is located a stone's throw from Rue Sainte-Catherine and Place des Arts. The former home of Emma Tassé (the wife of Guillaume-Alphonse Nantel, a lawyer and politician who was also Anathase David's father-in-law) was converted into a five-room bed and breakfast. The establishment's two floors can also be rented as private apartments that include a bedroom, a living room, a kitchen, a dining room and a private bathroom. This bed and breakfast also offers an extra gourmet touch: its Chic Choc Belgian chocolates are handmade on site.

Novotel Montréal Centre
$$$$
⚓))) 🍴 ≡ ⚖ ☓ @
1180 Rue de la Montagne
☎ (514) 861-6000 or 800-221-4542
▤ (514) 861-0992
www.novotelmontreal.com
Novotel is a French hotel chain. The pleasant rooms in its downtown Montréal establishment are equipped with numerous extras, including a large desk and outlets for computers. Special packages are available for guests travelling with children. The emphasis here seems to be on security. Some rooms are reserved for smokers.

Hôtel Godin
$$$$$ bkfst incl.
≡ 📠 ⚓ @ ☓
10 Rue Sherbrooke Ouest
☎ (514) 843-6000 or 866-744-6346
▤ (514) 843 6810
www.hotelgodin.com
Hôtel Godin's 126 rooms and 10 suites were designed for 21st-century globetrotters, with a focus on functionality that is rarely found in other hotel establishments. Business travellers will appreciate the long wooden mural panels and flat-screen televisions with integrated computers that can transform each room into an office. The hotel has managed to retain the former Godin building's original cachet while favouring a 1960s design with a minimalist touch that gives the establishment a very modern look. Hôtel Godin is ideally located between the "Main" and the downtown area, and offers a few interesting accommodation/tourism packages such as its *City Smart*, *Relaxation* and *The Main!* packages.

Hilton Montréal Bonaventure
$$$$$
≋ ⚓ 🍴 ≡ ⚖ 📠 @
1 Place Bonaventure
☎ (514) 878-2332 or 800-267-2575
▤ (514) 878-3881
www.hiltonmontreal.com
The Hilton Montréal Bonaventure is located between downtown and Old Montréal. Its 395 rooms offer a number of little extras (coffee maker, hair dryer) that make this hotel the perfect place to relax. The hotel has a heated outdoor swimming pool, where guests can swim all year, as well as a lovely garden and access to the underground city. Some rooms are reserved for smokers.

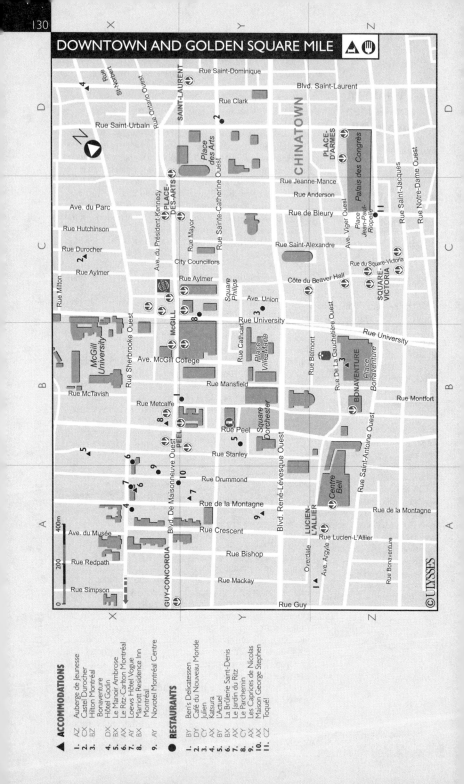

Loews Hôtel Vogue
$$$$
◎ ➤ ♨ ≡ ᵬ @ ⚡

1425 Rue de la Montagne
☎ (514) 285-5555 or 800-465-6654
🖥 (514) 849-8903
www.loewshotels.com/vogue.html
At first glance, the Loews Hôtel Vogue, a glass-and-concrete building with no ornamentation, looks bare. The lobby, however, embellished with warm-coloured woodwork, gives a more accurate idea of the luxury and elegance of this establishment. The 142 large rooms, with their elegant furniture, reveal the comfort of this hotel. Modems and hypoallergenic bedding in the rooms.

Marriott Residence Inn Montréal
$$$$$ bkfst incl.
➤ ≋ ≡ ᵬ ➤ @ ❄

2045 Rue Peel
☎ (514) 982-6064 or 800-999-9494
🖥 (514) 844-8361
This hotel was completely renovated before it re-

opened in early 1997. It has 190 suites and studios, each with a kitchenette complete with stove, microwave oven, refrigerator and dishwasher. These may be rented for a single night or for months at a time. Twenty-four-hour laundry service, a large outdoor terrace and a roof-top swimming pool are all available to guests.

Le Ritz-Carlton Montréal
$$$$$
➤ ♨ ≡ ◎ ⬠ ➤ ⚡

1228 Rue Sherbrooke Ouest
☎ (514) 842-4212 or 800-363-0366
🖥 (514) 842-3383
www.ritzcarlton.com
The Ritz Carlton opened in 1912 and has been renovated over the years in order to continue offering its clientele exceptional comfort; it has managed, however, to preserve its original elegance. Worthy of a high-end establishment, the 229 rooms are decorated with superb antique furniture and are very comfortable. In addition, an excellent

restaurant (Café de Paris) features, in summer, a lovely garden where you can have a bite (**Jardin du Ritz**, see p 135).

Quartier Latin

Pierre et Dominique
$$ bkfst incl.
sb @
271 Rue du Square St-Louis
☎ (514) 286-0307
www.gitescanada.com/928.html
Square Saint-Louis (see p 108) is a quaint park surrounded by beautiful Victorian houses. This private home is located by the square and stands out with its five extremely comfortable and tastefully decorated rooms. Non-smoking.

Hôtel de l'Institut
$$$-$$$$ bkfst incl.
≡ ♨ ᵬ @
3535 Rue St-Denis

Montréal - Accommodations - Quartier Latin

ACCOMMODATIONS
1. BY Hôtel de l'Institut
2. AY Pierre et Dominique

RESTAURANTS
1. BZ Le Pèlerin-Magellan
2. BY Restaurant de l'Institut

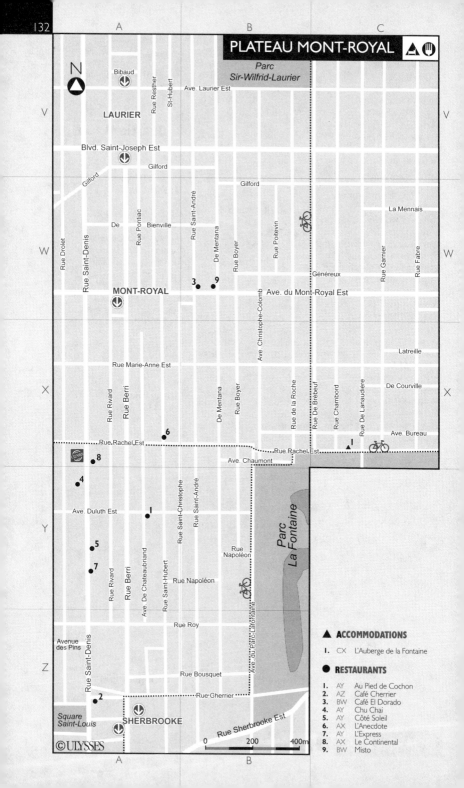

PLATEAU MONT-ROYAL

▲ ACCOMMODATIONS
1. CX L'Auberge de la Fontaine

● RESTAURANTS
1. AY Au Pied de Cochon
2. AZ Café Cherrier
3. BW Café El Dorado
4. AY Chu Chai
5. AY Côté Soleil
6. AX L'Anecdote
7. AY L'Express
8. AX Le Continental
9. BW Misto

© ULYSSES

☎ (514) 282-5120 or 800-361-5111
🖷 (514) 873-9893
www.ithq.qc.ca
The Hôtel de l'Institut occupies the upper floors of the Institut de Tourisme et d'Hôtellerie du Québec (ITHQ). It is ideally located across from Square Saint-Louis and at the limits of the Plateau Mont-Royal, "Main" and Quartier Latin neighbourhoods. It reopened in 2005, following major renovations that lasted two years. Its 42 rooms and two suites have undergone a much-needed rejuvenation, with splendid results. The architects have even managed to add balconies to almost every room, a noteworthy asset for a Montréal hotel. The now resolutely modern Hôtel de l'Institut offers very comfortable accommodations and all the major services you would expect from a quality hotel. The hotel is run by students in training who are followed closely by their professors to ensure the top-notch service that is expected from a four-star establishment such as this.

Plateau Mont-Royal

L'Auberge de la Fontaine
$$$$-$$$$$ bkfst incl.
◎ ≡ ✳ ⌂

1301 Rue Rachel Est
☎ (514) 597-0166 or 800-597-0597
🖷 🖷 (514) 597-0496
www.aubergedelafontaine.com
The Auberge de la Fontaine stands opposite the lovely Parc Lafontaine. Designed with a great deal of care, it has a lot of style. A feeling of peace and relaxation emanates from the 21 rooms, all of which are attractively decorated. These

features have made this a popular place, so it is best to make reservations. Dry-cleaning service.

Near the Airport

Hôtel Best Western Montréal Aéroport
$$$-$$$$ bkfst incl.
⇌))) ≈ ⛵ ≡ ✈

13000 Chemin de la Côte-de-Liesse
☎ (514) 631-4811 or 800-361-2254
🖷 (514) 631-7305
www.bestwestern.com
The 110 rooms at the Hôtel Best Western Montréal Aéroport are pleasant and affordable. The hotel also offers an interesting service: after spending the night, guests can park their car here for up to three weeks, free of charge. Free airport shuttle to Montréal-Trudeau service also available.

Restaurants

Vieux-Montréal

Olive + Gourmando
$
351 Rue St-Paul Ouest
☎ (514) 350-1083
This Saint-Paul street bistro-bakery's two owners used to ply their trade at Toqué!, Montréal's most celebrated restaurant over the last few years. Start your meal off with a mushroom soup, then move onto the beet salad served with a smoked-trout sandwich, and top it all off with a double chocolate and cherry biscuit. You won't be disappointed. This charming bistro is a good choice for an unpretentious

gourmet meal in Vieux-Montréal.

Le Bonaparte
$$$
443 Rue St-François-Xavier
☎ (514) 844-4368
The varied menu of French restaurant Le Bonaparte always includes some delicious surprises. Guests can savour them in one of the establishment's three rooms, all richly decorated in the Empire style. The largest offers the warmth of a fireplace in winter, while another, named "La Serre" (the greenhouse), reveals a subdued ambiance thanks to its many potted plants.

Le Vieux Saint-Gabriel
$$$
426 Rue St-Gabriel
☎ (514) 878-3561
The attraction of the Vieux Saint-Gabriel lies above all in its enchanting decor reminiscent of early New France; the restaurant is set in an old house that was home to an inn in 1754. The French and Italian selections from the somewhat predictable menu are adequate.

Chez Queux
$$$
158 Rue St-Paul Est
☎ (514) 866-5194
Ideally located in Old Montréal and overlooking Place Jacques-Cartier, Chez Queux serves classic French cuisine in the finest tradition. Refined service in an elegant setting guarantee a positive culinary experience.

Cube
$$$$
355 Rue McGill
☎ (514) 276-2823

Cube came close to becoming a featureless shape following a conflict between the restaurant's owners. Fortunately, the famous polygon managed to retain its purity with the arrival of Éric Gonzalez, one of the most talented chefs this city has had the privilege of welcoming. Since then, the establishment has maintained its chic, well-kept allure, with impeccable service, a tasteful decor and furnishings that provide the perfect setting for the real reason food aficionados come here: to revel in an unforgettable culinary experience that compares favourably with any of the world's top gourmet dining establishments. If money is no object, don't hesitate to choose the seven-course meal. The combination of marvellous flavours will leave you breathless. Among the many splendid offerings are roasted veal sweetbread and asparagus with hazelnut-butter juice; simply prepared sea salt-seasoned duck foie gras; melt-in-your-mouth, slow-cooked salmon, as light as mousse and served with a stunning veal stock and lobster sauce; and Angus beef filet served with truffle-flavoured egg-yolk ravioli. The wine list and the wine steward's judicious suggestions round out an exquisite meal.

Auberge-Restaurant Pierre du Calvet
$$$$
401 Rue Bonsecours
☎ (514) 282-1725

The old jewel among Montréal restaurants, the **Auberge-Restaurant Pierre du Calvet** (see p 127) inn boast one of the best dining rooms in the city. The establishment is particularly recommended for its delicious and imaginative French cuisine. Its menu, based on game, poultry, fish and beef, changes every two weeks. The elegant surroundings, antiques, ornamental plants and discrete service further add to the pleasure of an evening meal at the Maison Pierre du Calvet, which was built in 1725.

Downtown and Golden Square Mile

Ben's Delicatessen
$
900 Boulevard De Maisonneuve Ouest
☎ (514) 844-1000

In the beginning of the 20th century, a Lithuanian immigrant modified a recipe from his native country to suit the needs of workers and thus introduced the smoked-meat sandwich to Montréal, creating in the process Ben's Delicatessen. Over the years, the restaurant has become a Montréal institution, attracting a motley crowd. This is where people come when the bars close. The worn Formica tables and yellowed photographs give the restaurant an outdated appearance. Don't expect much from the service either.

La Brûlerie Saint-Denis
$
2100 Rue Stanley, in the Maison Alcan
☎ (514) 985-9159

This Brûlerie Saint-Denis branch serves the same delicious coffee blends, light meals and desserts as the other Brûleries. Even though the coffee is not roasted on the premises, it does come fresh from the roasters on Rue Saint-Denis.

Café du Nouveau Monde
$$
84 Rue Ste-Catherine Ouest
☎ (514) 866-8669

The Café du Nouveau Monde is a lovely addition to this part of town. Sip a glass of wine or a cup of coffee, sample a dessert in the deconstructionist decor of the ground-floor dining room, or enjoy a good meal upstairs in the atmosphere of a Parisian brasserie. The menu matches the decor: classic French bistro cuisine. Impeccable service, beautiful presentation and excellent food.

L'Actuel
$$-$$$
closed Sundays
1194 Rue Peel
☎ (514) 866-1537

L'Actuel, the most authentic Belgian restaurant in Montréal, is always full for lunch and dinner. It has two large dining rooms, one of which is lively and fairly noisy, where affable waiters rush to serve a clientele of business people. The restaurant serves mussels, of course, as well as a number of other specialties.

Julien
$$$
closed Sundays
1191 Rue Union
☎ (514) 871-1581
Julien is a Montréal institution, thanks largely to its *bavette à l'échalote*, or steak with shallots, which is one of the best in the city. But it isn't just the *bavette* that attracts patrons, since each dish is more succulent than the next. For that matter, everything here is impeccable, from the service to the decor to the wine list.

Katsura
$$$
2170 Rue de la Montagne
☎ (514) 849-1172
At Katsura, located in the heart of downtown, visitors can savour refined Japanese cuisine. The main dining room is furnished with long tables, making this a perfect place for groups. Smaller, more intimate rooms are also available.

Le Parchemin
$$$
closed Sundays
1333 Rue University
☎ (514) 844-1619
Occupying the former rectory of the Christ Church Cathedral, Le Parchemin is distinguished by its stylish decor and smooth atmosphere. Guests enjoy carefully prepared French cuisine, suitable for the finest of palates. The four-course table d'hôte, with its wide range of choices, is an excellent option.

Maison George Stephen
$$$
1440 Rue Drummond
☎ (514) 849-7338
Founded in 1884, the **Maison George Stephen** (see p 105) houses the Mount Stephen

Club, which only opens its restaurant to the public on Sundays, when it serves a musical brunch. The decor dates back to another era, with superb panelled walls adorned with 19th-century stained glass. You will have the privilege of treating both your taste buds and your ears to a feast, as classical music interpreted by conservatory students wafts through the air.

Le Jardin du Ritz
$$$$
1228 Rue Sherbrooke Ouest
☎ (514) 842-4212
Le Jardin du Ritz is the perfect escape from the summer heat and the fast pace of downtown. Classic French cuisine is featured on the menu, with tea served on a patio surrounded by flowers and greenery, next to the pond with its splashing ducks. Only open during the summer months, the Jardin is an extension of the hotel's other restaurant, the Café de Paris.

Les Caprices de Nicolas
$$$$
2072 Rue Drummond
☎ (514) 282-9790
Les Caprices de Nicolas is one of the very best restaurants in Montréal, with highly innovative and sophisticated French cuisine. There is an interesting arrangement whereby, for the price of a bottle of wine, you can sample different wines by the glass to accompany every course of the meal. The service is friendly and impeccable, and the decor is like an indoor garden. Non-smoking establishment.

Toqué!
$$$$
closed Sundays and Mondays
Centre CDP Capital
900 Place Jean-Paul Riopelle (on the western side of Rue De Bleury, between Avenue Viger and Rue St-Antoine)
☎ (514) 499-2084
If you're looking for a new culinary experience, Toqué is without a doubt the place to go. Chef Normand Laprise insists on the freshest ingredients, and prepares and serves dishes with great care. And then there are the desserts, which are veritable modern sculptures. The service is exceptional, the wine list good, the new decor elegant, and the high prices do not seem to deter anyone. One of the most original dining establishments in Montréal.

Quartier Latin

Le Pèlerin-Magellan
$
330 Rue Ontario Est
☎ (514) 845-0909
Located near Rue Saint-Denis, Le Pèlerin-Magellan's young and friendly ambiance attracts a disparate crowd that comes here to meet friends and have a bite. Wooden furniture, made to look like mahogany, and works of modern art create a friendly atmosphere.

Restaurant de l'Institut
$$$
3535 Rue St-Denis
☎ (514) 282-5120 or 800-361-5111
www.ithq.qc.ca
Recent major renovations have given the Institut de Tourisme et d'Hôtellerie du Québec's restaurant a

Montréal – Restaurants – Quartier Latin

much needed facelift, and provided the institute's students with splendid new digs where they can practice what they have been taught. Located on the ground floor of the institute, behind large bay windows that face Square Saint-Louis, the restaurant is a daytime haven of light and a nighttime hot spot in the heart of one of Montréal's liveliest districts. The atmosphere is warm and unhurried here, with a suspended ceiling that recalls a pergola, and oak and maple walls and ceilings. Chef William Chacon and his students prepare six menus per year, and always favour local products. Be it for breakfast, lunch or dinner, the institute's restaurant offers one of the best values for your money in Montréal.

Plateau Mont-Royal

L'Anecdote
$
801 Rue Rachel Est
☎(514) 526-7967
L'Anecdote serves burgers and vegetarian club sandwiches made with quality ingredients. The place has a 1950s-style decor, with movie posters and old Coca-Cola ads on the walls.

Café El Dorado
$$
921 Avenue du Mont-Royal Est
☎(514) 598-8282
Locals in the know head over to Café El Dorado for a coffee or a quick, tasty bite in its spectacular, curvilinear decor. The desserts here are particularly tasty.

Chu Chai
$$
4088 Rue St-Denis
☎(514) 843-4194
Chu Chai deserves praise for breaking the monotony and daring to be innovative. The Thai vegetarian menu is quite a surprise: vegetarian shrimp, vegetarian fish, and even vegetarian beef and pork. The resemblance to the real thing is so extraordinary that you'll spend the evening wondering how they do it! The chef affirms that they really are made of vegetable-based products like seitan and wheat. The delicious results delight the clientele that squeezes into the modest dining room or onto the terrace. The establishment also has inexpensive lunch specials. Next door is Chu Chai's little sister, **Chuch**, which offers ready-made delicacies of the same quality to enjoy in tasteful, relaxing surroundings.

Côté Soleil
$$
3979 Rue St-Denis
☎(514) 282-8037
Coté Soleil offers consistently fresh items from a menu that changes every day and never misses the mark. Excellent, occasionally inventive French cuisine is served at prices so affordable that this is probably the best value in the neighbourhood. The service is attentive and friendly, and the setting, although simple, is quite warm. In summer, there are two sunny terraces: one on the busy street and the other in the lovely garden.

Café Cherrier
$$-$$$
3635 Rue St-Denis
☎(514) 843-4308
The meeting place *par excellence* for many fifty-something professionals, the terrace and dining room at Café Cherrier are always packed. The atmosphere is reminiscent of a French *brasserie*, highly animated and busy, which can lead to fortuitous meetings. The menu features bistro-type meals that are generally quite tasty, but the service can be uneven.

Misto
$$-$$$
929 Avenue du Mont-Royal Est
☎(514) 526-5043
Misto is an Italian restaurant patronized by a hip clientele that comes here to savour delicious and imaginative Italian cooking. The decor features exposed brick walls and shades of green, and the noisy atmosphere and crowded tables only add to the ambiance and the attentive and friendly service.

Au Pied de Cochon
$$$
536 Avenue Duluth Est
☎(514) 281-1114
This bistro is located in the heart of the Plateau and serves delicious and resolutely hearty meals. Try the "happy pig" (*cochon heureux*) pork chops or the candied lamb shanks, or, if you're feeling adventurous, order the *poutine* with duck *foie gras*. Some may call this dish a culinary sacrilege, but wait till you've tried it!

Le Continental
$$$
4169 Rue St-Denis
☎ (514) 845-6842

The staging is very subtle at the Continental. Some evenings, the restaurant is positively charming, with its attentive, courteous staff, stylish clientele and modern 1950s-style decor. The varied menu always includes nice surprises. The cuisine can be sublime, and the presentation is always excellent.

L'Express
$$$
3927 Rue St-Denis
☎ (514) 845-5333

A yuppie gathering place during the mid-1980s, L'Express is still highly rated for its locomotive dining-car decor and lively Parisian-bistro atmosphere, which few restaurants

have managed to recreate. In addition to the consistently appealing menu, the above-mentioned factors have earned this restaurant a solid reputation over the years.

Outremont and Mile-End

Café Souvenir
$
1261 Avenue Bernard Ouest
☎ (514) 948-5259

Maps of large European cities like Paris decorate the walls of the Café Souvenir. The ambiance of a French café pervades this comfortable little restaurant, which is open 24 hours a day on weekends. Rainy Sundays bring out droves of locals for a quick coffee and a chat. The menu is not extraordinary, but the meals are well prepared.

Cyclo
$$
5136 Avenue du Parc
☎ (514) 272-1477

Many consider Cyclo one of the best Vietnamese restaurants in its category. Indeed, this establishment always delights its clientele thanks to delicious, classic Vietnamese cuisine. The dining-room decor is sober and elegant, bathed in shades of white. Excellent value for your money.

Leméac Café Bistrot
$$$
1045 Avenue Laurier Ouest
☎ (514) 270-0999

This classic Outremont café-bistro was designed by architect Luc Laporte, and is named after the famous Montréal publishing house that used to occupy this pleasant spot on Avenue Laurier. The woodwork, garden terrace and large bay windows

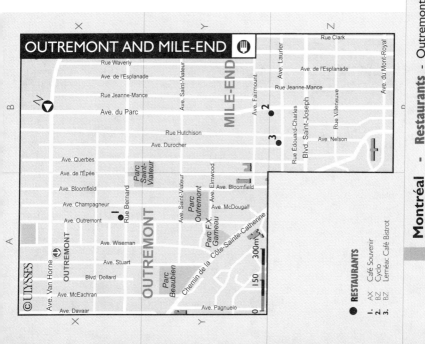

Montréal – Restaurants – Outremont and Mile-End

● **RESTAURANTS**

1. BY   Hélène de Champlain
2. BX   Le Festin du Gouverneur
3. AZ   Nuances

ÎLE SAINTE-HÉLÈNE AND ÎLE NOTRE-DAME

Lac des Dauphins
La Ronde
Fort de l'Île Sainte-Hélène
Quai de l'Horloge
ÎLE SAINTE-HÉLÈNE
Pont Jacques Cartier
Vieux-Port
Parc Jean-Drapeau
Biosphère
JEAN-DRAPEAU
Pont de la Concorde
Passerelle du Cosmos
20
ÎLE NOTRE-DAME
Parc Jean-Drapeau
Olympic Basin
St. Lawrence Seaway
Longueuil
© ULYSSES
Casino de Montréal
0   500   1000m

Montréal - Restaurants - Outremont and Mile-End

give this typical European café a particularly luminous ambiance. A vast selection of excellent wines accompanies a classic menu of French fare (including calf's liver, flank steak and duck confit).

Île Sainte-Hélène and Île Notre-Dame

Hélène de Champlain
$$$
☎ (514) 395-2424
Located on Île Sainte-Hélène, Hélène de Champlain lies in an enchanting setting, without question one of the loveliest in Montréal. The large dining room, with its fireplace and view of the city and river, is extremely pleasant. Each corner has its own unique charm, overlooking the season-changing surround-

ing landscape. Though the restaurant does not serve the fanciest of gastronomic cuisine, the food is very good. Service is courteous and attentive.

Le Festin du Gouverneur
$$$$
Fort de l'Île Ste-Hélène
☎ (514) 879-1141
Festin du Gouverneur creates feasts like those prepared in New France at the beginning of colonization. Characters in period costumes and traditional Québec dishes transport diners to a bygone era. The restaurant only serves groups and reservations are required.

Nuances
$$$$
Casino de Montréal, Île Notre-Dame
☎ (514) 392-2708
On the fifth floor of Montréal's casino, Nuances

is one of the best dining establishments in the city, perhaps even the country. Refined and imaginative cuisine is served in a decor bathed in mahogany, brass, leather and views of the city lights. Of particular note on the menu are the lobster *chartreuse* with green-asparagus appetizer, as well as roast-duck magret, Québec lamb tenderloin and pan-seared duck foie gras in its own juice. The delectable desserts are always exquisitely presented. The plush and classic ambiance of this award-winning restaurant is perfect for business meals or special occasions. The casino also has three less expensive restaurants: **Via Fortuna (*$$*)**, **La Bonne Carte (*$$*)**, a buffet with *à la carte* service and **L'Entre-Mise (*$*)**, a snack bar.

Entertainment

■ Bars and Nightclubs

Downtown

Altitude 737
1 Place Ville-Marie
☎ (514) 397-0737
If you are one of those people who love reaching high places, you must ascend to the top of Place Ville-Marie. Altitude 737 is jam-packed on weeknights, especially on Thursdays and Fridays, when a clientele of thirty-something professionals comes here for drinks before dinner. The comfortable room and two terraces offer breathtaking views of the city and the river that unquestionably justify the place's popularity. Later at night, clubbers have to climb another storey to the hip club.

Hurley's Irish Pub/ Hurley's Medieval
1225 Rue Crescent
☎ (514) 861-4111
Discreetly tucked away south of Rue Sainte-Catherine among innumerable Crescent Street restaurants and bars, Hurley's Irish Pub and Hurley's Medieval succeed in recreating an atmosphere worthy of traditional Irish pubs. This is largely due to excellent amateur Irish folk musicians (The Paddingtons, Jim & Gary) and the quality of the world-famous Guinness beer.

Newtown
1476 Rue Crescent
☎ (514) 284-6555
Owned by Québec's favourite Formula 1 pilot, Jacques Villeneuve, Newtown draws crowds of patrons who feel the urge to see and be seen. Guests can eat in the beautiful restaurant, dance at the nightclub or have a drink in the lush ambiance of the lounge in this huge, splendidly designed complex.

Quartier Latin

Café Chaos
2031 Rue St-Denis
☎ (514) 844-1301
The cooperatively run Café Chaos attracts a packed crowd of young, energetic students who like to chat about music and life. The music here includes every imaginable style: garage, rock, surf, alternative, techno-industrial, etc. Local musicians present their newest creations beginning at about 9pm. Local groups such as Caféine and WD-40 made their debuts here.

Les 3 Brasseurs
1660 Rue St-Denis
☎ (514) 845-1660
A stone's throw from Théâtre Saint-Denis, Les 3 Brasseurs is a Montréal franchise of a French chain of establishments that has gained quite a reputation. Thanks to its rustic decor and friendly service, the place welcomes a crowd of students and young executives who come here to quench their thirst. You can sample delicious Alsatian specialties, such as *flams* (flambéed pie topped with pieces of chicken, lardoons or vegetables). In summer, the two terraces (one on the roof, and the other at street level) are the ideal spot to sip a cold beer and watch passersby on Rue Saint-Denis.

Le P'tit Bar
3451 Rue St-Denis
☎ (514) 281-9124
Facing Square Saint-Louis, the P'tit Bar is the perfect place to discuss literature, philosophy, photography, etc. The former hangout of the late Gérald Godin, celebrated Québec poet, this place will appeal to fans of French music. Photo exhibits make up the sober decor and Québécois and French singers sometimes perform here..

Quartier Latin Pub
318 Rue Ontario Est
☎ (514) 845-3301
Is the Quartier Latin Pub overshadowed by its neighbours, L'Île Noire and Le Pèlerin-Magellan? Maybe not, since the bar has, on more than one occasion, been chosen as a filming location for several Québec television shows. Perhaps it's the meticulously designed but rather cold decor that brings it so much attention, or maybe it's the clientele, as prim as the surroundings: clean-cut "preppies" in their early 30s that seem right out of a beer commercial. Terrace in summer.

Plateau Mont-Royal

Bily Kun
354 Avenue du Mont-Royal Est
☎ (514) 845-5392
The second bar opened by the Cheval Blanc microbrewery, Bily Kun offers a wide selection of beers, including the excellent and good-value house brand. With an original decor of mounted ostrich necks, this hip place has a friendly and very lively atmosphere and is always packed.

Montréal - Entertainment

Le Réservoir

9 Avenue Duluth Est

☎ (514) 849-7779

A microbrewery at night and a bistro at lunch time, Le Réservoir also offers a tasty brunch menu on Saturday and Sunday mornings. We like the bar's location on charming little Avenue Duluth, its second-floor terrace and its quality micro-brewed beer.

Mile-End

BU

5245 Boulevard St-Laurent

☎ (514) 276-0249

This Mile-End wine bar has a distinctly laid back atmosphere. The wine menu offers a daily selection of some 30 wines sold by the glass. An array of antipasti is served until 2am, for those who would also like a quick bite to eat.

■ Gay Bars and Nightclubs

Le Cabaret Mado

1115 Rue Ste-Catherine Est

☎ (514) 525-7566

Frequented by a mixed, lively clientele, Le Cabaret Mado presents, among other things, drag shows. Guaranteed fun with the famous Mado!

Sky Pub and Sky Club

1474 Rue Ste-Catherine Est

☎ (514) 529-6969

This busy gay bar boasts an elaborate decor that lacks a certain unity, and the loud, uninspired music leaves a bit to be desired. The ground-floor Sky Pub attracts a crowd of young dancers, while the Sky Club is spread over the two upper floors and is one of the city's main gay nightspots where revellers dance to a variety of musical styles.

The atmosphere can seem rather cold in such a vast space, but the young crowd makes the most of it and doesn't let this get in the way of their partying. In summer, however, its huge, wonderful roof-top terrace allows guests to observe the hustle and bustle of Sainte-Catherine Street. Another sore spot is the unusually high cover charge that seems to vary for no apparent reason.

La Track

1574 Rue Ste-Catherine Est

☎ (514) 521-1419

This lively gay disco welcomes men of all ages.

Unity II

1171 Rue Ste-Catherine Est

☎ (514) 523-4429

Unity is a large gay club that is mainly frequented by a young masculine crowd. Its architecture is very interesting, with different levels, including a mezzanine from which you can watch the dance floor and the entrancing light show. In addition to the main dance floor, there are also two other dance floors, including the Bamboo, where the music tends to be quieter, and another featuring the trendiest of tunes. On the main floor, there is a lovely bar decorated with plenty of woodwork and carefully thought-out lighting. For warm summer nights there is a huge rooftop terrace.

Sky Pub and Sky Club

1474 Rue Ste-Catherine Est

☎ (514) 529-6969

This busy gay bar boasts an elaborate decor that lacks a certain unity, and the loud, uninspired music leaves a bit to be desired. The ground-floor Sky Pub attracts a crowd of young dancers, while the Sky Club

is spread over the two upper floors and is one of the city's main gay nightspots where revellers dance to a variety of musical styles. The atmosphere can seem rather cold in such a vast space, but the young crowd makes the most of it and doesn't let this get in the way of their partying. In summer, however, its huge, wonderful roof-top terrace allows guests to observe the hustle and bustle of Sainte-Catherine Street. Another sore spot is the unusually high cover charge that seems to vary for no apparent reason.

Unity II

1171 Rue Ste-Catherine Est

☎ (514) 523-4429

Unity is a large gay club that is mainly frequented by a young masculine crowd. Its architecture is very interesting, with different levels, including a mezzanine from which you can watch the dance floor and the entrancing light show. In addition to the main dance floor, there are also two other dance floors, including the Bamboo, where the music tends to be quieter, and another featuring the trendiest of tunes. On the main floor, there is a lovely bar decorated with plenty of woodwork and carefully thought-out lighting. For warm summer nights there is a huge rooftop terrace.

■ Cultural Activities

Ticket Sales

Two major ticket agencies sell tickets for shows, concerts and other events in Montréal over the telephone or Internet. You'll need to pay by credit card to buy tickets online, though various ticket outlets where you can pay cash can be found throughout the city. Service charges, which vary according to the show, are added to the price of tickets.

Admission
☎ (514) 790-1245 or 800-361-4595
www.admission.com

Ticketpro
☎ (514) 908-9090 or 866-908-9090
www.ticketpro.ca

Movie Theatres

Montréal has many movie theatres. Special rates are offered on Tuesdays, Wednesday and matinees. Here is a list of the major downtown theatres.

AMC
2313 Rue Ste-Catherine Ouest
☎ (514) 904-1250

Cinéma du Parc
3575 Avenue du Parc
☎ (514) 281-1900

Cinéma IMAX
Centre des Sciences de Montréal, Old-Port
☎ (514) 496-4629

ONF Montréal
(National Film Board)
1564 Rue St-Denis
☎ (514) 496-6895

Paramount
977 Rue Ste-Catherine Ouest
☎ (514) 842-5828

Theatres and Concert Halls

Le Cabaret Music-Hall
2111 Boulevard St-Laurent
☎ (514) 845-2014

La Tulipe
4530 Avenue Papineau
☎ (514) 529-5000

Centaur Theatre
453 Rue St-François-Xavier
☎ (514) 288-3161

Place des Arts
175 Rue Ste-Catherine Ouest
☎ (514) 842-2112
The complex contains five performance spaces: Salle Wilfrid-Pelletier, Théâtre Maisonneuve, Théâtre Jean-Duceppe, Studio-théâtre and the Cinquième Salle. The Orchestre Symphonique de Montréal *(☎514-842-9951)*, Opéra de Montréal *(☎514-985-2258)*, Compagnie Jean-Duceppe *(☎514-842-8681)*, Grands Ballets Canadiens *(☎514-849-0269)* and the Festival International de Jazz de Montréal hold performances here.

Spectrum
318 Rue Ste-Catherine Ouest
☎ (514) 861-5851
Shows usually begin around 9pm.

Théâtre Saint-Denis
1594 Rue St-Denis
☎ (514) 849-4211

Saidye Bronfman Centre
5170 Chemin de la Côte-Ste-Catherine
☎ (514) 739-2301

■ Festivals and Cultural Events

During summer, festival fever takes hold of Montréal and its visitors. From May to September, the city hosts a whole series of festivals, each with a different theme. One thing is certain: there is something for everyone. As the summer season draws to a close, the events become less frequent but remain just as interesting.

Winter's cold does not hinder the festival spirit;

it merely provides an opportunity to organize another festival in Montréal, this time to celebrate the pleasures and activities of the frosty season. The **Fête des Neiges** *(☎514-872-6120, www.fetedesneiges.com)* takes place in Parc Jean-Drapeau from late January to early February. Skating rinks and giant toboggans are available for the enjoyment of Montréal families. The snow-sculpture competition also attracts a number of curious onlookers.

The **Montréal High Lights Festival** (Festival Montréal En Lumière) *(☎514-288-9955, www.montrealenlumiere.com)* brings a bit of magic to the deepest frost of Québec's winter. In mid-February, light shows draw attention to the city's architecture and fireworks are presented outdoors. In the *Art de la Table* part of the festival, top chefs from all over the world prepare samples, meals and workshops. The festival also showcases concerts, dance and theatre.

L'International des Feux Loto-Québec (international fireworks competition) *(☎514-397-2000, www.internationaldesfeuxloto-quebec.com)* starts around mid-June and ends in late July. The world's top pyrotechnists present at La Ronde (île Sainte-Hélène) high-quality pyro-musical shows every Saturday in June and every Wednesday and Saturday in July. Montrealers head to the La Ronde amusement park (where admission fees must be paid), Pont Jacques-Cartier or along the river in the Old Port (both at no cost) to admire the spectacular fireworks display that col-

ours the sky above the city for over 30min.

During the **Festival International de Jazz de Montréal** (☎514-871-1881, www. montrealjazzfest.com), hundreds of shows set to the rhythm of jazz and its variations are presented on stages around Place des Arts. From late June to mid-July, this part of the city and a fair number of theatres are buzzing with activity. The event offers people an opportunity to take to the streets and be carried away by the festive atmosphere of fantastic, free outdoor shows that attract Montrealers and visitors in large numbers. The FIJM also presents various concerts outside the festival season.

Humour and creativity are highlighted during the **Festival Juste pour Rire / Just for Laughs Festival** (☎514-845-3155), which is held in mid-July. Theatres host comedians from a variety of countries for the occasion. Outdoor activities take place in the Quartier Latin, on Rue Saint-Denis south of Rue Sherbrooke, which is closed to traffic, while indoor shows are presented at the Théâtre Saint-Denis.

From the end of August until early September, the **Festival des Films du Monde de Montréal** (**World Film Festival**) (☎514-845-3883, www. ffm-montreal.org) takes over various Montréal movie theatres. During this competition, films from different countries are presented to Montréal audiences. At the end of the competition, prizes are awarded to the best films. The most prestigious category is the Grand Prix des Amériques. During the festival, films are shown from 9am to midnight, much to the delight of movie-goers across the city. An outdoor screening also takes place at Place des Arts during the festival.

■ Gaming and Amusement Parks

The **La Ronde** (see p 120) amusement park is chock-full of world-class roller coasters, Ferris wheels and rides that will delight thrill-seekers young and old.

With 2,700 slot machines and 100 gaming tables (blackjack, roulette, baccarat, poker, etc.), the **Casino de Montréal** (free admission; every day 9am to 5am; ☎514-392-2746) is without a doubt a major player in the city's nightlife. The casino is now one of the 10 largest in the world in terms of gaming equipment. Its concert hall, the **Cabaret du Casino**, presents colourful variety acts.

■ Sporting Events

Car Racing

Circuit Gilles-Villeneuve
☎(514) 350-0000 (tickets)
www.grandprix.ca
The month of June is marked by an international-scale event that captivates a massive crowd of Formula 1 amateurs who come from all over the world: the **Grand Prix of Canada**, held in the middle of June at the Circuit Gilles-Villeneuve of Parc Jean-Drapeau, on Île Notre-Dame. Without a doubt, this is one of the most popular events of the summer. For three days, you can attend various car races, notably the high-energy and spectacular Formula 1 race.

Cycling

Montréal Bike Fest
(**Féria du vélo de Montréal**)
☎(514) 521-8687 or
800-567-8356 (tickets)
www.velo.qc.ca/tour
The Montréal Bike Fest is held in late May-early June, and ends with the **Tour de l'Île** on the first Sunday in June. This cycling tour attracts some 30,000 cyclists who travel over approximately 50km. During the Bike Fest, three other events are also presented: the Défi Métropolitain, the Tour de l'Île des Enfants and Un Tour La Nuit.

Football

Percival-Molson Stadium
475 Avenue des Pins Ouest
☎(514) 871-2255 (tickets)
www.montrealalouettes.com
The **Montréal Alouettes** (Canadian Football League) have been playing at the Percival-Molson Stadium since 1998. Regular season begins in late May and ends in late October. You should attend at least one Alouettes games to enjoy the breathtaking view of downtown Montréal and, of course, to support the team, along with 20,000 other spectators!

Hockey

Bell Centre
1260 Rue De La Gauchetière Ouest
☎(514) 790-1245 or
800-361-4595 (tickets)
www.canadiens.com
The world-famous **Montreal Canadiens** National Hockey League team plays at the Bell Centre. There are 82

games during the regular season, 41 of which are played at home, then come the playoffs, at the end of which the winning team takes home the legendary Stanley Cup.

Tennis

Stade Uniprix
285 Rue Faillon Ouest
☎ (514) 790-1245 or
800-361-4595 (tickets)
www.tenniscanada.com
At Parc Jarry, located at the corner of Saint-Laurent Boulevard and Jarry Street, the best tennis players in the world participate, each year in early August, in the **Rogers Cup** competition. Even years are reserved to women's competitions.

Shopping

Die-hard shoppers will find much to love about Montréal. Among the many hunting grounds they can choose from are Rue Sainte-Catherine, the city's shopping mecca and main commercial artery, the maze-like halls of the underground city and its myriad boutiques, the Mile-End area where local designers have set up shop to sell their wares, Vieux-Montréal and its antique shops, and Avenue du Mont-Royal, where they'll find several funky second-hand clothing, book and music stores. To help you organize your shopping expeditions, we have chosen shops and boutiques that stand out for the quality, originality or value of their products. You're likely to encounter the phrases *"en vente"* or *"en solde"* in Montréal shops; both mean "on sale."

■ Bookstores

General

Chapter's
(French and English)
1171 Rue Ste-Catherine Ouest
☎ (514) 849-8825

Indigo
(French and English)
1500 Avenue McGill
☎ (514) 281-5549

Coles
(French and English)
Place Ville-Marie
☎ (514) 861-1736
Promenades de la Cathédrale
625 Rue Ste-Catherine Ouest
☎ (514) 289-8737

Paragraphe
(English)
2220 McGill College
☎ (514) 845-5811

Specialty

Librairie C.EstC. Michel Fortin
(education and languages)
3714 Rue St-Denis
☎ (514) 849-5719

Canadian Centre for Architecture Bookstore
(architecture)
1920 Rue Baile
☎ (514) 939-7028

Librairie Italiana
(Italian books)
6792 Boulevard St-Laurent
☎ (514) 277-2955

Librairie Las Américas
(Spanish, Latin American books)
10 Rue St-Norbert
☎ (514) 844-5994

Librairie-Bistrot Olivieri
(foreign literature, humanities)
5219 Chemin de la Côte-des-Neiges
☎ (514) 739-3639

Librairie Olivieri (Musée d'Art Contemporain Bookstore)
(art)
185 Rue Ste-Catherine Ouest
☎ (514) 847-6903

Librairie Ulysse
(travel)
4176 Rue St-Denis
☎ (514) 843-9447
560 Avenue du Président-Kennedy
☎ (514) 843-7222
Ulysses has a large selection of city and road maps, as well as travel guides.

■ Chocolate

Chocolats Geneviève Grandbois
162 Avenue St-Viateur Ouest
☎ (514) 394-1000
Marché Atwater,
138 Rue Atwater, 2nd floor
☎ (514) 933-1331
Geneviève Grandbois is renowned for her devilishly divine chocolates. Each little cube is a marvel, with stunningly creative varieties running the gamut from Chai tea and *fleur de sel*-flavoured caramel (homemade, of course) to black truffle and olive oil. Connoisseurs will appreciate the refined choice of ingredients and the high-quality cocoa beans. The pure pleasure of discovering your new favourite can be enjoyed again and again, as delicious new creations are presented each season.

Montréal - Shopping

■ Crafts

Le Chariot
448 Place Jacques-Cartier
☎ (514) 875-6134
Le Chariot exhibits fantastic artworks by Inuit and other native peoples, which are also sold here. It is really worth visiting just to take a look.

L'Empreinte Coopérative
272 Rue St-Paul Est
☎ (514) 861-4427
Set up in a historic building in Vieux-Montréal, L'Empreinte is a Québec artisan co-op that sells fashion accessories, clothing, artwork and decorative household objects. This is a good spot to discover the latest trends in Québec arts and crafts.

Canadian Guild of Crafts
1460 Rue Sherbrooke Ouest
☎ (514) 849-6091
The Canadian Guild of Crafts has a shop that sells hand-crafted Québécois and Canadian objects. As well, there are two small galleries that deal in Inuit and other native art.

Bonsecours Market
390 Rue St-Paul Est
☎ (514) 878-2787
The Bonsecours Market is the place to shop for crafts and exclusive designer items. Among the boutiques-galeries to visit, keep in mind the Galerie des métiers d'art (☎514-878-2787) and the Galerie de l'Institut de Design Montréal (☎514-866-2436).

Each year in December at Place Bonaventure (901 Rue De La Gauchetière Ouest) artists from Québec display and sell their work in a giant exposition hall during the **Salon des Métiers d'Art du Québec**. If you miss the show, the **Le Rouet** (1500 Avenue McGill College, ☎514-843-5235) boutique sells sculptures, pottery and ceramics by several Québec artists.

■ Fashion

The fashion industry is flourishing in Montréal. The city is a multi-ethnic crossroads where Québécois and Canadian designers show their latest creations alongside those from the United States, Italy, France and the world. Streets like Rue Saint-Denis, Avenue Laurier, Boulevard Saint-Laurent and Rue Sherbrooke stand out for the numerous fashion boutiques that line their sidewalks. A visit to the shops is sure to turn up something that is just your style.

Shopping Centres and Department Stores

Several downtown shopping centres and department stores offer a good selection of clothing by well-known fashion designers, including Jean-Claude Chacok, Cacharel, Guy Laroche, Lily Simon, Adrienne Vittadini, Mondi, Ralph Lauren and many others.

Les Ailes de la Mode
677 Rue Ste-Catherine Ouest
☎ (514) 282-4537

The Bay
585 Rue Ste-Catherine Ouest
☎ (514) 281-4422

Eaton Centre
705 Rue Ste-Catherine Ouest
☎ (514) 288-3759
The largest urban mall in Montréal, the Eaton Centre features 175 shops, services and restaurants, a foreign-exchange office and indoor parking.

Les Cours Mont-Royal
1445 Rue Peel
☎ (514) 842-7777

Ogilvy
1307 Rue Ste-Catherine Ouest
☎ (514) 842-7711

Simons
977 Rue Ste-Catherine Ouest
☎ (514) 282-1840
Established in Québec City in 1840, the Simons retail chain has long been a staple among many Quebecers. In 1999, Simons finally opened in Montréal, an event that had long been awaited by the city's most avid shoppers. In this large department store with lovely designer decor, you'll find head-to-toe clothing for men, women and children in a wide range of styles, as well as fashion accessories and bedding.

■ Gifts

Montréal's museum gift shops are almost like museums in themselves, and sell various reproductions lovely enough to embellish any home. Here are two to keep in mind:

Boutique du Musée d'Art Contemporain
185 Rue Ste-Catherine Ouest
☎ (514) 847-6904

Montreal Museum of Fine Arts Boutique and Bookstore
1390 Rue Sherbrooke Ouest
☎ (514) 285-1600

Céramique
4201B Rue St-Denis
☎ (514) 848-1119
If you're looking for an original gift, at Céramique Art-Café you can paint a clay object yourself while com-

fortably seated and enjoying a light meal or a drink. The experienced staff is there to help you.

Mortimer Snodgrass
209 Rue St-Paul Ouest
☎ (514) 499-2851
5737 Avenue Monkland
☎ (514) 485-9777

There's something for everyone in Mortimer Snodgrass' boutiques. You'll find every delightfully useless and strikingly original gift idea you could imagine here, from colourful electrical switch plates to neoprene wine bags to a unique collection of items for kids. For the humorous gift-giver in search of that perfect catch.

■ Music

The following megastores have the largest selection of compact discs of all musical genres at the lowest prices:

Archambault
500 Rue Ste-Catherine Est
☎ (514) 849-6201
Place des Arts
175 Rue Ste-Catherine Ouest
☎ (514) 281-0367

HMV
1020 Rue Ste-Catherine Ouest
☎ (514) 875-0765

■ Newspapers and Magazines

Maison de la Presse Internationale
550 Rue Ste-Catherine Est
☎ (514) 842-3857

■ Outdoor Equipment

Atmosphere
1610 Rue St-Denis
☎ (514) 844-2228

Located in the gleaming Quartier Latin movie theatre, Atmosphere offers all kinds of outdoor accessories in a large, airy space. Among other goods, you will find the top Québec brand for clothing and accessories, Chlorophylle. Atmosphere specializes in watersports and sells canoes and kayaks.

La Cordée
2159 Rue Ste-Catherine Est
☎ (514) 524-1106

La Cordée opened in 1953 to outfit the Boy Scouts and Girl Guides of Québec. Now they serve just about anyone who wants the best quality outdoor equipment. Renovated and expanded in 1997, the store is the largest of its kind in Montréal, and its layout and design make it a very pleasant place to shop.

Kanuk
485 Rue Rachel Est
☎ (514) 527-4494

Kanuk makes backpacks, sleeping bags and outdoor clothing and accessories. You can buy their merchandise at their huge outlet, located right above the factory on Rue Rachel. Kanuk winter coats come in various styles and are extremely warm.

■ Public Markets

Montréal still has public markets where local farmers come to sell their produce. Imported products are also available in some of these markets.

Les Marchés Publics de Montréal
www.marchespublics-mtl.com

Marché Atwater
138 Avenue Atwater
☎ (514) 937-7754

Marché Jean Talon
7075 Rue Casgrain
☎ (514) 277-1588

Montréal - Shopping

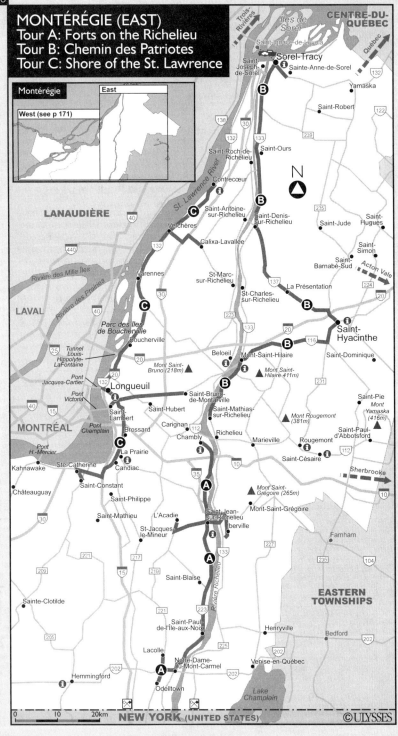

MONTÉRÉGIE (EAST)
Tour A: Forts on the Richelieu
Tour B: Chemin des Patriotes
Tour C: Shore of the St. Lawrence

Montérégie

East

West (see p 171)

CENTRE-DU-QUÉBEC

Trois-Rivières

Îles de Sorel

Québec

Saint-Ignace-de-Loyola

Sorel-Tracy

Saint-Joseph-de-Sorel

Sainte-Anne-de-Sorel

Yamaska

B

Saint-Robert

LANAUDIÈRE

St. Lawrence River

Saint-Roch-de-Richelieu

Saint-Ours

Contrecœur

N

Saint-Antoine-sur-Richelieu

C

Saint-Denis-sur-Richelieu

B

Saint-Jude

Saint-Hugues

Verchères

Calixa-Lavallée

Saint-Simon

Saint-Barnabé-Sud

Acton Vale

St-Marc-sur-Richelieu

La Présentation

Varennes

St-Charles-sur-Richelieu

B

LAVAL

Rivière des Mille Îles

C

Saint-Hyacinthe

Parc des îles de Boucherville

Boucherville

Saint-Dominique

Rivière des Prairies

Tunnel Louis-Hippolyte-LaFontaine

Mont Saint-Bruno (218m)

Beloeil

Mont-Saint-Hilaire

Mont Saint-Hilaire 411m

Pont Jacques-Cartier

Longueuil

B

Saint-Pie

Mont Yamaska (416m)

Pont Victoria

Saint-Bruno-de-Montarville

Saint-Mathias-sur-Richelieu

Mont Rougemont (381m)

Saint-Lambert

Saint-Hubert

Saint-Paul-d'Abbotsford

MONTRÉAL

Brossard

Carignan

Richelieu

Marieville

Rougemont

Pont H.-Mercier

Pont Champlain

C

Chambly

Saint-Césaire

La Prairie

Ste-Catherine

Candiac

Saint-Constant

Sherbrooke

Kahnawake

Châteauguay

Saint-Philippe

Mont Saint-Grégoire (265m)

A

Saint-Mathieu

L'Acadie

Saint-Jean-sur-Richelieu

Mont-Saint-Grégoire

St-Jacques-le-Mineur

Iberville

Farnham

A

EASTERN TOWNSHIPS

Saint-Blaise

Sainte-Clotilde

Henryville

Bedford

Saint-Paul-de-l'Île-aux-Noix

Venise-en-Québec

Lacolle

Rivière Richelieu

A

Notre-Dame-du-Mont-Carmel

Hemmingford

Odelltown

Lake Champlain

0   10   20km

NEW YORK (UNITED STATES)

©ULYSSES

Montérégie

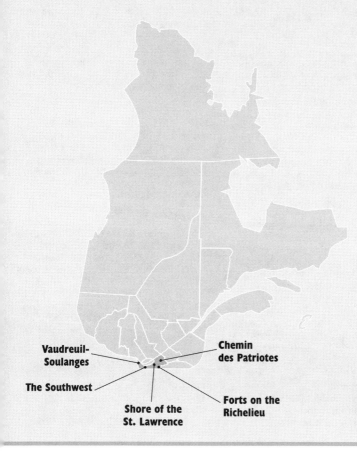

Vaudreuil-Soulanges

Chemin des Patriotes

The Southwest

Shore of the St. Lawrence

Forts on the Richelieu

Rich in history and agriculture, the Montérégie region is a beautiful plain located between Ontario, New England and the foothills of the Appalachians in the Eastern Townships. Located just south of Montréal, with many natural transportation routes, such as the majestic Rivière Richelieu, Montérégie has always played an important military and strategic role.

The seven hills in Montérégie, Mont Brome, Mont Saint-Bruno, Mont Saint-Hilaire, Mont Yamaska, Mont Rigaud, Mont Saint-Grégoire and Mont Rougemont, are the only large hills in this otherwise flat region.

The hills, which do not rise much over 400m, are spread out and were long considered ancient volcanoes. Actually, they are metamorphic rocks that did not break through the upper layer of the earth's crust and became visible as the neighbouring land eroded over a long period of time.

The many fortifications that can now be visited in the area were once outposts that served to protect the colony from the Iroquois, the British and the Americans. It was also in Montérégie that the United States experienced its first military defeat, in 1812. It was here, too, in Saint-Charles-sur-Richelieu and Saint-Denis-sur-Richelieu, that the Patriotes (French for patriots, those who supported Papineau in the Rebellion of Lower Canada) fought the British during the 1837-1838 rebellion.

Getting There and Getting Around

From the island of Montréal, the bridges across the St. Lawrence River lead to Montérégie. There are two distinct parts of this region: the Rive-Sud (south shore), a large plain punctuated by rivers south and east of Montréal, and the western point of the mainland leading from the Ontario border to the island of Montréal, bordered by Lac Saint-François and the Ottawa River. Five tours are outlined:

Tour A: Forts on the Richelieu ★★
Tour B: Chemin des Patriotes ★★
Tour C: Shore of the St. Lawrence ★
Tour D: Vaudreuil-Soulanges ★
Tour E: The Southwest ★

■ By Car

Tour A: Forts on the Richelieu

From Montréal, take the Champlain Bridge, then Aut. 10 to Chambly, on the western shore of the Rivière Richelieu, to the Boulevard Fréchette exit. From Chambly, take Rte. 223 S., then follow routes 202 and 221 to complete the tour.

Tour B: Chemin des Patriotes

From Montréal, take the Champlain Bridge, then Aut. 10 across the Rivière Richelieu, then take Rte. 133 N., also called "Chemin des patriotes." Drive along the eastern shore of the Richelieu, from St-Mathias-sur-Richelieu to Mont-St-Hilaire. From there, take Rte. 116 and then Rte. 231 to St-Hyacinthe. From there, Rte. 137 N. leads to St-Denis-sur-Richelieu and Rte. 133 to Sorel.

Tour C: Shore of the St. Lawrence

From Montréal, take the Honoré-Mercier Bridge toward La Prairie, then Rte. 132 E., the main road for this tour. When you reach Ste-Catherine, drive along the river until Contrecœur. You can also make a detour to St-Bruno-de-Montarville and Calixa-Lavallée.

Tour D: Vaudreuil-Soulanges

From Montréal, take Aut. 20 W. to Vaudreuil-Dorion, the start of the tour. By taking Rte. 342, you can reach Como, Hudson, Rigaud and Pointe-Fortune (to get to Saint-Lazare, head south from Hudson). Take either Rte. 342 or Aut. 40 to Rte. 201 to Coteau-du-Lac. From there, head east along the St. Lawrence River to Pointe-des-Cascades, then north to Île Perrot.

Tour E: The Southwest

From Montréal, cross the Honoré-Mercier Bridge and take Rte. 138 to the intersection of Rte. 132. Take Rte. 132 to St-Timothée (Salaberry-de-Valleyfield is a few kilometres further). Then go south on Rte. 132, cross the Canal de Beauharnois, and continue to Rivière Châteauguay. Drive south along the river to Ormstown, from where Rte. 201 follows Rte. 202 and will lead you through to the end of the tour.

■ Ferries

Tour A: Forts on the Richelieu

Saint-Paul-de-l'Île-aux-Noix – Île-aux-Noix
mid-May to mid-Nov
☎ (450) 291-5700

Tour B: Chemin des Patriotes

Saint-Denis-sur-Richelieu – Saint-Antoine-sur-Richelieu
mid-May to mid-Nov
☎ (450) 787-2759

Saint-Marc-sur-Richelieu – Saint-Charles-sur-Richelieu
mid-May to mid-Nov
☎ (450) 584-2813

Saint-Roch-de-Richelieu – Saint-Ours
mid-May to mid-Nov
☎ (450) 785-2161

Sorel-Tracy – Saint-Ignace-de-Loyola
year-round
☎ (450) 743-3258 or 836-4600

Tour C: Shore of the St. Lawrence

Longueuil – Île Charron
mid-May to early Oct
☎ (450) 442-9575

Longueuil – Montréal
mid-May to early Oct
☎ (514) 281-8000

Tour D: Vaudreuil-Soulanges

Hudson – Oka
mid-May to mid-Nov
☎ (450) 458-4732

■ Bus Station

Tour A: Forts on the Richelieu

Saint-Jean-sur-Richelieu
600 Boulevard Pierre-Caisse
☎ (450) 359-6024

Tour B: Chemin des Patriotes

Saint-Hyacinthe
1330 Rue Calixa-Lavallée
☎ (450) 773-3287

Sorel-Tracy
191 Rue du Roi
☎ (450) 743-4411

Tour C: Shore of the St. Lawrence

Longueuil
120 Place Charles-Lemoyne
☎ (450) 670-3422

Longueuil
RTL
(métro and bus terminal: Longueuil–Université-de-Sherbrooke métro station)
100 Place Charles-Lemoyne
☎ (450) 463-0131

■ Train Station

Tour B: Chemin des Patriotes

Saint-Hyacinthe
1450 Rue Sicotte
☎ 888-842-7245

Useful Information

■ Tourist Information

Regional Office

Tourisme Montérégie
11 chemin Marieville, Rougemont, J0L 1M0
☎ (450) 469-0069, (514) 990-4600 or 866-469-0069
🖷 (450) 469-1139
www.tourisme-monteregie.qc.ca

Tour A: Forts on the Richelieu

Office de Tourisme et des Congrès du Haut-Richelieu
31 Rue Frontenac, Saint-Jean-sur-Richelieu, J3B 7X2
☎ (450) 542-9090 or 888-781-9999
🖶 (450) 542-9091
www.tourismehautrichelieu.org

Tour B: Chemin des Patriotes

Tourisme Vallée-du-Richelieu
1080 Chemin des Patriotes Nord, Mont-Saint-Hilaire, J3H 5W1
☎ (450) 536-0395 or 888-736-0395
🖶 (450) 536-3147
www.vallee-du-richelieu.ca

Bureau de Tourisme et des Congrès de Saint-Hyacinthe
Parc des Patriotes, 2090 Rue Cherrier, Saint-Hyacinthe, J2S 8R3
☎ (450) 774-7276 or 800-849-7276
🖶 (450) 774-9000
www.tourismesainthyacinthe.qc.ca

Office de Tourisme du Bas-Richelieu
92 Chemin des Patriotes, Sorel-Tracy, J3P 2K7
☎ (450) 746-9441 or 800-474-9441
🖶 (450) 746-0447
www.tourismesoreltracyregion.qc.ca

Tour C: Shore of the St. Lawrence

Office du Tourisme de la Rive-Sud de Montréal
205 Chemin Chambly, Longueuil, J4H 3L3
☎ (450) 670-7293
🖶 (450) 670-5887

Tour D: Vaudreuil-Soulanges

Vaudreuil-Dorion
seasonal office
331 Rue Saint-Charles (Maison Valois)
☎ (450) 424-8620

Tour E: The Southwest

Office de Tourisme du Suroît
1155 Boulevard Mgr-Langlois, Salaberry-de-Valleyfield J6S 1B9
☎ (450) 377-7676 or 800-378-7648
🖶 (450) 377-3727
www.tourisme-suroit.qc.ca

Exploring

Tour A: Forts on the Richelieu
★ ★

 2 days

This tour goes from Chambly all the way to the U.S. border and gives visitors the opportunity to explore the defence network built along the Rivière Richelieu under the French Regime, which was reinforced following the British Conquest. This string of forts served to control access to the Richelieu, which, for a long time, was the main communication route between Montréal, New England and New York, via Lake Champlain and the Hudson River.

Chambly ★ ★ (pop. 20,923)

The town of Chambly occupies a privileged site alongside the Richelieu. The river widens here to form the Bassin de Chambly at the end of the rapids, which once hindered navigation on the river and made the area a key element in New France's defence system.

In 1665, the Carignan-Salières regiment, under the command of Captain Jacques de Chambly, built the first pile fort to drive back the Iroquois, who made frequent incursions into Montréal from the Mohawk River (Richelieu River). In 1672, the captain

★ **ATTRACTIONS**

1.	DX	Rue de Richelieu
2.	DX	Maison John-Yule
3.	DX	Atelier du Peintre Maurice Cullen
4.	DX	Manoir de Salaberry
5.	DX	Maison Ducharme
6.	DX	Corps de Garde (guardhouse)
7.	DX	St. Stephen Anglican Church
8.	CY	Fort Chambly National Historic Site
9.	BZ	Place de la Mairie
10.	BZ	Maison Culturelle de Chambly
11.	BZ	Église Catholique Saint-Joseph
12.	EX	Maison Thomas-Whitehead

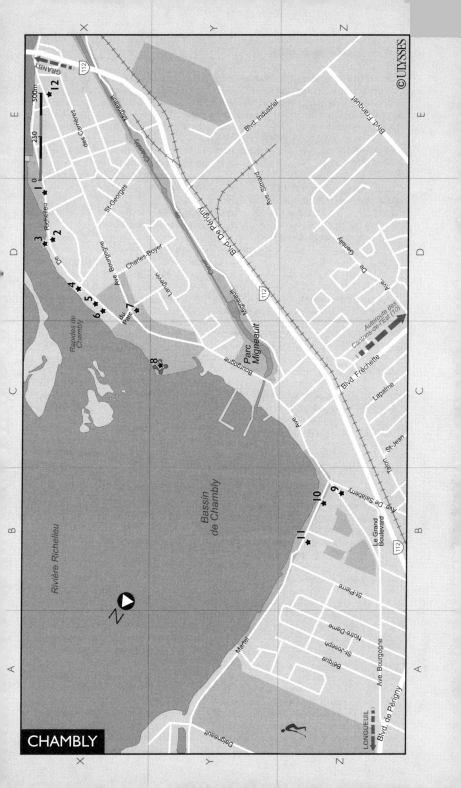

CHAMBLY

©ULYSSES

was granted a seigneury in his name for services rendered to the colony.

The town that gradually formed around the fort flourished during the War of 1812, while a sizeable British garrison was stationed there. Then, in 1843, the Canal de Chambly opened, allowing boats to bypass the Richelieu Rapids and thereby facilitating commerce between Canada and the United States.

Follow Avenue Bourgogne to the narrow **Rue de Richelieu ★**, which leads to the fort. Travel along the Parc des Rapides, where the Barrage de Chambly can be admired from up close. Imposing homes built in the first half of the 19th century line both sides of the road.

The comfortable Palladian-style house known as **Maison John-Yule** (27 Rue de Richelieu) was built in 1816. John Yule, of Scottish descent, emigrated to Canada with his brother William in the late 18th century. A few years later, William became seigneur of Chambly. John Yule prospered from his local flour and carding mills.

The **Atelier du Peintre Maurice Cullen** (28 Rue de Richelieu) was built in 1920 on the foundations of William Yule's seigneurial manor. The house served as a studio for Canadian painter Maurice Cullen (1866-1934).

Colonel Charles-Michel d'Irumberry de Salaberry is known for his decisive victory over the American Army during the War of 1812-1814. Salaberry and his wife, Julie Hertel de Rouville, were descendants of French nobility who chose to stay in Canada despite the British Conquest of 1760. They moved into the **Manoir de Salaberry** (18 Rue de Richelieu), built around 1814, in order to govern the seigneury of Chambly, one third of which belonged to them at that time. The Manoir de Salaberry is one of the most elegant properties in the region, mixing French and Palladian architectural styles.

Following the War of 1812, several military infrastructures were built in the vicinity of Fort Chambly. Many have since been demolished, while others have been renovated. This is the case with the **Maison Ducharme** (no visiting, 10 Rue de Richelieu), a former soldiers' barracks, built in 1814 and transformed into a private residence at the end of the 19th century.

The former **Corps de Garde (guardhouse)** (8 Rue de Richelieu), built in 1814, is next to the Maison Ducharme to the north. It is adorned with a wooden Palladian-style portico, the only element that truly distinguishes it from French Regime architecture. It houses an exhibit on the British presence in Chambly. At the end of Rue de Richelieu, Fort de Chambly can be seen in the middle of a park.

Turn left on Rue du Parc, and take Avenue Bourgogne to the right.

Many British people, both civilian and military, as well as American Loyalists, settled in Chambly during the first half of the 19th century. The **St. Stephen Anglican Church ★** (2004 Avenue Bourgogne) was built in 1820 to serve this community, as well as the fort's garrison. The exterior, designed by local entrepreneur François Valade, is reminiscent of the Catholic churches of that era, while its sober white interior is closer to the style of the Anglican churches of the time.

Fort Chambly National Historic Site ★★★ ($5.75; Apr to mid-Mar Wed-Sun 10am to 5pm, mid-May to late Jun every day 10am to 5pm, late Jun to early Sep every day 10am to 6pm, early Sep to mid-Oct weekends; 2 Rue de Richelieu, ☎450-658-1585, www.pc.gc.ca/fortchambly) is the largest remaining fortification of the French Regime. It was built between 1709 and 1711 according to plans drawn by engineer Josué Boisberthelot de Beaucours at the request of the marquis of Vaudreuil. The fort, defended by the Compagnies Franches de la Marine, had to protect New France against a possible British invasion. It replaced the four pile forts that had occupied this site since 1665.

At the time of the British Conquest, the fort, considered outdated, was given over to the British without a fight. It was kept in use until 1860 before being abandoned. A citizen of Chambly, Joseph-Octave Dion, took it over during the 1880s and restored it sufficiently to make it his home.

The military complex is located in a spectacular setting along the Bassin de Chambly, where the rapids begin. It is a rectangular building of rubble stone, with fortified bastions and completed by small wooden watchtowers. The interior of the fort houses an interesting interpretation centre describing the strategic importance of the Rivière Richelieu throughout history, the activities of the French garrison, the settlement of the Chambly seigneury and numerous objects found during archaeological digs, providing insight into the daily life of the inhabitants.

Place de la Mairie, built in 1912, can be found at the intersection of Avenue Bourgogne and Rue Martel. In front of it stands a bronze statue by Louis-Philippe Hébert, commemorating the hero of the battle of Châteauguay, Charles-Michel d'Irumberry de Salaberry.

Take Rue Martel, which runs along the Bassin de Chambly.

The **Maison Culturelle de Chambly** *(56 Rue Martel)*, Chambly's community centre, is located in the former convent of the Dames de la Congrégation de Notre-Dame, erected in 1885. The building, with its two-sided roof and long wooden gallery, is typical of the convents that sit imposingly in the heart of most Québec cities and towns.

The **Église Catholique Saint-Joseph** *(164 Rue Martel)* was built in 1881 from the remains of the walls of the first church (1784) after it was seriously damaged by fire. In front of the church is the last known piece of artwork by sculptor Louis-Philippe Hébert, the statue of parish priest Migneault.

Return to Rue Martel, then take Avenue Bourgogne toward Saint-Jean-sur-Richelieu.

When leaving Chambly, you'll spot a blue wooden house. The **Maison Thomas-Whitehead** *(2592 Avenue Bourgogne)* was built in 1815 for an employee of the fort barracks. Few of these wooden houses, once very popular in villages and suburbs of large cities, survived the many fires that ravaged Québec during the 19th century. A 1934 painting by Robert Pilot showing the Thomas-Whitehead home in winter (*The Blue House*, Musée des Beaux-Arts de Montréal) served as a reference during its restoration in 1985.

East of Chambly is the town of **Rougemont**. Though it is part of the Montérégie region,

we have included it in the "Orchards" tour of the **Eastern Townships** (see p 195).

Follow Rte. 223 South to Saint-Jean-sur-Richelieu.

Saint-Jean-sur-Richelieu ★ (pop. 82,400)

This industrial city was, for a long time, an important gateway into Canada from the United States, as well as an essential rest stop on the road from Montréal. Three features made this city important: its port on the Richelieu, active from the end of the 18th century onwards; its railway, the first in Canada, which linked the town to La Prairie as of 1836; and the opening of the Canal de Chambly in 1843. In the mid-19th century, many businesses in Saint-Jean-sur-Richelieu related to or dependent on these transportation routes prospered, such as pottery and earthenware manufacturers (teapots, jugs and plates were to become the region's specialties). The city's architecture reflects its industrial past, with its factories, commercial buildings, working-class areas and beautiful Victorian homes.

Saint-Jean's roots, however, are much older. It developed around Fort Saint-Jean, built in 1666. In 1775, it was attacked many times by the American rebel army, which finally had to beat a retreat upon the arrival of British troops. The fort has been rebuilt many times and was home to the Collège Militaire Royal de Saint-Jean until 1994. Today, it houses the university campus of Fort Saint-Jean. Since January 2001, Saint-Jean-sur-Richelieu, Saint-Luc, Iberville, L'Acadie and Saint-Athanase have merged to form the single municipal entity of Saint-Jean-sur-Richelieu.

Take **Rue de Richelieu**, the main commercial road, into Saint-Jean. The street was devastated by fire on two occasions during the course of its history. It was rebuilt immediately after the last fire in 1876, giving it an architectural homogeneity that is unusual in Québec.

The city's tourist attractions are located in a limited area that can be covered on foot from Rue Richelieu. Return to Rue Saint-Jacques and continue to the corner of Rue de Longueuil.

The body of the **Cathédrale Saint-Jean-L'Évangéliste** *(corner Saint-Jacques and de Lon-*

Montérégie ◾ Exploring ◾ Forts on the Richelieu

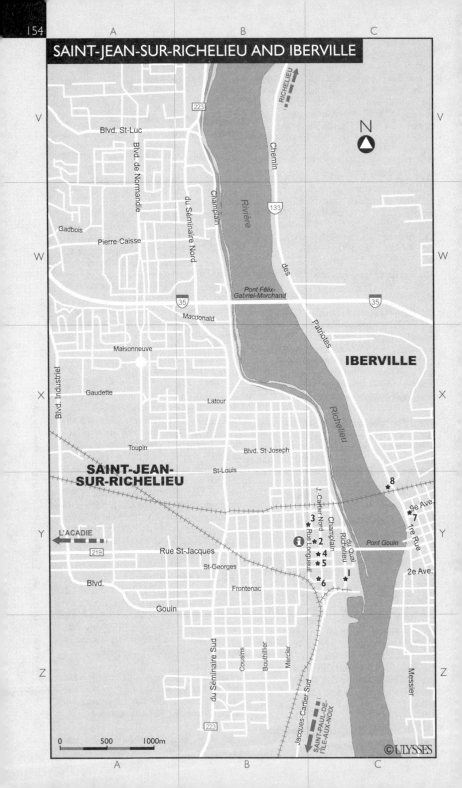

SAINT-JEAN-SUR-RICHELIEU AND IBERVILLE

Blvd. St-Luc

223

Blvd. de Normandie

du Séminaire Nord

Champlain

Chemin

RICHELIEU

Rivière

133

N

V

Gadbois

Pierre-Caisse

W

des

Pont Félix-
Gabriel-Marchand

Blvd. Industriel

35

Macdonald

35

Patriotes

Maisonneuve

IBERVILLE

Gaudette

Latour

X

Richelieu

Toupin

Blvd. St-Joseph

St-Louis

SAINT-JEAN-
SUR-RICHELIEU

8

J.-Cartier Nord

9e Ave.

3

Champlain

7

L'ACADIE

Rue Longueuil

2

du Quai Richelieu

1re Rue

219

Rue St-Jacques

i

4

5

Pont Gouin

Y

St-Georges

1

2e Ave.

Blvd.

Frontenac

6

Gouin

du Séminaire Sud

Cousins

Bouthillier

Mercier

Messier

Z

Jacques-Cartier Sud

223

SAINT-PAUL-DE-
L'ÎLE-AUX-NOIX

0   500   1000m

©ULYSSES

gueuil) dates back to 1827, but the exterior was completely redone in 1861, when the facade and the chevet were switched. The current facade, with its copper bell, dates from the early 20th century.

The neoclassical **Palais de Justice** *(109 Rue St-Charles)* is located at the north end of Rue de Longueuil, and was built in 1854 in a grey limestone that was very popular at the time.

Take Rue de Longueuil south to Place du Marché.

The **Musée du Haut-Richelieu** ★ *($4; Tue, Thu, Fri and Sun 11am to 5pm, Wed 11am to 8pm, Sat 9am to 5pm; 182 Rue Jacques-Cartier Nord, ☎450-347-0649, www.museeduhaut-richelieu. com)* is located inside the former public market, built in 1859. Apart from various objects relating to the history of *Haut-Richelieu*, the upper-Richelieu, the museum holds an interesting collection of pottery and earthenware produced in the region during the 19th century, including beautiful pieces from the Farrar and St. Johns Stone Chinaware companies.

The construction date of the bourgeois **Maison Macdonald** *(166 Rue Jacques-Cartier Nord)* is not known, but it appeared on maps for the first time in 1841. What is known, however, is that its current design is the result of the addition of a mansard roof and Second Empire styling around 1875.

St. James Church *(148 Rue Jacques-Cartier Nord, corner Rue Saint-Georges)*, built in 1817, is one of the oldest Anglican churches in Montérégie. Its American-inspired architecture reminds us that, during this period, Saint-Jean was home to a large community of Loyalist refugees from the United States.

Iberville

Across from Saint-Jean, on the other bank of the Richelieu, is Iberville, a sector that is now merged to the city of Saint-Jean-sur-le-Richelieu, and is accessible via the Gouin bridge.

This optional excursion begins at the exit from the Gouin Bridge. Turn left on 1re Rue, which runs along the Richelieu.

The Saint-Athanase-de-Bleury Catholic parish, founded in 1822, built **Église Saint-Athanase** *(500 1re Rue)*, their third church, in 1914. The presbytery, however, dates back to 1836. There is a panoramic view of Saint-Jean-sur-Richelieu from the front steps of the church.

In 1835, William Plenderleath Christie inherited the family seigneury. During the same year, he began construction on the imposing **Manoir Christie** ★ *(closed to the public; 375 1re Rue)*, done in a Georgian style and visible through the trees. It is a large stone house, whose roof is topped with an elegant lantern. The Christies only lived in their Iberville property sporadically, as they found themselves in London, then in Bath. Their former home remains one of the most evocative of the seigneurial regime.

Return toward Saint-Jean-sur-Richelieu by the Gouin Bridge then take Rue Saint-Jacques to the junction with Rte. 219 S. Follow the directions toward L'Acadie. Temporarily inland from the Richelieu shore, this other optional excursion takes you to one of the area's most charming villages.

L'Acadie ★

During the Seven Years War between France and England, Acadia (part of present-day Nova Scotia and New Brunswick) was conquered, and in 1755, the Acadians, who owned the best properties, were deported to faraway lands. Between 1764 and 1768, some of them returned from exile and established themselves on the shore of Petite Rivière. They formed "Petite Acadie," which later became the village of L'Acadie. In the early 19th century, a contingent of

Montérégie – Exploring – Forts on the Richelieu

Swiss families joined the community, settling in the locality of Grande-Ligne.

In L'Acadie, the **Église Sainte-Marguerite-de-Blairfindie** ★ ★ *(308 Chemin du Clocher)*, the presbytery and the old school are some of the most picturesque and best-kept institutional buildings in the Montérégie area. The Catholic parish of Sainte-Marguerite was canonically constituted in 1784, but it wasn't until 1801 that the present-day stone church was completed. With its Latin-cross style, twin lantern bell-tower and windows built according to the precepts of Father Conefroy, the church is a fine example of traditional Québec architecture. Note the covered passageway (1822), which shelters churchgoers from bad weather as they walk from the presbytery to the church.

The lovely wood Louis-XV-style interior decor was completed between 1802 and 1809 under the supervision of Jean-Georges Finsterer, a local artisan. In addition, the church features several paintings, including *Marie au tombeau* and *Saint René*, by Louis Dulongpré (circa 1802). The cemetery features another interesting work, a Madonna and Infant Jesus by sculptor Philippe Hébert (Monument Roy, 1897).

Several years ago, a certain Mr. Bertrand acquired the hobby of reconditioning old farm equipment. What was at first simply a hobby soon became a passion. Faced with the problem of storing his large collection of machines, he decided to buy a small farmhouse on the banks of Rivière l'Acadie. This is how the **Musée René Bertrand** *($6; late Jun to early Sep, every day 9am to 4pm, Sep and Oct, Sat and Sun 1pm to 5pm; 2864 Rte. 219,* ☎*450-346-1630)* was born. In addition to numerous ploughing implements, there is a large collection of antique objects that will stir the memories of the older generation and arouse the curiosity of the younger one. There is also a small amusement park that offers tractor rides, an excellent little restaurant that serves dishes made with old recipes, as well as a picnic area.

Take Rte. 219 N. towards Saint-Jean-sur-Richelieu, then Rte. 223 S., which follows the Richelieu River.

Saint-Paul-de-l'Île-aux-Noix (pop. 1,969)

This village is known for its fort, built on Île aux Noix (literally, island of nuts) in the middle of the Richelieu. Farmer Pierre Joudernet was the first occupant of the island, and he payed his seigneurial rent in the form of a bag of nuts, hence the island's name. Towards the end of the French Regime, the island became strategically important because of its proximity to Lake Champlain and the American colonies. The French began to fortify the island in 1759, but had such poor resources that the fort was taken by the British without difficulty. In 1775, the island became the headquarters for the American revolutionary forces, who attempted to invade Canada. Then, during the War of 1812, the reconstructed fort served as a base for the attack on Plattsburg (New York State) by the British.

Visitors must leave their cars at the information centre (61ᵉ Avenue) to take the ferry to the island.

Fort-Lennox National Historic Site ★ ★ *($3.50; &; mid-May to late Jun, Mon-Fri 10am to 5pm, Sat and Sun 10am to 6pm; late Jun to early Sep, every day 10am to 6pm, early Sep to early Oct Sat and Sun 10am to 6pm; 1 61ᵉ Avenue,* ☎*450-291-5700, www.pc.gc.ca/fortlennox)* takes up the whole of Île aux Noix. The fort, which has significantly alters the islands face on a third of its territory, was built on the ruins of previous forts between 1819 and 1829 by the British, prompting the construction of Fort Montgomery by the Americans just south of the border. Behind the wall of earth and surrounded by large ditches are a powder keg, two warehouses, the guardhouse, the officers' residence, a barracks and 17 blockhouses. This charming cut-stone ensemble is a good example of the colonial neoclassical architecture style of the British Empire.

British forces left the fort in 1870. Today, Parks Canada presents an interesting reconstitution of military life during the 19th century, as well as two exhibits on the history of the fort. Musical groups and theatre troupes take visitors back in time during **Les Beaux Dimanches au Fort Lennox**, held on Sundays in July and August.

Saint-Bernard-de-Lacolle (pop. 1,559)

The two-storey **Blockhaus de la Rivière-La-colle** ★ *(free admission; mid-May to mid-Jun and early Sep to early Oct Sat-Sun 9am to 5pm, mid-Jun to early Sep every day 9am to 5:30pm; 1 Rue Principale, ☎450-246-3227)*, a squared wooden building with loopholes, is found at the southernmost point of the Saint-Paul-de-l'Île-aux-Noix municipality. It dates back to 1782, making it one of the oldest wooden structures in Montérégie. It is also one of the few buildings of this type to survive in Québec.

From here, it is only about 10km to the American border. Although Canada-U.S. relations have been very cordial for many decades now, this was not always the case. In the late 18th century, the blockhouse acted as a sentry at the forefront of the Richelieu's river defence system. The occupants had to warn soldiers in neighbouring forts of the imminent arrival of troops from the other side of the border. During the 1930s, the blockhouse was restored by Richard Patterson, a citizen of Lacolle, who turned it into a museum dedicated to the military history of the region.

Turn right on Rte. 202 W. to connect with Aut. 15 N. Two short optional excursions can be taken to the village of Lacolle (Rte. 221 N.) and the Église d'Odelltown in Notre-Dame-du-Mont-Carmel (Rte. 221 S.).

Lacolle (pop. 2,422)

Behind the village of Lacolle is the former Napierville Junction Railway station (Canadian National), the **Gare de Lacolle**, built in 1930 in the style of a French provincial manor. As the first stop on the Canadian side of the border, the station became more important than the size of the town might have warranted.

Odelltown

This small hamlet with only a few dozen inhabitants is now part of the Notre-Dame-du-Mont-Carmel municipality. Odelltown was the scene of a decisive episode during the rebellion of 1837-38, when the Patriotes, who took refuge in the nearby United States, attempted to make a break-

through by taking the region of Lacolle by storm. They declared the area the *République du Bas-Canada* (Republic of Lower Canada). This lasted only seven days, however, since the Patriotes were forced to retreat when faced with the arrival of British troops led by Colborne.

The many Dutch Loyalist families who settled in the area became Methodists upon their arrival in Canada. The small Methodist **Odelltown Church** *(243 Rte. 221)* was built in 1823, making it one of the oldest Methodist churches in Québec.

Return to Rte. 202 W., which leads to Hwy. 15 N., toward Montréal.

Tour B: Chemin des Patriotes
★ ★

 3 days

The Vallée du Richelieu was the second area of settlement in New France, after the banks of the St. Lawrence, and many traces remain of the former seigneuries granted along the river in the 17th and 18th centuries. In the early 19th century, it was one of the most populous regions in Québec, and as such, the aftershocks of the 1837-1838 armed rebellion were keenly felt in the area. Meaningful testimonies of these events, among the most tragic in the history of Québec, are numerous throughout the valley.

Saint-Mathias-sur-Richelieu (pop. 4,266)

Saint-Mathias-sur-Richelieu was the site of significant events during the American War of Independence, as Ethan Allen and his Green Mountain Boys from Vermont took over the village in order to convince its inhabitants to join the United States. Saint-Mathias experienced a new period of intense activity during the 1837-38 rebellion, when the Patriotes' militia established their headquarters here.

The **Magasin Franchère** *(54 Chemin des Patriotes)* is the only remaining evidence of commercial activity in Saint-Mathias during the 19th century. The store was built in 1822 for brothers Joseph and Timothée Franchère. Timothée was jailed in 1838 for participating in the rebellion. The store originally housed two apartments where many Patriote meetings took place.

Noted for its outstanding interior decor and its stone cemetery enclosure, the **Église Saint-Mathias ★★** *(79 Chemin des Patriotes)* also boasts a charming exterior that reflects traditional Québec architecture. It was built in 1784 by mason François Châteauneuf.

Continue heading north along Chemin des Patriotes. The silhouette of Mont Saint-Hilaire, the highest hill in Montérégie (403m), comes into view as you approach.

Mont-Saint-Hilaire ★ (pop. 14,788)

This small town, located at the foot of Mont Saint-Hilaire, was originally part of the seigneury of Rouville, granted to Jean-Baptiste Hertel in 1694. It remained in the hands of the Hertel family until 1844, when it was sold to Major Thomas Edmund Campbell, secretary to the British governor, who ran an experimental farm that remained in operation until 1942.

Though scarred by the addition of parking lots and an ostentatious gate, the **Manoir Rouville-Campbell ★** *(25 Chemin des Patriotes Sud)* remains one of the most magnificent manor houses in Québec. It was built in 1854 by British architect Frederick Lawford, who also contributed to the interior decor of the Église de Saint-Hilaire. During the 1980s, the house and the stables were transformed into an inn (see p 180). Facing the Manoir Rouville-Campbell, stands Mont-Saint-Hilaire's **Monument aux Patriotes**.

The facade of the **Église Saint-Hilaire ★★** *(260 Chemin des Patriotes Nord)* was originally supposed to have two towers topped with spires. As a result of internal arguments, only the bases of the towers were erected in 1830, and a steeple, placed in the centre of the facade, was later installed. The interior decor, done in the Gothic Revival style, was completed over a long period of time, between 1838 and 1928. The masterpiece of this interior is the work of painter Ozias Leduc (1864-1955), and was completed at the end of the 19th century.

The presbytery (1798) is north of the church, while the **Couvent des Sœurs des Saints Noms de Jésus et de Marie**, with its odd rounded wing, is located behind the church.

The **Musée d'Art de Mont-Saint-Hilaire ★** *($4; &; Tue 10am to 8:30pm, Wed-Sat 10am to 5pm, Sun 1pm to 5pm; 150 Rue du Centre-Civique, ☎450-536-3033, www.mamsh.qc.ca)* promotes the development of contemporary visual arts and highlights the works of famous artists who have lived in Mont-Saint-Hilaire, including Ozias Leduc, Paul-Émile Borduas and Jordi Bonet.

Follow Rte. 133 N. Turn right onto Rte. 116 E. (follow the directions for the Centre de la Nature du Mont Saint-Hilaire). Take Rue Fortier to the right, which turns into Chemin Ozias-Leduc. Finally, turn right onto Montée des Trente to get to the Maison des Cultures Amérindiennes.

The goal of the **Maison des Cultures Amérindiennes ★** *($4; &; Mon-Fri 9am to 5pm, Sat-Sun 1pm to 5pm; 510 Montée des Trente, ☎450-464-2500, www.maisonamerindienne.com)* is to familiarize visitors with Québec's first inhabitants. The Abenakis called Mont Saint-Hilaire the "wigwam-shaped hill." They would climb to its summit to offer sacrifices to their divinities, but also to enjoy its wildlife, vegetation and the spectacular view of the Richelieu river below. Visitors can discover these native traditions through the Maison des Cultures Amérindiennes' many activities. The permanent exhibit explains the extraction and transformation techniques involved in making maple syrup, activities that represented not only hard work, but also a festive occasion for these first inhabitants of the region; in springtime, visitors even get to participate in the process in the maple grove adjacent to the building. Temporary exhibits present works by native artists from the area and visitors also get to taste authentic native cuisine.

The **Centre de la Nature du Mont Saint-Hilaire ★★** (see p 175).

*The tour leaves the Vallée du Richelieu for a short while in order to pass through Saint-Hyacinthe, known as the "farm-produce capital of Québec." To get there, return to Rte. 116 E. for approximately 20km. Enter the city by Rue Girouard, passing under the **Porte des Anciens Maires**, a medieval-style monument located along the Rivière Yamaska.*

Saint-Hyacinthe ★ ★
(pop. 51,402)

Saint-Hyacinthe was settled in the late 18th century, around the mills on the Rivière Yamaska and the estate of Jacques-Hyacinthe Delorme, seigneur of Maska. The surrounding fertile soil helped the town expand rapidly, attracting several religious institutions, businesses and industries. The processing and distribution of agricultural products still plays a leading role in the town's economy. Saint-Hyacinthe also has the only French-language veterinary medicine program in North America, as well as farm-produce research and insemination institutes. A large regional agricultural fair is held here every July.

The town also specializes in the construction of large pipe organs. The Casavant brothers set up their famous organ factory outside the city in 1879 *(900 Rue Girouard Est)*. Approximately 15 electro-pneumatic organs are made here every year and are installed throughout the world by the house experts. Guided tours are sometimes organized. Guilbault-Thérien organ-builders have been building mechanical traction organs since 1946 according to 18th-century French and German models *(2430 Rue Crevier)*.

Rue Girouard Ouest ★ is the main street in the upper part of Saint-Hyacinthe. This opulent residential neighbourhood reflects the success of local entrepreneurs.

Église Notre-Dame-du-Rosaire ★ *(2000 Rue Girouard Ouest)* was designed by famous architect Victor Bourgeau in 1858 to replace the previous church that had been built on the same spot in 1785. One of the original church's bells serves as a monument near the main entrance. The church is characteristic of Bourgeau's style, a hybrid of the Baroque design of the churches that were built under the French regime (consoles) and the Neoclassical style of the early 19th century (Tuscan pilasters).

The two rusticated-stone buildings that for many years housed the Saint-Hyacinthe **Bureau de Poste** (post office) *(1915 Rue Girouard Ouest)*, as well as the former **Douane** *(1995 Rue Girouard Ouest)*, or customs house, are two of the rare buildings of this type to have survived the wave of modernization that took place during the 1960s.

The buildings are now used for offices and housing.

The **Cathédrale Saint-Hyacinthe-le-Confesseur ★** *(&; 1900 Rue Girouard Ouest)* is a squat building despite its 50m-high spires. It was built in 1880 and modified in 1906 according to designs by Montréal architects Perrault and Venne. They contributed the Romanesque Revival style and interesting rococo interior.

Continue along Rue Girouard heading east.

The **Parc Casimir-Dessaulles** *(Rue Girouard Ouest at the corner of Avenue du Palais)*, named after an important mayor of Saint-Hyacinthe, was laid out in 1876 on the ruins of the seigneurial estate. It quickly became the favourite place of the local bourgeois class, who had imposing homes built near here. Today, it hosts various outdoor activities (contests, concerts, etc.). To the east is the city hall or **Hôtel de Ville** *(700 Avenue de l'Hôtel-de-Ville)*, located in the former Hôtel Yamaska, remodelled and enlarged in 1923, and to the north is the new **Palais de Justice** *(courthouse; 1550 Rue Dessaules)*.

Go to the lower part of town via Avenue Mondor. Turn right on Rue des Cascades Ouest.

Rue des Cascades ★ is the main commercial artery in Saint-Hyacinthe. It fell victim to fire in 1876, but was quickly rebuilt. The street is lined with many pleasant shops and cafés. The **Place du Marché**, demarcated in 1796 by the seigneur of Maska, can be found at number 1555. The market building (1877) remains the real heart of town, as agriculture is still the largest industry here.

The **Allée du Marché**, west of Place du Marché, is a modern reconstruction built after a devastating fire in 1970 that destroyed several dozen buildings between Rue Saint-François and Rue Sainte-Anne. Architects Courchesne and Bergeron created a multipurpose group of buildings linked by a pedestrian walkway, helping to revitalize the downtown area.

A testimony to the 19th century, the **Vieux Marché de Saint-Hyacinthe** *(1555 Rue des Cascades Ouest)* is the oldest market in Québec and the symbol of the city's farm-producing industry. Market-gardeners bring their

Montérégie ▪ Exploring - Chemin des Patriotes

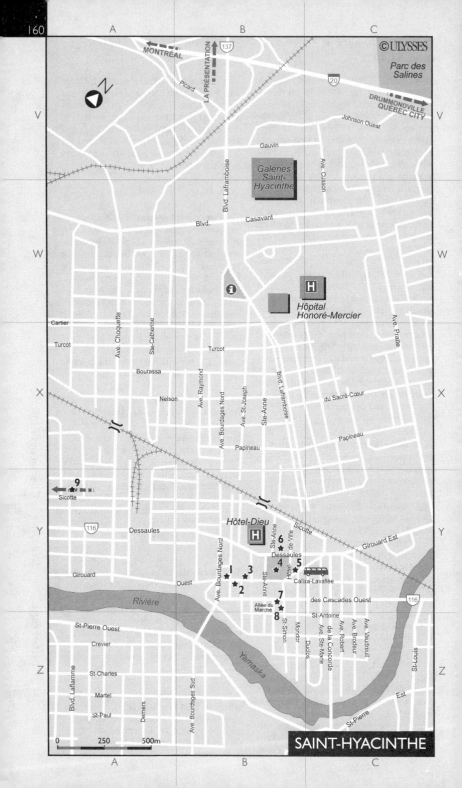

★ **ATTRACTIONS**

produce here in the summer and, inside, there are some specialty shops that are open year-round.

Expression *(year-round, Tue-Fri 10am to 5pm, Sat and Sun 1pm to 5pm; 495 Rue St-Simon, first floor,* ☎*450-773-4209, www.expression.qc.ca),* an organization whose mission is to promote contemporary art, is located above the Marché Central de Saint-Hyacinthe. The gallery, considered one of the most beautiful in Québec, hosts approximately 10 exhibitions each year.

Originally created for scholastic purposes (a practice site for landscape-management students of the Institut Agroalimentaire is just across the street), the **Jardin Daniel-A.-Séguin** ★ *($7; mid-Jun to early Sep, every day 10am to 5pm; 3215 Rue Sicotte,* ☎*450-778-6504, ext. 215, or 778-0372, www.itasth.qc.ca/jardindas/),* has been open to the public since 1995. With the help of guided tours, information panels and workshops, amateur horticulturalists can improve their knowledge to better tend their own gardens.

Continue on Rue Sicotte and turn left onto Boulevard Choquette. On Choquette, go to Boulevard Casavant Ouest and turn right. Continue to Boulevard Laframboise (Rte. 137), turn left and head to La Présentation and Saint-Denis-sur-Richelieu.

La Présentation (pop. 1,882)

The **Église de La Présentation** ★ ★ *(551 Chemin de L'Église)* is unique among other temples built in Montérégie during the same era because of its finely sculpted stone facade, completed in 1819. Note the inscriptions written in Old French above the entrances. The vast presbytery, hidden in the greenery, as well as the modest sexton house, complete this landscape typical of Québec rural parishes.

Follow Rte. 137 N. to Saint-Denis. Turn left on Chemin des Patriotes, which runs along the Richelieu (Rte. 133 S.).

Saint-Denis-sur-Richelieu ★ (pop. 2,242)

Throughout the 1830s, Saint-Denis was home to large political gatherings as well as the headquarters of the *Fils de la Liberté* (Sons of Freedom), a group of young French Canadians who wanted Lower Canada (Québec) to become an independent country. But even more important, Saint-Denis was the site of the only Patriotes victory over the British during the 1837-38 rebellion. On November 23, 1837, General Gore's troops were forced to withdraw to Sorel after a fierce battle against the Patriotes, who were poorly equipped but determined to defeat the enemy. The British troops took revenge a few weeks later, however, by surprising the inhabitants while they slept, pillaging and burning the houses, businesses and industries of Saint-Denis-sur-Richelieu.

The town of Saint-Denis, founded in 1758, experienced an intense period of industrialization in the early 19th century. Canada's largest hat industry was located here, which produced the famous beaver-pelt top hats worn by men throughout Europe and America. Other local industries in Saint-Denis included pottery and earthenware. The repression that followed the rebellion put an end to this economic expansion, and from then on, the town became a small agricultural village.

A monument was unveiled in 1913 in **Parc des Patriotes** to honour the memory of the Saint-Denis Patriotes. It is located in the middle of the square that was known as Place Royale before becoming Place du Marché, or market place, and then a public park in the early 20th century.

The **Maison Nationale des Patriotes** ★ *($6; May to late Aug Tue-Sun 10am to 5pm; Sep Tue-Fri 10 am to 6pm, Sat and Sun 1pm to 5pm; Nov Tue-Fri 10am to 4pm; 610 Chemin des Patriotes,* ☎*450-787-3623, www.mndp.qc.ca).* To the south of the park stands a former stone inn built in 1810. The building's irregular shape is characteristic of urban homes of the late

Montérégie - Exploring - Chemin des Patriotes

18th century (firebreak walls with corbels, veranda on the main floor, optimum usage of the land). It is one of the rare examples of this type found outside Montréal and Québec City.

Since 1988, the building has housed an informative interpretation centre on the 1837-38 rebellion and the history of the Patriotes. The main battles of the rebellion are described, as are the causes of these revolts, which had a great impact on the Richelieu region and the entire province of Québec. Two interesting festivals take place here: the **Fête du Vieux Marché** *(mid-Aug, Parc des Patriotes,* ☎*450-787-3939)*, a recreation of an old public market with approximately 100 craftspeople in historical costume that visitors get to see at work; and the **Commémoration de la Bataille du 23 Novembre 1837** *(third Sun of Nov;* ☎*450-787-3623)*, a popular gathering in commemoration of the 1837 Patriotes victory.

Return to Rte. 133 N. (Chemin des Patriotes) heading toward Saint-Ours.

The site of the 1837 battle at Saint-Denis is located near Rue Phaneuf, at the edge of town. The **Maison Pagé** at 553 Chemin des Patriotes was the scene of the first skirmishes between the Patriotes and the British troops. Six wounded British soldiers were treated by the young Dormicour women at the **Maison Dormicour** *(549 Chemin des Patriotes)*.

Saint-Ours (pop. 1,663)

Descendants of the Saint-Ours seigneurs still inhabit the seigneurial manor on land granted by Louis XIV in 1672 to their ancestor Pierre de Saint-Ours, captain in the Carignan-Salières regiment. The small village that neighbours the seigneur's house was once an active port on the Richelieu. The only surviving reminder of this activity is the lock, the **Écluse de Saint-Ours** *($1.50; mid-May to mid-Oct; 2930 Chemin des Patriotes,* ☎*450-785-2212)*, built in 1849, was refurbished in 1933.

Continue along Rte. 133 N. (Chemin des Patriotes) to Sorel-Tracy, where it first becomes Chemin Saint-Ours, and then Rue de la Reine.

Sorel-Tracy (pop. 34,562)

In Sorel-Tracy, the Richelieu flows into the St. Lawrence. Heavy industry and naval construction are still the town's main economic activities. Sorel got its name from Pierre de Saurel, captain of the Carignan-Salières regiment, to whom the land was granted in 1672. The town itself owes its current layout to British governor Frederick Haldimand, who wanted to make a model town populated by the British. He tried to attract American Loyalists to Sorel (once named William-Henry) in several different ways. First, the town joined the Domaine Royal in 1781, then adopted a checkerboard plan in 1783 when the streets were named in honour of members of the British royal family at that time (Augusta, Charlotte, George, etc.), and an Anglican mission was opened in 1784. Despite all this, his plan was a resounding failure.

During the 1860s, Sorel experienced phenomenal growth with the opening of several naval building sites that are still in operation. At the same time, the town adopted its original name, but changed the spelling. In 2000, it merged with the town of Tracy.

The white stucco **Maison des Gouverneurs** ★ *(90 Chemin Saint-Ours)* was built in 1781 to accommodate the Brunswick regiment's major, who was stationed in Sorel to counter the threat of an American invasion. The regiment, made up of German and Swiss mercenaries, was under the command of General von Riedesel, who immediately enlarged the house to make it more comfortable. For Christmas 1781, Riedesel and his family set up the first Christmas tree in America, in the Maison des Gouverneurs. A sculpture in the shape of a Christmas tree now stands in front of the home to commemorate the event.

From 1784 to 1860, the house served as a summer residence for the Governor Generals of Canada. During those years, it accommodated many famous people, such as Lord Dorchester, the Duke of Kent (father of Queen Victoria) and Prince William-Henry (the future William IV).

Continue along Rue de la Reine toward the downtown area.

The **Carré Royal** *(corner Charlotte and de la Reine)* is a pleasant green space in the centre of Sorel, incorrectly named "Carré Royal," an improper translation of the Royal Square. It was demarcated in 1791 and landscaped along the lines of the British Union Jack.

To the east of the square is the Anglican **Christ Church** *(79 Rue du Prince)* and its presbytery, built in the Gothic Revival style in 1842. The Sorel mission, whose foundation dates back to 1784, is the dean of the Anglican churches of Québec.

Place du Marché *(at the end of Rue de la Reine)* includes the original market (rebuilt in 1937 in the Art Deco style) in its centre, and several interesting shops and cafés on the periphery. The neighbourhood has a strange port atmosphere, with cranes, sheds and ships.

The Sorel Catholic parish was created in 1678 by Monseigneur de Laval. Construction of the **Église Saint-Pierre ★** *(170 Rue George)* began in 1826, but the building has been considerably modified over the years. Among the original elements are the cut-stone portals of the facade and, inside, the division of the nave into three vessels, supported by beautiful Corinthian pillars, an unusual sight during this era. Also of interest are the choir stalls, taken from the old Église Notre-Dame in Montréal, demolished in 1830.

An optional excursion is possible to Sainte-Anne-de-Sorel and the islands of Sorel to explore the Pays du Survenant (named after a famous Québec novel). From Rue George, take Boulevard Fiset south. Turn left onto Rue de l'Hôtel-Dieu, which becomes Rue de la Rive. Take Chemin du Chenal-du-Moine through Sainte-Anne-de-Sorel.

Sainte-Anne-de-Sorel ★ (pop. 2,758)

This village is more oriented towards hunting and fishing than other communities in Montérégie because of its proximity to the Sorel islands. Writer Germaine Guèvremont (1893-1968), who lived on one of these islands, introduced this archipelago, located in the middle of the St. Lawrence, to the literary world in her novel *Le Survenant*.

The best way to explore the **Îles de Sorel ★** is by taking one of the cruise boats that cross the archipelago of approximately 20 islands *(two types of cruises are offered: Croisière des Îles de Sorel, 1665 Chemin du Chenal-du-Moine, and canoe excursions, ☎450-743-7227 or 800-361-6420)*. The hour-and-a-half-long cruises begin at the Chenal du Moine.

The islands are an excellent place to observe aquatic birds, especially during the spring and fall. A few houses on piles with individual piers dot the flat landscape, which offers views of the vast expanse of Lac Saint-Pierre downstream. There are two restaurants at the end of the Île d'Embarras (accessible by car) that serve *gibelotte*, a fish fricassee typical of this region.

Return to Sorel-Tracy. To reach Montréal, take Rue de l'Hôtel-Dieu heading west. Turn left on Rue du Roi, then right onto Chemin Saint-Ours which leads to Aut. 30; follow it to Montréal.

Tour C: Shore of the St. Lawrence ★

 2 days

The shores of the St. Lawrence surrounding the island of Montréal have become bedroom communities of the metropolis. Once farming villages or small industrial towns, they have experienced tremendous growth over the past 40 years with the exodus of urban populations to the suburbs. In some cases, these towns have preserved their interesting urban cores where churches, museums and old houses can be found. Throughout this tour, Montréal looms across the river and can be admired from many different perspectives.

Saint-Constant (pop. 23,627)

The **Musée Ferroviaire Canadien ★★** *($12; late Jun to early Sep every day 10am to 6pm, Sep and Oct Wed-Sun 10am to 5pm, Nov to Apr Sat and Sun 10am to 5pm; 110 Rue Saint-Pierre, ☎450-632-2410, www.exporail.org)* displays an impressive collection of railway memorabilia, locomotives, freight cars and maintenance vehicles. The famous *Dorchester* locomotive, put into service in 1836 on the country's first railway, between Saint-Jean-sur-Riche-lieu and La Prairie, is worth noting, as are many luxurious passenger cars of the 19th century that belonged to Canadian Pacific. Also on display are foreign locomotives, such as the powerful *Châteaubriand* from the SNCF (French Railway System), put into service in 1884.

Return toward Sainte-Catherine. Take Boulevard Marie-Victorin east. You will travel along the St. Lawrence seaway and cross the town of Candiac before reaching La Prairie. Take Boulevard Salaberry and turn left onto Rue Desjardins, which becomes Rue Saint-Laurent in Vieux-La Prairie. Turn left on Chemin de Saint-Jean.

La Prairie ★ (pop. 19,731)

The seigneury of La Prairie was granted to the Jesuits in 1647, who turned the land into a retreat for their missionaries and a village for converted Iroquois. More and more French settlers began populating the surrounding area, forcing the Jesuits to move their mission in order to shield their protégés from the bad influence of Europeans. La Prairie's strategic location led the authorities to fortify the village in 1684. Very little remains today of the stone-and-wood enclosure that was dismantled by the Americans during the 1775 invasion.

La Prairie experienced a new era of prosperity in the early 19th century when it became an important link in the transportation route that brought merchandise to the United States, and in particular to the American port of Portland, Maine, which is ice-free during winter. A pier was built in 1835, allowing steamships linking the South Shore to Montréal to dock. The following year saw the inauguration of Canada's first railway, linking Saint-Jean-sur-Richelieu to La Prairie. Unfortunately, a fire started in a locomotive in 1846 destroyed the village and obliterated almost all traces of French Regime buildings. The event put an end to a promising future. However, the economy recovered with the opening of the brickyards and of a new working-class neighbourhood established in 1880 in the Rue Sainte-Rose area. It was called *Fort Neuf* (new fort) to distinguish it from the old fortified village.

La Prairie's first church, built in 1687, is long gone. Construction of the **Église de**

la Nativité de la Sainte Vierge ★ *(155 Chemin de Saint-Jean)* began in 1840. It has a high neoclassical facade designed by architect Victor Bourgeau, and is topped with an elegant peristyle steeple that dominates the surrounding area.

The corner building across from the church *(120 Chemin de Saint-Jean)* and the **Maison Aubin** *(150 Chemin de Saint-Jean)*, built in 1824, are good examples of the persistence of French Regime architecture following the British Conquest of 1760.

An interpretive trail across from the church leads behind the old market building (1863). In addition to the market, this brick building originally housed the fire department on the main floor and a theatre upstairs. An interesting museum dealing with the history of La Prairie, the **Musée du Vieux-Marché** *(free admission; Mon-Fri 9am to 5pm, Sat and sun 1pm to 5pm; 249 Rue Sainte-Marie, ☎450-659-1393)*, now occupies the building.

The streets of Vieux-La Prairie ★★ have an urban character rarely found in Québec villages during the 19th century. Several houses were carefully restored after the Québec government declared the area a historic district in 1975. A stroll along Saint-Ignace, Sainte-Marie, Saint-Jacques and Saint-Georges streets reveals this distinctive flavour. Some of the wood houses are reminiscent of those once found in Montréal districts *(240 and 274 Rue Saint-Jacques)*. Other homes draw their inspiration from French Regime architecture (two-sided roofs, firebreak walls, dormer windows), except for the fact that they are partially or totally built of brick instead of stone *(234 and 237 Rue Saint-Ignace, 166 Rue Saint-Georges)*. Lastly, the stone house covered with wood at number 238 Rue Saint-Ignace is the only surviving testimony of the French Regime in Vieux-La Prairie.

Return to Chemin de Saint-Jean.

At the end of the streets on the left is a square with a bandstand and a plaque commemorating the battle of La Prairie (1691), which pitted French settlers against Aboriginal peoples, who were loyal to the British army.

Return to Chemin de Saint-Jean, but take it in the opposite direction. Turn right onto Rue Saint-

Laurent, then right again onto Rue Saint-Henri. Take Aut. 15 (Rte. 132), which passes through Brossard before reaching Saint-Lambert (exit Boulevard Simard). Turn left onto Chemin Riverside (also called Riverside Drive).

Saint-Lambert

The development of Saint-Lambert was closely linked to the construction of the Victoria Bridge during the 19th century. The railway attracted a large anglophone community, which imparted a British flavour to the town. There are a few old farm houses along the St. Lawrence that have been well restored by their owners. Today, Saint-Lambert is part of the municipality of Longueuil.

The **Victoria Bridge** ★ is the oldest bridge linking the island of Montréal to the mainland. It was built with difficulty by hundreds of Irish and French-Canadian workers between 1854 and 1860 for the Grand Tronc railway company. It started out as a tubular bridge, designed by famous British engineer Robert Stephenson, known for the Menai Strait bridge in Wales. He was the son of George Stephenson, inventor of steam traction on railways. The bridge has since been modified several times, mainly to allow for automobile traffic. The only remaining original structures are the pointed pillars, for breaking up the ice. The bridge's 2,742m length was exceptional for the time—journalists called it the eighth wonder of the world!

The **Écluse de Saint-Lambert** ★ *(free admission; mid-Apr to late Sep, every day sunrise to sunset; at the trunk road of Boulevard Sir-Wilfrid-Laurier* ☎*450-672-4110)* locks are the gateway to the seaway, which begins here and ends 3,800km downstream, at the tip of the Great Lakes. The seaway allows ships to bypass the natural obstacles posed by the St. Lawrence and provides a direct route to the centre of the continent. Its opening in 1959 led to the closing of the Canal de Lachine in 1970 (it was reopened to pleasure boating in 2002) and contributed to the economic decline of southwestern Montréal.

Saint-Lambert residents are proud of the distinctly British atmosphere that permeates **Avenue Victoria** and its buildings. A good example of this is **Maison Dawson** *(581-585 Avenue Victoria)*. The surrounding streets also feature several Victorian houses, such as **Maison Terroux** *(15 Avenue Upper-Edison)*, built in 1890.

The **Musée Marsil** *($3; Tue-Fri 10am to 5pm, Sat and Sun 11am to 5pm; 349 Chemin Riverside,* ☎*450-923-6601)* presents temporary art and history exhibits, as well as an interesting collection of costumes and textiles. It is located in the Marsil house, whose stone foundation probably dates back to 1750.

Similar houses can still be seen along Chemin Riverside, buried amongst suburban cottages. At number 405, the **Maison Auclair** (circa 1750), has undergone fewer changes than the Maison Marsil, and better illustrates the humble rural architecture of the French Regime. The **Maison Mercille**, at number 789 (circa 1775), is more imposing than its neighbours of the same era. The dairy adjoining the main building has a window protected by rather ominous-looking bars called *étripe-chats* ("cat strangler") in French.

An optional excursion to the municipality of Saint-Bruno-de-Montarville further inland explores Mont Saint-Bruno, one of Montérégie's hills. To get there, take Boulevard Sir-Wilfrid-Laurier and turn left onto Chemin de la Rabastalière. If you do not want to take this excursion, continue toward Longueuil on Chemin Riverside, which turns into Rue Saint-Charles Ouest. One kilometre before arriving downtown, the road runs through overpasses leading to the Pont Jacques-Cartier, as well as a neighbourhood of modern high-rises grouped around the Longueuil-Université-de-Sherbrooke métro station.

Parc National du Mont-Saint-Bruno ★ *(330 Chemin des 25 Est)*, see p 175.

Longueuil ★ (pop. 380,580)

Since 2002, the new merged city of Longueuil comprises eight former municipalities: Boucherville, Brossard, Greenfield Park, Saint-Bruno-de-Montarville, Saint-Hubert, Saint-Lambert, Le Moyne and the old city of Longueuil (now known as the borough of Vieux-Longueuil).

Located across from Montréal, the old city of Longueuil is the most populous city in Montérégie. It once belonged to the Longueuil seigneury, granted to Charles Le

Montérégie – **Exploring** – Shore of the St. Lawrence

★ ATTRACTIONS

1.	CZ	Town hall
2.	CZ	Église Cathédrale Saint-Antoine-de-Padoue
3.	CZ	Maison Rollin-Brais

4.	CZ	Couvent des Sœurs des Saints-Noms-de-Jésus-et-de-Marie
5.	CZ	Maison Labadie

Moyne (1624-1685) in 1657. He headed a dynasty that played a key role in developing New France. Many of his 14 children are famous, such as Pierre Le Moyne d'Iberville (1661-1706), first governor of Louisiana, Jean-Baptiste Le Moyne de Bienville (1680-1768), founder of New Orleans, and Antoine Le Moyne de Châteauguay (1683-1747), governor of Guyana.

The oldest son, Charles Le Moyne de Longueuil, inherited the seigneury upon the death of his father. Between 1685 and 1690, he had a fortified castle built on the site of the current Église Saint-Antoine-de-Padoue. The castle had four corner towers, a church and many wings. In 1700, Longueuil was raised to the rank of baron by Louis XIV, the only such case in the history of New France. The baron of Longueuil saw to the development of his land, which continued to expand until it reached the banks of the Richelieu.

Longueuil experienced continuous growth during the 19th century with the introduction of the railway (1846) and the arrival of many summer vacationers who built beautiful villas along the river banks. At the beginning of the 20th century, the town welcomed a small Pratt and Whitney factory, which created an important industrial centre specializing in engineering and airplane technology. The construction of the Jacques-Cartier Bridge between Montréal and the south shore, inaugurated during the 1930s, made Longueuil one of Montréal's first suburbs.

Rue Saint-Charles is Longueuil's main commercial artery. Many lovely cafés and restaurants can be found east of the **town hall** *(300 Rue Saint-Charles Ouest)*. Near the Catholic church, the former **Foyer Saint-Antoine des Sœurs Grises**, designed in 1877 by Victor Bourgeau, now houses artistic and social organizations.

The site of the **Cathédrale Saint-Antoine-de-Padoue** ★★ *(55 Rue Ste-Elizabeth)* was once occupied by a 17th-century castle known as the Château de Longueuil. After being besieged by American rebels during the 1775 invasion, it was requisitioned by the British army. A fire broke out while a garrison was stationed here in 1792, destroying a good part of the building. In 1810, the ruins were used as a quarry during the building of a second Catholic church. A few years later, Rue Saint-Charles was built right through the rest of the site, forcing the complete destruction of this unique North American building. Archaeological excavations took place during the 1970s, tracing the castle's exact site and unearthing part of its foundations, visible to the east of the church.

The 1810 church was demolished in 1884 to make room for the present building, the largest church in Montérégie. The exterior is inspired by flamboyant Gothic art, but remains close to Victorian eclecticism.

The Office du Tourisme de la Rive-Sud de Montréal Longueuil (the tourism office for the south shore of Montréal) is located in the **Maison Rollin-Brais** *(205 Chemin de Chambly)*, an 18th-century stone house. Throughout its history, the house has accommodated an inn and a forge.

The **Couvent des Sœurs des Saints-Noms-de-Jésus-et-de-Marie** ★ *(tours by appointment; 80 Rue Saint-Charles Est, ☎450-651-8104)*, has been beautifully restored and is still inhabited by the Saints-Noms-de-Jésus-et-de-Marie nuns, a religious community founded in Longueuil in 1843 by the blessed Mother Marie-Rose. The building includes a residence built in 1769, but the main construction work was carried out between 1844 and 1851.

East of the convent is the **Maison Labadie** *(90 Rue Saint-Charles Est)*, built in 1812 on land that was once part of the seigneurial estate. The Saints-Noms-de-Jésus-et-de-Marie religious order, devoted to the education of young girls, was founded in this house. The neighbouring house *(100 Rue Saint-Charles Est)* was built in 1749.

Continue heading east towards Boucherville along Rue Saint-Charles Est, which becomes Boulevard Marie-Victorin. Breathtaking views of the Jacques-Cartier Bridge can be seen along the way.

Boucherville ★

Unlike many seigneuries in New France that were granted to servicemen or tradesmen, the Boucherville seigneury was handed over by Intendant Talon to a settler from Trois-Rivières, Pierre Boucher, in 1672. Rather than speculate or use it as a hunting reserve, Boucher made sustained efforts to develop his seigneury, an act that earned him a title of nobility from the king. By the end of the 17th century, Boucherville already consisted of a fortified village, a couple of mills and a church. Few buildings of this period survived the major fire of 1843 that destroyed a large part of the town. The seigneury of Boucherville remained in the hands of the Boucher family until the abolition of the seigneurial regime in 1854. The town is now part of Longueuil.

Parc National des Îles-de-Boucherville, see p 175.

Like its two neighbours, the **Maison Louis-Hippolyte-La Fontaine** *(free admission; Thu, Sat and Sun 1pm to 5pm; 314 Boulevard Marie-Victorin, ☎450-449-8347)* was moved to the Parc de la Brocquerie in 1964. It had previously been located in the heart of the village of Boucherville. Louis-Hippolyte Lafontaine, an ardent defender of French Canadians and Prime Minister of United Canada in 1842 and from 1848 to 1850, grew up here. The building, whose construction dates back to 1766, now houses an exhibition centre with a section dedicated to the house's history.

The **Manoir de Boucherville** ★ *(468 Boulevard Marie-Victorin)* is one of the rare manors dating back to the French Regime to have survived in the Montréal area. The large stone house was built in 1741 for François-Pierre Boucher, the third seigneur of Boucherville. The Boucher family lived in the manor until the end of the 19th century.

The harmonious ensemble of the **Église Sainte-Famille** ★★ *(560 Boulevard Marie-Victorin)*, the convent (1890) and the presbytery (1896), surrounds a public square, created during the 17th century. The church is an important piece of vernacular architectural work in Québec. It was built in 1801, according to plans by parish priest Pierre Conefroy. He was not content with sketching the outlines, so he drew up a detailed plan. Thus the Boucherville church, with three portals at the front and its large Latin-cross layout, served as a model for religious architecture in Québec villages up until 1830. Damaged by fire in 1843, it was restored the same year.

Montérégie – Exploring – Shore of the St. Lawrence

Varennes ★ (pop. 20,369)

For a long time, this town was a small, isolated agricultural community specializing in market gardening. Since the 1950s, however, many chemical and petroleum industries have moved in just east of the old part of town. Hydro-Québec also opened a research centre here in 1967, known as IREQ.

Located at the entrance to the old village, the wooden **Calvary** *(2511 Rue Sainte-Anne)* is one of the oldest monuments of this type to survive in Québec. In 1829, the current cross replaced the 18th-century cross, though some of the original statues were salvaged.

The **Basilique** and **Chapelles Votives** ★ *(Rue Sainte-Anne)*, or votive chapels, serve mainly as altars of repose during Corpus Christi processions. At one time, many of them lined the roads of Québec, but several disappeared following a decline in religion. The chapels in Varennes are still visited by pilgrims and are open for worship during the summer. The oldest one, in neoclassical style, was built in 1832 to replace a building from the early 18th century. The second one was erected in 1862 according to plans by Victor Bourgeau in the Gothic Revival style, identifiable by its spire and pointed arches. It has very elaborate ornamentation for this type of building. The vast Romanesque Revival–style church that dominates the village was elevated to the rank of minor basilica by Rome in 1993. Beyond its high facade with two steeples, visitors will discover a richly decorated interior.

Verchères (pop. 4,849)

In 1692, heroine Madeleine de Verchères took charge of the pile fort and village, defending it against Iroquois attacks from all sides. News of her brilliant victory resonated throughout the colony and lifted the settlers' spirits during a time of war and food shortages. Afterward, the town of Verchères developed slowly, following the ups and downs of the harvest. However, like Varennes, it has experienced massive industrialization over the past few decades.

Up until the mid-19th century, Verchères boasted seven mills (*moulins*) to grind its grain. Today, only two remain, including the **mill** on Rue Madeleine, built in 1730 and transformed by the municipality into an exhibition centre. It served as a lighthouse from 1913 to 1949, which explains its appearance.

The imposing **Monument à la Mémoire de Madeleine de Verchères**, cast in bronze by Louis-Philippe Hébert, proudly stands facing the river beside the mill, commemorating the town's heroine. The statue is a testimony to the feelings of Verchères residents for this frail but courageous adolescent of the 17th century who has become an almost mythic figure over the years.

The **Église Saint-François-Xavier** *(Rue Madeleine)* was built in 1787 on the site of the first church (1724). The facade was updated in the late 19th century, giving it a Romanesque Revival style. The interior, decorated by Louis-Amable Quévillon, is more interesting, including the flat-bottomed chancel with a flat backdrop and adorned with a triumphal arch (1808), as well as French paintings from the 18th century, sold off by Parisian churches during the French Revolution.

Calixa-Lavallée (pop. 492)

Near Verchères is this town that was named after musician Calixa Lavallée (1842-1891), the composer of Canada's national anthem.

Contrecœur (pop. 5,305)

Steel industry giants like Sidbec-Dosco haunt the landscape of this town located in the heart of the "steel region." The downtown area has luckily managed to preserve some interesting rural buildings.

Maison Lenoblet-duPlessis *(free admission; late Jun to early Sep, every day 10am to 7pm; 4752 Boulevard Marie-Victorin, ☎450-587-5750 or 587-5988)* is a 1794 house that was extensively transformed in the late 19th century to give it a Victorian feeling. For a long time it belonged to lawyer Alexis Le Noblet-du-Plessis (1780-1840). He welcomed Patriotes during many secret meetings, which led to the armed rebellion of 1837-38. Today the house is municipal property and accommodates a museum that retraces the history of both the building and the town. It is located in the middle of the pretty **Parc Cartier-Richard**, where a walkway and lookout provide great views of the St. Lawrence.

To reach Montréal, take Aut. 30, then head towards the Pont-Tunnel Louis-Hippolyte-LaFontaine, Pont Jacques-Cartier or Pont Champlain. On the way, you can stop at the Hydro-Québec Électrium, located inside the city limits of Sainte-Julie (Exit 128).

Hydro-Québec's **Électrium** ★ *(free admission; early Jun to late Aug, every day 9:30am to 4pm; rest of the year, Mon-Fri 9:30am to 4pm and Sun 1pm to 4pm; Aut. 30, Exit 128; ☎450-652-8977 or 800-267-4558)* is especially interesting for younger visitors. It offers interactive games, as well as examples of the various uses for electricity.

Tour D: Vaudreuil-Soulanges
★

 1 day

This region forms a triangular point of land isolated from the rest of Montérégie. It is demarcated to the west by the Ontario border, to the north and east by the Ottawa River, the beautiful Lac des Deux-Montagnes and Lac Saint-Louis, both areas known for excellent water sports, and lastly, to the south, by the St. Lawrence, which widens here to form Lac Saint-François. Don't be surprised if you hear the name Suroît mentioned—the region is sometimes referred to by this name for a wind from the southwest.

Vaudreuil-Dorion (pop. 21,176)

The western tip of the region was once part of the network of old seigneuries under the French Regime. As a result, it was considered part of Québec rather than the neighbouring province of Ontario during the creation of Upper and Lower Canada (1791). The seigneuries of Vaudreuil and Soulanges, granted in 1702, developed with difficulty since they were located upstream from the impassable Lachine Rapids. Thus, despite its proximity to Montréal, the area was sparsely populated until the end of the 18th century.

The **Maison Trestler** ★ *($3.50; Mon-Fri 10am to 4pm, Sun 1pm to 4pm; concerts Wed 8pm in summer; 85 Chemin de la Commune, ☎450-455-6290, www.trestler.qc.ca)* is ideally located on the shores of Lac des Deux-Montagnes. This unusual stone house is 44m long and was built in stages between 1798 and 1806. The owner of the house, Jean-Joseph Trestler, a mercenary in the Hesse-Hanau regiment, arrived in Canada in 1776. Ten years later, he settled in Dorion and became involved in the fur trade. In 1976 the house was partially converted into a cultural centre by the current owners. Concerts and conferences are now held here, and it also features a tearoom.

Return to Boulevard Saint-Henri. Turn right in the direction of Vaudreuil, where the road becomes Avenue Saint-Charles.

Built between 1783 and 1789, the **Église Saint-Michel** ★★ *(14 Avenue St-Charles)* was given a new Gothic Revival–style facade in 1856 in an effort to modernize it. The Latin-cross layout and apse with cut-off corners are similar to the first churches of the French Regime. The most complete collection of liturgical furniture sculpted by Philippe Liébert in the 18th century (pulpit, high altar, candelabra, statues) is located inside. Also of particular note, because they were eliminated from most other Québec churches during the restorations that took place in the 1960s, are the seigneurial bench and the polychromatic decor painted in trompe-l'œil by F. E. Meloche in 1883.

The **Musée Régional de Vaudreuil-Soulanges** ★ *($5, free admission on Fri nights; Mon-Fri 9:30am to 4:30pm, Tue also 7pm to 9:30pm, Sat and Sun 1pm to 4:30pm; 431 Avenue St-Charles, ☎450-455-2092)*, founded in 1953, is one of Québec's oldest regional museums, and a testimony to Vaudreuil's cultural vitality at the time. It is located in the former Collège Saint-Michel (1857), once run by the clerics of Saint-Viateur. The beautiful building, covered with a mansard roof, houses collections of everyday items, craft tools from the 18th and 19th century, as well as interesting religious art, antique paintings and carvings.

Continue along Avenue Saint-Charles towards Vaudreuil-sur-le-Lac. You will follow the shore of Lac des Deux Montagnes to Hudson.

Hudson ★ (pop. 4,960)

Hudson is a lovely, mostly English-speaking town. Its well-off residents live in comfortable homes, both modern and old. Whatever the season, exploring this small New England-style town, with its many shops, charming little restaurants and small, tree-lined streets, is a pleasure.

On Saturdays from spring to the end of October, don't miss **Finnegan's Market** *(775 Main Road, ☎450-458-4377)*, a bustling market in a mostly outdoor setting. Antiques, crafts, and plants are among the items on offer—a real "country-style" market rather than a flea market.

Rigaud (pop. 6,319)

The sons of the Marquis of Vaudreuil were granted the Rigaud seigneury in 1732. However, the village did not develop until after the arrival of the clerics of Saint-Viateur, who opened **Collège Bourget** in 1850. In addition to its educational vocation, Rigaud welcomes pilgrims to its hilltop sanctuary.

Follow Rue Saint-Jean-Baptiste (Rte. 342). Turn left onto Rue Saint-Pierre. Follow the directions to the sanctuary.

The **Sanctuaire Notre-Dame-de-Lourdes** ★ *(early Jun to late Sep, every day 9am to 5pm; 20 Rue de Lourdes, ☎450-451-4631)* was founded when, suffering from illness in 1874, Brother Ludger Pauzé carved a small hole in a rock and placed a statuette of the Virgin Mary there as a demonstration on his faith. And so, worship of Mary began in Rigaud. First, an eight-sided chapel, from which visitors can enjoy a beautiful view of the region, was built in 1887. Later, various additions were made so that outdoor celebrations could be organized for large crowds. These included a new chapel, where mass has been celebrated since 1954. Not far from the sanctuary is a strange pile of stones left on this site after the ebb of the Champlain Sea during glaciation. Legend has it that this bed of stones was once a potato field and God, appalled to see its owner working on a Sunday, changed it to a field of stones now known as "devil's field."

Head back onto Aut. 40 E. until Rte. 201 S., which will take you to Coteau-du-Lac.

Coteau-du-Lac ★ (pop. 5,882)

A narrowing of the river combined with a series of rapids makes sailing impossible here; the St. Lawrence reaches its lowest level after a change in altitude of 25m over just 12.8km. Coteau-du-Lac therefore became a rallying and portage point even before the arrival of the Europeans. Many vestiges of Aboriginal civilization have been found here, namely three skeletons including 6,000 years old. At the end of the French Regime (1759), authorities set up a sort of channel at the end of a small point, a simple reinforced dyke made with piles of rocks and parallel to the shore. Through this first canal, boatmen pulled flat-bottomed boats filled with furs. In 1779, the British constructed the first lock in North America here. A fort built by military engineer William Twiss was added to the canal in 1812.

Relics of the British and French canals can be seen from the **Coteau-du-Lac National Historic Site** ★ *($4; mid-May to early Sep, Wed-Sun 10am to 5pm; early Sep to mid-Oct, weekends 10am to 5pm, closed on holidays except July 1st; 308A Chemin du Fleuve, ☎450-763-5631, www.pc.gc.ca)*, as can ruins of the fort erected to defend this important passageway. Visitors first reach the welcome centre, where an instructive model fort recreates the area at the peak of its activity. Then, a trail through the site provides a closer look at the ruins of the facilities, as well as an outdoor reconstruction of the blockhouse, built by the British at the end of the point. There is also a beautiful view of the St. Lawrence rapids from here.

Return to Chemin du Fleuve heading east (towards Les Cèdres and Pointe-des-Cascades). Three kilometres from Coteau-du-Lac, a hydroelectric power station designed to resemble a German castle can be seen to the left, set back from the road; it has now been transformed into a residence (not open to the public). This rare building, erected in 1899, supplied electricity to the Canal de Soulanges facility. The canal stretches along the north bank of the river between Coteau-Landing and Pointe-des-Cascades.

Follow Chemin du Fleuve to Pointe-des-Cascades. Turn left onto Rue Centrale, then make an immediate right onto Chemin du Canal.

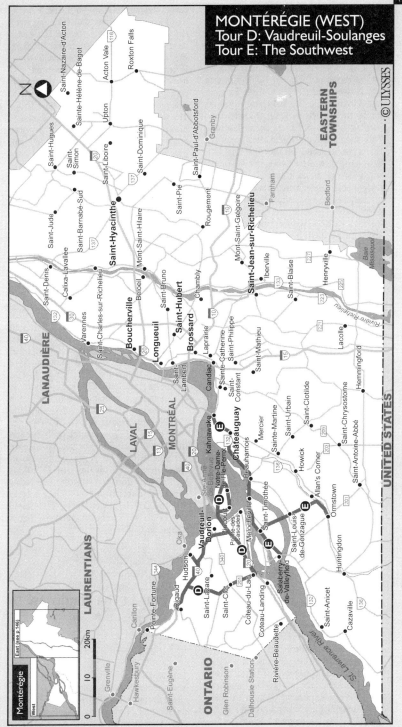

MONTÉRÉGIE (WEST)
Tour D: Vaudreuil-Soulanges
Tour E: The Southwest

© ULYSSES

Pointe-des-Cascades (pop. 952)

Located at the mouth of the Ottawa River, this town owes its existence to the Canal de Soulanges, which is now closed. Pointe-des-Cascades was visited as early as 1684 by the Baron of Lahontan, while a bloody war between the French and the Iroquois raged in the area. The first channel was set up by the French in 1749, followed by a small lock in 1805, named Canal Cascades. This canal and the Canal de Coteau-du-Lac were replaced by the first Canal de Beauharnois, which opened in 1845 on the south side of the St. Lawrence. The Canal de Soulanges, set up on the site of the Canal Cascades, succeeded the Canal de Beauharnois in 1899; it ceased operating when the St. Lawrence Seaway opened (current Canal de Beauharnois) in 1959.

The **Théâtre des Cascades** *(at the eastern trunk road of Chemin du Canal;* ☎450-455-8855 or 866-494-8855*)*, a summer theatre in a lumber warehouse, now occupies the former command station of the Canal de Soulanges at the **Pointe des Cascades** ★. Beautiful brick buildings designed by engineer Thomas Monroe in 1900 can be seen throughout the site, as can two lighthouses and three of the five locks. There are also lovely views of the Ottawa River, Lac Saint-Louis and Île Perrot from the entrance of the canal. There is a campground on site.

Return to Rue Centrale. Turn right onto Rte. 338 E., then right again onto Aut. 20. Cross the bridge over the Ottawa River to Île Perrot (Exit Boulevard Don Quichotte). Follow Boulevard Perrot and turn left onto Boulevard Don Quichotte.

Notre-Dame-de-l'Île-Perrot (pop. 8,964)

In 1672, the seigneury of Île Perrot was granted to the governor of Montréal, François-Marie Perrot, who set up a fur-trading post at the fief of Brucy. The seigneury then passed onto the hands of Charles Le Moyne, before being sold in 1703 to Joseph Trottier Desruisseaux, who set up a farm on the point near the mill. His widow began construction of Île Perrot's first church in 1740. Because it is closer to Montréal and not cut off by the rapids that hamper river traffic, the seigneury of Île Perrot experienced more extensive development than other lands in the area granted under the French Regime.

Parc Historique de la Pointe-du-Moulin ★ *(week-days $3, weekends $5; mid-May to late Aug, every day 9am to 8pm; late Aug to mid-Oct week-ends noon to 5pm; 2500 Boulevard Don Quichotte,* ☎514-453-5936, *www.pointedumoulin.com).* Beyond the modern reception area, visitors can reach the wooded park, which on clear days provides beautiful views of downtown Montréal across Lac Saint-Louis. The windmill, built in 1708, and the miller's house are located at the end of the point. Guides explain how the mill works (it is still in working order today), and the history of the area. A heritage information centre and picnic areas are also set up on site.

Return to Boulevard Perrot. Turn left, then left again onto Rue de l'Église.

The **Église Sainte-Jeanne-de-Chantal** ★★ *(1 Rue de l'Église)* is often described as the perfect example of a French-Canadian church in the Montréal region. In fact, its modest dimensions, reminiscent of the first churches of the French Regime, as well as its interior decor in the Louis XV and Louis XVI styles, make the church an excellent example of traditional Québec architecture. The building was completed in 1786, and embellished between 1812 and 1830 under the direction of Joseph Turcault and Louis-Xavier Leprohon. A commemorative chapel, with its back to the river, was built in 1953, using the stones from the first church of Pointe-du-Moulin (1753). The chapel walls contain Intendant Hocquart's plaque, which gave the seigneur of Île Perrot permission to establish a parish on this land (1740), as well as strange red sandstone mascarons (masks) brought over from France around 1945 by Colonel Roger Maillet. The chapel towers above a terraced cemetery that is unique in Québec.

Return to Montréal via Aut. 20.

- -

Tour E: The Southwest ★

 1½ days

This tour covers the southwestern part of Montérégie. It winds through the region along the shores of Lac Saint-Louis, through the foothills of the Appalachians along the New York State border and into the valley of the Rivière Châteauguay. The southwest is an agricultural region, perfect for autumn strolls, fruit-picking and market-going. The old seigneuries established along the lake and the Rivière Chateauguay are mostly French-speaking, while the townships that developed in the interior at the beginning of the 19th century are still mostly English-speaking.

Kahnawake (pop. 7,768)

In 1667, the Jesuits set up a mission for the converted Iroquois at La Prairie. After moving four times, the mission settled permanently in Sault-Saint-Louis in 1716. The Saint-François-Xavier mission has now become Kahnawake, a name that means "where the rapids are." Over the years, Iroquois Mohawks from the State of New York joined the mission's first inhabitants, so English is now the first language on the reserve, even though most inhabitants still use the French names given to them by the Jesuits.

Here you will find the **Enceinte**, **Musée** and **Église Saint-François-Xavier** ★★ *(Main St.)*, or the Saint-François-Xavier wall, museum and church. Villages and missions were required under the French Regime to surround themselves with fortifications. Very few of these walls have survived. The wall of the Kahnawake mission, still partially standing, is the kind of ruin rarely found north of Mexico. It was built in 1720 according to plans of the King's engineer, Gaspard Chaussegros de Léry, to protect the church and the Jesuit convent, built in 1717. The guardroom, powder magazine and officers' residences (1754) are also still standing.

The church was modified in 1845 according to the plans of Jesuit Félix Martin, and redecorated by Vincent Chartrand (1845-47), who also made some of the furniture. Guido Nincheri designed the polychromatic vaulted ceiling in the 20th century. Also found here is the tomb of Kateri Tekakwitha, a young Aboriginal. The convent houses the museum of the Saint-François-Xavier mission, where visitors can see some of the objects that belonged to the Jesuits, who still lead the parish.

Take Chemin Saint-Bernard towards Châteauguay (near the metallic cross and the school).

Turn left onto Chemin Christ-Roi (after the water-purification plant), then right onto Rue Dupont. Turn left onto Boulevard Salaberry Nord, follow the Rivière Châteauguay until the Pont Laberge. Cross the bridge to get to the Église Saint-Joachim. Turn right onto Boulevard D'Youville behind the church, where the parking lot is located.

Châteauguay (pop. 41,994)

The Châteauguay seigneury was granted to Charles Le Moyne in 1673. He immediately had Château de Guay built on Île Saint-Bernard, at the mouth of the Rivière Châteauguay. One hundred years later, a village stood around the Église Saint-Joachim. The roads and boulevards that run along the river and Lac Saint-Louis are still dotted with pretty farmhouses built between 1780 and 1840, when the seigneury belonged to the Sœurs Grises (the Grey Nuns).

When the first church in Châteauguay was built in 1735, it was the westernmost parish on the south shore of the St. Lawrence. Work on the present **Église Saint-Joachim** ★★ *(Boulevard D'Youville)* began in 1775 in order to better serve a growing number of parishioners. The **Hôtel de Ville** neighbours the church to the north. It is located in the former convent of the Congrégation de Notre-Dame (1886).

Continue along Boulevard D'Youville and travel along the Châteauguay river to Lac Saint-Louis.

Île Saint-Bernard, which still belongs to the Sœurs Grises, can be seen on the right; it is not open to visitors. The large stone house sitting on the shore is the seigneurial estate, the **Manoir D'Youville**, built by the nuns in 1774 on the site of the Château de Guay.

Chemin du Lac-Saint-Louis joins Rte. 132 W. at Maple Grove. Follow this road toward Beauharnois.

Beauharnois (pop. 11,722)

The seigneury of Villechauve was granted to the Marquis of Beauharnois, 15th governor of New France, in 1729. At the end of the 18th century, tradesman Alexander Ellice announced his intention to purchase it. He then had a saw mill built on the Rivière Saint-Louis, vestiges of which still remain.

Montérégie – Exploring – The Southwest

In 1863, the Kilgour family opened a large furniture factory in Beauharnois, turning the village into a small industrial city. The large brick buildings still dominate the river's west bank.

The **Église Saint-Clément** ★ *(at the top of the hill on Chemin Saint-Louis)* is very picturesque when seen from the Rivière Saint-Louis. Its Romanesque Revival–style facade, attributed to Victor Bourgeau, is built in front of a simple nave, completed in 1845.

Melocheville (pop. 2,366)

The locks that control the Beauharnois canal and hydroelectric station (the third most important in Québec) are located here.

The **Centrale Hydroélectrique de Beauharnois** ★★ *(free admission; mid-May to early Sep, every day; tours at 9:30am, 11:15am, 1pm, 2:45pm; 80 Boulevard Edgar-Hébert, ☎800-365-5229)* was once the jewel of the large Montréal Light, Heat and Power Company, owned by the uncompromising Sir Herbert Holt. Built in stages between 1929 and 1956, the power plant is a sprawling 864m long. The electricity produced in Beauharnois is distributed throughout Québec and to the United States during the summer, when local demands are not as high. The power plant now belongs to Hydro-Québec. It is open to visitors; guided tours include the very long turbine room, as well as the computers used in the control room.

Rte. 132 runs in front of the power plant before disappearing under the Canal de Beauharnois, opened in 1959. It is the last in a series of canals set up along the St. Lawrence. The canals are used to bypass the many rapids found in the area, and resolve the navigational problem posed by a 25m drop between Lac Saint-Louis and Lac Saint-François.

The **Parc Archéologique de la Pointe-du-Buisson** ★ *($4; mid-May to early Sep; ☎450-429-7857)*. The Buisson headland was inhabited sporadically for thousands of years by Aboriginals, leaving the area rich with artifacts (arrowheads, cooking pots, harpoons, etc). During the summer, different areas of the archaeological park can be visited, such as the excavation site, active since 1977, the information centre and the reconstructed

prehistoric fishing camp. Nature paths and picnic areas are also found here.

The **Parc Régional des Îles de Saint-Timothée**, see p 176.

Take Aut. 30 E. to Salaberry-de-Valleyfield.

Salaberry-de-Valleyfield (pop. 39,829)

This industrial city came into being in 1845 around a saw and paper mill purchased a few years later by the Montréal Cotton Company. This growing industry led to an era of prosperity in the late 19th century in Salaberry-de-Valleyfield, making it one of Québec's main cities at the time. The old commercial and institutional centre on Rue Victoria recalls this prosperous period, and gives the city more of an urban atmosphere than Châteauguay, whose population is higher. The city is cut in half by the old Canal de Beauharnois, in operation from 1845 to 1900 (not to be confused with the current Canal de Beauharnois located south of the city).

A diocese since 1892, Salaberry-de-Valleyfield was graced with the current **Cathédrale Sainte-Cécile** ★ *(31 Rue de la Fabrique)* in 1934, following a fire in the previous church. The cathedral is a colossal piece of work. Architect Henri Labelle designed it in the late Gothic Revival style, narrower and closer to the historical models, added with elements of Art Deco. The facade is adorned with a statue of Sainte Cécile, patron saint of musicians, and the bronze entrance doors are decorated with many bas-reliefs done by Albert Gilles, depicting the life of Jesus.

The Pont Monseigneur-Langlois, west of Salaberry-de-Valleyfield, connects the Southwest tour to the Vaudreuil-Soulanges tour. To continue on the Southwest tour, return to Saint-Timothée. Turn right and head towards the village of Saint-Louis-de-Gonzague to get to the banks of the Rivière Châteauguay.

The **Battle of the Châteauguay National Historic Site** ★ *($4; ♿; mid-May to late Aug, Wed-Sun 10am to 5pm; late Aug to mid-Oct, Sat and Sun 10am to 5pm; closed on holidays except Jul 1st; 2371 Chemin Rivière-Châteauguay Nord, ☎450-829-2003, www.pc.gc.ca)*. During the U.S. War of Independence (1775-76), the

Americans attempted their first takeover of Canada, a British colony since 1760. They were forced back by the majority French population. In 1812-13, the Americans tried once again to take over Canada. This time, it was loyalty to the Crown of England and the decisive battle of Châteauguay that bungled the Americans' attempt. In October 1813, the 2,000 troops of U.S. General Hampton gathered at the border. They entered Canadian territory during the night along the Rivière Châteauguay. But Charles Michel d'Irumberry de Salaberry, seigneur of Chambly, was waiting for them along with 300 militiamen and a few dozen Aboriginals. On October 26, the battle began. Salaberry's tactics got the better of the Americans, who retreated, putting an end to a series of conflicts and inaugurating a lasting friendship between the two countries.

There is an **interpretation centre** near the battlefield, where a model of the site, uniforms and artifacts unearthed during excavations are on display, as well as a miniature model of the site that shows troop positions during the battles.

Travel along the Rivière Châteauguay until Ormstown.

Ormstown ★ (pop. 3,687)

Founded by British settlers, Ormstown is, without a doubt, one of the prettiest villages of Montérégie. Many churches of various denominations are found here, such as the stone **St. James Anglican Church** (1837). Note the colourful homes on the west shore, with their red bricks, white wooden accents and green (or black) shutters. Ormstown specializes in horse-breeding. There is a **racetrack** here, as well as a few riding schools (breeding and boarding), owned by long-standing families of British origin.

Parks

Tour B: Chemin des Patriotes

Situated on the upper half of Mont Saint-Hilaire the **Centre de la Nature du Mont-Saint-Hilaire** ★ ★ *($4; every day 8am until one hour*

before sundown; 422 Chemin des Moulins, Mont-Saint-Hilaire, ☎450-467-1755) is a former estate that brigadier Andrew Hamilton Gault passed on to Montréal's McGill University in 1958. Scientific research is conducted at this nature conservation centre and recreational activities (hiking, cross-country skiing) are permitted throughout the year on half of the estate, which covers 11km². The Centre was also recognized as a Biosphere Reserve by UNESCO in 1978 for its untouched forest. An information centre on the formation of the Montérégie hills and a garden of indigenous plants can be found at the park's entrance.

The small **Lac Hertel**, visited by migrating birds, is located at the bottom of a valley. The surrounding peaks are criss-crossed by a 24km-long network of paths. One of these peaks, called "Pain de Sucre" or "Sugarloaf," offers an exceptional panoramic view of the Richelieu valley.

Tour C: Shore of the St. Lawrence

Parc National du Mont-Saint-Bruno ★ *($3.50 parking included; every day 8am until sundown; 330 Rang des 25 Est, St-Bruno-de-Montarville, ☎450-653-7544 or 800-665-6527, www.sepaq. com)* was once a holiday resort frequented by upper-class, English-speaking Montrealers. Many families, such as the Birks, the Drummonds and the Merediths, had beautiful second homes built here, in what is now a park. There are two lakes at the top of the mountain, Lac Seigneurial and Lac du Moulin, next to a 19th-century water mill. The park is a pleasant place to walk and relax. Self-guided trails and guided walks help familiarize visitors with the park. Cross-country skiing is possible during the winter, with almost 27km of trails set up and small heated cabins along the way.

To get to the **Parc National des Îles-de-Boucherville** *($3.50; year-round, every day 8am to sundown; 55 Rue de l'Île-Sainte-Marguerite, Boucherville, ☎450-928-5088 or 800-665-6527, www.pc.gc.ca)*, take Aut. 20, Exit 89, or take the ferry from Longueuil *(Promenade René-Lévesque)* or Montréal *(Promenade du Parc Bellerive)*. Some of the islands are still farmland, but the archipelago, linked by cable-ferries, is accessible to visitors. The

Montérégie - Parks

park is devoted to outdoor activities, mainly cycling and hiking in the summer. There is also a golf course and a picnic area frequented by birds of all kinds; the park is a favourite among ornithologists. You can also get a completely different perspective of the park by exploring it in a canoe; there are four tours totalling 28km.

Tour E: The Southwest

On the banks of the St. Lawrence, close to the town of Salaberry-de-Valleyfield, is the tourist-recreation complex on the **beach** of the **Parc Régional des Îles de Saint-Timothée** *($5 weekdays, $7 weekends; mid-Jun to early Sep Mon-Fri 10am to 5pm, Sat and Sun 10am to 7pm; Jul every day 10am to 7pm; 240 Rue St-Laurent, ☎450-377-1117).* Popular for a number of years, this spot offers all sorts of activities: swimming, in-line skating, kayaking lessons, volleyball competition, canoe and pedal-boat rental, etc. It's an interesting place for families and groups but not recommended for those seeking peace and quiet.

Take Rte. 132 W. and follow the signs starting at St-Anicet to **Lac Saint-François National Wildlife Area** ★★ *(free admission; early May to early Sep; Chemin de la Pointe Fraser Dundee, ☎450-370-6954),* also called Réserve Nationale de Faune du Lac-St-François. On the south shore of the St. Lawrence River, this park is a wetland recognized by the Ramsar Convention (a worldwide list of protected sites). Visitors can observe 220 species of birds, 600 types of plants and over 40 species of mammals. From May to September, excursions in Rabaska canoes and hikes, both with guides, are offered.

Outdoor Activities

■ Cycling

Cycling has become very popular over the last few years. For this reason, Montérégie, along with the Eastern Townships, established an amazing network of bicycle trails. **Tourisme Montérégie** *(☎866-469-0069, www.tourismemonteregie.qc.ca)* offers two free maps for cycling enthusiasts, one detailing the 12 bike paths and various cyclable roads in the area.

Here are a few other suggestions for paths in the region:

Tour A: Forts on the Richelieu

Chambly Canal National Historic Site *(1751 Avenue Bourgogne, ☎450-447-8888; 39km from Chambly to St-Jean-sur-Richelieu).* While riding alongside the historic Chambly Canal and Richelieu River, you'll see lock-keepers at work, daysailors and magnificent views of the Richelieu. If you're lucky, you might even spot a mallard or a heron. Near the bike trail, **Vélo Chambly** *(1731 Avenue Bourgogne, ☎450-447-3450)* rents bicycles by the day or the hour.

Tour C: Shore of the St. Lawrence

A welcome trek through nature between the St. Lawrence river and the municipalities of the south shore is provided by the **Circuit des Riverains** *(☎450-670-7293; 55km).* Cyclists get to enjoy a unique view of Montréal and the St. Lawrence from here.

Tour D: Vaudreuil-Soulanges

The **Circuit des Deux Lacs** *(☎450-377-7676; 70km)* borders Lac des Deux-Montagnes and crosses the charming town of Hudson before reaching the St. Lawrence, near Melocheville.

■ Cross-Country Skiing

Centre de la Nature du Mont Saint-Hilaire *($4; 422 Chemin des Moulins, ☎450-467-1755; 3 trails, 10km)*

Parc National du Mont-Saint-Bruno *($10.50 including access to the park; rental; 330 Rang des 25 Est, Saint-Bruno, ☎450-653-7544; 9 trails, 35km)*

Base de Plein Air des Cèdres *($7; rental; 1677 Chemin St-Dominique, Les Cèdres, ☎450-452-4736; 6 trails, 50km)*

■ Cruises

Tour A: Forts on the Richelieu

Croisières Richelieu
$18: 90min cruise
late Jun to early Sep Tue-Sun 1:30pm to 3:30pm
Rue du Quai, St-Jean-sur-Richelieu
☎ (450) 346-2446 or 800-361-6420
This cruise follows the Richelieu river to Saint-Paul-de-l'Île-aux-Noix and provides excellent views of the many sumptuous houses that line the riverside.

Tour D: Vaudreuil-Soulanges

Croisières Bellevue
$19: 90min cruise; $22: 2hr cruise
early Jun to early Sep, departures every day at 1pm and 3pm
Ste-Anne-de-Bellevue
☎ 888-455-5245
Leaving from the Sainte-Anne canal, these cruises take visitors on Lac Saint-Louis and Lac des Deux Montagnes.

■ Hiking

The Montérégie region includes six hills that were, for a long time, thought to be old volcanos. They actually consist of metamorphic rock that didn't break the surface of the earth's crust. These hills are great for day hikers, and most are accessible from the highways. Here are some of the best places:

Parc National des Îles-de-Boucherville *(55 Rue de l'Île Ste-Marguerite, Louis-Hippolyte-Lafontaine tunnel, Exit 89, ☎ 450-928-5088)*, located on an island in the middle of the St. Lawrence River, has a lot to offer in terms of flora and fauna. Over 170 species of fish and 40 species of birds have been spotted here.

Parc National du Mont-Saint-Bruno *(330 Rang des 25 Est, ☎ 450-653-7544)*, nestled in the middle of the charming municipality of Saint-Bruno, offers a network of pleasant trails that lead to a number of lakes. Many picnic and rest areas have been set up to accommodate hikers.

The **Centre de la Nature du Mont-Saint-Hilaire** *(422 Chemin des Moulins, ☎ 450-467-1755)* is 400m high, has many trails that offer great hiking possibilities, and rewards your efforts with fantastic views, notably along the "Pain de Sucre" trail.

The **Étangs Garand** *(834 Route 104, ☎ 450-346-8580)*, in Saint-Grégoire, offer wonderful hiking in maple groves and orchards.

The **Lac-Saint-François National Wildlife Area** *(☎ 450-370-6954)* is not to be missed. The marsh environment, canals and ponds are home to unique vegetation and wildlife; certain species aren't found anywhere else in the country.

■ Kayaking

Tour A: Forts on the Richelieu

Kayak Etc. *(1577 Boulevard Bourgogne, Chambly, behind the Maison Culturelle, ☎ 450-658-2031)* offers kayak and canoe rentals. Classes are available for young people, 12 years old and up, and for adults of all levels.

Montérégie - Outdoor Activities

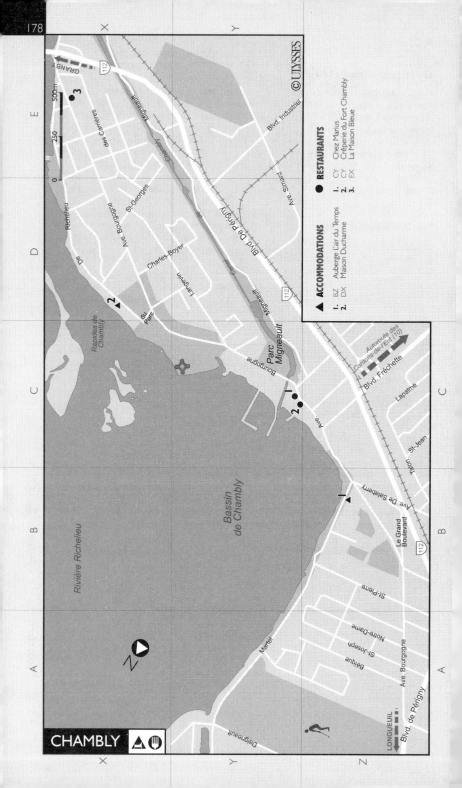

CHAMBLY

178

© ULYSSES

ACCOMMODATIONS

1. BZ   Auberge L'air du Temps
2. DX   Maison Ducharme

RESTAURANTS

1. CY   Chez Marius
2. CY   Crêperie du Fort Chambly
3. EX   La Maison Bleue

▲ Accommodations

Tour A: Forts on the Richelieu

Chambly

Auberge L'air du Temps
$$ bkfst incl.
124 Rue Martel
☎ (450) 658-1642 or 888-658-1642
▤ (450) 658-2830
www.airdutemps.qc.ca
This charming house right across from the Bassin de Chambly has been tastefully decorated despite the slight overabundance of pastels. There is one large guest room on the ground floor and four others in the old attic. Friendly welcome.

Maison Ducharme
$$$ bkfst incl.
▧
10 Rue De Richelieu
☎ (450) 447-1220
▤ (450) 447-1018
This pleasant B&B occupies a 19th-century barracks (see p 152), right near Fort Chambly. Tastefully decorated, the house is steeped in the antique luxury of another era, when people took the time to make every detail in their home immaculate. A lovely English garden and pool add to this large property next to the Rivière Richelieu rapids.

Saint-Jean-sur-Richelieu

Please note that accommodation rates may be slightly higher during the Festival des Montgolfières *(hot-air balloon festival, mid to late August)*.

SAINT-JEAN-SUR-RICHELIEU AND IBERVILLE ▲ ⍟

IBERVILLE

SAINT-JEAN-SUR-RICHELIEU

L'ACADIE

▲ **ACCOMMODATIONS**
Saint-Jean-sur-Richelieu
1. BY Auberge Harris
2. BY Relais Gouverneur

● **RESTAURANTS**
Saint-Jean-sur-Richelieu
1. CZ Le Samuel II
2. CZ Chez Noeser
3. CZ Manneken Pis

Iberville
4. CZ Al Paradiso

©ULYSSES

0   500   1000m

Auberge Harris
$$-$$$ bkfst incl.

≡ ✈ ⊚ ⊶ ⊜ ⅲ @

576 Rue Champlain
☎ (450) 348-3821 or 800-668-3821
🗐 (450) 348-7725
www.aubergeharris.com
Located on the shore of the
Richelieu river, Auberge
Harris has 77 modern and
comfortable rooms spread
over two distinct areas,
one of which features mo-
tel-type accommodations.
Courteous service.

Relais Gouverneur
$$$-$$$$

≡ ≋ ❄ ♨ ⅲ

725 Boulevard du Séminaire
Nord
☎ (450) 348-7376 or 800-667-3815
🗐 (450) 348-9778
www.relaisgouverneurst-jean.com
The Relais Gouverneur
stands at the entrance to
the city, along the Rivière
Richelieu. The rooms are
spacious and bright. Fa-
cilities include an indoor
swimming pool, a bar and
a non-smoking floor. Ser-
vice is courteous.

Tour B: Chemin
des Patriotes

Beloeil

Hostellerie Rive Gauche
$$$-$$$$

≡ ⚲ ♨ ⊚

1810 Boulevard Richelieu
☎ (450) 467-4477 or 888-608-6565
🗐 (450) 467-0525
www.hostellerierivegauche.com
Hôtellerie Rive Gauche is
located off Aut. 20 (Exit
112), along the shore of the
Rivière Richelieu. This inn
has 22 rooms decorated
in warm tones and linens,
and offers a view of the
water. A cozy dining room
is available for guests.

Mont-Saint-Hilaire

Auberge Montagnard
$$-$$$

≡ ✈ ≋ ♨ ⊚

439 Boulevard Laurier
☎ (450) 467-0201 or 800-363-9109
🗐 (450) 467-0628
Auberge Montagnard is
located on a noisy boule-
vard across from Mont
Saint-Hilaire. It offers old-
fashioned but comfortable
rooms, with a friendly staff.

Manoir Rouville-Campbell
$$$$

≡ ≋ ♨

125 Chemin des Patriotes Sud
☎ (450) 446-6060 or 866-250-6060
🗐 (450) 446-4878
www.manoirrouvillecampbell.com
Manoir Rouville-Campbell
has a mystical air about it;
as you enter the manor it's
as though time has stopped
or even gone back a cen-
tury. This place, now near-
ly 150 years old, has seen
many chapters of Québec
history unfold. It was con-
verted into a luxury hotel
in 1987 and is now owned
by Québec comedian Yvon
Deschamps. The dining
room, bar and gardens
overlooking the Rivière
Richelieu complement this
lordly manor.

Saint-Hyacinthe

Hôtel des Seigneurs
$$$$

≡ ⊶ ✈ ≋ ❄ ♨ ⊚

1200 Rue Johnson Ouest
☎ (450) 774-3810 or 866-734-4638
🗐 (450) 774-6955
www.hoteldesseigneurs.com
Located by the highway,
the Hôtel des Seigneurs
offers attractive rooms and
many services to ensure its
guests a pleasant stay. Ten-
nis and squash courts are
available.

Saint-Marc-sur-Richelieu

Auberge Handfield
$$-$$$$

≡ △ ⊶ ✈ ≋ ♨ ⅲ ❤ ⊚

555 Boulevard Richelieu
☎ (450) 584-2226
🗐 (450) 584-3650
www.aubergehandfield.com
Located in a beautiful home
across from the Richelieu,
Auberge Handfield is a true
escape. It offers its guests
many amenities and ser-
vices, including the *Escale*
theatre-boat and a spa.
The garden is well kept
and offers a great view.
The rooms are modest, but
nevertheless comfortable.

Hostellerie Les Trois Tilleuls
$$$$-$$$$$ bkfst incl.

≡ △ ⊶ ❄ ♨ ⅲ ❤ ⊚

290 Boulevard Richelieu
☎ (450) 856-7787 or 800-263-2230
🗐 (450) 584-3146
www.lestroistilleuls.com
Hostellerie les Trois Tilleuls
belongs to the prestigious
Relais et Châteaux asso-
ciation. Built next to the
Rivière Richelieu, it enjoys
a tranquil rural setting. The
name of the establishment
comes from the three grand
linden trees, called *tilleuls*
in French, which shade the
property. The rooms are
decorated with rustic furniture and each has a balcony overlooking the river.
Outside, guests have access
to gardens, a lookout and a
heated pool.

© ULYSSES

Parc des Salines

MONTRÉAL

LA PRÉSENTATION

137

20

DRUMMONDVILLE
QUÉBEC CITY

Picard

Johnson Ouest

Gauvin

Ave. Cusson

Galeries
Saint-
Hyacinthe

Blvd. Laframboise

Blvd. Casavant

Blvd.

Hôpital
Honoré-Mercier

Cartier

Turcot

Ave. Choquette

Ste-Catherine

Turcot

Ave. Pratte

Bourassa

Ave. Raymond

Ave. St-Joseph

Ste-Anne

Blvd. Laframboise

du Sacré-Cœur

Nelson

Papineau

Papineau

Sicotte

116

Dessaules

Hôtel-Dieu

Ave. Bourdages Nord

Sicotte

Girouard Est

Girouard

Dessaules

Ste-Anne

Ste-Anne

Hôtel de-Ville

Calixa-Lavallée

Ouest

des Cascades Ouest

116

0   250   500m

Rivière

3
Allée du
Marché

2

St-Antoine

1

St-Simon

Mondor

Duclos

Ave. Ste-Marie

de la Concorde

Ave. Robert

Ave. Brodeur

Ave. Vaudreuil

Yamaska

Est

St-Pierre

St-Louis

Ave. Bourdages Sud

Z

SAINT-HYACINTHE ▲ ⊕

Tour D: Vaudreuil-Soulanges

Vaudreuil-Dorion

Château Vaudreuil Suite Hôtel
$$$$$
≡ ▲ ⛱ ✕ ♨ ⑂ ◎ ㋕

21700 Transcanadienne
☎ (450) 455-0955 or 800-363-7896
▤ (450) 455-6617
www.chateau-vaudreuil.com
Located on Lac des Deux-Montagnes, this modern, imposing-looking hotel, which has very comfortable rooms, is a good choice in this region.

Sainte-Marthe

Auberge des Gallant
$$$$ bkfst incl.
≡ ⛵ ◎ ⛱ ▲ ♨ ❦ ♨ ⑂

1171 Chemin St-Henri
☎ (450) 459-4241 or 800-641-4241
▤ (450) 459-4667
www.gallant.qc.ca
Located in the heart of a bird and deer sanctuary, Auberge des Gallant offers luxury accommodations in a superb country setting. The rooms are comfortable though rather ordinary, but the extremely attentive service ensures a memorable stay.

Hudson

Auberge Willow Place
$$ bkfst incl.
≡ ⑂

208 Main Rd.
☎ (450) 458-7006
▤ (450) 458-4615
www.willowplaceinn.com
Auberge Willow Place is pleasantly located on the shores of Lac des Deux-Montagnes. Old-fashioned charm and a grand yet mellow British-style atmosphere.

Restaurants

Tour A: Forts on the Richelieu

Carignan

Au Tournant de la Rivière
$$$$
Wed-Sun
5070 Rue de Salaberry
☎ (450) 658-7372
Au Tournant de la Rivière has a critically acclaimed gourmet menu. In business for more than 20 years, the establishment's succulent French cuisine has helped it maintain its standing among the best restaurants in Québec. A must for gourmet palates.

Chambly

Chez Marius
$-$$
1737 Avenue Bourgogne
☎ (450) 658-6092
The Chez Marius snack bar is a local favourite. While savouring a delicious hamburger and *poutine* combo, you can look at old photographs documenting the history of the restaurant, as well as that of Chambly. During summer, you can eat outdoors on the riverside terrace.

Crêperie du Fort Chambly
$-$$
1717 Avenue Bourgogne
☎ (450) 447-7474
Crêperie du Fort Chambly, on the edge of Bassin de Chambly, occupies a wooden house with a maritime atmosphere. They serve crêpes, of course, but also cheese fondue. Waterfront terrace and friendly service. Brunch on Sundays.

La Maison Bleue
$$$-$$$$
2592 Avenue Bourgogne
☎ (450) 447-1112
What was once the large, wood-framed home of Thomas Whitehead (see p 153) now houses a luxurious restaurant with a country feel: large fireplaces, creaky floors and antiques. Upstairs, private rooms can be reserved, except in summer, for family gatherings or business meetings. Classic French cuisine and a warm reception.

Richelieu

Aux Chutes du Richelieu
$$$-$$$$
486 1ʳᵉ Rue
☎ (450) 658-6689
Aux Chutes du Richelieu prepares excellent French and Italian cuisine. Their crêpes Suzette are truly sinful. What's more, you can admire the Richelieu falls while you eat.

Saint-Jean-sur-Richelieu

Manneken Pis
$
320 Rue de Champlain
☎ (450) 348-3254
With a name like that, Belgian waffles are sure to be nearby—and what delicious waffles they are, with such fine chocolate! The coffee, roasted on site, is also excellent. A pleasant terrace faces a little marina.

They also serve sandwiches and salads.

Le Samuel II
$$-$$$
291 Rue Richelieu
☎ (450) 347-4353

Much loved by locals, Le Samuel II has always had a faithful following of connoisseurs. Large bay windows overlooking the canal offer a view of the boats going by. A delight.

Chez Noeser
$$$$
bring your own wine
236 Rue de Champlain
☎ (450) 346-0811

Chez Noeser offers particularly courteous service and deliciously creative French cuisine. There is a terrace during the summer months.

Iberville

Al Paradiso
$$$
437 1ʳᵉ Rue
☎ (450) 347-0600

A resolutely unique restaurant, Al Paradiso occupies every room of a charming Victorian home that dates from 1840. The warm decor, with its crimson wall covering and reproductions of classic artworks, provides an enjoyable setting in which to savour delicious antipasti, penne Romanoff and other Italian classics. The terrace that looks out on the Richelieu river makes for a superb dining spot at sunset.

Lacolle

Brochetterie Pharos
$$-$$$
7 Rue de l'Église
☎ (450) 246-3897

Brochetterie Pharos would be a Greek restaurant like any other were it not located in a church—a sign of the changing times in Québec, where many churches are being turned into restaurants, luxury apartments, condos and other businesses.

Tour B: Chemin des Patriotes

Saint-Bruno-de-Montarville

La Rabastalière
$$$
125 de la Rabastalière
☎ (450) 461-0173

La Rabastalière occupies a warm, century-old home; the restaurant offers classic French cuisine plus a gourmet six-course menu that varies each week. There is a sunroom for quiet meals. The staff is friendly and the food excellent.

Saint-Hyacinthe

Le Bouffon Resto-Pub
$-$$
485 Rue Ste-Anne
☎ (450) 778-9915

Le Bouffon Resto-Pub is a typical Irish-style pub and a very popular hangout in the area. In a warm decor that features attractive woodwork, Le Bouffon stands out thanks to more than 150 varieties of imported beers, scotches and ports. Lunch-time specials, festive happy hours, hearty dinners and entertaining evenings are a few of the reasons why locals keep coming back to Le Bouffon. In summer, the restaurant's two floors feature three tree- and flower-lined terraces. In winter, patrons get

to relax on couches next to the cozy fireplace.

Andréa Café
$$-$$$
1485 Rue St-Antoine
☎ (450) 774-3620

This pleasant restaurant is a good choice for lunch or dinner. The food is unpretentious, fresh and creative, and house specialties include grilled meats and seafood.

L'Auvergne
$$$
478 Avenue Saint-Simon
☎ (450) 774-1881

L'Auvergne has long offered one of the best French cuisines in the region in its two small dining rooms. Brunch is served on Sundays from 10am, except during the summer.

Beloeil

Le Trait d'Union
$-$$
919 Boulevard Wilfrid-Laurier
☎ (450) 446-5740

Le Trait d'Union is an unpretentious, hip little bistro where local residents come to meet. With its relaxed atmosphere and charming terrace, you're sure to have a pleasant time. They serve healthy little dishes at affordable prices. Open for breakfast on weekends.

Crêperie du Vieux-Belœil
$$
Tue-Sun
940 Boulevard Richelieu
☎ (450) 464-1726

The Crêperie du Vieux-Beloeil offers generous portions of their house crêpes, made of white flour or buckwheat, served with seafood, ham or cheese.

Danvito
$$$-$$$$
154 Boulevard Wilfrid-Laurier
☎ (450) 464-5166
Hidden in Beloeil's commercial district, Danvito attracts a business clientele with its fine Italian cuisine and Mediterranean character. They serve traditional Italian fare as well as veal sweetbread and succulent shrimp.

Saint-Marc-sur-Richelieu

Auberge Handfield
$$$-$$$$
555 Boulevard Richelieu
☎ (450) 584-2226
Auberge Handfield houses a large dining room decorated with wood beams. The country atmosphere and delicious Québec cuisine complement each other. In the spring you can also sample sweets from the sugar shack.

Hostellerie Les Trois Tilleuls
$$$$
290 Boulevard Richelieu
☎ (450) 856-7787 or 800-263-2230
The restaurant at Hostellerie des Trois Tilleuls serves up some gems of fine French gastronomy. The artfully prepared menu offers traditional and sophisticated meals, and the dining room has a nice view of the river. The beautiful terrace is open to guests during the summer.

Saint-Antoine-sur-Richelieu

Le Champagne
$$$$
1000 Chemin du Rivage
☎ (450) 787-2966
Le Champagne looks like an old Moroccan castle. The interior is magnificently decorated with panelling, while the tables are set with silverware, fine glassware, original dishes and embroidered tablecloths. Delicious French cuisine. Reservations required.

Tour C: Shore of the St. Lawrence

Saint-Lambert

Café-Passion
$
476 Rue Victoria
☎ (450) 671-1405
Café-Passion, located in the heart of Saint-Lambert, has quite a following. Although it is a pleasant place, the food does not quite live up to all the fuss. The decor is trendy and the food somewhat bland. Nevertheless, it's an acceptable choice for an inexpensive meal.

Au Vrai Chablis
$$$-$$$$
52 Rue Aberdeen
☎ (450) 465-2795
The food-service professionals here invite you to partake of a fabulous fine-dining experience. The menu changes daily and lists French specialties, superbly prepared by renowned chef Bernard Jacquin.

Longueuil

Charcuterie du Vieux-Longueuil
$
193 Rue St-Charles Ouest
☎ (450) 670-0643
For a good sandwich, Charcuterie du Vieux Longueuil is an excellent choice, despite the slightly rushed service.

Relais Terrapin
$$
295 Rue St-Charles Est
☎ (450) 677-6378
Located in a well-preserved inn that was built in 1856, Relais Terrapin is a longstanding favourite in Longueuil. Diners come here for quality French cuisine.

Lou Nissart
$$
260 Rue St-Jean
☎ (450) 442-2499
Lou Nissart is a charming little restaurant located in the heart of Vieux-Longueuil. Friends and family gather here to savour classic Provençale cuisine. There is a pleasant terrace in summertime.

Restaurant l'Incrédule
$$-$$$
288 Rue St-Charles Ouest
☎ (450) 674-0946
L'Incrédule offers an interesting choice of bistro-style meals, as well as an excellent selection of imported beer, scotch and port.

Saint-Hubert

Bistro des Bières Belges
$-$$
2088 Rue de Montcalm
☎ (450) 465-0669
Bistro des Bières Belges, as its alliterative name reveals, has a selection of about 60 Belgian beers. The menu is also in the Flemish trad-

● **RESTAURANTS**

1. CZ Charcuterie du Vieux-Longueuil
2. CZ Lou Nissart
3. CZ Relais Terrapin
4. CZ Restaurant l'Incrédule

---

ition. Reservations required on the weekend.

Tour D: Vaudreuil-Soulanges

Rigaud

Pierre de Rigaud
$$$
Jan to Mar
bring your own wine
437 Grande Ligne
☎ (450) 451-4205
Pierre de Rigaud offers fine regional cuisine in a relaxed and warm atmosphere. A special gourmet dinner is prepared for groups of 30 or more. Year-round catering service.

Sucrerie de la Montagne
$$$$
300 Rang St-Georges
☎ (450) 451-5204
The Sucrerie de la Montagne is practically an attraction in itself. It serves traditional sugaring-off dishes, such as those perennial favourites *oreilles de Christ* (literally Christ's ears, but actually deep-fried lard) and *œufs dans le sirop* (eggs in syrup). A folk group livens up the atmosphere with rigadoons and quadrille tunes. Open year-round.

Hudson

Clémentine
$$-$$$
398 Rue Principale
☎ (450) 458-8181
Chez Clémentine is easily one of the finest restaurants in Québec. A member of Toques Blanches Internationales, this small restaurant, located in a magnificent little country house in the heart of town, serves innovative Québécois cuisine. The service is courteous and friendly.

Auberge Willow Place
$$$
208 Main Rd.
☎ (450) 458-7006
On the shores of Lac des Deux-Montagnes, Auberge Willow Place serves steak and grilled specialties. With its English-style decor and cozy atmosphere, this place is irresistible. Courteous young staff and a lovely lakefront location add to its charm. The pub-style fare and beer is rather expensive, but the setting makes it more than worth the splurge.

♪
♪
🎁

Entertainment

■ Bars and Nightclubs

Saint-Hyacinthe

Le Bilboquet
1850 Rue des Cascades Ouest
☎ (450) 771-6900
Le Bilboquet is a comfortable spot. It's a microbrewery (they brew Métayer Blonde, Brune and Rousse), a fun place for a meal with friends, and also a centre for the promotion of the arts. They invite musicians to play, decorate the premises with works by local artists, present plays and poetry readings and host literary discussions.

Le Bouffon Resto-Pub
485 Avenue Ste-Anne
☎ (450) 778-9915
Le Bouffon Resto-Pub is another good spot for a lively night out in Saint-Hyacinthe (see also p 183).

Saint-Mathias-sur-Richelieu

Super 9
9 Rue Dufour
☎ (450) 658-5170
It's not every day that you come across a dance club in an old barn, and this one has been a popular weekend spot for young people from all over the region for many generations. Essentially, this place is a typical, small-town club with lasers, sports cars and all the other hoopla. Nonetheless, there's no lack of ambiance here.

■ Festivals and Cultural Events

Chambly

The **Fête Bières et Saveurs** *(late Aug and early Sep;* ☎ *450-447-2096, www.bieres etsaveurs.com)* is a beer festival whose popularity has exceeded all expectations, with attendance rising year after year. Beers from all over the world can be sampled at Fort Chambly.

Kahnawake

Various traditional Aboriginal events (dances, songs, etc.) are organized as part of the **Pow Wow** *(second weekend of Jul;* ☎ *450-632-8667)*, held in Kahnawake every year during the second weekend of July. Most of the activities are held on Kateri Tekakwitha island.

Saint-Jean-sur-Richelieu

The **Festival de Montgolfières** *(second or third week of Aug;* ☎ *450-347-9555, www.mont golfieres.com)*, a hot-air-balloon festival, fills the sky over Saint-Jean-sur-Richelieu with approximately 100 multicoloured hot-air balloons. Departures take place every day from 6am to 6pm, weather permitting. Exhibitions and shows make up some of the other activities that take place during the festival.

Salaberry-de-Valleyfield

Salaberry-de-Valleyfield hosts the **Régates Internationales de Valleyfield** *(early Jul;* ☎ *450-371-6144 or 888-371-6144, www.regates.ca)*. The competition involves several categories of hydroplane races, with speeds reaching

240km/h. The regattas always attract a large number of visitors.

■ Theatre

Upton

Unique in North America, the concept of **Théâtre de la Dame de Coeur** *(Jun to early Sep Wed-Sun; 611 Rang de la Carrière,* ☎ *450-549-5828, www.damedecoeur.com)* is sure to fascinate young and old alike. Located in a magnificent historic site, the "Queen of Hearts" puts on terrific marionette shows, complete with striking visual effects. The outdoor theatre has an immense roof and pivoting seats that are heated on chilly evenings.

🎁

Shopping

The Montérégie region's reputation among shoppers has grown steadily over the last few years. Montrealers come here regularly to pick their own fruit in summertime, to uncover hidden treasures in the region's many antique shops and to buy and savour some of the many delicious farm products that are produced in the area.

■ Antiques

Hudson

Finnigan's Market *(shop: Sun 11am to 5pm; public market: May to Nov Sat only 9am to 4pm; 775 Rue Principale,* ☎ *450-458-4377)*. This famous outdoor antique market also has loads of other great finds and is one place in the region not to be missed. It's a joy to wander around all these treasures. A hot spot for collectors!

■ Food

Otterburn Park

Chocolaterie La Cabosse d'Or
(Sat-Wed 9am to 5pm, Thu-Fri 9am to 10pm; 973 Chemin Ozias-Leduc, ☎450-464-6937, www.lacabossedor.com) has earned its reputation not only for selling Belgian chocolate of the finest quality but also for its enchanting fairy-tale ambiance. It's a splendid house with a shop, terrace and tearoom. The hostesses always greet you with a smile.

Saint-Antoine-Abbé

Vins Mustier Gerzer, Hydromel
(year-round; 3299 Rte. 209, ☎*450-826-4609).* Light and fresh, mead is the perfect drink for those wonderful summer days, and Vins Mustier, in the splendid St-Antoine-Abbé region, is an expert in the field. This place is also devoted to bee-keeping and offers a wide variety of honey-based products. Sampling available.

Saint-Hyacinthe

L'Épicière des Terroirs
Mon-Wed and Sat 10am to 5:30pm, Thu-Fri until 7:30pm, open Sun in summer
1630 Allée du Marché
☎ (450) 778-3030
Originally from France, Patricia Dinard was so knocked over by the quality of Québec's local food products that she opened this charming little stall in Saint-Hyacinthe's Allée du Marché. Delicious ready-made meals and various treats from every region of Québec can be savoured on the spot or bought to go.

■ Home Decor

Iberville

La Maison sous les Arbres
(2024 Route 133 Sud, ☎*450-347-1639).* Imagine an art gallery set up in a private home; you can shop for your bathroom articles in the bathroom, kitchen articles in the kitchen, and so on. Great for people who love to poke around in other people's houses.

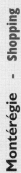

Montérégie - Shopping

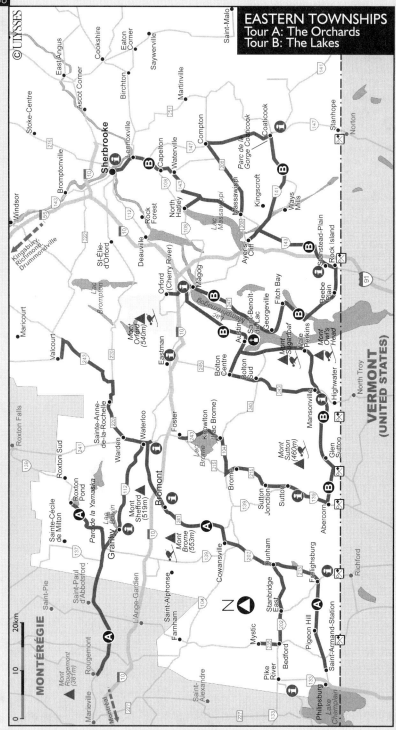

© ULYSSES

EASTERN TOWNSHIPS
Tour A: The Orchards
Tour B: The Lakes

MONTÉRÉGIE

VERMONT
(UNITED STATES)

The Eastern Townships

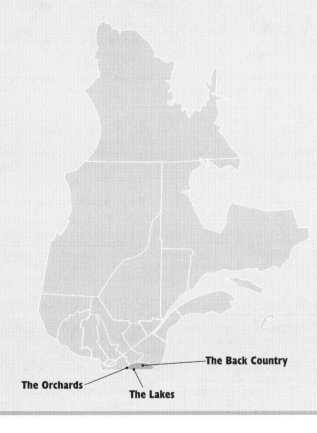

The Back Country

The Orchards

The Lakes

M ountainous countryside and a rich architectural heritage give the Cantons-de-l'Est (Eastern Townships), also referred to as Estrie, a distinctive character reminiscent in many ways of New England. Located in the southernmost part of the province, near the Appalachian foothills, they comprise one of the most beautiful regions in Québec.

Picturesque villages marked by what is often typically English architecture lie nestled between mountains with rounded summits and lovely little valleys.

As may be gathered from many place names, such as Massawippi and Coaticook, this vast region was originally explored and inhabited by the Abenaki First Nation. Later, when New France came under British control and the United States declared its independence, many American colonists still loyal to the British monarchy (known as Loyalists) settled in the Eastern Townships.

Throughout the 19th century, these settlers were followed by waves of immigrants from the British Isles, mainly Ireland, and French colonists from the overpopulated St. Lawrence lowlands.

Though the local population is now over 90% French-speaking, the area still bears obvious traces of its British past, most notably in its architecture. Many towns and villages are graced with majestic Anglican churches surrounded by beautiful 19th-century Victorian or vernacular American-style homes. The Townships are still home to a handful of prestigious English institutions, like Bishop's University in Lennoxville.

Though dairy farms still grace the countryside, the Eastern Townships is now a dynamic region with two universities and a number of high-technology businesses.

Located about an hour's drive from Montréal, this is cottage country and vacation land for many. The mountains are great for winter skiing, and the lakes and rivers perfect for summer water sports. But visitors also come to the Eastern Townships for its fine food and wineries, or simply to take part in one of its various festivals and family activities.

In terms of territorial division, the townships (*cantons*) are different from seigneuries. Not only are they more or less square, rather than oblong, but their administrative system was based on a British model. Instead of being granted to a single individual, a township was established at the request of the community wishing to settle there.

Most townships were founded in the 19th century, filling spaces left vacant by the French seigneurial system, usually mountainous sites removed from the already populated banks of the St. Lawrence and its tributaries, which at the time were the colony's main transportation routes. Nowhere in Québec was this means of populating the territory more widespread that in the Eastern Townships.

Getting There and Getting Around

Located southeast of Montréal, the Eastern Townships region is in competition with the Laurentians, to the northwest, for the honour of being Montréalers' favourite "playground." The three tours below will help you explore the Eastern Townships:

Tour A: The Orchards ★
Tour B: The Lakes ★ ★ ★
Tour C: The Back Country ★

■ By Car

Tour A: The Orchards

From Montréal, cross the Champlain Bridge and the Autoroute des Cantons de l'Est (Aut. 10) to Exit 29, then head south on the

133. Near Philipsburg and the U.S. border, keep left in order to turn onto the small road leading to Saint-Armand and Frelighsburg. Rte. 213 takes over until you reach Dunham, where you can either turn left on Rte. 202 to go to Mystic or head north on Rte. 202, then Rte. 241, to reach Waterloo. From there, Rte. 112 leads to Rougemont via Granby, while Rte. 220 meets Rte. 243, towards Valcourt.

Tour B: The Lakes

From Montréal, take the Autoroute des Cantons de l'Est (Aut. 10) to Exit 90, then head south on Rte. 243. Make sure to turn left towards Knowlton in order to follow the eastern shore of Lac Brome. In Knowlton, Rte. 104 leads to the intersection with Rte. 215. Turn left towards Brome and Sutton. By following Rte. 139, then Rte. 243 from here, you will reach Bolton Sud, where you can pick up Rte. 245 to Saint-Benoît-du-Lac. By continuing around the northern tip of Lac Memphrémagog on Rte. 247, you will end up in Rock Island. The last portion of the tour follows Rte. 143, with a detour on Rte. 141 to Coaticook, and then Rte. 208 to Sherbrooke.

Tour C: The Back Country

From Sherbrooke, take Rte. 108 to Birchton and then Rte. 210 to Eaton Corner. The heart of the village is located on either side of Rte. 253. Follow Rte. 253 to Cookshire, where you will take Rte. 212 to Saint-Augustin-de-Woburn. From here, head north via Rte. 161, following the eastern shore of Lac Mégantic to Ham-Nord where you will take Rte. 216, and then Rte. 255, to Danville.

■ Bus Stations

Tour B: The Lakes

Sutton
28 Rue Principale Nord (Esso station)
☎ (450) 538-2452

Magog
768 Rue Sherbrooke (Terminus Café)
☎ (819) 843-4617

Sherbrooke
80 Rue du Dépôt
☎ (819) 569-3656

Tour C: The Back Country

Lac-Mégantic
6630 Rue Salaberry (Dépanneur 6630 Fatima)
☎ (819) 583-2717

Useful Information

■ Tourist Information

Regional Office

Tourisme Cantons-de-l'Est
20 Rue Don-Bosco S., Sherbrooke, QC, J1L 1W4
☎ (819) 820-2020 or 800-355-5755
🖷 (819) 566-4445
www.cantonsdelest.com

Tour A: The Orchards

Bromont
15 Boulevard Bromont
☎ (450) 534-2006 or 877-276-6668
www.granby-bromont.com

Granby
650 Rue Principale
☎ (450) 372-7273 or 800-567-7273
www.granby-bromont.com

Rougemont
11 Chemin Marieville
☎ (450) 469-0069 or 866-469-0069

Tour B: The Lakes

Magog
55 Rue Cabana
☎ (819) 843-2744 or 800-267-2744
www.tourisme-memphremagog.com

Sherbrooke
2964 Rue King Ouest
☎ (819) 821-1919 or 800-561-8331
www.sdes.ca

Sutton
11-B Rue Principale Sud
☎ (450) 538-8455 or 800-565-8455
www.sutton-info.qc.ca

Tour C: The Back Country

Lac-Mégantic
3295 Rue Laval N.
☎ (819) 583-5515 or 800-363-5515
www.tourisme-megantic.com

Exploring

Tour A: The Orchards
★

 1 day

There are three clusters of orchards in the countryside surrounding Montréal, one in the Saint-Joseph-du-Lac region, another in the Saint-Antoine-Abbé region, and a third, which is both larger and more spread out, in the western part of the Eastern Townships. In recent years, vineyards have sprung up alongside the traditional apple orchards, turning a part of this tour into a sort of miniature wine route. In the fall, city dwellers come here on Sundays to admire the brilliant foliage, watch the grape harvest and pick their own MacIntosh apples in one of the many pick-your-own orchards. Apple growers also sell their products (apple butter, cider, juice, pies) by the side of the road, while viticulturists (wine growers) offer guided tours of their properties and provide visitors with an opportunity to taste and purchase their wine.

Frelighsburg ★ (pop. 1,104)

The Eastern Townships' architecture differs from that of the rest of Québec due to its Anglo-American origins, which account for the frequent use of red brick and white clapboard and the predominance of sash windows, composed of two vertically sliding panels. In houses built prior to 1860, the window panes are usually separated into little squares (three or four squares wide and four to eight squares high), while windows in the more recent Victorian houses contain large, undivided plates of glass.

The charming village of Frelighsburg grew up around its stone **mill** (*private, no visitors allowed; 12 Rte. 237 N.*), built in 1790 by two Loyalist pioneers. In 1839, the structure was enlarged by its new owner, Abram Freligh of New York State, for whom the village was named. The mill, which was converted into a residence in 1967, is visible through the trees on the left.

Frelighsburg's **Anglican Church ★** is very well situated atop a hill overlooking the village. Both its oblong structure and its steeple, which is at the side of the nave and marks the main entrance, are uncommon architectural features in the Eastern Townships. The church was built in 1884 in the Gothic Revival style advocated by the Church of England. Its red brick walls, yellow brick casings and slate roof create a polychromatic effect not unlike that of village churches in Ontario.

Take Rte. 213 N. toward Dunham.

Dunham ★ (pop. 3,299)

Traditionally, a single, somewhat imposing church lies at the centre of towns founded by Catholic French Canadians. As villages in the Eastern Townships were often inhabited by Anglicans, Presbyterians, Methodists, Baptists and Lutherans, little churches of various denominations abound. Accordingly, a number of churches are sprinkled among the well-kept residences lining Dunham's main street (*Rue Principale*). The oldest township in Lower Canada, Dunham is home to some of the first houses ever built in the Eastern Townships. **All Saints Anglican Church**, built of stone between 1847 and 1851, looks straight down the center of Rte. 202, known as the wine route.

Turn left on Rte. 202 W. to start the wine route. It is also possible to visit Stanbridge East, Bedford and Mystic from this road. Afterward, continue on the 213 N. towards Cowansville.

The Wine Route ★

European visitors might consider it quite presumptuous to call the road between Dunham and Stanbridge East (*Rte. 202 W.*) the "Wine Route," but the concentration of vineyards in this region is unique in the province, and Québec's attempts at winemaking have been so surprisingly successful that people have been swept away by their enthusiasm. There are no châteaux or distinguished old counts here, only growers who sometimes have to go as far as renting helicopters to save their vines from freezing. The rotor blades cause the air to circulate, preventing frost from forming on the ground during crucial periods in May. The region is, however, blessed with a microclimate and soil favourable for grape growing (slate). Most of the local wines are sold only at the vineyards where they are produced.

You can visit the **L'Orpailleur** (*1086 Rte. 202, Dunham,* ☎*450-295-2763, www.orpailleur. ca*) winery, whose products include a dry white wine and Apéridor, an apéritif similar to Pineau des Charentes. They also produce a delicious fortified white wine called La Marquise, La Part des Anges, a white wine and brandy mixture with a nutty flavour, as well as a highly acclaimed ice wine. A wine museum was also opened on the premises.

The **Domaine des Côtes d'Ardoises** (*879 Route 202, Dunham,* ☎*450-295-2020*) is one of the few Québec vineyards that produces red wine. Here, as at other wineries, the owner will give you a warm welcome.

Les Blancs Coteaux (*1046 Chemin Bruce, Route 202, Dunham,* ☎*450-295-3503*) not only makes quality wine but also has a lovely craft shop.

Stanbridge East (pop. 903)

This charming village is known mainly for its regional museum. Along its shady streets, visitors can also see large houses surrounded by gardens. **St. James the Apostle** (circa 1880), an Anglican church made of multicoloured brick, is particularly noteworthy, as its cruciform structure is somewhat unusual in Québec.

The **Musée Missisquoi** ★ (*$3.50; late May to mid-Oct, every day 10am to 5pm; 2 Rue River,* ☎*450-248-3153*) is devoted to preserving the region's essentially Loyalist heritage. The 12,000 objects displayed are housed in three period buildings, the **Cornell Mill** (1832), **Bill's Barn**, which houses antique cars and ploughing implements, and the **Magasin Général Hodge**, a general store whose counters date back to the beginning of the 20th century.

Continue on Rte. 202 W. to Bedford.

Bedford (pop. 2,684)

Another little town with American and Loyalist characteristics, Bedford is renowned for its grey and green slate extracted from surrounding quarries. Visitors can see lovely red-brick houses surrounded by greenery, most built during the second half of the 19th century, as well as the pretty **St. James Anglican Church** (circa 1840), also made of brick. The **Pont des Rivières**, to the northwest, is a 41m covered bridge, built in 1884. One of a few rare examples of wooden Howe-style bridges to be found in Québec, it is characterized by girders assembled in the shape of a cross.

To get to Mystic, turn right on Rte. 235 N. The village is located off the main road, to your left.

Mystic ★

Mystic is like a little piece of New England in Québec. Its population is still mainly anglophone.

Blink, and the village is gone: its central focus is the dodecagonal (12-sided) Walbridge Barn, built by American industrialist A.S. Walbridge around 1885. Unfortunately, the barn and its surrounding 40ha domain are not open for visits.

You can, however, visit the old general store. Built around 1860, the pink clapboard building is now a chocolatier known as **L'Oeuf** (*229 Chemin Mystic;* ☎*450-248-7529*). Chocoholic or not, step inside, as the interior has been well preserved. Adjoining the chocolatier is a restaurant and inn of the same name.

Head back towards Dunham to continue the main tour.

Cowansville (pop. 12,342)

Another Loyalist community, Cowansville has lovely Victorian homes made of wood and brick, as well as a few interesting public and commercial buildings, which bear witness to the town's prosperous past. Especially interesting is the former **Eastern Townships Bank** (*225 Rue Principale*), built in

1889, which has been converted into a community centre. The edifice's mansard roof is characteristic of the Second Empire style, which was popular both among the English and French. Not far away lies the small Anglican **Trinity Church**, a Gothic Revival structure erected in 1854 and surrounded by a cemetery.

Take Rte. 241 N., located east of Cowansville.

Bromont (pop. 5,085)

Developed in the 1960s, Bromont has become a favourite vacation area among Montréalers. It is renowned for its downhill ski resort, its sports facilities, and also for having hosted the 1976 Olympic equestrian competitions.

Visiting the **Musée du Chocolat** *($1.25; Mon-Fri 10am to 6pm, Sat and Sun 9am to 5:30pm; 679 Rue Shefford,* ☎ *450-534-3893)* is a golden opportunity for gourmands with discriminating palates to indulge in sinfully delicious chocolate. The museum presents the history of chocolate since the arrival of the Spanish in South America, the process of changing cocoa beans into powder and a few art works featuring... chocolate, of course! If your taste buds become overly sated, you can purchase all kinds of delicious sweets made right on the premises. Light meals are also served here.

Waterloo (pop. 4,140)

Waterloo is a charming little town with opulent homes on Western, Clark Hill, Lewis and Foster streets. Ironically, Anglo-Saxon homes here are much larger than their French-Canadian counterparts, even though their families were usually much smaller. **St. Luke Church** *(400 Rue de la Cour)* dates from 1821, making it one of the oldest Gothic Revival churches in Canada.

From here, visitors can make an optional detour to Valcourt, the village where Joseph-Armand Bombardier developed and began marketing the snowmobile.

To get there, take Rte. 241 to Warden. Turn right on Rte. 220, in the direction of Sainte-Anne-de-la-Rochelle, then left on Rte. 243, and follow the signs for Valcourt.

Valcourt (pop. 3,436)

Joseph-Armand Bombardier was not the only mechanic in Québec to develop a motor vehicle for use on snow-covered surfaces. Residents had to come up with something, since many roads in the province were not cleared of snow until the beginning of the 1950s. As automobiles were, for all practical purposes, somewhat unreliable, people had to depend on the same means of transportation as their ancestors, namely, the horse-drawn sleigh. Bombardier, however, was the only individual to make a profit from his invention, most notably because of a lucrative contract with the army during World War II. Though the company later diversified and underwent considerable expansion, it never left the village of Valcourt—which is to this day the site of its head office.

The **Musée J.-Armand-Bombardier** ★ *($5; early May to early Sep every day 10am to 5pm, early Sep to early May Tue-Sun 10am to 5pm; 1001 Avenue Joseph-Armand-Bombardier;* ☎ *450-532-5300)* is a museum that traces the development of the snowmobile and explains how Bombardier's invention was marketed all over the world. Different prototypes are displayed, along with a few examples of various snowmobiles produced since 1960.

From Waterloo, take Rte. 112 W. to Granby.

Granby (pop. 45,264)

A few kilometres from the verdant **Parc National de la Yamaska** (see p 204), Granby, the "princess of the Eastern Townships," basks in the fresh air of the surrounding countryside. In addition to its Victorian homes, this city boasts grand avenues and parks graced with fountains and sculptures. Transected by the Yamaska Nord river, it is also the point where the Montérégiade and Estriade bicycle trails converge. The city's youth and dynamism are reflected in its multiple festivals, notably the Festival International de la Chanson, an international festival of song that has exposed the French-speaking world to a number of excellent performers.

Visitors to the **Granby Zoo** ★ ★ *($23.45; ⅏; early Jun to end Aug, every day 10am to 7pm; beg Sep to mid-Oct every day 10am to 6pm; take*

Exit 68 or 74 from Aut. 10 and follow the signs; 525 Rue St-Hubert, ☎450-472-6299, www.zoogranby.ca) can see some 800 animals from 163 species from around the world. It is an interesting place to visit, particularly for young children. The admission fee provides access to the Amazoo, a water park that has been added to the site.

Continue on Route 112 W. towards Rougemont.

Roxton Pond (pop. 3,586)

Zoo et Sanctuaire d'Oiseaux Exotiques Icare *($9; Jun to Oct every day 10am to 5pm; 2699 Route 139, ☎450-375-6118, www.zooicare.com).* In response to the persistent curiosity of passers-by, the owners of a local bird-breeding farm have set up a 1km walking trail where visitors get to admire 125 different species of multicoloured birds from all over the world and see the breeders hand-feed the chicks. The sanctuary's nursery also sells various exotic birds, including spectacular blue and gold macaws.

Rougemont (pop. 2,641)

Though it is located outside of the Eastern Townships tourist area, Rougemont attracts visitors because of its status as Québec's apple capital. The village lies at the base of the smallest hill in the Montérégie region, Mont Rougemont.

The **Cidrerie Michel Jodoin** *(free admission; Mon-Fri 9am to 5pm, Sat and Sun 10am to 4pm; 1130 Rang de la Petite Caroline, ☎450-469-2676, www.cidrerie-michel-jodoin.qc.ca)* produces high-quality hard ciders and lovely sparkling apple juice. The secret lies in the aging process, which takes place in oak barrels, with delicious results. Visitors have the opportunity to taste, and of course buy, the various products produced on site, as well as tour the facility.

This is the end of the Orchards Tour. To return to Montréal, take Rte. 112 W. until it intersects with Rte. 227 S., then turn left to reach Aut. 10. To reach Tour B, continue eastward on Route 112 until Waterloo. From there, turn right and take Route 220 South to Knowlton.

Tour B : The Lakes
★ ★ ★

 2 days

This tour winds around the three most popular lakes (Brome, Memphrémagog and Massawippi) in the Eastern Townships and includes sweeping views, charming villages and friendly New England-style inns. It is an ideal excursion just a short distance from Montréal. Here, visitors can enjoy a variety of water sports, go rock-climbing, hiking, skiing or snowshoeing.

Knowlton ★ ★

When the Townships are compared to New England, Knowlton is often given as an example. Quaint shops and restaurants welcome visitors strolling through this well-to-do little village. In contrast to traditional French-Canadian villages, where the accent is on the parish church and its presbytery, civic buildings are the highlight in Knowlton. A notable example is the **Old Courthouse** (*15 Rue St. Paul*), designed in the Greek Revival style by Timothy E. Chamberlain and built in 1859. The building is now home to the Brome County Historical Society. All around, visitors will see examples of Loyalist architecture, characterized by red brick, white trim and dark-green shutters. Pick up a copy of the *Historic Walking Tour* brochure at **Auberge Knowlton/Restaurant Le Relais** (see p 210 and 217) for more information on Knowlton's many historic buildings.

Lac Brome ★ is popular among windsurfers, who can enjoy a parking lot and a small beach on the side of the road near Knowlton.

The **Brome County Museum** ★ (*$5; mid-May to mid-Sep, Mon-Sat 10am to 4:30pm, Sun 11am to 4:30pm; 130 Rue Lakeside; ☎450-243-6782*) occupies five Loyalist buildings and traces the lives and history of the region's inhabitants. In addition to the usual furniture and photographs, visitors can see a reconstructed general store, a 19th-century court of justice and, what's more unusual, a collection of military equipment, including a World War I airplane.

*The village of Knowlton is now part of the municipality of **Lac-Brome** (pop. 5,562), which en-*

The Eastern Townships – Exploring - The Lakes

circles the lake. To reach Sutton, turn right onto Rte. 104 W. at the end of Chemin Lakeside, and then left onto Rte. 215 S. in the direction of Brome and Sutton Junction.

Sutton ★ (pop. 3,582)

Sutton, which is located at the base of the mountain of the same name, is one of the major winter resorts in the Eastern Townships. The area also has several well-designed golf courses. Among the local houses of worship, the Gothic Revival **Grace Anglican Church**, built out of stone in 1850, is the most noteworthy. Unfortunately, though, its steeple no longer has its pointed arch.

Take Rte. 139 S. towards the tiny village of Abercorn, located less than 3km from the U.S. border (Vermont). From there, turn left on the secondary road that runs along the beautiful valley of the Missisquoi River and passes through Glen Sutton and Highwater before reaching Mansonville.

Lac Memphrémagog ★★

Lac Memphrémagog, which is 44.5km long but only 1 to 2km wide, will remind some visitors of a Scottish loch. It even has its own equivalent of the Loch Ness monster, named "Memphré," sightings of which go back to 1798. The southern portion of the lake, which cannot be seen from Magog, is located in the United States. The name Memphrémagog, like Massawippi and Missisquoi, is an Abenaki word (meaning "vast lake").

Sailing enthusiasts will be happy to learn that the lake is one of the best places in Québec to enjoy this sport.

Turn right on Rte. d'Austin, and right again on Chemin Fisher, which leads to the Abbaye de Saint-Benoît-du-Lac.

Saint-Benoît-du-Lac ★★ (pop. 46)

This municipality consists solely of the estate of the **Abbaye de Saint-Benoît-du-Lac**, an abbey founded in 1913 by Benedictine monks who were driven away from the Abbaye de Saint-Wandrille-de-Fontenelle in Normandy. Aside from the monastery,

there are guest quarters, an abbey chapel and farm buildings. However, only the chapel and a few corridors are open to the public. Visitors will not want to miss the Gregorian chants sung at vespers at 5pm every day.

Anyone who needs to meditate may stay in the guest quarters, where men and women are separated. The monks also raise Charolais cattle, run a dairy (where they make Ermite and Mont Saint-Benoît cheeses) and have two orchards, which are used for producing cider.

Make sure to stop by the abbey shop, in the basement of the main building, for a selection of up to 10 excellent cheeses, as well as apple products like hard cider, vinegar and sauces that rival homemade ones *(Mon-Sat 9am to 10:45am and 11:45am to 4:30pm; ☎819-843-4080, www.st-benoit-du-lac.com)*.

Backtracking along Chemin Fisher, a little road on the left leads to a handsome **round barn**, built in 1907 by Damase Amédée Dufresne. It is not open to the public, but its exterior qualifies it all the same as one of the province's best examples of this style of barn, developed in the United States to withstand strong winds (and also to prevent the devil from hiding in a corner!).

Austin's **Église Saint-Augustin-de-Cantorbéry**, formerly an Anglican church, stands at the intersection, along with a monument honouring the hamlet's most famous citizen, Reginald Aubrey Fessenden, who worked out the principle behind the transmission of the human voice by radio waves.

Turn right on the road leading to Magog. Between the houses, there are some lovely views of the lake and the abbey. Turn right on Rte. 112.

Magog ★ (pop. 23,085)

Equipped with more facilities than any other town between Granby and Sherbrooke, Magog has a lot to offer sports enthusiasts. It is extremely well situated on the northern shore of Lac Memphrémagog, and its cultural scene is also worth noting. Visitors can go to the theatre or the music complex, set in the natural mountain surroundings. The textile industry, once of great importance in the lives of local residents, has declined, giving way to tourism. Visitors will enjoy strolling down Rue Principale, which is lined with shops and restaurants.

The **Parc National du Mont-Orford ★★**, see p 206.

The **Centre d'Arts Orford ★** see p 221.

To get to Georgeville, take Rte. 247 S., which runs along the east coast of Lac Memphrémagog.

Georgeville ★

Most of director Denys Arcand's *Le Déclin de l'Empire américain* (*The Decline of the American Empire*, 1986) was shot in the heart of this area's rolling countryside, synonymous with relaxing vacations. For a long time now, the little village of Georgeville has been a favourite resort area among English-speaking families. The Molsons, for example, own an island in the vicinity. Various celebrities in search of seclusion have also purchased houses on the lake. In the 19th century, ferryboats from Newport, on the southernmost American part of the lake, and from Knowlton's Landing, on the western shore, would all stop in Georgeville, where a number of large wooden hotels once stood. All of these unfortunately burned to the ground; only the pleasant **Auberge Georgeville** and **Maison McGowan sur le Lac** remain. The **Vieille École** (Old School), the **Centre Culturel** (Cultural Centre) and **St. George's Church** (1866) are other buildings of significant historical interest. The quay offers a lovely view of the Abbaye de Saint-Benoît-du-Lac.

Fitch Bay

The **Narrows Covered Bridge** lies further along on Rte. 247 *(turn right on Chemin Merril, then left on Chemin Ridgewood)*. Though more expensive to build, covered bridges lasted much longer because they were protected from bad weather. Consequently, there are a number of them in Québec. This particular one, built in 1881, spans 28m across Fitch Bay. Just next to it, there is a small park with picnic tables.

The surrounding roads are pleasant to explore, especially **Magoon Point Road**, which offers sweeping views of the lake, and

Route de Tomifobia, which could be straight out of a painting by Grant Wood or one of his fellow American Regionalists. Rte. 247 S. leads to **Beebe Plain**, a town known for its granite quarries, which have enjoyed a revival in popularity in recent years, as granite, either bluish or pinkish, has been used for the facing of many postmodern skyscrapers all over North America.

Rock Island ★

Note that the villages of Rock Island, Stanstead Plain and Beebe Plain now form one municipality known as Stanstead (pop. 3,101). Straddling the American border, Rock Island is one of the strangest villages in the province. Walking down its streets, visitors will find themselves in the United States in certain spots and in Canada in others. Notices written in French give way suddenly to signs in English. The flagpole on Monsieur Thériault's lawn flies the Canadian maple leaf, while the Stars and Stripes unfurls in a patriotic and peaceable manner right next door. Its many beautiful stone, brick and wooden buildings make Rock Island a pleasant place to explore on foot.

The **Haskell Free Library and Opera House ★** *(at the corner of Church and Caswell Sts.)*, which dates from 1904, is both a library and a theatre. Straddling the Canadian-American border, it was built as a symbol of the friendship between the two nations. The architect, James Ball, drew his inspiration from Boston's opera house, which is no longer standing. A black line running diagonally across the interior of the building marks the exact location of the border, which corresponds to the 45th parallel.

Head north to Stanstead Plain on Rte. 143 N. (Rue Main, then Rue Dufferin).

Stanstead Plain ★

Some of the most beautiful houses in the Eastern Townships are located in this prosperous community. The distilleries of the 1820s, and later, the granite quarries, enabled a number of the area's inhabitants to amass large fortunes in the 19th century. Particularly noteworthy is the Renaissance Revival **Maison Butters** (1866), in the style of a Tuscan villa, and the **Maison Colby**, which is described below. The **Collège de Stanstead**

The Eastern Townships - Exploring - The Lakes

(1930), the **Couvent des Ursulines** (a French-Canadian order of nuns from Québec City and an unusual institution in these parts), and the Methodist and Anglican churches all merit a leisurely visit.

The **Musée Colby-Curtis** ★ *($4; mid-Jun to mid-Sep, Tue-Sun 11am to 5pm; rest of the year, Tue-Fri 10am to noon and 1pm to 5pm, Sat and Sun 12:30pm to 4:30pm; 535 Rue Dufferin; ☎819-876-7322)* is located in the Colby house, which includes all of its original furnishings, and provides an excellent indication of how the local bourgeoisie lived during the second half of the 19th century. The residence, which has a grey granite facade, was built in 1859 for a lawyer named James Carroll Colby, who called it "Carrollcroft."

Continue on Rte. 143 N. To make an optional detour to Coaticook and Compton, continue east on the 141.

Coaticook (pop. 9,191)

Coaticook, which means "River of the Land of Pine" in the language of the Abenakis, is a small industrial town. It is surrounded by a large number of dairy farms, making it Québec's dairy capital. Its old railroad station is quite interesting.

Located in the heart of Coaticook's residential area, the **Musée Beaulne** ★ *($5; mid-May to mid-Sep, Tue-Sun 10am to 5pm; mid-Sep to mid-May, Wed-Sun 1pm to 4pm; 96 Rue de l'Union; ☎819-849-6560, www.museebeaulne.qc.ca)* is located in a large wooden mansion built in 1912 for the Norton family. The house was designed in a mixture of the Queen Anne and Shingle styles, then popular in the United States. It stands amidst a large English garden. Some of its rooms have been kept in the style typical of bourgeois homes at the dawn of the 20th century, while others contain textile and costume displays.

The **Parc de la Gorge de Coaticook** ★ see p 206.

Head back toward Compton on Route 147 N.

Compton (pop. 2,991)

This village's main claim to fame is the fact that it is the birthplace of Louis-Ste-phen Saint-Laurent, Prime Minister of Canada from 1948 to 1957. He is remembered above all for his role in establishing NATO. There are also many orchards in the area.

Louis S. Saint-Laurent National Historic Site *($4; ♿; mid-May to late Sep, every day 10am to 5pm; 6790 Route Louis-S.-St-Laurent, ☎819-835-5448 or 800-463-6769, www.pc.gc.ca)* preserves the house where Saint-Laurent was born and the general store alongside it, which belonged to his father, providing a glimpse into early-20th-century rural life. Visitors can also listen to snatches of conversation around the stove and enjoy a multimedia show recounting the major achievements of Louis S. St-Laurent and the main events in the history of Canada and the world. A tour of the family home will allow you to discover the lifestyle of bygone days and admire over 2,500 objects that once belonged to the St-Laurent family. Plays and various special activities are offered throughout the summer. The Louis S. St-Laurent National Historic Site is located in a dynamic region with a charming setting that is the delight of many visitors. There is also a beautiful garden and gift shop on the premises.

To return to the main tour, take Rte. 208 to Massawippi, then turn right on Rte. 243, which leads to North Hatley.

North Hatley ★★ (pop. 754)

Attracted by North Hatley's enchanting countryside, wealthy American vacationers built luxurious villas here between 1890 and 1930. Most of these still line the northern part of Lac Massawippi, which, like Lac Memphrémagog, resembles a Scottish loch. Beautiful inns and gourmet restaurants add to the charm of the place, ensuring its reputation as a vacation spot of the utmost sophistication. In the centre of the village, visitors will notice the tiny Shingle-style **United Church**, which looks more Catholic than Protestant.

Manoir Hovey ★ *(575 Chemin Hovey)*, a large villa built in 1900, was modelled on Mount Vernon, George Washington's home in Virginia. It used to be the summer residence of an American named Henry Atkinson, who entertained American artists and politicians here every summer. The house has since been converted into an inn (see p 215).

Continue on Route 108 to Lennoxville.

A former copper mine, **Mines Capelton** *($20.50 including all the necessary equipment for the visit; reservations needed; 800 Rte. 108,* ☎*819-346-9545,   www.minescapelton.com)* was, around the 1880s, one of the most impressive and technologically advanced mining complexes in Canada and in the Commonwealth. Dug by hand, it runs 135m below the surface of Capel mountain. In addition to its geological interest, the 2hr tour reveals the fascinating way in which miners lived and aspects of the first industrial revolution. Temperatures hover around 9°C, so wear warm clothing. There is also a nice hiking trail offering lookouts and interpretive signs.

Head towards Lennoxville via Rte. 143.

Lennoxville ★

This little town, whose population is still mainly English-speaking and is now part of Sherbrooke, is home to two prestigious English-language educational institutions: Bishop's University and Bishop's College. Established alongside the road linking Trois-Rivières to the U.S. border, the town was named after Charles Lennox, the fourth Duke of Richmond, who was governor of Upper and Lower Canada in 1818. Once off the main road (Rte. 143), explore the town's side streets to see the institutional buildings and lovely Second Empire and Queen Anne houses nestled in greenery.

Thanks to changes made to it between 1847 and 1896, **St. George's Anglican Church** *(Rue Queen)* is one of the most charming and picturesque churches in the Eastern Townships.

Bishop's University ★ *(College Road)*, one of three English-language universities in Québec, offers 1,300 students from all over Canada a personalized education in an enchanting setting. It was founded in 1843 thanks to the efforts of a minister named Lucius Doolittle. Upon arriving at the university, visitors will see **McGreer Hall**, built in 1876 by architect James Nelson and later modified by Taylor and Gordon of Montréal to give it a medieval look. **St. Mark's Anglican Chapel**, which stands to its left, was rebuilt in 1891 after a fire. Its long, narrow interior has a lovely oak trim, as well as stained-glass windows by Spence & Sons of Montréal.

Head back towards Rte. 143, which leads to Sherbrooke.

Sherbrooke ★ ★ (pop. 142,958)

Sherbrooke, the Eastern Townships' main urban area, is nicknamed the "Queen of the Eastern Townships." It spreads over a series of hills on both sides of the Rivière Saint-François, accentuating its disorderly appearance. An industrial city, it nevertheless has a number of interesting buildings, the majority of which are located on the west bank.

Sherbrooke's origins date back to the beginning of the 19th century; like so many other villages in the region, it grew up around a mill and a small market. However, in 1823, it was designated as the site of a courthouse intended to serve the entire region, which set it apart from the neighbouring communities. The arrival of the railroad here in 1852, as well as the downtown concentration of institutions, such as the head office of the Eastern Township Bank, led to the construction of prestigious Victorian edifices that transformed Sherbrooke's appearance. Today, the city is home to a large French-language university, founded in 1952 in order to counterbalance Bishop's University in Lennoxville. Despite the city's name, chosen in honour of Sir John Coape Sherbrooke, governor of British North America at the time it was founded, the city's population has been almost entirely French-speaking (95%) for a long time.

Rte. 143 leads to Rue Queen, inside the Sherbrooke city limits. Turn left on Rue King Ouest, then right on Rue Wellington, where we recommend parking in order to continue the tour of the city on foot.

The **Hôtel de Ville ★** *(145 Rue Wellington Nord)*, or city hall, occupies the former Courthouse (the city's third), and is a granite building dating from 1904 that was designed by Elzéar Charest, head architect of the Department of Public Works. It is an example of Quebecers' enduring fondness for Second Empire architecture, with its French spirit. Visitors will recognize the segmental arches, the corner pavillions topped by false mansard roofs with wrought-iron

The Eastern Townships – Exploring - The Lakes

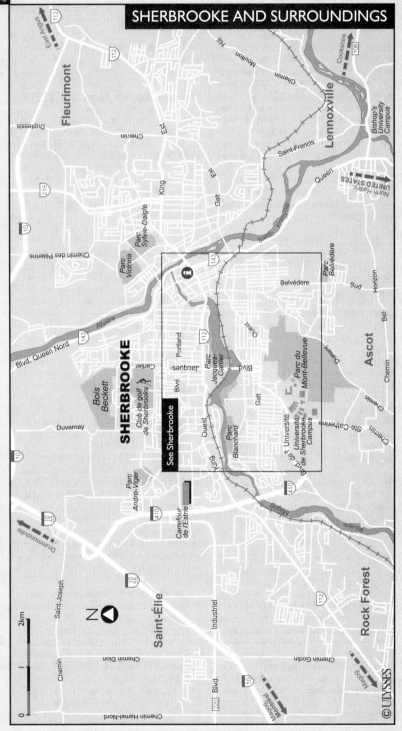

SHERBROOKE AND SURROUNDINGS

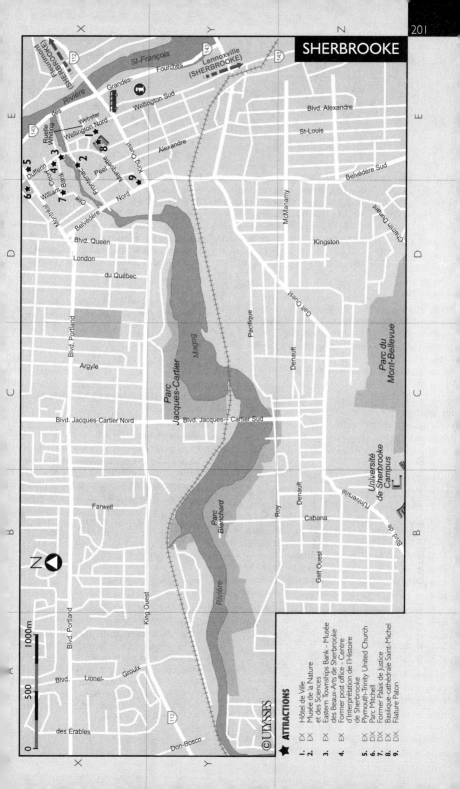

SHERBROOKE

Lennoxville (SHERBROOKE)

St-François

Fourches

Grandes-

Wellington Sud

Blvd. Alexandre

St-Louis

Webster

Wellington Nord

Ruelle Whiting

Alexandre

Belvédère Sud

Dufferin

Peel

King Ouest

McManamy

Kingston

Montréal

William

Bank

Court

Frontenac

Marquette

Nord

Chemin Duhnam

Belvédère

Blvd. Queen

London

du Québec

Galt Ouest

Parc du Mont-Bellevue

Blvd. Portland

Argyle

Magog

Parc Jacques-Cartier

Pacifique

Denault

Blvd. Jacques-Cartier Nord

Blvd. Jacques- Cartier Sud

Farwell

Parc Blanchard

Denault

Roy

Cabana

Université de Sherbrooke Campus

l'Université

Blvd. de

King Ouest

Rivière

Galt Ouest

Blvd. Portland

Groulx

Lionel-

Blvd.

des Érables

Don-Bosco

N

1000m

500

0

© ULYSSES

★ ATTRACTIONS

1. EX Hôtel de Ville
2. EX Musée de la Nature et des Sciences
3. EX Eastern Townships Bank - Musée des Beaux-Arts de Sherbrooke
4. EX Former post office - Centre d'interprétation de l'Histoire de Sherbrooke
5. EX Plymouth-Trinity United Church
6. DX Parc Mitchell
7. DX Former Palais de Justice
8. DX Basilique-cathédrale Saint-Michel
9. DX Filature Paton

cresting and the bull's-eye characteristic of the style. Strathcona Square, the garden in front of the Hôtel de Ville, marks the exact site of the market square that played such an important role in Sherbrooke's early development.

Head to Rue Frontenac and turn right to reach the Musée de la Nature et des Sciences.

The Musée du Séminaire de Sherbrooke was created in 1879. It was set up in the heart of a Sherbrooke seminary with an aim to promote natural sciences. Some 125 years later, the **Musée de la Nature et des Sciences** ★ ★ *($7.50; late Jun to early Sep every day 10am to 5pm, early Sep to late Jun Tue-Sun 10am to 5pm; 225 Rue Frontenac, ☎819-564-3200, www.mnes.qc.ca)* takes up the same mission in its new 10-million-dollar facilities. The museum's permanent exhibit explains the seasonal changes in southern Québec. The museum also features various temporary exhibits, as well as an interesting collection of 65,000 objects that was assembled over the years by the seminary's priests.

Turn left on Rue Frontenac, then right on Rue Dufferin, which crosses the frothy rapids of Rivière Magog, whose force was harnessed in the 19th century in order to provide power for the many mills located along the river.

An important financial institution in the 19th century, now merged with the CIBC (Canadian Imperial Bank of Commerce), the former **Eastern Townships Bank** ★ ★ *(241 Rue Dufferin)* was established by the region's upper class, who were unable to obtain financing for local projects from the banks in Montréal. Its Sherbrooke head office, erected in 1877, was designed by Montréal architect James Nelson, involved at the time in building Bishop's University. It is considered the finest Second Empire building in Québec outside of Montréal and Québec City.

Following a donation from the CIBC and major renovations carried out in the middle of the 1990s, the building now houses the **Musée des Beaux-Arts de Sherbrooke** *($6; Tue-Sun 12am to 5pm, late Jun to early Sep Tue-Sun 10am to 5pm; 241 Rue Dufferin, ☎819-821-2115, www.mbas.qc.ca)*. Gérard Gendron's work, which greets visitors in the main hall, reflects the building's former tenants and its present vocation. Besides the museum's large collection of folk art, there

are several works by local contemporary artists. Volunteers are available to answer questions on the exhibitions, which usually change every two months.

The bank and the **former post office** *(275 Rue Dufferin)* next door, designed by François-Xavier Berlinguet (1885), form a fine architectural ensemble. The post office houses the offices of the **Centre d'Interprétation de l'Histoire de Sherbrooke** *($6; Tue-Fri 9am to noon and 1pm to 5pm, Sat-Sun 1pm to 5pm; Jul and Aug, Tue-Fri 9am to 5pm, Sat and Sun 10am to 5pm; 275 Rue Dufferin, ☎819-821-5406, http://shs.ville.sherbrooke.qc.ca)*, an interpretive centre on Sherbrooke's history. The centre organizes architectural and historical tours of the city, and rents audio tapes *($6)* for walking or driving tours.

Designed in 1851 by William Footner, the **Plymouth-Trinity United Church** *(380 Rue Dufferin)* seems to come straight out of a New England village due to its size, as well as the building materials (red brick and wood painted white). Originally used by the Congregationalists, it was given its present name after several Protestant denominations united to form the United Church in 1925.

Continue on to Parc Mitchell.

Some of the loveliest houses in Sherbrooke are located around **Parc Mitchell** ★ ★, which is adorned with a fountain by sculptor George Hill (1921). **Maison Morey** *(not open to visitors; 428 Rue Dufferin)* is an example of the bourgeois Victorian style favoured by merchants and industrialists from the British Isles and the United States. It was built in 1873 for Thomas Morey.

Walk around the park, then down Rue Montréal, and turn left on Rue Williams.

Facing straight down the centre of Rue Court, the **former Palais de Justice** ★ *(Rue William)*, Sherbrooke's second courthouse, was converted into a drill hall for the city's Hussards regiment at the end of the 19th century. Built in 1839 according to a design by William Footner, the edifice has a lovely neoclassical facade similar to another of his designs, the **Marché Bonsecours** (see p 94) in Montréal.

Head back toward Rue Dufferin on Rue Bank. Turn right on Rue Marquette and climb the hill in the direction of the seminary and the cathedral.

Seen from a certain distance, the **Basilique-cathédrale Saint-Michel** *(130 rue de la Cathédrale, corner of Rue Marquette, ☎819-563-9934)* looks like a European abbey church perched on a promontory. The cathedral's medieval air contrasts with the city's neoclassical past. Up close, however, it becomes apparent that the structure was built very recently and never completed. Begun by architect Louis-Napoléon Audet in 1917, this Gothic Revival cathedral wasn't consecrated until 1958.

Continue on Rue Marquette towards the former Filature Paton, located on Rue Belvédère Nord.

Sherbrooke's former textile industry started up in the second half of the 19th century, and was very profitable, as it was in many New England towns. The **Filature Paton ★** *(at the end of Rue Marquette)*, once the most important textile mill in the Eastern Townships, operated from 1866 to 1977. It was scheduled for demolition the year it closed, but after a few visits over the border, notably to Lowell, Massachussetts, where many such factories have been converted into housing and businesses, the municipal authorities decided to preserve a number of the buildings for a multi-functional complex. Today, the mill is not only a model of how an area's industrial heritage may be preserved and such spaces transformed, but also a new focus for downtown Sherbrooke.

To return to Montréal, take Rte. 143 N. to Aut. 10 and head west.

- -

Tour C: The Back Country
★

 2 days

This most isolated part of the Eastern Townships is composed of an alternating series of mountains and plains. Long, deserted stretches of road link the local Loyalist villages. Far from the urban centres, these communities have in many cases remained primarily English-speaking and have retained their old-fashioned charm. The area around Mont Mégantic was col-

onized in the early 19th century by Scottish settlers from the Hebrides, and Gaelic was commonly spoken here 100 years ago. French Canadians from the Rivière Chaudière valley (Beauce) began arriving at the end of the 19th century.

Eaton Corner ★

Eaton, or Eaton Corner, takes its name from its location at the crossing of two roads that played an important role in the settling of the region, Chemin Sherbrooke and the road that brought Loyalist settlers who were fleeing the United States. The settlers starting clearing the lands of Eaton Township in 1793. These were prosperous times for the village of Eaton Corner, up until 1850 when local industry started being diverted towards towns that had access to waterways. Bypassed by the various railroads of the Eastern Townships, the town was slowly deserted, leaving behind an important architectural heritage.

The **Musée de la Société d'Histoire du Comté de Compton ★** *($2; early Jun to early Sep Wed-Sun 1pm to 5pm, Sep Sat-Sun 1pm to 5pm; Route 253, ☎819-875-5256)* is located in an old Congregationalist Church that was built in 1841. The pretty neoclassical building contains Loyalist-era furniture as well as documents and photos that bear witness to the lives of the first settlers who ventured east of Sherbrooke. The city hall facing the church is located in Eaton Corner's old school academy, where English Eastern Township village school teachers were trained between 1863 and 1899.

Take Rte. 153 N. to Cookshire, where you can pick up Rte. 212 E., which leads through the villages of Island Brook, West Ditton and La Patrie, offering beautiful views of Mont Mégantic. Continue on to Notre-Dame-des-Bois.

Notre-Dame-des-Bois (pop. 784)

Located in the heart of the Appalachians at an altitude of over 550m, this little community acts as a gateway to Mont Mégantic and its observatory, as well as Mont Saint-Joseph and its sanctuary, both located in Parc National du Mont-Mégantic.

From Notre-Dame-des-Bois, take the road in front of the church toward Val Racine. After 3.3km, turn left (past the Rivière aux Saumons). On the left, before the road starts heading upward, there is a tourist-information booth. Several kilometres further, you will reach a junction. The road on the left leads to the observatory while the unpaved road on the right leads to the Sanctuary.

The **ASTROlab du Mont-Mégantic** ★★ *(from $10.50; late May to late Jun Sat noon to 5pm and 8pm to 11pm, Sun noon to 5pm; late Jun to late Aug every day 10am to 7pm and 8pm to 11pm; late Aug to early Oct Sat noon to 5pm and 8pm to 11pm, Sun noon to 5pm; 189 Route du Parc, ☎819-888-2941 or 866-888-2941, www.astro-lab.qc.ca)* is an interpretive centre focusing on astronomy. The interactive museum's various rooms and multimedia show reveal the workings of astronomy from its beginnings to the latest technology. A guided tour to the summit of Mont Mégantic, lasting approximately 1hr 15min, takes visitors through the facilities. Famous for its observatory, Mont Mégantic was chosen for its strategic location between the universities of Montréal and Laval, as well as its distance from urban light sources. The second-highest summit in the Eastern Townships, it stands at 1,105m.

During the **Festival d'Astronomie Populaire du Mont Mégantic**, a local astronomy festival held the second week of July, astronomy buffs can observe the heavens through the most powerful telescope in eastern North America. Otherwise, the latter is only available to researchers. However, a new observatory with a 61cm telescope is now open to the public. In summer, basic celestial mechanics workshops are also given.

Head back to Rte. 212 E. At Woburn, take Rte. 161 N., which runs along beautiful Lac Mégantic.

A vast expanse of crystal-clear water stretching 20km and spanning 7km at its widest point, **Lac Mégantic** ★★ is teeming with all sorts of fish, especially trout, and attracts a good many vacationers eager to go fishing or simply enjoy the local beaches. Five municipalities around the lake, Lac-Mégantic being the best-known, welcome visitors lured by the lovely mountainous countryside.

Lac-Mégantic ★ (pop. 6,029)

The town of Lac-Mégantic was founded in 1885 by Scottish settlers from the Hebrides. Unable to make enough money

from the relatively poor soil, the residents soon turned to forestry. Today, thousands of people come to the region every year to enjoy a wide variety of sporting activities. The town is beautifully located on the shores of Lac Mégantic.

In the **Église Sainte-Agnès** ★ *(4872 Rue Laval)*, erected in 1913, visitors will discover a beautiful stained-glass window designed in 1849 for the Catholic Church of the Immaculate Conception in Mayfair, London.

*The road then leads through the villages of Nantes and Stornoway, Stratford and Saint-Gérard, passing alongside the **Parc National de Frontenac** ★ (see p 421) and skirting round Lac Aylmer before connecting with Rte. 216 and Rte. 255, which lead to Asbestos.*

Asbestos (pop. 6,671)

Asbestos, as its name indicates, is one of the foremost asbestos-mining centres in the world. But asbestos releases harmful particles when improperly handled, which led to it being banned by the United States and a subsequent decline in mining activity in the town of Asbestos.

The **Musée Minéralogique et d'Histoire Minière** *($2; late Jun to mid-Aug Wed-Sun 11am to 5pm; 341 Boulevard St-Luc, ☎819-879-6444 or 879-5308)*, a museum outlining mineralogy and the history of mining, includes samples of asbestos from various mines, both in Québec and abroad.

Danville ★ (pop. 4,288)

This attractive, shady village has preserved a number of noteworthy Victorian and Edwardian residences, which bear witness to a time when wealthy Montréal families summered in Danville.

Parks

Tour A: The Orchards

The **Parc National de la Yamaska** *($3.50; every day 8am until sundown; 1780 Boulevard David-Bouchard, Roxton Pond, ☎450-776-7182 or 800-665-6527, www.sepaq.com)* was laid out

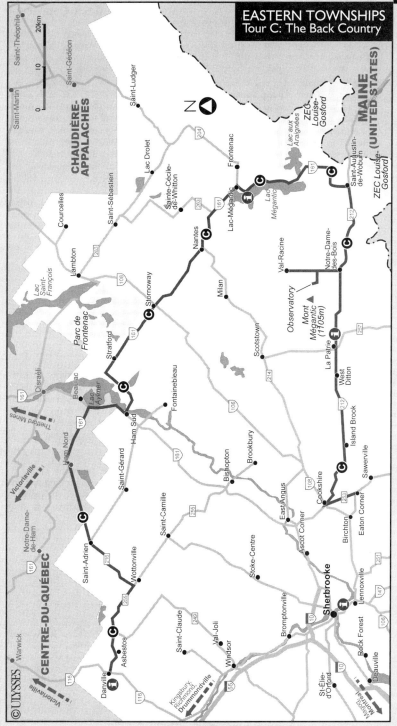

205

EASTERN TOWNSHIPS
Tour C: The Back Country

CHAUDIÈRE-
APPALACHES

MAINE (UNITED STATES)

20km

N

Saint-Théophile
Saint-Gédéon
Saint-Martin
Saint-Ludger
Courcelles
Lambton
Saint-Sébastien
Sainte-Cécile-de-Whitton
Lac Drolet
Saint-Théophile
Frontenac
ZEC Louise-Gosford
Lac aux Araignées

Parc de Frontenac
Lac Saint-François
Disraëli
Beaulac
Lac Aylmer
Ham Nord
Ham Sud
Stratford
Nantes
Stornoway
Milan
Scotstown
Lac-Mégantic
Lac Mégantic
Val-Racine
Notre-Dame-des-Bois
Saint-Augustin-de-Woburn
ZEC Louise-Gosford

Observatory
Mont Mégantic (1105m)
La Patrie
West Ditton
Island Brook
Sawerville
Cookshire

Thetford Mines
Victoriaville
Notre-Dame-de-Ham
Saint-Gérard
Saint-Camille
Fontainebleau
Bishopton
Brookbury
East Angus
Ascot Corner
Birchton
Eaton Corner

Saint-Adrien
Wottonville
Stoke-Centre
Bromptonville
Sherbrooke
Lennoxville
Rock Forest
Deauville
St-Élie-d'Orford

CENTRE-DU-QUÉBEC
Warwick
Victoriaville
Danville
Asbestos
Saint-Claude
Val-Joli
Windsor
Kingsbury, Richmond, Drummondville
Saint-Martin
Montréal

around the Réservoir Choinière, now a pleasant swimming area. There are 28km of cross-country ski trails available for public use in winter, and 18km of bike paths in summer.

Just a few kilometres from downtown Granby, the **Centre d'Interprétation de la Nature du Lac Boivin** *(free admission; Mon-Fri 8:30am to 4:30pm, Sat-Sun 9am to 5pm; 700 Rue Drummond, Granby, ☎450-375-3861, www.cinlb.org)* offers four trails for a total of 13km. An observation tower and blind offer good vantage points to spot aquatic plants and a variety of water birds. Mornings, when the trails are less busy, are the best time for birding. The paths are also open in the winter. There are temporary exhibits throughout the year at the information centre.

Tour B: The Lakes

The **Parc National du Mont-Orford** ★ ★ *($3.50; 3321 Chemin du Parc, Canton d'Orford, ☎819-843-9855 or 800-665-6527, www.sepaq. com)* stretches over 58km² and includes—in addition to the mountain—the area around lakes Stukely and Fraser. During the summer, visitors can enjoy the beach, the magnificent golf course *($30 per round)*, back-country campsites, and some 50km of hiking trails (the most beautiful path leads to Mont Chauve). The park also attracts winter-sports lovers with its cross-country ski trails and 33 downhill ski runs.

The **Parc de la Gorge de Coaticook** ★ *(fees vary according to activities; early May to late Jun, every day 10am to 5pm; late Jun to early Sep, every day 9am to 8pm; early Sep to late Oct, every day 10am to 5pm; Nov to May, Thu and Fri 6pm to 9pm, Sat 1pm to 4pm and 6pm to 9pm, Sun 11am to 5pm; 135 Rue Michaud or 400 Rue St-Marc, Coaticook, ☎819-849-2331 or 888-524-6743, www.gorgedecoaticook.qc.ca)* protects the part of the impressive 50m gorge created by the Rivière Coaticook. Trails wind across the entire area, enabling visitors to see the gorge from different angles. Cross the suspension bridge over the gorge, the longest in the world made for pedestrians, if you dare!

Tour C: The Back Country

Known mainly for its famed observatory (see p 204), the **Parc National du Mont-Mégantic** *($3.50; every day 9am to 5pm, until 11pm during astronomy evenings; no pets allowed; 189 Route du Parc, Notre-Dame-des-Bois, ☎819-888-2941 or 800-665-6527, www.sepaq. com)* covers an area of 58.8km². It displays the different types of mountainous vegetation characteristic of the Eastern Townships and contains the Mont St-Joseph and Mont Mégantic hills. Heavy infrastructure has not been able to disturb the tranquillity of this park, whose purpose is educational. Hikers and skiers can take advantage of the park's interpretive trails, cabins and campsites and, if lucky, observe up to 125 species of migrating birds. Enjoy snowshoeing in winter and mountain-biking in summer.

Outdoor Activities

■ Adventure Packages

Tour B: The Lakes

A young and dynamic enterprise, the **Adrénaline** *(☎819-843-0045 or 888-475-3462, www.adrenaline-adventure.com)* outdoor-adventure school has an experienced staff and offers different activities, such as dogsledding expeditions, ice climbing, ice fishing and snowshoeing in winter, and anything from beginners' rock climbing and river kayaking to panoramic rafting. In short, a host of activities for thrill-seekers! Prices include instructors and the required equipment. Personalized activities are also available upon request.

■ Cross-Country Skiing

Tour B: The Lakes

The Sutton region is not only ideal for downhill skiing and hiking, but is also home to a superb network of cross-country ski trails. The **Sutton-en-Haut** *($6.95; 297 Rue Maple, Sutton-en-Haut, ☎450-538-2271)* network includes 15 interconnected trails that allow skiers to switch tracks and levels of difficulty throughout the day.

Parc National du Mont Orford *($10; Canton d'Orford, ☎819-843-9855 or 800-665-6527)* also has a network of cross-country trails with a good reputation. Thirteen trails cover some 80km of terrain that will please all levels of skiers.

Tour C: The Back Country

The 50km-long **Centre de Ski de Fond Bellevue** *($9.50; 70 Chemin Lay, Melbourne, ☎819-826-3869)* is a pleasant surprise, with 15 trails for all levels.

Besides its famed observatory and excellent snow conditions, Parc du Mont-Mégantic has eight cross-country ski trails. The **Sentiers du Mont-Mégantic** *($8; Chemin de l'Observatoire, 189 Route du Parc, Notre-Dame-des-Bois, ☎819-888-2941 or 866-888-2941)* offers one of the longest ski seasons in the province. Because of its altitude, skiing sometimes lasts into the month of May.

■ Cruises

Croisières Memphrémagog *(regular cruises $20, one-day cruises $68; mid-May to late Sep: regular cruises from 10am, reservations required for one-day cruises; Quai de Magog, ☎819-843-8068 or 888-842-8068, www.croisiere-memphremagog. com)* offer 2hr cruises on magnificent Lac Memphrémagog, whose shores form part of both the Québec and U.S. borders. At around 9am, a second, one-day cruise leaves the wharf for Vermont where it makes a brief call at Newport. These cruises are all the more spectacular in the fall when the Appalachian colours are at their brightest. Fares include a light snack. Reservations required.

■ Cycling

Tour A: The Orchards

The **Estriade** bicycle path runs along an old railway line. It covers 21km, linking Granby, Bromont and Waterloo.

La Station de Vélo de Montagne de Bromont *(150 Rue Champlain, Bromont, ☎450-534-2200)* has close to 100km of intermediate and expert level trails. Bikers can also use the chairlift.

Tour B: The Lakes

The **Parc National du Mont-Orford** *($3.50; Canton d'Orford, ☎819-843-9855 or 877-843-9855)* may not be as popular as Bromont for mountain biking, but it nevertheless offers three trails for a total of 40km of easy, difficult and very difficult workouts.

■ Downhill Skiing

Tour A: The Orchards

The **Station de Ski Bromont** *($44; 150 Rue Champlain, Bromont, ☎450-534-2200 or 866-276-6668, www.skibromont.com)* has 56 runs, 40 of which are lit for night-skiing *(Sun-Thu to 10pm, Fri and Sat to 10:30pm)*. The mountain has a vertical drop of 385m.

Tour B: The Lakes

The **Station de Ski du Mont Sutton** *($46; 671 Chemin Maple, Sutton, ☎450-538-2545, www. montsutton.com)* has 53 downhill ski runs and a vertical drop of 460m. It is known for its magnificent glade runs.

Mont Orford *($44; Canton d'Orford, ☎819-843-6548 or 800-567-2772, www.orford.com)*, among the most attractive ski centres in Québec, offers 54 trails that will please everyone. It has a vertical drop of 540m.

Owl's Head *($36; Chemin du Mont Owl's Head, Mansonville, ☎450-292-3342, ski conditions: 450-292-5000, www.owlshead.com)* is one of the most beautiful ski resorts in the Eastern Townships region, with sweeping views of Lac Memphrémagog and the surrounding mountains. Owl's Head will mainly please beginners and intermediate skiers, as there are no trails to challenge experts.

■ Golf

Tour B: The Lakes

The courses at **Club de Golf Venise** *($32; 1519 Chemin de la Rivière, Magog, ☎819-864-9891)* are rigorously maintained, making it one of the best golfing spots in the region. The Blue *(Bleu)* course is particularly recommended for golfers who appreciate a challenge.

The Eastern Townships - Outdoor Activities

Much valued for its quality greens, the **Owl's Head** *($45; 181 Chemin Owl's Head, Mansonville, ☎450-292-3666 or 800-363-3342, www.owlshead.com)* golf course is easily the favourite amongst local golfers. Moreover, it is endowed with a very posh clubhouse and offers a superb view of the mountain after which it was named. Chances of teeing off are better on weekdays.

The mountainside golf course at **Manoir des Sables** *($29-$37; 90 Avenue des Jardins, Orford, ☎819-847-4299, www.manoirdessables.com)* provides a moderate challenge. Though relatively recent, it's one of the region's most promising courses.

The **Dufferin Heights** *($40; 4115 Route 143, Stanstead, ☎819-876-2113)* golf course, in operation for more than 75 years, puts even the staunchest of golfers to the test. Its undulating terrain offers splendid views of the Appalachian Mountains and lakes Massawippi and Memphrémagog.

■ Hiking

Tour A: The Orchards

The **Sentier de l'Estrie** *(☎819-864-6314, www.lessentiersdelestrie.qc.ca)* is a network of more than 160km of trails through the Chapman, Kingsbury, Brompton, Orford, Bolton, Glen, Echo and Sutton areas. You can obtain a topographical map of the trail and the membership card necessary to hike it for $40. Keep in mind that most of the trail runs across private property, and landowners have accorded an exclusive right of way to members.

Tour B: The Lakes

Parc d'Environnenment Naturel de Sutton *(4$; ☎450-538-4085 or 800-565-8455, www.parc-sutton.com)* is just as popular in the summer as it is in winter, thanks to its 77km trail system. The **Roundtop** hike, with its spectacular panoramas, attracts hikers from far and wide.

Parc National du Mont-Orford *(☎819-843-9855 or 800-665-6527)* is a prized hiking spot in

the Townships. Several sections of the **Sentier de l'Estrie** traverse it. It is an excellent choice for hikers as it contains a network of nearly 80km of trails of varying degrees of difficulty. The **Mont Chauve** and **Mont Orford** hikes are particularly interesting.

Tour C: The Back Country

Eight trails crisscross the **Parc National du Mont-Mégantic**, totalling 60km of hiking trails. The Trois Sommets trail, traversing Mont Mégantic and the crests of Monts Victoria and St. Joseph, is certainly among the most beautiful in the region. This network is also connected to the **Sentiers Frontaliers** *(☎819-583-6313 or 800-363-5515, www.sentiersfrontaliers.qc.ca)*, which encompass an area straddling the U.S. border.

■ Horseback Riding

The **Centre Équestre de Bromont** *(100 Rue Laprairie, ☎450-534-3255)* hosted the 1976 Olympic equestrian events, for which a variety of stables and rings, both exterior and interior, were built. Some of these facilities are now used for riding classes.

■ Ice Skating

Tour A: The Orchards

Lac Boivin becomes a skating rink during winter (1km loop). A musical backdrop is provided and the rink is lit to permit night skating. You can check the rink's ice conditions before heading out by contacting the **Centre d'Interprétation de la Nature du Lac Boivin (CINLB)** *(☎450-375-3861, www.cinlb.org)*. The rink's entrance is located at 700 Rue Drummond in Granby.

Tour B: The Lakes

Domaine Howard *(1300 Boulevard Portland, Sherbrooke)* is surrounded by quaint old houses and is home to Sherbrooke's most charming skating rink. Youngsters can also slide down the small hills that surround the estate.

⚠ Accommodations

Tour A:
The Orchards

Dunham

Au Temps des Mûres
$$ bkfst incl.
pb/sb ≋
2024 Chemin Vail
☎ (450) 266-1319 or 888-708-8050
▤ (450) 266-1303
www.tempsdesmures.qc.ca
Located on a 160ha maple-tree farm on a scenic road lined with towering trees, Le Temps des Mûres could be just the spot you've dreamt of—that is, if you dream of authentic country atmosphere at a very reasonable price. This handsome gabled brick farmhouse offers five cozy guest rooms, each with a planked wood floor and a duvet to snuggle under. A full breakfast is served at a long, communal wooden table. Children are welcome.

Cowansville

Le Passe-Partout
$$ bkfst incl.
pb/sb
167 Route Pierre-Laporte
☎ (450) 260-1678
www.passepartout.ca
Although you probably won't be spending much time in the industrial town of Cowansville, this bed and breakfast, with helpful, easygoing hosts and a casual atmosphere, has all the makings for a pleasant stay within easy reach of every point of interest on this tour. A former farmhouse built in 1865, each of its four smallish guest rooms

has wide-plank wood floors, a ceiling fan and a unique decor, which ranges from a red-and-black Japanese-themed room to a cheery little blue-and-yellow number.

Bromont

Camping Bromont
$
≋
24 Rue Lafontaine
☎ (450) 534-2712
www.campingbromont.com
Camping Bromont has every convenience, including showers, laundry room, a swimming pool, hiking trails—even miniature golf! Most sections are wooded, providing campers with some privacy.

Casa Bromont
$$ bkfst incl.
1208 Rue Shefford
☎ (450) 534-2429
www.casabromont.com
Enthusiastic young hosts Mélanie and Sassan have transformed their *casa*, located on a tranquil 1ha property with access to their own swimming hole, into a welcoming B&B with three guest rooms. The burgundy Zen room has an in-room clawfoot tub and toilet (not for shy types), the Sahara has a big in-room tub and separate toilet, and the serene and cozy Green Dream has wide-plank wood floors and a private bathroom down the hall. Breakfasts may include eggs from the owners' hens, as well as home-baked goods, a hot dish and espresso.

Auberge du Château
$$$
≡ ≋ ♨
95 Rue Montmorency
☎ (450) 534-3433 or 888-276-6668

www.aubergebromont.com
Auberge du Château is located on the town's golf course. Purchased by the owners of the Château Bromont in 2002, Auberge du Château and its 50 rooms have since been renovated. The place has loads of potential: it's beautifully set on grounds surrounded by mature trees, and the reception is friendly.

Château Bromont
$$$$
≡ ▲ ⚓ ≋ ❄ ♨ ⑉ ♈ ⚐ ◎
90 Rue Standstead
☎ (450) 534-3433 or 888-276-6668
▤ (450) 534-0514
www.chateaubromont.com
Those looking for comfort and elegance should head to the Château Bromont. There is a variety of room configurations and styles, ranging from split-level rooms with the bed either at the top or bottom of a spiral staircase (unfortunately the decor of some of these is rather cold) to elegant suites and junior suites. The latter, featuring elegant neutral tones and balconies, are among the most attractive. All guest rooms feature robes and a pillow menu that allows you to choose the type that's just right for your noggin. The **Pavillon des Sens** spa is attached to Château Bromont by a walkway and offers eight rooms and four suites.

Granby

Parc National de la Yamaska
$
1780 Boulevard David-Bouchard
☎ 450-776-7182 or 800-665-6527
www.sepaq.com
Parc National de la Yamaska has campsites available to those with tents. The ar-

rangement doesn't offer much privacy, but they are located close to the pleasant beach, an ideal spot for family relaxation.

Le Granbyen
$$-$$$

≡ ◎ ≋ ⚇

700 Rue Principale
☎ (450) 378-8406 or 800-267-8406
www.legranbyen.com

A typical roadside hotel for travellers on the move, Le Granbyen has decent but nondescript rooms.

Tour B: The Lakes

Around Lac Brome

Camping Domaine des Érables
$

688 Chemin Bondville, Rte. 215, Lac Brome
☎ (450) 242-8888

Located on the shores of Lac Brome, the well-kept Camping Domaine des Érables offers all the comforts of life with its laundromat, showers, convenience store and other services.

Auberge Joli Vent
$$ bkfst incl.

≋ ⚇

667 Chemin Bondville, Foster
☎ (450) 243-4272 or 866-525-4272
🖷 (450) 242-1943
www.aubergedujolivent.com

Auberge Joli Vent is a lovely inn with a pleasant setting, despite its roadside location. The modestly furnished rooms have a rustic charm.

Knowlton

La Venise Verte
$$ bkfst incl.

pb/sb ≋

58 Rue Victoria
☎ (450) 243-1844
www.laveniseverte.com

This handsome brick home (1884) is a good alternative to its much pricier next-door neighbour, Auberge Lakeview Inn. Hosts Sylvie and Pierre have four guest rooms, three of which have wide-planked wood floors. All are attractive and simply furnished with a mixture of antique and modern accessories; beds have cozy duvets and walls are painted soothing shades of blue, beige or ginger. Breakfasts feature organic products.

Auberge Knowlton
$$$ bkfst incl.

⚇

286 Chemin Knowlton
☎ (450) 242-6886
🖷 (450) 242-1055
www.aubergeknowlton.ca

A 12-room inn smack dab in the centre of town, Auberge Knowlton, built in 1849, has stood the test of time. The recently renovated guest rooms are on the small side, but large enough to open the hideabed provided in each. The main sour note is that the inn is situated on a busy road and trucks pass as of early morning; if you plan on sleeping until a reasonable hour, ask for a room at the rear, such as our favourite, no. 3, which has a high cathedral ceiling and sage-green walls.

Auberge Lakeview Inn
$$$$$ ½b

≡ ≋ ⚇ ◎

50 Rue Victoria
☎ (450) 243-6183 or 800-661-6183
🖷 (450) 243-0602
www.aubergelakeviewinn.com

Ideally located right in the village of Knowlton but off the main drag, Auberge Lakeview Inn offers a thoroughly Victorian atmosphere. Indeed,

renovations have restored some of the noble antiquity to this historic monument, built in the latter half of the 19th century. Cozy and romantic, the place is all oak and Victorian-style flowered wallpaper. Unfortunately, the standard guest rooms are absolutely miniscule; the bathrooms are barely large enough to contain a shower stall. Though pricier, the studios, furnished with rustic, antique-style furniture, are a much better idea. There's a cozy pub on site, as well as a formal dining room.

Sutton

Auberge Le St-Amour
$$-$$$

⚇ ● ≡

1 Rue Pleasant
☎ /🖷 (450) 538-6188
☎ 888-538-6188
www.auberge-st-amour.com

Occupying an imposing green-clapboard Second Empire residence (1902) right in the centre of town, Auberge Le St-Amour offers eight guest rooms and a two-bedroom suite with kitchenette, each decorated with murals that recall the French Impressionists. Unfortunately, most of the rooms are very dark and sombre, despite the flowery murals; most have cheap carpetting, others rough plywood floors. Room no. 8 is among the most attractive, with a Van Gogh–sun mural and a window seat; no. 9 and no. 7 are also good choices.

Dessine-Moi un Mouton
$$$ bkfst incl.

▲ ≋

212 Chemin Maple
☎ (450) 538-1515

If you don't mind paying a trifle more than for an average B&B after a day on (or off) the slopes, look no further. Dessine-Moi un Mouton ("draw me a sheep," a line from *The Little Prince*), a blue-and-white clapboard house on a large plot of land outside the village, is the perfect spot to spoil yourself. Chef Marc and artist Ginette (the latter is the painter of the B&B's whimsical sheep portraits) have created an elegant yet understated haven that is nothing like the bland ski condos along this road. The two romantic and cozy guest rooms and one studio are decorated with flair in cream and white and have their own private patios. The "Courrier Sud" room covers two floors: the first features a window seat that doubles as a bed while the second floor's bedroom offers a view on the outdoor pool. All bathrooms feature a deep soaker tub, all beds lovely linens. Marc serves intimate dinners on Saturdays (bring your own wine) in an airy dining room with six tables. Children are welcome.

Mansonville

La Chouette de Mansonville
$$ bkfst incl.
≋
560 Route de Mansonville
☎/▤ (450) 292-3020 or
888-304-3020
www.lachouette.ca
La Chouette de Mansonville is set on a huge estate. The charming house includes a common living room where guests can relax next to a cozy fireplace and an indoor pool.

Vale Perkins (Knowlton's Landing)

Aubergine Relais de Campagne
$$ bkfst incl.
♨
160 Chemin Cooledge
☎ (450) 292-3246
www.laubergine.com
The Aubergine Relais de Campagne occupies a former post house dating from 1816. Built out of red brick, it has a long wooden veranda perfect for summer evenings. This inn is all the more pleasant for the gorgeous view it offers of Lac Memphrémagog.

Eastman

Spa Eastman
$$$$ fb
pb/sb ⛄ ≋ ♨ △ ≡ ⚓ ♿
895 Chemin des Diligences
☎ (450) 297-3009 or 800-665-5272
▤ (450) 297-3370
www.spa-eastman.com
Nestled in the countryside, Spa Eastman is considered by some to be one of the best establishments of its kind. The whole gamut of body-care treatments is available here, either individually or in a package, by the day or during an extended stay, but always with the utmost in professionalism. Guests can also stay simply for the beauty and tranquility of the setting, without availing themselves of the spa.

Bolton Centre

L'Iris Bleu
$$-$$$ bkfst incl.
♨
895 Chemin Missisquoi
☎ (450) 292-3530 or 877-292-3530
www.irisbleu.com

L'Iris Bleu is a charming bed and breakfast. The lace curtains, flowered wallpaper and antique furniture decorating the three rooms exude a warm atmosphere. You will be welcomed by the friendly owners, who go out of their way to make your stay a pleasant one. A Mediterranean-style evening meal is served in the lovely dining room.

Magog

À Tout Venant
$$ bkfst incl.
624 Rue Bellevue Ouest
☎ (819) 868-0419 or 888-611-5577
www.atoutvenant.com
À Tout Venant was purchased by a couple from Lyon, France. Their five guest rooms are all located very close to one another, so soundproofing is not guaranteed. Our choice is the smallish and least expensive Soleil room, which has a wood floor and antiques. Abricot, with its own solarium, is also a pleasant option. Lovely, sunny breakfast room.

Au Virage
$$ bkfst incl.
pb/sb
172 Rue Merry Nord
☎ (819) 868-5828
Situated in the heart of Magog and surrounded by many other B&Bs, Au Virage is a very acceptable option. Hosts Louise and Jean live in the attached house. The five guest rooms are rather small (those with private bathrooms are larger) but a few antiques, wood floors and flowered fabrics warm them up. Elaborate breakfasts are served at a common table to encourage guests to socialize.

L'Ancestrale
$$-$$$
pb/sb ◎
200 Rue Abbott
☎ (819) 847-5555 or 888-847-5507
www.ancestrale.qc.ca

L'Ancestrale offers a simple, somewhat cluttered and very homey decor. The best of the four guest rooms is La Rêveuse, an intimate, ground-floor mini-suite with whirlpool bath and private patio. Simple, nutritious breakfasts are served, such as cereal with soy milk and scrambled eggs with vegetables. The host is very helpful and professional.

L'Auberge L'Étoile-sur-le-Lac
$$$
≡ ● ⚊ ≈ Ⓦ ◎ ▲ Ⓨ
1200 Rue Principale Ouest
☎ (819) 843-6521 or 800-567-2727
www.etoile-sur-le-lac.com

Located on the highway just outside of Magog, this large hotel doesn't look like much from the outside, but its 50-odd guest rooms are entirely acceptable. Each of the new "luxury" rooms has a large patio overlooking the lake, as well as duvets, deep soaker tubs and new furniture—nice, but not quite luxurious. All standard rooms offer lake views.

Austin

Aux Jardins Champêtres
$$-$$$ bkfst incl.
≈ Ⓦ ⚊
1575 Chemin des Pères
☎ (819) 868-0665 or 877-868-0665
www.auxjardinschampetres.com

This inn's six guest rooms are clearly an adjunct to the dining room—if you're not dining here, be aware that there will probably be noise until midnight. The country-style guest rooms, each with wood floors,

were recently renovated and private bathrooms were added.

Orford

Camping Stukely
$
3321 Chemin du Parc, Aut. 10 or 55, Exit 118, heading toward Parc National du Mont Orford
☎ (819) 843-9855 or 800-665-6527
www.sepaq.com

Located in Mont Orford national park, Camping Stukely occupies a site on the lake of the same name. Dense forest surrounds the campground and mountain—biking trails are close by. At night, during summer, the community centre becomes a movie theatre. The campground also has a beach and rents small boats.

Auberge du Centre d'Arts Orford
$-$$
3166 Chemin du Parc
☎ (819) 843-8595 or 800-567-6155
www.arts-orford.org

The Centre d'Arts d'Orford's inn has 87 rooms in its main building as well as 17 rustic chalets available for rent during the summer. There is also a restaurant and bar on the premises, five conference rooms and 30 multifunctional studios.

Gîte de la Maison Hôte
$$ bkfst incl.
≈
2037 Chemin du Parc
☎ (819) 868-2604

Christiane and Bernard skilfully transformed this clapboard house into a B&B in 1999 and have been the perfect hosts ever since. Their four impeccable guest rooms feature wood floors, attractive bed-

ding and plenty of country cachet; some offer a view of Mont Orford. Guests rave about the absolutely sublime five-course breakfasts, which feature edible flowers and a seat on the patio (both in season, of course). An excellent place to base yourself in the Magog/Orford area and a definite step above many of the options in downtown Magog, which is just a short drive away.

Auberge Estrimont
$$$$
≡ ▲ ⚊ ● ≈ Ⓦ ⫸ ◎
44 Avenue de l'Auberge
☎ (819) 843-1616 or 800-567-7320
www.estrimont.qc.ca

Located near Mont Orford, Auberge Estrimont features rooms and small condos. Made entirely of wood, the condos are equipped with balconies and fireplaces. Forest surrounds the property.

Manoir des Sables
$$$$-$$$$$
≡ ▲ ⚊ ● ≈ Ⓦ ⫸ Ⓨ ◎ &
90 Avenue des Jardins
☎ (819) 847-4747 or 800-567-3514
▤ (819) 847-3519
www.manoirdessables.com

In the shadow of Mont Orford is the very opulent and modern Manoir des Sables. The hotel features a multitude of services and facilities such as indoor and outdoor swimming pools, an 18-hole golf course, tennis courts and a health spa. Guest rooms on the top floor offer magnificent views of the lake and of the 60ha property. Rooms in the "Privilège" wing come with exemplary service and include continental breakfasts.

Village Mont Orford
$$$$$
≋ ☕ ◬

4969 Chemin du Parc
☎ (819) 847-2662 or 800-567-7315
▤ (819) 847-3635
www.village-mont-orford.com
The Village Mont Orford is comprised of several buildings, each containing a few lovely, fully equipped condos. Approximately 200m from there, a quadruple chair lift takes skiers up to Mont Orford's runs.

Georgeville

Maison McGowan sur le Lac
$$-$$$
♨

51 Carré Copp
☎ (819) 843-2126
Maison McGowan sur le Lac is located within a stone's throw of Memphémagog lake. Its 12 unpretentious rooms are warm and charmingly old-fashioned. A terrace provides guests with a beautiful view of the sailboats and spectacular sunsets on the lake. The dining room serves up tasty meals and the inn even has a sailboat; captain Robert Blondin takes guests out onto the lake twice a day when weather permits.

Auberge Georgeville
$$$$$ bkfst incl.
♨

71 Chemin Channel
☎ (819) 843-8683 or 888-843-8686
▤ (819) 843-5045
www.aubergegeorgeville.com
Auberge Georgeville, situated in the tiny lakeside village of the same name, occupies an imposing pink-clapboard Victorian mansion (1898). Its friendly welcome, wraparound veranda, wooden staircases, antiques and heavenly aromas emanating from the kitchen and cozy dining rooms create a warm

atmosphere that oozes historic cachet. Its 10 tiny guest rooms have wood floors and are decorated à la Laura Ashley; each has a private bathroom with shower. The inn's dining room has been much acclaimed over the years (see p 218).

Ayer's Cliff

Auberge Ripplecove Inn
$$$$-$$$$$
≡ ◬ ≋ ♨ ◉

700 Rue Ripplecove
☎ (819) 838-4296 or 800-668-4296
▤ (819) 838-5541
www.ripplecove.com
Located on a 6ha property facing Lac Massawippi, the Ripplecove Inn is wonderfully peaceful. Its elegant Victorian-style dining room and tasteful guest rooms ensure comfort in unparalleled, intimate surroundings. Moreover, the more luxurious rooms have their own fireplaces and whirlpool baths. A variety of outdoor activities are offered. The place becomes absolutely magical in winter. The inn's restaurant serves quality French cuisine (see p 218).

Coaticook

La Brise des Nuits
$$ bkfst incl.
142 Rue Cutting
☎ (819) 849-4667
La Brise des Nuits is a good bed and breakfast to keep in mind. The rooms are pleasantly decorated and the service is very friendly.

Ways Mills

L'Eau Vive
$$-$$$ bkfst incl.
sb/pb, ♨
698 Chemin Madore
☎ (819) 838-5631
www.eauvive.ca
A 10min drive along country roads leads to the small village of Ways Mills, with its two dozen or so houses set amidst two churches. The village is also home to the L'Eau Vive bed and breakfast, located on the edge of the charming Niger river. The inn is located in a heritage house and offers comfortable rooms, a warm welcome and some excellent dining in a relaxed setting.

North Hatley

Le Chat Botté B&B
$$-$$$ bkfst incl.
◬ ≡
550 Chemin de la Rivière
☎ (819) 842-4626
www.lechatbotte.ca
Allergic types will have to give this lovely B&B a wide berth, as its very welcoming owner, Nico, is crazy about cats (the name of the B&B is French for "puss 'n' boots"). An artist in her spare time, she has adorned her Victorian home with some of her striking canvases and has decorated her three guest rooms with character and originality. The smallest (and it is small) is successfully done up in terra cotta, while the largest is a romantic little number decorated in cream, with a gas fireplace and an in-room tub. All three have wood floors, sumptuous linens, feather beds and a sense of the romantic. Three-course breakfasts are served in a cozy, wainscotted breakfast

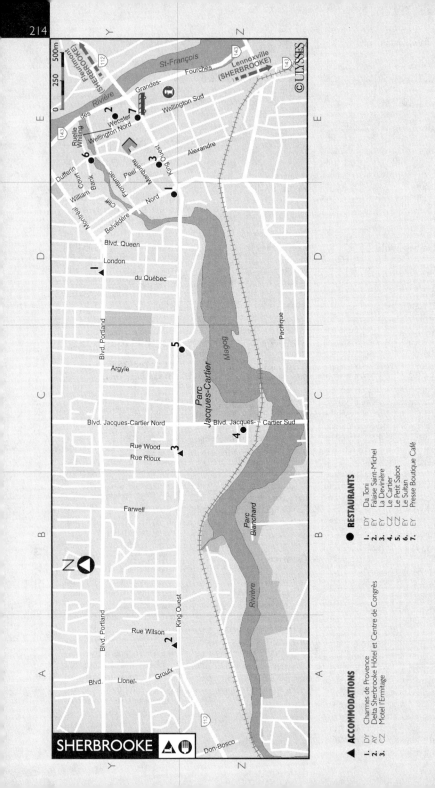

SHERBROOKE

St-François

Grandes-Fourches

Lennoxville (SHERBROOKE)

141

Fleuronne (SHERBROOKE)

112

143

Webster

Wellington Nord

Wellington Sud

Ruelle Whiting

Dufferin

William Court

Bank

Montréal

Cliff

Frontenac

Peel

Marquette

King Ouest

Alexandre

Nord

Belvédère

Blvd. Queen

London

du Québec

Pacifique

Blvd. Portland

Argyle

Parc Jacques-Cartier

Magog

Blvd. Jacques-Cartier Nord

Blvd. Jacques- Cartier Sud

Rue Wood

Rue Rioux

Parc Blanchard

Farwell

Rivière

Blvd. Portland

Rue Wilson

King Ouest

Groulx

Blvd. Lionel-

Don-Bosco

112

© ULYSSES

0 250 500m

N

room with individual tables for intimacy.

Auberge La Raveaudière
$$$ bkfst incl.
11 Hatley Centre
☎ (819) 842-2554
🖩 (819) 842-1304
www.laraveaudiere.com
La Raveaudière is a renovated farmhouse built around 1870 on a large plot of land, a short walk from the village centre. The grand yet inviting living room features burgundy walls and a Persian carpet on dark wood floors and large windows offering a view of the garden. The seven guest rooms feature plenty of interesting angles and sunny colours. A full breakfast with homemade goodies can be enjoyed on the rear patio. Warm welcome.

Tapioca
$$$ bkfst incl.
680 Chemin Sherbrooke
☎ (819) 842-2743
www.tapioca.qc.ca
The moment you cross the threshold of this lovely white-clapboard mansion, you'll feel right at home, and that's due in large part to Marielle, your warm, easygoing host. She has simply but tastefully decorated her five guest rooms to make the most of their natural features, like wood floors and huge window frames. Two share a spacious patio, while a third has its own "Romeo & Juliette" balcony. Gentle hues and wicker give the place an airy, cheerful atmosphere. Each guest room has a full, ensuite bathroom.

Manoir Hovey
$$$$$
◎ ⬥ △ ≈ ♨
575 Chemin Hovey
☎ (819) 842-2421 or 800-661-2421
🖩 (819) 842-2248
www.manoirhovey.com
Built in 1900, Manoir Hovey (see p 198) reflects the days when wealthy families spent their vacations in the beautiful country houses of the Townships. Converted into an inn 40 years ago, it is still extremely comfortable. The 40 rooms are decorated with lovely antique furniture and most offer a magnificent view of Lac Massawippi. A wide expanse of lakeside lawn behind the property is perfect for carefree lounging in the summer months. In short, this charming place has cachet to spare, and it's perfect for a romantic weekend.

Lennoxville

Motel La Paysanne
$$
≡ ⛽ ≈
42 Rue Queen
☎ (819) 569-5585
🖩 (819) 569-4294
www.paysanne.com
Motel La Paysanne is easily accessible on the way into town. The rooms are spacious and simply decorated and the building's black and white exterior is attractive. Inexpensive breakfast.

Sherbrooke

Charmes de Provence
$$ bkfst incl.
sb
350 Rue du Québec, at the corner of Boulevard Portland
☎ (819) 348-1147
www.charmesdeprovence.com

True to form, the blue shutters and yellow walls of Charmes de Provence proudly display the colours of Provence, and the breakfasts also have a Mediterranean flavour. You can even play "pétanque" in the backyard of this friendly B&B.

Motel L'Ermitage
$$
≡ ⬥ ⛽ ≈ ◎ △
1888 Rue King Ouest
☎ (819) 569-5551 or 888-569-5551
🖩 (819) 569-1446
L'Ermitage, a wood and brick motel located on the way into the city, is one of the most attractive lodging establishments in its category. The rooms are fairly comfortable, but starkly decorated. Parking available.

Delta Sherbrooke Hôtel et Centre de Congrès
$$$$$
♿ ≡ ⛽ ◎ ⬥ ≈ ⅄ ♨ ⫶⫶⫶
2685 Rue King Ouest
☎ (819) 822-1989 or 800-268-1133
🖩 (819) 822-8990
www.deltasherbrooke.com
The pinkish Delta Hotel is located on the way into town. It offers its guests a wide range of facilities, including an indoor pool, a whirlpool and an exercise room.

Tour C:
The Back Country

Notre-Dame-des-Bois

Camping Altitude
$
🐾
121 Route du Parc
☎ (819) 888-1129
Situated less than 2km from Mont Mégantic, the quiet Camping Altitude

offers nature-lovers about 15 gravelled campsites at some distance from each other. Rudimentary facilities include outhouses and spring-water taps.

Aux Berges de l'Aurore
$$-$$$ bkfst incl.
early May to late Oct
▥

139 Route du Parc
☎/▤ (819) 888-2715
www.auberge-aurore.qc.ca

Aux Berges de l'Aurore is a charming little house in a peaceful, natural setting, with four simple rooms.

Lac-Mégantic

L'Eau-Berge
$$
≡

3550 Boulevard Stearns
☎ (819) 583-1340 or 800-678-1340

L'Eau Berge is located on the shores of Lac Mégantic and provides an attractive accommodation option right in the centre of town. The inexpensive rates more than make up for the rather basic comfort of the rooms.

Restaurants

Tour A:
The Orchards

Frelighsburg

Aux Deux Clochers
$-$$
Tue-Sun
2 Rue de l'Église, corner Rue Principale
☎ (450) 298-5086

Aux Deux Clochers is a bistro located in the centre of this attractive little village.

Guests can enjoy consistently good classic cuisine or simply order a light meal. Breakfast is served on Saturdays and Sundays.

Dunham

La Rumeur Affamée
$
Wed-Sun
3809 Rue Principale
☎ (450) 295-2399

Diners come to La Rumeur Affamée to partake in the (pricey) cheese counter, pâtés and home-baked goodies. Adjoining Bistrot Seeley (see below).

Le Tire-Bouchon de l'Orpailleur
$-$$
end Jun to mid-Oct
1086 Rte. 202
☎ (450) 295-3335

The restaurant at the L'Orpailleur vineyard, open only in the summer, has a short but high-quality menu. A pleasant patio looks out on the vineyard so guests can enjoy the lovely countryside while eating. The service is extremely friendly. Reservations required.

Bistrot Seeley
$$$
Wed-Fri (dinner)
Tue-Sat (lunch)
3809 Rue Principale
☎ (450) 295-1512

Located in a handsome redbrick 19th-century building that was originally a stagecoach stopover, Bistrot Seeley is an attractive restaurant of which its owners are justifiably proud. The interior has retained its brick walls, which serve as a backdrop for a changing roster of local artists. Pasta features heavily on the menu, as does a wide range of salads. Rear court-

yard patio in season. Good selection of local microbrews.

Bedford

La Table Tournante
38 Rue Principale
☎ (450) 248-4664

This inviting little spot, with wood floors and tables, brick walls and plenty of plants, is a recent addition to Bedford's main drag. For dinner, a daily four-course table d'hôte is offered, featuring seafood, lamb, duck, poultry, beef and veal; vegetarians, eat your heart out! Also open for lunch and weekend brunch.

Cowansville

McHaffy
$$$-$$$$
351 Rue Principale
☎ (450) 266-7700

A must in the region, McHaffy, whose menu changes every two months, offers fine, international cuisine made with local ingredients. At lunch, patrons enjoy lighter meals on a pleasant terrace. Not to be missed is the duck festival, from the end of September to mid-October, when chef Pierre Johnson creates excellent dishes for the occasion.

Bromont

L'Étrier
$$$
Tue-Sun dinner only
547 Rue Shefford
☎ (450) 534-3562

L'Étrier Rest-O-Bar serves excellent cuisine to an established clientele. The restaurant is located a short distance outside the city in a pleasant, though little-visited spot.

Les Délices de la Table
$$$
Thu-Mon lunch only
641 Rue Shefford
☎ (450) 534-1646

Les Délices de la Table is a small country-style caterer with bright yellow walls, lace curtains and tablecloths with floral and fruit motifs. It's the kind of place where you feel right at home as soon as you open the door. Sample some tasty dishes, which are made with local products and carefully prepared by the chef/owner. Filled with regular customers, this tiny restaurant is quite popular, so reservations are recommended.

Les Quatre Canards
$$$$
90 Rue Stanstead
☎ (450) 534-3433 or 888-276-6668

The restaurant at **Château Bromont** (see p 209) boasts the same excellent reputation as the hotel. The attractive dining room features large picture windows that provide the perfect setting for its delicious meals. The chef's specialty is duck, which is also the Eastern Townships' major culinary calling card. Various French and local dishes complete a memorable dining experience.

Granby

Ben la Bédaine
$
599 Rue Principale
☎ (450) 378-2921

The name Ben la Bédaine, which means "Potbelly Ben," is certainly evocative; this place is a veritable shrine to French fries.

Chez Plumet
$$$-$$$$
Tue-Sat
1507 Rue Principale
☎ (450) 378-1771

Though rather blandly decorated, Chez Plumet has been a culinary institution in Granby for the last 40 years or so. Quality French cuisine is served here, and a particularly mouth-watering *magret de canard* (duck breast) provides a highlight.

La Maison Chez Nous
$$$-$$$$
Wed-Sun
bring your own wine
847 Rue Mountain
☎ (450) 372-2991

The owner of La Maison de Chez Nous gave up his wine cellar so that his customers, who may now bring their own wine, could save a little money. The menu offers Québec cuisine in its best and most refined form.

Tour B: The Lakes

Knowlton

Café Inn
$$
264 Chemin Knowlton
☎ (450) 243-0069

Café Inn is a good spot for breakfast or lunch, especially in the summer when a patio seat will get you a lake view, a rare find in Knowlton. The specialty is *tartines*—open-face sandwiches—and thin-crust pizzas. Dinner served on Friday and Saturday nights.

Knowlton Pub
$
267 Chemin Knowlton
☎ (450) 242-6862

The Knowlton Pub is without question one of the most popular spots in the Eastern Townships. The loud music hardly suits the rural setting, but it's a favourite nonetheless. During busy periods, service is extremely slow. When business is slower, however, the English-pub atmosphere and large terrace are pleasant.

Au Trois Canards
$$$
May to Oct, every day
Nov to Apr, Wed-Sun
78 Lakeside
☎ (450) 242-5801

It is gratifying to learn that the cuisine at Au Trois Canards is as appealing as the irresistible yellow-and-blue clapboard house it occupies. And nobody will be surprised to find out that the specialty here is duck—the duck *à l'orange* is particularly sublime—but the menu also includes other French specialties. In addition to the nightly table d'hôte, there's also a very inexpensive lunch and dinner bistro-style menu with comfort food like minced-duck pie.

Le Relais
$$$
Auberge Knowlton
286 Chemin Knowlton
☎ (450) 242-2232

As is only proper in these parts, Brome Lake duck is the specialty at Le Relais, the restaurant at **Auberge Knowlton** (see p 210): *confit, magret, brochettes* or an excellent warm-duck salad, for a light, refreshing change. Its casual, sunny dining room

The Eastern Townships - Restaurants - The Lakes

is encased in windows and decorated with a clutter of country bric-a-brac. There's also a huge selection of duckless main dishes, like burgers, quiches, steaks and vegetarian pastas, and local wines. A good bet.

Sutton

L'International Pâtisserie Café
$
10-D Rue Principale Sud
☎ (450) 538-1717
Ask anyone in town where to go for a bite and it's a good bet they'll send you here. The lunch offerings, such as soups, salads and sandwiches, are good and reasonably priced, and the service is pleasant.

Tartinizza
$$
Fri-Sun
19-A Rue Principale Nord
☎ (450) 538-5067
Tartinizza specializes in thin-crust pizzas and sandwiches, served in a cozy little spot with planked wood floors and yellow walls. A selection of microbrews rounds out the offerings.

À la Fontaine
$$$
30 Rue Principale Sud
☎ (450) 538-3045
At À la Fontaine visitors can enjoy succulent French cuisine while sitting on a pretty terrace.

Il Duetto
$$$-$$$$
227 Chemin Élie
☎ (450) 538-8239 or 888-660-7223
Il Duetto serves fine Italian cuisine in a quiet country setting in the hills around Sutton. The pasta is homemade and the main dishes are inspired by the regional cuisines of Italy. The five-course menu is a good

sampling of the variety of Italian cooking. Terrace.

Magog

La Grosse Pomme
$$
276 Rue Principale Ouest
☎ (819) 843-9365
La Grosse Pomme is a friendly restaurant serving good bistro-style food. In the evening, the ambiance is livened up by chatty patrons both young and old.

Le Saint-Tropez
$$$$
Wed-Sun, dinner only
211 Rue Merry Sud
☎ (819) 843-2017
Located next to the marina on Lac Memphrémagog, Le Saint-Tropez offers the best in lakeside dining. In fact, the lake is such an attraction here, particularly at sunset, that the owner has made sure that a seat in any of the three elegant, if somewhat sterile, dining rooms will provide a view. Its international-style cuisine is also popular, and the seasonal, four-course table d'hôte offers good value. Lakeside patio in season.

Les Toits Bleus
$$$-$$$$
bring your own wine
1321 Chemin Gendron, 12km south of Magog
☎ (819) 847-0988 or 888-847-0988
If there's one restaurant that Townshippers are talking about, it's Les Toits Bleus. Run by a transplanted French couple—he from Orléans, she from Périgord—, this 1880s farmhouse is the kind of place that whisks you in an instant to the French countryside. In summer, you can dine on the patio beneath the stars, while in winter,

make sure to reserve a spot by the fireplace in the original dining room, which is much cozier than the annex. This is a very popular spot so reserve well in advance—and don't forget your wine.

Georgeville

Auberge Georgeville
$$$$
71 Chemin Channel (Route 247)
☎ (819) 843-8683 or 888-843-8686
Gourmet food lovers are invariably charmed by the meals served in **Auberge Georgeville**'s (see p 213) dining room. The chef favours local products for his deliciously fresh culinary creations, and the lakeside century-old home provides a remarkable setting.

Ayer's Cliff

Auberge Ripplecove Inn
$$$$
700 Rue Ripplecove
☎ (819) 838-4296 or 800-668-4296
The dining room at the **Auberge Ripplecove Inn** (see p 213) offers fine gourmet cuisine of great distinction. Its Victorian atmosphere and elegant decor make it an excellent place for a romantic meal. Excellent selection of wines.

North Hatley

Pilsen
$$-$$$
55 Rue Principale
☎ (819) 842-2971
Take a reasonably priced, upgraded pub-style menu with something for everyone, add street-side tables with a lake view and a narrow patio on the lower level that literally floats

above the river and you've got the formula for a long-standing favourite. Good salads and burgers.

Manoir Hovey
$$$$
575 Chemin Hovey
☎ (819) 842-2421 or 800-661-2421
Graced with antique furniture and a fireplace, Manoir Hovey's lovely dining room exudes peace and quiet, which makes for a lovely evening. The refined cuisine has also earned a lot of praise.

Café Massawippi
$$$$
mid-May to early Sep every day, early Sep to mid-May Wed-Sun
3050 Chemin Capelton
☎ (819) 842-4528
This little house just beyond the centre of North Hatley is home to a real find. An inspired daily three-course table d'hôte introduces giant shrimp to passion fruit, medallions of caribou to cocoa and rabbit to fig marmelade, always with great success. Eclectic music and decor, with a *soupçon* of funkiness. Excellent wine list and service to match.

Lennoxville

Pub Le Lion d'Or
$
2 Rue du Collège
☎ (819) 565-1015
The terrace at Pub Le Lion d'Or is both lovely and noisy—especially when the students are celebrating! Three beers are brewed on site, a pale beer, a dark ale and a dark bitter. The food is simple, essentially

the standard fare of English pubs.

Sherbrooke

Presse Boutique Café
$-$$
4 Rue Wellington Nord
☎ (819) 822-2133
A laid-back clientele frequents the Presse Boutique Café. In addition to visual-art exhibitions and shows by local and other musicians, patrons can enjoy a wide variety of imported beers, a simple menu (salads, *croque-monsieur*, sandwiches, etc.) and vegetarian dishes. Moreover, two Internet stations are available (*$6/hr, $1/10min*).

Le Cartier
$$
255 Boulevard Jacques-Cartier Sud
☎ (819) 821-3311
It did not take long for Le Cartier to become a very popular restaurant. Overlooking Parc Jacques-Cartier and only a short drive from the university, this small restaurant feels airy and comfortable because of its large bay windows. Its healthy and affordable food makes it a popular family spot; however, it is intimate enough for dinner with friends. There is a good selection of beers from Québec microbreweries.

Le Sultan
$$
205 Rue Dufferin
☎ (819) 821-9156
Le Sultan specializes in Middle Eastern cuisine, in this case Lebanese food. The grilled meats are excellent.

La Devinière
$$-$$$
Tue-Fri 11am to 2pm and 5pm to 10pm, Sat 5pm to 10pm
17 Rue Peel
☎ (819) 822-4177
Diners in the mood for savoury seasonal French cuisine can head to La Devinière.

Le Petit Sabot
$$-$$$
1410 Rue King Ouest
☎ (819) 563-0262
The Petit Sabot is located inside an attractively decorated blue house with loads of character. The food is pleasantly different, game being the specialty.

Falaise Saint-Michel
$$$
100 Rue Webster
☎ (819) 346-6339 or 877-340-6339
Falaise Saint-Michel is a hidden treasure on a small, somewhat dreary street. Its specialty being refined regional cuisine, the restaurant serves a variety of excellent dishes, and also has a particularly well-stocked wine cellar.

Da Toni
$$$$
15 Belvédère Nord
☎ (819) 346-8441
Located right in the heart of the new downtown area, the opulent Da Toni has a well-established reputation. Indeed, for over 25 years now, patrons have been enjoying its fine French and Italian cuisine, served with a wide selection of wines in a classic decor. The table d'hôte features five excellent, reasonably priced main courses. Though somewhat noisy, the terrace allows guests to enjoy a drink outside during the summer.

The Eastern Townships - Restaurants - The Lakes

Tour C:
The Back Country

Danville

Le Temps des Cerises
$$$$
79 Rue du Carmel
☎ (819) 839-2818 or 800-839-2818
Le Temps des Cerises
serves elegant, inventive
cuisine in the distinctive
and unique atmosphere of
a former Protestant church.

Notre-Dame-des-Bois

L'Extra sur la Rive
$$
3502 Rue Agnès
☎ (819) 583-2565
Critically acclaimed L'Extra
sur la Rive is a French bis-
tro-style restaurant. The
gourmet food and friendly
atmosphere have made this
a local favourite.

Aux Berges de l'Aurore
$$$$
early May to late Oct Thu-Sat,
except late Jun to early Sep,
every day
139 Route du Parc
☎ (819) 888-2715
Located close to lush Mont
Mégantic, the intimate and
very charming Aux Berges
de l'Aurore serves excellent
Québec cuisine. Seasoned
with wild herbs gathered in
the surrounding country-
side, its dishes are most
original. From the very first
bite, guests will appreciate
why it received the *Mérite
de la Fine Cuisine Estrienne*
award.

Entertainment

■ Bars and Nightclubs

Knowlton

Knowlton Pub
267 Chemin Knowlton
☎ (819) 242-6862
The Knowlton Pub has
earned itself such a reputa-
tion that even Montrealers
in search of a change of
scenery go there to while
away an evening among
friends.

Magog

Le Chat du Moulinier
101 Rue du Moulin
☎ (819) 868-5678
For jazz and a great atmos-
phere, look no further.

Café St-Michel
50 Rue Principale Ouest
Café St-Michel offers a nice
variety of imported beers
and provides two comput-
ers for those who would
like to surf the Internet or
write home *($4 per half-
hour)*. Live music on week-
ends.

Microbrasserie La Memphré
12 Rue Merry Sud
☎ (819) 843-3405
This cozy, dimly lit brew-
pub, with sofas arranged in
front of a roaring fire come
the rigours of winter, of-
fers up rather good pints of
India Pale Ale and Scotch
Ale.

North Hatley

Pilsen
55 Rue Principale
☎ (819) 842-2971

The Pilsen is frequented by
vacationers who come to
chat and have a beer while
gazing out at Lac Massa-
wippi.

Sherbrooke

Au Café du Palais
184 Rue Wellington Nord
☎ (819) 566-8977
The favourite dance bar of
vacationers is Au Café du
Palais. Shows are presented
on certain evenings.

King Hall
286 Rue King Ouest
King Hall is a comfortable
bar with an interesting
selection of international
beers.

■ Festivals and Cultural Events

Brome

The **Brome Fair** *(☎450-242-
3976)* has been drawing
crowds each Labour Day
weekend (the weekend
prior to the first Monday
in September) since 1856.
A genuine agricultural fair,
complete with local prod-
ucts, livestock exhibitions,
contests and games.

Knowlton

Among the not-to-be-
missed festivals in the
Townships is **Le Canard est
en Fête!** *(☎450-242-6886)*, a
duck festival held for sev-
eral weekends from the
end of September to mid-
October.

Magog

A few days of festivities are
organized as part of the
**Traversée Internationale du
Lac Memphrémagog** *(late Jul;*

819-847-3007 or 800-267-2744), including performances by Québec theatrical artists, exhibits of all kinds and shows by folk singers. The highlight of the celebrations is the arrival of swimmers from Newport, U.S.A. The 42km swim is undertaken by athletes considered among the best in the world.

Orford

For more than 50 years each July and August, the **Festival Orford** *(3165 Chemin du Parc, ☎819-843-9871 or 800-567-6155)* has been offering a series of concerts featuring ensembles and world-famous virtuosos. Several excellent free concerts are also presented by young musicians, who come here for the summer to hone their skills at the Centre d'Arts Orford. This high-calibre festival is an absolute must for all music-lovers.

Sherbrooke

Townshippers Day *(mid-Sep; Sherbrooke, ☎866-566-5717)*, an annual celebration of the culture and heritage of English-speaking Townshippers, is an occasion for music, history, art, dance, children's activities and regional culinary delights.

■ Theatres and Concert Halls

Magog

Le Vieux Clocher
64 Rue Merry Nord
☎(819) 847-0470
Located inside an old Protestant church built in 1887, Le Vieux Clocher has staged many shows that

later became very successful in both Québec and France. Those interested in attending a show should reserve well in advance. The theatre is attractive but small.

Orford

Centre d'Arts Orford

3165 Chemin du Parc
☎ (819) 843-9871 or 800-567-6155
The Centre d'Arts Orford provides advanced training courses to young musicians during the summer. An annual festival also takes place at the centre, which is made up of several buildings designed in the 1960s by Paul-Marie Côté. The exhibition room that completes the centre was originally the Man and Music (*l'Homme et la Musique*) pavilion at Expo 67, and was designed by Desgagné and Côté.

Sherbrooke

Two free monthly publications (*Visages* and *Fusions*) provide all the necessary information on the area's entertainment events.

Salle Maurice-O'Bready
2500 Boulevard Université
☎ (819) 820-1000 or 821-7742
The Université de Sherbrooke's cultural centre houses the Salle Maurice-O'Bready, where concerts, from classical to rock and theatre plays, are put on.

Vieux Clocher
1590 Galt Ouest
☎ (819) 822-2102
A former church converted to a concert hall, the Vieux Clocher now welcomes music-lovers and entertainment-seekers. Performance listings can be found in

the Sherbrooke daily *La Tribune*.

■ Shopping

■ Clothing

Knowlton

For a small village, Knowlton has a surprising number of shopping options, particularly for fashion.

■ Crafts

Magog

Les Trésors de la Grange
early May to early Nov, Fri 1pm to 4pm, Sat and Sun 10am to 4pm
790 Chemin des Pères
☎ (819) 847-4222
This 130-year-old barn outside Magog on the way to the abbey is a most atmospheric—and drafty—place to showcase local crafts. Reasonably priced woodwork, stained glass, jewellery and tasty tidbits, as well as paintings and antiques.

■ Food

Knowlton

Canards du Lac Brome
Mon-Fri 8am to 5pm, Sat and Sun from 10am
40 Chemin Centre
☎ (450) 242-3825
It's a little disillusioning to learn that the duck on the menu of the region's fine restaurants is not plucked out of Brome Lake by an intrepid hunter and his pointer; instead of spending their days frolicking

carelessly on Lac Brome, these ducks are raised by the thousands in a dozen aluminum barns just beyond the town centre. For duck sausage, foie gras or confit, head to Brome Lake Ducks, where they process 1.7million of them each year.

Rougemont

Cidrerie Michel Jodoin
see p 195.

Vinaigrerie Artisanale Pierre Gingras
Mon-Fri 9am to 5pm, Sat-Sun 10am to 5pm
1132 Rang de la Grande-Caroline
☎ (450) 469-4954 or 888-469-4954
Some say apple-cider vinegar has miraculously therapeutic powers and that a small daily dose mixed with water can cure stiff joints. Be that as it may, there is no doubt that the variously flavoured apple-cider vinegar products that are made at Vinaigrerie Artisanale Pierre Gingras

will make your home-made salad dressings stand out.

Sutton

Chocolaterie Belge Muriel
Tue-Sat
8 rue Principale Sud
☎ (450) 538-0139
Funny how every chocolatier worth his sugar is trying to make an educational experience out of what was once purely a sensual one. But if it helps to justify our indulgence, then why not? Here, Monsieur Henquin creates true works of art, like chocolate marquetry boxes that look almost too good to eat. Free demonstrations *(mid-Jun to late Oct Fri-Sun 1:30pm)*.

■ Music

Sherbrooke

Le Juke Box
87 Rue Wellington Nord
☎ (819) 564-2070
Le Juke Box is a second-hand music store that car-

ries a nice selection of alternative titles and American comic books.

■ Outdoor Equipment

Sherbrooke

La Randonnée
2325 Rue King Ouest
☎ (819) 566-8882
Located at the top of Rue King, La Randonnée is the perfect stop for those who wish to purchase outdoor gear before setting out on a hike in the area.

■ Shopping Centres

Sherbrooke

Sherbrooke has several shopping centres. **Carrefour de l'Estrie** on Boulevard Portland, in the western part of town, is the most popular.

Lanaudière

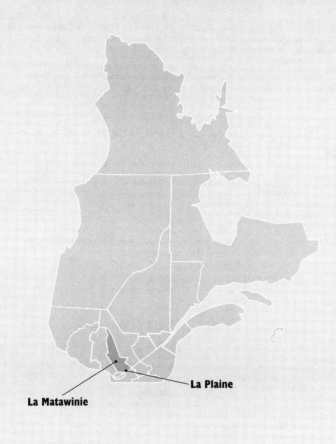

La Plaine

La Matawinie

A peaceful area of lakes, rivers, farmland, wild forests and huge open spaces, Lanaudière extends north of Montréal, from the plains of the St. Lawrence to the Laurentian plateau. Your visit to this region, one of the first colonized areas in New France, will take you through a place with a rich architectural heritage that has managed to retain many of its long-standing popular traditions.

In summer, Lanaudière plays host to an important event: Le Festival de Lanaudière. Music lovers from across Québec converge on the region for classical and popular music concerts performed by artists from around the globe.

The city of Joliette is also home to one of Québec's most interesting regional museums, the Musée d'Art de Joliette, which boasts an impressive collection of Québec art, including many pieces of religious art.

Getting There and Getting Around

Once a countryside of seigneurial manors and farmland that stretched from the shores of the St. Lawrence to the wild, mountainous land of the Aboriginals, the Lanaudière region has today been engulfed by the Montréal urban area. In keeping with this split personality, we suggest two very different routes from Montréal: **Tour A: La Plaine** ★★ and **Tour B: La Matawinie** ★.

■ By Car

Tour A: La Plaine

Aut. 25 is the extension of Boulevard Pie-IX and leads towards Terrebonne, the first stop on this tour. It continues east to L'Assomption on Rte. 344 E. Next take Rte. 343 N. to Joliette and Rte. 158 E. to Berthierville. To return to Montréal, follow lovely Rte. 138 W., also known as the Chemin du Roy, along the St. Lawrence River, with stops in Lanoraie, Saint-Sulpice and Repentigny.

Tour B: Matawinie

Aut. 25 N., the extension of Boulevard Pie-IX, joins Rte. 125 N., which leads to Rawdon, Chertsey, Notre-Dame-de-la-Merci and Saint-Donat. From there Rte. 347 leads to Saint-Gabriel-de-Brandon. To reach Saint-Michel-des-Saints and the Rouge-Matawin and Mastigouche reserves, head north on Rte. 131.

■ Bus Stations

Tour A: La Plaine

Terrebonne
Galeries de Terrebonne
☎ (450) 654-2315

Joliette
250 Rue Richard (Point d'Arrêt restaurant)
☎ (450) 759-1524

Repentigny
435 Boulevard Iberville (facing city hall)

Tour B: La Matawinie

Rawdon
3228 1ʳᵉ Avenue (facing Patate à Gogo)
☎ (450) 834-2000

Saint-Donat
751 Rue Principale (Dépanneur Boni-Soir)
☎ (819) 424-1361

■ Train Station

Tour A: La Plaine

Joliette
380 Rue Champlain
☎ 888-742-7245

The Seasons in Québec

Québec folksinger Gilles Vigneault said it best: "Mon pays ce n'est pas un pays, c'est l'hiver" (my country is not a country, it is winter). Though this long, cold season is most closely associated with Québec, all four seasons leave their mark on the province: the cold freezes waterfalls into walls of ice in winter, waters rise and plants come to life with the spring thaw, bright sun and sometimes unbearable heat waves last through the summer until Indian summer, the final hurrah before the brilliant spectacle of the fall colours. Quebecers have learned to make the most of the many incarnations of their home, heading to the mountains, forests, lakes and mighty rivers no matter what the season...

Félix Leclerc, a beloved Québécois folksinger, honoured the simple pleasures of spring in *L'hymne au printemps*: the calls of frogs and robins herald the arrival of spring: tiny buds on trees and bushes slowly grow into leaves and flowers, dandelions blanket the fields and the fresh smell of the earth returns to the air...

The St. Lawrence lowlands still bear the stamp of the old French seigneurial system, which divided the land into long, narrow rectangular plots in order to give the greatest possible number of colonists access to the waterways. Beyond the farmhouses that line the *rangs* (country roads), fields run on as far as the eye can see.

A fisher's life is a hard one, requiring backbreaking work, endurance and patience. The bounty of those fishing in the Gulf of St. Lawrence includes crab, shrimp, scallops, turbot, halibut, herring and mackerel.

Québec is very rich in wildlife. Those who quietly explore the country's parks and other rural areas may be delighted to encounter anything from racoons to moose, the latter often found near bodies of water, as pictured here.

The remote and mysterious Îles de la Madeleine (Magdalen Islands) have been sculpted by the wind and the sea.

A land of lakes and rivers, Québec is a choice spot for a slew of water sports: canoeing, kayaking, sailing, windsurfing, fishing, rafting... and the list goes on.

Country house, summer cottage or lakefront chalet...call it what you will, it is the dream of many an urban dweller in this province. What better way to pass the summer than out in the country, far from the heat and humidity of the city?

When fall arrives, the forests of Québec ignite with colour. This blaze of red, orange and gold transforms the countryside and is best experienced during those last warm days of Indian summer.

As soon as the waterways and lakes freeze over, the shacks go up, the hole in the ice is drilled and the ice fishing, or *pêche blanche*, season begins.

These two huskies and their team members lead the way to adventure across Québec's winter landscape. Several companies have revived this traditional Inuit mode of transportation and today make it available to the public.

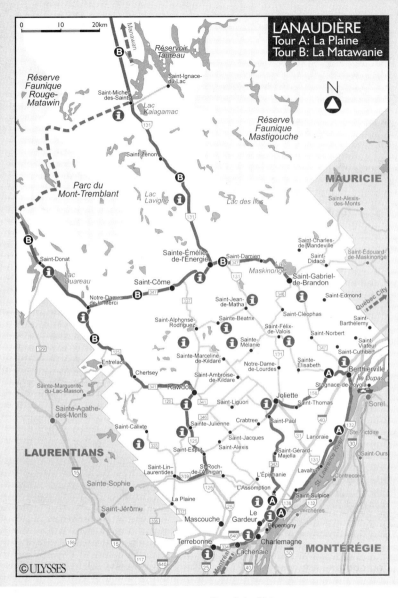

LANAUDIÈRE
Tour A: La Plaine
Tour B: La Matawanie

© ULYSSES

Useful Information

■ Tourist Information

Regional Office

Tourisme Lanaudière
3645 Rue Queen, Rawdon, JOK 1S0
☎ (450) 834-2535 or 800-363-2788
🖶 (450) 834-8100
www.tourisme-lanaudiere.qc.ca

Tour A: La Plaine

Berthierville
750 Rue Lambert
☎ (450) 836-7336

Joliette
5000 Côte Terrebonne
☎ (450) 759-5013 or 800-363-1775

Terrebonne
1091 Boulevard Moody
☎ (450) 964-0681

Tour B: La Matawinie

Rawdon
3590 Rue Metcalfe
☎ (450) 834-2282

Saint-Donat
536 Rue Principale
☎ (819) 424-2883 or 888-783-6628

Exploring

Tour A: La Plaine
★ ★

 2 days

In 1813, Marie-Charlotte Tarieu Taillant de Lanaudière, daughter of the seigneur of Lavaltrie, married Barthélémy Joliette. These two figures were much more than a couple of newlyweds, however, for their union left behind a precious heritage to the inhabitants of this region: the name of the region, Lanaudière, and the name of its main city, Joliette. But far beyond that, they also inspired an enterprising spirit rarely found amongst French Canadians at the time. This stimulated the creation of a manufacturing base, locally controlled banks and the development of specialized farming.

Take Aut. 25, the extension of Boulevard Pie-IX. Turn right at the Terrebonne–Centre-Ville Exit (Exit 22). Turn right immediately on Boulevard Moody then left on Rue Saint-Louis. Park on Rue des Braves, facing Île des Moulins.

Terrebonne ★ ★ (pop. 83,792)

Located along the banks of the rushing Rivière des Mille Îles, this municipality gets its name from the fertile soil (*terre* meaning earth and *bonne* meaning good) from which it grew. Today, it is part of the ribbon of suburbia surrounding Montréal, yet the old town, divided into an *haute-ville* and *basse-ville* (upper and lower towns), has preserved some of its residential and commercial buildings. Terrebonne is probably one of the best places in Québec to get an idea of what a prosperous 19th-century seigneury was really like.

The city was founded in 1707 and shortly thereafter the first flour and saw mills were built. In 1802 the seigneury of Terrebonne was purchased by Simon McTavish, director of the Northwest Company, which specialized in the fur trade. Terrebonne became a departure point for his lucrative commercial expeditions into northern Québec. Carding mills for wool were soon added to those built under the French Regime, creating a veritable pre-industrial complex. In 1832, the Masson family took over the running of the seigneury and rebuilt most of the mills.

The 20th century began promisingly, until a large section of the lower town was destroyed by fire on December 1, 1922. Only the buildings on Rue Saint-François-Xavier and Rue Sainte-Marie were spared.

Joseph Masson, a powerful Montréal banker, purchased the Terrebonne seigneury in 1832 during an auction sale, but the troubled following years (which included the 1837-1838 Patriots' rebellion) prevented him from developing it as he had wished. In 1848, his widow, Sophie Raymond, oversaw the construction of the imposing **Manoir Masson ★** *(901 Rue St-Louis)*, which was designed by French architect Pierre-Louis Morin (1811-1886). The attractive neoclassical grey limestone-covered building is the largest seigniorial residence in Québec. The Saint-Tharcisius chapel was added to the manor in 1912, after it had become the property of a religious order. The manor is now home to the Saint-Sacrement high school.

Rue Saint-Louis is the main artery of the upper-town bourgeois area. Besides the Manoir Masson, several other stately residences line the streets in particular the **home of Roderick Mackenzie** *(906 Rue Saint-Louis)*.

Return to Rue des Braves, heading towards l'Île des Moulins.

Île des Moulins ★ ★ *(free admission, $5 for guided tours Wed-Sun 10:30am to 5pm; late Jun to early Sep; at the end of Boulevard des Braves, ☎ 450-471-0619, www.ile-des-moulins.qc.ca)* is an impressive concentration of mills and other pre-industrial equipment from the Terrebonne seigneury. Most of the buildings, located in a park, have been renovated and now serve as community and ad-

TERREBONNE

★ ATTRACTIONS

1.	BZ	Manoir Masson
2.	BZ	Home of Roderick Mackenzie
3.	BZ	Maison de Pays

ministrative buildings. Upon entering, the first building on the left is the old flour mill (1846), then the sawmill (restored in 1986), which houses the municipal library. Next is the Centre d'Accueil et d'Interprétation de l'Île des Moulins (information centre) in what used to be the seigneurial office. This cut-stone building was constructed in 1848 according to plans by Pierre-Louis Morin.

The three-storey building on the left is the old bakery, built in 1803 for the Northwest Company, which used it to make cookies and *galettes* for the voyageurs collecting furs in the northern and western regions of the country. This bakery was one of the first large-scale bakeries in North America, and is also the oldest building left on the island. At the end of the walk is the new, larger mill, built in 1850 for Sophie Raymond. It produced wool fabrics sold throughout the region. The Terrebonne cultural centre is now located there.

*On your way back, follow the small **Rue Saint-François-Xavier** east of Boulevard des Braves, where picturesque homes escaped the fire of 1922, now housing various restaurants and galleries.*

Built in 1760, the **Maison de Pays** ★ *(late May to mid-Jun Thu-Sun 10am to 5pm, mid-Jun to early Sep Wed and Sun 10am to 5pm, Thu-Sat 10am to 9pm, rest of the year Sat-Sun 1pm to 5pm; 844 Rue St-François-Xavier, ☎450-471-0619, www.ile-des-moulins.qc.ca)* claims to be the oldest faithfully preserved house in Québec. Today it is used to promote regional products such as agrotourism and local arts and crafts, as well as Lanaudière's historical heritage and traditional music.

Leave Terrebonne on Rte. 344 E. (the continuation of Rue Saint-Louis) towards Lachenaie, then Le Gardeur, to eventually arrive in L'Assomption.

L'Assomption ★ (pop. 16,062)

This small city owes its growth in part to a portage route established in 1717 by the Sulpician Pierre Le Sueur, who used to spend time paddling on the Rivière L'Assomption. The trail, used by voyageurs transporting their canoes from one river to the next, avoids a 5km detour by water. Originally simply called Le Portage, the settlement was a crossroads frequented by fur trappers and traders on the northern route. It was eventually included in the Saint-Sul-

Lanaudière - Exploring - La Plaine

pice seigneury, conceded to the Messieurs de Saint-Sulpice of Paris in 1647.

The proximity of the carding mills in Terrebonne, as well as the frequent visits by the *coureurs des bois*, prompted the women of L'Assomption to design a special wool sash to be worn by French Canadians to distinguish them from the Scottish, many of whom were employees of the Northwest Company. Hence was born the famous *ceinture fléchée* (arrow sash), now a symbol of Québec. L'Assomption had the monopoly on arrow sash production from about 1805 to 1825.

Enter L'Assomption by Rue Saint-Étienne. Parking is available opposite the church.

The monumental facade of the **Église de L'Assomption-de-la-Sainte-Vierge** ★ *(153 Rue du Portage)* was designed by Victor Bourgeau (1863). The chancel was undertaken in 1819 and contains the tabernacle, the altar and the Baroque pulpit by Urbain Brien dit Desrochers in 1834. The artistry of the vault is the work of Bourgeau, modelled after the one in La Prairie.

Take Rue du Portage alongside the presbytery. This road follows Pierre Le Sueur's original portage route. At the corner of Boulevard L'Ange-Gardien stand the old seigneurial office of the Sulpiciens (402 Boulevard L'Ange-Gardien) and the building that once housed the store known as the Magasin Le Roux, specializing in the sale of the "ceinture fléchée" (arrow sash) (195 Rue du Portage). Turn right on Boulevard L'Ange-Gardien.

The **Maison Archambault** *(351 Boulevard L'Ange-Gardien)* is one of a few examples left around Montréal of this type of house, where the main floor served as a workshop and the second, accessible by a long staircase, was for the living quarters. This particular example, built in 1780, was the birthplace of Francis Archambault (1880-1915), an opera star in London, New York and Boston at the turn of the 20th century.

The **Collège de L'Assomption** ★ *(270 Boulevard L'Ange-Gardien)* for boys was founded in 1832 by the town's elite. The building is a fine example of 19th-century institutional architecture in Québec, with its fieldstone exterior (1869), mansard roof and superb silver dome, added in 1882. The eclectic wing to the east was built in 1892. Among the notable personalities who attended the college is Sir Wilfrid Laurier, Prime Minister of Canada from 1896 to 1911.

The **Oasis du Vieux Palais de Justice** *(free admission; year-round, variable schedule; reserve for guided tours; 255 Rue Saint-Étienne; ☎450-589-3266, www.vieuxpalais.com)*, or old courthouse, was originally three separate houses, constructed between 1811 and 1822. This rather long building housed a court of law and a registration office for many years. Victor Bourgeau, who designed the courtroom on the second floor, was not content with just modifying the openings; he also designed the furniture and woodwork. The courtroom remains intact, even though court has not been located here since 1929.

The site of the first church in L'Assomption (1724), the remains of the seigneurial manor and the **Maison Séguin** *(284 Rue Saint-Étienne)*, a bourgeois residence in the Second Empire style built in 1880, are all located across from the old courthouse.

Get back on Rue Saint-Étienne heading west (towards the church). At number 349 is the **Maison Le Sanche** (1812), an interesting example of a typical urban dwelling of the era with firebreak walls and built right up against the sidewalk.

Follow Boulevard L'Ange-Gardien, then Rte. 343 N., which follows the Rivière L'Assomption. Alongside the road there are several houses with mansard roofs, all oriented perpendicularly to the road to protect them from the prevailing winds.

Continue along Rte. 343 N., which becomes Boulevard Manseau in Joliette and passes some beautiful Victorian residences. Park your vehicle near the large Place Bourget in order to explore the streets of Joliette on foot. The downtown area extends around Boulevard Manseau.

Joliette ★ (pop. 18,263)

At the beginning of the 19th century, notary Barthélémy Joliette (1789-1850) opened up logging camps in the northern section of the Lavaltrie seigneury, which was at the time still undeveloped land. In 1823 he founded "his" town around the sawmills and called it "L'Industrie," a name synonymous with progress and prosperity. The settlement grew so rapidly that in just a few years it had eclipsed its two rivals,

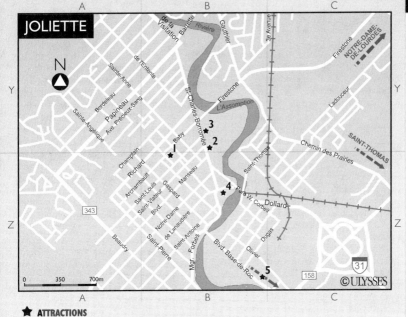

JOLIETTE

N

Berthier and L'Assomption. In 1864 it was renamed Joliette in honour of its founder. Barthélémy Joliette completed many other ambitious projects, most notably the construction of the first railroad belonging to French Canadians, and a bank where money bearing the Joliette-Lanaudière name was printed.

The market building and the *hôtel de ville* (city hall), both donated by Monsieur Joliette, used to stand in the middle of **Place Bourget**. Since their demolition, shops have been built and the area has been turned into a pedestrian strip. The **Palais de Justice**, at the far end, follows the neoclassical model proposed by the Minister of Public Works at the time. Its construction in 1862 confirmed Joliette's status as capital of the region.

Follow Boulevard Manseau towards the cathedral.

The interesting white building at number 400 was built in 1858 and used to house the **Institut**, the first cultural centre in Québec to house a municipal library and a performance hall. The Greek Revival style of the facade was chosen as a display of defiance against the British colonial power. Today, the building is home to a gourmet restaurant, **Le Fil d'Ariane** (see p 238).

The **Cathédrale Saint-Charles-Borromée** *(2 Rue Saint-Charles-Borromée N.)*, with its modest facade and single steeple, was originally just a simple parish church. The exterior of the church, constructed between 1888 and 1892, is plain yet impressive. The plans, drawn by architects Perrault and Mesnard, called for large proportions of the same scale as the Romanesque Revival churches built in Montréal at the time.

Joliette owes its cultural vibrance to the clerics of Saint-Viateur who established themselves at the **Maison Provinciale des Clercs de Saint-Viateur ★** *(132 Rue Saint-Charles-Borromée N.)* in the mid-19th century. In 1939, they undertook the construction of their new house. Its design, by Montréal architect René Charbonneau, was inspired by a sketch done by Father Wilfrid Corbeil. The building's massive Romanesque Revival arches and heavy stone tower are reminiscent of German monasteries of the Middle Ages. The chapel at the centre is

Lanaudière – Exploring – La Plaine

often described as a modern version of the German church in Frielingsdorff. The magnificent stained-glass windows, designed by Marius Plamondon, the sculptures on the pews and the stations of the cross all create an ethereal atmosphere of mystery and contemplation.

Father Wilfrid Corbeil founded the exceptional **Musée d'Art de Joliette ★★** *($4; &; summer Tue-Sun 11am to 5pm, rest of the year, Wed-Sun noon to 5pm; 145 Rue Wilfrid-Corbeil, ☎450-756-0311, www.musee.joliette.org)* with works collected during the 1940s by the clerics of Saint-Viateur that show Québec's place in the world. This is the most important regional museum in Québec. Since 1976, it has been located in a rather off-putting building on Rue Corbeil. On display are major pieces from Québec and Canadian artists like Marc-Aurèle de Foy Suzor-Côté, Jean-Paul Riopelle and Emily Carr, as well as works by European and American artists like Henry Moore and Karel Appel. One section of the museum is devoted to Québec religious art, while another contains religious art from the Middle Ages and Renaissance periods, with some excellent examples from France, Italy and Germany.

The Amphithéâtre de Lanaudière is on the outskirts of town. To get there, follow Rue Saint-Charles-Borromée Sud, then Rue Saint-Antoine, and turn left on Boulevard Base-de-Roc.

The **Festival de Lanaudière** (see p 239) was begun by Father Fernand Lindsay. Each year during the months of July and August, a variety of music concerts and opera performances are presented as part of the festival. In 1989 the 2,000-seat open-air **Amphithéâtre de Lanaudière** *(1575 Boulevard Base-de-Roc, ☎450-759-2999)* was constructed in order to increase the capacity and accessibility of the event.

Take the on-ramp to Rte. 158 E. close to the amphitheatre, and follow it toward Berthierville.

Berthierville ★ (pop. 4,014)

The modest Autray Seigneury was conceded to Jean Bourdon, an engineer of the King of France, in 1637. The land corresponds to the sector Berthier-en-Bas, or Berthierville, along the shores of the St. Lawrence. The Berthier Seigneury, which was much more

extensive, was conceded to Sieur de Berthier in 1672 before passing through several hands. It corresponds in part to Berthier-en-Haut, or Berthier. In 1765 both these tracts of land were acquired by James Cuthbert, aide-de-camp to General Wolfe during the battle of the Plains of Abraham in Québec City, as well as friend of the Duke of Kent. He developed the land mainly for use as a vacation spot.

The **Pont Couvert Grandchamps** *(on the right near Rte. 158)* crosses the Rivière Bayonne. This covered wooden bridge was constructed in the Town style in 1883, making it one of the first of this kind of structure popularized in the United States in the 19th century.

The **Église Sainte-Geneviève ★★** *(780 Avenue Montcalm)* is a Lanaudière treasure. Built in 1781, it is one of the oldest churches in the region. The interior's Louis XVI styling was designed by Amable Gauthier and Alexis Millette between 1821 and 1830. Many elements in the decor combine to make this building truly exceptional. The decor has a richness rarely seen at that time, comprising elements such as the original high altar, crafted by Gilles Bolvin in 1759, the shell-shaped retable and the diamond pattern ornamenting the vault.

The seigneurial **Chapelle des Cuthbert** *(free admission; every day early Jun to early Sep 10am to 6pm; entrance on Rue de Bienville, ☎450-836-7336)*, which belonged to the Cuthbert family (1786) and was known officially as St. Andrew's, was the first Protestant church built in Québec. In the years following the British Conquest of 1760, French-inspired architecture remained the dominant style, as there were few British architects and workers. This explains the Catholic configuration of the church. Since 1978, the building has served as a cultural centre for the residents of Berthierville.

Gilles Villeneuve, the championship racecar driver who was tragically killed during the qualifying trials for the 1982 Grand-Prix of Belgium, was from Berthierville. The **Musée Gilles-Villeneuve** *($7.50; every day 9am to 5pm; 960 Avenue Gilles-Villeneuve, ☎450-836-2714 or 800-639-0103, www.gilles-villeneuve.com)* is dedicated to the illustrious career of the Ferrari Formula 1 driver.

Farther on, take Rte. 158 to Île Dupras and the village of **Saint-Ignace-de-Loyola**, from which a ferry leads to Sorel on the south shore of the St. Lawrence *($5.35 per vehicle plus a $2 fee for each adult passenger; in summer, departures every half hour during the day, every hour in the evening; crossing takes 10min;* ☎ *450-836-4600).*

Follow Rte. 138 W. towards Lanoraie and Saint-Sulpice.

Lanoraie (pop. 3,961)

Rte. 138 follows the original Chemin du Roy, laid out in 1734 between Montréal and Québec City. Before then, people had to travel by canoe along the St. Lawrence. Several old houses still stand along the road between Berthierville and Lavaltrie.

Coteau-du-Sable, located to the northeast of the village of Lanoraie, has an important Aboriginal archaeological site. The foundations of a longhouse built by Iroquois in the 14th century were discovered here. Numerous handcrafted artifacts have also been found at the site since the beginning of the 20th century.

Continue on Rte. 138 to Repentigny.

Repentigny (pop. 74,259)

The city of Repentigny was named after its first seigneur, Pierre Le Gardeur de Repentigny. It is pleasantly located at the confluence of the Rivière L'Assomption and the mighty St. Lawrence.

Construction of the **Église de la Purification-de-la-Bienheureuse-Vierge-Marie** ★ *(445 Rue Notre-Dame Est)* began in 1723, making it the oldest church in the diocese of Montréal. It has many characteristics of New France churches, such as the apse with the corners cut off and the orientation of the building, parallel to the river. The facade was redone in 1850 with two towers instead of the original one steeple. The interior was restored to its original simplicity in 1984 following a fire which almost destroyed the whole church. The beautiful Louis XV-style high altar was designed by Philippe Liébert in 1761.

The **Moulins à Vent** *(460 and 861 Rue Notre-Dame Est)* are quite a sight. These two windmills, built around 1820, seem out of place amidst the gas stations and post-war bungalows of modern-day Repentigny.

To return to Montréal, follow Rue Notre-Dame in Repentigny, which is actually the continuation of the Montréal street of the same name.

Tour B: La Matawinie
★

 4 days

The colonization of the hinterland of Lanaudière was undertaken around 1860 by Catholic missionaries concerned about the mass exodus of French-Canadian farmers to the cotton textile mills of New England. Matawinie is not only well supplied with forests but also has an abundance of lakes, mountains and rivers, which attract hunters, fishers and vacationers. The northern part of the region has long been inhabited by the Attikamekw Nation, a small Aboriginal group that used to be nomadic but is now settled around the village of Manawan.

This tour is long and rugged. A vehicle in good condition and camping equipment are strongly recommended since hotels and service stations are rare or nonexistent along the more remote gravel roads.

Take Highway 25 N. to Route 125 N. Follow Route 125 N. to Route 337 N. and turn left, heading towards Rawdon.

Saint-Lin-des-Laurentides (pop. 12,676)

Take Route 339 west for a small side trip to Saint-Lin-des-Laurentides. This is where Parks Canada has set up the **Sir Wilfrid Laurier National Historic Site** *($4; early May to mid-Jun every day 9am to 5pm, mid-Jun to early Sep every day 10am to 6pm; 205 12ᵉ Avenue,* ☎ *450-439-3702, www.pc.gc.ca),* in the home that was the birthplace of Canada's first Prime Minister (he served from 1896 to 1911). This interpretation centre gives an overview of Laurier's life and political career and provides visitors with a snapshot of rural life in Québec during the middle of the 19th century.

Head back to Route 125 N. Turn right on Route 337 N. to get to Rawdon.

Rawdon ★ (pop. 9,028)

After the Conquest of 1760, the British established a more familiar means of dividing the territory, namely the township. Governed by residents, townships were established to accommodate American Loyalists and British immigrants. These townships were usually located on the periphery of land already conceded as seigneuries under the French Regime. The townships of Lanaudière were established in the foothills of the Laurentians, between the 17th-century seigneuries and the new territories opened up by the clergy after 1860. The township of Rawdon, at the centre of which is the town of Rawdon, was established in 1799.

The **Centre d'Interprétation Multiethnique de Rawdon** *(free admission, donations welcome; reserve ahead for guided tours; Sat and Sun 1pm to 4pm; 3588 Rue Metcalfe,* ☎*450-834-3334)* describes the short history of the many ethnic groups that have settled in the region since the establishment of the township. The centre is located in a wood house painted in the typical style of the region. A stroll through the neighbouring streets to see the different community churches is a pleasant way of completing a tour of the centre. The Anglican Church and the Russian Orthodox Church are the most interesting.

Two pleasant parks can be found around Rawdon. The first is **Parc des Chutes-Dorwin** ★ *(free admission; every day 9am to 7pm;* ☎*450-834-2282)*, located on Route 337, just before entering the village. Two scenic lookouts provide spectacular views of the Ouareau river's 30m-high waterfall. A wooded picnic area is located nearby.

The other spot of interest in the vicinity is **Parc des Cascades** ★ *($6/car; mid-May to mid-Oct every day;* ☎*450-834-4149)*, which can be reached on Route 341, the extension of Boulevard Pontbriand. Located on the bank of Rivière Ouareau, which runs in lovely cascades over the rocky riverbed here, this park includes a picnic area

where sunbathers stretch out during the hot months of summer.

Saint-Donat ★ (pop. 3,562)

Minutes away from Mont-Tremblant, tucked between mountains reaching up to 900m and the shores of Lac Archambault, the small town of Saint-Donat extends east to the shores of Lac Ouareau. Saint-Donat is also a departure point for the **Parc National du Mont-Tremblant** (see p 253).

Though Saint-Michel-des-Saints is accessible via a long trip through Parc du Mont-Tremblant, it is best to retrace your steps on Rte. 125 to Notre-Dame-de-la-Merci. Once there, follow Rte. 347 towards Sainte-Émélie-de-l'Énergie and then Rte. 131 N. towards Saint-Michel-des-Saints. Continue on Rte. 347 to reach Saint-Gabriel-de-Brandon.

Saint-Gabriel-de-Brandon (pop. 2,594)

The town of Saint-Gabriel-de Brandon borders magnificent Lac Maskinongé. In fact, this 10km² lake is pretty much the town's only attraction; its beautiful **municipal beach** is very popular (see below) with watersports enthusiasts.

Manawan ★

Manawan is one of the three hubs of the Atikamek nation (the others being Wemotaci and Obedjiwan). Certain traditional objects are still made here, such as canoes, snowshoes, moccasins and birchwood baskets.

Parks

Tour B: La Matawinie

The **Réserve Faunique Rouge-Matawin** *(26km west of Saint-Michel-des-Saints;* ☎*450-833-5530 or 800-665-6527, www.sepaq.com)* is 1,394km² of greenery, through which flow some 450 lakes and waterways. It is home to an abundant and fertile wildlife. There is no lack of things to do, from hiking, hunting, fishing, canoe-camping and wild-berry-picking, to snowmobiling in the winter.

Saint-Donat is one of the entry points to **Parc National du Mont-Tremblant ★ ★** (see p 253), which is generally associated with the Laurentians.

The same goes for Saint-Michel-des-Saints and the **Réserve Faunique Mastigouche** (see p 315), which is considered part of the Mauricie region.

Outdoor Activities

■ Cross-Country Skiing

Tour B: La Matawinie

The **Station Touristique de la Montagne Coupée** *($10; 204 Chemin de la Montagne-Coupée, Saint-Jean-de-Matha,* ☎*450-886-3845 or 800-363-8614, www.montagnecoupee.com)* offers outdoor activities year-round. In winter there are 65km of cross-country ski trails, with 43km of wider trails designed for "skating" techniques. Skis are available for rent on site. In the summer, there are trails for horseback riding and hiking.

There are many cross-country ski trails in the Saint-Donat area, in **Secteur La Donatienne** of **Parc des Pionniers** *(Chemin Hector-Bilodeau)*, in **Montagne Noire** and in **Secteur La Pimbina** of **Parc National du Mont-Tremblant** (see p 253).

■ Downhill Skiing

Tour B: La Matawinie

Station Touristique de Val Saint-Côme *($38; 501 Chemin Val St-Côme,* ☎*450-883-0701 or 800-363-2766, www.valsaintcome.com)* is one of the largest downhill ski centres in the Lanaudière region. It has 21 runs, some of which are lit for night skiing, and a vertical drop of 300m. Accommodations are also available.

Station de Ski Mont-Garceau *($32; 190 Chemin du Lac Blanc,* ☎*819-424-2784, www.skigarceau.com)* is located near Saint-Donat, has a vertical drop of 305m and features 17 runs, one of which is reserved for snowboarders.

■ Golf

Tour A: La Plaine

Terrebonne's **Centre de Golf Le Versant** *($34.95/half day; 2075 Côte Terrebonne,* ☎*450-964-2251, www.golfleversant.com)* has four 18-hole courses.

Club de Golf Base-de-Roc *($36; 2870 Boulevard Base-de-Roc,* ☎*450-759-1818)* in Joliette offers a par-72, 18-hole course.

Tour B: La Matawinie

Among the many golf courses in the area, two that stand out are the 18-hole, par-73 course at **Club de Golf de Rawdon** *($29; 3999 Lakeshore Dr.,* ☎*450-834-2320 or 800-363-8655, www.clubgolfrawdon.pj.ca)* and the 18-hole, par-72 course at **Club de Golf Saint-Jean-de-Matha** *($42.50-$65; 945 Chemin Pain de Sucre,* ☎*450-886-9321, www.golfmatha.com)*.

■ Hiking

Tour B: La Matawinie

At **Parc des Sept-Chutes** *($4.50; May to Nov every day 9am to 5pm; Rte. 131,* ☎*450-884-0484)* in Saint-Zénon, some 12km of hiking trails, arranged so as to offer spectacular view points, line some scenic waterfalls.

The **Sentier de la Matawinie** *(about 5km from Sainte-Émélie-de-l'Énergie along Rte. 131 N.,* ☎*450-835-5441, www.mrcmatawinie.qc.ca)* provides the opportunity to observe the Sept-Chutes from the Rivière Noire, as well as some of the other sights of the region. The trail zigzags between various lookout points and reaches an altitude of 565m before leading along a steep section of the trail to the Sept-Chutes in Saint-Zénon.

Parc Régional des Chutes-Monte-à-Peine-et-des-Dalles *($5; accessible from Rtes. 131, 337 and 343,* ☎*450-883-6060, www.parcdeschutes.com)* is jointly managed by the municipalities of Saint-Jean-de-Matha, Sainte-Béatrix and Sainte-Mélanie. Many walking trails, totalling 12km, have been laid out in this 300ha park. Among the sights are three beautiful waterfalls on Rivière L'Assomption.

Lanaudière - Outdoor Activities

■ Snowmobiling

Tour B: La Matawinie

La Cuillère à Pot *(41 Rte. 329, ☎819-424-2252 or 800-567-6704, www.cuillere-pot.com)*, in Saint-Donat, is a favourite rest stop for snowmobilers; it offers various packages and snowmobile rental to its guests.

In Saint-Michel-des-Saints, **Location de Motoneiges Haute-Matawinie** *(Mon-Wed 8:30am to 6pm, Thu and Fri 8:30am to 8pm, Sat and Sun 8:30am to 3pm; 180 Rue Brassard, ☎450-833-1355 or 800-833-6015, www.locationhaute matawinie.com)* has a fleet of approximately 300 snowmobiles for rent.

■ Swimming

Tour B: La Matawinie

The **Rawdon municipal beach** *($4; ☎450-834-8121)*, on the lake of the same name, is very popular during the summertime. Picnic area, fast-food stand, private parking and pedal boats and kayaks are available for rent *($8)*.

On the shores of superb Lac Maskinongé, the **Saint-Gabriel-de-Brandon municipal beach** *(free admission; ☎450-835-2105)* constitutes the main attraction in this little town. This large, beautiful beach can accommodate up to 5,000 bathers. Amenities include a picnic area, a fast-food stand and private parking, as well as pedal-boat, canoe, sailboard and personal watercraft rentals.

A
Accommodations

Tour A: La Plaine

Joliette

Château Joliette
$$$
≡ ♨ ◉
450 Rue St-Thomas
☎ (450) 752-2525 or 800-361-0572
🖷 (450) 752-2520
www.chateaujoliette.com
A large red-brick building by the river, Château Joliette is the largest hotel in town. Though the long corridors are cold and bare, the modern rooms are large and comfortable.

Repentigny

La Villa des Fleurs
$-$$ bkfst incl.
sb ≡ ⭐ 🛏
45 Rue Gaudreault
☎ (450) 654-9209 or 866-654-9209

🖷 (450) 654-1220
Located on the outskirts of Montréal, where a maple grove once stood, La Villa des Fleurs has four attractively decorated rooms. Friendly service and generous breakfasts.

Saint-Liguori

Le Liguori
$$ bkfst incl.
sb
1321 Rang Camp Notre-Dame
☎ (450) 834-6804
www.giteleliguori.com
Le Liguori is a gorgeous bed and breakfast located in a century-old three-storey house. Each of its three adorable rooms has its own unique decor. The common bathroom is a veritable jewel that includes everything guests might need: razor, cream, soap, lotions, etc. In summertime, the reassuring sound of the Ouareau river, which

flows just beside the inn, provides a relaxing ambiance. Small chalets can be rented on the premises. The generous breakfast is delicious and always features local products.

Tour B: La Matawinie

Rawdon

Le Gîte du Catalpa
$$ bkfst incl.
sb 🔺
3730 Rue Queen
☎ (450) 834-5253
The owners of this lovely Victorian house on Rue Queen have converted their home into a five-room bed and breakfast, Le Gîte du Catalpa. In good weather, a five-course breakfast is served on the terrace or in the garden.

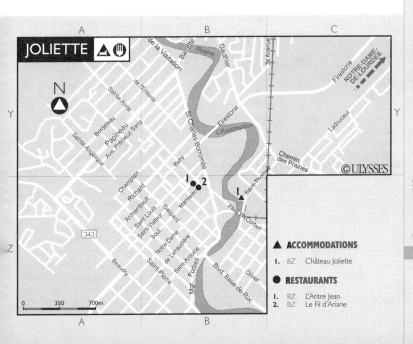

▲ **ACCOMMODATIONS**

1. BZ Château Joliette

● **RESTAURANTS**

1. BZ L'Antre Jean
2. BZ Le Fil d'Ariane

Lanaudière - Accommodations - La Matawinie

Saint-Ambroise-de-Kildare

La Bergerie des Neiges
$$ bkfst incl.
♨ ✗

1401 Rang 5
☎/▤ (450) 756-8395
www.bergeriedesneiges.com

Owned by a music teacher and a friendly ex-lawyer, La Bergerie des Neiges provides visitors with a distinctly warm welcome. The owners have remodelled this old rural schoolhouse to create an inn with five charmingly cozy rooms, each of which features a unique decoration theme. Guests get to savour excellent home cooking in the inn's dining room, visit the adjoining sheepfold, and, weather permitting, take a dip in the heated outdoor pool.

Saint-Alphonse-Rodriguez

Le Cheval Bleu
$$ bkfst incl.
✗

☎ (450) 883-3080
▤ (450) 883-3443
www.lechevalbleu.com

Located some 25km north of Joliette, Le Cheval Bleu bed and breakfast is owned by a couple from Brussels. It features four attractive rooms with private bathrooms. The inn's small restaurant serves a few delicious Belgian classics: mussels, fries, black pudding and homemade mayonnaise.

Auberge sur la Falaise
$$$-$$$$ bkfst incl.
≡ ◎ ➰ ▲ ☰ ✗ ✗ ⁑⁑

324 Avenue du Lac Long Sud
☎ (450) 883-2269 or 888-325-2473
▤ (450) 883-0143
www.auberge-falaise.com

Ten kilometres from the village of Saint-Alphonse-Rodriguez, after a long climb past peaceful Lac Long and into what seems like another world, is the marvellous Auberge sur la Falaise. The inn, perched on a promontory, dominates this serene landscape, reserving exceptional views for its guests. The 26 rooms in this modern building are luxurious, and the hotel does double duty as a spa and also offers many sports activities. Finally, the cuisine served in the dining room is among the best in the area (see p 238).

Saint-Jean-de-Matha

Auberge de la Montagne Coupée
$$$$
≡ ▲ ➰ ≋ ✗ ⁑⁑ ✗ ◎

1000 Chemin de la Montagne-Coupée
☎ (450) 886-3891 or 800-363-8614
▤ (450) 886-5401
www.montagnecoupee.com

Another exceptional establishment, Auberge de la Montagne Coupée appears after what seems like an interminable climb. Reward is at hand though in this immense white building with huge bay windows. The hotel has approximately 50 comfortable, modern rooms bathed in natural light, some of which have fireplaces. In the dining room and the lounge, large windows reveal a breathtaking panorama. There is

an equestrian centre and a summer theatre at the bottom of the grounds, and the hotel has a remarkable restaurant (see p 239).

Saint-Donat

Parc National du Mont-Tremblant
$

2951 Route 125 Nord
☎ (819) 424-7012 or 877-688-2289

The Pimbina section of Parc National du Mont-Tremblant, near Saint-Donat and accessible via Rte. 125, offers 340 campsites.

Auberge Havre du Parc
$$ bkfst incl.
▲ ➰ ✗ ◎

2788 Rte. 125 Nord
☎ (819) 424-7686
▤ (819) 424-3432
www.havreduparc.qc.ca

Located 10km just north of the village, the Auberge Havre du Parc is a haven of tranquillity. The magnificent location, on the shores of Lac Provost, and the comfort of the accommodations, make it easy to relax and forget the daily grind. Five minutes away from Mont Tremblant's cross-country ski trails.

Manoir des Laurentides
$$
▲ ➰ ≋ ✗ ◎

290 Rue Principale
☎ (819) 424-2121 or 800-567-6717
▤ (819) 424-2621
www.manoirdeslaurentides.com

The Manoir des Laurentides, well located by Lac Archambault, offers good value for your money. The rooms in the three-storey main building are comfortable but ordinary, though each has its own balcony. There are also two rows of motel rooms that stretch to the lakefront and about 40 cottages equipped with kitchenettes. Since this spot is often quite lively, visitors who value peace and quiet should opt for the motel rooms or cottages. A beach and a small marina are available to guests.

Sainte-Émélie-de-l'Énergie

Auberge du Vieux Moulin
$$$-$$$$ bkfst incl.
♨))) ◎ ≋
200 Chemin du Vieux-Moulin
☎ (450) 884-0211 or 866-884-0211
▤ (450) 884-0702
www.aubvieuxmoulin.com
Auberge du Vieux-Moulin is renowned both for its high-quality accommodations and for its excellent restaurant. Its 18 impeccable rooms are well equipped and will please families as well as couples. All provide direct outdoor access. Several summer and winter activities are offered on site.

Saint-Côme

Auberge Aux Quatre Matins
$$-$$$$
♨ ≋ ⌂ ◎ �
155 Rue des Skieurs
☎ (450) 883-1932 or 800-929-1932
www.auxquatrematins.ca
The friendly Auberge Aux Quatre Matins is located within a stone's throw of the Station Touristique Val Saint-Côme resort. The inn has 11 bright rooms and three suites. All are spacious and impeccably maintained. For guests who may wish to open their pocketbooks a little wider to offer themselves a real treat, we recommend the room with a cathedral roof, fireplace and therapeutic

tub. Small apartments with kitchenettes can also be rented. The inn is extremely busy in wintertime, so reservations should be made well in advance for this period. In summertime, various outdoor activity packages are offered, including golf, fishing and all-terrain-vehicle excursion packages.

Saint-Michel-des-Saints

Auberge CanadAventure
$$ bkfst incl.
Lac Taureau
☎ (450) 833-1478
▤ (450) 755-6568
www.canadaventure.net
Auberge CanadAventure is a fishing and hunting outfitter located 25km north of Saint-Michel-des-Saints. The handsome white pine lodge features cozy rooms with hardwood floors. In addition to hunting and fishing trips, various other activities are offered on site, including Jet Ski, seaplane and all-terrain-vehicle excursions, dogsled and snowmobile expeditions and off-track skiing.

Auberge du Lac Taureau
$$$
⌂ ≋ Y ♨))) ◎
1200 Chemin Baie du Milieu
☎ (819) 833-1919 or 877-822-2623
▤ (819) 833-1870
www.lactaureau.com
Luxurious hotels located right in the heart of a forest have become more and more popular lately in Québec. L'Auberge du Lac Taureau is one of these establishments. Visitors come here to be close to nature and to pamper themselves while taking advantage of the inn's many services. Magnificent wood lodges with large picture windows have been built on the edge

of Lac Taureau, placing guests right in the middle of a stunning natural environment. The three main buildings contain 100 or so comfortable rooms. Various activities are organized on site and the inn's fine restaurant serves excellent meals.

Restaurants

Tour A: La Plaine

Terrebonne

Le Jardin des Fondues
$$-$$$$
186 Rue Ste-Marie
☎ (450) 492-2048
Terrebonne's Le Jardin des Fondues, where the chic ambiance adds to a delicious assortment of fondues and traditional French dishes, is sure to please fondue fans from far and wide.

L'Étang des Moulins
$$$
888 Rue St-Louis
☎ (450) 471-4018
L'Étang des Moulins occupies a magnificent stone house that dominates Terrebone's historic district. Inside, an inviting, romantic ambiance dominates, with tables draped in lace and French music wafting through the air. Large windows and a glassed-in terrace out back maximize the view of Île des Moulins. On the menu are French classics successfully reinvented. Foodies will be happy to loosen the purse strings and splurge on the seven-course *"menu inspira-*

● **RESTAURANTS**

1. L'Étang des Moulins
2. Le Folichon
3. Le Jardin des Fondues

tion." Service is attentive yet discreet. This is without a doubt one of the best restaurants in Lanaudière.

Le Folichon
$$$-$$$$
Tue-Sun
804 Rue St-François-Xavier
☎ (450) 492-1863
Le Folichon, which means playful and lighthearted, lives up to its name. Occupying a lovely, two-storey wood-framed house in the historic quarter of Terrebonne, the restaurant's warm atmosphere is powerful enough to make one forget the coldest days of winter. In the summer, the shaded terrace is the spot of choice. The five-course table d'hôte is generally memorable, and there is an impressive wine list as well.

L'Assomption

Le Prieuré
$$$$
402 Boulevard L'Ange-Gardien
☎ (450) 589-6739
Located in a historic 18th-century building, Le Prieuré has developed an excellent reputation over the years. The chef prepares savoury

French cuisine with local products.

Joliette

Le Fil d'Ariane
$$-$$$
400 Boulevard Manseau
☎ (450) 755-3131
A gourmet restaurant with a cozy atmosphere, Le Fil D'Ariane specializes in savoury Belgian cuisine and is without a doubt one of the best dining establishments in the region. The menu also includes a few classic French dishes. The dining room features soft lighting and unobtrusive music. In summertime, diners get to eat under the stars on the restaurant's terrace. A quality wine list and superior service round out a memorable meal.

L'Antre Jean
$$$
385 Boulevard St-Viateur
☎ (450) 756-0412
Amongst the many fine restaurants in town, L'Antre Jean seems to be the unofficial favourite of locals. French specialties, prepared as they are in France, are served as part of the table-d'hôte menu. The

decor is warm and inviting and the atmosphere is unpretentious.

- - - - - - - - - - - - - - - - -
Tour B:
La Matawinie

Saint-Alphonse-Rodriguez

Auberge sur la Falaise
$$$$
324 Avenue du Lac Long Sud
☎ (450) 883-2269
At the extraordinary **Auberge sur la Falaise** (see p 236), meals are served in a setting of perfect tranquillity. Nestled deep in the forest, overlooking the calm surface of a lake, this establishment is the perfect retreat from the hectic pace of modern life (even if it is just for a meal). The chef skillfully adapts French cuisine to Québec flavours. The obvious choice for epicureans is the five-course gourmet menu—a memorable experience, indeed!

Saint-Jean-de-Matha

Auberge de la Montagne Coupée
$$$$
1000 Chemin de la Montagne-Coupée
☎ (450) 886-3891 or 800-363-8614
Auberge de la Montagne Coupée (see p 236), another spot famous for its peaceful setting, offers an exciting menu of innovative Québec cuisine. The dining room is surrounded by two-storey bay windows that look out on an absolutely breathtaking scene. And this is just the beginning—the best part of the evening (the meal) is yet to come. Imaginatively presented game dishes are enhanced by succulent treasures. The service is attentive; the wine list is excellent. Very copious breakfasts are also served.

Saint-Donat

La Petite Michèle
$-$$$
327 Rue St-Donat
☎ (819) 424-3131
La Petite Michèle is just the place for travellers looking for a good family restaurant. The atmosphere is relaxed, the service friendly and the menu traditional Québécois.

Maison Blanche
$$
515 Rue Principale
☎ (819) 424-2222
The food is always delicious at Maison Blanche. The house specialty, a divine, juicy, rare steak, is known far and wide.

Auberge Havre du Parc
$$$-$$$$
2788 Route 125 Nord
Lac-Provost
☎ (819) 424-7686
Auberge Havre du Parc not only boasts an exceptionally peaceful setting, it also has an excellent selection of French specialties:

Sainte-Émélie-de-l'Énergie

Auberge du Vieux Moulin
$$$
200 Chemin du Vieux-Moulin
☎ (450) 884-0211 or 866-884-0211
Run by a chef who once taught at the Institut de tourisme et d'hôtellerie du Québec (where many of the province's top chefs are trained), l'Auberge du Vieux Moulin offers quality dining in a warm country environment. The menu features a few surprises, but you can always be sure to find exquisite game dishes such as red deer paupiettes (rolled cutlets) and locally bred boar. Reservations required.

Entertainment

■ Bars and Nightclubs

Joliette

L'Alchimiste
536-A Boulevard Manseau
☎ (450) 760-2945
Colourful and lively L'Alchimiste attracts a large crowd of locals, including many students and professors. Eight tasty beers are brewed on site and various live concerts provide entertainment.

■ Festivals and Cultural Events

Joliette

The most important event on the regional calendar is the **Festival de Lanaudière** (*☎450-759-7636 or 800-561-4343, www.lanaudiere.org*). During the most beautiful weeks of the summer, dozens of classical, contemporary and popular music concerts are presented in the churches of the area and outdoors at the superb Amphithéâtre de Lanaudière.

The **Festival Mémoire et Racines** *(late Jul; St-Charles-Borromée, near Joliette, ☎450-752-6798 or 888-810-6798, www.memoireracines.qc.ca)* is a major festival of traditional music, dance and storytelling.

Repentigny

At the annual **Internationaux de Tennis Junior du Canada** *(late Aug; ☎450-470-3001, ext. 3483, www.tennis-junior-repentigny.com)*, tennis fans might discover tomorrow's Venus Williams or Roger Federer.

Saint-Donat

When autumn arrives, the forests of the Saint-Donat region turn into a multicoloured natural extravaganza. To celebrate this spectacular burst of colour, various family activities are organized during the **Weekends des Couleurs** (*☎819-424-2833 or 888-783-6668*).

■ Theatres and Concert Halls

Joliette

There is nothing more pleasant than attending an open-air concert at the **Amphithéâtre de Lanaudière** (*1575 Boulevard Base-de-Roc,* ☎ *450-759-2999 or 800-561-4343*), ideally located in a small, tree-ringed valley. The best of this acoustically privileged site's summer program is presented during the Festival de Lanaudière.

Terrebonne

Tiny but cozy, **Théâtre du Vieux-Terrebonne** (&; *867 Rue Saint-Pierre,* ☎ *450-492-4777 or 866-404-4777*) has earned the respect of the Québec artistic community over the years and now draws some of the biggest names in song and comedy, who use it as a sort of testing ground before they bring their act to Montréal. Touring theatre troupes also stop in regularly.

The Laurentians

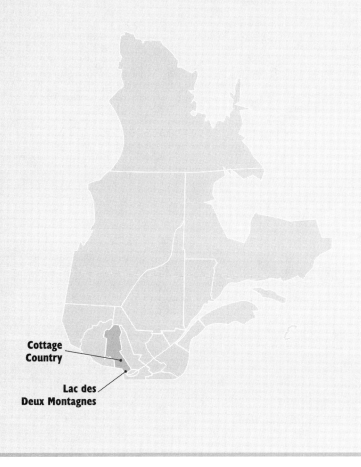

Cottage Country

Lac des Deux Montagnes

The most renowned resort area in Québec, the beautiful Laurentians region, or "Laurentides" in French, attracts a great many visitors all year round. For generations, people have been "going up north" to relax and enjoy the beauty of the Laurentian landscape. The lakes, mountains and forests provide a particularly good setting for a variety of physical activities or outings.

Since the region boasts the highest concentration of ski resorts in North America, skiing gets top billing here when winter rolls around. The villages scattered at the foot of the mountains are both charming and friendly.

The southern part of the region, known as the "Basses-Laurentides" (Lower Laurentians), was settled early on by French colonists, who came here to cultivate the rich farmland. A number of local villages reveal this history through their architectural heritage. The settling of the Laurentian plateau, initiated by the now-legendary Curé Labelle, began much later, toward the middle of the 19th century. The development of the "Pays d'En Haut," or Upper Laurentians, was part of an ambitious plan to colonize the outlying areas of Québec in an effort to counter the exodus of French Canadians to industrial towns in the northeastern United States. Given the poor soil, farming here was hardly profitable, but Curé Labelle nevertheless succeeded in founding some 20 villages and attracting a good number of French-Canadian colonists to the region.

Getting There and Getting Around

Vacationers of all types have been coming to this region since the start of the 20th century, making tourism the most important local industry. The following two tours have been laid out for you to discover this vast area: **Tour A: Lac des Deux Montagnes ★** and **Tour B: Cottage Country ★ ★**.

■ By Plane

Tour B: Cottage Country

Mont-Tremblant International Airport *(150 Roger-Hébert, Rivière Rouge,* ☎*819-425-7919 or 877-425-7919, www.mtia.ca)* is Canada's most recent international airport. It is located 30min north of the Mont-Tremblant resort. The airport welcomes most major airlines and offers all the usual services that are expected from an international airport. The terminal's singular log building houses a hotel-reservation service, a car-rental agency, restaurants and limousine and taxi services.

■ By Car

Tour A: Lac des Deux Montagnes

From Montréal, follow Aut. 13 N. Take the exit for Rte. 344 W. towards Saint-Eustache. This road continues to Oka. A ferry from Oka leads to Hudson (see p 170) in the Montérégie region.

Tour B: Cottage Country

From Montréal, take Aut. 15 N. (*Autoroute des Laurentides*) to Saint-Jérôme (Exit 43). Landmarks along the way include the imposing Collège de Sainte-Thérèse (1881) and its church. A little further, before Saint-Jérôme, is Mirabel Airport (for cargo planes only). Hwy. 15 and then Rte. 117 lead to Mont-Tremblant.

■ Bus Stations

Tour B: Cottage Country

Piedmont
770 Boulevard des Laurentides
☎ (450) 227-2487

Sainte-Adèle
1208 Rue Valiquette (Pharmacie Brunet)
☎ (450) 229-6609

The Laurentians

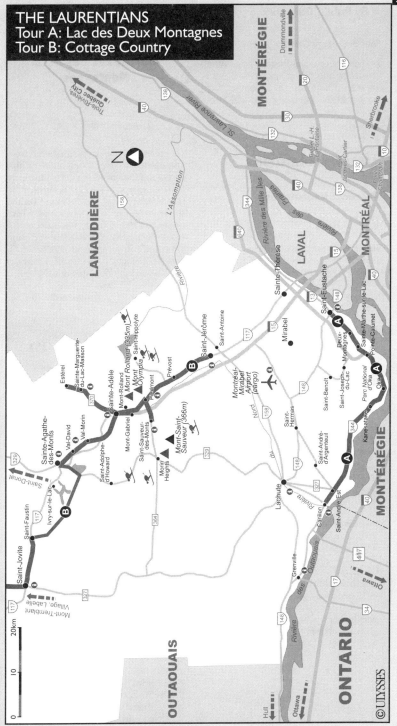

243

THE LAURENTIANS
Tour A: Lac des Deux Montagnes
Tour B: Cottage Country

■ By Public Transport

Tour B: Cottage Country

A shuttle links Saint-Jovite, Village Mont-Tremblant and the mountain itself (Mont Tremblant) from April to December. Tickets cost $1. To check schedules call ☎866-253-0097.

Useful Information

■ Tourist Information

Regional Office

Maison du Tourisme des Laurentides
14142 Rue de la Chapelle, Mirabel, QC, J7J 2C8
☎ (450) 436-8532 or 800-561-6673
📄 (450) 436-5309
www.laurentides.com

Tour A: Lac des Deux Montagnes

Saint-Eustache
600 Rue Dubois
☎ (450) 491-4444

Tour B: Cottage Country

Saint-Sauveur-des-Monts
605 Chemin Des Frênes
☎ (450) 227-3417

Sainte-Adèle
1490 Rue Saint-Joseph
☎ (450) 229-3729

Village Mont-Tremblant
5080 Montée Ryan
☎ (819) 425-2434

Labelle
7404 Boulevard du Curé-Labelle
☎ (819) 686-2606

Mont-Laurier
177 Boulevard Albiny-Paquette
☎ (819) 623-4544

Exploring

- - - - - - - - - - - - - - - - - - - -
Tour A: Lac des Deux Montagnes
★

 1 day

The priests of the Sulpician order were instrumental to the colonization of this part of the Laurentians right from the early days of the French Regime. Vestiges of the seigneurial era can still be found on the shores of Lac des Deux Montagnes, where nearly half the stops on this tour are located. Highlights of this short excursion through the lower Laurentians, just a half-hour from Montréal, are beautiful views of the lake and the opportunity to sample a wide variety of fresh produce at roadside stands along the way during the summer and fall.

Saint-Eustache (pop. 41,635)

In the early 19th century, Saint-Eustache was a prosperous farming community that had produced a French-Canadian intellectual and political elite. These individuals played a major role in the Patriote Rebellion of 1837-38, making Saint-Eustache one of the main arenas of the tragic events that took place at the time. The village used to be the centre of the Mille-Îles seigneury, which was granted to Michel Sidrac du Gué de Boisbriand in 1683. It was the Lambert-Dumont family, however, that undertook the development of the seigneury in the middle of the 18th century. From 1960 on, Saint-Eustache became one of the suburbs of Montréal.

The **Église Saint-Eustache** ★★ (♿; *123 Rue Saint-Louis*) is remarkable mainly for its high Palladian facade built out of cut stone between 1831 and 1836. Its two bell towers bear witness to the prosperity of local residents in the years leading up to the rebellion. The church still bears traces of the fierce fighting that took place within its walls on December 19, 1837, when 150 Patriotes led by Jean-Olivier Chénier shut themselves up in the building to resist General Colborne's British troops. The British leader had his men bombard the church, and by the end of the battle, only its walls were left standing. The troops were then ordered to burn most of the houses in the village. It took Saint-Eustache more than 30 years to recover from these events.

Beside the church, visitors will find the presbytery, the convent (1898) and a monument to the Patriotes.

Take Rue Saint-Eustache, directly in line with the centre of the church, to Manoir Globensky.

Manoir Globensky *($3; Tue-Sun 10am to 5pm; 235 Rue Saint-Eustache,* ☎*450-974-5170)* is a large white house that once belonged to Charles-Auguste-Maximilien Globensky, husband of the heiress of the Saint-Eustache seigneury, Virginie Lambert-Dumont. Though it was built in 1862 after the abolition of the seigneurial system (1854), local residents have always referred to it as the "manor." Today, it houses the city hall and cultural centre of Saint-Eustache.

The stone walls of the **Moulin Légaré** *($3; mid-Oct to mid-May Mon-Fri 9am to 5pm, mid-May to mid-Oct every day 9am to 5pm; 232 Rue St-Eustache,* ☎*450-974-5400)* date back to 1762. However, modifications made in the early 20th century have robbed the building of some of its character. This flour mill has been in continuous operation since it was built, making it the oldest water-powered mill still in use in Canada. Visitors can purchase wheat and buckwheat flour on the premises.

Return to Rte. 344 W., which leads through Deux-Montagnes, Sainte-Marthe-sur-le-Lac and Pointe-Calumet before reaching Oka, the next stop on the tour.

Oka ★ (pop. 4,681)

The Sulpicians, like the Jesuits, established missions in the Montréal area with the goal of converting local natives to Catholicism. The disciples of Ignatius Loyola settled permanently in Kahnawake in 1716 (see p 173), and those of Jean-Jacques Olier followed in their footsteps in 1721, settling on the shores of Lac des Deux Montagnes in a lovely spot named Oka, which means "golden fish." Here, the Sulpicians welcomed Algonquins, Hurons and Mohawks, all allies of the French. While the Kahnawake mission was supposed to remain isolated from

European-born inhabitants, a village of French colonists developed simultaneously around the Sulpician church.

At the end of the 18th century, a number of Iroquois from New York State supplanted the original Aboriginal inhabitants of the mission, giving an English character and, more recently, a new name (Kanesatake) to a whole section of territory located upriver from the village. Today, Oka is a centre for both recreational activities and tourism, as well as a distant suburb of Montréal. In 1990, during what has come to be known as the "Oka Crisis," the Mohawk Warriors of Kanesatake barricaded Rte. 344 at the western edge of Oka for several long months in an effort to affirm territorial rights and prevent a portion of the land from being turned into a golf course. Unfortunately, a police officer lost his life during the standoff.

Abbaye Cistercienne d'Oka ★ *(1600 Chemin d'Oka,* ☎*450-479-8361, www.abbayeoka.com)* is run by the Cistercian order, founded at the Abbaye de Citeaux by Robert de Molesme, Albéric and Étienne Harding at the end of the 11th century. It is a reformed branch of the Benedictine order. In 1881, a few Cistercian monks left the Abbaye de Bellefontaine in France in order to found a new abbey in Canada. The Sulpicians, who had already donated several pieces of their extensive territorial holdings in Montréal to various religious communities, granted the new arrivals a hillside in the seigneury of Deux-Montagnes. Within a few years, the monks had built the Abbaye d'Oka, also known as La Trappe. The famous Oka cheese is still made here, and can be purchased in the cheese dairy adjoining the monastery. The Romanesque Revival–style chapel in the centre of the abbey is also worth a short visit.

Parc National d'Oka ★, see p 252.

From the centre of Oka, turn left on Rue L'Annonciation to the church and the pier, which offers a beautiful view of Lac des Deux Montagnes. The pier serves as the landing stage for the tiny private ferryboat that links this tour to the **Vaudreuil-Soulanges** *tour in Montérégie (see p 169).*

The **Église d'Oka ★** *(181 Rue des Anges),* an eclectic church built in 1878 in the Romanesque Revival style, stands in front of the

The Laurentians – Exploring - Lac des Deux Montagnes

lake, on the same site once occupied by the church of the Sulpician mission (1733). It houses paintings belonging to the 18th-century French school, commissioned in Paris by Sulpician priests to adorn the stations of the cross (Calvaire) in Oka (1742). In 1776, these oil paintings were replaced by wooden bas-reliefs executed by François Guernon, which were better able to withstand the harsh Canadian climate. The bas-reliefs were severely damaged by vandals in 1970 before being removed from the oratories and chapels and hung in the Chapelle Kateri Tekakwitha, adjacent to the Église d'Oka.

Continue along Rue des Anges, then turn right on Rue Sainte-Anne before taking a left back on to Rte. 344 and heading towards Saint-André-d'Argenteuil.

The road then leads through **The Pines**, planted in 1886 to counter the erosion of the sandy soil. It was here, in this forest of 50,000 pine trees, that tensions peaked during the 1990 "Oka Crisis," when the provincial police force, the Sûreté du Québec, and then the Canadian Army, faced the Mohawk Warriors in an armed standoff.

On the edge of the village of Saint-Placide, further to the west, is the **Maison Routhier** *(3320 Rte. 344)*, childhood home of Basile Routhier, author of the lyrics to Canada's national anthem.

Turn left on Rue Saint-André, which leads to Carillon (Rte. 344).

Carillon

Charged with defending the colony against attacks from First Nations allied with the Dutch and later the English, Dollard des Ormeaux and 17 fellow soldiers were killed during a battle with the Iroquois in 1660. Their deaths prevented the Iroquois from taking Montréal. A plaque and a monument commemorate this bloody episode in the early history of New France. Known for many years as Long-Sault, Carillon is a peaceful village that was populated by Loyalists in the early 19th century. Visitors will find a hydroelectric dam here, as well as a vast park with a pleasant picnic area.

The **Musée Régional d'Argenteuil** *($3; early Jun to early Oct Tue-Sun 10:30am to 5pm, early*

Oct to early Dec and early Mar to early Jun Tue-Sat 10:30am to 5pm; 44 Route du Long-Sault, ☎450-537-3861) exhibits local antiques, as well as a collection of 19th-century clothing, in a handsome Georgian-style stone building erected in 1836. Originally intended to serve as an inn, it was converted the following year into a military barracks for the British troops who had come to put down the Patriote Rebellion in the Saint-Eustache region.

To return to Montréal, take Rte. 640 E., then Rte. 13 S. and finally Rte. 20 E.

Tour B: Cottage Country
★ ★

This part of the Laurentians has been the favourite playground of Montrealers since the 1930s. Located less than 1.5hrs from the big city, it encompasses a multitude of lakes, wooded mountains and villages equipped to accommodate visitors. Montrealers "go up north" to their cottages to relax, go canoeing—in short, to enjoy the natural surroundings. In winter, visitors from Ontario, New York and other parts of eastern North America join Montrealers in the charming local inns and luxury hotels. They come here not only to go downhill skiing, but also to snowshoe, cross-country ski or snowmobile across the snow-covered landscape, and spend pleasant evenings by the fireside. The Laurentians boast the largest concentration of ski resorts in North America.

Saint-Jérôme (pop. 62,684)

This administrative and industrial town is nicknamed "La Porte du Nord" (The Gateway to the North), because it marks the passage from the St. Lawrence valley into the mountainous region that stretches north of Montréal and Québec City.

To this day, much of the population of the region around Saint-Jérôme is of French-Canadian extraction. Indeed, the all-powerful clergy of Québec tried a number of tactics to halt the exodus to the United States in the years following the rebellion of 1837-38, the most important being the colonization of the upper Laurentians be-

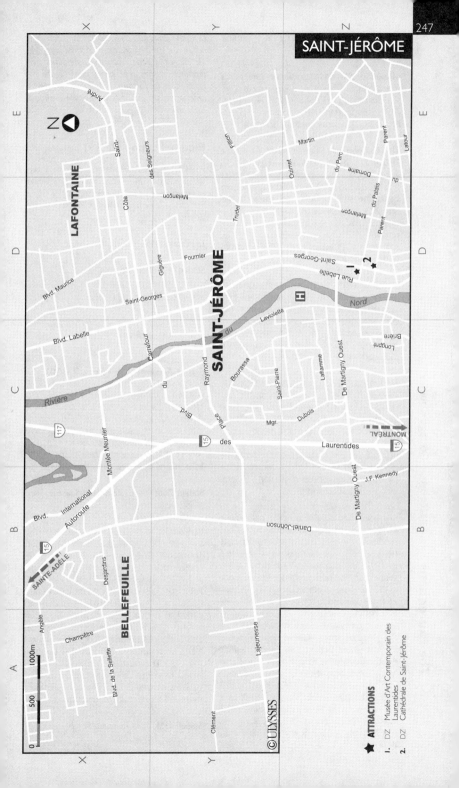

★ ATTRACTIONS

1. DZ Musée d'Art Contemporain des Laurentides
2. DZ Cathédrale de Saint-Jérôme

©ULYSSES

tween 1880 and 1895, led by Curé Antoine Labelle of Saint-Jérôme.

The **Musée d'Art Contemporain des Laurentides** *(free admission; Tue-Fri and Sun noon to 5pm, Sat 9am to 5pm; 185 Rue du Palais,* ☎*450-432-7171)* is located in Saint-Jérôme's old courthouse and presents contemporary art.

The **Cathédrale de Saint-Jérôme** ★ *(every day 7:30am to 4:30pm; 355 Rue St-Georges,* ☎*450-432-9741)*, a simple parish church when it was erected in 1899, is now a large Roman Byzantine–style edifice reflecting Saint-Jérôme's prestigious status as the "headquarters" of the colonization of the Laurentians. A bronze statue of Curé Labelle, sculpted by Alfred Laliberté, stands in front of the cathedral.

Saint-Jérôme is also the starting point of the **Parc Linéaire du P'tit Train du Nord** ★★. This extraordinary bike path, which becomes a cross-country ski trail in winter, stretches over 200km, from Saint-Jérôme to Mont-Laurier, along the same route once followed by the Laurentian railroad.

This railroad was built between 1891 and 1909 and played a crucial role in the colonization of the Laurentians. It came to be known as the P'tit Train du Nord, or "Little Train of the North," a nickname immortalized in a song by Félix Leclerc. Later, right up until the 1940s, the railroad fostered the development of the region's tourist industry by providing access to all sorts of summer and winter resort areas.

Roads and then highways eventually made the Laurentians more and more accessible, rendering the P'tit Train du Nord obsolete by the 1980s. The railroad was dismantled in 1991, and the park was laid out a few years later. The park has since become one of the area's major attractions. It is punctuated from one end to the other with information panels, enabling visitors to learn more about the region's rich history, particularly the original train stations (Saint-Jérôme, Prévost, Mont-Rolland, Val-Morin, Sainte-Agathe-des-Monts, Saint-Faustin–Lac-Carré, Mont-Tremblant, Labelle, L'Annonciation and Mont-Laurier), which are still standing. Some have even been restored, as is the case with the **Saint-Jérôme station**, which was not only overhauled in 1997 but now has a lovely square next to it called **Place de la Gare**.

Continue along Aut. 15 N. toward Saint-Sauveur-des-Monts. On the way, the road runs alongside the village of Prévost, where the Laurentians' first downhill ski trails were opened in 1932. The following year, the first mechanical chairlift in North America was installed here. Take the Piedmont Exit (58).

Piedmont (pop. 2,219)

Unlike other villages in the vicinity, Piedmont has not undergone much large-scale development. Mostly residential, it is a jumping-off point for fun water slides and downhill skiing.

La Pente des Pays-d'en-Haut, see p 257

Station de Ski Mont-Olympia, see p 255

Station de Ski Mont-Avila, see p 255

Follow the signs for Rte. 364 and Saint-Sauveur, located right nearby, west of Aut. 15.

Saint-Sauveur ★ (pop. 7,000)

Located perhaps a little too close to Montréal, Saint-Sauveur has been overdeveloped in recent years, and condominiums, restaurants and art galleries have sprung up like mushrooms. Rue Principale is very busy and is the best place in the Laurentians to mingle with the crowds.

Station Touristique Mont-Saint-Sauveur, see p 255.

Pavillon 70, located at the bottom of the same-numbered hill that leads to Station Touristique Mont-Saint-Sauveur, is justly considered Canada's first post-modern architectural work (1977). Its architect, Peter Rose, also designed Montréal's Centre Canadien d'Architecture. Post-modernism aimed to rejuvenate modern 1970s architecture, which was considered repetitive and boring, by adding decorative elements taken from various architectural styles from the past. The pavilion boasts a colourful wood exterior with Victorian details and massive stylized chimneys that recall those found on traditional Québec houses.

Station de Ski Mont-Habitant, see p 255.

Parc Aquatique Mont-Saint-Sauveur, see p 257.

From Saint-Sauveur-des-Monts, you can make a loop through charming Morin-Heights, with its two small white churches, one Catholic and the other Anglican, and pretty Saint-Adolphe-d'Howard. Rte. 364 O. and Rte. 329 N. ultimately lead to Saint-Agathe-des-Monts. Alternatively, get back on Aut. 15 N., then take the exit for Sainte-Adèle and Sainte-Marguerite-du-Lac-Masson (69).

Sainte-Adèle ★ (pop. 9,997)

The Laurentians were nicknamed the "Pays-d'En-Haut" (the Highlands) by 19th-century colonists heading for these northern lands, far from the St. Lawrence Valley. Writer and journalist Claude-Henri Grignon, born in Sainte-Adèle in 1894, used the region as the setting for his books. His famous novel, *Un homme et son péché* (A Man and his Sin), depicts the wretchedness of life in the Laurentians back in those days. Grignon asked his good friend, architect Lucien Parent, to design the village church, which graces Rue Principale to this day.

Today, Sainte-Adèle is a bustling modern city with many attractions, whose citizens enjoy a high standard of living. Among the many activities that can be enjoyed in the area are several ski resorts, including Mont-Gabriel and Les Pentes 40-80, which caters to novice skiers; golf courses such as La Vallée, Alpine Inn, Mont-Gabriel and Chantecler; a portion of the P'tit Train du Nord trail; and several opportunities for canoeing, kayaking and hiking.

Au Pays des Merveilles *($15; mid-Jun to late Aug every day 10am to 6pm; 3595 Chemin de la Savane,* ☎*450-229-3141)* is a small, modest amusement park that will appeal mainly to young children. Slides, a wading pool, a miniature golf course and a maze, among other things, have all been laid out in a setting reminiscent of Alice's Adventures in Wonderland (*Alice au Pays des Merveilles* in French).

Station de Ski Le Chantecler, see p 255.

Station de Ski Mont-Gabriel, see p 255.

Take Rte. 370 to Sainte-Marguerite-du-Lac-Masson. On the way, you'll see the charming Pavillon des Arts de Sainte-Adèle.

Sainte-Marguerite–Estérel ★ (pop. 2,466)

All year round, vacationers come to the lovely rolling countryside of the Lac Masson area to unwind, far from the hustle and bustle of Montréal. Two villages have sprung up on the shores of the lake, the elegant L'Estérel and the more modest but more populated Sainte-Marguerite-du-Lac-Masson, which is located on the westernmost part of the lake. These two villages have merged into one municipality.

Rte. 370 will take you to Sainte-Marguerite, on the shores of Lac Masson. A little square next to the church, in front of the renowned **Bistro à Champlain** (see p 266), offers a good view of the lake. The road then turns right, skirting around the lake on its way to Ville d'Estérel.

In Belgium, the name Empain is synonymous with financial success. Baron Louis Empain, who inherited the family fortune in the early 20th century, was an important builder, just like his father, who was responsible for the construction of Heliopolis, a new section of Cairo (Egypt). During a trip to Canada in 1935, Baron Louis purchased Pointe Bleue, a strip of land that extends out into Lac Masson. In two years, from 1936 to 1938, he erected about 20 buildings on the site, all designed by Belgian architect Antoine Courtens. Empain named this entire development **Domaine de l'Estérel**. The onset of World War II thwarted his plans, however, and after the war, the land was divided up. In 1958, a portion of it was purchased by a Québec businessman named Fridolin Simard, who began construction of the present **Hôtel L'Estérel** (see p 259) along Rte. 370, and then divided the rest of the property into lots.

Return to Aut. 15 N. and get off at Exit 76, which leads to Val-Morin and Val-David.

Val-Morin (pop. 2,346)

Val-Morin is a modest village that has attracted cottage-goers who want to avoid the overdevelopment prevalent in some Laurentian villages. It is located in a mountainous region traversed by cross-country ski trails, where a number of outdoor activities can be enjoyed.

Return to Rte. 117 N. and continue to Val-David.

Val-David (pop. 4,128)

Val-David attracts visitors not only because it is located near the Laurentian ski resorts, but also for its craft shops, where local artisans display their work. The village, made up of lovely houses, has managed to retain its own unique charm.

Every year, the **Village du Père-Noël** *($10; early Jun to late Aug every day 10am to 6pm; 987 Rue Morin, ☎819-322-2146 or 800-287-6635, www. noel.qc.ca)*, or Santa's Village, attracts children eager to meet Saint Nicholas at his summer retreat. A number of activities are organized, ensuring memorable days for the kids.

From Aut. 15 (Exit 86), turn right onto Rte. 117 N. Keep left and turn onto Rte. 329 S. (Rue Principale).

Sainte-Agathe-des-Monts ★ (pop. 9,396)

Set in the heart of the Laurentians, this is a business- and tourism-oriented town, which sprang up around a sawmill in 1849. When the railway was introduced to the region in 1892, Sainte-Agathe-des-Monts became the first resort area in the Laurentians. Located at the meeting point of two movements of colonization, the British settling of the county of Argenteuil and the French-Canadian settling of Saint-Jérôme, the town succeeded in attracting wealthy vacationers, who, lured by Lac des Sables, built several beautiful villas around the lake and near the Anglican church. The region was once deemed a first-class resort by important Jewish families from Montréal and New York. In 1909, the Jewish community founded the Mount Sinai Sanitarium (the present building was erected in 1930) and in the following years, built synagogues in Sainte-Agathe-des-Monts and Val-Morin.

There are two ways to discover the many observation points that provide magnificent views of **Lac des Sables** ★ and its surroundings. The first is to follow Chemin du Lac around the lake by car or bicycle (11km). The second is to take a short cruise on the lake aboard one of **Croisières Alouette's**

boats *($12; mid-May to late Jun and late Aug to late Oct every day 11:30am, 1:30pm, 2:30pm and 3:30pm; additional departures Jun to Aug at 5pm at 7:30pm; Rue Principale pier, ☎819-326-3656, www.croisierealouette.com).*

Take the winding Rte. de Saint-Faustin through the mountains and around the lakes. Turn left on Rte. 117 (caution: dangerous intersection), which leads to Saint-Jovite. Near the church, turn down Rue Limoges (327) in the direction of Mont Tremblant, which is already visible on the horizon. The road passes through Mont-Tremblant Village before reaching the Station Mont-Tremblant resort (open year-round).

Station Mont-Tremblant ★★★

Some of the largest resorts in the Laurentians were built by wealthy American families with a passion for downhill skiing. They chose this region for the beauty of the landscape, the province's French charm and, above all, the northern climate, which makes for a longer ski season than in the United States. Station Mont-Tremblant was founded by Philadelphia millionaire Joseph Ryan in 1938. Since 1991, the resort has been owned by Intrawest, which also owns Whistler Resort in British Columbia, and which has invested over $1 billion in Tremblant over the past decade in order to put it on a par with the huge resorts of Western Canada and the United States. At the height of the season, some 100 trails,

Whither Tremblant?

Because of the fusion fever that has hit Québec of late, many independent towns, villages and cities have merged. In keeping with the trend toward "bigger is better," St-Jovite, Mont-Tremblant village and the resort at the foot of the mountain are now all part of "Ville de Mont-Tremblant." They are now known respectively as "Secteur St-Jovite," "Secteur du Village" and "Station Mont-Tremblant." We have adopted these names in our text.

including several new ones, attract downhill skiers to Tremblant's slopes (875m). In the summer, the two magnificent golf courses are just as popular. Not only does this place have the longest and most difficult vertical drops in the region, it also boasts a brand-new resort complex set in an ersatz, yet extremely attractive, little village of traditional Québec-style buildings at the base of the mountain.

Place Saint-Bernard is surrounded by hotel complexes as well as many shops, restaurants and bars. Vieux-Tremblant preserves a more authentic feel; several of the original and more traditional buildings have been renovated. No motor vehicles are permitted anywhere in the village, so you'll have to get around on foot, skis or snowshoes.

Charming **Chapelle Saint Bernard** (1942), a replica of Église Saint-Laurent, which once stood on Île d'Orléans, greets visitors on the way to the resort beside Lac Tremblant. The road on the right leads to the public parking lot, a panoramic chairlift and, 10km further north, to the entrance to **Parc National du Mont-Tremblant** ★ ★ (see p 253).

Village Mont-Tremblant ★ (pop. 764)

On the other side of Lac Tremblant lies the charming Mont-Tremblant Village, not to be confused with the resort area. Here, in a more authentic setting, visitors will find attractive shops and restaurants, as well as a number of other places to stay.

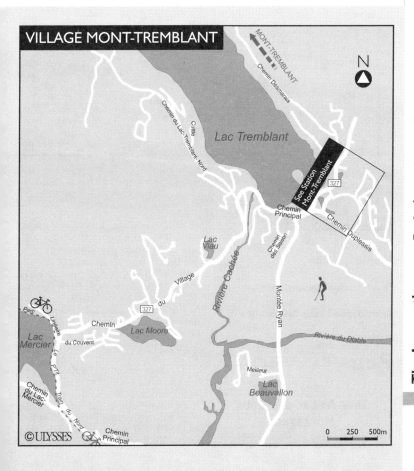

VILLAGE MONT-TREMBLANT

Lac Tremblant

See Station Mont-Tremblant

327

MONT-TREMBLANT

Chemin Desmarais

Chemin du Lac-Tremblant-Nord

Chemin Duplessis

Chemin Principal

Lac Viau

Rivière Cachée

Chemin des Saison

Village

du

327

Chemin

Lac Moore

Montée Ryan

Rivière du Diable

Parc

Le P'tit Train du Nord

Lac Mercier

du Couvent

Chemin du Lac Mercier

Meilleur

Lac Beauvallon

©ULYSSES

Chemin Principal

0   250   500m

The Laurentians - **Exploring** - Cottage Country

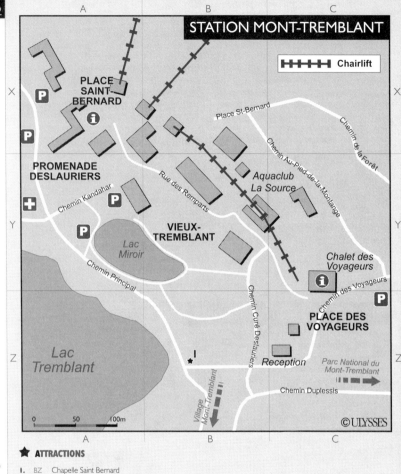

STATION MONT-TREMBLANT

⊬⊢⊣⊨ Chairlift

PLACE SAINT-BERNARD

Place St-Bernard

Chemin de la Forêt

PROMENADE DESLAURIERS

Chemin Kandahar

Rue des Remparts

Chemin Au-Pied-de-la-Montange

Aquaclub La Source

VIEUX-TREMBLANT

Lac Miroir

Chemin Principal

Chalet des Voyageurs

Chemin des Voyageurs

PLACE DES VOYAGEURS

Lac Tremblant

Chemin Curé Deslauriers

Reception

Parc National du Mont-Tremblant

Village Mont-Tremblant

Chemin Duplessis

©ULYSSES

0   50   100m

★ **ATTRACTIONS**

1.   BZ   Chapelle Saint Bernard

The Laurentians - Exploring - Cottage Country

Labelle (pop. 2,395)

The town of Labelle is the gateway to Parc du Mont-Tremblant.

Réserve Faunique Papineau-Labelle, see p 279.

Réserve Faunique Rouge-Matawin, see p 253.

Parks

Tour A: Lac des Deux Montagnes

The **Parc National d'Oka and the Calvaire d'Oka** ★ *($3.50; Oka,* ☎*450-479-8365 or 800-*

665-6527, www.sepaq.com) encompasses some 50km of trails for hikers in the summer and cross-country skiers in the winter. Most of the trails lie south of Rte. 344, crisscrossing a relatively flat area. North of Rte. 344, there are two other trails that lead to the top of the Colline d'Oka (168m), where visitors can drink in a view of the entire region. The longer trail (7.5km) ends at a panoramic viewing area, while the shorter one (5.5km) guides visitors past the oldest stations of the cross in the Americas. This calvary was set up by the Sulpicians back in 1742, in an effort to stimulate the faith of Aboriginals recently converted to Catholicism. Humble and dignified at the same time, the calvary is made up of four trapezoidal oratories and three rectangular chapels built of whitewashed stone. These little buildings, now empty, once housed wooden bas-reliefs depicting the Passion of Christ. The park also has campsites *($23/day, ☎450-479-8365 or 800-665-6527)*, an interpretation centre and the **Le Littoral** service centre, located on the shore of Lac des Deux Montagnes and featuring a restaurant, shops and a beach.

Tour B: Cottage Country

The **Parc Linéaire du P'tit Train du Nord** ★★ *($5 in summer, $7 in winter)* follows the old Laurentian railroad, spreading over 200km between Saint-Jérôme and Mont-Laurier. Since its inauguration during the mid-1990s, the park has become one of the region's main attractions. It welcomes thousands of cyclists in summertime, while cross-country skiers and snowmobilers (north of Sainte-Agathe) take advantage of its trails come winter.

Parc National du Mont-Tremblant ★★ *($3.50; ☎819-688-2281 or 800-665-6527, www.sepaq.com)*, created in 1894, was originally known as Parc de la Montagne Tremblante (Trembling Mountain Park) in reference to an Algonquian legend. It covers an area of 1,510km², encompassing the mountain, six rivers and about 400 lakes. The ski resort opened in 1938 and has been welcoming skiers ever since. The park also offers 16 cross-country ski trails, which stretch over 80km. The resort caters to sports enthusiasts all year round. Hikers can explore up to 100km of trails here; two of these, La Roche and La Corniche, have been rated among the most beautiful in Québec. The park also has bicycle paths and mountain-bike circuits, and offers water sports like canoeing and windsurfing.

The **Réserve Faunique Rouge-Matawin** *(accessible via the La Macaza or the Saint-Michel-des-Saints entrances; ☎819-424-3026 or 800-665-6527, www.sepaq.com)* is a wildlife reserve and home to a number of different species of animals, including the highest concentration of moose in the province. Bridle paths and hiking trails have been laid out. The rivers running through the park are suitable for canoeing.

Réserve Faunique Papineau-Labelle, see p 279.

Outdoor Activities

■ Cross-Country Skiing

Tour A: Lac des Deux Montagnes

Park National d'Oka *($8.50; Chemin d'Oka, ☎450-479-8365)* has eight trails covering a total of about 50km. Three are ranked easy, three difficult and two very difficult. Those who prefer snowshoes to skis will be pleased to learn that the park also has two snowshoeing trails (6.5km in all).

Tour B: Cottage Country

The **Parc Linéaire du P'tit Train du Nord** *($7; ☎450-436-8532)*, which stretches over some 200km, becomes a wonderful cross-country ski and snowmobile trail in the winter. The section from Saint-Jérôme to Sainte-Agathe is reserved for skiers; the rest, as far as Mont-Laurier, is snowmobile territory.

The **Réseau de Morin-Heights et Corridor Aérobique** *($8; 50 Chemin du Lac Écho, Morin-Heights, ☎450-226-1220 or 226-3232, www.mssi.ca)* is one of the oldest cross-country ski resorts in Canada. It's the perfect place for "adventure skiing," that is, taking longer trips on ungroomed, back-country trails.

The **Centre de Ski de Fond L'Estérel** *($8; 39 Boulevard Fridolin-Simard, Sainte-Marguerite–Estérel, ☎450-228-2571 or 888-378-3735, www.esterel.com)* is one of the best-organized cross-country resorts in the region. It is located at an altitude of 330m, so the snow conditions are excellent. Furthermore, this is truly a resort for skiers of all levels. Most of the trails are short, though not necessarily easy. There are 13 in all, four of which are easy, five difficult and four very difficult.

The **Centre Far Hills** *($10; Chemin du Lac La-Salle, Val-Morin, ☎819-322-2014, 514-990-4409 or 800-567-6636, www.farhillsinn.com)* maintains over 90km of cross-country trails. These run through a hilly, forested region, so skiers can enjoy some lovely scenery. This is where you'll find the famous **Maple Leaf Trail**, cleared by none other than Jack Rabbit Johanssen.

Jack Rabbit Johannsen

Born in Norway in 1875, Herman Smith-Johannsen emigrated to Canada in 1901. An engineer by profession, he started selling railroad equipment, which enabled him to visit a number of remote areas. He would ski to these places, meeting many Aboriginals along the way, who dubbed him "Wapoos," or Jack Rabbit. This nickname was then picked up by Smith-Johannsen's friends at the Montréal Ski Club.

Jack Rabbit Johannsen explored the Laurentians throughout the 1920s and 1930s. He even set up residence here and managed to develop an excellent network of cross-country ski trails. It took him four years to clear a 128km trail known as the Maple Leaf, which stretches between the towns of Prévost and Labelle. Unfortunately, this lovely trail has since been interrupted by Autoroute 15 (Autoroute des Laurentides).

By founding a number of cross-country ski centres and opening numerous trails, Jack Rabbit Johannsen is remembered as a pioneer of sorts. This living legend hung up his skis, so to speak, at the age of 106 and passed away in 1987, at the ripe old age of 111. His legacy is the history of cross-country skiing in Québec.

Another popular spot with cross-country skiers is the **Centre de Vacances et de Plein Air Le P'tit Bonheur** *($7; 1400 Chemin du Lac-Quenouille, Lac-Supérieur,* ☎*819-326-4281 or 800-567-6788, www.ptitbonheur.com)*, which maintains 57km of ski trails, with one reserved for snowshoers.

With its 35 trails covering 100km, 25km of which are set up for skate-style cross-country skiing, the **Centre de Ski de Fond Mont-Tremblant–Saint-Jovite** *($12; 539 Chemin St-Bernard, Mont-Tremblant,* ☎*819-425-5588)* is one of the largest cross-country ski centres in the Laurentians. Snowshoeing trails can also be found here, and skis can be rented on site.

Parc National du Mont-Tremblant, see p 253.

■ Cycling

Tour B: Cottage Country

The former railway line of the **Parc Linéaire du P'tit Train du Nord** *(*☎*450-436-8532)*, which carried Montréalers up north for many years, has been transformed into a superb 200km bike path from Saint-Jérôme to Mont-Laurier. It leads through a number of little villages where accommodations and restaurants in all price ranges can be found.

The **Station Mont-Tremblant** has a dozen mountain-bike trails. To reach them, you and your bike will need to take a specially designed chairlift. There are several trails: La Cachée *(novice)*; Le Labyrinthe *(intermediate)*; La Nord-Sud, La Chouette and La Grand Nord *(advanced)*; and La Sasquatch *(expert)*.

Parc National du Mont-Tremblant *(*☎*819-688-2281)* maintains some 59km of bike paths.

Bikes can be rented from the following outfits:

Boutique Phénix
2444 Rue de l'Église, Val-David
☎ (819) 322-1118

Parc National du Mont-Tremblant
☎ (819) 688-2281

Station Mont-Tremblant
☎ (819) 681-3000, ext. 45564

■ Dogsledding

Tour B: Cottage Country

Hôtel Estérel *(*☎*450-228-4722 or 888-588-4722)* organizes 20min and 1hr dog-sledding excursions. Guests who do not wish to take part in these outings should none-theless visit the dog pens that adjoin the hotel, where 115 magnificent beasts await. A must for the kids!

■ Downhill Skiing

Tour B: Cottage Country

There are two ski resorts in the mountains around Piedmont; **Station de Ski Mont-Olym-pia** *($35; 330 Chemin de la Montagne, Piedmont, ☎450-227-3523 or 800-363-3696, www.mssi. ca)* which has 23 trails and a total vertical drop of 200m, and **Station de Ski Mont-Avila** *($36; Chemin Avila, Piedmont, ☎450-227-4671 or 514-871-0101, www.mssi.ca)* where vis-itors will find some 10 trails, the longest of which runs 1,050m.

A small mountain with a vertical drop of only 210m, **Station Touristique Mont-Saint-Sauveur** *($43; 350 Rue St-Denis, St-Sauveur; ☎450-227-4671, www.mssi.ca)* attracts lots of skiers because of its proximity to Montréal. It offers 38 downhill ski trails, a few of which are lit for night-skiing.

As Mont-Saint-Sauveur is often over-crowded, some might prefer the slopes of the neighbouring mountains, which have fewer trails but shorter lift lines. The **Sta-tion de Ski Mont-Habitant** *($33; 12 Boulevard des Skieurs, ☎450-227-2637 or 866-227-2637, www.monthabitant.com)*, with 11 runs, is one of these.

We should also mention **Station de Ski Morin-Heights** *($35; Chemin Bennett, ☎450-227-2020)*, which has 23 trails, 16 of which are lit for night-skiing; and the modest (12 trails) **Station de Sports Mont Avalanche** *($26; 1657 Chemin de l'Avalanche, ☎819-327-3232, www.mont-avalanche.com)* ski centre, located near Saint-Adolphe-d'Howard.

The Sainte-Adèle region also attracts ski-ers with its two good-sized ski resorts. The **Station de Ski Mont-Gabriel** *($30; 1501 Montée Gabriel, Ste-Adèle, ☎450-227-1100, www.mssi. ca)* has 18 trails (12 lit for night-skiing) for skiers of all different levels. The hand-some Chantecler tourist complex was built near the **Station de Ski Le Chantecler** *($35; 1474 Chemin du Chantecler, ☎450-229-3555 or 888-916-1616, www.lechantecler.com)*, with 25 trails, including 17 that are lit in the even-ing.

In Val-Morin, skiers can head to **Centre de Ski Belle Neige** *($28; Rte. 117, ☎819-322-3311 or 877-600-3311, www.belleneige.com)*, which has 14 trails of all different levels of dif-ficulty. In the Val-David area, you'll find **Mont-Alta** *($20; Rte. 117, ☎819-322-3206)* and the **Station de Ski Vallée-Bleue** *($25; 1418 Chemin Vallée-Bleue, ☎819-322-3427, www. vallee-bleue.com)*, with 22 and 17 trails, re-spectively.

The **Station de Ski Mont-Blanc** *($37; Rte. 117, ☎819-688-2444 or 800-567-6715, www. skimontblanc.com)*, in Saint-Faustin, has 39 runs and the second-highest vertical drop in the Laurentians (300m).

Station Mont-Tremblant *($53.30; 1000 Chemin des Voyageurs, Mont-Tremblant, ☎888-736-2526, www.tremblant.com)* forms a large ski area of 94 runs at an altitude of 875m, with snow parks and half-moons for lovers of glide sports. The 6km Nansen run will ex-haust beginners, the challenging Zig Zag and Vertige runs will delight experts, and the 77ha of undergrowth will thrill the ad-venturous.

Gray Rocks *($33; 2322 Rue Labelle, Mont-Trem-blant, ☎819-425-2771 or 800-567-6767, www. grayrocks.com)* is another resort in the re-gion. It has 22 trails, with a vertical drop of 191m (much lower than at Mont-Trem-blant).

■ Golf

Tour A: Lac des Deux Montagnes

The **Club de Golf Carling Lake** *($70, $35 after 3pm; 2235 Rte. 327 N., Brownsburg-Chatham, ☎450-533-5333, www.golfcarlinglake.com)*, established near Lachute in 1961, is one of the most beautiful public golf courses in Canada, according to *Golf Digest U.S.* maga-zine. Furthermore, the elegant **Hôtel du Lac Carling** (see p 258) is located right nearby.

Tour B: Cottage Country

Among the dozens of golf courses scattered across the Laurentians, one of the more renowned is the **Club de Golf L'Estérel** *($48; 44 Boulevard Fridolin-Simard, Sainte-Marguer-ite–Estérel, ☎450-228-4532, www.esterel.com)*.

The Laurentians - Outdoor Activities

The Station Mont-Tremblant resort also boasts some good golf courses: **Le Géant** *(3005 Chemin Principal, Mont-Tremblant, ☎819-681-4653 or 888-857-8253, www. golftremblant.com)*, which experts have ranked among the 10 best in Canada, and **Le Diable**. Reservations accepted no more than seven days in advance.

Club de Golf Gray Rocks *($55; 2322 Rue Labelle, Mont-Tremblant, ☎819-425-2771 or 800-567-6767, www.grayrocks.com)* has one 18-hole course.

■ Hiking

Tour A: Lac des Deux Montagnes

Parc National d'Oka, see p 252.

Tour B: Cottage Country

Near Saint-Faustin, the **Centre Touristique et Éducatif des Laurentides** *($5.50; late Apr to late Oct, every day; 5000 Chemin du Lac du Caribou, ☎819-326-1606)* has eight trails, which range in length from one to 10km, covering a total of 35km. Among these, Le Panoramique (3km) offers the loveliest views of the area. L'Aventurier, the longest trail (10km), leads to the top of a 530m-high mountain.

At Station Mont-Tremblant, the Tremblant Express chairlift will take you up to the new **ÉcoZone** centre, which has trails designed specifically for families, as well as others for more seasoned hikers. All along the trails, there are markers containing information on the Laurentian wildlife.

Parc National du Mont-Tremblant is an excellent place for hiking, since it has trails of all levels of difficulty. La Roche and La Corniche are both short, delightful hikes, while the 47.6km Diable trail is sure to satisfy even the most fanatical hiking buffs.

■ Rafting

Thanks to the thrilling Rivière Rouge, the Laurentians offer excellent conditions for whitewater rafting—among the best in Canada, according to some experts. Of course, there is no better time to enjoy this activity than during the spring thaw.

Rafting during this period can prove quite a challenge, however, so previous experience is recommended. The best season for novices is summer, when the river is not too high and the weather is milder. For further information, contact **Nouveau Monde, Expéditions en Rivière** *($95 on weekdays, $99 on weekends; 25 Chemin Rourke, Calumet; ☎819-242-7238 or 800-361-5033, www.newworld.ca)*, which offers group outings every day.

■ Rock-Climbing

Tour B: Cottage Country

The **Val-David** area is renowned for its rock faces. A number of mountains here are fully equipped to accommodate climbers' needs; **Mont King**, **Mont Condor** and **Mont Césaire** are among the most popular. For more information, equipment rentals or guide services, contact **Passe Montagne** *(1760 Montée 2ᵉ Rang, Val-David; ☎819-322-2123 or 800-465-2123)*, a trail-blazing rock-climbing outfit in the Val-David region. Their team of experts offers excellent advice.

■ Snowmobiling

Tour B: Cottage Country

Scores of snowmobile trails crisscross the Laurentians. Snowmobile rentals are available at the following places:

Randonneige
25 Rue Brisette, Sainte-Agathe-des-Monts
☎ (819) 326-0642 or 800-326-0642

Location Constantineau
1117 Boulevard Albiny-Paquette, Mont-Laurier
☎ (819) 623-1724

Hôtel L'Estérel
39 Rue Fridolin-Simard, Sainte-Marguerite–Estérel
☎ (450) 228-4722 or 888-588-4722

■ Swimming

Tour A: Lac des Deux Montagnes

The **Park National d'Oka** *($3.50; Jun to Sep; ☎450-479-8365)* has a very popular beach where canoes, sailboards and pedalboats are all available for rent. Picnic area, snack bar and restrooms are found on site.

Tour B: Cottage Country

Among the region's other public beaches, we should mention those in **Sainte-Adèle** *($7; Chemin du Chantecler,* ☎*450-229-2921, ext. 212)*, which is small but pleasant; in **Saint-Adophe-d'Howard** *(free admission; 2000 Chemin du Village,* ☎*819-327-2044)*; in **Sainte-Agathe-des-Monts** *($5; Lac des Sables)*; in **Sainte-Marguerite–Estérel** *(free admission;* ☎*450-228-2545)* and the one in **Mont-Tremblant** *($5; Chemin Principal,* ☎*819-425-8614)*, as well as the **Club Plage et Tennis** *(1000 Chemin des Voyageurs, Mont-Tremblant,* ☎*819-681-2000 or 888-243-6836)*, which rents out canoes, kayaks, rowboats, sailboards and pedal boats.

■ Waterslides and Tobogganing

Tour A: Lac des Deux Montagnes

There are no fewer than 45 waterslides at the **Super Aqua Club** *($27; mid-Jun to late Aug every day 10am to 7pm; 322 Montée de la Baie,* ☎*450-473-1013)* in Pointe-Calumet, as well

as a wave pool and inner-tube "rivers." The water park is on the shores of Lac des Deux Montagnes and has a lovely sandy beach. Pedal-boat and canoe rentals available.

Tour B: Cottage Country

During the winter, those who are interested in spending a pleasant day in the fresh air but don't want to ski can head over to **La Pente des Pays-d'en-Haut** *($27/day, hourly rates also available; mid-Dec to late Mar Mon-Thu 9am to 5pm, Fri and Sat 9am to 10pm; 440 Chemin Avila, Piedmont,* ☎*450-224-4014 or 800-668-7951, www.pente-des-pays-den-haut.qc.ca)* and try the 38 different toboggan slides. In the summer, visitors can opt for the **Cascades d'Eau** *($22; mid-Jun to late Aug every day 10am to 7pm; Exit 58 off Aut. 15, Piedmont,* ☎*450-227-4671 or 800-363-2426)*, which has 17 waterslides.

Another waterslide option is the **Parc Aquatique du Mont-Saint-Sauveur** *($29; mid-Jun to early Sep every day 10am to 7pm; Exit 60 off Aut. 15, 350 Rue St-Denis, Saint-Sauveur,* ☎*450-227-4671)*, with a wave pool and six slides, plus three more especially designed for children.

▲ Accommodations

Tour A: Lac des Deux Montagnes

Oka

Parc National d'Oka
$
May to Sep
☎ (450) 479-8365
Park d'Oka has a magnificent campground with about 880 sites laid out in the middle of the forest.

Grenville-sur-la-Rouge

Hôtel du Lac Carling
$$$$ bkfst incl.
≡ ▲ ➟ ≋ ⩲ ♨))) ⅄ ⅙ ⊚ ❄
2255 Rte. 327 N.
☎ (450) 533-9211 or 800-661-9211
🖷 (450) 533-9197
www.laccarling.com
Hidden away on the shores of a lake just northwest of Lachute lies the remarkable but little-known Hôtel du Lac Carling. Made of stone and pale wood, and graced with tall windows, this is a lovely, luxurious hotel. Inside, a sumptuous decor enhanced by numerous works of art and antiques awaits. The huge guest rooms are bathed in natural light. Some have a whirlpool bath, a patio or a fireplace. The hotel also has a sports centre complete with indoor tennis courts, an exercise room, an indoor pool, a sauna and an excellent restaurant, **L'If** (see p 264). The renowned **Club de Golf Carling Lake** tops off the amenities (see p 255).

Tour B: Cottage Country

Saint-Sauveur

Le Bonnet d'Or
$$-$$$ bkfst incl.
⊚ ▲ ➟
405 Rue Principale
☎ (450) 227-9669 or 877-277-9669
Le Bonnet d'Or features three guest rooms with wood-planked walls painted in deep colours and decorated in a Victorian style that is either cute or cloying, depending on your taste. Two suites, one with whirlpool bath, offer a more romantic setting. Friendly, pleasant proprietors, but the main-street location may be bad news for light sleepers.

Manoir Saint-Sauveur
$$$$$ bkfst incl.
⅙ ≡ ➟ ≋ ♨)))
246 Chemin du Lac Millette
☎ (450) 227-1811 or 800-361-0505
🖷 (450) 227-8512
www.manoir-saint-sauveur.com
Manoir Saint-Sauveur, with some 300 rooms, focuses on athletic activities, offering lots of summer and winter packages with downhill skiing, golf or horseback riding, as well as a wide variety of facilities including tennis and squash courts. A more recent section has attractive new rooms sporting a warm beige hue and lovely duvets. Opt for these for a small extra charge (and ask for one on the mountain side). Manoir Saint-Sauveur manages to combine the coziness of a ski lodge and the elegance of a fine hotel. It is conveniently located within walking distance of the town of Saint-Sauveur.

Sainte-Adèle

Auberge de la Gare
$$ bkfst incl.
sb ≡
1694 Chemin Pierre-Péladeau
☎ (450) 228-3140 or 888-825-4273
www.aubergedelagare.com
Located a few kilometres outside Sainte-Adèle, Auberge de la Gare occupies a lovely Victorian house with elegant common areas and simple, country-style guest rooms decorated with pastel colours and a few antiques. There is a comfortable games room in the basement. Choice of sweet or savoury breakfast.

Motel Chantolac
$$-$$$
≡ ➟ ▲ ≋ ❄
156 Rue Morin
☎ (450) 229-3593 or 800-561-8875
🖷 (450) 229-4393
www.chantolac.com
Motel Chantolac is a comfortable, well-located establishment with reasonable rates. The rooms may not be spectacular, but they're a real bargain. Furthermore, the place boasts a lovely location on the street leading to the Hôtel Le Chantecler, near lots of pleasant restaurants and just steps away from Lac Rond and its small beach.

Le Chantecler
$$$$
≡ ➟ ≋ ♨))) ⅄ ⊚ ▲
1474 Chemin du Chantecler
☎ (450) 229-3555 or 800-363-2420
🖷 (450) 229-5593
www.lechantecler.com
At Hôtel Le Chantecler, whose name and emblem (a rooster) were inspired by Edmond Rostand's play, guests can enjoy a multitude of activities in a pristine lakeside setting at the foot of Mont Chantecler. The golf course is picturesque, with mountains

on either side. The guest rooms themselves, however, are small and ultra-ordinary, their decor a dreary reminder of the 1980s.

L'Eau à la Bouche
$$$$
≡ ◎ ⚐ ﹌ ⚒

3003 Boulevard Ste-Adèle
☎ (450) 229-2991 or 888-828-2991
🖨 (450) 229-7573
www.leaualabouche.com

A member of the prestigious Relais & Châteaux association, L'Eau à la Bouche is known for its excellent gourmet restaurant (see p 265) and extremely comfortable rooms. Don't be fooled by the building's rustic appearance; the rooms *are* elegantly furnished. The hotel itself dates from the mid-1980s and is set back from the road. It offers a splendid view of the ski slopes of Mont Chantecler. The restaurant is in a separate building. The complex is located on Rte. 117, a fair distance north of the village of Sainte-Adèle.

Sainte-Marguerite–Estérel

L'Estérel
$$$$$
≡ ⚓ ﹌ Y ⚒ ⫶⫶⫶

39 Boulevard Fridolin-Simard
☎ (450) 228-2571 or 888-378-3735
🖨 (450) 228-4977
www.esterel.com

At L'Estérel, a large resort located on the shores of Lac Masson, guests can enjoy a variety of water sports and diverse athletic activities such as tennis, golf and cross-country skiing. Those who appreciate a lake view will be overjoyed by the lake-facing rooms, whose balconies literally overhang the lake—if you got any closer, you'd be swimming.

Val-Morin

Hôtel Far Hills Inn
$$$$
≡ ﹌ ⚒ ⫶⫶⫶

3399 Chemin Far Hills
☎ (514) 990-4409 or 800-567-6636
🖨 (819) 322-1995
www.farhillsinn.com

Making the most of its extensive grounds, the Far Hills Inn has an extremely peaceful country setting. Its clientele includes cross-country skiers, who come to enjoy over 100km of trails. The rooms are pleasantly decorated and the welcome is friendly. Furthermore, the hotel's restaurant gets top marks as one of the best in the area (see p 266).

Val-David

Chalet Beaumont
$
⚓ ⚒ ⫶⫶⫶

1451 Rue Beaumont: from the bus stop, take Rue de l'Église across the village to Rue Beaumont and turn left; it's about a 2km walk
☎ (819) 322-1972
🖨 (819) 322-3793
www.chaletbeaumont.com

Chalet Beaumont, located in a peaceful mountain setting, is one of only two youth hostels in the Laurentians. A log building with two fireplaces, it's a very appealing, comfortable place and an excellent option for outdoor enthusiasts on a tight budget. It is wise to ask who you'll be sharing a room with, as groups of young students often stay here on field trips to Val-David.

Le Temps des Cerises
$$ bkfst incl.
1347 Chemin de la Sapinière
☎ (819) 322-1751 or 866-322-3528

🖨 (819) 322-3636

Le Temps des Cerises is a good choice in the B&B category. The people who run it are very friendly, which makes for a pleasant stay. The rooms are beautifully decorated, and each has a distinctive charm about it.

La Maison de Bavière
$$ bkfst incl.
1472 Chemin de la Rivière
☎ (819) 322-3528
www.maisondebaviere.com

La Maison de Bavière provides visitors with a pleasant stay. The owners meticulously decorated their rooms, each of which is named after a renowned composer: Mozart, Strauss, Haydn and Beethoven. Guests enjoy the splendid setting near a waterfall and can expect a particularly warm welcome. Reservations should be made well in advance.

Hôtel La Sapinière
$$$$$ ½b
≡ ⚓ ⚐ ﹌ ⚒

1244 Chemin de la Sapinière
☎ (819) 322-2020 or 800-567-6635
🖨 (819) 322-6510
www.sapiniere.com

La Sapinière is a rustic log building dating from 1936 (and still under the original ownership). It's nothing luxurious at this price, and the faded yet cheery decor in each room features variations on the theme of pink carpeting, flowered wallpaper and lace curtains. Still, it makes for a comfortable place to stop during a tour of the region, especially for its beautiful location by a calm lake and surrounded by mountains and cross-country ski trails. Boats are available for use.

Sainte-Agathe-des-Monts

Auberge Le Saint-Venant
$$ bkfst incl.
≡ ⚫ ❄ ◎

234 Rue St-Venant
☎ (819) 326-7937 or 800-697-7937
🖨 (819) 326-4848
www.st-venant.com

Auberge Le Saint-Venant is one of the best-kept secrets in Sainte-Agathe. A big, beautiful, yellow house perched atop a hill, it has nine large, tastefully decorated rooms with big windows that let lots of light flood in. The service is friendly yet discreet.

Auberge Chez Girard
$$ bkfst incl.
🍴 ◎ ⚘

18 Rue Principale Ouest
☎ (819) 326-0922 or 800-663-0922
🖨 (819) 326-3386
www.aubergechezgirard.com

Auberge Chez Girard is a charming inn set in a century-old house near Lac

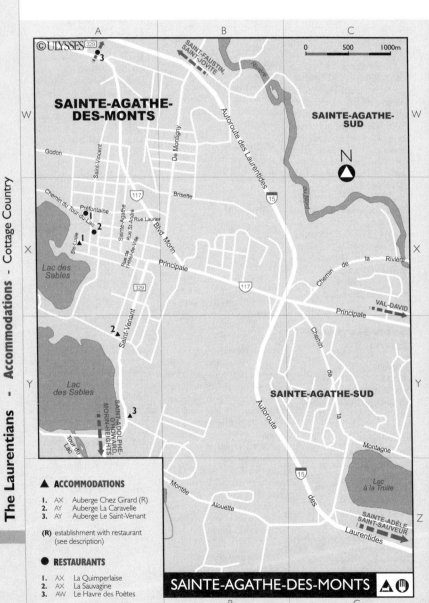

▲ ACCOMMODATIONS

1.	AX	Auberge Chez Girard (R)
2.	AY	Auberge La Caravelle
3.	AY	Auberge Le Saint-Venant

(R) establishment with restaurant
(see description)

● RESTAURANTS

1.	AX	La Quimperlaise
2.	AX	La Sauvagine
3.	AW	Le Havre des Poètes

SAINTE-AGATHE-DES-MONTS ▲🍴

des Sables. A significant number of regular customers come back here year after year for the pleasant atmosphere.

Auberge La Caravelle
$$$ bkfst incl.

92 Rue Major
☎ (819) 321-2444 or 800-661-4272
🖷 (819) 326-0818
www.aubergelacaravelle.com
Auberge La Caravelle, a pretty blue-and-red house, defines itself as a "small, romantic inn." Appropriately, it is surrounded by a lovely garden full of flowers. Furthermore, half of its 16 rooms, including the bridal suite, are equipped with a whirlpool bath. The inn also has bicycles for its guests.

Lac-Supérieur

Centre de Vacances et de Plein Air Le P'tit Bonheur
$$$$/pers for two nights incl. five meals and activities
sb ⚊
1400 Chemin du Lac Quenouille
☎ (819) 326-4281 or 800-567-6788
🖷 (819) 326-9516
www.ptitbonheur.com
Le P'tit Bonheur is nothing less than an institution in the Laurentians. Once a children's summer camp, it now caters to families looking for an outdoor vacation. Set on a vast property on the shores of a lake, right in the heart of the forest, it has four buildings containing a total of nearly 430 beds, most in dormitories. About 20 of the beds are in separate rooms, each equipped with a private bathroom and able to accommodate up to four people. Of course, this is the perfect place to enjoy all sorts of outdoor activities: sailing,

hiking, cross-country skiing, skating, etc.

Auberge Caribou
$$$$$ bkfst incl.
⚊
141 Chemin du Tour du Lac
☎ (819) 688-5201 or 877-688-5201
🖷 (819) 688-2393
www.cariboulodge.qc.ca
Keep this one under your hat: a rustic log chalet (built in 1945) within spitting distance of a lake with 14 cozy, affordably priced rooms (some with a lake view) and an excellent restaurant (see p 267) located in the Tremblant region. No two rooms are quite alike, but all feature knotty-wood panels, hand-painted leaf motifs and duvets. Most are cozy, rather than spacious, but there is a suite that can accommodate a small group or family. There are canoes available, and both a dock and a deck for lounging in summer. In the winter, the cross-country ski trails in Parc national du Mont-Tremblant are right nearby. Delicious breakfasts and fantastic dinners. A real gem.

Station Mont-Tremblant

Station Mont-Tremblant
1000 Chemin des Voyageurs
☎ 866-836-3030 or 888-857-8043
🖷 (819) 681-5990
www.tremblant.ca
The Station Mont-Tremblant directly manages a whole assortment of lodgings. Visitors may rent a room or an apartment in the **Country Inn and Suites by Carlson** *($$$$ bkfst incl.; ⚊ ∆ ≋))) ☎; ☎819-681-5555 or 800-461-8711)* located near Lac Miroir, or in the luxurious **Deslauriers**

and **Johanssen** *($$$-$$$$; ≋ ∆ ≋ ☎; ☎819-681-5555 or 800-461-8711)* complexes, which face onto Place Saint-Bernard. Families will be better off with a fully equipped condo in **La Chouette** *($$$; ∆ ☎; ☎866-836-3030)*. These units are small but flooded with natural light. What's more, they offer excellent value for the money, making them an option well worth considering in this area.

Westin Resort Tremblant
$$$$$ bkfst incl.
≡ ∆ ☎ ● ≋)))
100 Chemin Kandahar
☎ (819) 681-8000
🖷 (819) 681-8001
www.westin.com/tremblant
Opened in 2000, the Westin continues to set the bar high in terms of luxury and comfort. The lobby has the grandness and warmth of a country manor house, and the rooms, furnished with Westin's trademark "Heavenly Bed" and "Heavenly Bath," are boldly done up in red and gold and offer every comfort. Even the standard rooms are equipped with a kitchenette. While the service is generally excellent, it is unfortunately uneven.

Marriott Residence Inn Mont-Tremblant
$$$$$ bkfst incl.
≡ ⚊K ∆ ≋ ⚊
170 Chemin Curé-Deslauriers
☎ (819) 681-4000 or 888-272-4000
🖷 (819) 681-4099
www.marriott-tremblant.com
The prestigious international Marriot chain has joined in the action at Tremblant, with its Marriott Residence Inn Mont-Tremblant, a large building located right at the entrance to the village. The place rents out

The Laurentians - Accommodations - Cottage Country

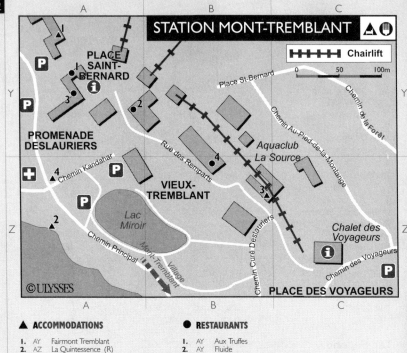

STATION MONT-TREMBLANT

⊞⊞⊞⊞⊞ **Chairlift**

0   50   100m

PLACE SAINT-BERNARD

PROMENADE DESLAURIERS

Place St-Bernard

Chemin Au-Pied-de-la-Montagne

Chemin de la Forêt

Rue des Remparts

VIEUX-TREMBLANT

Aquaclub La Source

Chemin Kandahar

Lac Miroir

Chemin Principal

Mont-Tremblant Village

Chemin Curé Deslauriers

Chalet des Voyageurs

Chemin des Voyageurs

© ULYSSES

PLACE DES VOYAGEURS

▲ **ACCOMMODATIONS**

1.	AY	Fairmont Tremblant
2.	AZ	La Quintessence (R)
3.	BZ	Marriott Residence Inn Mont-Tremblant
4.	AZ	Westin Resort Tremblant

● **RESTAURANTS**

1.	AY	Aux Truffes
2.	AY	Fluide
3.	AY	Le Shack
4.	BZ	Microbrasserie la Diable

(R) establishment with restaurant (see description)

studios and one- or two-bedroom apartments, each equipped with a kitchenette. Some units even have a fireplace.

Fairmont Tremblant
$$$$$
♿ ≡ ◎ ⚓ ⊙ ⌂ ☷ ♨)))

3045 Chemin de la Chapelle
☎ (819) 681-7000 or 800-441-1414
🖷 (819) 681-7099
www.fairmont.com

Overlooking Station Mont-Tremblant, the Fairmont is one of only two additions to have been made to the prestigious Canadian Pacific hotel chain in a century, the other being located in Whistler, British Columbia. This imposing 316-room hotel manages to combine a genuine rustic warmth, well-suited to the surroundings, with all the comforts one expects from a top-flight establishment. It also houses a large convention centre and numerous conference rooms. The atmosphere and the decor are definitely more casual than that of the Westin, the newest Tremblant resort.

La Quintessence
$$$$$
☷ ⚓))) ♨ ≡ ≋ ⍟

3004 Chemin de la Chapelle
☎ (819) 425-3400 or 866-425-3400
🖷 (819) 425-3480
www.hotelquintessence.com

Though the name may seem pretentious, this hotel definitely lives up to its moniker. The first boutique hotel to set up at Mont-Tremblant, La Quintessence is located on the shores of Lac Tremblant and a stone's throw from the Mont-Tremblant Pedestrian Village. The hotel has 30 elegant and luxurious suites of various sizes, all of which enjoy views of the lake. Room amenities include teak furniture, raised fireplaces, high-speed Internet connection, bathrooms with heated marble floors and therapeutic spa bathtubs. The hotel's ambiance and decor is also heightened by a judicious use of marble, wrought iron, stone, woodwork and panelling. The hotel's restaurant (see p 268) is one of the region's better gourmet establishments. Friendly, thoughtful service.

Village Mont-Tremblant

Parc National du Mont-Tremblant
$
☎ (819) 688-2281 or 877-688-2289
🖷 (819) 688-1169
www.sepaq.com
There are nearly 600 camp-sites in the Diable sector of Parc National du Mont-Tremblant. Restrooms and showers are found on site.

Auberge de Jeunesse Internationale de Mont-Tremblant
$
♨
2213 Chemin du Village
☎ (819) 425-6008 or 866-425-6008
🖷 (819) 425-3760
www.hostellingtremblant.com
The Auberge de Jeunesse Internationale de Mont-Tremblant youth hostel has 84 beds, either in private rooms or dormitories. The common areas include a kitchen, a café/bar/restaurant and a living room with a fireplace.

Auberge Sauvignon
$$$ bkfst incl.
≡ ◉ ♨ &
2723 Chemin du Village
☎ (819) 425-5466 or 888-669-5466
🖷 (819) 425-9260
www.aubergesauvignon.com
The Auberge Sauvignon is a refreshing alternative to Mont-Tremblant's larger hotels. Francine's seven guest rooms are carefully decorated with country charm in neutral colours. Breakfast is continental, with homemade breads and fruit salad, and can be enjoyed in a cozy foyer with plenty of woodwork and dried flowers.

La Petite Cachée
$$$ bkfst incl.
≡ ▲ ≋
2681 Chemin du Village
☎ (819) 425-2654 or 866-425-2654
🖷 (819) 425-6892
www.petitecachee.com
La Petite Cachée, named after the nearby river, has impeccably decorated rooms maintained by fas-

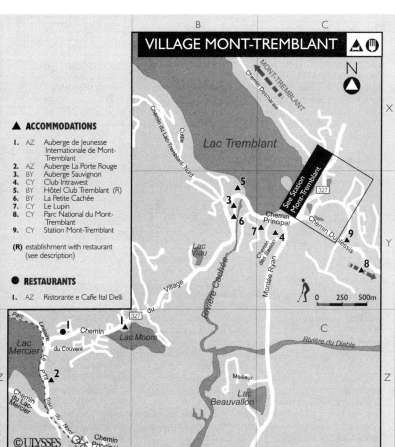

VILLAGE MONT-TREMBLANT ▲ ⑪

N

Lac Tremblant

See Station Mont-Tremblant

▲ ACCOMMODATIONS

1.	AZ	Auberge de Jeunesse Internationale de Mont-Tremblant
2.	AZ	Auberge La Porte Rouge
3.	BY	Auberge Sauvignon
4.	CY	Club Intrawest
5.	BY	Hôtel Club Tremblant (R)
6.	BY	La Petite Cachée
7.	CY	Le Lupin
8.	CY	Parc National du Mont-Tremblant
9.	CY	Station Mont-Tremblant

(R) establishment with restaurant (see description)

● RESTAURANTS

| 1. | AZ | Ristorante e Caffe Ital Delli |

0   250   500m

Lac Viau

Rivière Cachée

Lac Moore

Lac Mercier

du Couvent

Rivière du Diable

Meilleur

Lac Beauvallon

Chemin Principal

©ULYSSES

The Laurentians - Accommodations - Cottage Country

tidious owners Manon and Normand. Some have balconies. But the best part about this B&B has to be its quality breakfasts. Normand gave up his cooking career to become an innkeeper, and every morning he returns to his first love and creates refined little dishes. Have a seat by one of the large mountain-facing windows in the dining room and let your taste buds come alive.

Le Lupin
$$$ bkfst incl.
≡ △ ♨

127 Rue Pinoteau
☎ (819) 425-5474 or 877-425-5474
▤ (819) 425-6079
www.lelupin.com

Built in 1945, this nineroom B&B has preserved the country atmosphere that reigned in Tremblant in the pre-Intrawest days. Country-style guest rooms range from the small, simply furnished standard and superior rooms, with wood floors, wood-planked walls and quilts, to a more romantic version, with deep soaker tub, fireplace, CD player, wall-to-wall carpeting and bubble bath. Convenient location in a quiet spot just 1km from the ski hill, restaurants and bars of Station Mont-Tremblant. Allergy sufferers should note that a dog and a cat also call this place home.

Hôtel Club Tremblant
$$$$ ½b
≡ ⚓ ● △ ≈ ❄ ♨ ☰

121 Rue Cuttle
☎ (819) 425-2731 or 800-567-8341
▤ (819) 425-9903
www.clubtremblant.com

Hôtel Club Tremblant wins the prize for best view in Tremblant. Located just outside Station Mont-Trem-

blant, off the road leading to the village, its every room (120 in 10 buildings) offers a tremendous view of the lake and mountain, as well as a balcony. Good thing, because the rooms themselves are rather dreary and outdated, in the manner typical of ski condos built (or last renovated) in the 1980s. One of the earliest Tremblant inns, the current property grew out of a log house built in the early 1900s.

Auberge La Porte Rouge
$$$$ ½b
≡ ⊛ ● △ ≈ ❄ ♨

1874 Chemin du Village
☎ (819) 425-3505 or 800-665-3505
▤ (819) 425-6700
www.aubergelaporterouge.com

Auberge La Porte Rouge offers 14 standard rooms with balconies in its main, motel-style building, as well as "deluxe" rooms and chalets in separate buildings, some of which are converted old houses on the village's main street. Rooms are spacious and comfortable and have balconies, some facing the lake. Rates include breakfast and dinner in the hotel restaurant, Le Saint-Louis.

Club Intrawest
$$$$$
≈ ● △ ≈ Y ⟩⟩⟩

200 Chemin des Saisons
☎ (819) 681-3535 or 800-799-3258
▤ (819) 681-3559
www.clubintrawestresorts.com

Primarily a time-share property, Club Intrawest also rents out studio (sleeps two) and one-bedroom apartments (sleeps four) in a number of low-rise buildings. Unfortunately, none offer much in the way of a view but inside, a pleasant surprise: an imaginative decor that is colourful and

lighthearted. Reservations are a must.

Restaurants

Tour A: Lac des Deux Montagnes

Saint-Eustache

L'Impressionniste
$$$
245 Chemin de la Grande Côte
☎ (450) 491-3277

L'Impressionniste is renowned in the area for its quality fare. The varied and creative selection is sure to please.

Deux-Montagnes

Les Petits Fils d'Alice
$$$$
1506 Chemin d'Oka
☎ (450) 491-0653

Les Petits Fils d'Alice serves fine French cuisine in a pleasant, intimate setting. During summer, you can eat outside on the terrace.

Grenville-sur-la-Rouge

L'If
$$$$
2255 Rte. 327 Nord
☎ (450) 533-9211 or (514) 990-7733

The splendid **Hôtel du Lac Carling** (see p 258) has a remarkable restaurant, L'If, located in the rotunda of the main building, looking out onto the lake. Gourmet menu, luxurious decor and romantic atmosphere.

Tour B:
Cottage Country

Saint-Hippolyte

Auberge des Cèdres
$$$-$$$$
26 305ᵉ Avenue
The restaurant at Auberge des Cèdres offers some of the region's best fare. French cuisine is served here, with several Norman specialities featured on the menu.

Saint-Sauveur

Boulangerie Pagé
$
7 Rue de l'Église
☎ (450) 227-2632
This bakery can tide travellers over till dinner with its wide variety of breads, buns, fritters and other pastries.

Au Petit Café Chez Denise
$-$$
338 Rue Principale
☎ (450) 227-5955
Had your fill of croissants and capuccino? Follow the locals to Denise's place for *la grosse bouffe*—eggs, bacon, ham, sausage, *fèves au lard* (pork and beans)... Breakfast is served until late, but if it's really late, tuck into a hot chicken sandwich, a club sandwich or a heaping plate of beef liver served with a dollop of mashed potatoes.

Crêperie à la Gourmandise Bretonne
$$
396 Rue Principale
☎ (450) 227-5434
Diners come to Crêperie à la Gourmandise Bretonne for the crepes, cheese fondues and salads. The country atmosphere is perfect for a quiet meal.

La Marmite
$$-$$$
314 Rue Principale
☎ (450) 227-1554
La Marmite serves succulent dishes in an extremely pleasant setting. It also has a lovely terrace, which you can enjoy during the summer.

Papa Luigi
$$-$$$
155 Rue Principale
☎ (450) 227-5311
The menu at Papa Luigi is made up of—you guessed it—Italian specialties, as well as seafood and grilled dishes. Set up inside a lovely, wooden house, this restaurant draws big crowds, especially on weekends. Reservations are strongly recommended.

Le Vieux Four
$$$
252 Rue Principale
☎ (450) 227-6060
Always packed with regulars, Le Vieux Four owes its popularity to its pasta dishes and delicious pizza, baked in a wood-burning oven. Its pleasant decor makes it a cozy place to go after a day of skiing.

Le Mousqueton
$$$-$$$$
120 Rue Principale
☎ (450) 227-4330
Located in a green house facing Papa Luigi, Le Mousqueton serves innovative, contemporary Québec cuisine in a warm, unpretentious atmosphere. Game and fish appear on the menu.

Sainte-Adèle

La Clef des Champs
$$$-$$$$
875 Chemin Pierre-Péladeau
☎ (450) 229-2857
The Clef des Champs serves French cuisine fit for even the most discerning palates. The warmly decorated dining room is just right for an intimate dinner for two. The wine cellar is excellent.

Auberge La Biche au Bois
$$$$
100 Boulevard Ste-Adèle
☎ (450) 229-8064
The enchanting natural setting of Auberge La Biche au Bois is sure to stir up your appetite. The menu is made up of Québec and French specialties. Romantic ambiance.

L'Eau à la Bouche
$$$$
3003 Boulevard Ste-Adèle
☎ (450) 229-2991
One of the finest restaurants not only in the Laurentians but in all of Québec can be found at the hotel **L'Eau à la Bouche** (see p 259). Chef Anne Desjardins takes pride in outdoing herself day after day, serving her clientele outstanding French cuisine made with local ingredients. Two menus, one with three courses, the other with six, are offered each evening. Excellent wine list. An unforgettable gastronomic experience!

The Laurentians – Restaurants - Cottage Country

Sainte-Marguerite–Estérel

Bistro à Champlain
$$$$
75 Chemin Masson
☎ (450) 228-4988

Don't be put off by the uninspired exterior of the Bistro à Champlain. The place is actually one of the best restaurants in the Laurentians, serving excellent nouvelle cuisine made with fresh local ingredients. The interior is extraordinary—a veritable art gallery where you can admire a number of paintings by the late Jean-Paul Riopelle, a close friend of the owner's, as well as works by other artists like Joan Mitchell and Louise Prescott. The restaurant also boasts one of the province's most highly reputed wine cellars, which may be toured by appointment. Everyone can sample some of the wines in this impressive stock, since even the finest are available by the glass. Reservations strongly recommended.

Morin-Heights

Clos Joli
$$$
$$$$ - gourmet seven-course dinner
19 Chemin Clos-Joli
☎ (450) 226-4501

The restaurant at the Clos Joli inn is justifiably renowned. The eclectic menu features several creative options, and an excellent staff of wine waiters can help diners select the right bottle for their meal. One bite and you'll understand what the fuss is all about.

Val-Morin

Hôtel Far Hills Inn
$$$$
3399 Chemin Far Hills
☎ (819) 322-2014 or
(514) 990-4409

Hôtel Far Hills Inn (see p 259) still has one of the finest restaurants in the Laurentians. The gourmet cuisine is positively world-class.

Val-David

La Vagabonde
$
1262 Chemin de la Rivière
☎ (819) 322-3953

Primarily a bakery offering wholesome and delicious organic breads and treats, La Vagabonde is also a tiny café and tea room with a few tables and a patio in the conifers, where patrons wearing socks in their sandals sit around discussing yoga. A variety of unusual teas is lovingly served in Japanese tea sets.

Le Nouveau Continent
$
2301 Rue de l'Église
☎ (819) 322-6702

Le Nouveau Continent serves simple, inexpensive food. The restaurant doubles as an exhibition space and a meeting place for artists, so the interior is decorated with works of art.

Au Petit Poucet
$$
1030 Route 117
☎ (819) 322-2246 or 888-334-2246

Au Petit Poucet has been serving traditional family-style Québécois cuisine since 1945. Don't miss out on the house speciality, maple-smoked ham. The relaxed ambiance is perfect for a meal among friends. Breakfasts here are particularly generous: those with

a big appetite can opt for the "Ogre," but may want to loosen their belts.

Hôtel La Sapinière
$$$$
1244 Chemin de La Sapinière
☎ (819) 322-2020

The restaurant in **Hôtel La Sapinière** (see p 259) has been striving for over 60 years now to create innovative dishes inspired by the culinary repertoires of both Québec and France. Among the house specialties, the game dishes and the gingerbread are particularly noteworthy. Very good wine list.

Sainte-Agathe-des-Monts

Le Havre des Poètes
$$
55 Rue St-Vincent
☎ (819) 326-7770

At Le Havre des Poètes, singers perform French and Québec classics. The food is well-rated, but people come here mainly for the ambiance.

Auberge Chez Girard
$$-$$$
18 Rue Principale Ouest
☎ (819) 326-0922

At Auberge Chez Girard, set back a little from the road and not far from Lac des Sables, guests can enjoy delicious French cuisine in an extremely pleasant setting. It has two floors, the first being the noisiest. A good stop after a day spent in the outdoors.

La Quimperlaise
$$-$$$
11 Tour du Lac
☎ (819) 326-1776

Housed in a little building, La Quimperlaise specializes in Breton dishes, especially crepes filled with a wide variety of ingredients. The decor is charming, the atmosphere relaxed.

La Sauvagine
$$$$
1592 Rte. 329 Nord
☎ (819) 326-7673
La Sauvagine is a French restaurant cleverly set up inside what used to be the chapel of a convent. Extremely well thought-out, it is decorated with large pieces of period furniture.

Lac-Supérieur

Auberge Caribou
$$$-$$$$
141 Chemin Tour du Lac
☎ (819) 688-5201 or 877-688-5201
Leave aside any reservations you may have about hotel restaurants. At Auberge Caribou, chef Suzanne Boulianne, who always seems to be smiling (even when she's serving tables), just may treat you to the best meal you'll have during your trip to Québec. The unpretentious dining room provides a nice view of the lake, especially at sunset. Chef Boulianne favours local ingredients and everything she prepares is a testament to her talent and enthusiasm: from the flower pot filled with bread rolls to the mixed green salad and the generous helping of caribou served with Saskatoon berries. A different selection of appetizers and main courses is served every evening (although the house specialty, caribou, is always on the menu) and the wine list features a few reasonably priced wines that are available by the glass. Reserva-

tions should be made well in advance.

Saint-Jovite

Le Brunch Café
$
814 Rue Ouimet
☎ (819) 425-8233
Le Brunch Café offers simple, unpretentious fare. The various savoury pizzas and tasty desserts are the highlights of the menu. Relaxed, friendly atmosphere.

Verre Bouteille
$$-$$$
888 Rue Ouimet
☎ (819) 425-8776
This cute little bistro was a welcome addition to St-Jovite when it opened a few years back, but its reputation has suffered since the departure of its original chef. Still, it's worth a try for its reasonable lunch specials.

La Table Enchantée
$$-$$$
1842 Rte. 117 Nord
☎ (819) 425-7113
La Table Enchantée, an inviting place with an understated decor, serves delectable Québec specialties. The chef does wonders with the *cipaille* and venison, among others.

Chez Roger
$$$
444 Rue St-Georges
☎ (819) 429-6991
Located in an attractive old house just off Saint-Jovite's main drag, Chez Roger offers a short, changing menu of fine cuisine featuring such meaty items as *médaillons de cerf forestière* and osso buco *milanaise*. Outdoor seating on a cozy, covered terrace.

Le Cheval de Jade
$$$-$$$$
688 Rue Ouimet
☎ (819) 425-5233
The Tremblant region's uncontested favourite spot for a splurge with your sweetie is certainly Cheval de Jade. Occupying a white shingled house just beyond Saint-Jovite's commercial centre, its simple yet elegant decor consists of brick and wood with dark-green walls and white-lace curtains. There is outside dining, beneath a canopy, during the summer. The specialties of the house are fish (walleye with lobster sauce, sole with truffled hollandaise sauce, bouillabaisse) and flambées, and the service is attentive and friendly—no pretensions despite its star rating. A sure hit for a special night out.

Station Mont-Tremblant

Fluide
$
3005 Chemin Principal Le Johannsen
☎ (819) 681-4681
This juice bar, tucked into one of the sloping streets at the base of the mountain, is ideally located to restore the energy you spend skiing or walking. The fluids in question are delicious fresh juices and smoothies boosted with various natural ingredients known for their restorative properties. Soups, sandwiches and "energy" bars are also offered.

Microbrasserie La Diable
$
3005 Chemin du Village
☎ (819) 681-4546
In the summer, you can take in the action on the

The Laurentians - Restaurants - Cottage Country

pedestrian street from the lovely outdoor seating area of the Microbrasserie La Diable. The interior, with tables set up on two floors, is a lot bigger than you'd think. Here, people savour spare ribs, sausages and smoked meats, washed down with one of the beers brewed on the premises, such as Extrême Onction, which has an 8.5% alcohol content.

Le Shack
$-$$
3035 Chemin du Village
☎ (819) 681-4700

Le Shack's overloaded decor, which parodies a traditional sugar shack with its rustic furniture, artificial maple trees with the red leaves of an Indian summer, and wild geese hanging from the ceiling, is sure to bring a smile to your face. Its big outdoor seating area is very popular in the summertime. The menu features simple fare like steak, roast chicken and burgers. Le Shack also has a morning buffet, where you can concoct a copious breakfast for yourself.

Aux Truffes
$$$$
3035 Chemin du Village
☎ (819) 681-4544

Aux Truffes is the best restaurant in the Mont-Tremblant Resort. In an inviting modern decor, guests dine on succulent nouvelle cuisine. Truffles, foie gras and game are among the predominant ingredients.

La Quintessence
$$$$
3004 Chemin de la Chapelle
☎ (819) 425-3400

The restaurant at hotel **La Quintessence** (see p 262) serves delicious fare that favours local products. The

wine bar is perfect for a quick appetizer before sitting down for dinner. As a matter of fact, wine lovers will be pleased to know that the restaurant's wine cellar holds some 5,000 carefully selected bottles and that a fine selection of scotches and ports is also offered. Comfortable setting and attentive service.

Village Mont-Tremblant

Ristorante e Caffe Ital Delli
$$-$$$
1920A Chemin du Village
☎ (819) 425-3040

Ask anyone in the know for an unpretentious eatery serving honest food at honest prices within close proximity to Tremblant, and chances are they'll send you here. A range of interesting pasta dishes (as well as veal and other meat dishes) is served in a simple decor of woodwork, brick and homey plaid tablecloths.

Hôtel Club Tremblant
$$$-$$$$
121 Rue Cuttle
☎ (819) 425-2731

The dining room at **Hôtel Club Tremblant** (see p 264) offers a panoramic view of the lake and Mont Tremblant. The chef prepares traditional French gastronomic cuisine. On Thursday and Saturday nights, the restaurant serves a lavish buffet; the Sunday brunch is also very popular. Reservations are strongly recommended.

♪
Entertainment

Tour B: Cottage Country

■ Bars and Nightclubs

Sainte-Adèle

Bourbon Street Club
195 Boulevard Sainte-Adèle
Bourbon Street hosts live music and is frequented by a relatively young clientele.

Saint-Sauveur

Les Vieilles Portes
185 Rue Principale
☎ (450) 227-2662
Bar Les Vieilles Portes is a nice place to get together with friends for a drink. It has a pleasant outdoor terrace open during the summer.

Bentley's
235 Rue Principale
☎ (450) 227-1851
Bentley's is often full of young people, who come here to have a drink before going out dancing.

Station Mont-Tremblant

Petit Caribou
The Petit Caribou is a young, energetic bar that really fills up after a good day of skiing.

■ Festivals and Cultural Events

The **Festival des Couleurs** *(☎450-436-8532 or 800-561-6673)* takes place from

Summer Theatres

There is a strong tradition of summer theatre in the Laurentians. A number of well-known, well-loved theatres present quality French-language productions throughout the season. These include the **Théâtre Saint-Sauveur** *(22 Rue Claude,* ☎*450-227-8466)*, **Le Patriote de Sainte-Agathe** *(260 Rue Saint-Venant,* ☎*819-326-3655)* and the **Théâtre Sainte-Adèle** *(1069 Boulevard Sainte-Adèle,* ☎*450-227-1389)*.

mid-September to early October, when the landscape is ablaze with flamboyant colours. Countless family activities are organized in Saint-Sauveur, Sainte-Adèle, Sainte-Marguerite–Estérel, Sainte-Adolphe-d'Howard, Sainte-Agathe and Mont-Tremblant to celebrate this time of the year.

Station Mont-Tremblant

In mid-July, blues greats gather at the Mont-Tremblant resort for the **Festival de Blues de Tremblant** *(*☎*888-857-8043)*. The shows are presented outdoors, as well as in local bars and restaurants.

The **Fête de la Musique** *(*☎*888-857-8043)*, a classical-music festival run by renowned violinist Angèle Dubeau, is held at the Mont-Tremblant resort in late August or early September. The concerts are held outdoors and in the Chapelle Saint-Bernard (see p 251).

■ Theatres

Sainte-Adèle

The **Pavillon des Arts de Sainte-Adèle** *(1364 Chemin Pierre-Péladeau,* ☎*450-229-2586)* is a 210-seat concert hall in a former chapel. Twenty-five classical concerts are presented here annually. Wine and cheese are offered to music lovers after each concert in the adjoining gallery.

Shopping

■ Miscellaneous Goods

Saint-Jovite

Le Hameau
816 Rue Ouimet
Le Hameau shopping centre features a few charming boutiques where shoppers can purchase jewellery, perfume, clothing, shoes and various fashion accessories.

Saint-Sauveur

Rue Principale in Saint-Sauveur is lined with boutiques that will delight shoppers. Among these are various fashion outlets as well as a few furniture makers who specialize in reproductions of antique Québec furnishings.

Visitors will find all sorts of treasures at **La Petite École** *(153 Rue Principale,* ☎*450-227-4227)*, ranging from Christmas decorations to dried flowers, not to mention kitchen utensils and beauty products.

Station Mont-Tremblant

Station Mont-Tremblant features many little boutiques and shops. Large Canadian chain stores like Roots and La Cache share space with smaller exclusive boutiques. Everything from ready-to-wear clothing, household items and beauty products to tasty treats and fine pastries can be found here.

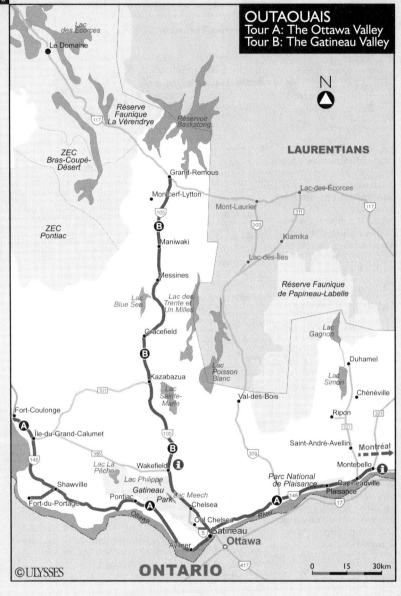

OUTAOUAIS
Tour A: The Ottawa Valley
Tour B: The Gatineau Valley

N

Lac des Écorces

Le Domaine

Réserve Faunique La Vérendrye

Réservoir Baskatong

ZEC Bras-Coupé-Désert

Grand-Remous

Montcerf-Lytton

LAURENTIANS

Lac-des-Écorces

Mont-Laurier

ZEC Pontiac

B

Maniwaki

Kiamika

Messines

Lac-des-Îles

Lac Blue Sea

Lac des Trente et Un Milles

Réserve Faunique de Papineau-Labelle

Gracefield

Lac Gagnon

B

Duhamel

Kazabazua

Lac Sainte-Marie

Lac Poisson Blanc

Lac Simon

Chénéville

Fort-Coulonge

Val-des-Bois

Ripon

A

Île-du-Grand-Calumet

Saint-André-Avellin

Montréal

B

Wakefield

Montebello

Shawville

Lac La Pêche

Gatineau Park

Parc National de Plaisance

Papineauville

Plaisance

Fort-du-Portage

Pontiac

Lac Philippe

Lac Meech

Chelsea

A

Old Chelsea

Ottawa *River*

A

© ULYSSES

Aylmer

Gatineau

Ottawa

ONTARIO

0   15   30km

Outaouais

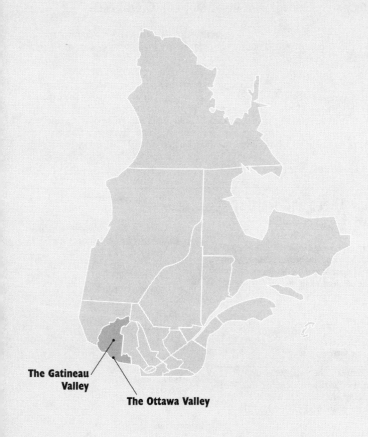

The Gatineau Valley

The Ottawa Valley

Explorers and trappers discovered the Outaouais region early on, but it was not settled by Europeans until the arrival of Loyalists from the United States in the early 19th century. Forestry was long the region's main economic activity. Of particular importance to the industry were red and white pine trees used for ship building. The logs were sent down the Ottawa River and the St. Lawrence to Québec City, where they were loaded onto ships headed for Great Britain.

Forestry still plays an important role here, but service industries and government offices are also a major source of jobs, a situation resulting from the proximity of Canada's capital region.

Directly north of the recently created large city of Gatineau (the result of a merger of the cities of Gatineau, Hull, Buckingham, Masson-Angers and Aylmer) lies an expanse of rolling hills, lakes and rivers, which includes the magnificent Gatineau Park. The park is the location of the official summer residence of the Canadian Prime Minister and is a wonderful place for cycling, canoeing and cross-country skiing. The city of Gatineau has one of the best museums in the country, the Canadian Museum of Civilization. For its part, Ottawa, just across the river, is home to Canada's beautiful Parliament Buildings and a plethora of excellent museums.

Getting There and Getting Around

Two tours of the region, following the Ottawa and Gatineau rivers, respectively, are outlined in **Tour A: The Ottawa Valley ★** and **Tour B: The Gatineau Valley ★**.

■ By Car

Tour A: The Ottawa Valley

From Montréal, there are two ways of reaching the departure point of the tour; one through the Ottawa River valley (1), and a faster way through Ontario (2).

1. Take Aut. 13 N., then Rte. 344 W., which corresponds to part of the Laurentians region's **Lac des Deux-Montagnes ★** tour (see p 242). Finally take Rte. 148 W. toward Ottawa.

2. Take Aut. 40 W., which becomes Rte. 17 W. across the Ontario border. In Hawkesbury, cross the Ottawa River to return to Québec. Turn left on Rte. 148 W., toward Montebello and Ottawa.

Tour B: The Gatineau Valley

Driving and cycling are the best ways to tour the whole valley. Follow Promenade de la Gatineau from Boulevard Taché in the Hull sector of Gatineau. You will almost immediately enter Gatineau Park, created in 1938 by Canadian Prime Minister William Lyon Mackenzie King.

■ Bus Stations

Tour A: The Ottawa Valley

Montebello
535 Rue Notre-Dame
☎ (819) 423-6311

Gatineau (Hull sector)
238 Boulevard Saint-Joseph
☎ (819) 771-2442

Ottawa (Ontario)
265 Catherine St.
☎ (613) 238-5900

■ Train Station

Tour A: The Ottawa Valley

Ottawa (Ontario)
200 Tremblay Rd.
☎ 888-842-7245

Tour B: The Gatineau Valley

The **Hull-Chelsea-Wakefield Steam Train** is a great way to see part of the rural Gatineau valley. The 64km trip takes approximately five hours and stops for two hours in Wakefield.

Useful Information

■ Tourist Information

Regional Office

Association Touristique de l'Outaouais
103 Rue Laurier, Gatineau, J8X 3V8
☎ (819) 778-2222 or 800-265-7822
▤ (819) 778-7758
www.tourisme-outaouais.org

Tour A: The Ottawa Valley

Montebello
502A Rue Notre-Dame
☎ (819) 423-5602

Gatineau (Hull sector)
103 Rue Laurier
☎ (819) 778-2222 or 800-265-7822

Ottawa (Ontario)
90 Wellington St.
☎ (613) 239-5000 or 800-465-1867

Tour B: The Gatineau Valley

Maniwaki
156 Rue Principale Sud
☎ (819) 449-6627

Exploring

Tour A: The Ottawa Valley
★

 1 to 3 days

All that remains of the Ottawa First Nation, slaughtered by the Iroquois in the 17th century, is its name. Ottawa, or in French, Outaouais, is used to denote the beautiful river that forms the border between Québec and Ontario, a vast region of lakes and forests, as well as Canada's capital city. The Ottawa River was once the main route of fur-trappers travelling to the Canadian Shield. These *voyageurs*, who worked for large trading companies, used this river each spring, returning in the fall with their precious cargo of pelts (beaver, seal, mink), which were then shipped to London and Paris from Montréal.

Montebello ★ (pop. 1,066)

The Outaouais region did not experience significant development under the French Regime. Located upstream from the Lachine Rapids, the area was not easily accessible by water, and was thus left to hunters and trappers until the early 19th century and the beginning of the forestry operations. The Petite-Nation seigneury, granted to Monseigneur de Laval in 1674, was the only attempt at colonization in this vast region. It was not until 1801, when the seigneury passed into the hands of notary Joseph Papineau, that the town of Montebello was established. Papineau's son, Louis-Joseph Papineau (1786-1871), head of the French-Canadian nationalist movement in Montréal, inherited the Petite-Nation seigneury in 1817. Returning from an eight-year exile in the United States and France following the rebellion of 1837-38, disillusioned and disappointed by the stand taken by the Catholic clergy during the rebellion, Papineau retired to Montebello, where he built an impressive manor.

Manoir Papineau National Historic Site ★ ★ *($7; mid-May to mid-Jun and early Sep to early Oct Wed-Sun 10am to 5pm, late Jun to late Aug every day 10am to 5pm; 500 Rue Notre-Dame, ☎819-423-6965)* was erected between 1846 and 1849 in the monumental neoclassical villa style. The manor was designed by Louis Aubertin, a visiting French architect. The towers added in the 1850s give the house a medieval appearance. One of the towers houses a precious library that Papineau placed here to protect it from fire. The house has approximately 20 staterooms, through which visitors can now stroll, and features a rich Second Empire decor. It is located on lovely tree-shaded grounds. A small wooden walkway leads to the **Chapelle Funéraire des Papineau** (1853), where 11 members of the family are buried. Note that this is an Anglican chapel.

Papineau's son joined the Church of England when his father died and was refused a Catholic burial. A bust of the elder Papineau, made from the funeral mask of the deceased by Napoléon Bourassa, is one of the interesting objects found in the chapel.

The **Château Montebello** ★★ (&; *392 Rue Notre-Dame;* ☎*819-423-6341*) is a large resort hotel (see p 281) on the Papineau estate. It is the largest log building in the world. The hotel was erected in 1929 (Lawson and Little, architects) in a record 90 days. The impressive lobby has a central fireplace with six hearths, each facing one of the building's six wings that contain the rooms and a restaurant.

The **Gare de Montebello** (*free admission; open year-round; 502-A Rue Notre-Dame,* ☎*819-423-5602*) (former train station; 1931) houses an information centre. It includes a roadside rest area with picnic tables.

Spread over 600 ha, **Parc Oméga** ★ (*$13 in winter, $16 in summer; summer every day 9:30am to 6pm, winter every day 10am to 4pm; Rte. 323 N.,* ☎*819-423-5487, www.parc-omega. com*) is home to many animal species that can be observed from one's vehicle, including bison, wild sheep, elk, wild goats, wild boar and deer (a map is provided and visitors can tune into the park's radio station to get information on each species).

Rte. 321 heads north from Papineauville to Duhamel, providing access to the **Sentier d'Interprétation du Cerf de Virginie** *(see p 279) and the* **Réserve Faunique de Papineau-Labelle** *(see p 279). Continuing east of Papineauville on Rte. 148, you'll soon reach the* **Parc National de Plaisance** ★ *(see p 279) and the* **Chutes de Plaisance** *(Rang Malo), (see p 279). Continue east on Rte. 148 to the Hull sector of Gatineau.*

Gatineau (pop. 234,679)

While most of Ottawa's English-speaking civil servants live in Ontario suburbs such as Nepean, Uplands and Kanata, their French-speaking counterparts mainly live on the Québec side of the Ottawa river, in the sectors of Hull, Aylmer and Gatineau.

Hull Sector

Although the road leading into the Hull sector of Gatineau is named after an important post-war town planner, the former city is certainly not a model of enlightened urban development. Its architecture is very unlike that of Ottawa, just across the river. Hull is a mixture of old factories, typical working-class houses, tall, modern government office buildings, and barren land awaiting future government expansion. The town was founded in 1800 by American Loyalist Philemon Wright, who introduced forestry operations to the Ottawa Valley.

The modest wood-frame houses that line the streets of Hull are nicknamed "matchboxes" because they once housed many employees of the Eddy match factory, and because they have had more than their fair share of fires. In fact, Hull has burned so many times throughout its history that few of the town's historic buildings remain. The former town hall and beautiful Catholic church burned down in 1971 and 1972, respectively.

Ottawa has the reputation of being a quiet city, while Gatineau, particularly its Hull sector, is considered more of a fun town, essentially because the legal drinking age is a year younger than in Ontario and the bars stay open later in Québec. It is not uncommon to see crowds of Ontarians along the **Promenade du Portage** on Saturday nights.

Turn left onto Rue Papineau. The Canadian Museum of Civilization parking lot is at the end of this street.

The **Canadian Museum of Civilization** ★★★ (*$10; early May to mid-Oct every day 9am to 6pm, Thu to 9pm; early Jul to early Sep also Fri to 9pm; mid-Oct to late Apr Tue-Sun 9am to 5pm, Thu to 9pm; 100 Rue Laurier,* ☎*819-776-7000 or 800-555-5621, www.civilization.ca*) is one of many parks and museums that were established along this section of the Québec-Ontario border as part of a large redevelopment program in the National Capital Region between 1983 and 1989. Hull became the site of the magnificent Canadian Museum of Civilization, dedicated to the history of Canada's various cultural groups. If there is one museum that must be seen in Canada, it is this one. In fact, it's the most frequented museum in the country. Douglas

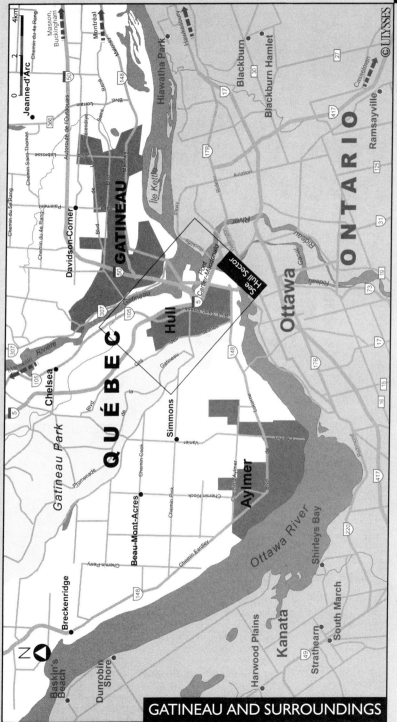

GATINEAU AND SURROUNDINGS

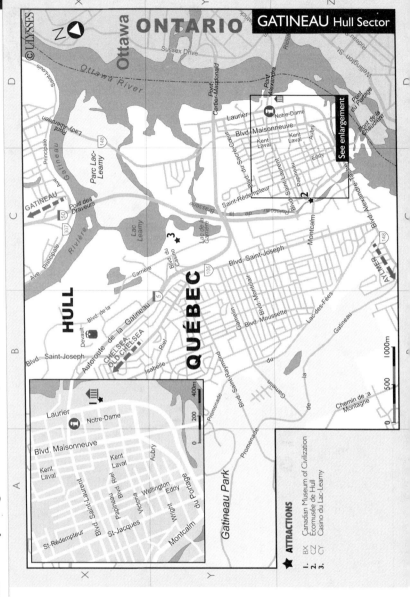

ATTRACTIONS

1. BX Canadian Museum of Civilization
2. CZ Écomusée de Hull
3. CY Casino du Lac-Leamy

Outaouais - Exploring - The Ottawa Valley

Cardinal, a First Nations architect from Alberta, drew up the plans for the museum's two striking curved buildings, one housing the administrative offices and restoration laboratories, and the other the museum's collections. Their undulating design brings to mind rock formations of the Canadian Shield, shaped by wind and glaciers. There is a beautiful view of the Ottawa River and Parliament Hill from the grounds behind the museum.

The Great Hall houses the most extensive collection of totem poles in the world. Another collection brilliantly recreates different periods in Canadian history, from the arrival of the Vikings around 1000 CE to life in rural Ontario in the 19th century and French Acadia in the 17th century. Contemporary Aboriginal art, as well as popular arts and traditional crafts, are also on display. In 2003, the museum inaugurated its **First Peoples Hall**, dedicated to the First Nations of Canada. In the **Canadian Children's Museum**, young visitors choose a theme before being led through an extraordinary adventure. There is also an IMAX cinema.

Continue south on Rue Laurier. At Rue Montcalm, turn right.

The **Écomusée de Hull** (*$5; Tue-Sun 10am to 4pm; 170 Rue Montcalm at Rue Papineau, ☎819-595-7790*), which used to focus on educating the public about environmental issues, is now concentrating on the region's industrial history.

Take Aut. 50, then Rte. 5 north to the "Boulevard du Casino" exit. Then take Rue Saint-Raymond, which becomes Boulevard du Casino.

The **Casino du Lac-Leamy** ★ ★ (*every day 11am to 3am; 1 Boulevard du Casino, ☎819-772-2100 or 800-665-2274, www.casino-du-lac-leamy.com*) has an impressive location between two lakes; Leamy Lake, in the park of the same name, and Lac de la Carrière, which is in the basin of an old limestone quarry. The theme of water is omnipresent around the superb building, completed in 1996. The magnificent walkway leading to the main entrance is dotted with towering fountains, and the harbour has 20 slips for boaters. The gambling area, which covers 6,563m², includes 1,800 slot machines and 64 playing tables spread around a simulated tropical forest. Attached to the casino is the Théâtre du Casino, a modern concert hall, two bars and some excellent restaurants, among which is the **Baccara** (see p 283).

Aylmer Sector ★

Aylmer was once the administrative centre of the Outaouais region. The city was founded by Charles Symmes, an American from Boston who arrived in Canada in 1814. The Hudson's Bay Company, then a major player in the fur trade, centered its activities in this region. Today, Aylmer, with its residential streets lined with middle-class homes, is part of the city of Gatineau.

Prompted by his uncle, Philemon Wright, Charles Symmes settled in the Aylmer region in 1824. In 1830, he built the **old Symmes inn** ★ (*1 Rue Front, ☎819-685-5033*), which became very popular with fur-trappers heading out to the Canadian Shield. The building, which has been completely

restored and is now a performance hall, shows how widespread the urban architectural styles of the French Regime had become, even among Americans like Symmes. Perhaps Symmes had the inn built this way for purely commercial reasons, i.e. to appeal to a predominantly French-Canadian clientele.

To go to Ottawa, turn right onto Rue Laurier and head to the Alexandra Bridge, visible from the grounds of the Canadian Museum of Civilization.

Crossing the Ottawa River, visitors enter Ontario, the most populous province in Canada, with 12.5 million inhabitants.

Ottawa (Ontario) ★ ★ ★

Canada has one federal capital and 13 provincial or territorial capitals corresponding to its 10 provinces and 3 territories. Ottawa, the federal capital, was founded in 1827 by Colonel By, who first named the city Bytown. Following the 1849 Montréal riots and the lack of consensus on a location for a permanent capital for the British colony, Queen Victoria decided in 1857 to place the seat of the colonial government on the border of Anglophone Upper Canada and Francophone Lower Canada. Specifically, she chose the small Ontario city of Ottawa, on the Ottawa River. Ten years later, in 1867, the agreement that created the independent Dominion of Canada was finally signed, and the House of Commons sat for the first time in the new Parliament Buildings.

Ottawa has several interesting museums, including the **National Gallery of Canada**, located on the left when coming off the Alexandra Bridge. Also of interest in the city are the Gothic Revival buildings on **Parliament Hill** (*Wellington St.*), and the **Parliament Buildings**, dominated by the **Peace Tower**. For more information on Ottawa and its surroundings, please consult the **Ulysses Travel Guide Ontario**.

Return to Québec by crossing the Pont du Portage Bridge, a continuation of Wellington St. Turn left onto Boulevard Alexandre-Taché toward Aylmer (Rte. 148 W.). The Eddy factory can be seen on the left. Further down on the right is Promenade de la Gatineau, the starting point for the Gatineau Valley tour (see below).

Tour B: The Gatineau Valley
★

 1 day

The Gatineau Valley runs perpendicular to the Ottawa Valley. The Algonquins who once lived in the region were heavily involved in the fur trade with the French and later the English of the Hudson's Bay Company, before being driven out of the area by increasing development in the 19th century. Today the valley is a peaceful rural region dotted with villages founded by American Loyalists and Scottish settlers. The architecture, influenced by that of nearby Ontario, is characterized by simple neoclassical buildings built between 1830 and 1860. The forestry industry plays a significant role in the valley's economy, particularly farther north. At one time, wood was floated to the former city of Hull on the Gatineau River.

Gatineau Park ★ ★

Gatineau Park (see p 279) is the starting point for this tour. The park, established in 1934, is an area of rolling hills, lakes and rivers that covers more than 35,000ha.

To get to the Gatineau Park Visitor Centre from Hull, take Aut. 5 N. to Exit 12. Turn left and follow the road signs. For the Mackenzie-King Estate, take Chemin Kingsmere heading west, and turn left onto Rue Barnes.

Mackenzie-King Estate ★ ★ *($8, parking included; &; mid-May to mid-Oct Mon-Fri 11am to 5pm, Sat, Sun and holidays 10am to 6pm; Rue Barnes, Chelsea, ☎819-827-2020 or 800-465-1867 from Québec, ☎613-239-5100 from Ontario)* was William Lyon Mackenzie King's summer residence. He was Prime Minister of Canada from 1921 to 1930, and again from 1935 to 1948. His love of art and horticulture rivalled his interest in politics and he was always happy to get away to his summer home near Lac Kingsmere, which today is part of Gatineau Park. The estate consists of two houses (one of which is now a charming tea room), a landscaped garden and follies, false ruins that were popular at the time. However, unlike most follies that were designed to imitate ruins, those on the Mackenzie-King estate are authentic building fragments. Most were taken from the original Canadian House of Parliament, destroyed by fire in 1916, and from Westminster Palace, damaged by German bombs in 1941.

Return to Chemin Kingsmere and head east to Chelsea, where the Gatineau Park Visitor Centre is located, then turn right to reach Rte. 105N towards Wakefield.

Wakefield ★ (pop 6,595)

Founded around 1830 by Scottish, British and Irish settlers, Wakefield is a charming little town located at the mouth of Rivière La Pêche. It is quite pleasant to stroll down its main avenue, with shops and cafés on one side and the beautiful Gatineau River on the other. The **Gendron covered bridge**, painted a striking brick red, stands out in the distance, particularly in summer, when it is surrounded by trees in foliage. Wakefield is also the arrival point of the popular **Hull-Chelsea-Wakefield Steam Train ★** (see p 273). Even if you don't take the trip, you can watch the train being manually turned in the small park where the ride ends.

Val-des-Monts (pop. 8,301)

The Canadian Shield's largest known cave can be found east of Wakefield, in the heart of some gorgeous countryside: **Caverne Laflèche** *($14; year-round, every day 9am to 4pm; reservations required; 255 Route Principale, ☎819-457-4033 or 877-457-4033, www.aventurelafleche.ca).* No need to be a speleology expert to visit the cave: the guided tour, which lasts over an hour, provides a fine introduction to the subject and may leave you wanting to learn more. Travellers with children five years and older should not hesitate to bring them along, as kids are generally fascinated by this unique environment.

*Beyond Gatineau Park, Rte. 105 cuts a path through mountains and forests all the way to Rte. 117 at Grand-Remous. Rte. 117 leads eventually to the **Réserve Faunique La Vérendrye ★**, see p 294.*

Parks

Tour A: The Ottawa Valley

The 26km-long **Sentier d'Interprétation du Cerf de Virginie** *(RR1, Duhamel, ☎819-449-6666)* is a trail that crosses an area frequented by white-tailed deer, called *cerf de Virginie* or *chevreuil* in French, during the winter. The trails are open to hikers, snowshoers and cross-country skiers and allows visitors to observe these graceful animals. Fed by the inhabitants of Duhamel, the deer come here every year. The herd is estimated to number 3,000.

Located in both the Laurentians and Outaouais regions, the **Réserve Faunique Papineau-Labelle** *(mid-May to mid-Nov; 443 Rte. 309, Val-des-Bois; accessible by Rte. 311 coming from Kiamika, by Rte. 321 coming from Lac-Nominingue, or by Rte. 117 coming from La Minerve; ☎819-454-2011, ext. 33, ☎819-428-7510 off-season)* stretches over almost 1,600km² of land and is home to a multitude of animals, including deer and moose. Hunting and fishing are permitted, and the hiking trails are well maintained. Canoe-camping enthusiasts can plan long trips here, though these usually require many portages. Long cross-country ski trails (100km) are also maintained, and skiers can stay in the huts along the way *($17.50 per person per day)*. Approximately 120km of snowmobile trails crisscross the reserve.

The **Parc National de Plaisance** ★ *($3.50; mid-Apr to mid-Oct every day; Route 148, Plaisance, ☎819-427-5334 or 800-665-6527, www.sepaq.com)* is one of the smallest parks in Québec. It borders the Ottawa River for some 27km and its goal is to introduce visitors to the animal and plant life of the region. To better observe birds and aquatic plants, wooden footbridges have been built above the marshes along the river. The park can also be explored by canoe, bicycle or hiking trails. Excursions guided by naturalists are organized.

During the 1980s, the former village of North Nation Mills was the site of several archaeological digs. Nearby is the **Centre d'Interprétation du Patrimoine et des Chutes de Plaisance** *($4; late Jun to early Sep every day 10am to 5pm; 100 Chemin Malo, ☎819-427-6400)*. This is the perfect area for picnics and hikes. The interpretation centre presents four different exhibits on the area's history.

Tour B: The Gatineau Valley

Gatineau Park ★ ★ *(free admission, $8 parking for Mackenzie-King Estate and the beaches; 33 Chemin Scott, Chelsea, ☎819-827-2020 or 800-465-1867)*, a 35,000ha park, was founded during the Depression in 1934 to protect the forests from people looking for firewood. It is crossed by a 34km-long road dotted with panoramic lookout points, including **Belvédère Champlain**, which offer superb views of the lakes, rivers and hills of the Pontiac region. Outdoor activities can be enjoyed here throughout the year. Hiking and mountain-biking trails are open during the summer. There are many lakes in the park, including Meech Lake, which was also the name of the Canadian constitutional agreement drawn up nearby but never ratified. Watersports such as windsurfing, canoeing and swimming are also very popular and the park rents small boats and camp sites. **Lusk Cave**, formed some 12,500 years ago by water flowing from melting glaciers, can be explored. Some 200km of cross-country ski trails are maintained during winter.

Outdoor Activities

■ Canoeing

Canoeing is a unique and pleasant way to contemplate the magnificent landscape of the Outaouais. **Trailhead** *(1960 Rue Scott, ☎613-722-4229, www.trailhead.ca)*, a company located in Ottawa, organizes single-day canoe trips and longer excursions in Gatineau Park. These tours are guided, allowing you to head deep into the forest in complete safety.

Expédition Eau Vive LAQS *(8 Chemin Hudson, Chelsea, ☎819-827-4467 or 888-820-4467, www.canot.qc.ca)* organizes trips on the rivers of the Outaouais for people who are completely inexperienced but still dream of canoe-tripping. More accomplished canoeists can choose a seven- to 15-day trip.

Outaouais - Outdoor Activities

■ Cycling

Whether you're going cycling on one of the Gatineau region's trails or mountain biking in Parc de la Gatineau, the one address you should keep in mind in the Hull area is **Maison du Vélo** *(every day 11:30am to 7pm; 350 Rue Laurier Nord,* ☎*819-997-4356)*. It's the perfect place to either rent a bike or have yours repaired, and you can get all the necessary information on the Outaouais region's many bike trails here.

■ Cross-Country Skiing

In winter, when there's a thick layer of snow, **Gatineau Park** *($9;* ☎*819-827-2020 or 800-465-1867)* maintains an impressive 200km of cross-country ski trails. These trails, 47 in all, are sure to delight skiers of all levels.

Bolder skiers who dream of going deep into the woods, far away from any signs of civilization, will find what they're looking for at the **Réserve Faunique Papineau-Labelle** *($5/day; $20 for overnight cabins;* ☎*819-454-2011, ext. 33, www.sepaq.com)*, with its 120km-long ski trail. There are heated cabins all along the route. Definitely a memorable adventure, but only for experienced skiers.

■ Downhill Skiing and Snowboarding

The Outaouais region's mostly flat urban landscape doesn't provide skiers with many hills. But those who just can't shake the call of the slopes can head to Wakefield, where they'll find two rather small downhill ski resorts: **Edelweiss** and **Vorlage**.

■ Forest Adventure Courses

Tour B: The Gatineau Valley

The Outaouais region has the largest treetop adventure course in North America:

Aventure Laflèche *($30, $39 including tour of Caverne Laflèche; every day 9am to 4pm; reservations required; 255 Route Principale, Val-des-Monts,* ☎*819-457-4033 or 877-457-4033, www.aventurelafleche.ca)*, located near **Caverne Laflèche** (see p 278). Starting out 30m above ground, visitors get to zip 200m over a lake via a Tyrolean traverse, cross 80 or so suspended bridges that provide breathtaking views of the surrounding Laurentian forest, swing on "Tarzan" ropes and manoeuvre across several cleverly installed ramps and nets, among many other challenges. Snacks can be purchased on site.

■ Hiking

Gatineau Park *(*☎*819-827-2020 or 800-465-1867)* offers many hiking trails, over 125km in all, and just as many chances to discover its beauty. You can explore Lac Pink, a beautiful but polluted lake (you can't swim in it), on a 1.4km-trail. If you prefer splendid panoramic views, choose Mont-King, a 2.5km-long trail that leads to the summit and to gorgeous views of the Ottawa River Valley. And finally, if you have a bit more time and are interested in a fascinating excursion, the Lusk Cave trail is 10.5km long and leads to a 12,500-year-old marble cave.

Covering 1,628km², the immense **Réserve Faunique Papineau-Labelle** *(443 Route 309, Val-des-Bois,* ☎*819-454-2011, ext. 33 in season,* ☎*819-428-7510 off-season)* is a veritable hikers' paradise

Walking tours through marshlands have been created at the **Parc National de Plaisance** (see p 279) to help people understand the significant role that these wetlands play in maintaining an ecological balance. The 1km-long path, La Zizanie des Marais, is fully accessible and particularly captivating. It leads to the heart of the marsh by way of wooden footbridges that pass over Petite Presqu'île bay.

Accommodations

Tour A: The Ottawa Valley

Montebello

Auberge Suisse Montevilla
$$$-$$$$ bkfst incl.
≋ ◎ ● ⚓ ≡

☎ (819) 423-6692 or 800-363-0061
🖨 (819) 423-5420
www.auberge-montevilla.com
Located a little outside the village of Montebello, Auberge Suisse Montevilla is a good choice for travellers who want to spend a few days relaxing in a country setting without sacrificing comfort. The inn offers several outdoor-activity options, such as fishing and tennis, and guests can go for a swim in the pool or in one of two artificial lakes. Chalets can also be rented on site.

Fairmont Le Château Montebello
$$$$$
≡ ⚓ ≋ ⚓))) ⛛ & ◎

392 Rue Notre-Dame
☎ (819) 423-6341 or 800-441-1414
🖨 (819) 423-5283
www.fairmont.com
This beautiful pine and cedar building stands next to Ottawa River. It is the largest log building in the world and is equipped with several facilities, including an indoor and outdoor swimming pool, squash courts and fitness centre.

Hull (Gatineau)

Auberge Un Pied à Terre
$$ bkfst incl.
● ⚓

245 Rue Papineau
☎/🖨 (819) 772-4364
www.3.sympatico.ca/unpiedaterre
Auberge Un Pied à Terre is located near the Canadian Museum of Civilization and offers both quality accommodations and tasty meals.

Auberge de la Gare
$$$-$$$$ bkfst incl.
≡ ◎

205 Boulevard St-Joseph
☎ (819) 778-8085 or 866-778-8085
🖨 (819) 595-2021
www.aubergedelagare.ca
Auberge de la Gare is a simple, conventional hotel that offers good value. The service is both courteous and friendly, and the rooms are clean and well-kept, albeit nondescript.

Hilton Lac-Leamy
$$$$$
& ≡ ◎ ⚓ ≋ ⛛ ⚓)))

3 Boulevard du Casino
☎ (819) 790-6444 or 866-488-7888
🖨 (819) 790-6408
www.hiltonlacleamy.com
This imposing hotel adjoins the casino on the shores of Lac Leamy. The twenty-storey establishment's rooms are comfortable and provide beautiful views of two neighbouring lakes and their surroundings. Business travellers will appreciate the hotel's many amenities.

Aylmer (Gatineau)

Le Gîte Enchanté
$$ bkfst incl.
32 Promenade Lakeview
☎ (819) 682-0695
www.giteenchante.ca
Le Gîte Enchanté is located a mere 10min away from Ottawa. Guests will appreciate the comfortable,

peaceful accommodations and the inn's splendid backyard. The house features the superb art work of its friendly owner, Rita Rodrigue, and a gourmet breakfast provides the perfect start to a sight-seeing day in the area.

Château Cartier Relais Resort
$$$$-$$$$$
≡ ◎ ⚓ ⚓ ≋ ⛛ ⚓)))

1170 Chemin Aylmer
☎ (819) 778-0000 or 800-807-1088
🖨 (819) 777-2518
www.chateaucartier.com
Château Cartier occupies a relatively recent pink and green building. The rooms offer basic comfort and a modern decor.

Tour B: The Gatineau Valley

Gatineau Park

La Pêche Lake Campground
$
Rte. 366
☎ (819) 456-3016
Without a doubt, one of the most beautiful places in the area to camp is Gatineau Park, which offers more than 350 campsites, some of which are equipped to receive RVs.

Wakefield

Les Trois Érables
$$$-$$$$ bkfst incl.
≡ ⚓

801 Chemin Riverside
☎ (819) 459-1118 or 877-337-2253
www.lestroiserables.com
The small Les Trois Érables inn is set in a beautifully restored house that dates from 1896. The marvellous setting and warm welcome ensure a memorable stay.

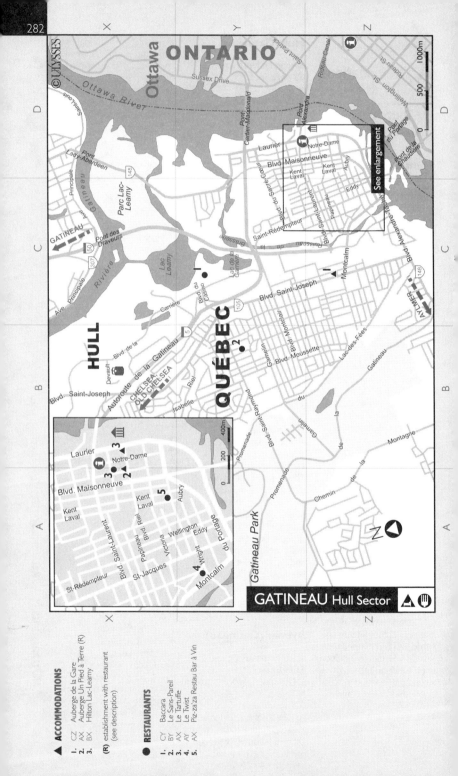

GATINEAU Hull Sector

ACCOMMODATIONS

1. CZ Auberge de la Gare
2. AX Auberge Un Pied à Terre (R)
3. BX Hilton Lac-Leamy

(R) establishment with restaurant (see description)

RESTAURANTS

1. CY Baccara
2. BY Le Sans-Pareil
3. AX Le Tartuffe
4. AY Le Twist
5. AX Piz-za'za Restau Bar à Vin

ONTARIO

Ottawa

HULL

QUÉBEC

Gatineau Park

Laurier
Notre-Dame
Blvd. Maisonneuve
Kent Laval
Eddy
See enlargement

Montcalm
Blvd. Saint-Joseph

AYLMER

Messines

Maison La Crémaillère
$$ bkfst incl.
≋ ◎
24 Chemin de la Montagne
☎ (819) 465-2202 or 877-465-2202
▤ (819) 465-5368
www.lacremaillere.qc.ca
A warm welcome awaits at Maison La Crémaillère's charming little bed and breakfast. The quiet little village of Messines is the perfect spot to relax and watch the days go by in the Outaouais countryside.

Restaurants

- - - - - - - - - - - - - - - - -

Tour A: The Ottawa Valley

Papineauville

La Table de Pierre Delahaye
$$$$
Wed-Fri and Sun 11:30am to 2pm and Wed-Sun 5:30pm to 9pm; closed Mon-Tue
247 Rue Papineau
☎ (819) 427-5027
La Table de Pierre Delahaye is worth a stop. This restaurant is sure to linger in your memory. It's run by a couple—Madame greets the guests and Monsieur takes care of the food. The welcome is always warm and cordial, the Norman-style cuisine succulent. If the thought of sweetbreads makes your mouth water, look no further. The rooms in this historic house (1880) are oozing with atmosphere. Parties of eight or more can even have a room all to themselves.

Hull (Gatineau)

Auberge Un Pied à Terre
$
245 Rue Papineau
☎ (819) 772-4634
The little café at **Auberge Un Pied à Terre** (see p 281) serves inexpensive, tasty fare and offers a nice selection of specialized coffees.

Piz-za'za Restau Bar à Vin
$-$$
36 Rue Laval
☎ (819) 771-0565
At Pi-za'za Restau Bar à Vin, you can sample an excellent variety of fine pizzas in a pleasant, relaxed atmosphere.

Le Twist
$$
88 Rue Montcalm
☎ (819) 777-8886
Le Twist provides a terrific setting in which to satisfy your cravings for a good burger and homemade fries. In the summer, you can sit outside on a large terrace.

Le Tartuffe
$$$-$$$$
Mon-Sat
133 Rue Notre-Dame
☎ (819) 776-6424
Le Tartuffe is a marvellous gourmet French restaurant located just steps from the Canadian Museum of Civilization. With its friendly, courteous service and delightful, intimate ambiance, this place is sure to win your heart.

Le Sans-Pareil
$$$-$$$$
Mon-Sat
71 Boulevard St-Raymond
☎ (819) 771-1471
Le Sans-Pareil is located 5min from Casino du Lac-Leamy, and right near the shopping centres. This is a Belgian restaurant, so it's only normal that chef Luc Gielen offers mussels (prepared in 12 different ways) on Tuesday nights. The sinfully good menu usually changes every three weeks, and the focus is on fresh products from various parts of Québec. The chef has a flair for combining ingredients in innovative ways, so don't hesitate to try the *menu gourmand*, which includes several courses, complete with the appropriate wines to wash them down. This place may be small, but it's truly charming.

Baccara
$$$$
dinner only
1 Boulevard du Casino
☎ (819) 772-6210
Located in **Casino du Lac-Leamy** (see p 277), has won itself a place among the best restaurants of the region. The set menu always consists of superb dishes that you can enjoy along with spectacular views of the lake. The well-stocked wine cellar and impeccable service round out this memorable culinary experience.

Aylmer (Gatineau)

À l'Échelle de Jacob
$$$
open for dinner only; closed Mon-Tue and mid-Jul to mid-Aug
27 Boulevard Lucerne
☎ (819) 684-1040
The delightful À l'Échelle de Jacob is located in a charming stone house. The delicious French cuisine and warm atmosphere make this a perfect spot for a quiet, romantic night out.

Outaouais - Restaurants - The Ottawa Valley

Messines

Maison La Crémaillère
$$$$
closed Sun
24 Chemin de la Montagne
☎(819) 465-2202 or 877-465-2202
One of the region's best restaurants is located in **Maison La Crémaillère** (see p 283). The magnificent heritage house's small dining room offers deliciously creative fare while providing personalized, courteous service. Reservations required.

- - - - - - - - - - - - - - - -

Tour B: The Gatineau Valley

Gatineau Park

L'Orée du Bois
$$$-$$$$
Tue-Sun, Tue-Sat in winter
15 Chemin Kingsmere, Chelsea
☎ (819) 827-0332
It would be unheard of to visit the Outaouais without going to Gatineau Park—if only for a meal. L'Orée du Bois occupies a rustic house in the country, and its crocheted curtains and wood and brick interior add to the ambiance. This is the kind of family business that you find all over France. For years now, Manon has been welcoming guests and overseeing the dining rooms, while Guy focuses his expertise on the food. He has developed a French cuisine featuring ingredients from the various regions of Québec, so the menu lists dishes made with wild mushrooms, fresh goat cheese, Lac Brome duck, venison and fish smoked on the premises, using maple wood. The prices are very

reasonable, and the portions generous. A pleasant evening is guaranteed!

♪ Entertainment

■ Bars and Nightclubs

Hull (Gatineau)

Café Aux Quatre Jeudis
44 Rue Laval
☎771-9557
For many years now, Aux Quatre Jeudis has been the place for the café crowd. It has lots of atmosphere, and there's a big, attractive terrace to hang out on in the summer.

Le Bop Bar
5 Rue Aubry
☎777-3700
Le Bop Bar is a fun little place at Place Aubry. You can kick off your evening with a reasonably priced, decent meal. The music ranges from techno and disco to soft rock and even a little hard rock.

Le Fou du Roi
253 Boulevard St-Joseph
☎778-0516
Le Fou du Roi is where the thirty-something crowd hangs out. There's a dance floor, and the windows open onto a little terrace in the summertime. This place is also a popular after-work gathering place.

Le Troquet
41 Rue Laval
☎ (819) 776-9595
Le Troquet is a small bistro-style bar located on busy Rue Laval where patrons come for a drink among friends. In summertime,

front and back terraces provide the perfect setting for a quick afternoon bite or a pleasant night out.

The **Casino du Lac-Leamy** *(1 Boulevard du Casino)* has two beautiful bars: the **777** and **La Marina**, which serve no fewer than 70 Canadian microbrews.

■ Casino

Hull (Gatineau)

Casino du Lac-Leamy *(&; every day 9am to 4am; 1 Boulevard du Casino, ☎819-772-2100 or 800-665-2274).* This huge casino has slot machines, Keno, blackjack and roulette tables, as well as two restaurants.

■ Festivals and Cultural Events

Aylmer

The **Fête de l'Été d'Aylmer** is centered around the Aylmer marina. For a few days in August, you can watch or take part in various competitions and activities out on the water. In the evening, well-known Québec singers take turns entertaining the crowd.

Gatineau

During the **Festival des Montgolfières** *(☎819-243-2330 or 800-668-8383)*, held in Gatineau on Labour Day weekend, the sky is filled with colourful hot-air balloons, a real feast for the eyes. This well-organized event has earned itself an enviable reputation in just a few years and is the largest of its kind in Canada. A number of prominent singers perform here in the evening.

Hull (Gatineau)

The inauguration of the Casino du Lac-Leamy also marked the start of the popular **Les Grands Feux du Casino** (☎*819-771-3389 or 888-429-3389*) fireworks display, held every year in August.

■ Theatres and Live Entertainment

Aylmer (Gatineau)

The **Centre Culturel du Vieux-Alymer** (*1 Rue Front,* ☎*819-685-5033*) is located in the old Auberge Symmes inn. An interesting and varied selection of cultural events are presented in this historic building.

Next door is the **Centre d'Exposition l'Imagier** (*9 Rue Front,* ☎*819-684-1445*) and the adjoining Parc de l'Imaginaire, an open-air art gallery where various concerts and shows are presented in summer.

Hull (Gatineau)

The **Théâtre du Casino** (☎*819-772-2100*), a recent

addition to the casino, presents various musical productions and comfortably seats 1,000.

Wakefield

In Wakefield, you will never be bored. There are several pubs for your entertainment, including the famous **Black Sheep Inn** (*753 Riverside Dr.,* ☎*819-459-3228*), which stages a surprising variety of shows for such a small town; from Sunday-afternoon folk to African nights, a good time is always guaranteed. The artists who play here, whether local or internationally renowned, are usually quite worthwhile and entertain the entire village.

Shopping

■ Arts and Crafts

Wakefield

The small village of Wakefield has a few treats in store for those who wish to stroll down the avenue and visit a shop or two. The village is home to a community of artists and artisans

and offers a good selection of shops.

■ Gifts

Hull (Gatineau)

The **Canadian Museum of Civilization** gift shop (*100 Rue Laurier*) is, in a way, part of the exhibit. Although the craft pieces aren't of the same quality as those exhibited in the museum, you'll find all sorts of reasonably priced treasures and lots of great little curios. The museum also has a **bookstore** with a wonderful collection on the history of crafts in many different cultures.

ABITIBI-TÉMISCAMINGUE
Tour A: Abitibi
Tour B: Témiscamingue

Abitibi-Témiscamingue

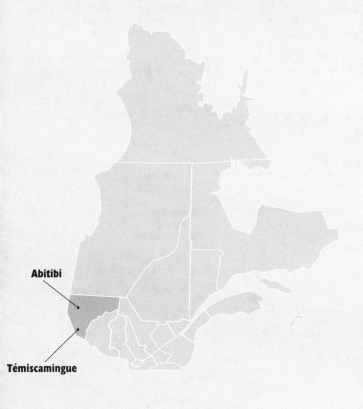

Abitibi

Témiscamingue

A region of 100,000 lakes and 150,000 inhabitants, Abitibi-Témisca-mingue, together with Nord-du-Québec (Northern Québec) and the James Bay area, forms the province's last frontier. While the rich fertile land bordering Lac Témiscamingue and the Ottawa River was cleared in the 19th century, agricultural development in the rest of the region, where the soil is not as good, did not begin in earnest until the 1930s.

The discovery of gold deposits in the 1920s provoked a second wave of migration, a true gold rush. Today, the region has preserved its boomtown atmosphere as the mining industry still employs one fifth of the local workforce. Forestry and farming are also important to the regional economy.

Nowadays, people come here to relive the great adventure of the gold rush, but most of all to enjoy the wide-open spaces and explore the huge forests and countless lakes that are a hunter's, fisher's and snowmobiler's paradise.

Getting There and Getting Around

Although Abitibi and Témiscamingue are considered part of the same general region, both are areas with unique identities. Thus, two separate tours are suggested: **Tour A: Abitibi** ★ and **Tour B: Témiscamingue** ★.

■ By Car

Tour A: Abitibi

Since Abitibi is located approximately 500km from Montréal, it is best to plan an overnight stop along the way. Take Aut. 15 N. from Montréal, which turns into Rte. 117 at Sainte-Agathe. The Abitibi tour can be combined with the **Cottage Country** tour in the Laurentians tourist region (see p 246) and the **Témiscamingue** tour (see p 292).

Tour B: Témiscamingue

Témiscamingue can be reached from either Abitibi or various places in the province of Ontario. In the first case, follow Rte. 391 S. from Rouyn-Noranda. From Ontario, take Rtes. 17, 533 and 63 (on the south shore of the Ottawa River) to Témiscaming and follow the tour in reverse.

■ Bus Stations

Tour A: Abitibi

Val-d'Or
1420 4e Avenue
☎ (819) 874-2200

Rouyn-Noranda
52 Rue Horne
☎ (819) 762-2200

Tour B: Témiscamingue

Ville-Marie
19 Rue Sainte-Anne
☎ (819) 629-2166

■ Train Station

Tour A: Abitibi

Senneterre
4e Rue Ouest
☎ (819) 737-2979

■ By Boat

Tour B: Témiscamingue

Another way to reach Témiscamingue is via the **Voie Navigable du Témiscamingue et de l'Outaouais**. This water route runs along the Ottawa River and ends at Lac Témisca-mingue, the same route once used to float wood down to the sawmills and pulp and paper factories in Hull. For more information, contact the regional tourist-information offices listed below.

Useful Information

■ Tourist Information

Regional Office

Tourisme Abitibi-Témiscamingue
170 Avenue Principale, Bureau 103
Rouyn-Noranda, J9X 4P7
☎ (819) 762-8181 or 800-808-0706
▤ (819) 762-5212
www.48nord.qc.ca

Tour A: Abitibi

Val-d'Or
1070 3ᵉ Avenue Est
☎ (819) 824-9646 or 877-582-5367
www.ville.valdor.qc.ca

Amos
892 Rte. 111 Est
☎ (819) 727-1242 or 800-670-0499
▤ (819) 727-3437
www.ville.amos.qc.ca

Rouyn-Noranda
191 Avenue du Lac
☎ (819) 797-3195 or 888-797-3195
▤ (819) 797-7134
www.ville.rouyn-noranda.qc.ca

Tour B: Témiscamingue

Ville-Marie
1 Rue Industrielle
☎ (819) 629-2918
www.temiscamingue.net

Exploring

Tour A: Abitibi
★

 2 days

The development of the Abitibi region began in 1912 with the arrival of the rail-road. Because the region is isolated from the rest of Québec by the Cadillac fault (which marks the northern limit of the St. Lawrence River basin), it was virtually impossible to reach via water. At one time Abitibi was thought of as a promised land by the Catholic clergy, who began to direct farmers from the overdeveloped St. Lawrence Valley into the area to stop emigration to the United States. Discovery of copper and gold deposits in the early 1920s sped up the development of towns such as Val-d'Or, but the rest of the region has remained sparsely inhabited.

During the Depression, developing Abitibi for agriculture became a way of reducing the desperate unemployment situation in large cities to the south. Measures taken by the Québec government between 1932 and 1939 resulted in a doubling of Abitibi's population and the creation of 40 new villages and towns.

The rolling countryside of Abitibi has countless lakes and rivers and is blanketed by extensive forests, making it ideal for hunting and fishing. In the Algonquin language, the word "Abitibi" means "area of high lands."

Val-d'Or (pop. 31,798)

The search for gold in Québec under the French Regime ended after explorers who believed they had discovered the precious metal in the colony sent samples of their exciting find back to King François I. As it turned out, they had uncovered a worthless deposit of fool's gold. Following this embarrassing incident, further processing was abandoned as a waste of time. In 1922, however, prospectors discovered a tremendous deposit of actual gold along the Cadillac fault. Shortly afterward, the town of Val-d'Or, literally "Valley of Gold," quickly sprang to life. Throughout the 1930s, Val-d'Or was the premier gold-mining town in the world, and today, it is still an important mining centre.

You can climb to the summit (18m) of the **Tour d'Observation Rotary** (*☎819-824-9646*), an observation tower located at the corner of Boulevard des Pins and Boulevard Sabourin, for a breathtaking view of Québec's northern landscape.

Abitibi-Témiscamingue - Exploring - Abitibi

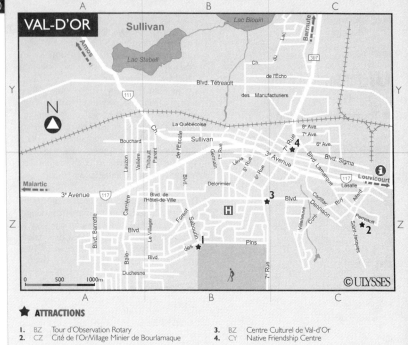

★ ATTRACTIONS

| I. | BZ | Tour d'Observation Rotary | 3. | BZ | Centre Culturel de Val-d'Or |
| 2. | CZ | Cité de l'Or/Village Minier de Bourlamaque | 4. | CY | Native Friendship Centre |

The Canadian-American company Teck-Hughes Gold Mines began exploiting the Lamaque mine in 1932, a welcome initiative during a period of high unemployment. The **Village Minier de Bourlamaque** ★ *($3; late Jun to early Sep every day 9am to 6pm, rest of year by appointment; 90 Avenue Perreault, ☎819-825-7616)* was established in the spring of 1935 to accommodate the miners and their families. This gold-rush town has been preserved down to the smallest detail, first by the Lamaque company, which built it, and then by the town of Val-d'Or, which has had control of the town since 1965. This village is composed of 54 authentic mining houses built from unhewn timber, which exemplify the typical rugged Canadian log cabin. The buildings are well maintained and still inhabited. The house at 123 Avenue Perreault has been converted into an information centre devoted to the history of Val-d'Or and the mining industry in Abitibi.

At **La Cité de l'Or** ★ ★ *($25; mid-Jun to early Sep every day 9am to 6pm, Sep to May Mon-Fri 9am to 5pm by appointment only; 123 Avenue Perreault, ☎819-825-7616 or 877-582-5367)*, you can head 90m underground into an old mine and learn about various gold-mining techniques. The tour, which lasts nearly 2hrs, offers a chance to see the incredible working conditions of the miners. Temperatures at the bottom of a mine are completely different from those outside, so bring along a warm sweater. After the tour, you can take a look at the above-ground facilities of the old Lamaque mine. This is definitely a must.

Works of art from the Val-d'Or region and beyond are shown at the **Centre Culturel de Val-d'Or** *(free admission; hours vary; 600 7ᵉ Rue, ☎819-825-0942)*.

Native culture, including an annual Cree hockey tournament, is important in Val-d'Or and the **Native Friendship Centre** *(free admission; year-round; 1272 7ᵉ Rue, ☎819-825-6857)* offers insights to the history, legends and traditions of local First Nations. At the shop you can see works by Aboriginal craftspeople.

Continue along Rte. 117 to Malartic.

Malartic (pop. 3,653)

Gold mining is no longer an important economic activity in Malartic, but the buildings from the gold rush era have survived, giving the town an interesting Far West appearance.

The **Musée Minéralogique de Malartic** ★ *($4; Jun to mid-Sep every day 9am to 5pm, mid-Sep to late May Mon-Fri 9am to noon and 1pm to 5pm, weekends by appointment; 650 Rue de la Paix, ☎819-757-4677, www.museemalartic.qc.ca)* was founded by a group of miners who wanted to share their experiences with the public. Today, it is firmly planted in the 21st century, with very educational exhibits. Here, you'll learn about the process that led to the creation of Earth and the uses of its minerals in our everyday lives. There is also a multimedia show.

At Rivière-Héva take Rte. 109 to Amos.

Amos (pop. 12,846)

After an exhausting voyage, the first settlers arrived in Abitibi in the summer of 1912. They set up camp along the banks of the Rivière Harricana, founding the village of Amos. The original village, with its rustic cabins built from the trees that were cut to clear the site, quickly gave way to a modern town. Amos was the first settlement in Abitibi and is still the administrative and religious centre of the region.

The **Cathédrale Sainte-Thérèse-d'Avila** ★ *(11 Boulevard Mgr-Dudemaine, ☎819-732-2110)*, promoted to the rank of cathedral in 1939, was built in 1923 from a design by Montréal architect Aristide Beaugrand-Champagne. Its unusual circular structure, large dome and Roman Byzantine appearance are reminiscent of the Église Saint-Michel-Archange in Montréal, designed by the same architect. The interior is decorated with Italian marble, beautiful mosaics and French stained-glass windows.

The **Refuge Pageau** ★★ *($12; early Jun to late Aug Tue-Sun 10am to 4pm, rest of the year by appointment; 4241 Chemin Croteau, ☎819-732-8999, www.refugepageau.ca)* takes in wounded animals, treats their injuries, then sets them free again. Unfortunately, not all of these animals can safely return to the wilderness, so they stay on the reserve,

much to the delight of visitors. In autumn, you can take in the magnificent spectacle presented by the migratory birds that stop here. With a little luck, you'll spot Michel Pageau playing with these wild animals, which no other person can approach, in their cages. It is always impressive to see a man getting his face licked by a wolf or struggling with a bear! Aside from bears and wolves, there are foxes, raccoons, owls and various other members of Québec's animal population.

*Rte. 109 then passes through Pikogan, and 620km farther, reaches James Bay and its massive hydroelectric installations (see **Côte-Nord and Northern Québec**, p 547). To continue the Abitibi tour, take Rte. 111 from Amos, then Rte. 393 N. to La Sarre.*

La Sarre (pop. 7,426)

The village of La Sarre is located in a remote area crossed by long straight roads, where you must often drive 20km or more to buy a litre of milk. Forestry, an industry developed during the economic crisis of the 1930s, is still the main source of income in the region.

The **Centre d'Interprétation de la Foresterie** *(free admission; late Jun to late Aug every day 9:30am to 7:30pm; guided tours Tue-Sat 9:30am to noon and 1pm to 4:30pm, Sun noon to 5pm; 600 Rue Principale, ☎819-333-3318)*, at the local tourist-information centre, describes the development of La Sarre's forestry industry.

But there's more to La Sarre than wood. Cultural expression finds its home at the **Maison de la Culture** *(Mon-Fri 1pm to 4:30pm and 7pm to 9pm, Sat and Sun 1pm to 5pm; 195 Rue Principale; ☎819-333-2294)*, where you'll find both the Richelieu municipal library and the Centre d'Art Rotary, which present travelling and permanent exhibits by artists from the Abitibi-Témiscamingue region and elsewhere. Notice the **fresco** at the entrance of the Maison; if you look closer, you'll be able to read about 70 years of local history!

Retrace your steps south on Rte. 393 and continue to Duparquet, the site of an abandoned gold mine. Turn left onto Rte. 388 E., then right onto Rte. 101 S. to D'Alembert. At D'Alembert, turn left toward Saint-Norbert-de-Mont-Brun, where the

Abitibi-Témiscamingue - Exploring - Abitibi

*entrance to **Parc National d'Aiguebelle** ★ ★ is located (see p 294).*

Take Rte. 101 S. to Rouyn-Noranda

Rouyn-Noranda (pop. 39,512)

Rouyn-Noranda was once two separate towns, Rouyn and Noranda, respectively located on the south and north shores of Lac Osisko (also called Trémoy). The town was established following the discovery of large gold and copper deposits in the region. In 1921, all there were there were a forest and rocks. Five years later, however, a town, complete with churches, factories and houses, had developed. Historically, Rouyn has been the more commercial and industrial of the two cities. In contrast, the Noranda mining company carefully developed the village of Noranda as a predominately residential and institutional settlement. Even though the Rouyn-Noranda mines are now depleted, the town remains an important ore-processing centre.

The **Maison Dumulon** *($3; late Jun to early Sep every day 9am to 7pm, early Sep to late Jun Mon-Fri 8:30am to noon and 1pm to 4:30pm; 191 Avenue du Lac,* ☎*819-797-7125, www. maison-dumulon.ca)* is a log house built by shopkeeper Joseph Dumulon in 1924; the property includes an adjoining general store. The Dumulon family played a central role in the development of Rouyn by opening a store, an inn and a local post office. The building, made of spruce blocks, now houses a tourist-information centre and a small information centre on the history of Rouyn-Noranda.

The **Russian Orthodox church** *($5; late Jun to early Sep every day 10am to noon and 1pm to 5pm; 201 Rue Taschereau Ouest,* ☎*819-797-7125)* pays homage to the many Eastern European immigrants who played an important role in the development of Abitibi's mining towns in the 1930s and 1940s. While the communities they established have declined in recent years, vestiges such as synagogues and other temples remain, though most are being used for other purposes.

The **Noranda, Fonderie Horne** ★ foundry *(free admission; early Jun to early Sep every day 8:15am to 4pm; 101 Avenue Portelance,* ☎*819-762-7764)* provides an opportunity to visit one of the world's major producers of copper and other precious metals. The foundry opened in 1927 and is still in operation.

The **Centre Éducatif Forestier du Lac-Joannès** *(free admission; late Jun to early Sep every day 10am to 6pm; 703 Chemin des Cèdres, McWatters; accessible via Rte. 117, heading towards Rouyn-Noranda;* ☎*819-762-8867)* offers activities that will please the whole family. Inaugurated in 1972, the centre provides information on the forest industry's activities through interpretative walking and fitness trails and a huge 3.5km maze. Guides supply visitors with information on the flora and fauna of the region's forests. Reservations are required for groups.

The enchanting **"À Fleur d'eau" botanical park** *(free admission, guided tours $2; Jun to Aug every day 10am to 4pm; reservations required 24hrs ahead for guided tours; 250 Avenue Dallaire,* ☎*819-797-8753)* features a trail skirting Lac Édouard that allows you to admire its aquatic flora and fauna. Ornithologists take note: the park is home to a great variety of birds.

The **Jardin Géologique** *(free admission, guided tours available upon request $2; summer 9am to 10pm; Rue Pinder Est, in the botanical park)* of Rouyn-Noranda is one of the few of its kind in the world. The geological garden's 17 blocks of minerals acquaint visitors with the region's geology. Explanatory panels provide interesting information about Abitibi-Témiscamingue's mining and geological history.

- -

Tour B: Témiscamingue
★

 1½ days

Beautiful Lac Témiscamingue, the namesake of the entire region, feeds the Ottawa River. Témiscamingue, which means "place of deep waters," was once the heart of

Abitibi-Témiscamingue - Exploring - Abitibi

 ATTRACTIONS

1.	CY	Maison Dumulon
2.	BY	Russian Orthodox church
3.	CX	Noranda, Fonderie Horne

4.	DZ	Centre Éducatif Forestier du Lac-Joannès
5.	CZ	"À Fleur d'eau" botanical park/Jardin Géologique

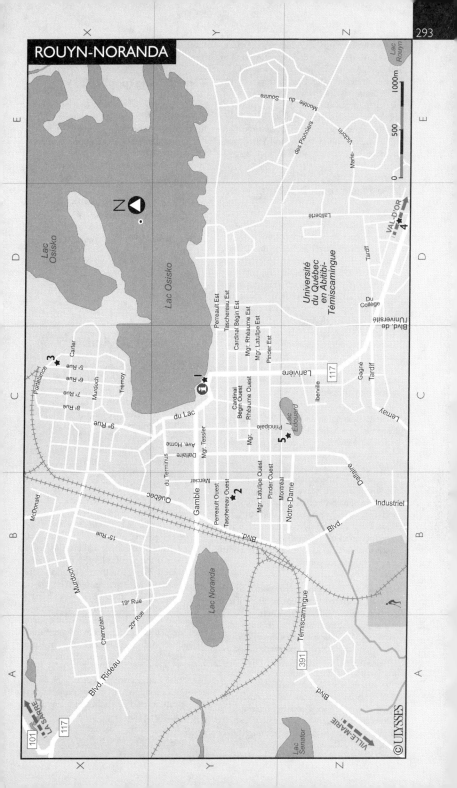

ROUYN-NORANDA

293

Algonquin territory. For 200 years before the region started to become an important forestry area, the only non-Aboriginals in Témiscamingue were French trappers. By 1850, lumberjacks from the Outaouais region began travelling in the area to cut a seemingly endless supply of wood. In 1863, priests of the Oblate religious order settled in the region and helped found Ville-Marie in 1888, the first town in Témiscamingue.

Ville-Marie (pop. 2,762)

Due to its strategic location between southern Québec and Hudson Bay, Lac Témiscamingue entered regional colonial history in the 17th century. In 1686, the French Knight of Troyes stopped here briefly on an expedition to expel the British from the Hudson Bay region. During the same year, a trading post was set up along the lake. The opening of lumber camps in Témiscamingue during the 19th century brought a seasonal population to the area. Soon, permanent settlers and priests from an Oblate mission established the town of Ville-Marie. The town has a beautiful lakeside location that is highlighted by the surrounding parklands.

Located 8km south of Ville-Marie, the **Fort Témiscamingue National Historic Site** ★★ *($5 to $14.50; &; early Jun to early Sep; 834 Chemin du Vieux-Fort, ☎819-629-3222 or 800-463-6769)*, which was in service from 1720 to 1902, commemorates the important role the fur trade played in the Canadian economy. From the North West Company and the French regime to the Hudson's Bay Company, Fort-Témiscamingue was a meeting point for different cultures and religions—that is to say, between Europeans and First Nations peoples.

An interpretive centre showcases a collection of regional archaeological artifacts, placing them within a historical framework, while an outdoor interpretive tour takes visitors to the site of various scenographies, which are scenic reproductions of the location and function of the former trading post's buildings. Right nearby stands the captivating "enchanted forest," studded with eastern thujas deformed by the harsh winters. Bordered by majestic Lac Témiscamingue, this coniferous forest has borne witness to several thousand years of history.

Follow Rte. 101 S. to Témiscaming.

Témiscaming (pop. 2,883)

This one-industry town was founded in 1917 by the Riordon paper company. The result was a "new town" along the lines of the British garden cities. The pretty homes are mostly Arts & Crafts in style; note the attractive, but somewhat out-of-place, marble fountain in the residential area.

Paper and carboard production are demystified at the **Tembec factory** ★ *(free admission; Mon-Fri 9am to 3pm, reservations required 24hrs in advance; 33 Rue Kipawa, ☎819-796-3329)*.

Parks

Tour A: Abitibi

Parc National d'Aiguebelle ★★ *($3.50; &; 1737 Rang Hudon, Mont-Brun, ☎819-637-7322 or 800-665-6527, www.sepaq.com)* covers 243km². In addition to many lakes and rivers, the park features the region's highest hills. Several outdoor activities are possible, including canoeing, fishing, cycling and hiking (69km) during the summer, and cross-country skiing (35km) and snowshoeing during the winter.

The **Réserve Faunique La Vérendrye** ★★ *(reception at northern entrance; ☎819-736-7431; you can also get information from the Sépaq: ☎819-354-4392 or 800-665-6527, www.sepaq. com)* covers 13,615km², making this wildlife reserve the second-largest natural area in Québec. There are three entrances: the north entrance, which is 60km south of Val-d'Or, the Domaine, which is indicated on the TransCanada Highway, and an entrance to the south. At the Domaine there is a gas station, garage, convenience store, restaurant and a place to rent boats and cottages. Picnic tables are set up by the lake. Every summer, enthusiasts flock here to canoe, camp, fish and cycle. This is one of Québec's most popular canoe-camping locations and a number of routes have been mapped out.

Outdoor Activities

In terms of tourism, Abitibi-Témiscamingue is still uncharted territory, so modern explorers will discover incredible richness, abundant unspoiled places and a seemingly infinite number of waterways. Although hunters and fishers have been coming to these fertile forests and waters for years, there's a lot more to this region than game and fish. Countless adventures await, from the simple to the extreme, in the untamed spaces and on the rivers and lakes.

■ Aboriginal Adventure Packages

Tour A: Abitibi

Société de Développement Économique AMIK
10 Rue Tom Rankin, Pikogan
☎ (819) 732-3350
www.pikogan.com
Winner of the 2000 award for outdoor and adventure tourism, the AMIK Economic Development Service offers customized excursion packages on the Harricana River. Aboriginal guides offer participants the chance to experience the Algonquin way of life as it was during the time of the great Aboriginal canoe expeditions. Excursionists will also get the opportunity to sample traditional food and spend the night in a tipi or at a campsite. Reservations are required at least one week in advance. The excursion costs about $100 per person, but varies according to the package.

Tour B: Témiscamingue

Association Faunique Kipawa
7C Rue des Oblats Nord, Ville-Marie
☎ (819) 629-2002
▤ (819) 629-3285
The Kipawa wildlife association manages the ZEC (controlled zone of exploitation) in the Témiscamingue region (2,500km²) with regard to hunting, fishing, wilderness camping and outfitters. The ZEC's territory includes four outfitters that offer clients a range of activities depending on the season and the package chosen. For information on current rates, activities and regulations, contact the Kipawa association. Note that wilderness camping is free.

■ Adventure Packages

Tour A: Abitibi

ÉCOaventures
99 5ᵉ Avenue Est, La Sarre
☎ (819) 339-3300 or 866-326-9453
www.ecoaventures.ca
ÉCOaventures organizes several activities to promote the area's natural environment, including the Raid des Conquérants mountain-bike race and the Traversée de la Baie James and Traversée du Lac Abitibi Nordic ski races. Winter-sports equipment can also be rented here.

Wawatè *(104 Avenue Perreault, Val-d'Or,* ☎*819-824-7652 or 825-9518, www.aubergeorpailleur.com)* is an Algonquin word meaning "northern lights." This establishment is located at L'Orpailleur and offers all kinds of outdoor activities focusing on the natural and human riches of the Abitibi-Témiscamingue region.

■ Cross-Country Skiing

Tour A: Abitibi

Camp Dudemaine *($6; mid-Dec to mid-Apr every day 10am to 5pm; Rte. 395, Amos,* ☎*819-732-2781)* offers 22km of trails, a waxing room, ski rental and a restaurant. Both the skating and standard techniques are practized here. In the summer the trails are used for hiking and mountain biking.

The **Centre Quatre-Saisons Mont-Vidéo** *(every day 9:30am to 5pm; Chemin Mont-Vidéo, Barraute,* ☎*819-734-3193)* ski resort maintains 10km of cross-country ski trails. A restaurant and a waxing room can be found on site.

The **Club de Ski de Fond de Val-d'Or** *($7; Mon, Wed, Thu and Fri 10am to 8pm; Tue 10am to 7pm; Sat and Sun 9am to 5pm; Chemin de l'Aéroport, Val-d'Or,* ☎*819-825-4398)* has 40km of trails, including an "international" trail with lights (4km). There's a waxing room, a rental shop, a heated hut and a snack bar.

■ Cycling

Tour A: Abitibi

A 5km bike trail runs between Amos and La Ferme *(May 15th to August 30th, every day 9am to 9pm)*, an outdoor activity centre for the whole family. The forest trail features several rest stops and a lookout provides a magnificent view of the surrounding area. The trailhead is located at the intersection of Route 111 Ouest and Chemin du Cimetière in Amos and can also be run in the opposite direction, starting out at the La Ferme municipal campgrounds.

At **Parc Linéaire Rouyn-Noranda–Taschereau** *(100 Avenue du Lac, Rouyn-Noranda,* ☎*819-762-0500 or 866-306-0500, www.groupevelo. com)*, a 71km trail takes cyclists (or snowmobilers in winter) from Rouyn-Noranda to Taschereau.

Bicycle Rental

Autopro Les P'tits Roberge
$15/day
67 Rue Ste-Anne, Ville-Marie
☎ (819) 629-2548

■ Fishing and Hunting

Tour A: Abitibi

Hunting and fishing rule in this realm of lakes and rivers, wide-open spaces and endless forests. The outfitter **Pourvoirie du Balbuzard Sauvage** *(Trévet Lake, Senneterre,* ☎*819-737-8681, www.balbuzard.com)* was awarded a Québec tourism prize for the excellence of its restaurant and the comfort of its facilities. Its rates depend on the season and activity.

The **Pourvoirie du Lac Faillon** *(Senneterre,* ☎*819-737-4429, www.pourvoiriedulacfaillon. com)* is another very popular outfitter offering hunting and fishing. It also boasts a lovely beach.

Tour B: Témiscamingue

The internationally renowned **Réserve Beauchêne** *(*☎*819-627-3865 or 888-627-3865,*

www.beauchene.com) offers sport fishing with a twist: the fish must be thrown back into the water. Superior quality fishing is guaranteed. The rooms, furthermore, are very comfortable, and the restaurant has an excellent reputation.

■ Hiking

Tour A: Abitibi

Parc National d'Aiguebelle *(*☎*819-637-7322)* is a local favourite hiking spot. It covers some of the Canadian Shield's oldest landscapes.

In the Rouyn-Noranda region, hikers can head to the Kekeko hills, located 11km out of town. Parking is available off Route 391. Eight trails lead hikers through a gorgeous natural environment with rock shelters, stunning observation decks and splendid waterfalls. A trail guide is sold *($5)* at **Maison Dumulon** (see p 292) and in local bookstores.

Tour B: Témiscamingue

The **Sentier de la Grande Chute** trail starts off 10km north of Témiscaming. It provides interesting views of the Kipawa river and its waterfalls, rapids and potholes.

■ Snowmobiling

This region is a veritable paradise for snowmobilers in winter, as 3,540km of snowmobile trails cover the most beautiful areas of Abitibi-Témiscamingue. With the abundant snow, mild weather (cold but never damp) and the warm welcome from the people in the area, those who appreciate enchanting landscapes and nordic adventures are sure to be satisfied.

Location Blais
280 Avenue Larivière, Rouyn-Noranda
☎ (819) 797-9292

Moto Sport du Cuivre
175 Boulevard Évain Est, Évain
☎ (819) 768-5611

Accommodations

Tour A: Abitibi

Val-d'Or

Camping Sagittaire
$
451 Chemin Lac-Lemoyne
☎ (819) 829-4011
This campground has approximately 100 campsites.

Auberge de l'Orpailleur
$$ bkfst incl.
104 Avenue Perreault
☎ (819) 825-9518
🖷 (819) 824-7653
www.aubergeorpailleur.com
The Auberge de l'Orpailleur, located in the mining village of Bourlamaque, was once a bunkhouse for unmarried miners. Not only is the place of historical interest, but its rooms are also attractively decorated,

each in its own style. The warm welcome and generous breakfasts make for an unforgettable stay. The owner of the inn also runs an outfit that offers adventure packages (**Wawatè**, see p 295).

Motel L'Escale Hôtel Suite
$$-$$$
≡ 🖈 ⚏ ◎
1100 Rue de l'Escale
☎ (819) 824-2711 or 800-567-6572
🖷 (819) 825-2145
www.lescale.qc.ca
L'Escale is a comfortable place with lots of atmosphere.

Val-Senneville

Au Soleil Couchant
$$-$$$ bkfst incl.
sb
301 Val-du-Repos
☎ (819) 856-8150
🖷 (819) 874-0426
This establishment's five rooms are all marvellously decorated. Guests are treat-

ed to a delicious breakfast and get to relax in the whirlpool tub, go for a swim on the private beach or enjoy the view from one of three terraces that overlook Lac Blouin. The perfect stop for travellers who want to relax and recharge their batteries.

Amos

L'Aubergine
$
May to Oct
pb/sb
762 10ᵉ Avenue Ouest
☎ (819) 732-4418
L'Aubergine is a large residence that has a sitting room with a fireplace and a lovely terrace.

Hotel-Motel Amosphère
$$-$$$
≡ 🖈 ◎ ❄ ⚏ ⦚
1031 Rte. 111 Est
☎ (819) 732-7777 or 800-567-7777
🖷 (819) 732-5555
www.amosphere.com
Hotel-Motel Amosphère is a hotel complex that pro-

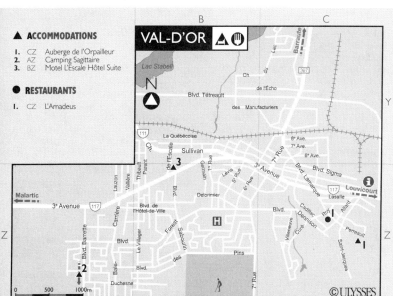

▲ ACCOMMODATIONS
1. CZ Auberge de l'Orpailleur
2. AZ Camping Sagittaire
3. BZ Motel L'Escale Hôtel Suite

● RESTAURANTS
1. CZ L'Amadeus

Abitibi-Témiscamingue – Accommodations - Abitibi

ROUYN-NORANDA

ACCOMMODATIONS
1. BY Hôtel Albert
2. BY Hôtel-Motel de Ville
3. CY Le Passant B&B

RESTAURANTS
1. BY OeufOrie
2. BY Olive et Basil

---

vides high-class accommodation; in the evening the dining room offers steak and seafood specialities. Amosphère is also a stopover for snowmobilers in the winter, and offers heated garages for snowmobiles. It also has a lively dance club frequented by Abitibi-Témiscamingue's night owls.

natural setting to get away from it all. The inn features three comfortable rooms, while the numerous services (including balneotherapy and three types of massages) are sure to leave guests feeling well-rested and rejuvenated. Several health packages are offered, for one or several overnight stays.

Located on the way into La Sarre, the Motel Le Bivouac has an unusual characteristic: the rooms are dedicated to the soldiers who served under Montcalm during the battle on the Plains of Abraham (1759), who have had townships and certain Abitibi-Temiscamingue municipalities named after them. The place is lovely.

Preissac

Le Héron Bleu
$$
sb ☙ ⫸
40 Chemin de la Baie
☎ (819) 759-4772
This health centre provides guests with a spectacular

La Sarre

Motel Le Bivouac
$$
≡ ❋
637 2ᵉ Rue Est
☎/🖶 (819) 333-2241
www.motellebivouac.com

Motel Villa Mon Repos
$$
≡ ⛵ ❋ ⫸
32 Rte. 111 Est
☎ (819) 333-2224 or 888-417-3767
🖶 (819) 333-9106
www.motelvillamonrepos.qc.ca
The biggest hotel in the La Sarre area, the Motel Villa Mon Repos offers a var-

iety of rooms close to the centre of town.

Rouyn-Noranda

Le Passant B&B
$-$$ bkfst incl.
pb/sb
489 Rue Perreault Est
☎ (819) 762-9827
▤ (819) 762-3820
www.lepassant.com
Four charming rooms (one with a private bathroom and three with shared bathrooms) await visitors at the friendly Le Passant Bed and Breakfast. Renowned for the quality of its meals, Mr. Michel Bellehumeur's establishment offers guests a fortifying breakfast made of garden-fresh products.

Hotel-Motel de Ville
$$-$$$ bkfst incl.
≡ ⚓ ♨
95 Avenue Horne
☎ (819) 762-0725 or 888-828-0725
▤ (819) 762-7243
The Hotel-Motel de Ville offers comfortable, reasonably priced rooms. Every room also offers Internet access.

Hôtel Albert
$$-$$$
≡ ♨
84 Avenue Principale
☎ (819) 762-3545 or 888-725-2378
▤ (819) 762-7157
The Hôtel Albert, located downtown, is a real bargain. Its convenient location, impeccable service and simple yet comfortable rooms make this a reliable option in town.

Tour B:
Témiscamingue

Ville-Marie

Gîte Touristique Marcelle Aubry
$ bkfst incl.
≋
341 Route 101 Sud
☎ (819) 629-3360
Marcelle Aubry's bed and breakfast provides comfortable accommodations. Guests can choose from one of four rooms, including a double room, and can enjoy a private living room, a pool and a terrace.

Motel Caroline
$$
≡ ⚓ ♨
2 Chemin de Fabre
☎ (819) 629-2965
▤ (819) 629-3363
Motel Caroline has 16 simple rooms, some with a lovely view of Lac Témiscamingue. Good value.

Laniel

Chalets Pointe-aux-Pins
$$$$$
🍴 ⌂
3 chalets with 1 to 3 rooms with a maximum capacity of 15 people
1955 Chemin du Ski
☎/▤ (819) 634-5211
www.temiscamingue.net/pointe-aux-pins
The Chalets Pointe-aux-Pins overlook Kipawa Lake and are located on the former site of a field entomology station where novelist Margaret Atwood's father once worked. Guests who rent these attractively decorated cottages can enjoy the restful country setting and practice several outdoor activities in the area.

Témiscaming

Auberge Témiscaming
$$
≡ ⚓ ♨ ❄
1431 Chemin Kipawa
☎ (819) 627-3476 or 800-304-9469
▤ (819) 627-1387
www.auberge-temis.com
The Auberge Témiscaming has a solid reputation in these parts. Its modern decor and courteous service have earned it regional prizes. Avoid the rooms near the staircases; they can be noisy.

Restaurants

Tour A: Abitibi

Amos

Café Folie
$
11 1re Avenue Ouest
☎ (819) 727-2848
Excellent coffee and tasty sandwiches are served in a modern, tasteful decor. The perfect spot for a quick lunch or a yummy desert.

Restaurant Le Moulin
$$$
100 1re Avenue Ouest
☎ (819) 732-8271
Restaurant Le Moulin prepares refined French and local cuisine. Be sure to try the trout, which will delight the most demanding of palates.

Rouyn-Noranda

OeufOrie
$
33 Rue Perreault Est
☎ (819) 797-4867

Located in the town centre, this eatery has an original breakfast menu, offering lavish little dishes such as omelets, stuffed crepes and traditional eggs with home fries and choice meats. Modern, pleasant ambiance.

Olive et Basil
$-$$
164A Rue Perreault Est
☎ (819) 797-6655
A breath of fresh air for jaded palates, Olive et Basil offers a delicious, reasonably priced table d'hôte. The menu is composed of delectable Mediterranean specialties.

Val-d'Or

L'Amadeus
$$
166 Avenue Perreault
☎ (819) 825-7204
L'Amadeus serves excellent French cuisine. The service is impeccable and the decor very pleasant.

- - - - - - - - - - - - - - - -

Tour B:
Témiscamingue

Ville-Marie

Brassette 101
$-$$
38 Rue des Oblats Nord
Brassette 101 serves simple, generous meals in a warm environment. Nothing fancy, just tasty, honest pub fare such as chicken, pizza, steak and a variety of daily specials.

Restaurant-Bar La Bannik
$$
862 Chemin du Vieux-Fort
☎ (819) 622-0922

Restaurant-Bar La Bannik is set on a hill that overlooks the Fort-Témiscamingue-Duhamel National Historic Site. A terrace provides an exceptional view of the surroundings. Unfortunately, the food doesn't quite match up to the view.

Entertainment

■ Bars and Nightclubs

Rouyn-Noranda

Cabaret de la Dernière Chance
146 8ᵉ Avenue
☎ (819) 762-9222
The "last chance saloon" is a good spot for a night out among friends.

Val d'Or

Super Club Le Vegas
784 3ᵉ Avenue
☎ (819) 825-9417
If you're a billiards or bowling enthusiast, head to Super Club Le Vegas. You can also dance to the latest hits on the bar's large dance floor.

■ Festivals and Cultural Events

Rouyn-Noranda

During the non-competitive **Festival du Cinéma International en Abitibi-Témiscamingue** *(late Oct;* ☎*819-762-6212, www.lino.com/festivaldu cinema)*, films from various countries make their North American (and sometimes even world) premieres.

Shopping

■ Art Galleries and Native Art

Rouyn-Noranda

Makonigan
153 Avenue Principale
☎ (819) 764-9497
Makonigan is a small Native arts and crafts shop that sells traditional objects from across Canada. The prices are reasonable and the shop's owner is a good source of information on Algonquin culture.

Val-d'Or

Boutique Wachiya
145 Avenue Perreault
☎ (819) 825-0434
The Wachiya shop offers a fine range of traditional Cree arts and crafts for all tastes and budgets. The dream-catchers and moccasins here are particularly refined.

■ Chocolate

Ville-Marie

Les Chocolats Martine
$2 guided tour (reservations required)
5 Rue Sainte-Anne
☎ (819) 622-0146
www.chocolatmartine.com
The 30min guided tour of this small chocolate shop and its adjacent small-scale factory offers chocoholics an opportunity to discover the many fascinating secrets behind the chocolate-making process. The tour ends on a high note with a sampling of treats. Reservations required at least one week in advance.

Mauricie and Centre-du-Québec

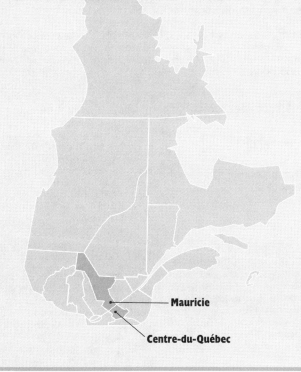

Mauricie

Centre-du-Québec

Forming a north-south axis located about halfway between Montréal and Québec City, the two regions of Mauricie and Centre-du-Québec feature the three types of terrain that make up the province: the Canadian Shield, the St. Lawrence plains and the Appalachian Mountain range.

The city of Trois-Rivières, the second city founded in New France (1634), is generally considered the heart of Mauricie. First a fur-trading post, it became an industrial centre with the founding of the Saint-Maurice ironworks in 1730.

Further up the Rivière Saint-Maurice, the town of Shawinigan serves as a centre for the production of hydroelectric power. To the north lies a vast untamed expanse of lakes, rivers and forests. This land of hunting and fishing also contains the magnificent La Mauricie National Park, reserved for outdoor activities such as canoeing and camping.

To the south of the St. Lawrence River lie the rural zones of Centre-du-Québec. Opened up very early to colonization, the land is still divided according to the old seigneurial system. In the extreme south of the region, the gently rolling hills of this countryside herald the Appalachian Mountains.

Getting There and Getting Around

Two tours are suggested, one for the north shore of the St. Lawrence, the other for the south: **Tour A: Mauricie ★ ★ and Tour B: Centre-du-Québec ★**.

■ By Car

Tour A: Mauricie

From Montréal, take Aut. 40 (Aut. Félix-Leclerc), followed by Aut. 55 S. for a short while, and then turn onto Rte. 138 E. as far as Trois-Rivières. Take Boulevard Royal and continue along Rue Notre-Dame to the downtown area. This part of town is best visited on foot.

Next, you'll drive inland to Saint-Tite on Rte. 159 then head to Grand-Mère on Rte. 153. Once at Grand-Mère, those who want to explore the Haute-Mauricie (Upper Mauricie) can make a detour to La Tuque on the 155. To continue the main tour, stay on the 153, which leads through the Shawinigan region, among others. The portion of the tour between Trois-Rivières and Sainte-Anne-de-la-Pérade, which runs along Rte. 138 E., can be incorporated into an excursion along the St. Lawrence and up to Québec City.

From Montréal, it is also possible to get to Trois-Rivières via the south shore of the St. Lawrence on Aut. 20. You can also take the Chemin du Roy (Rte. 138), which leads to Québec City. The first road suitable for motor vehicles in Canada, the Chemin du Roy is the scenic route, with views of the countryside and the river. On the other hand, it takes quite a bit longer, so your decision will have to be based on how much time you have.

Tour B: Centre-du-Québec

This tour focuses on the St. Lawrence plains, where the main towns of the region are located. From Montréal or from Québec City, take Aut. 40 and then Aut. 55 S. Cross the Pont Laviolette in Trois-Rivières.

Opened in 1967, this bridge is the only one that links the two shores between Montréal and Québec City. Once across, take Rte. 132 E. to Deschaillons. From there, follow Rte. 256 to Plessisville, then Rte. 116 to Victoriaville. Rte. 122 W. will take you to Drummondville. Complete the loop by taking Rtes. 255, 226 and then 132 Est. Note that the region is easily accessible via Aut. 20 as well.

Mauricie and Centre-du-Québec

By Boat

Tour A: Mauricie

There is a pleasant and relatively fast way to get to Trois-Rivières from Montréal or Québec City: by boat with **Les Dauphins du Saint-Laurent**, (*514-288-4499 or 877-648-4499, www.dauphins.ca)*. The boat drop passengers off in the heart of Vieux-Trois-Rivières.

Bus Stations

Tour A: Mauricie

Trois-Rivières
275 Rue St. Georges
(819) 374-2944

Grand-Mère
800 6ᵉ Avenue
(819) 533-5565

Shawinigan
1563 Boulevard Saint-Sacrement
(819) 539-5144

Tour B: Centre-du-Québec

Victoriaville
475 Boulevard Jutras Est
(819) 752-5400

Drummondville
330 Rue Heriot
(819) 477-2111 or 472-5252

Train Stations

Tour A: Mauricie

La Tuque
550 Rue Saint-Louis
(819) 523-3257

Shawinigan
1560 Chemin du CN
(819) 537-9007

Tour B: Centre-du-Québec

Drummondville
263 Rue Lindsay
(819) 472-5383

Useful Information

Tourist Information

Tour A: Mauricie

Tourisme Mauricie
777 4ᵉ Rue, Shawinigan, G9N 1H1
(819) 536-3334 or 800-567-7603
(819) 536-3373
www.icimauricie.com

Chambre de Commerce de Trois-Rivières
168 Rue Bonaventure, Trois-Rivières, G9A 2B1
(819) 375-9628

Office de Tourisme et de Congrès de Trois-Rivières
1457 Rue Notre-Dame
(819) 375-1122 or 800-313-1123
(819) 375-0022

Tour B: Centre-du-Québec

Tourisme Centre-du-Québec
20 Boulevard Carignan Ouest, Princeville, G6L 4M4
(819) 364-7177 or 888-816-4007
www.tourismecentreduquebec.com

Bécancour
3689 Boulevard Bécancour
(819) 298-2070 or 866-441-0404
www.cldbecancour.qc.ca

Bois-Francs
231-A Rue Notre-Dame Est, Victoriaville, G6P 4A2
(819) 758-9451 or 888-758-9451
www.tourismeboisfrancs.com

Drummondville
1350 Rue Michaud
(819) 477-5529 or 877-235-9569
www.tourisme-drummond.com

Nicolet-Yamaska
20 Rue Notre-Dame, Nicolet, J3T 1G0
(450) 293-6960 or 866-279-0444
www.tourismenicolet-yamaska.net

Mauricie and Centre-du-Québec - Useful Information

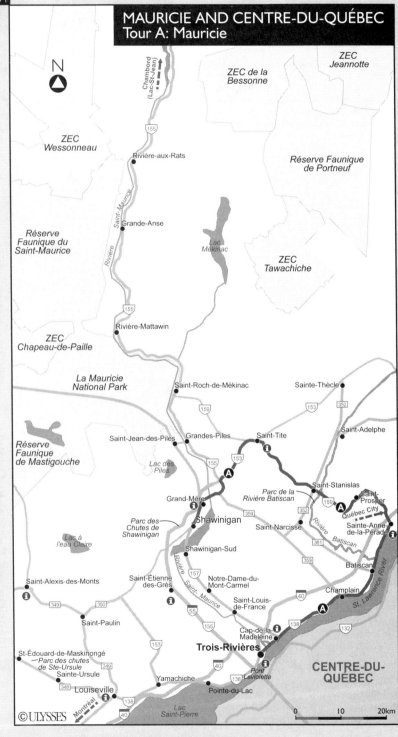

MAURICIE AND CENTRE-DU-QUÉBEC
Tour A: Mauricie

Exploring

- -

Tour A: Mauricie
★ ★

 2 to 3 days

The valley of the Rivière Saint-Maurice is located halfway between Montréal and Québec City, on the north shore of the St. Lawrence River. The cradle of Canada's first major industry, Mauricie has always been an industrial region. Its towns feature fine examples of architecture from Québec's industrial revolution. Nevertheless, the vast countryside surrounding the towns remains primarily an area of mountain wilderness covered in dense forest, perfect for hunting, fishing, camping and hiking.

Trois-Rivières ★ ★ (pop. 125,086)

The appearance of Trois-Rivières, once similar to Vieux-Québec, was completely changed by a fire in June 1908. Now, it resembles more a town of the American Midwest.

Often considered simply a place to stop for a break between Montréal and Québec, Trois-Rivières is unfortunately underestimated by most tourists. However, it remains a city redolent with Old World charm, with its many cafés, restaurants and bars on Rue des Forges, and the terrace overlooking the St. Lawrence River.

Located at the confluence of the St. Lawrence and Saint-Maurice rivers, where the latter divides into three branches, giving the town its name, Trois-Rivières was founded in 1634 by Sieur de Laviolette. From the outset, the town was surrounded by a stone wall that now marks the city's historic area.

In the 17th century, there were three regional governments in the St. Lawrence valley apart from the Governor of New France: that of Québec City, Montréal, and Trois-Rivières. More modest than its two sister cities, the latter boasted a population of a mere 600 and a total of 110 houses. The real boom took place in the middle of the 19th century with the advent of the pulp and paper industry. For a time, Trois-Rivières was the world's leading paper producer.

Park near the intersection of Notre-Dame and Laviolette streets. Walk up Rue Bonaventure (one street west of Laviolette) as far as the old Manoir de Boucher-de-Niverville, now the tourist information centre.

The **Manoir Boucher-de-Niverville** ★ *(free admission; Mon-Fri 8:30am to 4:30pm; 168 Rue Bonaventure, ☎819-375-9628)* was fortunately spared in the 1908 fire. It is a unique example of 17th-century architecture, with few adaptations to the local environment. Inside the manor are a display of antique furniture and a diorama on local history.

A statue of Maurice Le Noblet Duplessis (1890-1959), Premier of Québec from 1936 to 1939, and from 1944 to 1959, stands in front of the manor. Duplessis was a conservative whose power was closely linked to the Catholic clergy of the time. His term of office is often referred to as the great darkness that preceded the Quiet Revolution. His former home can still be seen at 240 Rue Bonaventure, on one of the more posh streets in Trois-Rivières.

Cross Rue Hart and walk along Parc Champlain to the cathedral.

The **Cathédrale de l'Assomption** ★ *(Mon-Sat 9am to 11:30am and 2pm to 6pm, Sun 9:30am to 11:30am and 2pm to 6pm; guided tours on the first Sun of each month; 362 Rue Bonaventure ☎819-374-2409)* was built in 1858 according to the plans of architect Victor Bourgeau, well known for the many churches he designed in the Montréal region. The cathedral's massive Gothic Revival style is vaguely reminiscent of London's Westminster Abbey, also designed in the mid-19th century. Guido Nincheri's stained-glass windows, executed between 1923 and 1934, are certainly the most interesting element of what is otherwise an austere interior.

At the other end of Parc Champlain is Trois-Rivière's modern **Hôtel de Ville** (city hall; 1965) and the **Maison de la Culture ★ ★** *(1425 Place de l'Hôtel-de-Ville)*, which houses the **Bibliothèque Gatien-Lapointe** (library), the **Centre d'Exposition Raymond-Lasnier** (art gallery) and the **Salle de Spectacle Anaïs-Allard Rousseau** (theatre and concert hall).

Mauricie and Centre-du-Québec - Exploring - Mauricie

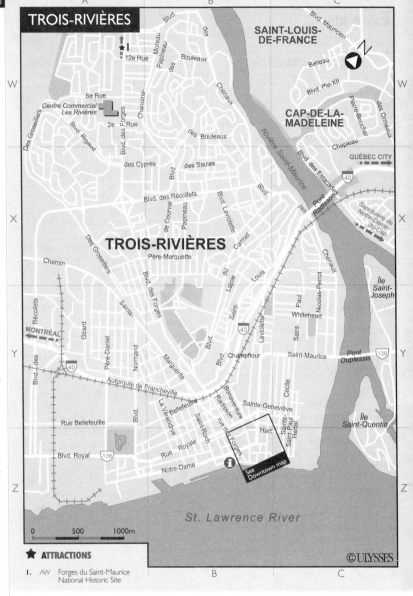

TROIS-RIVIÈRES

SAINT-LOUIS-
DE-FRANCE

CAP-DE-LA-
MADELEINE

QUÉBEC CITY

Rivière Saint-Maurice

TROIS-RIVIÈRES

Père-Marquette

Île
Saint-
Joseph

MONTRÉAL

Pont
Duplessis

Île
Saint-Quentin

See
Downtown map

St. Lawrence River

0   500   1000m

© ULYSSES

★ ATTRACTIONS

1. AW   Forges du Saint-Maurice
         National Historic Site

Retrace your steps down Rue Bonaventure and turn left on Rue Hart.

South of Rue Hart is the **Musée Québécois de Culture Populaire ★ ★** (*$6.50, $9.50 including admission to the prison; Sep to May Tue-Sun 10am to 5pm; Jun to Aug every day 9:30am to 6:30pm; 200 Rue Laviolette,* ☎*819-372-0406, www.culturepop.qc.ca*). The museum provides an interesting overview of Québec popular culture, from its social context and products to its unique traits and heritage. The permanent exhibit presents historically significant everyday objects and various temporary exhibits cover different themes associated with Québec popular culture.

The **Vieille Prison de Trois-Rivières ★** has been restored to welcome visitors and allow them to see how prisoners lived here

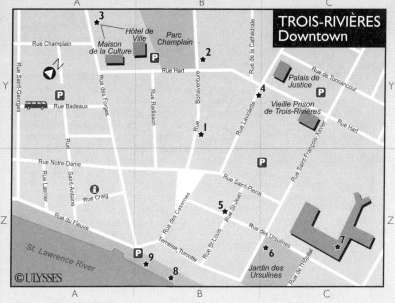

Mauricie and Centre-du-Québec - Exploring - Mauricie

★ ATTRACTIONS

1.	BY	Manoir Boucher-de-Niverville
2.	BY	Cathédrale de l'Assomption
3.	AY	Hôtel de Ville and Maison de la Culture
4.	BY	Musée Québécois de Culture Populaire
5.	BZ	Manoir de Tonnancour
6.	CZ	Couvent des Récollets
7.	CZ	Monastère and Musée des Ursulines
8.	BZ	Parc Portuaire
9.	BZ	Centre d'Exposition sur l'Industrie des Pâtes et Papiers

in the 1960s and 1970s. Guided tours are provided by ex-inmates, making for a very authentic experience.

Turn right on Rue Saint-Pierre and then left at Place Pierre-Boucher. Walk up Rue des Ursulines, the only street to have been spared from the fire of 1908.

The **Manoir de Tonnancour** *(free admission; Tue-Fri 10am to noon and 1:30pm to 5pm, Sat and Sun 1pm to 5pm; guided tours by reservation, $2/pers.; 864 Rue des Ursulines,* ☎*819-374-2355)* was built in 1725 for René Godefroy de Tonnancour, Lord of Pointe-du-Lac and the King's prosecutor. After successive 19th-century incarnations as a fire station, a presbytery and a school, it is today an art gallery, the **Galerie d'Art du Parc**. The Place d'Armes is located opposite the manor.

The former **Couvent des Récollets** ★ *(811 Rue des Ursulines)* is the only Récollet convent still standing in Québec. The building has been preserved thanks to its conversion into an Anglican church following the demise of the last member of the Trois-

Rivières branch of the Récollet Order in 1776.

The **Monastère** and **Musée des Ursulines** ★ *($3; Mar and Apr Wed-Sun 1pm to 5pm, May to early Nov Tue-Fri 9am to 5pm, Sat and Sun 1pm to 5pm, Nov to Feb by appointment only; 734 Rue des Ursulines,* ☎*819-375-7922)* is where the Ursulines first settled in 1697, in the house of Claude de Ramezay, who left Trois-Rivières after being named Governor of Montréal. The museum presents thematic displays featuring items from the collection of the Ursulines (paintings, liturgical garments, needlework, etc.).

Walk across the lovely park in front of the Monastère des Ursulines to Terrasse Turcotte and Parc Portuaire.

In the port area, **Parc Portuaire** *(&; along the St. Lawrence River)*, formerly known as Terrasse Turcotte, was, until the 1920s, the favourite meeting place of the local upper class. It later fell into disrepair, and was replaced by a new, tiered terrace between 1986 and 1990. Now the starting point for mini-cruises on the St. Lawrence, it also features a café and an exhibit on the pulp and paper industry.

The pulp and paper industry was the main economic activity in the Mauricie for many years and still occupies a prominent place in the lives of the people of the region. It's not surprising, then, that the **Centre d'Exposition sur l'Industrie des Pâtes et Papiers** *($3; early Jun to early Sep every day 9am to 6pm, Sep Mon-Fri 9am to 5pm, Sat and Sun 11am to 5pm; 800 Parc Portuaire, facing Rue des Forges,* ☎*819-372-4633)* is located here. Situated in the lovely harbour park, the centre has a permanent exposition describing all the facets of the pulp and paper industry, as well as the way in which it influenced the development of the region. A guided tour is recommended to get the most out of your visit, since the models are rather dull without any explanation.

The Forges Saint-Maurice are 10km from downtown along Boulevard des Forges.

The **Forges du Saint-Maurice National Historic Site** ★★ *($4, guided tours; mid-May to late Aug, every day 9:30am to 5pm; Sep and Oct 9:30am to 4pm; reservations required for groups; 10000 Boulevard des Forges,* ☎*819-378-5116)* is known in French as the "Lieu Historique National Les Forges du Saint-Maurice." These ironworks began in 1730, when Louis XV granted permission to François Poulin de Francheville to work the rich veins of iron-ore that lay under his land. The presence of dense wood lots from which charcoal is made, limestone, and a swift-running waterway, favoured the production of iron. The workers of this first Canadian ironworks mostly came from Burgundy and Franche-Comté in France. They were kept busy making cannons for the king and wood-burning stoves for his subjects in New France.

After the British Conquest (1760), the plant passed into the hands of the British colonial government, who in turn ceded it to a private enterprise. The works were in use until 1883. At that time, the plant included the smelter and forges, as well as the Grande Maison, the foreman's house, at the centre of a worker's village. Following the 1908 fire, the residents of Trois-Rivières recuperated the material necessary to rebuild their town from the forge, leaving only the foundations of most buildings. In 1973, Parks Canada acquired the site and

rebuilt the foreman's house to serve as an information centre. They set up a second, very interesting centre on the site of the smelting forge.

Trois-Rivières hosts the **Festival International de la Poésie** (International Poetry Festival) every fall, which has given it the well-deserved title of the poetry capital of Québec. The town had the brilliant idea of building a walkway, which it named "**Promenade de la Poésie**," with 300 plaques featuring excerpts from the works of poets from across Québec

Go back toward Trois-Rivières along Boulevard des Forges. Turn left on Boulevard des Récollets, which then becomes Boulevard des Chenaux. Turn left again on Rte. 138 E., cross the Rivière Saint-Maurice and turn right onto Rue Notre-Dame in Cap-de-la-Madeleine, which is now part of the city of Trois-Rivières.

Cap-de-la-Madeleine

The heartland of Catholicism in North America, Québec is home to a number of major pilgrimage destinations visited every year by millions from all over the world. The **Sanctuaire Notre-Dame-du-Cap** ★★ *(free admission; guided tours for groups upon reservation; 626 Rue Notre-Dame,* ☎*819-374-2441, www.sanctuaire-ndc.ca)*, a shrine under the auspices of the Oblate Missionaries of the Virgin Mary, is consecrated to the worship of the Virgin.

Built between 1714 and 1717, the sanctuary is one of the oldest churches in Canada. Today, visitors meditate before the statue of the Virgin. It is said that in 1888, the statue opened its eyes in front of several witnesses.

Take Notre-Dame Est to Rte. 138 (Boulevard Sainte-Madeleine). Along the way are the villages of Champlain, and then Batiscan, the site of an old presbytery.

Sainte-Anne-de-la-Pérade ★ (pop. 2,170)

In the winter, this pretty farming village hosts a second village that springs up in the middle of the Rivière Sainte-Anne, which runs through the village. Hundreds of multicoloured shacks, heated and lit by electricity, shelter families that come from all over the world to fish for tomcod, also known as *petit poisson des chenaux*, which means "little channel fish." Ice-fishing in Sainte-Anne has become part of Québécois folklore over the years, along with trips to sugar shacks and corn-roasts. The village is dominated by an imposing Gothic Revival church (1855) based on the basilica of Notre-Dame in Montréal.

Take Rte. 159 inland toward Saint-Prosper, Saint-Stanislas and Grand-Mère.

Grand-Mère ★

The town was named after a rock bearing a strong resemblance to the profile of an old woman ("grandmother"). Found on an island in the middle of the Saint-Maurice, the rock was transported piece by piece to a park in downtown Grand-Mère when the hydroelectric dam was constructed in 1913. The town and its neighbour Shawinigan (the two cities merged in recent years and now make up the city of Shawinigan) are good examples of "company towns" where life revolves around one or two factories. The omnipresence of the factories extends to the residential patterns, the towns being divided into two distinct sections, one for management (mostly Anglophone at first) and one for workers (almost exclusively Francophone).

The **Pont de Grand-Mère** ★ (bridge) was built in 1928 across the swift-running Rivière Saint-Maurice by American engineers Robinson and Steinman, who would become famous in the 1950s for their reconstruction of the Brooklyn Bridge in New York and the Mackinac Bridge in Michigan. On the left are the facilities of the Stone Consolidated Company, the descendant of the Laurentide Pulp and Paper. The hydroelectric centre of the vast industrial complex straddles the Saint-Maurice. It was designed in 1914 by New York architect George F. Hardy, who looked to the Cathedral of Albi in France for inspiration.

Chemin Riverside leads to an exclusive residential neighbourhood and an attractive municipal golf course. The sod for the course was taken from the renowned St. Andrews golf course in Scotland. A left on 3ᵉ Avenue leads up a street with charming houses designed for the executives

of the paper companies in the early 20th century. At the corner of 4ᵉ Avenue and 1ʳᵉ Rue is the handsome Anglican Church of St. Stephen by Le Boutillier and Ripley of Boston (1924). Standing opposite, between 5ᵉ and 6ᵉ avenues, is the **Rocher de Grand-Mère** with its famous profile of an old woman.

La Mauricie National Park ★, see p 315.

Réserve Faunique du Saint-Maurice ★, see p 315.

Shawinigan (pop. 52,057)

In 1901, Shawinigan became the first city in Québec to be laid out according to the principles of urban planning, thanks to the powerful Shawinigan Water and Power Company, which supplied electricity to all of Montréal. The name of this hilly town means "portage at the peak" in Algonquian. The town itself was hard hit by the recession of 1989-93, which left indelible marks on its urban landscape: abandoned factories, burnt-out buildings, empty lots and so on. Nevertheless, Shawinigan boasts many architecturally interesting buildings from the first third of the 20th century. Some of its residential streets resemble those of interwar English suburbs.

Inaugurated in the spring of 1997, the **Cité de l'Énergie** ★ ★ *($15; ; mid-Jun to early Jul Tue-Sun 10am to 5pm, mid-Jul to early Sep every day 10am to 6pm, Sep to mid-Oct Tue-Sun 10am to 5pm; 1000 Avenue Melville, ☎819-536-8516 or 866-900-2483)* acquaints visitors, children and adults alike, with the history of industrial development in Québec in general and Mauricie in particular. The hub of this development is the town of Shawinigan, singled out by aluminum factories and electric companies a century ago thanks to the strong currents in the Rivière Saint-Maurice and the 50m-high falls nearby. A huge theme park, the Cité de l'Énergie features several attractions: two hydroelectric power stations, one of which, the Centrale Shawinigan 2, is still in operation; a science pavilion and a 115m-high observation tower, which, needless to say, offers a sweeping view of the area, including the frothy Shawinigan Falls.

The Cité de l'Énergie provides transportation (by trolley or boat) to make it easier

Mauricie and Centre-du-Québec — Exploring - Mauricie

MAURICIE AND CENTRE-DU-QUÉBEC
Tour B: Centre-du-Québec

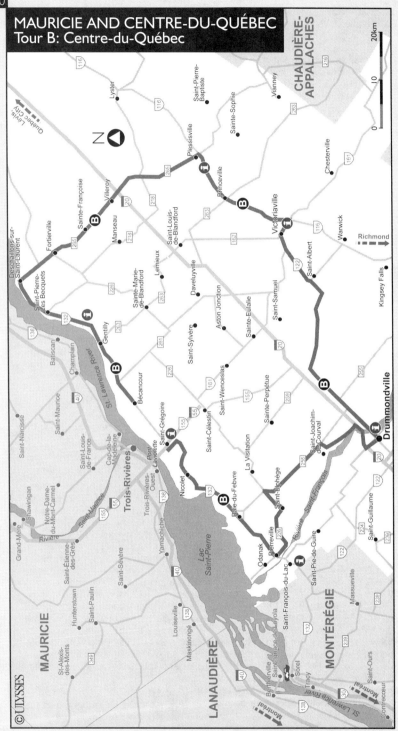

to visit its attractions. A multimedia show is also presented. During your tour of the Cité, you will learn how various regional industries, such as hydroelectricity, pulp and paper, aluminum, etc., have evolved over the past 100 years. The development of innovations that led to scientific advances in these fields is explained step by step. Interactive exhibitions are presented in the Centre des Sciences, which also has a restaurant and a shop.

The Cité de l'Énergie associated itself with the National Gallery of Canada in 2003 to set up the magnificent **Former Shawinigan Aluminum Smelting Complex National Historic Site** ★★ *($15; mid-Jun to late Jun and early Sep to early Oct Tue-Sun 10am to 5pm, late Jun to early Sep every day 10am to 6pm; 1882 Rue Cascade,* ☎*819-537-5300 or 866-900-2483),* where major world-class contemporary art exhibits are presented. The quality and success of recent exhibits bodes well for this impressive brick building's new vocation. With its huge halls and high ceilings, it's perfectly suited for visual arts. The complex was originally built in 1900 and is the oldest aluminum-production facility in North America. It was run by Alcan until 1986, when the company relocated its smelting operations to Shawinigan's industrial park.

Parc des Chutes de Shawinigan ★, see p 315.

Réserve Faunique Mastigouche, see p 315.

Tour B: Centre-du-Québec ★

 1 to 2 days

The population of Centre-du-Québec is a mix of French, British, Acadian and Loyalist colonists. Up until the mid-19th century, there was not much going on here. However, the arrival of the Grand Trunk Railway began a process of industrialization that has yet to taper off. In the course of the last quarter century, some of Canada's largest and most modern factories have been built here. Paradoxically, nothing remains of the railway but the strip of land it occupied. The railbed is now a bike path.

Victoriaville (pop. 40,105)

The economic heartland of the Centre-du-Québec, Victoriaville owes its development to the forestry and steel industries.

Arthabaska ★, the southern portion of Victoriaville, means "place of bulrushes and reeds" in the native language. It has produced or welcomed more than its share of prominent figures in the worlds of art and politics. Its residential sectors have always boasted a refined architecture, notably in the European and American styles. The town is especially known for its Victorian houses, particularly those along Avenue Laurier Ouest. In 1859, Arthabaska became the judicial district of the township. Construction of the courthouse, the prison and the registry office, which would make the fortune of the town, followed. Arthabaska was superseded by Victoriaville at the turn of the 20th century, and though these buildings have now been demolished, it still retains a good part of its Belle Époque charm.

The **Maison Suzor-Coté** *(not open to the public; 846 Boulevard des Bois-Francs Sud)* is the birthplace of landscape painter Marc-Aurèle de Foy Suzor-Coté (1869-1937). His father had built the humble home 10 years earlier. One of Canada's foremost artists, Suzor-Coté began his career decorating churches, including Arthabaska's, before leaving to study at the École des Beaux-Arts in Paris in 1891. After taking first prize at both the Julian and Colarossi academies, he worked in Paris before moving to Montréal in 1907. From then on, he returned annually to the family home, gradually turning it into a studio. His impressionist winter scenes and red summer sunsets are well-known. The house is still a private residence.

Turn right on Rue Laurier Ouest (Rte. 161).

The **Sir Wilfrid Laurier National Historic Site** ★ *($3.50; Jul and Aug Mon-Fri 9am to 5pm, Sat and Sun 1pm to 5pm, Sep to Jun Tue-Fri 9am to noon and 1pm to 5pm, Sat and Sun 1pm to 5pm; 16 Rue Laurier Ouest,* ☎*819-357-8655, www.museelaurier.com)* occupies the house of the first French-Canadian Prime Minister (1896 to 1911), Sir Wilfrid Laurier (1841-1919). Born in Saint-Lin in the Basses-Laurentides, Laurier moved to Arthabaska as soon as he finished his legal studies. His house was turned into a museum in 1929 by two ad-

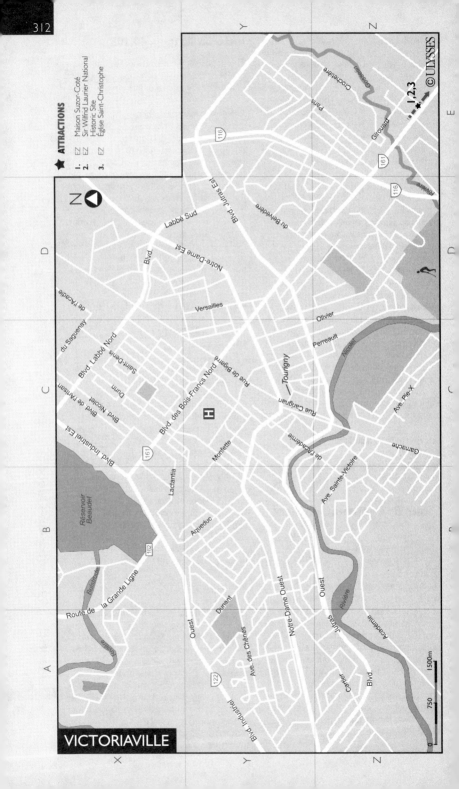

VICTORIAVILLE

★ **ATTRACTIONS**

1. EZ Maison Suzor-Coté
2. EZ Sir Wilfrid Laurier National Historic Site
3. EZ Église Saint-Christophe

© ULYSSES

312

mirers. The ground-floor rooms retain their Victorian furniture, while the second floor is partly devoted to exhibits. Paintings and sculptures by Québec artists encouraged by the Lauriers are on view throughout the house. Of particular interest are the portrait of Lady Laurier by Marc-Aurèle de Foy Suzor-Coté and the bust of Sir Wilfrid Laurier by Alfred Laliberté.

The **Église Saint-Christophe** ★ *(40 Rue Laurier Ouest, ☎819-357-2376)* was designed in 1871 by Joseph-Ferdinand Peachy from Québec City. It is best known for its polychromatic interior, completed by architects Perrault et Mesnard in 1887, and for its decoration by painters Marc-Aurèle de Foy Suzor-Coté and J. O. Rousseau from Saint-Hyacinthe. The church was declared a historic site in 2001.

Drummondville (pop. 65,891)

Drummondville was founded in the wake of the War of 1812 by Frederick George Heriot, who gave it the name of the British Governor of the time, Sir Gordon Drummond. The colony was at first a military outpost on the Rivière Saint-François, but the building of mills and factories soon made it a major industrial centre.

Turn right on Rue Montplaisir.

The **Village Québécois d'Antan** ★★ *($16.95; early Jun to Sep every day 10am to 5:30pm, Sep to mid-Oct Fri-Sun 10am to 5:30pm; 1425 Rue Montplaisir, ☎819-478-1441 or 877-710-0267, www.villagequebecois.com)* traces 100 years of history, from 1810 to 1910. Some 70 colonial-era buildings have been reproduced to evoke the atmosphere of village life during this era. People in period costumes make *ceintures fléchées* (arrow sashes), candles and bread. Many historical television shows are shot on location here.

Continue along the east shore of Rivière Saint-François toward Saint-Joachim-de-Courval. Continue toward Pierreville and the nearby Odanak reserve.

Odanak (pop. 449)

Marguerite Hertel, the owner of the Saint-François seigneury at the beginning of the 18th century, ceded a portion of her land on the east bank of the Saint-François to the government of Trois-Rivières for the creation of an Aboriginal village. The goal of resettling the Abenaki nation of Maine, who were allies of the French, was attained in 1700. Subsequently, at the time of the British conquest in 1759, the village was laid to waste by the British in reprisal. Odanak is still a reserve today.

The **Musée des Abénaquis** ★ *($4; Mon-Fri 10am to 5pm, Sat and Sun 1pm to 5pm, Nov to Apr closed weekends; 108 Waban-Aki, Rte. 132, ☎450-568-2600)* was founded in 1962, and allows visitors to explore Abenaki culture. A permanent exhibit depicts the ancestral way of life of the Abenakis and their relations with the French. The museum's animators bring to life the artifacts on display with traditional songs, legends and dances. The **village church**, with its native carvings, is also well worth a visit.

Continue along Rte. 132 E. to the former village of Saint-Grégoire, now part of Nicolet.

Saint-Grégoire

The **Église Saint-Grégoire** ★★ *(4200 Boulevard Port-Royal)* is located in the middle of the old village of Saint-Grégoire, founded in 1757 by a group of Acadians originally from Beaubassin. The parishioners began the construction of the present church in 1803. Since then the church has been touched up by two famous Québécois architects, Thomas Baillargé, who designed the 1851 neoclassical facade, and Victor Bourgeau, who remodelled the bell towers before decorating the arch of the nave.

In 1811, the church council acquired the precious retable and tabernacle from the Récollet church in Montréal, which used to stand at the corner of Sainte-Hélène and Notre-Dame. Well-placed at Saint-Grégoire, the retable is the oldest in Québec, dating from 1713, and made by Jean-Jacques Bloem, known as Le Blond. The Louis-XIII style tabernacle is a major work executed by the carver Charles Chaboulié in 1703. The paintings by Parisian artist Joseph Uberti are much more recent (circa 1910).

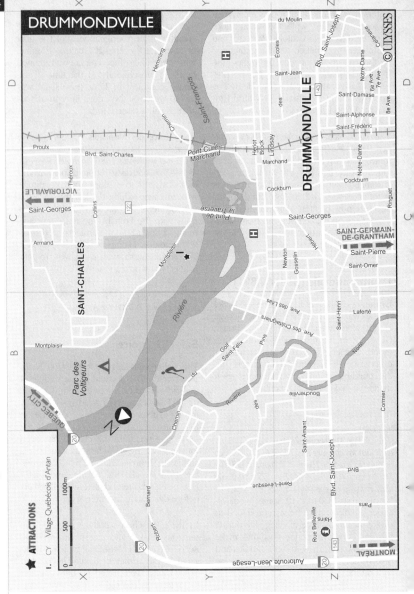

Parks

Tour A: Mauricie

Situated at the mouth of the Rivière Saint-Maurice is the **Parc de l'Île Saint-Quentin** *($3.50; &; every day 9am to 10pm; ☎819-373-8151)*. This island of tranquillity and nature is ideal for strolling or swimming in summer and for skating and cross-country skiing in winter. There are also picnic grounds.

The **Parc de la Rivière-Batiscan** ★ *($5/pers., up to $15/car; early May to mid-Oct every day 9am to 9pm; 200 Chemin du Barrage, Saint-Narcisse, ☎418-328-3599, www.parcbatiscan.com)* is devoted to wildlife conservation and the preservation of natural habitats. It is also a pleasant place for all kinds of activities, from walking and mountain biking to camping and fishing. The park also offers nature and historical tours. In the middle of the park stands one of Québec's first hydroelectric plants; constructed in 1897, the Saint-Narcisse station still provides power.

La Mauricie National Park ★ ★ *($5/person, $12.50/family; ♿; ☎819-538-3232)* is known in French as "Parc National de La Mauricie." It was created in 1970 to preserve a part of the Laurentians. It is the perfect setting for outdoor activities such as canoeing, walking, mountain biking, snowshoeing and cross-country skiing. Hidden among the woods are several lakes and rivers, as well as natural wonders of all kinds. Visitors can stay in dormitories year-round. Reservations can be made at ☎(819) 537-4555.

The **Réserve Faunique du Saint-Maurice ★** *(3773 Rte. 155, Rivière-Mattawin,* ☎819-646-5687) is accessible via a toll bridge *($12)* on the Rivière Saint-Maurice. Covering more than 750km², it includes several hiking trails equipped with huts. In the fall, moose- and game-hunting are allowed. Reservations for campsites and other accommodations: ☎(819) 646-5687.

Parc des Chutes de Shawinigan ★ *(admission fees and schedules vary according to activities;* ☎819-536-0222) is located next to **Cité de l'Énergie** (see p 309) on Route 157. The riverside park's stunning landscape includes two islands on the majestic Saint-Maurice river. It provides a countryside getaway from the nearby town of Shawinigan and attracts many visitors who come here to camp *($17 and up)*, canoe, fish, hike, cycle and enjoy the scenery and wildlife, including some 30 white-tailed deer. The river's falls are only visible during certain parts of the year, especially in spring. An inn is located on Île Melville.

The **Réserve Faunique Mastigouche** *(Rte. 349, St-Alexis-des-Monts,* ☎819-265-2098 or 800-665-6527) covers 1,600km². Dotted with lakes and rivers, it is a prized canoe-camping spot. Hunting and fishing are also allowed. In winter, 180km of cross-country-ski trails and 130km of snowmobile trails are maintained. Visitors can sleep in shelters *(reservations:* ☎819-265-3925) or small chalets

that can accommodate four to eight people *(reservations:* ☎800-665-6527).

Picnic areas and playgrounds can be found at **Parc des Chutes Sainte-Ursule** *($5; every day 10am to 6pm; Route 348, 2575 Rang des Chutes, Ste-Ursule,* ☎819-228-3555 or 800-660-6160), but the 70m-high waterfalls are the main attraction here. Cross-country ski trails are set up in the park in winter.

Tour B: Centre-du-Québec

In 2000, Lac Saint-Pierre was declared a UNESCO Biosphere Reserve. It is now protected by the **Réserve de la Biosphère du Lac Saint-Pierre** *(*☎450-746-9441, www.biospherelac-st-pierre.qc.ca). The largest flood plain, largest rest stop for migrating wildfowl, first spring rest stop for migrating snow geese on the St. Lawrence and largest heron site in North America, Lac Saint-Pierre includes the largest archipelago in the St. Lawrence River (with some 100 islands), 20% of all its marshes and half its wetlands. Here, you can observe rare plants, nearly 300 bird species (over 100 of which are nesting species) and a dozen endangered species.

Outdoor Activities

■ Canoeing

Tour A: Mauricie

La Mauricie National Park is perfect for canoe trips. Strewn with lakes of all sizes, as well as a number of rivers, it has long been renowned among canoe-campers. Let yourself glide down narrow channels from one lake to another beneath luxuriant vegetation, accompanied by friendly water birds. You can rent a boat at the park and plan your own itinerary.

The region's two wildlife reserves, the **Réserve Faunique du Saint-Maurice** and the **Réserve Faunique Mastigouche**, are also good places to explore by canoe.

Mauricie and Centre-du-Québec - Outdoor Activities

Cross-Country Skiing

Tour A: Mauricie

In winter, the **Réserve Faunique Mastigouche** has 200km of well-maintained trails. The **Réserve Faunique du Saint-Maurice** (see p 315) and **La Mauricie National Park** (see p 315) are also lovely places to go cross-country skiing.

Tour B: Centre-du-Québec

Cross-country skiers in the Centre-du-Québec region will enjoy the **Courvalloise** ski trail *(30km; Mon-Fri 9am to 4pm, Sat-Sun 8am to 4pm; 526 Rang Ste-Anne, Saint-Joachim-de-Courval, ☎819-397-2666)*, which follows the Saint-François river. They can also ski through the **Village Québécois d'Antan** (see p 313) on trails maintained by the **Club de Ski de Fond Saint-François** *(☎819-478-5475)*.

Cruises

Tour A: Mauricie

Croisières M/S Jacques-Cartier—M/V Le Draveur
$16
Departures from Parc Portuaire in Trois-Rivières
☎(819) 375-3000 or 800-567-3737
Have a seat aboard a luxury 92-passenger catamaran and enjoy a cruise with commentary on the main points of interest in Trois-Rivières: the port, Laviolette bridge, Pointe des Ormes, Rivière St-Maurice and the archipelago of the Îles Saint-Quentin. Several other longer cruises are also offered.

Cycling

Tour B: Centre-du-Québec

In Québec, more and more bike paths are being laid out where railway lines used to be. One of these is the 77km **Parc Linéaire des Bois-Francs** *(33 Avenue Pie-X, Victoriaville, ☎819-758-6414)*, which runs between Tingwick and Lyster.

The **Circuit des Traditions de la MRC de Drummond** *(La Plaine rest stop, Aut. 20, Exit 179; ☎819-475-1164)* features a 57.5km marked trail along the Route Verte, including 25km in the forest, along a former railroad track. Several tree species embellish this flat region. Don't miss the 7.5km portion of the trail that crosses the Forêt Drummond, along the Saint-François river. A building with a large parking lot has been converted into a rest area for cyclists.

Dogsledding

Tour A: Mauricie

At the **Réserve Faunique du Saint-Maurice**, you can experience the thrill of racing along a snowy trail with a team of dogs at your command. All winter long, this park maintains nearly 270km of marked trails laid out expressly for dogsledding.

Ice Fishing

Tour A: Mauricie

From December to February, thousands of **ice-fishing** enthusiasts converge on the Rivière Sainte-Anne to fish for tomcod. The river is covered with fishing huts in the winter. These can be rented, along with the necessary equipment, from the **Comité de Gestion de la Rivière Sainte-Anne** *(Sainte-Anne-de-la-Pérade, ☎418-325-2475)*, the river's management committee. The price is around $20/pers. per day (maximum four per cabin), and $24 on weekends.

Snowmobiling

Tour A: Mauricie

In winter, the **Réserve Faunique Mastigouche** (see p 315) is a playground for snowmobilers, with 130km of marked trails studded with heated shelters.

Tour B: Centre-du-Québec

The Centre-du-Québec region has over 1,200km of well-maintained, marked snowmobile trails, including several Trans-Québec trails. For more information or to order a map of the region's trails, contact **Tourisme Centre-du-Québec** (see p 303).

▲ Accommodations

Tour A: Mauricie

Trois-Rivières

Stretching from the Ursuline convent to the Monument du Flambeau, Rue des Ursulines has about a half-dozen exceptionally charming bed and breakfasts that offer enchanting accommodations well within reach of activities in the town centre. Contact the local tourist office to make reservations, as rooms in these establishments fill up quickly.

Auberge de Jeunesse La Flottille
$
497 Rue Radisson
☎ (819) 378-8010

▤ (819) 378-4334
The Auberge de Jeunesse La Flotille is a pleasant little youth hostel close to Trois-Rivières' nightlife. There are some 40 beds in the summer season, 30 in the winter.

L'Émérillon
$$
890 Terrasse Turcotte
☎ (819) 375-1010
▤ (819) 373-5843
Housed in a colonial-style home built in the early 20th century, this elegant bed and breakfast overlooks the St. Lawrence River.

Les Suites de Laviolette
$$-$$$
& ≡ ◎ ≈ ✳
7201 Rue Notre-Dame, Trois-Rivières Ouest
☎ (819) 377-4747 or 800-567-4747
▤ (819) 377-2331
www.suiteslaviolette.com

Les Suites Laviolette are set up in a handsome red brick building with white window panes. They offer quality accommodations in spacious, tastefully decorated rooms.

Hôtel Delta
$$$-$$$$
≡ ⇐ ⇒ ≈ ♨ ⫴ & ◎
1620 Rue Notre-Dame
☎ (819) 376-1991 or 800-268-1133
▤ (819) 372-5975
The high tower of the Hôtel Delta is easy to spot in the downtown area. The rooms are spacious. The hotel also has sports facilities and a convention centre.

Cap-de-la-Madeleine

Motel Jacques
$$
≈ ✳ ≡
2050 Rue Notre-Dame, Sainte-Marthe-du-Cap
☎ (819) 378-4031 or 378-4032

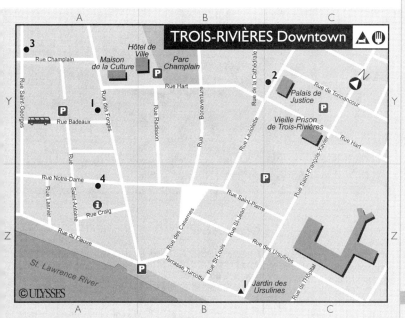

TROIS-RIVIÈRES Downtown ▲ ⑪

©ULYSSES

▲ **ACCOMMODATIONS**

1. BZ L'Émérillon

● **RESTAURANTS**

1. AY Angéline
2. CY Au Four à Bois
3. AY Le Lupin

4. AZ Maison des cafés, Le Torréfacteur

Mauricie and Centre-du-Québec - Accommodations - Mauricie

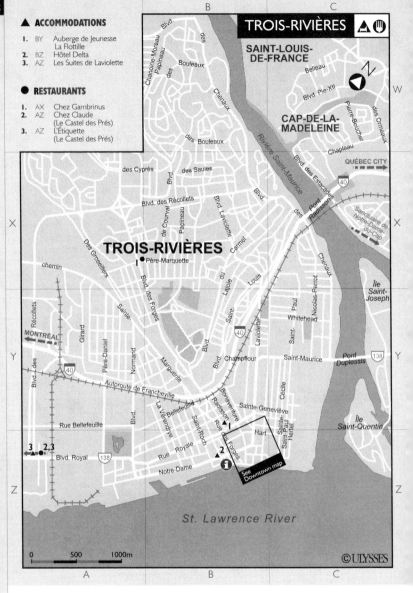

▲ ACCOMMODATIONS

1.	BY	Auberge de Jeunesse La Flottille
2.	BZ	Hôtel Delta
3.	AZ	Les Suites de Laviolette

● RESTAURANTS

1.	AX	Chez Gambrinus
2.	AZ	Chez Claude (Le Castel des Prés)
3.	AZ	L'Étiquette (Le Castel des Prés)

TROIS-RIVIÈRES ▲ ⌾

▤ (819) 693-1938

www.moteljacques.com

Motel Jacques provides inexpensive, comfortable accommodations. The pool, which overlooks the St. Lawrence river, makes up for the rather bland decor.

Grand-Mère

L'Auberge Santé Lac des Neiges
$$-$$$$

pb/sb ▲ ≈ ♨ ⑅ ¥ ⊚

100 Chemin du Lac-des-Neiges

☎ (819) 533-4518 or 800-757-4519

▤ (819) 533-4727

www.aubergesantelacdesneiges.qc.ca

The stress of the daily grind immediately melts away

upon reaching the Auberge Santé Lac des Neiges. Nestled on a peninsula, the building's modern architecture is tempered by white stucco, wooden beams and stairs, somewhat reminiscent of the baroque style. The common lounge is particularly inviting, with its many couches, windows with a view of the lake and, above all, a fire in the hearth. In this relaxing setting, guests often lounge about in their bathrobes between treatments. The inn's restaurant offers elegantly presented French cuisine. Many packages are available in order to cater to everyone's needs. In short, the staff does everything possible to make you feel at home and ensure that you leave feeling like a new person—completely refreshed and invigorated.

Auberge Le Florès
$$$
≡ ⚑ ≋ ♨))) Y

4291 50e Avenue
☎ (819) 538-9340 or 800-538-9340
🗏 (819) 538-1884

The Auberge Le Florès is a superb period house. Though not spectacular, the rooms are quite comfortable.

Saint-Jean-des-Piles

Maison Cadorette
$$ bkfst incl.
pb/sb ♨

1701 Rue Principale
☎ (819) 538-9883 or 888-538-9883
🗏 (819) 538-2299
www.cdit.qc.ca/cadoret

The Maison Cadorette accommodates guests just a few minutes from the entrance to La Mauricie National Park. The rooms are attractively decorated and the service is impeccable.

Grandes-Piles

Auberge Le Bôme
$$$ bkfst incl.
♨))) @

720 2e Avenue
☎ (819) 538-2805 or 800-538-2805

🗏 (819) 538-5879
www.auberge-le-bome.qc.ca

The Auberge Le Bôme is an excellent option in this region. The 10 rooms are beautifully decorated, and the friendly service makes for a very inviting atmosphere. There is also a superb sitting room, ideal for fascinating discussions with other travellers.

Shawinigan

Auberge Escapade Inn
$$-$$$ bkfst incl.
≡ ♨ @

3383 Rue Garnier
☎ (819) 539-6911 or 800-461-6911
🗏 (819) 539-7669
www.aubergeescapade.qc.ca

A well-kept place on the way into town, the Escapade Inn has several different personalities. The choice of accommodations here ranges from basic, inexpensive rooms to luxurious rooms decorated with period furniture. In between the two, there are attractive, comfortable rooms that offer good value for the money. What's more, the restaurant serves tasty food.

Gouverneur Shawinigan
$$$$
≡ ▲ ≋ ♨ ♿ @

1100 Promenade St-Maurice
☎ (819) 537-6000 or 888-922-1100
🗏 (819) 537-6365
www.gouverneurshawinigan.com

Located right near Shawinigan's town centre, Gouverneur Shawinigan meets the needs of both business and leisure travellers.

Saint-Élie-de-Caxton

Station Touristique Floribell
$$
▲ ➔ ♨

95 Chemin Lac Bell
☎ (819) 221-5731

🗏 (819) 221-3347
www.floribell.com

The Floribell holiday resort is perfect for sociable travellers or families on vacation. The resort rents out campsites and condos looking out on a lake with crystal-clear waters, where you can enjoy swimming, boat rides or simply building sand castles with your family. What's more, right nearby is a bike path that winds through the surrounding countryside leading right to the gates of La Mauricie National Park. In short, this place offers the ambiance of a holiday camp. The spotless, modern condos, furnished with double beds and sofa beds, can accommodate up to four people.

Saint-Paulin

Le Baluchon
$$$$
▲ ➔ ➔ ≋ ♨))) Y @

3550 Chemin des Trembles
☎ (819) 268-2555 or 800-789-5968
🗏 (819) 268-5234
www.baluchon.com

During the 1980s, seven adventurous students obtained the rights to the land surrounding the former Damphousse mill from Hydro-Québec. The land features a few waterfalls and the Sabot de la Vierge archipelago. The outdoor activity/health resort they set up on the land was inaugurated in 1990 with 12 rooms and some 20 employees. A few years later, after having won several tourism awards and managed to overcome a disastrous fire that destroyed the resort's first inn, Le Baluchon's clever mix of tourism and ecology has become one of the region's more remarkable success stories. The resort's vast estate features several installations that take full advantage of the splendid natural setting. Riverside and forest trails await hikers and cross-country skiers, while water-sports enthusiasts can rent canoes or kayaks to explore the river. The resort's 91 rooms are located in three elegantly understated buildings, and all have whirlpool baths. A well-equipped spa and a gourmet restaurant (see p 323) round out the amenities.

Saint-Alexis-des-Monts

Hôtel Sacacomie
$$$
△ ♨))) ◎

4000 Rang Sacacomie
☎ (819) 265-4444 or 888-265-4414
🖷 (819) 265-4445
www.sacacomie.com

Hôtel Sacacomie is a magnificent establishment with log cabins nestled in the middle of the forest near the Mastigouche reserve. Overhanging the majestic Lac Sacacomie, the facility has an idyllic location with a beach nearby. There's a great range of activities all year round.

Pointe-du-Lac

Auberge du Lac Saint-Pierre
$$$
≡ ♨ ♨))) ◎

1911 Rue Notre-Dame
☎ (819) 377-5971 or 888-377-5971
🖷 (819) 377-5579
www.aubergelacst-pierre.com

Auberge du Lac Saint-Pierre is located in Pointe-de-Lac, a small village at the north end of Lac Saint-Pierre, which is actually just a widening in the St. Lawrence. The flora and fauna that make their home in and around the "lake" are characteristic of marshy areas. Perched atop a promontory that slopes down to the

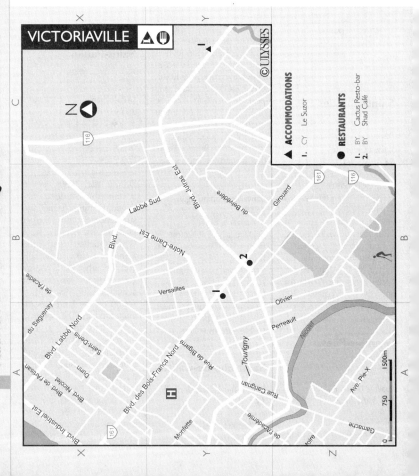

Mauricie and Centre-du-Québec - Accommodations - Mauricie

shore, this large inn boasts an outstanding location. It has comfortable, modern rooms, some of which have a mezzanine for the beds, leaving more space in the main room. The dining room serves excellent cuisine (see p 323). There are bicycles on hand if you feel like exploring the area.

Tour B: Centre-du-Québec

Bécancour

Auberge Godefroy
$$$$
≡ ⚠ ⛱ ☎ ≋ 🍴 ⫝̸ ⋎ ◎
17575 Boulevard Bécancour
☎ (819) 233-2200 or 800-361-1620
▤ (819) 233-2288
www.aubergegodefroy.com
Auberge Godefroy is an imposing building with lots of windows. In winter, a crackling fire greets guests in the stately lobby. The 70-odd rooms are spacious and offer all the comforts one would expect from an establishment of this calibre. The hotel also has a spa and offers a variety of packages to pamper yourself. Go ahead and indulge yourself in the dining room, as well (see p 323).

Victoriaville

Le Suzor
$$$
≡ ⫝̸ ◎
1000 Boulevard Jutras Est
☎ (819) 357-1000 or 866-357-8967
▤ (819) 357-5000
www.hotelsuzor.com
The modern Le Suzor hotel is located in a quiet part of town. The pleasant, spacious rooms have new furniture.

Kingsey Falls

Auberge Kingsey
$$
≡ ⫝̸
2141 Route 16
☎ (819) 839-2362
▤ (819) 839-3800
Auberge Kingsey is located at the limits of the Centre-du-Québec and Eastern Townships regions. Comfortable rooms and a friendly atmosphere ensure a pleasant stay.

Drummondville

Hôtel-Motel Blanchet
$$
≡ ⚠ ⛱ ⟆ ✳ ⫝̸ ◎
225 Boulevard St-Joseph Ouest
☎ (819) 477-0222 or 800-567-3823
▤ (819) 478-8706
www.hotelblanchet.com
The Hôtel-Motel Blanchet has a good location and attractive, reasonably priced rooms.

Comfort Inn
$$$
≡ ⟆
1055 Rue Hains
☎ (819) 477-4000 or 800-465-6115
▤ (819) 477-0930
This branch of the Comfort Inn chain offers the usual comfortable though somewhat plain rooms.

Restaurants

Tour A: La Mauricie

Trois-Rivières

Maison des Cafés, Le Torréfacteur
$
1465 Rue Notre-Dame
☎ (819) 694-4484

Coffee has now replaced alcohol as the social beverage of choice. It's therefore not surprising to see coffee houses popping up like mushrooms. Trois-Rivières is no exception; the locals' favourite place to meet is in a coffee house. In addition to a variety of hot beverages, this establishment also offers light fare and desserts.

Chez Gambrinus
$$
3160 Rue des Forges
☎ (819) 691-3371
Located outside of town near the university, the Chez Gambrinus restaurant and microbrewery attracts a clientele of regulars who are not shy to tell you how great the place is. It's one of those rare establishments where beer and oysters are elevated to unparalleled heights. Game and hamburgers are also served. The place is located in an old home surrounded by a terrace. The atmosphere and welcome are warm.

Au Four à Bois
$$
329 Rue Laviolette
☎ (819) 373-3686
Au Four à Bois, a regional institution, has been open for many years. The varied menu, which has evolved with time, offers seafood, grilled meats and gourmet pizza at reasonable prices. Located in a large two-storey house with a wood stove in the middle of the main floor, the atmosphere is elegant but relaxed.

Angéline
$$
313 Rue des Forges
☎ (819) 372-0468
There are several interesting restaurants on Rue Des Forges near the harbour park. Frequented by an

Mauricie and Centre-du-Québec - Restaurants - Mauricie

eclectic crowd, Angéline's menu and audacious decor are inspired by Italy. There are scrumptious pasta dishes, a variety of pizzas and other Italian specialties. It isn't gourmet dining, but the place is unpretentious and has a large clientele.

Le Castel des Prés
$$-$$$$
5800 Boulevard Royal
☎ (819) 375-4921

Auberge Castel des Prés actually has two separate dining rooms: the bistro-style **Étiquette** *($$)* and the popular **Chez Claude**

($$$-$$$$), which serves traditional French fare. The renowned chef at Chez Claude has won several awards for his quality cuisine, which features pasta, meat and fish served with sinfully rich sauces. In summer, a covered terrace provides a nice setting for a romantic meal.

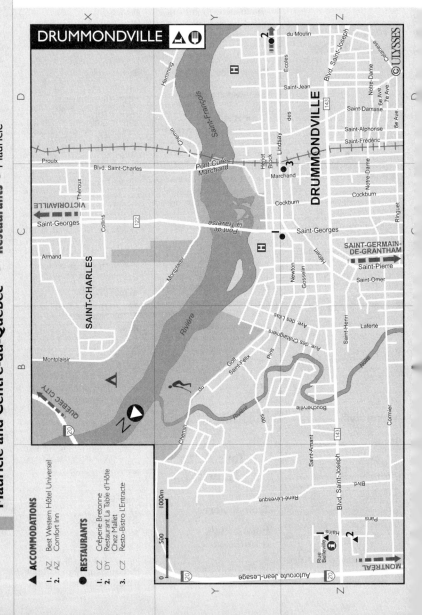

DRUMMONDVILLE

▲ **ACCOMMODATIONS**

1. AZ Best Western Hôtel Universel
2. AZ Comfort Inn

● **RESTAURANTS**

1. CZ Crêperie Bretonne
2. DY Restaurant La Table d'Hôte Chez Mallet
3. CZ Resto-Bistro L'Entracte

Le Lupin
$$$
bring your own wine
376 Rue St-Georges
☎ (819) 370-4740
Located in a charming ancestral home, Le Lupin serves some of the finest cuisine in the entire region. In addition to excellent *crêpes bretonnes*, it offers game and perch, considered the region's specialities.

Grand-Mère

Crêperie de Flore
$$-$$$
3580 50ᵉ Avenue
☎ (819) 533-2020
The Crêperie de Flore has a simple, informal ambiance and specializes in Breton crepes and veal.

Grandes-Piles

Auberge Le Bôme
$$$$
720 2ᵉ Avenue
☎ (819) 538-2805
In addition to being charming and comfortable, the Auberge Le Bôme serves French cuisine combined with regional specialties like venison and Arctic trout, with sensational results. An absolute must!

Saint-Jean-des-Piles

Maison Cadorette
$$$
1701 Rue Principale
☎ (819) 538-9883
Maison Cadorette serves refined Québécois cuisine in an unpretentious, friendly setting.

Shawinigan

La Pointe à Bernard
$$-$$$
692 4ᵉ Rue
☎ (819) 537-5553
This laid-back bistro-style restaurant is a good spot for dinner among friends or colleagues. The house specialty is mussels. Friendly and efficient service.

Restaurant La Piñata
$$-$$$
902 Promenade du Saint-Maurice
☎ (819) 537-7806
Quality Mexican fare is served in this restaurant located across from Cité de l'Énergie. The simple but tasteful decor, generous portions and very reasonable prices make this a good choice. Mariachis occasionally provide entertainment.

Pointe-du-Lac

Auberge du Lac Saint-Pierre
$$$-$$$$
1911 Rte. 138
☎ (819) 377-5971 or 888-377-5971
If you go to the **Auberge du Lac Saint-Pierre** (see p 320) for dinner, start your evening with a short walk on the shore to work up an appetite, or perhaps have an apéritif on the terrace, with its view of the river. The modern decor of the dining room is a bit cold, but there's nothing bland about the presentation of the dishes, much less their flavour. The menu, made of French and Québec cuisine, includes trout, salmon, lamb and pheasant, all artfully prepared. Reservations required.

Saint-Paulin

Le Baluchon
$$$-$$$$
3550 Chemin des Trembles
☎ (819) 268-2555 or 800-789-5968
Located on a magnificent estate, **Le Baluchon** (see p 319) offers choice French and Québec cuisine, as well as a more health-conscious menu that will leave you feeling anything but deprived. The dining room has a soothing decor and a view of the river.

Tour B: Centre-du-Québec

Bécancour

Auberge Godefroy
$$$-$$$$
17575 Boulevard Bécancour
☎ (819) 233-2200 or 800-361-1620
The spacious dining room at **Auberge Godefroy** (see p 321) looks out onto the river. The delicious French cuisine varies from classic to original creations made with regional produce. Succulent desserts!

Victoriaville

Shad Café
$
309 Rue Notre-Dame Est
☎ (819) 751-0848
The Shad Café is probably the only place in town where you can enjoy a light meal along with an imported beer or European coffee. The place is very pleasant both day and night, when it essentially turns into a bar whose clientele appreciates its unpretentious café ambiance.

Mauricie and Centre-du-Québec - Restaurants - Centre-du-Québec

Cactus Resto-bar
$$
139 Boulevard des Bois-Francs Sud
☎ (819) 758-5311
At Cactus, orange hues, brickwork and wainscotting create a warm, slightly intimate ambiance despite the high turnout. Generous portions of good Mexican food draw a mixed crowd. Like several establishments in Victoriaville, this restaurant turns into a laid-back pub, complete with a pool table, at night.

Drummondville

Resto-Bistro L'Entracte
$-$$
247 Rue Lindsay
☎ (819) 477-4097
Inexpensive fare and a central location make this a popular dining spot in Drummondville. The creative menu features salads, sausages, *"pizzelles"* and a few other tasty surprises.

Restaurant La Table d'Hôte Chez Mallet
$$-$$$
1320 Boulevard Mercure
☎ (819) 475-6965
Though Drummondville initially seems devoid of good restaurants, visitors need only dig a little deeper. Located away from the town centre, this restaurant is a great gastronomic option for lovers of French cuisine. As its name indicates, this establishment offers tables d'hôte, ranging from lamb to poultry to ostrich.

Crêperie Bretonne
$$-$$$
131 Rue St-Georges
☎ (819) 477-9148
Set up in the Mitchell house, Crêperie Bretonne is an attraction in itself. Indeed, this Victorian house was restored by its Breton-born owner, who put as much care into the renovations as she does into the preparation of her delicious crepes. The classy decor, which combines original wallpaper and tasteful innovations, exudes a muted ambiance. Moreover, patrons can browse through documents dealing with architectural influences and portfolios of photographs tracing the history of the house's restoration. And the crepes? They're exquisite. Several types of menus are offered that introduce diners to a variety of flavours. Of particular note is the buckwheat crepe with seafood and cognac sauce—absolutely delicious. On a healthier note, all crepes are made with organic flour.

Entertainment

■ Bars and Nightclubs

Saint-Élie-de-Caxton

La Pierre Angulaire
cover charge for shows
39 Chemin des Loisirs
☎ (819) 268-3393
La Pierre Angulaire café-showbar is run by a co-op that brings together several young local talents. The collective organizes shows, activities and entertainment of all kinds, but primarily devotes itself to the preservation of local traditions and folklore by hosting evenings of storytelling and traditional Québécois music. Set in the middle of the woods, this café offers the warmest of ambiances, where you are welcomed like one of the family.

Trois-Rivières

Downtown Trois-Rivières' reputation for its nightlife is well established and you need only stroll around to discover its captivating bars and nightclubs. This is particularly true in summer, when jam-packed terraces spill out onto the streets.

Café Bar Le Zénob
171 Rue Bonaventure
☎ (819) 378-9925
Hot summer nights are very lively and enjoyable beneath the large trees of Zénob's front and rear terraces. This café-bar welcomes a fair share of local artists and regularly hosts exhibitions and art events.

Café Galerie l'Embuscade
1571 Badeaux
☎ (819) 374-0652
Café Galerie l'Embuscade is a popular meeting place where artists, students and others gather to sip a beer or snack on a light meal. It also acts as a gallery to promote the works of many talented artists. Artistic events, such as live painting, are presented on the outdoor terrace in the summer.

Nord Ouest Café
1441 Rue Notre-Dame
☎ (819) 693-1151
Nord Ouest Café is a laid-back spot with several floors, including a bar on the main floor, a private lounge, pool tables and games. It serves a variety of imported beer, as well as light fare.

■ Festivals and Cultural Events

Drummondville

In mid-July, Drummondville hosts the **Mondial des Cultures** (*☎819-472-1184 or 800-265-5412*). The goal of this festival is to encourage exchanges between the different traditions and cultures of the world.

Saint-Tite

The **Festival Western de Saint-Tite** (*☎819-365-7524*) is the biggest country music festival in all of Eastern Canada. Every year during the second week of September, the city attracts hordes of country and western fans who come here for live concerts, a rodeo and a parade that features several animals.

Trois-Rivières

The **Grand Prix de Trois-Rivières** (*late Jul; ☎819-373-9912, ticket sales: ☎819-380-9797 or 866-416-9797, www.gp3r.com*), an Atlantic Championship race, is held in the city streets. Now-famous drivers like Jacques Villeneuve have participated in this event in the past.

Victoriaville

The **Festival International de Musique Actuelle de Victoriaville** (*☎819-752-7912, www.fimav.qc.ca*) takes place each year during the third week of May. This festival is an exploration of new musical forms. Of course, the event won't appeal to everyone, but it is an adventure for musicians and spectators alike. The festival's international reputation has grown since it started over 20 years ago, and it now attracts a large number of music fans from the northeastern United States and Ontario. Quite a feat for a festival held outside the province's large urban centres of Montréal and Québec City.

Shopping

■ Clothing

Bécancour

Chèvrerie l'Angélaine
12285 Boulevard Bécancour (Rte. 132)
☎ (819) 222-5702 or 877-444-5702
www.langelaine.com

Chèvrerie l'Angélaine specializes in the breeding of Angora goats and makes a line of quality mohair clothing. The collection consists of a great selection of sweaters, vests, shawls, jackets and fashion accessories.

■ Food

Bécancour

Fromagerie L'Ancêtre
1615 Boulevard Port-Royal
☎ (819) 233-9157
Both a shop and a restaurant, the Fromagerie L'Ancêtre makes delicious homemade dairy products, including three kinds of cheese, butter and ice cream. All are made using natural manufacturing processes. Sample its products along with home-brewed wine and beer.

Trois-Rivières

Le Muscadin
60 Rue des Forges
☎ (819) 691-9080
Stop by Le Muscadin's gourmet shop to satisfy your sweet tooth with a few mouth-watering goodies or to fill your picnic basket before setting out for a day in the countryside.

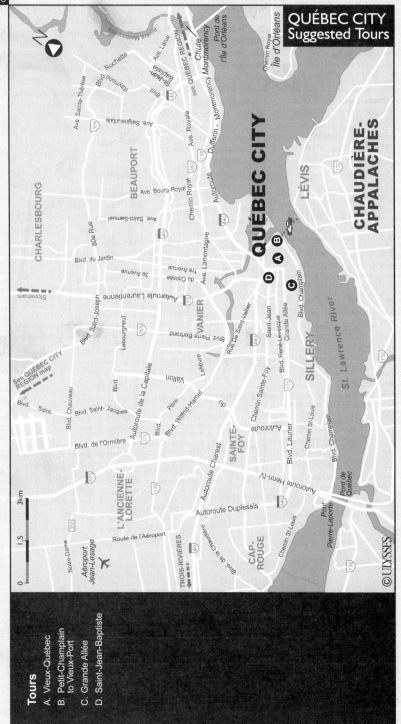

QUÉBEC CITY
Suggested Tours

Tours

A. Vieux-Québec
B. Petit-Champlain to Vieux-Port
C. Grande Allée
D. Saint-Jean-Baptiste

© ULYSSES

Québec City

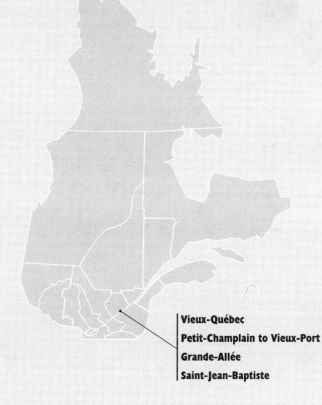

Vieux-Québec

Petit-Champlain to Vieux-Port

Grande-Allée

Saint-Jean-Baptiste

A lthough it is a magical place whatever the season, meandering through the winding streets of **Québec City** ★ ★ ★ on a winter evening is a particularly enchanting experience: the snow sparkles under the light of the street lamps and the whole city looks like a scene from *A Christmas Carol*. Diners savouring hearty fare appear through the window panes of restaurants, illuminated by the light dancing from the hearth. They've come to join the carnival, or maybe they're setting off on an excursion to the ski slopes of Mont Sainte-Anne.

In the spring and summer, the terraces of Grande Allée shelter their thirsty patrons under a sea of multicoloured parasols, while out on the Plains of Abraham, elderly women perform Tai Chi exercises. Fall keeps in reserve its own treasure of special moments to be shared with the inhabitants of the jewel of French America: the spectacular display of leaves rustling in the fresh breeze; the sight of students dawdling to arrive just in time for the start of their university courses, while politicians and civil servants pursue their debates over one last coffee before returning to the Parliament buildings.

Québec City stands out as much for the stunning richness of its architectural heritage as for the beauty of its location. The Haute-Ville quarter covers a promontory that is over 98m high, known as Cap Diamant, and juts out over the St. Lawrence River, which narrows here to a mere 1km. In fact, it is this narrowing of the river that gave the city its name: in Algonquian, *kebec* means "place where the river narrows." Affording an impregnable vantage point, the heights of Cap Diamant dominate the river and the surrounding countryside. From the inception of New France, this rocky peak played a strategic role and was the site of major fortifications early on. Dubbed the "Gibraltar of North America," today Québec is the only walled city north of Mexico.

The cradle of New France, Québec City's atmosphere and architecture are more reminiscent of Europe than of America. The stone houses that flank its narrow streets and the many spires of its churches and religious institutions evoke the France of the Old Regime. In addition, the old fortifications of Haute-Ville, the Parliament and the grandiose administrative buildings attest eloquently to the importance of Québec City in the history of the country. Indeed, its historical and architectural richness are such that the city and its historic surroundings were recognized by UNESCO in 1985 as a World Heritage Site, the first in North America.

With over 95% of the population being of French ancestry, the capital of Québec is home to an impressive number of excellent restaurants and cafés. It is a lively city all year round, distinguished in the fall by the changing colours of the leaves, in the winter by its famous carnival, in the spring by the musicians who take to the streets and the newly opened terraces, and in the summer by its summer festival. What's more, the region offers lovely mountainous landscapes within reach of the city.

This chapter contains suggestions for four different walking tours of the city, while the next chapter explores the surrounding area.

A **Brief History of Québec City**

During his second expedition in 1535, Jacques Cartier stopped at Stadacona, a native village located on land that would later become Québec City. Hoping to find precious stones, he christened the sheer and stony escarpment that overlooks the river Cap Diamant, or "Cape of Diamonds." At the time, Cartier was on a mission for the King of France, François I, to discover gold, as well as a passage to the Orient. After Cartier's three expeditions turned up neither of these, the King declined to finance further voyages to North America.

A few decades later, the significant profits to be made in the fur trade rekindled

France's interest in this far-off land. After the failure of many trading posts both on the coast and in the interior, the area where Québec City now stands was chosen for the establishment of a permanent trading post. In 1608, Samuel de Champlain and his men erected and fortified a series of buildings at the foot of the cape. This first settlement was known as *Abitation*. Despite the extreme harshness of the first winter and the deaths of 20 of the 28 men from scurvy and malnutrition, 1608 marked the beginning of a permanent French presence in North America. Québec City was founded for the fur trade, therefore it initially attracted the interest of French merchants. Little by little, a few peasant families began to establish themselves. Basse-Ville became the centre of commercial activity and the residential area of the colonists. In fact, Québec's lower-town remained its urban and commercial centre until the middle of the 19th century because the religious institutions of Haute-Ville opposed commercial development.

Early on, New France's capital became a prize in the rivalry that pitted France against England. Québec City was captured by the Kirke brothers in 1629, before being returned to France in 1632. Although the city held out against the English siege led by Admiral Phipps in 1690, pressure from England continued to build throughout the 18th century. The outcome was decided in the famous battle of the Plains of Abraham in 1759, in which British troops led by General Wolfe defeated those of the Marquis de Montcalm. When New France was ceded to the British under the terms of the Treaty of Paris in 1763, the population of Québec City had reached almost 9,000.

Because of its geographic location, Québec City served as the entrance to the colony, as well as its principal economic centre.

The goods of the commercial triangle linking Canada, the West Indies and London were transhipped in the port of Québec City, which naturally developed an important shipyard. Nevertheless, Québec City began to rapidly lose ground with the growth of Montréal in the 19th century. Following the dredging of the St. Lawrence up to Montréal and the construction of a railway system with Montréal as its centre, Québec City was usurped as the focus of trade and foremost economic centre

of Canada. Though Montréal became the Canadian metropolis, Québec City nonetheless retained an important role as the provincial capital and as a strategic military base. In the 1920s, it even enjoyed a certain prosperity based largely on the shoemaking industry.

The growth of Québec City in the 1960s paralleled that of the scope and power of Québec's provincial government. Today, the economy of the sole francophone capital of North America revolves around civil service.

Getting There and Getting Around

Four walking tours of Québec city are suggested: **Tour A: Vieux-Québec ★ ★ ★**, **Tour B: Petit-Champlain to Vieux-Port ★ ★ ★**, **Tour C: Grande Allée ★ ★** and **Tour D: Saint-Jean-Baptiste ★** .

For more information on Québec City, consult the *Ulysses Travel Guide Québec City*.

■ By Car

Québec City can be reached from Montréal along either shore of the St. Lawrence River. Aut. 40 East runs along the north shore, becoming Rte. 440 on the outskirts of Québec City and then Boulevard Charest once you get downtown. On the south shore, Aut. 20 runs east until the Pierre-Laporte bridge. Across the bridge, Boulevard Laurier continues to Québec City, becoming Grande Allée Est as you enter the downtown area.

Car Rental

Budget
7300 Boulevard Wilfrid-Hamel Ouest
☎ (418) 872-9885
Vieux-Québec: 29 Côte du Palais
☎ (418) 692-3660
Sainte-Foy: 2481 Chemin Sainte-Foy
☎ (418) 651-6518
www.budgetmtl.com

Discount
12 Rue Sainte-Anne
☎ (418) 655-2206
www.discountcar.com

Hertz
Jean-Lesage Airport
☎ (418) 871-1571
580 Grande Allée
☎ (418) 647-4949
Vieux-Québec: 44 Côte du Palais
☎ (418) 694-1224
2800 Boulevard Laurier, Hôtel Carillon
☎ (418) 658-6795
www.hertz.com

National
Jean-Lesage Airport
☎ (418) 877-9822
Beauport: 301 Rue Seigneuriale
☎ (418) 663-8681
www.nationalcar.com

Via Route
2605 Boulevard Wilfrid-Hamel
☎ (418) 682-2660
450 Rue de la Gare-du-Palais
☎ (418) 694-1727
www.viaroute.com

■ By Plane

Aéroport International Jean-Lesage (see p 48), though smaller than Montréal's airports, does receive international flights.

■ By Ferry

Even if you have no reason to go to Lévis, on the south shore of the St. Lawrence River, you should take the ferry trip just for the view. The ferry dock is across from Place-Royale; you should have no trouble finding it. The return trip from Lévis gives you a magnificent view of Québec City. A one-way trip costs $2 during winter and $2.50 in summer for adults, and $8.50 per car in winter and $9.85 during summer (maximum six passengers). The timetable varies from one season to the next so it is best to check directly for departure times.

Société des Traversiers du Québec
10 Rue des Traversiers
☎ (418) 643-8420 or 877-787-7483
www.traversiers.gouv.qc.ca

■ By Boat

There is now a great new way to reach Québec City from Montréal or Trois-Rivières. **Les Dauphins du Saint-Laurent**

(☎514-288-4499 or 877-648-4499, www.dauphins.ca) links these three cities on its daily summer runs by hydroplane, travelling at 65km/h. You can leave Montréal in the morning and be in Québec City 4½hrs later—a longer trip than it would take by car (about 2½hrs), but it makes for a pleasant, scenic trip.

■ By Bus

A network of bus routes covers the entire city. A $63.40 monthly pass allows unlimited travel. A single trip costs $2.50 (exact change only) or $2.20 with the purchase of tickets (sold at newspaper stands). You can also buy a day pass for $5.65. Students and senior citizens have reduced rates, while children five years of age and under travel free of charge. Transfers, if needed, should be requested from the driver upon boarding. For more information: ☎(418) 627-2511.

■ Taxis

Taxi Coop
☎ (418) 525-5191

Taxi Québec
☎ (418) 525-8123

■ Ride Sharing

Rides are organized to Québec City by **Allo-Stop Québec** (membership card required: passengers $6/year, drivers $7/year; 665 Rue St-Jean, ☎418-522-0056; see also p 50).

■ Train Stations

ViaRail
☎888-842-7245
www.viarail.com

Gare du Palais
450 Rue de la Gare-du-Palais

Gare de Charny
2326 Rue de la Gare Est

Gare de Sainte-Foy
3255 Chemin de la Gare

■ Bus Stations

Gare d'autocars de Québec
320 Rue Abraham-Martin (Gare du Palais)
☎ (418) 525-3000

Gare d'autocars Sainte-Foy
3001 Chemin des Quatre-Bourgeois
☎ (418) 650-0087

Useful Information

■ Banks

Banque Royale
700 Place d'Youville
☎ (418) 692-6800

Caisse Populaire Desjardins du Vieux-Québec
19 Rue Desjardins
☎ (418) 522-6806

Banque Nationale
150 Boulevard René-Lévesque Est
☎ (418) 647-6100

■ Guided Tours

The **Société Historique de Québec** *($12; 72 Côte de la Montagne,* ☎*418-692-0556)* offers guided tours of Vieux-Québec. There are a number of themes from which to choose. These walking tours usually last around 2hrs and cover various aspects of the history of Québec City.

■ Post Offices

300 Rue St-Paul
☎ (418) 694-6176
59 Rue Dalhousie
☎ (418) 694-6190
5 Rue du Fort
☎ (418) 694-6102

■ Tourist Information

Tourist information is available from Tourisme Québec, the Délégations Générales du Québec abroad and the various offices of the Office du Tourisme et des Congrès de la région de Québec. A tourist-information service is also available from guides on mopeds in Vieux-Québec during the summer. The mopeds are painted green and feature a flag with a question mark.

Office du Tourisme de Québec
399 Rue St-Joseph Est, Québec, G1K 8E2
☎ (418) 641-6654
www.quebecregion.com

Centre Infotouriste
12 Rue Sainte-Anne
☎ 877-266-5687
The Centre Infotouriste provides detailed information and supplies road maps, travel brochures and lodging guides for all of Québec's tourist regions.

Tourisme Québec
PO Box 979, Montréal, H3C 2W3
☎ (514) 873-2015 or 877-266-5687
www.bonjourquebec.com

Exploring

Arriving in Québec City by car, the most common route is via Grande Allée. After passing through a typical North American-style suburb, you come to a rather British-looking part of town with tree-lined streets. Next come the government buildings of the provincial capital, and finally, the imposing medieval-looking gates, and behind them the historic streets of the old city, Vieux-Québec.

Tour A: Vieux-Québec
★ ★ ★

   2 to 3 days

Haute-Ville, or upper town, covers the plateau atop Cap Diamant. As the administrative and institutional centre, it is adorned with convents, chapels and public buildings whose construction dates back, in some cases, to the 17th century. The walls of Haute-Ville, dominated by the citadel, surround this section of Vieux-Québec and give it the characteristic look of a fortress. These same walls long contained the development of the town, yielding a densely built-up bourgeois and aristocratic milieu. With time, the picturesque urban planning of the 19th century contributed to the present-day image of Québec City through the construction of such fantastical buildings as

Québec City - Exploring - Vieux-Québec

the Château Frontenac and the creation of public spaces like Terrasse Dufferin, in the *belle époque* spirit.

The Haute-Ville walking tour begins at Porte Saint-Louis, near the parliament buildings.

The **Porte Saint-Louis** *(at the top of the street of the same name)* gateway is the result of Québec City merchants' pressuring the government between 1870 and 1875 to tear down the wall surrounding the city. The Governor General of Canada at the time, Lord Dufferin, was opposed to the idea and instead put forward a plan drafted by Irishman William H. Lynn to showcase the walls while improving traffic circulation. The design he submitted exhibits a Victorian romanticism in its use of grand gateways that bring to mind images of medieval castles and horsemen. The pepper-box tower of Porte Saint-Louis, built in 1878, makes for a striking first impression upon arriving in downtown Québec City.

The **Fortifications of Québec National Historic Site** ★ *($3.50; early May to mid-Oct every day 9am to 5 pm, rest of the year every day 10am to 5pm; 100 Rue Saint-Louis,* ☎*418-648-7016)* displays models and maps outlining the development of Québec City's defense system; you can also visit the **Poudrière de l'Esplanade**. Booklets are available with a complete tour of the city's fortifications, and the **Centre d'Initiation aux Fortifications** offers two guided tours *($10)*. Information plaques have been placed along the wall, providing another means of discovering the city's history. The walkway on top of the wall can be reached by using the stairs next to the city gates.

Québec City's first wall was made of earth and wooden posts. It was erected on the

west side of the city in 1693, according to the plans of engineer Dubois Berthelot de Beaucours, to protect Québec City from the Iroquois. Work on much stronger stone fortifications began in 1745, designed by engineer Chaussegros de Léry, when England and France entered a new era of conflict. However, the wall remained unfinished when the city was seized by the British in 1759. The British saw to the completion of the project at the end of the 18th century. Some work on the Citadelle began in 1693; however, the structure as we now know it was essentially built between 1820 and 1832. Nevertheless, the Citadelle is largely designed along the principles advanced by Vauban in the 17th century—principles that suit the location admirably.

Continue along Rue Saint-Louis and turn right on Rue Sainte-Ursule.

Until the end of the 19th century, Québec City had a small but influential community of Scottish Presbyterians, most of whom were involved in shipping and the lumber trade. The **Chalmers-Wesley United Church** *(78 Rue Ste-Ursule,* ☎*418-692-2640)*, an attractive Gothic Revival structure, is presently used by a variety of groups, testifying to the decline of the Scottish Presbyterian community. The church was built in 1852 and designed by John Wells, an architect known for a number of famous buildings, including the Bank of Montreal headquarters.

Turn left on Avenue Sainte-Geneviève and then turn left.

In addition to the city's major historical landmarks, Québec's appeal lies in its smaller, less imposing buildings, each of which has its own separate history. It is enjoyable to simply wander the narrow

★ **ATTRACTIONS**

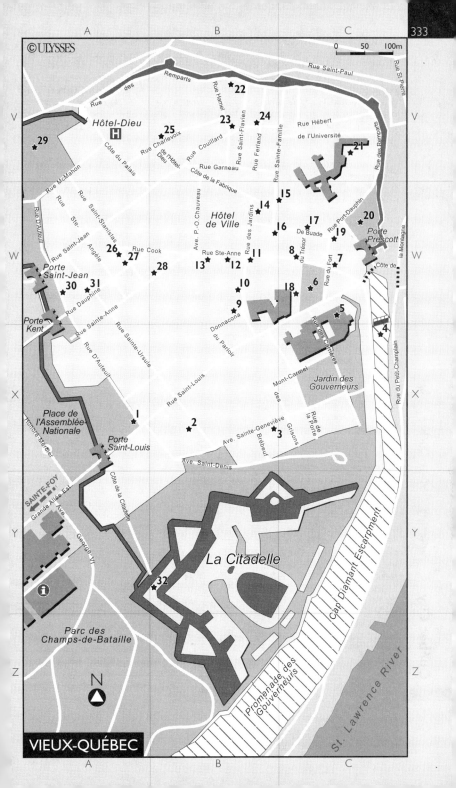

streets of the old city, taking in the subtleties of an architecture so atypical of North America. The **Maison Cirice-Têtu** ★ *(25 Avenue Ste-Geneviève)* was built in 1852. It was designed by Charles Baillargé, a member of a celebrated family of architects who, beginning in the 18th century, left an important mark on the architecture of Québec City and its surroundings.

The charming square known as **Jardin des Gouverneurs** ★ was originally the private garden of the governor of New France. The square was laid out in 1647 for Charles Huault de Montmagny to the west of Château Saint-Louis, the residence of the governor. A monument to opposing military leaders Wolfe and Montcalm, both of whom died on the battlefields of the Plains of Abraham, was erected during the restoration of the garden in 1827.

A walk on the wooden planks of the **Terrasse Dufferin** ★★★, overlooking the St. Lawrence River, provides a different sensation than the pavement we are used to. It was built in 1879 at the request of the governor general of the time, Lord Dufferin. The boardwalk's open-air pavilions and ornate street lamps were designed by Charles Baillargé and were inspired by the style of French urban architecture that was common under Napoleon III. Terrasse Dufferin is one of Québec City's most popular sights and is the preferred meeting place of young people. The view of the river, the south shore and Île d'Orléans is magnificent. During the winter months, a huge ice slide is set up at the western end of the boardwalk.

There are two **monuments** at the far end of Terrasse Dufferin. One is dedicated to the memory of Samuel de Champlain, the founder of Québec City and father of New France. It was designed by Parisian sculptor Paul Chevré and erected in 1898. The second monument informs visitors that Vieux-Québec was recognized as a World Heritage Site by UNESCO in 1985. Québec City is the first city in North America to be included on this list. A staircase just to the left of the Champlain monument leads to the Place Royale quarter in Basse-Ville.

The first half of the 19th century saw the emergence of Québec City's tourism industry, when the romantic European nature of the city began to attract growing numbers

of American visitors. In 1890, the Canadian Pacific Railway company, under Cornelius Van Horne, decided to create a chain of distinguished hotels across Canada. The first of these hotels was the **Château Frontenac** ★★★ *(1 Rue des Carrières)*, named in honour of one of the best-known governors of New France, Louis de Buade, Comte de Frontenac (1622-1698).

The magnificent Château Frontenac, symbol of the province's capital city, is probably the most famous sight in Québec. Ironically, the hotel was designed by an American architect, Bruce Price (1845-1903) who was known for his New York skyscrapers. The look of the hotel, which combines certain elements of Scottish manors and the châteaux of the Loire Valley in France, has come to be considered a national archetype style called "Château Style." Bruce Price, who also designed Montréal's Windsor train station and the famous Tuxedo Park development near New York, was inspired by the picturesque location that was chosen for the hotel and by the mix of French and English cultures in Canada.

Château Frontenac was built in phases. Price's initial wing overlooked Terrasse Dufferin and was completed in 1893. Three sections were later added, the most important of these being the central tower (1923), the work of architects Edward and William Sutherland Maxwell. To fully appreciate the château, one must go inside to explore the main hall, decorated in a style that was popular in 18th-century Parisian *hôtels particuliers*, and visit the Bar Maritime in the large main tower overlooking the river.

Château Frontenac has been the site of a number of important events in history. In 1944, the Québec Conference was held here. At this historic meeting, U.S. President Franklin D. Roosevelt, British Prime Minister Winston Churchill and Canadian Prime Minister Mackenzie King met to discuss the future of post-war Europe. On the way out of the courtyard is a stone with the inscription of the Order of Malta, dated 1647, the only remaining piece of Château Saint-Louis. **Tours** *($8; May to mid-Oct every day 10am to 6pm, mid-Oct to late Apr Sat and Sun 1pm to 5pm; ☎418-691-2166)* of Château Frontenac are given by guides dressed in period costumes.

Until the construction of the citadel, **Place d'Armes** ★ was a military parade ground. It became a public square in 1832. In 1916, the *Monument de la Foi* (Monument of Faith) was erected in Place d'Armes to mark the tricentennial of the arrival of the Récollet religious order in Québec. Abbot Adolphe Garneau's statue rests on a base designed by David Ouellet.

*At the other end of the square are the Centre Info-touriste (the tourist-information centre) and two museums. The back of the **Holy Trinity Anglican Cathedral** ★ ★ (see p 336) is also visible from here.*

The **Centre Infotouriste de Québec** *(12 Rue Ste-Anne)* is located in the former Union Hotel, a white building with a copper roof. A group of wealthy Quebecers saw the need for a luxury hotel in Québec City and commissioned British architect Edward Cannon to head the project, which was completed in 1803.

On either side of the Centre Infotouriste are two popular tourist attractions. Using an elaborate model of the city along with a sound and light show, the **Musée du Fort** *($7.50; Feb and Mar Thu-Sun 10pm to 4pm, Apr to mid-Jan every day 10am to 5pm, mid-Jan to Feb closed; 10 Rue Ste-Anne, ☎418-692-2175)* recreates the six sieges of Québec City, starting with the capture of the town by the Kirke brothers in 1629 and ending with the American invasion of 1775.

The **Musée de Cire de Québec** *($3; May to Oct every day 8:30am to 9pm, rest of the year every day 9am to 4pm; 22 Rue Ste-Anne, ☎418-692-2289)* displays wax likenesses of some 60 individuals grouped in 16 settings that depict Québec City's history and recent events. You will see contemporary Québécois pop-music stars alongside Churchill, Champlain and Wolfe.

Return to Rue St-Louis and turn right on Rue du Parloir.

At the corner of Rue Donnacona, you will find the **Monastère des Ursulines** ★ ★ ★ *(18 Rue Donnacona)*. In 1535, Sainte Angèle Merici founded the first Ursuline community in Brescia, Italy. After the community had established itself in France, it became a cloistered order dedicated to teaching (1620). With the help of a benefactor, Madame de la Peltrie, the Ursulines ar-

rived in Québec City in 1639 and, in 1641, founded a monastery and convent where generations of young girls have received a good education. The Ursulines' convent is the longest running girls' school in North America.

Only the museum and chapel, a small part of the huge Ursulines complex where several dozen nuns still live, are open to the public.

The Sainte-Ursuline chapel was rebuilt in 1901 on the site of the original 1722 chapel. Part of the magnificent interior decoration of the first chapel, created by Pierre-Nöel Levasseur between 1726 and 1736, survived and is present in the newer structure. The work includes a pulpit surmounted by a trumpeting angel and a beautiful altarpiece in the Louis XIV style. The tabernacle of the high altar is embellished with fine gilding applied by the Ursulines. The Sacred Heart tabernacle, a masterpiece of the genre, is attributed to Jaques Leblond, also known as Latour, and dates from around 1770.

The chapel was the burial site of the Marquis de Montcalm until 2001, when his remains were transferred to the Hôpital Général military cemetery. General of the French troops during the decisive Battle of the Plains of Abraham, he was fatally wounded during the conflict, as was his rival General Wolfe. The tomb of blessed Mère Marie de l'Incarnation, the founder of the Ursulines monastery in Québec, is still there.

The entrance to the **Musée des Ursulines** *($6; May to Sep Tue-Sat 10am to noon and 1pm to 5pm, Sun 1pm to 5pm, Oct to Dec and Feb to Apr Tue-Sun 1pm to 4:30pm; 12 Rue Donnacona, ☎418-694-0694)* is located across from the chapel. The museum outlines nearly four centuries of Ursuline history. On display are various works of art, Louis XIII furniture, impressive embroideries made of gold thread, and 18th-century altar cloths and church robes.

Continue on Rue Donnacona, and turn left on Rue des Jardins. Note the tiny little house on your left.

After the British Conquest of Québec, a small group of British administrators and military officers established themselves in Québec City. These men wanted to mark their presence through the construction of prestigious buildings with typically British designs. However, their small numbers resulted in the slow progress of this project until the beginning of the 19th century, when work began on the **Holy Trinity Anglican Cathedral** ★ ★ *(31 Rue des Jardins)* by Majors Robe and Hall, two military engineers inspired by St. Martin's Church in London Fields. The Palladian-style church was completed in 1804. This significant example of non-French architecture changed the look of the city. The church was the first Anglican cathedral built outside Britain and, in its elegant simplicity, is a good example of British colonial architecture. The roof was made steeper in 1815 so that it would not be weighed down by snow.

The cathedral's interior, soberer than that of most Catholic churches, is adorned with various generous gifts from King George III, including several pieces of silverware and pews made of English oak from the forests of Windsor. The bishop's chair is said to have been carved from an elm tree under which Samuel de Champlain liked to sit. There are stained-glass windows and commemorative plaques that were added over the years. There is also a Casavant organ dating from 1909 that was restored in 1959. Its set of eight bells is one of the oldest in Canada.

Continue along Rue des Jardins. To the right is a cobblestone section of Rue Sainte-Anne and on the left is the Hôtel Clarendon and the Price building.

The **Hôtel Clarendon** *(57 Rue Ste-Anne)* began welcoming guests in 1870 in the former Desbarats print shop (1858). It is the oldest hotel still operating in Québec. The Charles Baillargé-designed restaurant on the main floor is also the oldest restaurant in Canada. The Victorian charm of the somber woodwork evokes the *belle époque*. The Hôtel Clarendon was enlarged in 1929 by the addition of a brick tower featuring an Art Deco entrance hall designed by Raoul Chênevert.

The design of **Édifice Price** ★ *(65 Rue Ste-Anne)* manages to adhere to traditional North-American skyscraper architecture and yet does not look out of place among the historic buildings of Haute-Ville. Architects Ross and MacDonald of Montréal gave the building a tall yet discreet silhouette when they designed it in 1929. It features

a copper roof typical of Château architecture. The main hall of the building, a fine example of Art Deco design, is covered in polished travertine and bronze bas-reliefs depicting the various activities of the Price company, which specialized in the production of paper.

Walk back up to Rue des Jardins, and turn right on Côte de la Fabrique.

Place de l'Hôtel-de-Ville ★, a small square, was the location of the Notre-Dame market in the 18th century. A monument in honour of Cardinal Taschereau, created by André Vermare, was erected here in 1923.

During the 17th century, the **Séminaire de Québec** ★ ★ ★ *(late Jun to late Aug; 1 Côte de la Fabrique, ☎418-692-3981)* religious complex was an oasis of European civilization in a rugged and hostile territory. To get an idea of how it must have appeared to students of the day, go through the old gate (decorated with the seminary's coat of arms) and into the courtyard before proceeding through the opposite entryway to the reception desk.

The seminary was founded in 1663 by Monseigneur François de Laval, on orders from the Séminaire des Missions Étrangères de Paris (seminary of foreign missions), with which it remained affiliated until 1763. As headquarters of the clergy throughout the colony, it was at the seminary that future priests studied, that parochial funds were administered, and that ministerial appointments were made. Louis XIV's Minister, Colbert, further required the seminary to establish a smaller school devoted to the conversion and education of native people. Following the British Conquest and the subsequent banishing of the Jesuits, the seminary became a college devoted to classical education. It also served as housing for the bishop of Québec after his palace was destroyed during the invasion. In 1852, the seminary founded the Université Laval, the first French-language university in North America. The Séminaire's vast ensemble of buildings now includes the priests' residence, a private school for boys and girls, the faculty of architecture of Université Laval, and the Musée de l'Amérique Française (see below), which manages these historic buildings.

Fauna

Québec's vast natural spaces are populated by a tremendously diverse collection of birds and mammals. The beaver, a symbol of the colonization of the New World, chomps his way through forests to create his abode; the mighty moose, which prefers the cover of a stand of firs, reigns over the forest, with its velvety crown; in deciduous and coniferous forests, listen and watch for the call of the blue jay. One of the province's most striking riches is certainly its wildlife.

nowy Owl

nlike other members of its species, this great owl
diurnal. It is common to arctic tundra around the
orld, but can also be found in the southern United
ates. It feeds primarily on small mammals; lemmings
e its favourite.

Snow Goose

Snow geese pause in the St. Lawrence Valley every spring and fall during their migratory journey of several thousand kilometres, and literally cover the shoreline around Cap Tourmente.

nada Goose

nd throughout Canada, the eponymous goose is
ly identified by its long black neck, black head and
conspicuous white cheek patches. This bird nests
small islets or on muskrat or beaver dams.

Northern Gannet

Northern gannets inhabit Île Bonaventure, and the sight of a whole colony taking flight is like a flurry of snowflakes on a sunny day. These birds are not shy and can be easily observed up close.

Great Cormorant

With its glistening black plumage, this bird can reach 1m in height. An excellent diver, it can hold its breath for up to 30 seconds, time enough to catch some food.

Belted Kingfisher

This sturdy little bird is found throughout the America and in Australia. You might be lucky enough to spot o asit gets ready to plunge into waters teeming with fish search of its next meal.

Great Blue Heron

This wader, which can reach 132cm, can be found throughout southern Québec. Hunted for many years, it is now protected by Canadian law. The great blue heron feeds by standing still in open water and waiting for its unsuspecting prey to approach.

Common Loon

Shortly after the spring thaw, this bird returns to Québec to nest. They are usually seen in solitar pairs on lakes.

American Robin

The robin's song announces the start of spring. This bird, which is found throughout Québec, pokes about grassy areas for its diet of small fruits, insects and worms.

Northern Cardinal

The cardinal can be spotted year-round in southern Québec. The male's brilliant red plumage makes him easy to spot.

Black-capped Chickadee

The chickadee is one of those cheerful little birds that flits about, even in winter, without a care for the cold. This bird is easily attracted to feeders. It eats insects, small fruit and seeds.

Blue Jay

This crested bird is found across southern Canada. Practically carnivorous, the blue jay eats the eggs and chicks of other birds, as well as fruits, seeds, acorns and insects.

Red-winged Blackbird

The red spots on each wing of the male are visible in flight. The blackbird nests in marshes where frogs and bulrushes are plentiful. Considered a pest by farmers, it consumes grain from cultivated fields.

Beaver

Known as a skilful and tireless dam builder, the beaver is Canada's national symbol. It has a stout body, short, webbed hind feed and a large, flat, scaly tail used as a rudder when it swims. Its powerful lower incisors allow it to cut down trees for its shelter.

Skunk

This small mammal is mostly known for its defence mechanism; it sprays its attackers with a foul-smelling liquid. The first European settlers called it *bête puante* or stinking beast. This animal is common to eastern North America, even to some cities and, while it is attractive, it is a good idea to keep your distance.

Porcupine

Found in significant numbers in both deciduous and coniferous forests, the porcupine is famous for the way it defends itself. When threatened, the quills covering its body stand on end, turning the porcupine into a kind of unassailable pin cushion.

Racoon

The racoon is a nocturnal and particularly crafty animal found in southeastern Canada. It has a reputation for cleanliness because of its habit of plunging its food underwater before eating it.

Ungava Caribou (Arctic Reindeer)

This large species of deer can weigh up to 250kg when fully grown. It lives in the tundra, and its name comes from the Algonquian language.

White-tailed Deer

The white-tailed deer is the smallest species of deer in eastern North America, attaining a maximum weight of about 150kg. This graceful creature lives at the forest's edge and is one of the most commonly hunted animals in Québec. The male's antlers fall off each winter and grow back in the spring.

Moose

This is the largest member of the deer family; it can measure more than 2m in height and weigh up to 600kg. The male is distinguished by its broad, flattened antlers, large head, rounded nose and the hump on its back.

Black Bear

Most often found in forests, this is the most common species of bear in eastern Canada. It can weigh up to 150kg when fully grown, yet it is Canada's smallest bear. Be careful—the black bear is unpredictable and dangerous.

Wolf

This predator lives in packs. It measures between 67 and 95cm, and weighs no more than 50kg. Wolves attack their prey (often deer) in packs, and their viciousness makes them rather unsympathetic creatures. Wolves keep their distance from humans.

Red Fox

This small animal has striking auburn fur and is found throughout the forests of eastern Canada. A cunning creature, it keeps its distance from humans and is rarely seen. It hunts small animals and also feeds on nuts a berries.

Coyote

Smaller than the wolf, the coyote adapts easily to various surroundings; it can be spotted throughout southeastern Canada. If meat is unavailable, this carnivore can survive as a vegetarian.

Today's seminary is the result of rebuilding efforts following numerous fires and bombardments. Across from the old gate, the wing devoted to the offices of the Procurator can be seen, complete with sundial. During the 1690 attack of Admiral Phipps, it was in the vaulted cellars of this wing that the citizens of Québec City took refuge.

It also contains the private chapel of Monseigneur Briand (1785), decorated with sculpted olive branches by Pierre Emond. Forming a right angle with the chapel is the beautiful parlor wing, constructed in 1696. The use of segmented arch windows in this attractive building betrays the direct influence of French models, which were used prior to making adaptations to Québec's climate. Guided tours leave from the Musée de l'Amérique Française.

The **Musée de l'Amérique Française** ★★ *($5, $13 with admission to Musée de la Civilisation and Centre d'Interprétation de la Place-Royale; late Jun to early Sep every day 9:30am to 5pm; early Sep to late Jun Tue-Sun 10am to 5pm; 2 Côte de la Fabrique,* ☎*418-692-2843 or 866-710-8031, www.mcq.org)* is dedicated to the seven North-American communities that were formed by French immigration. Other than the Québécois, they include the Acadians, the Franco-Ontarians, the Francophones from the West, the Metis and the Francophones from Louisiana and New England. It contains over 450,000 artifacts, including silverware, paintings, oriental art and numismatics, as well as scientific instruments collected for educational purposes over the course of the last three centuries by the priests of the seminary. The museum occupies five floors of what used to be the residences of the Université Laval. The first Egyptian mummy brought to America is on view, as are several items that belonged to Monseigneur de Laval. Temporary exhibitions are also held here, presenting various figures from history.

On returning to Place de l'Hôtel-de-Ville, turn left on Rue de Buade.

The old **Holt Renfrew** store *(43 Rue de Buade),* which opened in 1837, faces the cathedral. Originally dedicated to the sale of furs, which they supplied by appointment to Her Majesty the Queen, Holt's held the exclusive rights for the Canadian distribution of Christian Dior and Yves Saint-Laurent designs for a long time. Holt's is now closed, having given way to the boutiques of the **Promenades du Vieux-Québec**.

The history of Québec City's cathedral underscores the problems faced by builders in New France and the determination of the Québécois in the face of terrible circumstances. The **Basilique-Cathédrale Notre-Dame-de-Québec** ★★★ *(guided tours and "Feux sacrés" sound and light show; 20 Rue de Buade,* ☎*418-694-0665, www.patrimoine-religieux.com)* as it stands today is the result of numerous phases of construction and a number of tragedies that left the church in ruins on two occasions. The first church on this site was built in 1633 under the orders of Samuel de Champlain, who was buried nearby four years later. This wooden church was replaced in 1647 by the Église Notre-Dame-de-la-Paix, a stone church in the shape of a Roman cross that would later serve as the model for many rural parish churches. In 1674, New France was assigned its first bishop in residence. Monseigneur François de Laval (1623-1708) decided that this small church, after renovations befitting its status as the heart of such an enormous ministry, would become the seat of the Catholic Church in Québec. A grandiose plan was commissioned from architect Claude Baillif, which, despite personal financial contributions from Louis XIV, eventually had to be scaled down. Only the base of the west tower survives from this period. In 1742, the bishop had the church remodelled by engineer Gaspard Chaussegros de Léry, who is responsible for its present layout, featuring an extended nave illuminated from above. The cathedral resembles many urban churches built in France during the same period.

During the siege of Québec in 1759, the cathedral was bombarded and reduced to ruins. It was not rebuilt until the status of Catholics in Québec was settled by the British crown. The oldest Catholic parish north of Mexico was finally allowed to begin the reconstruction of its church in 1770, using the 1742 plans. The work was directed by Jean Baillargé (1726-1805), a member of the well-known family of architects and craftsmen. This marked the beginning of the Baillargé family's extended, fervent involvement in the reconstruction and renovation of the church for almost a century. In 1959, a mausoleum was added in the basement of the church. It holds the remains of Québec bishops and various governors (Frontenac, Vaudreuil, de Callière). In recent years, several masterpieces that were hanging in the church have been stolen, leaving bare walls and increasing the need to safeguard the remaining paintings, including the beautiful *Saint-Jérôme* by Jacques-Louis David (1780).

Québec Expérience *($7.50; mid-May to mid-Oct every day 10am to 10pm, mid-Oct to mid-May every day 10am to 4:45pm; 8 Rue du Trésor, third floor, ☎418-694-4000)* is an elaborate show depicting the history of Québec City. This lively three-dimensional multimedia presentation takes viewers back in time to relive the great moments in the city's history through its important historical figures. A wonderful way to learn about Québec City's past, these half-hour shows are a big hit with kids. Presented in both French and English.

Québec City's old central post office, or **Bureau de Poste** ★ *(3 Passage du Chien-d'Or)*, was built between 1871 and 1873 on the former site of the Hôtel du Chien d'Or, a solid dwelling built around 1735 for a wealthy Bordeaux merchant, who ordered a bas-relief depicting a dog gnawing a bone installed above the doorway. The following inscription appeared underneath the bas-relief, which was relocated to the pediment of the present post office in 1872: *"Je suis un chien qui ronge l'os, en le rongeant je prends mon repos. Un temps viendra qui n'est pas venu où je mordrai qui m'aura mordu."* ("I am a dog gnawing a bone, as I gnaw, I rest at home. Though it's not yet here there'll come a time when those who bit me will be paid in kind.") It is said that the message was destined for Intendant Bigot, a man known for being a swindler and who was so outraged he had the Bordeaux merchant killed.

The dome of the post office and the facade overlooking the river were added at the beginning of the 20th century. The building was renamed **Édifice Louis-S.-Saint-Laurent**, in honour of the former Prime Minister of Canada. Besides the traditional post and philatelic services, a **Parks Canada** information service office *(free admission; Mon-Fri 8am to 4:30pm, Sat and Sun 10am to 5pm; 3 Passage du Chien-d'Or, ☎418-648-4177)* was added to illustrate Canada's natural and historical heritage.

Facing the post office stands a **monument to Monseigneur François de Montmorency Laval** (1623-1708), the first bishop of Québec, whose diocese covered two thirds of the North-American continent. Designed by Philippe Hébert and erected in 1908, the monument features an attractive staircase leading to Côte de la Montagne and, from there, to Basse-Ville.

Parc Montmorency ★ was laid out in 1875 after the city walls were lowered along Rue des Remparts and the governor general of Canada, Lord Dufferin, discovered the magnificent view from the promontory. George-Étienne Cartier, prime minister of the Dominion of Canada and one of the Fathers of Confederation, is honoured with a statue here, as are Louis Hébert, Guillaume Couillard and Marie Rollet, some of the original farmers of New France. These last three disembarked in 1617 and were granted the fiefdom of Sault-au-Matelot, on the future site of the seminary, in 1623. These attractive bronzes are the work of Montréal sculptor Alfred Laliberté.

Continue along Rue des Remparts.

The halls of the **old Université Laval** ★ can be seen through a gap in the wall of the ramparts. Built in 1856 in the gardens of the seminary, they were completed in 1875 with the addition of an impressive mansard roof surmounted by three silver lanterns. When the spotlights shine on them at night, it creates the atmosphere of a royal gala. Note that Université Laval is now located on a large campus in **Sainte-Foy** (see p 385).

Following **Rue des Remparts**, Basse-Ville (lower town) comes into view and you'll see several old cannons. The patrician manors on the street along the ramparts provide a picturesque backdrop for the old Latin quarter that extends behind them. The narrow streets and 18th-century houses in this neighbourhood are worth the detour.

Maison Montcalm *(45 to 51 Rue des Remparts)* originally was a single, very large residence constructed in 1727; it is now divided into three houses. Home to the Marquis de Montcalm at the time of the Battle of the Plains of Abraham, the building subsequently housed the officers of the British army before being subdivided and returned to private use. In the first half of the 19th century, many houses in Québec were covered in the sort of imitation stone boards that still protect the masonry of the Montcalm house. It was believed that this type of covering lent a more refined look to the houses.

Take Rue Saint-Flavien.

At the corner of Rue Couillard is **Maison François-Xavier-Garneau** *($5; May to Feb Sun 1pm to 4pm, tours every hour; 14 Rue St-Flavien, ☎418-692-2240)*. Québec City businessman Louis Garneau recently bought this neo-classical house (1862) where historian and poet François-Xavier-Garneau lived during the last years of his life. Throughout the summer, an actor dressed in period costume is on site to make the past come alive as you visit the rooms and admire the objects on display.

Nearby, on Rue Couillard, is the **Musée Bon-Pasteur** ★ *($2; Tue-Sun 1pm to 5pm; 14 Rue Couillard, ☎418-694-0243)*. Founded in 1993, it tells the story of the Bon Pasteur (Good Shepherd) community of nuns, which has been serving the poor of Québec City since 1850. The museum is located in the Béthanie house, an eclectic brick structure built around 1887 to shelter unwed mothers and their children.

Walk back on Rue Couillard. Go down Rue Hamel until Rue Charlevoix, where you will turn left.

The **Musée des Augustines de l'Hôtel-Dieu de Québec** ★ *(free admission, $3 guided tours; Tue-Sat 9:30am to noon and 1:30pm to 5pm, Sun 1:30pm to 5pm; 32 Rue Charlevoix, ☎418-692-2492)* is a museum that traces the history of the Augustinian community in New France through pieces of furniture, paintings and medical instruments. On display is the chest that contained the meagre belongings of the founders (pre-1639), as well as pieces from the Château Saint-Louis, the residence of the first governors under the French Regime, including portraits of Louis XIV and Cardinal Richelieu. Upon request, visitors can see the chapel and the vaulted cellars. The remains of Blessed Marie-Catherine de Saint-Augustin, the founder of the community in New France, lie in an adjoining chapel, as is a beautiful gilded reliquary in the Louis XIV style, sculpted in 1717 by Noël Levasseur.

Follow the small street opposite the chapel (Rue Collins). At the corner of Rue Saint-Jean is a pleasant view of Côte de la Fabrique, with the Hôtel de Ville on the right and Cathédrale Notre-Dame in the background on the left. Turn right on Rue Saint-Jean, a lovely commercial street in the heart of Vieux-Québec.

A short detour to the left down Rue Saint-Stanislas provides a view of the old **Methodist Church**, a beautiful Gothic Revival building dating from 1850. Today it houses the **Institut Canadien** *(42 Rue St-Stanislas)*, a centre for literature and the arts. Before the Quiet Revolution of the 1960s, this centre was the focus of many a contentious dispute with the clergy over its "audacious" choice of books. The institute is home to a theatre and a branch of the municipal library.

The neighbouring building, number 44, is the **Ancienne Prison de Québec** (former jail) built in 1808 by François Baillargé. In 1868, it was renovated to accommodate Morrin College, affiliated with Montréal's McGill University. This venerable institution of English-speaking Québec also houses the library of the **Québec Literary and Historical Society**, a learned society founded in 1824. The building on the corner of Rue Cook and Rue Dauphine surmounted by a Palladian steeple is **St. Andrew's Presbyterian Church**, completed in 1811.

Return to Rue Saint-Jean, which you'll cross. Turn left on Rue McMahon, and continue on to the reception and information centre at the Artillery Park.

The **Site Patrimonial du Parc-de-l'Artillerie** ★ ★ *($4; early Apr to mid-Oct every day 10am to 5pm, rest of the year reservations required; 2 Rue d'Auteuil, ☎418-648-4205)* takes up part of an enormous military installation running alongside the walls of the city. The reception and information centre is located in the old foundry where munitions were manufactured until 1964. On display is a fascinating model of Québec City, which was built between 1795 and 1810 by military engineer Jean-Baptiste Duberger for strategic planning. The model was returned to Québec City after having been sent to England in 1813. It is an unparalleled source of information on the layout of the city in the years following the British Conquest.

Walk back up Rue D'Auteuil.

Québec City - **Exploring** - Vieux-Québec

The most recent of Québec City's gates, **Porte Saint-Jean** ★, has rather ancient origins. As of 1693 it was one of only three entrances to the city. It was reinforced by Chaussegros de Léry in 1757, and then rebuilt by the British. To satisfy merchants who were clamouring for the total destruction of the walls, a "modern" gate equipped with tandem carriage tunnels and corresponding pedestrian passageways was erected in 1867. However, this structure did not fit in with Lord Dufferin's romantic vision of the city and was eliminated in 1898. The present gate did not replace it until 1936.

Number 29, on the left, is an **old Anglican orphanage** built for the Society for Promoting Christian Knowledge in 1824, and was the first Gothic Revival style building in Québec City. Its architecture was portentous, as it inaugurated the romantic current that would eventually permeate the city.

The last of Québec's Jesuits died in 1800, his community having been banished by the British and then, in 1774, by the Pope himself. The community was resuscitated in 1814, however, and returned to Québec City in 1840. Since their college and church on Place de l'Hôtel-de-Ville were no longer available, they were welcomed by the Congregationists, a brotherhood founded by the Jesuit Ponert in 1657 with a mission to propagating the cult of the Virgin. These latter parishioners built the **Chapelle des Jésuites** ★ *(20 Rue Dauphine, ☎418-694-9616)*. François Baillargé designed the plans for the church, which was completed in 1818. The facade was redone in 1930. The decoration of the interior began with the construction of the counterfeit vaulting, and its centrepiece is Pierre-Noël Levasseur's altar (1770). Since 1925, the Jesuit church has been Québec's sanctuary for the worship of Canada's martyred saints.

Porte Kent ★, like Porte Saint-Louis, is the result of Lord Dufferin's romantic vision of the city. The plans for this gate, Vieux-Québec's prettiest, were drawn up in 1878 by Charles Baillargé, based on the ideas of Irishman William H. Lynn.

Climb the stairway to the top of Porte Kent and walk along the wall towards Porte Saint-Louis. Then, climb down from the wall at Porte Saint-Louis. Côte de la Citadelle is on the other side of Rue Saint-Louis.

Québec City's **Citadelle** ★ ★ ★ *(at the far end of the Côte de la Citadelle, www.lacitadelle.qc.ca)* represents three centuries of North-American military history and is still in use. Since 1920, it has housed the Royal 22nd Regiment of the Canadian Army, a regiment distinguished for its bravery during World War II. Within the circumference of the enclosure are some 25 buildings, including the officers' mess, the hospital, the prison and the official residence of the governor general of Canada, as well as the first observatory in Canada. The Citadelle's history began in 1693, when engineer Dubois Berthelot de Beaucours had the Cap Diamant redoubt built at the highest point of Québec City's defense system, some 100m above the river. Today, this solid construction is included inside the King's bastion.

Throughout the 18th century, French and then British engineers developed projects for a citadel that remained unfulfilled. Chaussegros de Léry's powderhouse of 1750, which now houses the Museum of the Royal 22nd Regiment, and the temporary excavation works to the west (1783) are the only works of any scope accomplished during this period. The citadel that appears today was built between 1820 and 1832 by Colonel Elias Walker Durnford. Dubbed the "Gibraltar of America," and built according to principles expounded by Vauban in the 17th century, the citadel has never borne the brunt of a single cannonball, though it has acted as an important element of dissuasion.

The **Musée du Royal 22e Régiment** *($8; Nov to March with reservations only, Apr every day 10am to 4pm, May and Jun every day 9am to 5pm, Jul every day 9am to 6pm, Sep every day 9am to 4pm, Oct every day 10am to 3pm; ☎418-694-2815, www.lacitadelle.qc.ca)* is a museum that offers an interesting collection of weapons, uniforms, insignia and military documents spanning almost 400 years. It is possible to take a guided tour of the whole installation, where you'll witness the changing of the guard, the retreat and the firing of the cannon. The changing of the guard lasts 30min and takes place every day from the end of June until the beginning of September at 6pm, weather permitting. The retreat lasts 30min and occurs according to a variable schedule during the summer.

Tour B: Petit-Champlain to Vieux-Port
★ ★ ★

 1 to 2 days

Québec's port and commercial area is a narrow U-shaped piece of land wedged near the waters of the St. Lawrence River. This area is sometimes called the Basse-Ville of Vieux-Québec because of its location at the foot of the Cap Diamant escarpment. The cradle of New France, Place-Royale is where Samuel de Champlain (1567-1635) founded the settlement he called *"Abitation"* in 1608, which would eventually become Québec City. In the summer of 1759, three quarters of the city were badly damaged by British bombardment. It took 20 years to repair and rebuild the houses. In the 19th century, the construction of multiple embankments allowed the expansion of town and enabled the area around Place-Royale to be linked by road with the area around the intendant's palace. The port's decline at the beginning of the 20th century led to the gradual abandonment of Place-Royale; restoration work began in 1959. The Petit-Champlain district has been reclaimed by artisans who have set up shop here, especially on the Rue du Petit-Champlain. This area now caters mostly to tourists, who visit the numerous studios to watch the craftspeople at work and to buy their wares.

This walking tour begins at Porte Prescott, which straddles Côte de la Montagne. Those who do not enjoy walking would be well advised to take the funicular from Terrasse Dufferin and to begin the tour at the start of Rue Petit-Champlain.

The **Funiculaire** (funicular) *($1.50; ☎418-692-1132, www.funiculaire-quebec.com)* began operating in November 1879. It was installed by entrepreneur W. A. Griffith in order to link the lower and upper towns. When the funicular was first built, water was transferred from one reservoir to another to make it function. It was converted to electricity in 1906, at the same time that Terrasse Dufferin was illuminated. The funicular is an outdoor elevator that eliminates the need to take the *Escalier Casse-Cou,* or "break-neck stairway," or to go around Côte de la Montagne. The funicular was completely overhauled in 1998. It operates from 7:30am until at least 11pm.

Porte Prescott *(Côte de la Montagne)* can be reached from Côte de la Montagne or from Terrasse Dufferin by means of a stairway and a charming footbridge on the left of the funicular's entryway. This discreetly postmodern structure was built in 1983 by the architectural firm of Gauthier, Guité, Roy, which sought to evoke the 1797 gate by Gother Mann. It allows pedestrians to cross directly from Terrasse Dufferin to Parc Montmorency.

Descend Côte de la Montagne and take the Escalier Casse-Cou on the right.

The **Escalier Casse-Cou** *(Côte de la Montagne),* which literally means "break-neck stairway," has been here since 1682. Until the beginning of the 20th century, it had been made of planks that were in constant need of repair or replacement. It connects the various businesses situated on different levels. At the foot of the stairway is **Rue du Petit-Champlain**, a narrow pedestrian street flanked by charming craft shops and quaint cafés located in 17th- and 18th-century houses. Some of the houses at the foot of the cape were destroyed by rock slides prior to the cliff's reinforcement during the 19th century.

At the foot of the Escalier Casse-Cou, a small *économusée* (economuseum) unveils the secrets of glass-blowing. At the **Verrerie La Mailloche** *(free admission; late Jun to early Nov Wed-Sun 10am to noon and 1:30pm to 4:30pm, rest of the year Mon-Fri 10am to noon and 1:30pm to 4:30pm; 58 Rue Sous-le-Fort, ☎418-694-0445, www.lamailloche.com)*, visitors can observe the fascinating spectacle of artisans shaping molten glass according to traditional techniques. The finished products are sold in a shop on the second floor.

Maison Louis-Jolliet ★ *(16 Rue du Petit-Champlain)* is one of the earliest houses of Vieux-Québec (1683) and one of the few works of Claude Baillif still standing. The house was built after the great fire of 1682, which destroyed Basse-Ville. It was this tragedy that prompted the authorities to require that stone be used in all buildings. The fire also paved the way for some improvements in urban planning: roads were straightened and Place-Royale was created.

Québec City – Exploring – Petit-Champlain to Vieux-Port

Louis Jolliet (1645-1700) was the man who, along with Father Marquette, discovered the Mississippi and explored Hudson Bay. During the last years of his life, he taught hydrography at the Séminaire de Québec. The interior of the house was completely gutted and now contains the lower platform of the funicular (see above).

Follow Rue du Petit-Champlain until the end, where it meets Boulevard Champlain. You will see a colourful fresco on the facade of the last house.

You will probably need a few minutes to admire the many details that make up the beautiful **Fresque du Petit-Champlain** *(102 Rue du Petit-Champlain)*. Some 35 characters, both famous and unknown, who shaped the history of the province of Québec, and most particularly of Québec City and the Petit-Champlain district, come to life in six rooms. From the first floor to the attic, they are presented in various settings, such as artisan workshops and an inn. You'll feel as though the walls suddenly open up on different chapters in history!

Retrace your steps and take the stairway that leads to Boulevard Champlain. At the foot of the stairway, make sure to turn around and admire the exceptional view from below of the Château Frontenac.

Maison Demers ★ *(28 Boulevard Champlain)* was built in 1689 by mason Jean Lerouge. This impressive residence is an example of the bourgeois style of Québec's Basse-Ville. A two-storey residential facade looks on to Rue du Petit-Champlain while the rear, which was used as a warehouse, extends down another two storeys to open directly onto l'Anse du Cul-de-Sac.

The cove called l'**Anse du Cul-de-Sac**, also known as the Anse aux Barques, was Québec City's first port. In 1745, Intendant Gilles Hocquart ordered the construction of a major shipyard in the western part of the cove. Several French battleships were built there using Canadian lumber. In 1854, the terminus of the Grand Trunk railway was built on the embankments, and in 1858 the Marché Champlain went up, only to be destroyed by fire in 1899. The location is presently occupied by administrative buildings and by the **terminal of the Québec-Lévis ferry**. A short return trip on the ferry provides a spectacular view of Vieux-Québec in its entirety. Taking the ferry (see

p 330) in the winter affords a rare chance to come face to face with the ice floes on the St. Lawrence River.

Follow Boulevard Champlain east as far as Rue du Marché-Champlain. The ferry boards from the south end of this road.

Hôtel Jean-Baptiste-Chevalier ★ ★ *(60 Rue du Marché-Champlain)* is not a hotel but rather the townhouse of a wealthy family. The first building in the Place-Royale area to be restored, the hôtel is really three separate houses from three different periods: **Maison de l'Armateur Chevalier** (home of Chevalier the shipowner), built in a square in 1752; **Maison Frérot**, with a mansard roof (1683); and **Maison Dolbec**, dating from 1713. These houses were all repaired or partially rebuilt after the British Conquest. As a group, they were rescued from deterioration in 1955 by Gérard Morisset, the director of the Inventaire des Oeuvres d'Art, who suggested that they be purchased and restored by the government of Québec. This decision had a domino effect and prevented the demolition of Place-Royale.

Take Rue Notre-Dame, and turn right onto Rue Sous-le-Fort.

With no walls to protect Basse-Ville, other means of defending it from the cannon-fire of ships in the river had to be found. Following the attack by Admiral Phipps in 1690, it was decided to set up the **Batterie Royale** ★ *(at the far end of Rue Sous-le-Fort)*, according to a plan drawn up by Claude Baillif. The strategic position of the battery allowed for the bombardment of any enemy ships foolhardy enough to venture into the narrows in front of the city. The ruins of the battery, long hidden under storehouses, were discovered in 1974. The crenellations, removed in the 19th century, were reconstructed, as was the wooden portal, discernible in a sketch from 1699.

Continue along Rue Saint-Pierre, and turn left on Rue de la Place to go up to Place-Royale.

Place-Royale ★ ★ ★ is the most European quarter of any city in North America. It resembles a village in northwestern France. Place-Royale is laden with symbolism, as it was on this very spot that New France was founded in 1608. After many unsuccessful attempts, this became the official departure point of French exploits in America. Under

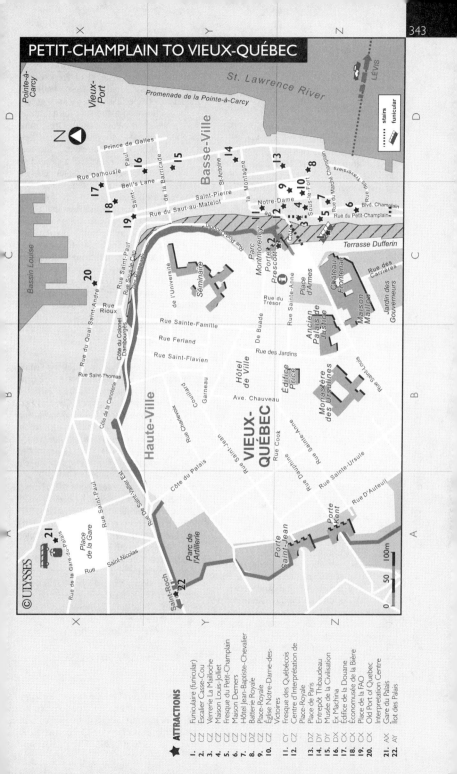

PETIT-CHAMPLAIN TO VIEUX-QUÉBEC

St. Lawrence River

LÉVIS

Promenade de la Pointe-à-Carcy

Pointe-à-Carcy

Vieux-Port

Basse-Ville

stairs
funicular

Prince de Galles

Rue Dalhousie

Bell's Lane

Rue du Saut-au-Matelot

Rue Saint-Pierre

St-Antoine

Notre-Dame

Sous-le-Fort

Rue du Marché Champlain

Blvd. Champlain

Rue du Petit-Champlain

Terrasse Dufferin

Bassin Louise

Rue Saint-André

Rue du Quai Saint-André

Rue Rioux

Rue Saint-Paul

Rue Sous-le-Cap

Rue des Remparts

Côte du Colonel Dambourgès

Séminaire

de l'Université

Rue Sainte-Famille

Rue Ferland

Rue Saint-Flavien

Rue Saint-Thomas

Parc Montmorency

Porte Prescott

Place d'Armes

Château Frontenac

Rue des Carrières

Jardin des Gouverneurs

Rue du Trésor

Rue Sainte-Anne

De Buade

Rue des Jardins

Maison Maillou

Ancien Palais de Justice

Monastère des Ursulines

Rue Saint-Louis

Hôtel de Ville

Édifice Price

Ave. Chauveau

HAUTE-VILLE

VIEUX-QUÉBEC

Rue Garneau

Rue Couillard

Rue Christie

Rue Saint-Jean

Côte de la Canoterie

Rue Saint-Paul

Rue Des Prairies

Rue Saint-Villier Est

Côte du Palais

Rue Cook

Rue Dauphine

Rue Sainte-Anne

Rue Sainte-Ursule

Rue d'Auteuil

Place de la Gare

Rue de la Gare-du-Palais

Rue Saint-Paul

Rue Saint-Nicolas

Parc de l'Artillerie

Porte Saint-Jean

Porte Kent

0   50   100m

©ULYSSES

the French Regime, Place-Royale was the only densely populated area in a vast, untamed colony. Today, it contains the most significant concentration of 17th- and 18th-century buildings in the Americas north of Mexico.

The square itself was laid out in 1673 by Governor Frontenac as a market. It replaced the garden of Champlain's Abitation, a stronghold that went up in flames in 1682, along with the rest of Basse-Ville. In 1686, Intendant Jean Bochart de Champigny erected a **bronze bust of Louis XIV** in the middle of the square, hence the name of the square, Place-Royale. In 1928, François Bokanowski, then French Minister of Commerce and Communications, presented Québécois Athanase David with a bronze replica of the marble bust of Louis XIV in the Gallerie de Diane at Versailles to replace the missing statue. The bronze, by Alexis Rudier, was not set up until 1931, for fear of offending England.

The small, unpretentious **Église Notre-Dame-des-Victoires** ★★ *(free admission; early May to mid-Oct every day 9am to 4:30pm, rest of the year every day 10am to 4:30pm; closed during weddings, baptisms and funeral ceremonies; 32 Rue Sous-le-Fort;* ☎*418-692-1650)* is the oldest church in Canada. Designed by Claude Baillif, it dates from 1688. It was built on the foundations of Champlain's *Abitation* and incorporates some of its walls. Beside the church, black granite marks the remains of the foundations of the second Abitation de Champlain. These vestiges were discovered in 1976.

Initially dedicated to the Infant Jesus, it was rechristened Notre-Dame-de-la-Victoire after Admiral Phipp's attack of 1690 failed. It was later renamed Notre-Dame-des-Victoires (the plural) in memory of the misfortune of British Admiral Walker, whose fleet ran aground on Île-aux-Oeufs during a storm in 1711. The bombardments of the Conquest left nothing standing but the walls of the church, spoiling Levasseur's lovely interior. The church was restored in 1766, but was not fully rebuilt until the current steeple was added in 1861.

If you continue on Rue Notre-Dame towards Côte de la Montagne and then turn around, you will be surprised by the colourful sight. On the blind wall of Maison Soumande, in front of Parc de La Cetière,

are displayed the colours of the **Fresque des Québécois** ★★. In fact, if they're not careful, passersby may actually miss the fresco: it is a *trompe l'œil*! A team of French and Québec artists created this fresco with the guidance of specialists (historians, geographers, etc.) who made sure the painting was realistic and educational. On a surface area of $420m^2$, they brought together Québec City's architecture and famous sites, such as Cap Diamant, the ramparts, a bookshop, houses of Vieux-Québec—in short, the different places that the town's inhabitants encounter every day. Just like the crowd of admiring onlookers that gathers rain or shine, you can amuse yourself for quite a while trying to identify the historical figures and the role they played. From top to bottom and from left to right, you will see Marie Guyart, Catherine de Longpré, François-Xavier Garneau, Louis-Joseph Papineau, Jean Talon, the Comte de Frontenac, Marie Fitzbach, Marcelle Mallet, Louis Jolliet, Alphonse Desjardins, Lord Dufferin, Félix Leclerc and, finally, Samuel de Champlain, who started it all.

Return to Place-Royale and visit the **Centre d'Interprétation de Place-Royale** ★★ *($4, free admission on Tue from early Nov to late May and on Sat from 10am to noon during Jan and Feb; $13 includes admission to Musée de la Civilisation and Musée de l'Amérique Française; early Sep to late Jun Tue-Sun 10am to 5pm, late Jun to early Sep every day 9:30am to 5pm; 27 Rue Notre-Dame,* ☎*418-646-3167, www.mcq.org),* which was inaugurated in the fall of 1999. To accommodate the centre, both the Hazeur and Smith houses, which had burned down, were rebuilt in a modern style while using a large portion of the original materials. The omnipresent glass lets you admire the exposed rooms as well as the buildings' architecture from all angles. Along the glass walls between the two houses, a stairway goes down Côte de la Montagne to Place-Royale. From the staircase, you can see some of the centre's treasures. On each of the three levels, an exhibition presents chapters of Place-Royale's history.

Continue along Rue de la Place until it opens onto Place de Paris.

Place de Paris ★ *(along Rue du Marché-Finlay)* is an elegant and sophisticated combination of contemporary art and traditional surroundings conceived by Québécois architect Jean Jobin in 1987. A large sculpture by French artist Jean-Pierre Raynault dominates the centre of the square. The work was presented by Jacques Chirac, who was then mayor of Paris, on behalf of his city, when he visited Québec City. Entitled *Dialogue avec l'Histoire* (Dialogue with History), the black granite and white marble work is said to evoke the first human presence in the area and forms a pair with the bust of Louis XIV, visible in the background. The Québécois have dubbed it the Colossus of Québec because of its imposing dimensions. From the square, which was once a market, there is a splendid view of the Batterie Royale, the Château Frontenac and the St. Lawrence River.

Entrepôt Thibaudeau *(215 Rue du Marché-Finlay)* is a huge Second Empire building whose stone facade fronts onto Rue Dalhousie. It represents the last prosperous days of the area before its decline at the end of the 19th century.

Head back up the street towards Rue Saint-Pierre and turn right, and right again onto Rue Saint-Jacques. The entrance to the Musée de la Civilisation is on Rue Dalhousie, on the right.

The **Musée de la Civilisation ★ ★** *($8, Tue free admission, except in summer; $13 includes admission to Musée de l'Amérique Française and Centre d'Interprétation de la Place-Royale; early Sep to late Jun Tue-Sun 10am to 5pm, late Jun to early Sep every day 9:30am to 6:30pm; 85 Rue Dalhousie, ☎418-643-2158, www.mcq.org)* is housed in a building that was completed in 1988 in the traditional architectural style of Québec City, with its stylized roof, dormer windows and a bell tower like those common to the area. Architect Moshe Safdie, who also designed the revolutionary Habitat 67 in Montréal, Ottawa's National Gallery and Vancouver's Public Library, designed a sculptural building with a monumental exterior staircase at its centre. The lobby provides a charming view of Maison Estèbe and its wharf while preserving a contemporary look that is underlined by Astri Reuch's sculpture, *La Débâcle*.

The Musée de la Civilisation presents a great variety of temporary exhibitions. Themes such as humour, circus and song, for example, have been the object of very lively displays. Travelling exhibitions also recount the world's great civilizations, while permanent exhibitions provide a portrait of the local culture. *Mémoires* recounts the history of the Québec people; *Nous les Premières Nations*, developed in collaboration with First Nations peoples, is a large exhibition tracing the history of the 11 Aboriginal nations that originally inhabited Québec. You can view many objects here, as well as audiovisual materials like the work of filmmaker Arthur Lamothe. Some of the more remarkable items are the Aboriginal artifacts, the large French Regime fishing craft unearthed during excavations for the museum itself, some highly ornate 19th-century horse-drawn hearses, and some Chinese *objets d'art* and pieces of furniture, including an imperial bed, from the collection of the Jesuits. A gift shop is located in the museum's vaulted cellar, which dates from the 18th century.

Head northeast, towards the Vieux Port, through Rue Dalhousie.

Beside the Musée de la Civilisation is a lavish *Beaux-arts* fire station dating from 1912 that now houses **Ex Machina** *(103 Rue Dalhousie)*, a multi-disciplinary artistic production centre founded by Robert Lepage. Note the high tower with a copper dome rising on the southeast corner like a church spire, which was inspired by the tower of the Hôtel du Parlement. Firefighters used to hang their hoses in the tower to dry and to prevent damage, since in those days hoses were made of fabric. The building has been expanded and in order to keep its character, a false wall similar to the original stone wall, but made of plastic, has been erected in front of the new part.

The **Vieux-Port ★** *(160 Rue Dalhousie)* (old port) is often criticized for being overly American in a city with such a pronounced European sensibility. It was refurbished by the Canadian government on the occasion of the maritime celebration *Québec 1534-1984*. Various metallic structures were designed to enliven the promenade, at the end of which is the handsome **Édifice de la Douane** *(2 Quai St-André)* (customs house). With its dome and columns, it features a lovely neoclassical architecture. At the time the structure was built (1856-1857), the river actually flowed right next to it.

The entire port area between Place-Royale and the entrance of **Bassin Louise** is known as **Pointe-à-Carcy**. A pleasure boat harbour was added here in 2002.

Québec City - Exploring - Petit-Champlain to Vieux-Port

The **Économusée de la Bière** *(free admission; every day noon to 3am; 37 Quai St-André, ☎418-692-2877)* (beer economuseum) has been set up in an established Vieux-Port bar, L'Inox. Since L'Inox is a microbrewery, it is possible to have the master brewer take you behind the scenes, which are visible from the bar through a glass wall (reservations required). And not only will he explain how he makes the beer, he will offer you a taste of his work.

Take Rue Saint-Pierre on your left.

Place de la FAO is located at the intersection of Saint-Pierre, Saint-Paul and Sault-au-Matelot streets. This square honours the United Nations Food and Agriculture Organisation (FAO), whose first meeting was held at the Château Frontenac in 1945. The sculpture at the centre of the square represents the prow of a boat as it emerges from the waves, its female figurehead, *La Vivrière*, firmly grasping all kinds of fruit, vegetables and grains.

In the square at the corner of Rue Saint-Pierre stands an imposing building with a large round portico that formerly housed the **Imperial Bank of Commerce**.

Take Rue Sault-au-Matelot to Rue de la Barricade. This street is named in honour of the barricade set up against invading revolutionaries coming from what was to become the United States. They attempted to take Québec City on December 31, 1775.

On the right, Rue de la Barricade leads to **Rue Sous-le-Cap**. This narrow passage was once wedged between the St. Lawrence and the Cap Diamant escarpment. At the end of the 19th century, the street housed working-class families of Irish origin. Today's inhabitants, finding the houses too small, have renovated the little cottages on the side of the cliff and connected them to their houses by walkways crossing the street at clothesline height. One almost enters Rue Sous-le-Cap on tiptoe because of the feeling that you're walking into another world. At the end of the street is Côte du Colonel-Dambourgès and then Rue Saint-Paul.

Rue Saint-Paul is a most pleasant street, lined with antique shops overflowing with beautiful Québec heritage furniture.

To get to the Centre d'Interprétation du Vieux-Port-de-Québec, take Rue Rioux or Rue des Navigateurs, which both meet up with Quai Saint-André.

In the days of sailboats, Québec City was one of the most important gateways to America, since many vessels could not make their way any farther against the current. Its bustling port was surrounded by shipyards that made great use of plentiful and high-quality Canadian lumber. The first royal shipyards appeared under the French Regime in the cove known as l'Anse du Cul-de-Sac. The Napoleonic blockade of 1806 forced the British to turn to their Canadian colony for wood and for the construction of battleships. This was a great boost for a number of shipyards and made fortunes for many of their owners. The **Old Port of Quebec Interpretation Centre** *($3.50; early May to early Sep every day 10am to 5pm, early Sep to mid-Oct noon to 4pm; 100 Rue St-André, ☎418-648-3300)* is a national historic site that concentrates on those flourishing days of navigation in Québec. You can also take part in guided tours *($8)* of the Vieux-Port accompanied by characters in period costumes.

Take the promenade that runs along the basin to the Vieux-Port market.

Most of Québec City's public markets were shut down in the 1960s because they had become obsolete in an age of air-conditioned supermarkets and frozen food. However, people continued to want farm-fresh fruits and vegetables, as well as contact with the farmers. Moreover, the market was one of the only non-aseptic places people could congregate. Thus, the markets gradually began to reappear at the beginning of the 1980s. **Marché du Vieux-Port ★** *(corner of Rue St-Thomas and Rue St-André)* was built in 1987 by the architectural partners Belzile, Brassard, Galienne and Lavoie. It is the successor to two other markets, Finlay and Champlain, that no longer exist. In the summer, the market is a lovely place for a stroll and to take in the view of the Marina Bassin Louise at the edge of the market.

Continue along Rue Saint-Paul. Turn right on Rue Abraham-Martin and then left on Rue de la Gare-du-Palais until you reach the train station.

For over 50 years, the citizens of Québec City clamoured for a train station worthy of their city. Canadian Pacific finally fulfilled their wish in 1915. Designed by New York architect Harry Edward Prindle in the same style as the Château Frontenac, the **Gare du Palais** ★ *(Rue de la Gare-du-Palais)* gives visitors a taste of the romance and charm that await them in Québec City. The 18m-high arrival hall that extends behind the giant window of the facade is bathed in sunlight from the leaded glass skylight on the roof.

Return to Rue Saint-Paul by Boulevard Jean-Lesage, which becomes Rue Vallière. At the corner of Rue Saint-Nicolas and Rue Saint-Paul, you will be in the heart of the Quartier du Palais, so named because it surrounds the Palais de l'Intendant. To reach it, head west on Rue de Saint-Vallier.

The block bordered by Ruelle de l'Ancien-Chantier, Rue Saint-Vallier Est, Rue Saint-Paul and Rue Saint-Nicolas is known as **L'Îlot Saint-Nicolas**. It was restored with verve by architects De Blois, Côté, Leahy.

The handsome stone building on the corner and the two others behind it on Rue Saint-Nicolas housed the famous **Cabaret Chez Gérard** from 1938 to 1978. It was here that Charles Trenet, Rina Ketty and many other famous French singers performed. Charles Aznavour actually got his start here; in the bohemian days of the 1950s, he sang here every night for several months for a mere pittance.

The **Îlot des Palais** *($3; late Jun to early Sep every day 10am to 5pm, rest of the year upon reservation only; 8 Rue Vallière,* ☎ *418-641-6173)* . The Intendant oversaw the day-to-day affairs of the colony, so the royal stores, the few state enterprises and the prison were all located near his residence. With so many opportunities to enrich himself, it was only natural that his should be the most splendid mansion in New France. The remains of one wing of the palace can still be seen in the shape of the segment of brown-brick foundation wall that is now above ground. The location was originally the site of the brewery that was set up by the first intendant, Jean Talon (1625-1694). Talon took great effort to populate and develop the colony. For his trouble, he was made secretary of the king's cabinet upon his return to France. His brewery was replaced by a palace designed by engineer La Guer Morville in 1716. This elegant building had a classical cut-stone entrance that led to a horseshoe-shaped staircase. Twenty or so

ceremonial rooms were used for receptions and the meetings of the Conseil Supérieur.

The palace was spared British cannon-fire only to be burned to the ground during the American invasion of 1775-76. The arches of its cellars were used as the foundation of the Boswell brewery in 1872, bringing the site full circle. Visitors are free to inspect the cellars where the archeological information centre is located. The centre displays artifacts and ruins from the site itself.

To return to Haute-Ville, climb Côte du Palais at the end of Rue Saint-Nicolas.

Tour C: Grande Allée
★ ★

 1 day

Grande Allée appears on 17th-century maps, but it was not completed until the first half of the 19th century, when the city grew beyond its walls. Grande Allée was originally a country road linking the town to Chemin du Roi, and then to Montréal. At that time, it was bordered by the large agricultural properties of the nobility and clergy of the French Regime. After the British Conquest, many of the domains were turned into country estates by English merchants who set their manors well back from the road. The neoclassical town then spilled over into the area before the Victorian city had a chance to stamp the landscape with its distinctive style. Today's Grande Allée is the most pleasant route into the old city and the focus of extramural Haute-Ville. Although it links the capital's various ministries, a portion of it is a cheerful street, as many of its bourgeois houses have been converted into restaurants and bars.

This walking tour starts at Porte Saint-Louis and gradually works its way away from the walled city.

On the right is Paul Chevré's monument to historian François-Xavier Garneau. On the left is the *Croix du Sacrifice*, where Remembrance Day services are held every year on November 11.

The **Hôtel du Parlement** ★ ★ ★ *(free admission; guided tours late Jun to early Sep Mon-Fri 9am to 4:30pm, Sat and Sun 10am to 4:30pm, early Sep to Jun Mon-Fri 9am to 4:30pm; at the corner of Honoré-Mercier and Grande Allée Est,* ☎*418-643-7239, www.assnat.qc.ca)* is known to the Québécois as the Assemblée Nationale, or National Assembly. The seat of the government of Québec, this imposing building was erected between 1877 and 1886. It has a lavish French Renaissance Revival exterior intended to reflect the unique cultural status of Québec in the North-American context. Eugène-Étienne Taché (1836-1912) looked to the Louvre for inspiration in both the plan of the quadrangular building and its decor. Originally destined to incorporate the two houses of parliament characteristic of the British system of government, as well as all of the ministries, it is today part of a group of buildings on either side of Grande Allée.

The numerous statues of the parliament's main facade constitute a sort of pantheon of Québec. The 22 bronze statues of important figures in the history of Québec were cast by such well-known artists as Louis-Philippe Hébert and Alfred Laliberté. A raised inscription on the wall near the central passage identifies the statues. In front of the main entrance a bronze by Hébert entitled *La Halte dans la Forêt* (The Pause in the Forest) depicts an Aboriginal family. The work, which is meant to honour the original inhabitants of Québec, was displayed at Paris' World's Fair in 1889. *Le Pêcheur à la Nigog* (Fisherman at the Nigog), by the same artist, hangs in the niche by the fountain. The building's interior is a veritable compendium of the icons of Québec's history. The handsome woodwork is done in the tradition of religious architecture.

In front of the Assemblée Nationale, you'll notice the beautiful **Place de l'Assemblée-Nationale**, divided in two by the handsome Avenue Honoré-Mercier. On the wall's side, many events are hosted throughout the year. In February, the Ice Palace, the focus of carnival festivities, is located here.

Since the spring of 2002, the offices of the Conseil Exécutif and the Premier's cabinet have been located in the beautiful **Édifice Honoré-Mercier** *(835 Boulevard René-Lévesque Est)*, on the north side of the Hôtel du Parlement. In fact, this is actually a homecoming since the building housed the Premier's offices up until 1972. Before the move, the building was entirely renovated but the beauty of its architecture was preserved, including its marble features, plaster mouldings and woodwork. It was built between 1922 and 1925 according to the designs of architect Chênevert.

Take Grande Allée westward, leaving Vieux-Québec. On the left you will come to Rue Place-George-V, which runs along the square of the same name. Take this street to Avenue Wilfrid-Laurier.

Place George-V and the **Manège Militaire** ★ *(Avenue Wilfrid-Laurier)*, an expanse of lawn, is used as the training area and parade ground of the military's equestrians. There are cannons and a statue in memory of the two soldiers who perished attempting to douse the flames of the 1889 fire in the suburb of Saint-Sauveur. Otherwise, the grounds serve mainly to highlight the amusing Château-style facade of the Manège Militaire, (military riding academy) built in 1888 and designed by Eugène-Étienne Taché, who also designed the Hôtel du Parlement.

The Centre d'Interprétation du Parc des Champs-de-Bataille is on Avenue Wilfrid-Laurier behind the H and J Buildings, which border the Plains of Abraham. Housed in one of the Citadelle buildings, the **Maison de la Découverte des Plaines d'Abraham** ★ *(free admission; late Jun to mid-Oct every day 8:30am to 5:30pm, mid-Oct to late Jun every day 8:30 to 5pm; 835 Avenue Wilfrid-Laurier,* ☎*418-648-4071)* should please Québec City natives as much as visitors. On the ground floor, questions are answered about the Parc des Champs-de-Bataille, its history and the many activities that go on here. A multimedia show and an exhibit on the battle of the Plains of Abraham are presented. Various guided tours leave from here. One of them takes place on board the "Bus d'Abraham," guided by Abraham Martin himself.

Go back towards Grande Allée and continue west along its liveliest section.

A little further to the west, the fabric of the old city is again in evidence. **Terrasse Stadacona** *(nᵒˢ 640 to 664)*, on the right, is a neoclassical row of English-style townhouses; the multiple houses share a common facade. These houses date from 1847 and have been converted into bars and restaurants with terraces sheltered by multitudes

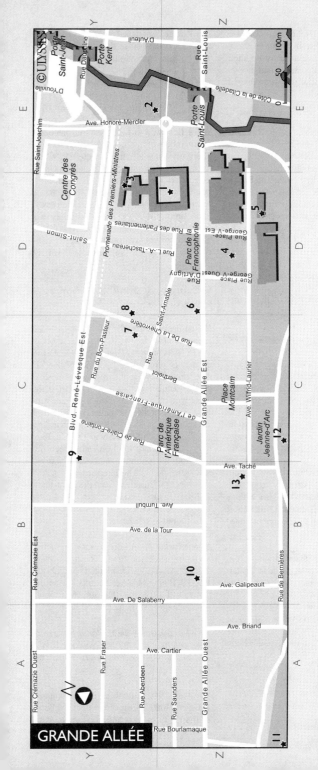

GRANDE ALLÉE

349

Rue Crémazie Ouest · **Rue Crémazie Est**

Rue Fraser · Rue Aberdeen · Rue Saunders · Grande Allée Ouest · Rue Bourlamaque

Ave. Cartier · Ave. Briand · Ave. De Salaberry · Ave. Galipeault · Rue de Bernières

Ave. Turnbull · Ave. de la Tour · Ave. Taché · Ave. Wilfrid-Laurier

Blvd. René-Lévesque Est · Rue de Claire-Fontaine · Rue de l'Amérique-Française · Berthelot · Rue · Rue du Bon-Pasteur · Rue De La Chevrotière · Saint-Amable · Grande Allée Est

Parc de l'Amérique Française

Place Montcalm

Jardin Jeanne-d'Arc

Rue Place-George-V Ouest · Rue George-V Ouest · Rue D'Artigny · Parc de la Francophonie · Rue Place-George-V Est · Rue L.-A.-Taschereau · Promenade des Premiers-Ministres · Rue des Parlementaires

Saint-Simon · Saint-Jean · Rue Saint-Joachim

Centre des Congrès

Ave. Honoré-Mercier

Porte Kent · Rue Dauphine · Porte Saint-Jean · D'Youville · D'Auteuil

Rue Saint-Louis · Porte Saint-Louis · Côte de la Citadelle

© ULYSSE

0 50 100m

★ ATTRACTIONS

1. DZ   Hôtel du Parlement
2. EY   Place de l'Assemblée-Nationale
3. DY   Édifice Honoré-Mercier
4. DZ   Place George-V / Manège Militaire
5. DZ   Maison de la Découverte des Plaines d'Abraham
6. DZ   Terrasse Stadacona
7. CY   Chapelle Historique Bon-Pasteur

8. DY   Édifice Marie-Guyart / Complexe G /
         Observatoire de la Capitale
9. CY   Grand Théâtre
10. BZ Maison Henry-Stuart
11. AZ Musée National des Beaux-Arts du Québec
12. CZ Parc des Champs-de-Bataille
13. BZ Tour Martello no. 2

of parasols. Opposite (n°s 661 to 695) is a group of Second Empire houses that dates from 1882, a period when Grande Allée was the most fashionable street in Québec City. These houses show the influence of the parliamentary buildings on the residential architecture of the area.

In the small **Parc Montcalm**, next to the **Hôtel Loews Le Concorde** (see p 363), is a statue commemorating the general's death on September 13, 1759, at the Battle of the Plains of Abraham. The **statue of French General Charles de Gaulle** (1890-1970), which faces away from Montcalm, created quite a controversy when it was erected in the spring of 1997. Farther along, at the entrance to the Plains of Abraham, **Jardin Jeanne-d'Arc ★★** boasts magnificent flowerbeds and a statue of Joan of Arc astride a spirited charger. Note that you are now standing on a huge drinking-water reservoir located under this part of the Plains of Abraham.

Return to Grande Allée and go east, then turn left on Rue de La Chevrotière.

Behind the austere facade of the mother house of the Soeurs du Bon-Pasteur, a community devoted to the education of abandoned and delinquent girls, is the charming, Baroque Revival-style **Chapelle Historique Bon-Pasteur ★★** *(free admission; Mon-Fri 1pm to 5pm; 1080 Rue de La Chevrotière, ☎418-522-6221)*. Designed by Charles Baillargé in 1866, this tall, narrow chapel houses an authentic baroque tabernacle dating from 1730. Pierre-Noël Levasseur's masterpiece of New France carving is surrounded by devotional miniatures hung on pilasters by the nuns.

Atop the 31 storeys of **Édifice Marie-Guyart** in Complexe G, the **Observatoire de la Capitale** *($5; late Jun to mid-Oct every day 10am to 7pm, mid-Oct to late Jun Tue-Sun 10am to 5pm; 1037 Rue de La Chevrotière, ☎418-644-9841, www.observatoirecapitale.org)*, provides a splendid **view ★★** of Québec City and its surrounding area. At 221m in altitude, it is the highest observation point in the city. For an even better view, use the telescopes.

Go back and turn right on Rue Saint-Amable. Walk as far as the Parc de l'Amérique-Française.

The **Parc de l'Amérique-Française** is centered around a collection of flags of the various francophone communities of America.

The **Grand Théâtre** *(269 Boulevard René-Lévesque Est, ☎418-643-8131)* is located at the far end of the park. Inaugurated in 1971, this theatre designed by Polish architect Victor Prus was to be a meeting place for the members of Québec City's high society. There was quite a scandal, therefore, when Jordi Bonet's mural was unveiled and the assembled crowd read the lines from a poem by Claude Péloquin: *"Vous êtes pas tannés de mourir, bande de caves"* (Aren't you idiots tired of dying?). The theatre has two halls (Louis-Fréchette and Octave-Crémazie) and presents symphony orchestra concerts as well as theatre, dance and variety shows.

Go down Rue de Claire-Fontaine to return to Grande Allée.

Maison Henry-Stuart *($5; late Jun to early Sep every day 11am to 5pm; 82 Grande Allée Ouest, ☎418-647-4347 or 800-494-4347)*, at the corner of Cartier and Grande Allée, is one of the few remaining Regency-style Anglo-Norman cottages in Québec City. This type of colonial British architecture is distinguished by a large pavilion roof overhanging a low veranda surrounding the building. The house was built in 1849 and used to mark the border between the city and the country; its original garden still surrounds it. The interior features several pieces of furniture from the Saint-Jean-Port-Joli manor and has been practically untouched since 1911. Tea is served here on summer afternoons.

Avenue Cartier is one of the most attractive shopping streets in town. The main artery in the Montcalm residential neighbourhood, it is lined with restaurants, shops and specialty food stores that attract the well-to-do clientele strolling around here.

Turn left on Avenue Wolfe-Montcalm, which is one of the entrances to both Parc Champs-de-Bataille and the Musée National des Beaux-Arts du Québec.

Located at the roundabout is the **Monument to General Wolfe**, victor of the decisive Battle of the Plains of Abraham. It is said to stand on the exact spot where he fell. The 1832 monument has been the object of count-

Riopelle

Jean-Paul Riopelle was one of Québec's most renowned painters, and its best-known internationally. Many of the impressive number of paintings he created are exhibited throughout the world. This legendary character, an abstract painter famous for his huge mosaics, left his mark on the world of contemporary art. He was born in Montréal in 1932, and his career took off with the Automatism movement in the 1940s. He was also a co-signatory of the *Refus Global*, an artistic manifesto. He lived in Paris for several years but returned to the province of Québec during the last years of his life. He died on March 12, 2002, in his manor on Île aux Grues, on the St. Lawrence River, in the migration path of the snow geese he held so dear to his heart.

less demonstrations and acts of vandalism. Toppled again in 1963, it was rebuilt, this time with an inscription in French.

The **Musée National des Beaux-Arts du Québec ★ ★ ★** *($10, free admission to the permanent exhibits; early Jun to early Sep every day 10am to 6pm, Wed to 9pm, early Sep to late May Tue-Sun 11am to 5pm, Wed to 9pm; Parc des Champs de Bataille, ☎418-644-6460 or 866-220-2150, www.mnba.qc.ca)* was renovated and expanded in 1992. The older, west-facing 1933 Classical Revival building is on the right. The entrance, parallel to Avenue Wolfe-Montcalm, is dominated by a glass tower similar to that of the Musée de la Civilisation. The first building is subterraneously linked with the old prison on the left. The latter has been cleverly restored to house exhibits and has been rebaptized "Édifice Ballargé" in honour of its architect. Some of the cells have been preserved.

A visit to this important museum allows one to become acquainted with the painting, sculpture and silverwork of Québec from the time of New France to today. In 2000, the museum inaugurated a gallery (Salle 3) in honour of painter Jean-Paul Riopelle, who died in 2002, in which his huge mural (42m), *Hommage à Rosa Luxembourg*, is displayed. The collections of religious art gathered from Québec's rural parishes are particularly interesting. Also on display are official documents, including the original surrender of Québec (1759). The museum frequently hosts temporary exhibits from the United States and Europe. Many cultural activities are held here, such as conferences, films and concerts.

Turn left on Avenue Georges VI and right on Avenue Garneau.

The **Parc des Champs-de-Bataille ★ ★ ★** *(free admission; ☎418-648-4071)* takes visitors back to July 1759: commanded by General Wolfe, the British fleet arrives in front of Québec City. An attack is launched almost immediately. Almost 40,000 cannonballs crash down on the besieged city. As the summer draws to a close, the British must make a decision before they are surprised by French reinforcements or trapped in the December freeze. On the 13th of September, under cover of night, British troops scale the Cap Diamant escarpment west of the fortifications. The ravines, which here and there cut into the otherwise uniform mass of the escarpment, allow them to climb while remaining concealed. By morning, the troops have taken position in the fields of Abraham Martin, hence the name given to the park, **Plains of Abraham**. The French are surprised, as they had anticipated a direct attack on the citadel. Their troops, with the aid of a few hundred Aboriginal and French-Canadian warriors, throw themselves against the British. The generals of both sides are slain, and the battle draws to a close in bloody chaos. New France is lost.

Parc des Champs-de-Bataille, where the battle took place, was created in 1908 to commemorate the event. With its 101ha, the park is a superb recreational space. Previously occupied by a military training ground, the Ursulines and a few farms, the park was laid out between 1929 and 1939 by landscape architect Frederick Todd. This project provided work for thousands of Québécois during the Depression. To-

Québec City - Exploring - Grande Allée

day, the plains are a large green space crisscrossed by paths that were used for all kinds of winter and summer activities. You will find beautiful landscaping here as well as historical and cultural sites such as the **Kiosque Edwin-Bélanger**, which presents outdoor entertainment. At the park's eastern entrance, the **Maison de la Découverte des Plaines d'Abraham** (see p 348) presents a fine introduction to the Plains, as various exhibitions and activities interpret its history and natural environment.

The **Tours Martello no. 1 and no. 2 ★** (martello towers) *(www.ccbn-nbc.gc.ca)* are characteristic of British defenses at the beginning of the 19th century. Tower number 1 (1808) is visible from the edge of Avenue Ontario; number 2 (1815) blends into the surrounding buildings on the corner of Avenue Laurier and Avenue Taché. Inside the first tower, an exhibition recounts some of the military strategies used in the 19th century *($4; late Jun to late Sep every day 10am to 5:30pm)*. At Tour Martello no. 2, you can enjoy "Conseil de guerre" (war council) evenings, which consist of murder-mystery dinners. Reservations are required. A third tower is located further north, in the Saint-Jean-Baptiste district.

*This marks the end of the Grande Allée walking tour. To return to the walled city, follow Avenue Ontario east to Avenue Georges-VI or take Avenue du Cap-Diamant (in the hilly part of the park) to **Promenade des Gouverneurs**. The promenade follows the Citadelle and overlooks the Cap Diamant escarpment, winding up at Terrasse Dufferin. This route affords stunning views of the city, the St. Lawrence River and the south shore.*

- -

Tour D: Saint-Jean-Baptiste ★

 2 hours

A hangout for young people, complete with bars, cafés and boutiques, the Saint-Jean-Baptiste area is perched on a hillside between Haute-Ville and Basse-Ville. The abundance of pitched and mansard roofs is reminiscent of parts of the old city, but the orthogonal layout of the streets is quintessentially North American. Despite a terrible fire in 1845, this old Québec City suburb retains several examples of wooden constructions, which were forbidden inside the city's walls.

The Saint-Jean-Baptiste tour begins at Porte Saint-Jean, on Place d'Youville. It threads along Rue Saint-Jean, the neighbourhood's main artery.

Place d'Youville, also called "Carré d'Youville" (square), is the public space at the entrance of the old section of town. Formerly an important market square, today it is a bustling crossroads and cultural forum. Redevelopment has given the square a large promenade area with some trees and benches. The counterscarp wall, part of the fortifications that were removed in the 19th century, has been highlighted by the use of black granite blocks. In winter, part of the square is covered in ice, much to the delight of skaters who twirl around to the sound of cheerful tunes.

At the beginning of the 20th century, Québec City was in dire need of a new auditorium, its Académie de Musique having burnt to the ground in March 1900. With the help of private enterprise, the mayor undertook the search for a new location. The Canadian government, owner of the fortifications, offered to provide a strip of land along the walls of the city. Although narrow, the lot grew wider toward the back, permitting the construction of a suitable hall, the **Capitole de Québec ★** *(972 Rue St-Jean, www.lecapitole.com)*. W. S. Painter, the ingenious Detroit architect who was already at work on the expansion of the Château Frontenac, devised a plan for a curved facade, giving the building a monumental air despite the limited size of the lot. Inaugurated in 1903 as the Auditorium de Québec, the building is one of the most impressive *Beaux-arts* realizations in the country.

In 1927, the famous American cinema architect Thomas W. Lamb converted the auditorium into a sumptuous 1,700-seat cinema. Abandoned for a few years, the Capitole was entirely refurbished in 1992. The building now houses a dinner-theatre

★ **ATTRACTIONS**

1.	DY	Place d'Youville
2.	DY	Capitole de Québec
3.	CY	Church and Cemetery of Saint Matthew

4.	BY	Épicerie J.-A.-Moisan
5.	BY	Choco-Musée Érico
6.	BY	Église Saint-Jean-Baptiste

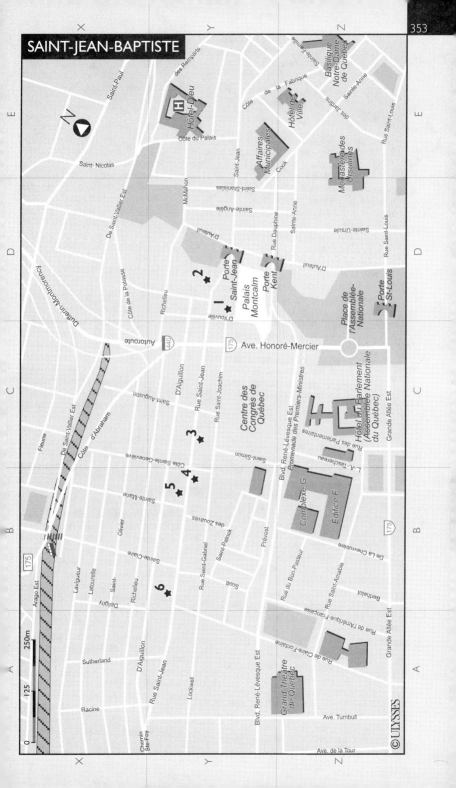

SAINT-JEAN-BAPTISTE

© ULYSSES

in the hall, a luxury hotel (**Hôtel du Capitole**, see p 363) and a restaurant (**Il Teatro**, see p 370) in the curved facade.

From Rue Saint-Joachim, take Rue Saint-Augustin, which will lead you to Rue Saint-Jean, where you turn left.

There has been a cemetery on the site of the **Church and Cemetery of Saint Matthew ★** *(755 Rue St-Jean)* since 1771, when Protestants, whether French Huguenot, English Anglican or Scottish Presbyterian, banded together to establish a Protestant graveyard. Several 19th-century tombstones are still standing. The gravestones were recently carefully restored, and the cemetery is now a public garden.

Located in the cemetery, along Rue Saint-Jean, is a lovely Anglican church. Its Gothic Revival architecture was influenced by the Ecclesiologists, an influential school of Anglican thought that sought to re-establish ties with the traditions of the Middle Ages. In its design, and even in its materials, it looks more like an ancient village church than a Victorian church with a Gothic decor. The church is now a branch of the municipal library.

Continue along Rue Saint-Jean.

Épicerie J.-A.-Moisan *(699 Rue St-Jean)* was founded in 1871 and claims to be the "oldest grocery store in North America." It does in fact look like a general store from yesteryear, with its wooden floor and shelves, old advertisements and array of tin cans.

The owner of the Érico chocolate shop, a favourite among "chocoholics," had the great idea of adding a small chocolate museum to his shop. If this interests you, stop by the **Choco-Musée Érico** *(free admission; 634 Rue St-Jean, ☎418-524-2122, www.chocomusee. com)* to learn how the Mayans used cocoa, find out how this fruit grows, discover different recipes and more.

The **Église Saint-Jean-Baptiste ★** *(410 Rue St-Jean, corner of Rue de Ligny)* stands out as Joseph Ferdinand Peachy's masterpiece. A disciple of French eclecticism, Peachy was a whole-hearted admirer of the Église de la Trinité in Paris. The resemblance here is striking, as much in the portico as in the interior. Completed in 1885, the building caused the bankruptcy of its architect, who was, unfortunately for him, held responsible for cracks that appeared in the facade during construction. In front of the church is now an attractive little square.

For a beautiful view of the city, take the Rue Claire-Fontaine stairs up to the corner of Rue Lockwell on the right. The climb is steep but the view is worth the effort, especially in the evening when the Basse-Ville lights dance at your feet behind the imposing church. When strolling through this neighbourhood's attractive streets, you will have many opportunities to catch a glimpse of this great view. For example, you can go down Rue Sainte-Claire to the stairs leading to the Saint-Roch neighbourhood, which you will be able to see with the Laurentian mountains in the background.

Wedged between Rue Saint-Vallier Est and Côte d'Abraham, slightly north of the Saint-Jean-Baptiste neighbourhood, **Méduse** *(541 Rue de Saint-Vallier Est, ☎418-640-9218, www.meduse.org)* houses various artists' associations that support and promote Québec culture. Encompassing restored houses and modern buildings that integrate the city's architecture, the complex is perched on the side of Cap Diamant, linking Haute-Ville and Basse-Ville. Running along the east side is a stairway that links Côte d'Abraham to Rue de Saint-Vallier Est.

Parks

The **Parc des Champs-de-Bataille ★ ★ ★** (see p 351), better known as the **Plains of Abraham**, is Québec City's undisputed park of parks. This immense green space covers about 100ha and stretches all the way to the Cap Diamant, which slopes down to the river. It is a magnificent place for local residents to enjoy all sorts of outdoor activities.

With its big trees and lawns, **Domaine Maizerets** *(free admission; 2000 Boulevard Montmorency, ☎418-691-2385)* is the perfect place for a leisurely stroll. Gardening buffs will love the arboretum and the landscaping; the Domaine also belongs to the Association des Jardins du Québec. In the heart of the arboretum is a butterfly aviary. Weather permitting (it is closed when it rains), visitors can walk into this world of butterflies, which features some 30 species from eastern Canada. Not only will you be amazed, but you will also learn about the different stages of their development. A number of historic buildings can also be found here, including the château that houses a small exhibition on the history of the estate. All sorts of outdoor activities can be enjoyed here in both summer and winter. Outdoor concerts, plays and conferences on ornithology and other subjects are held at Domaine Maizerets all year round.

Outdoor Activities

■ Cross-Country Skiing

The snow-covered **Plains of Abraham** provide an enchanting setting for cross-country skiing. Trails crisscross the park from one end to the other, threading their way through the trees or leading across a headland with views of the icy river. And all in the heart of the city!

Some extremely pleasant cross-country ski trails can also be found at **Domaine Maizerets** *(free admission; 2000 Boulevard Montmorency, ☎418-641-6335)*. At the starting point, there is a little heated chalet with a wood-burning stove. Equipment rentals *($4; mid-Dec to mid-Mar every day 10am to 4pm)* are available.

■ Cruises

Croisières AML *(124 Rue St-Pierre, ☎418-692-1159 or 800-563-4643, www.croisieresaml.com)* organizes cruises all summer, providing a great view of Québec City and its surroundings from a different angle. One of the ships owned by this company is the **M/V Louis-Jolliet** *($25; departures at 11am, 2pm and 4pm)*, which sails from Québec City, its port of registry. Day cruises last 1hr 30min and go as far as the Montmorency Falls. At night, you can go up to Île d'Orléans and enjoy dinner in one of the ship's two dining rooms. These evening cruises last a few hours and feature musicians and dancing.

Croisières du Groupe Dufour *(22 Quai St-André, ☎800-463-5250, www.familledufour.com)* take passengers to the lovely Charlevoix region, to Pointe-au-Pic, Île-aux-Coudres and even

to the heart of the breathtaking Saguenay fjord, among other destinations, aboard a big modern catamaran.

■ Cycling

Québec City is developing its cycling infrastructure. Today, more than 100km of cycling paths stretch out around the city and its surroundings. The many marked or shared routes make Québec City and its neighbouring communities enjoyable places to discover by bicycle.

A bike path called the **Corridor des Cheminots** *(☎418-641-6415)* enables cyclists and other sports enthusiasts to travel 22km through various municipalities to Val-Bélair, not far from the beginning of the Jacques-Cartier–Portneuf path.

The **Promo-Vélo** association *(C.P. 700, Succ. Haute-Ville, Québec, G1R 4S9, ☎418-522-0087)* offers a great deal of information on the various kinds of tours available in the region. Furthermore, this organization publishes a map of bike paths in the Québec City area.

Bicycle Rentals

You can rent mountain bikes at Station Mont-Sainte-Anne and in Parc de la Jacques-Cartier.

Cyclo Services
$25/day
Marché du Vieux-Port
160 Quai St-André
☎ (418) 692-4052
Cyclo Services also organizes excursions in the city and its surrounding area.

Vélotek
$30/day
463 Rue St-Jean
☎ (418) 648-6022

■ Ice Skating

Each winter, an ice rink is laid out on **Terrasse Dufferin**, enabling skaters to swirl about at the foot of Château Frontenac with a view of the icy river. You can don your gear at the kiosk *($2; mid-Dec to mid-Mar every day 11am to 11pm; ☎418-692-2955)*, which also rents out skates *($5/day)*.

On beautiful winter days, **Place d'Youville** turns into a magical place, with skaters, snow, frost-covered Porte-Saint-Jean, the illuminated Capitole and Christmas decorations hanging from lampposts. In the centre of the square is a skating rink with music, and even if you don't feel like joining in the ice waltz, you can still enjoy the sights. The skating rink opens early in the season, around the end of October, and shuts down in late spring, ensuring that Québec City residents can skate for as long as possible. There are restrooms for skaters *(free admission, skate rentals $5/hr; Mon-Thu noon to 10pm, Fri-Sun 10am to 10pm;* ☎*418-641-6256).*

A lovely skating rink winds beneath the trees of **Domaine Maizerets** *(free admission; 2000 Boulevard Montmorency,* ☎*418-641-6335).* There's a small chalet nearby where you can take off your skates and warm up next to a wood stove. Skate rentals are available *($4; mid-Dec to mid-Mar every day 10am to 9pm).*

■ In-Line Skating

On the **Plains of Abraham**, in front of the Musée National des Beaux-Arts du Québec, is a large paved rink for in-line skating. Scores of children and adults wearing protective helmets can be seen blading around the track on fine summer days. Equipment rentals are available at a small stand by the rink. This is the only spot on the Plains of Abraham where this activity is allowed.

■ Jogging

Again, the place to go is the **Plains of Abraham**. The big flat track in front of the Musée National des Beaux-Arts du Québec is a good place for a run, though people also go jogging on the paved streets and trails.

■ Tobogganing

During winter, the **Glissades de la Terrasse** appear on **Terrasse Dufferin**, which you can slide down on a toboggan. First purchase your tickets at the stand in the middle of the terrace *($2/ride; mid-Dec to mid-Mar every day 11am to 11pm; 52 Rue St-Louis, Vieux-Québec,* ☎*418-694-9487 or 829-9898 or 692-2955),* then grab a toboggan and climb to the top of the slide. Once you get there, make sure to take a look around: the view is magnificent!

The hills of the **Plains of Abraham** are wonderful for sledding. Bundle up and follow the kids pulling toboggans to find the best spots.

Accommodations

Québec City has all kinds of accommodations to offer: two youth hostels and plenty of bed and breakfasts, inns and luxury hotels. You will certainly find a suitable place to stay, whether it's for one night or one week. Although comfort may be a little rudimentary in the smaller inns, most hotels offer very comfortable conditions and many services. There are quite a few bed and breakfasts in Québec City. They are reasonably priced and offer the advantages of a home-style atmosphere. In Québec, bed and breakfasts are known as *gîtes du passant*.

Hospitalité Canada *(124 Rue St-Pierre, Vieux-Port,* ☎*418-694-1602 or 866-363-6674)* is a free reservation service for accommodations and tourist attractions in Québec and Canada. Depending on the kind of accommodations you're looking for, the staff can suggest various establishments belonging to the network and even make reservations for you.

Tour A:
Vieux-Québec

Auberge de la Paix
$ bkfst incl.
$3 bedding surcharge for the first night if you don't bring your own
sb ☜ @
31 Rue Couillard
☎ (418) 694-0735
www.aubergedelapaix.com
Behind its lovely white facade in Vieux-Québec, Auberge de la Paix offers a youth-hostel atmosphere. It has 60 beds in rooms able to accommodate from two to eight people, as well as a kitchenette and a living room. This inn lives up to its name by providing a friendly and fun place to relax. In the summer, a lovely garden is filled with flowers. Children are welcome.

Manoir LaSalle
$
pb/sb ☜
18 Rue Ste-Ursule
☎ (418) 692-9953
Manoir LaSalle is a small hotel with 11 rooms, one of which has a private bathroom. This red-brick building is exemplary of the architectural style of some of the first homes built in the city. Visitors who are allergic to cats should stay away, however.

La Maison Demers
$-$$ bkfst incl.
68 Rue Ste-Ursule
☎ (418) 692-2487 or 800-692-2417
This beautiful home dating from 1898 is filled with charmingly mismatched furnishings and travel souvenirs. The reception is warm and charming.

Auberge Internationale de Québec
$$
pb/sb
19 Rue Ste-Ursule
☎ (418) 694-0755 or
(514) 252-3117 from Montréal
The Auberge Internationale de Québec is a youth hostel with 280 beds for young people. The rooms can accommodate from two to five people, the dormitories from four to 12, and there are also private double rooms.

Au Petit Hôtel
$$
3 Rue des Ursulines
☎ (418) 694-0965
Located in the heart of Vieux-Québec, this large red-and-yellow house with a green roof, tucked away on Rue des Ursulines, offers 16 rooms that inspire happiness and tranquillity. Parking is available.

Marquise de Bassano
$$-$$$ bkfst incl.
sb @
15 Rue des Grisons
☎ (418) 692-0316 or 877-692-0316
www.marquisedebassano.com
Vieux-Québec has been home to some colourful characters throughout its history. At the corner of Rue des Grisons and Avenue Sainte-Geneviève is a small Victorian house that, it is said, was built for one such character. The dark panelling that decorates the interior surely guards the secrets of the Marquise de Bassano. The house has been transformed into a welcoming bed and breakfast, with charming rooms and a cheerful sitting room with a piano and fireplace. During breakfast, which sometimes lasts into the afternoon, the young hosts take pleasure in animating the discussions. Parking is available. No smoking.

Hôtel Acadia
$$-$$$$
sb/pb @ ≡ ☜ ❋ @
43 Rue Ste-Ursule
☎ (418) 694-0280 or 800-463-0280
▤ (418) 694-0458
www.hotelacadia.com
A number of old houses on Rue Sainte-Ursule have been transformed into hotels. Among these, Hôtel Acadia stands out with its large, white facade. In the basement are luxury

Québec City — Accommodations — Vieux-Québec

suites with stone walls and beautiful woodwork.

Hôtel du Vieux-Québec
$$$ bkfst incl.
≡ ◎ ⚓ @

1190 Rue St-Jean
☎ (418) 692-1850 or 800-361-7787
▤ (418) 692-5637
www.hvq.com

Hôtel du Vieux-Québec is a modern establishment that exudes the kind of cool ambiance that is often associated with modernism. Although the decor is not extravagant, it is quite comfortable and friendly.

Château de Pierre
$$$
≡ @

17 Avenue Ste-Geneviève
☎ (418) 694-0429 or 888-694-0429
▤ (418) 694-0153

The Château de Pierre is set in an old colonial-style house. The ostentatious entrance of this hotel is quite striking and somewhat flashy. The rooms are comfortable.

Château de Léry
$$$
≡ ◎ ↩

8 Rue de la Porte
☎ (418) 692-2692 or 800-363-0036
▤ (418) 692-5231

Located next to Parc des Gouverneurs and overlooking the river, the Château de Léry has comfortable rooms. Rooms facing the street offer a good view. This hotel is in a quiet neighbourhood in the old part of the city, just a few minutes' walk from the bustle of downtown.

Hôtel Cap-Diamant
$$$-$$$$ bkfst incl.
≡ ◍ ▵ @

39 Avenue Ste-Geneviève
☎ (418) 694-0313
▤ (418) 692-1375
www.hcapdiamant.qc.ca

Hôtel Cap-Diamant is located in an old house in Vieux-Québec. This is the kind of house where even the walls have secrets, and many stories to tell. It is the perfect place to immerse yourself in the family life of bygone days. The long staircase, the creaking floors, and even the wallpaper contribute to its charm and quaint appearance. You can enjoy the porch or wander in the flower-filled garden and sit by the stream.

Hôtel Maison du Fort
$$$-$$$$ bkfst incl.
≡ ☛ ◎

21 Avenue Ste-Geneviève
☎ (418) 692-4375 or 888-203-4375
▤ (418) 692-5257
www.hotelmaisondufort.com

This renovated Georgian-style house was designed by architect Charles Baillargé in 1851. The service is quite welcoming and there are two cats on the premises.

Hôtel Château Bellevue
$$$-$$$$
≡ @

16 Rue de la Porte
☎ (418) 692-2473 or 800-463-2617
▤ (418) 692-4876
www.vieux-quebec.com

Hôtel Château Bellevue offers an impressive view of the river. The rooms are attractive and equipped with modern-style furniture.

Hôtel Clarendon
$$$$
≡ ◍ ◎ ⚲ ↩ ⚙

57 Rue Ste-Anne
☎ (418) 692-2480 or 888-554-6001
▤ (418) 692-4652
www.hotelclarendon.com

Built in 1870, Hôtel Clarendon is one of the oldest hotels in the city (see p 336). The hotel has an

unpretentious exterior while the elegant interior is decorated in Art Deco style. The entrance hall is very attractive. The rooms in this hotel have been renovated many times over the years and are spacious and comfortable, making this a very good place to stay in Vieux-Québec. Its restaurant, **Le Charles-Baillargé** (see p 366), serves elegant meals, and there is also a lively bar, **L'Emprise** (see p 371), which presents live jazz shows.

Le Clos Saint-Louis
$$$$-$$$$$ bkfst incl.
◎ ≡ ▵ @

71 Rue St-Louis
☎ (418) 694-1311 or 800-461-1311
▤ (418) 694-9411
www.clossaintlouis.com

Le Clos Saint-Louis comprises two imposing Victorian houses dating from 1844 on Rue St-Louis. Located close to Vieux-Québec and its attractions, this hotel has 18 rooms with Internet access spread out on four floors. The rooms have all been decorated to make their historic aspect especially welcoming: some have four-poster beds with canopies, others old-fashioned bookcases or fireplaces. The rooms on the second floor are particularly attractive, with their stone walls and exposed wooden beams. The bathrooms are all modern and well equipped. Coffee and croissants are served in the morning. No smoking.

Château Frontenac
$$$$$
◍ ≡ ⚙ ◎ ⌘ ↩ @

1 Rue des Carrières
☎ (418) 692-3861 or 800-441-1414
▤ (418) 692-1751
www.fairmont.com

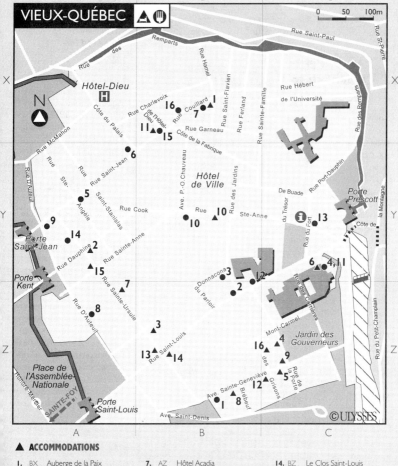

VIEUX-QUÉBEC

0   50   100m

▲ ACCOMMODATIONS

1.	BX	Auberge de la Paix
2.	AY	Auberge Internationale de Québec
3.	BZ	Au Petit Hôtel
4.	CZ	Château de Léry
5.	CZ	Château de Pierre
6.	CY	Château Frontenac

7.	AZ	Hôtel Acadia
8.	BZ	Hôtel Cap-Diamant
9.	CZ	Hôtel Château Bellevue
10.	BY	Hôtel Clarendon (R)
11.	BX	Hôtel du Vieux-Québec
12.	CZ	Hôtel Maison du Fort
13.	BZ	La Maison Demers

14.	BZ	Le Clos Saint-Louis
15.	AY	Manoir LaSalle
16.	CZ	Marquise de Bassano
(R)		establishment with restaurant (see description)

● RESTAURANTS

1.	BZ	À la Bastille Chez Bahüaud
2.	BZ	Aux Anciens Canadiens
3.	BY	Café de la Paix
4.	CY	Café de la Terrasse
5.	AY	Café d'Europe
6.	AY	Casse-Crêpe Breton

7.	BX	Chez Temporel
8.	AZ	L'Élysée-Mandarin
9.	AY	L'Entrecôte Saint-Jean
10.	BY	La Crémaillère
11.	CY	Le Champlain
12.	BZ	Le Continental

13.	CY	Le Gambrinus
14.	AY	Le Petit Coin Latin
15.	BX	Les Frères de la Côte
16.	BX	Portofino Bistro Italiano

The Château Frontenac is by far the most prestigious historic hotel in Québec City (see p 334). Enter its elegant lobby with its wood panelling and warm colours and let yourself be transported back in time. The Château Frontenac was built in 1893 and, over the years, has been the setting of several historic events. The decor exudes a classic, refined richness that is truly worthy of a castle. Its restaurant also offers a taste of luxury (see **Le Champlain**, p 366). The sumptuous rooms provide the most comfortable environment possible, and although the size and amenities of the hotel's 618 rooms greatly vary, all are quite lovely. The rooms overlooking the river have beautiful bay windows and, of course, the view is magnificent.

Tour B: Petit-Champlain to Vieux-Port

Hôtel Belley
$$-$$$
⬤ ≡

249 Rue St-Paul
☎ (418) 692-1694 or 888-692-1694
🖨 (418) 692-1696

The pleasant Hôtel Belley stands opposite the market in the Vieux-Port. A hotel since 1877, this handsome building will leave you with fond memories for years to come. It has eight simply decorated cozy rooms, some with exposed brick walls, others with wooden beams and skylights. The ground floor is home to the **Taverne Belley** (see p 371) bar, whose breakfasts and lunches, served in two lovely rooms, are very popular with locals. A number of extremely comfortable and attractively decorated lodgings, some with terraces, are also available in another house across the street. These may be rented by the night, the week or the month.

Le Priori
$$$$ bkfst incl.
◎ ♨ ⚠ ⬤ ≡ 🕭 @

15 Rue Sault-au-Matelot
☎ (418) 522-8108 or 800-351-3992
🖨 (418) 692-0883

Le Priori is located on a quiet street in the Basse-Ville. The building is very old but has been renovated in a modern style. The decor successfully contrasts its old stone walls with up-to-date furnishings. Its ap-

pearance is striking and even the elevator is distinctive. Le Priori is highly recommended.

Hayden's Wexford House
$$$ bkfst incl.
sb/pb ≡

450 Rue Champlain
☎ (418) 524-0524
🖨 (418)648-8995
www.haydenwexfordhouse.com

Located on a magnificent street between Cap Diamant and the river, Hayden's Wexford House has proudly displayed its facade since 1832. Its name, in fact, is inscribed in the brickwork. This house has managed to maintain all of its period charm. The four small rooms nestled on the top floor provide lovely views from the dormer windows and are tastefully decorated with wood trim and floral patterns.

Auberge Saint-Pierre
$$$$-$$$$$ bkfst incl.
◎ ≡ @

79 Rue St-Pierre
☎ (418) 694-7981 or 888-268-1017
🖨 (418) 694-0406
www.auberge.qc.ca

This lovely inn is located in a building that had housed Canada's first insurance company since the end of the 19th century. The historic charm of Auberge Saint-Pierre was retained when the building was renovated. The rooms are similar to the neighbouring apartments, with their various landings and narrow hallways. Each room has beautiful, dark hardwood floors and sumptuously coloured walls. Those on the lower floors have lovely high ceilings, while those higher up provide a wonderful view.

Hôtel Dominion 1912
$$$$$ bkfst incl.
≡ 🕭 @

126 Rue St-Pierre
☎ (418) 692-2224 or 888-833-5253
🖨 (418) 692-4403
www.hoteldominion.com

Dating from 1912, as its name indicates, this beautiful building on Rue Saint-Pierre has been transformed into a hotel that enchants its chic clientele. The luxurious Hôtel Dominion 1912 has a modern aspect with materials such as glass and wrought iron, but still maintains its original character. Elements of interior decoration, such as cream-and-sand-coloured draperies and cushions, and luxuriously soft sofas and bedspreads, add an extremely comfortable touch. Black-and-white photographs of the neighbourhood hang in each room, inviting you to go out and visit. The upper floors have magnificent views of the river on one side and the city on the other.

Auberge Saint-Antoine
$$$$$
◎ ≡ ⬤ ⚠ ♨ @

8 Rue St-Antoine
☎ (418) 692-2211 or 888-692-2211
🖨 (418) 692-1177
www.saint-antoine.com

Auberge Sainte-Antoine is located near the Musée de la Civilisation. This lovely hotel is divided into two buildings. The old rooms are wonderfully decorated according to different themes and each has its own unique charm. The hotel features 64 new, more modern rooms and an already famous restaurant, Panache.

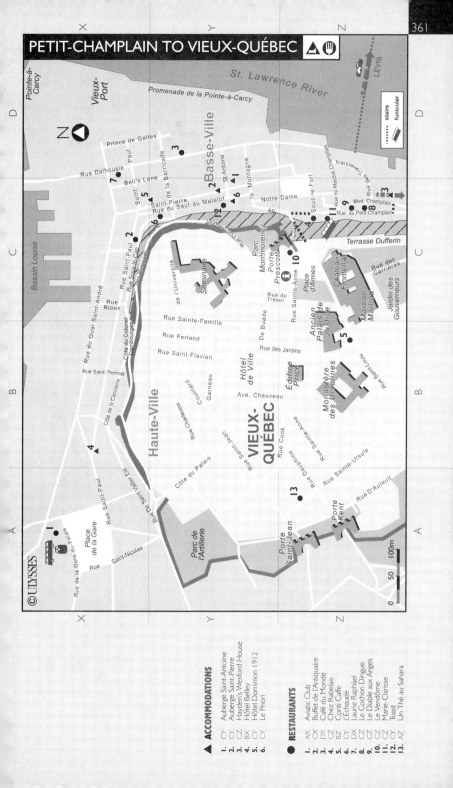

PETIT-CHAMPLAIN TO VIEUX-QUÉBEC ▲ ⏍

▲ **ACCOMMODATIONS**

1.	CY	Auberge Saint-Antoine
2.	CY	Auberge Saint-Pierre
3.	DY	Hayden's Wexford House
4.	BX	Hôtel Belley
5.	CY	Hôtel Dominion 1912
6.	CY	Le Priori

● **RESTAURANTS**

1.	AX	Aviatic Club
2.	CX	Buffet de l'Antiquaire
3.	DY	Café du Monde
4.	BZ	Chez Rabelais
5.	BZ	Conti Caffe
6.	CY	L'Échaudé
7.	DX	Laurie Raphaël
8.	CZ	Le Cochon Dingue
9.	CZ	Le Diable aux Anges
10.	CZ	Le Vendôme
11.	CZ	Marie-Clarisse
12.	CZ	Toast
13.	AZ	Un Thé au Sahara

© ULYSSES

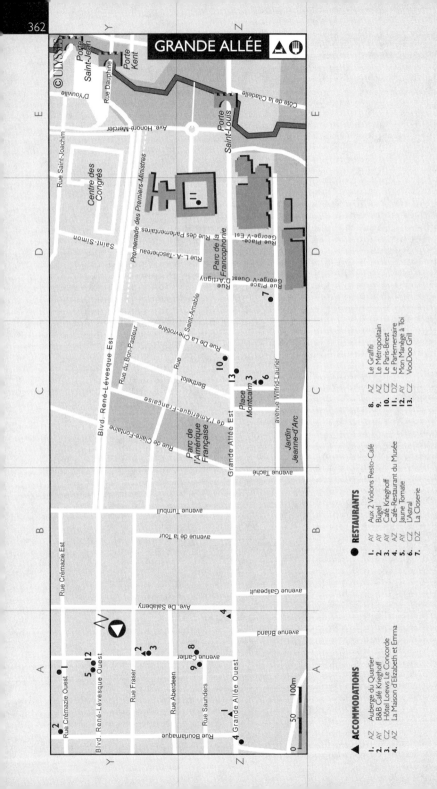

362

GRANDE ALLÉE

Tour C: Grande Allée

B&B Café Krieghoff
$$ bkfst incl.
♨ ❅ ≡ @
1091 Avenue Cartier
☎ (418) 522-3711
🖨 (418) 647-1429
www.cafekrieghoff.com
B&B Café Krieghoff offers travellers a bed-and-breakfast combination. The novelty, however, is that breakfast is served in the café itself (see p 368), which guarantees both good food and pleasant surroundings. The friendly staff makes sure that guests feel right at home in the family-like atmosphere. The six rooms nestled above the restaurant are modest and clean.

La Maison d'Elizabeth et Emma
$$ bkfst incl.
10 Grande Allée Ouest
☎ (418) 647-0880
This lovely B&B features three charming, peaceful rooms decorated with mahogany wood and beautiful drapes. Each is fitted with a pretty and well-lit bathroom. In the morning, a hearty breakfast is served in a sun-bathed dining room. The whole package is simple and refined, and hosts Jacinthe and François take marvellous care of their guests.

Auberge du Quartier
$$$ bkfst incl.
≡ @
170 Grande Allée Ouest
☎ (418) 525-9726 or 800-782-9441
🖨 (418) 521-4891
www.aubergeduquartier.com
Looking for a quaint little neighbourhood inn? Facing the imposing Église Saint-Dominique, just 5min from the Plaines d'Abraham and the Musée national des beaux-arts du Québec, Auberge du Quartier should do the trick. This large house has some 15 clean, well-lit, attractive and modern rooms. They are spread out on three floors, with a suite in the attic. There is a charming terrace on the rooftop and the reception is very friendly.

Hôtel Loews Le Concorde
$$$-$$$$
♿ ≡ ≋ ⚓))) ♨ @)
1225 Cours du Général-De Montcalm
☎ (418) 647-2222 or 800-463-5256
🖨 (418) 647-4710
www.loewshotels.com
Just outside Vieux-Québec is the Hôtel Loews Le Concorde. It is part of the Loews hotel chain and has spacious, comfortable rooms with spectacular views of Québec City and the surrounding area. There is a revolving restaurant on top of the hotel (see **L'Astral** p 369).

Tour D: Saint-Jean-Baptiste

Chez Pierre
$$ bkfst incl.
pb/sb ≡ ☛ ❅
636 Rue d'Aiguillon
☎ (418) 522-2173
www.chezpierre.qc.ca
Chez Pierre is a bed and breakfast with three rooms. Two of them are situated on the second floor and offer all the charm of a Faubourg Saint-Jean-Baptiste apartment. The first floor presents a studio-style room that includes a kitchenette. Pierre, your host, is a painter, and his large coloured canvases brighten up the house. He serves a generous breakfast in the morning. No smoking.

Hilton Québec
$$$$
≡ ≋ ⚓))) ♨ ♿ @
1100 Boulevard René-Lévesque Est
☎ (418) 647-2411 or 800-447-2411
🖨 (418) 647-6488
www.hiltonquebec.com
Located just outside Vieux-Québec, the Hilton Québec offers rooms with the kind of comfort one expects from an international hotel chain. The Place Québec shopping mall is located in the lobby, which is connected to the Centre des Congrès.

Delta Québec
$$$$
≋ ≡ ⚓ ♿))) ♨ @
690 Boulevard Rene-Lévesque Est
☎ (418) 647-1717 or 888-884-7777
🖨 (418) 647-2146
www.deltahotels.com
The Delta Québec is linked to the Centre des Congrès. This hotel has over 375 rooms, all attractively decorated. Standard rooms are furnished with slightly rustic but elegant pine furniture. The hotel's heated outdoor pool is open all year.

Hôtel du Capitole
$$$$-$$$$$
♨ ≡ @) @
972 Rue St-Jean
☎ (418) 694-9930 or 800-363-4040
🖨 (418) 647-2146
www.lecapitol.com
Adjoining the theatre (see p 352), the Hôtel du Capitole is not exactly luxurious, but its rooms are amusing, with a decor that resembles a stage set. At the entrance is the **Il Teatro** (see p 370) restaurant.

Québec City - Accommodations - Saint-Jean-Baptiste

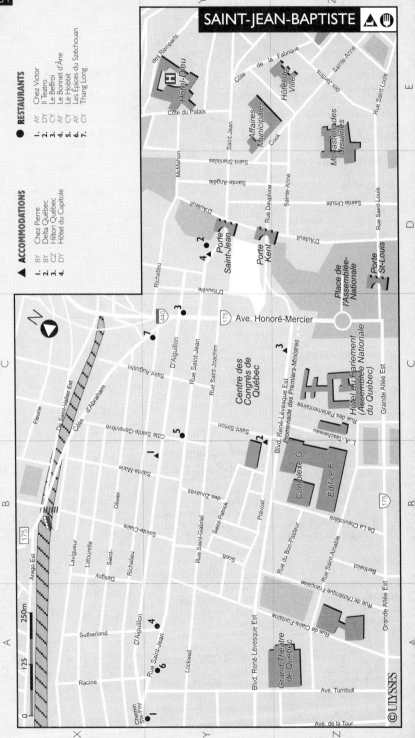

SAINT-JEAN-BAPTISTE

▲ ACCOMMODATIONS

1. BY Chez Pierre
2. BY Delta Québec
3. CZ Hilton Québec
4. DY Hôtel du Capitole

● RESTAURANTS

1. AY Chez Victor
2. DY Il Teatro
3. CY Le Beffroi
4. AY Le Bonnet d'Âne
5. CY Le Hobbit
6. AY Les Épices du Széchouan
7. CY Thang Long

Ave. Honoré-Mercier

Centre des Congrès de Québec

Hôtel du Parlement (Assemblée Nationale du Québec)

Hôtel des Ministres

Promenade des Premiers-Ministres

Rue des Parlementaires

Blvd. René-Lévesque Est

Complexe G

Édifice F

Place de l'Assemblée-Nationale

Porte St-Louis

Porte St-Louis

Porte Kent

Porte Saint-Jean

Hôtel-Dieu

Côte du Palais

des Remparts

Hôtel de Ville

Affaires Municipales

Monastère des Ursulines

Côte de la Fabrique

Grand Théâtre de Québec

Ave. Turnbull

Ave. de la Tour

Restaurants

Tour A:
Vieux-Québec

Casse-Crêpe Breton
$
1136 Rue St-Jean
☎ (418) 692-0438
Little Casse-Crêpe Breton is a popular spot that draws big crowds. Though it has been expanded, patrons still have to line up for a taste of its delicious crepes. Prepared right before your eyes, these delights are filled with your favourite ingredients by waitresses who manage to keep smiling in the midst of the hubbub. High-backed, upholstered seats help lend the place a warm atmosphere.

Chez Temporel
$
25 Rue Couillard
☎ (418) 694-1813
At Chez Temporel, the food is prepared right on the premises. Whether you opt for a rich butter croissant, a *croque-monsieur*, a salad or the special of the day, you can be sure it will be fresh and tasty. To top it all off, this establishment serves the best espresso in town. Tucked away on the narrow Rue Couillard, the two-storey Chez Temporel has been welcoming people of all ages and stripes for over 30 years now. Open early in the morning to late at night.

Le Petit Coin Latin
$
8½ Rue Ste-Ursule
☎ (418) 692-2022
Le Petit Coin Latin serves homestyle cooking in an ambiance reminiscent of a Parisian café. The decor is dominated by parlour chairs and mirrors, creating a relaxed, convivial atmosphere. The menu includes *croûtons au fromage*, quiche and salads. You can also snack on *raclette* served at your table on small burners with potatoes and cold cuts. Delicious! During summer, a lovely outdoor seating area enclosed by stone walls is open out back; to get there from the street, use the carriage entrance.

L'Entrecôte Saint-Jean
$$
1011 Rue St-Jean
☎ (418) 694-0234
L'Entrecôte Saint-Jean is renowned for its steaks, prepared in a variety of ways and accompanied with matchstick potatoes. Try the walnut salad and the chocolate *profiteroles*, which make a perfect ending to your meal. Great value for your money.

Les Frères de la Côte
$$
1190 Rue St-Jean
☎ (418) 692-5445
Les Frères de la Côte serves delicious bistro fare, including pasta, grilled meats and thin-crust pizzas baked in a wood-burning oven and topped with delicious fresh ingredients. All-you-can-eat mussels and fries are also available on certain evenings. The atmosphere is lively yet relaxed and the place is often packed, in keeping with the bustling activity of Rue St-Jean. Guests can take in the action through the restaurant's large windows.

Café de la Paix
$$-$$$
44 Rue des Jardins
☎ (418) 692-1430
Café de la Paix occupies a narrow space a few steps from the sidewalk on the small Rue des Jardins. It has been around for years and enjoys a solid reputation among Québec City residents. The menu features traditional French cuisine such as frog's legs, beef Wellington, rabbit in mustard sauce and grilled salmon.

Portofino Bistro Italiano
$$-$$$
54 Rue Couillard
☎ (418) 692-8888
Portofino was designed to resemble a typical Italian trattoria. A long bar, blue glasses, mirrors on the wall and soccer banners on the ceiling help create a warm, lively atmosphere. To top it all off, the mouth-watering Italian aromas will whet your appetite for the upcoming delights.

Le Gambrinus
$$-$$$
15 Rue du Fort
☎ (418) 692-5144
Le Gambrinus is a beautiful restaurant that has a good reputation with the people of Québec City. The welcoming dining room is adorned with small-paned windows. The entire room is decorated with ivy, and elegant ornamental plates hang on the walls. The atmosphere could not be more enjoyable in this warm and appealing room. On certain summer evenings guests are entertained by a singer, making the ambiance even more inviting. The terrace overlooks Château Frontenac. The French

and Italian cuisine features a large selection of fish and seafood dishes.

L'Élysée-Mandarin
$$-$$$

65 Rue d'Auteuil

☎ (418) 692-0909

L'Élysée-Mandarin, which also boasts prime location in Paris, serves excellent Szechuan, Cantonese and Mandarin cuisine in a decor that features a small indoor garden and Chinese sculptures and vases. The food is always succulent and the service is extremely courteous. If you are with a group, try the sampler menu: it would be a shame not to sample as many dishes as possible.

Le Charles-Baillargé
$$-$$$$

57 Rue Ste-Anne

☎ (418) 692-2480

The Charles-Baillargé restaurant is located on the main floor of the beautiful **Hôtel Clarendon** (see p 358). Discriminating diners come here for excellent, traditional French cuisine served in comfortable surroundings.

Café d'Europe
$$$

27 Rue Ste-Angèle

☎ (418) 692-3835

Café d'Europe has a sober, slightly outdated decor. There is a limited amount of space, and when the place is busy, the noise level gets pretty high. The service is courteous with a personal touch. Sophisticated European cuisine is presented in a traditional manner and served in generous portions. The flambéed dishes are expertly prepared, and the smooth,

flavourful sauces make for an unforgettable culinary experience.

À la Bastille Chez Bahüaud
$$$

47 Avenue Ste-Geneviève

☎ (418) 692-2544

À la Bastille Chez Bahüaud is located near the Plains of Abraham and is surrounded by trees. The wonderfully quiet terrace makes this the ideal spot for an intimate moonlit dinner. Inside, the decor is both elegant and comfortable. There is also a charming downstairs bar with a more intimate atmosphere. Fine French cuisine awaits you.

La Crémaillère
$$$-$$$$

73 Rue Ste-Anne

☎ (418) 692-2216

Friendly service and exquisite cooking with a European flavour await you at La Crémaillère. A great deal of attention is given here to make your meal memorable. The attractive decor adds to the charm of this inviting restaurant.

Aux Anciens Canadiens
$$$-$$$$

34 Rue St-Louis

☎ (418) 692-1627

Located in one of the oldest houses in Québec City, Aux Anciens Canadiens serves upscale versions of traditional Québécois specialties and specializes in wild game. Try the pork and beans and the blueberry or maple sugar pie.

Le Continental
$$$-$$$$

26 Rue St-Louis

☎ (418) 694-9995

Le Continental, located just steps away from Château Frontenac, is one of the oldest restaurants in Québec City. Its continental cuisine includes seafood, lamb and duck, among other dishes. Service is *au guéridon* (pedestal table) in a large, comfortable dining room.

Café de la Terrasse
$$$$

1 Rue des Carrières

☎ (418) 692-3861

The Café de la Terrasse, in the Château Frontenac, has picture windows looking out onto Terrasse Dufferin. Attractive decor and delicious French cuisine.

Le Champlain
$$$$

1 Rue des Carrières

☎ (418) 692-3861

Le Champlain is the Château Frontenac's main restaurant. Needless to say, its decor is extremely luxurious, in keeping with the opulence of the rest of the hotel. The outstanding French cuisine also does justice to the Château's reputation. Chef Jean Soular, whose recipes have been published, adds a unique touch to the classic dishes. Impeccable service.

- - - - - - - - - - - - - - - - - - -

Tour B: Petit-Champlain to Vieux-Port

Buffet de l'Antiquaire
$

95 Rue St-Paul

☎ (418) 692-2661

Buffet de l'Antiquaire is a good snack bar that serves homestyle cooking. As its name suggests, it is located in the heart of the antique dealers' quarter and is a good spot for a break from treasure-hunting. It is also one of the first restaurants to open in the morning (6am) in the area.

Le Cochon Dingue
$$
46 Boulevard Champlain
☎ (418) 692-2013
Le Cochon Dingue is a charming café-bistro located between Boulevard Champlain and Rue du Petit-Champlain. Mirrors and a checkerboard floor create a fun, attractive decor. The menu features bistro-style dishes such as *steak-frites* and *moules-frites* combos (steak and fries or mussels with fries). The desserts are heavenly.

Un Thé au Sahara
$$
bring your own wine
7 Rue Ste-Ursule
☎ (418) 692-5315
Located in a basement on small Rue Sainte-Ursule, this cozy Moroccan restaurant is very friendly and romantic. The heady fragrances of couscous, tajines, merguez and harissa that seep from the kitchen take patrons to another world.

Le Diable aux Anges
$$-$$$
28 Boulevard Champlain
☎ (418) 692-4674
Le Diable aux Anges, located in an 18th-century French house, features a diverse menu that is simply heavenly. The all-you-can-eat mussels and fries are served with a selection of 14 sauces.

Le Vendôme
$$-$$$
36 Côte de la Montagne
☎ (418) 692-0557

Le Vendôme is located halfway up Côte de la Montagne, and is one of the oldest restaurants in Québec City. It serves classic French dishes like *Chateaubriand*, *coq au vin* and *canard à l'orange* in an intimate setting.

Toast
$$$
17 Rue Sault-au-Matelot
☎ (418) 692-1334
Located in the beautiful stone building that houses **Le Priori** hotel (see p 360), Toast stands out from the exterior thanks to its lovely red lighting. Inside, a mixture of stone walls and red neon lights make for a stunning decor. The cuisine is classic but inspired by flavours from the world over. Summer terrace at the back.

Conti Caffe
$$$
32 Rue St-Louis
☎ (418) 692-4191
The Conti Caffe serves trendy Italian cuisine in an equally trendy and lively ambiance. In the middle of the dining room sits a large, crescent-shaped bar that welcomes many regulars.

L'Échaudé
$$$
73 Rue Sault-au-Matelot
☎ (418) 692-1299
L'Échaudé is an appealing restaurant with an Art Deco interior featuring a mirrored wall. Relaxed atmosphere. A sophisticated cuisine is prepared daily with fresh market ingredients.

Aviatic Club
$$$
450 De la Gare-du-Palais
☎ (418) 522-3555

The magnificent Gare du Palais is home to the Aviatic Club, which takes you back in time with its mid-19th-century English-style decor featuring leather armchairs, beige curtains and a Euro-Asian menu. No smoking. Adjacent to the Le Charbon steak house, also in the Gare du Palais.

Café du Monde
$$$-$$$$
84 Rue Dalhousie
☎ (418) 692-4455
Café du Monde is a large Parisian-style brasserie that serves dishes one would expect from such a place, including *magret de canard* (duck filet), *tartare* (raw minced steak with herbs), *bavette* (flank steak) and of course, *moules-frites* (mussels and french fries). The lunch menu is also interesting, with its delicious *profiteroles* (cream puffs) served for dessert. On the weekend there are great brunches as well. The bright decor is conducive to relaxation and discussion: there are black-and-white tiles on the floor, leather seats, large windows overlooking the river and a long bar adorned with an imposing copper coffee machine. There is also a bar at the entrance. The waiters, dressed in long aprons, are quite helpful.

Two good restaurants are perched on the picturesque Escalier Casse-Cou, which leads to Rue du Petit-Champlain. On the top floor, **Chez Rabelais** *($$$; 2 Rue du Petit-Champlain, ☎418-694-9460)* serves French fusion cuisine with an emphasis on seafood, game and local products. A little lower down is **Marie-**

Clarisse (*$$$$*; *12 Rue du Petit-Champlain,* ☎*418-692-0857)*, where everything, except for the stone walls, is as blue as the sea—and with good reason: seafood is the house specialty. The divine dishes are served in a lovely dining room that has been very ornately decorated. When the cold weather sets in, a crackling fire warms you up.

Laurie Raphäel
$$$$
17 Rue Dalhousie
☎ (418) 692-4555
Chef and co-owner Daniel Vézina is well known as one of the best chefs in Québec. When creating his mouth-watering dishes, Vézina draws inspiration from culinary traditions from all over the world, preparing local products with a creativity that guarantees a memorable dining experience. The menu features *foie gras*, mussels, Atlantic halibut, Ecuador tuna, venison and piglet. It goes without saying that the food at Laurie Raphäel is simply exquisite.

Tour C:
Grande Allée

Bügel
$
164 Rue Crémazie Ouest
☎ (418) 523-7666
Craving a bagel? You'll find all different kinds at Bügel, a bagel bakery on the quaint Rue Crémazie. In a warm atmosphere enhanced by the aroma of the wood oven, you can snack on bagels with salami, cream cheese or veggie

pâté and stock up on goodies to take back home.

Aux 2 Violons Resto-Café
$
bring your own wine
122 Rue Crémazie Ouest
☎ (418) 523-1111
Nestled on Rue Crémazie Ouest, Aux 2 Violons is exactly the kind of tiny place that regulars like to keep secret and visitors love to discover. This small restaurant offers Maghrebi and Lebanese cuisine and is quite exotic, thanks to a colour scheme that recalls the contrast between the desert and the sea. Here, the owners serve *fayrouz* (a malted beverage) and mint tea while diners take their time and relax. On the Mediterranean menu, you'll find an ingenious exotic *poutine* that includes *shish taouk*, onions and green peppers.

Le Parlementaire
$-$$
Mon-Fri
at the corner of Avenue Honoré-Mercier and Grande Allée
☎ (418) 643-6640
Visitors who might want to rub shoulders with members of Québec's National Assembly should have breakfast at Le Parlementaire. The menu features Québécois dishes. The restaurant is often packed, particularly at lunch, but the food is worth the wait. Open only for breakfast and lunch.

Café Krieghoff
$-$$
1089 Avenue Cartier
☎ (418) 521-3711
Named after the Dutch-born artist whose former home is located at the end of Avenue Cartier, Café

Krieghoff occupies an old house on the same street. It serves light tasty meals (quiche, salads, etc.), a fine daily menu and a more elaborate *table d'hôte*. The café is famous for its delicious espresso. Have a cup with one of their very good breakfast offerings, like the eggs benedict. The casual, convivial atmosphere is reminiscent of a North European café. During summer, its two outdoor seating areas are often packed. No smoking.

Mon Manège à Toi
$$
102 Boulevard René-Lévesque Ouest
☎ (418) 649-0478
Mon Manège à Toi offers a taste of Gaspésie in every meal. Its specialty, as you'll have guessed, is seafood. The menu includes mussels served with a choice of 25 different sauces, but you can also choose from many other regional dishes. The establishment's ambiance is a little theatrical, with large burgundy tablecloths, high, light-coloured ceilings and an array of paintings by Québécois artists.

Jaune Tomate
$$-$$$
120 Boulevard René-Lévesque Ouest
☎ (418) 523-8777
This pretty yellow and red restaurant on Boulevard René-Lévesque near Avenue Cartier serves good Italian cuisine in a country-style decor. Come here on Saturday and Sunday mornings to sample the delicious and inventive brunches. The eggs benedict with a hollandaise sauce flavoured with a zest of orange or teriyaki will make your weekend mornings a delight.

Café-Restaurant du Musée
$$-$$$
same hours as the museum
1 Avenue Wolfe-Montcalm
☎ (418) 644-6780

Inside the **Musée National des Beaux-Arts du Québec** (see p 351) you'll find the lovely Café-Restaurant du Musée. The restaurant's top priority is offering well-prepared food and outstanding service. Guests can gaze out at the Plains of Abraham and the river through large windows; in summer, the same view can be enjoyed from the patio.

Le Métropolitain
$$-$$$
1188 Avenue Cartier
☎ (418) 649-1096

Le Métropolitain is *the* place for sushi in Québec City. Its delicious Japanese morsels are a real feast, prepared before your very eyes by expert hands behind a glass counter. Other Oriental specialties, including fish and seafood dishes, are available here as well.

VooDoo Grill
$$$
575 Grande Allée Est
☎ (418) 647-2000

This old house was once the social club of the Union Nationale, the political party of the notorious Maurice Duplessis. This explains the name of the nightclub, **Maurice** (see p 370), occupying the building's two upper floors and where you can end the evening after your meal. Located on the second floor, the restaurant has kept some of the building's original architectural features and displays a most ingenious decor. *Djumbé* players occasionally perform in the evening, adding a bit of

rhythm to the already lively atmosphere. The VooDoo Grill menu has grilled food, of course: meat, fish, fowl and wild Nunavut salmon, as well as dishes sautéed in a wok and served on spicy rice or satay with a choice of sauces. All are tasty, but far from exquisite. The kitchen is open late.

Le Paris-Brest
$$$
590 Grande Allée Est, at the corner of de La Chevrotière
☎ (418) 529-2243

At Le Paris-Brest, French cuisine is the specialty. Prepared with care, the food here will satisfy the most demanding gourmets. In summer, the restaurant opens its small terrace, which looks out onto Grande Allée.

L'Astral
$$$
Hotel Loews Le Concorde, 1225 Cours du Général-De Montcalm
☎ (418) 647-2222

A rotating restaurant located atop one of the city's largest hotels, L'Astral serves excellent French food and provides a stunning view of the river, the Plains of Abraham, the Laurentian mountains and the city. It takes about one hour for the restaurant to make a complete rotation. This is a particularly good place for Sunday brunch.

Le Graffiti
$$$
1191 Avenue Cartier
☎ (418) 529-4949

Revamped as a "Resto-Cité," Le Graffiti has managed to maintain, in addition to its lovely wood beams and brick walls, a warm ambiance. It is a bit surprising, in such as modern

environment, to feel both enveloped by its beautiful interior and, thanks to a magnificent terrace, connected to the outdoors. The fine cuisine features French and Italian accents. On the menu, salmon or beef tartare is the top choice.

La Closerie
$$$$
1210 Place George-V
☎ (418) 523-9975

La Closerie serves fine French cuisine. The chef, who has a well-established reputation, creates meals from fresh, prime quality ingredients.

Tour D: Saint-Jean-Baptiste

Chez Victor
$
145 Rue St-Jean
☎ (418) 529-7702

Located in a basement with a retro decor, Chez Victor serves salads and hamburgers—and not just any old hamburgers! The menu offers several different kinds (including four delicious veggie versions), all big, juicy and served with fresh toppings. The homemade peanut-oil fries are sublime. Cordial service.

Thang Long
$-$$
bring your own wine
869 Côte d'Abraham
☎ (418) 524-0572

Thang Long may be tiny, but its menu will transport you to Vietnam, Thailand, China and even Japan. The decor of this neighbourhood restaurant is simple and unpretentious; the cuisine is truly up to the mark, and the service, very atten-

Québec City - Restaurants - Saint-Jean-Baptiste

tive. Don't miss the *Chakis*, a Hanoï specialty that you can only find in this establishment. Try one of the meal-size soups—comfort food at bargain prices.

Le Bonnet d'Âne
$$
298 Rue St-Jean
☎ (418) 647-3031
The theme here is elementary school and the menu is as varied as the subjects after which the dishes are named. Hamburgers, pizza and light meals are served on big beautiful plates that will delight both young and old. The theme extends to the decor, which includes blackboards, school desks and old toys, as well as some lovely wood trim. There is a pretty terrace in the summer.

Le Hobbit
$$
700 Rue St-Jean
☎ (418) 647-2677
Le Hobbit has occupied an old house in the Saint-Jean-Baptiste neighbourhood for years, and its stone walls and big windows overlooking bustling Rue St-Jean have not lost their appeal. Here you can linger over an espresso and have a light meal or enjoy the *table d'hôte*'s delicious menu that changes daily and is never disappointing. Works by local artists are displayed here regularly.

Les Épices du Széchouan
$$-$$$
215 Rue St-Jean
☎ (418) 648-6440
For exotic cuisine with succulent flavours and enticing aromas, try Les Épices du Széchouan, which occupies an old house in the Saint-Jean-Baptiste quarter.

Its pretty decor is enhanced by a thousand and one Chinese trinkets. One table with a banquette is nestled beneath a corbelled wall. The house is a little ways from the street, so be careful not to miss it.

Le Beffroi
$$$
775 Avenue Honoré-Mercier
☎ (418) 694-2000
Le Beffroi offers a menu where beef is the main staple, but which also provides a good selection of seafood dishes. The big bay window, which overlooks the entrance to the fortified town, and the lovely woodwork make this dining room a most charming spot. The edible flowers (pansies, orchids and, especially, nasturtiums) will delight your taste buds!

Il Teatro
$$$
Capitole de Québec
972 Rue St-Jean
☎ (418) 694-9996
Il Theatro, located inside the magnificent **Capitole de Québec** (see p 352), serves excellent Italian cuisine in a lovely dining room with a long bar and big, sparkling windows all around. The courteous service is on par with the delicious food. During summer, guests can dine in a small outdoor seating area sheltered from the hustle and bustle of Place d'Youville. Valet service.

♪ Entertainment

■ Bars and Nightclubs

There is no cover charge at most bars and nightclubs in Québec City, except when they are hosting a special event or a show. During winter, most places require customers to check their coats, which costs a dollar or two.

Grande Allée

Le Dagobert
600 Grande Allée Est
☎ (418) 522-0393
Better known as Le Dag, Le Dagobert is one of the largest clubs in town. According to the regulars, it is the best nightclub for flirting. Taking up three floors of an old house, Le Dag is actually very chic-looking, as is its somewhat young clientele. The dance floor is quite large and a horseshoe-shaped mezzanine is ideal for those who prefer to watch rather than join the dancing crowd.

Maurice
575 Grande Allée Est
☎ (418) 647-2000
The Maurice nightclub resembles no other in town. The decor is so original that it is difficult to describe. A predominantly red colour scheme highlights some amazing avant-garde furniture. Comfortable sofas are nestled in the various cozy corners of the establishment, and the large central dance floor is lined with small bars. Here, the doormen cleverly handpick the customers, who are always hip, beautiful and aged be-

tween 20 and 35. On the upper floor, you can relax in the **Charlotte Lounge** or the **Société Cigare** cigar room. Some nights feature Latino music. Cover charge.

Jules et Jim
1060 Avenue Cartier
☎ (418) 524-9570
The small Jules et Jim has graced Avenue Cartier for several years now. It offers a smooth atmosphere, with banquettes and low tables reminiscent of Paris in the 1920s.

Le Turf Pub
1179 Avenue Cartier
☎ (418) 522-9955
On lively Avenue Cartier, Le Turf is the place to be for the "beautiful" crowd (30 and over).

Petit-Champlain to Vieux-Port

L'Inox
37 Rue St-André
☎ (418) 692-2877
L'Inox is a bistro-style brewery and the last bastion of the brewing tradition in Québec City. The decor is original and the stainless-steel central bar is quite eye-catching. The clientele is young and varied. As well as serving beer, they also have hot-dogs to satisfy your growling stomach. Many different activities are held throughout the year, so you should inquire; for example, it might be fun to attend a session of *peinture en direct*, where artists create paintings on the spot and then auction their works, or take part in one of the CD launches that are regularly held here.

Le Pape Georges
8 Rue Cul-de-Sac
☎ (418) 692-1320

Le Pape Georges is a charming wine bistro. Beneath the vaults of an old house in Petit Champlain, guests can sample a wide variety of wines while nibbling on snacks like cheese and *charcuteries* (cold cuts). The atmosphere is warm, especially when there are folk and blues musicians to liven things up.

Taverne Belley
249 Rue St-Paul
☎ (418) 692-4595
The Taverne Belley, located in front of the Marché du Vieux-Port, has a few typical tavern features, such as a pool table and small, round, metal tables. The decor of its two rooms is both warm and fun, with colourful paintings hanging on exposed brick walls.

Pub de L'Oncle Antoine
29 Rue St-Paul
☎ (418) 694-9176
Located near Place-Royale, Pub de L'Oncle Antoine is nestled beneath a vaulted ceiling. This place is entirely made of stone, which, in addition to the long white candles placed in bottles on the wooden tables, makes you feel as if you've stepped back in time to the Middle Ages. During winter, a crackling fire helps banish the cold.

Saint-Jean-Baptiste

Le Fou-Bar
525 Rue St-Jean
☎ (418) 522-1987
Le Fou-Bar is an appealing place with a regular clientele who comes here to drink, chat with friends or check out the current works of art on display.

Le Temps Partiel
698 Rue d'Aiguillon
☎ (418) 522-1001

For over a decade, the Fourmi Atomik club in Vieux-Québec was the haunt of a colourful, underground crowd. Forced to shut down in the summer of 2001, it more or less reopened under this new name in the Saint-Jean-Baptiste district. The music includes a wide variety of styles, from worldbeat to punk rock, alternative and 1980s techno, as well as the latest tunes.

Vieux-Québec

Le Chantauteuil
1001 Rue St-Jean
☎ (418) 692-2030
Le Chantauteuil is a quaint bistro. The pretty decor is reminiscent of Paris, with its attractive paintings hanging on stone walls. This café has lots of character, the service is friendly and communication is easily established between staff and customers. Le Chantauteuil used to be a *boîte à chanson* where renowned Québécois artists like Félix Leclerc and Claude Gauthier performed in the 1960s.

L'Emprise
57 Rue Ste-Anne
☎ (418) 692-2480
The oldest hotel in the city (see **Hôtel Clarendon** p 358) houses L'Emprise. This elegant bar is recommended to jazz fans. There is a long *L*-shaped bar and, in the centre of the room, a magnificent black grand piano. While relaxing comfortably in an armchair, you can listen to one of the informal shows that are frequently presented here. There is no cover charge.

Le Saint-Alexandre
1087 Rue St-Jean
☎ (418) 694-0015

Québec City - Entertainment

Le Saint-Alexandre is a typical English pub. The Scottish-green colour scheme and stone walls blend perfectly with the mahogany wood panelling and furniture. Here, great care is given to detail and authenticity. The impressive line-up of imported beers behind the bar is eye-catching and will give you a taste of the exotic. In fact, 200 varieties of beer are served, including about 20 on tap, their handles decorating the long bar. Good light meals are also served.

Bar Fixion
811 Rue St-Jean
☎ (418) 694-9669
Passion dominates in this bar, all decorated in red. A lovely spiral wrought-iron staircase stands right in the middle of the dance floor, where patrons can groove to their heart's content to the sounds of Latin and tropical music. Hip hop, percussion and "karibe" (Caribbean) evenings.

■ Gay and Lesbian Nightclubs

L'Amour Sorcier
789 Côte Ste-Geneviève
☎ (418) 523-3395
L'Amour Sorcier is a small bar in the Saint-Jean-Baptiste quarter, where the atmosphere can sometimes really heat up. During summer, it features a pretty patio.

Le Drague – Cabaret Club
815 Rue St-Augustin
☎ (418) 649-7212
This gay bar, which attracts a large number of regulars, is livened up by drag shows and wild karaoke evenings.

■ Festivals and Cultural Events

Carnaval de Québec (*☎418-626-3716 or 866-422-7628, www.carnaval.qc.ca*), Québec City's winter carnival, takes place annually during the first two weeks of February. It is an opportunity for visitors and residents of Québec City to celebrate the beauty of winter. It is also a good way to add a little life to a cold winter that often seems without end. Various activities are organized. Some of the most popular include night-time parades, canoe races over the partially frozen St. Lawrence River as well as the international ice and snow sculpture contests held on the Plains of Abraham and in front of the carved ice castle at Place du Parlement. This can be a bitterly cold period of the year, so dressing very warmly is essential.

The **Festival d'été de Québec** (*early Jul; ☎418-523-4540 or 888-992-5200, www.info festival.com*) is generally held over 10 days in early July when music, songs, dancing and other kinds of entertainment from all over the world liven up Québec City. The festival has everything it takes to be the city's most important cultural event. The outdoor shows are particularly popular. For most theatres' indoor shows, you must buy tickets. However, those presented outdoors are free.

Parc de la Francophonie plays host to the **Plein Art** (*first two weeks of Aug every day 10am to 11pm; ☎418-694-0260*) exhibit. All kinds of arts and crafts are displayed and sold.

People from the Québec City region have been enjoying themselves at **Expo-Québec** (*Parc ExpoCité, 250 Boulevard Wilfrid-Hamel, ☎418-691-7110*) every August for close to 100 years. This huge fair, complete with an amusement park, is held in front of the Colisée Pepsi for about 10 days at the end of the month.

■ Theatres and Performance Halls

The Québec City edition of the French-language magazine *Voir* is distributed free of charge and provides information on the main events of the city.

Concert Halls

Auditorium Joseph-Lavergne
Bibliothèque Gabrielle-Roy
350 Rue St-Joseph Est
☎ (418) 529-0924
All kinds of shows are presented in this intimate theatre.

Grand Théâtre de Québec
269 Boulevard René-Lévesque Est
☎ (418) 643-8131 or 877-643-8131
The Orchestre Symphonique de Québec, the oldest symphony orchestra in Canada, often performs at the Grand Théâtre de Québec. See also p 350.

Maison de la Chanson/ Théâtre Petit Champlain
68-78 Rue du Petit-Champlain
☎ (418) 692-4744
Excellent concerts are held in this intimate hall.

Le Capitole de Québec
972 Rue St-Jean
☎ (418) 694-4444
First inaugurated in 1903, this theatre was restored in 1992. It is now one of the most beautiful venues in Québec City.

Movie Theatres

Place Charest
500 Rue du Pont
☎ (418) 529-9745

Cinéma Cartier
1019 Avenue Cartier
☎ (418) 522-1100
For unpretentious repertoire cinema.

Theatres

Théâtre Périscope
2 Rue Crémazie Est
☎ (418) 529-2183
This theatre presents experimental plays.

Théâtre de La Bordée
315 Rue St-Joseph Est
☎ (418) 694-9631

Théâtre du Trident
Grand Théâtre de Québec
269 Boulevard René-Lévesque Est
☎ (418) 643-8131

Le Petit Théâtre de Québec
190 Rue Dorchester
☎ (418) 529-9711

🏠 Shopping

■ Arts and Crafts

Galerie d'Art Indien Cinq Nations
20 Rue Cul-de-Sac
Boutique Cinq Nations
25½ Rue du Petit-Champlain
☎ (418) 692-1009
Aboriginal art and crafts.

Boutique Métiers d'Art
29 Rue Notre-Dame
Place Royale
☎ (418) 694-0267
Québec-made crafts.

L'Oiseau du Paradis
80 Rue du Petit-Champlain
☎ (418) 692-2679
Paper and paper objects.

Pot-en-Ciel
27 Rue du Petit-Champlain
☎ (418) 692-1743
Ceramics.

Verrerie La Mailloche
Escalier Casse-Cou (see p 341)
☎ (418) 694-0445
Workshop-made glass objects.

Sculpteur Flamand
49 Rue du Petit-Champlain
☎ (418) 692-2813
In the boutique-workshop of Alain Flamand, you can watch wood sculptors at work. Its two floors are filled with traditional and contemporary Québécois sculptures.

Peau sur Peau
85 Rue du Petit-Champlain
☎ (418) 694-1921
In this shop you'll find shoes, handbags and hats made from quality leather. There are also leather sculptures and 3-D paintings, as well as a famous belt made from, among other things, a "mysterious braid" invented by a Native American from the eastern United States.

Galerie d'Art Buade
43 Rue de Buade, third floor
☎ (418) 694-4443
Galerie d'Art Buade, a co-op that brings together some 10 artists, painters and sculptors, allows you to buy directly from the artists.

■ Books

La Maison Anglaise
Place de la Cité, Sainte-Foy
☎ (418) 654-9523
The best selection of English books in Québec City.

■ Food

La Cuisine du Quartier
1191 Avenue Cartier
Halles du Petit-Quartier
☎ (418) 524-4185
For some fine take-out, head to La Cuisine du Quartier, which offers duck, boar and rabbit prepared with international flavours.

■ Jewellery and Decorative Arts

Lazuli
774 Rue St-Jean
☎ (418) 525-6528

Origines
54 Côte de la Fabrique
☎ (418) 694-9257

Pierres Vives
23½ Rue du Petit-Champlain
☎ (418) 692-5566

■ Music

Here are two good places to buy CDs. They both sell all kinds of music and can advise you on the latest releases.

Sillons Le Disquaire
1149 Avenue Cartier
☎ (418) 524-8352

Archambault Musique et Livres
1095 Rue St-Jean, Vieux-Québec
☎ (418) 694-2088

■ Outdoor Equipment

Azimut
1194 Avenue Cartier
☎ (418) 648-9500
Clothing and accessories.

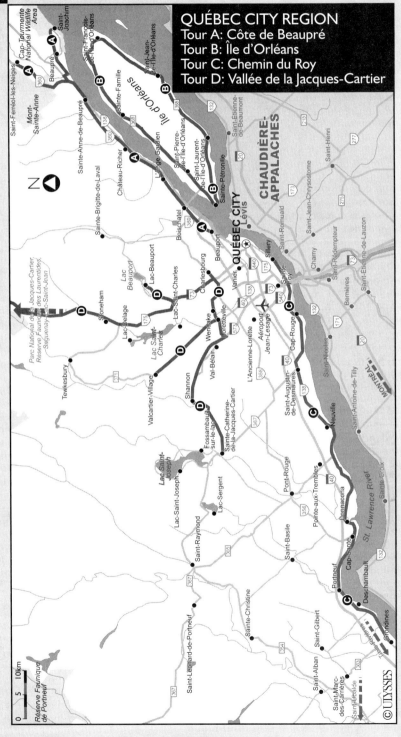

QUÉBEC CITY REGION
Tour A: Côte de Beaupré
Tour B: Île d'Orléans
Tour C: Chemin du Roy
Tour D: Vallée de la Jacques-Cartier

© ULYSSES

The Québec City Region

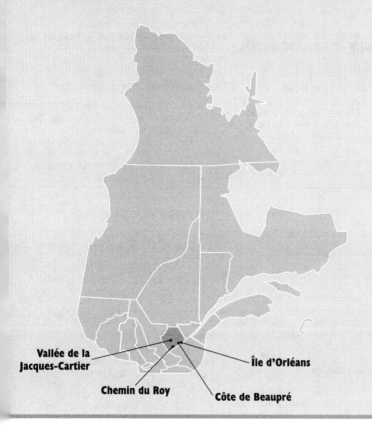

Vallée de la Jacques-Cartier

Île d'Orléans

Chemin du Roy

Côte de Beaupré

The seat of colonial administration under the French Regime, Québec City was the main urban centre of New France. To supply produce to the city and its institutions, farms were introduced to the area in the middle of the 17th century. The farming region on the periphery of the city was the first populated rural zone in the St. Lawrence Valley.

Traces of the first seigneuries granted to settlers in New France are still visible in this historically rich rural area. The farmhouses are the oldest of New France, and the descendants of their first residents are now scattered across the American continent.

Getting There and Getting Around

Four tours are suggested for the area surrounding Québec City: **Tour A: Côte de Beaupré ★★**, **Tour B: Île d'Orléans ★★**, **Tour C: Chemin du Roy ★★** and **Tour D: Vallée de la Jacques-Cartier ★**. With the exception of the Jacques-Cartier tour, which is longer and extends further into the wilderness, these excursions can all be enjoyed as day trips from Québec City.

■ By Car

Tour A: Côte de Beaupré

From Québec City, take the Autoroute Dufferin-Montmorency (Aut. 440) towards Beauport (Exit 24), then take Rue d'Estimauville. Turn right on Chemin Royal (Rte. 360), which becomes Avenue Royale and will lead you throughout the tour.

Tour B: Île d'Orléans

From Québec, take Autoroute Dufferin-Montmorency (Rte. 440) to the Pont de l'Île. Cross the river and turn right on Rte. 368, also called Chemin Royal, which circles the island.

Tour C: Chemin du Roy

From Québec City, head west on Grande-Allée, which eventually becomes Chemin Saint-Louis from Bagatelle to Sillery. After following Chemin St-Louis to Cap-Rouge, take Rte. 138, which you will follow for the rest of the tour. It is also possible to follow this tour in the opposite direction; in other words, starting in Montréal (Exit 236 off Rte. 40), or to add a visit to the village

of **Sainte-Anne-de-La-Pérade** included in the **Mauricie** tour (see p 308).

Tour D: Vallée de la Jacques-Cartier

From Québec City, take Côte d'Abraham, turn right on Rue de la Couronne, then follow Autoroute Laurentienne (Aut. 73) to Exit 150. Turn right on 80ᵉ Rue Ouest, which leads to the heart of the Trait-Carré in Charlesbourg. Rte. 175 leads to Parc national de la Jacques Cartier.

■ Public Transportation

Tour A: Côte de Beaupré

Bus no. 53 leaves Place Jacques-Cartier (*$2.50; Rue du Roi, at the corner of Rue de la Couronne*) and drops visitors near the Montmorency Falls.

Tour B: Île d'Orléans

There is no public transportation or bus service on or to Île d'Orléans. Some private companies organize tours of the island; to explore the island on your own and at your own pace, you will need a car or bicycle.

Tour D: Vallée de la Jacques-Cartier

To reach Charlesbourg from Québec City, take bus no. 801 (*métrobus*), whose stops are clearly indicated (for example, at Place d'Youville). From the Charlesbourg terminus, take bus no. 72 to Wendake. The historic village of Onhoüa Chetek8e is north of the reserve and accessible by taxi.

The Québec City Region

■ By Bus

Tour A: Côte de Beaupré

Sainte-Anne-de-Beaupré *(9687 Boulevard Ste-Anne, Olco convenience store,* ☎ *418-827-3621)* is accessible by bus from Québec City *(320 Rue Abraham-Martin,* ☎ *418-525-3000).*

If you do not have a car at your disposal, the only way to reach the Parc du Mont-Sainte-Anne, the Grand Canyon des Chutes Sainte-Anne and the Cap-Tourmente National Wildlife Area is by bus from Québec City to Sainte-Anne-de-Beaupré, and then by taxi for the remaining 6km in each case.

Tour C: Chemin du Roy

Sainte-Foy bus station
3001 Chemin des Quatre-Bourgeois
☎ (418) 650-0087

■ Train Station

Tour C: Chemin du Roy

Sainte-Foy
3255 Chemin de la Gare (corner Chemin St-Louis)
☎ 800-835-3037

Useful Information

■ Tourist Information

Regional Office

Centre d'Information de l'Office du Tourisme et des Congrès de Québec
835 Avenue Wilfrid-Laurier, Québec, G1R 2L3,
☎ (418) 641-6290
🖶 (418) 522-0830
www.quebecregion.com

Tour A: Côté de Beaupré

Sainte-Anne-de-Beaupré
5490 Boulevard Ste-Anne
☎ (418) 822-0122

Tour B: Île d'Orléans

Saint-Pierre-de-l'Île-d'Orléans
490 Côte du Pont
☎ (418) 828-9411

Tour C: Chemin du Roy

Deschambault-Grondines
12 Rue des Pins
☎ (418) 286-3002

Tour D: Vallée de la Jacques-Cartier

Charlesbourg
7960 Boulevard Henri-Bourassa
☎ (418) 641-6290

Exploring

Tour A: Côte de Beaupré
★ ★

 1 day

This long, narrow strip of land, nestled between the St. Lawrence and the undeveloped wilderness of the Laurentian massif, is the ancestral home of many families whose roots go back to the beginning of the colony. This illustrates how the spread of the population was limited to the riverside in many regions of Québec and recalls the fragility of development in the era of New France. From Beauport to Saint-Joachim, the colony's first road, the Chemin du Roy (king's road), built under orders from Monseigneur de Laval during the 17th century, follows the Beaupré shore. A typical style characterized by a raised main floor covered in stucco, long balconies with intricately carved wooden balusters and lace-curtained windows is repeated in houses along this road. Since about 1960, however, the suburbs of Québec City have gradually taken over the shore, marring the simple beauty of the area. Nevertheless, the Chemin du Roy is still an extremely pleasant route; whether rounding a cape, making one last jaunt in the Laurentians or exploring the plains of the St. Lawrence, this route offers magnificent views of the mountains, fields, the river and Île d'Orléans.

The Québec City Region - Exploring - Côte de Beaupré

Beauport ★

Three types of urban development have shaped Beauport over the course of its history. Originally an agricultural settlement, in the 19th century it became an important industrial town, finally evolving into one of the main suburbs of Québec City in the 1960s. In 1634, the Beauport seigneury, from which the present city grew, was granted to Robert Giffard, a doctor and surgeon from the Perche region of France. In the next few years, he enthusiastically set about building a manor house, a mill and a small village, establishing one of the largest seigneuries in New France. Unfortunately, wars and fires have claimed several of these buildings, notably the huge fortified manor house built in 1642, containing a chapel and a prison, which burned down in 1879.

The **Chemin Royal** ★ *(Route 360 Est)* corresponds to the original 17th-century Chemin du Roy, and follows both the upper and lower sections of the Côte de Beaupré. It traverses the former Beauport seigneury diagonally, which explains the angled placement of the buildings along the road. Many of these houses are ancestral homes, such as the **Maison Marcoux** *(588 Avenue Royale)*, constructed in the 18th century.

Turn right on Rue du Couvent to find parking.

The **Bourg du Fargy** ★ district of Beauport was set up as a fortified village in the middle of the 17th century. In 1669, Seigneur Giffard drew up an ambitious plan for the town, which even included a market square. The **Maison Girardin** *(600 Avenue Royale,* ☎ *418-666-2199)*, built in 1727 by the Marcoux family on land granted to Nicolas Bellanger of Normandy, is one of the last remaining vestiges of the original town. The house, designed for the harsh Canadian climate, has just a few small windows and thick doors. The building now houses the **Centre d'Interprétation de l'Arrondissement Historique de Beauport**. A group of Edwardian houses on Rue du Couvent (circa 1910) offers an interesting contrast to the French Regime–era style.

The large white house known as **Manoir Montmorency** *(2490 Avenue Royale,* ☎ *418-663-3330)* was built in 1780 for British governor Sir John Haldimand. At the end of the 18th century, the house became famous as the residence of the Duke of Kent, son of George III and father of Queen Victoria. The manor, which was once a hotel, was severely damaged by fire in 1993. It has been restored according to the original plans and now hosts an information centre, a few shops and a restaurant (see p 400) that offers an exceptional view of the Montmorency Falls, the St. Lawrence and Île d'Orléans. The small Sainte-Marie chapel on the property and the gardens are open to the public.

The Manoir Montmorency is nestled in the **Parc de la Chute-Montmorency** ★★ *(free admission, parking $8.75, cablecar $8 return;* ♿ *; accessible year-round, check parking opening hours;* ☎ *418-663-3330 or 800-665-6527, www.sepaq. com)*. The Rivière Montmorency, which has its source in the Laurentians, flows along peacefully until it reaches a sudden 83m drop, at which point it tumbles into a void, creating one of the most impressive natural phenomena in Québec. One and a half times the height of Niagara Falls, the Montmorency Falls flow at a rate that can reach 125,000 litres-per-second during the spring thaw. Samuel de Champlain, the founder of Québec City, was impressed by the falls and named them after the viceroy of New France, Charles, Duc de Montmorency. During the 19th century, the falls became a fashionable leisure area for the well-to-do of the region, who would arrive in horse-drawn carriages or sleighs.

A park has been created to preserve this magnificent spectacle for the public and tours of the falls are available. From the manor, follow the beautiful cliff walk, location of the Baronne lookout. You'll soon reach two bridges, the Pont Au-dessus de la Chute and the Pont Au-dessus de la Faille, which pass over the falls and the fault, respectively, with spectacular views. Once in the park you'll find picnic tables and a playground. The bottom of the falls is reached by the 487-step panoramic staircase or the trail. The cable-car provides a relaxing and picturesque means of reaching the top. In winter, steam freezes into a cone of ice, called a sugar-loaf, making for an ice wall that anyone feeling adventurous can climb.

The lower part of the park is also accessible by car, though a complicated detour is required: continue along Avenue Royale, turn right on Côte de l'Église, then right again on Aut. 40. The parking lot is on the right. To get back to Avenue Royale, take Boulevard Sainte-Anne west, Côte Saint-Grégoire and finally Boulevard des Chutes to the right.

Take Chemin Royal heading east.

The **Maison Laurent-dit-Lortie** ★ *(3200 Chemin Royal)* was originally constructed at the end of the 17th century. At the beginning of the following century, it was acquired by Jean Laurent-dit-Lortie. His descendants still live in the house. The imposing size of the building is the result of successive additions, while the steep slope of the roof is indicative of the age of the original structure. The finely carved wood of the balcony, typical of the region, was probably installed around 1880.

Boischatel (pop. 4,480)

The **Manoir de Charleville** ★ *(5580 Avenue Royale)* is one of the oldest standing buildings in Canada. It was built in 1670 for the farmer hired by the capital administration. The building's low profile, high gabled roof and small windows are typical of very old buildings in Québec. Unfortunately, the neighbouring property has recently been built up, partially obscuring this venerable site.

Château-Richer ★ (pop. 3,478)

Under the French Regime, Château-Richer was the nerve centre of the immense Beaupré seigneury, which extended from Saint-Jean-de-Boischatel to Baie-Saint-Paul in the Charlevoix region. Conceded in 1636 by the Compagnie des Cents Associés, this seigneury was granted to the Séminaire de Québec 30 years later, and stayed in its hands until the abolition of seigneurial tenure in 1854. In the 17th century, the directors of the seminary constructed Château Richer, a veritable castle endowed with a tower used as a prison. The building, which was bombarded during the British conquest, was practically in ruins when it was finally demolished around 1860.

The village's location is charming and picturesque, highlighted by the striking placement of the church on a promontory. Throughout the village, small wooden signs have been posted in front of historic buildings indicating their distinctive architectural features and the date they were built.

The **Centre d'Interprétation de la Côte-de-Beaupré** ★ *($5; summer every day 10am to 5pm, rest of the year Mon-Fri 9:30am to 4:30pm; 7976 Avenue Royale,* ☎*418-824-3677)* is located in the centre of town, in a former four-storey school house. An information centre, it has an interesting exhibition on the history and geography of the Côte de Beaupré, as well as some temporary exhibits.

Take Boulevard Sainte-Anne (Rte. 138), which runs parallel to the river, to Chemin Royal.

For those who are curious about bees and honey, here's an interesting little museum. The **Musée de l'Abeille** *(free admission, "bee safari" $4.50; late Jun to early Sep every day 9am to 6pm, early Sep to late Jun every day 9am to 5pm; 8862 Boulevard Ste-Anne,* ☎*418-824-4411, www.musee-abeille.com)* offers a brief look into the lives of these tireless workers. Visitors can stroll through at their leisure or receive an introduction to the art of beekeeping by participating in a "bee safari." A beekeeper explains the steps involved in making honey and even mead (honey wine). There's also a pastry shop and a gift shop.

Continue on Chemin Royal.

Sainte-Anne-de-Beaupré ★ (pop. 2,781)

This long, narrow village is one of the largest pilgrimage sites in North America. In 1658, the first Catholic church on the site was dedicated to Saint Anne after sailors from Brittany, who had prayed to the Virgin Mary's mother, were saved from drowning during a storm on the St. Lawrence. Soon, a great number of pilgrims began to visit the church. The second church, built in 1676, was replaced in 1872 by a huge temple, which was destroyed by fire in 1922. Finally, work began on the present basilica, which stands at the centre of a virtual complex of chapels, monasteries and facilities as varied as they are unusual. They include the Bureau des Bénédictions, or blessings office, and the Cyclorama. Each year, Sainte-Anne-de-Beaupré welcomes more than a million pilgrims, who stay in the hotels and visit the countless gift shops, many of which purvey items of a rather kitschy nature, along Avenue Royale.

The **Basilique Sainte-Anne-de-Beaupré ★★★** *(every day 8:30am to 4:30pm; 10018 Avenue Royale,* ☎*418-827-3781, www.ssadb.qc.ca)*, towering over the small, metal-roofed wooden houses that line the winding road, is surprising not only for its impressive size, but also for the feverish activity it inspires all summer long. The church's granite exterior, which takes on a different colour depending on the ambient light, was designed in the French Romanesque Revival style by Parisian architect Maxime Roisin, who was assisted by Quebecer Louis Napoléon Audet. Its spires rise 91m into the sky above the coast, while the nave is 129m long and the transepts over 60m wide. The wooden statue gilded with copper sitting atop the church's facade was taken from the 1872 church. When the fire destroyed the former basilica, the statue stayed in place while everything collapsed around it.

The basilica's interior is divided into five naves supported by heavy columns with highly sculpted capitals. The vault of the main nave is adorned with sparkling mosaics designed by French artists Jean Gaudin and Auguste Labouret, recounting the life of Saint Anne. Labouret also created the magnificent stained glass, found all along the perimeter of the basilica. The left transept contains an extraordinary statue of Saint Anne cradling Mary in her right arm. Her tiara reminds the visitor that she is the patron saint of Québec. In a beautiful reliquary in the background, visitors can admire the Great Relic, part of Saint Anne's forearm sent over from the San Paolo Fuori le Mura in Rome. Finally, follow the ambulatory around the choir to see the 10 radiant chapels built in the 1930s, whose polychromatic architecture is inspired by Art Deco.

Material retrieved after the demolition of the original church in 1676 was used to build the **Chapelle Commémorative ★** *(free admission; early May to mid-Oct every day 8am to 4:30pm; alongside Avenue Royale,* ☎*418-827-3781)* in 1878. The steeple (1696) was designed by Claude Bailiff, an architect whose numerous other projects in 17th-century New France have all but disappeared, victims of wars and fires. The water from the

Fontaine de Sainte-Anne, at the foot of the chapel, is said to have healing properties.

La Scala Santa ★ *(free admission; early May to mid-Oct every day 8am to 4:30pm; to the right of the Chapelle du Souvenir,* ☎*418-827-3781)*, a strange yellow and white wooden building (1891), houses a staircase that pilgrims climb on their knees while reciting prayers. It is a replica of the Scala Santa, the sacred staircase conserved in Rome at San Giovanni in Laterano, which Christ climbed to get to the court of Pontius Pilate. An image of the Holy Land is inlaid in each riser.

The **Cyclorama de Jérusalem ★★** *($7; early May to late Oct every day 9am to 6pm, Jul and Aug every day 8am to 8pm; 8 Rue Régina, near the parking lot,* ☎*418-827-3101, www.cyclorama.com)*, a circular building with oriental features, houses a 360° panorama of Jerusalem on the day of the crucifixion. This immense *trompe l'œil* painting, measuring 14m by 110m, was created in Munich between 1878 and 1882 by French artist Paul Philippoteaux and his assistants. A specialist in panoramas, Philippoteaux produced a work of remarkable realism. It was first exhibited in Montréal before being moved to Sainte-Anne-de-Beaupré at the very end of the 19th century. Very few panoramas and cycloramas, so popular a century ago, have survived to the present day.

The **Musée de Sainte Anne ★** *($2;* ♿*; Easter to mid-Oct every day 10am to 5pm; 9803 Boulevard Ste-Anne,* ☎*418-827-3781, ext. 754)* is dedicated to sacred art honouring the mother of the Virgin Mary. These interestingly diverse pieces were acquired over many years from the basilica but have only recently been put on display for the public. The exhibition is attractively presented and covers two floors.

Other recommended destinations in the region include the **Mont-Sainte-Anne** *ski resort (see p 393) and the charming village of Saint-Ferréol-les-Neiges on Rte. 360 E., which branches off Avenue Royale at Beaupré.*

*Follow Avenue Royale to Saint-Joachim (Cap Tourmente). Cross Rte. 138, and go through the municipality of Beaupré. Turn right on Rue de l'Église in Saint-Joachim. Beyond the church (***Église Saint-Joachim ★***, worth visiting for its beautiful interior), turn left on Chemin du Cap.*

Saint-Ferréol-les-Neiges (pop. 2,098)

At the east end of Saint-Ferréol-les-Neiges is **Les Sept Chutes** hydroelectric complex *($7; mid-May to late Jun every day 10am to 5pm, late Jun to early Sep every day 9am to 6pm, Sep to mid-Oct every day 10am to 5pm; 4520 Avenue Royale, ☎418-826-3139 or 877-724-8837, www. septchutes.com)*, which was active from 1916 to 1984 and has since been transformed into an information centre. You can learn about the stages of hydroelectric production and the lives of people who worked in such power stations. There are also paths along the Sainte-Anne-du-Nord river to the impressive 130m-high falls.

On your way back to Québec City, take Rte. 138 W., which provides beautiful views of Île d'Orléans, the Côte de Beaupré and, when weather permits, Québec City itself, located 25km west.

Canyon Sainte-Anne, see p 391.

Cap-Tourmente ★ ★

The pastoral and fertile land of Cap-Tourmente is the easternmost section of the St. Lawrence plain, before the mountains of the Laurentian Massif reach the shores of the St. Lawrence. The colonization of this area at the beginning of the 17th century represented one of the first attempts to populate New France. Samuel de Champlain, the founder of Québec City, established a farm here in 1626, the ruins of which were recently unearthed. Following the British conquest, the seminary, who then owned the land, moved the seat of its Beaupré seigneury to Cap-Tourmente, leaving behind the ruins of the Château Richer. The **Château Bellevue** ★ was built between 1777 and 1781. This superb building is endowed with a neoclassical cut-stone portal. The property's Saint-Louis-de-Gonzague chapel (1780) is well hidden in the trees.

Cap-Tourmente National Wildlife Area ★ ★ see p 391.

*To return to Québec City, continue along the loop formed by the Cap-Tourmente road leading to Saint-Joachim and continue towards Beaupré before taking Rte. 138 W. It is possible to combine the Côte de Beaupré tour with the visit to the **Charle-***

voix region described on p 492. To do this, head to Rte. 138 E. via the steep, winding road northeast of the village of Saint-Joachim. Turn right towards Baie-St-Paul.

Tour B: Île d'Orléans ★ ★

 1 day

Located in the middle of the St. Lawrence River, downstream from Québec City, this 32km-by-5km island is famous for its old-world charm. Of all the regions of Québec, this island is the most evocative of life in New France. When Jacques Cartier arrived in 1535, the island was covered in wild vines, which inspired its first name: Île Bacchus. However, it was soon renamed in honour to the Duc d'Orléans. With the exception of Sainte-Pétronille, the parishes on the island were established in the 17th century. The colonization of the entire island followed soon after. In 1970, the government of Québec designated Île d'Orléans a historic district. The move was made in part to slow down the development that threatened to turn the island into yet another suburb of Québec City, and also as part of a widespread movement among Quebecers to protect the roots of their French ancestry by preserving old churches and houses. Since 1936, the island has been linked to the mainland by a suspension bridge, the Pont de l'Île.

To get to the island from Québec City take the Autoroute Dufferin-Montmorency (Aut. 440) to the Pont de l'Île. Cross the river and turn right on Rte. 368, also called Chemin Royal, which circles the island.

Sainte-Pétronille ★ (pop. 1,071)

Paradoxically, Saint-Pétronille was the site of the first French settlement on Île d'Orléans and is also its most recent parish. In 1648, François de Chavigny de Berchereau and his wife Éléonore de Grandmaison established a farm and a Huron mission here. However, constant Iroquois attacks forced the colonists to move further east, to a spot facing Sainte-Anne-de-Beaupré. It was not until the middle of the 19th century that Sainte-Pétronille was consolidated as a village, as its beautiful location began attracting numerous summer visitors. Anglophone merchants from Québec City built beautiful second homes here, many of which still line the road.

Turn right on Rue Horatio-Walker, which leads to the river banks and to a promenade.

Maison Horatio-Walker ★ *(11 and 13 Rue Horatio-Walker)*. The red brick building and the stucco house beside it were, respectively, the workshop and residence of painter Horatio Walker from 1904 to 1938. The British-born artist liked the French culture and the meditative calm of Île d'Orléans. His workshop, designed by Harry Staveley, is a good example of English Arts and Crafts architecture.

The Porteous family, of English origin, settled in Québec City at the end of the 18th century. In 1900, they had the **Domaine Porteous** ★ *(253 Chemin Royal)* built. This vast country house surrounded by superb gardens was christened "La Groisardière." Designed by Toronto architects Darling and Pearson, the house revived certain aspects of traditional Québec architecture. The most notable of these are the Louis XV–inspired woodwork, and the general proportions used in the design of the house. The building also incorporates Art Nouveau features. The property, which today belongs to the Foyer de Charité Notre-Dame-d'Orléans, a seniors' residence, was expanded between 1961 and 1964 when a new wing and a chapel were added.

Saint-Laurent-de-l'Île-d'Orléans (pop. 1,634)

Until 1950, Saint-Laurent's main industry was the manufacturing of *chaloupes*, boats and sailboats that were popular in the United States and Europe. Though production of these boats has ceased, some traces of the industry, such as abandoned boatyards, can still be seen off the road, near the banks of the river. The village was founded in 1679 and still has some older buildings, such as the beautiful **Maison Gendreau** built in 1720 *(2387 Chemin Royal, west of the village)* and the **Moulin Gosselin**, which now houses a restaurant *(758 Chemin Royal, east of the village)*.

At the little **Forge à Pique-Assaut** *(free admission; Jun to Oct every day 9am to 5pm, Nov to May Mon-Fri 9am to noon and 1:30pm to 5pm; 2200 Chemin Royal, ☎418-828-9300)*, you can learn about the blacksmith trade by watching artisans at work in front of a large forge or by taking a guided tour. There's a shop on the second floor (see p 402).

Saint-Jean-de-l'Île-d'Orléans ★★ (pop. 881)

In the mid-19th century, Saint-Jean was the preferred home base of nautical pilots who made a living guiding ships through the difficult currents and rocks of the St. Lawrence. Some of their neoclassical or Second Empire houses remain along Chemin Royal and provide evidence of the privileged place held by these seamen, who were indispensable to the success of commercial navigation.

The most impressive remaining manor from the French Regime is in Saint-Jean. The **Manoir Mauvide-Genest** ★★ *($5; 1451 Chemin Royal, ☎418-829-2630)* was built in 1734 for Jean Mauvide, the Royal Doctor, and his wife, Marie-Anne Genest. This beautiful stone building has a rendering coat of white roughcast, in the traditional Norman architectural style. The property officially became a seigneurial manor in the middle of the 18th century, when Mauvide, who had become rich doing business in the Caribbean, bought the southern half of the Île d'Orléans seigneury.

Saint-François-de-l'Île-d'Orléans ★ (pop. 485)

Saint-François, the smallest village on Île d'Orléans, retains many heritage buildings. Some, however, are far from Chemin Royal and are therefore difficult to see from Rte. 368. The surrounding countryside is charming and offers several pleasant panoramic views of the river, Charlevoix and the coast. The famous wild vine that gave the island its first name, Île Bacchus, can also be found in Saint-François.

On the roadside as you leave the village is an **observation tower** ★★, which offers excellent views to the north and east. Visible are the Îles Madame et au Ruau, which mark the meeting point of the fresh water of the St. Lawrence and the salt water of the gulf. Mont Sainte-Anne's ski slopes, Charlevoix on the north shore and the Côte-du-Sud seigneuries on the south shore can also be seen in the distance.

You can get a close look at some majestic buffaloes at the unique **Parc des Bisons de l'île d'Orléans** ★★ *(adults $11, children $4-$6; add $3 for a 45min guided tour, late Jun to early Sep tours leave at noon and 3:30pm; mid-May to late Oct every day 10am to 6pm, early Nov to mid-Mar every day 10am to 3pm; 156 Chemin Royal,* ☎*418-829-1234, www.parcdesbisons. com).* Both an outdoor activity centre (featuring a hiking trail and three lakes set up for canoeing, kayaking, pedal-boating and rafting) and a 120ha ranch, the Parc des Bisons has the largest herd in Québec, with over 400 heads. Furthermore, the park also has a museum, a small farm, a log building with food services, picnic areas and a gift shop. The park's restaurant, **Le Bison Futé**, serves excellent buffalo-based meals. All in all, the park provides a total change of scenery, right on Île d'Orléans.

Sainte-Famille ★ (pop. 879)

The oldest parish on Île d'Orléans was founded by Monseigneur de Laval in 1666 in order to establish a settlement across the river from Sainte-Anne-de-Beaupré for colonists who had previously settled around Sainte-Pétronille. Sainte-Famille has retained many buildings from the French Regime. Among them is the town's famous church, one of the greatest accomplishments of religious architecture in New France, and the oldest two-towered church in Québec.

The beautiful **Église Sainte-Famille** ★★ *(3915 Chemin Royal)* was built between 1743 and 1747 to replace the original church built in 1669. Inspired by the Église des Jésuites in Québec City, which has since been destroyed, Father Dufrost de la Jemmerais ordered the construction of two towers with imperial roofs. This explains the single steeple sitting atop the gable. Other unusual elements, such as five alcoves and a sun dial by the entrance (since destroyed), make the building even more original. In the 19th century, new statues were installed in the alcoves, and the imperial roofs gave way to two new steeples, bringing the total number of steeples to three.

Most of the French Regime farm homes on Île D'Orléans were built some distance away from the road. Today, they are distinguished estates whose secluded character is jealously guarded by their owners, which means a visit is highly unlikely. Fortunately, thanks to a citizen's organization, **Maison Drouin** ★★ *(free admission, fee for activities; mid-Jun to mid-Aug every day 10am to 6pm, mid-Aug to late Sep Sat and Sun 1pm to 5pm; 4700 Chemin Royal,* ☎*418-829-0330)* opens every summer, to the delight of curious visitors. Originally built in 1675 and later expanded in 1725, it is one of the oldest homes on the island and even in all of Québec. Located on a curve of Chemin Royal, it was built using large stones and wood beams. The guides, who are dressed in period costume, talk about the history of the home as they re-enact the everyday life of its former residents.

Situated far from its motherland across the Atlantic, this rustic house was not designed with the harsh climate in mind. The low stone blocks are buried in snow in the wintertime. The entrances are small and the gables are covered with cedar shingles to protect the masonry. The three rooms on the main floor and the third floor exude the bygone era of the first settlers. The house is also full of antiques, furniture and tools, which clearly depict the life of the pioneers. A magnificent place to visit!

Saint-Pierre-de-l'Île-d'Orléans (pop. 1,874)

The most developed parish on Île d'Orléans had already lost some of its charm before the island was declared a historic site. Saint-Pierre is particularly important to Quebecers as it was for many years the home of renowned poet and singer Félix Leclerc (1914-1988). The singer and songwriter was the first musician to introduce Québec music to Europe. He is buried in the local cemetery.

At the end of the village is a new site honouring the poet's memory. The **Espace Félix-Leclerc** ★ *($5/person, $4/person for groups; mid-Feb to mid-Dec every day 9am to 6pm; 682 Chemin Royal,* ☎*418-828-1682)* includes a wide array of interesting features: a building housing an exhibit on the life and work of Félix Leclerc, a *boîte à chansons* (music venue for singer-songwriters) where young and old alike can belt out Leclerc's famous tunes or come up with some new ones of their own, and hiking trails to explore the heart of the island, as Leclerc did so many times.

Unassuming **Église Saint-Pierre** ★ *(1249 Chemin Royal)* was built in 1716, making it the oldest village church still standing in Canada. It is also one of the rare surviving French Regime churches of its kind, characterized by its single exterior doorway topped with a bull's eye window. Most of these small churches were destroyed during the 19th century and replaced by more elaborate structures. The church's interior was ransacked following the British Conquest and rebuilt at the end of the 18th century.

The tour is now completed. Head back to the Pont de l'Île to return to the mainland.

- -
Tour C: Chemin du Roy
★ ★

 1 day

With the exception of Sillery, near Québec City, the towns and villages on this tour are all located along the Chemin du Roy, the first maintained road between Montréal and Québec City, built in 1734. This road, running along the St. Lawrence (some parts parallel to Rte. 138) and lined with beautiful 18th-century French-style houses, churches and windmills, is one of the most picturesque drives in Canada.

Sillery ★ ★

This well-to-do suburb of Québec City retains many traces of its varied history, influenced by the town's dramatic topography. There are actually two sections to Sillery, one at the base and the other at the top of a steep cliff that runs from Cap Diamant to Cap-Rouge. In 1637, the Jesuits built a mission in Sillery on the shores of the river, with the goal of converting the Algonquins and Montagnais who came to fish in the coves upriver from Québec City. They named the fortified community for the mission's benefactor, Noël Brûlart de

Sillery, an aristocrat who had recently been converted by Vincent de Paul.

By the following century, Sillery was already sought after for its beauty. The Jesuits converted their mission to a country house, and the bishop of Samos built Sillery's first villa (1732). Following the British Conquest, Sillery became the preferred town of administrators, military officers and British merchants, all of whom built luxurious villas on the cliff, in architectural styles then fashionable in England. The splendour of these homes and their vast English gardens were in stark contrast to the simple houses lived in by workers and clustered at the base of the cliff. The occupants of these houses worked in the shipyards, where a fortune was being made building ships out of wood coming down the Outaouais region to supply the British navy during Napoleon's blockade, which began in 1806. The shipyards, set up in Sillery's sheltered coves, had all disappeared before Boulevard Champlain, now running along the river's edge, was built in 1960.

The **Siège Social de L'Industrielle-Alliance** *(1080 Chemin Saint-Louis)* looks like a modern villa, but was actually built as the headquarters of a large insurance company. It is one of the best examples of post-war architecture in Québec. The work of architects Pierre Rinfret and Maurice Bouchard (1950-52) was inspired by houses from the 19th century and is accentuated by a beautiful garden.

The **Parc du Bois-de-Coulonge** ★ *(free admission; every day; 1215 Chemin St. Louis,* ☎*418-528-0773)* to the east borders Chemin Saint-Louis. This English park once surrounded the residence of the lieutenant-governor of Québec, the King or Queen's representative in Québec. The stately home was destroyed in a fire in 1966, though some of its outbuildings have survived, notably the guard's house and the stables. The Saint-Denys stream flows through the eastern end of the grounds at the bottom of a ravine. British troops gained access to the Plains of Abraham, where a historic battle decided the future of New France, by climbing through this ravine. Now Bois de Coulonge, member of the Jardins du Québec association, has magnificent gardens and a well-arranged arboretum to walk through.

Villa Bagatelle ★ *(free admission; Tue-Sun 11am to 5pm; 1563 Chemin Saint-Louis ☎418-654-0259)* was once home to an attaché of the British governor who lived on the neighbouring property of Bois-de-Coulonge. Built in 1848, the villa is a good example of 19th-century Gothic Revival residential architecture, as interpreted by American Alexander J. Davis. The house and its Victorian garden were impeccably restored in 1984, and they are now open to the public. On the grounds, there is an interesting information centre providing background on the villas and large estates of Sillery.

On Avenue Lemoine, which runs along the south side of Bagatelle, is the **Spencer Grange Villa** *(1321 Avenue Lemoine)*, built in 1849 for Henry Atkinson. During the Second World War, the building was home to Zita de Bourbon-Parme, the dethroned Empress of Austria.

The Gothic Revival **St. Michael's Church** *(1800 Chemin St-Louis)*, built in 1852, serves the Anglican congregation of Sillery. Nearby is the **Mount Hermon Protestant Cemetery** and the **Couvent des Soeurs de Sainte-Jeanne-d'Arc** (1917), a huge convent that looks like an imposing castle.

Turn left onto Côte de l'Église.

A short side trip leads to the **Cimetière de Sillery**, Sillery's Catholic cemetery, where René Lévesque, founder of the Parti Québecois and Premier of Québec from 1976 to 1984, is buried. To get there, turn right on Avenue Maguire, then left on Boulevard René-Lévesque Ouest.

The **Église Saint-Michel** ★ *(at the corner of Chemin du Foulon and Côte de l'Église)*, Sillery's Catholic church, has many points in common with its Anglican counterpart, St. Micheal's Church: its patron saint, its Gothic Revival style and its date of construction, 1852. The Catholic church, designed by architect George Browne, is, however, much larger. Inside are five paintings from the famous Desjardins collection. These originally hung in Parisian churches until they were sold in 1792 following the French Revolution and brought to Québec by Abbé Desjardins.

The **Maison des Jésuites de Sillery** ★★ *(donations accepted; Jun to Sep Tue-Sun 11am to 5pm, Oct to May Tue-Sun 1pm to 5pm; 2320 Chemin du Foulon, ☎418-654-0259)*, built of stone and covered with white plaster, occupies the former site of a Jesuit mission, a few ruins of which are still visible. In the 17th century, the mission included a fortified stone wall, a chapel, a priest's residence and Aboriginal housing. As European illnesses, such as smallpox and measles, devastated the indigenous population, the mission was transformed into a hospice in 1702. At the same time, work began on the present house, a building with imposing chimney stacks. In 1763, the house was rented to John Brookes and his wife, writer Frances Moore Brookes, who immortalized it as the setting for her novel, *The History of Emily Montague*, published in London in 1769. It was also during this time that the structure was lowered and the windows were made smaller in size, in the New England saltbox tradition. The house now has two stories in front and one in back and is covered with a catslide roof.

By 1824, the main building was being used as a brewery and the chapel had been torn down. The house was later converted into offices for various shipyards. In 1929, the Maison des Jésuites became one of the first three buildings designated as historic by the government of Québec. Since 1948, it has housed a museum detailing the 350-year history of the property.

Continue along Chemin du Foulon, then take Côte à Gignac up the embankment on the right. Turn right to head west on Chemin Saint-Louis.

Sainte-Foy

The **Maison Hamel-Bruneau** *(free admission; Tue-Sun 12:30pm to 5pm, Wed to 9pm; 2608 Chemin St-Louis, ☎418-654-4325)* is a beautiful example of Regency architecture, popular in British colonies at the beginning of the 19th century. This style is characterized by hip roofs with flared eaves covering low wraparound verandas. Graced with French windows, the Maison Hamel-Bruneau has been carefully restored and transformed into a cultural centre by the town of Sainte-Foy.

Turn left on Avenue du Parc to get to the Parc Aquarium du Québec.

The **Parc Aquarium du Québec** *(Jun to Sep adults $25, children $7-$16, Oct to May adults $15, chil-*

dren $5-$10; May to Oct every day 10am to 5pm, Oct to May every day 10am to 4pm;1675 Avenue des Hôtels, ☎418-659-5264 or 866-659-5264, www.spsnq.qc.ca), which reopened in late 2002 after lengthy renovations, is a magnificent site. The "Pont de Québec" aquarium, as it was once known, was founded in 1959. Since then, it has welcomed over eight million visitors.

Now home to over 3,500 fish species, the Parc Aquarium du Québec features over 16ha of the St. Lawrence River and polar ecosystems. When you first walk in, you can attend a multimedia presentation that plunges you (virtually, of course) into the river to take you to the North Pole. Outside, all you have to do is follow the tours to meet various mammal species. You will also walk through a rocky valley along the shores of the St. Lawrence in a natural-like decor. Another must-see is the polar world of the North. In this reconstituted Arctic, polar bears and harp seals will undoubtedly impress you.

In addition, in the main building, you'll be transported from the marine universe of the Laurentian Plateau to the waters of the Northern Atlantic. Visitors will finally be able to head into laboratories, then to a huge circular basin where they can admire the sub-arctic Pacific Ocean in all its splendour: the Grand Océan, in which you'll be surrounded by 350,000 litres of water inhabited by 650 marine specimens. You can even watch feedings and handle small invertebrates, such as starfish and sea urchins. The Parc Aquarium du Québec features rest areas, play areas for children, food services (a restaurant with a panoramic terrace and a view of the St. Lawrence River and the bridges; daily and kids' menus), as well as two souvenir shops, one in the reception pavilion and the other in the main building's atrium.

At press time, we learned that the Jardin Zoologique du Québec was closing and that part of its animal population would be relocated to the Parc Aquarium du Québec. Furthermore, the Aquarium will henceforth be run by Société des établissements de plein air du Québec (Sépaq).

Take Chemin Saint-Louis west towards Cap-Rouge, then take Rue Louis-Francœur to the right before turning left down Côte de Cap-Rouge.

Cap-Rouge

Jacques Cartier and the Sieur de Roberval tried to establish a French colony at Cap-Rouge in 1541. They called their encampments Charlesbourg-Royal and France-Roy. The unfortunate souls who came with them, having no idea how cold Canada could get in January, built frail wood buildings with paper windows. Most died during the winter, victims of the cold or of scurvy, a disease caused by lack of vitamin C. The others returned to France in the spring.

A plaque has been placed at the **Site Historique de Cap-Rouge** *(at the end of Côte de Cap-Rouge)*, a historic site commemorating the first French colony in America. Cartier and Roberval had intended to make the site a base camp for expeditions heading out in search of a passage to the Orient.

Take Rue Saint-Félix heading west, turn left on Chemin du Lac, then left again on Rang de la Butte, which becomes Rte. Tessier. Turn left on Rte. 138 towards Saint-Augustin-de-Desmaures. Continue along Rte. 138 to Neuville.

Neuville ★ (pop. 3,436)

A vein of limestone, traversing the region from Neuville to Grondines, has been tapped for the construction of prestigious buildings across the province since the French Regime. This explains the large number of field-stone houses dotting the villages in the area. Today, most of the jobs related to the extraction and cutting of this grey stone are concentrated in the town of Saint-Marc-des-Carrières, west of Deschambault.

The village of Neuville was formerly part of the Pointe-aux-Trembles seigneury, granted to the royal engineer Jean Bourdon in 1653. The houses of Neuville are built into the hills at varying elevations so that most of them have a view of the St. Lawrence. This terraced layout lends this section of the Chemin du Roy a certain charm.

The **"Château" de Neuville** *(205 Route 138)*, on the left as you enter the village, is a fanciful home built between 1964 and 1972 with materials gathered from the demolition of about 100 homes along the Grande-Allée in Québec City.

The **Maison Darveau** *(210 Route 138)* was built in 1785 for one of the most important stonemasons in Neuville, which explains the presence of the more elaborate stone frames around the windows and doors. In addition to these, the house has a classical portal, which, though common in France, was quite exceptional in Québec.

Turn right on Rue des Érables.

Rue des Érables ★★ *(guided tours in summer,* ☎ *418-286-3002)* has one of the largest concentrations of old stone houses outside Québec's large urban centres. This is explained by the abundance of the necessary raw material and the homowners' desire to make use of the talents of local builders and stonemasons. Number 500 on Rue des Érables was built for Édouard Larue, who acquired the Neuville seigneury in 1828. The huge house is representative of traditional rural Québec architecture, with its raised stone foundation and gallery covered with flared eaves running the whole length of the facade.

In 1696, the villagers undertook the construction of the simple **Église Saint-François-de-Sales** ★★ *(guided tours available; 644 Rue des Érables,* ☎ *418-286-3002)*. It was added to and altered during the following centuries, to the point where the original elements of the building have all but disappeared. A newer chancel was built in 1761, the nave was expanded in 1854 and, finally, a new facade was added in 1915. The present church is the result of these transformations. The interior of the church houses an impressive piece of baroque art from the period of the French Regime: a wooden baldaquin (a richly ornamented canopy over the altar) ordered in 1695 for the chapel of the episcopal palace in Québec City.

At the western end of Rue des Érables, take Rte. 138 to the right. Follow Rte. 138 W. to Pointe-aux-Trembles, then Donnacona.

Turn left on Rue Notre-Dame to get to Donnacona, then cross the bridge over the Rivière Jacques-Cartier.

Cap-Santé ★ (pop. 2,567)

This farming village enjoys an enviable setting overlooking the St. Lawrence. For- merly part of the Portneuf seigneury, Cap-Santé came into being at the end of the 17th century and grew slowly. If there is such a thing as a typical Québécois village, Cap-Santé is probably it.

A plaque by the side of the road indicates the site of **Fort Jacques-Cartier** *(near 15 Rue Notre-Dame)*. Erected hastily in 1759, at the peak of the Seven Years War, the fort was meant to slow down the English on their march towards Montréal. The courageous Chevaliers de Lévis tried desperately to save what remained of New France with these measures. The eventual attack on the fort lasted barely an hour, before the ill-equipped French surrendered. Only archaeological remains of the wood fort have survived. The **Cap-Santé seigneurial manor**, built around 1740 on the same site, is, however, still standing, well concealed in the woods.

Return to Rte. 138 on the left.

Construction of the **Église de la Sainte-Famille** ★★ *(guided tours late Jun to early Sep;* ☎ *418-285-2311)* went on between 1754 and 1764 under the auspices of curate Joseph Filion, but was seriously disrupted by the British conquest. In 1759, materials intended for the finishing touches on the building were requisitioned for the construction of Fort Jacques-Cartier. Nevertheless, the completed church, with its two steeples and high nave lit by two rows of windows, is an ambitious piece of work for its time, and was possibly the largest village church built under the French Regime. The three beautiful wooden statues placed in the alcoves of the facade in 1775 have miraculously survived Québec's harsh climate. The imitation cut stone done in wood covering the stone walls was added in the 19th century. Before stepping inside the church, be sure to visit the wooded cemetery and presbytery built by Thomas Baillargé in 1850.

Today the **Vieux Chemin** ★, the old road, is nothing more than a simple road passing in front of the church, but it was once part of the Chemin du Roy, which linked Montréal and Québec City. Numerous well-preserved 18th-century houses facing the river can still be seen along the road, making this one of the most picturesque drives in Canada.

Drive through Portneuf before stopping in Deschambault.

Deschambault ★★

The charming tranquillity of this agricultural village on the banks of the St. Lawrence was a bit disturbed recently by the development of an aluminum smelter. Deschambault was founded thanks to the efforts of Seigneur Fleury de la Gorgendière, who previously had a church built in nearby Cap Lauzon in 1720. Because the village has grown slowly, it retains its small-town charm.

The **Maison Deschambault** *(128 Chemin du Roy)* is visible at the end of a long tree-lined lane. The stone building equipped with fire-break walls was probably built in the late 18th century. It was practically in ruins in 1936, when the Québec government, which owned the building at the time, undertook its restoration, a rarity in an era when many elements of Québec's heritage had already been lost. The building now houses a charming inn (see p 398) and a fine French restaurant (see p 401).

Turn left on Rue de l'Église, which leads to the village square.

With its large facade adorned with two massive towers set back slightly from the front of the church, the **Église Saint-Joseph** ★ (&; *120 Rue St-Joseph)* is unlike no other church in Québec. Instead of the usual gable, the roof of the church has a hipped end adorned with a statue. This solid building, erected between 1835 and 1841, is the work of architect Thomas Baillargé. The original neoclassical steeples were destroyed and replaced in the 20th century with poor imitations of typical New France steeples.

The **Vieux Presbytère** *(donations accepted; Jun to Aug every day 9am to 5pm, May, Sep and Oct Sat and Sun 10am to 5pm; 117 Rue St-Joseph,* ☎*418-286-6891)* occupies a prime location behind the church and offers a beautiful panoramic view of the river and the south shore. The small presbytery building, set apart in the centre of a large lawn, was built in 1815 to replace the first presbytery dating from 1735. The foundations of the original building are visible near the entrance. In 1955, an antique dealer saved

the presbytery from destruction, then, in 1970, a residents' association began using the building as an exhibition centre, demonstrating a dynamic community commitment to preserving its heritage.

Get back on Rte. 138 W. This section of the Chemin du Roy is lined with many well-preserved traditional Québec homes. Turn right onto Rue de Chavigny.

The magnificent **Moulin de La Chevrotière** ★ *(free admission; late Jun to Sep every day 10am to 6pm, rest of the year by appointment; 109 Rue de Chavigny,* ☎*418-286-6862)*, a former mill, now houses a facility where traditional building skills are taught. Every summer, young artisans from around Québec come to learn pre-industrial techniques of working with wood, iron and stone. The imposing building is located on a former section of the Chemin du Roy, renamed Rue de Chavigny in honour of Joseph de Chavigny de La Chevrotière, owner of the fief of the same name, who had this mill built in 1802. The roughcast structure just beside the mill, which houses the forge, is in fact the original mill, built in 1766.

Get back on Rte. 138 heading towards Grondines.

Grondines ★

In the 18th century, the village of Grondines was situated on the banks of the St. Lawrence. In 1831, it was relocated inland to facilitate access and avoid flooding. Traces of the original village, found between the river and Rte. 138, show French architectural influences, whereas the core of the present village, centred around Rue Principale, displays decidedly more Victorian influences. The citizens of Grondines showed great concern for their environment during the 1980s, when they fought plans to run hydroelectric lines across the river. The people of Grondines finally won their case. The lines run under the river, keeping the picturesque countryside intact.

The remains of the first stone church in Grondines, the **Église Saint-Charles-Borromée** ★ *(490 Route 138)* (1716), are visible near the mill. When the village was moved, a new church had to be built. Admired for the churches he designed in the neighbouring parishes, Thomas Baillargé was asked to design a magnificent church. However, funds became very scarce, so much so that the neoclassical structure begun in 1832 remained incomplete. The church steeples were not added until 1894, by which time neoclassicism was no longer in vogue, having given way to Victorian architecture. As a result, the towers, windows and doors were designed in the Gothic Revival style.

Inside, several interesting paintings are displayed, notably *La Madone du Rosaire* (The Rosary Madonna) by Théophile Hamel (above the right lateral altar), and *Saint Charles Borromée* by Jean-Baptiste Roy-Audy. The tabernacle of the high altar was sculpted in 1742 by Levasseur. Also of interest is the neoclassical presbytery from 1842, with its beautiful dormer-window-pediment.

Though it lost its imposing presence when it was converted into a lighthouse (a fate shared by many similar buildings), the **Moulin de Grondines** *(770 Rue du Moulin)* is still important for being the oldest building of its type still standing. The mill was built in 1672 for the Religieuses Hospitalières de l'Hôtel-Dieu, nuns working as nurses in the main hospital of Québec City, to whom the Grondines seigneury was granted in 1637.

The Chemin du Roy tour ends in Grondines, but can be combined with a visit to the Mauricie region in Sainte-Anne-de-la-Pérade, see p 308.

Tour D: Vallée de la Jacques-Cartier
★

 3 days

After a quick tour through some of the first settlements of New France, this itinerary enters the resort regions of the Laurentides, before plunging into the wilderness of the Rivière Jacques-Cartier valley and the Réserve Faunique des Laurentides. Ideal for camping, river rafting and other outdoor activities, the untouched forest of the Rivière Jacques-Cartier is surprisingly close to the city.

Charlesbourg ★

The Notre-Dame-des-Anges seigneury was granted to the Jesuits in 1626, making it one of the first permanent settlements inhabited by Europeans in Canada. Despite this early settlement and original seigneurial design, few buildings built before the 19th century remain in Charlesbourg. The fragility of early buildings and the push to modernize are possible explanations for this void. Since 1950, Charlesbourg has become one of the main suburbs of Québec City, and has lost much of its original character.

It is best to park near the church and explore the Trait-Carré on foot.

The **Église Saint-Charles-Borromée** ★ ★ *(135 80e Rue Ouest)* revolutionized the art of building in rural Québec. Architect Thomas Baillargé, influenced by the Palladian movement, showed particular innovation in the way he arranged the windows and doors of the facade, to which he added a large pediment. Construction of the church began in 1828 and was uninterrupted. The original design has remained intact since. The magnificent interior decor by Baillargé was done in 1833.

At the corner of Boulevard Henri-Bourassa is the old Moulin des Jésuites.

The **Moulin des Jésuites** ★ *(free admission; mid-Jun to Aug every day 10am to 6pm, early Sep to mid-Jun Sat and Sun 10am to 5pm; 7960 Boulevard Henri-Bourassa,* ☎*418-624-7720, www.traitcarre.org)*, a handsome mill in roughcast fieldstone, is the oldest building in Charlesbourg. It was built in 1740 by the Jesuits, who were the landowners at the time. After several decades of neglect, the two-storey building was restored in 1990 and now houses the **Centre d'Interprétation de l'Histoire du Trait-Carré** and a tourist bureau. Concerts and exhibits are also presented here.

Lac-Beauport (pop. 5,781)

The Lac-Beauport region is a popular year-round resort area. There are downhill ski centres in the region, including **Le Relais** (see p 394). Vacationers can also enjoy the lake's beautiful beaches.

Route 175 passes the **Lac-Delage**, **Stoneham** and **Tewskesbury** resort areas. It also leads to **Parc National de la Jacques-Cartier** (see below) and the **Réserve Faunique des Laurentides** (see below).

The Jacques-Cartier tour ends here. To return to Québec City, follow Rte. 175 S. You could also continue north into the Saguenay–Lac-Saint-Jean tourist region (see p 511).

Wendake ★ (pop. 1,613)

Forced off their land by the Iroquois in the 17th century, 300 Huron families moved to various places around Québec before settling in 1700 in Jeune-Lorette, today known as Wendake. Visitors will be charmed by the winding roads of the village in this native reserve located on the banks of the Rivière Saint-Charles. The museum and gift shop provide a wealth of information on the culture of this peaceful and sedentary people.

The **Église Notre-Dame-de-Lorette** ★ *(140 Boulevard Bastien)*, the Huron church, whose sacred objects and art works date from the original chapel (1730), is reminiscent of the first churches of New France. This humble building with a white plaster facade conceals unexpected treasures in its chancel and in the sacristy. Some of the objects on display were given to the Huron community by the Jesuits, and come from the first chapel in Ancienne-Lorette (late 17th century). Among the works to be seen are several statues by Pierre-Noël Levasseur, created between 1730 and 1740, an altar-facing depicting an Aboriginal village by Huron sculptor François Vincent (1790) and a beautiful *Vierge à l'Enfant* (Madonna and Child) sculpture, by a Parisian goldsmith (1717). In addition, the church features a reliquary that was made in 1676, 18th-century chasubles and various liturgical objects by Paul Manis (circa 1715). However, the most interesting element is the small, Louis XIII–style gilded tabernacle on the high altar, sculpted by Levasseur in 1722.

Onhoüa Chetek8e *($8; ᴦ; late Apr to Oct every day 8:30am to 6pm, Nov to late Apr every day 9am to 5pm; 575 Rue Stanislas-Koska, ☎418-842-4308, www.huron-wendat.qc.ca)* is a replica of a Huron village from the time of early colonization. The traditional design includes wooden longhouses and fences. Visitors are given an introduction to the lifestyle and social organization of the Huron nation. Various Aboriginal dishes are also served and are worth a taste.

Parc de la Falaise et de la Chute Kabir Kouba, see p 392.

From Wendake, you can reach the Lac Saint-Joseph region, to the northwest. This is a popular resort area for Québec City residents who swim and practice watersports in this lake all summer long and enjoy, among other things, its beach.

Sainte-Catherine-de-la-Jacques-Cartier (pop. 4,920)

Before reaching Lac Saint-Joseph, you'll pass Sainte-Catherine-de-la-Jacques-Cartier and the **Station Touristique Duchesnay** ★ (see p 391), a lovely park that, come wintertime, features the famous **Ice Hotel** ★ *(guided tours $14 every day hourly from 10am to 8pm; ☎418-875-4522 or 877-505-0423, www.icehotel-canada.com)*. The Québec **Ice Hotel** (see p 399), a spectacular, Swedish-inspired structure, is unique in North America and is definitely one of Québec's "hottest" attractions. Its lifespan is obviously limited (early Jan to late Mar), but every year, builders return to the site to erect this stunning complex using several tonnes of ice and snow. And not only is the ice used for building, it also serves as decoration. Indeed, the hotel houses an art gallery showcasing unusual snow and ice sculptures, as well as an exhibit room, a small movie theatre, a chapel and a bar where vodka is served in ice glasses. You'll simply be amazed!

Take Rte. 73, which becomes Rte. 175 and leads to Lac-Beauport.

Parks

Tour A: Côte de Beaupré

Parc de la Chute-Montmorency, see p 378.

Mont-Sainte-Anne ★ *(2000 Boulevard Beau-Pré, Beaupré, ☎418-827-4561, www.mont-sainte-anne.com)* covers 77km² and includes a 800m-high peak that is one of the most beautiful downhill-ski sites in Québec (see p 393). Various other outdoor activities are possible since the park has 200km of mountain-bike trails, which become 200km of cross-country trails in winter. Sports equipment can be rented on site.

The **Canyon Sainte-Anne** ★ ★ *($9; early May to late Jun and early Sep to late Oct every day 9am to 5pm, late Jun to early Sep every day 8:30am to 5:45pm; 206 Route 138, Beaupré, ☎418-827-4057, www.canyonste-anne.qc.ca)* was created by the rushing Rivière Sainte-Anne, which carves a deep path through the hills near Beaupré and plunges 74m into a large pothole 22m in width, formed by the resulting water current. Visitors can take in this impressive site from lookouts and a suspension bridge.

The **Cap-Tourmente National Wildlife Area** ★ ★ *($6; 570 Chemin du Cap-Tourmente, Saint-Joachim, ☎418-827-4591)* is located on pastoral, fertile land. Each spring and autumn, its sandbars are visited by countless snow geese, who stop to gather strength for their long migration. The reserve also has bird-watching facilities and naturalists on hand to answer your questions about the 250 species of birds and 45 species of mammals you might encounter on the hiking and walking trails that traverse the park.

Tour C: Chemin du Roy

Northwest of Québec, the **Réserve Faunique de Portneuf** *(mid-May to mid-Mar; 229 Rue du Lac Vert, Rivière-à-Pierre, ☎418-323-2021 or 800-665-6527, www.sepaq.com)* offers many kilometres of trails for various outdoor activities, including snowmobiling, cross-country skiing and snowshoeing. Lakes and rivers abound in the area. Pleasant little chalets *(reservations: ☎800-665-6527)*, well equipped for two to eight people, are available for rent.

Tour D: Vallée de la Jacques-Cartier

The **Réserve Faunique des Laurentides** *($3.50; Rte. 175 N., Km93, Mercier entrance, ☎418-848-2422 or 800-665-6527, www.sepaq.com)* covers 8,000km². This huge wilderness is home to a diversified wildlife, including black bears and moose. Hunting and fishing (spotted trout) are permitted at certain times of the year; check with the information desk regarding permits. The reserve has beautiful cross-country ski trails, one-day and overnight hiking trails, small chalets for two to 12 people; rates for two are around $90 *(reservations: ☎800-665-6527)*. In the summer, canoeists can ply the waters of the Rivière Métabetchouane and the Rivière Écorces.

Throughout the year, hordes of visitors come to **Parc National de la Jacques-Cartier** ★ ★ *($3.50; Route 175 Nord, ☎418-848-3169 or 800-665-6527, www.sepaq.com)*, located in the Réserve Faunique des Laurentides, 40km north of Québec City. The area is called Vallée de la Jacques-Cartier after the river that runs through it, winding between steep hills. Benefiting from the microclimate caused by the river being hemmed in on both sides, the site is suitable for a number of outdoor activities. The vegetation and wildlife are abundant and diverse. The winding and well-laid-out paths sometimes lead to interesting surprises, like a moose and its offspring foraging for food in a marsh. Before heading out to discover all the riches the site has to offer, you can get information at the nature centre's reception area. Campsites (see p 399), chalets and equipment are all available for rent (see "Outdoor Activities" section).

At the park, specialists organize **moose and other wildlife observation safaris** from mid-September to mid-October *($21.30)*. Reservations are required for this excursion, which usually lasts 3hrs and requires that you walk through the forest.

About 45km from Québec City, on the shore of the region's largest lake, Lac Saint-Joseph, the **Station Touristique Duchesnay** ★ *(143 Route Duchesnay, Ste-Catherine-de-la-Jacques-Cartier, ☎418-875-2122 or 877-511-5885, www.sepaq.com)* allows visitors to familiarize themselves with the Laurentian forest. Located on an area of 90km², this centre is dedicated to researching the fauna and flora of forests and is now one of Sépaq's tourism and recreation centres. Long famous for its cross-country ski trails, it is also ideal for practicing all kinds of outdoor activities, such as hiking on 16km of maintained footpaths. There are also ample opportunities for water sports. The Jacques-Cartier–Portneuf bike path also

The Québec City Region – Parks

traverses Duchesnay. In addition, you will find an interpretation centre that hosts educational and awareness-raising activities. The installations have been entirely renovated to offer visitors comfortable lodging and dining. In winter, the site is home to the **Ice Hotel** (see p 399).

The **Parc de la Falaise et de la Chute Kabir Kouba** is in the Wendake Aboriginal village. A few small trails go along the edge of the 40m cliff, at the bottom of which flows the Rivière Saint-Charles.

Outdoor Activities

■ Bird-Watching

Tour A: Côte de Beaupré

One of the best places for bird-watching in the region is definitely the **Cap-Tourmente National Wildlife Area** *($6; 570 Chemin du Cap-Tourmente, Saint-Joachim,* ☎*418-827-3776)* (see p 391). During spring and autumn, the thousands of migrating snow geese that overtake the area are a fascinating sight to behold. Any questions you might have after seeing these creatures up close and in such great numbers can be answered here. The reserve is also home to many other avian species who are drawn here throughout the year by a number of bird houses and feeders.

■ Canoeing

Tour D: Vallée de la Jacques-Cartier

You can canoe on the rivers and lakes of the **Réserve Faunique de Portneuf** (see p 391), down the river at **Parc National de la Jacques-Cartier** *(rental $36/day; Rte. 175 Nord,* ☎*418-848-3169; see p 391)* or at **Rivière Bras-du-Nord** *(*☎*418-337-2900 or 800-321-4992)*, in Portneuf. All have canoes for rent and Parc de la Jacques-Cartier also rents river kayaks.

■ Canyoning

Tour A: Côte de Beaupré

The **Canyoning Québec** association organizes canyoning excursions from June to October *(reservations required; special reduced rates for students and groups;* ☎*418-998-3859 or 827-8110, www.canyoning-quebec.com)*. Adventurous climbers who've made reservations for an excursion meet their guides at Station de Ski et de Villégiature Mont-Saine-Anne's visitor centre. The outings generally last three to four hours and take place in the morning or afternoon. Participants form groups of five to eight people, and each group is led by two experienced guides. Some of the association's favourite climbing sites are the **Jean-Larose waterfall** *($80 including equipment rental for a half-day excursion)* at the foot of Mont Sainte-Anne, **Vieille Rivière** and **Les Éboulements** *($120 including equipment rental for a full day excursion; meals and transport cost extra)*. Two-day beginner's training courses are also offered.

■ Cross-Country Skiing

Tour A: Côte de Beaupré

Centre de Ski de Fond Mont-Sainte-Anne *($17; Mon-Fri 9am to 3:45pm, Sat and Sun 8:30am to 4pm; 2000 Boulevard Beau-Pré, Beaupré,* ☎*418-827-4561, www.mont-sainte-anne.com)* features 212km of well-maintained cross-country ski trails with heated huts set up along the way. The Sports Alpins ski shop on Rang Saint-Julien rents the necessary equipment *($14.80/day;* ☎*418-826-3153)*.

Tour D: Vallée de la Jacques-Cartier

Nestled in the heart of the Réserve Faunique des Laurentides, **Camp Mercier** *($9.78; every day 8:30am to 4pm; Route 175 N., Réserve Faunique des Laurentides,* ☎*418-848-2422 or 800-665-6527, www.sepaq.com)* is crisscrossed by 192km of well-maintained trails in an extremely tranquil landscape. Given its ideal location, you can ski here from fall to spring. Long routes (up to 68km) with heated huts offer some interesting opportunities. There are also cottages for rent that can accommodate from two to 12 people *($85 for two people, $250 for 12)*.

In winter, **Station Touristique Duchesnay** (*$9.78; every day 8:30am to 4pm; 143 Route Duchesnay, Ste-Catherine-de-la-Jacques-Cartier, ☎418-875-2122 or 877-511-5885*) is very popular with skiers in the area. There are 182km of well-maintained trails in this vast forest.

■ Cycling

Located in the Vieux-Port de Québec, **Cyclo-Services** (*160 Rue du Quai St-André, Marché du Vieux-Port, ☎418-692-4052, www.cycloservices. net*) offers a series of cycling excursions around the city. They also offer bike rentals (*$10/hr*).

Tour A: Côte de Beaupré

A bicycle path runs from the Vieux-Port of Québec City to Parc de la Chute Montmorency, passing through Beauport on the way. Also, roads such as Chemin du Roy, on the Côte de Beaupré and Île d'Orléans (*bike rental at **Le Vieux-Presbytère** guesthouse, see p 398*), are meant to be shared between motorists and cyclists. Caution is always in order, but these trips are definitely worth the effort.

Mountain bikers can head to **Station de Ski et de Villégiature Mont-Saine-Anne** (*$7.80/ day, $16.50 for one ski-lift climb or $22.60 for unlimited climbs; 2000 Boulevard Beau-Pré, ☎418-827-4561, www.mont-sainte-anne.com*) where 200km of trails await. They can either climb to the summit of the mountain via the ski trails or use the bicycle-adapted ski lifts to get to the top. Some 20 challenging trails can be found here, and the mountain hosts a world-class championship race every year.

Tour D: Vallée de la Jacques-Cartier

In 1997, a brand new bicycle path was inaugurated in the Québec City region. Following the route of old railway lines, the **Piste Jacques-Cartier/Portneuf** (*$5; 100 Rue St-Jacques, St-Raymond, ☎418-337-7525 or 800-321-4992*) crosses through the Réserve Faunique Portneuf and the Station Touristique Duchesnay (where you can park your vehicle and rent bicycles), and runs alongside certain lakes in the area. Including the most recent additions, it is 68km in length, stretching from Rivière-à-Pierre

to Saint-Gabriel-de-Val-Cartier. Its magical setting and safe conditions have already attracted many cyclists. In winter, the path is used for snowmobiling.

In **Parc National de la Jacques-Cartier** (*$3.50; Route 175 Nord, ☎418-848-3169*), the trails are for both hikers and mountain-biking enthusiasts. Bike rental is available.

The **Station Touristique Stoneham** (*1420 Avenue du Hibou, Stoneham, ☎418-848-2411 or 800-463-6888, www.ski-stoneham.com*) ski resort maintains 30km of mountain-biking trails in summer. Bikes can be rented on site.

■ Dogsledding

Tour D: Vallée de la Jacques-Cartier

La Banquise des Chukchis (*228 Rang St-Georges, St-Basile, ☎418-329-3055*) is a company that offers various day or evening dogsledding packages where you lead the team yourself; one of the packages includes dinner. Friendly atmosphere.

The **Domaine de la Truite du Parc** (*$79/half-day; 4 Rue des Anémones, Stoneham, ☎418-848-3732*) is an outfitter that lets you drive your own dogsled team. In the summer you can fish for trout.

■ Downhill Skiing

Tour A: Côte de Beaupré

Mont-Sainte-Anne (*$53; day skiing Mon-Fri 9am to 4pm, Sat-Sun 8:30am to 4pm, night skiing late Dec to early Jan Wed-Sun 4pm to 10pm, late Feb to late Mar every day 4pm to 10pm; 2000 Boulevard Beau-Pré, Beaupré, ☎418-827-4561, www. mont-sainte-anne.com*) is one of the biggest ski resorts in Québec. Among the 64 runs, some reach 625m in height and 17 are lit for night skiing. It's also a delight for snowboarders. Instead of buying a regular ticket, you can buy a pass worth a certain number of points, valid for two years, and each time you take the lift, points are deducted. Equipment rentals are also available from Sports Alpins on Rang Saint-Julien (*$29/day for skis, $36/day for snowboards; ☎418-826-3153*).

The Québec City Region - Outdoor Activities

Tour D: Vallée de la Jacques-Cartier

Le Relais *($31; Mon-Thu 9am to 10pm, Fri 9am to 10:30pm, Sat 8:30am to 10:30pm, Sun 8:30am to 9pm; 1084 Boulevard du Lac, Lac-Beauport,* ☎*418-849-1851 or 866-373-5247, www.skirelais.com)* has 27 downhill-ski trails, all of which are lit for night skiing.

The **Station Touristique Stoneham** *($43; Mon-Fri 9am to 10pm, Sat 8:30am to 10pm, Sun 8:30 to 9pm; 1420 Avenue du Hibou, Stoneham,* ☎*418-848-2411 or 800-463-6888, www.ski-stoneham. com)* welcomes visitors year-round. In the winter there are 32 runs, 17 of which are lit for night skiing. For cross-country skiers, there are 30km of maintained trails.

■ Golf

Tour A: Côte de Beaupré

Mont-Sainte-Anne's golf course, **Le Grand Vallon** *($69 Mon-Thu, $80 Fri-Sun; 100 Rue Beau-Mont, Beaupré,* ☎*418-827-4653, www. legrandvallon.com)* was entirely redesigned in 1999. Today, it offers a par-72 course with several sand traps and four lakes, and is known as one of the most interesting courses in eastern Canada.

■ Hiking

Tour A: Côte de Beaupré

At the **Cap-Tourmente National Wildlife Area** *(570 Chemin du Cap-Tourmente, St-Joachim,* ☎*418-827-4591 or 827-3776; see p 391)*, if your legs allow it, you can take one of the trails up the cape, where you'll get a magnificent view of the river and surrounding countryside. You can also take an equally enjoyable stroll on wooden walkways along the shore, which are adapted for people with disabilities.

Station de Ski et de Villégiature Mont-Saine-Anne *(2000 Boulevard Beau-Pré,* ☎*418-827-4561, www.mont-sainte-anne.com)* and the **Les Sept Chutes** hydroelectric complex in Saint-Férréol-les-Neiges (see p 381) both have several hiking trails.

Tour D: Vallée de la Jacques-Cartier

The trails in **Parc National de la Jacques-Cartier** *($3.50; Rte. 175 N.,* ☎*418-848-3169; see p 391)* are favoured by locals. Whether leisurely or steep, the trails lead you to lovely little spots in the forest and reveal magnificent views of the valley and its river.

The **Réserve Faunique de Portneuf** (see p 391) and the **Station Touristique Duchesnay** (see p 391) both offer several great hiking trails.

■ Horseback Riding

Tour A: Côte de Beaupré

Ranch des Pionniers *(2140 Avenue Royale, St-Férréol-les-Neiges,* ☎*418-826-2520)* has been organizing riding excursions in the foothills of Mont Sainte-Anne for the last 30 years.

Tour D: Vallée de la Jacques-Cartier

Excursions Jacques-Cartier *(860 Avenue Jacques-Cartier Nord, Tewkesbury,* ☎*418-848-7238, www.excursionsj-cartier.com)* organizes riding excursions on the banks of the Jacques-Cartier river and in the surrounding forest. A quick lesson is provided for beginners. The spectacular winter landscape provides a unique riding experience, with riders bundled up in warm long coats to ward off the cold.

■ Hunting and Fishing

In the Québec City area, you can hunt and fish at the **Cap-Tourmente National Wildlife Area** *(*☎*418-827-3776 or 827-4591)*, the **Réserve Faunique de Portneuf** *(*☎*418-323-2021)* and **Réserve Faunique des Laurentides** *(*☎*418-848-2422)*, among other places.

■ Rafting

Tour D: Vallée de la Jacques-Cartier

In spring and summer the Rivière Jacques-Cartier gives adventurers a good run for their money. Two long-standing companies offer well-supervised rafting expeditions with all the necessary equipment. At **Village Vacances Valcartier** *($56 including* *wetsuit rental; 1860 Boulevard Valcartier, St-Gabriel-de-Valcartier,* ☎*418-844-2200 or 888-384-5524, www.valcartier.com/aventure),* they promise lots of excitement on an 8km ride. With **Excursions Jacques-Cartier** *(860 Avenue Jacques-Cartier Nord, Tewkesbury,* ☎*418-848-7238, www.excursionsj-cartier.com),* you can also experience some very exciting runs. Rafting excursions are also offered on the Rivière Batiscan in the **Réserve Faunique de Portneuf** (see p 391).

■ **Tobogganing and Waterslides**

Tour D: Vallée de la Jacques-Cartier

You can zip down the hill in winter on an inner-tube at **Club Mont-Tourbillon** *(55 Montée*

du Golf, Lac-Beauport, ☎*418-849-4418 or 866-949-4418).* They also offer all sorts of other activities, including cross-country skiing. There is a restaurant and a bar on site.

In both winter and summer, the **Village Vacances Valcartier** *($19.13; mid-Dec to late Mar; 1860 Boulevard Valcartier, St-Gabriel-de-Valcartier; from Québec City, take Rte. 371 N.;* ☎*418-844-2200 or 888-384-5524, www.valcartier. com)* outdoor-activity centre is the undisputed authority when it comes to slides. In winter, ice slides will help you forget the cold for a little while. There is also snow rafting *($20)* and skating *($4.35)* on a 2.5km-long ice rink that snakes through the woods. Restaurant and bar on site.

The Québec City Region - Outdoor Activities

Accommodations

Tour A: Côte de Beaupré

Beauport

Ramada Hôtel Ambassadeur
$$-$$$
≡ ⛅ 🍴 ◎)))
321 Boulevard Ste-Anne
☎ (418) 666-2828 or 800-363-4619
▤ (418) 666-2775
www.hotelambassadeur.ca
This hotel is on the outskirts from the sights. The rooms are large and pleasant, and there is a Chinese restaurant on the main floor.

Journey's End
$$$
♿ ≡ 🛏
240 Boulevard Ste-Anne
☎ (418) 666-1226 or 800-465-6116
▤ (418) 666-5088
This member of the Journey's End hotel chain lives up to company standards. It offers travellers comfortable rooms where they can relax. Journey's End is better known for its low prices than for its variety of services. No smoking.

Château-Richer

Auberge du Petit Pré
$$ bkfst incl.
🍴
7126 Avenue Royale
☎ (418) 824-3852
▤ (418) 824-3098
At the Auberge du Petit Pré, which occupies an 18th-century house, you will be warmly received and well treated. Their four guest rooms are cozy and

tastefully decorated. There is a large picture window, which is open when the weather is nice, two lounges, one with a TV and the other with a fireplace, as well as two bathrooms with clawfoot tubs. Breakfasts are generous and finely prepared. Also, if requested in advance, the owner will prepare one of his delicious dinners for you. The splendid aroma of the food fills the house and adds to its overall warmth.

Auberge du Sault-à-la-Puce
$$-$$$ bkfst incl.
◎ 🍴
8365 Avenue Royale
☎ (418) 824-5659
▤ (418) 824-5669
Marie-Thérèse Rousseau and Michel Panis left the city to settle in a beautiful 19th-century residence with a sloping roof on the Côte-de-Beaupré. They named the place Auberge du Sault-à-la-Puce after the tiny rapids in a nearby stream. The hotel has five rooms that are decorated with elegant iron furniture. Excellent restaurant (see p 400).

Auberge Baker
$$-$$$ bkfst incl.
≡ ⛺ 🍴 ◎ @
8790 Avenue Royale
☎ (418) 824-4478 or 866-824-4478
▤ (418) 824-4412
www.auberge-baker.qc.ca
For over 50 years, Auberge Baker has existed in this century-old Côte-de-Beaupré house. Its stone walls, low ceilings, wood floors and wide-frame windows enchant visitors. The seven bedrooms are on the dimly lit upper floor but there is also a kitchenette, a bathroom and an adjoining terrace on the same floor.

The rooms are meticulously decorated in authentic fashion and furnished with antiques. They serve delicious food (see p 400).

Sainte-Anne-de-Beaupré

Auberge La Bécassine
$-$$
🍴 ≡
9341 Boulevard Ste-Anne
☎ (418) 827-4988 or 877-727-4988
www.labecassine.com
La Bécassine is located less than 10min from Mont Sainte-Anne. It is actually a motel since most of the rooms are next to the main building. The rooms are simply but quite pleasantly decorated. The main building's dining room specializes in game meat dishes.

Beaupré (Mont-Sainte-Anne)

Camping Mont-Sainte-Anne
$
Rang St-Julien, St-Ferréol-les-Neiges
☎ (418) 826-2323 or 800-463-1568
Camping Mont-Sainte-Anne has 166 campsites in a wooded area traversed by the Rivière Jean-Larose. Essential services are offered, and, because the campground is close to all the park's outdoor activities, the location is great.

Hôtel Val des Neiges
$$-$$$
≡ ⛺ ⛅ ≋ 🍴))) ⓨ ◎
201 Val des Neiges
☎ (418) 827-5711 or 888-554-6005
▤ (418) 827-5997
www.hotelvaldesneiges.com
Many chalets have been built around the base of Mont-Sainte-Anne, in newly developed areas. Among these is the Hôtel Val des Neiges. The decor

is rustic and the rooms are comfortable. The complex also includes small, well-equipped condos. Cruise packages are offered.

La Camarine
$$$
≡ ☀ ♨ ☺ ♿

10947 Boulevard Ste-Anne
☎ (418) 827-5703 or 800-567-3939
🖷 (418) 827-5430
www.camarine.com
La Camarine faces the St. Lawrence River. This charming high-quality inn has 30 rooms. The decor successfully combines the rustic feel of the house with the more modern wooden furniture. A delightful spot.

Château Mont-Sainte-Anne
$$$-$$$$$
≋ ⚓))) ♨ ☺ ✗ ♿ ≡ ☀

500 Boulevard Beau-Pré
☎ (418) 827-5211 or 800-463-4467
🖷 (418) 827-3421
www.chateaumontsainteanne.com
Château Mont-Sainte-Anne is located at the foot of the slopes—you couldn't get much closer to the mountain. The rooms are spacious and equipped with kitchenettes that can be used for an extra $10. The establishment also has a spa.

Tour B:
Île d'Orléans

There are about 50 bed and breakfasts on Île d'Orléans, a list of which can be obtained from the tourist office. There are also a few guesthouses with solid reputations, as well as a campground. Therefore, there are plenty of options for getting the most out of your stay on this enchanting island.

Sainte-Pétronille

Au Toit Rouge au Bord de l'Eau
$$

43 Rue Horatio-Walker
☎ (418) 828-9654 or 800-430-9946
Located near the water, this former rest home for nuns offers three charming rooms providing a superb view of Château Frontenac and the Montmorency falls.

La Goéliche
$$$ bkfst incl.
♨ ≋ ☀ ● ♨

22 Chemin du Quai
☎ (418) 828-2248 or 888-511-2248
🖷 (418) 828-2745
www.goeliche.ca
La Goéliche has managed to give a certain country-style charm to its modern facilities. Its 12 rooms are comfortable and offer a lovely view of Québec City. There is a small living room with a fireplace and games. Small chalet-stye condos can also be rented by the night or for longer stays, and the restaurant (see p 400) is definitely worth the trip.

Saint-Laurent-de-l'Île-d'Orléans

Le Canard Huppé
$$$-$$$$ bkfst incl.
♨ ♨ ☀

2198 Chemin Royal
☎ (418) 828-2292 or 800-838-2292
🖷 (418) 828-0966
www.canard-huppe.com
Le Canard Huppé has enjoyed a very good reputation over the last several years. Its clean, comfortable, country-style rooms are situated in two old houses, each with decorative wooden ducks scattered throughout. The restaurant is also just as renowned and appealing

(see p 400). The service is conscientious, and the surroundings are beautiful.

Saint-Jean-de-l'Île-d'Orléans

Auberge Le P'tit Bonheur
$-$$ bksft incl.
sb

186 Côte Lafleur
☎ (418) 829-2588
www.leptitbonheur.qc.ca
Auberge Le P'tit Bonheur, situated on Île d'Orléans, is named after a song by Félix Leclerc, who fell in love with this island located in the middle of the St. Lawrence River. This youth hostel offers an affordable alternative to those who wish to discover this part of the region. Both the 300-year-old house and the site offer a most friendly atmosphere. Several outdoor activities are available in summer and winter, when guests can go for dog-sleigh rides.

Saint-François-de-l'Île-d'Orléans

Camping Île d'Orléans
$
≋

357 Chemin Royal
☎ (418) 829-2953
🖷 (418) 829-2563
Camping Orléans has close to 150 campsites, most of which are shaded and offer a view of the river. Many services are offered. There is access to the river bank where you can go for a lovely walk.

The Québec City Region - Accommodations - Île d'Orléans

The Québec City Region - Accommodations - Île d'Orléans

Auberge Chaumonot
$$$$ bkfst incl.
≈ ♨

425 Chemin Royal
☎ (418) 829-2735 or 800-520-2735
🖹 (418) 829-0483
www.aubergechaumonot.specialistes.com

This small inn only has eight rooms and is open exclusively in the summer. Located on the south shore of the island, Auberge Chaumonot was built near the banks of the river and is surrounded by charming countryside, far from the village and the road. The country-style rooms are comfortable.

Saint-Pierre-de-l'Île-d'Orléans

Le Vieux-Presbytère
$$$ bkfst incl.
pb/sb ♨
1247 Avenue Monseigneur-D'Esgly
☎ (418) 828-9723 or 888-282-9723
🖹 (418) 828-2189
www.presbytere.com

Le Vieux-Presbytère is in fact located in an old presbytery just behind the village church. The structure is predominantly made out of wood and stone. Low ceilings with wide beams, wide-frame windows and antiques such as woven bed-covers and braided rugs take you back to the days of New France. The dining room and the lounge are inviting in this tranquil spot with rustic charm.

Tour C: Chemin du Roy

Sainte-Foy

Hôtel Germain-des-Prés
$$$-$$$$
♨ ≡
1200 Avenue Germain-des-Prés
☎ (418) 658-1224 or 800-463-5253
🖹 (418) 658-8846
www.germaindespres.com

Hôtel Germain-des-Prés is a classic in the Québec City region. Established a few years ago, it was the first of what is now a chain of five extremely well-reputed boutique hotels. Its rooms, decorated with utmost care, are very welcoming and offer all the amenities you need for total relaxation: bathrobes, comfy armchairs, duvets and feather pillows... not to mention the little extras that are typical of this type of establishment, which provides personalized service despite its 126 rooms. The rooms will please business travellers, with its work desks and Internet access, as well as leisure travellers. There are also meeting rooms and the restaurant **Le Bistango** (see p 401), whose reputation is already firmly established.

Deschambault

Auberge Chemin du Roy
$$-$$$ bkfst incl.
♨
106 Rue St-Laurent
☎ (418) 286-6958 or 800-933-7040
www.cheminduroy.com

The old Victorian house that has been reborn as Auberge Chemin du Roy is set on a beautiful property with waterfalls and gardens, where good vegetables and lots of flowers grow. There are eight rooms, decorated with lace and antiques, along a narrow, winding hallway of the type often found in this type of old house. In the warmly decorated dining room, wonderful varied meals are served. The owners take great care of the property, the house and the guests, right down to the tiniest details.

Maison Deschambault
$$$
♨
128 Chemin du Roy
☎ (418) 286-3386
🖹 (418) 286-4064
www.quebecweb.com/deschambault

Maison Deschambault offers five luxurious rooms, decorated with flower patterns and pastel colours. There is also a small bar, a dining room that serves fine cuisine (see p 401), a conference room and massage therapy, all in an enchanting old manor house. Relaxing in this peaceful setting is not difficult at all.

Cap-Santé

La Maison de Mlle Bernard
$$ bkfst incl.
pb/sb
56 Vieux Chemin
☎ (418) 285-3149
www.mllebernard.ca

Cap-Santé's picturesque Vieux Chemin is home to a charming bed and breakfast. La Maison de Mlle Bernard's splendid historical setting ensures a memorable stay in a wood house surrounded by wild flowers. The pretty rooms are comfortable and tastefully furnished with antiques.

Tour D: Vallée de la Jacques-Cartier

Parc National de la Jacques-Cartier

Camping Stoneham
$

101 St-Edmond
☎ (418) 848-2233
Right in the heart of Parc de la Jacques-Cartier you can camp in magnificent surroundings. Along the river, there are numerous campsites, some rustic, others with some facilities. And, of course, there's no lack of things to do.

Lac-Delage

Manoir du Lac Delage
$$$

40 Avenue du Lac
☎ (418) 848-2551 or 888-202-3242
▤ (418) 848-1352
www.lacdelage.com
Manoir du Lac Delage will please both summer and winter sports enthusiasts. The resort has a skating rink in winter and is located near cross-country ski trails and tobogganing sites. Various water sports can be enjoyed in summer, thanks to the inn's lakeside location. The rooms are comfortable and feature attractive wood furnishings.

Lac-Beauport

Château du Lac Beauport
$$-$$$

154 Chemin Tour-du-Lac
☎ (418) 848-1811 or 800-463-2692
▤ (418) 849-2895
www.chateaulacbeauport.com
Château du Lac Beauport resembles a large ski chalet and offers comfortable accommodations and several activities. The hotel faces Lac Beauport and provides access to a pretty beach. The lake is perfect for wind surfing, kayaking, canoeing and sailing in summer, and a skating rink is set up in winter. Another good choice for outdoor enthusiasts.

Sainte-Catherine-de-la-Jacques-Cartier

Chaumière Juchereau-Duchesnay
$$

5050 Route de Fossambault
☎ (418) 875-2751 or 800-501-2122
▤ (418) 875-2752
Not far from Station Touristique Duchesnay, where you can take part in a variety of outdoor activities, Chaumière Juchereau-Duchesnay offers room and board. Its nine pastel-coloured rooms are all similarly decorated. They are very comfortable despite the fact that they do not have the same antique elegance as the dining room. This inn, with its trees, swimming pool and terrace, will allow you to relax in peace and quiet.

Station Touristique Duchesnay
$$$

pb/sb
143 Route Duchesnay
☎ (418) 875-2122 or 877-511-5885
▤ (418) 875-2868
www.sepaq.com/duchesnay
Nestled in the heart of a $90km^2$ forest, on the shores of Lac Saint-Joseph, several cottages and log cabins were renovated to welcome visitors. A number of packages are available, all providing nature and comfort. Whether you wish to rent a cabin for the entire family and enjoy the lake and footpaths, or rent a romantic room for two and take advantage of the many cross-country ski trails, you will undoubtedly be seduced by this place.

Ice Hotel
$$$$$ ½b

sb
143 Route Duchesnay, Pavillon L'Aigle
☎ (418) 875-4522 or 877-505-0423
▤ (418) 875-2833
www.icehotel-canada.com
It's hard to believe a hotel could actually be made of ice…but it really is (see also p 390). This magnificent structure is built from thousands of tonnes of ice and snow. Adventurous travellers come from all over the continent to spend the night in this chilly castle. Note, however, that because the ice provides natural insulation, the temperature always remains between -2ºC and -6ºC within the hotel's walls. So you can snooze quite comfortably in one of its 32 rooms, all wrapped up in a thick sleeping bag. And if you're new to winter camping, don't worry: the hotel's staff is available day and night. Furthermore, the shared bathrooms are heated, and breakfast and dinner are served in a warm chalet. On site, guests can enjoy a multitude of outdoor activities. An unforgettable experience is guaranteed!

Restaurants

Tour A: Côte de Beaupré

Beauport

Manoir Montmorency
$$-$$$$
Manoir Montmorency
2490 Avenue Royale
☎ (418) 663-3330
Manoir Montmorency (see p 378) benefits from a superb location above the Montmorency Falls. From May to late October, the restaurant's menu features *grillades* served on the magnificent covered and heated terrace. The rest of the year, eight luxurious rooms can hold banquets or meetings. It goes without saying that the environment is enchanting. The executive chef, Martin Côté, prepares refined Québécois cuisine from the freshest local products. From the dining room surrounded by bay windows, there's an absolutely magnificent view of the falls, the river and Île d'Orléans. The entrance fee to the Parc de la Chute Montmorency (where the restaurant is located) and the parking fees are waived upon presentation of your restaurant receipt or by mentioning your reservation.

Château-Richer

Auberge du Sault-à-la-Puce
$$$$
8365 Avenue Royale
☎ (418) 824-5659

The chef at Auberge du Sault-à-la-Puce carefully prepares each meal with fresh fruit and vegetables from his garden. He also uses local products, such as meat and fowl from neighbouring villages. This establishment also has five guest rooms (see p 396) and offers a limited menu of three or four dishes inspired by French or Italian cuisine. The salmon tartare is delicious.

Auberge Baker
$$$$
8790 Avenue Royale
☎ (418) 824-4478
Auberge Baker (see p 396) has two dining rooms. One has stone walls and a fireplace, whereas the decor of the other is somewhat cold. They serve fine traditional Québec cuisine: game, meat and fowl are all well prepared and presented with care.

Beaupré (Mont-Sainte-Anne)

La Camarine
$$$$
10947 Boulevard Ste-Anne
☎ (418) 827-5703
La Camarine also houses an excellent restaurant that serves Québec nouvelle cuisine. The dining room is peaceful, with a simple decor. The innovative dishes are a feast for the senses. In the basement of the inn is another small restaurant, the **Bistro**, which offers the same menu and prices as upstairs but is only open in the winter. Equipped with a fireplace, it is a cozy spot for après-ski and is open in the evening for drinks.

Tour B: Île d'Orléans

Sainte-Pétronille

La Goéliche
$$$-$$$$
22 Chemin du Quai
☎ (418) 828-2248 or 888-511-2248
The dining room at **La Goéliche** (see p 397) is a pleasant spot that offers one of the most beautiful views of Québec City. This restaurant serves fine French cuisine: calf's sweetbread, loin of venison and *filet mignon* in morel sauce.

Saint-Laurent-de-l'Île-d'Orléans

Le Canard Huppé
$$$-$$$$
2198 Chemin Royal
☎ (418) 828-2292
The dining room at **Le Canard Huppé** (see p 397) serves fine regional cuisine. Prepared with fresh ingredients, locally abundant in the area—island specialties such as duck, trout and maple products—these little dishes will delight the most demanding of palates. Although the room is somewhat dark, with forest green being the predominant colour, the country decor is, on the whole, pleasant. Reservations required.

Tour C: Chemin du Roy

Sillery

Brynd
$
1360 Avenue Maguire
☎ (418) 527-3844

Byrnd is the place to go for smoked meat and has a variety for all tastes and appetites. There are also items on the menu for those, and too bad for them, who don't want to try the house specialty. The meat is smoked and sliced in front of your eyes, just like at a real delicatessen!

Paparazzi
$$$
1363 Avenue Maguire
☎ (418) 683-8111
Paparazzi serves refined Italian cuisine and also features a sushi bar. The decor is modern and pleasant with pretty tables covered in ceramic tiles set up on various levels.

Montego
$$$
1460 Avenue Maguire
☎ (418) 688-7991
In Sillery, the restaurant-club Montego promises a "sunny experience." The warmly decorated interior, large colourful plates and food presentation are a pleasure to behold. And the cooking will delight your taste buds with sweet, hot and spicy flavours inspired by cuisine from California and other sunny places.

Sainte-Foy

Mille-Feuilles
$$
Mon-Fri 11am to 11pm, Sat-Sun 11am to 2pm
1405 Chemin Ste-Foy
☎ (418) 681-4520
Mille-Feuilles is a vegetarian restaurant where you can find good food that is healthy, delicious and carefully prepared. Located on

a section of Chemin Ste-Foy that has a few shops and restaurants, the decor is a bit cool, but the ambiance is relaxed.

Le Bistango
$$$
Hôtel Germain-des-Prés
1200 Avenue Germain-des-Prés
☎ (418) 658-8780
Located in the **Hôtel Germain-des-Prés** (see p 398) complex, Le Bistango combines savoir-faire and casual ambiance. The good-sized dining room is decorated with taste and originality, and is very busy both at lunch and dinner. Comfortably seated in a chair or booth, you can savour fine dishes prepared and served with care. The menu changes with the seasons and the arrival of fresh local products promises delicious surprises. This is a great spot if you find yourself in Sainte-Foy. On certain evenings, musicians liven up the atmosphere.

Michelangelo
$$$-$$$$
3111 Chemin St-Louis
☎ (418) 651-6262
Michelangelo serves fine Italian cuisine that both smells and tastes wonderful. The classically decorated dining room, although busy, is warm and intimate. The courteous and attentive service adds to the pleasure of the food.

La Fenouillère
$$$$
3100 Chemin St-Louis
☎ (418) 653-3886
At La Fenouillère, the menu of refined and creative

French cuisine promises a succulent dining experience. This restaurant is also proud to possess one of the best wine cellars in Québec. The decor is simple and comfortable.

La Tanière
$$$$
Wed-Sun
2115 Rang St-Ange
☎ (418) 872-4386
La Tanière specializes in wild game (a *tanière* is a den or lair). Although located in Sainte-Foy, this restaurant is slightly off the tour, near the airport. Here you can experience tasty and delicious specialties from the forests of Québec.

Deschambault

Maison Deschambault
$$$
128 Chemin du Roy
☎ (418) 286-3386
The restaurant in the Maison Deschambault inn (see p 398) is well known for its excellent menu, which consists mainly of fine French cuisine as well as various specialties of the region. The setting is particularly enchanting.

Tour D: Vallée de la Jacques-Cartier

Charlesbourg

Da Cortina
$$$
615 80ᵉ Rue Ouest
☎ (418) 622-3833
Da Cortina is a big, beautiful white house whose dining room features large windows overlooking a country setting. The fine Italian cuisine includes

pasta and seafood. Service is attentive.

Wendake

Nek8arre
$$-$$$
9am to 5pm, with reservations for dinner
575 Rue Stanislas-Kosca
☎ (418) 842-4308

At the Huron Village (see p 390), there is a pleasant restaurant whose name means "the meal is ready to serve." Nek8arre (pronounced "Nekwaray") introduces you to traditional Huron cooking. Wonderful dishes such as clay trout, caribou or venison brochettes with mushrooms accompanied by wild rice and corn are some of the items on the menu. The wooden tables have short texts explaining the diet of Aboriginal peoples embedded in them. Numerous objects scattered here and there will arouse your curiosity, and luckily, the waitresses act as part-time "ethnologists" and can answer your questions. All this in a pleasant atmosphere. The entry fee to the village will be waived if you are only going to the restaurant.

Sagamité
$$-$$$
10 Boulevard Maurice-Bastien
☎ (418) 847-6999

At Sagamité, beautiful sculpted columns depicting hunting and war scenes remind guests that they are in the Huron-Wendat community. Among other things, it serves *potence*, a traditional grilled dish, and *sagamité*, a salty soup consisting of squash, beans, corn and ground beef.

♪ Entertainment

■ Festivals and Cultural Events

Beauport

On Wednesday and Saturday nights throughout the summer, the Parc de la Chute Montmorency comes to life with the **Grands Feux Loto-Québec** *(☎418-523-3389 or 800-923-3389, www. lesgrandsfeux.com)*. This magical fireworks display takes place over the falls. Fleets of small boats gather on the river to admire the show.

■ Theatres and Concert Halls

L'Ancienne-Lorette

Théâtre de la Fenière *(1500 Rue de la Fenière, ☎872-1424)*.

Pont-Rouge

The **Moulin Marcoux** *(1 Boulevard Notre-Dame, ☎873-3425)* presents various shows and exhibitions.

Sainte-Foy

The **Salle Albert-Rousseau** in the Sainte-Foy Cegep *(2410 Chemin Ste-Foy, ☎659-6710)* presents excellent plays and shows throughout the year.

🛍 Shopping

■ Arts and Crafts

Île d'Orléans

Île d'Orléans has a handful of craft shops, antique dealers and cabinet-making studios. One of these, the **Corporation des Artisans de l'Île** *(☎418-828-2519)*, is located in the Saint-Pierre church. There are also about half a dozen art galleries on the island, many in the village of Saint-Jean.

The shop at the **Forge à Pique-Assaut** *(2200 Chemin Royal, St-Laurent-de-l'Île-d'Orléans, ☎418-828-9300)* (see p 382) sells various forged-metal objects, from candle holders to furniture. They also sell other crafts.

In the former Saint-Jean presbytery *(2001 Chemin Royal)* in front of the church overlooking the river are two shops that deserve a visit: **Les Échoueries** sells a variety of crafts made by talented artists, and the **country-style bakery** bakes homemade breads and pastries.

■ Food

Château-Richer

Musée de l'Abeille
8862 Boulevard Sainte-Anne
☎ (418) 824-4411

Adjoining the Musée de l'Abeille is a small shop that sells a host of objects related to bees, such as honey-based beauty products, mead and, of course, honey. There's also a pastry shop that offers sweet deli-

cacies made with honey instead of sugar.

Île d'Orléans

The **Chocolaterie de l'Île d'Orléans** *(150 Chemin Royal for the factory and 196 Chemin Bout-de-l'Île for the shop, Ste-Pétronille, ☎418-828-2252 or 828-2250)* offers a whole range of delectable treats. Their homemade ice cream is also delicious.

■ Native Arts and Crafts

Wendake

You'll find a large selection of Native arts and crafts in Wendake. Among these, **Raquettes et Artisanat Gros Louis** *(30 Boulevard Maurice-Bastien, ☎418-843-2503)* offers snowshoes for all tastes. You can find traditional styles and more modern ones, which, unfortunately, are not as charming as the authentic handmade snowshoes.

■ Shopping Centres

Charming boutiques can be found on Rue du Campanile in **Sainte-Foy** and Avenue Maguire in **Sillery**, while Sainte-Foy's Boulevard Laurier is shopping centre central: **Place Laurier, Place Sainte-Foy, Place de la Cité** and **Place Belle-Cour** can all be found here.

Sainte-Anne-de-Beaupré

Shoppers will find creations by the biggest names in fashion as well as outdoor clothing and accessories at the **Promenades Sainte-Anne** factory outlet centre *(10909 Boulevard Ste-Anne, ☎418-827-3555)*.

The Québec City Region - Shopping

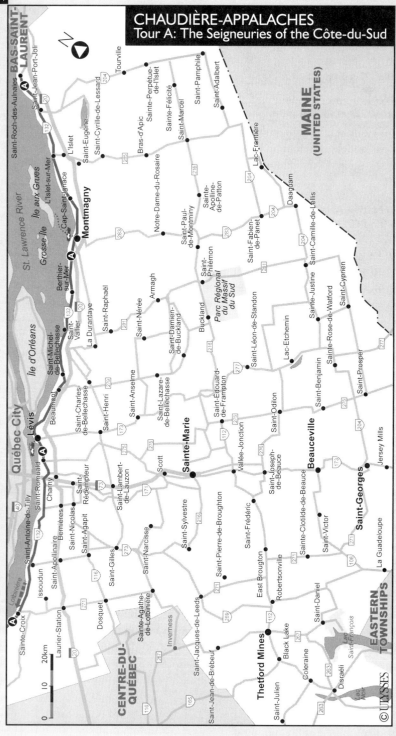

© ULYSSES

Chaudière-Appalaches

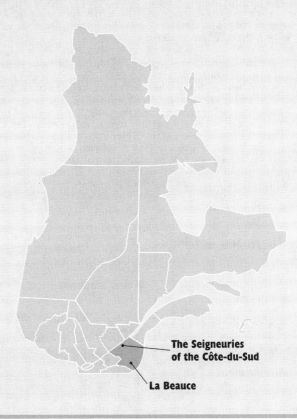

**The Seigneuries
of the Côte-du-Sud**

La Beauce

Charming cities with very distinct geographical features make up the Chaudières-Appalaches region. Located opposite Québec City, on the south shore of the St. Lawrence River, it stretches across a vast fertile plain before slowly climbing into the foothills of the Appalachian Mountains, all the way to the U.S. border. The Rivière Chaudière, which originates in Lac Mégantic, runs through the centre of this region, then flows into the St. Lawrence across from Québec City.

A pretty, pastoral landscape unfolds along the river between Leclercville and Saint-Roch-des-Aulnaies, an area occupied very early on by the French. There are attractive villages, including Saint-Jean-Port-Joli, an important provincial craft centre. Out in the gulf, adventure awaits in the Archipel de l'Isle-aux-Grues.

Farther south, the picturesque Beauce region extends along the banks of the Rivière Chaudière. The river rises dramatically in the spring, flooding some of the villages along its banks almost every year, lending muddied local inhabitants the nickname *"jarrets noirs,"* which translates somewhat inelegantly as "black hamstrings." The discovery of gold nuggets in the river bed attracted prospectors to the area in the 19th century, and farms have prospered in the rolling green hills of the Beauce for hundreds of years. Church steeples announce the presence of little villages, scattered evenly across the local countryside. The Beauce region is also home to Québec's largest concentration of maple groves, making it the true realm of the *cabane à sucre* or sugar shack. The spring thaw gets the sap flowing and signals the sugaring-off season. Local inhabitants, "Beaucerons," are also known for their sense of tradition and hospitality. The "asbestos" region, located a little farther west of the Rivière Chaudière, around Thetford Mines, has a fairly varied landscape, punctuated with impressive open-cut mines.

Getting There and Getting Around

Two tours have been laid out for the Chaudière-Appalaches region:

Tour A: The Seigneuries of the Côte-du-Sud ★ ★ runs along the St. Lawrence from Leclercville to Saint-Roch-des-Aulnaies, **Tour B: La Beauce** ★ leads through the valley of the Rivière Chaudière and the asbestos region.

■ By Car

Tour A: The Seigneuries of the Côte-du-Sud

From Montréal, take Hwy. 20 to Exit 253, then follow the 265 N. to Deschaillons-sur-Saint-Laurent, and turn right on Rte. 132 E. From Québec City, cross the river to take Rte. 132 in either direction.

Tour B: La Beauce

From Québec City, take Hwy. 73 S. (use the Pierre-Laporte bridge). The Rivière Chau-dière falls are on the right. Take Exit 101 to Rte. 173 and follow this to Saint-Georges.

■ Bus Stations

Tour A: The Seigneuries of the Côte-du-Sud

Lévis
5401 Boulevard de la Rive-Sud
☎ 837-5805

Montmagny
20 Boulevard Taché Est (Irving)
☎ (418) 248-1850

Saint-Jean-Port-Joli
10 Avenue de Gaspé Est (Épicerie Pelletier)
☎ 598-6808

Tour B: La Beauce

Saint-Georges
11655 Promenade Chaudière
☎ (418) 228-4040

Thetford Mines
127 Rue Saint-Alphonse Ouest
☎ (418) 335-5120

Useful Information

■ Train Station

■ Tourist Information

*Tour A: The Seigneuries of the
Côte-du-Sud*

Montmagny
4 Rue de la Station
☎ 888-842-7245

■ By Ferry

*Tour A: The Seigneuries of the
Côte-du-Sud*

The ferry between Québec City and Lévis
*($2.50 pedestrian or cyclist; $5.60 car plus extra
charge for passengers,* ☎ *418-644-3704 in Québec City, 418-837-2408 in Lévis, www.traversiers.
gouv.qc.ca)* takes only 15min. The schedule
is subject to change, but there are frequent
crossings.

The ferry to Île aux Grues, the **Grue des Îles**
(free; ☎ *418-643-2019 in Montmagny, 418-248-
6869 in l'Isle-aux-Grues)*, leaves from the
Montmagny dock and takes about 20min.
The schedule varies with the tides.

Croisières Lachance *(prices vary according to
cruise packages; cruises to Grosse Île and the Montmagny archipelago; 110 de la Marina, Berthier-
sur-Mer;* ☎ *418-259-2140 or 888-476-7734,
www.croisiereslachance.qc.ca)* offers daily
cruises from Berthier-sur-Mer.

■ By Plane

The Île aux Grues ferry's schedule varies
greatly according to the tides and seasons,
making it somewhat complicated to get to
the island. Getting there by plane is a practical alternative that also provides a unique
aerial view of the area. **Air Montmagny**'s
Cessna *($20/person, minimum three people;
640 Boulevard Taché Est, Montmagny,* ☎ *418-
248-3545)* takes passengers to the island in
less then 5 min.

Regional Office

Association Touristique Chaudière-Appalaches
800 Autoroute Jean-Lesage, St-Nicolas, G7A 1C9
☎ 831-4411 or 888-831-4411
▤ 831-8442 www.chaudapp.qc.ca

*Tour A: The Seigneuries of the
Côte-du-Sud*

Lévis
5995 Rue St-Laurent
☎ 838-6026

Montmagny
45 Avenue du Quai
☎ 248-9196 or 800-463-5643
▤ 248-1436 www.montmagny.com

Cap-St-Ignace
100 Place de l'Église
☎ 246-5390
▤ 246-3350

Saint-Jean-Port-Joli
20 Route 132 Ouest
☎ 598-3747
▤ 598-6488

Tour B: La Beauce

Saint-Georges
11700 Boulevard Lacroix
☎ 227-4642 or 877-923-2823
▤ 228-2255

Thetford Mines
2600 Boulevard Frontenac
☎ 423-3333 or 877-335-7141
▤ 423-3331
www.tourisme-amiante.com

Chaudière-Appalaches – Useful Information

Exploring

Tour A: The Seigneuries of the Côte-du-Sud
★ ★

 2 days

This tour is dotted with charming villages at regular intervals along the majestic St. Lawrence. It encompasses both the Rive-Sud of Québec City and the Côte-du-Sud (the southern shore and coast), gradually taking on a maritime flavour as the river widens. Visitors will enjoy stunning views of this vast stretch of water as its colour varies with the time of day and temperature, as well as Île d'Orléans and the mountains of Charlevoix. The tour also features some of the loveliest examples of traditional architecture in Québec, including churches, seigneurial manors, mills and old houses, whose windows overlook wide-open spaces. It is perhaps this region that best represents rural Québec.

Lotbinière (pop. 912) ★

Granted to René-Louis Chartier de Lotbinière in 1672, the seigneury of Lotbinière is one of the few estates to have always remained in the hands of the same family. Because he had a seat on the Conseil Souverain (sovereign council), the first seigneur did not actually live on the premises. Nevertheless, he saw to it that the land and the village of Lotbinière were developed. At the heart of Lotbinière, which quickly became one of the most important villages in the region, visitors will find a number of old houses made of stone and wood. This area is now protected by the provincial government.

Turn right on Route du Vieux-Moulin.

Moulin du Portage ★ (*Rang Saint-François*), a flour mill built in 1815 for Michel-Eustache-Gaspard-Alain Chartier de Lotbinière, lies in a pastoral setting on the banks of the Rivière du Chêne. Visitors can enjoy a pleasant walk or a picnic in the park surrounding the mill.

Along with its presbytery and former convent, the monumental **Église Saint-Louis** ★ ★ (*7510 Rue Marie-Victorin*), set parallel to the St. Lawrence, provides a lovely setting from which to enjoy a view of the river. The present building is the fourth Catholic church to be built in the seigneury of Lotbinière. Designed by François Baillargé, it was begun in 1818. The spires, as well as the crown of the facade, are the result of modifications made in 1888. Its polychromatic exterior—white walls, blue steeples and red roof—creates a surprising (and very French) tricolour effect.

The decor of the church is a masterpiece of traditional religious art in Québec. Without question, the key piece is the neoclassical reredos shaped like a triumphal arch, sculpted by Thomas Baillargé in 1824. In the middle of it hang three paintings dating back to 1730, which are attributed to Frère François Brékenmacher, a Récollet monk from the Montréal monastery. The organ in the jube, originally intended for the Anglican cathedral in Québec City, was built in London by the Elliott Company in 1802. Too high for the Anglican church, it was put into storage before being acquired by Père Faucher, the parish priest, in 1846. A century later, it was restored and equipped for electric power by the Casavant Company of Saint-Hyacinthe.

Before reaching the village of Sainte-Croix, turn left on Route de la Pointe-Platon to the Domaine Joly-De Lotbinière.

Sainte-Croix (pop. 2,444)

The Chartier de Lotbinière lineage dates back to the 11th century. In the service of French kings for many generations, the family preserved its contacts with the motherland even after it established itself in Canada, despite the British conquest and the distance between the two lands. In 1828, Julie-Christine Chartier de Lotbinière married Pierre-Gustave Joly, a rich Huguenot merchant from Montréal. In 1840, Joly purchased a part of the Sainte-Croix land from the Québec City Ursulines in order to build a seigneurial manor there, which would come to be known as the Manoir de la Pointe Platon, or Domaine Joly-De Lotbinière.

Domaine Joly-De Lotbinière ★★ *($10; early May to late Oct every day 10am to 5pm; Route de Pointe-Platon,* ☎*418-926-2462, www.domainejoly.com)* is part of the Jardins de Québec association. The main attraction here is the superb setting on the banks of the St. Lawrence. It is especially worthwhile to take the footpaths to the beach in order to gaze out at the river, the slate cliffs and the opposite shore, where the Église de Cap-Santé is visible. Numerous rare century-old trees, floral arrangements and an aviary adorn the grounds of the estate. There is also a boutique and café with a patio. The manor, which was built in 1840 to overlook the river, is designed as a villa with wrap-around verandas.

Inside is a small exhibition on the family of the Marquis de Lotbinière. Visitors will learn, for example, that Henri-Gustave, the son of Pierre-Gustave Joly, was born in Épernay (France), and later became Premier of Québec (1878-79), federal Revenue Minister and finally Lieutenant-Governor of British Columbia. The Domaine Joly de Lotbinière came under the care of the provincial government in 1967, when the last seigneur, Edmond Joly de Lotbinière, had to vacate the premises.

Upon leaving the parking lot, turn left on the road leading to Rte. 132 E.

Église Sainte-Croix *(alongside Rte. 132 E.).* The Université Laval's agronomical centre is the economic mainspring for the village of Sainte-Croix. The village is dominated by its granite Baroque Revival church, built in 1911. The church has a coffered ceiling that is typical of the Belle Époque.

Continue along Rte. 132 E. Turn left on Chemin de Tilly, which leads to the centre of Saint-Antoine-de-Tilly.

Saint-Antoine-de-Tilly ★ (pop. 1,427)

In 1702, Noël Legardeur de Tilly acquired the seigneury of Auteuil, which now bears his name. The hamlet has evolved into the peaceful village looking over the river that visitors will find today. Saint-Antoine-de-Tilly still has a few small ship-building companies.

The present facade of **Église Saint-Antoine** ★ *(3870 Chemin de Tilly),* added in 1902, adorns the building erected at the end of the 18th century. The interior, decorated by André Pâquet between 1837 and 1840, highlights several beautiful paintings purchased at sales after the French Revolution, including *La Sainte Famille* (The Holy Family), or *Intérieur de Nazareth* (Inside Nazareth), by Aubin Vouet, which once adorned the abbey church of Saint-Germain-des-Prés in Paris, and *La Visitation* (The Visitation), by A. Oudry. Other noteworthy works include *Jésus au Milieu des Docteurs* (Jesus Surrounded by Doctors) by Samuel Massé and *Saint François d'Assise* (St. Francis of Assisi), by Frère Luc. A stroll through the neighbouring cemetery offers a lovely view of the St. Lawrence and the church in silhouette.

Four generations of the Tilly family lived in the **Manoir de Tilly** *(3854 Chemin de Tilly),* built at the end of the 18th century. The building, now an inn, has a low veranda with delicate wood trellises. A little farther along lies the Manoir Dionne, with a veranda decorated with wrought iron. This was the residence of Henriette de Tilly, wife of merchant Charles François Dionne, whose family owned a number of seigneuries on the Côte-du-Sud (south coast).

*Continue along Rte. 132 E., through **Saint-Nicolas**, a former resort area. Follow the signs for Rte. 132 E. to **Saint-Romuald**, then **Lévis**. Drivers should pay particular attention near the **Pont de Québec** bridge, where the interchanges are frequent.*

Lévis ★★ (pop. 126,396)

Lévis developed rapidly during the second half of the 19th century due to the introduction of the railroad (1854) and the establishment of several local shipyards, supplied with wood by sawmills owned by the Price and Hamilton families. Because there was no railway line on the north shore of the St. Lawrence at the time, some of Québec City's shipping activities were transferred to Lévis. Originally known as Ville d'Aubigny, Lévis was given its present name in 1861, in memory of Chevalier François de Lévis, who defeated the British in the Battle of Sainte-Foy in 1760. The upper part of the city, consisting mostly of administrative buildings, offers some interesting views of Vieux-Québec, located on the

Chaudière-Appalaches – Exploring – The Seigneuries of the Côte-du-Sud opposite side of the river, while the very narrow lower part welcomes the trains and the ferry linking Lévis to the provincial capital.

Turn left on Côte du Passage to get to Lévis' old town (Vieux-Lévis), which can be visited on foot. Turn left on Rue Desjardins, and then left again on Rue William-Tremblay to get to the Terrasse de Lévis.

Built during the stock market crash of 1929, the **Terrasse de Lévis** ★★ *(Rue William-Tremblay)* offers spectacular views of downtown Lévis and Québec City. From here, you can admire Vieux-Québec's Place Royale, located along the river, and the Château Frontenac and Haute-Ville above. A few modern skyscrapers stand out in the background, the tallest being the Édifice Marie-Guyart, located on Québec City's Parliament Hill.

Turn right on Rue Carrier. The Maison Alphonse-Desjardins, former home of the founder of the Mouvement Desjardins credit union, stands at the corner of Rue Mont-Marie and Rue Guénette.

Maison Alphonse-Desjardins *(free admission; &; Mon-Fri 10am to noon and 1pm to 4:30pm, Sat and Sun noon to 5pm; 6 Rue du Mont-Marie, ☎418-835-2090 or 866-835-8444 ext. 2090).* Alphonse Desjardins (1854-1920) was a stubborn man. Eager for the advancement of the French-Canadian people, he struggled for many years to promote the concept of the *caisse populaire* (credit union), a cooperative financial institution controlled by its members, and by all the small investors who hold accounts there. Today, Desjardins forms the largest financial cooperative in Canada.

The Gothic Revival house where the Desjardins lived for nearly 50 years was built in 1882. It was beautifully restored on its 100th anniversary and converted into an information centre that focuses on Desjardins' career and achievements. Visitors can watch a documentary and see several restored rooms. The offices of the Société Historique Alphonse-Desjardins are located on the second floor.

Église Notre-Dame-de-la-Victoire ★ *(18 Rue Notre-Dame).* In 1851, a parish priest named Joseph Déziel proposed building a large Catholic church to serve the flourishing town. Thomas Baillargé, the architect of so many churches in the Québec City area,

drew up the plans. His buildings express a complete mastery of the neoclassical vocabulary of Québec, where French and English styles converge. The interior, divided into three naves, has high-columned galleries. On the grounds of the church, there is a plaque marking the exact location of the English cannons that bombarded Québec City in 1759.

Those interested in visiting the Lévis Forts National Historic Site should take Rte. 132 E., then turn left on Chemin du Gouvernement. Otherwise, take Côte du Passage (away from the river) and turn left on Rue Saint-Georges, which becomes Rue Saint-Joseph in Vieux-Lauzon.

The **Lévis Forts National Historic Site** ★ *($3.50; early May to late Aug every day 10am to 5pm, late Aug to late Sep Sat-Sun 1pm to 4pm; 41 Chemin du Gouvernement, ☎418-835-5182 or 800-463-6769, www.pc.gc.ca/levis).* Fearing a surprise attack from the Americans at the end of the Civil War, the British (and later Canadian) government built three separate forts in Lévis between 1865 and 1872, which were incorporated into Québec City's defence system. Only Fort No.1 remains intact. Made of earth and stone, it illustrates the evolution of fortified structures in the 19th century, when military techniques were advancing rapidly. Visitors will be particularly interested in the rifled bore, an imposing piece of artillery, as well as the vaulted pillboxes and the caponiers, masonry structures intended to protect the moat. The site also includes an exhibition on the history of the fort.

Finally, from the top of the wall, visitors can enjoy a lovely view of Québec City and Île d'Orléans. A little farther along are the remnants of **Fort de la Martinière** *($2; May to Oct, every day 9am to 4pm; Nov to Apr, Mon-Fri 9am to 4pm; 9805 Boulevard de la Rive-Sud),* which also offers an exhibition of various implements of war. The grounds feature picnic areas.

Église Saint-Joseph-de-Lauzon ★ *(Rue Saint-Joseph).* Lauzon was once the nucleus of the seigneury of the same name, granted to Jean de Lauzon, Governor of New France, in 1636. The parish of Saint-Joseph, founded in 1673, is the oldest on Québec City's entire south shore. At the time, it encompassed the territory now occupied by Lévis, Saint-Romuald and Saint-Nicolas. The original church, destroyed by a fire in

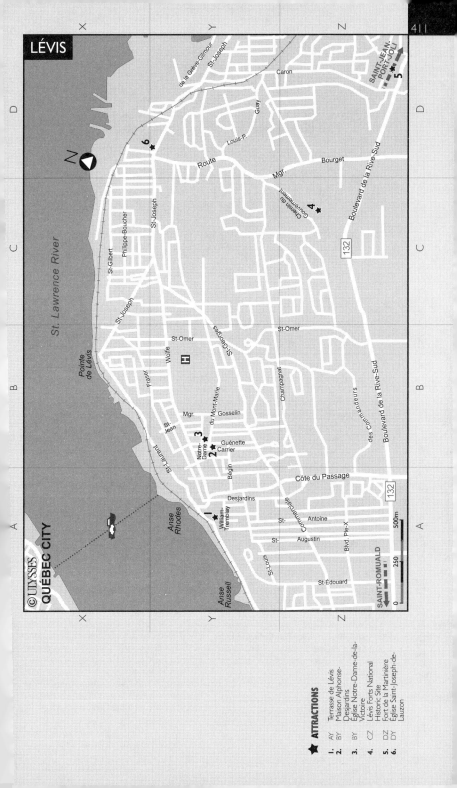

St. Lawrence River

QUÉBEC CITY

© ULYSSES

ATTRACTIONS

1. AY Terrasse de Lévis
2. BY Maison Alphonse-Desjardins
3. BY Église Notre-Dame-de-la-Victoire
4. CZ Lévis Forts National Historic Site
5. DZ Fort de la Martinière
6. DY Église Saint-Joseph-de-Lauzon

Alphonse Desjardins
(1854-1920)

Alphonse Desjardins was born in Lévis in 1854, where 46 years later he founded the Caisse Populaire de Lévis, the first in an important movement of credit unions that has grown into the present-day Caisses Populaires Desjardins.

The injustice of the loan system of the day prompted Desjardins to create a savings organization that would meet the needs of small-scale investors. Credit unions already existed in Europe; by adapting their methods to the Québec context, Desjardins realized his idea of a cooperative system in which community solidarity could benefit all of its members.

Desjardins spent three years refining his project when he took time off from his position as a House of Commons reporter in Ottawa. During parliamentary breaks, he returned to his home in Lévis. At the end of the year 1900, he convinced certain town notables that his project was viable and, on December 6, the men held a meeting during which the establishment of a new savings and loan company was proposed.

During the first years of this new institution, members came to deposit their nest eggs right at the Desjardins family home, on Rue du Mont-Marie, where Alphonse, or his wife Dorimène, would advise them and record their deposits.

Initially, the founders of the Caisses Populaires insisted that the credit union's activities be limited to the parish, but when they encouraged the creation of new unions, requests came in from all over the province. Since these were cooperatives, they were created by the demand of citizens who were interested in working together to get better savings and fairer credit.

Desjardins toured Québec for several years, explaining his idea to volunteers. In 1909, 22 Caisses were active across the province; the 100th was inaugurated in 1912. Each credit union functioned independently under Desjardins's guidance.

At the end of his life, Alphonse Desjardins was as involved as ever in the activities of the Caisses Populaires. He who had so much faith in the human spirit of cooperation left behind a popular movement that today has close to five million members in 500 Caisses across Québec.

1830, was replaced soon after by the present one, yet another design by the Baillargé family. Particularly notable are the two procession chapels located on either side of the church, the **Chapelle Sainte-Anne** (1789) and the **Chapelle Saint-François-Xavier** (1822). The **MIL Davie shipyard** lies opposite the latter.

Rue Saint-Joseph leads back to Rte. 132 E. (also known as Boulevard de la Rive-Sud). Continue on to Beaumont. A road on the left leads to the centre of the village.

Beaumont ★ (pop. 2,264)

The Côte-du-Sud corresponds to the south coast (*côte sud*) of the St. Lawrence estuary and technically begins in Beaumont. With its silver-roofed churches, procession chapels for Corpus Christi and manors set in a landscape that seems larger than life, this is true French-Canadian country. The seigneury of Beaumont (1672) is a fine example of the regional heritage.

The beautiful little **Église Saint-Étienne ★★** *(Chemin du Domaine)*, built in 1733, is one of the oldest churches still standing in Québec. It looks straight down the axis of the main road, which curves inland just afterwards, forming a small triangular plaza in front of the church square. This formation is typical of classical 18th-century French town planning. In 1759, during the British conquest, the British posted General Wolfe's proclamation decreeing the fall of New France on Beaumont's church. The villagers hastened to tear up the document. To punish them, General Moncton, who was responsible for the deportation of the Acadians in 1755, ordered his soldiers to set fire to the church. They held flaming torches to the door three times, but with no success. According to legend, each attempt was thwarted when a mysterious hand "miraculously" extinguished the flames.

Inside, the tabernacle of the high altar, sculpted around 1715, stands amidst a lovely Louis XV-style decor designed by Étienne Bercier in the early 19th century. In the middle of the retable is *Mort de Saint Étienne* by Antoine Plamondon (1826), and to the left, behind the pulpit, is a side chapel that was added in 1894. On the right, as you leave the church, you will find both the present-day presbytery and the old stone presbytery-chapel that was built in 1721 and later converted to a library.

Two French Regime procession chapels, one at the village entrance (De Sainte-Anne, 1734) and the other at the exit (De la Vierge, around 1740), add to the old-fashioned charm of Beaumont.

Follow Chemin du Domaine east, until it intersects with Rte. 132 E. The Moulin de Beaumont lies a little farther on the left.

The **Moulin de Beaumont** ★ *($7; early May to late Jun, Sat and Sun 10am to 4:30pm; late Jun to early Sep, Tue-Sun 10am to 4:30pm; early Sep to late Oct, Sat and Sun 10am to 4:30pm; 2 Rue du Fleuve, Rte. 132, ☎833-1867)* was built in 1821 on a plateau halfway down the waterfall in Maillou, and only its upper floors are visible from the road. The grounds of the mill, which include a picnic area, slope gradually down toward the St. Lawrence, offering lovely views of Île d'Orléans and the mountains on the opposite shore. There is even a staircase leading down to the tidal flats and the ruins of an older mill, the Moulin Péan. Visitors can purchase

muffins and bread made with flour milled on the premises. Both are baked using traditional methods. A video relates the history of the mill as well as an account of the archaeological digs that have been carried out on the site.

Saint-Michel-de-Bellechasse ★ (pop. 1,661)

The shady streets of Saint-Michel-de-Bellechasse are lined with colourfully decorated white wood houses, some of which feature American and British-inspired architectural touches. You'll cross the **Chapelle Votive Notre-Dame-de-Lourdes** (early 20th century) on your way into town. A little further is the **Église Saint-Michel**, a neoclassical church built in 1858 and its presbytery, which was rebuilt in 1789, 30 years after British Conquest. The town had been completely destroyed in 1759 as the advancing British army razed every village it encountered on its way to Québec City. Behind the presbytery is a little marina that welcomes watersports enthusiasts and sailboats.

The village's main road ends at Route 132 Est, which you can take to get to Berthier-sur-Mer.

Berthier-sur-Mer ★ (pop. 1,319)

This village is aptly named (Berthier by the Sea) because on arriving here from the west, visitors catch their first whiff of sea air. Here, Île d'Orléans has faded into the background, and the river, with its blue waves, starts to look like the ocean. On a clear day, typical sights include the mountains of Charlevoix, just opposite, and the fully equipped sailing harbour of this small summer resort founded back in the seigneurial era. Seigneur Dénéchaud's manor, built in the early 19th century, was destroyed by fire in 1992 after nearly 40 years of neglect.

From Berthier-sur-Mer, visitors can set off on a cruise of the St. Lawrence, around the Archipel de l'Isle-aux-Grues, also known as the Archipel de Montmagny. The trip includes a visit to the Grosse Île and the Irish Memorial National Historic Site and Île aux Grues itself (see descriptions below).

Next to the Motel-Restaurant de la Plage is a road that leads to a small beach. It's

Chaudière-Appalaches – Exploring – The Seigneuries of the Côte-du-Sud

a nice spot to relax and enjoy the view of the St. Lawrence and the islands that face the beach (Île Madame, Île aux Ruaux and Grosse Île). The western end of the beach is closed off by large rocks that you can climb to get an even better view.

Montmagny (pop. 11,814)

The **Centre Éducatif des Migrations** ★ *($6; Jun to Nov every day 9:30am to 5pm; 53 Rue du Bassin-Nord, ☎418-248-4565 or 248-9334)* is located on the Pointe-aux-Oies campsite. This information centre on bird migrations deals with the *sauvagine*, or snow goose; it also has a theatre presenting documentaries, exhibits, conferences and shows.

Cross Boulevard Taché and pick up Rue du Bassin-Sud, which soon connects with Rue Saint-Ignace. After crossing one bridge, turn right on Rue de la Fabrique. Go over another bridge, then just before the church, turn left on Rue Saint-Jean-Baptiste.

Visitors will notice that the centre of Montmagny, like that of most towns in Québec (as opposed to Europe), faces neither of the rivers that run alongside it. This is because waterways are a source of cold wind in the winter, and of flooding and ice-jams during the spring thaw. In the past, rivers were viewed from a strictly utilitarian angle and valued only for the purposes of transportation, industry and dumping waste. This means their banks were not graced with promenades.

Rue Saint-Jean-Baptiste and Rue Saint-Thomas meet at a point west of the church and are lined with a number of cafés, terraces and attractive shops in old houses. Avenue Sainte-Marie provides access to the beautiful and historic Taché house, hidden behind commercial buildings. The **Maison Historique Sir Étienne-Pascal-Taché** *($4; Jun to Sep, Mon-Fri 10am to 5pm, Sat and Sun 10am to 4pm; Sept to late Oct, Sat and Sun, 10am to 4pm; 37 Avenue Sainte-Marie, ☎418-248-0993)*, built in 1759, was the home of Sir Étienne Pascal Taché (1795-1865), who was Prime Minister of United Canada for a few years. He had the two picturesque towers looking out over the river added to the building.

Head back to Rue de la Fabrique and turn left, then take a right on Boulevard Taché, and another left on Avenue du Quai.

Before Avenue du Quai is the **Manoir Couillard de L'Espinay**, built in 1817 and now a luxury hotel (see **Manoir des Érables**, p 424). The pier street runs along a beautifully landscaped walking path for the entire length of the Montmagny basin. This is a great spot to have a picnic or simply to relax before departing on a boat trip. The **Montmagny pier** is an exceptional spot to see snow geese in spring and fall, and is one of the departure points to Grosse Île and Île aux Grues. The harbour station is situated just before the pier.

Grosse Île and the Irish Memorial National Historic Site ★★ *(independent or guided visits; May to Oct; a restaurant is located on site or bring your own lunch for a picnic by the shore; ☎418-248-8888 or 800-463-6769, www.pc.gc.ca/grosseile)* is called the Lieu Historique National de la Grosse-Île-et-le-Mémorial-des-Irlandais in French. An excursion to Grosse Île is to step back into the sad history of North American immigration. Fleeing epidemics and famine, Irish emigrants to Canada were particularly numerous from the 1830s to the 1850s. In order to limit the spread of cholera and typhus in the New World, authorities required transatlantic passengers to submit to a quarantine before allowing them to disembark at the port of Québec. Grosse Île was the logical location for this isolation camp, far enough from the mainland to sequester its residents effectively, but close enough to be convenient. On this "Quarantine Island" each immigrant was inspected with a fine-tooth comb. Travellers in good health stayed in "hotels," the luxury of which depended on the class of the berths they had occupied on the ships. The sick were immediately hospitalized.

A total of four million immigrants from 42 different countries passed through the port of Québec between 1832 and 1937. It is impossible to ascertain how many of these spent time on Grosse Île, but close to 7,000 people perished there. In 1847, the year of the Great Potato Famine, a principle cause of Irish emigration, the typhus epidemic was particularly virulent and especially hard on Irish immigrants. Of the 7,000 deaths registered over 105 years, 5,434 were counted in this tragic year. In memory of this sad year, people of Irish descent have made pilgrimages to Grosse Île every year since 1909. A Celtic cross stands on the island, in memory of those who came here and of those unfortunates who did not survive. On March 17, 1997, Saint Patrick's Day, Minister of Canadian Heritage Sheila Copps commemorated the tragedy, renaming the site Grosse Île and the Irish Memorial National Historic Site.

The guided tour of Grosse Île, part of which is done on a small motorized train, reveals the natural beauty of the island and its built structures. Among the 30 or so buildings still standing, a few are now open to the public: the disinfection building informs visitors about Canadian technology at the end of the 19th century and gives them a glimpse inside a lazar house (a hospital for people with infectious diseases). This is where victims of the 1847 typhoid epidemic were quarantined. These precious remnants of a tragic page in Canadian history give the place a particular allure.

Île aux Grues ★★ is the only island in the Isle-aux-Grues archipelago that is inhabited throughout the year. It is an excellent spot for watching snow geese in the spring, for hunting in autumn, and for walking in summer. In winter, the island is locked in by ice and residents can only access the mainland by airplane. A few rural inns dot this 10km-long agricultural island. A bicycle trip through its golden wheat fields along the river is one of the most pleasant ways to explore the area. The island is also accessible by car thanks to the **Grue des Îles** ferry (see p 407). At the centre of the island is the village of **Saint-Antoine-de-l'Isle-aux-Grues**, with its little church and lovely houses. There is a craft shop, a cheese store that sells a delicious, locally produced cheese, and a small museum that reveals past and present traditions of island life. To the east is the **Manoir Seigneurial McPherson-LeMoine**, which was rebuilt for Louis Liénard Villemonde Beaujeu after the island was sacked by the British army in 1759. This attractive house, fronted by a long balcony, was the summer home of historian James McPherson-LeMoine at the end of the 19th century. It later became the haven of painter Jean-Paul Riopelle until his death in 2002.

At the end of the dock is a small tourist-information stand that is staffed during high season. If you plan to spend a few days on the island, bring enough cash, since there is only one small bank on the island and it does not have an automatic teller machine.

Continue along Rte. 132 E. to Cap-Saint-Ignace. Turn right on the village road (Rue du Manoir).

Cap-Saint-Ignace (pop. 3,176)

The **Manoir Gamache** ★ *(not open to visitors; 120 Rue du Manoir, to the right on the way into the village)* was built in 1744 as a chapel and presbytery. Miraculously spared during the British Conquest, it became the residence of Seigneur Gamache shortly thereafter. The manor, with its thick, low square masonry and its high roof with dormer windows, is typical of rural architecture under the French Regime. The only unconventional element is the main door, which faces inland instead of the river. Its landscaping showcases this extremely well-restored manor.

Église Saint-Ignace ★ *(in the centre of the village)* was rebuilt between 1880 and 1894 as a replacement for the original church erected in 1772. Its long nave, lack of transepts, corner pinnacles and magnificent gilded interior with columned side galleries make it one of the most interesting buildings ever designed by David Ouellet. This Québec City architect did a great deal of work in the Beauce, Bas-Saint-Laurent and Gaspésie regions.

Continue along the old village road, then turn left to get back on Rte. 132.

L'Islet-sur-Mer ★

As its name ("Islet by the Sea") suggests, this village's activities centre on the sea. Since the 18th century, local residents have been handing down the occupations of sailor and captain on the St. Lawrence from father to son. Some have even become highly skilled captains and explorers on distant seas. In 1677, Governor Frontenac granted the seigneury of L'Islet to two families, the Bélangers and the Couillards, who quickly developed their lands. They turned both L'Islet-sur-Mer, on the banks of the St. Lawrence, and L'Islet, farther inland, into prosperous communities that still play an important role in the region.

The sea breeze, both strong and mild, gives a good indication of the immensity of the nearby river. A good place to breathe in this sea air is the front step of the **Église**

Joseph-Elzéar Bernier (1852-1934)

Joseph-Elzéar Bernier, one of Québec's most famous sailors, was born into a long line of captains in 1852, in the lovely village of L'Islet-sur-Mer.

In 1869, at the age of 17, Joseph-Elzéar was named captain of a ship called the *Saint-Joseph*, which had been previously piloted by his father, making him the youngest captain in the world. During the following years, he navigated all of the oceans and seas on Earth, setting speed records along the way.

In 1904, he made the first of his exploratory voyages to the Arctic Ocean, financed by the Canadian government. A plaque on the Melville Peninsula commemorates his crowning achievement, the appropriation of this arctic territory in the name of the government of Canada.

Bernier then returned to commercial navigation in the Arctic and on the St. Lawrence River. Until the end of his life, at the age of 82, he maintained a close relationship with the sea.

Notre-Dame-de-Bonsecours ★★ *(15 Chemin des Pionniers Est, Rte. 132)*. The present church, the construction of which began in 1768, is a large stone building with no transepts. The interior decor, executed between 1782 and 1787, reflects the teachings of the Académie Royale d'Architecture in Paris, where designer François Baillargé had recently been a student. Consequently, unlike earlier churches, the reredos mimics the shape of the semicircular chancel, itself completely covered with gilded Louis XV and Louis XVI–style wood panelling. The coffered ceiling was added in the 19th century, as were the spires on the steeples, which were redone in 1882. The tabernacle was designed by Noël Levasseur and came from the original church in 1728. Above it hangs *L'Annonciation* (The Annunciation), painted by Abbé Aide-Créquy in 1776. The glass doors on the left open onto the former congregationist chapel, added to the church in 1853, where occasional summer exhibitions with religious themes are presented.

With objects related to fishing, ship models, an interpretive centre and two real ships, the **Musée Maritime du Québec** ★★ *($8.15; mid-May to late Jun and mid-Sep to mid-Oct, every day 10am to 5pm; late Jun to early Sep, every day 9am to 6pm; the rest of the year, Tue-Fri, 10am to noon and 1:30pm to 4pm; 55 Chemin des Pionniers Est,* ☎*418-247-5001, www.mmq.qc.ca)* recounts the maritime history of the St. Lawrence from the 17th century to the present day. The institution, founded by the Association des Marins du Saint-Laurent, occupies the former Couvent de l'Islet-sur-Mer (1877) and bears the name of one of the village's most illustrious citizens, Captain J.-E. Bernier (1852-1934). Bernier was one of the first individuals to explore the Arctic, thus securing Canadian sovereignty in the Far North.

Heading towards Saint-Jean-Port-Joli, visitors will see the **Chapelle des Marins** *(Route des Pionniers)* of L'Islet (1835) on the left, along with the *Croix de Tempérance*, perched atop a hillock. These symbolic structures are used during the Corpus Christi procession, a tradition over three centuries old, revived a few years ago following the restoration of a number of chapels in villages along the Côte-du-Sud. This celebration takes place in the early evening on the second Sunday in June. It involves parish guards in costume, the penance of the Vatican and the Sacred Heart, and the monstrance and the Blessed Sacrament. The priest in all his finery is sheltered by a gold-embroidered baldachin and followed by the congregation carrying candles, as he makes stops in front of the procession chapels. This event, dedicated to the Adoration of the Blessed Sacrament, is particularly spectacular in L'Islet-sur-Mer.

Saint-Jean-Port-Joli ★
(pop. 3,395)

Saint-Jean-Port-Joli has become synonymous with handicrafts, specifically wood carving. The origins of this tradition go back to the Bourgault family, which made its living carving wood in the early 20th century. On the way into the town, Rte. 132 is lined with an impressive number of shops where visitors can purchase a wooden pipe-smoking grandfather or knitting woman. A museums exhibit the finest pieces. Though the handicraft business is now flourishing more than ever, the village is also known for its church and for Philippe Aubert de Gaspé's novel *Les Anciens Canadiens* (Canadians of Old), written at the seigneurial manor.

On the way into the village, the **seigneurial mill** is visible on the right. Farther, on the left, the lovely **Maison Saint-Pierre**, built around 1820, precedes a lookout by the river.

The original manor of Saint-Jean-Port-Joli was destroyed during the British conquest. Another manor was built in 1764 on the same foundations and based on the same design as the first, but it unfortunately burned down in 1909. All that remains of **Philippe Aubert de Gaspé's Manor** *(710 Avenue de Gaspé Ouest)* is the bread oven by the side of the road. Philippe Aubert de Gaspé (1786-1871), Seigneur de Saint-Jean-Port-Joli, withdrew to his manor to write *Les Anciens Canadiens*, published in 1863. Considered the first French-Canadian novel, the book's literary significance is as great as its ethnological interest, since it describes daily life at the end of the seigneurial era. Plans are currently under way to rebuild the manor.

The **Musée des Anciens Canadiens** *($4; May, Jun, Sep, Oct every day 8:30am to 5:30pm; Jul and Aug, every day 8:30am to 9pm; 332 Avenue de Gaspé Ouest, ☎418-598-3392 or 866-598-3392)* exhibits a series of wood carvings depicting local traditions.

Maison Médard-Bourgault ★ *(free admission; mid-Jun to early Sep, every day 9am to 5pm; 322 Avenue de Gaspé Ouest, ☎418-598-3880)* once belonged to Médard Bourgault (1877-1967), the first of a line of famous sculptors from Saint-Jean-Port-Joli. When he bought this house in 1920, the master-mariner gave up navigating in order to devote himself entirely to woodcarving. As the years went by, he carved the walls and the furniture, producing a highly personal work of art. The house now belongs to his son, also a sculptor, who has his studio in the house. If you want to see his work, and that of his father, just ask.

The charming **Église Saint-Jean-Baptiste ★ ★** *(2 Avenue de Gaspé Ouest)*, built between 1779 and 1781, is recognizable by its bright red roof topped by two steeples, placed in a way altogether uncommon in Québec architecture: one in the front, the other in the back at the beginning of the apse. The church has a remarkable interior made of carved, gilded wood. Pierre Noël Levasseur's rocaille tabernacle, crowned with a wood shell supported by columns, comes from the original chapel and dates back to 1740. The side balconies added to the nave in order to increase the number of pews are also somewhat rare in Québec. Those in Saint-Jean-Port-Joli, dating back to 1845, are the only ones to have survived the waves of renovation and restoration of the past 40 years.

Continue along Rte. 132 to Saint-Roch-des-Aulnaies.

Saint-Roch-des-Aulnaies ★ ★
(pop. 1,023)

This pretty village on the banks of the St. Lawrence is actually made up of two neighbourhoods. The one around the church is called Saint-Roch-des-Aulnaies, while the other, not far from the manor, is known as the Village des Aulnaies. The name "Aulnaies" refers to the abundance of alder trees *(aulnes)* that grow along the Rivière Ferrée, which powers the seigneurial mill. Nicolas Juchereau, the son of Jean Juchereau, Sieur de Maur from Perche, was granted the seigneury in 1656. Most of the old residences in Saint-Roch-des-Aulnaies are exceptionally large, a sign that local inhabitants enjoyed a certain degree of prosperity in the 19th century.

Seigneurie des Aulnaies ★ ★ *($9.50; mid-Jun to early Sep every day 9am to 6pm, early Jun to mid-Jun and early Sep to mid-Oct Sat-Sun 10am to 4pm; 525 Chemin de la Seigneurie, ☎418-354-2800 or 877-354-2800, www.laseigneuriedesaulnaies.qc.ca)*. The Dionne estate has been transformed into a fascinating information centre focusing on the seigneurial era. Visitors are greeted in the former miller's house, converted into a shop and café whose menu includes pancakes and muffins made with flour ground in the neighbouring mill, a large stone structure rebuilt in 1842 on the site of an older mill. Guided tours of the mill in operation enable visitors to understand its complex gearing system, set in motion by the Rivière Ferrée. Its main wheel is the largest in Québec.

The manor house, built on a promontory, is accessed by a long stairway. Like the manor house at the **Domaine Joly-De Lotbinière** (see p 409), the Dionne home lacks the austerity of typical seigneurial manors. It was designed by Charles Baillargé, a member of Québec's famous architectural dynasty, at the beginning of the Victorian era. His trademark is the Greek Revival ornamentation around the doorways (see **Maison Cirice-Têtu**, Québec City, p 334). In the basement, interactive displays explain in detail the principals of the seigneurial system and its impact on the landscape of rural Québec. The reception rooms on the main floor are plainly furnished in 19th-century style. A lovely garden, part of the Jardin du Québec association, as well as nature paths, surround the manor house. Guides and characters in period costume animate the site.

The Chaudière-Appalaches tourist area ends here, but the Côte-du-Sud continues all the way up to Rivière-du-Loup. We recommend combining this tour with the one entitled **The Kamouraska Region ★★**, which leads through the Bas-Saint-Laurent region (see p 433).

To rapidly return to Québec City or Montréal, head west on Hwy. 20, located just behind the village of Saint-Roch-des-Aulnaies.

- -

Tour B: La Beauce
★

 2 days

After the French Regime's timid attempts at colonization, Beauce, or Nouvelle-Beauce as it was frequently called in the 18th century, enjoyed a boom due to the opening of the Kennebec road (between 1810 and

1830), and then the railway (1870-1895). Both linked Québec and its capital to New England, passing through the valley of the Rivière Chaudière on the way. Agricultural hamlets all along this route flourished, becoming prosperous little industrial towns by the end of the 19th century. Known for their enterprising spirit and favoured by fortune, Beaucerons founded a number of businesses whose names, such as Vachon-Culinar and Canam-Manac, are now well known in Québec.

Continue on Hwy. 73 and then Rte. 173, which runs alongside the Rivière Chaudière to the U.S. border. This road was named Route du Président-Kennedy in honour of the man whose memory is dear to the tens of thousands of Americans who take Rte. 173 each year to Québec City. Near Saint-Joseph-de-Beauce, leave Rte. 173 in order to drive along the river to the centre of town.

Saint-Joseph-de-Beauce ★ (pop. 4,528)

In Saint-Joseph, visitors will find a plaque commemorating **Route du Président-Kennedy**, which was renamed in 1970 *(347 Avenue du Palais)*. This major artery's modest origins date back to 1737, when the Beauce's first seigneurs were asked to open a road between the newly cleared lands and Lévis, located on the south shore of Québec City. In 1758, this original road was replaced by the wider, straighter Route Justinienne. It was not until 1830 that the road was extended across the border to Jackman, Maine.

Saint-Joseph is renowned for its extremely well-preserved group of religious buildings erected at the end of the 19th century on a hillock a good distance from the river, safe from floods. The first houses built along the Chaudière have long since been destroyed or, in some cases, moved to higher ground. This explains why the banks of the river are only slightly developed today.

The Romanesque Revival **Église Saint-Joseph** and its **Presbytery ★** *(Rue Sainte-Christine)*, built out of stone in 1865, are the work of François-Xavier Berlinguet and Joseph-Ferdinand Peachy, two architects from Québec City. The presbytery was designed by George-Émile Tanguay upon his return from a trip to France in the 1880s, an era marking the peak of the French Renais-

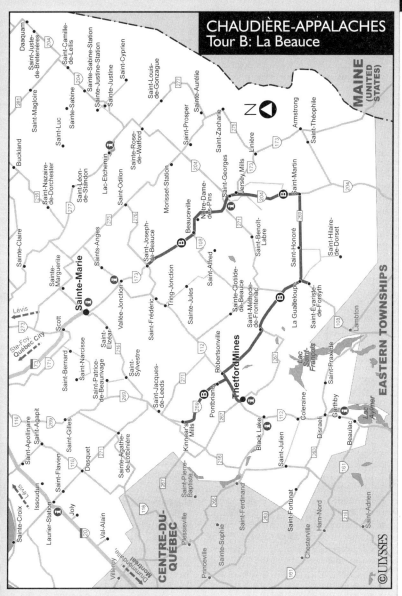

sance Revival style in the Paris region. Tanguay drew his inspiration from this style for the brick and stone presbytery, a veritable little palace for the parish priest and his curates.

The **Musée Marius-Barbeau** ★ *($5; &; winter Mon-Fri 9am to 4:30pm, Sat-Sun 1pm to 4:30pm; summer Mon-Fri 9am to 5pm, Sat-Sun 10am to* *5pm; 139 Rue Sainte-Christine, ☎418-397-4039, www.museemariusbarbeau.com)* focuses on the history of the Beauce region and explains the different stages of development in the Vallée de la Chaudière, from the first seigneuries, to the 19th-century gold rush to the building of major communication routes. The arts and popular traditions studied by Beauceron ethnologist and folklorist Marius Barbeau are also prominently displayed. The building itself is the former convent of the Sisters of Charity (1887), a handsome polychromatic brick edifice built in the Second Empire style. Its neighbour to the south is the former orphanage, now used by social organizations.

Continue to Saint-Georges.

Saint-Georges (pop. 28,946)

Divided into Saint-Georges-Ouest and Saint-Georges-Est, on either side of the Rivière Chaudière, the industrial capital of the Beauce region is reminiscent of a New England manufacturing town. A German-born merchant by the name of Georges Pfotzer is considered the true father of Saint-Georges for having taken advantage of the opening of the Lévis-Jackman route in 1830 to launch the forest industry here. In the early 20th century, the Dionne Spinning Mill and various shoe manufacturers established themselves in the region, leading to a significant increase in population. Today, Saint-Georges is a sprawling city. Though the outskirts are somewhat grim, there are a few treasures nestled in the centre of town.

The **Église Saint-Georges** ★ ★ *(1ʳᵉ Avenue, in Saint-Georges-Ouest)* stands on a promontory overlooking the Rivière Chaudière. Begun in 1900, it is unquestionably Québec City architect David Ouellet's masterpiece (built in collaboration with Pierre Lévesque). The art of the Belle Époque is beautifully represented here by the central steeple towering 75m and the magnificent three-level interior, which has been lavishly sculpted and gilded. In front of the church stands an imposing statue titled **Saint Georges Terrassant le Dragon** *(St. George Slaying the Dragon)*. This is a fibreglass copy of the fragile original. Louis Jobin's original metal-covered wooden statue (1909) is now exhibited at the Musée National des Beaux-Arts du Québec in Québec City.

The **Barrage Sartigan** *(on the way out of town)* was built in 1967 in order to regulate the flow of the Rivière Chaudière and limit spring flooding.

Take Rte. 173 S. to Jersey Mills, and bear right on Rte. 204 to drive along the Rivière Chaudière to Saint-Martin. Turn right on Rte. 269, which leads to La Guadeloupe and Saint-Évariste-de-Forsyth, and get back on Rte. 108, in the heart of Haute-Beauce.

Saint-Évariste-de-Forsyth (pop. 599)

Haute-Beauce is an isolated region, made up of high plateaus that were cultivated for the first time at the end of the 19th century. Its villages are new and sparsely populated, but residents are friendly and warm-hearted. Saint-Évariste looks out over the surrounding landscape, offering lovely views of neighbouring farms and maple groves.

Get back on Rte. 269 and head north toward Saint-Méthode-de-Frontenac. In Robertsonville, turn left onto Rte. 112 to visit the asbestos region.

Thetford Mines (pop. 26,403)

Asbestos is a strange ore with a whitish, fibrous appearance that is valued for its insulating properties and resistance to heat. It was discovered in the region in 1876, promoting the development of a portion of Québec that had previously been considered extremely remote. Large American and Canadian companies developed the mines in Asbestos, Black Lake and Thetford Mines (before the mines were nationalized in the early 1980s), building industrial empires that made Québec one of the highest-ranking producers of asbestos in the world.

The **Musée Minéralogique et Minier de la Région de Thetford Mines** *($6; ᗝ; late Jun to early Sep, every day 9.30am to 6pm; low season every day 1pm to 5pm; closed Jan and Feb; 711 Boulevard Smith Sud, ☎418-335-2123)* houses superb collections of rocks and minerals from all over the world, including samples of asbestos taken from 25 different countries. There are also exhibits explaining the development of the mines and the different characteristics of rocks and minerals found in Québec.

Mine Tours ★ ★ *($17; reservations required; late Jun to early Sep every day departure at 1:30pm; Jul and Aug departures at 10:30am, 1:30pm and 3:30pm; 682 Rue Mofette N., ☎418-423-3333 or 877-335-7141, www.tourisme-amiante.com)* provide a unique opportunity to see an asbestos mine in operation. Two types of tours are offered. The **open-pit mine tour** *($17, includes admission to the Musée Minéralogique; late Jun to early Sep, reservations required; tours leave from the museum;* ☎*418-423-3333 or 877-335-7141)* take visitors 354m underground, where they get to visit the place asbestos is extracted, bagged and shipped and the equipment that is used while mining the ore. On the **Galerie Souterraine de la Mine Bell** tour *($46, includes admission to the Musée Minéralogique; late Jun to early Sep Mon-Tue and Fri-Sun 9am to noon; visitors must be 14yrs or older; tours leave from the museum;* ☎*418-423-3333 or 877-335-7141)*, visitors travel 316m below ground and learn about the different aspects of a miner's work. Protective clothing is provided, and visitors must be comfortable in enclosed spaces.

Parc National de Frontenac ★, see below.

The neighbouring municipality of **Black Lake** *(8km southwest of Thetford Mines, along Rte. 112)* has one of the most impressive mining landscapes in North America.

Return to Rte. 269 and head north toward Kinnear's Mills and Saint-Jacques-de-Leeds. The isolated hamlet of Kinnear's Mills, located off the main road, is worth a short visit.

Kinnear's Mills (pop. 359)

Between 1810 and 1830, the British colonial government established townships with English-sounding names on territory that hadn't yet been distributed under the seigneurial system. The village of Kinnear's Mills, located on the banks of the Rivière Osgoode, was founded by Scottish settlers in 1821. It is home to a surprising number of churches of different denominations reflecting the region's ethnic diversity—a Presbyterian church (1873), a Methodist church (1876), an Anglican church (1897) and a more recent Catholic church.

Continue on to Saint-Jacques-de-Leeds to visit a few more charming churches before heading back to Québec City via Rte. 269 N. and Rte. 116.

Parks

Tour A: The Seigneuries of the Côte-du-Sud

Parc des Chutes-de-la-Chaudière ★ *(330 Avenue Joseph-Hudon, Charny,* ☎*418-838-6026)*. Head out of Québec City via the Pont Pierre-Laporte. Once across the river, follow the signs for the Chutes (waterfalls; Exit 130). The Rivière Chaudière originates in Lac Mégantic. Covering 185km, it flows into the St. Lawrence just after the falls, which are the result of an unusual geological formation: a highly resistant layer of sandstone lies within a series of sedimentary rocks formed over 570 million years ago. The area around the falls was set aside as a park by the provincial government. From the footbridge stretching over the Rivière Chaudière, visitors can enjoy an impressive view of the falls. In the spring, the rate of flow reaches nearly 1,700,000 litres per second, 15 times more than usual, making this the most magnificent time to see the falls.

Tour B: La Beauce

The **Parc des Rapides-du-Diable** *(free admission; Route du Président-Kennedy, Beauceville, to the west when leaving Beauceville;* ☎*418-774-9137)* is equipped with trails leading to the Chaudière and the Diable rapids. You will have the opportunity to see the remains of a mill dating back to the Beauce gold rush.

Located on the shores of Lac Saint-François, the **Parc National de Frontenac** ★ *($3.50; 599 Chemin des Roy, Saint-Daniel-Lambton,* ☎*418-286-2300 or 800-665-6527, www.sepaq.com)* has a number of picnic areas, beaches and hiking trails. Most of the park's territory is located in the Eastern Townships region.

Parc de la Chute Sainte-Agathe *($5/car, $15/camping; 342 Rang Gosford Ouest, Sainte-Agathe-de-Lothinière,* ☎*418-599-2661)* is a wonderful place for swimming and hiking. In certain spots, you have to be pretty resourceful and hop from rock to rock to get to the water, but there is a little beach where everyone can enjoy the refreshing waterfalls and pools of Rivière Palmer. From the shore there is a charming view of a covered bridge across the falls.

Outdoor Activities

■ Bird-Watching

Tour A: The Seigneuries of the Côte-du-Sud

Ornitour *(prices vary but include binoculars, transportation and guide; reservations required; individual or group tours; 35 Chemin du Vieux-Quai, Montmagny,* ☎*418-241-5368, www. ornitour.net)* is the only private company in Québec that offers bird-watching packages. There are various excursions depending on the season: in the spring, trips to see the snow geese; from May to November, bird-watching excursions focusing on the history of the birds on Île-aux-Grues (departures from the Montmagny pier); in the winter, excursions on the Bombardier B-12 multi-passenger snowmobile, which allows you to go into the forest to watch and even feed the birds. (The blue tit will feed right out of your hand!).

■ Canoeing

Tour B: La Beauce

In Sainte-Marie, the tourist-information kiosk is located at Manoir Taschereau and rents canoes *($10/hour, $20/half-day, $30/ day; late Jun to late Aug)*. Why not explore the area by paddling along the Chaudière river?

At **Parc National de Frontenac**, visitors can enjoy great canoeing excursions on Lac Saint-François (boat rental available).

■ Cruises

Tour A: The Seigneuries of the Côte-du-Sud

Croisière Lachance *($42, 5hr cruise; 110 Rue de la Marina, Berthier-sur-Mer,* ☎*418-259-2140 or 888-476-7734, www.croisiereslachance.ca)* offers cruises on a comfortable boat. Discover an archipelago rich in history (Archipel de l'Isle aux Grues) with the Lachance family, members of which have been sailors for three generations. Their stories will take you back to island life as it was in the early 20th century.

■ Cycling

Tour A: The Seigneuries of the Côte-du-Sud

Île aux Grues is ideal for cycling. Its small, flat roads follow the river and run through vast wheat fields, offering breath-taking views.

Tour B: La Beauce

A beautiful bicycle path begins in **Saint-Georges** and runs along the west and east sides of the Rivière Chaudière, all the way to Notre-Dame-les-Pins and Saint-Jean-de-la-Lande, uncovering hidden treasures of the Beauce that are well worth a pedal push or two. And if you run into a snag along the way, Saint-Georges is home to Procycle, the largest bicycle manufacturer in Canada.

■ Golf

Tour A: The Seigneuries of the Côte-du-Sud

Golf de l'Auberivière *($33 weekdays, $37 weekends; 777 Rue Alexandre, Lévis,* ☎*418-835-0480)* is located a few minutes from the bridges to Québec City in a lovely green space crisscrossed by two rivers and dotted with little lakes. This course is easily and quickly accessible.

■ Hiking

Tour B: La Beauce

At **Parc de la Chute Sainte-Agathe** *(342 rang Gosford Ouest, Sainte-Agathe-de-Lotbinière,* ☎*418-599-2661)*, hikers can stroll along the banks of Rivière Palmer and through the surrounding woods.

Lovely forest walks and strolls on the shore of Lac Saint-François await at **Parc National de Frontenac** *(599 Chemin des Roy, Saint-Daniel-Lambton,* ☎*418-486-2300 or 800-665-6527, www.sepaq.com)*.

■ Kayaking

Tour A: The Seigneuries of the Côte-du-Sud

Dedicated kayakers run the **Kayaks et Nature** *($40 for 3hrs with guide; early May to late Oct; 3962 Rue des Champs, Saint-Antoine-de-Tilly,* ☎*418-886-2218)* outfit. Every day, they accompany excursionists along the banks of the river, introducing them to its peaceful beauty. Here, safety comes first (fun being a close second, of course), so supervision and initiation are done in the best possible conditions, at a pace that is comfortable for everyone.

Montmagny's bay is sheltered from the strong winds and currents of the river. It is the perfect spot for beginners to test the water and gradually familiarize themselves with their craft before heading for deeper water, and it is the departure point for excursions along the banks of the river and to the islands of the Isle-aux-Grues archipelago offered by the team at **Aventures Kayak-Eau-Fleuve** *($89/day, $45/half-day, $35/ evening; 25 Boulevard Taché Ouest, Montmagny,* ☎*418-248-3173).*

Chaudière-Appalaches - Outdoor Activities

Accommodations

- - - - - - - - - - - - - - -

Tour A: The Seigneuries of the Côte-du-Sud

Sainte-Croix

Camping Belle-Vue
$
⚲ ≈ ♨

6939 Route Marie-Victorin
☎/▤ (418) 926-3482
www.quebecweb.com/camping-bellevue
Camping Belle-Vue provides spectacular views, thanks to its location right on the edge of the St. Lawrence, near **Domaine Joly-De Lotbinière** (see p 409). The campground offers all the usual services, as well as several activities like tennis, cycling and swimming.

Saint-Antoine-de-Tilly

La Maison Normand
$$ bkfst incl.
3894 Chemin de Tilly
☎ (418) 886-1314
La Maison Normand is located in the heart of the village of Saint-Antoine-de-Tilly. This former Victorian-style general store was converted into a pleasant bed and breakfast. The spacious high-ceilinged living room is a good spot to relax with a good book, while the house's pretty library is stacked with books on various parts of the world, a reminder that its owners are also dedicated travellers who know how to please road-weary guests. Reasonable rates, four comfortable rooms and a generous breakfast make this a good choice.

Manoir de Tilly
$$$-$$$$ bkfst incl.
≡ ▲ ⚲ ⚿ Ⓦ Ⓨ ◎
3854 Chemin de Tilly
☎ (418) 886-2407 or 888-862-6647
▤ (418) 886-2595
www.manoirdetilly.com
Manoir de Tilly is a historic home that dates from 1786. The guest rooms are not, however, in the older part of the building, but rather a modern wing that nonetheless offers all of the comfort and peace one could desire. Each room has a fireplace and a beautiful view. The service is attentive and the dining room offers fine cuisine (see p 426). The inn also has a spa and conference rooms.

Beaumont

Manoir de Beaumont
$$$ bkfst incl.
≈
485 Route du Fleuve
☎ (418) 833-5635 or 800-302-5634
▤ (418) 833-7891
www.manoirdebeaumont.qbc.net
Perched high on a hill and surrounded by trees, the Manoir de Beaumont offers bed-and-breakfast accommodations in perfect peace and comfort. Its five rooms are attractively decorated in period style, matching the house itself. A large, sunny living room and a swimming pool are at guests' disposal.

La Belle Époque Inn
$$
⚲ Ⓦ
100 Rue St-Jean Baptiste Est
☎ (418) 248-3373 or 800-490-3373
▤ (418) 248-7957
www.epoque.qc.ca
The warm, elegant atmosphere of La Belle Époque Inn leaves a lasting impression. The charming house dates from 1850, features attractive furnishings and provides a high level of comfort.

Montmagny

Manoir des Érables
$$$-$$$$
≡ ▲ ⚲ ≈ Ⓦ ◎
220 Boulevard Taché Est
☎ (418) 248-0100 or 800-563-0200
▤ (418) 248-9507
www.manoirdeserables.com
The Manoir des Érables is an old, English-style seigneurial abode. The opulence of its period decor and the warm, courteous welcome make guests feel like royalty. The rooms are beautiful and comfortable, and many of them have fireplaces. On the ground floor is a lovely cigar lounge decorated with hunting trophies where guests can choose from a wide variety of scotches and cigars. There is also a dining room (see p 427) and a bistro, both of which serve excellent cuisine. Also available are motel rooms under the maples, set off from the hotel, and a few rooms in a lodge that is just as inviting as the manor itself.

Île aux Grues

On Île aux Grues, two inns, a few campgrounds and some bed and breakfasts can accommodate visitors who want to stay overnight and witness the archipelago's magnificent sunsets.

Gîte Chez Bibiane
$ bkfst incl.

sb
270 Chemin du Roi
☎ (418) 248-6173
Guests at Chez Bibiane receive a warm welcome from the live-in hosts who are discreet but not averse to conversation with guests who want to learn more about islanders and island life. The four small guestrooms are simply decorated. Breakfast, served in a room overlooking the river, includes fresh island cheese. The hosts also run a dairy farm on their land and, come autumn, a snowgoose hunting outfitter.

Saint-Eugène-de-L'Islet

Auberge des Glacis
$$-$$$ bkfst incl.
≡ ♨

46 Route de la Tortue
☎ (418) 247-7486 or 877-245-2247
🖹 (418) 247-7182
www.aubergedesglacis.com
Set in an old seigneurial mill at the end of a tree-lined lane, Auberge des Glacis has a special charm about it. Each of the comfortable rooms has a name and its own unique decor. Delicious French cuisine is featured in the dining room (see p 427). The stone walls and wood-framed windows of the mill have been preserved as part of the finery of the establishment, whose property includes a lake, bird-watching trails, a small terrace, and, of course, the river. This is an especially peaceful spot, perfect for relaxation.

L'Islet-sur-Mer

Gîte Les Pieds Dans L'Eau
$$ bkfst incl.

pb/sb ≡
549 Chemin des Pionniers Est
☎ (418) 247-5575
🖹 (418) 247-7772
Solange offers a warm welcome at her bed and breakfast located right on the edge of the St. Lawrence. Basic accommodations are provided and the heavenly breakfast does not disappoint.

Auberge La Marguerite
$$-$$$ bkfst incl.
≡ ❈ ♨

88 Chemin des Pionniers Est
☎ (418) 247-5454 or 877-788-5454
🖹 (418) 247-7725
www.aubergelamarguerite.com
A renovated house that dates back to 1754, the Auberge La Marguerite has managed to retain the charm of days gone by. The eight rooms, named after the schooners that were once this region's claim to fame, are comfortable and tastefully decorated. Make sure not to miss breakfast!

Saint-Jean-Port-Joli

Camping de la Demi-Lieue
$
🛶 ≋

589 Avenue de Gaspé E.
☎ (418) 598-6108 or 800-463-9558
🖹 (418) 598-9558
www.quebecweb.com/demilieue
La Demi-Lieue campground extends along the grounds of a former seigneury that is exactly one half-league long (a half league, the literal translation of the campground's name, is equivalent to about 2.4km or 1.5mi), providing ample space for all to enjoy this beautiful riverside spot. All necessary services are provided, including a security guard.

Maison de L'Ermitage
$$ bkfst incl.

pb/sb ❈
56 Rue de l'Ermitage
☎ (418) 598-7553
In an old, red-and-white house with four corner towers and a wraparound porch with a view of the river, the inn at Maison de L'Ermitage offers five cozy rooms and a tasty breakfast. The house is full of sunny spots furnished for reading and relaxing, and its yard slopes down to the river. An annual sculpture festival is held just next door (see p 429).

Tour B: La Beauce

Saint-Joseph-de-Beauce

Camping Municipal Saint-Joseph
$
🛶 ≋

221 Route 276
☎ (418) 397-5953
🖹 (418) 397-5715
This campground has 60 campsites next to a river and rapids. Swimming and many other activities are possible in this lovely setting.

Motel Bellevue
$-$$
≡ 🛶 ♨ ◎

1150 Avenue du Palais
☎ (418) 397-6132 or 866-666-5585
🖹 (418) 397-5050
Motel Bellevue is located on the outskirts of town. Very ordinary looking, it has rooms decorated with plywood furniture. The adjacent restaurant serves good breakfasts.

Chaudière-Appalaches - Accommodations - La Beauce

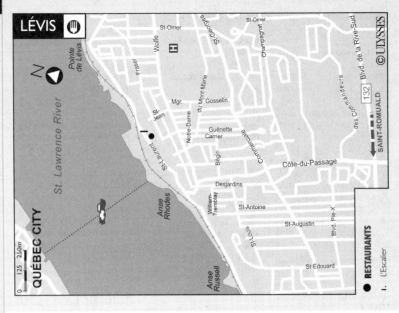

LÉVIS

St-Omer
St-Omer
Wolfe
Fraser
Pointe de Lévis
St-Jean
Mgr.
du Mont-Marie
Gosselin
Notre-Dame
Guénette Carrier
Bégin
Commerciale
Desjardins
William-Tremblay
St-Antoine
St-Louis
St-Augustin
Blvd. Pie-X
St-Édouard
Côte-du-Passage
Champagnat
Blvd. de la Rive-Sud
des Commandeurs
132
SAINT-ROMUALD
Anse Rhodes
Anse Russell
St. Lawrence River
St-Laurent
QUÉBEC CITY
0 125 250m
© ULYSSES

RESTAURANTS
1. L'Escalier

Saint-Georges

Gîte La Sérénade
$$
sb
8835 35ᵉ Avenue (via 90ᵉ Rue)
☎ (418) 228-1059
www.gitelaserenade.com
This friendly family home is surrounded with mature trees and offers a restful stay just outside the centre of town.

Auberge-Motel Benedict-Arnold
$$-$$$ bkfst incl.
≡ ⛽ ⋇ ❄ ♨ ⫸ ◎
18255 Boulevard Lacroix
☎ (418) 228-5558 or 800-463-5057
🖨 (418) 227-2941
www.aubergearnold.qc.ca
Auberge-Motel Benedict-Arnold has been a well-known stopover near the U.S. border for many generations. The inn has more than 50 rooms, each of them decorated with privacy in mind. Motel rooms are also available. Two dining rooms offer quality fare, and the staff is quite courteous.

Restaurants

Tour A: The Seigneuries of the Côte-du-Sud

Lotbinière

La Romaine
$$
7406 Route Marie-Victorin
☎ (418) 796-2723
Set in a Victorian house, La Romaine offers a good menu for lunch and dinner, featuring fresh, locally produced ingredients. In the summertime, the set menu always includes fish and seafood. Service is friendly and unpretentious.

Saint-Antoine-de-Tilly

Manoir de Tilly
$$$$
3854 Chemin de Tilly
☎ (418) 886-2407 or 888-862-6647
Manoir de Tilly's dining room serves refined French cuisine based on local products such as lamb and duck or, for more imaginative dishes, ostrich and deer. The renovated dining room preserves not even a hint of the historic building, but is pleasant nonetheless. Here, diners savour carefully prepared and finely presented dishes, complemented by the view through the large windows on the north wall.

Lévis

L'Escalier
$$

6120 Rue St-Laurent
☎ (418) 835-1865

This friendly little restaurant has been serving tasty fare to Lévis diners for over 20 years. Located near the Lévis ferry terminal, L'Escalier faces Québec City's Château Frontenac and fortifications and takes its name from the nearby steep stairway that links Vieux-Lévis to the riverfront. The restaurant's interior and terrace are both attractively decorated, and the setting is even more alluring at sunset. Notable house specialties include veal cutlets served with a delicious blue-cheese sauce.

Beaumont

Moulin de Beaumont
$

late Jun to late Aug
2 Route du Fleuve
☎ (418) 833-1867

This charming little café offers a splendid view of the St. Lawrence river and the Beaumont mill. Tasty light meals such as *croquemonsieur* and meat pie are served with delicious homemade bread made with flour produced at the mill. You can also stock up on bread at the mill's adjoining bakery.

Berthier-sur-Mer

Café du Havre
$$

120 Rue de la Marina
☎ (418) 259-2364

This café is located in Berthier-sur-Mer's marina. The usual hamburgers and pizza are served here, and the daily menu usually features a few fish, seafood and chicken selections. The dining room and terrace both provide stunning views of the St. Lawrence.

Montmagny

L'Épi d'Or
$

117 Rue St-Jean-Baptiste Est
☎ (418) 248-3021

The region's best croissants and crepes can be found in this friendly little café. A good choice to start the day off on the right foot.

La Belle Époque
$$-$$$

100 Rue St-Jean-Baptiste Est
☎ (418) 248-3373 or 800-490-3373

La Belle Époque Inn (see p 424) boasts a shaded terrace and an attractive dining room. The reasonably priced French cuisine-inspired daily menu provides good value.

Manoir des Érables
$$$$

220 Boulevard Taché E.
☎ (418) 248-0100 or 800-563-0200

The dining room at **Manoir des Érables** (see p 424) features fish and game. Goose, sturgeon, burbot, lamb and pheasant are lovingly prepared in traditional French style. Served in the inn's magnificent dining room, these local foods enchant guests, who, in fall and winter, dine in the warm glow of a fireplace. One of the finest restaurants in the region.

Île aux Grues

Visitors to Île aux Grues can replenish themselves either at the good fast-food stand near the dock or in the dining room of one of the island's two inns. On the west side of the island, the hull of a large, beached ship proclaims: "*Oh! que ma quille éclate, Oh! que j'aille à la mer*" ("Oh! my keel is bursting, Oh! I must go to sea"). The **Bateau Ivre**, literally "the drunken ship," *($$; May to early Sep; 118 Chemin Basse-Ville, ☎418-248-0129)* has been feeding and entertaining islanders and visitors alike. Honest family cooking is served, and on some evenings a small band serenades diners. All of this takes place in the ship's interior, which has been left pretty much as it was when it sailed the seas. Needless to say, the place has a beautiful view of the river!

Saint-Eugène-de-L'Islet

Auberge des Glacis
$$$$

46 Route de la Tortue
☎ (418) 247-7486 or 877-245-2247

Auberge des Glacis serves fine French cuisine that is likely to become one of the best memories of any trip. The dining room, in a historic mill, is bright and pleasantly laid out. Diners savour meat and fish dishes as easy on the eyes as they are on the taste buds. The restaurant also serves a light lunch, which may be enjoyed on a riverside terrace. Brunch on Saturday and Sunday.

L'Islet-sur-Mer

La Paysanne
$$-$$$$

497 Chemin des Pionniers Est
☎ (418) 247-7276 or 877-660-7276

La Paysanne is set right on the riverbank and of-

Chaudière-Appalaches - Restaurants - The Seigneuries of the Côte-du-Sud

fers a spectacular view of the St. Lawrence and the north shore. Its fine French cuisine plays on regional flavours and is attractively presented.

Saint-Jean-Port-Joli

La Boustifaille
$
547 Avenue de Gaspé Ouest
☎ (418) 598-3061 or 877-598-7409
Generous Canadian cuisine is served at La Boustifaille, which is located in a barn that also hosts theatre productions in summer. Tasty meals are served in a picturesque setting and quality homemade goods, such as bread, mustard and jam, can also be bought to go.

Boulangerie Sibuet
$
22 Avenue de Gaspé Ouest
☎ (418) 598-7890
The owner of this pretty bakery comes from a long line of French artisan bakers, much to the delight of his faithful Saint-Jean-Port-Joli customers. Delicious breads and pastries await and tasty soup and sandwich combos are served at lunch time.

Café La Coureuse des Grèves
$$-$$$$
300 Route de l'Église
☎ (418) 598-9111
This café consistently offers visitors quality all around. Inside, enjoy memorable coffee in a warm ambiance enhanced by blond wood; in summer it's the terrace, which is decked out in flowers, that makes a great impression. Don't forget to ask about the legend of the *Coureuse des Grèves*.

Tour B: La Beauce

Saint-Georges

Il Mondo
$$-$$$
11615 1ʳᵉ Avenue
☎ (418) 228-4133
A restaurant-bar, Il Mondo is attractively decorated in the latest style, with ceramic, wood and wrought-iron elements. Internationally inspired cuisine, including nachos and paninis, is featured, as is delicious coffee.

La Table du Père Nature
$$$
10735 1ʳᵉ Avenue
☎ (418) 227-0888
La Table du Père Nature is definitely one of the best restaurants in town. Guests enjoy innovative French cuisine prepared with skill and sophistication. Just reading the menu is enough to make your mouth water. Game is occasionally served.

Entertainment

■ Bars and Nightclubs

Montmagny

L'Autre Bar
118 Rue Saint-Jean-Baptiste
L'Autre Bar is set in a former post office. This nightclub with a black and blue decor and terrace attracts an over-25 crowd on weekends. An attractive fresco on the bar's western wall brightens the terrace.

Le Pub du Lys
135 Rue St-Jean-Baptiste Est
☎ (418) 248-4088
The Pub du Lys is a pleasant spot to sip a Guinness while chatting with friends. The cheerful owner livens up the atmosphere every night with his special surprises. The terrace, a popular meeting place for a younger crowd, overflows during the summer season.

Saint-Georges

Le Vieux Saint-Georges
11655 1ʳᵉ Avenue
Le Vieux Saint-Georges is located inside a big, beautiful house. Its magnificent terrace is a great place to have a drink on a lovely summer evening.

Saint-Jean-Port-Joli

Café La Coureuse des Grèves
300 Route de l'Église
☎ (418) 598-9111
A small bar is located on the upper floor of Café La Coureuse des Grèves. Leather and wood furnishings and a shaded terrace provide a cozy atmosphere.

■ Festivals and Cultural Events

Montmagny

In the fall, snow geese leave the northern breeding grounds where they have spent the summer and head south toward more clement climates. On the way, they stop on the banks of the St. Lawrence River, especially in spots that provide abundant food for them, like the sand bars of Montmagny. These avian visitors are the perfect excuse to celebrate the **Festi-**

val de l'Oie Blanche *(two weeks in early to mid-Oct,* ☎*418-248-3954, www.festivaldeloie. qc.ca)*, which features all sorts of activities related to watching and learning about these beautiful migratory birds.

Saint-Jean-Port-Joli

Every year at the end of June, Saint-Jean-Port-Joli welcomes sculptors from all over the world to the lively **Internationale de la Sculpture** *(*☎*418-598-7288)*. Renowned artists create works before your eyes, some of which are then exhibited throughout the summer.

🏛 Shopping

■ Food

Lévis

Les Chocolats Favoris /

La Glacerie à l'Européenne 32 Avenue Bégin, Vieux-Lévis ☎ (418) 833-2287 Here they make and sell delicious, irresistable chocolate treats and ice cream that can be enjoyed on their terrace.

■ Arts and Crafts

Cap-Saint-Ignace

Les Créations du Berger 1008 Chemin des Pionniers Ouest ☎ (418) 246-3400 Les Créations du Berger offers a wide array of acces-

sories made of sheepskin that are most welcome in wintertime!

Montmagny

Boutique Suzette-Couillard 70 Rue St-Jean-Baptiste Est ☎ (418) 248-9642 This is a good place to find all sorts of small items for your home, as well as antiques and jewellery.

Saint-Jean-Port-Joli

Saint-Jean-Port-Joli is renowned for its crafts and many of its shops sell the work of local artisans. If this sort of shopping interests you, this town has much to offer.

There are also a few second-hand stores here, to the delight of treasure hunters, many of them along Rte. 132.

Art lovers will enjoy the charming **Sculptures en Jardin** *(768 Avenue de Gaspé Ouest,* ☎*418-598-6005)* outdoor art gallery on Route 132, between L'Islet and Saint-Jean-Port-Joli. This sculpture garden is open year-round and features some 30 works set up on the riverside. The artist's workshop and an arts-and-crafts shop are located in the adjoining house.

Boutique Jacques-Bourgault *(326 Avenue de Gaspé Ouest,* ☎*418-598-6511)* is located between Musée des Anciens Canadiens and Maison Médard-Bourgaut and sells contemporary and religious art.

Entr'Art *(812 Avenue de Gaspé Ouest,* ☎*418-598-9841)*, which is both a gallery and a shop, offers a lovely selection of sculptures, paintings and stained glass.

Saint-Vallier

Artisanat Chamard *(mid-Mar to Dec every day 8am to 5pm, mid-Jun to mid-Sep every day 8am to 9pm; 601 Avenue de Gaspé Est,* ☎*418-598-3425)* has enjoyed a great reputation for nearly half a century. Here, you can purchase woven pieces and ceramic objects, as well as First Nations and Inuit art.

At the **"Village des Artisans"** *(mid-Jun to early Sep; 329 Avenue de Gaspé Ouest,* ☎*418-598-6829)*, you will find a series of shops offering a good selection of crafts, such as pottery, wood toys, paintings, leather goods, woven pieces and sculptures.

Chaudière-Appalaches - Shopping

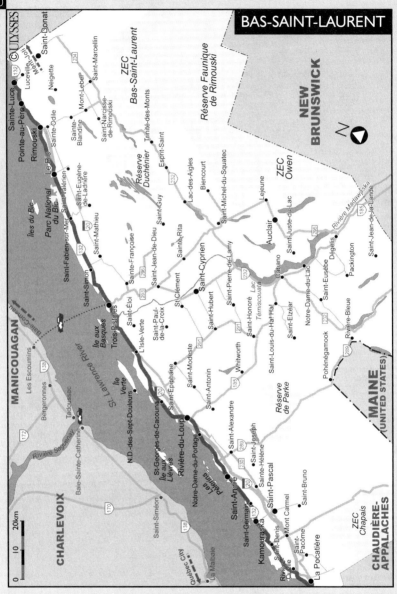

BAS-SAINT-LAURENT

Bas-Saint-Laurent

The Kamouraska Region

T he picturesque Bas-Saint-Laurent region extends east along the
St. Lawrence River from the little town of La Pocatière to the village of Sainte-Luce and south to the borders of the United States
and New Brunswick.

Aside from the particularly fertile agricultural land next to the river, much of the Bas-Saint-
Laurent is composed of farming and forestry development areas covering gently rolling
hills sparkling with lakes and streams.

A permanent European presence in the Bas-Saint-Laurent region began with the founding
of New France and continued in stages that corresponded to the development of different
economic activities. Before the end of the 17th century, colonists attracted by the fur trade
founded trading posts at Rivière-du-Loup, Bic, Cabano and Notre-Dame-du-Lac.

Much of the fertile land along the St. Lawrence River Valley was cleared and cultivated at
the beginning of the following century. The layout of farms in the region still reflects the
seigneurial system originally used to divide land among peasant farmers. Inland areas,
used for agriculture and forestry, were first colonized around 1850.

There was a final wave of settlers during the Depression of the 1930s, when unemployed
city dwellers took refuge in the country. The various periods of colonization are reflected
in the area's rich architectural heritage.

The Bas-Saint-Laurent region is located at the eastern extremity of the St. Lawrence River
Valley and was settled under the French Regime. Like elsewhere in New France, the
land along the banks of the St. Lawrence was populated first. During the 19th century,
the region became a popular vacation spot with wealthy Montrealers who had luxurious
Victorian residences built in the area.

Getting There and Getting Around

The tour of the **Kamouraska region** ★ ★ follows the St. Lawrence River from La Pocatière to Sainte-Luce and features sweeping
views of the river and the mountains of the
Charlevoix and Saguenay regions.

■ By Car

Turn off Hwy. 20 and take Rte. 132 East.
Hwys. 232, 185 and 289 run through the
Bas-St-Laurent, taking you to the heart of
this region and providing views of its spectacular forests and valleys.

■ By Ferry

Rivière-du-Loup

Cost: $12; bicycle $4.40, car $30.50
Duration: 1hr
☎ (418) 862-5094 (from Rivière-du-Loup)
☎ (514) 849-4466 (from Montréal)

☎ (418) 638-2856 (from St-Siméon)
*This ferry links Rivière-du-Loup and Saint-
Siméon in Charlevoix.*
www.travrdlstsim.com

L'Isle-Verte

The *La Richardière* ferry (*$5; bicycle $6,
car $30; May to Nov;* ☎*418-898-2843*) trans-
ports passengers from L'Isle-Verte to Notre-
Dame-des-Sept-Douleurs in 30min.

If you don't have a car, you can take a taxi-
boat (*$6;* ☎*418-898-2199*).

Trois-Pistoles

A ferry runs between Trois-Pistoles and Les
Escoumins (*$14.25 round-trip, no vehicles per-
mitted;* ☎*418-851-4676 or 866-851-4676, www.
info-basques.com*). The crossing takes 90min
and, if you're lucky, you might see some
whales. Reserve in advance for summer.

■ Bus Stations

Rivière-du-Loup
83 Boulevard Cartier
☎ (418) 862-4884

Rimouski
90 Rue Léonidas
☎ (418) 723-4923

■ Train Stations

La Pocatière
95 Avenue de la Gare
☎ (418) 856-4774 or 888-842-7245

Rimouski
57 de l'Évêché Est
☎ 800-361-5390

Rivière-du-Loup
615 Rue Lafontaine
☎ 888-842-7245

Trois-Pistoles
231 Rue de la Gare
☎ 800-361-5390

Useful Information

■ Tourist Information

Regional Office

Maison Touristique du Bas-Saint-Laurent
148 Rue Fraser, Rivière-du-Loup, G5R 1C8
☎ (418) 867-3015 or 800-563-5268
🖷 (418) 867-3245
www.tourismebas-st-laurent.com

The Kamouraska Region

Rivière-du-Loup
189 Rue Hôtel-de-Ville
☎ (418) 862-1981 or 888-825-1981

Saint-Fabien
33 Route 132 Ouest
☎ (418) 869-3333
www.parcdubic.com

Rimouski
50 Rue St-Germain Ouest
☎ (418) 723-2322 or 800-746-6875

Exploring

The Kamouraska Region
★ ★

 2 days

This tour begins near Kamouraska, but leads much further afield. However, since the region is best known as the setting of Anne Hébert's novel *Kamouraska*, this name also graces this tour, which is a logical extension of the Seigneuries of the Côte-du-Sud tour through the **Chaudière-Appalaches** region (see p 408). Together, these two tours give a good overall picture of the Côte-du-Sud region.

Take Rte. 132 E. to La Pocatière.

La Pocatière (pop. 4,468)

In 1672, the former La Pocatière seigneury was granted to Marie-Anne Juchereau, the widow of François Pollet de la Combe-Pocatière, an officer in the Carignan-Salières regiment. The land later fell into the hands of the d'Auteuil family, and then the Dionne family. The opening of a college in La Pocatière in 1827, followed by the creation of Canada's first agricultural school in 1859, transformed the town into a centre of higher education, a role it still plays today. A factory of the multinational Bombardier corporation is also located here.

Turn left on 4ᵉ Avenue, which leads to the cathedral and the former seminary, an imposing Beaux-Arts building that dates from 1922 and now houses a college (CÉGEP de la Pocatière).

Musée François-Pilote ★ *($4.50; ♿; Mon-Sat 9am to noon and 1pm to 5pm, closed Sat from Oct to May; 100 4ᵉ Avenue, ☎418-856-3145)* is located in a former convent and was named for the founder of La Pocatière's agricultural training college. It presents various collections that bring the Québec rural experience at the turn of the 20th century to life (a doctor's office, ploughing equipment, items used in the making of maple syrup, etc.).

Take Avenue Painchaud to Rte. 132 E. to Rivière-Ouelle.

Bas-Saint-Laurent - Exploring - The Kamouraska Region

Rivière-Ouelle (pop. 1,180)

This charming village, straddling the river after which it is named, was founded in 1672 by Seigneur François de la Souteillerie. In 1690, a naval detachment under the command of British admiral William Phipps tried to land at Rivière-Ouelle, but was immediately driven back by about 40 colonists led by the Abbé Pierre de Francheville.

The **Église Notre-Dame-de-Liesse** ★ and its presbytery *(early Jul to mid-Aug Tue-Fri 9am to noon and 1pm to 5pm; 100 Rue de l'Église, ☎418-856-2603)* was rebuilt in 1877 on the foundations of the previous church that had been built in 1792. It was designed by La Pocatière resident David Ouellet. The church's interior boasts a few interesting features, such as the high altar, which was imported from France, and the seven paintings by Louis Dulongpré. The next-door presbytery, which was built in 1881, is a good example of the Second Empire style, as characterised by its high sloping roof. It was sub-divided to create residential apartments in 1978.

Take Rte. 132 E. to Saint-Denis.

Saint-Denis (pop. 476)

A typical village in the heart of the Kamouraska region, Saint-Denis is dominated by its church, next to which is a monument honouring Abbé Édouard Quertier (1796-1872), the founder of the "Croix Noire de la Tempérance" (Black Cross of Temperance). It was Monseigneur de Forbin-Janson's tour of Canada in 1840-41 that led him to found the movement. He solemnly awarded a black cross to each person who promised to stop drinking.

Kamouraska ★ ★ (pop. 716)

On January 31, 1839, the young Seigneur of Kamouraska, Achille Taché, was murdered by a former friend, Doctor Holmes. The Seigneur's wife had plotted with Holmes, her lover, to do in her husband and flee to distant lands. The incident inspired Anne Hébert's novel *Kamouraska*, which was made into a film by prominent Québécois director Claude Jutra. The novel, and later the film, brought fame to the village. Kamouraska, an Algonquin word meaning

"bulrushes by the water," earned a place in the colourful history of rural Québec. For many years, the village was the eastern-most trading post on the Côte-du-Sud. Kamouraska stands on several ranges of rocky hillocks that provide a striking contrast to the adjacent coastal plain. The unusual rugged terrain is a remnant of ancient mountains long worn down by glaciers typical of the area.

The former **Palais de Justice** *($3; Jun to Sep, every day 9am to noon and 1pm to 5pm; 111 Avenue Morel, ☎418-492-9458)*, designed by architect Élzéar Charest, was built in 1888 on the site of the first courthouse in eastern Québec. Its medieval-style architecture sets it apart from other North-American courthouses, which are usually neoclassical in style. The five islands of the Kamouraska archipelago can be seen in the distance from the front steps of the Palais.

To fully appreciate the charm of the village, head down the street facing the Palais de Justice and take narrow Avenue Leblanc to the pier.

The **Musée de Kamouraska** *($5; early Jun to mid-Oct every day 9am to 5pm, mid-Oct to late May Tue-Fri 9am to 5pm, Sat-Sun 1pm to 4pm; 69 Avenue Morel, ☎418-492-9783)*, which focuses on ethnology, history and local traditions, is housed in the former Couvent de Kamouraska. A number of historic artefacts from the region are on display, including a beautiful retable designed by François-Noël Levasseur (1734); it was taken from the present village church. The present **church**, facing the museum, was built in 1914 by Joseph-Pierre Ouellet.

Maison Amable-Dionne *(no visitors; located east of the church)* was the residence of Amable Dionne, a merchant who acquired a number of seigneuries in the Côte-du-Sud area during the first half of the 19th century. His manor house in La Pocatière is gone, but his residence in Kamouraska, built in 1802, is still standing. Located east of the church, it is a long building with a neoclassical decor that was added around 1850.

For a look at the interior of the region, take the road between Kamouraska and Saint-Pascal.

Domaine Seigneurial Taché, now a bed and breakfast, once belonged to the Taché family, who acquired the Kamouraska seigneury in 1790. Shortly thereafter, they built this manor, the scene of the now-famous local drama, the murder of Achille Taché (described in the introduction to the town).

If you're interested in learning about eels, stop by the **Site d'Interprétation de l'Anguille** ★ (*$5; early Jun to mid-Oct, every day 9am to 6pm; 205 Avenue Morel,* ☎*418-492-3935*), which offers guided tours and fishing trips. The tours last about 30min. Eel fishing plays an important role in the local economy: 78% of all eels fished in the Bas-Saint-Laurent are caught in Kamouraska. These snakelike fish account for 97% of the local fishing industry. The fishing season runs from September to the end of October.

Head back to Rte. 132 and turn right.

Saint-Pascal ★ (pop. 3,669)

The little town of Saint-Pascal enjoyed a prosperous period during the 19th century thanks to the powerful current of the nearby Rivière aux Perles, which attracted entrepreneurs who built flour mills, sawmills and carding mills on the banks of the river. You'll find a few luxurious homes and a church that dates from 1845 here.

Berceau de Kamouraska (*Rte. 132 E., 3km east of Kamouraska*) is where a small chapel marks the site of the original village of Kamouraska, founded in 1674 by Sieur Morel de la Durantaye. In 1790, a powerful earthquake destroyed the village, which was rebuilt on the present site. Just off Rte. 132 is Saint-Germain-de-Kamouraska and the ruins of the Manoir de la Pointe-Sèche (1835), one of the oldest and most elegant Regency cottages in Québec.

Saint-André ★ (pop. 670)

The countryside around Saint-André is a dramatic mix of steep hills plunging straight into the river and expansive fields. The tidal flats are typically lined with tall wooden fences strung with eel nets. The nearby rocky slopes of the Îles Pèlerins provide a striking backdrop. The islands are home to thousands of birds (including cormorants and black guillemots) and a penguin colony, and if you're lucky, you might even catch a glimpse of a beluga whale or peregrine falcon.

The **Église Saint-André** ★ ★ (*late Jun to early Sep every day 9am to 11:30am and 1pm to 5pm; 128 Rue Principale,* ☎*418-493-2152*), built between 1805 and 1811, is one of the oldest churches in the region. Its Récollet design, characterized by an absence of side chapels, a narrowing of the nave around the chancels and a flat caveat, differs from the Latin-cross design usually found in Québec churches.

Halte Écologique des Battures du Kamouraska, see p 440.

Falaises d'Escalade de Saint-André, see p 442.

The tour now leaves the Kamouraska region and enters the former seigneury of Rivière-du-Loup. The first village you'll cross is **Notre-Dame-Portage**, followed by **Saint-Patrice**, whose tree-lined streets feature attractive summer residences. Vacationers came to the windy banks of the St. Lawrence to escape the hot summers of the Eastern United States. Among these houses is **Les Roches**, the former summer residence of Sir John A. Macdonald, Prime Minister of Canada from 1867 to 1873 and 1878 to 1891. The residence is now a bed and breakfast and a plaque commemorates the house's prestigious former occupant.

Rivière-du-Loup ★ (pop. 18,374)

Rivière-du-Loup is situated on several ranges of rolling hills. It has become one of the most important towns in the Bas-Saint-Laurent region, its strategic location made it a marine communication centre for the Atlantic, the St. Lawrence, Lac Témiscouata and the St. John River in New Brunswick. Later, it was an important railway centre, when the town became the eastern terminus of the Canadian train network. Rivière-du-Loup is the turn-off point for the road to New Brunswick and is linked by ferry to Saint-Siméon, on the north shore of the river.

In order to fully enjoy your visit to Rivière-du-Loup, park your car on Rue Fraser and explore the town on foot. In addition to the tour suggested here, the local tourist office has put up a series of signs explaining the history of the town and its buildings.

Manoir Fraser ★ (*$4; late Jun to mid-Oct every day 10am to 5pm; 32 Rue Fraser,* ☎*418-867-*

Bas-Saint-Laurent - **Exploring** - The Kamouraska Region

Bas-Saint-Laurent - Exploring - The Kamouraska Region

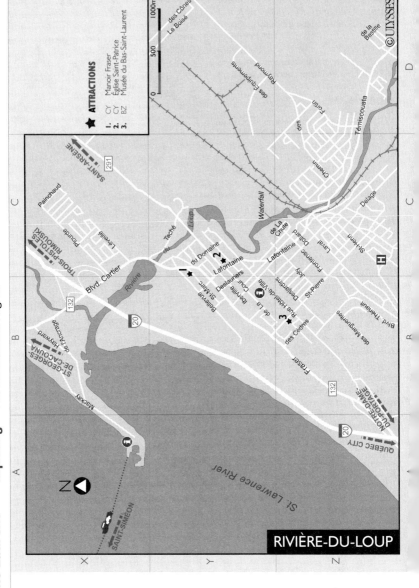

ATTRACTIONS

1. CY Manoir Fraser
2. CY Église Saint-Patrice
3. BZ Musée du Bas-Saint-Laurent

RIVIÈRE-DU-LOUP

St Lawrence River

©ULYSSES

3906, *www.manoirfraser.com*). The Rivière-du-Loup seigneury was granted to a wealthy Québec merchant named Charles Aubert de la Chesnaye in 1673. It was later passed to several owners, all of whom showed little interest in the remote region. The house, originally built for Timothy Donahue in 1830, became the Fraser family residence in 1835. In 1888, it was modified to suit contemporary tastes by Québec architect Georges-Émile Tanguay. The house was renovated in 1997 with the help of local residents, and is now open to the public with guided tours, as well as a multimedia presentation of an official dinner of the time.

Turn right on Rue du Domaine, then left on Rue Lafontaine.

Église Saint-Patrice ★ *(121 Rue Lafontaine)* was rebuilt in 1883 on the site of an earlier church erected in 1855. It houses several treasures, including a representation of the Stations of the Cross designed by Charles Huot, stained-glass windows created by the Castle company (1901) and statues by Louis Jobin. Rue de la Cour, in front of the church, leads to the **Palais de Justice** *(33 Rue de la Cour)*, the courthouse constructed in 1882 by architect Pierre Gauvreau. A number of judges and lawyers built beautiful houses on the shady streets nearby.

Head back toward Rue Fraser on Rue Deslauriers from the Palais de Justice.

The **Musée du Bas-Saint-Laurent** ★ *($5; early Jun to mid-Oct every day 10am to 6pm, off-season every day 1pm to 5pm, year-round Mon and Wed also 6pm to 9pm; 300 Rue Saint-Pierre, ☎418-862-7547, www.mbsl.qc.ca)* displays objects that are characteristic of the region, and holds contemporary art exhibits (these are often more interesting). The building itself, made of concrete, is a perfect example of not-so-attractive modern architecture.

Saint-Georges-de-Cacouna ★ (pop. 1,138)

Cacouna is an Algonquin word meaning "land of the porcupine." The Victorian mansions scattered throughout the village are reminders of a golden age of vacationing in Québec, when Cacouna was a favourite summer resort among the Montréal elite. People began to spend summers in the village in 1840, drawn by the scenery and the saltwater of the St. Lawrence (which was said to have healing properties). While the grand hotels of the 19th century, such as St. Lawrence Hall, have disappeared, Cacouna is still geared towards tourism and recreational activities.

Built for shipowner Sir Hugh Montague Allan and his family, **Villa Montrose** ★ *(no visitors allowed; 700 Rue Principale)* is now a prayer house. Its American Colonial Revival architecture demonstrates the influence of New England's seaside resorts on their Canadian counterparts.

Another of Cacouna's noteworthy houses is **Pine Cottage** *(no visitors allowed; 520 Rue Principale)*, also known as Château Vert. It was built in 1867 for the Molsons (a family of

brewers, bankers and entrepreneurs from Montréal) and is an excellent example of Gothic Revival residential architecture, little of which remains in Québec.

Église Saint-Georges and its Presbytery ★ *(455 Route de l'Église, ☎418-862-4338)* built in 1838, boasts an architecture that is typical of farmhouses in the Montréal region, characterized by decorative firebreak walls, a roof with a fairly gentle pitch and straight eaves. The Église Saint-Georges, designed by Louis-Thomas Berlinguet, was built in 1845. The church represents the culmination of a long architectural tradition in Québec that disappeared when new building styles inspired by the past were introduced to rural parishes. Visitors won't want to miss its richly decorated interior containing a number of particularly interesting pieces, including gilded altars, stained-glass windows and paintings by Italian artists Porta (over the high altar) and Pasqualoni (in the right chapel).

Site Ornithologique du Marais du Gros-Cacouna, see p 441.

L'Isle-Verte ★ (pop. 1,507)

The village of L'Isle-Verte was once an important centre of activity in the Bas-Saint-Laurent region; several buildings remain from this period. Meanwhile, life in the surrounding countryside follows a traditional pattern that keeps time with the continuing rhythm of the tides. Just off shore lies Île Verte, the island named by the explorer Jacques Cartier who, upon spotting the lush island, exclaimed, *"Quelle île verte!"*, literally "What a green island!". The only island in the Bas-Saint-Laurent inhabited year-round, Île Verte is more easily accessible than the other islands in the area.

Île Verte ★★ *($6 for access to the lighthouse, school and Musée du Squelette; late Jun to mid-Sep every day 9am to noon and 1pm to 5pm, May to late Jun and mid-Sep to mid-Oct by appointment; Route du Phare, ☎418-898-2730, www.ileverte. net)*, though 12km long, is only inhabited by 40 people. Its isolation and constant winds have discouraged many would-be colonists over the years. Basque fishers (Île aux Basques lies nearby), however, made use of the island from very early on. French missionaries were also a presence on the island; they were there to convert the Malecite First Nation who came to the island every year to trade and fish.

Around 1920, the island enjoyed an economic boom when the region became a source of a type of sea moss that was dried and used to stuff mattresses and carriage seats.

Visitors to the island get the opportunity to watch sturgeon and herring being salted in small smokehouses, taste excellent local lamb, watch beluga and blue whales and photograph the waterfowl, black ducks and herons. The **lighthouse**, located on the eastern tip of the island, is the oldest on the St. Lawrence (built in 1806). Five generations of the Lindsay family tended the lighthouse from 1827 to 1964. From the top of the tower, the view can seem almost endless.

Baie de L'Isle-Verte National Wildlife Area ★, see p 441.

Continue on Rte. 132 E. to Trois-Pistoles.

Trois-Pistoles (pop. 3,601)

According to legend, a French sailor passing through the region in the 17th century dropped his silver tumbler, worth three pistols, in the nearby river, giving it its unusual name. The name was adopted by the small industrial town that sprang up next to the river.

When the colossal **Église Notre-Dame-des-Neiges** ★★ *(late Jun to early Sep every day 9am to 4pm; 30 Rue Notre-Dame Est, ☎418-851-4949)* was built in 1887, the citizens of Trois-Pistoles believed their church would soon be named the cathedral of the diocese. This explains the size and splendour of the building, topped by three silver steeples. The honour eventually fell to the Rimouski church, the masterpiece of architect David Ouellet, to the great dismay of the congregation of Notre-Dame-des-Neiges.

Île aux Basques ★★, see p 441.

Continue on Rte. 132 E. After Saint-Simon, turn left on Rte. de Saint-Fabien-sur-Mer to approach the water, or right on Rte. Saint-Fabien.

Saint-Fabien-sur-Mer / Le Bic ★★ (pop. 2,889)

Here, the landscape suddenly becomes more rugged, giving visitors a taste of the Gaspé region farther east. In Saint-Fabien-sur-Mer, a line of cottages is wedged between the beach and a 200m-high cliff.

An octagonally shaped barn built around 1888 is located inland, in the village of Saint-Fabien. This type of farm building originated in the United States and, while interesting, proved relatively impractical and enjoyed limited popularity in Québec.

*To get to the beautiful **Parc National du Bic** ★★ (see p 441), continue along Rte. 132 E., then turn left on Chemin de l'Orignal.*

The road skirts the village of Le Bic before reaching Rimouski, the largest urban centre in the Bas-Saint-Laurent.

Rimouski (pop. 42,460) ★

At the end of the 17th century, a French merchant named René Lepage, originally from Auxerre, France, undertook the monumental task of clearing the Rimouski seigneury. The land thus became the easternmost area on the Gulf of St. Lawrence to be colonized under the French regime.

In 1919, the Abitibi-Price company opened a factory here, turning the town into an important wood-processing centre. Today, Rimouski is considered the administrative capital of eastern Québec, and prides itself on being on the cutting edge of the arts. Rimouski means "land of the moose" in Micmac.

The **Musée Régional de Rimouski** ★ *($4; Jun to Sep Wed-Fri 9:30am to 8pm, Sat-Tue 9:30am to 6pm; rest of the year Wed-Sun noon to 5pm, Thu to 9pm; 35 Rue Saint-Germain Ouest, ☎418-724-2272, www.museerimouski.qc.ca)*, a museum of art and ethnology, is housed in the former Église Saint-Germain, built between 1823 and 1827. The simple church, with its belltower set in the centre of the roof, is reminiscent of churches built under the French regime. The town's **Cathédrale St-Germain** *(111 Rue St-Germain Ouest)*, which houses a Casavant organ, and immense **Palais Épiscopal**, built in 1901, are located

RIMOUSKI

★ ATTRACTIONS

1.	BX	Musée Régional de Rimouski
2.	BX	Cathédrale St-Germain
3.	AV	Maison Lamontagne
4.	CZ	Canyon des Portes de l'Enfer

St. Lawrence River

Pier
SAINTE-FLAVIE
★ 3
132
Montée
Industrielle
Ave. Léonidas
Rue Saint-Germain Est
Blvd. Jasson
Saint-Pierre
Sasseville
Corneau
Léonard
Fiset
Blais
132
Julien-Réhel
Lepage
Saint-Jean-Baptiste Est
René-
Rue Saint-Germain Est
Saint-Pierre
Notre-Dame Est
Ave. Belzile
Lepage
St-Paul
2 ★
1 ★
Ave. de la Cathédrale
2e Rue Est
4e Rue
7e Rue
9e Rue
11e Rue
13e Rue
15e Rue
Hupé
du Père Nouvel
Saint-Louis
de l'Évêché
Sainte-Marie
Lavoie
Saint-Jean-Baptiste Ouest
Notre-Dame Ouest
Saint-Laurent
Potvin
Ave. Rouleau
Blvd.
Blvd. Arthur-Buies
Blvd.
132
Germain Ouest
de
Rimouski
Michaud
Saint-René
2e Rue Ouest
Ave. Sirois
de la Normandie
La Salle
Laval Nord
Dollard Nord
Saint-
Tessier
la
Rivière
Ross
des Geais
des Fauvettes
des Passereaux
des
LE BIC
Blvd.
de Lausanne
Tessier
Rivière
Chemin Ste-Odile
232
4 ★
20
du Coteau

| 0 | 500 | 1000m |

nearby. In the neighbouring park is a monument honouring Seigneur Lepage.

Continue on Rte. 132 E., which is known by different names here: Boulevard Saint-Germain Ouest, then Boulevard René-Lepage, and finally Boulevard du Rivage.

The **Maison Lamontagne** ★ *($3; mid-Jun to mid-Oct every day 9am to 6pm; 707 Boulevard du Rivage, Rimouski-Est, ☎418-722-4038)* is one of the only buildings east of Kamouraska dating back to the French regime, and is one of the rare examples of half-timber architecture found in Canada. The left part of the house, an alternating sequence of posts and rough masonry filler made of stones and clay, dates from 1745, while the right part was added at the beginning of the 19th century. There is an exhibition on the architecture and antique furniture of the house inside.

The **Canyon des Portes de l'Enfer** *($6.50; late Jun to early Sep every day 8:30am to 6:30pm, mid-May to late Jun and early Sep to mid-Oct every day 9:30am to 5pm; 1280 Chemin Duchénier, Saint-Narcisse-de-Rimouski, 5.6km from Saint-Narcisse-de-Rimouski along a dirt road; ☎418-735-6063, www.canyonportesenfer.qc.ca)* is a fascinating natural spectacle, especially in winter. Literally the "gates of hell," this canyon starts at the 18m Grand Saut falls, and stretches nearly 5km on either side of the Rivière Rimouski, with cliffs reaching as high as 90m in places. You can rent bicycles here.

The next stop on the tour is Pointe-au-Père. Turn left on Rue Père-Nouvel, then right on Rue du Phare.

Pointe-au-Père

The **Musée de la Mer** and the **Pointe-au-Père Lighthouse National Historic Site** ★ ★ *($10.50; early Jun to late Aug every day 9am to 6pm, early Sep to mid-Oct every day 9am to 5pm, off-season by reservation; 1034 Rue du Phare Ouest, ☎418-724-6214, www.museedelamer.qc.ca)* is also known as the Lieu National Historique du Phare-Pointe-au-Père. It was off the shores of Pointe-au-Père that the *Empress of Ireland* sank in 1914, claiming the lives of 1,012 people. The Musée de la Mer houses a fascinating collection of objects recovered from the wreck and provides a detailed account of the tragedy. The nearby light-house, which is open to the public, marks the exact spot where the river officially becomes the Gulf of St. Lawrence.

The **monument to the *Empress of Ireland*** *(on the old road, by the shore)*. On the night of May 23, 1914, more than 1,000 people perished when the *Empress of Ireland*, a Canadian Pacific ocean liner that provided service between Québec City and England, went down in the middle of the St. Lawrence. The liner had collided with a coal ship in the thick fog that occasionally blankets the river. This monument marks the burial place of just a few of the tragedy's many victims.

Sainte-Luce (pop. 2,895)

The little town of Sainte-Luce boasts some of the Bas-Saint-Laurent region's prettiest beaches. Visitors can enjoy a superb view while strolling on the banks of the St. Lawrence on the **Promenades de l'Anse-aux-Coques**. A sand-castle building contest is held here in summer and a few inns provide accommodations.

Église Sainte-Luce ★ *(20 Route du Fleuve / Route 132 Est)* was built in 1840 and received a new facade in 1914. The interior was completed between 1845 and 1850 and presents an attractive decor, with its lovely stained-glass windows (added in 1917) and a painting by Antoine Plamondon (1842).

Parks

The **Halte Écologique des Battures du Kamouraska** *($3, $8 for guided tours; early May to late Jun every day 10am to 6pm, late Jun to early Sep every day 8am to 9pm, early Sep to late Oct every day 10am to 6pm; 273 Route 132 Ouest, St-André, ☎418-493-9984, www.sebka.ca)* explains the importance of the wetlands, or *battures*, along the river, which are home to many species of birds and a number of invertebrates. Visitors can have a picnic or explore the surroundings on foot to view the salt marshes and local plants and animals. There are lookouts that command unobstructed views of the river. Sea-kayak and chalet rentals, as well as campsites are available.

Parc des Chutes et de la Croix Lumineuse ★ *(year-round, every day; from Chemin Raymond in Rivière-du-Loup, turn left on Rue Alexandre, right on Rue Bernier and left Rue Ste-Claire)* features a cliff-top belvedere that offers a splendid view of the city, river and nearby islands. Footbridges overlook the spectacular waterfall, which was once used to produce Rivière-du-Loup's electricity.

The **Baie de L'Isle-Verte National Wildlife Area ★** *(mid-Jun to mid-Sep; guided tour approx. 2hrs, reservations required; 371 Rte. 132, l'Isle-Verte, ☎418-898-2757)* protects extensive grasslands that are ideal breeding grounds for black ducks, and marshes teeming with tiny aquatic animals. Trails provide an opportunity to better enjoy this exceptional site.

The Société Provancher offers excursions to **Île aux Basques ★★** *(consult the Web site for up-to-date information on prices and activities; reservations required; Trois-Pistoles Marina, ☎418- 877-6541, www.provancher.qc.ca)*, which it safeguards as an ornithological preserve. Bird-watchers will certainly enjoy a trip here. The island is also of historical interest: a few years ago, facilities used by Basque fishers were discovered. They came here on whaling expeditions in the 15th century, over 100 years before the explorer Jacques Cartier ever set foot on the island. The remains of ovens used to melt whale blubber are also visible at several places on the riverbanks. There are 2km of trails on the island.

Parc National du Bic ★★ *($3.50; closed to cars in winter; for a schedule of summer activities, contact reception, Le Bic, ☎418-736-5035 or 800-665-6527, www.sepaq.com or www. parcdubic.com)* covers 33km² and features a jumble of coves, jutting shoreline, promontories, hills, escarpments and marshes, as well as deep bays teeming with a wide variety of plant and animal life. The park is a good place for hiking (26km of trails), cross-country skiing and mountain biking, and also has an information centre *(Jun to mid-Oct every day 9am to 5pm)*.

Outdoor Activities

■ Bird-Watching

The **Site Ornithologique du Marais du Gros-Cacouna** is a lovely place to go birding (some 130 species can be spotted here). Located at the port of Cacouna, the ornithological centre was created to harmonize local port activities with the natural riches of this marshy environment. If you'd like to take part in a 2hr guided tour of the area, contact the **Société de Conservation de la Baie de l'Isle-Verte** *(☎418-898-2757)*. There are 3km of intermediate-level hiking paths.

Île Verte and its marshes are perfect for bird-watching. Thanks to the extraordinarily rich plant and animal life here, all sorts of pleasant surprises await visitors. The **Baie de L'Isle-Verte National Wildlife Area** (see p 441), crisscrossed by hiking trails, is particularly well-suited to wildlife observation.

The **Parc National du Bic** (see p 441) is also frequented by several species of water and forest birds. You're sure to see some if you take a hike on the park's trails.

■ Cross-Country Skiing

The **Parc du Mont-Comi** *($6; RR2, Saint-Donat, 31km southeast of downtown Rimouski, ☎418-739-4858)* has 18km of cross-country trails.

■ Cruises and Whale-Watching

The **Duvetnor** *(early Jun to mid-Sep, every day; 200 Rue Hayward, Rivière-du-Loup, ☎418-867-1660, www.duvetnor.com)* company offers a variety of cruises. You can visit the Îles du Bas-Saint-Laurent and see black guillemots, eider ducks and razorbills. The cruises start at the Rivière-du-Loup marina and last anywhere from 1.5 to 8hrs, depending on your destination. You can even stay overnight in a lighthouse on one of the islands (**Phare de l'Île du Pot à l'Eau-de-Vie**, see p 444).

Croisières AML *($50; mid-Jun to mid-Oct every day 9am to 1pm, 3;30pm in high season; Exit 507 off Hwy. 20, 200 Rue Hayward, Rivière-du-Loup, ☎800-563-4643, www.croisieresaml.com)* takes visitors on whale-watching excursions aboard the *Cavalier des Mers*. You'll get to observe beluga whales, minke whales and maybe even a blue whale. Don't forget to bring along some warm clothing. Cruises last approximately three hours.

■ Cycling

The **Parc National du Bic** (*Rte. 132, 21km west of downtown Rimouski, in Saint-Fabien and Le Bic,* ☎*418-736-5035*) is without question the most beautiful place in the region to go mountain biking. It has 15km of maintained trails. Unfortunately, it is not possible to bike up the Pic Champlain. You can hike up to take in the sunset, though.

The **Parc Beauséjour** (*Boulevard de la Rivière, Route 132, Rimouski,* ☎*418-724-3167*) has several bike paths. The **Sentiers du Littoral et de la Rivière Rimouski** (*less than 2km from downtown Rimouski,* ☎*418-723-0480*) offer 7km of superb mountain-bike trails along the Rivière Rimouski and through a swamp.

■ Kayaking

The **Société Écologique des Battures du Kamouraska (SEBKA)** (*St-André,* ☎*418-493-9984,*

www.sebka.ca) offers sea-kayaking expeditions in the Kamouraska archipelago with interpretive guides. Departures from the Kamouraska pier.

Rivi-Air Aventure (*mid-May to mid-Oct every day departures at 8pm, 1pm and 5:30pm; Le Bic marina, Route 132,* ☎*418-723-5252, www.rivi-air.qc.ca*) arranges solo and group sea-kayaking excursions, helping visitors explore the Parc du Bic, its beaches, ponds and cliffs.

■ Rock-Climbing

There is a magnificent place to go climbing in Saint-André-de-Kamouraska. The climbing cliffs known as the **Falaises d'Escalade de Saint-André** (*for information contact the SEBKA:* ☎*418-493-9984, www.sebka.ca*) are composed of an extremely hard stone that makes them safe to climb. Those daring enough to scale them will be rewarded with an extraordinary view of the area. Follow the signs to get there.

Accommodations

The Kamouraska Region

Kamouraska

Gîte chez Jean et Nicole
$$ bkfst incl.
pb/sb
81 Avenue Morel, Route 132
☎ (418) 492-2921
www3.sympatico.ca/titesouris/gite.
html
Jean and Nicole opened a four-room B&B in their lovingly maintained cen-tury-old home for the sheer pleasure of meeting people. They serve memor-able breakfasts, are located near the village and, more importantly, near the sea. Non-smoking.

Saint-André

La Solaillerie
$$$ bkfst incl.
♨
112 Rue Principale
☎ (418) 493-2914
🖷 (418) 493-2243
www.aubergelasolaillerie.com
A large house dating from the late 19th century, La Solaillerie has a magnifi-cent white facade and a big wraparound porch on the second storey. Inside, the sumptuous decor evokes the era in which the house was built. The five guest rooms are cozy, comfort-able and tastefully decorat-ed in classic "old inn" trad-ition. An extra pavilion with six extra rooms was later added, with warmly decor-ated rooms that are more intimate. As far as the food is concerned, gourmets can expect some delightful sur-prises (see p 446).

Bas-Saint-Laurent - Accommodations - The Kamouraska Region

Rivière-du-Loup

Auberge de Jeunesse Internationale
$ bkfst incl.
46 Rue de l'Hôtel-de-Ville
☎ (418) 862-7566
▤ (418) 862-1843
www.hihostels.ca

The Auberge de Jeunesse Internationale in Rivière-du-Loup is a youth hostel that offers the most affordable accommodations in town. The rooms are dorm-style and simple but clean.

Auberge de la Pointe
$$-$$$
🛏🚗🏊⛱♨🍴☕◎
closed Nov to Apr
10 Boulevard Cartier
☎ (418) 862-3514 or 800-463-1222
▤ (418) 862-1882
www.auberge-de-la-pointe.qc.ca

The Auberge de la Pointe is particularly well-located. In addition to comfortable rooms, guests can indulge in a hydrotherapy, algotherapy or massage-therapy session, and enjoy spectacular sunsets from the balcony. There is also a summer theatre.

Hôtel Lévesque
$$$
≡◎🛏🏊❄🍴♨≈
171 Rue Fraser
☎ (418) 862-6927 or 800-463-1236
▤ (418) 867-5827
www.hotellevesque.com

Hôtel Lévesque takes full advantage of its natural setting and is surrounded by a superb landscaped garden. The rooms are spacious and cozy, and some provide nice views of the St. Lawrence River.

Île du Pot à L'Eau-de-Vie

Phare de l'Île du Pot à l'Eau-de-Vie
$$$$/person, incl. fb and cruise
sb
200 Rue Hayward, Rivière-du-Loup
☎ (418) 867-1660 or 877-867-1660
▤ (418) 867-3639
www.duvetnor.com

The Phare de l'Île du Pot à L'Eau-de-Vie, a lighthouse on an island in the middle of the St. Lawrence, exposes its white facade and red roof to the four winds. Owned by Duvetnor, a non-profit organization dedicated to protecting birds, the Pot à L'Eau-de-Vie archipelago is swarming with water birds. Duvetnor offers package rates that include accommodations, meals and a cruise on the river with a naturalist guide. The lighthouse, over a century old, has been carefully restored. It has three cozy guest rooms and delicious food is served. If you're looking for a peaceful atmosphere, this is the place to stay.

Saint-Antonin

Camping chez Jean
$
🚗≈
434 Rue Principale, Exit 499 off Hwy. 20
☎ (418) 862-3081

Camping Chez Jean is a campground with 119 sites, a swimming pool, laundry facilities and a snack bar.

Île Verte

Les Maisons du Phare
$$ bkfst incl
sb
28B Chemin du Phare
☎ (418) 898-2730
▤ (418) 898-4002
www.ileverte.net

On lovely Île Verte, La Maison des Phares offers you the pleasure of staying in one of the two former lighthouse-keeper houses. There is a beach.

Trois-Pistoles

Camping Plage Trois-Pistoles
$
🚗≈
late May to late Sep
130 Route 132 Est
☎ (418) 851-2403
▤ (418) 851-4890

Camping Plage Trois-Pistoles is a 5min drive from Trois-Pistoles. Its unique setting on the banks of the St. Lawrence offers some of the most beautiful panoramic views of the region. You can go hiking along the beach or in the nearby woods. In August, at low tide, you can see eel-catching nets stretched out along the river, adding a picturesque touch to the scenery. Laundry facilities on site.

La Ferme Paysagée
$ bkfst incl.
sb
from Trois-Pistoles, turn right onto Rte. 293 S. and continue 4km past the church of St-Jean-de-Dieu
☎ (418) 963-3315
▤ (418) 963-2903

La Ferme Paysagée, a bed and breakfast on a farm, is popular with families and animal lovers. Deer, goats, sheep and even llamas are all kept on the farm.

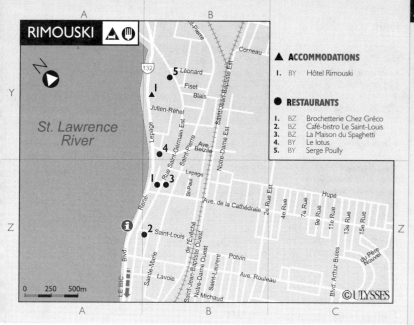

RIMOUSKI

▲ ACCOMMODATIONS

1. BY Hôtel Rimouski

● RESTAURANTS

1. BZ Brochetterie Chez Gréco
2. BZ Café-bistro Le Saint-Louis
3. BZ La Maison du Spaghetti
4. BY Le lotus
5. BY Serge Poully

©ULYSSES

Motel Trois-Pistoles

$$

≡ ☞ ♨

64 Route 132 Ouest
☎ (418) 851-2563
🖷 (418) 851-0893

The Motel Trois-Pistoles has 30 or so comfortable rooms, some affording a lovely view of the river; the sunsets from this spot are absolutely magnificent.

Saint-Simon

Auberge Saint-Simon

$$

♨

early Jun to mid-Oct
18 Rue Principale
☎ (418) 738-2971
🖷 (418) 736-4902

Built in 1830, the charming Auberge Saint-Simon is a large house with a mansard roof typical of this period. The nine tastefully decorated rooms are rich in historical atmosphere.

Le Bic

Camping du Bic

$

3382 Route 132 Ouest, Parc National du Bic
☎ (418) 736-5035 or 800-665-6527
www.parcdubic.com

Camping du Bic has approximately 100 campsites in magnificent Parc National du Bic, where all kinds of outdoor activities are possible. Unfortunately, the noise from the highway can be heard at most of these campsites, even though the road is not visible.

Auberge du Mange Grenouille

$$-$$$ bkfst incl.

pb/sb ♨ ✕

148 Rue Ste-Cécile
☎ (418) 736-5656
🖷 (418) 736-5657
www.aubergedumangegrenouille.
qc.ca

The Auberge du Mange Grenouille has a good reputation in Québec and beyond. Guests are warmly welcomed, served succulent food (see p 447), and stay in 22 cozy rooms decorated with antiques. The inn also hosts murder-mystery evenings.

Rimouski

Hôtel Rimouski

$$-$$$

≡ ☞ ☼ ✳ ♨ ◎

225 Boulevard René-Lepage Est
☎ (418) 725-5000 or 800-463-0755
🖷 (418) 725-5725
www.hotelrimouski.com

Hôtel Rimouski has a unique design; its big staircase and long swimming pool in the lobby will appeal to many visitors. Children under 18 can stay in their parents' room for free.

Pointe-au-Père

Auberge La Marée Douce
$$$ bkfst incl.
Ⓦ

1329 Boulevard Ste-Anne
☎ (418) 722-0822
🖷 (418) 723-4512
www.giteetaubergedupassant.com/
mareedouce

The Auberge La Marée Douce is a riverside inn located in Pointe-au-Père, near the Musée de la Mer. Built in 1860, it has comfortable rooms, each with its own decor. There are also some extra rooms in a modern pavilion, as well as a beach.

Sainte-Luce

Auberge Sainte-Luce
$$
🍽 Ⓦ

46 Route du Fleuve Ouest
☎ (418) 739-4955
🖷 (418) 739-4923

Auberge Sainte-Luce is a converted century-old house with simple but comfortable rooms. Guests also have access to a lookout and a beach.

Ⓦ
Restaurants

The Kamouraska Region

Saint-André

La Solaillerie
$$$-$$$$
112 Rue Principale
☎ (418) 493-2914

The dining room at La Solaillerie has been carefully

decorated to highlight the historic character of the old house in which it is located. In this inviting setting, guests savour excellent cuisine lovingly prepared and served by the owners of the inn. Drawing his inspiration from a French culinary repertoire, the chef uses fresh regional ingredients like quail, lamb, and fresh and smoked salmon to create new dishes according to his fancy. Reservations required.

Notre-Dame-du-Portage

L'Estran Auberge sur Mer
$$$-$$$$
363 Route du Fleuve
☎ 888-622-0642

The dining room at l'Estran Auberge sur Mer has a marvellous view of the river, which really does begin to resemble the sea here. The fine cuisine will enrapture the most exacting customers. Fish and seafood are served all summer long, accompanied by whatever is in season. In autumn, game is featured on the menu. Reservations required.

Rivière-du-Loup

La Terrasse
$$-$$$
171 Rue Fraser
☎ (418) 862-6927

The restaurant at Hôtel Lévesque serves a variety of delicious Italian and regional dishes, as well as smoked salmon prepared according to a traditional method in the hotel's smokehouse. Children's menu available.

Le Saint-Patrice
$$$
169 Rue Fraser
☎ (418) 862-9895

Le Saint-Patrice is one of the best restaurants in town. Fish, seafood, rabbit and lamb are its specialties. At the same address, **Le Novelo** *($$)* serves pasta and thin-crust pizza in a bistro setting, and **La Romance** *($$$)* specializes in fondue.

Trois-Pistoles

L'ensoleillé
$$-$$$
138 Rue Notre-Dame Ouest
☎ (418) 851-2889

The vegetarian café/restaurant L'ensoleillé has a very simple à-la-carte menu, featuring healthy vegetarian meals.

Le Michalie
$$$
55 Rue Notre-Dame Est
☎ (418) 851-4011

Le Michalie is a charming little restaurant serving some of the best regional cuisine, as well as gourmet Italian food.

Saint-Fabien

Auberge Saint-Simon
$$$
18 Rue Principale
☎ (418) 738-2971

In the warm, traditional atmosphere of the Auberge Saint-Simon, guests will enjoy another excellent Bas-Saint-Laurent dining experience. Rabbit, lamb, halibut and seafood are paired with fresh vegetables grown in the restaurant's garden.

Le Bic

Auberge du Mange Grenouille
$$$-$$$$
148 Rue Ste-Cécile
☎ (418) 736-5656

The Auberge du Mange Grenouille is one of the best restaurants in the Bas-Saint-Laurent. It was once a general store and is decorated with old furniture carefully chosen to complement the architecture. Guests are offered a choice of six daily *tables d'hôte* that include fowl, game, lamb and fish dishes. Everything served here is delicious, and the service is always attentive.

Rimouski

La Maison du Spaghetti
$$-$$$
35 Rue St-Germain Est
☎ (418) 723-6010

La Maison du Spaghetti's eclectic menu attracts its fair share of Rimouski students, residents and tourists.

Brochetterie Chez Gréco
$$-$$$
40 Rue St-Germain Est
☎ (418) 724-2804

Brochetterie Chez Gréco is a typical Greek restaurant. You can expect to eat tasty brochettes and huge seafood platters served with pasta.

Le Lotus
$$$
143 Avenue Belzile
☎ (418) 725-0822

If you're in the mood for Thai, Vietnamese or Cambodian food, head to Le Lotus, were delicious, exotic and well-presented dishes are served. Every day, in addition to the *à la carte* menu, guests have a

choice between a Mandarin dinner, a gastronomic dinner and a "super gastronomic" dinner, each of which includes four or five courses. Reservations recommended.

Café-Bistro Le Saint-Louis
$$$
97 Rue St-Louis
☎ (418) 723-7979

The Café-Bistro Le Saint-Louis looks just like its Parisian cousins and is filled with all the same aromas. It offers a large selection of imported beer and microbrews. The menu, which changes daily, is delicious, and the dishes are served in a pleasant atmosphere.

Serge Poully
$$$-$$$$
284 Rue St-Germain Est
☎ (418) 723-3038

Serge Poully serves game, seafood, steak and French specialties. The relaxed atmosphere and attentive service make this the perfect place for an intimate dinner for two.

Pointe-au-Père

Auberge La Marée Douce
$$$
1329 Rue Ste-Anne
☎ (418) 722-0822

Auberge La Marée Douce is located in a beautiful ancestral home. Its dining room's specialties include delicious seafood and various French classics.

Sainte-Luce

Café-Bistro L'Anse-aux-Coques
$$$
31 Route du Fleuve Ouest
☎ (418) 739-4815

This pleasant little café enjoys a superb riverside setting in Sainte-Luce and

serves steaks, submarines, quiches, fish and seafood.

Entertainment

■ Bars

Rimouski

Chiffre de Nuit
204 Avenue de la Cathédrale

The Chiffre de Nuit nightclub spreads over two floors and attracts a large crowd of Rimouski students.

Sens Unique
160 Avenue de la Cathédrale
☎ (418) 722-9400

The music and outdoor seating at the Sens Unique make this one of the most appealing places in Rimouski. The very diverse clientele ranges in age from 18 to 45.

■ Festivals and Cultural Events

Rimouski

The **Festi-Jazz** *(☎418-724-7844, www.festijazzrimouski.com)* is a series of some 20 shows by jazz musicians from Québec and abroad. Some shows are presented in bars and theatres, others on the street. The festival lasts four days and is always held on Labour Day weekend (the first weekend of September).

The **Carrousel International du Film de Rimouski** *(☎418-722-0103, www.carrousel.qc.ca)* is a film festival for the younger generation. It takes place the third week of September and lasts

Bas-Saint-Laurent - Entertainment

seven days, during which about 40 films are shown.

■ Theatres

Le Bic

The **Théâtre Les Gens d'en Bas** (*50 Route du Golf, 16km west of downtown Rimouski, ☎418-736-4141*) puts on at least one play each summer. The theatre boasts a magnificent natural setting.

Shopping

■ Arts and Crafts

Rimouski

La Samare (*84 Rue St-Germain Ouest, ☎418-723-0242*) has a large array of articles made of fish skin, as well as a wide selection of carvings, vases and other objects, all handcrafted by Inuit artisans.

Québec Architecture

Québec architecture is at once the result of a population adapting to
a difficult climate and a synthesis of French, British and American
influences. The photos in this section illustrate the evolution of Québec
architecture, including both simple buildings erected by farmers and
elaborate works designed by world-renowned architects.

For many years, Québec invested all of its creative energies in the interior decors of its churches, which resulted in veritable woodworking masterpieces. The choir of Église de la Visitation du Sault-au-Récollet (Montréal), designed by Philippe Liébert and David-Fleury David between 1764 and 1818, skillfully combines Louis XV and Louis XVI styles. The traditional combination of white and gold is embellished with bright colours.

Marché Bonsecours, erected between 1845 and 1850, reflects mid-19th-century British colonial ambitions in Montréal. Its metallic dome, formidable portico, Tuscan pillars and sash windows are typically neoclassical—a very popular style throughout the British Empire during the first half of the 19th century.

The inhabitants' sense of insecurity, along with the king's desire to better protect his colony, resulted in the towns and villages of New France being surrounded by wood or stone fortresses. A number of forts designed to slow down the enemy were also established. Indeed, the fortresses had to resist both the surprise attacks of hostile Aboriginal peoples as well as the British army, which would arrive by sea on war ships.

Throughout the 19th century, Quebecers endeavored to adapt to the climatic extremes of the St. Lawrence Valley by developing what was to become a traditional Québec architecture. For example, they raised the masonry foundation and adorned their houses with long verandas to prevent snow from piling on window sills. The decreased pitch of the roof kept snow from falling off, so it could serve as insulation.

What makes Vieux Québec so charming is not only its great monuments but also its houses, each of which has its own story to tell. It is enjoyable to stroll through its narrow streets and observe the minute details of this compact architecture, losing oneself in an urban landscape that is quite unusual to most North Americans.

Colourful Victorian homes such as these, with impossibly steep or contorted exterior staircases, have become emblematic of Montréal.

The Château Frontenac, a magnificent hotel, symbolizes Québec City. Designed by American architect Bruce Price, its style was influenced both by the castles of Scotland and those of the Loire region of France.

In 1851, Father Joseph Déziel decided to build a large Catholic church for his rapidly expanding city. It was Thomas Baillargé, the architect who designed many of Québec City's churches, who drew up the plans. The architecture featured at the Notre-Dame de Lévis church is a beautiful example of the Québécois neoclassical tendency, combining the French and English styles. The interior, divided into three naves, features high galleries with columns, and outside, a plaque marks the place where English cannons bombarded Québec City in 1759.

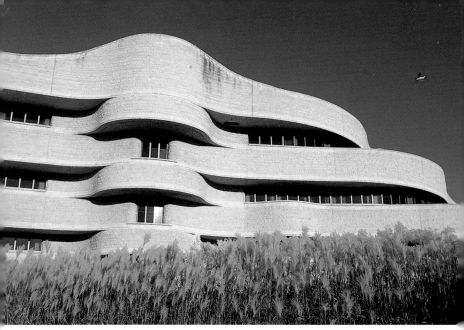

The unique architecture of the Canadian Museum of Civilization in Gatineau was designed by Douglas Cardinal, an Aboriginal architect from Alberta. This museum is composed of two unusual, organically shaped structures.

The unique architecture of Montréal's Habitat '67, designed by Moshe Safdie, makes these posh condominiums resemble a pile of blocks.

Gaspésie

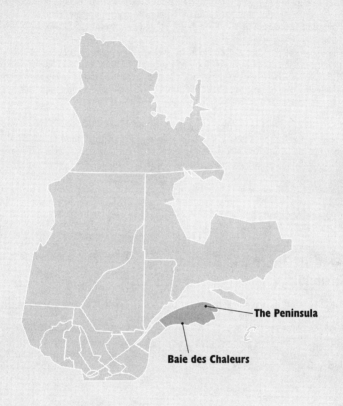

The Peninsula

Baie des Chaleurs

U nforgettable memories are cherished by the many Quebecers who have travelled to the mythical land of Gaspésie, in the easternmost part of Québec.

People dream of touring Gaspésie and discovering its magnificent coastal landscape, where the Chic-Chocs mountains plunge abruptly into the cold waters of the St. Lawrence. They dream of going all the way to the famous Percé rock, heading out to sea toward Île Bonaventure, visiting the extraordinary Forillon National Park, and then slowly returning along Baie des Chaleurs and through the valley of Rivière Matapédia in the hinterland.

This beautiful part of Québec, with its strikingly picturesque scenery, is inhabited by friendly, fascinating people, who still rely mainly on the sea for their living. The majority of the 85,000 Gaspesians live in small villages along the coast, leaving the centre of the peninsula covered with dense Boreal forest. The highest peak in southern Québec lies here, in the part of the Appalachians known as the Chic-Chocs.

The word *Gaspé* means "land's end" in the language of the Micmacs, who have been living in this region for thousands of years. Despite its isolation, the peninsula has attracted fishers from many different places over the centuries, particularly Acadians driven from their lands by the British in 1755. Its population is now primarily Francophone.

Gaspésie's main attractions are its rugged, mountainous landscapes and the Gulf of St. Lawrence, which is so huge that it might as well be the ocean. The coastline is studded with a string of fishing villages, leaving the interior devoid of towns and roads, much as it was when Jacques Cartier arrived in 1534.

Getting There and Getting Around

The two tours in this chapter, **Tour A: The Peninsula** ★★ and **Tour B: Baie des Chaleurs** ★, follow the coastline.

■ By Car

Tour A: The Peninsula

To start this tour, head to Sainte-Flavie via Aut. Jean-Lesage (Aut. 20). From there, Rout 132 hugs the shore of the St. Lawrence River all the way to Percé, passing through Matane, Sainte-Anne-des-Monts and Gaspé. Once in L'Anse-Pleureuse, you can take a detour through Murdochville.

Tour B: Baie des Chaleurs

This tour follows the road along the shore of the Baie des Chaleurs. In Matapédia, the tour heads inland to Causapscal.

■ By Ferry

Tour A: The Peninsula

Baie-Comeau - Matane *($12.75, cars $29.95, motorcycles $22.45;* ☎*418-562-2500 or 877-562-6560)*: the crossing takes 2hrs 30min. The schedule varies from year to year so be sure to check when planning your trip. Reservations are a good idea during summer.

Godbout - Matane *($12.75, cars $29.95, motorcycles $22.45;* ☎*418-562-2500 or 877-562-6560)*: the crossing takes 2hrs 10min. Reservations are a good idea during summer.

■ Bus Stations

Tour A: The Peninsula

Matane
521 Avenue du Phare Est (Irving station)
☎ (418) 562-4085

Sainte-Anne-des-Monts
90 Boulevard Sainte-Anne
☎ (418) 763-9176

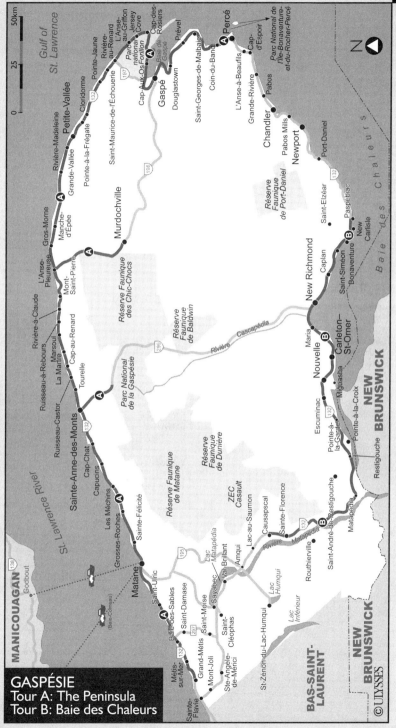

451

Gaspé
20 Rue Adams
☎ (418) 368-1888

Percé
L'Anse-à-Beaufils (Ultramar station)
☎ (418) 782-5417

Tour B: Baie des Chaleurs

Bonaventure
118 Avenue Grand-Pré (Motel Grand-Pré)
☎ (418) 534-2053

Carleton-Saint-Omer
561 Boulevard Perron
☎ (418) 364-7000

Amqui
219 Boulevard Saint-Benoit Est
☎ (418) 629-6767

■ Train Stations

Tour A: The Peninsula

Gaspé
8 Boulevard Marina
☎ (418) 368-4313

Percé
44 L'Anse-à-Beaufils
☎ 800-361-5390

Tour B: Baie des Chaleurs

Via Rail
☎ 800-361-5390
www.viarail.ca

Bonaventure
Rue de la Gare (near Avenue Grand-Pré)

Carleton
Rue de la Gare

Matapédia
10 Rue MacDonnell

Useful Information

■ Tourist Information

Regional Office

Association Touristique de la Gaspésie
357 Route de la Mer, Sainte-Flavie, G0J 2L0
☎ (418) 775-2223 or 800-463-0323
🖶 (418) 775-2234
www.tourisme-gaspesie.com

Tour A: The Peninsula

Sainte-Flavie
see above

Matane
968 Avenue du Phare Ouest
☎ (418) 562-1065

Gaspé
27 Boulevard York Est
☎ (418) 368-6335

Tour B: Baie des Chaleurs

Percé
142 Route 132 Ouest
☎ (418) 782-5448

Carleton-Saint-Omer
629 Boulevard Perron
☎ (418) 364-3544

Pointe-à-la-Croix
1830 Rue Principale
☎ (418) 788-5670

Exploring

Tour A: The Peninsula
★ ★

 2 to 3 days

Europeans were fishing in the Gulf of the St. Lawrence before they even set foot on the North-American continent. Today, not a trace remains of the camps they set up along the coast, but it is possible to imagine their reaction to this unknown continent and their encounters with the Aboriginal population. While touring the peninsula, visitors will pass alongside steep cliffs before reaching the hospitable areas where Jacques Cartier took possession of the land in the name of the king of France.

Grand-Métis ★ (pop. 279)

Grand-Métis is blessed with a micro-climate that once attracted wealthy summer visitors to the area, and also made it possible for horticulturist Elsie Reford to plant a landscape garden here. The garden is now the town's main attraction. It contains a number of species of trees and flowers that cannot be found anywhere else at this latitude in North America. The word "Métis" is derived from the Malecite name for the area, "Mitis," meaning "little poplar."

The **Jardins de Métis** ★★★ *($14; &; early Jul to late Aug every day 8:30am to 6:30pm; Jun, Sep and Oct every day 8:30am to 5pm; 200 Route 132, ☎418-775-2221, www.jardinsmetis.com)* are among Québec's most beautiful gardens, and their name is world-renowned. The gardens are also a national historic site. In 1927, Elsie Stephen Meighen Reford inherited an estate from her uncle, Lord Mount Stephen, who had made his fortune by investing in the Canadian Pacific transcontinental railroad. The following year, she began laying out a landscape garden that she maintained and expanded until her death in 1954. Seven years later, the government of Québec purchased the estate and opened it to the public. The gardens are now owned by the grandson of their founder, Alexander Reford, who has endowed them with new energy thanks to achievements like the International Garden Festival.

The garden is divided into eight distinct ornamental sections: the Floral Massif, the Rock Garden, the Rhododendron Garden, the Royal Walkway, the Primrose Garden, the Crab Apple Garden, the *Muret* (low wall) overlooking Baie de Mitis, and the Underbrush, which contains a collection of indigenous plants. The mosquitoes are voracious here, so don't forget your insect repellent.

Villa Reford ★★ *(mid-Jun to mid-Oct every day 9am to 5pm; in the Jardins de Métis, ☎418-775-3165)*, a 37-room villa set in the midst of

the Jardins de Métis, offers a glimpse of what life was like for early 20th-century Métissiens. Visitors can tour a number of rooms, the servants' quarters, the chapel, the general store, the school and the doctor's office. There is also a restaurant and gift shop.

Continue along Rte. 132 E. towards Matane. A brief detour through Métis-sur-Mer provides an opportunity to get closer to the water.

Métis-sur-Mer ★ (pop. 614)

At the turn of the 20th century, this resort area, also known as Métis Beach, was a favourite among the professors of Montréal's McGill University, who rented elegant seaside cottages here for the summer vacation. Wealthy British families also built large New England–style homes in the area, attracted by the beauty of the landscape and the presence of a small Scottish community, established here in 1820 by John Mc-Nider, the seigneur of Métis. The village's harmonious appearance and high-quality wooden architecture set it apart from the surrounding municipalities.

Most Scots are members of the Presbyterian Church, the official church of Scotland, though a number of communities merged with the Methodists in the early 20th century to form the United Church; Métis-sur-Mer was one of these. Erected in 1874, the **Presbyterian Chapel** *(on the way into the village)* resembles a colonial Catholic church due to the shape of its doors, windows and belltower.

The road then leads through Les Boules and the charming village of Baie-des-Sables before reaching Saint-Ulric and Matane.

Matane (pop. 14,862)

The main attraction in Matane, whose name means "beaver pond" in Micmac, is salmon and famous local shrimp, which are celebrated at an annual festival. The town is the region's administrative centre and economic mainspring thanks to its diversified industry based on fishing, lumber, cement-making, oil refining and shipping. During World War II, German submarines came all the way to the town pier.

Gaspésie - Exploring - The Peninsula

MATANE

© ULYSSES

ATTRACTIONS

1.	CX	Old lighthouse
2.	DY	Barrage Mathieu-D'Amours and migratory passage
3.	DX	Église Saint-Jérôme

St. Lawrence River

GODBOUT

BAIE-COMEAU

RIMOUSKI

Ave. du Phare Est

GASPÉ

0   350   700m

Ave. du Phare Ouest

de Matane-sur-Mer

du Barachois

St-Robert

du Vallon

Simard

Meunier

du Buisson

Blvd. Jacques-Cartier

de Courtemanche

Dionne

Ave. D'Amour

Champlain

de la Marée

Boutard

du Sault

Boucher

Blvd. du Père-Lamarche

Ave. St-Rédempteur

du Bosquet

St-Joseph

Côté

Bélanger

Bouillon

Collin

Matane

Ave. St-Jérôme

Gagnon

Fournier

Ave. de la Fabrique

Fraser

St-Christophe

St-Pierre

Soucy

Bergeron

Price

Ave. St-Jérôme

Parc des Îles

Rivière Matane

Ave. D'Amour

Ave. Desjardins

Belvédère

Ave. Ruisseau

des Pins

Trembles

de Bois-Joli

W. Russel

St-Aubin

Grant

Paradis

Blvd. Dion

Dion

Fournier

St-Pierre

St-Jean

Blvd. Dion

Quimper

Goyer

St-Jean

Gaspé

Ave. Henri-Dunant

Ave. Henri-Dunant

du Parc Industriel

Brillant

Duette

Savard

du Port

du Port

Réserve Faunique de Matane

195

132

132

195

195

The **old lighthouse** *(968 Avenue du Phare)*, built in 1911 and no longer in use, greets visitors on their way into town. The lighthouse keeper's house now serves as a tourist office and small museum of local history.

The Rivière Matane runs through the centre of town. Here, visitors will find the **Barrage Mathieu-D'Amours ★** *(near Parc des Îles)*, a dam, along with a **migratory passage** *($2)* intended to help salmon swim upriver to spawn. From an observation area located below water level, visitors can take in the fascinating spectacle of the salmon struggling furiously against the current. At nearby **Parc des Îles**, there is a beach, a picnic area and an outdoor theatre.

Religious architecture in Québec was greatly influenced by a French monk and architect named Dom Bellot. However, before this man had even made his first trip to Canada in 1934, two architects by the name of Paul Rousseau and Philippe Côté had the **Église Saint-Jérôme ★** *(527 Avenue St-Jérôme)* built, one of the precursors of modern religious art in Québec. The architects re-used the walls of the town's former church, which was consumed by flames in 1932. Because the ruins of the devastated church were too fragile to support the new structure, the full weight of the roof was placed on large, concrete parabolic arches. In the chancel, visitors will see a large mural by painter Lucien Martial.

Visitors can take an optional trip inland to the **Réserve Faunique de Matane** *(see p 464), a wildlife reserve located about an hour's drive from town.*

Return to Rte. 132 E. On the way to Cap-Chat and Sainte-Anne-des-Monts, the road runs alongside charming fishing villages with evocative names like Sainte-Félicité, L'Anse-à-la-Croix (Cross Cove), Grosses-Roches (Big Rocks) and Les Méchins (a derivative of the French word for "mean," "méchant").

Cap-Chat (pop. 2,821)

According to some, this little town owes its name to Champlain, who christened the area "Cap de Chatte" in honour of Commander de Chatte, the King's Lieutenant-General. Still others maintain that the name was inspired by a rock near the lighthouse that is shaped like a crouching cat (*chat* is the French word for cat). Erected in 1916, **Église Saint-Norbert** is the only sizable monument in the centre of town. Romanesque Revival in style, it is one of only a few churches east of Matane that is not built out of wood.

Electricity can be produced in a variety of ways. One of the most original and least employed methods is without question the wind turbine, or *éolienne* in French. The village of Cap-Chat is an ideal location for the production of wind energy, and its many turbines create a somewhat supernatural landscape. The **Centre d'Interprétation de l'Énergie Éolienne Éole ★** *($12; early Jun to Oct every day 8:30am to 5pm; Route 132, ☎418-786-5719)* is home to a 110m-high turbine, the tallest and strongest in the world, as well as the largest concentration of turbines in eastern Canada.

The **Centre d'Interprétation du Vent et de la Mer Le Tryton** *($8; Jun to Sep every day 9am to 5pm; 9 Route du Phare, near Cap-Chat, ☎418-786-5543)*, located alongside a lighthouse built in 1871, traces the history of Cap-Chat and its ties to the wind and the Gulf of St. Lawrence. There are pleasant trails leading to the sea. The centre also houses the **Musée Germain-Lemieux**, a naval history museum.

Sainte-Anne-des-Monts ★ (pop. 6,986)

There are several interesting buildings in this town, including **Église Sainte-Anne**, built by Louis-Napoléon Audet in 1939, and the former Palais de Justice (courthouse), erected in 1885. Visitors will also find a number of lovely homes, built for various ship captains and industrialists. Sainte-Anne-des Monts is the point of departure for excursions to Rivière Sainte-Anne and the forests of Parc National de la Gaspésie and the Réserve Faunique des Chic-Chocs.

At **Centre de Découverte Explorama ★** *($10; Jun to Oct every day 9am to 6pm; 1 Rue du Quai, ☎418-763-2500, www.explorama.org)*, visitors can learn more about the Gaspé peninsula and its close links to the sea and the mountains through interpretive activities. Gift shop onsite.

From here, it is possible to set off on a side trip into the heart of the peninsula. To do so, take Rte. 299, *which leads to the entrance of **Parc National de la Gaspésie*** ★ ★ ★ *(see p 464).*

Back on Rte. 132, visitors will pass through the villages of Tourelle, Ruisseau-Castor and Cap-au-Renard on the way to La Martre.

From La Martre to L'Anse-Pleureuse ★ ★

With its **wooden church** (1914) and **lighthouse** (1906), La Martre is a typical fishing village, located on the edge of the coastal plain. Beyond this point, the coast becomes much steeper and more jagged. The road zigzags into deep bays and out onto windswept capes. In a number of places, it passes so close to the sea that the waves lap at the asphalt in rough weather. It is worth exploring some of the few roads leading inland from the villages, especially the gravel ones alongside Rivière à Claude and Rivière Mont-Saint-Pierre, to fully appreciate the ruggedness of the landscape and the might of the rivers.

Musée des Phares ★ *($3; early Jun to late Sep every day 9am to 5pm; 10 Avenue du Phare, ☎418-288-5698),* in the red octagonal former lighthouse and the equally colourful lighthouse keeper's house, presents an interesting exhibit on the history and operation of lighthouses in Gaspésie.

*The road then leads through Marsoui, Ruisseau-à-Rebours, Rivière-à-Claude, Mont-Saint-Pierre, where you will find launching pads for hang-gliding, and finally, a village whose name is like something out of a ghost story, **L'Anse-Pleureuse** (Weeping Cove). From here, it is possible to take a side trip to **Murdochville**, the so-called "copper capital" of Québec, and the only sizable inland town in Gaspésie (Rte. 198).*

Murdochville (pop. 836)

Murdochville is located in the middle of the forest, 40km away from civilization. It dates back only to 1951, when a company named Gaspésie Mines decided to mine the extensive copper deposits in this isolated region. The company built the town according to a relatively precise plan. In 1957, the Murdochville miners went on a difficult strike, demanding recognition of their right to form a union and thus marking one of the most important chapters in the history of trade unionism in Québec.

Unfortunately, a sad page in the history of the town was written in 2002, when the mine closed. After 50 years of working underground, the workers were laid off and the mining of copper ceased its operations.

Nevertheless, visitors can still take in the **Centre d'Interprétation du Cuivre** ★ *($6; early Jun to mid-Sep every day 10am to 4pm; 345 Rte. 198, ☎418-784-3335 or 800-487-8601),* an unusual experience because visitors are required to don a miner's uniform supplied by the centre before heading into a real underground gallery. The objects on display illustrate the history of copper mining and the techniques involved in extracting the metal from the earth.

*Head back towards Anse-Pleureuse. Turn right onto Rte. 132, which leads through a number of other little villages with colourful names, such as **Gros-Morne** (Big Hill), **Manche-d'Épée** (Sword Handle), **Pointe-à-la-Frégate** (Frigate Point) and **L'Échouerie** (in French, "échouer" means to run aground).*

L'Anse-au-Griffon ★

Starting after the British conquest of New France in 1760, a small group of Anglo-Norman merchants from the island of Jersey took control of commercial fishing in the Gaspésie. One of these individuals, John LeBoutillier, built warehouses for salt, flour and dried cod in L'Anse-au-Griffon around 1840, and then began exporting cod to Spain, Italy and Brazil.

Centre Socioculturel Manoir LeBoutillier ★ *($4; early Jun to mid-Oct every day 9am to 5pm; 578 Boulevard Griffon, ☎418-892-5150),* a beautiful wooden house painted bright yellow, was built in 1840 to serve as a residence and office for the managers of LeBoutillier's company, which employed up to 2,500 people in the region 20 years later. Its roof has arched eaves, like those found on houses in **Kamouraska** (see p 434). Inside is a café, a craft shop and an information centre.

After passing through Jersey Cove, you'll reach Cap-des-Rosiers, gateway to the southern portion of Forillon National Park, where the landscape is more uneven and the sea makes its existence even more conspicuous.

Cap-des-Rosiers ★

Located in a magnificent setting, Cap-des-Rosiers has been the scene of many shipwrecks. Two monuments have been erected in memory of one in particular—that of the *Karrik* sailing ship, which claimed the lives of 87 of the 200 or so Irish immigrants aboard. The victims were buried in the local cemetery, while most of the survivors settled in Cap-des-Rosiers, giving the community a surprising new character. Irish names, such as Kavanagh and Whalen, are still common in the area. It was also from atop this cape that the French spotted General Wolfe's fleet heading for Québec City in 1759.

Forillon National Park ★ ★ ★, see p 464.

The road skirts round Cap Gaspé, then leads to the bay of the same name, where jagged cliffs suddenly give way to gentle valleys traversed by rivers.

Gaspé ★ (pop. 14,979)

It was here that Jacques Cartier claimed Canada for King Francis I of France in early July 1534. However, it was not until the beginning of the 18th century that the first fishing post was established in Gaspé, and the town itself did not develop until the end of that century.

Throughout the 19th century, the lives of an entire population of poorly educated, destitute French-Canadian and Acadian fishers were regulated by the large fishing companies run by merchants from the island of Jersey. During World War II, Gaspé prepared to become the Royal Navy's main base in the event of a German invasion of Great Britain, which explains why there are a few military installations around the 0bay. Today, Gaspé is the most important town on the peninsula, as well as the region's administrative centre. The city follows the waterfront in a narrow ribbon of development.

The long building that towers over the city is Gaspé's **former sanatorium** *(in the*

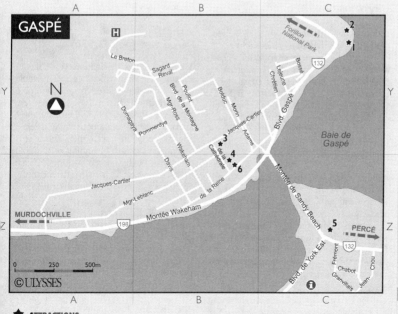

GASPÉ

MURDOCHVILLE

PERCÉ

© ULYSSES

0   250   500m

★ ATTRACTIONS

1.	CY	Musée de la Gaspésie
2.	CY	Monument to Jacques Cartier
3.	BY	Cathédrale du Christ-Roi
4.	BZ	Croix de Gaspé
5.	CZ	Monument à Jacques de Lesseps
6.	BZ	The Ash Inn

Gaspésie - Exploring - The Peninsula

city's surrounding hills). The hybrid post-war modernist structure features a Beaux-Arts design characterized by symmetrical lines, classic composition with a few grandiose touches and pavilions located at the building's extremities.

In 1977, upon the initiative of the local historical society, the **Musée de la Gaspésie ★ ★** *($4; late Jun to early Sep every day 9am to 5pm, early Sep to late Jun Tue-Fri 9am to 5pm, Sat and Sun 1pm to 5pm; 80 Boulevard Gaspé, ☎418-368-1534)* was erected on Pointe Jacques Cartier, overlooking Baie de Gaspé. A museum of history and popular tradition, it houses a permanent exhibit entitled *Un Peuple de la Mer* (A People of the Sea), tracing life in Gaspésie from the first Aboriginal inhabitants, members of the Micmac nation, all the way to the present day. Temporary exhibits are also featured at the museum.

Next to the museum lies a superb **monument to Jacques Cartier**, executed by the Bourgault family of Saint-Jean-Port-Joli. The six bronze steles are inscribed with descriptions of Cartier arriving in Canada, taking possession of the land, and meeting the Aboriginal people for the first time.

Take Boulevard Gaspé to Rue Jacques-Cartier.

Cathédrale du Christ-Roi ★ *(20 Rue de la Cathédrale)*, the only wooden cathedral in North America, has a contemporary design characteristic of Californian "shed" architecture, which is foreign to the east coast of the continent. Designed by Montréal architect Gérard Notebaert, it was erected in 1968 on the foundations of an earlier basilica, which was begun in 1932 to commemorate the 400th anniversary of Jacques Cartier's arrival in Canada, but was never completed due to a lack of funds. The interior is bathed in soft light from a lovely stained-glass window by Claude Théberge, who made it with antique glass. Visitors will also find a fresco showing Jacques Cartier taking possession of Canada. The fresco was received as a gift from France in 1934. The **Croix de Gaspé** (cross) faces the cathedral and commemorates Jacques Cartier's arrival to Canada.

The Gaspé cemetery features the **Monument à Jacques de Lesseps** *(Boulevard Gaspé)*. The monument honours Jacques de Lesseps and his friend Theodor Chicheko, who both perished in a plane crash in 1927.

Lesseps, the son of Ferdinand de Lesseps, who built the Suez Canal, was an adventurer and a renowned pilot who garnered many honours during the First World War and was the first pilot to fly over Montréal. Upon his discharge from the army, he relocated to the Gaspésie region to provide aerial geographical surveys.

The Ash Inn ★ *(186 Rue de la Reine)*, a former residence built in 1885 for Dr. William Wakeham, the famous Arctic explorer, is one of the only 19th-century stone houses in all of Gaspésie.

Heading out of Gaspé, visitors will get back on Rte. 132, leading to Percé. On the way, the road runs along the southern side of Baie de Gaspé, with its charming villages, some of which were settled by small communities of American Loyalists, others by British immigrants. The British colonial government intentionally populated these distant regions with settlers who were staunchly loyal to the king of England in the hopes of strengthening its position throughout Québec and promoting the rapid assimilation of the French-Canadian population.

Continue along Rte. 132 to Percé.

Percé ★ ★ (pop. 3,550)

A famous tourist destination, Percé lies in a beautiful setting, which has unfortunately been somewhat marred by the booming hotel industry. The majestic scenery features several natural phenomena, the most important being the famous Rocher Percé, which is to Québec what the Sugar Loaf is to Brazil. Since the beginning of the 20th century, artists have been flocking to Percé every summer, charmed by the beautiful landscapes and the local inhabitants.

Percé was an important gathering place for the Aboriginals until the Denys family established a seasonal fishing camp here in the 17th century, attracting French and Basque fishers. In 1781, Charles Robin, a powerful merchant from the island of Jersey, founded a fishing business in L'Anse du Sud, at which point a number of Loyalists, Irish and immigrants from Guernsey joined the French-Canadian population. At the time, the area's permanent population was still very small compared to the sea-

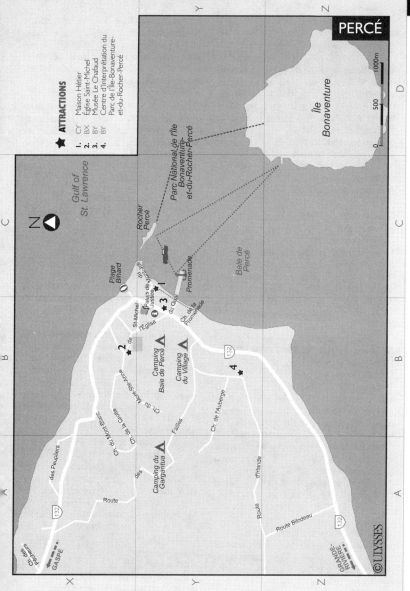

PERCÉ

★ **ATTRACTIONS**

1. CY Maison Hétier
2. BX Église Saint-Michel
3. BY Musée Le Chafaud
4. BY Centre d'interprétation du Parc de l'île-Bonaventure-et-du-Rocher-Percé

Gulf of St. Lawrence

Île Bonaventure

Parc National de l'île Bonaventure-et-du-Rocher-Percé

Rocher Percé

Baie de Percé

Plage Bihard

Promenade

Camping Baie de Percé

Camping du Village

Camping du Gargantua

GASPÉ

GRANDE-RIVIÈRE

Route Bilodeau

© ULYSSES

sonal population working in Robin's flimsy buildings. Percé was also the main fishing port on Québec's coast throughout the 19th century. The tourist industry took over in the 20th century, especially after Rte. 132 was built in 1929. Life in Percé nevertheless retains a precarious, seasonal quality.

Upon arriving in Percé, visitors are greeted by the arresting sight of the famous **Rocher Percé ★★★**, a wall of rock measuring 400m in length and 88m in height at its tallest point. Its name, which translates into "pierced rock," comes from the two entirely natural arched openings at its base. Only one of these openings remains today, since the eastern part of the rock collapsed in the mid-19th century. At low tide, starting from Plage du Mont Joli, it is possible to walk to the rock and admire the majestic surroundings and the thousands of fossils trapped in the limestone (*inquire about the time of day and duration of the tides beforehand*).

Maison Hétier ★ *(27 du Mont-Joli).* American painter Frederick James was one of the first artists to be drawn by the beauty of the Percé landscape. His summer residence was built around 1900 and is located on the headlands of Mont Joli, which is actually a cape that juts into the sea and is said to be the site where Canada's first chapel was built. More rock formations can be seen to the northwest, including **Pic de l'Aurore, Les Trois Soeurs** and **Cap Barré**.

Percé's Catholic **Église Saint-Michel** ★ *(57 Rue de l'Église)* was built using local pink-hued stone in 1898. It was designed by Montréal architect Joseph Venne and is a good example of his picturesque, eclectic style. It's one of the Gaspésie region's rare stone churches and certainly the largest. The Mont Sainte-Anne trail, which leads to a cave, starts out behind the church.

The **Musée Le Chafaud** ★ *($2; Jun to Oct every day 10am to 5pm; 145 Rte. 132, ☎418-782-5100)* occupies the largest building at Charles Robin's old plant in Percé. The *chafaud* is a building where fish was processed and stored. Today, it houses an exhibition on local heritage and is also used for various activities linked to the visual arts. The icehouse and salt shed still stand near the quay. On the other side of the street are the "Bell House," topped by a bell once used to call employees to work, the former company store, with its gabled roof and wood ornaments, and finally an old barn, which serves as the local arts centre.

At the Percé docks, there are a number of boats that take people out to **Île Bonaventure** (see p 465). During the high season, there are frequent departures from 8am to 5pm. Often, the crossing includes a short ride around the island and Rocher Percé, so that passengers can get a good look at the park's natural attractions. Most of these outfits let you spend as long as you want on the island and come back on any of their boats, which travel back and forth regularly between the island and the mainland.

The **Centre d'Interprétation du Parc de l'Île-Bonaventure-et-du-Rocher-Percé** *($3.50; early Jun to mid-Oct, every day 9am to 5pm; 343 Route de l'Irlande, ☎782-2721)* shows a short film

on the history of Île Bonaventure and the gannets that nest there. Visitors will also find an exhibition area, saltwater aquariums and two short footpaths. Finally, there is a shop run by local bird-watchers, which sells books and souvenirs.

*The tour of the peninsula ends at Percé. To make a complete circle and return to Québec City or Montréal without having to double back, the most pleasant way is to combine the tour of the peninsula with the following tour of **Baie des Chaleurs**.*

Tour B: Baie des Chaleurs ★ ★

 2 days

In 1604-06, Samuel de Champlain and Sieur de Monts founded the settlements of Île Sainte-Croix and Port-Royal, which were then populated by colonists from Poitou (France), marking the origins of Acadie (Acadia), a vast colony corresponding to the territory now occupied by Nova Scotia, Prince Edward Island and New Brunswick. In 1755, during the Seven Years War, the British captured the Acadians, whom they subsequently deported to faraway regions. A number of those who survived the trip attempted to return to their land, which had been confiscated and granted to new British colonists. Some settled in Louisiana, while others went to Québec and settled mostly in the Baie des Chaleurs area. Ironically, these Acadians were soon joined by Irish, Scottish and English immigrants, with whom they lived in relative peace, turning the area into a patchwork of French and English villages.

This tour leads through gentler landscapes and more farmlands than the tour of the peninsula. Visitors will also discover sandy beaches washed by calmer, warmer waters than those off Percé. The bay itself penetrates deep into the territory, creating a natural border between New Brunswick to the south and Québec to the north. This route can serve as a springboard for a tour of the Îles de la Madeleine or Canada's Atlantic provinces.

Take Rte. 132 to Paspébiac.

Paspébiac (pop. 3,341)

This little industrial town used to be the headquarters of the Robin company, which specialized in processing and exporting cod. The business was founded in 1766 by Charles Robin, a merchant from the island of Jersey, and then expanded to several spots along the coast of Gaspésie and even along the Côte-Nord. In 1791, Robin added a shipyard to his facilities in Paspébiac to build vessels to transport fish to Europe. Around 1840, the company began to face fierce competition from an enterprise owned by John LeBoutillier, one of Robin's former employees. Then, the failure of the Bank of Jersey in 1886 had a severe impact on fishing enterprises in Gaspésie, which never regained their former power.

The **Site Historique du Banc-de-Paspébiac** ★ ★ *($5; Jun to Sep every day 9am to 5pm; 3e Rue, Route du Quai, ☎418-752-6229).* A *banc* is a strip of sand and gravel used for drying fish. Paspébiac's *banc*, along with the town's deep, well-protected natural port, lent itself to the development of a fishing industry. In 1964, there were still some 70 buildings from the Robin and LeBoutillier companies on the *banc*. That year, however, most of them were destroyed by a fire. The eight surviving buildings have been carefully restored in this historic site and are open to the public.

Most of these buildings were erected in the 19th century. Particularly noteworthy sights include the forge, the former carpenter's shop, the kitchens, the Robin company offices, a powder magazine and the "B.B." (LeBouthillier and Brothers; 1850), a structure with a high pointed roof used for storing cod. Some of the buildings house thematic exhibitions on shipbuilding, the international fish market and the history of the Jersey companies. The site also includes a shop and a restaurant with typical regional dishes.

New Carlisle ★ (pop. 1,430)

The New Carlisle region was settled by American Loyalists who came here after the 1783 signing of the Treaty of Versailles, under which Great Britain recognized the independence of the United States. The charming village, with its four churches of different denominations, is not unlike those of New England. A visit to New Car-

lisle wouldn't be complete without a tour of its three **Protestant churches** ★, which are a great source of pride for the villagers. They are located along Rte. 132, which becomes Rue Principale, in the centre of the village.

Gothic Revival in style, **St. Andrew's Anglican Church** was built around 1890. Larger than most churches of its denomination in villages of comparable size, it bears witness to the importance of the Anglican community in New Carlisle. The **Zion United Church**, which hardly has any members left, has a curious shape, while the **Knox Presbyterian Church**, in the Scottish tradition, has a typical 1850s design.

There are only a few 19th-century bourgeois residences in Gaspésie, a region of fishers and forestry workers. **Maison Hamilton** ★ *($3.50; mid-May to mid-Nov every day guided tours at 1pm and 2pm; 115 Rue Principale, ☎418-752-6498)* is one of them. Its stone foundations make it even more remarkable and its somewhat austere facade adheres to the neoclassical style of the period. Erected in 1852 for lawyer and deputy John Robinson Hamilton, the house is still occupied but the present owners have opened it to the public. Inside, visitors will discover a lovely assortment of Victorian furniture, including a piano dating back to 1840. The owners plan to open a bed and breakfast on the premises in the near future.

Much humbler than Maison Hamilton is the **birthplace of René Lévesque** (1922-1987) *(not open to visitors; 16 Mount Sorel).* Premier of Québec from 1976 to 1985, Lévesque was the driving force behind the nationalisation of electricity in Québec and the founder of the Parti Québécois. This house bears witness to the cultural intermingling between the French and the English that took place in the region during the 19th century, when New Carlisle was the administrative centre of Baie des Chaleurs.

Continue along Rte. 132 to Bonaventure.

Bonaventure ★ (pop. 2,842)

This village was founded by Acadians taking refuge at the mouth of the Rivière Bonaventure (one of the best salmon rivers in North America) after Restigouche fell to the British in 1760. Today, Bonaventure is a bastion of Acadian culture in the Baie des Chaleurs area, as well as being home to a small seaside resort with a sandy beach and a deep-water port. It is also one of the only places in the world where visitors will find goods made out of fish skin (like wallets and purses).

An estimated one million Quebecers are of Acadian descent. The **Musée Acadien du Québec** ★ *($5; ⚕; late Jun to early Sep, every day 9am to 6pm; early Sep to mid-Oct, every day 9am to 5pm; rest of the year, Mon-Fri 9am to noon and 1pm to 5pm, Sat and Sun 1pm to 5pm; 95 Avenue Port-Royal, ☎418-534-4000, www.museeacadien.com)* recounts the odyssey of Acadians living in Québec and elsewhere in North America. The permanent collection includes 18th-century furniture, period paintings and photographs, and an audiovisual presentation of Acadian ethnography, which gives visitors an excellent idea of the spread of Acadian culture in North America. The museum occupies the village's old church hall, a large wooden building painted blue and white, dating back to 1914.

The construction of **Église Saint-Bonaventure** ★ *(100 Avenue Port-Royal)* began in 1860, the same year the Catholic clergy finally started establishing parishes in the Baie des Chaleurs region, considered very remote in those days. The building's facade was modified in 1919 according to a design by architect Pierre Lévesque. Its very colourful interior is decorated with remounted paintings by Georges S. Dorval of Québec City, as well as a number of wooden ornaments made to look like marble.

The **Bioparc de la Gaspésie** *($12.50; Jul and Aug every day 9am to 6pm; Jun and Sep 9am to 5pm, rest of the year by appointment; 123 Rue des Vieux-Ponts, ☎418-534-1997 or 866-534-1997, www.bioparc.ca)* is an ideal spot for families. With the aid of multimedia presentations and guides, discover the secret world of Gaspésien animals: bears, seals, otters, lynx and caribou. Their natural habitats are recreated along a 1km path: tundra, river, *barachois,* forest and bay. The tour lasts 2hrs.

Grotte de Saint-Elzéar, see p 465.

Return to Rte. 132 and turn right, towards New Richmond. Take a left off the main road, onto Boulevard Perron Ouest.

New Richmond ★ (pop. 3,750)

The first English colonists in Gaspésie settled here after the Conquest of 1760. They were soon joined by Loyalists, and then Irish and Scottish immigrants. This strong British presence is evident in the architecture of New Richmond, with its tidy streets dotted with small Protestant churches of various denominations.

Located on Pointe Duthie, on the way into the village, the **Village Gaspésien d'Héritage Britannique** ★ *($10, including shuttle service; early Jun to early Sep, every day 9am to 6pm; early Sep to mid-Oct every day 9am to 5pm; 351 Boulevard Perron Ouest, ☎418-392-4487)* is made up of buildings from the Baie des Chaleurs area, which were saved from demolition, transported to the grounds of the former Carswell estate and restored to house thematic exhibitions on Gaspesians of British extraction. Each structure illustrates a different group's arrival in the area: the vestiges of the Carswell residence are devoted to the British settlers; a Loyalist camp to those faithful subjects who came here in August 1784; a house and a grain warehouse to the Scottish immigrants, and another house to the Irish. Finally, in the last clearing, visitors will find the Willet house, which evokes the region's industrial development at the end of the 19th century.

St. Andrew's Presbyterian Church ★ *(211 Boulevard Perron Ouest)*, in the centre of New Richmond, is one of the oldest churches in the Baie des Chaleurs area, built in 1839 by Robert Bash. After a number of Protestant communities merged in the 20th century, St. Andrew's became part of the United Church of Canada.

Carleton-Saint-Omer ★ (pop. 4,070)

Carleton-Saint-Omer, like Bonaventure, is a stronghold of Acadian culture in Québec, and a seaside resort with a lovely sandy beach washed by calm waters that are warmer than elsewhere in Gaspésie and account for the name of the bay (*chaleur* means warmth). The mountains rising up behind the town give it a distinctive character. Carleton was founded in 1756 by Acadian refugees, who were joined by deportees returning from exile. Originally known as Tracadièche, the little town was renamed in the 19th century by the British elite, in honour of Sir Guy Carleton, Canada's third governor.

Église Saint-Joseph ★ *(764 Boulevard Perron)* is one of the oldest Catholic churches in Gaspésie. Begun in 1849, it wasn't actually finished until 1917. It houses a tabernacle attributed to François Baillargé (1828), which was given to the parish at an undetermined date. The main vault is adorned with remounted paintings by Charles Huot.

Follow Rue du Quai (perpendicular to Rte. 132) toward the sea; after the ***Saint-Barnabé*** (a beached boat) take the gravel road and stop near the **observation tower**. Climb to the top of the tower, equipped with a telescope for bird-watching. A guide is on hand to provide visitors with information on ornithology.

Nouvelle (pop. 2,100)

Palaeontology buffs will surely be interested in **Parc National de Miguasha** ★ ★ *($10; early Jun to early Sep, every day 9am to 6pm; early Sep to mid-Oct, every day 9am to 5pm; off-season Mon-Fri 8:30am to noon and 1pm to 4:30pm; 231 Miguasha Ouest, ☎418-794-2475 or 800-665-6527, www.sepaq.com)*, a UNESCO World Heritage Site, and the second-largest fossil site in the world. The park's **palaeontology museum** *(占)* displays fossils discovered in the surrounding cliffs, which formed the bottom of a lagoon 370 million years ago. The information centre houses a permanent collection of many interesting specimens. In the laboratory, visitors can learn the methods used to remove fossils from the rock and identify them.

West of Miguasha, Baie des Chaleurs narrows considerably as it approaches the mouth of the Rivière Restigouche, which flows into it.

Pointe-à-la-Croix (pop. 1,559)

On April 10, 1760, a French fleet set off from Bordeaux on its way to Canada, with the goal of liberating New France from the

English. Only three ships reached Baie des Chaleurs, the others having fallen victim to English cannons as they headed out of the Gironde. The *Machault*, *Bienfaisant* and *Marquis-de-Malauze*, vessels weighing an average of 350 tonnes, survived, but the English troops caught up with the French at the mouth of the Restigouche in Baie des Chaleurs. A battle broke out, and the English defeated the French fleet within a few hours.

At the **Battle of the Restigouche National Historic Site** ★ *($5; early Jun to mid-Oct, every day 9am to 5pm; Route 132, ☎418-788-5676)*, also called the Lieu Historique National de la Bataille de la Restigouche, visitors can see a collection of objects recovered from the wreckage of the battle between these ships, as well as a few pieces of the frigate *Machault*. An interesting audiovisual presentation illustrates the different stages of the confrontation.

Between Pointe-à-la-Croix and Restigouche, there is a bridge that stretches across Baie des Chaleurs, linking Québec to New Brunswick.

Causapscal (pop. 2,545)

The Matapédia, one of the best salmon rivers in North America, flows through the centre of Causapscal, with its towering sawmills. Every year, fans of sport fishing come to the area. Salmon fishing and exclusive rights to the river have been a source of longstanding conflict between the local population and private clubs. Causapscal, whose name means "rocky point" in Micmac, was founded in 1839 after a post house known as La Fourche (The Fork) was opened at the junction of the Matapédia and the Causapscal.

Site Historique Matamajaw ★ *($5; early Jun to mid-Aug, every day 9am to 5pm; 53C Rue Saint-Jacques, ☎418-756-5999)*. In 1873, Donald Smith, the future Lord Mount Stephen, acquired the fishing rights to the Matapédia. A few years later, he sold the rights to the Matamajaw Salmon Club. In general, members of clubs like this were American or English-Canadian businessmen, who spent three or four days a year here in the middle of the woods, in a relaxing, holiday atmosphere. These individuals were offered the ultimate luxury of sending their catch home in refrigerated railway cars that waited for

Gaspésie - Exploring - Baie des Chaleurs

them at the Causapscal station. The club stopped operating around 1950, and the buildings on the Matamajaw property were listed as historic monuments and opened to the public in 1984. Here, visitors can see an exhibition on club life and the history of salmon fishing. Salmon can be observed on site, thanks to the addition of a pool. There are trails leading to **Parc Les Fourches**, where the Matapédia and Causapscal rivers meet and you can see fishers at work.

*The road then leads through **Mont-Joli**, which offers a lovely view of the St. Lawrence River, before coming full circle at the departure point of Tour A.*

Parks

Tour A: The Peninsula

The **Réserve Faunique de Matane** *(257 Rue Saint-Jérôme, Matane, ☎418-562-3700 or 800-665-6527)* is a series of wooded hills and mountains, stretching over an area of 1,284km², and strewn with lakes and rivers excellent for salmon fishing. The **Auberge de Montagne des Chic-Chocs** was added in 2005 *(transport to the inn is provided from the Cap-Chat visitor centre, ☎800-665-3091, www.sepaq.com)*, inn welcoming the many outdoor sports enthusiasts who come to the park for its many ski mountaineering, snowshoeing, hiking, fishing and wildlife-observation opportunities.

Parc National de la Gaspésie ★★★ *($3.50; early Jun to mid-Oct and mid-Dec to mid-Apr; northern entrance at 40km from Sainte-Anne-des-Monts by route 299, ☎418-763-7494 or 800-665-6527, www.sepaq.com)* covers an area of 800km² and encompasses the famous Monts Chic-Chocs. It was established in 1937 in an effort to heighten public awareness regarding nature conservation in the Gaspésie. The park is composed of conservation zones devoted to the protection of the region's natural riches, and an ambient zone, made up of a network of roads, trails and lodgings. The Chic-Chocs form the northernmost section of the Appalachian Mountains and stretch over 90km, from Matane to the foot of Mont Albert. The McGerrigle Mountains lie perpendicular to the Chic-Chocs, covering an area of 100km². The park's trails run through

three levels of terrain, leading all the way to the summits of the four highest mountains in the area, **Mont Jacques-Cartier**, **Mont Richardson**, **Mont Albert** and **Mont Xalibu**. This is the only place in Québec where white-tailed deer (in the rich vegetation of the first level), moose (in the Boreal forest) and caribou (in the tundra, at the top of the mountains) co-exist. Hikers are required to register before setting out.

The **Gîte du Mont-Albert** (see p 469) lies in the centre of the park. A very comfortable inn, it is known for its fine cuisine, delicate wooden architecture inspired by the French Regime, and stunning panoramic view.

The motto of **Forillon National Park** ★★★ *($6; Penouille and Anse-au-Griffon reception centres open from mid-Jun to early Sep; Parcs Canada, 122 Boulevard Gaspé, Gaspé, ☎418-368-5505 or 800-463-6769, www.pc.gc.ca)* is "harmony between man, land and sea." Many an outdoor enthusiast dreams about this series of forests, mountains and cliff-lined shores all crisscrossed by hiking trails. Home to a fairly wide range of animals, this national park abounds in foxes, bears, moose, porcupines and other mammals. Over 200 species of birds live here, including herring gulls, cormorants, finches, larks and gannets. Depending on the season, visitors might catch a glimpse of whales or seals from the paths along the coast. A variety of rare plants also lie hidden away in Forillon National Park, contributing to a greater understanding of the soil in which they grow. Visitors will find not only natural surroundings here in the park, but also traces of human activity. Indeed, this vast area (245km²) once included four little villages. The 200 families inhabiting them were relocated—not without a fight—when the park was established in 1970. The buildings of great ethnological interest were kept and restored, namely the 10 or so **Maisons de Grande-Grave**, the **Phare de Cap-Gaspé** (the lighthouse), the **former Protestant Church** of Petit-Gaspé and the **Fort Péninsule**, part of the fortifications erected during World War II to protect Canada from attacks by German submarines.

Particularly notable buildings in Grande-Grave, originally populated by Anglo-Norman immigrants from the Island of Jersey in the English Channel, include the **Magasin Hyman** (1845). The store's interior has been carefully reconstructed to evoke the early 20th century, while the seaside **Ferme Blanchette** could easily grace a postcard. All of these are either fully or partly open to the public.

At **Parc National de l'Île-Bonaventure-et-du-Rocher-Percé ★ ★** *($3.50 plus transportation fee; access to Île Bonaventure by ferry from Percé; late May to mid-Oct 9am to 5pm, ☎418-782-2240 or 800-665-6527, www.sepaq.com)*, visitors will find large bird colonies, as well as numerous footpaths lined with rustic houses. The trails range from 2.8 to 4.9km in length, and cover a total of 15km. Due to the aridity of the surroundings, there are no stinging insects on the island. There is also no water along the trails, so be sure to bring a canteen. All trails end at an impressive bird sanctuary, where some 250,000 birds, including about 80,000 gannets, form a wildlife exhibition.

Created in 1953, the **Réserve Faunique de Port-Daniel ★** *(8km from Rte. 132 from Port-Daniel, ☎418-396-2789 or 396-2232 off-season)* is teeming with wildlife. Covering an area of 57km², it is laced with trails and strewn with lakes and cabins. To top it all off, there are some gorgeous views to drink in from some of its lookouts.

The **Grotte de Saint-Elzéar** *($22-$35, children 6 and older only; early Jun to early Sep, first tour leaves at 8am; 198 Rue de l'Église, Saint-Elzéar, ☎418-534-4335)* introduces visitors to 500,000 years of Gaspesian history. This speleological and geomorphological journey offers participants the opportunity to visit the two largest caves in Québec. Warm clothing and a good pair of shoes are required, as the temperature is a steady 4°C.

Outdoor Activities

■ Bird-Watching

Tour A: The Peninsula

The **Jardins de Métis**, in Grand-Métis, are teeming with bird life—in the clearings, on the lawns, in the gardens, in the wooded area and near the river.

The **Baie des Capucins**, a saltwater marsh, is home to a multitude of birds that can be observed by taking a stroll along the path that follows its shores.

The **Parc National de la Gaspésie** boasts over 150 avian species who nest in different climates. You can observe them easily from the trails running through the park. Every Monday, Parc Ami Chic Chocs organizes a 4hr-bird-watching excursion, which starts at 7am at the shop in the interpretive centre.

Île Bonaventure (see above), a protected nesting ground for cormorants and gannets, is a wonderful place to go birding.

Tour B: Baie des Chaleurs

The **Carleton** *barachois* is an excellent place to observe wildfowl, terns and great herons. There is a large colony of terns on the south end of the Carleton bank. A small observation tower, complete with information panels, makes it easy to get a good look at the birds.

■ Cross-Country Skiing

Tour A: The Peninsula

The **Station de Ski Val-d'Irène** *($10; 115 Route Val-d'Irène, ☎418-629-3450, www.val-direne. com)* boasts the best snow conditions in Québec. There are 15km of maintained trails here.

■ Cruises and Whale-Watching

Tour A: The Peninsula

Croisières Baie de Gaspé *($40; 64 Boulevard de la Montagne, Gaspé, ☎418-892-5500 or 866-617-5500, www.baleines-forillon.com)* offers whale-watching cruises a board a ship that plies the waters around Forillon National Park. Seals and dolphins also visit these waters so keep your eyes peeled.

Observation Littoral Percé *($40 for a 2½ to 3hr excursion, Jun to Oct; near the Hôtel Normandie; 240 Route 132, Percé, ☎782-5359)* hosts whale-watching excursions. With a little luck, you might also meet up with a school of white dolphins. Don't expect to see whale tails like those in photographs; usually, only the whale's back is visible, and often the animal is far away. The companies that organize these excursions must adhere to strict laws and have to pay large fines if they don't keep their distance. The outings start early in the morning. Make sure to bundle up and wear a good windbreaker.

■ Downhill Skiing

The **Station Val d'Irène** *($23; 115 Route Val d'Irène, ☎418-629-3450 or 629-3101 for ski conditions, www.val-direne.com)* ski resort has 26 runs and a 274m vertical drop.

■ Fishing

Tour A: The Peninsula

The **Réserve Faunique de Port-Daniel** *(8km from Rte. 132 from Port-Daniel, ☎396-2789 or 396-2232 off-season)* is dotted with about 20 lakes where you can go trout fishing. You have the choice between day-tripping it to the reserve or staying in one of the lakeshore cabins, which must be reserved 48hrs in advance. In the latter case, you'll have a rowboat at your disposal.

Tour B: Baie des Chaleurs

In **Causapscal**, the visitor's reception centre *(☎418-756-6174, for reservations: 888-730-6174, www.cgrmp.com)* in front of the Site Historique Matamajaw issues fishing permits for the Matapédia and Causapscal rivers.

■ Hiking

Tour A: The Peninsula

Parc National de la Gaspésie *($3.50; ☎418-763-3301 or 866-727-2427 or 800-665-6527, www.*

sepaq.com) has an outstanding network of hiking trails. On the same outing, you can pass through four different kinds of forests: boreal, coniferous, subalpine (made up of miniature trees), and finally, the tundra on the mountaintops. We especially recommend the Mont Jacques-Cartier (difficult) and Mont Albert (very difficult) trails. The Lac aux Américains trail is an excellent choice for novice hikers.

Forillon National Park *($4; $6 family; ☎368-5505)*, with its cliffs sculpted by the sea and its extraordinary landscapes, is a wonderful place to go hiking. Some of the trails are suitable for children.

■ Kayaking

Tour A: The Peninsula

Carrefour Aventure *($10/hr; 106 Rue Cloutier, ☎418-797-5033)*, in Mont-Saint-Pierre, rents out sea kayaks (accessories included).

Tour B: Baie des Chaleurs

In Bonaventure, **Cime Aventure** *(200 Chemin Athanas-Arsenault, ☎418-534-2333 or 800-790-2463, www.cimeaventure.com)* organizes kayak trips ranging in length from a few hours to six days.

Gaspésie - Outdoor Activities

Accommodations

Tour A: The Peninsula

Sainte-Flavie

Motel Gaspésiana
$$-$$$
≡ ☞ ⊌ ◎
460 Route de la Mer
☎ (418) 775-7233 or 800-404-8233
🖷 (418) 775-9227
www.gaspesiana.com
Motel Gaspésiana has well-equipped, soundproofed rooms that are actually quite pleasant, thanks to their big windows.

Grand-Métis

Motel Métis
$$
◎ ≈
mid-Jun to mid-Oct
220 Rte. 132
☎ (418) 775-6473
The Motel Métis offers simple, modern rooms.

Métis-sur-Mer

Camping Annie
$
≈
1352 Rte. 132
☎ (418) 936-3825
🖷 (418) 936-3035
www.campingannie.com
Camping Annie has 150 sites, 58 of which are equipped with RV hook-ups. There are hiking trails and bike paths right nearby. Located 8km from the Jardins de Métis, this is a very friendly, welcoming place.

Au Coin de la Baie
$$-$$$
☛ ⊌
mid-May to mid-Sep
336 Rte. 132
☎ (418) 936-3855
🖷 (418) 936-3112
www.aucoindelabaie.com
Au Coin de la Baie is a motel with 14 lovely rooms.

Auberge du Grand Fleuve
$$$ bkfst incl.
⊌
47 Rue Principale
☎ (418) 936-3332
www.aubergedugrandfleuve.qc.ca
This unique inn is run by a French and Québécois couple of book lovers. You'll find books in your bedroom, in the living room, in the dining room… The stunning seaside setting and fine cuisine are sure to please, but if you just want to get away from it all and relax, set your sights on Auberge du Grand Fleuve and prepare to catch up on your reading.

Matane

Auberge La Seigneurie
$$ bkfst incl.
pb/sb
621 Avenue St-Jérôme
☎ (418) 562-0021 or 877-783-4466
🖷 (418) 562-4455
www.aubergelaseigneurie.com
Visitors will find the perfect place to relax at the confluence of the St. Lawrence and Matane rivers: Auberge La Seigneurie. Located on the former site of the Fraser seigneury, this inn has comfortable rooms.

Motel La Vigie
$$
≡ ⊌ ◎
1600 Avenue du Phare Ouest
☎ (418) 562-3664 or 888-527-3664
🖷 (418) 566-2930
www.lavigie.com
Located near the snow-mobile route, Motel La Vi-

gie offers simple rooms in a modern setting.

Riotel Matane
$$-$$$
≡ ⇓ ≈ ⊌))) ◎
250 Avenue du Phare Est
☎ (418) 566-2651 or 888-427-7374
🖷 (418) 562-7365
www.riotel.qc.ca
The Riotel Matane makes a charming first impression. Upon their arrival, visitors will notice the care that has been given to make the place both attractive and comfortable. The wooden spiral staircase and leather armchairs are just a hint of what is to come. On their way through the restaurant and bar, guests will enjoy an exquisite view of the St. Lawrence. The rooms on the third floor are among the newest in the hotel, which also has a tennis court and a golf course.

Sainte-Anne-des-Monts

Auberge Internationale Sainte-Anne-des-Monts
$
295 1ʳᵉ Avenue Est
☎ (418) 763-7123
🖷 (418) 763-7138
www.aubergesgaspesie.com
Travellers on a budget can head to this laid-back hostel. Laundry facilities and Internet access are available.

Réserve Faunique de Matane

Auberge de Montagne des Chic-Chocs
$$$$$ fb
⊌)))
transport to the inn is provided from the Cap-Chat visitor centre
☎800-665-3091

Gaspésie - Accommodations - The Peninsula

MATANE

St. Lawrence River

N

BAIE-COMEAU
GODBOUT

Ave. du Phare Ouest

RIMOUSKI

132

195

du Parc Industriel

de Matane-sur-Mer

Brillant
Dureté
Savard
du Port

Ave. Henri-Dunant

Quimper
Goyer
St-Jean
Dion
Blvd. Dion
Fournier Blvd.
St-Pierre
Grant
St-Aubin
W. Russel
Paradis

Gaspé
St-Jean

Gagnon
Fournier
Ave. Fraser
de la Fabrique
St-Pierre
St-Christophe
Soucy
Bergeron
Price
St-Jérôme

Ave. St-Jérôme

Matane

du Barachois
132

Ave. D'Amour
de la Marée
Champlain

Ave. du Phare Est
GASPÉ

St-Robert
du Vallon
Simard
de Courtemanche
Dionne
Boutrand

Meunier
du Buisson
Blvd. Jacques-Cartier

du Sault
Boucher
Ave. St-Rédempteur
du Basque
St-Joseph
Côté

Blvd du Père-Lamarche
Bélanger
Bouillon
Collin

Parc des Îles
Ave. St-Jérôme
Rivière
Ave. Desjardins
Ave. D'Amour
Ave. Ruisseau
Belvédère
des Pins
des Trembles
de Bois-Joli

195
du Port

Réserve
Faunique
de Matane

© ULYSSES

350   700m

ACCOMMODATIONS
1. DX   Auberge la Seigneurie
2. AZ   Motel La Vigie
3. DX   Riotel Matane

RESTAURANTS
1. DX   La Table du Capitaine Gourmand
2. AY   Le Vieux Rafiot
3. DX   Pizzeria Italia

This major addition to the Réserve Faunique de Matane was inaugurated in December 2005. The inn is located at an altitude of 600m, in the heart of an untamed environment that attracts outdoor-sports enthusiasts who come here to enjoy the reserve's many activities. The inn favours an intimate atmosphere and only contains 18 rooms, as well as a common living room with a fireplace, a sauna, an outdoor whirlpool bath and a dining room. A team of guides helps visitors take full advantage of the reserve's vast landscape and numerous outdoor activities.

Parc National de la Gaspésie

There are a number of different **campgrounds** (*$*; *mid-Jun to late Sep*) in Parc National de la Gaspésie, as well as 20 or so **cabins** (*$$-$$$*) that can accommodate four, six or eight people (*☎866-727-2427 or 800-665-6527, www.sepaq. com*).

Gîte du Mont-Albert
$$$$
$$$$$ ½b
△ ➡ ⚒ ♨ ⋙ &
☎ (418) 763-2288 or 866-727-2427
▤ (418) 763-7803
www.sepaq.com
For panoramic views, head to the Gîte du Mont-Albert, located in Parc National de la Gaspésie. The building is *U*-shaped, so each comfortable room offers a sweeping view of Mont Albert and Mont McGerrigle. Cabins are also for rent.

Forillon National Park

You'll find three basic campgrounds in the park, as well as the **Camping de Groupe de Petit-Gaspé** (*☎418-892-5911 in summer, 418-638-5505 rest of the year*), which is open year-round and is reserved for groups of 10 people or more. To reserve (*$11*) one of the park's 367 campsites, call ☎877-737-3783 or visit www.pccamping.ca. Note that only half of the park's campsites can be reserved in advance; the others are allocated on a first-come, first-serve basis.

Cap-aux-Os

Auberge de Jeunesse de Cap-aux-Os
$
♨
2095 Boulevard Grande-Grève
☎ (418) 892-5153
Located at the entrance to Forillon National Park, the Auberge de Jeunesse de Cap-aux-Os is the perfect hostel for visitors on a tight budget. The atmosphere is truly convivial in both the cafeteria and the large living room. Activities are organized.

Gaspé

Résidence du CÉGEP de la Gaspésie et des Îles
$
➡ &
94 Rue Jacques-Cartier
☎ (418) 368-2749
www.cgaspesie.qc.ca
The residence hall of the CÉGEP de la Gaspésie et des Îles rents out its rooms between June 15 and August 15. Guests are provided with a kitchenette, bedding, towels and dishes.

Motel Camping Fort Ramsay
$-$$
➡ ⛟ ❄ ♨
254 Boulevard Gaspé
☎/▤ (418) 368-5094
www.fortramsay.com
Situated between Forillon National Park and downtown Gaspé, the Motel Camping Fort Ramsay offers simple rooms that are somewhat noisy due to the proximity of the road. Tents can also be planted on the premises.

Hôtel des Commandants
$$$
≡ ♨ ⊚ &
178 Rue de la Reine
☎ (418) 368-3355 or 800-462-3355
▤ (418) 368-1702
www.hoteldescommandants.com
Formerly the Quality Inn, the Hôtel des Commandants is downtown, next to a shopping centre. The rooms are pleasant and comfortable.

Fort Prével

Auberge Fort-Prével
$$-$$$$
≋ ♨
mid-Jun to mid-Sep
2053 Boulevard Douglas
Saint-Georges-de-Malbaie
☎ (418) 368-2281 or 888-377-3835
▤ (418) 368-1364
Like the Gîte du Mont-Albert, the Auberge Fort-Prével is run by the Société des Établissements de Plein Air du Québec (SEPAQ). The Fort Prével battery was used during the second World War, and an interpretive trail tells its story. The inn has six rooms. Nearby are a pavilion with 12 rooms and a motel with 40 rooms. Twelve equipped cottages and a large house that can accommodate 12 people can also be rented. Finally, there are 28 RV sites.

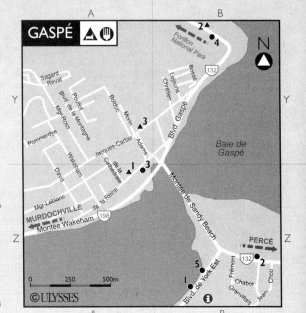

GASPÉ

Baie de Gaspé

MURDOCHVILLE

PERCÉ

Montée Wakeham

©ULYSSES

0 250 500m

▲ **ACCOMMODATIONS**

1.	AZ	Hôtel des Commandants
2.	BY	Motel Camping Fort Ramsay
3.	AY	Résidence du Cégep de la Gaspésie et des Îles

● **RESTAURANTS**

1.	BZ	L'Ancêtre
2.	BZ	Le Bourlingueur
3.	AZ	Le Brise Bise
4.	BY	Le Café des Artistes
5.	BZ	Restaurant Bar Latini

Percé

Camping du Gargantua
$
222 Route des Failles
☎ (418) 782-2852

Camping du Gargantua is definitely the most beautiful campground in the Percé area. It offers a view not only of Rocher Percé and the ocean, but also of the verdant surrounding mountains.

Auberge du Gargantua
$$
♨
Jun to mid-Oct
222 Route des Failles
☎ (418) 782-2852
▤ (418) 782-5229

L'Auberge du Gargantua has been looking out over Percé from atop its promontory for 30 years now, and it is well known to anyone familiar with the Gaspé peninsula. Its restaurant (see p 473) is one of the best in the region, and

its location and view are unforgettable. The small, motel-style rooms are simply decorated but comfortable.

Chalets au Pic de l'Aurore
$$-$$$
▲●🛏
mid-Jun to mid-Sep
1 Rte. 132
☎ (418) 782-2166 or 800-463-4212
▤ (418) 782-5323
www.resperce.com

The Chalets au Pic de l'Aurore are located above the coast north of Percé, overlooking the entire town. Each of the 17 cottages has an attractive terrace, a kitchenette, a bedroom and a living room with a fireplace.

Hotel-Motel La Normandie
$$$-$$$$
♨
221 Rte. 132
☎ (418) 782-2112 or 800-463-0820
▤ (418) 782-2337
www.normandieperce.com

The Hotel-Motel La Normandie has a well-established reputation in Percé. During high season, this luxury establishment is full most of the time. Both the restaurant and the rooms offer a view of the famous Rocher Percé.

Tour B: Baie des Chaleurs

Paspébiac

Auberge du Parc
$$$
♨ ♨))) ⅄ ◎
early Feb to late Nov
68 Boulevard Gérard-D.-Lévesque Ouest
☎ (418) 752-3355 or 800-463-0890
▤ (418) 752-6406
www.aubergeduparc.com

The Auberge du Parc occupies a 19th-century manor erected by the Robin company. It stands in the midst of a wooded area, provid-

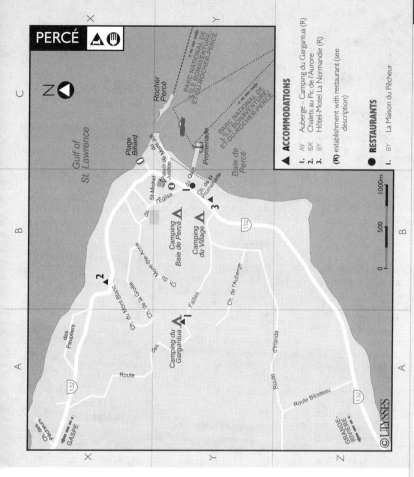

PERCÉ ⛺🖐

ACCOMMODATIONS

1. AY   Auberge – Camping du Gargantua (R)
2. BX   Chalets au Pic de l'Aurore
3. BY   Hôtel-Motel La Normandie (R)

(R) establishment with restaurant (see description)

RESTAURANTS

1. BY   La Maison du Pêcheur

PARC NATIONAL DE L'ÎLE-BONAVENTURE-ET-DU-ROCHER-PERCÉ

Rocher Percé

Gulf of St. Lawrence

Plage Bihard

Baie de Percé

Camping Baie de Percé

Camping du Village

Camping du Gargantua

Route

©ULYSSES

---

ing a perfect place to relax. Whirlpools, body wraps, therapeutic massages, acupressure and a saltwater pool will enhance your stay.

Carleton-Saint-Omer

Camping Carleton
$
mid-Jun to late Sep
Banc de Larocque
☎ (418) 364-3992
Camping Carleton is located near the sea and the beach. Despite the lack of shady sites, this is a very quiet and pleasant place.

Hotel-Motel Baie Bleue
$$-$$$
≈ ⅏ ◎
482 Boulevard Perron
☎ (418) 364-3355 or 800-463-9099
🖷 (418) 364-6165
www.baiebleue.com
The Hotel-Motel Baie Bleue has 100 modern and well-maintained rooms.

Aqua-Mer Thalasso
$$$ bkfst incl.
early May to late Oct
≈ ⅄
868 Boulevard Perron
☎ (418) 364-7055 or 800-463-0867
🖷 (418) 364-7351
www.aquamer.ca
Aqua-Mer Thalasso, located in an enchanting setting,

offers a number of week-long thalassotherapy (seawater treatment) packages.

Pointe-à-la-Garde

Auberge de Jeunesse / Château Bahia de Pointe-à-la-Garde
$ bkfst incl.
⅏
152 Boulevard Perron
☎ / 🖷 (418) 788-2048
Auberge de Jeunesse / Château Bahia de Pointe-à-la-Garde is set back from the road, halfway between Carleton-Saint-Omer and Matapédia. This youth hostel is a great place to relax. Guests are offered high-quality regional dishes

such as fresh salmon and maple-flavoured ham, all at modest prices, and may sleep either in the hostel or in the chateau behind it.

Causapscal

Camping de Causapscal
$

Jun to Aug
601 Rte. 132 Ouest
☎ (418) 756-5621
▤ (418) 756-3344
The Causapscal campground has 48 sites for tents and trailers.

Auberge La Coulée Douce
$$
≡ ♨
21 Rue Boudreau
☎ (418) 756-5270 or 888-756-5270
▤ (418) 756-5271
www.lacouleedouce.com
Auberge La Coulée Douce is open from spring to autumn, as well as during the winter, depending on demand. The former residence of a parish priest, this lovely little family inn lies in the heart of the Matapédia valley. The rooms are cozily decorated with old-fashioned furniture.

Restaurants

Tour A: The Peninsula

Grand-Métis

Le Café-Jardin
$-$$
Jardins de Métis, 200 Route 132
☎ (418) 775-2221
Le Café-Jardin serves inexpensive soups, sandwiches, salads and a few

more elaborate meals made from local products.

Métis-sur-Mer

Auberge Métis-sur-Mer
$$-$$$
late Jun to late Oct
1301 Route 132
☎ (418) 936-3563
If you're in the mood for some perfectly prepared fresh seafood, the dining room at Auberge Métis-sur-Mer is a good choice.

Matane

Pizzeria Italia
$-$$
101 Rue Saint-Pierre, corner of Avenue Saint-Jérôme
☎ (418) 562-3646
The Pizzeria Italia serves pizza made with fresh, top-quality ingredients and an interesting choice of toppings.

Le Vieux Rafiot
$$-$$$
1415 Avenue du Phare Ouest, alongside Rte. 132
☎ (418) 562-8080
Le Vieux Rafiot attracts lots of visitors to its incredible dining room, which is divided into three sections by partitions with portholes and decorated with paintings by local artists. In addition to the novel decor, guests can enjoy a variety of delicious dishes.

La Table du Capitaine Gourmand
$$-$$$
260 Rue du Barachois
☎ (418) 562-3131
La Table du Capitaine Gourmand serves up generous portions and attracts a clientele fond of fish and fresh seafood. It has a live lobster tank and is furnished with an assorted collection of objects, such as a treas-

ure chest and a lobster pot. The seafood pizza is a real treat. Friendly service.

Réserve Faunique de Matane

Auberge de Montagne des Chic-Chocs
$$$$$
The dining room at **Auberge de Montagne des Chic-Chocs** (see p 467) offers healty fare that features local products such as fish, duck, caribou, moose and deer.

Cap-Chat

Fleur de Lys
$$-$$$
184 Rte. 132 Est
☎ (418) 786-5518
The Fleur de Lys invites visitors to savour dishes freshly prepared every day. Warm welcome.

Parc National de la Gaspésie

Gîte du Mont-Albert
$$$$
☎ (418) 763-2288
The restaurant at **Gîte du Mont-Albert** (see p 469) offers innovative seafood dishes that are definitely worth a try. During the Game Festival in September, you can sample more unusual meats like guinea hen, bison and partridge.

Gaspé

Le Bourlingueur
$-$$
39 Montée de Sandy Beach
☎ (418) 368-4323
Varnished wooden tables and chairs make Le Bourlingueur look like an old English pub. This is a large

place where visitors can enjoy a relaxing meal of Canadian or Chinese food.

Le Brise-Bise
$-$$
135 Rue de la Reine
☎ (418) 368-1456
The bistro/bar Brise-Brise is probably the finest café in Gaspé. The menu includes sausages, seafood, salads and sandwiches. The place also features an assortment of beer and coffee, an enjoyable happy hour, live shows all summer long, and dancing late into the evening.

Restaurant Bar Latini
$$
35 Boulevard York Est
☎ (418) 386-7447
If you plan on spending the day at Forillon National Park, stop by Restaurant Bar Latini, where you can buy ready-made meals to go. The menu features fresh pasta, salads and homemade soup.

L'Ancêtre
$$-$$$
55 Boulevard York Est
☎ (418) 368-4358
The specialties here are grilled steak and seafood, and meals are served in a beautiful Anglo-Norman-style house with a splendid view of the ocean. You'll find Gaspé's best Sunday brunch here.

Le Café des Artistes
$$-$$$
249 Boulevard de Gaspé
☎ (418) 368-2255
The owners of Café des Artistes, who are obviously artists themselves, offer a completely original and attractive concept. In this art centre, you can linger over a delicious table d'hôte and then admire the works of various artists. The home-

made ice cream (particularly the avocado) and sorbets are delightful.

Fort Prével

Auberge Fort-Prével
$$$-$$$$
2053 Boulevard Douglas
Saint-Georges-de-Malbaie
☎ (418) 368-2281 or 888-377-3835
At **Auberge Fort-Prével** (see p 469), guests are plunged into a historic atmosphere and get to savour delicious French and Québec cuisine. These skillfully prepared and elegantly presented dishes are served in a huge dining room. The menu includes fish and seafood, of course, as well as all sorts of specialties that will satisfy any gourmet.

Percé

La Maison du Pêcheur
$$$-$$$$
155 Place du Quai
☎ (418) 782-5331
La Maison du Pêcheur lies right in the heart of the village. It is two restaurants in one; on the first floor, there is a *crêperie* that looks out on the sea and also serves breakfast, while the second floor is reserved for dinner guests. The prices are a little high, but everything is first-rate.

La Normandie
$$$-$$$$
221 Rte. 132 Ouest
☎ (418) 782-2112
Regarded by many as one of the best restaurants in Percé, La Normandie serves delicious food in an altogether charming spot. Diners rave about the *feuilleté de homard au champagne*

(lobster in puff pastry with champagne) and the *pétoncles à l'ail, au miel et aux poireaux* (scallops with garlic, honey and leeks). The restaurant also features an extensive wine list.

Auberge du Gargantua
$$$$
222 Rue des Failles
☎ (418) 782-2852
The decor of the **Auberge du Gargantua** (see p 470) is reminiscent of the French countryside where the owners were born. The dining room offers a splendid view of the surrounding mountains, so be sure to arrive early enough to enjoy it. The dishes are all gargantuan and delicious, and usually include an appetizer of periwinkle, a plate of raw vegetables, and soup. Guests choose their main dish from a long list, ranging from salmon to snow crab and a selection of game.

- - - - - - - - - - - - - - -
Tour B: Baie des Chaleurs

Bonaventure

Café Acadien
$$-$$$
early Jun to mid-Sep
168 Rue Beaubassin
☎ (418) 534-4276
Café Acadien serves good food in a charming setting. Open throughout the summer season, this place is very popular with locals and tourists alike, which might explain why the prices are a little high.

New Richmond

Les Têtes Heureuses
$-$$
104 Chemin Cyr
☎ (418) 392-6733
This café-bistro has both a charming atmosphere and an attractive menu with a vast selection of entrees, croissants, bagels, breads, pasta, quiches and rice. Everything is scrumptious, especially the homemade breads and desserts. A selection of imported and microbrewed beer is also available.

Carleton-Saint-Omer

La Seigneurie
$$-$$$
482 Boulevard Perron
☎ (418) 364-3355
La Seigneurie, the restaurant of the Hotel-Motel Baie Bleue, serves a wide variety of delicious dishes based on game, fish and seafood. The view from the dining room is superb.

Causapscal

Auberge La Coulée Douce
$$-$$$
21 Rue Boudreau
☎ (418) 756-5270
The dining room at the Auberge La Coulée Douce serves delicious meals, such as *bouillabaisse gaspésienne* and fresh salmon prepared a number of different ways. Pleasant service.

Entertainment

■ Bars and Nightclubs

Gaspé

La Voûte
114 Rue de la Reine
☎ (418) 368-1219
La Voûte caters mainly to students. The bar is busiest from 6pm to midnight. *Chansonniers* (folk singers) perform here regularly. On the second floor is a bar for people aged 25 and over.

Matane

Billbard
366 Avenue St-Jérôme
☎ (418) 562-3227
Billbard is a popular bar in Matane. Jazz and blues music play while patrons enjoy espresso, microbrewed beer and a few European sausage dishes. There is a terrace.

Le Vieux Loup de Mer
389 Avenue St-Jérôme
☎ (418) 562-2577
Another popular spot in Matane is Le Vieux Loup de Mer. The bar attracts an eclectic crowd and live entertainment is provided by folk singers on weekends.

Sainte-Anne-des-Monts

Chez Bass
170 1ʳᵉ Avenue
☎ (418) 763-2613
Chez Bass is a local institution where tourists and locals come for a drink and conversation among friends.

■ Festivals and Cultural Events

Carleton-Saint-Omer

Festival International Maximum Blues
early Aug
Carleton municipal beach
☎ (418) 364-6008
www.maximumblues.net
This festival offers a nice variety of live blues concerts on a stage located right on the city's municipal beach.

Mont-Saint-Pierre

Mont-Saint-Pierre's **Fête du Vol Libre** (☎418-797-2222) celebrates the town's vocation as a sky-diving centre. Sky-divers come here from all over to swoop over the bay all summer long, but at the end of July, when this activity-filled festival takes place, they really turn up in droves.

■ Theatres

Carleton-Saint-Omer

The **Théâtre La Moluque** (*mid-Jul to late Aug Tue-Sat 8:30pm; 586 Boulevard Perron,* ☎418-364-7151) puts on professional stage productions. New and classic plays are both performed here.

Petite-Vallée

The **Théâtre de la Vieille Forge** (*Jun to late Aug; 4 Longue-Pointe,* ☎418-393-2222) stages plays with a Gaspésian or Québécois flavour performed by local actors. Touring professional comedians and singers also perform here throughout the summer.

🏠 Shopping

■ Arts and Crafts

Grand-Métis

Les Ateliers Plein Soleil (♿; *Jardins de Métis, 220 Route 132, ☎418-775-2222)*, a group of artisans from Grand-Métis, runs this shop. They make all sorts of hand-woven tablecloths, doilies and napkins, which may be purchased in their shop, along with herbs, locally produced honey and homemade tomato ketchup.

■ Miscellaneous

Percé

Thanks to its central location, you can't miss the **Place du Quai**, a cluster of over 30 shops and restaurants, as well as a laundromat and an SAQ (liquor store).

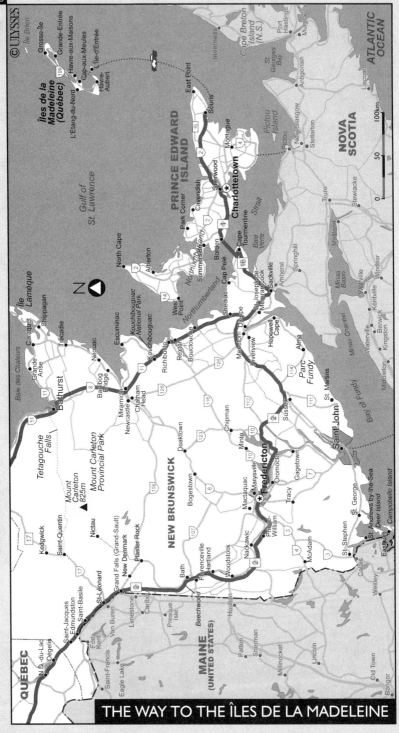

THE WAY TO THE ÎLES DE LA MADELEINE

Îles de la Madeleine

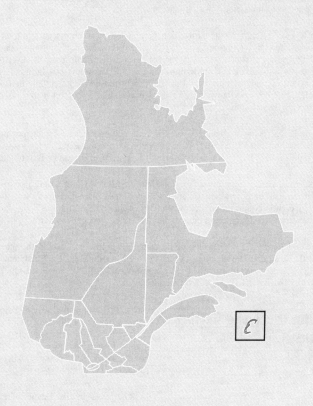

Rising from the Gulf of St. Lawrence more than 200km from the Gaspé Peninsula, the Îles de la Madeleine are sometimes referred to in English as the Magdalen Islands. They constitute a 65km-long archipelago of about a dozen islands, many of which connected to one another by long sand dunes. Swept by winds from the open sea, these small islands offer superb, colourful scenery.

The golden dunes and long, untouched beaches blend with the red sandstone cliffs and the blue sea. Villages with brightly painted houses, lighthouses and harbours add the finishing touches to the islands' beautiful scenery.

The islands' 13,000 *Madelinots* (as the residents are called) have always earned their livelihood from the sea, and continue to do so today by fishing for crab, bottom-feeding fish, mackerel and lobster. The population, mostly of French origin, lives on seven of the archipelago's islands: Île de la Grande Entrée, Grosse-Île, Île aux Loups, Île du Havre aux Maisons, Île du Cap aux Meules, Île du Havre Aubert and Île d'Entrée. Only Île d'Entrée, where a few families of Scottish ancestry live, is not linked by land to the rest of the archipelago.

The Îles de la Madeleine archipelago was first inhabited sporadically by Micmac peoples, also called the "Indians of the Sea." As of the 15th century, the islands were visited regularly by walrus and seal hunters, fishers and whalers, most of Breton or Basque descent.

In 1534, Jacques Cartier came upon the islands during his first North American expedition. Permanent settlers did not arrive until after 1755, when Acadian families took refuge here after having escaped deportation. Following the British conquest, the Îles de la Madeleine were annexed to Newfoundland before being integrated into Québec territory in 1774.

A few years later, in 1798, King George III granted Admiral Isaac Coffin the title of seigneur of the Îles de la Madeleine, ushering in a dismal period for the inhabitants of the archipelago. He and his family ruled the land despotically until 1895, when a Québec law allowed the Madelinots to buy back their land.

Getting There and Getting Around

■ By Car

From Québec

Approximately 1,420km separate Montréal from Souris, on Prince Edward Island, where a ferry (from April 1 to January 31) takes travellers on a 105km (5hr) ride to Cap-aux-Meules.

There are two ways to get to the islands from continental Québec:

1) Route 185 in the Bas-Saint-Laurent region (starting off in Rivière-du-Loup). Follow the road to Dégelis. You'll cross the New Brunswick border a few kilometres further, and Route 185 will become Highway 2. Follow this highway to Edmunston and then Moncton, where you'll turn onto Highway 15 to get to Shediac, and then Routes 15 and 16 towards Cape Tormentine. Expect to drive about 500km between Edmunston and Shediac.

2) Route 132 in the Gaspésie region. A bridge spans the Restigouche river in Pointe-à-la-Croix, linking the town to Campbellton, New Brunswick. After crossing the bridge you'll find yourself on Route 11. Follow this road from Campbellton to Bathurst, where you'll take Route 8 to Miramichi and then Route 11 again to Shediac and Routes 15 and 16 to Cape Tormentine. Some 285km separate Campbellton from Shediac.

Both these routes lead to the end of New Brunswick Route 16, where you'll reach **Confederation Bridge** *(cars $40.50 return-trip; pedestrians and cyclists not admitted on the bridge;* ☎ *902-437-7300 or 888-437-6565, www.*

confederationbridge.com). Cross the bridge to get to Prince Edward Island. Head to Souris, where the **N.M. Madeleine** ferry *($40 per person plus $75 per car)* will take you to the islands.

On the Islands

Of the seven inhabited islands of the Îles de la Madeleine, six are linked together by Rte. 199. The proposed tour takes visitors to each island to discover some of their hidden treasures.

The seventh island, Île d'Éntrée, is only accessible by boat, and is a trip in itself. The **S.P. Bonaventure** *($16; ☎418-986-5705 or 986-8452)* shuttles between Havre-Aubert, Cap-Aux-Meules and Île d'Entrée from Monday to Saturday, and the trip takes approximately 1hr.

Car rentals are available for visitors who want to drive around the islands.

Cap-aux-Meules Honda
1090 Chemin de Lavernière, L'Étang-du-Nord
☎ (418) 986-4085
This establishment also rents motorcycles.

National Tilden
205 Chemin de l'Aéroport, Havre-aux-Maisons
☎ (418) 969-4209 or 888-657-3036

Thrifty
188 Chemin de l'Aéroport, Havre-aux-Maisons
☎ (418) 969-9006 or 800-367-2277

Location du Berceau
701 Rte. 199, Havre-Aubert
☎ (418) 937-5614

■ By Plane

Air Nova - Air Alliance (Air Canada) *(☎418-969-2888 or 800-630-3299)* offers daily flights to the Îles de la Madeleine. Departures are from Halifax, Québec City and Montréal. Most flights make stopovers in Québec City, Mont-Joli or Gaspé, so count on a 4hr trip. Considerable price reductions can be found by booking well in advance.

■ By Ferry

The **N/M Madeleine** ferry *($40, car $75, motorcycle $26, bicycle $9.50; ☎418-986-3278*

or 888-986-3278, www.ctma.ca) leaves from Souris (Prince Edward Island) and reaches Cap-aux-Meules in about 5hrs. Try to reserve in advance if possible; if not, arrive at the pier a few hours before departure, or to be extra sure, go to Souris the day before your departure and reserve seats. Ask for the ferry-crossing schedule, as it changes from one season to the next.

CTMA Vacancier
☎ (418) 986-3278 or 888-986-3278
www.ctma.ca

■ By Bicycle

Bikes are definitely the best way to get around on the islands. Here is a bike-rental outfit:

Le Pédalier
800 Chemin Principal, Cap-aux-Meules
☎ (418) 986-2965

Useful Information

■ Tourist Information

Regional Office

Tourisme Îles de la Madeleine
128 Chemin Principal, Cap-aux-Meules, G4T 1C5
☎ (418) 986-2245 or 877-624-4437
🖷 (418) 986-2327
www.tourismeilesdelamadeleine.com

Exploring

Île du Cap aux Meules
★

Our tour begins on Île du Cap aux Meules, since it is the archipelago's most populated island as well as the docking point for all ferries (Cap-aux-Meules). Home to the region's major infrastructures, (hospital, high school, college), this island is the centre of local economic activity. This activity does not take away from the island's charm, however, with its brightly painted houses that some say allow sailors to see their homes from the sea.

Cap-aux-Meules

Cap-aux-Meules, the only urban centre of the archipelago, has experienced major development over the past few years. Since many buildings were constructed quickly, aesthetics were not a primary consideration. A few of the traditional houses still stand, however.

A climb to the top of the **Butte du Vent** ★★ reveals a superb panorama of the island and the gulf.

The beautiful **Chemin de Gros-Cap** ★★, south of Cap-aux-Meules, runs along the Baie de Plaisance and offers breathtaking scenery. If possible, stop at the **Pêcherie Gros-Cap**, where the employees can be seen at work in this fish-processing plant.

Head back and take Chemin de L'Étang-du-Nord to L'Étang-du-Nord.

You'll notice the imposing **Église de la Vernière** ★ along the way. It features an interesting wood architecture and was declared a historical monument.

L'Étang-du-Nord

For a long time, L'Étang-du-Nord was home to almost half the population of the Îles de la Madeleine and constituted the largest fishing village. With the foundation of Cap-aux-Meules (1959) and Fatima (1954), however, it lost a significant part of its population, and now only has just over 3,000 inhabitants. The municipality, with its beautiful port, welcomes many visitors every year who come to take advantage of the region's tranquillity and natural beauty.

North of L'Étang-du-Nord, visitors can take in the splendid view by walking along the magnificent **Belle Anse cliffs** ★★. The violent waves crashing relentlessly along the coast are an impressive sight from the top of this rocky escarpment.

Return to L'Étang-du-Nord and take Chemin de L'Étang-du-Nord to the Aut. 199 junction; take this road toward Havre-Aubert, crossing the Dune du Havre aux Basques.

Île du Havre Aubert
★ ★ ★

Beautiful Île du Havre Aubert, dotted with beaches, hills and forests, has managed to keep its picturesque charm. From early on, it was home to various colonies. Even today, buildings testify to these early colonial years. Prior to this, it was populated by Micmac communities, and relics have been discovered.

Havre-Aubert

The first stop on the island, Havre-Aubert, stretches along the sea and benefits from a large bay that is ideal for fishing. Apart from the magnificent scenery, the most interesting attraction is without a doubt the **La Grave** ★★★ area, which has developed along a pebbly beach and gets its charm from the traditional cedar-shingled houses. It lies at the heart of a lively area, and is home to several cultural events. Boutiques and cafés line the streets, which are always enjoyable, even in bad weather. The few buildings along the sea were originally stores and warehouses that received the fish caught by locals.

For anyone interested in the fascinating world of marine life, the **Aquarium des Îles** ★ *($5; early Jun to mid-Aug every day 10am to 6pm, mid-Aug to mid-Oct every day 10am to 5pm; 982 Rte. 199, La Grave, ☎418-937-2277)* is a real treat. Here, visitors can observe (and even touch) many various marine species, such as lobsters, crabs, sea urchins, eels, a ray, as well as a multitude of other fish and crustaceans. The second floor has more of an educational atmosphere with exhibits explaining the various fishing techniques used by the islands' fishers throughout the years.

The **Musée de la Mer** ★ *($5; mid-Jun to mid-Sep every day 9am to 6pm, mid-Sep to late Oct Mon-Fri 9am to noon and 1pm to 5pm, Sat-Sun 1pm to 5pm, early Nov to mid-Jun Tue-Fri 9am to noon and 1pm to 5pm; 1023 Pointe Shea, at the end of Rte. 199, ☎418-937-5711)* recounts the history of the populating of the islands as well as the relationship that links Madelinots to the sea. Visitors also have the opportunity to explore the world of fishing and navigation, as well as discover some of the myths and legends that surround the sea.

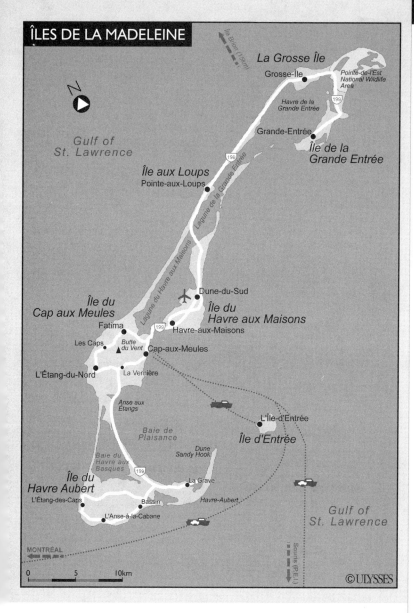

ÎLES DE LA MADELEINE

When leaving Havre-Aubert, follow Chemin du Sable to Sandy Hook Dune.

Sandy Hook Dune ★★★, see p 483.

Return along Chemin du Sable and take Chemin du Bassin to L'Étang-des-Caps.

The road that runs along the sea between the Pointe à Marichite and L'Étang-des-Caps offers a magnificent **view** ★★ of the Gulf of St. Lawrence. From the small village of **L'Étang-des-Caps**, the small Île Corps Mort is visible in the distance on clear days.

Return via Chemin de la Montagne, and follow Chemin du Bassin, then return towards Île du Cap

The *Blanchons*

The symbol of the ecotourism industry on the Îles de la Madeleine, the *blanchon* is a young seal or *loup-marin* (sea-wolf), as the islanders call this mammal. During the first weeks of March, after a long journey along the shores of Labrador and through the Gulf of St. Lawrence, the seals give birth on the ice floes around the Îles de la Madeleine. Nearly three million seals make this trip each year. Once the young have been weaned, the animals head back up to the Arctic, where they spend the greater part of their lives.

The seals actually reach the islands in January, after swimming south along the shores of Labrador for about four months. They stay in the gulf for two or three months, building up their fatty tissue. The month of March is marked by the birth of thousands of these adorable little fur-balls, which have raised international awareness since the 1970s, when environmental groups demonstrated against seal-hunting. The *blanchons* have to be a month and a half old before they can take their first dive, which makes them easy to observe. During this period, the *blanchons* grow at an astonishing rate; during the 12 days during which they are suckled by their mothers, their weight triples. Seal's milk is actually five times as rich as cow's milk.

The *blanchons* are no longer threatened by hunting, but adult seals are still hunted. Madelinots and Newfoundlanders kill nearly 50,000 seals every year. When it comes to fish, these animals are formidable predators. Some fishers even hold them responsible for depleted fish stocks. Seals are far from being an endangered species, and in fact their population has grown considerably in recent years. In response to pressure from the fishers, the federal government has revived seal hunting by setting the quota at 200,000 per year.

aux Meules by taking Rte. 199, which leads to Île du Havre aux Maisons.

Île du Havre aux Maisons
★ ★

Île du Havre aux Maisons is characterized by its bare landscape and its small, attractive villages with pretty little houses scattered along winding roads. The steep cliffs at the southern end of the island overlook the gulf and offer a fascinating view of this immense stretch of water.

Havre-aux-Maisons

The Dune du Nord and the Dune du Sud are two long strips of sand found at both extremities of the island and feature beautiful beaches. In the centre of the village of Havre-aux-Maisons stand the Vieux Couvent (old convent) and the presbytery; the village is also the island's main centre of activity.

The **La Méduse** ★ *(Jun to Aug Mon-Sat 10am to 5pm, Mar to May and Sep-Oct Mon-Fri 10am to 5pm; 37 Chemin de la Carrière,* ☎*418-969-4681)* glass-blowing factory opens its doors to visitors, allowing them to see glassblowers at work. Next to the workshop is a small boutique that sells the factory's products.

The scenic Chemin de la Pointe-Basse crosses the south of the island along the Baie de Plaisance and offers beautiful views. A small path along the road, between the Cap à Adrien and the Cap à Alfred, descends towards the sea, revealing the charming natural haven of Pointe-Basse.

Don't miss the **Fumoir d'Antan** (traditional smokehouse) and the **Économusée du Hareng Fumé** (smoked herring economuseum) *(27 Chemin du Quai,* ☎*418-969-4907).*

Continue along Rte. 199, which leads to Grosse-Île, by crossing Île aux Loups.

Grosse-Île

The rocky coasts of Grosse-Île have caused numerous shipwrecks, the survivors of which have settled here. A good number of these accidental colonists were Scottish, and approximately 500 of them still live here today. Most earn their living from fishing and agriculture; some also work in the Seleine saltworks, which opened in 1983.

Rte. 199 continues until the **Pointe-de-l'Est National Wildlife Area** ★ (see below).

Follow Rte. 199 to Île de la Grande Entrée.

Île de la Grande Entrée
★

Île de la Grande Entrée, colonized in 1870, was the last of the Îles de la Madeleine to be inhabited. Upon arriving, cross Pointe Old-Harry to check out a striking view of the gulf. This tip of the island was named in honour of Harry Clark, who was the area's only inhabitant for many years. The island's main town, **Grande-Entrée**, has an active port that serves as a departure point for many brightly painted fishing boats, usually for lobster fishing.

To learn more about the lives of seals, visit the **Centre d'Interprétation du Phoque** ★ *($5.75; Jun to Sep every day 10am to 6pm; 377 Rte. 199;* ☎*418-985-2833)* where various exhibits explain the lifestyle of these mammals.

To get to Île d'Entrée, which can be toured in one day, take the ferry from the Cap-aux-Meules dock.

Île d'Entrée
★★

Île d'Entrée differs from the rest of the islands not only because of its geographic location (it is the only inhabited island that is not linked to the others), but also because of its population of some 200 residents all of Scottish descent.

This small community lives almost entirely from the sea, and has managed to settle on this land despite the waves and the wind. The island has its own infrastructure to meets the needs of its residents (electricity, roads, and telephone). An incredible feeling of serenity prevails here.

Parks

Grosse-Île

The eastern tip of Grosse-Île, made up of dunes and beaches, is home to the diverse bird life that is characteristic of these islands. It is one of the best sites for spotting various species, such as the rare piping plover (which only nests on the islands), the northern pintail, the betted kingfisher, the Atlantic puffin and the horned lark. Take care not to damage the nesting sites (generally clearly marked). This entire zone is protected by the **Pointe-de-l'Est National Wildlife Area** ★, also known as the Réserve Nationale de Faune de la Pointe-de-l'Est. The **Grande Échouerie beach** is also located here (see below).

Beaches

Île du Cap aux Meules

The **Plage de l'Hôpital**, located along the Dune du Nord, is a good place to go for a dip and watch the seals. It should be noted that the currents become dangerous toward Pointe-aux-Loups. The Anse, l'Hôpital, Cap de l'Hôpital, Plage de l'Hôpital and Étang-de-l'Hôpital are all named after a boat that came into the cove (*anse*) carrying passengers suffering from a contagious illness (typhus). The boat was quarantined, and only doctors and nurses were allowed on board.

Île du Havre Aubert

Like a long strip of sand stretching into the gulf, **Sandy Hook Dune** ★ ★ ★ is several kilometres long and its beach is among the finest on the islands.

The **Plage de l'Ouest** ★ stretches from the northwest part of Île du Havre Aubert to the southwest part of Île du Cap aux Meules. Perfect for swimming and shell collecting, it is renowned for its magnificent sunsets.

Île du Havre aux Maisons

The **Plage de la Dune du Sud** ★ offers several kilometres of beach, which is great for swimming.

Grosse-Île

One of the most beautiful beaches on the islands, the **Plage de la Grande Échouerie** ★ ★, stretches for about 10km in the Pointe-de-l'Est wildlife area.

Outdoor Activities

■ Bird-Watching

During the "échouerie" (two mornings per week) nature walks organized by the **Club Vacances Les Îles** *(377 Rte. 199, Grande-Entrée, ☎418-985-2833 or 888-537-4537, www. club iles.qc.ca)*, you'll have a chance to see the nests of whistling plovers, an endangered species. It is important that observers spend no more than 10 or 15min near the nests to avoid disturbing the birds. At the beach, you'll see guillemots soaring through the air.

The **Pointe de la Cormorandière**, on the northern side of Big Hill on Île d'Entrée, is another good spot for birding enthusiasts.

■ Fishing

Visitors can take part in fishing trips organized by **Excursions en Mer** *(early Jun to mid-Sep; Cap-aux-Meules pier, ☎418-986-4745, www.excursionsenmer.com)*, which also offers boat trips to Île d'Entrée and Île du Havre Aubert. All fishing equipment and instructions are provided on the boat.

■ Hiking

The **Club Vacances Les Îles** *(Grande-Entrée, ☎418-985-2833 or 888-537-4537, www.club iles.qc.ca)* organizes nature walks to help visitors discover the various ecosystems found on the Îles de la Madeleine.

■ Horseback Riding

La Chevauchée des Îles *(year-round every day 9am to 9pm; L'Étang-des-Caps, Île du Havre Aubert, ☎418-937-2368)* organizes riding excursions in the forest and on the beach. Reservations required.

Les Calèches du Havre
784 Rte. 199, Havre-Aubert
☎(418) 937-2586

■ Kayaking

L'Istorlet *(100 Chemin L'Istorlet, Havre-Aubert, ☎418-937-5266 or 888-937-8166)* offers the chance to join kayaking excursions that take you to grottos and cliff bottoms. Other nautical activities are also offered.

Aérosport Carrefour d'Aventures *(1390 Chemin Lavernière, L'Étang-du-Nord, ☎418-986-6677 or 866-986-6677, www.aerosport.ca)* offers sea-kayaking trips and training.

■ Sailing and Windsurfing

L'Istorlet *(weekly rentals available; 100 Chemin L'Istorlet, Havre-Aubert, ☎418-937-5266 or 888-937-8166)* offers sailing and windsurfing courses and rents out small boats. Its safe, sheltered location near the Bassin makes it the ideal spot for first-timers to try this sport. Expect to spend $30/hr for sailing and $25/hr for windsurfing.

■ Scuba Diving

The waters around the islands make for great scuba diving. Encounters with schools of fish, lobsters and coral are guaranteed.

Le Repère du Plongeur
18 Allée Léo Leblanc, L'Étang-du-Nord
☎(418) 986-3962
www.repereduplongeur.com

Îles de la Madeleine - Beaches

Accommodations

Île du Cap aux Meules

Fatima

Camping Le Barachois
$
🐾

early May to late Oct
87 Chemin du Rivage
☎ (418) 986-6065
Le Barachois campground can accommodate tents or campers in its 180 wind-sheltered sites. Located in the middle of a small wooded area along the sea, it has a peaceful atmosphere and a beach.

La Maison du Cap-Vert
$$ bkfst incl.
pb/sb
202 Chemin L.-Aucoin
☎ (418) 986-5331
www.maisonducapvert.ca
La Maison du Cap-Vert is a family inn with five absolutely charming rooms with comfy beds and a unique decor. This place has made a name for itself in just a short period of time. With its delicious, all-you-can-eat breakfasts, it is definitely a good deal.

Château Madelinot
$$$
🛏≈ ♨ ⁇ ◎
323 Rte. 199
☎ (418) 986-3695 or 800-661-4537
🖨 (418) 986-6437
Visitors might first be surprised to find that the Château Madelinot is not a *château*, but rather a large house. But the comfortable rooms and superb view of the sea make it easy to get over the disappointment. The place offers many services and is without a doubt the best-known accommodation on the islands. Its interior features temporary exhibits of works by artists from the islands and elsewhere in Québec.

L'Étang-du-Nord

Auberge Chez Sam
$$ bkfst incl.
pb/sb
1767 Chemin de L'Étang-du-Nord
☎ (418) 986-5780
The very warm welcome at Auberge Chez Sam will quickly make guests feel et home. The place has five attractive, well-kept rooms.

Île du Havre Aubert

Camping Plage du Golfe
$
🐾

535 Chemin du Bassin
☎ (418) 937-5224
🖨 (418) 937-5115
The Plage du Golfe camground features more than 70 sites, some of which accommodate trailers.

B&B L'Aquarelle
$$ bkfst incl.
sb
66 Chemin des Fumoirs
☎ (418) 937-5908
Miche and Louis are the affable artists who run this bed and breakfast. The warm atmosphere they provide is typical of the famous friendly vibe of the islands.

La Marée Haute
$$-$$$ bkfst incl.
sb/pb ♿ ♨
25 Chemin des Fumoirs
☎/🖨 (418) 937-2492
Located close to La Grave, La Marée Haute is a lovely little inn where guests are warmly welcomed. The rooms are cozy and attractively decorated. One of the owners also cooks; you won't regret trying one of these lovingly and meticulously prepared dishes. The view from the inn is absolutely awesome.

Auberge Havre sur Mer
$$-$$$ bkfst incl.
◎

May to mid-Oct
1197 Chemin du Bassin
☎ (418) 937-5675
🖨 (418) 937-2540
www.havresurmer.com
The Havre Sur Mer, near the cliff's edge, enjoys a magnificent location. The rooms have a communal terrace from which everybody can enjoy the beautiful view. The inn is furnished with antiques and attracts many visitors.

Île du Havre aux Maisons

Auberge de la Petite Baie
$$ bkfst incl.
♨
187 Route 199
☎ (418) 969-4073
🖨 (418) 969-4900
Réjeanne Langford is proud to welcome visitors to her cozy inn, which is located in an early 20th century customhouse and has four rooms for rent. The dining room, which features beautiful old English tableware, offers some of the islands' delicious traditional fare, such as *loup marin*

Îles de la Madeleine - Accommodations - Île du Havre aux Maisons

Îles de la Madeleine - Accommodations - Île du Havre aux Maisons

(seal) and *pot-en-pot* (which resembles a seafood pie).

Île de la Grande Entrée

Camping Grande-Entrée du Club Vacances Les Îles
$
🚐 👘
377 Rte. 199
☎ (418) 985-2833 or 888-537-4537
🖳 (418) 985-2226
www.clubiles.qc.ca
The Grande-Entrée campground at the Club Vacances Les Îles has 24 sites, eight of which are set up for trailers. A dormitory is available for visitors on rainy days.

Club Vacances Les Îles
$$$$ fb
377 Rte. 199
☎ (418) 985-2833 or 888-537-4537
www.clubiles.qc.ca
In addition to offering spacious, comfortable rooms, the Club Vacances Les Îles organizes several activities and excursions so that visitors can discover the area's natural riches. Guests can also take advantage of the cafeteria for varied and flavourful meals.

Île d'Entrée

Chez McLean
$ bkfst incl.
sb
Chemin de l'École
☎ (418) 986-4541
Chez McLean was built over 60 years ago and has managed to keep its character of yesteryear.

Restaurants

Île du Cap aux Meules

Fatima

Le P'tit Café
$$$
mid-May to mid-Sep
☎ (418) 986-2130
Le P'tit Café, located in the **Château Madelinot** (see p 485), serves Sunday brunch from 10am to 1:30pm. Those with a taste for novelty can order seafood, red meat or chicken cooked on a hot stone. The menu includes a large selection of appetizers, soups and charbroiled dishes.

L'Étang-du-Nord

La Table des Roy
$$$$
Jun to Sep; closed Sun
1188 Chemin Lavernière
☎ (418) 986-3004
Since 1978, La Table des Roy has offered refined cuisine to delight every visitor's taste buds. The tempting menu features seafood, prepared in a multitude of ways, such as grilled scallops and lobster with *coralline* sauce. The dining room is charming and adds a particular style to this excellent restaurant, which also offers dishes adorned with edible flowers and plants of the islands. Reservations recommended.

Île du Havre Aubert

Le Régal II
$$
mid-May to mid-Sep
591 Route 199, La Grave
☎ (418) 937-2492
Located in the seaside La Grave area, Le Régal II occupies the former site of the islands' first restaurant, Le Régal. This friendly little café serves simple but delicious local fare like fish & chips. A good spot to meet the locals.

Café de la Grave
$$
May to Sep
969 Rte. 199
☎ (418) 937-5765
Decorated like an old general store, the Café de la Grave has a very pleasant atmosphere. When the weather is bad, you can spend hours here chatting. In addition to muffins, croissants and a wide variety of coffees, the menu offers healthy and sometimes unusual dishes, such as *tourtière de loup marin*, which are always good. This café is delightfully welcoming and will leave you with lasting memories.

La Saline
$$-$$$
1009 Rte. 199
☎ (418) 937-2230
A former salting shed in La Grave, La Saline serves excellent regional cuisine. *Loup-marin*, cod, mussels, shrimp and other saltwater treats appear on the menu. Guests also have a splendid view of the sea.

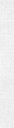

La Marée Haute
$$$$
25 Chemin des Fumoirs
☎ (418) 937-2492

The chef and co-owner of La Marée Haute knows how to bring out the best in fish and seafood. In this lovely inn, you can sample sea perch, shark or mackerel while drinking in the magnificent view. You can taste the ocean in these dishes, whose expertly enhanced flavour will send you into raptures. The menu also includes a few equally well-prepared meat dishes and some succulent desserts.

Île du Havre aux Maisons

La Moulière
$$$
11am to 10pm
292 Rte. 199
☎ (418) 969-2233

There are two restaurants in the Hôtel Au Vieux Couvent. **La Moulière**, located on the main floor, occupies a large room that formerly served as a chapel. It serves excellent dishes in a lively atmosphere. **Rest-O-Bar** *($$)* is found on the same floor, in the former parlour that extends onto a terrace overlooking the sea. Hamburgers and mussels are among the dishes served in this restaurant, which is as popular as La Moulière.

La Petite Baie
$$$$
Jun to mid-Sep
187 Rte. 199
☎ (418) 969-4073

La Petite Baie serves well-prepared grilled dishes, seafood and fish, as well as a number of beef, pork and chicken dishes. *Loup-marin* is served here in season. In addition to the à-la-carte menu, there is a table-d'hôte with a choice of two main dishes. The service is courteous, and a great deal of care has gone into the decor.

Grosse-Île

Chez B&J
$$
126 Chemin Principal
☎ (418) 985-2926

Chez B&J serves fresh scallops, halibut, lobster salad and fresh fish.

Île de la Grande Entrée

Le Délice de la Mer

$$
May to Sep
907 Chemin Principal
☎ (418) 985-2364

Le Délice de la Mer specializes in simply prepared seafood dishes; the lobster is delicious. Affordable prices and homemade desserts are also in store.

Entertainment

■ Bars and Nightclubs

Île du Cap aux Meules

Les Pas Perdus
169 Chemin Principal, Cap-aux-Meules
☎ (418) 986-5151

Whether you're looking for a drink, a cup of coffee, a place to meet the locals, a spot to curl up with a book, an Internet fix or some live entertainment, head to Les Pas Perdus. A unpretentious and creative menu awaits, and there are even six rooms for rent on the upper floor.

Le Barachois
Fatima
☎ (418) 986-3130

This nightclub features a large dance floor and a long enclosed terrace. It attracts a young crowd and is a favourite meeting place for the local gay community.

Île du Havre Aubert

Quality micro-brewed beer is served at the laid-back **Pub Chez Brophy**, in the La Grave area.

Île du Havre aux Maisons

The **Chez Gaspard** bar at the Domaine du Vieux Couvent *(292 Rte. 199, ☎418-969-2233)* occupies a former convent dining hall. Musicians play on some evenings, making the bar lively and noisy.

■ Festivals and Cultural Events

Île du Havre Aubert

The **Concours des Châteaux de Sable** takes place every August on the Havre-Aubert beach as participants work for hours to build the best sandcastle. Visitors wanting to put their talent to the test can register by calling ☎(418) 986-6863.

■ **Theatre and Performance Hall**

Île du Havre Aubert

Located in La Grave, **Au Vieux Treuil** *(Jul and Aug;* ☎*418-937-5138)* is a venue for theatre, jazz and classical music. Temporary exhibitions are also presented here.

Shopping

■ **Arts and Crafts**

Île du Havre Aubert

Les Artisans du Sable *(907 Rte. 199, La Grave, Havre-Aubert,* ☎*418-937-2917)* sells items made of sand according to a special technique used only by Madelinot artisans. These items, which vary from decorations to lampshades, are wonderful souvenirs of the islands. You can also visit the **Économusée du Sable** to learn more about sand.

Île du Havre aux Maisons

La Méduse
37 Chemin de la Carrière, Havre-aux-Maisons
☎ (418) 969-4681
The **La Méduse** glass factory (see p 482) features a small gift shop.

■ **Food**

Île du Cap-aux-Meules

Boulangerie Madon
353 Chemin Petitpas, Cap-aux-Meules
☎ (418) 986-3409

In addition to bread and pastries, this bakery offers ready-made meals, cheese and coffee. A good stop before setting out on a picnic.

Île du Havre Aubert

La Chocolaterie Diane
2026 Étang-des-Caps, L'Étang-des-Caps
☎ (418) 937-5757
This chocolate shop will appeal to both gourmets and gluttons who'll want to try handmade orange chocolates, strawberry chocolates, wild-berry chocolates, pralines…

Charlevoix

The unique beauty of the Charlevoix region has been captivating artists for years. From the town of Saint-Joachim to the mouth of the Rivière Saguenay, the dramatic mountainous countryside contrasts sharply with the expansive open water of the St. Lawrence.

Ascattering of charming villages and towns dots the coastline, dwarfed by mountains that recede into the salt water of the river and steep-sided valleys. Away from the river, Charlevoix is a wild, rugged region where the Boreal forest sometimes gives way to the tundra.

The old houses and churches found throughout the region are vestiges of Charlevoix's history as a French colony. In addition, the division of farmland in the area still reflects the seigneurial system of land grants used under the French Regime.

The rich architectural heritage and exceptional geography are complemented by a dazzling variety of flora and fauna. The Charlevoix region was declared a UNESCO World Biosphere Reserve in 1988 and is home to many fascinating animal and plant species. A number of whale species feed at the mouth of the Rivière Saguenay during the summer.

In the spring and fall, hundreds of thousands of snow geese make migratory stops in the region, creating a remarkable sight near Cap-Tourmente, farther west. Deep in the hinterland, the territory has all the properties of the tundra, a remarkable occurrence at this latitude. This area is home to a variety of animal species, such as caribou and the large Arctic wolf. Charlevoix also has many types of plants not found in other parts of eastern Canada.

The Charlevoix region's beautiful landscape has been attracting vacationers since the late 18th century. During the early 20th century, well-to-do members of Québec, Canadian and American society would meet at the elegant Manoir Richelieu in Pointe-au-Pic after a cruise on the St. Lawrence. This long tradition of hospitality has stood the test of time, and you'll find several charming inns and excellent restaurants during your travels in Charlevoix.

Getting There and Getting Around

The **Charlevoix** ★★★ tour follows the St. Lawrence shoreline and includes some inland excursions. Before leaving, make sure your car is in good condition and remember to have the brakes checked: Charlevoix roads are often steep and winding.

■ By Car

To get to Charlevoix from Québec City, take Route 138, the main road in the region. For a more complete look at the region, consider combining this tour with the **Côte de Beaupré** tour (see p 377). After crossing a low-lying area close to the St. Lawrence, Route 138 veers into the rolling Charlevoix countryside. This is the southwest extremity of the Laurentians Mountains. The north side of the river valley is bordered by the Laurentians for hundreds of miles to the

east. Île d'Orléans and Québec City can be seen from here on clear days.

■ Bus Stations

Baie-Saint-Paul
2 Route de l'Équerre (Le Village shopping centre)
☎ (418) 435-6569

Saint-Hilarion
354 Route 138
☎ (418) 457-3855

Clermont
83 Boulevard Notre-Dame
☎ (418) 439-3404

La Malbaie–Pointe-au-Pic
46 Rue Ste-Catherine
☎ (418) 665-2264

Saint-Siméon
775 Rue St-Laurent
☎ (418) 638-2671

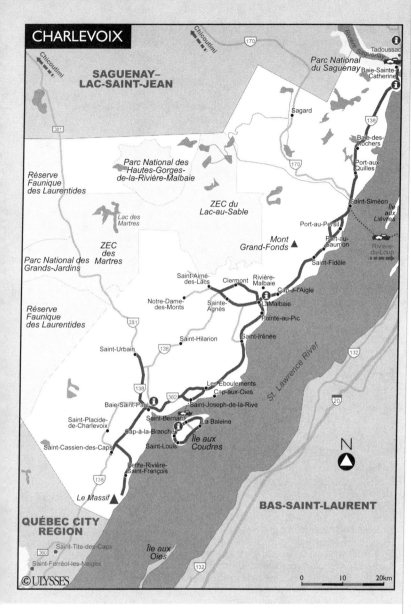

CHARLEVOIX

SAGUENAY–
LAC-SAINT-JEAN

Parc National
du Saguenay

Tadoussac

Baie-Sainte-
Catherine

Sagard

Baie-des-
Rochers

Port-aux-
Quilles

Réserve
Faunique
des Laurentides

Parc National des
Hautes-Gorges-
de-la-Rivière-Malbaie

ZEC du
Lac-au-Sable

Saint-Siméon

Île
aux
Lièvres

Port-au-Persil

Lac des
Martres

Mont
Grand-Fonds

Port-au-
Saumon

Rivière-
du-Loup

ZEC
des
Martres

Parc National des
Grands-Jardins

Saint-Fidèle

Saint-Aimé-
des-Lacs

Clermont

Rivière-
Malbaie

Cap-à-l'Aigle

Réserve
Faunique
des Laurentides

Notre-Dame-
des-Monts

Sainte-
Agnès

LaMalbaie

Pointe-au-Pic

Saint-Hilarion

Saint-Irénée

St. Lawrence River

Saint-Urbain

Les Éboulements

Cap-aux-Oies

Baie-Saint-Paul

Saint-Joseph-de-la-Rive

Saint-Placide-
de-Charlevoix

Saint-Bernard

La Baleine

Cap-à-la-Branche

Île aux
Coudres

Saint-Cassien-des-Caps

Saint-Louis

Petite-Rivière-
Saint-François

Le Massif

QUÉBEC CITY
REGION

BAS-SAINT-LAURENT

N

Saint-Tite-des-Caps

Île aux
Oies

Saint-Ferréol-les-Neiges

©ULYSSES

0   10   20km

Charlevoix – Getting There and Getting Around

■ By Ferry

Saint-Siméon

The ferry *($12, cars $30.50; Apr to Jan; ☎418-638-2856, www.travrdlstsim.com)* from Rivière-du-Loup travels to Saint-Siméon in just over an hour.

Baie-Sainte-Catherine

The ferry *(free; ☎418-235-4395)* travels between Tadoussac and Baie-Sainte-Catherine in approximately 10min.

Île aux Coudres

The car ferry to Île aux Coudres *(free; ☎418-438-2743)* leaves from Saint-Joseph-de-la-Rive. There is usually a half-hour wait before boarding during the summer months.

Useful Information

■ Tourist Information

Regional Office

Association Touristique de Charlevoix
495 Boulevard de Comporté, C.P. 275
La Malbaie, G5A 1T8
☎ (418) 665-4454 or 800-667-2276
▤ (418) 665-3811
www.tourisme-charlevoix.com

Baie-Saint-Paul

Bureau de Tourisme de Charlevoix
444 Boulevard Monseigneur-De Laval, Route 138
☎ (418) 435-4160

Exploring

Charlevoix
★ ★ ★

 2 days

The Charlevoix countryside could have been created for giants—the villages tucked into bays or perched atop summits look like dollhouses left behind by a child. Rustic farmhouses and luxurious summer houses are scattered about, and some have been converted into inns. Although Charlevoix was one of the first regions in North America where tourism flourished, the area further inland is still a wilderness area of valleys and tranquil lakes.

Petite-Rivière-Saint-François (pop. 732)

Petite-Rivière-Saint-François is nestled between the mountains and the St. Lawrence and features a spectacular landscape sprinkled with charming wood cottages. Author Gabrielle Roy (1909-1983) had a summer

residence here, where she would retire to write. A nice view of the surroundings can be had from the town pier.

Le Massif ★ ★ ★ (see p 500).

Follow Route 138 to Baie-Saint-Paul.

Baie-Saint-Paul ★ ★ (pop. 7,387)

Charlevoix's undulating geography has proved a challenge to agricultural development. Under the French Regime, only a few attempts at colonisation were made in this vast region which, along with parts of the Beaupré coast, was overseen by the Séminaire de Québec. Baie-Saint-Paul, at the mouth of the Rivière du Gouffre valley, was home to a few settlers.

Although Charlevoix has some of the planet's oldest rock formations, several major earthquakes have rocked the pastoral region since it was first colonized. The following description by Baptiste Plamondon, then vicar of Baie-Saint-Paul, appeared in the October 22, 1870 edition of the *Journal de Québec*:

"It was about half an hour before noon...a tremendous explosion stunned the population. Rather than simply tremble, the earth seemed to boil, such that it caused vertigo.... The houses could have been on a volcano, the way they were tossed about. Water gushed fifteen feet into the air through cracks in the ground...."

A bend in the road reveals Baie-Saint-Paul in all its charm, and a slope leads to the heart of the village, which has maintained a quaint small-town atmosphere. Set out on foot along the lovely Rue Saint-Jean-Baptiste, Rue Saint-Joseph and Rue Sainte-Anne, where small wooden houses with mansard roofs now house boutiques and cafés. For over a century, Baie-Saint-Paul has attracted North-American landscape artists, inspired by the mountains and a quality of light particular to Charlevoix. There are many art galleries and art centres in the area, which display and sell beautiful Canadian paintings and sculptures (see p 509).

Belvédère Baie-Saint-Paul *(444 Boulevard Mgr-De Laval, Route 138,* ☎*418-435-6275)* occupies a rest stop off Route 138. The lookout offers a spectacular vantage point

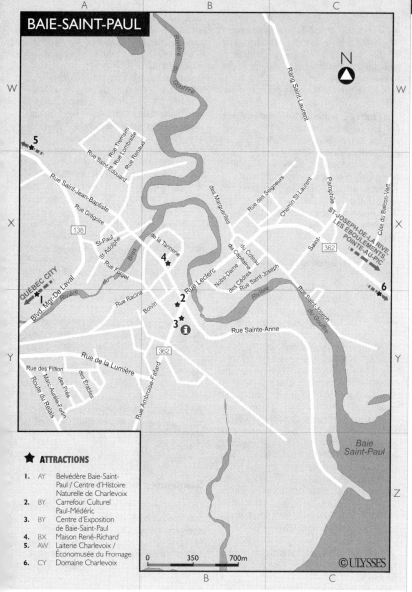

BAIE-SAINT-PAUL

N

★ 5

Rue Tremblay
Rue Saint-Édouard
Rue Lombrette
Rue Renaud

Rivière du Gouffre

Rang Saint-Laurent

Rue Saint-Jean-Baptiste

Rue Grégoire

des Marguerites

Rue des Seigneurs

Chemin St-Laurent

Pamphile

Côte du Balcon-Vert

138

St-Paul
St-Adolphe

de la Tannerie

Bras

du Coteau
du Capitaine
des Cèdres

ST-JOSEPH-DE-LA-RIVE
LES ÉBOULEMENTS,
POINTE-AU-PIC

Saint-

362

Rue Forget

★ 4

Rue Leclerc

Notre-Dame

Rue Saint-Joseph

QUÉBEC CITY

Blvd. Mgr-De Laval

Rivière

★ 1

Rue Racine

Bolvin

★ 2

★ 3 ℹ

Rue Sainte-Anne

Rivière

Rue Saint-Joseph
du Gouffre

★ 6

362

Rue de la Lumière

Rue des Fillion
Marc-Aurèle-Fortin
Route du Relais
des Prés
des Érables

Rue Ambroise-Fafard

Baie
Saint-Paul

★ ATTRACTIONS

1. AY   Belvédère Baie-Saint-
        Paul / Centre d'Histoire
        Naturelle de Charlevoix
2. BY   Carrefour Culturel
        Paul-Médéric
3. BY   Centre d'Exposition
        de Baie-Saint-Paul
4. BX   Maison René-Richard
5. AW   Laiterie Charlevoix /
        Économusée du Fromage
6. CY   Domaine Charlevoix

0   350   700m

©ULYSSES

Charlevoix - Exploring

from which you can enjoy a view of the Gouffre river valley, Baie-Saint-Paul and Île aux Coudres. A visitor centre supplies information on the area's various attractions, outdoor activities, accommodations and restaurants. The Centre d'Histoire Naturelle de Charlevoix presents **Charlevoix, Un Destin Venu du Ciel ★ ★** here *(voluntary contribution, guided tours for groups $1.75/person; late Jun to early Sep every day 9am to 5pm, late May to late Jun and early Sep to mid-Oct every day 10am* to 4pm). The exhibit covers the geological history of the Charlevoix region and the extraordinary meteor impact that shaped its landscape some 350 million years ago.

A selection of paintings by Charlevoix artists is displayed in the **Carrefour Culturel Paul-Médéric ★** *(free admission; early Apr to late Jun every day 10am to 5pm, late Jun to mid-Nov Tue-Sun 10am to 7pm, mid-Nov to early Apr*

Fri-Sun 10am to 5pm; 4 Rue Ambroise-Fafard, ☎418-435-3681 or 435-5654, www.centredart-bsp.qc.ca), designed in a modern style in 1967 by architect Jacques DeBlois. A painting and sculpture symposium, where works by young artists are displayed, is held by the centre every August.

The **Centre d'Exposition de Baie-Saint-Paul** ★★ *($3; late Jun to late Aug Tue-Sun 10am to 6pm, late Aug to late Jun Tue-Sun 10am to 5pm; 23 Rue Ambroise-Fafard, ☎418-435-3681)* is a museum and gallery, completed in 1992 according to blueprints by architect Pierre Thibault. It houses travelling exhibits from around the world, as well as the René Richard gallery, where several paintings by this Swiss-born artist are on display (see below).

The **Maison René-Richard** ★ *(voluntary contribution; every day 10am to 6pm; 58 Rue Saint-Jean-Baptiste, ☎418-435-5571)* was inherited in the early 20th century by François-Xavier Cimon, along with the grounds that extended to the Rivière du Gouffre. Portrait painter Frederick Porter Vinton struck up a friendship with the Cimon family, who let him set up a painting workshop on their property. The facility was later used by important artists, including Clarence Gagnon, A. Y. Jackson, Frank Johnston, Marc-Aurèle Fortin and Arthur Lismer. These artists' works can be found in a number of Canadian museums. In 1942, painter René Richard took ownership of the house when he married one of the Cimon daughters. Since his death in 1983, the property and house have been open to the public. A tour of the grounds provides a fascinating glimpse into the Charlevoix of the 1940s, when artists and collectors from New York and Chicago congregated here during the summer.

The **Centre d'Histoire Naturelle de Charlevoix** ★ *(voluntary contribution, $1.75/person for groups; late May to late Jun and early Sep to mid-Oct every day 10am to 4pm, late Jun to early Sep every day 9am to 5pm, mid-Oct to late May by appointment; 444 Boulevard Mgr-De Laval / Route 138, ☎418-435-6275)* explores geological history, flora, fauna, climate and human history through a slide show. The centre also offers a 2hr bus tour to the back country to discover the meteorological origins of Charlevoix.

The **Laiterie Charlevoix** ★ is home to the **Économusée du Fromage** *(free admission; late Jun to early Sep every day 8am to 7pm, Sep to late Jun Mon-Fri 8am to 5:30pm, Sat and Sun 9am to 5pm; 1167 Boulevard Mgr-De Laval, ☎418-435-2184, www.fromagescharlevoix. com)*, a museum dedicated to the production of cheese. Founded in 1948, this dairy still makes its cheddar cheese the old-fashioned way, that is, by hand. Every day before 11am, visitors can see cheese makers in action and get a rudimentary grasp of how cheese is made and ripened. Since 1994, the Laiterie Charlevoix has been producing the delicious "Migneron de Charlevoix" cheese, winner of many prizes. They also produce a tasty blue cheese called "Ciel de Charlevoix."

Leave Baie-Saint-Paul by Route 362 (Rue Leclerc) toward Saint-Joseph-de-la-Rive, Les Éboulements and La Malbaie. A scenic lookout on a mountainside provides the opportunity to take in the view. A little farther, you will reach the entrance to **Domaine Charlevoix** (see p 499).

From Baie-Saint-Paul, you can take an optional excursion along routes 138 and 381 towards Saint-Urbain and the Charlevoix hinterland.

Parc National des Grands-Jardins ★★ (see p 499).

Return toward Baie-Saint-Paul and take Route 362 heading east. A steep hill leads to the village of Saint-Joseph-de-la-Rive on the right, below Les Éboulements.

Saint-Joseph-de-la-Rive ★

The rhythm of life in this village on the St. Lawrence followed the rhythm of the river for many generations, as the boats beached along the shore eloquently testify. In recent decades, however, tourism and handicrafts have replaced fishing and shipbuilding as the staples of the economy. East of the dock where the ferry to Île aux Coudres lands, a fine sandy beach tempts swimmers into the chilly saltwater. A little wooden building in front of the church is a reminder of the fragility of human endeavours within the immense marine landscape of Charlevoix.

The dimensions and white-painted wooden exterior of the **Église Catholique Saint-Joseph** ★ *(Chemin de l'Église)* are reminiscent of the Anglican churches found in Québec's Eastern Townships region. Its interior is decorated with various objects from the sea. For example, the altar is supported by anchors, and the baptismal fountain is actually an immense seashell, retrieved off the coast of Florida. A recorded presentation on the church's liturgical ornaments is activated by a button on the right-hand side of the entrance.

The **Papeterie Saint-Gilles** ★ *(free admission; Mon-Fri 8am to 5pm, Sat and Sun 9am to 5pm; 304 Rue Félix-Antoine-Savard, ☎418-635-2430 or 866-635-2430, www.papeteriesaintgilles. com)* is a traditional papermaking workshop founded in 1966 by priest and poet Félix-Antoine Savard (1896-1982, author of *Menaud Maître-Draveur*) with the help of Mark Donohue, member of a famous Canadian pulp and paper dynasty. Here, museum guides explain the different stages involved in making paper using 17th-century techniques. Saint-Gilles paper has a distinctive thick grain and flower or leaf patterns integrated into each piece, producing a high-quality writing paper sold on site in various packages.

The **Musée Maritime de Charlevoix / Économusée de la Goélette** ★ ★ *($3; mid-May to mid-Jun and early Sep to mid-Oct Mon-Fri 9am to 4pm, Sat and Sun 11am to 4pm, late Jun to Sep every day 9am to 5pm; 305 Rue de l'Église, ☎418-635-1131 or 635-2803, www.musee-maritime-charlevoix.com)*, located in a shipyard, recaptures the golden era of the schooner. Visitors are welcome to climb aboard the boats on the premises.

The **Santons de Charlevoix** *(free admission, groups $1/person; May to Oct every day 10am to 5pm; 303 Rue de l'Église, ☎418-635-2521 or 635-1632 off-season)*. For a few years now, craftspeople in Saint-Joseph-de-la-Rive have been making *santons*, terra-cotta figurines representing the Christian nativity scene, including the villagers who gathered around the manger. Setting them apart from other figurines of this kind, the characters are dressed in traditional Québécois garb and the buildings are miniature representations of traditional houses typical of Charlevoix and Île aux Coudres.

Île aux Coudres ★ ★ (pop. 1,352)

Visitors are sometimes surprised to learn that a number of whale species live in the St. Lawrence River. For several generations, the economic livelihood of Île aux Coudres centred around whale hunting, mainly belugas, and whale blubber was melted to produce lamp oil. Ship building, mainly small craft, was also an important regional industry.

L'Isle-aux-Coudres is the municipality that was formed when the villages of La Baleine, Saint-Bernard and Saint-Louis merged *(arrival and departure point on Île-aux-Coudres)*. The ferry docks at the Quai de Saint-Bernard, where the following tour of the island begins. The dock is the best place to appreciate the view of the Charlevoix mountains. One of the last shipyards still in operation in the region can be seen from here.

Follow Chemin Royal to Saint-Louis, where it becomes Chemin des Coudriers. Many old schooners are beached along the shore in the area, vestiges of a bygone era. Baie-Saint-Paul can be seen from Cap à Labranche on clear days. Île aux Coudres can be visited by bicycle but be aware that the sea breeze makes for challenging conditions.

The **Musée Les Voitures d'Eau** ★ *($3; late May to mid-Jun and mid-Sep to mid-Oct Sat-Sun 10am to 5pm, mid-Jun to mid-Jul and mid-Aug to mid-Sep every day 10am to 5pm, mid-Jul to mid-Aug every day 9:30am to 6pm; 203 Chemin des Coudriers, St-Louis, ☎418-438-2000 or 800-463-2118)* presents exhibits on the history, construction and navigation of the small craft once built in the region. The museum was founded in 1973 by Captain Éloi Perron, who recovered the wreck of the schooner *Mont-Saint-Louis*, now on display.

Turn left onto Chemin du Moulin.

It is extremely rare to find a water mill and a windmill operating together. Indeed, the **Moulins de l'Île-aux-Coudres** ★ ★ *($2.75; late May to mid-Jun and mid-Aug to mid-Oct every day 10am to 5pm, mid-Jun to mid-Aug every day 9am to 6:30pm; 36 Chemin du Moulin, St-Louis, ☎418-438-2184)* are a unique pair in Québec. Erected in 1825 and 1836 respectively, the mills complement one another by alternately generating power according to prevailing climatic conditions. Along with a forge and milling house, the mills were restored by the Québec government, which has also established on-site information centres. The machinery necessary for operation is still in perfect condition, and

Charlevoix - Exploring

is now back at work grinding wheat and buckwheat into flour. Bread is made in an antique wood oven.

Take the ferry to Saint-Joseph-de-la-Rive and head to Les Éboulements.

Les Éboulements ★ (pop. 1,266)

In 1663, a violent earthquake in the region caused a gigantic landslide; it is said that half a small mountain sank into the river. The village of Les Éboulements is named after the event (*éboulements* means "land-slide" in English).

At the entrance to the grounds of the **Manoir de Sales-Laterrière / Camp Le Manoir** *(free admission; every day 9am to 11am and 2pm to 4pm; 159 Rue Principale,* ☎*418-635-2666)* and the **Moulin Banal** ★★ *($3; mid-Jun to late Sep every day 10am to 5pm; 157 Rue Principale,* ☎*418-635-2239)* is a wooden processional chapel (circa 1840). Once located in the village of Saint-Nicolas on the south shore of the St. Lawrence, it stands beside the entrance to the grounds. The chapel was reconstructed in 1968, under the auspices of a heritage organization that also owns the nearby late-18th-century seigneurial mill. Visitors cannot enter the red-shuttered manor house, as it is currently used as a school by the Brothers of the Sacré-Coeur.

Return to Route 132. After a spectacular descent, the road leads to Saint-Irénée. Once at river level, the entrance to the Forget estate is ahead on the left.

Saint-Irénée ★ (pop. 683)

Saint-Irénée, or Saint-Irénée-les-Bains, as it was known during the Belle Époque, is the gateway to the part of Charlevoix usually considered the oldest vacation spot in North America. In the late 18th century, British sportsmen were the first Europeans to enjoy the pleasures of the simple life the wild region had to offer. They were followed by wealthy Americans escaping the heat of summer in the United States. Wealthy English- and French-Canadian families also had summer houses with lovely gardens built in Charlevoix. Saint-Irénée is renowned for its picture-perfect landscapes and classical-music festival.

Domaine Forget ★ *(prices and schedules vary according to activities; 5 Rang Saint-Antoine,* ☎*418-452-8111 or 888-336-7438, www.domaineforget.com)* was home to Sir Rodolphe Forget (1861-1919), a prominent French-Canadian businessman in the early 20th century. The vast property had its own power plant, in addition to a dozen interesting secondary buildings. Unfortunately, the main house, known locally as "Le Château," was destroyed by fire in 1961. Inaugurated in the summer of 1996, the Salle Françoys-Bernier, at Domaine Forget, can accommodate 600 music lovers, who are sure to be delighted with its wonderful acoustics.

Since 1977, the property has been home to the **Académie de Musique et de Danse de Saint-Irénée**, which holds summer sessions. Every summer a classical-music festival is held here; it is a major social event in the lives of Charlevoix summer residents.

Before arriving in Pointe-au-Pic, the road runs next to the **Club de Golf Fairmont le Manoir Richelieu**, one of the highest rated golf resorts in the world. The club features an 18-hole course, a clubhouse and restaurants. Turn right onto Rue Principale at the bottom of Côte Bellevue.

La Malbaie ★ (pop. 9,334)

On his way to Québec City in 1608, Samuel de Champlain anchored in a Charlevoix bay for the night. To his surprise, he awoke the next morning to find his fleet resting on land and not in water. Champlain learned that day what many navigators would come to learn as well: the water recedes a great distance in this region and will trap any boat not moored in deep enough water. In exasperation, he exclaimed *"Ah! La malle baye!"* (Old French that translates roughly to "Oh what a bad bay!"), inadvertently providing the name for many sites in the region. The towns of Pointe-au-Pic, La Malbaie and Cap-à-l'Aigle now form a continuous web of streets and houses lining the bay.

The Malbaie seigneury passed through three seigneurs (lords) before being seriously developed. Jean Bourdon received the land for services rendered to the French crown in 1653. Too busy with his job as prosecutor for the king, he did noth-

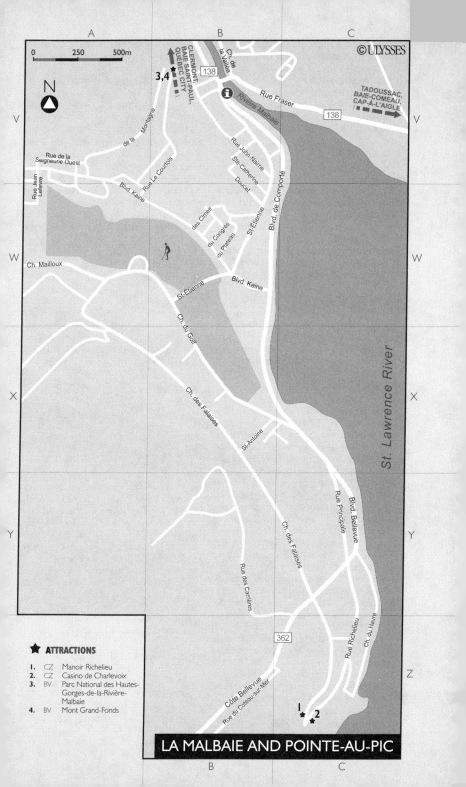

LA MALBAIE AND POINTE-AU-PIC

ing with it. The seigneury was then granted to Philippe Gaultier de Comporté in 1672. Following his death, it was sold by his family to merchants Hazeur and Soumande, who harvested wood on the property for the construction of ships in France. The seigneury became crown property in 1724. Exceptionally, it was then granted, under English occupation, to Captain John Nairne and Officer Malcolm Fraser in 1762, who began colonizing it.

Seigneurs Nairne and Fraser initiated a long-standing tradition of hospitality in Charlevoix. They hosted, in their respective manors, friends and even strangers from Scotland and England. Following the example of these seigneurs, French Canadians began welcoming visitors from Montréal and Québec during the summer months.

Eventually, larger inns had to be built to accommodate the increasing number of urban vacationers now arriving on steamships that moored at the dock in Pointe-au-Pic. Among the wealthy visitors was U.S. President Howard Taft and his family, who were very fond of Charlevoix.

In the early 20th century, a wave of wealthy Americans and English Canadians built summer houses along **Chemin des Falaises**, a street well worth exploring. The houses reflect popular architectural styles of the period, including the charming Shingle-style characteristic of seaside resorts on the U.S. east coast, which is distinguished by a cedar shingle exterior. Another popular trend at the time was to build houses that resembled 17th-century French manor houses, complete with turrets and shuttered casement windows. Beginning in 1920, the architecture of summer residences started to incorporate traditional local building styles. La Malbaie architect Jean Charles Warren (1869-1929) became known for designing a style of rustic furniture, inspired by local traditions and the English Arts and Crafts movement. Owning one of his creations became a must among summer residents. The most important and impressive building from the turn-of-the-century construction boom is the Manoir Richelieu, at the west end of Chemin des Falaises.

La Malbaie is now the regional administrative centre and has confirmed its position

of strength within the region's tourist industry.

The **Manoir Richelieu** ★★ *(181 Rue Richelieu)*, the only grand hotel in Charlevoix to survive, was built of wood in 1899. Destroyed in a fire, it was replaced by the current cement building in 1929. The hotel was designed by architect John Smith Archibald in the Château style. Many famous people have stayed at the hotel, from Charlie Chaplin to the King of Siam and the Vanderbilts of New York City. Visitors not staying at the Manoir can nevertheless discreetly walk through its hallways, elegant salons and gardens overlooking the St. Lawrence.

The region's number-one attraction is the **Casino de Charlevoix** *(183 Rue Richelieu, ☎418-665-5300 or 800-665-2274, www.casino-de-charlevoix.com)*, an attractively designed European-style casino located next to the Manoir Richelieu. Proper dress is required.

Parc National des Hautes-Gorges-de-la-Rivière-Malbaie ★★ (see p 499).

Mont Grand-Fonds ★ (see p 500).

Return to the main tour at Cap-à-l'Aigle.

Cap-à-l'Aigle

From Boulevard de Comporté in La Malbaie, visitors can catch a glimpse of a stately stone house sitting high on the Cap-à-l'Aigle escarpment. The building is the old manor house of the Malcolm Fraser seigneurs, a property also known as Mount Murray. It is matched to the east of Rivière Malbaie by the John Nairne seigneury, established west of the waterway and simply named Murray Bay in honour of James Murray, British Governor at the time. Cap-à-l'Aigle, whose tourism industry dates back to the 18th century, forms the heart of the Mount Murray seigneury.

Manoir Fraser ★ *(private property, no visits; Rte. 138)*. Malcolm Fraser, like his compatriot John Nairne, belonged to the Fraser Highlanders, a Scottish regiment sent to Canada to help capture Louisbourg. After the signing of the Treaty of Paris in 1763, putting an end to the Seven Years War, Nairne and Fraser settled in their seigneuries. Both spoke French; Nairne's family lived in exile in France because they sympathized with the Stuarts. Meanwhile, the Fraser family was of French origin, descendants of Jules de Berry, who served exquisite strawberries to Charles III, and so created their family name (in French, strawberries are called *fraises*, which later turned into Fraser). The Manoir Fraser was built for the son of Malcolm Fraser in 1827, according to plans by architect Jean-Baptiste Duléger. Damaged during a fire in 1975, the manor was restored by the Cabot family, which has held the title to the Cap-à-l'Aigle seigneury since 1902.

Turn right onto Chemin Saint-Raphaël and continue to the junction with Route 138 Est, which travels through Saint-Fidèle and Port-au-Saumon.

Port-au-Persil ★

This small but charming harbour town is set apart by its waterfall, Anglican chapel and winding road that leads through beautiful mountain landscapes.

Saint-Siméon (pop. 1,470)

From Saint-Siméon, roads lead to the Saguenay region, Côte-Nord and Québec City. A ferry links the town of Rivière-du-Loup on the south shore of the St. Lawrence.

Baie-Sainte-Catherine ★ (pop. 275)

A tiny village on the north shore of the St. Lawrence, Baie-Sainte-Catherine borders a bay on the Saguenay estuary and has a picturesque sandy beach.

Parks

Domaine Charlevoix (*$10, including the shuttle to the river; late May to late Oct every day 9:30am to 6pm; 340 Route 362, Baie-Saint-Paul, ☎418-435-2626 or 877-435-2627*), just outside Baie-Saint-Paul, is a sports centre devoted to various outdoor activities such as cross-country skiing, hiking and mountain biking. Classical music is played along the short trails, creating a lovely atmosphere. Its magnificent lookouts overhang the St.

Lawrence and the Félix-Antoine-Savard terrace, from where you can admire beautiful Île aux Coudres. There is a good restaurant on the property as well as a lakeside tearoom.

Located at the eastern edge of the Réserve Faunique des Laurentides, the **Parc National des Grands-Jardins** ★ ★ (*$3.50; mid-May to late Jun and Aug to late Oct Mon, Wed, Fri 8am to 10pm, Sun, Tue, Thu, Sat 8am to 6pm; Jul every day 8am to 10pm; Centre de Services Thomas-Fortin, Route 381, Km31, ☎418-439-1227 or 800-665-6527, www.sepaq.com*) is rich in flora and fauna characteristic of taiga and tundra, a very unusual occurrence this far south. Situated north of Saint-Urbain, this park covers 310km². Hikes led by naturalists are organized throughout the summer, and caribou have been spotted on some of the trails. The park's Mont du Lac des Cygnes (Swan Lake Mountain) trail is among the most beautiful in Québec. Visitors can also go on canoe-camping trips, and winter activities are offered.

Parc National des Hautes-Gorges-de-la-Rivière-Malbaie ★ ★ (*$3.50; late May to mid-Oct Mon-Fri 8am to 5pm, Sat-Sun 8am to 7pm; from Baie-Saint-Paul, take Route 138 to Saint-Aimé-des-Lacs, then cross the village on Rue Principale; ☎418-439-1227 or 800-665-6527, www.sepaq.com*), which covers over 233km², was created to protect the area from commercial exploitation. Over 800 million years ago, a crack in the earth's crust formed the magnificent gorges after which the park is named; later, the terrain was shaped by glaciers. The park features an incredible diversity of vegetation, ranging from maple stands to alpine tundra. The rock faces, some of which are 800m high, tower over the river and are used for rock-climbing. The best known climb, "Pomme d'Or," is a 350m-high expert-level trail. Other park activities include snowmobiling, hiking (the Acropole trail is particularly scenic), and canoe-camping. The park's rental centre has mountain bikes (*$26.50/day*) and canoes (*$32/day*). **River boat cruises** (*$24; duration: 1hr 30min; ☎418-439-1227*) are also offered. A trip down the river is the best way to truly appreciate the park.

On the entrance road to the park, look for a sign on the right-hand side that says "ZEC des Martres, secteur 7, Lac des Américains." Nearby, a suspension foot bridge spans Rivière Malbaie. There are some decent restaurants

Charlevoix – Parks

here, as well as a pleasant tea room by a lake, which is inhabited by swans. An enchanting, pastoral setting.

Outdoor Activities

■ Cross-Country Skiing

Mont Grand-Fonds *($12 weekdays, $13 weekends; Mon-Fri 10am to 3:45pm, Sat and Sun 9am to 3:45pm; 1000 Chemin des Loisirs, La Malbaie,* ☎*418-665-0095 or 877-665-0095)* has some 160km of cross-country ski trails.

The **Génévrier activity centre** *($4.50; 1175 Boulevard Mgr-De Laval, Baie-Sainte-Paul,* ☎*418-435-6520 or 877-435-6520, www. genevrier.com)* is located a few kilometres north of Baie-Saint-Paul. It has 15km of cross-country skiing and snowshoeing trails. There are four runs: two beginners, one intermediate and one advanced. A skating rink and tobogganing hills have also been set up.

At **Parc National des Grands-Jardins** *($3.50; Thomas-Fortin Service Centre, Rte. 381,* ☎*418-439-1227)*, during the winter, 40km-long hiking trails become cross-country skiing and snowshoeing trails. Chalets and shelters are available but reservations are required *(*☎*800-665-6527)*.

■ Cycling

A good way to explore Île aux Coudres is by bicycle. The terrain is mostly flat and cyclists get to explore the landscape at a leisurely pace. Pointe de l'Islet, on the western extremity of the island, offers a spectacular view of the St. Lawrence.

In La Baleine, on the east coast of the island, **Vélo-Coudres** *(743 Chemin des Coudriers,* ☎*418-438-2118)* rents out bikes of all kinds.

■ Dogsledding

Le Chenil du Sportif *($140/day per pers., $80/ half-day per pers.; 65 Rang Ste-Marie, Les Éboulements,* ☎*418-635-2592)* organizes excursions that last from half a day to three days

and can include ice-fishing and snowshoeing expeditions. Le Chenil du Sportif lets dog-sledders lead their own team themselves through spectacular natural surroundings between Les Éboulements and Saint-Hilarion. Guides are experienced and friendly. Day packages include breakfast in a log cabin. There are cabins and trailers for longer stays.

■ Downhill Skiing

Le Massif *($40; 1350 rue Principale, Petite-Rivière-St-François,* ☎*418-632-5876 or 877-536-2774, www.lemassif.com)* is one of the finest ski centres in Québec. At 770m, it has the highest slopes in eastern Canada, and receives abundant snow each winter, which is enhanced with artificial snow to create ideal ski conditions. The mountain, which almost rises up from the river, has a breathtaking view from the summit. Since 2001, the Massif's infrastructure has been significantly upgraded without harming the skiing experience. It now offers some 42 trails for every level of expertise, and a comfortable chalet graces the summit.

Mont Grand-Fonds *($31 weekdays, $35 weekends; Mon-Fri 10am to 3:45pm, Sat and Sun 9am to 3:45pm; 1000 Chemin des Loisirs, La Malbaie,* ☎*418-665-0095 or 877-665-0095, www.montgrandfonds.com)* has 14 runs and a vertical drop of 355m. The longest one runs 2,500m.

■ Hiking

In addition to the magnificent parks in the region (see p 499), hikers also flock to Charlevoix's beautiful **Sentier des Caps** *($5/ day; 1 Rue Leclerc, St-Tite-des-Caps,* ☎*418-823-1117 ou 866-823-1117, www.sentierdescaps. com)*. The path stretches some 51km from Saint-Tite-des-Caps to Petite-Rivière-Saint-François, climbing 500 to 800m summits that drop off into the river. The mountain huts and campsites scattered along the trail allow you to take your time. Its slopes will challenge even experienced hikers. The views of the river, especially from the lookouts, will literally take your breath away.

■ Horseback Riding

Écurie des Deux Continents
83 Rang 2, La Malbaie
☎ (418) 439-4187
www.ecuriedeuxcontinents.com

Écurie des Deux Continents organizes riding excursions that last a few hours or several days. Multiple-day outings include overnight stays in local inns or campgrounds and provide a unique way to explore the Charlevoix backcountry.

■ Kayaking

K-IAC de Mer *(3043 Rue des Coudriers, La Baleine, ☎418-438-4388 or 866-438-8438)* offers several different excursions around the lovely Île aux Coudres. Short expeditions, one- or two-day group outings and romantic sunset excursions on the river are some of the options. Friendly guides ensure kayakers' safety.

Charlevoix - Outdoor Activities

Accommodations

Petite-Rivière-Saint-François

Auberge La Courtepointe
$$ bkfst incl.
$$$ ½b
♥ ♨ ♨

8 Rue Racine
☎ (418) 632-5858 or 888-788-5858
🖷 (418) 632-5786

Auberge La Courtepointe is located near the Le Massif ski resort. The inn's decor features a nice collection of paintings and kids will love sleeping in the pretty attic room. A delicious breakfast and tasty meals are served and the inn enjoys a view of the river.

Baie-Saint-Paul

Le Balcon Vert
$
sb ♨ ♨

22 Côte du Balcon Vert, Rte. 362
☎ (418) 435-5587
🖷 (418) 435-6669
www.balconvert.charlevoix.net

One of the least expensive places to stay in town is Le Balcon Vert. This youth hostel offers small chalets that can accommodate up to four people, as well as campsites.

Parc National des Grands-Jardins
$

entrance to the park via Route 381, in Saint-Urbain

The Parc National des Grands-Jardins rents out small cottages and shelters. This park is a popular place for fishing, so if you want to stay here during summer, you'll have to reserve early. To do so, reserve with the SÉPAQ at ☎ 800-665-6527.

Le Genévrier
$-$$$
△ ♨ ♨

1175 Boulevard Mrg-De Laval, Rte. 138
☎ (418) 435-6520 or 877-435-6520
www.genevrier.com

Le Genévrier's campground is a vast recreational-tourism complex in perfect harmony with its natural environment. Campers of all persuasions are sure to find what they are looking for here. The campground boasts 450 sites, mostly on forested land, for all types of lodging and shelter, from the biggest motorhomes to tents for wilderness camping. Several fully equipped, modern and comfortable cottages are situated by the river or lake. In summer, two more rustic but fully equipped log cabins with bedding and showers are also for rent. Every day, an extensive program of sports and leisure activities is offered. Hiking and mountain-biking trails along the river.

Auberge La Pignoronde
$$
≡ ≈ ♨

750 Boulevard Mgr-De Laval
☎ (418) 435-5505 or 888-554-6004
www.aubergelapignoronde.com

The strange circular building housing the Auberge la Pignoronde may be less than appealing from the outside, but the interior decor is quite charming, and the lobby features a welcoming fireplace. There is also an excellent view of the bay.

Auberge La Muse
$$-$$$ bkfst incl.
♨ ♨

39 Rue St-Jean-Baptiste
☎ (418) 435-6839 or 800-841-6839
🖷 (418) 435-6289
www.lamuse.com

Located in the heart of Baie-Saint-Paul, Auberge La Muse occupies both a period home beneath tall trees with a lovely balcony, and a former general store. The guest rooms are decorated in the Victorian style. Guests can sample the specialties that make this restaurant famous at the breakfast buffet.

Auberge Cap-aux-Corbeaux
$$-$$$ bkfst incl.
◎ ♈

2 Cap-aux-Corbeaux Sud
☎ (418) 435-5676 or 800-595-5676
🖷 (418) 435-4125
www.cap-aux-corbeaux.com

Nestled at the end of a little road along the cape overlooking Baie-Saint-Paul, Auberge Cap-aux-Corbeaux offers a breathtaking view. The inn itself is rather modern, but woodwork predominates. All the rooms are situated on the riverside so that guests can fully enjoy the view. In one of the rooms, the double whirlpool tub is surrounded by windows, allowing for moments of absolute relaxation. On some summer evenings, the innkeepers serve their guests cocktails while a painter creates a canvas before their eyes.

Auberge La Maison Otis
$$$$-$$$$$
△ ♨ ≈ ♨))) ♈ ◎

23 Rue St-Jean-Baptiste
☎ (418) 435-2255 or 800-267-2254
🖷 (418) 435-2464
www.maisonotis.com

Auberge La Maison Otis combines refined elegance, tasteful decor and exquisite cuisine. The inn's older section features small, cozy rooms with beds located on an upper level, while its newest section offers more spacious accommodations. Classic Québec architecture prevails in this former bank located in the heart of town.

BAIE-SAINT-PAUL

© ULYSSES

▲ **ACCOMMODATIONS**

I.	CY	Le Balcon Vert (R)
2.	AX	Parc National des Grands-Jardins
3.	AX	Le Genévrier
4.	AZ	Auberge La Pignoronde (R)
5.	BY	Auberge La Muse (R)
6.	CY	Auberge Cap-aux-Corbeaux
7.	BY	Auberge La Maison Otis (R)

(R) establishment with restaurant (see description)

● **RESTAURANTS**

I.	BY	Al Dente
2.	BY	Café des Artistes
3.	BZ	L'Orange Bistro
4.	BZ	Le Mouton Noir
5.	AX	Maison d'Affinage Maurice Dufour
6.	BY	Restaurant Les Deux Sœurs
7.	BY	Saint-Pub
8.	CY	Domaine Charlevoix

Saint-Hilarion

L'Aubergine
$$ bkfst incl.
🍴 ≋

179 Rang 6
☎ (418) 457-3018 or 877-457-3018
www.aubergineinn.com
With its beautiful name, L'Aubergine is the perfect place for tranquillity and the outdoors. The surrounding countryside is beautiful and offers numerous outdoor activities. Each of the six rooms has its own private entrance and bathroom, providing lots of privacy. The hosts prepare very good vegetarian evening meals, but reservations are required. Generous breakfasts.

Saint-Joseph-de-la-Rive

Auberge Beauséjour et Motels
$$
🍴 🛏 ≋ ♨

569 Chemin du Quai
☎ (418) 635-2895 or 800-265-2895
🖷 (418) 635-1195
www.aubergebeausejour.com
Located in a spacious residence with a superb terrace, Auberge Beauséjour et Motels enjoys a perfect

setting. The rooms, though rather plain, are comfortable.

Île aux Coudres

Note that all of the island's accommodations are closed in winter.

Auberge La Coudrière et Motels
$$ bkfst incl.

≋ ♨

2891 Chemin des Coudriers
☎ (418) 438-2838 or 888-438-2882
Auberge La Coudrière et Motels has very comfortable rooms. It is located near the river in a beautiful area perfect for quiet walks.

Hotel-Motel Cap-aux-Pierres
$$

⊯≋ ♨ ≈ ✝ ≡

246 Chemin La Baleine
☎ (418) 438-2711 or 888-554-6003
▤ (418) 438-2127
www.hotelcapauxpierres.com
A long building with several skylights, the Hotel-Motel Cap-aux-Pierres offers pleasant, rustic rooms.

Saint-Irénée

L'Eider Matinal
$$ bkfst incl.
310 Chemin des Bains
☎ (418) 452-8259
▤ (418) 452-8245
L'Eider Matinal is as lovely inside as it is outside. This bed and breakfast occupies a beautiful century-old residence with a red roof, right in the middle of an attractively landscaped property facing the river. Its four guest rooms are tastefully decorated and offer modern comforts and antique furnishings. A charming front terrace embellishes the inn, and a pleasant sitting room is also available to guests. What's more,

guests are greeted with a smile.

La Malbaie

Auberge La Châtelaine
$$$ bkfst incl.
pb/sb
830 Chemin des Falaises
☎ (418) 665-4064 or 888-840-4064
▤ (418) 665-4623
Auberge La Châtelaine occupies a large home where memories of days gone by seem to pop out of every corner. Antiques, attractive bedspreads, old-fashioned clawfoot bathtubs, dormer windows, lath walls and an imposing staircase provide a memorable setting. The long veranda, pleasant terrace and beautiful garden are perfect for sunny days.

Petit Manoir du Casino
$$$-$$$$ bkfst incl.
≡ ☜ ♨ ☛ △ ≋ ✝ ♨
525 Chemin des Falaises
☎ (418) 665-0000 or 800-618-2112
▤ (418) 665-4092.
This establishment is located near the casino and is the latest addition to Pointe-au-Pic's hotels. A family atmosphere prevails here. The 76 rooms all feature a fireplace and a balcony, and several offer superb views of the bay.

Auberge La Romance
$$$-$$$$ bkfst incl.
☜ △ ☛ ≡ ᵫ
415 Chemin des Falaises
☎ (418) 665-4865
▤ (418) 665-4954
www.aubergelaromance.com
Auberge La Romance, as its name indicates, is focused from top to bottom on romantic getaways. Every detail has been planned in order to make guests feel as though they are on cloud nine. For example, each room features a double door for soundproofing

and a speaker that plays romantic music day and night (guests have a remote control). This cedar-shingled home offers eight romantic rooms with Victorian decor and furnishings. Each one has a unique cachet, as well as several amenities that add an extra touch of romance, such as fireplace (gas or wood-burning), balcony, canopy bed or whirlpool tub.

Auberge des Falaises
$$$$ bkfst incl.
△ ☜ ≋ ≋ ♨ ☜ ᵫ
250 Chemin des Falaises
☎ (418) 665-3731 or 800-386-3731
▤ (418) 665-6194
www.aubergedesfalaises.com
Auberge des Falaises features several rooms with a spectacular view. The rooms are just the right size and quite comfortable, but guests will probably want to spend most of their time on their balcony if they stay in the most recent wing, since all of its rooms overlook the cliff and the river, in the distance.

Auberge Des 3 Canards
$$$$-$$$$$ ½b
△ ☜ ☛ ≋ ᵫ ☜
115 Côte Bellevue
☎ (418) 665-3761 or 800-461-3761
▤ (418) 685-4727
www.auberge3canards.com
Auberge Des 3 Canards has a magnificent view of the entire region. The inn offers nine rooms, each warmly decorated with a fireplace, thick carpets and a whirlpool tub. Its motel rooms are not as nice but still offer a great view of the water. The inn's restaurant is highly recommended (see p 508).

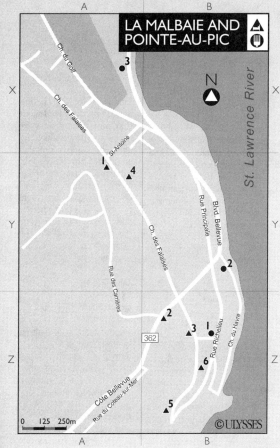

LA MALBAIE AND POINTE-AU-PIC

St. Lawrence River

▲ **ACCOMMODATIONS**

1. AY   Auberge des Falaises
2. BZ   Auberge Des 3 Canards (R)
3. BZ   Auberge La Châtelaine
4. AY   Auberge La Romance
5. BZ   Manoir Richelieu (R)
6. BZ   Petit Manoir du Casino

(R) establishment with restaurant (see description)

● **RESTAURANTS**

1. BZ   Auberge Les Sources
2. BY   Café de la Gare
3. AX   Crêperie Le Passe Temps

© ULYSSES

Manoir Richelieu
$$$$$
≋ ⬤ ♨ ⛵ ⛴ ≡ ◎ ▲ ⛾ ⑴⑴⑴

181 Rue Richelieu
☎ (418) 665-3703 or 800-441-1414
🖷 (418) 665-8131
www.fairmont.com/richelieu

A veritable institution in Québec, the Manoir Richelieu is a distinguished establishment that is still the choice holiday resort in Québec. Perched on a point overhanging the river, the century-old building is adorned with turrets, gables and a sloped roof. This jewel of Norman architecture has 405 rooms and suites. Some rooms are a little small, but all are comfortable. There are numerous boutiques on the main floor, as well as an underground passageway to the casino. Its restaurant, **Le Saint-Laurent** (see p 508), is sure to please all gourmet food lovers.

Cap-à-l'Aigle

Auberge Fleurs de Lune
$$$$ bkfst incl.
pb/sb ◎ ⬤ ▲

301 Rue St-Raphaël
☎ (418) 665-1090 or 888-665-1020
🖷 (418) 665-4458
www.fleursdelune.com

Auberge Fleurs de Lune offers a lovely bouquet in-deed: each room is named after a flower and is decorated with flowered fabrics and accessories by Laura Ashley. In addition, they are all equipped with a balcony, allowing for a view of the river. The living room, complete with roaring fire in winter, is warm and welcoming.

Auberge des Peupliers
$$$$-$$$$$
▲ ♨ ⑴⑴⑴ ⛾ ◎

381 Rue St-Raphaël
☎ (418) 665-4423 or 888-282-3743
🖷 (418) 665-3179

www.aubergedespeupliers.com

Auberge des Peupliers sits on a hillside overlooking the St. Lawrence. The rooms are decorated with wooden furniture that creates a warm, charming atmosphere. The inn also has pleasant, quiet living rooms.

La Pinsonnière
$$$$-$$$$$
≡ ▲ Ⴤ ≋ ♨ ⫯ ◉
124 Rue St-Raphaël
☎ (418) 665-4431 or 800-387-4431
🖷 (418) 665-7156
www.lapinsonniere.com

The luxurious La Pinsonnière, a member of the prestigious Relais & Châteaux association, boasts a wonderful location on a headland overhanging the river. The rooms are tastefully decorated, and each is different from the next. This is a very pleasant hotel and the restaurant is very popular (see p 508).

Restaurants

Baie-Saint-Paul

Le Balcon Vert
$
22 Côte du Balcon Vert
☎ (418) 435-5587

Le Balcon Vert is a youth hostel with a small cafeteria that serves good, simple dishes, including several vegetarian selections. Diners can also enjoy a terrace that offers a stunning view.

Restaurant Les Deux Sœurs
$
mid-Jun to early Sep every day, from Labour Day to Thanksgiving Wed-Sun, Feb to Jun Sat and Sun
48 Rue St-Jean-Baptiste
☎ (418) 435-6591

Restaurant Les Deux Sœurs is a quiet, pleasant establishment that serves healthy food.

Al Dente
$
30 Rue Leclerc
☎ (418) 435-6695

Behind the facade of this ordinary bungalow hides a lovely restaurant that is worth the detour for those who love fresh pasta. Al Dente, where you can also stock up on homemade pasta, sauce and other gourmet products, specializes in pasta, obviously, but also offers original dishes prepared with local products.

Café des Artistes
$-$$
25 Rue St-Jean-Baptiste
☎ (418) 435-5585

The Café des Artistes has a beautiful mahogany bar and wicker armchairs. European pizzas and panini are served with delicious garnishings. On a hot summer day, the large windows in the front and the few tables on the gallery are great places to pass the time.

Saint-Pub
$$-$$$
2 Rue Racine, corner Rue St-Jean-Baptiste
☎ (418) 240-2332

Saint-Pub is a charming restaurant that serves good bistro food. It is the flagship of the Charlevoix microbrewery, which makes excellent beers for all tastes. Saint-Pub is easy to spot on the charming Rue Saint-Jean-Baptiste thanks to its colourful, original architecture and its lively terrace in summer.

Maison d'Affinage Maurice Dufour
$$-$$$$
1339 Boulevard Mgr-De Laval
☎ (418) 435-5692

This is where the cheeses that are produced at **Laiterie Charlevoix** (see p 494) are ripened. The facilities include a dining room that is open from Wednesday to Saturday. The European chef prepares regional dishes, which spotlight the two excellent cheeses that are produced here (Le Migneron and Ciel de Charlevoix). Reservations required.

Auberge La Muse
$$$
39 Rue Saint-Jean-Baptiste
☎ (418) 435-6839 or 800-841-6839

The restaurant at **Auberge La Muse** (see p 502) offers refined and creative cuisine made from local ingredients. The dining room is pleasantly decorated and provides a view of the inn's pretty garden. A terrace and a garden pavilion offer a nice setting for an outdoor meal in summer.

Le Mouton Noir
$$$
closed Nov, Dec and Jan, except from Dec 20 to Jan 6
43 Rue Ste-Anne
☎ (418) 240-3030

Le Mouton Noir is one of the revelations of Baie-Saint-Paul. Its cuisine is a product of the seasons, making use of the local bounty. The menu is inventive and the dishes are both refined and good. During the summer, a large terrace provides *al fresco* dining near the river.

L'Orange Bistro
$$$
29 Rue Ambroise-Fafard
☎ (418) 240-1197
There are plenty of terraces along lovely Rue Ambroise-Fafard, but each one is unique. At L'Orange Bistro, just like in the cozy dining room, there is a menu that is mainly composed of meat and pasta, prepared with plenty of local products. If you enjoy burgers, don't miss the delicious veal hamburger.

Auberge La Maison Otis
$$$-$$$$
23 Rue St-Jean-Baptiste
☎ (418) 435-2255 or 800-267-2254
The finest and most sophisticated cuisine is featured at **Auberge La Maison Otis** (see p 502), which has developed an avant-garde gourmet menu where regional flavours adopt new accents and compositions. Guests are treated to a delightful culinary experience and a relaxing evening in the oldest part of the inn, which used to be a bank. The service is impeccable, and several ingredients on the menu are homemade. Fine selection of wines.

Auberge La Pignoronde
$$$$
750 Boulevard Mgr-De Laval
☎ (418) 435-5505 or 888-554-6004
Graced with an exceptional decor, the dining room at **Auberge La Pignoronde** (see p 502) looks out on the Vallée du Gouffre and Île aux Coudres. The restaurant serves absolutely delicious fare, where meat, fish and seafood share the spotlight with panache. Service is particularly attentive.

Domaine Charlevoix
$$$$
Rte. 362
☎ (418) 435-2626
If a breathtaking setting is what it takes to give you an appetite, then head to Domaine Charlevoix, where you can also enjoy several outdoor activities (see p 499). Whether you choose the Félix-Antoine-Savard terrace or the dining room with great big windows, the main attraction of your meal will be the extraordinary view unravelling before you: the cliff, the river below, Île aux Coudres, etc. But your plate will also grab your attention; for both lunch (sandwiches and salads) and supper (an elaborate table d'hôte), local products get top billing.

Saint-Joseph-de-la-Rive

La Maison Sous les Pins
$$$
352 Rue Félix-Antoine-Savard
☎ (418) 635-2583
The warm and intimate dining rooms at the inn La Maison Sous les Pins can accommodate about 20 guests, who come here to discover the refined aromas emanating from a medley of regional and French dishes, with an emphasis on local ingredients. Friendly reception and romantic ambiance. Non-smoking.

Île aux Coudres

La Mer Veille
$$-$$$
160 Chemin des Coudriers
☎ (418) 438-2149
La Mer Veille is a very popular restaurant that serves light meals and an appealing table d'hôte.

Les Éboulements

Les Saveurs Oubliées
$$$$
bring your own wine
350 Rte. 132
☎ (418) 635-9888
Les Saveurs Oubliées adjoins the Ferme Éboulmontaise, where lamb is raised and organic vegetables are grown. From the farm to your plate, literally! In a small, country-style room, sample fine cuisine prepared by experienced chef Régis Hervé and made from quality products, to which are added other local products. Homemade treats can be purchased in the shop located on the premises.

Saint-Irénée

Le St-Laurent Café
$$
128 Rue Principale
☎ (418) 452-3408
In Saint-Irénée, the friendly St-Laurent Café is perched on a hill (one of many in Charlevoix), right next to the church. Inside, the establishment is most charming, inviting you to take a seat at a lovely, ceramic-topped table. Outside, the terrace overlooks the cape and reveals a beautiful view. The menu features colourful dishes, such as chicken-liver salad and *sauté* of chicken with maple syrup. A real treat.

La Malbaie

Café de la Gare
$$
late Jun to mid-Oct every day, rest of the year Wed-Sat; closed Jan
100 Chemin du Havre
☎ (418) 665-4272
Despite its name (*gare* is French for "train station"),

this establishment is not located near the train station but rather near the dock. Built with a round architectural style, it stands next to the Quai de Pointe-au-Pic. Here, you can enjoy panini, hamburgers and other family-style dishes in a large room with big windows.

Crêperie Le Passe-Temps
$$-$$$
245 Boulevard de Comporté
☎ (418) 665-7660
With its pleasant atmosphere, the crêperie Le Passe-Temps constitutes an excellent choice for both lunch and dinner. The menu features a great variety of buckwheat or whole-wheat-flour crepes as main courses and desserts. The fresh pasta is exquisite, particularly the spaghetti with fresh tomatoes and Migneron cheese. The terrace is also a welcome treat.

Auberge Les Sources
$$$
8 Rue des Pins
☎ (418) 665-6952
The dining room at Auberge Les Sources is filled with light, thanks to large windows overlooking the garden. Diners can sample very flavourful cuisine prepared with regional products.

Auberge Des 3 Canards
$$$$
115 Côte Bellevue
☎ (418) 665-3761 or 800-461-3761
The chefs at the **Auberge Des 3 Canards** (see p 504) have always been daring and inventive in integrating local ingredients or game with their refined cuisine. Invariably succeeding, they have endowed the restaurant with an enviable nation-wide reputation. The service is outstanding, and the staff is genuinely cordial and knowledgeable about the dishes served. Good wine list.

Le Saint-Laurent
$$$$
181 Rue Richelieu
☎ (418) 665-3703 or 800-441-1414
The dining room at the **Manoir Richelieu** (see p 505) has improved so much over the past few years that it it now one of the best restaurants in the region—and it offers unbeatable view of the river to boot. The superb menu, generally composed of three meat choices and three fish choices, offers five courses. Sunday brunch here is a must, even if you aren't staying at the hotel.

Cap-à-l'Aigle

Auberge Petite Plaisance
$$$
310 Rue Saint-Raphaël
☎ (418) 665-2653 or 877-565-2653
Named after Marguerite Yourcenar's last residence, Auberge Petite Plaisance offers good cuisine made from local products. The tastes of Charlevoix blend harmoniously, resulting in a very decent table d'hôte, while the setting features an old-fashioned touch, thanks to various objects, furnishings and walls steeped in history.

Auberge des Peupliers
$$$$
381 Rue St-Raphaël
☎ (418) 665-4423 or 888-282-3743
The Auberge des Peupliers has many wonderful surprises in store for its guests, fruits of its chef's fertile imagination and audacity. Patrons have only to abandon themselves to these intoxicating French and regional flavours, sure to delight any palate.

La Pinsonnière
$$$$
124 Rue St-Raphaël
☎ (418) 665-4431 or 800-387-4431
The food at **La Pinsonnière** (see p 506) has long been considered the height of gastronomic refinement in Charlevoix and, despite increasingly fierce competition, is still worthy of the title in many respects. La Pinsonnière offers a very upscale, classic gourmet menu that should be savoured at leisure. The wine cellar remains the best stocked in the region and one of the finest in Québec.

Entertainment

■ Bars and Nightclubs

Baie-Saint-Paul

Saint-Pub
2 Rue Racine
☎ (418) 240-2332
A good spot for a taste of local microbrewed beer.

La Malbaie

On the road facing the Pointe-au-Pic dock are **Le Bambochard** and **Le Bar à Jazz**, two bars that have existed for several years. They are relatively lively during the weekend.

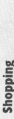

■ Casino

La Malbaie

The **Casino de Charlevoix** *(183 Rue Richelieu,* ☎*418-665-5300 or 800-665-2274, www. casino-de-charlevoix.com),* in La Malbaie, next to the Manoir Richelieu, is a European-style casino. Formal dress is required.

■ Festivals and Cultural Events

Enjoying greater success every year, **Rêves d'Automne Charlevoix** (☎*418-435-5875 or 800-761-5150, www.reves automne.com)* takes place during the last week of September and the first week of October. This multi-disciplinary festival allows the public to fully appreciate the beauty of Indian summer in Charlevoix, offering a whole series of musical and theatrical performances, as well as irresistible gastronomic treats.

Baie-Saint-Paul

The **Symposium International de la Nouvelle Peinture au Canada** (☎*418-435-3681)* is held annually in Baie-Saint-Paul. Throughout the month of August, visitors can admire huge works based on a suggested theme and created here by approximately 15 artists from Québec, the rest of Canada and abroad.

Saint-Irénée

Every summer, from mid-June to the end of August, the **Festival International du Domaine Forget** (☎*418-452-3535 or 888-336-7438, www.domaineforget.com)* brings together many classical musicians and vocalists, famous both at home and abroad, who perform on the stage at the Salle François-Bernier (hall), or during outdoor musical brunches every Sunday. You can request the programme by calling the number above. Season tickets are available.

🅿 Shopping

■ Art Galleries

Baie-Saint-Paul

Baie-Saint-Paul is particularly noteworthy for its **art galleries**. There is a little of everything here, as each shop has its own specialty. Oils, pastels, watercolours and etchings by big names and up-and-coming artists, originals and reproductions, sculpture and poetry—whatever your heart desires! Take an enjoyable stroll along Rue St-Jean-Baptiste and the neighbouring streets, where you'll find countless beautiful galleries staffed by friendly and chatty art dealers.

■ Food

Les Éboulements

Les Saveurs Oubliées
350 Rte. 132
☎ (418) 635-9888
Adjoining the restaurant (see p 507) and the farm, a small shop offers the creations (meat dishes, jelly, jam, etc.) of Régis Hervé, which are made from fresh local products. A tour of the farm is also a pleasant experience.

■ Stationery

Saint-Joseph-de-la-Rive

The wonderful paper made at the **Papeterie Saint-Gilles** (*304 Rue Félix-Antoine-Savard,* ☎*418-635-2613 or 866-635-2430, www.papeteriesaintgilles. com)* is sold on the premises. The quality of the cotton paper is remarkable, and some of it is decorated with maple or fern leaves. You can also purchase a collection of narratives, stories and Québec songs printed on these fine sheets.

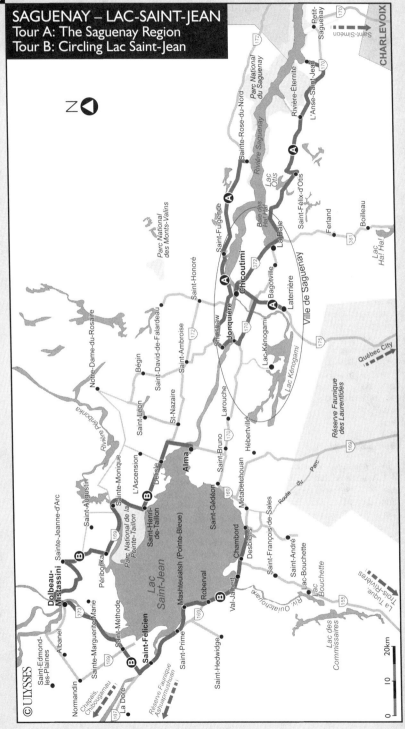

SAGUENAY – LAC-SAINT-JEAN
Tour A: The Saguenay Region
Tour B: Circling Lac Saint-Jean

Saguenay–Lac-Saint-Jean

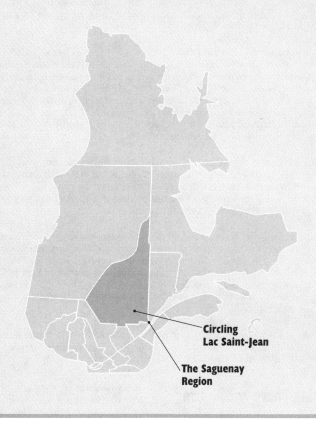

**Circling
Lac Saint-Jean**

**The Saguenay
Region**

A veritable inland sea, Lac Saint-Jean has a diameter of over 35km; from it flows the Rivière Saguenay, the location of the southern-most fjord in the world. In a way, these two impressive bodies of water form the backbone of this magnificent region.

Moving swiftly toward the St. Lawrence River, the Rivière Saguenay flows through a rugged landscape studded with cliffs and mountains. Aboard a cruise ship or from the banks of the river, visitors can enjoy a series of gorgeous panoramic views of this untouched natural setting. The Saguenay is navigable as far as Chicoutimi and governed by the eternal rhythm of the tides. Its rich marine-mammal life includes various species of whale in the summer. In the heart of the region, visitors will find the bustling city of Chicoutimi, the main urban centre in this part of Québec.

The region's first settlers came here in the 19th century, attracted by the beautiful fertile plains and excellent farmland around the lake. The hard life of these pioneers, who were farmers in the summer and lumberjacks in the winter, was immortalized in Louis Hémon's novel *Maria Chapdelaine*. Sweet, delicious blueberries abound in the area and have made the region of Lac Saint-Jean famous. The fruit is so closely identified with the region that Quebecers all over the province have adopted the term *bleuets*, blueberries, as an affectionate nickname for the local inhabitants. Residents of both the Saguenay and Lac Saint-Jean regions are renowned for their friendliness and spirit.

A considerable portion of the local work force is still involved in the same economic activities that brought the original settlers here towards the middle of the 20th century: forestry development in the Saguenay region and agriculture in the area around Lac Saint-Jean. Other industries have, however, developed since then, in particular aluminum smelters, due to the abundant supply of hydroelectric power.

Most settlers came from Charlevoix and the Côte-du-Sud regions in the middle of the 19th century, populating the twin regions of Saguenay and Lac-Saint-Jean, which were until then sporadically frequented by nomadic Montagnais peoples, Jesuit missionaries and trappers. The latter were connected with small trading posts established back in the 17th century, which lay sprinkled across densely wooded territory. Everything is large scale in the Saguenay–Lac-Saint-Jean—not only the rivers and the lakes, but also the industrial complexes, which are often open to the public.

A few French-Canadian families that originated in the Saguenay–Lac-Saint-Jean region actually became famous for their remarkable fertility. The Tremblays, for example, were so prolific that their surname is now closely linked to both areas.

Getting There and Getting Around

Two tours have been prepared for this region:

Tour A: The Saguenay Region ★ ★
Tour B: Circling Lac Saint-Jean ★ ★

■ By Car

Tour A: The Saguenay Region

From Québec City, take Route 138 east to Saint-Siméon. Turn left onto Route 170, which passes through the village of Sagard on its way to the Parc du Saguenay. This road continues on to Chicoutimi. It is possible and even recommended to combine this tour with a tour of the Charlevoix region, farther south (see p 492).

Tour B: Circling Lac Saint-Jean

This tour can easily be done after the Saguenay tour. From Jonquière, take Route 170 west to Saint-Bruno and then Route 169 around the lake.

Saguenay–Lac-Saint-Jean

■ Bus Stations

Tour A: The Saguenay Region

Chicoutimi
Autobus Tremblay et Tremblay
55 Rue Racine Est
☎ (418) 543-1403

Jonquière
Autocars Jasmin
2249 Rue St-Hubert
☎ (418) 547-2167

Tour B: Circling Lac Saint-Jean

Alma
430 Rue du Sacré-Cœur (Coq-Rôti restaurant)
☎ (418) 662-5441

■ Train Stations

Tour A: The Saguenay Region

Hébertville
15 Rue St-Louis
☎ 800-361-5390

Jonquière
2439 Rue St-Dominique
☎ 800-361-5390

Tour B: Circling Lac Saint-Jean

Chambord
78 Rue de la Gare
☎ 800-361-5390

Useful Information

■ Tourist Information Offices

Regional Office

**Association Touristique Régionale
du Saguenay–Lac-Saint-Jean**
455 Rue Racine Est, Bureau 101
Chicoutimi, G7H 1T5
☎ (418) 543-9778 or 877-253-8387
🖹 (418) 543-1805
www.tourismesaguenaylacsaintjean.qc.ca

Tour A: The Saguenay Region

La Baie
1171 7ᵉ Avenue
☎ (418) 697-5050 or 800-263-2243
🖹 (418) 697-5180

Chicoutimi
295 Rue Racine Est
☎ (418) 698-3167 or 800-463-6565
🖹 (418) 693-0084

Jonquière
2665 Boulevard du Royaume
☎ (418) 548-4004 or 800-561-9196
🖹 (418) 548-7348

Tour B: Circling Lac Saint-Jean

Alma
1682 Avenue du Pont Nord
☎ (418) 668-3611 or 877-668-3611
🖹 (418) 668-0031

Saint-Félicien
1209 Boulevard du Sacré-Cœur
☎ (418) 679-9888
🖹 (418) 679-0562

Exploring

Tour A:
The Saguenay Region
★ ★

 2 days

The "Kingdom of Saguenay," as its inhabitants often refer to it, proudly and without an ounce of modesty, extends on both sides of the Rivière Saguenay and its gargantuan fjord. This region is characterized above all by its grandiose scenery and extraordinary flora and fauna. It was originally exploited for fur, then wood, before eventually being permanently settled by such companies.

Since the beginning of the 20th century, the aluminum industry has flourished on the outskirts of local towns, taking advantage of the abundant supply of hydroelectric power provided by area rivers and the ports deep enough to accommodate ships carrying bauxite, the mineral from which aluminum is extracted.

L'Anse-Saint-Jean ★ (pop. 1,184)

In the spring of 1838, the first schooner chartered by the Société des Vingt-et-Un set off from the Charlevoix region to deposit settlers at various places along the banks of the Saguenay. The first stop was L'Anse-Saint-Jean, making this charming village, with its many handcrafted bread ovens the oldest municipality in the Saguenay–Lac-Saint-Jean region. Noteworthy attractions include a stone **church**, designed by architect David Ouellet (1890), and a covered bridge, known as **Pont du Faubourg**, built in 1929. The village and its bridge are depicted on the back of the Canadian thousand-dollar bill. The **Belvédère de l'Anse de Tabatière**, with its spectacular view of the sheer cliffs along the fjord, is also worth a visit. The village boasts a salmon river, a yacht club, and hiking and riding trails. It is also one of the many points of departure for river cruises on the Saguenay.

Return to Route 170 and head towards Rivière-Éternité.

Rivière-Éternité ★ (pop. 563)

With a poetic name that translates to Eternity River, how could anyone resist being carried away by the stunning beauty of the Saguenay? Rivière-Éternité is the gateway to **Parc National du Saguenay ★★★** (see p 522) and the marvelous **Parc Marin du Saguenay–Saint-Laurent ★★★** (see p 553), where whales can be observed in their natural habitat.

On the first of the three cliffs that form Cap Trinité is a statue of the Virgin Mary, christened **Notre-Dame-du-Saguenay**. Carved out of pine by Louis Jobin, it was placed here in 1881 in thanks for a favour granted to a travelling salesman, who was saved from certain death when he fell near the cape. The statue is tall enough (8.5m) to be clearly visible from the deck of ships coming up the river.

The **International Christmas Mangers Exposition ★** *($5; early Jul to early Sep every day 8:30am to 4:30pm, late Nov to early Jan every day noon to 7pm; 418 Rue Principale, ☎418-*

272-2414 off-season or 272-2807 during the exhibit, www.creches.qc.ca) is presented during high season in summer and the holiday season in winter. A permanent exhibit featuring a 6m-high Nativity scene statue created by Serge Claveau can be found on the mountain that is located in the heart of Rivière-Éternité. In summer, the exhibit presents more than 250 mangers from around the world. In winter, life-size mangers are set up in Parc des Artistes and an illuminated village with 150 mangers can also be found in town.

Head back to Route 170. The road leads through Saint-Félix-d'Otis, along the shores of the lake of the same name, before reaching the town of La Baie.

Saguenay ★ (pop. 148,339)

The new municipality of Saguenay is the region's largest city and includes three boroughs: **La Baie**, which occupies the territory of the former city of La Baie; **Chicoutimi**, which includes the former cities of Chicoutimi and Laterrière, as well as part of the former district of Tremblay; and **Jonquière**, which comprises the former cities of Jonquière, Shipshaw and Lac-Kénogami.

La Baie ★

La Baie is an industrial area occupying a beautiful site at the far end of the Baie des Ha! Ha! (old French for *impasse* or dead-end). The colourful term "Ha!Ha!" was supposedly employed by the region's first explorers, who headed into the bay thinking it was a river. The former town of La Baie is the result of the 1976 merging of three adjacent municipalities, Bagotville, Port-Alfred and Grande-Baie. The latter was founded in 1838 by the Société des Vingt-et-Un, making it the oldest of the three. At La Baie, the Saguenay is still influenced by the salt-water tides, giving the town a maritime feel. La Baie also has a large **sea port**, which is open to the public.

The Société des Vingt-et-Un was founded in La Malbaie (Charlevoix) in 1837 with the secret mission of finding new farmlands to ease overcrowding on the banks of the St. Lawrence. Under the pretext of cutting wood for the Hudson's Bay Company, the Société cleared the land around a number of coves along the Saguenay, and settled men, women and children there.

On June 11, 1838, Thomas Simard's schooner, with the first settlers on board, set anchor in the Baie des Ha! Ha! The colonists disembarked and, under the supervision of Alexis Tremblay, built the region's very first wood cabin (4m x 6m), marking the birth of the former town of La Baie.

At the **Palais Municipal** ★ *($45; late Jun to mid-Aug Wed-Sat 8pm; 591 5ᵉ Rue, ☎418-697-5151 or 888-873-3333)*, visitors can see *La Fabuleuse Histoire d'un Royaume*, an elaborate historical pageant similar to those presented in some provincial French towns. Bringing this colourful extravaganza to life involves over 200 actors and 1,400 costumes, along with animals, carriages, lighting effects and sets.

The **Passe Migratoire à Saumons de la Rivière-à-Mars** ★ *($3; mid-Jun to mid-Sep every day 8am to 8pm; 3232 Chemin St-Louis, ☎418-697-5093)*, built on a part of the river located right in the heart of town, was designed to facilitate the salmon's upriver migration during its spawning period. From the lovely park that has been laid out in the surrounding area, visitors can watch the salmon and occasionally fish them.

Take Route 372, west of La Baie, which leads into downtown Chicoutimi. Since it is better to visit this part of the city on foot, we recommend parking in the area around the cathedral, located on Rue Racine.

Chicoutimi ★

In the language of the Montagnais, "Chicoutimi" means "there where it is deep," a reference to the waters of the Saguenay, which are navigable as far as this city, the most important urban area in the entire Saguenay–Lac-Saint-Jean region. For over 1,000 years, nomadic Aboriginal peoples used this spot for meetings, festivities and trade. Starting in 1676, Chicoutimi became one of the most important fur-trading posts in New France. The post remained active up until the mid-19th century, when two industrialists, Peter McLeod and William Price, opened a sawmill nearby (1842). This finally enabled the development of a real town on the site, graced with the presence of three powerful rivers: the Moulin, the Chicoutimi and the Saguenay.

Religious and institutional buildings are predominant in downtown Chicoutimi, the main commercial thoroughfare of which is Rue Racine. Very little remained of the 19th-century Victorian town after most of Chicoutimi was destroyed by a raging fire in 1912; over the past 30 years, the rest has been "modernized," stripping it of its character. Along the streets, visitors will notice shop signs bearing typical Saguenay names, like Tremblay and Claveau, as well as English-sounding names, such as Harvey and Blackburn; this is indicative of a phenomenon found only in this part of the country: the assimilation of English-speaking families into French-speaking society.

The **Cathédrale Saint-François-Xavier** ★ *(514 Rue Racine Est)* was rebuilt on two different occasions, both times due to fire. The present building, erected between 1919 and 1922, was designed by architect Alfred Lamontagne. It is remarkable above all for its high facade, whose two towers, topped with silvered steeples, rise above the old port. In front of the cathedral, visitors will find the former post office, built of pink granite in the Second Empire style (1905).

Cruises on the Saguenay river leave from the **Vieux-Port de Chicoutimi** *(old port; Boulevard du Saguenay)*. A pleasant public market can also be found here.

Return to your vehicle in order to visit other attractions located beyond the downtown area. Drive up Rue Bégin, west of the cathedral, then turn right on Rue Price Est. Turn left on Boulevard Saint-Paul, then right on Rue Dubuc.

At the turn of the 20th century, several large-scale French-Canadian enterprises were established in the Saguenay–Lac-Saint-Jean region, the largest being the pulp mills in Val-Jalbert and Chicoutimi. The **Pulperie de Chicoutimi** ★★ *($10; late Jun to early Sep every day 9am to 6pm, early Jun to mid-Jun and early Sep to mid-Oct Wed-Sun 9am to 5pm, rest of the year Wed-Sun 10am to 4pm; 300 Rue Dubuc, ☎418-698-3100 or 877-998-3100)* was founded in 1896 by Dominique Guay and then expanded several times by the powerful North American Pulp and Paper Company, run by Alfred Dubuc. For 20 years, the company was the largest mechanical manufacturer of pulp and paper in Canada, supplying the French, American and British markets. This vast industrial complex, built alongside the turbu-

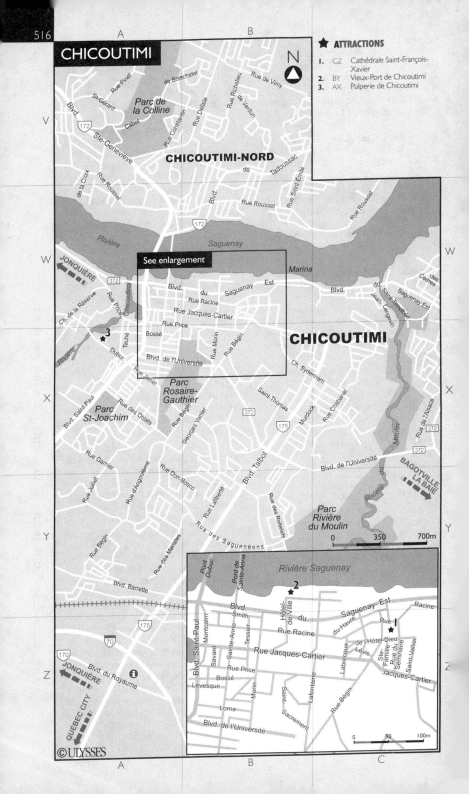

lent Rivière Chicoutimi, included four pulp mills equipped with turbines and digesters, two hydroelectric stations, a smelter, a repair shop and a railway platform. The decline of pulp prices in 1921 and the crash of 1929 led to the closing of the pulp mill. It remained abandoned until 1980. In the meantime, most of the buildings were ravaged by fire, which, if nothing else, showed the strength of their thick stone walls. Since 1996, the whole complex has become a gigantic museum covering an area of over 1ha. In addition to stopping by the Maison Arthur-Villeneuve, visitors can go on a 12-stop self-guided tour of the site and enjoy a thematic exhibition.

Jonquière

In 1847, the Société des Défricheurs du Saguenay (land-clearers) received authorization to set up shop alongside Rivière aux Sables. The name Jonquière was chosen in memory of one of the governors of New France, the Marquis de Jonquière. The town's early history is marked by the story of Marguerite Belley of La Malbaie, who escorted three of her sons to Jonquière on horseback to prevent them from being tempted to emigrate to the United States. In 1870, the territory between Jonquière and Saint-Félicien, in the Lac-Saint-Jean region, was destroyed by a major forest fire. It took over 40 years for the region to recover. Today, Jonquière is regarded as an essentially modern town, whose economic mainspring is the Alcan aluminum smelter.

This multinational company owns several factories in the Saguenay–Lac-Saint-Jean region, replacing the Price brothers and their wood empire as the largest local employer. The towns of Arvida and Kénogami had already merged with Jonquière in 1975, forming a city large enough to rival nearby Chicoutimi. Jonquière is known for its industrial tours.

The **Centrale Hydroélectrique de Shipshaw** ★ ★ *(free admission; Jun to Aug Mon-Fri 1:30pm to 4:30pm, reservations required; 1471 Route du Pont, ☎418-699-1547)*, which began operating in 1931, is a striking example of Art Deco architecture. It supplies electricity to the local aluminum smelters.

Cross the Aluminum Bridge and turn left on Rue Price.

The **Aluminum Bridge**, opened in 1948, weighs about 164 tonnes, a third of the weight of an identical steel bridge. It was built as a means of promoting aluminum, which was rarely used in construction at the time.

The contemporary-style **Église Notre-Dame-de-Fatima** ★ *(3635 Rue Notre-Dame)* is renowned as one of the most famous white churches in the Saguenay region. Designed by Paul-Marie Côté and Léonce Gagné, it was erected in 1963. The stained-glass windows by artist Guy Barbeau produce a lovely play of light on the bare concrete interior.

The **Parc et Promenade de la Rivière-aux-Sables** is the fruit of a major environmental restoration project carried out on the Rivière aux Sables, alongside the largest historic district in town. It links the Place des Nations de la Francité and Place Nikitoutagan to the immediate surroundings of the bridge on Boulevard Harvey. Here, visitors will find Les Halles, where many local market gardeners have stalls. There are a few places to eat as well, including an excellent *crêperie*. Both pedestrians and cyclists are permitted on the riverside promenade.

Usine Alcan d'Arvida. The former city of Arvida was expressly created for the aluminum industry and has been a part of Jonquière since 1976. Alcoa (Aluminium Company of America), which later became Alcan (Aluminium Company of Canada), built the world's largest aluminum smelter here in 1925, attracting several migrant workers from Eastern Europe and forever changing the ethnic makeup of the Saguenay–Lac-Saint-Jean region. Arvida quickly became the world's foremost aluminum producer and remained so for several decades. The city's strange name is the result of a contraction of the name of Alcoa's founder, Arthur Vinning Davis.

If you wish to explore the Lac-Saint-Jean region via tour B, follow Rue Saint-Dominique and turn left on Boulevard du Royaume (Route 170 Ouest) to get to Larouche and Alma. If you'd rather head to the northern bank of the Saguenay river to visit the **Tadoussac** *area (see p 539), cross the bridge on Rue Price that leads to Shipshaw. Turn right on Route 172 Est, which will take you to Saint-Fulgence and then Sainte-Rose-du-Nord.*

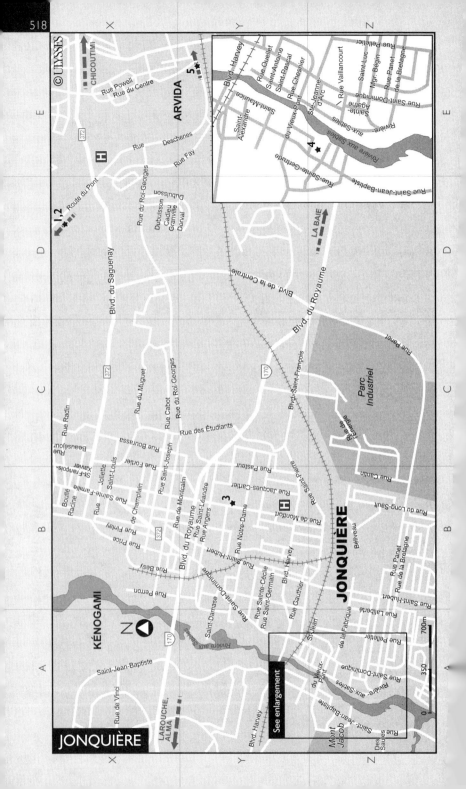

518

©ULYSSES

JONQUIÈRE

KÉNOGAMI

ARVIDA

JONQUIÈRE

See enlargement

Parc Industriel

0   350   700m

Streets and landmarks

Rue Powell
Rue du Centre
Route du Pont
Rue Deschenes
Rue Fay
Rue du Roi-Georges
Dubuisson
Cadieu
Granville
Dorval
Blvd. du Saguenay
Rue du Muguet
Rue Cabot
Rue du Roi-Georges
Rue des Étudiants
Rue Radin
Rue Beauséjour
St-François-Xavier
Boullé
Radine
Rue Sainte-Famille
Jollette
Saint-Louis
Rue Fortier
Rue Saint-Joseph
Rue Bourassa
Rue Pasteur
Rue Jacques-Cartier
Rue Price
Rue Finlay
de Champlain
Rue de Montcalm
Rue Saint-Léandre
Rue Angers
Rue Notre-Dame
Rue de Montfort
Rue Saint-Pierre
Rue Perron
Rue Besy
Saint-Dominique
Blvd. du Royaume
Rue Saint-Hubert
Blvd. Harvey
Rue Sainte-Cécile
Rue Saint-Germain
Rue Gauthier
Saint-Damase
Saint-Jean-Baptiste
Rue de Vinci
Rue Laliberté
Rue Saint-Hubert
Rue Panet
Rue de la Bretagne
Béliveau
Rue du Long-Sault
Rue Cantin
Rue Panet
Blvd. de la Centrale
Blvd. du Royaume
Blvd. Saint-François
Rue de la Fabrique
Rue Pelletier
Rue Saint-Dominique
Rivière-aux-Sables
St-Jean
Mont Jacob
Des Saules
Rue Roy
Saint-Jean-Baptiste
du Vieux-Pont

Enlargement:
Blvd. Harvey
Rue Ouellet
Saint-Antoine
Saint-Pascal
Rue Chesnier
Saint-Maurice
Saint-Alexandre
Ste-Jeanne-d'Arc
Rue du Vieux-Pont
Sainte-Agathe
Rue Saint-Dominique
Rue Vaillancourt
Saint-Luc
Mgr-Bégin
Rue Panet
Rue de la Bretagne
Rue Pelletier
Rue Sainte-Gertrude
Rivière aux Sables
Rue Saint-Jean-Baptiste

CHICOUTIMI

LAROUCHE, ALMA

LA BAIE

★ **ATTRACTIONS**

1.	DX	Centrale Hydroélectrique de Shipshaw	**4.**	EZ	Parc et Promenade de la Rivière-aux-Sables
2.	DX	Aluminum Bridge	**5.**	EY	Usine Alcan d'Arvida
3.	BY	Église Notre-Dame-de-Fatima			

Saint-Fulgence (pop. 2,035)

The little village of Saint-Fulgence is nestled in the valleys near Chicoutimi and the edge of the fjord, and offers several interesting options for outdoor-sports enthusiasts. It's the entry point to the **Parc National des Monts-Valins** ★ (see p 523) and bird lovers should make sure they head to the **Centre d'Interprétation des Battures et de Réhabilitation des Oiseaux CIBRO** *(sandbar interpretation centre and bird rehabilitation facility; $6; early May to late Jun Mon-Fri 9am to 4pm, late Jun to late Aug every day 8:30am to 6pm, late Aug to early Nov every day 9am to 4pm; 100 Rue Cap-des-Roches, ☎418-674-2425).* The sandbars that spread out in front of the centre are home to several different bird species. A walk along the trails that were set up here provides an opportunity to observe them while enjoying the magnificent scenery. Visitors can also get a close look at injured birds of prey that were found in the area and brought to the centre to be treated.

Sainte-Rose-du-Nord ★ (pop. 409)

Though it seems much older, the charming little village of Sainte-Rose-du-Nord was only founded some 60 years ago. The rocky scarp of the Saguenay provides a surreal backdrop that recalls the cardboard villages that are set at the foot of Christmas trees. Visitors can explore the village's arts and crafts shops and the **Église Sainte-Rose-de-Lima**, which features a unique interior forest-themed decor made of branches, roots and birch bark.

Croisières La Marjolaine (see p 523) offers cruises on the Saguenay river between Sainte-Rose-du-Nord and Chicoutimi.

The **Musée de la Nature** *($5; year-round every day 9am to 8:30pm; 199 Rue de la Montagne, ☎418-675-2348, www.musee-de-la-nature.com)* presents various stuffed wild animals and samples of the region's flora in six creatively designed exhibits.

Tour B: Circling Lac Saint-Jean ★ ★

 2 days

Various Montagnais nations, including the Nation du Porc-Épic (Porcupine Nation), were once attracted to the vast expanse of water known today as Lac Saint-Jean (1,350km²). Europeans were unaware of the lake's existence for many years; it wasn't until 1647 that a Jesuit missionary named Jean de Ouen discovered it on his way to nurse some ailing local inhabitants. Long regarded as an inexhaustible source of fur, this region, with its rich farmlands, sandy beaches and relatively mild climate, was not actually settled until much later, in the second half of the 19th century. In 1926, Lac Saint-Jean's water level increased significantly when dams were built on the Saguenay, leading to the loss of several square kilometres of farmland. The following tour takes visitors around the lake in the same direction as the area was settled, coming almost full circle.

Desbiens (pop. 1,148)

Located on either side of the Rivière Métabetchouane, this town is steeped in history. It was settled in 1652 by a Jesuit mission; a fur-trading post was added in 1676. The trading post consisted of a store, a chapel and several farm buildings. It prospered until 1880, when the buildings were dismantled and moved to Pointe-Bleue (Mashteuiatsh).

Many excavations have been conducted around the mouth of Rivière Métabetchouane, uncovering various archaeological traces of the Aboriginals' thousand-year-long habitation of the area, as well as remnants of the Jesuit mission and the fur-trading post. A number of the objects uncovered during these digs are on display at the **Centre d'Histoire et d'Archéologie de la Métabetchouane** ★ *($5; late Jun to early Sep every* day 9am to 5pm, early Sep to late Jun reservations required; 243 Rue Hébert, ☎418-346-5341).

Guides lead visitors through the granite cave known as the **Trou de la Fée** *($8.50; mid-Jun to late Aug every day 9am to 5pm, late Aug to early Sep every day 10am to 4pm, rest of the year by appointment; Chemin du Trou de la Fée,* ☎*418-346-1242 or 346-5632 off-season);* the name means "the fairy's hideaway."

Continue along Route 169 toward Chambord.

Chambord (pop. 1,720)

The **Village Historique de Val-Jalbert** ★★ *($16; mid-May to mid-Jun and late Aug to mid-Oct every day 9am to 4pm, mid-Jun to late Aug every day 9:30am to 5:30pm; 95 Rue St-Georges, Route 169,* ☎*418-275-3132 or 888-675-3132)* was established in 1901, when an industrialist by the name of Damase Jalbert built a pulp mill at the foot of the Rivière Ouiatchouane falls. The enterprise prospered quickly, becoming the most important industrial company run entirely by French Canadians. But the drop in pulp prices in 1921, followed by the shift to artificial pulp in the manufacturing of paper, forced the mill to close down in 1927, at which point the village was completely deserted by its inhabitants.

Val-Jalbert is a rich slice of North America's industrial heritage. Part of the village still looks like a ghost town, while the rest has been carefully restored to provide visitors with accommodations and an extremely informative interpretation centre. Various viewing areas, linked by a gondola *($3),* have been built to enable visitors to fully appreciate the surroundings. There is a campground beside the village, and accommodations are available in some of the restored houses.

Continue along Route 169 to Roberval.

Roberval (pop. 11,013)

This industrial town used to be the crossroads of the railway and the Lac Saint-Jean shipping routes. Today, it is the finishing point of the famous Traversée Internationale du Lac Saint-Jean, a swimming event held each year in July.

The Roberval region is well known for its reserves of granite, which is used in the facing of North-American skyscrapers. The city was named in honour of New France's viceroy Jean-François La Rocque de Roberval, who had (unsuccessfully) attempted to settle the Saguenay region as early as the 16th century. Roberval was developed at the turn of the 20th century when Philadelphia millionaire Horace Beemer made it the terminal of a railroad that linked Québec City to Lac-Saint-Jean.

Beemer also had an immense wood hotel built in Roberval to attract rich American sport fishers and outdoor excursionists. The hotel has since been destroyed. In 1920, the federal and provincial governments chose Roberval as the base camp from which geographical surveys of the northern territories of Québec, including mountainous regions and thousands of lakes, were carried out.

Turn right on Avenue Lizotte and head west on Boulevard Saint-Joseph at the intersection.

Most of Roberval's historic buildings are located on Boulevard Saint-Joseph. These include **Maison Donaldson** *(464 Boulevard St-Joseph)*, a former general store that was built in 1873 and, across the street, **Église Notre-Dame**, a modern tent-style church that was designed by architects Saint-Gelais, Tremblay and Tremblay in 1966.

Canada's first home-economics school (cooking and sewing classes) was founded in Roberval by the Ursulines religious community in 1881. The present **Couvent des Ursulines** *(720 Boulevard St-Joseph)* was designed by architects Joseph-Pierre and David Ouellet and built during the first part of the 20th century. Visitors can admire the pretty chapel under the church's silver dome. West of the convent is the city's **Palais de Justice** *(750 Boulevard St-Joseph)*. The courthouse tower's design was inspired by Québec City's National Assembly building.

Turn right on the narrow road that runs alongside the lake towards Mashteuiatsh (Pointe-Bleue).

Mashteuiatsh (Pointe-Bleue) ★ (pop. 1,868)

The Montagnais lived in nomadic communities all around Lac Saint-Jean for over

1,000 years. Advancing colonization and the forest industry eventually put an end to this way of life.

A sedentary reserve was created in Pointe-Bleue, on the western coast of Lac Saint-Jean, in 1856; 1,800 of Québec's total Innu population of 15,000 still live here today. First called Pointe-Bleue, the reserve was renamed Mashteuiatsh in 1983. Visitors shouldn't expect to find a traditional wigwam village as depicted in history books, though. Colourful aluminum-siding-covered houses are the norm here, and Mashteuiatsh has more in common with a suburban bedroom community than a stereotypical reserve. The city nonetheless offers several nice views of Lac Saint-Jean and, in the last few years, its Innu population has attempted to revive some of its traditions through an interesting museum, various events (such as powwows) and accommodation packages (*kukum*) that are sure to captivate visitors and provide a memorable stay.

The **Musée Amérindien de Mashteuiatsh** ★ *($7; ௸; mid-May to mid-Oct every day 10am to 6pm, rest of the year by appointment; 1787 Rue Amishk, ☎418-275-4842 or 888-875-4842, www.museeilnu.ca)* focuses on the customs of the first inhabitants of the Saguenay–Lac-Saint-Jean region. Its temporary exhibitions help acquaint visitors with Canada's other Aboriginal peoples as well. Significant objects on permanent display include a set of chairs and a table used by the band council, different types of snowshoes and examples of traditional clothing. Artisans skilled in the techniques of their ancestors occasionally gather on the grounds of the museum to pass on their know-how.

Saint-Félicien (pop. 10,674)

At the **Zoo Sauvage de Saint-Félicien** ★ ★ *($25; Jun to Aug every day 9am to 6pm, Sep to mid-Oct every day 9am to 5pm; in winter, hiking trails are accessible Mon-Fri 9am to 5pm; 2230 Boulevard du Jardin, ☎418-679-0543 or 800-667-5687, www.borealie.org)*, visitors can observe various species of Québec's indigenous wildlife in their natural habitat. What makes this zoo unusual is that the animals are not in cages, but roam about freely while visitors tour the zoo in small, screened buses. A lumber camp, fur-trading post, Inuit encampment and settler's farm have all been reconstructed and, along with the authentic buildings on site, add a historical feel to this unique zoo.

Dolbeau-Mistassini (pop. 15,076)

Mistassini and Dolbeau, which recently merged, are located on the banks of the Mistassini river, along Route 169. Be sure not to confuse Mistassini with the Cree village of Mistissini, located by Mistassini Lake some 300km away. Dolbeau-Mistassini is the self-declared blueberry capital of the world. Every year in August, the town hosts a blueberry festival (**Festival du bleuet**), which is as much a reunion of the *Bleuets*, residents of the region, who have scattered across America, as it is a culinary event, featuring delicious chocolate-covered blueberries, among other goodies.

Continue along Route 169 toward Sainte-Jeanne-d'Arc and Péribonka.

Péribonka ★ (pop. 567)

Louis Hémon was born in Brest, France in 1880. After attending the Lycée Louis-le-Grand in Paris, he obtained his law degree from the Sorbonne. In 1903, he settled in London, where he started his career as a writer. His adventurous spirit eventually led him to Canada. He lived in Québec City, then in Montréal, where he met some investors who wanted to build a railroad in the northern part of the Lac-Saint-Jean region. He headed off to scout out a location, but instead became fascinated with the local inhabitants' daily life. In June 1912, he met Samuel Bédard, who invited him to his home in Péribonka. Hémon helped out on the farm, secretly recording his impressions of the trip in a notebook. These impressions later formed the basis of his masterpiece, the novel *Maria Chapdelaine*.

Hémon did not, however, have time to enjoy his novel's tremendous success; on July 8, 1913, he was hit by a train while walking on the railroad tracks near Chapleau, Ontario, and died a few minutes later in the arms of his travelling companions.

Maria Chapdelaine was serialized in *Le Temps* in Paris, then published as a novel by Grasset in 1916, and finally translated into several languages. No other work of literature has done so much to make Québec known abroad. The novel was even adapted three times for the screen, by Jean Duvivier in 1934 (with Madeleine Renaud and Jean Gabin), Marc Allégret in 1949 (with Michèle Morgan in the title role) and Gilles Carle in 1983 (with Carole Laure in the title role). Péribonka is a charming village that serves as the starting point for the swimming race, the Traversée Internationale du Lac Saint-Jean.

Musée Louis-Hémon / Complexe Touristique Maria-Chapdelaine ★ ★ *($5.50; Jun to Sep every day 9am to 5pm, Sep to Jun Mon-Fri 9am to 4pm; 700 Route 169, ☎418-374-2177)* is located in the house where Louis Hémon spent the summer of 1912 with Samuel Bédard and his wife Eva (née Bouchard). It is still visible alongside Route 169 and is one of a few rare examples of colonial homes in the Lac-Saint-Jean region to have survived the improvements in the local standard of living. The extremely modest house that inspired Hémon was built in 1903. As it was converted into a museum in 1938, its furnishings have remained intact and are still laid out in their original positions in the humble rooms. A large postmodern building was erected nearby in order to house Hémon's personal belongings, as well as various souvenirs of the villagers who inspired his work, and memorabilia relating to the success of *Maria Chapdelaine*.

The road then leads through the villages of Sainte-Monique, Saint-Henri-de-Taillon (giving access to Parc de la Pointe-Taillon) and Delisle. On the way to Alma, visitors will cross the Saguenay by the Pont de l'Isle Maligne, which overlooks the Alcan hydro-electric dam.

Alma (pop. 30,579)

This industrial town lies along the edge of the Lac-Saint-Jean region. It is home to a large aluminum smelter and a paper mill, all surrounded by working- and middle-class neighbourhoods. Parc Falaise serves as a reminder that Alma has been the twin town of Falaise, Normandy since 1969.

The new **L'Odyssée des Bâtisseurs** ★ ★ theme park *($12 in high season, rest of the year $8; early Jun to late Sep every day 9am to 5pm, early Oct to early Jun Mon-Fri 9am to 4pm; 1671 Avenue du Pont Nord, ☎418-668-2606 or 866-668-2606, www.odysseedesbatisseurs.com)* was

created by the Société d'Histoire du Lac-Saint-Jean (historical society) and focuses on the important role that water played in the region's development. Permanent and temporary exhibits are shown in the Maison des Bâtisseurs and interpretive walking trails crisscross the historic L'Isle-Maligne sector, where visitors can take part in guided tours. The unique Parcours des Bâtisseurs trail is open until late October and leads to a belvedere and a water tower where multimedia presentations are shown in summer.

Tours of the **Papeterie Alma** ★ facilities *(late Jun to early Sep Tue-Thu 9:30am to 1:30pm; 1100 Rue Melançon, ☎418-668-9400, ext. 9348)* are available, including a visit to the pulp department and the machine room and an explanation of the manufacturing process.

Parks

Tour A: The Saguenay Region

Parc National du Saguenay ★ ★ ★ *($3.50; Baie Éternité sector, 91 Chemin Notre-Dame, Rivière-Éternité, ☎800-665-6527, www.sepaq.com)* extends across a portion of the shores of the Rivière Saguenay. It stretches from the banks of the estuary (located in the Manicouagan tourist region) to Sainte-Rose-du-Nord. In this area, steep cliffs plunge into the river, creating a magnificent landscape. The park has about 100km of hiking trails, providing visitors with an excellent opportunity to explore this fascinating region up close. A few of the more noteworthy trails include a short, relatively easy one along the banks of the Saguenay (1.7km) the Sentier de la Statue, which stretches 3.5km and includes a difficult uphill climb; and the superb, 25km Sentier des Caps, which takes three days (registration required). During winter, the trails are used for cross-country skiing. Lodging in the form of campsites and shelters is available. The park's two other sectors are located on the Saguenay river's left bank: Baie-du-Moulin-à-Baude sector, 750 Chemin Moulin-à-Baude, Tadoussac; and Baie-Sainte-Marguerite sector, 1121 Route 172 Nord, sector Sacré-Cœur.

Parc National des Monts-Valin ★ *($3.50; accessible via Route 172, 27km from Chicoutimi and 17km from Saint-Fulgence; 360 Rang St-Louis, Accueil Petit-Séjour,* ☎*418-674-1200 or 800-665-6527, www.sepaq.com)*, with its lofty summits, offers a whole slew of activities all year round. Hiking, mountain biking, canoeing, cabin stays and sport fishing are the summertime favourites.

During winter, snowfall reaches record levels of up to 5m. All this snow turns the trees into ghostlike figures, hence the legends of the "Vallée des Fantômes" (phantom valley) and the "Champs de Momies" (mummy fields). This wild and spectacular area, which looks out over the surrounding region, becomes a mecca for off-trail and cross-country skiing, snowshoeing and ice climbing.

Tour B: Circling Lac Saint-Jean

The **Réserve Faunique Ashuapmushuan** wildlife reserve *(May to Sep every day 7am to 9pm; access via Route 167, Km 33, La Doré,* ☎*418-256-3806)* covers a vast 3,400km² area and is favoured by hunters (moose and small game) who enjoy the reserve's comfortable chalets. A superb one-day discovery package includes a visit to the spectacular Chutes de la Chaudière waterfalls, a hike along former portage trails and an excursion on the rapids of the Ashuapmushuan river aboard traditional native rabaska canoes.

Parc National de la Pointe-Taillon ★ *($3.50; 825 3ᵉ Rang Ouest, St-Henri-de-Taillon,* ☎*418-347-5371 or 800-665-6527, www.sepaq.com)* lies on the strip of land formed by the Rivière Péribonka, which extends into Lac Saint-Jean. It is an excellent place to enjoy water sports, such as canoeing and sailing, and it also has magnificent sandy beaches. Bicycle paths and hiking trails provide access to the natural beauty of the park.

Outdoor Activities

■ Cycling

Tour B: Circling Lac Saint-Jean

The Lac-Saint-Jean region features one of the province's main cycling infrastructures: the **Véloroute des Bleuets** *(La Maison du Vélo de la Véloroute des Bleuets, 1692 Avenue du Pont Nord, Alma,* ☎*418-668-4541, www.veloroutebleuets.qc.ca)*. This cycling circuit goes all the way around Lac Saint-Jean on 256km of cycling trails and shared roads. The circuit's prettiest section leads from Saint-Gédéon to Roberval, closely hugging the banks of the lake. The Pointe-Taillon sector is also notable. A bike ferry provides shuttle service across the lake in Alma.

■ Cross-Country Skiing

Tour A: The Saguenay Region

Located alongside the Rivière à Mars, 7km from La Baie, the **Centre de Plein Air Bec-Scie** *($6.50; 7400 Chemin des Chutes,* ☎*418-697-5132)* has a network of 10 trails, four of which are easy, four difficult and two very difficult.

The **Club de Ski Le Norvégien** *($6; 4885 Chemin St-Benoît, Jonquière,* ☎*418-546-2344)* has 60km of trails for skiers of all levels.

■ Cruises

Tour A: The Saguenay Region

Croisières La Marjolaine *($46; Boulevard Saguenay, Port de Chicoutimi,* ☎*418-543-7630 or 800-363-7248)* organizes cruises on the Saguenay, one of the most enjoyable ways to take in the spectacular view of the fjord. The ship sets out from Chicoutimi, en route to Sainte-Rose-du-Nord. Passengers return by bus, except during June and September, when the return trip is by boat. Each cruise lasts an entire day. It is also possible to take the trip in the opposite direction, from Sainte-Rose-du-Nord to Chicoutimi.

See the **Manicouagan** chapter for more cruises on the Saguenay river, p 554.

Saguenay–Lac-Saint-Jean - Outdoor Activities

Downhill Skiing

Tour A: The Saguenay Region

The **Station Touristique du Mont-Édouard** ★ *($30; 67 Rue Dallaire, L'Anse-St-Jean, ☎418-272-2927, www.montedouard.com)* has the highest vertical drop in the region (450m). There are 20 runs for skiers of all levels.

In the Valin hills, where the park of the same name is located, there is also downhill skiing. **Le Valinouët** *($30; 200 Route du Valinouët, St-David-de-Falardeau, ☎418-673-6455 or 800-260-8254, www.valinouet.qc.ca)* has 25 runs with a vertical drop of 350m. It is renowned for the quality of its snow.

Hiking

Tour A: The Saguenay Region

The **Sentier des Caps** *(L'Anse-St-Jean; after the Pont du Faubourg, turn right on Chemin Thomas Nord and continue for 3km)* leads to the foot of one of the concrete pylons supporting Hydro-Québec's first 735kw line. There are two lookouts from which hikers can enjoy an extraordinary view of the fjord.

Horseback Riding

Tour A: The Saguenay Region

Centre Équestre des Plateaux
31 Chemin des Plateaux, L'Anse-Saint-Jean
☎ (418) 272-3231
Riders at Centre Équestre des Plateaux get to cross L'Anse-Saint-Jean's famous covered bridge before heading into the backcountry that borders the bay. Beginner's courses and various excursions are offered.

Ice Fishing

Tour A: The Saguenay Region

Parc National du Saguenay (see above) and the Rivière Saguenay attract hordes of ice-fishing enthusiasts. From December to mid-March, when the river is frozen, it is covered with fishers' colourful, little wooden shacks. The river is home to many species of fish, including cod, halibut and smelt. You can rent the necessary equipment in **Rivière-Éternité** *(only ice and seasonal fishing: equipment free of charge when you rent a cabin)* and in **La Baie** *(1352 Anse-à-Benjamin, ☎418-544-4176)*.

Kayaking

Tour A: The Saguenay Region

Fjord en Kayak *(359 Rue St-Jean-Baptiste, L'Anse-Saint-Jean, ☎418-272-3024, www.fjord-en-kayak.ca)* is located in the charming village of L'Anse-Saint-Jean and organizes kayaking excursions on the Saguenay fjord that will appeal to all tastes and levels of expertise. Kayakers get to live an unforgettable experience while admiring the cliffs that surround the river aboard their small watercraft.

Sea-kayaking excursions on the fjord are also offered at **Parc Aventure Cap Jaseux** *(Chemin de la Pointe-aux-Pins, Saint-Fulgence, ☎418-698-6673 or 877-698-6673, www.capjaseux.com)*, as well as "sport-yaking" outings on the Shipshaw river, aboard inflatable watercraft called "Sportyaks" that are stabler than kayaks but just as manoeuvrable.

Accommodations

Tour A: The Saguenay Region

L'Anse-Saint-Jean

Camping de L'Anse
$

325 Rue St-Jean-Baptiste
☎ (418) 272-2554 or
(418) 272-2633 (off-season)
🖷 (418) 272-3148
Camping de l'Anse not only faces the fjord, but also offers extremely well-equipped sites.

La Ferme des Trois Cours d'Eau
$$ bkfst incl.
sb
6 Rue de L'Anse
☎ (418) 272-2944
The three guest rooms in this small bed and breakfast occupy the second floor of a modest but superbly located farmhouse. The site is truly magnificent. Surrounded by pastures where cattles graze and crossed by a peaceful stream, the farm stands facing the bay where the Saint-Jean river meets the Saguenay river fjord. Guests have an unobstructed view of this meeting in a completely bucolic environment.

Auberge des Cévennes
$$
pb/sb
294 Rue St-Jean-Baptiste
☎ (418) 272-3180 or 877-272-3180
🖷 (418) 272-1131
www.auberge-des-cevennes.qc.ca
Auberge des Cévennes has held court on Rue Saint-Jean-Baptiste for many years. This huge century-old property reveals lovely and well-decorated guest rooms that look out over the long wraparound veranda. In addition to these relaxing rooms, a common living room is available to guests, who also have access to the spacious property around the house. The half-board option, which includes the evening table d'hôte (see p 529), is a good deal.

Les Gîtes du Fjord
$$$-$$$$$

344 Rue St-Jean-Baptiste
☎ (418) 272-3430 or 800-561-8060
🖷 (418) 272-3480
www.lesgitesdufjord.com
Perched atop a cliff along the fjord, Les Gîtes du Fjord rents out cottages and condominiums that are ideal for family vacations.

Rivière-Éternité

Centre de Villégiature du Parc National du Saguenay
$$$-$$$$$

91 Rue Notre-Dame
☎ (418) 272-1556 or 877-272-5229
🖷 (418) 272-3438
This outdoor recreation centre is part of the Parc National du Saguenay's facilities. The centre rents chalets located some 2km from the Saguenay river.

La Baie

Auberge de la Rivière Saguenay
$$-$$$ bkfst incl.

9122 Chemin de la Batture
☎ (418) 697-0222 or 866-697-0222
🖷 (418) 697-1178
www.aubergesaguenay.com
Auberge de la Rivière Saguenay lies in an enchanting setting, surrounded by beautiful greenery. Its peaceful atmosphere makes it a daydreamer's paradise. Here, you can enjoy unique, specialized packages focusing on regional and native gastronomy, wild plants, the outdoors, cultural activities, romance and alternative medicine. Comfortable rooms are designated by names taken from nature; 10 of them have private balconies with stunning views of the fjord. Warm welcome.

Auberge des 21
$$$

621 Rue Mars
☎ (418) 697-2121 or 800-363-7298
🖷 (418) 544-3360
www.aubergedes21.com
The charming Auberge des 21 offers magnificent, comfortable rooms with a view of the Baie des Ha! Ha!. There is a health and beauty centre to help travellers relax and an excellent restaurant, **le Doyen** (see p 530).

Auberge des Battures
$$$-$$$$

6295 Boulevard de la Grande-Baie Sud
☎ (418) 544-8234 or 800-668-8234
🖷 (418) 544-4351
www.battures.ca
L'Auberge des Battures not only offers a spectacular view of La Baie des Ha! Ha!, it also has wonderful accommodations and refined cuisine.

Chicoutimi

Hôtel du Fjord
$$-$$$ bkfst incl.
241 Rue Morin
☎ (418) 543-1538 or 888-543-1538
🖷 (418) 543-8253
www.hoteldufjord.qc.ca

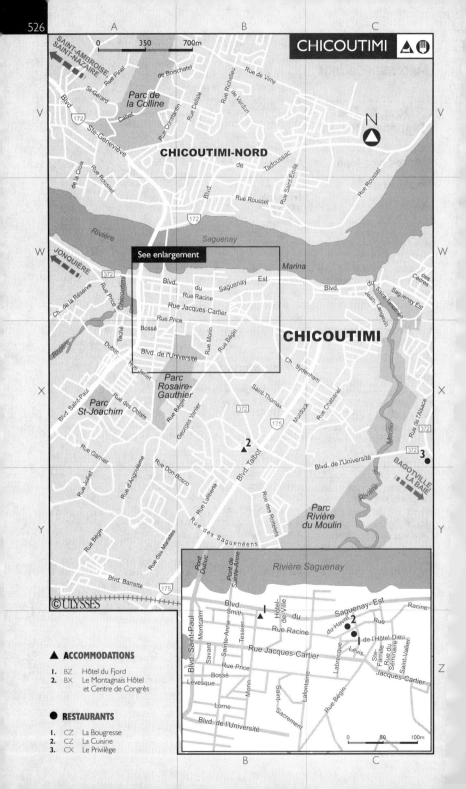

CHICOUTIMI

0   350   700m

SAINT-AMBROISE
SAINT-NAZAIRE

Rue Pinel
de Boischatel
Rue Richelieu
Rue de Vimy

Parc de
la Colline

St-Gérard

Blvd.

172

Ste-Geneviève

Rue Delisle
Rue de Verdun

Cabot

Rue Constantin

CHICOUTIMI-NORD

de
Tadoussac

Rue Roussel

de la Croix
Rue Roussel

Rue saint-Émilie

172

Rivière   Saguenay

N

See enlargement

Marina

JONQUIÈRE

372

Blvd.   du   Saguenay   Est

Blvd.

du   Saint-Timothée

Saguenay Est

des
Cèdres

Rue Price
Chicoutimi
Taché

Rue Racine

Rue Jacques-Cartier

Rue Price

Bossé

CHICOUTIMI

Jean-Langevin

Ch. de la Réserve

Rivière

Dubuc

Rue Jellet

Blvd. de l'Université

Rue Morin
Rue Bégin

Ch. Sydenham

Parc
Rosaire-
Gauthier

Saint-Thomas

Murdock

Rue Chatairel

Rue de l'Atsaca

372

Blvd. Saint-Paul

Parc
St-Joachim

Rue des Oblats

Rue Bégin

Georges Vanier

372

175

Rue Morin

372

372   3

BAGOTVILLE
LA BAIE

Rue Garnier

Rue Jolliet

Rue d'Angoulême

Rue Don-Bosco

2

Blvd. Talbot

Rue Laliberté

Rue des Roitelets

Blvd. de l'Université

Rivière du

Rue Bégin

Rue des Marais

Rue des Saguenéens

Parc
Rivière
du Moulin

Blvd. Barrette

175

©ULYSSES

Pont
Dubuc

Pont de
Sainte-Anne

Rivière Saguenay

Blvd.
Smith

Hôtel-
de-Ville

1

du

Saguenay-Est

Racine

Blvd. Saint-Paul

Montcalm

Sainte-Anne

Tessier

Rue Racine

du Havre

2

Rue

Labrecque

Lévis

de l'Hôtel-Dieu

Savard

Rue Jacques-Cartier

1

Ste-
Famille
Rue du
Séminaire

Saint-Vallier

Rue Price

Bossé

Lévesque

Morin

Lafontaine

Saint-Sacrement

Rue Bégin

Jacques-Cartier

Lorne

Blvd. de l'Université

0   50   100m

▲ ACCOMMODATIONS

1. BZ   Hôtel du Fjord
2. BX   Le Montagnais Hôtel
         et Centre de Congrès

● RESTAURANTS

1. CZ   La Bougresse
2. CZ   La Cuisine
3. CX   Le Privilège

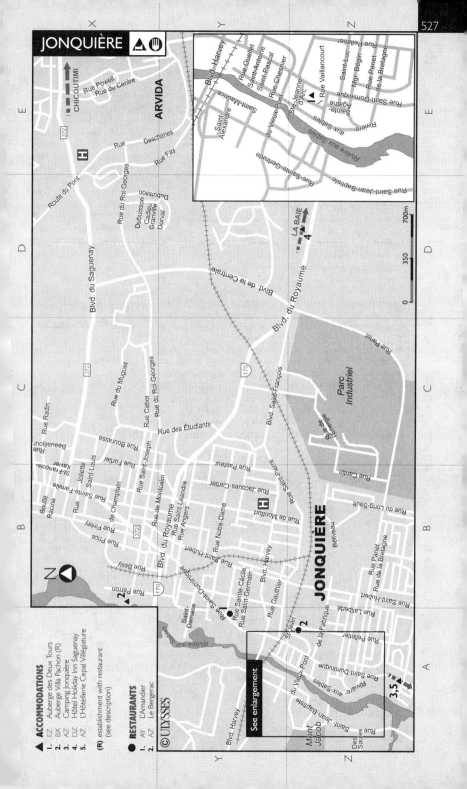

Hôtel du Fjord is located beyond the cluster of large hotels, near Parc du Vieux-Port, Rivière Saguenay and the town centre.

Le Montagnais Hôtel et Centre de Congrès
$$-$$$

≡ ◎ ❤ ≈ ❣ ♨ 〉〉〉

1080 Boulevard Talbot
☎ (418) 543-1521 or 800-463-9160
🖩 (418) 543-2149
www.lemontagnais.qc.ca

Le Montagnais Hôtel et Centre de Congrès occupies a large building and is ideally located for shoppers who wish to explore Chicoutimi's nearby malls.

Jonquière

Camping Jonquière
$

♨ 🐾

3553 Chemin du Quai
☎ (418) 542-0176

A small marina and a lakeside setting on Lac Kénogami make this campground a good choice for water-sports enthusiasts.

Auberge des Deux Tours
$$ bkfst incl.

pb/sb ≡

2522 Rue St-Dominique
☎ (418) 695-2022 or 888-454-2022
🖩 (418) 542-6489
www.aubergedeuxtours.qc.ca

Facing the church on this busy street stands a house that doesn't easily go unnoticed. Its two towers inspired its owners to turn this house into an inn and its corridors, stairs and common rooms retain the memory of its former residents. The simple guest rooms have been brightened up with new colours. Guests are welcome to get fresh air on the veranda and on the balconies in the summer.

Hôtel Holiday Inn Saguenay
$$-$$$$

≡ ❤ ≈ ♨ ⅌

2675 Boulevard du Royaume
☎ (418) 548-3124 or 800-363-3124
🖩 (418) 548-1638
www.saguenay.holiday-inn.com

Though outside the centre of town, the Hôtel Holiday Inn Saguenay is nevertheless very well located on the road between Jonquière and Chicoutimi, and has attractive rooms.

L'Hôtellerie Cepal Villégiature
$$$ bkfst incl.

≡ ♨ ≈

3350 Rue St-Dominique
☎ (418) 547-5728 or 800-361-5728
🖩 (418) 547-4882
www.cepalaventure.com

Surrounded by nature, by the shore of the Rivière aux Sables and not far from impressive Lac Kénogami, the Cepal resort offers outdoor holidays. There's something for the entire family to enjoy here, from snowmobiling to canoeing to fishing and hiking. The guest rooms are simple but comfortable. A variety of packages, including meals and activities, is available.

Auberge Villa Pachon
$$$ bkfst incl.

♨

1904 Rue Perron
☎ (418) 542-3568 or 888-922-3568
🖩 (418) 542-9667
www.aubergepachon.com

After it moved to Jonquière, the **Chez Pachon** restaurant (see p 530) became the Auberge Villa Pachon, a restaurant-inn. It has five rooms and a suite in one of the loveliest historic houses in all of Saguenay–Lac-Saint-Jean, the ancestral home of the Price Brothers.

Saint-Honoré

Gîte du Lac Docteur
$ bkfst incl.

sb

431 Rue Honoré, Lac Docteur
☎ (418) 673-4428
www.gitedulacdocteur.com

The Gîte du Lac Docteur provides an enchanting setting at the foot of Monts Valin, near a lake. The surrounding region provides many outdoor-activity opportunities all year long. Saint-Honoré is a short 15min drive north of the Chicoutimi sector of the city of Saguenay, via the Dubuc bridge.

Tour B: Circling Lac Saint-Jean

Hébertville

Auberge Presbytère Mont-Lac-Vert
$$ bkfst incl.
♨

335 Rang du Lac-Vert
☎ (418) 344-1548 or 800-818-1548
🖩 (418) 344-1013
www.aubergepresbytere.com

Auberge Presbytère Mont-Lac-Vert enjoys a beautiful setting and has a warm, relaxing atmosphere. The food, furthermore, has received rave reviews from many guests.

Métabetchouan

Auberge La Maison Lamy
$$ bkfst incl.

pb/sb

56 Rue St-André
☎ (418) 349-3686 or 888-565-3686

In a magnificent upper-class home in the heart of a quaint little town, Auberge La Maison Lamy has irresistible charm, a meticulous decor and offers a warm welcome. Near Lac Saint-Jean and the Véloroute des Bleuets cycling trail.

Chambord

Village Historique de Val-Jalbert
$ camping
$$-$$ apartment, hotel and chalet accommodations
sb/pb ➡ ♨
95 Rue St-Georges, Route 169
☎ (418) 272-3132 or 888-675-3132
🖷 (418) 275-5875
www.sepaq.com
The vast campground at Village Historique de Val-Jalbert is perfect for back-country campers who'll appreciate the site's many natural campsites. Apartments, hotel rooms and small chalets are also part of the village's facilities.

Mashteuiatsh (Pointe-Bleue)

Travellers who'd like to learn more about Innu culture can enjoy an immersive experience by staying in a private residence in Mashteuiatsh. Contact the city's tourist office *(every day mid-Jun to Sep; 1427 Rue Ouiatchouan, ☎888-222-7922)* for further information.

Saint-Félicien

Camping de Saint-Félicien
$
🦮 ≋ ♨
2206 Boulevard du Jardin
☎418-679-1719 or 866-679-1719
🖷418-679-5410
As you may have guessed, the Camping de St-Félicien is located beside the zoo, so you might be awakened by animal noises at night. It occupies a large property

and is equipped with all the necessary facilities.

Hôtel du Jardin
$$-$$$
≡ ⛱ 🦮 ≋ ♨))) Ⴤ ⊚
1400 Boulevard du Jardin
☎ (418) 679-8422 or 800-463-4927
🖷 (418) 679-4459
www.hoteldujardin.com
The Hôtel du Jardin offers standard, confortable rooms near the zoo.

Péribonka

Auberge de l'Île-du-Repos
$-$$
➡ ♨
105 Cercle de l'Île-du-Repos
☎ (418) 347-5649 or 800-461-8585
🖷 (418) 347-4810
Alone on an island, in the middle of the river, the Auberge de l'Île-du-Repos offers beautiful surroundings, an environment that stimulates conversation and a fascinating cultural programme. This is a large youth hostel that also has campsites available.

Alma

Complexe Touristique de la Dam-en-Terre
$$-$$$
≡ ➡ ≋ ❄ ♨
1385 Chemin de la Marina
☎ (418) 668-3016 or 888-289-3016
🖷 (418) 668-4599
www.damenterre.qc.ca
The Complexe Touristique de la Dam-en-Terre rents out well-designed cottages with a beautiful view of Lac Saint-Jean. Those with tents can opt for the more economical campsites.

Hôtel Universel
$$-$$$
≡ ♨
1000 Boulevard des Cascades
☎ (418) 668-5261 or 800-263-5261

🖷 (418) 668-9161
www.hoteluniversel.com
Hôtel Universel is located in the heart of town and offers 75 comfortable rooms.

Restaurants

Tour A: The Saguenay Region

L'Anse-Saint-Jean

Bistro de l'Anse
$
319 Rue St-Jean-Baptiste
☎ (418) 272-4222
Located in a former fishing camp, Bistro de l'Anse offers a warm ambiance. People come here to have a drink in the evening while enjoying musical performances, for an aperitif on the veranda or for a sandwich or salad. The extensive property behind the house gives way to the Saint-Jean river estuary, into which many a fishing line has been dipped.

Le Maringouinfre
$$-$$$$
212 Rue St-Jean-Baptiste
☎ (418) 272-2385 or 877-272-2385
Le Maringouinfre is grill and seafood restaurant. Fresh ingredients and an intimate atmosphere are the highlights here.

Auberge des Cévennes
$$$
294 Rue St-Jean-Baptiste
☎ (418) 72-3180 or 877-272-3180
The restaurant at **Auberge des Cévennes** (see p 525) offers a mouth-watering evening table d'hôte. On offer is classic French cuisine accented by local products,

to enjoy inside or al fresco, weather permitting.

La Baie

Le Doyen
$$$$
Auberge des 21
621 Rue Mars
☎ (418) 697-2121 or 800-363-7298
With its succulent game dishes, the restaurant at **Auberge des 21** (see p 525) boasts one of the region's best menus and its dining room commands a remarkable, sweeping view of the Baie des Ha! Ha!. The Sunday brunch is excellent. Run by renowned chef Marcel Bouchard, who has won numerous regional, national and international awards, Le Doyen is making a tangible contribution to the evolution and refinement of regional Québec cuisine.

Auberge de la Rivière Saguenay
$$$$
9122 Chemin de la Batture
☎ (418) 697-0222 or 866-697-0222
The head chef at Auberge de la Rivière Saguenay has developed a menu centered on Aboriginal traditions, regional dishes and international cuisine. This superb inn lies in an extremely pleasant setting, featuring a lovely view of the fjord.

Chicoutimi

La Bougresse
$$-$$$
260 Rue Riverin
☎ (418) 543-3178
La Bougresse distinguishes itself by the variety and quality of its cuisine, which is always good. The confidence and loyalty of La Bougresse's Chicoutimi patrons are the best possible indication of the quality of the cuisine served here. The restaurant has regular all-the-mussels-you-can-eat nights.

La Cuisine
$$$-$$$$
387-A Rue Racine Est
☎ (418) 698-2822
The scent of freshly ground coffee permeates the air at La Cuisine. We especially recommend the steak tartare, mussels, rabbit, sweetbreads and *steak-frites* (steak and fries).

Le Privilège
$$$$
1623 Boulevard St-Jean-Baptiste
☎ (418) 698-6262
Le Privilège ranks among the finest restaurants in the region, offering a feast for the senses in a picturesque century-old house. Intuitive cuisine with market-fresh ingredients is reserved for a lucky few at a time. Friendly, relaxed ambiance and service. Reservations required.

Jonquière

Le Bergerac
$$$-$$$$
Tue-Sat
3919 Rue St-Jean
☎ (418) 542-6263
One of the finest restaurants in Jonquière, Le Bergerac has developed an excellent repertoire of dishes. Lunchtime *menu du jour* and evening table d'hôte.

Chez Pachon
$$$$
1904 Rue Perron
☎ (418) 542-3568 or 888-922-3568
Chez Pachon, an institution in the town of Chicoutimi, moved to Jonquière in 1999. It is now part of **Auberge Villa Pachon** (see p 528), which occupies the magnificent heritage home of the Price brothers, in a wonderful countryside setting. Its chef, who is already famous in the region, concocts a gourmet extravaganza of French-style cuisine with regional flavours. His specialities include *cassoulet de Carcassonne* (a casserole dish from southwestern France), *confit de magret et foie de canard* (magret duck breast and liver confit), filet and loin of lamb, calf sweetbreads, as well as fish and seafood. Dinner only. Reservations required.

L'Amandier
$$$$
Tue-Sun
5219 Chemin St-André
☎ (418) 542-5395
L'Amandier has an astonishing dining room decorated with carved plaster and an overabundance of woodwork. The restaurant serves regional cuisine made with fresh ingredients. Good food is joined here by a unique ambiance that is well suited to dining among friends; the inviting decor and the hosts' hospitality create a festive mood. Reservations required. Somewhat removed from town, however, it is not easy to find.

Sainte-Rose-du-Nord

Café de la Poste
$
169 Rue du Quai
☎ (418) 675-1053
Café de la Poste is located a stone's throw away from a pier that offers a splendid view of the fjord. The café's warm decor features attractive woodwork and an enchanting terrace. Delicious homemade fare is served in this former post office, including fresh-from-the-oven bread, refreshing fruit-flavoured alcoholic beverages (blackcurrant and raspberry) and divine pastries.

Tour B: Circling Lac Saint-Jean

Saint-Félicien

Hôtel du Jardin
$$-$$$$
1400 Boulevard du Jardin
☎ (418) 679-8422 or 800-463-4927
The fine regional cuisine served at the Hôtel du Jardin never disappoints.

Roberval

Château Roberval
$$-$$$
1225 Boulevard Marcotte
☎ (418) 275-7511 or 800-661-7611
Château Roberval is a renowned restaurant. The menu, made up of regional specialties, is full of pleasant surprises.

Alma

Bar-Restaurant Chez Mario Tremblay
$$-$$$
534 Rue Collard Ouest
☎ (418) 668-7231

People don't come to Bar-Restaurant Chez Mario Tremblay to enjoy the meal of their life; they are attracted by the owner's reputation as a hockey player and coach, which earned him the nickname *"le bleuet bionique"* (the bionic blueberry). This brasserie-style restaurant is a popular gathering place for hockey fans.

Entertainment

■ Bars and Nightclubs

Chicoutimi

You'll find several bars and nightclubs on Rue Racine. **L'International** is a good place to meet some of the famously friendly locals as rock and blues play in the background, while the **Loft** attracts a younger crowd and is a good place to dance the night away.

Jonquière

Jonquière's nightspots are mostly located on **Rue Saint-Dominique**, between Boulevard Harvey and Rue Dupont. You'll find a good variety of bars and nightclubs in this area.

■ Festivals and Cultural Events

Chicoutimi

The **Carnaval-Souvenir de Chicoutimi** *(mid-Feb;* ☎*418-543-4438 or 877-543-4439)* celebrates the customs of winter in days gone by

with period costumes and traditional activities.

Roberval

Since 1955, the last week of July has been devoted to the **Traversée Internationale du Lac Saint-Jean** *(*☎*418-275-2851)*. Swimmers cover the 32km between Péribonka and Roberval in eight hours, and some even register for the marathon, making the return trip in 18 hours.

Shopping

■ Blueberry Patches

The Saguenay Region

Here in the land where three blueberries can just about fill a pie, you might want to check out one of the following blueberry patches:

Bleuetière Au Gros Bleuet
159 Rang 2, 3km from St-David-de-Falardeau
☎ (418) 673-3269

Bleuetière de Saint-François-de-Sales
Chemin du Moulin, 15km west of the village of Saint-François-de-Sales
☎ (418) 348-6548

■ Food

Chicoutimi

If you're craving healthy, natural food, **Le Garde-Manger** *(271 Rue Ste-Famille, corner Hôtel-Dieu,* ☎*418-696-1597)* is the perfect place to stock up for a picnic.

Côte-Nord and Northern Québec

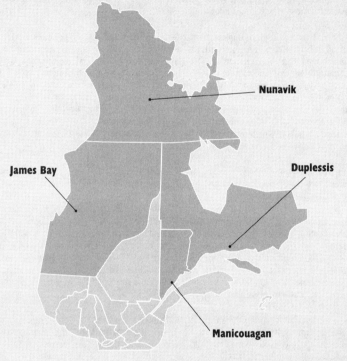

Nunavik

James Bay

Duplessis

Manicouagan

B ordering the St. Lawrence for some 300km, the **Manicouagan** region extends north into the Laurentian plateau to include the Monts Groulx and the Réservoir Manicouagan. It is also joined to the Duplessis region, forming what is called the **Côte-Nord**, or north shore.

One of the Manicouagan region's main attractions is the Parc Marin du Saguenay–Saint-Laurent, where a variety of whale species can be spotted during the summer months. Tourism, based mainly on whale watching, is playing an increasingly larger role in the region's economy, and the whales are now protected. In short, the Côte-Nord is an exceptional wilderness area with an interesting history.

A vast and remote region, **Duplessis** is bordered to the south for almost 1,000km by the Gulf of St. Lawrence and to the north by Labrador. Its small population of Francophones, Anglophones and the Montagnais First Nation is concentrated along the St. Lawrence coast and in a few inland mining towns. The Duplessis region is far from any large urban centre, and its economy has always been based on natural resources. Aboriginals have lived in the region for thousands of years. In the 16th century, Basque and Breton fishers and whalers set up seasonal posts in the area. Today, its important economic activities are fishing, forestry, and iron and titanium mining. Additional jobs are provided by a large aluminum smelter, which was built in Sept-Îles to take advantage of the availability of hydroelectricity.

A gigantic northern territory stretching from the 49th parallel to the 62nd parallel, **Nord-du-Québec (Northern Québec)** covers more than half the province's total area and includes the James Bay and Nunavik regions.

The singular beauty of this barren landscape, its harsh winter climate and its unique tundra vegetation giving way to taiga and then boreal forest create a region that is completely different from the rest of Québec, leading many southern Quebecers to imagine it as an inhospitable environment. After all, all roads and railways stop about halfway into the region and almost 2,000km separate Montréal and Ivujivik, the northernmost village in Québec. Some travellers do venture north, but for the most part this vast territory remains the land of northern Aboriginal peoples.

The 14 communities along the shores of Hudson Bay, Hudson Strait and Ungava Bay are home to some 9,500 people, 90% of whom are Inuit. In Inuktitut, the language of the Inuit, this territory is known as **Nunavik**. The territory is largely administered by the Inuit, the Cree, who number 12,000, live in nine villages on the taiga, mostly along the shores of James Bay.

From the first days of North-American colonization, English and French forces fought for the control of the fur trade in this vast region. Today, and for the last 30 or so years, it is the government of Québec that has taken a keen interest in the resources of these lands, namely the massive potential for hydroelectric power contained in certain rivers. Huge hydroelectric dams were constructed in the **James Bay** region, now capable of putting out 10,282 megawatts of power.

Increasingly, Northern Québec has been attracting tourists: its vast wilderness and wildlife are of interest nature and adventure lovers in growing numbers from all corners of the world. Similarly, "southern" city dwellers who want to experience a way of life that they consider to be closer to nature are fascinated by the culture of Québec's Cree and Inuit peoples, who are finding creative and exciting ways to respond to this demand. How about a dog-sledding expedition across the tundra or a night in a teepee?

Getting There and Getting Around

■ By Car

Côte-Nord

Manicouagan

From Beauport (near Québec City), take Route 138, which runs along the north shore of the St. Lawrence River, to Natashquan, in the Duplessis region. At Baie Sainte-Catherine, a ferry crosses the Rivière Saguenay to Tadoussac. To follow the Manicouagan tour, continue on Route 138; you can't go wrong—there is only one highway!

Duplessis

In 1996, Route 138 was extended to reach Pointe-Parent. However, during the summer, only hydroplanes and Relais Nordik's weekly supply boats from Havre-Saint-Pierre link the inhabitants of the scattered villages farther east to the rest of Québec. In the winter, snow and ice provide a natural route for snowmobiles between villages.

Northern Québec

James Bay

The region of Nord-du-Québec constitutes 51% of the territory of Québec but has only about 40,000 inhabitants (Inuit, Cree and non-Aboriginal). Route 109 penetrates part of this immense territory, travelling from Amos in Abitibi-Témiscamingue to Radisson. This 600km route is entirely paved and practically deserted. There is only one rest stop on this highway for you to fill up on food and gas, at Km 381. It is crucial to be prepared on this leg. In fact, although it is a long one, we recommend that you complete this trip in one day.

Another road heads east-west and accesses the hydroelectric installations of La Grande: LG-2 (renamed "Robert-Bourassa"), LG-3, LG-4, Brisay and Caniapiscau. However, it is impossible to travel past Km 323 without authorization from Hydro-Québec. The

section of the road from LG-2 to LG-4 is gravel. There is also a road linking Radisson to Chisasibi and LG-1.

The 437km-long Route du Nord runs east from Route 109, linking Chibougamau, Nemiscau, and, at the latitude of Rivière Rupert, Route de la Baie-James. Gasoline is available at the **Nemiscau Cree Construction station** *(Mon-Sat 7am to 9am and 3pm to 6pm)* and at a gas station at the entrance to the village of **Nemiscau** *(every day 9am to 3pm)*.

The Route du Nord is an earth-and-stone road that is especially difficult in summer and on which it is preferable to drive an all-terrain vehicle. There is constant traffic from heavy-weight trucks on this road, and they are not inclined to cede passage—drive defensively and keep to the right. When a truck comes barrelling down the middle of the road, pull over to the right and let it pass. Conditions on the Route du Nord are better in winter when the road surface, although icy, is harder and smoother.

Car Rental

Location Aubé
La Grande airport
☎ (819) 638-8353
🖷 (819) 638-7294

Nunavik

No roads or railroads link the Inuit communities of Nunavik, so car and train travel is out of the question. Flying is the only way to travel between villages in this area.

A small, unpaved road links the Naskapi village of Kawawachikamach to Schefferville, which is accessible by plane from Québec City's Jean Lesage International Airport (www.aeroportdequebec.com).

■ By Ferry

Côte-Nord

Manicouagan

Except for the Baie-Ste-Catherine–Tadoussac ferry, it is better to reserve a spot a few days in advance in the summer.

Baie-Sainte-Catherine–Tadoussac

The ferry ride from Baie-Sainte-Catherine to Tadoussac *(free; ☎418-235-4395)* takes only 10min. The schedule varies greatly from one season to the next, so make sure to double-check departure times before planning a trip.

Baie-Comeau–Godbout–Matane

The ferry *($12.75, car $29.95, motorcycle $22.45; ☎418-568-7575 from Godbout, ☎418-294-8593 from Baie-Comeau or ☎418-562-2500 from Matane)* serving Godbout, Matane and Gaspésie leaves from Baie-Comeau and takes 2hrs 20min.

■ By Boat

Côte-Nord

Duplessis

The **Relais Nordik** cargo boat *(rates vary according to destination; Apr to Jan, reservations required; ☎418-723-8787 or 800-463-0680, www.desgagnes.com)* leaves from Sept-Îles and travels to Port-Menier, Havre-Saint-Pierre, Natashquan, Kegaska, La Romaine, Harrington Harbour, Tête-à-la-Baleine, La Tabatière, Saint-Augustin and Blanc-Sablon. There is only one departure per week, so check the schedule before planning a trip.

■ Bus Stations

Côte-Nord

Manicouagan

Bus Stations

Tadoussac
443 Rue du Bateau-Passeur (Pétro-Canada station)
☎ (418) 235-4653

Baie-Comeau
212 Boulevard LaSalle
☎ (418) 296-6921

Duplessis

Intercar *(Gare du Palais, Québec City, ☎418-525-3000 or 888-861-4592)* links Québec City to Havre-Saint-Pierre, passing through all the major towns on the north shore of the St. Lawrence along the way.

Bus Stations

Sept-Îles
126 Rue Monseigneur Blanche
☎ (418) 962-2126

Havre-Saint-Pierre
843 Boulevard de l'Escale
☎ (418) 538-2033

■ By Plane

Côte-Nord

Duplessis

During the summer and the Christmas season, **Air Satellite** *(☎418-589-8923 or 800-463-8512, www.air-satellite.com)* offers daily flights from Rimouski, Sept-Îles, Baie-Comeau, Havre-Saint-Pierre, Longue-Pointe-de-Mingan and Île d'Anticosti.

Northern Québec

James Bay

Air Creebec
☎ (819) 825-8355 or 800-567-6567
www.aircreebec.ca
Air Creebec is the only airline that serves all of the Cree villages of Northern Québec, from Montréal and Val-d'Or. Mistissini, Oujé-Bougoumou and Waswanipi can be reached by taxi or rental car from the airport at Chibougamau. Air Creebec also offers flights to La Grande.

Nunavik

Air Inuit
☎ 800-361-2965
www.airinuit.com
This airline serves all the Inuit villages of Northern Québec.

First Air
☎ 800-267-1247
www.firstair.ca
First Air links Montréal and Kuujjuaq.

■ By Train

Côte-Nord

Duplessis

QNS&L Railway
☎ (418) 962-9411
The train links Sept-Îles to Schefferville, Fermont and Labrador City and runs three times a week in summer and twice a week in winter. The trip lasts from eight to 12hrs and crosses the Canadian Shield to the outlying tundra.

Useful Information

■ Tourist Information

Côte-Nord

Manicouagan

Association Touristique Régionale de Manicouagan
337 Boulevard Lasalle, Suite 304
Baie-Comeau, G4Z 2Z1
☎ (418) 294-2876 or 888-463-5319
▤ (418) 294-2345
www.routedesbaleines.ca

Tadoussac
197 Rue des Pionniers
☎ (418) 235-4744 or 866-235-4744
▤ (418) 235-4984

Baie-Comeau
3501 Boulevard Laflèche
☎ (418) 589-3610 (high season only)

Duplessis

Association Touristique Régionale de Duplessis
312 Avenue Brochu, Sept-Îles, QC, G4R 2W6
☎ (418) 962-0808 or 888-463-0808
▤ (418) 962-6518
www.tourismecote-nord.com

Port Cartier
Tourisme 50ième Parallèle
62 Route 138
☎ (418) 766-4414 or 888-766-6944
▤ (418) 766-4412
www.tourisme50parallele.com

Sept-Îles
Corporation Touristique de Sept-Îles
1401 Boulevard Laure Ouest
☎ (418) 962-1238 or 888-880-1238
▤ (418) 968-0022
www.ville.sept-iles.qc.ca

Havre-Saint-Pierre
Centre Culturel et d'Interprétation de Havre-Saint-Pierre
957 Rue de la Berge
☎ (418) 538-2512 or 538-2450
▤ (418) 538-1408

Île d'Anticosti
Sépaq Anticosti
C.P. 179, Port-Menier, QC, G0G 2Y0
☎ (418) 535-0156
▤ (418) 535-0289
www.sepaq.com
Sépaq Anticosti offers a few affordable vacation packages: a one-week stay at an inn (meals included); a one-week stay in a chalet or campground (meals not included); and a two-night stay at Auberge Port-Menier or Auberge Carleton (meals included). Other options include the North-South package (a three-night stay in the northern part of the island followed by a four-night stay in the southern part, or vice versa) and various hunting and fishing packages that include plane transportation to the island, accommodations and a rental vehicle. Reservations: ☎800-463-0863.

Natashquan
Corporation de Développement Touristique de Natashquan
55 Allée des Galets
☎ (418) 726-3054

Northern Québec

The tourism infrastructure in this region is relatively undeveloped. It is difficult to travel around the area, so it is recommended to make all reservations for both hotels and excursions in advance. For exploring this isolated territory, as well as for hunting and fishing trips, it is strongly recommended to hire the services of an outfitter.

Be aware that prices for goods and services are significantly higher in the North than they are in southern Québec. The vast majority of consumer goods have to be air freighted up to the North and the cost of living is relatively high, hence the price difference.

Côte-Nord and Northern Québec - Useful Information

MANICOUAGAN

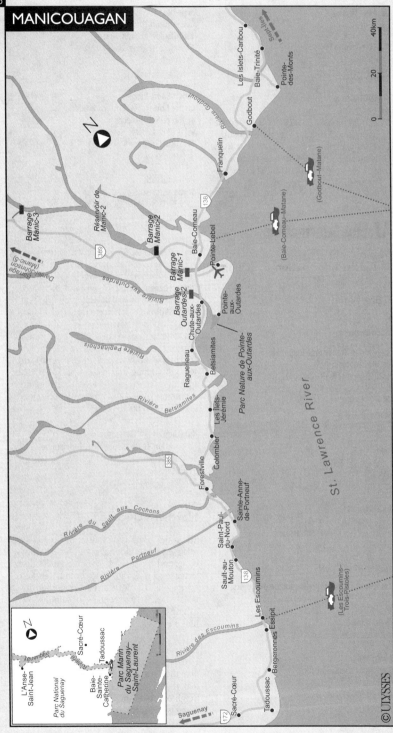

40km

20

0

Spruce Jets

Les Islets-Caribou

Baie-Trinité

Pointe-des-Monts

Godbout

Franquelin

Rivière Godbout

N

(Godbout–Matane)

138

Baie-Comeau

Pointe-Lebel

(Baie-Comeau–Matane)

Réservoir de Manic-2

Barrage Manic-3

389

Barrage Manic-2

Barrage Manic-1

Barrage Johnson (Manic-5)

Barrage Daniel

Rivière aux Outardes

Barrage Outardes-2

Chute-aux-Outardes

Pointe-aux-Outardes

Rivière Papinachois

Ragueneau

Betsiamites

Parc Nature de Pointe-aux-Outardes

Rivière Betsiamites

St. Lawrence River

Les Ïlets-Jérémie

Colombier

385

Forestville

Sainte-Anne-de-Portneuf

Rivière du Sault aux Cochons

Saint-Paul-du-Nord

Rivière Portneuf

Sault-au-Mouton

138

Les Escoumins

Essipit

(Les Escoumins–Trois-Pistoles)

Rivière des Escoumins

Bergeronnes

Sacré-Cœur

Tadoussac

Saguenay

172

Sacré-Cœur

N

L'Anse-Saint-Jean

Rivière Saguenay

Sacré-Cœur

Parc National du Saguenay

Baie-Sainte-Catherine

Tadoussac

Parc Marin du Saguenay–Saint-Laurent

© ULYSSES

James Bay

James Bay Tourism
Mon-Fri 8:30am to 4pm
166 Boulevard Springer, PO Box 1270
Chapais, QC, G0W 1H0
☎ (418) 745-3969 or 888-745-3969
🖷 (418) 745-3970
www.municipalite.baie-james.qc.ca

Chibougamau
Commission Économique et Touristique de Chibougamau
600 3ᵉ Rue, Bureau 2, Chibougamau, QC, G8P 1P1
☎ (418) 748-6060
🖷 (418) 748-4020

Matagami
Tourisme Matagami
100 Place du Commerce, C.P. 160
Matagami, QC, J0Y 2A0
☎ (819) 739-4566 or 739-4455
🖷 (819) 739-4805
www.matagami.com

Cree Territory
Association Crie de Pourvoirie et de Tourisme
203 Rue Opémiska Meskino, C.P. 266
Oujé-Bougoumou, QC, G0W 3X0
☎ (418) 745-2220 or 888-268-2682
🖷 (418) 745-2240
www.creetourism.ca

Mistissini
Tourisme Mistissini
187 Rue Principale
Mistissini, QC, G0W 1C0
☎ (418) 923-3253
🖷 (418) 923-3115
www.nation.mistissini.qc.ca

Oujé-Bougoumou
Tourisme Oujé-Bougoumou
203 Rue Opémiska Meskino
Oujé-Bougoumou, QC, G0W 3C0
☎ 888-745-3905
🖷 (418) 745-3544
www.ouje.ca

Nunavik

Association Touristique du Nunavik
C.P. 779
Kuujjuaq, QC, J0M 1C0
☎ 888-594-3424
🖷 (819) 964-2002
www.nunavik-tourism.com

Centre d'Information du Nunavik
1204 Cours du Général De-Montcalm
Québec City, QC, G1R 3G4
☎ (418) 522-2224
🖷 (418) 522-2636
www.nunavik.ca

Exploring

Manicouagan (Côte-Nord)

Tadoussac ★ ★ (pop. 883)

In 1600, eight years before Québec City was founded, Tadoussac was established as a trading post; it was chosen for its strategic location at the mouth of the Saguenay river. Tadoussac was the first permanent White settlement north of Mexico.

In 1615, the Récollet religious order established a mission that operated until the mid-19th century. The town's tourism trade received a boost in 1864 when the original Tadoussac Hotel was built to better accommodate the growing number of visitors coming to the area to enjoy the sea air and breathtaking landscape. Furthermore, the town is an excellent spot for whale-watching. Although it is old (by North-American standards), Tadoussac has a look of impermanence, as if a strong wind could sweep the entire town away.

Dominating the town, the **Hôtel Tadoussac ★** *(mid-Apr to late Oct; 165 Rue du Bord-de-l'Eau,* ☎*418-235-4421)* is to this community what the Château Frontenac is to Québec City: its symbol and landmark. The current hotel was built between 1942 and 1949 by Canada Steamship Lines, following the destruction of the first hotel. Reminiscent of the resort hotels built in New England during the second half of the 19th century, Hôtel Tadoussac is long and low and its weathered wood-siding exterior contrasts sharply with its bright red roof. The polished wood panelling and antique furniture that characterize the interior decor reflect traditional rural French-Canadian tastes.

The **Centre d'Interprétation des Mammifères Marins ★** *($6.25; mid-May to mid-Jun and late Sep to mid-Oct every day noon to 5pm, mid-Jun to late Sep every day 9am to 8pm; 108*

Côte-Nord and Northern Québec - **Exploring** - Manicouagan

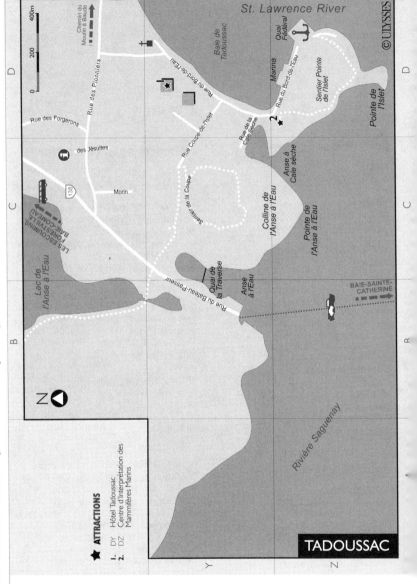

St. Lawrence River

Baie de Tadoussac

Marina

Quai Fédéral

Sentier Pointe de l'Islet

Pointe de l'Islet

Rue du Bord-de-l'Eau

Rue de la Cale-Sèche

Anse à Cale sèche

Colline de l'Anse à l'Eau

Pointe de l'Anse à l'Eau

Rue Coupe-de-l'Islet

Sentier de la Coupe

Rue des Pionniers

Chemin du Morin à Baude

Rue des Forgerons

des Jésuites

Morin

138

Lac de l'Anse à l'Eau

LE FORESTVILLE BAIE-COMEAU

Rue du Bateau-Passeur

Quai de la Traverse

Anse à l'Eau

BAIE-SAINTE-CATHERINE

Rivière Saguenay

400m 200 0

©ULYSSES

N

TADOUSSAC

★ **ATTRACTIONS**

DY Hôtel Tadoussac
DZ Centre d'Interprétation des Mammifères Marins

1.
2.

Rue de la Cale-Sèche, ☎418-235-4701, www. baleinesendirect.net) is an information centre that educates people about the whales that migrate to the region every summer. The centre features skeletons of various sea mammals, video presentations and an aquarium with specimens of fish species that live in the St. Lawrence; naturalists are on hand to answer questions.

Baie-Comeau (pop. 23,207)

In 1936, when Colonel Robert McCormick, publisher and senior editor of *The Chicago Tribune*, decided he no longer wanted to be dependant on foreign paper-making companies, he chose to build his own paper factory in Baie-Comeau, sparking the transformation of a quiet village into a bustling mill.

BAIE-COMEAU (EAST)
Marquette Area

© ULYSSES

ATTRACTIONS

★
1. BX Centrales Manic 2 and Manic 5
   (Barrage Daniel-Johnson)

MARQUETTE AREA

BAIE-COMEAU

MINGAN AREA

St. Lawrence

0   0.5   1km

N

MATANE

FERMONT,
SCHEFFERVILLE

GODBOUT
SEPT-ÎLES

Mingan
Area

Reynolds

Parc du
Lac Aber

Route Maritime

Maisonneuve

De Salaberry

Lac
Leven

Legendre

Legardeur

Maritime

Grain Company
Cargill

Route

Ave. Cartier

Maisonneuve

Marquette

Ave. Cabot

Parc des
Pionniers

Ave. Talon-Lévis

Mance

Mance

Mance

Lévis

Garnier

Laval

Plage
Champlain

Parc de
la Grotte
Ste-Amélie

Hébert

Fontaine

Tarhé

Étang
des Mandres

Laval

Lac
Comeau

138

Lac à la
Chasse

389

Babin

Blvd Comeau

Blvd LaSalle

Narcisse-Blais

Desjardins

Babel

Plessis

D'Iberville

Babel

Alfred-Poulin

Charles-Guay

Michel-Harmon

Samuel-Miller

Donald-Smith

Marcoux

Boisvert

Blvd Schman

Parc St-Nom-
de-Marie

Ave. du Parc

Parc
Bégin

Bégin

Damase-Potvin Ave.

Ave.
Garneau

Parent

Lajeunesse

Blvd LaSalle

Ave. Chapleau

Ave. Crémazie

Ave. Crémazie

Lac
Provencher

Rivière de la Chasse

138

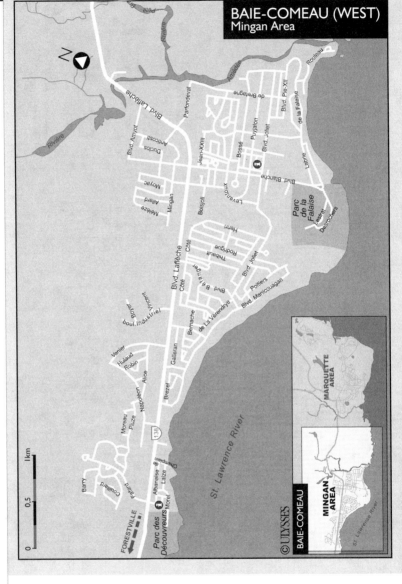

The first hydroelectric dams in Québec were built by private companies for industrial use and to provide electricity to nearby residents. Some of these companies held monopolies on the energy produced in large regions. Eventually, the Québec government nationalized most of the electric companies in 1964. From then on, Hydro-Québec took over and significantly expanded energy production to attract industries with large energy requirements and to export electricity to the United States.

The **Centrales Manic 2 and Manic 5 (Barrage Daniel-Johnson)** ★ ★ ★ *(free admission; late Jun to early Sep 90min tours every day at 9am, 11am, 1:30pm and 3:30pm; 1866 La Manic, via Rte. 389; Manic 2 is at Km 21 and Manic 5 at Km 211; ☎866-526-2642)*, the generating stations and dam, are located on the Rivière Manicouagan. A 30min drive through the beautiful Canadian Shield landscape leads to the first dam of the Manic 2 complex, the largest hollow-joint gravity dam in the world.

A guided tour of the dam brings visitors inside the imposing structure. A 3hr drive farther north leads to the more impressive Manic 5 and the Daniel-Johnson dam. Built in 1968, the dam is named after a Québec premier who died on the morning the dam was officially declared completed. With a 214m central arch and measuring 1,314m in length, it is the largest multiple-arch structure in the world. The dam regulates the water supply to the generating stations of the Manic-Outardes complex. Visitors can walk to the foot of the dam as well as to the top, where there is a magnificent view of the Vallée de la Manicouagan and the reservoir, which covers 2,000km².

- -
Duplessis (Côte-Nord)
★

Sept-Îles (pop. 25,541)

The **Musée Régional de la Côte-Nord** ★ *($4; summer every day 9am to 5pm, rest of the year Tue-Fri 10am to noon and 1pm to 5pm, Sat and Sun 1pm to 5pm; 500 Boulevard Laure, ☎418-968-2070)* displays some 40,000 objects of anthropological and artistic importance found during the many archaeological excavations carried out along the Côte-Nord, as well as mounted wildlife, Aboriginal objects and contemporary artistic works (paintings, sculptures and photographs) from various regions of Québec.

Parc Régional de l'Archipel des Sept-Îles ★★ see p 553.

Mingan (pop. 391)

Montagnais and non-Aboriginals live together in this village located on the mainland, opposite the Îles de Mingan. Mingan is a major salmon-fishing location.

Havre-Saint-Pierre ★ (pop. 3,301)

This small picturesque town was founded in 1857 by fishers from the Îles-de-la-Mad-

eleine. In 1948, following the discovery of large titanium deposits 43km inland, the town's economy was transformed overnight by the QIT-Fer-et-Titane company. It became an active industrial centre and port. Since the opening of the Mingan Archipelago National Park Reserve in 1983, Havre-Saint-Pierre has also developed a significant tourism industry. The town is an excellent starting point for visitors who want to explore the Îles de Mingan and the large Île d'Anticosti.

The **Centre Culturel et d'Interprétation de Havre-Saint-Pierre** ★ *($2; mid-Jun to mid-Sep every day 9am to 9pm; 957 Rue de la Berge, ☎418-538-2512 or 538-2450)* is an information centre in the Clarke family's former general store, which has been skilfully restored. Local history is recounted with an exhibit and slide show.

Centre d'Accueil et d'Interprétation de la Réserve de Parc National de l'Archipel-de-Mingan *(mid-Jun to late Aug; 975 Rue de l'Escale, ☎418-538-3285)* is the information centre for the Mingan Archipelago park. Here, visitors will find a photo exhibit as well as information concerning the flora, fauna and geology of the Mingan islands.

Mingan Archipelago National Park Reserve ★★ see p 553.

Île d'Anticosti ★★ (pop. 277)

The presence of Aboriginals on Île d'Anticosti goes back many years. The Montagnais made sporadic visits to the island, but the harsh climate discouraged permanent settlement.

In 1542, Basque fishers named the island "Anti Costa," which roughly means "anti-coast," or "after travelling all this way across the Atlantic, we still haven't reached the mainland!"

In 1679, Louis Jolliet was given the island by the King of France as thanks for leading important expeditions into the middle of the North-American continent. Jolliet's efforts to settle Anticosti were limited by the island's isolation, poor soil and high winds. To make matters much worse, British troops returning from a failed bid to take Québec City in 1690 were shipwrecked on the island and slaughtered most of the set-

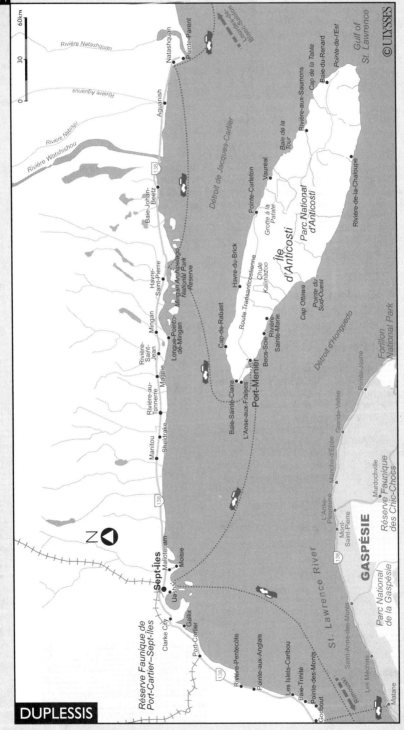

© ULYSSES

DUPLESSIS

Réserve Faunique de Port-Cartier–Sept-Îles

Parc National d'Anticosti

Île d'Anticosti

Gulf of St. Lawrence

St. Lawrence River

Forillon National Park

Parc National de la Gaspésie

Réserve Faunique des Chic-Chocs

GASPÉSIE

Mingan Archipelago National Park Reserve

Détroit de Jacques-Cartier

Détroit d'Honguedo

Route Transantcostienne

Rivière Natashquan

Rivière Aguanish

Rivière Nabispi

Rivière Watshishou

Natashquan
Pointe-Parent
Aguanish
Baie-Johan-Beetz
Havre-Saint-Pierre
Mingan
Rivière-Saint-Jean
Magpie
Rivière-au-Tonnerre
Manitou
Sheldrake
Longue-Pointe-de-Mingan
Sept-Îles
Maliotenam
Moisie
Uashat
Gallix
Clarke City
Port-Cartier
Rivière-Pentecôte
Pointe-aux-Anglais
Les Islets-Caribou
Baie-Trinité
Pointe-des-Monts
Godbout

Cap-de-Rabast
Havre-du-Brick
Pointe-Carleton
Vauréal
Grotte à la Patate
Chute Kalimazoo
Baie de la Tour
Rivière-aux-Saumons
Cap de la Table
Baie-du-Renard
Pointe-de-l'Est
Rivière-de-la-Chaloupe
Cap Ottawa
Pointe du Sud-Ouest
Becs-Scie
Rivière Sainte-Marie
Port-Menier
Baie-Sainte-Claire
L'Anse-aux-Fraises

Pointe-Jaune
Grande-Vallée
Manche-d'Épée
L'Anse-Pleureuse
Mont-Saint-Pierre
Murdochville
Sainte-Anne-des-Monts
Cap-Chat
Les Méchins
Matane
Rimouski

Traversier Blanc-Sablon–Rimouski

60km 30 0

N

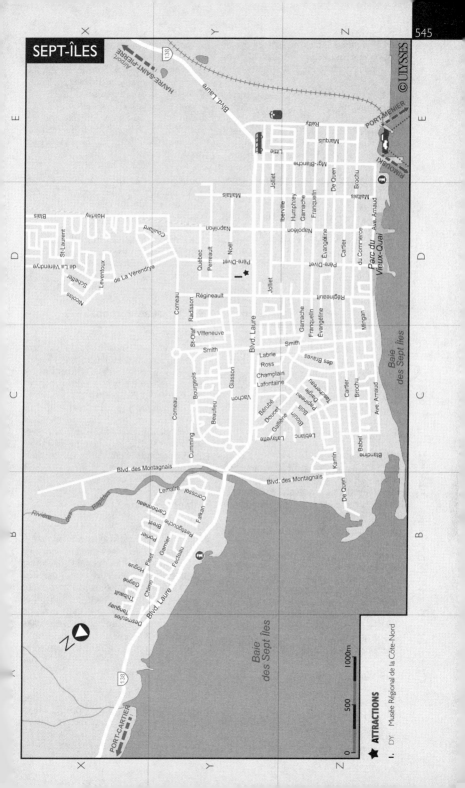

SEPT-ÎLES

© ULYSSES

ATTRACTIONS

1. DY Musée Régional de la Côte-Nord

0   500   1000m

tlers living there. Anticosti is feared by sailors, because more than 400 ships have run aground here since the 17th century.

In 1895, Île d'Anticosti became the exclusive property of Henri Menier, a French chocolate tycoon. The "Cocoa Baron" introduced white-tailed deer and foxes to the island to create a personal hunting preserve. In addition, he established the villages of Baie-Sainte-Claire (later abandoned) and Port-Menier, still the main settlement on the island.

Menier governed the island like an absolute monarch reigning over his subjects. He established forestry operations on the island and commissioned a cod-fishing fleet. In 1926, his heirs sold Anticosti to a consortium of Canadian forestry companies named Wayagamack, which continued operations until 1974, when the island was sold to the Québec government and became a wildlife reserve.

Not until 1983 were residents given the right to purchase land and houses on the island. Anticosti, still unexplored in parts, holds many surprises, such as the **Grotte à la Patate** cave, discovered in 1981.

Port-Menier

Port-Menier, where the ferry from Havre-Saint-Pierre docks, is the only inhabited village on the island. Most village houses were built during the Menier era, giving the village a certain architectural uniformity.

The foundations of **Château Menier** (1899), an elaborate wooden villa built in the American Shingle style, can be seen from Route de Baie-Sainte-Claire. Because the villagers could not adequately maintain the spectacular estate, they set fire to it in 1954, reducing an irreplaceable historic building to ashes. In **Baie-Sainte-Claire**, visitors can see the remains of a lime kiln built in 1897, the only vestige of the short-lived village that once stood on this site.

Parc National d'Anticosti ★★, see p 554.

Baie-Johan-Beetz ★ (pop. 88)

Maison Johan-Beetz ★ *($5; late Jun to late Aug every day 10am to 12:30pm and 1:30pm to 4pm; 15 Rue Johan-Beetz, ☎418-648-0557 or 877-393-0557, www.seigneuriedutriton/bjb)*. Johan Beetz was born in 1874 at the Oudenhouven castle in Brabant, Belgium. Grief-stricken over the death of his fiancée, he wanted to take off for the Congo, but a friend convinced him to emigrate to Canada instead. A hunting and fishing fanatic, he visited the Côte-Nord and soon set up residence there.

In 1898, he married a Canadian woman and built this charming Second Empire–style house, which can be visited by appointment. Beetz painted lovely still lifes on the doors inside. In 1903, he became something of a pioneer in the fur industry when he started breeding animals for their pelts, which he sold to the Maison Revillon in Paris.

Natashquan ★ (pop. 367)

This small fishing village, with its wooden houses buffeted by the wind, is where the famous poet and songwriter Gilles Vigneault was born in 1928. Many of his songs describe the people and scenery of the Côte-Nord. He periodically returns to Natashquan for inspiration and still owns a house here. In the Montagnais language, Natashquan means "place where bears are hunted." The neighbouring village of Pointe-Parent is mainly inhabited by Montagnais.

Blanc-Sablon

This isolated region was visited as early as the 16th century by Basque and Portuguese fishers. They established camps where they melted seal blubber and salted cod before shipping it to Europe. It has been suggested that Vikings, who are known to have established a settlement on the nearby island of Newfoundland, might have set up a village near Blanc-Sablon around the year 1000. However, archaeological digs have only just begun. Brador, a fishing camp used by French fishers from Courtemanche, has been reconstructed.

Blanc-Sablon is only 4km from Labrador, a large, mostly Arctic territory. Much of Labrador was once part of the province of Québec; it is now the mainland half of the province of Newfoundland and Labrador.

It is accessible by road from Blanc-Sablon. The former British colony of Newfoundland did not become a part of Canada until 1949. A ferry links Blanc-Sablon and the island of Newfoundland.

James Bay
(Northern Québec)
★ ★

Whether it's called Moyen-Nord, Radissonnie, Baie-James or Cree land, this region, as difficult to define as it is to name, represents the most northerly region of Québec accessible by road. These roads, laid out by dam builders and mine operators, truly opened up the heart of Québec to its southern population while simultaneously giving the native peoples of the north an entry, for better or for worse, to the world down south.

A whole universe opens up here to adventurous travellers who seek authenticity and a radical change of scene. Everything is different here: time, climate, wildlife, flora, space, people... No aspect of life resembles anything found anywhere else.

Nemiscau ★ (pop. 587)

The French began trading furs as early as 1661 in this historic crossroads, and commerce continued to play a determining role in the history of Nemiscau, mainly thanks to the Hudson's Bay Company, which maintained a post here until 1970. At that point, this centre of economic activity disappeared and the Cree dispersed to found a beautiful, brand-new village on the shores of marvellous Lac Champion in 1979. This relatively new, well-equipped village has become the administrative centre of the Grand Council of the Cree.

Radisson ★ ★

This town was built in 1974 to accommodate workers from the south who were arriving to take part in the James Bay hydroelectric project. During the boom years of construction on the hydro project, the population of Radisson was more than 3,000.

Radisson's main draw is its impressive hydroelectric complex. Visitors can tour the **Centrale Robert-Bourassa** ★ ★ ★, formerly known as La Grande-2 or LG-2 *(free admission; year-round Mon and Wed 1pm, Fri and Sat 3pm, summer every day 1pm, except Tue 3pm; reservations required 48hrs in advance; from anywhere in Québec:* ☎*800-291-8486, from outside Québec:* ☎*819-638-8486, www.hydroquebec.com/visitez)*. Visits to **La Grande-1** are also available *(year-round on availability, reserve 48hrs in advance; summer every day 8am except Tue)*. The tour lasts 4hrs and includes a tour of the exterior facilities and an information session.

During the 1960s, the Québec government envisioned a plan to tap the hydroelectric potential of the James Bay region by constructing dams along its rivers. It was not until the 1970s that a development project for the damming of the Rivière La Grande (Chisasibi in Cree), which runs 800km from east to west before flowing into James Bay, was proposed by then Québec premier Robert Bourassa. The project was divided into two phases, the first being the construction of three powerful damming centres along the river, namely La Grande-2 (LG-2), renamed "Robert-Bourassa," La Grande-3 (LG-3) and La Grande-4 (LG-4). Construction began in 1973 and spanned several years, since damming the river was an intense and complex project. To increase the flow of the Rivière La Grande, various waterways were diverted, namely the Eastmain and the Opinaca, as well as the Caniapiscau in the east. The source of the Rivière Caniapiscau was used to create the largest artificial lake in Québec, a reservoir covering more than 4,275km².

The construction of this hydroelectric complex has had very serious repercussions not only on the environment but also the Aboriginal populations living off the land in this region. To create the reservoirs, some 11,505km² of land were flooded, representing 6.5% of the hydrographic basin of the Rivière La Grande and 2.9% of Cree hunting grounds. During the whole construction of this hydroelectric mega-project, Hydro-Québec and its subsidiary SEBJ (Société d'Énergie de la Baie James), which administers all hydroelectric projects in the area, both carried out environmental-impact studies on this project, and they continue to follow up on their findings. Part of the flooded land was Aboriginal hunt-

Côte-Nord and Northern Québec - Exploring - James Bay

ing ground, and the Inuit and Cree who used these lands contested the provincial government's use of their ancestral lands. On November 11, 1975, the James Bay and Northern Québec Agreements were signed, but since then, 11 supplementary agreements and eight specific accords have been signed to better define each party's rights.

The entrance to the complex is like a terrifying descent into the belly of the earth. The cathedral-sized turbine room is surreal; megalomaniacs will be thrilled by the sheer size of this place.

Radisson – Brisay

The Route de la Baie-James does not end in Radisson. From Lac Yasinski (Km 544), the long gravel road continues to Réservoir Caniapiscau and the Brisay dam, the exact geographic centre of Québec.

Chisasibi ★ ★ (pop. 3,651)

A Cree word meaning "the big river," Chisasibi is a modern village that was built in 1981, after the Cree left Île de Fort George. This little village was laid out in keeping with the Cree's matriarchal society, so that the houses stand in small groups, with the mother's house surrounded by those of her daughters. The two-storey wooden houses are often accompanied by a tepee that serves as the kitchen, since the Cree prefer to cook their food over a fire rather than on an electric stove. You'll notice that the streets have no names and that many are dead ends. Don't let this discourage you—the Cree are very friendly and quick to help out. The cemetery is also interesting, as it contains examples of two different burial traditions. The Cree buried their dead where they passed away, facing the rising sun. Because many people died in the forest, the Cree would build a small fence around the tomb to make it easier to locate. Today, due to the influence of European religions, they bury the dead in a communal cemetery, but the fence tradition has endured. Chisasibi is a dry community, so don't bring any alcohol with you when you visit, and don't be surprised to see a roadblock a few kilometres before the village; it's a checkpoint.

Waskaganish (pop. 1,840)

Founded in 1668 by Médard Couart Des Groseillers, this village was first called Rupert, then Rupert's House and Fort Rupert, in honour of the first governor of the Hudson's Bay Company. Changing hands between the French and the English, this important trading post remained one of the most active until 1942, the same year the village's infrastructure was put in place.

The traditional campsite **Nuutimesaanaan** (Smokey Hill), where fish and fish eggs (*waakuuch*) were smoked, can be visited.

Chibougamau (pop. 7,904)

The name Chibougamau is derived from an Aboriginal language and has managed to retain its mystery over the years, as there is still no consensus as to its meaning. Located 250km northwest of Lac Saint-Jean, Chibougamau is the largest city in Northern Québec, with 25% of the region's population. It is also situated at the crossroads of major roads between Abitibi-Témiscamingue and Saguenay–Lac-Saint-Jean and, since the opening of the Route du Nord in 1993, is the gateway to Northern Québec. It is also a major entry point by air.

Oujé-Bougoumou ★ ★

This most recently established Cree village is in many ways also the most remarkable one. After a long, meandering journey from Mistissini to Chibougamau, Lac aux Dorés, Chapais and onward, a group of Cree chose Lac Opémiska for their permanent settlement. Through their determination they gained reservation status and were permitted to draw up plans for a unique and fascinating village. Architect Douglas Cardinal, the creative mind behind the Museum of Civilization in Gatineau, was entrusted with the task of designing the settlement. Oujé-Bougoumou's architecture is profoundly traditional despite the prevalence of symbolism and the emphasis on vanishing lines. Each residence evokes an ancient teepee, particularly in the slope of its roof. The main buildings are especially impressive. The village as a whole is laid out in the shape of a goose, at one end of which stands a reconstructed traditional village that is used for important community events and to accommodate tourists.

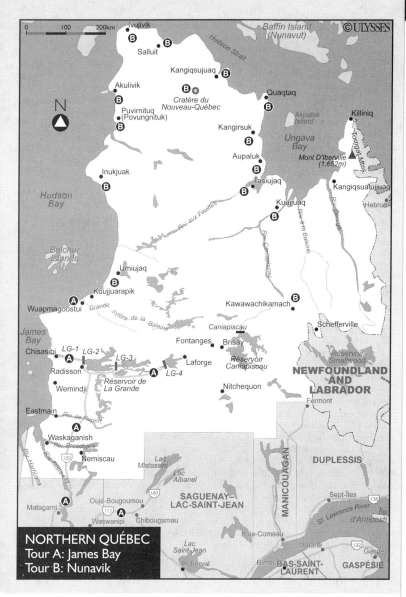

In 1995, Oujé-Bougoumou earned official recognition from the United Nations as one of 50 villages in the world that best represent the goals of social cooperation, respect for the environment and sustainable development, all which the UN seeks to promote.

At the village entrance, you will notice a unique building from which a column of smoke rises. This is the cogeneration plant, which provides heat to every building in the village with a hot-water system fuelled by the waste shavings from the Barrette de Chapais sawmill 26km away.

Mistissini ★★ (pop. 2,761)

At the heart of what was known as Le Domaine du Roi (the king's domain) during the fur trade, halfway between the St. Lawrence Valley and Hudson Bay, Mistissini, along with its immense lake, has been a tremendously important cultural crossroads for centuries. Mistissini is on the southwest tip of Lac Mistassini, on Presqu'île Watson (peninsula), between Baie du Poste and Baie Abatagouche.

With an area of 2,336km², **Lac Mistassini** was the largest expanse of water in Québec before the creation of the great reservoirs. It is 161km long, 19km wide and up to 180m deep in places. It is the main source of Rivière Rupert. Champlain knew of the lake's existence as early as 1603, but French explorers did not reach it until 1663, when Guillaume Couture accomplished that feat. The Jesuit Charles Albanel crossed it in 1672 during an expedition from Lac Saint-Jean to James Bay.

Whapmagoostui ★★ (pop. 804) and Kuujjuarapik ★★ (pop. 573)

Here is a truly unique community, as much for its history and geographic location as for its social makeup. The Cree village of Whapmagoostui (a Cree word meaning "place where there are whales") sits across from the Inuit village of Kuujjuarapik (an Inuktitut word meaning "the small large river") at the mouth of Grande Rivière de la Baleine on Hudson Bay. This coexistence has lasted for about two centuries around the trading post known as "Great Whale River" or "Poste-de-la-Baleine." These villages are actually only one agglomeration divided by what some locals call an imaginary border, which visitors cross completely obliviously. A closer look, however, reveals that the two communities share no public services whatsoever, regardless of the harmony between them. Even the new medical clinic (CLSC), which was built right on the boundary line, is partisan. The Inuit are cared for on one side of the corridor, the Cree on the other, and each group on a different day. The best example of integration is the bar, on the Inuit side of town, which is frequented by both communities simultaneously, although each has its own section.

Whapmagoostui is the northernmost Cree village, at the very edge of Cree territory and on the fringes of Inuit territory, which historically has extended all the way to the shores of the extraordinary Lac Guillaume-Delisle.

The villages are bordered by a large sandy beach that forms dunes from atop which the magnificent **Îles Manitounuk** are visible. These formations are called **Hudson cuestas**, which are characterized by sandy beaches and dunes facing the open water of the bay and spectacular towering cliffs facing the continent. They are refuges for countless birds, seals, whales and belugas.

- -
Nunavik (Northern Québec)
★★

Kuujjuarapik

See Whapmagoostui above.

Umiujaq ★ (pop. 372)

Situated 160km north of Kuujjuarapik, the village of Umiujaq was inaugurated in December 1986. The James Bay and Northern Québec Agreements offered the Inuit of Kuujjuarapik the option of moving to the region of Lac Guillaume-Delisle, in the eventuality of the completion of the Great Whale hydroelectric project. A portion of the residents, fearing the harmful effects of the dam project, voted in favour of a plan to create a new community further north, which became the little village of Umiujaq, after a referendum in October 1982.

Inukjuak ★ (pop. 1,327)

Nunavik's second-largest village, Inukjuak is set 360km north of Kuujjuarapik, at the mouth of the Innuksuac river, facing the Hopewell Islands.

The lives of the residents of Inukjuak remain strongly tied to traditional activities. Discovery of a steatite deposit has promoted sculpture-making; many of the most renowned sculptors in Nunavik live and work in small studios here.

The Hudson Bay Meteorite

If you look at a map of Québec, you will see that the east of Hudson Bay forms a perfect arc. You will also see the Belcher Islands in the centre of the bay. Some scientists attribute this geological formation to the impact of a meteorite. When a meteorite lands, it forms a perfectly round crater. In addition, the force of the impact creates a phenomenon of centrifugal and centripetal waves—a little like what happens when you throw a rock into the water. As these three elements are all present, it is possible to hypothesize that a meteorite hit the middle north of Québec. There are actually a number of sizeable meteoritic craters in Québec: the Cratère du Nouveau-Québec, the semi-crater in Charlevoix, which you can visit, and the largest crater in the province, the Réservoir Manicouagan.

If this hypothesis is accurate, the Hudson Bay meteorite was the largest ever to hit the face of the Earth. The impact would have been powerful enough to alter the planet's axis and thus cause major climatic changes. In fact, given all the potential repercussions, it could have led to the disappearance of dinosaurs!

There is insufficient evidence, however, to say for certain that this gigantic hollow was created by meteoritic impact. The presence of rocks similar to those collected on lunar expeditions made it possible to identify the meteorite responsible for the Réservoir Manicouagan. Yet various studies contradict each other when it comes to the Hudson Bay meteorite. Consequently, Québec cannot yet claim the largest meteoritic crater on earth, which is officially in the Gulf of Mexico, around the Yucatan Peninsula. Some scientists attribute Hudson Bay's geological formation to the movement of tectonic plates. Again, though, they have found no proof in the sea bed to support their theory. Perhaps it was caused by the glacier that raged its way through Québec 20,000 years ago. The mystery has yet to be solved.

Salluit ★★ (pop. 1,164)

Situated 250km north of Puvirnituq, 115km east of Ivujivik and 2,125km from Québec City, Salluit (an Inuktitut word meaning "the thin people") is nestled in a valley formed by steep mountains, about 10km from the mouth of the fjord of the same name.

The actual site of Salluit, dominated by jagged mountains and steep hills, is absolutely spectacular. Located between the sea and the mountains on a magnificent **fjord ★★**, it is one of the most picturesque villages in Nunavik. **Deception Bay**, which the Inuit call Pangaligiak, is famous for its hunting, its excellent fishing and the year-round richness of its wildlife and vegetation.

Kangiqsujuaq ★★ (pop. 550)

Surrounded by majestic mountains at the bottom of a superb valley, Kangiqsujuaq, an Inuktitut word that means "the large bay," stands proudly over the fjord of immense Wakeham Bay.

The most impressive natural tourist attraction of the area, and of Nunavik as a whole, is without question the **Cratère du Nouveau-Québec ★★**, which the Inuit call Pingualuit and is now protected by the **Parc National des Pingualuit**. Less than 100km from the village, this gigantic crater has imposing dimensions: its diameter measures 3,770m and it is 446m deep. Discovered by Chubb, an aviator who was intrigued by its perfectly round shape, the crater was formed by the fall of an enormous meteorite. The crater fills with water from the rain and the melting snow.

On the coastal islands east of the village, there are remains of ancient campsites that date from the Thule era.

Côte-Nord and Northern Québec - Exploring - Nunavik

Kuujjuaq ★ (pop. 2,015)

Situated 1,304km north of Québec City, the administrative, economic and political capital of Nunavik stretches over flat sandy ground on the western shore of Rivière Koksoak, 50km upstream from its mouth on Ungava Bay. With a population of over 2,000 residents, including a good number of non-natives, Kuujjuaq is the largest Inuit community in Québec.

Today, Kuujjuaq (Inuktitut for "big river") is the administrative centre of the territory of Nunavik and the headquarters of the Administration Régionale de Kativik. Various governmental and regional organizations have offices here, as well. The town's two large landing strips are part of the DEW (Distant Early Warning) line, and the village is the hub of air transport in Northern Québec and home to the head offices of many charter airlines.

Kuujjuaq is also known as Fort Chimo. In the 19th and early 20th centuries, it was a prosperous Hudson Bay Company (HBC) fur-trading post. Since then, the village has been moved to the other bank of the Koksoak river, where it was easier to build the landing strip that the Americans needed for the military base that they operated here in the 1940s. Today, you can visit "Old Chimo," where buildings dating from the HBC era still stand, now used for a children's summer camp.

Kuujjuaq has hotels, restaurants, stores, a bank and craft shops. It offers most of the services that are available in regional capitals of the south. Tulattavik Hospital provides top-of-the-line health-care services and constitutes the principal medical resource of the Ungava region.

Majestic **Rivière Koksoak** ★ is one of the marvels of the area. It adds a unique and very picturesque dimension to Kuujjuaq's setting, and its tides shape landscapes of fascinating beauty.

Kangiqsualujjuaq ★ ★ ★ (pop. 740)

Located 160km northeast of Kuujjuaq on the east coast of Ungava Bay, Kangiqsualujjuaq (Inuktitut for "the long bay") was once known as George River, a name more readily pronounced by non-Inuit people. Up until 1959 there was no real village here; summer camps were established on the coast and winter camps were about 50km into the interior. The hamlet was created on the initiative of local Inuit who founded the first cooperative in Nouveau-Québec here, with the goal of creating a commercial char fishery. Construction of the village began at the very beginning of the 1960s, and the first public services were organized here at that time.

Kangiqsualujjuaq made headlines around the world as a result of a tragedy that occurred on January 1, 1999. While nearly the entire village was gathered in the school gymnasium for New Year's celebrations, an avalanche suddenly crushed the building, which was situated at the foot of a steep hill. Fourteen inhabitants lost their lives, forever marking the tiny community.

The region attracts one of the largest herds of caribou in the world. In fact, the Rivière George herd is the most imposing in Nunavik, with approximately 600,000 heads. Kangiqsualujjuaq hunters supply Les Aliments Arctiques du Nunavik with a large proportion of the 3,000 kilograms of caribou meat that it puts on the market annually, both locally and in the south.

The **Torngat Mountains** ★ ★ ★, whose name means "mountains of bad spirits" in Inuktitut, are situated about 100km east of the village, between Ungava Bay and the Atlantic Ocean, at the Québec-Labrador border. At 300km long and about 100km wide, they are the tallest mountains in Québec, making the chain as important as the Alps. Many of the summits reach altitudes of nearly 1,700m, including majestic **Mont d'Iberville** ★ (the highest summit in Québec), which dominates the range with its height of 1,646m. The **Torngat Mountains National Park Reserve of Canada** was created in December 2005. It protects an area of some 9,600km^2 between fjord Saglek down south, to the extreme north end of Labrador, then in Québec to the west up to the Labrador sea on the east side.

Kawawachikamach ★ (pop. 576)

Situated 15km from Schefferville, some 1,000km north of Montréal and right next to the Labrador border, Kawawachikamach is the only Naskapi community in Québec. Related to the Cree and the Montagnais, the Naskapi are also part of the Algonkian language family. Kawawachikamach, a Naskapi word that means "the place where the sinuous river becomes a great lake," is located in a region of exceptional natural beauty and innumerable lakes and rivers.

In 1978, the Naskapi, encouraged by the treaty signed three years earlier with the Inuit and the Cree, signed the Northeastern Québec Agreement with the federal and provincial governments. The Naskapi thereby abandoned title to their ancestral lands and in return obtained finan cial compensation, inalienable rights over certain territories and new fishing, hunting and trapping rights. In addition, they decided to establish a community on the shores of Lake Matemace, 15km northeast of Schefferville. Inaugurated in 1984, the village of Kawawachikamach has modern equipment for collective use, a dispensary and a shopping centre.

Parks

Manicouagan

The **Parc National du Saguenay** ★ ★ ★ *($3.50; Baie-du-Moulin-à-Baude sector: 750 Chemin Moulin-à-Baude, Tadoussac; Baie-Sainte-Marguerite sector: 1121 Rte. 172 N., Sacré-Coeur; 800-665-6527, www.sepaq.com)* is located along the St. Lawrence between Tadoussac and Baie des Ha!-Ha! (for the **Saguenay** section, see p 522), near the gulf of the Rivière Saguenay. The park has three hiking trails that wind through the hilly countryside: the Fjord trail, the Colline de l'Anse à l'Eau trail and the Pointe de l'Islet trail. The latter offers a magnificent view of the St. Lawrence.

The **Parc Marin du Saguenay–Saint-Laurent** ★ ★ ★ *(&; 182 Rue de l'Église, Tadoussac, ☎418-235-4703 or 800-463-6769, www.pc.gc.ca)* features the fjord du Saguenay, the southern-most fjord in the world, and was created to protect the area's exceptional aquatic wildlife. The park covers 1,138km² and is under both federal and provincial jurisdiction. The fjord was carved out by glaciers; it is 276m deep near Cap Éternité and just 10m deep at the mouth. The dis-

tinctive geography in the fjord, created by glacial deposits, includes a basin where fauna and flora indigenous to the Arctic can be found. The top 20m of water in the Saguenay are fresh and their temperature varies between 15°C and 18°C, whereas the deeper water is saline and maintains a temperature of approximately 1.5°C. This environment, a remainder of the ancient Goldthwait sea, supports wildlife such as the arctic shark and the beluga, creatures otherwise found farther north.

A number of whale species frequent the region to feed on the marine organisms that proliferate here due to the constant oxygenation in the water. One of these, the blue whale, reaches lengths of 30m and is the largest mammal in the world. Seals and, occasionally, dolphins can be seen in the park as well.

From early on, European fishers took advantage of the abundance of marine life, with the result that some species were over-hunted. Today, visitors can venture out on the river to observe the whales at close range. However, strict rules have been set to protect the animals from being mistreated, and boats must maintain a certain distance.

Duplessis

The **Parc Régional de l'Archipel des Sept-Îles** ★ ★ is made up of several islands: Petite Boule, Grande Boule, Dequen, Manowin, Corossol, Grande Basque and Petite Basque. There is an abundance of shrimp in the area, making fishing a popular activity. Trails and campsites have been set up on Île Grande Basque. For cruises around the archipelago, see p 554.

A series of islands and islets stretching over a 152km-long area, the **Mingan Archipelago National Park Reserve** ★ ★ *(1340 Rue de la Digue, Havre-St-Pierre, ☎418-538-3285 or 800-463-6769, www.pc.gc.ca)* boasts incredible natural riches. The islands are characterized by distinctive rock formations, made up of very soft stratified limestone that has been sculpted by the waves.

The formations are composed of marine sediment that was swept into the area some 250 million years ago from equatorial

Côte-Nord and Northern Québec - Parks

regions before being washed up on land and covered by a mantle of ice several kilometres thick. As the ice melted some 7,000 years ago, the islands re-emerged with their impressive stone monoliths. In addition to this fascinating element, the marine environment encouraged the development of varied and unusual plant life. From mid-April to mid-August, some 35,000 pairs of sea birds from 12 different species can be observed nesting here, including the Atlantic puffin, the gannet and the Arctic tern. The river is also home to several whale species, including the blue whale.

There are two **visitor information centres**, one in Longue-Pointe-de-Mingan (*625 Rue du Centre*, ☎*418-949-2126*) and the other in Havre-Saint-Pierre (*975 Rue de l'Escale*, ☎*418-538-3285*). Both are only open in the summer. There are campsites near Havre-Saint-Pierre and some of the islands have hiking trails.

In addition to natural attractions, the park also contains the vestiges of a very old Aboriginal settlement dating back over 4,000 years. Montagnais from the village of Mingan were the first to visit this spot regularly, to hunt for whales and gather berries.

The twentieth addition to the Parcs Québec network of parks, **Parc National d'Anticosti** ★★ (*SÉPAQ Anticosti:* ☎*418-535-0156, www.sepaq.com*) was set up in the centre of Île d'Anticosti to protect the island's most beautiful sites, including the Vauréal canyon, the Grotte à la Patate («potato cave»), the Baie de la Tour, the Rivière Observation canyon, the Jupiter salmon river and the Chicotte river.

The park is big enough to accommodate a number of activities, including walking, swimming and fishing. The island has belonged to the Québec government since 1974, but was not open to hikers until 1986. Contributing to the magnificent scenery are breathtaking panoramas, long beaches, waterfalls, caves, cliffs and rivers.

The **Chute and Canyon de la Vauréal** ★★ are two of the major natural sites on Île Anticosti. The waterfall (*chute*) flows into the canyon from a height of 70m, offering a truly breathtaking spectacle. You can take a short (1hr) hike along the river, inside the canyon, to the base of the falls. This will give you a chance to see some magnifi-

cent grey limestone cliffs streaked with red and green shale. If you continue 10km on the main road, you'll come to the turn-off for **Baie de la Tour** ★★, which lies another 14km away. There, you'll find a long beach with majestic limestone cliffs rising up behind it.

Outdoor Activities

■ Cruises and Whale-Watching

Manicouagan (Côte-Nord)

Many agencies near Tadoussac's dock organize boat trips on the river:

Croisières AML (*$55; early May to late Oct; 177 Rue du Bord-de-l'Eau, Tadoussac, departure from the piers of Tadoussac and Baie-Sainte-Catherine;* ☎*418-235-4642 or 800-463-1292, www. croisieresaml.com*), offers whale-watching trips in large, comfortable boats that accommodate up to 300 people. The expedition lasts approximately 3hrs, with a selection of large, comfortable boats or rubber dinghies, which are very safe.

Groupe Dufour (*$50; May to Oct three departures per day, tours last 2.5hrs; 165 Rue du Bord-de-l'Eau, Tadoussac,* ☎*418-235-4421 or 800-561-0718, www.dufour.ca*) offers excursions on large, comfortable boats such as the wonderful **Famille Dufour II** catamaran. If you want to be closer to the action, the company also has a few large, powerful dinghies. Whale-watching excursions as well as cruises on the Saguenay river to Chicoutimi and on the St. Lawrence to Québec City are offered, and nature guides provide information on board.

Croisières Neptune (*$43.25; mid-May to mid-Oct; 2hr tours leave at 9am, 11:30am, 2pm and 4:30pm; 507 Rue du Boisé, Bergeronnes,* ☎*418-232-6716, www.croisieresneptune.com*) whisks thrill-seekers into the heart of the fjord aboard 8m-long, well-equipped rubber dinghies to watch magnificent sea mammals frolicking about.

Duplessis (Côte-Nord)

The **Tournée des Îles** (*$35; Marina Havre-Saint-Pierre, kiosk #2,* ☎*866-538-2547*), a 4hr

New Regulations for Whale-Watching Boats

In the Parc Marin du Saguenay–Saint-Laurent, priority is given to the conservation of animal and plant life. Due to the growing popularity of whale-watching activities, there is concern over the effect that a great number of boats in close proximity might have on these marine mammals. In 2002, new regulations were introduced to ensure that the disturbance to the whales is minimized. Boats are prohibited from getting closer than 200m (400m for belugas, which are more vulnerable) to whales and are obliged to adopt safe behaviour when they are within one nautical mile of a whale. These regulations are strictly enforced. If you will be operating a boat in the park, make sure you familiarize yourself with them.

cruise through the Archipel des Sept-Îles, offers a glimpse of the rich marine life of the St. Lawrence, home to many kinds of aquatic mammals, particularly whales. The boat goes to Île Corossol, a large bird sanctuary.

For whale-lovers, the most wonderful experience the Côte-Nord has to offer is to set out with the biologists of the **Station de Recherche des Îles Mingan** *($80/person; 378 Rue du Bord-de-la-Mer, Longue-Pointe-de-Mingan,* ☎ *418-949-2845, www.rorqual.com)* for a close encounter with humpback whales. Seated aboard 7m dinghies, passengers take part in a day of research, which involves identifying the animals by the markings under their tails. Biopsies are occasionally carried out as well, and useful data is compiled. These outings are not recommended for anyone prone to seasickness, however, as they start at the research station at 7am and last a minimum of 6hrs (sometimes much longer) in turbulent waters.

■ Hiking

Manicouagan (Côte-Nord)

The numerous short and medium-length trails that lace the Tadoussac area are fantastic, since they lead through radically different ecosystems.

Tadoussac is also the starting point of one of the most remarkable long trails in Québec: the strikingly beautiful **Sentier du Fjord** *(*☎*418-235-4238, for camping reservations:* ☎ *877-272-5229, www.sepaq.com)*. This 45km intermediate trail starts near Baie Sainte-Marguerite. For almost its entire length, it offers a view of the mouth of the Saguenay,

the cliffs, the capes, the river and Tadoussac. There is a rudimentary campground about 9km from the start. When you reach the end of the trail, you can continue hiking to Passe-Pierre, where you'll find another campground superbly laid out in an idyllic spot.

Camping de la Mer *(72 Rue Chouinard, Pointe-Lebel,* ☎ *418-589-6576)* is located near Baie-Comeau and features 5km of pleasant, wide hiking trails. Hikers can also head to the **Manicouagan peninsula** to walk along a 30km beach that leads to the **Pointe-aux-Outardes** nature park, where a superb landscape and an extra 6km of trails await.

■ Outdoor Activity Packages

Several outfitters and tourism associations in Northern Québec offer various outdoor-activity packages. The companies listed below provide visitors with an opportunity to discover this great untamed region and the native communities that inhabit it through activities such as fishing, hunting, dogsledding, snowmobiling, photo-safaris, wildlife-observation trips, cross-country skiing, snowshoeing and canoeing.

Radisson

Some dream of catching giant fish in untamed wilderness. Others long to hunt caribou in the taiga or simply observe it on snowmobile photo-safaris. Still others hope to have the family vacation of a lifetime in a comfortable cottage at the end of the world. **La Pourvoirie Mirage** *(99 5ᵉ Avenue Est, La Sarre, J9Z 3A8,* ☎ *819-339-3150,* 🗎 *819-339-3151, www.pourvoiriemirage.com)* has put

Côte-Nord and Northern Québec – Outdoor Activities

together very attractive packages that can make any of these dreams come true.

Chisasibi

The **Chisasibi Mandow Agency** *(PO Box 720, Chisasibi, J0M 1E0,* ☎*819-855-3373)* is the best organized and the most reliable tourism organization in the Cree territory, and it offers the greatest variety of outings. Under the aegis of the band council, Mandow offers fishing trips, photo-safaris, wildlife-observation trips, and snowmobiling, cross-country skiing and canoeing excursions.

Nadockmi *(PO Box 240, Chisasibi, J0M 1E0,* ☎*/* 🖳*819-855-3000)*, an outfitter located on the Kapsaouis river, organizes hunting (caribou and black bear) and fishing trips and arranges cultural visits with the Cree.

Oujé-Bougoumou

The tourism office (see "Tourist Information" at the start of this chapter) conducts 90min tours of this award-winning community and its cultural village. It will also help you plan lengthier tours and packages.

Nuuhchimi Wiinuu Tours
74 Opataca St., Oujé-Bougoumou, QC, G0W 3C0
☎800-745-2045
🖳(418) 745-3500
www.ouje.ca/tourism
David and Anna Bosum provide visitors with a first-hand experience of Cree culture. Snowshoeing trips in the bush, Cree cultural teaching, "country foods" like moose, beaver and ptarmigan, traditional handicrafts and storytelling are all part of the experience.

Nunavik Region

Québec law requires that anyone hunting in Nunavik must hire a guide. For more information, contact the **Association Touristique du Nunavik** (see "Tourist Information").

Arctic Adventures / Inuit Adventures
19950 Boulevard Clark Graham
Baie-d'Urfé, QC, H9X 3R8
☎(514) 457-6580 or 800-465-9474
🖳(514) 457-9834
www.arcticadventures.ca
Tour divisions of the **Fédération des Coopératives du Nouveau-Québec**, which is entirely owned by the Inuit of Nunavik, Arctic Adventures and Inuit Adventures have been offering excursions to Nunavik since 1969 and 1990, respectively. While Arctic Adventures handles hunting and fishing expeditions, Inuit Adventures offers cultural-adventure tours in locations all across Nunavut, including Inukjuak, Puvirnituq, Ivujivik, Kangiqsujuaq and Kangirsuk.

Kuujjuaq

Ungava Adventures
46 Rue Ste-Anne, Suite 3A
Pointe-Claire, QC, H9S 4P8
☎(514) 694-4424 or 866-444-3445
🖳(514) 694-4267
www.ungava-adventures.com
Many outfitters, like Ungava Adventures, organize trips in the Kuujjuaq area that feature caribou hunting, salmon and char fishing, and extraordinary photo-safaris.

Arctic Aventures (see above) organizes ptarmigan-hunting and ice-fishing excursions, as well as packages, with or without guides, that include caribou hunting or salmon and char fishing with nights spent in a camp.

Qimutsik Eco-Tours
284 Evans, Kirkland, QC, H9H 3L9
☎/🖳(514) 694-8264
☎888-297-3467
Qimutsik Eco-Tours is the dream-child of two young Inuit men from Nunavik, who, along with their Montréal-based partner, offer week-long dogsledding tours from Kuujjuaq during the winter and spring. Participants sleep in prospectors' tents and igloos, which they build with help from their guides.

Accommodations

Manicouagan (Côte-Nord)

Tadoussac

Camping Tadoussac
$

428 Rue du Bateau-Passeur
☎ (418) 235-4501 or 888-868-6666
🖶 (418) 235-4902
www.essipit.com

No place offers a more stunning panoramic view than Camping Tadoussac, which looks out over the bay and the village.

La Galouïne
$$ bkfst incl.
pb/sb 🍴
251 Rue des Pionniers
☎ (418) 235-4380
www.lagalouine.com

"*Galouïne*" is an Acadian word meaning a storm wind. Not to worry though—you'll be protected from the elements under the roof of this pleasant little B&B! This isn't Acadia, but the Madelinot (from the Îles de la Madeleine) origins of the kindly hosts explains the name given to this huge house made even bigger by long balconies. Marie-Line, who decorated the inviting guest rooms, gave them a creative, personal touch. The warm or bright colours that dominate inside and out add loads of charm. There are two guest rooms in the attic, for even more country cachet.

Hôtel Tadoussac
$$$$$
≈ 🍴

mid-Apr to late Oct
165 Rue du Bord-de-l'Eau
☎ (418) 235-4421 or 800-561-0718
🖶 (418) 235-4607
www.hoteltadoussac.com

Located by the river, the Hôtel Tadoussac resembles a late 19th century manor house and is distinguished by its bright-red roof. The hotel was made famous when it served as the setting for the movie *Hotel New Hampshire*. All of its rooms were refurbished in 2001. A solarium adjoins the gourmet dining room.

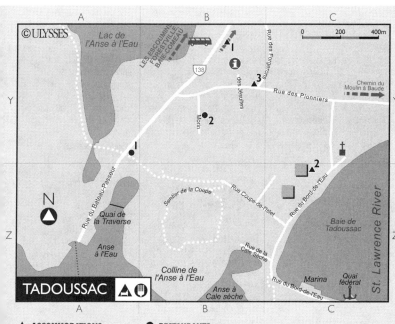

TADOUSSAC

▲ ACCOMMODATIONS

1.	BY	Camping Tadoussac
2.	CZ	Hôtel Tadoussac
3.	BY	La Galouïne

● RESTAURANTS

1.	AY	Café du Fjord
2.	BY	Restaurant La Bolée

Côte-Nord and Northern Québec – Accommodations – Manicouagan

▲ ACCOMMODATIONS

1. AY Auberge Le Petit Château

BAIE-COMEAU (WEST) ▲
Mingan Area

Baie-Comeau

Auberge Le Petit Château
$$-$$$ bkfst incl.
≡

2370 Boulevard Laflèche
☎ (418) 295-3100
🖹 (418) 295-3225

What, you might ask, is that splendid house in its own little Garden of Eden doing right in the middle of town? Auberge Le Petit Château, a bed and breakfast, has a simple, country atmosphere and is quite inviting.

Godbout

Gîte Aux Berges
$
May to mid-Sep
sb ♨
180 Rue Pascal-Comeau
☎ (418) 568-7816
🖹 (418) 568-7833
www.maisonnettes-chalets-quebec.com

Any way you look at it, Aux Berges is one of the

best bed and breakfasts on the Côte-Nord. The rooms are simple and the place is far from luxurious, but the graciousness of the hosts, the tourist services available to guests and the sophisticated regional cuisine make all the difference. This is a place to kick back and relax in the heart of a fascinating village. Aux Berges also rents out log cabins, located near the main building. There is a beach.

- - - - - - - - - - - - - -
Duplessis
(Côte-Nord)

Sept-Îles

Camping Municipal de Sept-Îles
$
mid-May to mid-Sep
Maison du Tourisme de Sept-Îles
1401 Boulevard Laure Ouest
☎ (418) 962-1238 or 888-880-1238
🖹 (418) 968-0022

Many city-dwellers dream of camping on an unspoiled island in the wilderness. Camping Municipal de Sept-Îles can make this dream a reality in the magnificent setting of the Baie de Sept-Îles. This island is the closest to the shore, making it a good stopping place for kayakers and canoeists. Firepits and firewood available. No drinking water.

Hôtel Sept-Îles
$-$$
❄ ♨ @
451 Avenue Arnaud
☎ (418) 962-2581 or 800-463-1753
🖹 (418) 962-6918
www.hotelseptiles.com

Hôtel Sept-Îles stands alongside the St. Lawrence river and has a lovely view. The rooms are simply decorated but quite comfortable.

Havre-Saint-Pierre

Auberge de la Minganie
$
May to Oct
sb ☛
3980 Rte. 138
☎ (418) 538-0084
The friendly Auberge de la Minganie youth hostel is located on the outskirts of town, beside the Mingan Archipelago National Park Reserve. Visitors arriving by bus can ask the driver to let them off here. Many cultural and outdoor activities are offered.

Hotel-Motel du Havre
$$-$$$
≡
970 Rue de l'Escale
☎ (418) 538-2800 or 888-797-2800
▤ (418) 538-3438
You can't miss the Hotel-Motel du Havre, located at the intersection of the main road and Rue de l'Escale, which runs through town to the docks. This place is definitely the big hotel in town. Friendly service.

Île d'Anticosti

Auberge Port-Menier
$$$
♨
Rue des Menier, Port Menier
☎ (418) 535-0122
▤ (418) 535-0204
The Auberge Port-Menier, a venerable institution on the island, offers clean rooms in a modest setting. The lobby is decorated with magnificent wooden reliefs from the Château Meunier. The inn serves as the starting point for a number of guided tours. Bicycle rentals.

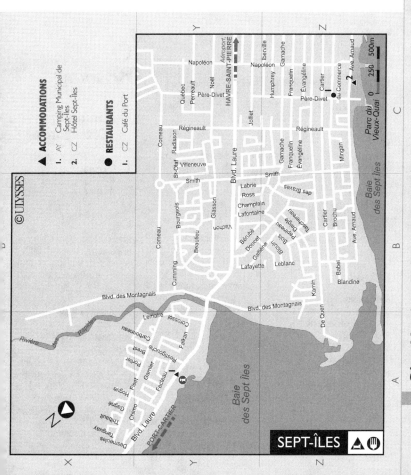

Côte-Nord and Northern Québec – Accommodations - Duplessis

Natashquan

Auberge La Cache
$$
183 Chemin d'En Haut
☎ (418) 726-3347 or 888-726-3347
▤ (418) 726-3508
Auberge La Cache has 10 or so pleasant rooms.

James Bay (Northern Québec)

Radisson

Hôtel-Motel Le Carrefour La Grande
$$
pb/sb ⌂ ☞
53 Avenue Des Groseillers
☎ (819) 638-6005
▤ (819) 638-7497
Hôtel-Motel Le Carrefour La Grande offers acceptable rooms, all of them equipped with kitchenettes.

Auberge Radisson
$$
☞ ♨
66 Avenue Des Groseillers
☎ (819) 638-7201 or 888-638-7201
▤ (819) 638-7785
Auberge Radisson rents modern, comfortable rooms. All have televisions and private bathrooms.

Chisasibi

Motel Chisasibi
$$$
above the shopping centre
☎ (819) 855-2838
▤ (819) 855-2735
The Motel Chisasibi offers 20 comfortable rooms with private washrooms and televisions. No food service.

Chibougamau

Camping Municipal
$
Jun to early Sep
500 Route 167 Sud
☎ (418) 748-7276
▤ (418) 748-4020
Chibougamau's municipal campground is located just outside town on the shores of Lac Sauvage. It includes some 40 campsites for tents and recreational vehicles, and offers several amenities and sports facilities.

Hôtel Chibougamau
$$
◎ ❀ ♨
473 3ᵉ Rue
☎ (418) 748-2669
▤ (418) 748-2107
www.hotelchibougamau.com
You'll easily spot Hôtel Chibougamau's stone-facade building and tower in the heart of town. The hotel has been offering basic accommodations and snowmobiling packages for over 40 years.

Oujé-Bougoumou

Auberge Capissisit
$$
♨
☎ (418) 745-3944
▤ (418) 745-3469
Twelve comfortable rooms are available at Auberge Capissisit. The furniture in the main room, the work of Native-American artisans from the southern United States, is particularly attractive.

Nunavik (Northern Québec)

The **Fédération des Coopératives du Nouveau-Québec (FCNQ)** operates most of the hotel establishments in Inuit communities. Reservations for FCNQ hotels should be made through the central number (☎866-336-2667).

Salluit

Qavvik Hotel
$$$$$
☎ (819) 255-8501
▤ (819) 255-8504
The Fédération des Coopératives du Nouveau-Québec does not operate any hotels here, but there is one private establishment where you can stay. The Qavvik Hotel offers 10 rooms, each with two small beds.

Restaurants

Manicouagan (Côte-Nord)

Tadoussac

Café du Fjord
$$
154 Rue du Bateau-Passeur
☎ (418) 235-4626
The Café du Fjord is very popular. A seafood buffet is offered for lunch, and nights are livened up with live shows or dance music.

Restaurant La Bolée
$$$-$$$$
164 Rue Morin
☎ (418) 235-4750
Try Restaurant La Bolée for simple but tasty meals, such as stuffed crepes. It is also a good place to come later on in the evening for a drink. There is a bakery below the restaurant.

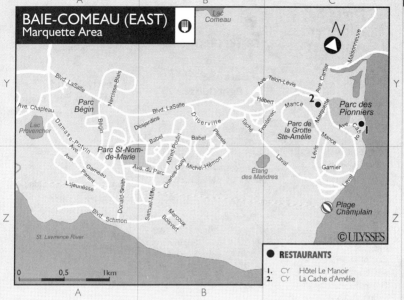

BAIE-COMEAU (EAST)
Marquette Area

RESTAURANTS

1. CY Hôtel Le Manoir
2. CY La Cache d'Amélie

Baie-Comeau

Hôtel Le Manoir
$$$
8 Rue Cabot
☎ (418) 296-3391

The dining room at **Hôtel Le Manoir** (see p 561) has a well-established reputation. In an extremely inviting and luxurious decor, guests dine on expertly prepared cuisine worthy of the most elaborate praise. A meeting place for business people and industrialists, it will also appeal to tourists, who will enjoy the unique view of the bay and the holiday atmosphere that pervades the outdoor seating area. Outstanding wine list.

La Cache d'Amélie
$$$$
37 Avenue Marquette
☎ (418) 296-3722

La Cache d'Amélie is *the* gourmet rendezvous in Baie-Comeau. This inn is located in a picturesque former presbytery and its dining room's intimate atmosphere marvellously complements the delicious cuisine.

Duplessis (Côte-Nord)

Sept-Îles

Café du Port
$$-$$$
495 Avenue Brochu
☎ (418) 962-9311

The charming Café du Port prepares simple, delicious dishes.

Havre-Saint-Pierre

Chez Julie
$-$$$$
1023 Rue Dulcinée
☎ (418) 538-3070

Chez Julie has an excellent reputation for seafood. The coffee-shop decor, including vinyl seat covers, does not seem to discourage the customers, who flock to the restaurant for seafood and smoked-salmon pizza.

Île d'Anticosti

Hôtel de l'Île
$$
143 Rue des Forestiers, Port Menier
☎ (418) 535-0279

Hôtel de l'Île offers excellent family-style cuisine with a different lunch menu every day. Located in the heart of town.

Côte-Nord and Northern Québec - Restaurants - Duplessis

James Bay (Northern Québec)

Radisson

Radis-Nord
57 Avenue Des Groseillers
☎ (819) 638-7255
Radis-Nord is a general store that sells foodstuffs and provisions. It is a good spot to keep in mind for those planning excursions into the surrounding wilderness.

Auberge Radisson
$$$-$$$$
66 Avenue Des Groseillers
☎ (819) 638-7201
The restaurant at Auberge Radisson features an excellent menu and courteous, congenial service.

Chibougamau

Hôtel Chibougamau
$$
5:30pm to 9:30pm
473 3ᵉ Rue
☎ (418) 748-2669
The dining room at **Hôtel Chibougamau** (see p 560) serves simple, unpretentious fare and is very popular with both locals and business people passing through the area.

Nunavik (Northern Québec)

Kuujjuaq

Kuujjuaq Inn
$$-$$$
☎ (819) 964-2903
The Kuujjuaq Inn offers restaurant service. The chef often prepares freshly caught fish or game.

Entertainment

■ Bars and Nightclubs

Kuujjuaq

Adjoining the Kuujjuaq Inn is the **Lounge**, a café where Kuujjuamiut gather after work or after a meal in the hotel restaurant.

Ikkaqivvik Bar
The music here is as eclectic as it gets, ranging from Inuktitut country to techno to throat singing to disco. They even give weekly salsa and merengue classes.

Port-Cartier

With its shows, exhibitions, bar and restaurant, the **Graffitti** *(Île McCormick,* ☎*418-766-3513)* dinner theatre is one of the liveliest and most popular places in town.

Sept-Îles

In the heart of town, right alongside the Parc du Vieux-Quai's magnificent promenade, the **Resto-Bar de l'O** *(451 Avenue Arnaud, Hôtel Sept-Îles, rear entrance)* is where locals and visitors go for happy hour and lively nights out. The atmosphere is conducive to talking, camaraderie and making new friends. Thirtysomething crowd.

Tadoussac

Find out what acts are booked at the **Café du Fjord** *(154 Rue du Bateau-Passeur,* ☎*418-235-4626),* where big names in rock, jazz and blues perform from June to the end of August. It's also a good spot for a drink and a bit of dancing.

■ Festivals and Cultural Events

Kuujjuaq

Aqpik Jam
mid-Aug
Named after the cloudberry *(aqpik)*, an edible, bitter-tasting amber fruit harvested in autumn, this annual music festival unites Inuit from Canada, Alaska and Greenland.

Easter Games
mid-Apr
Like Puvirnituq's Snow Festival, this festival is an occasion to participate in traditional Inuit games. The activities generally take place at the "Forum," the village sports centre, and at Stewart Lake, 5km north of the village. A snowmobile race between Kuujjuaq and Tasiuaq is one of the most popular events of the festival.

Shopping

■ Aboriginal Art

It would be a shame to return from a trip to the North without a handcrafted souvenir of your visit. A trip to Cree territory would not be complete without a tamarack goose—a decoy still made in the traditional way with aromatic tamarack pine twigs. A trip to Nunavik, on the other hand, demands a soapstone carving or a piece of caribou-antler jewellery.

You can also purchase delicious smoked Arctic char, local herbal teas and caribou sausages.

Chisasibi

A small, extremely interesting shop is set up in the large teepee. It has an excellent selection of products created by local artisans.

Kangiqsualujjuaq

Artisans create all sorts of crafts with caribou skin. They have preserved the ancestral art of making mittens and export a portion of their products to other Inuit villages. Other items of clothing are also made here, like *kamiks*, slippers, coats and *nasaks*, as well as caribou-antler jewellery.

Kuujjuaq

In addition to the cooperative, one other establishments exhibit the talents of Inuit artists here: **Tivi Galleries** *(844A Airport Rd., ☎819-964-2465 or 800-964-2465)*.

Kuujjuarapik

The great interest expressed by members in the village's well-established cooperative movement is evident in the quantity and quality of sculptures produced in Puvirnituq. Credit and debit (ATM) cards are accepted at the Northern store and at the co-op store.

Radisson

Inouis *(65 Avenue Des Groseillers, ☎819-638-6969)* sells magnificent carvings and lovely pendants.

■ Arts and Crafts

Île d'Anticosti

Les Artisans d'Anticosti *(mid-Jun to late Dec every day 8am to 6pm; Port-Menier, ☎418-535-0270)* boast a superb assortment of crafts and deerskin clothing, as well as jewellery made from antlers. T-shirts and maps are also sold here.

Sept-Îles

Local artists and craftspeople sell their creations at the **Boutique de Souvenirs de la Terrasse du Vieux-Quai** *(during high season)* and **Les Abris de la Promenade du Vieux-Quai**, located at the west end of the promenade. **Les Artisans du Platin** *(451 Avenue Arnaud, ☎418-968-6115)* is another place to check out. Fresh fish can be purchased in the two fish shops on the pier.

The **Musée Régional de la Côte-Nord** *(500 Boulevard Laure, ☎418-968-2070)* has a shop with an interesting selection of typical Montagnais crafts.

Tadoussac

In a village where you can find every kind of souvenir imaginable, **Boutique Nima** *(231 Rue des Pionniers, ☎418-235-4858)* stands out for its quality products, including magnificent Aboriginal art.

Appendix

Index

Bold numbers refer to maps.

Index - S

Notes

Notes

Notes

Our Guides

Fabulous
Fabulous Québec	CAD$ 29,95	USD$ 22,95

Ulysses Green Escapes
Cross-Country Skiing and Snowshoeing in Ontario	CAD$ 24,95	USD$ 22,95
Cycling in France	CAD$ 24,95	USD$ 17,95
Cycling in Ontario	CAD$ 24,95	USD$ 17,95
Hiking in Ontario	CAD$ 24,95	USD$ 19,95
Hiking in Québec	CAD$ 24,95	USD$ 19,95
Ontario's Bike Paths and Rail Trails	CAD$ 19,95	USD$ 17,95
The Trans Canada Trail in Québec	CAD$ 24,95	USD$ 19,95

Ulysses One-of-a-Kind Titles
Bed and Breakfasts in Ontario	CAD$ 17,95	USD$ 12,95
Inns and Bed and Breakfasts Québec 2004	CAD$ 17,95	USD$ 12,95

Ulysses Phrasebooks
Canadian French for Better Travel	CAD$ 9,95	USD$ 6,95
French for Better Travel	CAD$ 9,95	USD$ 6,95
Italian for Better Travel	CAD$ 9,95	USD$ 7,95
Spanish for Better Travel in Latin America	CAD$ 9,95	USD$ 7,95
Spanish for Better Travel in Spain	CAD$ 9,95	USD$ 7,95

Ulysses Travel Guides
Arizona and Grand Canyon	CAD$ 24,95	USD$ 17,95
Atlantic Canada	CAD$ 24,95	USD$ 19,95
Boston	CAD$ 17,95	USD$ 12,95
Canada	CAD$ 29,95	USD$ 22,95
Cancún-Riviera Maya	CAD$ 19,95	USD$ 17,95
Cape Cod, Nantucket and Martha's Vineyard	CAD$ 17,95	USD$ 12,95
Dominican Republic	CAD$ 24,95	USD$ 17,95
Montréal	CAD$ 24,95	USD$ 22,95
New England	CAD$ 29,95	USD$ 21,95
Ontario	CAD$ 29,95	USD$ 22,95
Panamá	CAD$ 27,95	USD$ 19,95
Puerto Vallarta	CAD$ 14,95	USD$ 10,95
Québec	CAD$ 29,95	USD$ 27,95
Québec City	CAD$ 24,95	USD$ 19,95
San Diego	CAD$ 17,95	USD$ 12,95
St. Lucia	CAD$ 17,95	USD$ 12,95
St. Martin - St. Barts	CAD$ 17,95	USD$ 12,95
Toronto	CAD$ 22,95	USD$ 17,95
Vancouver, Victoria and Whistler	CAD$ 19,95	USD$ 14,95
Washington D.C.	CAD$ 19,95	USD$ 14,95
Western Canada	CAD$ 29,95	USD$ 22,95

Ulysses Travel Journals
Travel Journal: The Lighthouse	CAD$ 12,95	USD$ 9,95

Titles	Quantity	Price	Total

Name:	Subtotal	
	Shipping	$4.85CAD/$5.75 USD
Address:	GST in Canada 7%	
	Total	
E-mail:		

Payment: ☐ Cheque ☐ Visa ☐ MasterCard

Card number _____ Expiry date _____

Signature _____

To place an order, please send this order form to one of our offices (the adresses appear on the following page), or visit our Web site: **www.ulyssesguides.com**.

Our Guides

Contact Information

Offices

Canada: Ulysses Travel Guides, 4176 St. Denis Street, Montréal, Québec, H2W 2M5, ☎(514) 843-9447, ▤(514) 843-9448, info@ulysses.ca, www.ulyssesguides.com

Europe: Les Guides de Voyage Ulysse SARL, 127 rue Amelot, 75011 Paris, France, ☎01 43 38 89 50, voyage@ulysse.ca, www.ulyssesguides.com

U.S.A.: Ulysses Travel Guides, 305 Madison Avenue, Suite 1166, New York, NY 10165, info@ulysses.ca, www.ulyssesguides.com

Distributors

U.S.A.: Hunter Publishing, 130 Campus Drive, Edison, NJ 08818, ☎800-255-0343, ▤(732) 417-1744 or 0482, comments@hunterpublishing.com, www.hunterpublishing.com

Canada: Ulysses Travel Guides, 4176 St. Denis Street, Montréal, Québec, H2W 2M5, ☎(514) 843-9882, ext. 2232, ▤514-843-9448, info@ulysses.ca, www.ulyssesguides.com

Great Britain and Ireland: Roundhouse Publishing, Millstone, Limers Lane, Northam, North Devon, EX39 2RG, ☎1 202 66 54 32, ▤1 202 66 62 19, roundhouse.group@ukgateway. net

Other countries: Ulysses Travel Guides, 4176 St. Denis Street, Montréal, Québec, H2W 2M5, ☎(514) 843-9882, ext.2232, ▤514-843-9448, info@ulysses.ca, www.ulyssesguides.com

Write to Us

The information contained in this guide was correct at press time. However, mistakes may slip by, omissions are always possible, establishments may move, etc. The authors and publisher hereby disclaim any liability for loss or damage resulting from omissions or errors.

We value your comments, corrections and suggestions, as they allow us to keep each guide up to date. The best contributions will be rewarded with a free book from Ulysses Travel Guides. All you have to do is write us at the following address and indicate which title you would be interested in receiving (please refer to the list provided in the previous pages).

Ulysses Travel Guides

4176, Saint-Denis Street
Montréal (Québec)
Canada H2W 2M5

305 Madison Avenue
Suite 1166, New York
NY 10165

www.ulyssesguides.com
E-mail: text@ulysses.ca

Contact Information - Write to Us

QUÉBEC'S TOURIST REGIONS

N

21

18

17

16

15

2

14

3

5

7

4

13

11

10

20

9

8

6

© ULYSSES

19

12

1.	Îles de la Madeleine	**9.**	Montérégie	**17.**	Côte-Nord: Duplessis
2.	Gaspésie	**10.**	Lanaudière	**18.**	Baie-James (James Bay)
3.	Bas-Saint-Laurent	**11.**	Laurentides (Laurentians)	**19.**	Laval
4.	Québec City Region	**12.**	Montréal	**20.**	Centre-du-Québec
5.	Charlevoix	**13.**	Outaouais	**21.**	Nunavik
6.	Chaudière-Appalaches	**14.**	Abitibi-Témiscamingue		
7.	Mauricie	**15.**	Saguenay–Lac-Saint-Jean		
8.	Cantons-de-l'Est (Eastern Townships)	**16.**	Côte-Nord: Manicouagan		

Table of Distances

Distances in kilometres, via the shortest route

Example: the distance between Québec City and Boston (Mass.) is 648km.

														Baie-Comeau
Boston (Mass.)														1040
Charlottetown (P.E.I.)													1081	724
Chibougamau												1347	1152	679
Gaspé											1214	867	1247	293
Gatineau / Ottawa										1124	775	1404	701	869
Halifax (N.S.)									1488	952	1430	265	1165	807
Montréal								1290	205	924	700	1194	512	674
New York (N.Y.)							608	1508	814	1550	1308	1421	352	1239
Niagara Falls (Ont.)						685	670	1919	543	1590	1298	1836	767	1334
Québec City					925	834	259	1056	461	700	521	984	648	414
Rouyn-Noranda				872	858	1246	636	1916	522	1551	517	1833	1136	1171
Saguenay			860	210	1126	1045	463	1076	666	636	363	992	849	316
Sherbrooke		445	786	240	827	657	157	1271	356	906	757	1187	426	656
Toronto (Ont.)	693	1000	606	802	141	823	546	1828	399	1476	1124	1746	906	1224
Trois-Rivières	688	155	334	742	130	814	750	138	1173	322	809	577	1089	566	544

Weights and Measures

Land Measure

1 acre = 0.4 hectare (ha)
1 hectare (ha) = 2.47 acres
10 square feet (ft²) = 1 square metre (m²)

Linear Measure

1 inch (in) = 2.5 centimetres (cm)
1 foot (ft) = 30 centimetres (cm)
1 mile (mi) = 1.6 kilometre (km)
1 kilometre (km) = 0.63 miles (mi)
1 metre (m) = 39.37 inches (in)

Volume Measure

1 U.S. gallon (gal) = 3.79 litres

Weights

1 pound (lb) = 454 grams (g)
1 kilogram (kg) = 2.2 pounds (lbs)

Temperature

To convert °F into °C:
subtract 32, divide by 9, multiply by 5.

To convert °C into °F:
multiply by 9, divide by 5, add 32.

100°F —	40℃
	30℃
70°F —	20℃
50°F —	10℃
32°F —	0℃
20°F —	-10℃
0°F —	-18℃
-20°F —	-30℃

Map Symbols

★	Attractions	⊘	Beach	◐	Metro station
▲	Accommodations	🚲	Bike path	▲	Mountain
●	Restaurants	⊠	Border crossing	🏛	Museum
▇	Sea, lake, river	▇	Building		Optional tour
▇	Forest or park	🚐	Bus station	P	Parking
▢	Place	🚗	Car ferry	⛴	Passenger ferry
✪	National capital	♱	Church	⛷	Ski resort
⊛	Provincial or state capital	H	Hospital	≡	Stairs
—··—··—	International border	✚	First aid	⤹	Suggested tour
·········	Provincial or regional border	⋔	Golf course	ⓘ	Tourist information
⊷⊷⊷	Train track	✈	International airport	⌂	Train station
▨▨▨	Tunnel	⛆	Lookout	⬡	ULYSSES bookstore
		⚓	Marina		

Symbols Used In This Guide

≡	Air conditioning
bkfst incl.	Breakfast included
♠	Casino
⋏	Fan
▤	Fax number
▲	Fireplace
🏋	Fitness centre
fb	Full board (lodging + 3 meals)
½b	Half board (lodging + 2 meals)
●	Kitchenette
@	Internet access in the room
#	Mosquito net
P	Parking
🐾	Pets allowed
≋	Pool
❄	Refrigerator
♨	Restaurant
⟩⟩⟩	Sauna
sb	Shared bathroom
✠	Spa
☎	Telephone number
🚴	Travel by bike
🚌	Travel by bus
🚗	Travel by car
🚶	Travel by foot
Ⓜ	Travel by metro
☺	Ulysses favourite
♿	Wheelchair access
@	Whirlpool

Attraction Classification

★★★	Not to be missed
★★	Worth a visit
★	Interesting

Accommodation Classification

Unless otherwise noted, all prices indicated in this guide apply to a standard room for two people in peak season.

$	less than $60
$$	from $60 to $100
$$$	from $101 to $150
$$$$	from $151 to $225
$$$$$	more than $225

Restaurant Classification

Prices in this guide are for a meal for one person, excluding taxes and tip.

$	less than $15
$$	$15 to $25
$$$	$26 to $50
$$$$	more than $50

All prices in this guide are in Canadian dollars.

This guide's practical section features a grey border and lists this destination's useful addresses. You can refer to the following pictograms to find the information you need:

▲	Accommodations
◐	Restaurants
♪	Entertainment
🎁	Shopping